POLICY-MAKING AND EXECUTIVE ACTION

McGraw-Hill Series in Management

Keith Davis and Fred Luthans, *Consulting Editors*

Allen: Management and Organization
Allen: The Management Profession
Argyris: Management and Organizational Development: The Path from XA to YB
Beckett: Management Dynamics: The New Synthesis
Benton: Supervision and Management
Brown: Judgment in Administration
Buchele: The Management of Business and Public Organizations
Campbell, Dunnette, Lawler, and Weick: Managerial Behavior, Performance, and Effectiveness
Cleland and King: Management: A Systems Approach
Cleland and King: Systems Analysis and Project Management
Cleland and King: Systems, Organizations, Analysis, Management: A Book of Readings
Dale: Management: Theory and Practice
Dale: Readings in Management: Landmarks and New Frontiers
Davis: Human Behavior at Work: Organizational Behavior
Davis and Newstrom: Organizational Behavior: Readings and Exercises
Davis, Frederick, and Blomstrom: Business and Society: Concepts and Policy Issues
DeGreene: Systems Psychology
Dunn and Rachel: Wage and Salary Administration: Total Compensation Systems
Edmunds and Letey: Environmental Administration
Feldman and Arnold: Managing Individual and Group Behavior in Organizations
Fiedler: A Theory of Leadership Effectiveness
Finch, Jones, and Litterer: Managing for Organizational Effectiveness: An Experiential Approach
Flippo: Personnel Management
Glueck: Business Policy and Strategic Management
Glueck: Readings in Business Policy and Strategy from *Business Week*
Glueck: Strategic Management and Business Policy
Hampton: Contemporary Management
Hicks and Gullett: Management
Hicks and Gullett: Modern Business Management: A Systems and Environmental Approach
Hicks and Gullett: Organizations: Theory and Behavior
Johnson, Kast, and Rosenzweig: The Theory and Management of Systems
Karlins: The Human Use of Human Resources
Kast and Rosenzweig: Experiential Exercises and Cases in Management
Kast and Rosenzweig: Organization and Management: A Systems and Contingency Approach
Knudson, Woodworth, and Bell: Management: An Experiential Approach
Koontz: Toward a Unified Theory of Management

POLICY-MAKING AND EXECUTIVE ACTION

SIXTH EDITION

Thomas J. McNichols

J. L. Kellogg Graduate School of Management
Northwestern University

McGRAW-HILL BOOK COMPANY

New York   St. Louis   San Francisco   Auckland   Bogotá
Hamburg   London   Madrid   Mexico   Montreal   New Delhi
Panama   Paris   São Paulo   Singapore   Sydney   Tokyo   Toronto

This book was set in Times Roman by A Graphic Method Inc.
The editors were Kathi A. Benson and Scott Amerman;
the production supervisor was Leroy A. Young.
New drawings were done by Burmar.
The cover was designed by Hermann Strohbach.
Halliday Lithograph Corporation was printer and binder.

POLICYMAKING AND EXECUTIVE ACTION

67890 HALHAL 898

ISBN 0-07-045680-1

Library of Congress Cataloging in Publication Data

McNichols, Thomas J.
    Policymaking and executive action.

    (McGraw-Hill series in management)
    Includes bibliographies.
    1. Industrial management.   2. Industrial manage-
ment—Case studies.   I. Title.   II. Series.
HD31.M386   1983   658.4'01   82-20891
ISBN 0-07-045680-1

To Willelene,
Margaret Ann, and Tom

CONTENTS

PART 7   MANAGING DIVERSIFICATION: EXPANSION, ACQUISITIONS, AND MERGERS

PART 8   DETERMINATION AND ANALYSIS OF MANAGEMENT RESPONSIBILITIES AND THEIR LIMITS

PART 9   CHARACTERISTICS OF THE CHIEF EXECUTIVE: HIS ROLE IN DEVELOPING THE CULTURE OF THE ORGANIZATION

   *Disguised Case
   (I)International Case—Describe Strategic Planning Problems and Opportunities of Multinational Companies

PREFACE

This sixth edition of *Policymaking and Executive Action* is designed to provide a comprehensive framework which delineates the process of strategic planning and policy formulation. The text represents a blend of concepts, theory, and current practice which is coordinated with selected cases drawn from actual dynamic business and other organizational situations. The broad range of cases provides a laboratory to test and extend the analytical and conceptual skills of the student.

This edition, like the previous editions, is intended to advance the teaching of strategic planning and business policy to students in undergraduate and graduate schools of business and management, and to serve the requirements of executive development programs. An effort has been made in coordinating the text and cases to recognize the possible variations in the teaching of strategic planning and business policy. A basic approach for developing the skill of strategic planning and policymaking was used in the arrangement of the text and cases. Although the cases are keyed to the text, the arrangement is not intended as an absolute guide and changes in the sequence of cases can readily be made to adapt the material to accommodate particular teaching methods or techniques. With the exception of some cases in Parts Eight and Nine, almost all cases have a sufficient variety of strategic issues to be effectively used under several topical headings.

Part One introduces the student to the complexities of the general management function and the demanding role of the chief executive. Chapter 1 emphasizes the necessity and importance for the general manager to develop an overall view of the organization and to grasp the totality of the firm as a single unit directed toward the attainment of specific objectives. A basic conceptual model of the strategic planning and policymaking process is developed in the chapter. This conceptual model is stressed throughout the book and is sequentially developed in the succeeding chapters.

The automotive industry with its rich background and extensive historical literature provides the backdrop for Chapter 2 to illustrate situational and institutional differences in strategic behavior. The strategic planning and policy formulation processes of Ford and General Motors are analyzed and contrasted over time as examples of the concept of strategy and of the response of management to environmental changes.

Part One includes introductory cases intended to provide direction and a framework for the analysis of business situations. The various functions and levels of the executive group should become apparent to students in their initial exposure to policy cases, and in this phase of case analysis they should also begin to cultivate a "feel" or "way of thinking" about the management job from the viewpoint of top-level executives. The importance of the role of the chief executive in shaping the corporate image and in charting the course of the business operation should become increasingly apparent as the student progresses from the simpler to the more complex cases. The need for policymaking—the "think" aspect of the top management role which leads to the setting of guiding principles for courses of action—should also become apparent to the student at this stage.

The student's ability to recognize the interrelationship of business functions in these early cases should mark the first step in a gradual development of unique conceptual skill—the ability to see the business enterprise as a whole and the awareness that the various functions of the business organization are interdependent and must be coordinated for successful operation. As students progress through the sequence of cases, it is not expected that they will perceive any abrupt change in the nature of the cases. Their experiences with each distinct business situation are more likely to meld together in easy stages eventually forming the whole structure of the policymaking skill.

Part Two develops one of the major management tasks, that is, the analysis of competitive threats and opportunities. Chapter 3 assesses and appraises the opportunities available for the business enterprise to effect profitability and growth and examines the threats from competition and environmental changes which affect its operations and in some cases its survival. The life cycle of the firm is described and analyzed to indicate expected management behavior of the typical pattern of events likely to be associated with each separate stage of the cycle. The chapter also emphasizes the importance of industry structure and the life cycle of industries as major factors which determine a company's competitive posture.

Chapter 4 examines management's response to environmental change. The potential impact of economic, political, and technological change on the firm is evaluated. Environmental forecasting is discussed and analyzed as a strategic aid to evaluate and prepare management's response to environmental change. The international dimensions of environmental scanning are also discussed to indicate the extent and importance of global competition and to delineate the opportunities and challenges it presents to the firm. Industry structure significantly affects a firm's competitive position. The importance of recognizing this vital factor in environmental scanning is also stressed in the chapter.

Chapter 5 outlines a pragmatic and conceptual approach to problem solving and situational analysis. The firm is analyzed as a system which comprises a number of interrelated functions which make up the whole. The need for continued recognition of the stated mission and purpose of the enterprise is emphasized in this chapter, as are key factors in internal analysis. The principle of functional dynamics—how decisions to change policies and operations of one functional area affect the other functions of the firm—is described and analyzed. The importance of taking into account the interrelatedness of all operations of the enterprise in internal analysis is stressed in this chapter. A series of probing questions for management consideration in conducting an audit and appraisal of the firm's internal problems and competitive position is also provided in the chapter.

The cases in Part Two provide the student with the opportunity to assess the impact of environmental change on the competitive position of the firm. The varied industries represented in the cases can be effectively utilized to acquaint the student with industry structure and the necessity for industry analysis in evaluating the competitive opportunities and threats to the enterprise. The life cycle of the company and the problems associated with the transition from one cycle to the next are clearly indicated in several of the cases.

Part Three defines the basic objectives that shape the image and character of the enterprise. Specific attention is directed in Chapter 6 to the overriding economic objectives which provide the initial guidelines for all strategic action and form the basis for control and accountability. Discussion of the first phase of the policymaking process—the formulation of a root strategy, which defines the kind and type of business the enterprise will engage in and the extent of its commitment of skills and resources—forms a large part of the chapter. The cases in Part Three provide issues and business situations to permit the analysis of basic objectives, root strategy formulation, and the application of the concept of profit maximization.

Parts Four and Five emphasize the successively more pragmatic phases of policymaking, implementation, organization, and interpretation, in which operating, organizational, and control strategies are developed. The chapters and cases in these parts are integral blocks in the development of the conceptual skill of the policymaker. Here students are presented with diverse business situations of increasing complexity, which serve as the raw materials for strengthening their analytical ability and for developing a conceptual action-oriented approach to the problems of business policy.

Operating strategy flows from the root strategy and defines the specific operational plans to accomplish the mission of the firm. Chapter 7 develops the process of implementation and analyzes a number of operating strategies which have proved effective or have been the cause of corporate problems. Specific strategic aids for developing operating strategies such as the experience curve, growth/share matrices, planning grids, and the PIMS data are described and analyzed in the chapter.

The organizational strategy of the firm follows the development of the root and operating strategies. Chapter 8 provides a number of examples of unique organization strategies which have been a significant factor in the success of prominent industrial companies. The process of organizational design and its relationship to the company's structure, objectives, and operating plans is emphasized in this chapter.

Part Six stresses the importance of the monitoring of the control system to determine when and if reformulation should be effected and to what extent the strategic plan should be revised. Chapter 9 discusses these vital elements of the strategic planning process and illustrates reformulation and the development of recovery strategies with examples drawn from industry. The importance of the cases in Part Six must be emphasized. These cases are very comprehensive and provide an opportunity to synthesize the elements of policy formulation and the strategic planning process. The cases also offer excellent examples of recovery strategies necessitated by a complete reformulation.

The importance of expansion, acquisitions, and mergers is stressed in Part Seven through the utilization of case examples of prominent business organizations. The concept of growth as a basic economic objective and the pressure for diversification and integration to attain organizational goals are described and analyzed in Chapter 10 and illustrated in the cases in this part.

Cases in Part Eight develop the external influences beyond the direct control of management which have a decided effect on the planning process of the firm. The cases in this part provide the student with an opportunity to examine the external, environmental problems of decision making associated with antitrust considerations, minority groups, and consumer pressures. While the cases describing these topics are not readily interchangeable with other parts of the book, they can be effectively used in sequence with cases in other parts, particularly in Parts Two, Three, Four, and Six.

The cases in Part Nine describe the importance of leadership and executive style in policy formulation. The nature of the human factor in day-to-day administration and in the development of the character and image of the enterprise is clearly illustrated in these cases.

The cases in this edition have retained the use of generic masculine pronouns in references to individuals whose gender is not otherwise established. I wish to emphasize, however, that I have done so solely for succinctness of expression and intend such references to apply equally to men and women.

ACKNOWLEDGMENTS

The collection of business policy cases in this book was made possible by the cooperation of many business executives who provided the opportunity to write cases about their companies and who generously shared their business experiences with the author and the case writers. I wish to thank Dean Donald P. Jacobs and the faculty of the J. L. Kellogg Graduate School of Management of Northwestern University for permission to use the Northwestern University cases which appear in this volume.

Many of the cases in this edition were written or supervised by the author, some represent joint efforts, and others were individual efforts of present or former professors or staff members of the J. L. Kellogg Graduate School of

Management. I wish to thank them for their contributions and cooperation in making this collection of cases available for publication. Present members include Professors Laurence G. Lavengood and Edward T. P. Watson. Former faculty and staff members who have contributed cases to this edition include Professors Anthony Akel (who is responsible for several cases), Kenneth Armstrong, Gwen Baker, Ram Charan, Charles W. Hofer, Robert D. Hamilton, Serge Oreal, Dominic Parisi, Lawrence C. Rhyne, Professor Robert C. Shirley, Richard Slovacek, Curt Stiles, and David M. Voorman. Additional contributions to case development was provided by Robert L. Campbell, Lawrence D. Chrzanowski, Judy Lipnick, Peter C. Pierce, Gerald A. Rolph, William Sandberg, James C. Shaffer, Frances Sheridan and Roger A. Wojtkiewitz. Former staff member William L. Dejon deserves special recognition for the many cases he has written which are a part of this and previous editions.

I wish to extend my gratitude and special thanks to Albert W. Isenman, of the staff of the Policy and Environment Department, in the J. L. Kellogg Graduate School of Management for his invaluable assistance in the preparation of this book. He has contributed new cases, aided in the revision of other cases, and provided editorial assistance.

I am grateful to staff member Gloria Liberthal for her very special and excellent secretarial assistance.

I would also like to express my thanks for the many useful comments and suggestions provided by colleagues who reviewed this text during the course of its development, especially to Sheila Adams, Arizona State University; Hale Bartlett, University of Illinois at Chicago Circle; Bruce Coleman, Michigan State University; John Faris, Loyola University, Baltimore; Fred Luthans, University of Nebraska; Clayton Reeser, University of Hawaii at Manoa; Earl Sage, University of North Carolina at Charlotte; John Stanley, University of Texas, Arlington; and Curt Stiles, University of Southern California.

I am most indebted to my wife, Willelene A. McNichols, for editorial assistance, counsel, encouragement, and patience during the preparation of this book. Without her help it would not have been possible.

Thomas J. McNichols

POLICY-MAKING AND EXECUTIVE ACTION

PART ONE

POLICY FORMULATION AND STRATEGIC PLANNING: THE GENERAL MANAGEMENT VIEWPOINT; THE ROLE OF THE CHIEF EXECUTIVE

CHAPTER 1

The Concept of Policy Formulation and Strategic Planning

RELATING STRATEGIC PLANNING TO POLICY FORMULATION

In this book we are concerned with *strategic planning as a part of the policy-making process.* The chief executive officer and the policymaking group determine the organization's strategic design by distinct or determined action or by *drift strategy* through the day-to-day decisions at the operating levels as managers seek to suboptimize their specific units, divisions, or departments. A company's strategic plan may be explicit or derived implicity from its pattern of operations. *Strategy is embedded in policy formulation;* it comprises a sequence of decisions reflecting the will and purpose of the organization, its basic economic and business objectives, and its operational plans to utilize its skills and resources. Strategic planning is related to the future, and to the external environment. The strategic planning process involves environmental scanning and reasoned projections to ascertain the most promising opportunities for the business entity to position it for future profitable growth. It is utilized to provide for the identification of the firm's future products and product market scope to meet real, assumed, or potential demand, and to keep pace with competitive threats and pressures.

Policy results from the institutionalization of strategic decisions. The choice of the kind and type of business to be engaged in sets the initial stage for the development of policies which may guide and direct a company for a long time period until reformulation changes its strategic thrust. The business firm and the not-for-profit organizations crystallize their purpose by defining the dimensions and scope of their efforts. Their strategy is directed toward accomplishing specific objectives; over time these strategic decisions evolve into policies which frame the culture of the organization and are reflected in their products and product market scope or in the range of services they perform. Over time the hierarchical policies become symbols and badges of identification which are frequently well recognized in the communities which the firms or organizations serve.

The proliferate use of the term *strategy* in management literature and in corporate annual reports has resulted in confusion and varied interpretations of the word. Strategy is used to identify single actions taken by organizations covering a wide range of decision choices, past and present, which resulted in establishing the image and culture of the firm, its role in the marketplace, and its day-to-day operations. It is infrequent that you find attempts to distinguish these decisions, to classify them, or to evaluate their significance to the organization's strategic design. The strategy of a firm cannot be isolated to a single all-encompassing decision which provides purpose and direction over a long-term horizon. The enterprise develops a strategic design based on a series of significant decisions which relate and delineate the interdependence of the formulation, implementation, organization, and control phases of the policymaking process. Strategic designs form a linking device which connects categories of decisions at the various stages of the policy process. Each class of decisions has separate and distinct characteristics which permit the various classes to be analyzed and studied separately. However, they must be taken as a whole, as a pattern of decisions, to form a strategic design which guides the firm in the marketplace. Each successive set of strategic decisions is derived and flows from the preceding set.

In the formulation phase of the policymaking process, a *root strategy* is developed to give the firm its basic guidelines in terms of the nature and scope of its business commitment and the extent of its skill and resource development and allocation. In the implementation phase an *operating strategy* is developed which flows from the *root strategy* and guides the enterprise in its action commitment in the marketplace. The blueprint for market penetration, coping with environmental changes, and directing day-to-day operations are part of a firm's *operating strategy*.

The organizational phase logically flows from the implementation phase: here management has a decision choice of alternative *organizational strategies* to provide the guidelines, framework, and communication network to complete and put into effect the operating strategy. In the interpretative phase, *control strategies* must be developed to determine the effectiveness of the organization's performance in relation to the predetermined objectives developed in the formulation and implementation phases. The interpretation of control data provides the basis for determining the necessity for reformulation or recycling of the policymaking process and the development of a *recovery strategy* with its consequent effects on *root strategy, operating strategy, organizational strategy, and control strategy.*

The interrelationship of this policymaking process and the concept of a strategic design are illustrated in Exhibit 1-1. This conceptual model stresses the interdependence of the five basic phases of a continuous flowing process which shapes the image and character of the business enterprise and provides it with basic guidelines for executive action.

The specific elements of the strategic design and the policymaking process are discussed in greater detail in Chapters 2 through 8.

THE ROLE OF THE CHIEF EXECUTIVE AS A POLICYMAKER AND STRATEGIC PLANNER

Functional Skills and the General Management Viewpoint

To understand the importance and significance of functional decisions and the relationship of the functional manager or staff specialist to the basic purpose, objectives, and strategic design of the organization, the student or manager must grasp the totality of the firm and recognize that the whole is greater than the sum of its parts (or specific functions). The all-encompassing role of the top decision makers must be analyzed and studied to be understood. The importance of the linkage of decisions at all levels of the organization to the strategic design and "overall master plan" should be comprehended in order to view the firm as a system and to gain an understanding of the significance and dimensions of the functional areas.

The hierarchy of management is confronted with a complex organization which may include separate divisions and companies as well as specialized functions and departments. The chief executive and the policymakers must possess more than a comprehensive knowledge of the operations of the multiple functions of the business entity; they must make judgments about the organization as a whole, and their strategic decision-making efforts must be directed toward the attainment of objectives designed to maximize the efforts of the enterprise as a single integrated unit. Top management has the advantage of perspective since they look down on the entire business operation; but the view may be distorted by their backgrounds and functional specialties. Most policymakers were at one time specialists in one function or another and most likely received recognition for performance at this level, thus earning the opportunity to direct and coordinate the efforts of the enterprise at the higher echelons of management.

The skills and abilities learned at the functional level may, in many instances, prove to be among the greatest handicaps of executives in their attempts to adapt to the overall viewpoint so necessary to the policymaker. It is not uncommon for top managers, particularly in the initial stages of their role as policymakers, to suffer from functional emotionalism—they may tend to see many corporate problems as stemming from poor financial policy, a failure to apply the "marketing concept," or ignorance of the ramifications of production difficulties. Others, trained and experienced in different specialties, may tend to approach the decision-making process through their own familiar channels. The tendency toward functional emotionalism is not unusual or unexpected in view of the career path of most executives. Their education, job assignments,

EXHIBIT 1-1

INTERRELATIONSHIP OF THE POLICYMAKING PROCESS AND THE STRATEGIC DESIGN

Strategic design

Policymaking process →

Formulation phase	Implementation phase	Organizational phase	Interpretative phase	Reformulation phase —recycling of the strategy design
Development of basic overall guiding policies—formulation of the character, culture, and image of the enterprise				
Determination of basic niche in the marketplace in terms of economic goods or services —allocation of skills and resources to specific objectives				
	Development of action strategy—defining the general and specific strategies which the firm intends to execute in the marketplace			
	Commitment of skills and resources			
	Testing of action strategies against environment and marketplace			
	Coordination of product flow with market demand. Development of functional strategies in finance, production, and marketing			

Root strategy →

Operating strategy →

Organization of skills and resources to effect root and operational strategies

Development of organizational design and structure to effect root and operational strategies

Choice and development of an appraisal system to measure the effectiveness of organizational performance in pursuit of company objectives

Interpretation of results from information systems to effect controls

What progress has been made toward goals and objectives?

Closing the system. What changes and refinements are necessary in the strategic design? Complete recycling of the policymaking process? Change root strategy? Recycle to operating strategy? Recycle to organizational strategy? Recycle to control strategy?

Organizational strategy ⟶ Control strategy ⟶ Recovery strategy and development are frequently directed toward a functional specialty. We still find considerable debate today in business circles over whether the "technically trained or functional expert" makes a better chief executive officer than the "general-manager type." Frequently we hear the story told that large firms pick a production person, a marketing person, or a specialist in finance as chief executive officer, depending on what they view as their most pressing functional problem at the time. We also find that many companies choose professional managers who owe no allegiance to a function or specialty. The usual reason given for this kind of selection is found in the explanation that the chief executive's concern is in guiding and directing the company as an integrated unit, not in managing its separate parts.

The internal functions of the firm also tend to obscure the necessity for the overall viewpoint so essential for the policymaker. Operating decisions and day-to-day decisions can command the greater part of the attention and energy of the average company's policymaking group. This is not surprising in view of the dynamic nature of business, which must respond to vagaries of the marketplace and environmental pressures. It can be argued that current operations must be dealt with on a day-to-day basis and that they form an integral part of the management process. It also must be stated that they have a tendency to absorb an inordinate amount of the time of policymakers who are charged with the responsibility of formulating strategic long-range decisions. Most executives concern themselves with operating decisions, with the implementation of preconceived or assumed strategies, and with reacting to the marketplace in attempting to maximize current operations.

The policymakers must initiate and bear the responsibility for the analysis of environmental trends, the nature and extent of competition, and the strategic thrust needed by the firm to cope with these factors. This task constitutes a constant on-going monitoring process that involves many facets and levels of the organization. Strategic direction must be provided by the chief executives, and as the final arbiters and decision makers, they must assume the ultimate responsibility for the firm's success or failure. The chief executive and the senior management group are in the most advantageous position to have the overall business perspective and to determine the firm's basic objectives and strategic planning efforts.

Defining the Chief Executive Role

Defining the role of the chief executive and the policymaking group constitutes a particularly difficult task because of the multifaceted nature of their functions. Attempts to find an all-inclusive definition of the chief executive's role has elicited a significant amount of management literature. Some works have stressed the qualities and skills needed to perform the chief executive's function, others have placed emphasis on their behavioral characteristics, and still others have defined the executive role in terms of what executives do or do not do in their day-to-day performance. There seems to be little question concerning the necessity for a chief executive to provide leadership as well as decision-making ability. Incorporated into most concepts of leadership is a recognized skill of instilling confidence into subordinates and the ability to unite varied managerial levels, groups, and coalitions into a management team that can work in concert toward a predetermined set of objectives. The traits and qualities of a leader have also received much attention in the literature. Frequently posed questions are: Are leaders made or born, or do leaders arise out of given situations or crises? Should leaders possess personal charisma or magnetism? Should they become symbols in their organizations? Should they possess specific professional skills related to the type and purpose of the organizations they lead?

Answers to these questions are not readily forthcoming since empirically we find leaders and chief executives who possess some of these traits and are sadly lacking in others. Nonetheless, they have established themselves as successful leaders of varied kinds of organizations. We also find that leadership styles and managerial styles vary significantly, although it is usually possible to find common characteristics which stand them apart from others who have not been accorded or have not accepted the mantle of leadership or chief executive responsibility. Contrasting leadership and managerial styles are clearly illustrated in the cases of Henry Ford and Alfred Sloan as discussed in Chapter 2 of this book. No one can doubt the success of these executives who have become legendary figures in the history of management. Henry Ford was imbued with the entrepreneurial spirit, and for decades he dominated his organization as a strong-willed pragmatic chief executive who dictated policy and procedure, sometimes involving himself in minor details of the management functions. Alfred Sloan, on the other hand, was not recognized as an entrepreneur, although the soft-spoken executive was a pioneer in modern managerial concepts and practices. Sloan was recognized as an organizer, one of the first so-called professional managers, who established order and system out of the crises created in the early stages of General Motors by its entrepreneurial founder Will Durant.

Despite the long list of desirable traits needed by the chief executive and the top management group to accomplish the all-inclusive functions of managing complex organizations, finding executives that possess these qualifications is recognized to be highly unlikely.

The human limitations of individual executives and their bounded rationality, as described by Simon,[1] points up the obvious human factors that militate against the likelihood of a chief executive successfully operating as a one-person show, although many have been accused of attempting this impossible task. The limits of an individual's intellectual capacity and reasoning power force the chief executive to seek the cooperation and expertise of a managerial group. While there are differences in managerial styles of chief executives, all

---

[1]H. A. Simon, *Administration Behavior* (New York: Macmillan, 1945) and J. G. March and H. Simon, *Organizations* (New York: Wiley, 1958).

are decision makers, and their effectiveness is reflected and judged in their performance record. It is assumed that good performance results from making "right decisions." We find that several academic disciplines or areas of study share an interest in the decision-making process. The areas of operations research and management science are concerned with how to improve decision making. Their models of decision making are aimed at providing a rational basis for selecting the "right decision or most acceptable decision" from among a number of alternatives or possible courses of action. The efforts of behavioral scientists, sociologists, and political scientists have been directed to the understanding of the decision maker as an individual in a leadership position, and the process of decision making followed in organizations. Efforts in these areas has led to the conclusion that an understanding of the decision maker and the decision-making process are central to understanding the behavior of an organization.[2]

March and Simon also concluded that because of bounded rationality, the unlimited number of possible alternatives, and the complexity of the managerial function, decision makers were constrained from reaching optimal or maximizing decisions which is assumed in the rational man role embedded in economic theory. Instead they contended that decision makers reached decisions which "satisfied" the best conditions possible within their purview; thus the firm or organization "satisfies" rather than maximizes.[3]

What executives do or do not do in relation to assumed or prescribed roles has also been given attention in the management literature. Just as March and Simon stated that reaching optimal decisions in an attempt to maximize revenues or utility is an unlikely or impossible task, others have stated that policymakers do not develop and operate from "overall master plans" and their policymaking is likely to emanate from fragmented or incremental decisions. Lindblom[4] contended that most managers make remedial decisions in an adaptive manner, proceeding in small incremental steps rather than in a sweeping grandiose manner that follows a clearly defined set of objectives. Lindblom calls this the "science of muddling through," which he has also termed "disjointed incrementalism." By this kind of action Lindblom maintained that the policymaker never strayed too far from the corporate culture and was able to keep some semblance of order in the complex environment of the organization.

Quinn[5] in much the same vein stated that managers did not operate with a precise cohesive package of strategic goals. He asserted that his research led him to believe that most managers announced only a few broad general goals and only rarely were they quantitative or measurably precise. Quinn maintained that these goals were arrived at through an incremental muddling pro-

[2] Ibid.

[3] Ibid.

[4] C. E. Lindblom, "Science of Muddling Through," *Public Administration Review, Journal of the American Society for Public Administration,* vol. 19, 1959, and C. E. Lindblom, *The Policy-Making Process* (Englewood Cliffs, N.J.: Prentice-Hall, 1968).

[5] J. B. Quinn, *Strategies For Change—Logical Incrementalism* (Homewood, Ill.: Irwin, 1980).

cess, which he termed "logical incrementalism," rather than through a structured analytical process. He asserted that these practices were purposeful, politically astute, and represented effective management, despite "dogma" to the contrary commonly found in the management literature.

Wrapp[6] also observed that executives engaged in purposeful muddling. His experience with top management groups led him to conclude that most executives seldom made formal statements of policy, did not make master plans, and did not spell out objectives for their organizations. He contended that general managers frequently were involved in a multitude of operating matters and did not limit themselves to the "big picture."

Mintzberg[7] also noted that executives did not follow a set pattern or managerial style. He concluded that while the manager's job was challenging there was no real science involved in the managerial function. Mintzberg contended that managers were opportunists who worked mainly with verbal information and intuitive processes as contrasted to the formal management information systems and preconceived master plans which is prominent in much of the management literature. He also observed that because of the open-ended nature of the manager's role, the manager usually assumed an excessive work load and as a result performed most of it superficially. The manager's work pace he considered to be unrelenting and characterized by brevity, variety, and fragmentation. Because of these factors, Mintzberg concluded that managing did not develop reflective planners but rather it bred adaptive information manipulators who preferred a stimulus-response milieu.

Cyert and March[8] suggested that the executive as a strategic planner and decision maker sought to avoid uncertainty and frequently focused attention on solving current pressing problems rather than developing formal long-range strategies. They maintained that executives in complex organizations were forced to negotiate with various coalitions which represented disparate views and interests. They found executive decisions were frequently made to reduce conflict and develop a strategy acceptable to the organization from a number of conflicting goals.

CONCEPTUALIZATION, POLICYMAKING, AND THE STRATEGIC PLANNING PROCESS

Despite these contrary views of the executive role, the cognitive limits of executives, and the extent of formality associated with policymaking and the strategic planning process, most authors would agree that the chief executive and

---

[6] H. E. Wrapp, "Good Managers Don't Make Policy Decisions," *Harvard Business Review,* vol. 45, September-October 1967, pp. 91–99.

[7] H. Mintzberg, *The Nature of Managerial Work* (Englewood Cliffs, N.J.: Prentice-Hall, 1980) and H. Mintzberg "Strategy Making in Three Modes," *California Management Review,* vol. XVI, no. 2, Winter 1973, pp. 44–53.

[8] R. M. Cyert and J. G. March, *A Behavioral Theory of the Firm* (Englewood Cliffs, N.J.: Prentice-Hall, 1963).

his or her counterparts must develop an ability to conceptualize and view the organization as an integrated unit. Whether the chief executive is working with a comprehensive formal plan or is utilizing fragmented information and strategies developed from the suboptimization of the separate units of the organization, an attempt must be made to relate them to the enterprise as a single unit seeking to attain some preconceived or assumed objectives.

In seeking to focus attention on the skills needed in the performance of the executive role, rather than on the personality traits, Katz[9] developed three major classifications of skills: technical, human, and conceptual. He indicated that all three skills were essential, some in varying degrees in terms of executive level, but concluded that the conceptual skill, the most difficult to acquire, was the most essential for the top executive function. Unlike the plethora of works describing functional specialties, the capacity and necessity of executives to conceptualize has only recently been subjected to study. Both in practice and in the literature, specialization of the management functions has received greater attention than the conceptualization of the executive's role. Since expertise in specific functions were easily recognized in the day-to-day operations of business, this emphasis seemed more pragmatic, measurable, and productive. The setting of objectives and the formulation of strategic plans were the less obvious functions of the executive. The writings of Henri Fayol[10] represented one of the first major efforts to direct attention toward the conceptualization of the management role. Fayol pioneered in setting the stage for the development of management principles reflecting the basic concepts of planning, organizing, and controlling. At a later date, Chester Barnard,[11] a business executive like Fayol, advanced the need for conceptualization in the management function by defining in practical terms the role of chief executives and their counterparts who directed business firms. Simon[12] combined some of his early writings in public administration with an extension of Barnard's basic work to develop an important contribution to the understanding of the general management function.

What can the chief executive and the management group do when faced with nonprogrammed complex business or organizational decisions? Is there any prescribed order of analysis or decision-making process which can be followed which will enable the executive to grasp the totality of any given situation? Are there any specific tools which will aid policymakers in developing effective strategic plans and guidelines for action? These significant questions have been posed in the past and are in the forefront of the minds of practitioners and scholars concerned with developing a general management concept or theory which will provide an approach to aid in the direction of the total enterprise.

[9] R. L. Katz, "Skills of an Effective Administrator," *Harvard Business Review,* January-February 1955, pp. 33–41, and R. L. Katz, "Retrospective Commentary," *Harvard Business Review,* September-October 1974, pp. 101–102.

[10] H. Fayol, *General and Industrial Administration* (New York: Pitman, 1949) (originally published in 1915).

[11] C. Barnard, *The Functions of the Executive* (Cambridge, Mass.: Harvard, 1938).

[12] H. A. Simon, op. cit.

This work, as part of the specialized field of business policy and strategic planning, responds to these questions. The following chapters represent an effort to develop a practical systematic methodology to serve as a conceptual framework for the study and analysis of general management problems and opportunities of the business enterprise and other purposeful organizations.

SUMMARY AND GENERAL COMMENTS

Relating Strategic Planning to Policy Formulation

In this book we are concerned with *strategic planning as a part of the policymaking process. Strategy* is embedded in policy formulation. *Policy* results from the institutionalization of strategic decisions. The strategy of a company or organization cannot be isolated to a single all-encompassing decision which provides purpose and direction over the long-term horizon. The enterprise develops a strategic design based on a series of significant decisions which relate and delineate the interdependence of the formulation, implementation, organization, and control phases of the policymaking process. Strategic designs form a linking device which connects categories of decisions at the various stages of the policymaking process. (See Exhibit 1-1.) The field of policy and strategic planning includes more than an analysis of the policymaker's role as the architect and designer of the organization's blueprint for action; it encompasses major elements of the management process beyond the formulation phase. It also includes the study and appraisal of decisions for implementation and action, the structuring and design of organizations, and the development of an interpretative mechanism to provide the information and control necessary to guide the organization.

Functional Skills and the General Management Viewpoint

It is not uncommon for top managers to suffer from "functional emotionalism"; they may tend to see many corporate problems as stemming from the specific functional area which provided their background prior to ascending to a top management role. While many chief executives have emanated from technical and functional backgrounds, the chief executive is usually defined as professional manager who owes no allegiance to a function or specialty.

To understand the importance and significance of functional decisions and the relationship of the functional manager or staff specialist to the basic purpose and strategic design of the organization, the student or manager must grasp the totality of the firm and recognize that the whole is greater than the sum of its parts (or specific functions).

The Chief Executive Role

Chief executives and their counterparts must initiate and bear the responsibility for the analysis of environmental trends, the nature and extent of competition, and the strategic thrust needed by the company to cope with these factors.

The chief executive provides the strategic direction, is the final arbiter, and has the ultimate yes or no as the final decision maker.

Management literature is replete with definitions of the role of chief executive. However, no single all-inclusive definition has been developed. Most authors agree that chief executives must exhibit leadership ability. Most agree that executives can be successful despite the fact that they may have different and contrasting managerial styles.

The human limitations of executives and their bounded rationality, as described by Simon, indicates that decision makers tend to reach decisions which "satisfied" rather than "maximized," as described by March and Simon.

Some authors stress the fact that most executives tend not to operate from "master plans" and that policymaking is likely to develop from fragmented or incremental decisions (Lindblom, Quinn, Wrapp, Mintzberg).

Conceptualization, Policymaking, and the Strategic Planning Process

Fayol, Barnard, and Simon provided some of the early concepts and writings which distinguished the need for conceptualization from functional expertise in the manager's role. Both in practice and in the literature, specialization of the management functions has received greater attention than the conceptualization of the executive's role. The student or executive needs to develop a systematic methodology to serve as a framework for the study and analysis of general management problems and opportunities.

SELECTED REFERENCES

The Concept of Policymaking and Strategic Planning

Ansoff, H. I.: *Corporate Strategy* (New York: McGraw-Hill, 1965).

Bower, R. A., and K. J. Gergen (eds.): *The Study of Policy Formulation* (New York: Free Press, 1968).

Cannon, J. T.: *Business Strategy and Policy* (New York: Harcourt, Brace & World, 1968).

Christensen, C. R., K. R. Andrews, and J. L. Bower: *Business Policy,* 8th ed. (Homewood, Ill.: Irwin, 1980).

Glueck, W. F.: *Business Policy and Strategic Management,* 3d ed. (New York: McGraw-Hill, 1980).

Henderson, B. D.: *Henderson on Corporate Strategy* (Cambridge, Mass.: Abt Books, 1979).

Hofer, C. W., and Dan Schandel: *Strategic Management: A New View of Business Policy and Planning* (Boston: Little, Brown, 1979).

———— and ————: *Strategy Formulation: Analytical Concepts* (St. Paul, Minn.: West, 1978).

Katz, R. L.: *Cases and Concepts in Corporate Strategy* (Englewood Cliffs, N.J.: Prentice-Hall, 1970).

Lorange, P., and R. F. Vancil: *Strategic Planning Systems* (Englewood Cliffs, N.J.: Prentice-Hall, 1977).

Mintzberg, H.: "Policy as a Field of Management Theory," *Academy of Management Review,* January 1979, pp. 88–103.

Porter, M. E. *Competitive Strategy* (New York: The Free Press, a Division of Macmillan, 1981).

Steiner, G., and J. Miner: *Management Policy and Strategy* (New York: Macmillan, 1977).

Uyterhoeven, E. R., R. W. Ackerman, and J. W. Roesenblum: *Strategy and Organization,* rev. ed. (Homewood, Ill.: Irwin, 1977).

The Role of the Chief Executive

Andrews K.: *The Concept of Corporate Strategy* (Homewood, Ill.: Dow Jones-Irwin, 1971).

———: *The Concept of Corporate Strategy,* rev. ed. (Homewood, Ill.: Irwin, 1980)

Arygris, C.: *Executive Leadership: An Appraisal of a Manager in Action* (New York: Harper & Row, 1953).

Bailey, J. C.: "Clues for Success in the President's Job," *Harvard Business Review,* vol. 45, May-June 1953, pp. 97–104.

Drucker, P. F.: *The Practice of Management* (New York: Harper & Row, 1954).

———: *The Effective Executive* (New York: Harper & Row, 1967).

Jennings, E. E.: *An Anatomy of Leadership* (New York: Harper & Row, 1960).

———: *The Executive: Autocrat: Bureaucrat: Democrat* (New York: Harper & Row, 1962).

Livingston, J. S.: "The Myth of the Well Educated Manager," *Harvard Business Review,* January-February 1971, pp. 79–89.

Mace, H. L.: "The President and Corporate Planning," *Harvard Business Review,* January-February 1965, pp. 49–62.

McKenney, J. L., and P. G. W. Keen: "How Managers' Minds Work," *Harvard Business Review,* May-June 1974, pp. 79–90.

Rockwell, W. F., Jr.: *The Twelve Hats of a Company President* (Englewood Cliffs, N.J.: Prentice-Hall, 1971).

Stieglitz, H.: "The Chief Executive's Job—and the Size of the Company," *The Conference Board Record,* vol. 7, September 1970, pp. 38–49.

CHAPTER 2

Developing a Strategic Design: Ford and General Motors

The development of the strategic designs of the Ford Motor Company and General Motors provides a practical illustration which can be utilized by the student to gain an understanding of strategic planning and the policymaking process. The progress of the firms, their difficulties and subsequent recoveries, encompass all phases of the strategic design and illustrate the interrelation of strategy and policymaking. The study and analysis of Ford and General Motors indicates significant differences in strategies, industry position, and leadership roles. The student is provided an opportunity to compare and contrast the decision-making process over a long time span of two of the nation's industrial giants.

THE FORD MOTOR COMPANY

Early Environment of the Automotive Industry

The origin and development of the Ford Motor Company provides a practical and graphic example of the concept of strategic planning. Ford, one of the leaders in the automobile industry, developed his strategic design over a long time period and successfully entrenched his organizations in a specific market position. The formulation stage, when Ford developed his root strategy, and the reformulation stage, when recovery strategies were effected, are particularly illustrative of the on-going policymaking process which is essential to the success of any business enterprise.

Environmental considerations played an important role in the fortunes of the automobile industry and particularly in establishing Detroit as the industry center. At the turn of the century the city was heavily involved in industrial production and was the recognized center of the bicycle, wagon, and carriage industries. The bicycle business turned downward in the 1890s and in the same time period the timber resources of northern Michigan were being depleted. As a result, the bicycle producers and the wagon and carriage manufacturers were seeking new outlets for their company efforts. Names which later became famous in the automobile industry—such as Studebaker, Nash, Durant, and the Fisher Brothers—came from wagon and carriage shops. Men like Alexander Winton, John Willys, W. E. Metzger, Charles Duryea, Barney Oldfield, and the Dodge Brothers left the declining bicycle industry to enter the fledgling field of automobiles. All these men had a common skill; they were all familiar with factory production and plant management. These skills, which were so essential in the early days of development, dominated the automotive industry for decades and were an important consideration in the design of their strategic plans. The initial factory production methods for automobiles were crude and unreliable, and the major consideration of those who pioneered in the industry was to produce a car which would run well enough to replace the horse and buggy. This "horseless carriage" philosophy dominated the early stages of the industry's development. The market was defined by the producers in terms of the well-to-do. The price of automobiles at that time was within the reach of only a small percentage of the population: the mass automotive market was not envisioned at this stage. In addition to high prices and the impracticability of early models, many social objections were raised to the automobile.

Development of a Root Strategy

This was the environment of the embryonic industry which Henry Ford entered in 1899. Ford was one of the true pioneers in the business; he had built three operating cars before he entered the industry on a full-time basis. His entrepreneurial and mechanical genius was recognized early, and he developed a company which captured 60 percent of the market in the United States before being overtaken by the surge of General Motors. Ford's initial success was predicated upon his conception of who the prospective customers were, what they wanted in basic automotive transportation, and what they could afford to pay. Ford did not conceive of the root strategy which was responsible for his success in his early ventures into the automobile industry. His first efforts in the industry with the newly formed Detroit Automobile Company ended in failure after a year. Ford was said to have expended a sizable budget attempting to produce a high-priced racing car which had no commercial value. In 1901 Ford reentered the business with a new group of promoters as manager of the Ford Automobile Company. Once again he attempted to manufacture an expensive high-speed racer, which also proved to be an unsalable product. The company was dissolved in 1902. Ford persisted, however, and took to racing a car he had developed with C. H. Wills. He eventually developed his famous "999" racing car, which attracted much attention in the automobile circles of that day. Through this publicity he attracted new investors for another try at the commercial automobile market. The Ford Motor Company was incorporated and in 1903 produced a commercial automobile designed by Ford and Wills. Unlike his previous cars, the new entry was practical and relatively inexpensive at $850. The automobile proved to be an immediate success, and the company sold over 1,700 cars in its first 15 months of operation. The profits of the firm were exceptional and in the first several years of operation had provided modest fortunes for the original group of promoters.

Defining the Root Strategy: Choosing the Market Niche

Despite this early success, the company's management was indecisive about the right model to produce to enhance their market share. Ford and other company executives fell victims to the traditions of the industry at that time, which defined the market in terms of a luxury product. In the first five years of operation, the Ford Motor Company experimented with eight different models. Despite the success of the original $850 model, the company changed direction in 1905-1906, producing cars ranging in price from $1,000 to $2,000. This entry into the luxury field proved to be a disaster. Business declined significantly, and the firm's profits fell to one-third of the previous year's total. At Ford's insistence, management lowered its prices the next year and recaptured its market and profits. This experience reinforced Ford's lingering conviction that lower prices produced higher profits and that the real potential was in the mass market, not the highly segmented luxury car market. It was at this stage that Henry Ford articulated his root strategy, which became a legend and symbol of unprecedented success in the automobile industry. At his demand, the company announced that henceforth it would produce only one basic model, a relatively low-priced, standardized automobile to appeal to the largely untapped mass market.

Ford, no doubt, nurtured this root strategy over a period of time and had significant evidence to indicate that the change to a low-priced fundamental car was the surest guarantee of success. This concept of a universal automobile eventually resulted in the production of the famous Model T. It was frequently referred to as the farmer's car because, at the time of its entry into the market, the nation was still basically agrarian, and Ford's product had special appeal to the rural population.

Ford was reputed to have envisioned the Model T as an all-purpose machine which would be able to get the farmer to the market and might also be used as a power source for sawing wood, pumping water, churning milk, or running farm machinery.

Development of Operating Strategy

In order to implement Ford's root strategy of supplying the mass market with a low-priced, standardized, all-purpose automobile, it logically followed that the design of the Model T would have to be as basic and as simple as possible. This meant conceiving a design which would permit the building of a rugged, serviceable, and mass-produced automobile. At the outset, Ford stated that all parts would have to be standardized and produced as much like pins or matches as possible. Despite the well-articulated, definitive, market-oriented root strategy conceived by Ford, the operating strategy eventually perfected by the company was a major factor in the success of the Model T. Production costs had to be kept to a minimum to have a price sufficiently low to appeal to the mass market. This meant pioneering an entirely new concept in automobile production. At the time the Model T came into existence, the production methods in force were hopelessly inadequate to supply a mass market. Automobile production, even in the advanced Ford plants, was based on the skills of mechanics who moved from station to station to complete the assembly of a car.

Mass Production as a Concept and Strategy

Ford and his associates assembled the best talent they could find to develop mass-production methods that would reduce factory costs and accelerate production runs. While the operating strategy based on production was determined by Ford when he conceived of the Model T, it took many years of experimentation and hard work to realize his goals. It was in Ford's new Highland Park plant, opened in 1910, that the company developed the most radical production changes in the automotive industry. The significant competitive advantages Ford Motor enjoyed for several decades were developed to a large extent through its innovations in assembly-line production.

By 1910 the company had set the pace for the industry. The Ford factories were the first to have straight-line production, with the product flowing from one machine operation to the next. Ford engineers eventually added the flow of materials for each assembly station which facilitated the continuity of the production process. The string of innovations, inventions, and new techniques continued through to the demise of the Model T in 1927. The Ford organization was responsible for specialization on the assembly line, the first continuous automatic conveyor, subassembly systems, automatic single-purpose machine tools, and a significant number of other advances in automobile manufacture. In 1925 the company turned out a new car for every 10 seconds of the working day, an accomplishment which was never again attained by the industry or the Ford Motor Company itself after that date.

Functional Strategies

Significant operating strategies developed by the Ford organization were not confined to the production area. James Couzens, Ford's business manager and number-two man in the company through its formative years, was credited with several strategic concepts which contributed to the company's early success. For example, Ford Motor Company developed the franchise dealership concept to a greater extent than any of its competitors in the early years of the industry. Couzens built a sales network of 7,000 dealers within a short time, giving the company a marked advantage over its competitors. He used a novel method of financing, which enabled Ford Motor Company to spread new dealerships across the country with a minimum investment of capital. The company would give a local bank a Ford account—a deposit of funds—with the proviso that the bank would aid in the financing of a new dealership in the area. The dealership network grew rapidly to cover practically every town in the country with a population of a thousand or more. This operating strategy proved to be an exceptional marketing device. The widespread dealerships not only provided sales outlets but also prompted many customers to purchase the Model T because they could be assured of repair and parts service in all areas of the country as well as a good resale market for their cars.

Couzens was also credited with developing a purchasing department which traded on the strength of the company's position as the largest single user of raw materials and automotive parts and accessories in the industry. The company's purchasing system, despite some coercive tactics, was one of the major factors in keeping the price of the Model T within the range of the mass market. Couzens's touch was also felt in the area of transportation, where he capitalized on the industry practice of collecting a freight charge from those buyers who required delivery at a distance from the place of manufacture. The company took full advantage of this charge and thus reduced its real freight bill to a bare minimum. Shipment by water was substituted for rail shipment whenever possible, and the cars were shipped stripped down to reduce freight rates. The company further reduced its cost by being the first in the industry to eliminate long-distance freight costs for complete cars by establishing the plants in key locations where separate parts were shipped for assembly.

Strategy in Crisis

The continuous drive for operating efficiency led to widespread worker dissatisfaction and to one of the most important strategic moves the company ever made. The repetitive assembly-line production methods proved to be dull and monotonous, and the craft skills which were formerly required in the plant were limited to a small group of workers. The constant changes in technology caused frequent speed-ups of routinized operations. The turnover of the working force increased significantly, and the hiring of new workers became an increasing problem. The company was threatened by union action and a growing number of dissident workers inside of the company.

Out of this crisis came the famous $5-a-day minimum wage for all workers in Ford plants, which was announced by Couzens in January of 1914. This proposal was far-reaching in its day; it not only solved the company's labor problems but also set the stage for distinct competitive advantages which lasted for over a decade. By this move the Ford Motor Company reduced rather than increased its overall costs. Labor flocked to the company's doors, and it was able to select the best production workers in the industry. With its new wage policy, management had no problem in introducing more efficient and faster production methods.

Effects of Operating Strategy on Design

The operating strategy which resulted from Ford's idea of restricting production and sales to the basic automobile, the Model T, determined specific mechanical and body features of the automobile. In accordance with the required standardization and low production costs, all the cars were built on the same chassis. There were three body styles, and all cars were painted black. There were no extras or frills, just basic transportation. Efforts were made to redesign the car so as to reduce costs and yet provide the durable, rugged transportation required in rural areas. These efforts led to the development of a unique ignition system with a magneto as part of the motor, a "splash" lubrication system, and the famous planetary transmission system.

Development of Organization and Control Strategies

As indicated in the previous chapter in Exhibit 1-1, organization and control strategies are sequential and flow from a company's defined root and operating strategies. In the case of Ford Motor, its highly centralized organization structure logically flowed from the business concept developed by Henry Ford to manufacture and market a basic, standardized, low-priced car for the mass market. This one-model concept—with a single chassis for a few body styles, all parts interchangeable, all cars one color (black), and no accessories—facilitated a centralized organization. This basic root strategy dictated the company's finely honed production process and made possible a simplified control system which monitored cost and quality of product. Like many industrial firms of its day, Ford Motor Company did not have a refined, formal organization structure. The company was organized along traditional functional lines such as sales, production, finance, and personnel. However, there was no evidence of decentralized functions or decentralized authority apart from the few executives who implemented Ford's policies.

Market Conditions and the Determination of Organization and Control Strategies

The organization structure and control system which developed under Ford was influenced by the favorable market conditions which existed for his incomparable Model T as much as it was by the product concept itself. The automobile industry was in its infancy when Ford conceived of his root strategy; the developing nation was still mainly agrarian and eagerly awaiting a low-priced utilitarian car. A seller's market developed for the company and continued for over a decade and a half. Consequently production and cost control dominated management's thinking throughout this period of spectacular success. As might be expected, the company became production-oriented and embodied its marketing concept in the manufacture and design of the Model T.

Ford never forgot the company's traumatic experience in the 1905-1906 period when it shifted from the low-price market to the higher-priced luxury car segment and lost its position. He considered the low price of the company's product to be its major marketing tool; since demand generally exceeded supply, the logical way to increase profits was through the adoption of advanced production techniques designed to decrease costs and increase output. In view of Ford's concept of strategy, the company's organization was dominated by the chief of production, who made many decisions which affected marketing, finance, and personnel.

The Influence of Production on Organization and Control

The driving force behind the sustained push for greater and greater production efficiency, however, was always Henry Ford. His energy and enthusiasm for the production task seemingly made up for the lack of a well-conceived, formal organization structure with appropriate channels of communication. The company's highly centralized, authoritative, ladderlike structure worked because of Henry Ford and the simplicity of his standardized product. There seemed to be no doubt that organization and control were built around one man and one function. Ford was said to have judged the caliber of managers at the workbench, and he built his organization with technicians. He made frequent trips to the assembly line, where he could detect flaws in production or utilize his mechanical genius to suggest innovations or improvements. This visual control and exceptional knowledge of the art of the automobile business was one of the company's main competitive advantages.

The Logic of Ford's Organization and Control System

Ford Motor was never in the true sense a public company, and Ford eventually bought out all the original stockholders. Therefore financial reporting and elaborate financial controls were not considered necessary. Ford placed his reliance on the control of production cost. The company's one-product concept eliminated the need for a decentralized organization and duplication of staff functions. This simplified organization structure and control system was logical, effective, and consistent with the company's strategic design in the formative and developmental period. After the spectacular growth of Ford Motor, however, the company's organization and control strategies did not provide the flexibility and information needed to detect those significant changes in the industry and the environment which signaled the need for reformulation.

Reformulation: Development of Recovery Strategies

Ideally, a well-defined control system provides the information management needs to appraise company performance and to indicate environmental trends which will affect the firm's future advance. It also provides warning signals which permit a recycling of the policymaking process and the development of needed recovery strategies. In the case of Ford Motor, its organization structure and control strategies were outmoded and did not reflect the danger signals in the changing environment which threatened the company. Henry Ford was still the central figure in the organization in the early 1920s, when it became evident that his root strategy, which had given the company unprecedented success, would soon jeopardize its survival.

There is no doubt that Ford was a major factor in blocking a change in the company's direction. He was enamored of his car—the Model T—and of his product concept which had provided him with industry leadership, fame, and fortune. Reluctance to reformulate and discard a tried and true business formula is commonplace in the industrial world. Like Ford, many policymakers become emotionally attached to successful strategies, particularly if they are the ones who conceived them. It usually takes a severe decline in earnings to initiate the reformulation process and launch an earnest search for a recovery strategy. Ford Motor reached an all-time high in production in 1923, when it manufactured 1.9 million cars. Production declined in 1924, 1925, and 1926; it reached the low of 359,000 in 1927, the year the Model T was discontinued. Volume was the foundation of Ford's strategy; when he saw the decline in his sales and the increase in the sales of his competition, he stopped the production of the Model T.

Environment and Competition

The demise of the Model T could have been foretold from trends in the environment and the automobile industry long before 1927. The country was rapidly shifting from an agrarian to an industrial economy, a middle class had developed along with higher average incomes, consumer tastes had changed, and automobile buyers had begun to seek style and comfort as well as economy. The roads had improved greatly, macadam and concrete having replaced dirt and rugged pavement. In addition, Chevrolet, the General Motors entry in the low-price field, was rapidly closing in on Ford's number-one position. Ford's competitors offered style and design, riding comfort, color choice, and model changes.

The rapid growth of the automobile industry, with sales of over 4 million in 1923 and for several succeeding years, had created a used-car market, and used cars at low prices made serious inroads into the basic transportation market which the Model T had served almost exclusively for over a decade.

Delay in Implementation of a Recovery Strategy

Ford's delayed action and apparent lack of preparation prevented the company from readily implementing a recovery strategy. The Model T was abruptly discontinued in May of 1927, and production was shut down for a year. This left the low-price field exclusively to Chevrolet.

Ford failed to realize how completely the market had changed; before giving up the Model T he tried several unsuccessful recovery strategies. For the first time in the company's history, he permitted a national advertising campaign. The company also tried to restyle the car through superficial changes, and the traditional black color gave way to a choice among four colors. Only when these attempts failed to recapture the lost position did Ford reluctantly submit to reformulation.

The company's hopes for recovery were based on a new car, the Model A, which was delayed over a year in entering the marketplace because of the lack of strategic planning on the part of Ford and his management group. The delay caused serious disruption in the company; over 100,000 employees were laid off for an extended period. The entire industry was affected as well, since Ford was the largest purchaser of parts and supplies. Despite the problems created by the shutdown of the Ford plants, the majority of the former employees applied for their old jobs when the plants were reopened for the production of the Model A. The $5 day and "profit-sharing plans" had created a reputation for the company as a benevolent employer despite the production speed-ups, reportedly tense working conditions, and the mass lay-off which lasted over a year.

The Recovery Strategy: Ford's Model A

The Model A's introduction received an unprecedented amount of publicity and was accompanied by an intensive advertising campaign that cost $2 million over five days. Dealers were eager to display the new car in their showrooms. Unlike the Model T, the new automobile came in a choice of four colors and 17 body styles; its standard equipment included most of the fundamental items competitors had offered the market for a period of years.

The Model A was judged a success in its early stages, and Ford Motor recaptured its leading market share, selling 719,000 cars in 1928, 1.2 million in 1929, and 1.6 million in 1930. The automobile market had expanded, however, and the Model A lost a significant number of potential buyers to its major competitor, the Chevrolet (made by General Motors), as well as to the cars made by Chrysler. Many of these purchasers grew tired of waiting for the new Ford; once they found a satisfactory competitor's product they not only purchased the competing automobile but also shifted their long-run consumer loyalties.

The delay in reformulation and development of the Model A (the company's recovery strategy) was too long, however. Despite the initial flush of success when the car was introduced, a toll had been taken. The long-run position of Ford Motor as the industry leader and dominant company in the automotive field was seriously eroded. Not only were sales lost, never to be recaptured, but a large number of valuable dealers in the enviable network of Ford dealerships went bankrupt.

Failure to Complete the Reformulation Process

The Ford organization never fully recovered from the dramatic turn of events which led to the demise of the Model T in 1927. The company did not complete the reformulation process—it engaged in only partial reformulation. A complete recycling of their policymaking process through formulation, implementation, organization, and control was not undertaken. Ford's original strategic design was changed only in terms of substituting the Model A, with a greater choice of variations in body styles, for the Model T. The prospects held out to the dealers when the much-heralded Model A was introduced never fully materialized. Instead of offering a variety of cars and annual model changes to keep pace with competition, the new Ford remained unchanged except for some minor variations for five years. General Motors introduced in this period a six-cylinder Chevrolet, which approached the price of the Model A in terms of value received. As a result, General Motors once again made serious inroads among the loyal customers of Ford. Chrysler entered the low-price field in 1931 with the Plymouth, which was highly stylized and offered innovations and advances in automotive engineering.

A Second Recovery Strategy

Once again, because Ford and his executive group had failed to recognize the full impact of environmental changes, the company found itself behind its competition in serving the customer. The Model A was discontinued in 1932, after five years of production. Like the Model T when it was discarded, it lacked style and progressive engineering. Ford conceived of a second recovery strategy—the production of a V8—to circumvent competition in the low-price field. Despite the experience of the model change from the T to the A, the company seemed to encounter the same organizational problems, and the changeover took almost six months. The authoritarian leadership of Ford and the highly centralized organization structure were once again stumbling blocks to a smooth transition. General Motors assumed the number-one position in the industry after 1930, and the 1932 crisis of Ford enabled Chrysler to assume the number-two position in the industry for a short period.

A complete reformulation and a new strategic plan were not effected until Henry Ford relinquished control of the company in 1945. After Henry Ford II assumed the leadership, he initiated a thorough reorganization. Contrary to his grandfather's precedent, he went outside the organization for talent, hiring, among others, several top General Motors executives, most notably Ernest R. Breech, who became the top operating officer next to the young Ford. The new executive team introduced modern management concepts and techniques and installed control procedures and financial systems which were common in industry but never employed at Ford Motor. Management, utilizing the new financial and control procedures, was able for the first time in the company's history to determine which operations were profitable and which were not. As a result, a number of inefficient and unprofitable operations were cut off, such as the soybean works at Dearborn and rubber plantations in Brazil. The topheavy, centralized, inflexible organization structure was also drastically changed. A decentralized structure was initiated, and the company's major operations were apportioned among numerous divisions. Appropriate control measures were devised, and a central staff was organized to help administer the various divisions. All these measures were necessary to gain control of an organization which had been guided by drift strategy since losing its number-one position in the industry in 1931.

Despite the introduction of scientific management and several changes in strategic plans, Ford Motor Company has not to this day been able to overtake General Motors and regain its leadership. Nor has the company been able to match General Motors' full line of cars directed to specific segments of the automotive market. Currently Ford is faced with a serious threat and challenge from foreign automotive producers, particularly the Japanese. The recovery of Ford in the 1980s is based on emulating the lines of foreign producers which have positioned their companies in today's market with quality, economy cars equipped with the latest technological improvements in the industry.

STRATEGIC PLANNING AT GENERAL MOTORS: COMPARISON AND CONTRAST WITH FORD MOTOR COMPANY

Strategic Development under Will Durant[1]

General Motors, by contrast with Ford, was formed as a holding company and was a large, decentralized organization from its inception. Will Durant started the original General Motors Company in 1908 and was the largest automobile manufacturer in the United States when Ford produced his first Model T. Durant, a pioneer in the automobile business, had a background of success as one of the major carriage producers. He and his partners organized and developed a high-volume, integrated carriage manufacturing business with a national sales organization. Durant's company was unique in the carriage trade in terms of the manufacturing process. Unlike other carriage makers of the time, Durant's company developed an assembly-line system, purchasing the carriage parts from outside suppliers. To assure adequate supply, Durant personally

---

[1] Of the sources indicated in the bibliography at the end of the chapter, see particularly Alfred P. Sloan, Jr., *My Years with General Motors*, and A. D. Chandler, Jr., *Strategy and Structure*.

organized a number of specialty producers in Flint, Michigan, the site of his company. Durant's entrepreneurship and flair for innovation in the manufacture of carriages was carried over into the automobile business, which he recognized as a threat to the carriage business but nevertheless as providing an excellent opportunity to create a new, challenging enterprise.

Durant took over the failing Buick Motor Company in 1904 and began immediately to plan a company similar in operation and structure to his carriage business. The Buick was redesigned, large new assembly plants were built, and a national distributing and dealer organization was formed. Durant granted franchises to distributors, who formed their own dealer and service organizations. He utilized the personnel and plants of the carriage business in the production and sales of the Buick. To ensure the supply of parts and accessories for his assembly-line operation, Durant converted a number of the companies that he had helped organize and finance for the carriage business into suppliers for his automobile company. Durant's ability was quickly reflected in the company's fortunes, and by 1908 the Buick was the best-selling car in the industry.

The success of the Buick prompted Durant to seek ways of quick expansion to take advantage of the growing automobile market. He concluded that the most expedient way would be to effect a combination of existing car manufacturers. With support from J. P. Morgan and Company, Durant and his associates formed General Motors as a holding company which acquired stock in Buick, Olds, and W. F. Stewart, a body-making firm of Flint, Michigan. He exchanged General Motors stock for the stock of Cadillac, Oakland, six other automobile companies, three truck manufacturers, and parts and accessory companies. Following the same strategy he had used with the carriage business and Buick, Durant based his new organization on volume and vertical integration.

Many of the companies he acquired were well established and had large manufacturing plants and good sales organizations. One of the significant contributions of the combination was the acquisition of the companies which produced essential automotive parts and accessories such as engines, bodies, steering mechanisms, transmissions, gears, lamps, and rims. This group of companies, put together by Durant to assure a reliable and sufficient supply of parts and accessories, is still an integral part of General Motors today.

In his efforts to organize and promote his new corporate giant, Durant banked on a continuing increase in the demand for automobiles and did not provide for an adequate cash reserve. He had also failed to build an organization and control system, so that such information and reporting as he received was insufficient to provide an early warning of the impending recession of 1910. Sales of General Motors, particularly of Buick, the company's leading seller, dropped. Durant was without sufficient cash to pay labor and suppliers. To save the company, Durant had to turn over management to bankers, after signing a five-year voting trust which left him as a vice-president and director with no direct voice in management. Under the new leadership of Storrow and

Nash, the company made significant moves to consolidate and integrate General Motors' wide span of operations.

Durant returned in 1916, after the expiration of the voting trust, as the chief executive officer. In the period of his absence from active management of the company, he acquired Chevrolet, a high-volume integrated producer. Supported by financial backing from the Du Ponts, he utilized his interest in this company to regain managerial control of General Motors. Because the Du Ponts were heavily involved in their own operations, Durant was left on his own to direct and formulate strategy for General Motors. He embarked on a vigorous campaign of expansion, producing a variety of moderately priced cars backed up by a national sales network and an integrated group of suppliers of parts and accessories. A large number of companies was added to the General Motors organization. With $50 million in additional capital provided by the Du Ponts, Durant accelerated his expansion program, adding such important units as Fisher Body, Hyatt Bearing, and gear and brake manufacturing units. In 1917 General Motors was converted from a holding company to an operating company, and the separate companies in the organization were made operating divisions. The company, however, remained essentially the same, operating as separate entities with a minimum of direction from the parent organization. Despite the influence of the Du Ponts and members of their executive group who joined General Motors, the company lacked an organization structure that provided administrative control over this automotive complex.

The lack of control of the separate divisions led to a financial crisis in 1920. In the early months of this year, the company continued its expansion, spending significant sums of money on plant and equipment and building up inventories. Division managers overrode attempts made by the hastily formed corporate Inventory Allocations Committee to curtail their spending. In August of 1920 the automobile market collapsed and General Motors suffered serious losses, which resulted in a drastic decline in its stock price. Durant made an effort to sustain the stock price by buying it on credit on the open market. This proved to be disastrous; Durant incurred serious losses and was forced to resign as president of the company he had formed, nurtured, and developed into a giant in the industry.

General Motors Strategic Development under Alfred Sloan[2]

Development of Root Strategy   Pierre S. Du Pont succeeded Durant as chief executive officer to protect the family's substantial interest in the company. It was understood that his tenure in office would be short and that his major objective in coming out of retirement, after his long service at Du Pont, was to lend his name and prestige to General Motors in a time of crisis when stability was sorely needed. Alfred Sloan at this time was already a prominent figure in

---

[2] See Sloan, op. cit.

General Motors' policymaking group. He was head of United Motors, an integral part of the company that controlled and managed a group of operating companies producing automotive parts and accessories. Sloan was a member of the company's executive committee and one of the top officers in the organization. Under Durant, Sloan was requested to study the organization of General Motors to seek possible solutions to the problem created by the rapid expansion of the company after World War I. He produced a detailed conceptual analysis simply entitled *Organization Study,* which defined the basis for operating a multiunit organization and established the principles for the management of a decentralized organization which are still basic in General Motors today. Although the study was submitted to Durant, it was not adopted until 1920, after he had left General Motors. *Organization Study* went beyond the analysis of operations and recommendations for changes in organizational structure; it also provided the impetus for the development of a strategic design.

Under Durant, General Motors operated as a loosely knit group of companies without a unifying concept of corporate strategy. Ford's distinct expression of a root strategy to produce a standardized, low-priced car for the mass market gave his company dominance of the automotive market for over a decade. Durant's General Motors, in the words of Sloan, "had no clear-cut concept of the business."[3] The closest Durant came to defining a strategic base was in terms of providing a pattern of variety in product which was expressed in two models of the Chevrolet, the Oakland, Olds, Scripps-Booth, Sheridan, Buick, and Cadillac models. Only two of these automobiles had distinct market niches: the Buick, with relatively high quality and high volume, and the Cadillac at the top of the line. The company did not have a position in the low-price segment of the market to compete with Ford, the industry leader. In 1921 all the cars in the line were losing money except Buick and Cadillac, the only General Motors products which had distinct markets.

In 1921 a special committee under Sloan was organized to study the company's product policy. The executive committee informed this special committee that the company intended to enter the low-price auto market and challenge the dominance of Ford in this field. They requested advice on entering two cars in the low price market, one to compete with Ford and another to be slightly higher in price, and they planned to review the range of other cars with the exception of Buick and Cadillac. Sloan took the initiative as the head of the committee to seek a concept of the business rather than to confine deliberations to the concept of a product line.[4] The basis for General Motors' long-standing root strategy evolved from the product policy recommended by Sloan's special committee, which stated:[5]

  1 The corporation should produce a line of cars in each price area, from the low-

---

[3] Ibid., p. 58.
[4] Ibid., p. 64.
[5] Ibid., p. 65.

est price up to that of a strictly high-grade quantity-production car. The company would not get into the fancy-price field, with small production.

2 The price steps should not leave wide gaps in the line but they should be great enough to keep their number within reason and to assure the greatest advantage of quantity production.

3 There should be no duplication by the corporation in the price fields or steps.

This first definitive statement of root strategy distinguished General Motors from the Ford organization and the other car manufacturers. Essentially the new statement of strategy placed General Motors in all those segments of the automobile market in which the company believed it could secure sufficient volume to employ its resources profitably, from the low-price end represented by Chevrolet to the high-price quality market of Cadillac. Despite some variance in this root strategy in terms of product line duplication and competition between models, General Motors has essentially retained this concept in the automotive field.

The root strategy proposed by Sloan's committee did not become "institutionalized" for some time after its adoption. The company's abortive efforts to produce and market in their cars an air-cooled engine, called the cooper-cooled engine, detracted from the implementation of the Sloan committee's recommendations. It was not until Sloan succeeded Pierre Du Pont as president in 1923 that significant efforts were made to formulate and implement a strategic design.

The changes in the United States economy and the consequent effects on the automobile market aided Sloan in effecting the adopted root strategy. In Sloan's words,[6] "The industry had evolved from a class market, in the early days of the automobile, to a mass market dominated by Ford, to the mass-class market of the middle 1920s," which matched General Motors' strategic design. The initial product policy determined for the Chevrolet also proved to be a market advantage. The company did not try to compete head-on with Ford in the low-price field but chose to offer a car in this segment of the market with greater quality and comfort than the basic stripped-down Model T yet within striking distance of the Ford price. The rising income of the consumer dictated a preference for the "more complete" automobile, with style and value at a price. This market change eventually forced Ford to abandon the Model T. The absence of a Ford product in the low-price field for almost a year before the introduction of the Model A gave Chevrolet a market advantage which allowed it to gain a significant number of Ford's loyal customers.

In addition to its entry into the low-price field, General Motors developed its product line to fill each segment and eliminate gaps in market coverage. The Scripps-Booth and the Sheridan cars were eliminated from the company's line in 1921 and, through the ensuing years of the 1920s, mainly under Sloan's direction, General Motors evolved its product line. The Oakland, which com-

[6] Ibid., p. 150.

peted directly with the Olds, was replaced by the Pontiac, which at the time of its introduction in 1926 filled a gap in the company's market coverage. With the exception of the LaSalle car, which lasted for about a decade, the basic General Motors line of Chevrolet, Pontiac, Olds, Buick, and Cadillac has remained intact over the years since the 1920s, when they were first given specific market niches to conform to the company's conceived root strategy.

Development of Operating Strategy   General Motors' operating strategy evolved over a long time span stemming from the stated root strategy of Sloan and the loose strategic design of Durant. Vertical integration was initially derived from Durant's incorporation of the varied manufacturing units of his carriage business into the newly formed General Motors. His concept of owning the basic supply of essential automotive parts and accessories originated in his carriage business, which was essentially an assembly operation. In the early days of automobile production, this was also the case; however, General Motors was the first producer to own any significant source of parts and accessory supply.

Sloan expanded Durant's original base and made his entry into the top levels of General Motors management through the presidency of United Motors, which was a consolidation of the many companies producing parts and equipment for the car manufacturing units. The addition of Fisher Body gave General Motors particular advantages other than owning its major single supplier of automotive bodies. It provided operating economics by coordinating body and chassis assembly, and it assured the company of control over the supply of the "closed bodies" which were becoming dominant in the industry in the early 1920s. There is no doubt that vertical integration provided advantages over competitors, who eventually followed this strategy but never attained the extensive network of suppliers owned by General Motors.

The Sloan special committee determined a pricing structure which proved to be an advantageous long-standing operating strategy of the company. The committee proposed that the General Motors cars be placed at the top of each previously determined price bracket and that the product be of such quality to attract sales below that price from customers who would be willing to pay a little more for additional quality. The plan was also to attract customers to move down a notch from competitors' higher prices to take advantage of a quality car in a lower price bracket.

As contrasted with Ford, who gained dominance in the industry by producing a static model, General Motors adopted an operating strategy of continuous change and improvement in its cars. The company is credited with introducing the annual model change into the industry in 1923. Although it did not become a formal policy until much later, it provided General Motors with a distinct advantage in the evolving mass-class automobile market and set the production cycle for all automobile manufacturers, even Henry Ford, who fell into line after his Model A was abandoned.

While Ford set the pace in the industry with his innovative mass-production development, General Motors developed an operating strategy to extend basic mass-production techniques to its five product lines and their variations. Because of the Model T and its success, it was generally assumed that mass production on a large scale had to be applied to a uniform product. With the introduction of the Pontiac line in 1926, however, General Motors coordinated production of one car in the product line with another in a different segment of the market. The Pontiac was constructed with Chevrolet parts to open the way for the company's higher-priced lines to benefit from the volume economies of the lower-priced classes and to extend mass production advantages to the entire car line of the company.

Because of its introduction of annual model changes, General Motors took an early interest in the importance of styling as an operating strategy in the automobile market. It was the first in the industry to organize styling as a staff function and to coordinate its activities with engineering. While Ford and other producers stressed engineering in automotive production, General Motors took advantage of the consumer's desire for style as well as engineering quality in an automobile. The company utilized styling to keep the appearance of the individual cars in their line distinctive; thus the customer could easily recognize each car as a separate product. Through the years, General Motors developed a large styling staff and utilized its skills to gain market advantages over its competitors.

General Motors employed a network of franchised dealers to distribute its products in much the same manner as Ford and other producers. It had become common practice to distribute automobiles through distributor-wholesalers who subcontracted to dealers; but after 1920 this arrangement faded from the industry and the method of distribution became fairly uniform throughout. Some differences were found in the attention and help given to dealers by the manufacturers and in the practice of determining sales quotas and rebate allowances. General Motors had some strategic advantage through GMAC (General Motors Acceptance Corporation), which was formed as a subsidiary in 1919 to finance car sales on an installment basis. GMAC developed into one of the largest financial institutions of its kind and gave General Motors definite competitive advantages in helping its dealers to sell cars.

Development of Organizational Strategies   Although Sloan's development of a root strategy was a major contribution to the corporation, it was probably overshadowed by his contribution to the development and implementation of organizational and control strategies. When Sloan entered the top management group of the company, the basic thrust of the organization had already been determined by Durant's strategy of providing a pattern of variety in product expressed in seven different automobile lines. Sloan and his special committee refined this concept and developed practical guidelines to give substance to Durant's loose strategic design.

While significant operating strategies, many of which had been carried over from his carriage business, had been developed under Durant, little had been done to effectively organize and control the company outside of the infusion of a committee structure from the Du Ponts. Sloan's *Organization Study* was a major contribution to the development of General Motors and set forth basic principles of decentralized management which have had a significant influence on industrial organization in the United States. Ford, which had a single standardized product through the stages of its rapid growth and development, was able to operate effectively with a simple, centralized organization and control system. General Motors, however, with its root strategy of multiple car lines to satisfy each market segment and an operating strategy which developed partial vertical integration and numerous subunits. required a highly decentralized organization and a highly developed control system to manage the company. This placed strong emphasis on the organization and interpretative phases of the policymaking process and on the formulation of organizational and control strategies. The concepts set forth in the Sloan study provided the company with a strong base on which to build its decentralized organization structure.

Sloan's approach to organization was based on two principles, which he defined in his *Organization Study* as follows:[7]

1 The responsibility attached to the chief executive of each operation shall in no way be limited. Each such organization headed by its chief executive shall be complete in every necessary function and enabled to exercise its full initiative and logical development.

2 Certain central organization functions are absolutely essential to the logical development and proper control of the Corporation's activities.

Sloan's aim in developing a new organizational strategy was primarily to retain the decentralization which prevailed under Durant. He also hoped, through the establishment of clear lines of authority and coordination and interrelation between the various groups and divisions, to establish an effective management team directed toward the attainment of predetermined objectives. Furthermore, Sloan provided the guidelines for activating his organizational proposals. He enumerated the goals of his study in the following terms:[8]

1 To definitely determine the functioning of the various divisions constituting the Corporation's activities, not only in relation to one another, but in relation to the central organization.

2 To determine the status of the central organization and to coordinate the operation of that central organization with the corporation as a whole to the end that it will perform its necessary and logical place.

3 To centralize the control of all the executive functions of the Corporation in the president as its chief executive officer.

4 To limit as far as practical the number of executives reporting to the president, the object being to enable the president to better guide the broad policies of the Corporation without coming in contact with problems that may safely be entrusted to executives of less importance.

[7] Ibid., p. 53
[8] Ibid., pp. 53–54.

5 To provide means within each executive branch whereby all other executive branches are represented in an advisory way to the end that the development of each branch will be along lines constructive to the Corporation as a whole.

These statements gave substance to the loosely knit organization structure which had existed in General Motors for some time. It reinforced Sloan's belief in decentralization but provided guidelines to effect the necessary coordination between divisions and the corporation. These proposals also clearly outlined, perhaps for the first time in corporate history, the functions and responsibilities of the chief executive officer in a highly decentralized organization.

Sloan's Committee Structure   Sloan also proposed to regroup the operating divisions, to expand the staff functions in the general office, and to bring together the officers performing these functions into an advisory staff. He stressed the need to expand the financial and accounting units to ensure the control which was lacking under Durant. Sloan assigned to the Finance Committee the responsibility for determining dividend rates, salaries to top management, the raising of funds, and other major financial policies. The Finance Committee also was given the authority to pass on the major appropriations recommended by the Executive Committee and to exercise general control over the corporation's finances and accounting. The Executive Committee was to retain much the same function it had under Durant: to exercise supervision over the entire operating staff and the operations of the corporation. Each operating division had representation on the Executive Committee, which was headed by the president and was the major policymaking unit of the corporation subject only to the Finance Committee for approval of large appropriations.

Sloan utilized the committee structure to provide coordination of the various functions of the company and yet retain decentralization. He was aware that the various units and divisions had suboptimized under Durant and would likely continue to do so unless some effective means could be devised to unify their efforts in pursuing the objectives of the corporation. Sloan relied heavily on the committee structure to accomplish this purpose. In addition to the Finance and Executive Committees, which were borrowed from the Du Pont organization under Durant, he developed a number of other important interdivisional committees to effect further coordination of divisional effort. A General Purchasing Committee was organized, with membership drawn from the divisions; an Institutional Advertising Committee was formed to effect coordination in advertising; and the General Technical Committee became the highest advisory body on engineering in the company. To effect coordination of sales, a General Sales Committee was formed, and Sloan activated an Operations Committee composed of all the general officers on the Executive Committee, as well as the general managers of the principal divisions, to appraise the performance of the divisions.

The combination of interdivisional and corporate committees provided the necessary coordinating influences to ensure the effective operation of the complex structure; it also gave expression to Sloan's philosophy of decentralization with coordinated control. This organizational strategy—which was innovative and far-reaching at the time of its inception—formed the basis for General Motors' successful operations through the past five decades. Exhibit 2-1 illustrates the initial organization structure which evolved from Sloan's *Organization Study;* except for developments and elaborations, it still basically describes the operation of the company today.

General Motors' control system was directly related to its decentralized divisionalized organization structure. Sloan was acutely aware of the crises caused in the company because of the lack of control over the decentralized divisions which existed when Durant was president. When Sloan became chief executive officer, he developed and refined a corporate control system introduced into the company by Donaldson Brown, a former treasurer of the Du Pont company. Sloan utilized the control system to provide the information base needed to effect divisional coordination through his committee structure. Brown and Alfred Bradley, an associate who eventually succeeded him as chief financial officer, not only defined General Motors' control strategy and developed its financial and accounting system but also were responsible for developing many new financial concepts that are widely used today.

Control of Capital Appropriations   The crisis of 1920 was a major factor in prompting the development of a comprehensive control system in General Motors. Division managers continued to make capital expenditures until well into the economic collapse of that year. This plus the abrupt slowdown in sales created a cash shortage, and the uncontrolled purchases of raw materials and semifinished materials by division managers resulted in an inventory glut which added to the liquidity crisis. To prevent this situation in the future and effect corporate control, a well-defined capital-appropriation procedure was instituted. All projects requiring capital expenditures were submitted to an appropriations committee functioning under the Finance and Executive Committees. Each request was given uniform treatment, and funds were approved for projects on the basis of their relative value to the corporation. In time, the appropriations committee was dropped, but the capital budgeting procedure started in the early 1920s is still followed—with modifications—in the company today.

Cash Control   Prior to 1922 each division handled its own cash and had no systematic procedure for remitting funds to corporate headquarters. To alleviate this situation and prevent a recurrence of the 1920 cash shortage, the corporation set up a consolidated cash control system. This system, a new concept for large decentralized organizations, called for the establishment of some hundred banks in the United States that would receive all incoming receipts of the organization and deposit them to the credit of General Motors Corporation. All withdrawals from the accounts were to be administered by the headquarters financial staff; the divisions had no control over cash transfers from the deposit

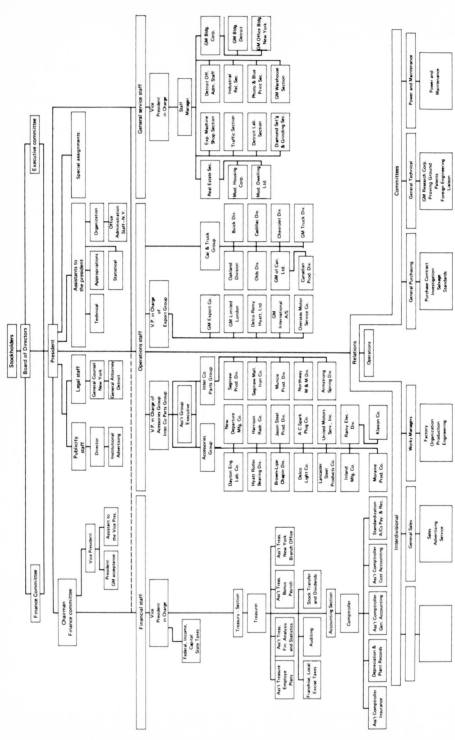

EXHIBIT 2-1
General Motors organization chart (from Sloan, p. 115).

36

accounts. This system permitted quick bank transfers and eliminated problems of deficient and excessive cash balances.[9]

Inventory Control   To solve the inventory crisis. the company set up an Inventories Committee, which exercised tight control over all purchases of raw material and semifinished goods. The Inventories Committee was eliminated as an acting unit after the crisis passed, and a new system was initiated which required divisional four-month forecasts of expected business. The division managers bought the materials, but they were restricted by their forecasts of the number of cars and trucks to be produced. The inventory control system tied in with production control, which was related to the level of production of cars and trucks. To provide information for control of these finished products, the four-month forecasts were expanded to include plan and investment, working capital, and inventory commitments as well as estimated sales, production, and earnings. These forecasts were submitted to corporate headquarters for approval on a monthly basis covering the current month and the next three months. From this beginning, the procedure was modified and elaborated to include annual divisional forecasts and developed into a comprehensive budgeting system.[10]

Control of Decentralized Divisions   While the establishment of controls over appropriations, cash inventory, and production was essential and important, these controls were not as significant or far-reaching as the strategy developed by Brown and Bradley to control and coordinate the decentralized divisions. In Sloan's words, "It was on the financial side that the last necessary key to decentralization with co-ordinated control be found. That key in principle, was the concept, if we had the means to review and judge the effectiveness of operations, we could safely leave the prosecution of those operations to the men in charge of them."[11] The principle of return on invested capital (ROI) was the base for measuring the division operations. The economic objective of the corporation was to elicit the highest average rate of return over a long period, consistent with attainable volume in the market and sound business growth. Brown utilized the system he brought with him from Du Pont to refine the concept of return on invested capital. He considered the rate of return to be a function of both profit margin and rate of turnover on invested capital. Multiplying one by the other equaled the percentage rate of return. This concept also directed attention to the various accounts which made up the margin and the turnover sides of the equation; thus, in effect, the analysis of all factors affecting the business was facilitated. This system made it possible to compare past, current, and projected results with determined standards of performance for working capital, fixed capital needs, and the detailed elements of cost.

[9] Ibid., pp. 121–123.
[10] Ibid., pp. 127–139.
[11] Ibid., p. 140.

Each division manager was required to submit monthly reports of the division's total operating results. The computed data were put on standard forms by the central finance office and were used as the basis for measuring and comparing the rate of return on investment for each division. The divisional return-on-investment reports were analyzed by top management and used as the basis for corrective action.

The utilization of the return-on-investment concept revealed to the company the importance and necessity of having an accurate and well-defined standardized accounting system. Management also became aware of the need for a well-defined objective against which to measure the return on investment. Because of the influence of changing volume in production and sales, financial results showed wide fluctuations. Brown developed a concept which related long-term return on investment to average or "standard volume" expectations over a period of years. This measure, which came to be known inside and outside General Motors as *the standard-volume concept,* gave top management a yardstick which was unaffected by short-term volume fluctuations and could be used to evaluate the extent of deviation from long-term profit objectives.

Purpose of Control Techniques   The foregoing description of financial techniques and methods developed by the management of General Motors is not in itself necessarily important to the policymaker or the student of business policy. The value of the techniques is to be found in the terms of the concepts of control they represent, their usefulness as instruments of interpretation to aid in the determination of the extent of progress being made toward the accomplishment of basic business objectives, and in highlighting operational problems and weaknesses to signal the need to initiate recovery strategies.

Reformulation: Development of Recovery Strategies   Both General Motors and Ford went through traumatic experiences and several crises before they reformulated and developed recovery strategies. Their experiences represented dramatic events which attracted considerable publicity and have been duly recorded in the annals of business history. As previously described, Ford lost its number-one position in the industry by waiting too long to begin reformulation and by failing to recycle fully through the reformulation process. The company relied on a single recovery strategy—the replacement of the Model T with the Model A—and did not effect needed changes in operating, organization, and control strategies. As a result, the company floundered and continued to lose market share. Its first complete reformulation did not occur until the immediate post-World War II period.

General Motors' First Reformulation Period   General Motors' experience in reformulation showed many similarities and sharp contrasts to Ford's. As indicated in the preceding review of the early history of General Motors, the company's first crisis occurred in 1910, when it experienced a severe cash shortage and was unable to pay labor and suppliers. Because of the lack of an adequate control system, management did not receive warning signals early enough to prevent serious difficulties due to the impending recession and the sharp drop in demand for automobiles. To save the company, Durant was forced to turn over management to bankers, who supplied the necessary financing. When Durant took control again five years later, the same difficulties and the lack of divisional controls precipitated a more serious crisis. In the early part of 1920, the company continued its postwar expansion, spending large sums of money on plant and equipment and building up inventories. The collapse of the automobile market in the latter half of that year forced Durant out of office and signaled an urgent need for a second reformulation.

Second Reformulation Period   The second reformulation period was under new leadership and was greatly influenced by Sloan's *Organizational Study*. This study went beyond the analysis of operations and recommendations for changes in organizational structure; it also provided the basis for the development of a strategic design. Unlike Ford, General Motors had never developed or articulated a distinct root strategy. Durant's concept of offering a pattern of variety of product provided little guidance to the corporate organization or the divisional operations. In contrast, Ford's concept of producing a standardized, low-priced car for the mass market was a distinct expression of a root strategy. Despite the number of cars in its product line, General Motors did not have any entry to compete with Ford, the industry leader, which had captured 60 percent of the total market. These factors, which were recognized by Sloan, in effect forced a complete reformulation and recycling of the policymaking process.

General Motors established its long-standing root strategy from the productline policy recommended by Sloan's special committee. In essence, it stated the corporate mission in terms of producing a line of cars in each price class where quantity production could be assured. To facilitate the implementation of the broad guidelines of this root strategy, management had to develop significant operating strategies. Innovations in styling and design, the initiation of annual model changes, the development of production synergy, and a unique pricing structure were some of the major operating strategies effected to build the company's share of each market segment.

Unifying Force of Sloan's Policies   The major unifying force of the reformulation under Sloan, however, was found in the development of the organizational design and the supporting control strategies which were described in some detail in the immediately preceding pages. Sloan's philosophy of decentralization with coordinated control formed the basis for General Motors' successful operations. His concept of coordinating committees to unify the divisional structure and the use of highly refined financial measures provided the necessary control to enable the policymaking group to manage the highly decentralized organization as a single corporate entity directed toward a set of common goals.

The reformulation under Sloan was effected over a period of years, but it was a complete reformulation, as contrasted with Ford's partial recycling. The strategic design established under Sloan has proved to be a lasting one, which has been improved over time rather than drastically changed. Unlike Ford, General Motors has not gone through a complete cycle of reformulation since the early 1920s. The closest the company has come to a significant reformulation of strategy since that date is in the current period. Petroleum shortages, ecological considerations, market erosion due to imports, and other environmental pressures and changes have forced a reformulation in General Motors and the entire automotive industry.

The history and description of the operations and policymaking processes of the two leaders in the automotive field, General Motors and Ford, were presented in this chapter to provide some basic understanding of the concept of strategic planning and its practical application. The description of the companies' operations was restricted to automobiles, their dominant product and the major concern of their managements. Automobiles are readily identifiable, and the strategic options open to management in the production and marketing of the product are relatively limited, thus permitting the student or manager to concentrate on the policymaking process rather than a multiplicity of products and decision alternatives. The more complex problems of strategic planning involving multiproduct lines and multiple strategic options will be discussed in chapters which follow.

SUMMARY AND GENERAL COMMENTS

Ford Motor Company

The development of strategic design in the Ford Motor Company and General Motors provides a history of strategic decisions of two major industrial organizations. The Ford case illustrates the distinct advantages of establishing a clear statement of purpose and building a strategic design to attain a leadership position in an emerging industry. Ford's root strategy of manufacturing and selling a low-priced quality economy car, aimed at the mass market, captured a market share of 50 to 58%. The company's operating strategy was easily recognizable. The objective of the company to serve the mass market required producing a standarized automobile of one basic model. This necessitated developing mass-production techniques and methods to assure the lowest manufacturing cost possible consistent with a durable car of quality.

Marketing efforts had to be directed to consumers who needed reliable transportation at low cost. This prompted Ford to build a national franchised dealer organization with emphasis in the rural areas to serve the farm population. The organization structure was flat and simple, designed to serve a single product line. The control structure followed the organization and was simple rather than complex. However, it apparently did not provide the signals needed to prompt reformulation when market shifts affected the sales of Ford's basic Model T. Reformulation and the change to new models came late and cost Ford its dominant market share.

General Motors

In contrast to Ford, General Motors was a corporate giant in its early stages of development under Will Durant. Its root strategy to serve all phases of the automotive market dictated its size and complexity. After serious problems under Durant, the company found a new leadership in Alfred Sloan. He developed a strategic design based on Durant's root strategy with the restrictions that the company would serve all *viable* automotive markets. If a car did not have a sales volume sufficient to produce a target return on investment, it was dropped from the line.

Marketing and production efforts were decentralized by product divisions. Market efforts were centered in franchised dealerships on a model basis. Some centralization of production was developed with the Fisher Body Shop and through staff assistance and direction emanating from Detroit.

Because of the numerous models and divisions which resulted from horizontal and vertical integration, the organization required decentralization. The complexity of managing a multimodel multidivisioned organization required a strong central staff and a highly developed control system. General Motors refined the ROI reporting system to aid in the management of its decentralized operations.

SELECTED REFERENCES

Ford Motor Company

Chandler, A. D.: *Giant Enterprise, Ford, G. M. and the Automobile Industry* (New York: Harcourt, Brace & World, 1964).

Ford, Henry: *My Life and Times* (Garden City, N. Y. : Doubleday, Page 1923).

———, with Samuel Crouther: *Today and Tomorrow* (Garden City, N. Y.: Doubleday, Page, 1926).

Forbes, Bertie Charles, and O. D. Foster: *Automotive Giants of America: Men Who Are Making Our Motor Industry* (New York: B. C. Forbes, 1926).

Griffin, Clare Elmer: *The Life History of Automobiles* (Ann Arbor, Mich.: University of Michigan, School of Business Administration, Bureau of Business Research, 1926).

Hollander, Stanley C., and Gary A. Marple: *Henry Ford: Inventor of the Supermarket?* (East Lansing: Bureau of Business and Economic Research, Graduate School of Business Administration, Michigan State University, 1960).

Jardin, Anne: *The First Henry Ford: A Study in Personality and Business Leadership* (Cambridge, Mass.: M.I.T., 1970).

McManus, Theodore F., and Norman Beasley: *Men, Money, and Motors: The Drama of the Automobile* (New York: Harper, 1929).

Norwood, Edwin P.: *Ford Men and Methods* (New York: Doubleday, Doran, 1931).

Pound, Arthur: *The Turning Wheel: the Story of General Motors through Twenty-five Years, 1908–1933* (Garden City, N.Y.: Doubleday, Doran, 1934).

Sward, Keith: *The Legend of Henry Ford* (New York: Rinehart, 1948).

General Motors

Boyd, T. A.: *Professional Amateur: The Biography of Charles F. Kettering* (New York: Dutton, 1957).

Chandler, A. D.: *Giant Enterprise, Ford. G. M., and the Automobile Industry* (New York: Harcourt, Brace & World, 1964).

————: *Strategy and Structure* (Cambridge, Mass.: M.I.T., 1962).

Forbes, Bertie Charles, and O. D. Foster: *Automotive Giants of America: Men Who Are Making Our Motor Industry* (New York: B. C. Forbes, 1926).

Griffin, Clare Elmer: *The Life History of Automobiles* (Ann Arbor, Mich.: University of Michigan, School of Business Administration, Bureau of Business Research, 1926).

McManus, Theodore F., and Norman Beasley: *Men, Money, and Motors. The Drama of the Automobile* (New York: Harper, 1929).

Pound, Arthur: *The Turning Wheel: The Story of General Motors through Twenty-five Years, 1908–1933* (Garden City, N.Y.: Doubleday, Doran, 1934).

Sloan, Alfred P., Jr.: *My Years with General Motors* (New York: Doubleday, 1963).

Some Notes on the Case Method

THE CASE METHOD OF TEACHING

The case method of teaching has long been used in schools of business and management. It has had its greatest use in the teaching of courses in business policy or strategic planning where the student is introduced to the complexities of the total management function. Most students taking a course in business policy have used cases in other disciplines. However, frequently they have had only minimum exposure to the case method, little or no formal preparation to the concept of case teaching, and no formal preparation for classroom discussions. These notes are intended to aid the student in the study and use of the cases which follow in this book. The cases all represent actual business situations which occurred at a point in time in the history of a particular organization or business entity. The actual names of the companies are used in many of the cases, and in others the case has been disguised at the request of the company. In the latter instances, names, sometimes locations, and minor details are disguised, but the major and general facts which describe the position of the company, its competitive position, its industry, and its problems and opportunities remain valid.

The cases presented in this volume have been selected to provide the student with a complete profile of the process of strategic planning and policy formulation. The cases are sequentially arranged to ease the student into the role of the general manager and the complexities of directing and guiding the whole organization. The multifaceted task of the strategic planner and of policymaking are developed and illustrated in cases that cover varied organizations—small, medium, and large businesses which operate in different industries representing an important cross section of United States and international firms.

The Concept of the Case Method

In business and other purposeful organizations the concept of learning by doing—on-the-job training—has long been practiced and is considered an integral and important part of management development. The case method is based on this concept of learning by doing, by participating in the educational process, not just acting as a receiver of information from the instructor, but also taking an active part in case discussions. We cannot assume that by the simple process of "telling" we can pass on knowledge. Conceptual understanding and the ability to analyze complex situations is not readily comprehended. It requires a more penetrating depth of understanding on the part of the student which is not transmitted by the instructor. Students must be active participants in the process, they must learn to think and act, to diagnose problems, to discern opportunities, and to formulate alternative courses of action. The case method is designed to provide this opportunity. It is a laboratory for decision making where students can test and develop their analytical abilities and acquire an understanding of the viewpoint of policymakers and general managers.

Each case presents a unique situation, it must be viewed and approached as a new challenge requiring the force of all of the student's analytical skills and perception to prepare and articulate judgments pertinent to the case situation. Students are not forewarned of what kinds of problems to expect in each case situation, just as the executive or manager cannot foresee with any degree of accuracy the dimensions of the problems likely to be encountered in the future. All organizations must deal with the future and make decisions under uncertainty without all of the facts or data that would facilitate the decision-making process. Ambiguity and uncertainty plague policymakers; they must learn to cope with these factors if their organizations are to survive and prosper. Since cases are the actual description of organizational situations, they present the student with the same challenges and perplexing problems faced by executives and general managers.

It must be remembered that in the use of policy cases the objective to impart knowledge, to instill the student with distinct facts, is less important than the development of analytical skills, attitudes, a point of view, and the ability to stretch the mind to grasp the significance of the general manager's role in relation to the organization and its external environment. The cases must be approached with the mind-set of the generalist, not the specialist. This frequently causes problems for some students and managers. It is not always easy to leave the comforts of single-problem analysis and the search for specific identifiable solutions and to wade into the morass of complex, multifaceted problems of policy cases which are not likely to lend themselves to incontestable right answers or single solutions. In case discussions the generalist viewpoint and the viewpoint of the specialist are very likely to come in conflict. Participants in the case discussions soon realize that the all-encompassing viewpoint which the general manager must assume is not any less penetrating or shallow than the in-depth, narrow view of the specialist, but is far more appropriate for formulating strategic plans for the organization as a whole.

Development of an analytical skill is essential for any manager. The analytical skills required for general managers may be difficult for those steeped in functional specialties to attain. In the analysis of policy cases, as in the analysis of business and other organizational situations, the student or manager has to approach problems and challenges without complete information. Participants in case analysis and decision making may become disappointed and frustrated because of the lack of data they consider pertinent to seeking alternative solutions and answers to the problems and questions raised in the cases. However, in most instances there are sufficient data to make an analysis and recommendations consistent with the purpose of the case assignment. Like the lack of a single correct solution to case problems, the lack of complete data, although not purposefully designed, is a reflection of "real world" situations, where general managers must live and make decisions.

Strategic planners and policymakers are never likely to have all the data they would like in a given situation to make judgments and decisions with certainty. The amount of information to support decision making is a function of availability, time, and money. Students and managers should learn through policy case discussions that risk taking and problem solving which will lead to action must take priority over the endless search for complete information to facilitate easy solutions. Uncertainty is a fact of life for the general manager, and he or she must develop an attitude and viewpoint to cope with this nagging factor which is present in all complex problem situations involving future commitments. Learning through the case method what constitutes the viewpoint and attitudes of professionals, general managers, is as important and integral a part of teaching policy by the case method as is the imparting of the knowledge of the strategic planning process.

There are other frustrations which may become evident in policy case discussions before the concept of the case method is understood by the participants. The number of issues contained in most policy cases, the listing of problems and opportunities, and the enumeration of possible solutions may frequently seem endless. The reiteration of case facts may at times seem boring and tiring to participants in case discussions. If they recognize, however, that each case represents an actual company situation which demanded at a point in time an analysis and decision on the part of management, they will recognize that each case presents a different challenge and there are practical alternative solutions which can be sought and evaluated in terms of each specific situation.

A participant in a policy course may ask "Why such an array of cases? Why a brewery, a clothing manufacturer, a petroleum company, an electronics firm?

Why small companies, medium-sized companies, and large companies?" Because all of the case situations require the art of analysis, problem identification, the development of alternative courses of action, and most importantly a conceptual understanding of strategic planning and policy formulation. Through the order of analysis of different challenging case situations, a commonality becomes evident that forms the basis for generalizations which can be applied with judgment to all organizational or business situations. Through this process the student of policy should develop an understanding of the concept of strategic planning and the policymaking process. This constitutes the intellectual basis for the study of this discipline and is a basic objective of policy case analysis and discussion.

HOW TO APPROACH CASE ANALYSIS

Developing a Knowledge of the Case Facts

In approaching a case the student must be prepared to spend sufficient time to understand all of the case facts and to analyze the firm or organization in terms of its skills and resources and position relative to its environment. The student should begin by reading each case thoroughly and becoming acquainted with all of the data in the case. To ensure that all of the pertinent information is captured, it is suggested that each case be read three times: The first reading should be for "familiarization"; in the second reading students should make notes on the important data and information contained in the case; and in the final reading students should make a thorough analysis of the case situation and direct their attention to the development of key discussion questions. In this reading students are in a position to skim certain sections of the case and move back and forth between specific areas which they have decided were most significant and reinforcing to their analysis. A series of guideline questions are contained in Chapter 5 and should prove helpful in conducting a case analysis.

Assuming a Point of View

Students analyzing policy cases must assume the viewpoint of the chief executive or general manager. In this role they are not likely to find a ready answer or solution to the problems presented in the cases. Students will bring to the study of policy cases their knowledge and skills acquired in the separate disciplines and functional areas. But in the comprehensive policy cases, they will be required to expand their analytical abilities to reach out to assume the chief executive's or general manager's role, just as practitioners are asked in policy case discussions to broaden the dimensions of their understanding beyond their functional specialties. The analysis of policy cases requires persistence on the part of participants in the case discussion to ferret out the germane—to isolate central problems from the myriad of data which describes the total organizational situation. They must constantly be alert to the totality of the firm or organization and recognize that it is a total entity comprising a system in itself.

Determining Major Problems and Key Issues

In the thorough review of the case facts the student should be constantly alert to discern the major problems and opportunities facing the organization. The relevant must be separated from the irrelevant, and key issues must be refir :d from the subissues. In most cases the major questions and problems are not likely to be explicitly stated. The cases are designed to objectively describe the situation of the firm or organization at a point in time and provide sufficient data to support a thorough analysis. This analytical searching, probing part of case analysis is the most important task of a case assignment just as it is of major importance in the executive role. Once the key problem or opportunities are clearly defined, the solution or action plan will follow. Most students and many executives tend to approach case situations or actual business problems by initially seeking a solution rather than defining the key issues and major problem areas. In the initial steps of case analysis the solution should be subordinated to problem analysis and the refinement of the key issues involved in the case situation.

Assessing the Firm's Competitive Position

In addition to appraising skills and resources in the analysis of business policy cases the student should form some judgments about the firm's competitive position. Where does it stand in terms of its life cycle? Is it in a growth stage? A defensive stage? Or a decline stage? This kind of analysis will set the base for judging competitive potential. Chapter 3 can be referred to for greater depth of analysis of companies' life cycles.

The industry or industries where the firm competes should be analyzed to ascertain the competitive environment before judgments can be made about market positions and the challenges and opportunities facing the company. A major consideration in any case analysis is the determination of the firm's position in relation to its industry environment. An analysis of the life cycle of the industry will aid in determining and judging whether or not it is growing, is in a stage of maturity, or is in a decline stage. For a more detailed description of industry analysis see Chapter 3.

Appraising Competitors' Positions

The industry analysis will lead to an appraisal of major competitors. What are their strengths and weaknesses? Where do they fit in the industry environment in relation to the company being analyzed? Are they dominant forces—market leaders—with superior products and resources? Do they have any apparent weaknesses which could be exploited? Does the description of their competitive behavior indicate any market signals, any signs which would provide clues to future strategic action? At this juncture the student will have made some judgments about the firm's market share, competitive behavior, product-line strengths and weaknesses, and corporate culture and management style. This kind of analysis combined with the industry appraisal will provide the student with sufficient information to make some determinations about the course of action to recommend for the firm.

The relationship of market share to profitability, the positioning of companies within industries, and the assessment of the firm's potential in relation to competitors is described in some detail in Chapter 6.

The foregoing suggested analytical procedure may not be possible to complete for all of the cases studied because of lack of sufficient information and data. This is also frequently true for managers in day-to-day business situations. They are often forced to make considered judgments about their market share, industry position, and competitors' market plans and prospects. Students will also need to make these kinds of judgments when complete information is lacking in the case.

Using Functional Analysis to Determine Specific Strengths and Weaknesses

In determining the company's competitive position, each functional area should be analyzed to determine specific strengths or weaknesses. In this process the students should keep uppermost in their minds the interrelatedness of functional area problems and the concept of functional dynamics—the force and impact that a change in one function has on all functions of the firm. These points for analysis are explained in greater detail in Chapters 1 and 5. Chapter 5 also contains a list of key questions relating to each functional area which should be considered in developing a profile of the firm's competitive strengths and weaknesses. Problem areas should be recognized and defined in terms of "root causes." They should be approached as symptoms of deeper underlying causes which can be traced to the strategic design of the organization. The interdependence of the strategic planning and policymaking process must be understood for the student to develop an appreciation of the organization as a single integrated system. Exhibit 5-1 can be utilized as an aid in identifying major organizational problems and in developing an understanding of the interrelatedness of the strategic planning and policymaking process.

In analyzing a business policy case the student should test for consistency of the firm's operating strategic planning process. The most important test should determine how consistent the operating strategy is with the basic economic and business objectives, the major forces which determine the root strategy and form the basis for the development of a strategic design. Chapter 6 describes and provides a basis for analysis of these significant measures.

Developing a Plan of Action

When students have familiarized themselves with all elements of the case and feel satisfied with their analysis of the major problems and opportunities that the company faces, they should be able to develop a plan of action. The plan may call for changes in any phase or in all phases of the strategic planning or policymaking process. Some cases may require a complete reformulation extending from the root strategy. Some case assignments may call for a detailed plan which would include not only a well-developed strategic design but also functional plans for each area such as production, marketing, finance, and personnel.

The student may also develop alternate plans of action on a "what-if" basis which extend beyond the case facts. The case situation may suggest a need for contingency plans to provide a backup to the primary plan of action based on assumptions about the projection of future events extending beyond the final date of the case. As previously stated, students should remember in cases, as in the on-going-business situation, there is no one correct solution, only a number of feasible alternatives which must be analyzed, evaluated, and acted upon. Commitments involve the future, and the "correct solution" chosen today may develop the problems of tomorrow.

CASE DISCUSSION

The above suggestions are appropriate for the preparation of written assignments and also apply for general class discussions. Class discussion of cases is a vital and necessary part of any policy course. As previously stated, it is here that the students "test" their ideas and concepts and evaluate their analyses and action plans. Thorough preparation on the part of each student is necessary to ensure fruitful classroom discussions. Students should look upon each case as a new challenge where they can utilize the skills acquired in other disciplines while they are engaged in learning a new skill. The success of their preparation for management through the educational process can be assessed in their analysis and discussion of business policy cases.

Students should come to the class with a number of key questions that will generate discussion and provide insights into areas that will expand their knowledge of the case situation. The key questions developed by the students or supplied by the instructor should represent the distillation of the case facts and the results of thorough analysis. The general discussion of the key issues and questions will give rise to new issues and questions generated by the pooling of the expertise and conclusions reached by a number of people working on a single case situation. To find the best possible solution to any case problem requires asking and discussing the right key questions which should emanate from the distillation process which results from general case discussions. The stimulus of the expressed thoughts of various group members will provoke and generate new thoughts, issues, and ideas. Many of these will be quickly dismissed by the force of group opinion, and others will incite intense discussion. The interaction of the group should invoke new insights and bring into focus new concepts and proposed solutions that withstand the pressure of general criticism of the group and forge some common opinions about the case situation. It must be remembered that each solution that is discussed and presented is but one of many possible solutions. General agreement on a single "class" solution is not sought, nor is likely to be attained. Reasonable alternative solutions that reflect the results of thorough preparation and well-reasoned analysis accomplish the objective of case discussions.

CASES ON BUSINESS POLICY FOR PART ONE

The cases in Part One stress the role of chief executives and their policymaking groups as the architects of their companies' strategic designs. All the cases in this section emphasize the necessity for general management to be constantly aware of the interrelationship of the functions of the firm and the need to coordinate these functions to attain preconceived objectives. Understanding the leadership role is also of paramount importance in gaining a knowledge and feel of policymaking and strategic planning. The role of the chief executive officer and the general management group must be understood in another context: they provide the main sources for inspiration in the organization, and the final decisions are made at this level. The ultimate authority—the final yes or no—rests with the chief executive officer.

The student should also be alerted to the need to conceptualize the opportunities and problems of the firm and to make judgments in their case analyses in terms of enterprise objectives, not functional subobjectives. Recognition of these basic factors is a necessary and preliminary step in understanding the description and analysis of the strategic planning process in the text and cases which follow.

ABC Construction

Bill Duncan, president and chief executive officer of ABC Construction stated:

Our organization is not large by most standards; however, except for the real big ones in our area, we aren't small. We take some fair-sized jobs in our home territory of Cleveland and the surrounding area, and we also have offices in Columbus and Dayton. Most of our business is right here in the Cleveland region, but we are in the process of developing Columbus and Dayton. The problem we really have is the lack of competent people to put in these offices. I try to get down to the branches as much as I can and give them a push. Charlie (Charles Jennings, vice president of operations) spends a little time visiting; but, on the whole, I guess we get busy in Cleveland and tend to neglect the branches. I just don't have the time to look after everything. We are outgrowing the reach of our executive group.

The ABC organization (see Exhibit 1) was not complex since the company was small and was composed mainly of engineers. The major part of ABC's business was in commercial construction projects with some work on civil projects for the county and townships within the Cleveland area and also in their branch areas of Columbus and Dayton. Total billings for the company were approximately $60 million and had increased on the average of $3 million each year for a 10-year period. Bill Duncan was well aware that a good part of the increase was due to inflation, which had been particularly acute in the building industry. The cost of labor and materials had gone up well over 12 to 15 percent for several years.

In an attempt to ascertain the bottlenecks in his organization and in hopes of relieving the stress on himself and the executive group, Bill Duncan engaged a management consulting firm to survey his organization. The consulting firm

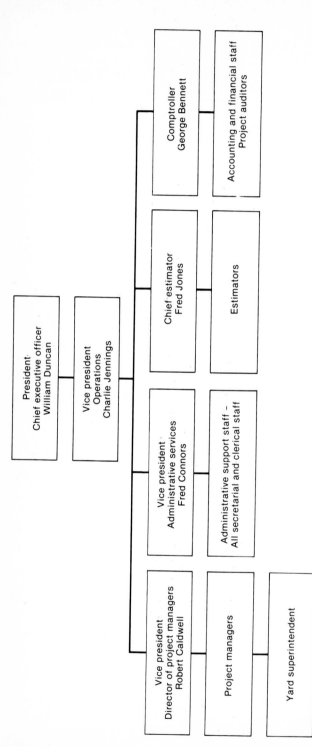

EXHIBIT 1
Organization chart as conceived by the president.

spent one week in ABC examining the nature of their business, inspecting their equipment, and appraising their yard operations. They also visited several of ABC's key accounts to ascertain the general quality of the company's work and their record of meeting completion schedules. The consulting firm found that with the exception of some work done in the branches, ABC received high marks from the customers surveyed.

The consultants concluded that the most significant problems were to be found in the organization and within the executive group. They hoped to find an answer to Bill Duncan's complaint about the lack of competent people and the great burden and long hours he and his executive group were experiencing trying to keep pace with the business. The first task they assumed in this vein was to gain an understanding of the company's XYZ process. This method of analyzing and organizing jobs was conceived by Bill Duncan. He got the idea for XYZ from a meeting of construction executives he had attended. Under the XYZ process, the job up for bidding was reviewed or scanned for a fit with ABC's skills and resources. This was done by Bill Duncan and/or Charlie Jennings, vice president of operations, and Fred Connors, the vice president of administrative services. If the job fit the ABC skills, the completion deadline and the fit into the overall ABC schedule was examined. This procedure was done rapidly, usually on Friday afternoon, unless the project was exceptionally large and important; then the procedure was started about as soon as it was received in the office. Many projects were completed in the X stage before any formal bid request was received because Bill, Charlie, or one of the other executives had frequent contacts with the client and may have been selling ABC to assure a favorable reception to a bid on a desired project.

The Y stage involved formal action by the estimators, who consulted very closely with Bill Duncan and Charlie Jennings on all major projects. Minor projects were estimated rapidly with only an occasional brief review by Bill and Charlie. Many of the engineers in the organization were of the opinion that estimating was the most important function performed since it could make or break a construction job. When the estimators completed their appraisal and reduced it to numbers, it was reviewed by Bill Duncan, usually with Charlie Jennings, in a conference with the estimators. If it was a particularly large project, several other key executives were included in the review.

When the job was awarded to ABC, a project manager was appointed. The project manager then chose a working team and had several conferences with the estimators to develop a plan that would assure meeting the specifications and deadline date for the project. Bill Duncan managed to attend at least one or two of all of the planning sessions. If it was a big project, he made an effort to be at all of the planning meetings. The yard superintendent or representative was included in all the project planning sessions to assure that ABC's equipment and other necessary equipment for the project would be available when needed. The project engineer then developed a PERT (program evaluation and review technique) chart, which outlined in detail each step in the project with alternative action to be taken as a result of unforeseen delays in material delivery, labor problems, late completion of particular segments, or work stoppages due to weather and conditions. The PERT chart developed a critical path which guided all the actions of the project manager in dealing with the subcontractors who were responsible for constructing the various external and internal parts of the building. After developing the PERT chart, the project manager let the specific jobs out for bidding to subcontractors. All the bids were reviewed with the project team and the estimators for the project. Any questions or problems encountered in the process of awarding the subcontracts were brought to Bill Duncan and/or Charlie Jennings.

Built into the XYZ process were bonuses based on the dollar amount of the project and the results produced by each group in the process. The estimators received a bonus based on the accuracy of their cost estimate for the project. The project managers received a bonus based on the cost of the project and the completion date of the project.

The consultants found the XYZ to be a good planning and working procedure for the company. They were not too sure how well it was implemented and could not account for the long hours and excessive work load of Bill Duncan. With this in mind, they decided to interview each of the engineers and executives in the Cleveland office to determine where the bottleneck was in the organization. The first one interviewed was Charlie Jennings, vice president of operations. After several leading questions by the consultants and repeated assurances of confidentiality, Charlie Jennings began to talk freely:

What is the major problem we have? I'd say it's one of communications. You know, I am the number-two guy in this organization, but you would be surprised how little Bill Duncan has to say to me. Sure he is quick to point out mistakes and to be critical, then he doesn't mind talking. But he sure isn't much for friendly chit chat, or really letting you know what's going on unless it is absolutely necessary. "Necessary" is always a reflection of his viewpoint. Communications are probably bad because we don't have a definitive organization chart. I think that Bill has a copy in his desk based on the way he thinks it works, but I don't believe anybody else thinks that way. We definitely need a more formal organization; we need to outline relationships so we can get communications down from the top and up from the bottom and most importantly laterally. Sure, we have a lot of meetings and a great number of discussions, but this doesn't help too much because Bill seems to do all of the talking at the executive committee sessions. When I get in that meeting room, it seems that all I do is listen to Bill. He is telling us what to do and how to do it. He reads all of the correspondence and interoffice memos that come in, and he will mark them with his initials. He may put on the memos, very good, fine idea, etc., but not much more. He also demands to receive a carbon of all letters that are sent out by anyone in the executive group.

You asked about our bonus and incentive system. I think it works very well. No, I don't think I would leave the job for more money; it would have to be something more than that. There has to be some kind of a plus to get me out of here. This organization, despite all things that Bill seems to do on his own, has a certain kind of integrity. It's really built in. It is a good company, it has a good reputation. But there still is a distinct need for good communications. There is just not enough of that in the organization. Our XYZ plan is OK. It seems to work very well. Our estimators and our project managers seem to get along well. They have to do a great deal on their own and still have to put up with Bill's stern hand coming down on them all too often. He works too long and too hard. You ask where the bottleneck is? When I stop to think about it, it may be Bill Duncan himself. He should be in the field more. He should pay more attention to what his executive committee says. We have to develop growth within the organization. We can't continue to have a one-man show any longer. There is a need for smooth growth to develop the organization for the future.

The next executive interviewed by the consulting group was Bob Caldwell, the vice president in charge of project managers. Prior to talking to the consultants, Bob had a conversation with Charlie Jennings and was convinced that the consulting group could help the organization, so he thought it was in his best interest to give as much information as he possibly could.

You asked what some of our major problems or difficulties are as I see them. First of all, I think that somehow or another, Bill has got to get into his mind the field should come first and the office detail should come second. Another factor that we must look into is that of the training. We definitely need a change. All of the personnel, particularly those in the branch offices, need more field experience, and they need someone to guide them and give them some of that experience. Bill tries to do it, but he certainly doesn't have enough time. He is a one-man show, and this company is going to go just as far as he wants it to go and it is going just where he is going to take it. He runs everything. You asked what the bottleneck is. I think it is Bill Duncan himself. Let me give you some examples. Our personnel selection is really all made by Bill. Sure he has some consultation with us and the executive committee, but he has the consultation with his mind made up. You get so after a while that you sort of ignore these meetings or conferences with Bill. You just go on. It is sort of playing games. Bill's meetings are all his. In our executive committee he tells us. He doesn't bother to listen.

Another example is that of Roy Swanson. Swanson was hired by Bill; he's one of Bill's wife's nephews. Checking up on this, we found that Bill made Roy Swanson a promise. He said that he would keep him in the organization some way or another. He sent him down to our Dayton office, and I think that has been a little bit of the problem in the Dayton office. Swanson really doesn't have the kind of experience or knowledge to be a head of an office and to go out into the field to seek contracts and to see that they are completed on time.

Bill has to have some kind of an outlet for his energies. If there is nothing going on he is going to go around and seek out problems. He has to keep busy; he can't stop long enough to really take a good, hard look at what the job of a CEO of a pretty good size construction company should be. He should be looking forward. We need to grow. We must grow and expand just to keep our key personnel. Just issuing a few shares of stock here and there and giving us a pretty decent bonus isn't going to do it. The men are all professionally trained. They need responsibility. They need something to aspire to on the job.

I think the branch offices we have recently established offers this kind of an opportunity. As a matter of fact, I would have liked to have gone to the Columbus office myself. I would have liked to run that office for a while to sort of have the feeling that I took something from the ground up and got it into business and developed the business in that area for the company. Actually, Fred Jones was the logical one to have gone to Columbus, but Bill was afraid to let him go.

The indication is that the young man who is in that office now may be good, but he is far too inexperienced. Sure, we run down there once in a while; and when Bill does, he just criticizes everything that has gone on for the last month or so since he has been in the office, and this really doesn't help the young man to grow any. The branch offices, I thought, would give Bill an opportunity to let go of some of the petty details that he consistently has to get into when he is here in the main office. But so far it hasn't worked out that way. Maybe sooner or later he will see the light and make an effort to develop the whole company. He is a very difficult man to change, and I doubt that he can change. Bill has to keep his hands on everything in the organization. Our growth is really restricted to what he can do, or what he can handle, or for that matter what he thinks he can handle. He will not delegate. That's not his style. Bill is very bright and is certainly a hard worker, and I have to admit that he is always two steps ahead of all the rest of us. He has ideas, and I think he is an exceptional engineer. The XYZ system that he initiated has worked very well. And in its time, it had a certain degree of originality attached to it. But right now I don't think there is anybody of any size at all that doesn't use some kind of a system that is very similar to the XYZ. We need something new. Bill is capable of conceptualizing; he has the ability. If he would only take the time to get rid of the petty details, get himself together with the organization, and listen to some of the people on the executive committee, and let the organization have some degree of independence, then I think we could grow. But I really have my doubts about this happening, at least not anytime soon.

The next executive interviewed by the consultants was Fred Jones, the chief estimator. It was generally understood that Fred was one of the best estimators in the Cleveland area. While most of the estimators technically reported to him, because of the confusion created by Bill Duncan, they often went directly to Duncan when they had specific kinds of problems. Fred was aware of this but didn't seem to get too excited about Bill's interference because he knew that Bill had a good opinion of his work. Fred said:

You ask, what kinds of problems and difficulties we have been having. Well, our estimators are all pretty good, and under the XYZ system, we have to work pretty closely with the project managers and the yard people before we can get anything really down on paper. We have had some problems. For example, the Reynolds shopping center was a good indication of what can frequently happen. We had made our estimations and had gotten together with the project manager. When Bill Duncan came back to town, he went over the figures very thoroughly and called a meeting of all of us, that is, the estimators and the project managers, and he berated us for making some mistakes. He went over each one of them and pinned them down to me. While they were of some significance, and I admit that we hadn't taken into consideration some difficult engineering problems that were likely to be encountered, I certainly didn't like being berated in the conference with the rest of the executives. On one occasion over in the Columbus area, he stated that we failed to prepare a bid for a pretty good sized project there. Actually, this wasn't the case at all. The individuals had already made up their minds that they were going to go with another contractor and they had put out the bids just as a perfunctory exercise, knowing that they would have to have a certain number of bids before they could accept the final. When this was explained to Bill, he apologized for his remarks. But he frequently jumps to conclusions. This is bad for morale. He also doesn't defend the project managers in the field when they are criticized by some of the customers for a particular petty kind of situation.

Our executive committee, I guess, is OK. It is one way of getting some communication. We certainly need that in this organization. But unfortunately Bill Duncan seems to be in charge of everything. He has to have his hands on everything and he pretty much runs the executive committee; we don't get a great deal of exchange of information. He has to keep busy all the time. I think he has a serious potential problem. You asked what I think about the organization and the jobs other than the things I'm griping about now. Well, it is a pretty good organization. I would say it is a good to fine organization. We have a good reputation; we have some good young people. They want to do something; they need some incentives in terms of responsibility, in terms of being able to do things on their own without interference. Sure, the pay, the compensation is good. Bill treats everybody well in this regard. In fact, I would say exceptionally well. I have no complaint here. You asked what the bottleneck is. I think it is probably Duncan himself. He wants to do too much. He controls everything here in one way or another. Sure it is a good place to work but sometimes you need something more than compensation and security. You need some kind of a challenge.

In an effort to get the opinions of some of the group closer to the work scene, two of the younger managers were interviewed by the consultants. John Presser explained that he was mainly an estimator but he also handled some projects. He reported to Fred Jones as an estimator and to Bob Caldwell as a project manager. Presser contended:

I find it somewhat confusing to be whipsawed between two bosses. I really think that all estimators and project managers should report to Charlie Jennings, vice president of operations. This would provide better coordination. The way Bill Duncan works, I don't know why we need a second tier of management.

ABC pays well, but that is not my major concern. I am mainly interested in gaining experience for the future, and I think I am getting some very valuable experience in this organization. Bill Duncan is an exceptional engineer and construction man. When he takes the time to explain some tough technical problems, you really learn something. But unfortunately, he doesn't spend much time in the field. He seems to be in the headquarters office all the time.

The next individual interviewed by the consultant was Art Murdock, an estimator who had been with the organization almost from its inception. He had come from one of the major contracting firms in the Cleveland area. He had been a friend of Bob Caldwell, and Bob had talked him into coming with him when the firm got under way.

What kind of problems do we have in the organization? What do I think could be done to improve it? It is not really all that bad an organization. I've been fairly well satisfied here. Maybe the estimator doesn't have it as good as the project manager. I have certainly noticed that. The project manager has a great deal more freedom and a better deal than the estimators. I think estimators are hemmed in. We are always working with the figures and the data. We are out there before we ever get a bid, and then if we don't get the bid, we get most of the criticism. If it is an important project and we lose it, Bill Duncan will come down on you like a ton of bricks. Despite all of this, it's not a bad organization to work for. The compensation is good, and the incentives are good. If I left ABC, it would have to be for more money and less work. We all put in long hours here. I guess it is because Bill Duncan does.

George Bennett, the comptroller, handled all the financial and accounting records through his office. Two auditors who worked on projects reported to him and provided financial data for the projects. On specific projects they were required to report all financial data to the project managers. In explaining the functions of his operation, Bennett stated:

No doubt we need a better system in this office. We are a bit antiquated in terms of the modern computerized systems we see today. Our payroll for example is still all done by hand and a simple check printer. Bill Duncan insists on signing all checks over $50 except when he is out of town. Then he leaves specific instructions. My two assistants could do these functions with ease. I believe my office also spends too much time on cost reports. I think they all go to Bill Duncan and end up on his desk. I don't believe anyone else looks at them.

We could make a lot of improvements here, but it's hard to get Bill to go along with them. Payroll accounting as well as other financial data should be put on the computer. Our computer time has been monopolized by the estimators and project managers.

I must state that despite some problems, this is still a good organization. We have a good reputation in the construction business in this area. The company pays very well, and we are rewarded with bonuses when the company does well. Bill Duncan is a hard man to work for sometimes. He is a tough taskmaster; but he is fair and he is a very hard worker and expects you to work as hard as he does.

Before discussing their findings with Bill Duncan, the consultants talked with Alice Ramsey, Duncan's secretary. When asked about her views of the organization, she stated:

I think we have a bad morale problem here. I know because I am the one who takes the notes at the executive committee meetings. Bill Duncan frequently berates the other executives in the meetings about minor errors they have made on specific jobs. They certainly don't like this, and they frequently express their displeasure to me. Of course, I don't put any of this in the transcript of the meetings. Bill is too quick to criticize, and he certainly does not give needed praise for a job well done.

He has to get into everything going on in the organization. Take the telephones, for example. I should be the one screening the calls and directing them to the proper persons. But as soon as I leave my desk he picks up the phone when it rings and gets himself involved in things that should be directed to someone else. He is into almost everything, not just telephone calls. He wants to see just about all of the correspondence. The other executives and managers have learned this, and they know they had better keep him informed even about minor details. But I don't think that's the way a president of a fairly good sized company should operate. He should be doing the planning, the big things, and not get himself into petty details.

After compiling their notes and studying the interviews with the executive group, the consultants made an appointment with Bill Duncan to give him their impression of ABC and to get his opinion of how the organization functioned.

The first question they asked was why the executives and office staff felt he kept such tight controls. Bill stated:

Well, I don't know that the controls are that tight. But on the other hand, I am afraid to let go of the controls I have because I think they are a very effective check. It keeps everybody on their toes. They know that I am doing it, so they are not so likely to slip into a rut or get slipshod in their functions, both in the office and in the field. I did give up the frequent trips to the field to get a hold on the operations here in the main office particularly from a cost standpoint. I monitor most bills, the club dues, the phone bills. I really don't go over them very thoroughly. I may pull one or two out of the pile and ask some questions if necessary. I am not spending all that much time reviewing the small items. I do sign all the job payments and sign all the checks if they are over $50. I really hate to give this up because it keeps me current on the cost of material and labor, and specific project costs. You must remember that the project manager and auditor must approve all the bills on specific projects before they reach me to be signed. An invoice must be initiated by the project manager with a purchase order number, subcontractor number, and a brief summary of the job the bill represents.

I feel that my check signing gives me an insight into the operation which I could not get any other way. I probably should give up signing the office payroll checks, but even here there is always something happening that I observe. For example, last month I caught some excessive overtime payments, and when I questioned the managers in charge, I found that most of the overtime could have been avoided. It's things like this that pay off if you will just spend some time checking on the payouts and keeping control of the finances. I don't spend much time doing this. I just thumb through the pile and try to pick out the bigger items; it's a good control device and I find it to be very helpful. I don't waste much time doing this. I usually do this after five o'clock. It doesn't take more than 15 minutes, may be 30 minutes. I am just making a spot check.

You ask me why I don't go out in the field. I love to, but I have delegated this to Charlie Jennings and Bob Caldwell. I guess that I should go out more often, but when I do, it seems to upset people in the field. They think I am on a spying trip.

I know that I should visit the branch offices more often. For example, in Columbus we have a young man, Chet Bailey. He is a good engineer, but very inexperienced. I should check on him more often. When I go out to the field, I try to get some idea of what is going on by checking the field reports on each job. This gives me some idea of what is going on that I may not see in the branch managers' weekly report.

You asked how long I work each day? You should ask how hard I work. Well, I start out about 7 A.M. each day, get to the office before 8 A.M., and stay to 6 sometimes 7 P.M. It depends on what my wife has set up for the evening. I work some on Saturdays and do some catching up reading on Sundays. I just leisurely read the mail and circulars, Dodge reports, and other material relating to the construction industry. But I think this is relaxing, not working.

You asked what I thought about growth? We have been growing, at least keeping up with inflation. But how big can you get if you have troubles when you grow too big, too fast? It's hard to get the personnel needed to grow. There aren't many good engineers that you can hire that are dependable. Growth is going to require more delegation on my part and on the part of the other executives. I don't think they are as good at delegation as they think they are. If we are going to grow at all, we need smooth and gradual growth that we can handle.

For example, one of the larger and better construction firms in this area went broke last year. I think it was mainly due to rapid expansion. They took on a number of projects and did not have the qualified managers to keep them in control and meet the completion dates. The principals were very good, but they couldn't do everything. They were running around trying to keep the big jobs going as well as their several branches. It's easy to build up overhead in this business through expansion, but it's very difficult to get rid of it. If you expand, you have to add project managers, estimators, expand the equipment yard, and enlarge the office force.

If we expand to any great extent, you have to cut up the pie into more pieces, and I am not so sure the rest of the group are eager to do this. In a way, you have to fight to keep small, and you just don't grow to satisfy your personnel. I would like to maintain our present image. We are a quality firm, and we do quality work. This gives us a certain amount of prestige in the area, and I think it is worth maintaining.

The Case of the Missing Time

It was 7:30 Tuesday morning when Chet Craig, general manager of the Norris Company's Central Plant, swung his car out of the driveway of his suburban home and headed toward the plant in Midvale, six miles away. The trip to the plant took about 20 minutes and gave Chet an opportunity to think about plant problems without interruption.

The Norris Company operated three printing plants and did a nationwide business in quality color work. It had about 350 employees, nearly half of whom were employed at the Central Plant. The company's headquarters offices were also located in the Central Plant building.

Chet had started with the Norris Company as an expeditor in its Eastern Plant 10 years ago, after his graduation from Ohio State. After three years he was promoted to production supervisor, and two years later he was made assistant to the manager of the Eastern Plant. A year and a half ago he had been transferred to the Central Plant as assistant to the plant manager, and one month later, when the manager retired, Chet was promoted to general plant manager. (See Exhibit 1.)

Chet was in good spirits this morning. Various thoughts occurred to him as he said to himself, "This is going to be the day to really get things done." He thought of the day's work—first one project, then another—trying to establish priorities. He decided that the open-end unit scheduling was probably the most important—certainly the most urgent. He recalled that on Friday the vice president had casually asked him if he had given the project any further thought. Chet realized that he had not been giving it any attention lately. He had been meaning to get to work on his idea for over three months, but something else always seemed to crop up.

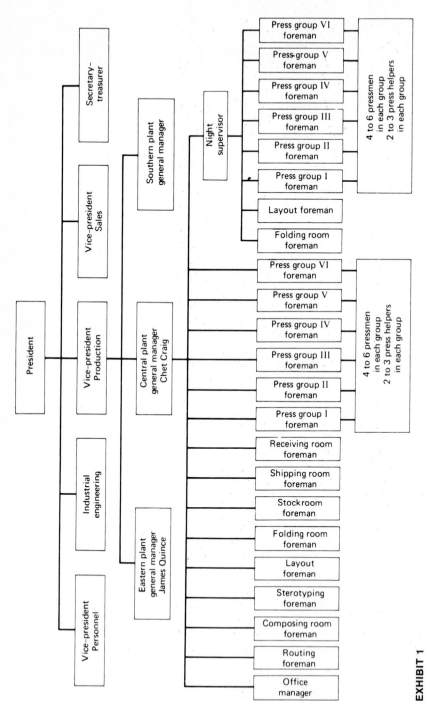

EXHIBIT 1
Norris Company organization chart.

The organization chart shows the following structure:

President

Reporting to the President:
- Vice-president Personnel
- Industrial engineering
- Vice-president Production
- Vice-president Sales
- Secretary-treasurer

Reporting to Vice-president Production:
- Eastern plant general manager James Quince
- Central plant general manager Chet Craig
- Southern plant general manager

Reporting to Central plant general manager Chet Craig:
- Office manager
- Routing foreman
- Composing room foreman
- Sterotyping foreman
- Layout foreman
- Folding room foreman
- Stockroom foreman
- Shipping room foreman
- Receiving room foreman
- Press group I foreman
- Press group II foreman
- Press group III foreman
- Press group IV foreman
- Press group V foreman
- Press group VI foreman (4 to 6 pressmen in each group, 2 to 3 press helpers in each group)

Reporting to Night supervisor:
- Folding room foreman
- Layout foreman
- Press group I foreman
- Press group II foreman
- Press group III foreman
- Press group IV foreman
- Press group V foreman
- Press group VI foreman (4 to 6 pressmen in each group, 2 to 3 press helpers in each group)

64

"I haven't had time to really work it out," he said to himself. "I'd better get going and finish it off one of these days." He then began to break down the objectives, procedures, and installation steps in the project. It gave him a feeling of satisfaction as he calculated the anticipated cost savings. "It's high time," he told himself. "This idea should have been completed a long time ago."

Chet had first conceived the open-end unit scheduling idea almost two years ago just prior to leaving the Eastern Plant. He had talked it over with the general manager of the Eastern Plant, and both agreed that it was a good idea and worth developing. The idea was temporarily shelved when Chet had been transferred to the Central Plant a month later.

His thoughts returned to other plant projects he was determined to get under way. He started to think through a procedure for the simpler transport of dies to and from the Eastern Plant. He thought of the notes on his desk: the inventory analysis he needed to identify and eliminate some of the slow-moving stock items; the packing controls which needed revision; and the need to design a new special order form. He also decided that this was the day to settle on a job printer to do the outside printing of simple office forms. There were a few other projects he could not recall offhand, but he felt sure that he could tend to them sometime during the day. Again he said to himself: "This is the day to really get rolling."

When he entered the plant, Chet was met by Al Noren, the stockroom foreman, who appeared troubled. "A great morning, Al," said Chet, cheerfully.

"Well, I don't know, Chet; my new man isn't in this morning," said Noren morosely.

"Have you heard from him?" asked Chet.

"No, I haven't."

"These stock handlers take it for granted that if they're not here, they don't have to call in and report. Better ask Personnel to call him."

Al hesitated a moment. "Okay, Chet," he said, "but can you find me someone? I have two cars to unload today."

Making a note of the incident, Chet headed for his office. He greeted some workers discussing the day's work with Marilyn, the office manager. As the meeting broke up, Marilyn took some samples from a clasper and showed them to Chet, asking if they should be shipped that way or if it would be necessary to inspect them. Before he could answer, Marilyn went on to ask if he could suggest another clerical operator for the sealing machine to replace the regular operator, who was home ill. She also told him that Gene, the industrial engineer, had called and was waiting to hear from him.

Chet told Marilyn to ship the samples, made a note of the need for a sealer operator, and then called Gene. He agreed to stop by Gene's office before lunch, and started on his routine morning tour of the plant. He asked each foreman the volumes and types of orders he was running, the number of people present, how the schedules were coming along, and the orders to be run next; he helped the folding-room foreman find temporary storage space for consolidating a carload shipment; discussed quality control with a pressman who had been running poor work; arranged to transfer four people temporarily to different departments, including two for A1 in the stockroom; and talked to the shipping foreman about pickups and special orders to be delivered that day. As he continued through the plant, he saw to it that reserve stock was moved out of the forward stock area; talked to another pressman about his requested change of vacation schedule; had a "heart-to-heart" talk with a press helper who seemed to need frequent assurance; and approved two type and one color okays for different pressmen.

Returning to his office, Chet reviewed the production reports on the larger orders against his initial projections and found that the plant was running slightly behind schedule. He called in the folding-room foreman, and together they went over the lineup of machines and made several changes.

During this discussion the composing-room foreman stepped in to cover several type changes and the routing foreman telephoned for approval of a revised printing schedule. The stockroom foreman called twice—first to inform him that two standard, fast-moving stock items were dangerously low, and later to advise him that the paper stock for the urgent Dillon job had finally arrived. Chet telephoned this information to the people concerned.

He then began to put delivery dates on important inquiries received from customers and salespersons. (The routine inquiries were handled by Marilyn.) While he was doing this he was interrupted twice, once by a sales correspondent calling from the west coast to ask for a better delivery date than originally scheduled, and once by the vice president of personnel, asking Chet to set a time when he could hold an initial induction interview with a new employee.

After dating the customer and salesperson inquiries, Chet headed for his morning conference in the executive office. At this meeting he answered the vice president for sales' questions in connection with "hot" orders, complaints, the status of large-volume orders, and potential new orders. Then he met with the vice president and general production manager to answer "the old man's" questions on several production and personnel problems. Before leaving the executive offices, he stopped at the office of the purchasing agent to inquire about the delivery of some cartons, paper, and boxes and to place an order for some new paper.

On the way back to his own office Chet conferred with Gene about two current engineering projects. When he reached his desk, he lit a cigarette and looked at his watch. It was ten minutes before lunch—just time enough to make a few notes of the details he needed to check in order to answer knotty questions raised by the vice president for sales that morning.

After lunch Chet started again. He began by checking the previous day's production reports, did some rescheduling to get out urgent orders, placed delivery dates on new orders and inquiries received that morning, and consulted with a foreman about a personal problem. He spent about twenty minutes at the TWX[1] going over mutual problems with the Eastern Plant.

[1] Leased private telegram communication system using a teletypewriter.

By midafternoon Chet had made another tour of the plant, after which he met with the vice president of personnel to review with him a touchy personal problem raised by one of the clerical employees, the vacation schedules submitted by his foremen, and the pending job evaluation program. Following this conference, Chet hurried back to his office to complete the special statistical report for Universal Waxing Corporation, one of Norris's biggest customers. When he finished the report he discovered that it was ten after six and he was the only one left in the office. Chet was tired. He put on his coat and headed for the parking lot. On the way out he was stopped by the night supervisor and the night layout foreman for approval of type and layout changes.

As he drove home Chet reviewed the day he had just completed. "Busy?" he asked himself. "Too much so—but did I accomplish anything?" The answer seemed to be "Yes, and no." There was the usual routine, the same as any other day. The plant kept going and it was a good production day. "Any creative or special project work done?" Chet winced. "I guess not."

With a feeling of guilt Chet asked himself: "Am I an executive? I'm paid like one, and I have a responsible assignment and the authority to carry it out. My superiors at headquarters think I'm a good manager. Yet one of the greatest returns a company gets from an executive is his innovative thinking and accomplishments. What have I done about that? Today was just like other days, and I didn't do any creative work. The projects that I was so eager to work on this morning are no further ahead than they were yesterday. What's more, I can't say that tomorrow night or the next night they'll be any closer to completion. This is a real problem, and there must be some answer to it.

"Night work? Yes, sometimes. This is understood. But I've been doing too much night work lately. My wife and family deserve some of my time. After all, they are the people for whom I'm really working. If I spend much more time away from them, I'm not meeting my own personal objectives. I spend a lot of time on church work. Should I eliminate that? I feel I owe that as an obligation. Besides, I feel I'm making a worthwhile contribution in this work. Maybe I can squeeze a little time from my fraternal activities. But where does recreation fit in?"

Chet groped for the solution. "Maybe I'm just rationalizing because I schedule my own work poorly. But I don't think so. I've studied my work habits, and I think I plan intelligently and delegate authority. Do I need an assistant? Possibly, but that's a long-time project and I don't believe I could justify the additional overhead expense. Anyway, I doubt whether it would solve the problem."

By this time Chet had turned off the highway into the side street leading to his home. "I guess I really don't know the answer," he said to himself as he pulled into his driveway. "This morning everything seemed so simple, but now—."

Ammco Tools, Inc.[1]

Ammco Tools, Inc., was a North Chicago–based, family-owned company specializing in the manufacture and marketing of automotive engine rebuilding and brake service and wheel alignment tools and equipment. Under the leadership of its president, Fred G. Wacker, Jr., Ammco enjoyed steady growth. Sales grew from $6.2 million in 1967 to $33.8 million in 1980. (Financial statements are shown in Exhibits 1 and 2.)

PRESIDENT AND CHIEF EXECUTIVE OFFICER: BUSINESS OBJECTIVES AND PHILOSOPHY

Fred Wacker, Jr., entered the company in 1947 and became president and chairman of the board of directors after his father's death in 1948. Sales at that time were $1 million. Wacker moved the company into brake service tools and further diversified in the 1950s in order to reduce the company's dependence on the automobile industry. He bought the patents for a newly invented positive displacement meter for measuring any liquid, including petroleum, chemicals, and food products. He organized the Liquid Controls Corporation (LCC) in 1954 to manufacture and sell these products.

Fred Wacker (62) graduated from Yale in 1940 with a B. A. in English. He worked in the machine shop at the AC Spark Plug Division of General Motors while simultaneously studying at General Motors Institute. He was later moved to the time-study department of the AC division. In 1943 he left Gener-

---

[1] This case was developed by Serge Oreal and Robert D. Hamilton, III, under the direction of Professor Thomas J. McNichols. It is intended to be used as a basis for class discussion rather than to illustrate effective or ineffective management of a situation.

al Motors for a four-year stint in the U. S. Navy. When he returned from the war, he formed the Fred Wacker Swing Band, which provided him with a comfortable income. In addition to his musical talents, Wacker was an ardent auto racer. He drove on the European Grand Prix Circuit as a member of the French racing team. He also raced with Phil Hill as his teammate in the Le Mans 24-hour race. In 1951 he won the first Sebring Endurance Race. He also sought unsuccessfully to break a motorcycle world speed record at the Bonneville Salt Flats in 1974 and again in 1975.

Fred Wacker possessed a distinct personal and business philosophy which guided Ammco. He considered his chief executive role as ideal in a company that was well positioned in the automotive after market. He noted that the company was technically oriented, and while "you don't have to be a technical genius, you don't have every Tom, Dick, and Harry trying to get into this business." He noted, "what is important to me is to be independent. I don't have to reach for the *Wall Street Journal* every morning to look at the stock quotes. I maintain a no-debt policy and operate a privately held company which assures me of protection from a takeover."

Wacker expressed his views on the common practice of management by committees in these terms: "I'm not much for committees where you tend to sit around and just talk about things." In discussing his philosophy of long-range planning, Wacker vowed that his long-range goal was to "make a profit every month." He was "not much for long-range planning" and he was absolutely opposed to making long-range commitments: "You shouldn't make promises you can't keep." Wacker singled out Henry Ford, Eddie Rickenbacker, and William Patterson (founder of United Airlines) as men he admired as entrepreneurs and managers. Wacker believed that the Bible was the best guide for business and personal behavior. He felt that the ten commandments were the most important laws to guide a person's life.

> We may not do formal strategic planning, but we have morning meetings of the key personnel to review our operations. We use the Arthur Young charts, which give us a good indication of what has been happening in the company in terms of production and cost trends; the charts allow us to track our product lines. We also have used the Strategic Planning Institute, which produces the PIMS data.
>
> But you have to be careful in using certain measures and should not go overboard on any single system. For example, too much adherence to the return on investment concept can lead you to do the wrong things. Our morning meetings may not last very long. We spend time on problems that need solving. We don't know what is going to come up each day. We try to remain flexible and take things as they come up. Our department heads meet once a month. We try to keep them informed and look at the problems they are encountering.

Fred Wacker, Jr., owned 9.6 percent of the outstanding shares of Ammco; the remainder was owned by the Wacker family. The board of directors was made up of Fred Wacker, Jr. as chairman, Mrs. Wacker, Sr., Fred Wacker's brother, his sister, and Mark Anderson, chairman of the board of Aro Corporation of Bryan, Ohio.

EXHIBIT 1
Ammco Tools, Inc.
Income Statements 1972–1980
($000)

	1972	1973	1974	1975
AUTOMOTIVE				
Gross shipments	$14,965.5	$16,206.9	$17,830.9	$21,150.9
Less returns/allowances	189.3	236.9	229.5	427.2
Net shipments	14,776.2	15,970.0	17,601.4	20,723.7
Cost of sales	6,301.1	7,197.1	8,825.9	9,727.2
GROSS PROFIT	8,475.1	8,772.9	8,775.5	10,996.5
Other costs				
Commissions	1,964.0	2,141.0	2,304.4	2,755.4
Freight out	211.8	256.3	306.1	308.7
Other	(33.9)	(32.5)	(46.8)	(60.5)
AUTOMOTIVE INCOME	6,333.2	6,408.1	6,211.8	7,992.9
LCC INCOME	2.9	4.2	4.2	4.9
TOTAL INCOME	$ 6,336.1	$ 6,412.3	$ 6,216.0	$ 7,997.8
DEPARTMENTAL EXPENSES				
Engineering expense	$ 215.1	$ 332.3	$ 396.0	$ 540.0
Selling expense	867.3	918.4	1,006.6	1,183.7
Administrative expense	1,813.1	1,956.8	2,065.4	2,420.6
Other expense, net	103.7	27.0	156.4	250.2
Total departmental	2,999.2	3,234.5	3,624.4	4,394.5
OPERATING INCOME	3,336.9	3,177.8	2,591.6	3,603.3
Interest expense	56.8	56.8	57.5	31.5
NET INCOME	3,280.1	3,121.0	2,534.1	3,571.8
Tax provision	1,619.0	1,508.0	1,280.0	1,800.0
NET PROFIT	$ 1,661.1	$ 1,613.0	$ 1,254.1	$ 1,771.8

Source: Corporate Records

Wacker maintained a personal interest in Ammco's employees. He kept 3 × 5 in. cards with pictures of each employee so that he would know them by name. He also tried to keep personal contact through the sponsorship of all-day company outings or parties that included employees and spouses.

Wacker had decided several years ago not to put a cap on the cost-of-living escalator clause. He felt certain that he could beat the inflation rate. The Ammco plant was the highest-paying plant in the area. The result was a "good atmosphere and employees that don't want to leave."

Ammco plant workers were, for the most part, members of the United Steelworkers of America. Twenty-five people in the plant were not members, however, and did not pay dues. Wacker felt strongly that the open shop concept

1976	1977	1978	1979	1980	1981 Budget
$23,336.4	$26,732.5	$30,537.1	$34,831.6	$34,713.2	$38,920.0
421.2	544.1	653.9	797.6	863.3	920.0
22,915.2	26,188.4	29,883.2	34,034.0	33,849.9	38,000.0
10,802.8	12,084.9	12,858.3	14,321.0	15,734.4	16,770.0
12,112.4	14,103.5	17,024.9	19,713.0	18,115.5	21,230.0
3,027.0	3,477.9	4,046.6	4,623.0	4,509.8	5,020.0
335.9	386.9	421.8	553.2	706.5	760.0
(51.5)	(36.7)	(25.8)	(30.9)	(45.5)	(50.0)
8,801.0	10,275.4	12,582.3	14,567.7	12,944.7	15,500.0
5.6	8.3	8.9	11.8	21.8	20.0
$ 8,806.6	$10,283.7	$12,591.2	$14,579.5	$12,966.5	$15,520.0
$ 710.2	$ 776.9	$ 890.2	$ 1,015.3	$ 935.5	$ 910.0
1,472.5	1,794.8	1,670.3	2,058.1	2,626.5	2,650.0
2,916.8	3,365.4	3,628.8	4,543.3	4,626.8	4,980.0
241.1	294.2	147.9	(81.2)	180.8	210.0
5,340.6	6,231.3	6,337.2	7,535.5	8,369.6	8,750.0
3,466.0	4,052.4	6,254.0	7,044.0	4,596.9	6,770.0
18.6	71.0	5.2	29.7	86.0	60.0
3,447.4	3,981.4	6,248.8	7,014.3	4,510.9	6,710.0
1,782.0	2,050.0	3,255.0	3,555.0	2,380.0	3,360.0
$ 1,665.4	$ 1,931.4	$ 2,993.8	$ 3,459.3	$ 2,130.9	$ 3,350.0

was a fundamental worker right and vowed "I'll take a strike on it. Membership in the union should not be a condition of employment." His father had fought a case based on this principle all the way to the Supreme Court. It was Wacker's belief that labor and management need not have an adversary relationship. "Labor doesn't win unless management makes a profit. They rise and fall together."

AMMCO'S EXECUTIVE GROUP

Wacker was always concerned with developing a good working executive group since the time he became the chief officer. Through the years he brought

EXHIBIT 2
Ammco Tools, Inc.
Balance Sheets for the Periods Ending December 31
($000)

	12-31-72	12-31-73	12-31-74	12-31-75
Cash	165.5	203.7	178.2	181.7
Securities	1050.0	325.0	325.0	1600.0
Accounts receivable-net	1691.9	1365.3	1930.6	1819.1
Due from Liquid Controls	5.6	76.6	116.1	14.7
Inventories	1554.7	2209.9	2830.4	2648.5
Inventory reserve-LIFO	–	–	(537.2)	(639.0)
Prepaid expenses	62.1	33.1	69.0	33.9
Total current assets	4529.8	4206.6	4912.1	5658.9
Investment-LCC	800.0	850.0	850.0	1450.0
Investment-rent-Ammco	–	–	–	1.0
Cash value of life insurance	174.9	236.9	297.2	351.6
Note receivable-Dayco	–	257.8	248.7	238.7
Other investments	36.4	36.4	36.4	36.4
Total investments	1011.3	1381.1	1432.3	2077.7
Property, plant, and equipment	6072.7	7408.0	7855.0	8552.7
Accumulated depreciation	(2429.1)	(2744.3)	(3359.0)	(3985.3)
Net plant and equipment	3643.6	4663.7	4496.0	4567.4
Patents and trademarks-net	11.2	13.1	13.0	13.1
Deferred federal income taxes	147.0	147.0	202.0	270.0
TOTAL ASSETS	9342.9	10411.5	11055.4	12587.1
Notes payable to bank	–	–	–	–
Accounts payable	366.2	448.8	459.9	410.4
Accrued expenses	774.6	610.9	692.2	730.6
Federal and state inc. taxes	411.1	197.1	(126.3)	603.2
Total current liabilities	1551.9	1256.8	1025.8	1744.2
Long-term debt–Prud/other	850.0	941.3	900.7	324.3
Capital stock	1000.0	1000.0	1000.0	1000.0
Earned surplus, Jan.	5519.5	5941.0	7214.4	8128.9
Year to date profit	1661.1	1613.0	1254.1	1771.8
Less: Dividends paid	(339.6)	(339.6)	(339.6)	(382.0)
Other	(900.0)	–	–	–
Total equity	6941.0	8213.4	9128.9	10518.7
TOTAL LIABILITIES AND EQUITY	9342.9	10411.5	11055.4	12587.2
Current ratio	2.7	3.1	4.8	3.0
Book value per share	81.76	96.75	107.53	123.89

Source: Corporate Records

12-31-76	12-31-77	12-31-78	12-31-79	12-31-80
11.9	171.4	158.7	768.8	229.5
–	900.0	4874.7	3555.3	4947.2
2513.2	2672.3	3355.5	3745.4	4480.0
11.9	35.1	39.6	20.3	–
3465.0	3782.9	3764.8	5834.9	5044.5
(744.0)	(1221.0)	(1033.0)	(1246.0)	(1296.0)
41.5	16.1	49.3	34.8	44.9
5299.5	6356.8	11209.6	12713.5	13450.0
1130.0	1977.4	1658.6	1329.2	1078.9
800.0	438.6	438.6	–	–
409.0	528.9	686.0	827.9	399.1
227.8	216.0	–	–	–
482.4	1.6	1.6	1.6	1.7
3049.2	3162.5	2784.8	2158.7	1479.7
9833.0	11078.8	11878.3	14539.1	17151.2
(4646.0)	(5410.5)	(6178.8)	(7022.8)	(7788.0)
5187.0	5668.2	5699.5	7516.3	9363.3
12.9	12.8	12.4	1396.3	1286.0
314.2	279.7	321.0	346.3	219.5
13862.8	15480.2	20027.3	24130.9	25798.5
–				
717.8	416.6	519.9	963.3	790.0
730.5	854.0	1233.6	1621.8	2002.9
262.9	536.1	1976.1	1091.2	1211.4
1711.2	1806.8	3729.6	3676.3	4004.3
392.1	322.1	292.6	1563.0	1034.9
1000.0	1000.0	1000.0	1000.0	1000.0
9518.6	10759.5	12350.9	14771.9	17891.6
1665.4	1931.4	2993.7	3459.3	2130.9
(424.5)	(339.6)	(339.6)	(339.6)	(263.2)
–	–	–	–	–
11759.5	13351.3	16005.1	18891.6	20759.3
13862.8	15480.2	20027.3	24130.9	25798.5
2.9	3.3	2.9	3.3	3.2
138.51	157.3	188.5	222.5	244.5

together his own operating staff. The group included:

J. Dragoni (55) joined Ammco in January 1956 as a New England district representative. After seven years he was promoted to be the New England regional manager. During his tenure, he built the New England sales force of 4 people up to 18. He was brought to the North Chicago office in February of 1979 as the vice president of sales to succeed L. Monteith. His mission was to increase export sales. Dragoni served as a B-29 navigator in the China-Burma-India theatre during World War II. He was married with two children.

L. Morrison (45) emigrated in 1950 from Israel where he worked for a racing car company and auto shop. Before joining Ammco in 1972 he worked for Northwestern University building x-ray equipment. He joined the engineering department of Ammco, performing a wide variety of different functions at the entry level. He was gradually given increased responsibility until he was named a vice president in 1977. Morrison succeeded Wally Mitchell, who retired in 1980 as head of research and development. He was married with no children.

A. D. Yankus (43) joined Ammco in 1959 shortly after obtaining a B.S. in accounting. His starting position was a junior accountant. He was promoted to assistant treasurer after eight years. He attended business school at night while he worked and was awarded an M.B.A. in 1967. He was married and had two children.

Tom McPherson joined Ammco in 1961 as a controller. He left the company at the age of 54. He had experience in a small printing company and with the Toni Company, a division of Gillette, before joining Ammco. McPherson came to the company with a good background in data processing and aided in developing Ammco's computer-based information system. He assumed the added position of treasurer in 1963 and during his tenure also served as treasurer and controller of Liquid Controls Corporation. In 1974 McPherson was promoted to general manager, a position he held until leaving in 1977.

Wally Mitchell was another important member of the executive group until 1980. He had served as vice president and director of manufacturing and engineering. Although Mitchell had only a seventh-grade education he had patented over 150 inventions, 20 of which were related to Ammco's business. Mitchell had worked in the 1930s under Fred Wacker, Sr. After leaving the company over some differences with Mr. Wacker, Sr., he returned under Fred Wacker, Jr. with whom he shared some common interests in the automotive field, including auto racing.

Mitchell was Fred Wacker, Jr.'s personal mechanic when Wacker was part of the French auto racing team. During his time with Ammco, he made many suggestions for streamlining Ammco's production system and designed some new items in the product line. Mitchell established a research group in Ammco to develop new products to solve problems encountered by large auto and brake companies which were customers of Ammco.

During Fred Wacker, Jr.'s tenure Mitchell was compensated as a consultant. He discontinued his activities with Ammco in 1980 at the age of 74.

AMMCO'S DEVELOPMENT

Problems started to develop in the mid-1950s at Ammco. Many new products were introduced before being properly tested, and, as a consequence, the product line declined in quality. Ammco's plant and equipment were becoming obsolete. There were numerous bottlenecks and tie-ups in production. The situation worsened until 1967, when the cost of goods sold reached 56 percent of sales and profits dropped to 1.4 percent of sales. At one point, Wacker was not sure he would be able to meet the company's weekly payroll. Inventories became greater than unfilled orders, sales dropped, and Ammco's debt-to-equity ratio peaked at 70 percent.

In the summer of 1967, drastic measures were taken to turn the company around. These included: (1) reduction of the work force, (2) improvement of the existing products, and (3) use of only one production shift to aid in the reduction of inventories. By 1973 Ammco had $16 million in sales with 319 employees, compared with $6 million in sales and 475 employees in 1967. The cost of goods sold was down to 44 percent of sales, and its after-tax profit was 10.6 percent of sales.

Throughout the 1970s, Ammco's sales (net shipments) increased at a fairly steady rate. Different elements converged to make the years 1971 to 1973 three profitable years for Ammco. During that period, the company's profit rate was above the company's 10 percent profit goal.

ORGANIZATIONAL CHANGES

Partly because of his firm's rapid expansion program, Wacker was concerned at the end of 1973. First there was the problem of his succession and the future of the company. What would happen should he become disabled or if he decided to retire? He knew that none of his other family shareholders was either able or willing to take the company over should such an event occur. Wacker's son was still very young and had not even decided which college he would like to attend.

In anticipation of a management succession problem, Wacker, early in 1974, modified his organization chart (Exhibit 3). At the same time, Tom McPherson was promoted from treasurer and controller to a newly created position of general manager. Although he was not a family member, McPherson, in Wacker's mind, was being tested and trained to eventually take over the company should that become necessary. In his position McPherson had been responsible for the design, development, and introduction of new, computerized management information, inventory control, and production scheduling systems. McPherson was considered by many people in the company to be a likeable person, who was respected in his job and who possessed important leadership abilities. As early as 1973 John Lauten, then industrial relations manager, said: "I think Tom McPherson could do a good job of running the company and keeping the same atmosphere that Fred has established."

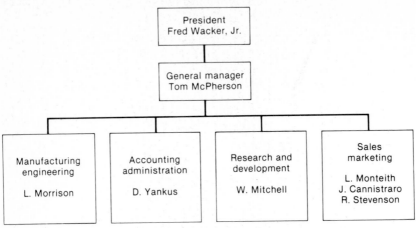

EXHIBIT 3
Ammco Tools, Inc. organization chart, 1974. (*Source:* Corporate records.)

Ammco's rapid increase in sales and profits prompted a new investment program which was decided on in 1973. In 1976 these new capital investment programs were being implemented in order to keep pace with increased demand.

There were two plants at that time:

1 Plant 1 in North Chicago, 108,330 square feet
2 Plant 8, also in North Chicago, 60,000 square feet

Plant 8 was enlarged by about 40,000 square feet at the cost of $19 a square foot. This increase in capacity was finished in 1977 and led to a major reorganization of Ammco's facilities. Machining was concentrated in Plant 1. The different parts were then transported the 3 miles to Plant 8 for assembly and shipping. (See Exhibit 3A and 3B.)

At Liquid Controls, a program of expansion was also undertaken: 23,400 square feet of space was added to the 49,000-square-foot plant at a cost of $36 a square foot. The difference in cost was due to the fact that office space was added, with a marble floor and expensive furniture. (See Exhibit 3C.)

All this was done, as Wacker was proud to say, "without going to the banks, but financed out of retained earnings." In fact, in September 1976, the company did not have any long-term debt, and had been completely out of the banks and insurance company since the end of July 1975, when the balance of the Prudential loan had been repaid.

This policy was also consistent with one of the company's basic objectives, which was "to finance growth through earnings rather than debt or public offerings." Wacker insisted on presenting this no-debt policy as one of the major elements of his business philosophy. (See Exhibit 4.) He said, "I do not want to be in anybody else's hands. In fact, I am not so much interested in growing fast as

EXHIBIT 3A Ammco Tools, Inc., Plant 1.

EXHIBIT 3B Ammco Tools, Inc., Plant 8.

EXHIBIT 3C Liquid Controls Corporation.

EXHIBIT 4
AMMCO TOOLS, INC.
AMMCO TOOLS, INC., BASIC OBJECTIVE

Our basic objective is to operate a profitable, growth, manufacturing, and sales corporation selling quality products, competitively priced, to the automotive aftermarket.

Supporting objectives are to broaden the line of products, diversify into other lines not necessarily related to the automotive aftermarket, and to put profits back into the business, which, with the overall objective, indicates a conservative dividend policy.

Our further policy is to finance growth through earnings rather than debt or public offering.

With respect to employees, our policy is to pay well, operate both an annual bonus and a deferred profit-sharing plan, and in return expect maximum performance.

Further, we will have no planned obsolescence.

We will try to be a model of what is right about the free, competitive enterprise system.

Source: Corporate Records.

I am in growing solidly and securely." According to him, internally generated cash would best allow a company to grow securely in the long run. A fair selling price should generate enough profits, which in turn should permit the company to expand. Although he recognized that his position was sometimes considered old-fashioned and too conservative, he was always eager to demonstrate that this policy was the only one which would enable a smaller-size company like Ammco to survive in case of a recession or a drastic economic downturn.

OPERATING CHANGES

In August 1976, after long discussions and negotiations, all plant workers were taken off the incentive plan. The incentive system had been established in the late 1940s, and the rates had not substantially changed in the past 10 years. More than once, McPherson had recommended that shop workers on the floor be taken off this incentive plan. His argument against the plan was that some of the employees working on very big, slow-moving pieces had difficulty earning incentive.

For example, on one particular part an average worker was able to produce 7 pieces a day; another one, by pushing hard was eventually able to come up with 7.2 or 7.3 pieces during the same period, which did not allow him to substantially benefit from the incentive plan. For these reasons, nobody wanted to work on those jobs, which as a consequence always created back orders, delays, and scheduling problems. McPherson's idea was to give these workers a compensating pay raise, and take them off the incentive plan.

Before the change, general supervisors met every morning in order to decide on the most important jobs, ones that had to be done during the day "to put out the fires." There was little scheduling in advance. Scheduling was complicated by the fact that there was often a shortage in certain critical small tools and accessories which were low-volume items.

McPherson had also remarked that workers were in fact metering their production and that there was significant group pressure not to go over the norms, so that the norms would not be revised: "What was supposed to be an incentive, was in fact a brake." Besides the problems created by the norms themselves, it was also difficult to find toolmakers. Although they were paid the highest hourly rate, they were not included in the incentive plan. Finally, Ammco was caught in a circular problem. It had the production capacity to turn out more units, but since the sales force was not selling enough, there was no pressure to produce more.

In 1976, after numerous lengthy discussions, McPherson finally convinced the plant manager and Wacker to shift to the new plan. Wacker agreed, but subject to the condition that the time-study person would go on doing his duties and "keep the old program going," just in case it would prove necessary to revert to the old system. As soon as the paycheck ended up being bigger than before, the union accepted the change, scheduling improved, and problems started to disappear.

At the same time, however, production went down. The standard hours efficiency rate (the ratio of hours worked to units produced) was always in the 52 to 54 percent range before August 1976. After the change it quickly went down and stabilized around 44 percent.

In terms of cost, the change did not cause any modification in the payroll for the workers who were included in the incentive plan previously. Their new rate was derived from their average weekly earnings divided into 40 hours. For the other workers, who were not directly included in the incentive plan before, there was a pay increase because they were in fact out of line with the other category.

AMMCO'S POSITION IN THE AUTOMOTIVE INDUSTRY

Ammco Tools, Inc., had six major product lines:

1 Heavy equipment: brake service—brake lathes and brake shoe grinders
2 Accessories: shop benches, facing sets, silencers, adaptors
3 Small tools: cylinder and brake hones, ridge reamers, torque wrenches, declerometers
4 Stones and cutters: tool bits, stone sets, and abrasive belts
5 Wheel service: wheel alignment, gauges, instrumentation, and drive-on racks
6 Parts: replacement parts for the heavy equipment

Sales and profitability by product line are shown in Exhibit 5. The heavy number of models and products is indicated in Exhibit 6. Ammco's heavy equipment line dominated the business. The company had approximately 60 to 70 percent market share in this area with five major competitors. In the small-

EXHIBIT 5
AMMCO TOOLS, INC.
INCOME STATEMENTS BY PRODUCT GROUP PERIODS ENDING DECEMBER 31 ($000)

	1972	1973	1974	1975	1976	1977	1978	1979	1980 (budget)
Sales by product group									
1 - Heavy equipment	$ 8,275	$ 9,140	$10,645	$12,293	$12,808	$15,028	$17,150	$19,763	$21,400
2 - Accessories	2,183	2,280	2,246	2,207	2,305	2,478	2,672	3,031	3,300
3 - Small tools	1,904	1,932	2,018	2,508	2,303	2,554	2,772	4,132	4,600
4 - Stones and cutters	1,698	1,839	1,867	2,358	2,729	3,086	3,543	2,725	2,900
5 - Wheel service	304	272	369	770	2,083	2,280	2,770	2,962	3,600
6 - Parts	398	505	456	587	684	757	967	1,093	1,200
9 - Other	15	2	–	–	3	5	9	329	–
Total	$14,777	$15,970	$17,601	$20,723	$22,915	$26,188	$29,883	$34,034	$37,000
Gross profit by group									
1 - Heavy equipment	$ 5,181	$ 5,233	$ 5,633	$ 6,084	$ 7,107	$ 8,425	$ 9,831	$11,580	$12,500
2 - Accessories	1,366	1,361	1,234	1,217	1,315	1,428	1,557	1,766	1,920
3 - Small tools	1,068	963	1,026	1,303	1,189	1,276	1,389	2,477	2,820
4 - Stones and cutters	1,000	1,068	1,110	1,383	1,610	1,781	2,298	1,763	1,840
5 - Wheel service	145	116	198	350	1,071	1,188	1,306	1,580	1,820
6 - Parts	290	348	310	374	423	452	607	649	700
9 - Other	2	2	–	–	1	3	5	161	–
Total	$ 9,002	$ 9,091	$ 9,511	$11,431	$12,716	$14,533	$16,992	$19,904	$21,600

EXHIBIT 6
AMMCO TOOLS, INC.
PRODUCT LINE 1981

	Models	Replacement parts/ accessories
Alignment rack	5	
Air jacks	1	
Camber/caster gauges	1	1
Toe gauge—optical	1	4
Wheel clamps	2	–
Storage cabinets	4	–
Alignment tool sets	2	–
Scuff detector	1	–
Portable alignment testor	2	–
Brake shops/lathes	7	32
Brake drum grinder	2	4
Brake shoe grinder	4	10
Brake service tools	6	1
Cylinder hones	9	24
Brake bleeder/washers	2	7
Miscellaneous tools	28	–

tool business, Ammco's share was more limited: between 10 and 15 percent of the market. Ammco faced many small competitors in various segments of the business. Snap-On Tools distributed various Ammco small tools through their direct-selling truck fleet.

Ammco was relatively new in the wheel service sector. Its major products were wheel alignment systems and drive-on racks. Although Ammco entered that line of business in 1963, sales remained rather flat and limited until 1974 (from $306,453 in 1966 to $369,487 in 1974). However, the sales of wheel service equipment started to increase rapidly after 1975. Ammco's share of this market was around 3 percent according to company estimates.

MARKETING PHILOSOPHY

The products that Ammco designed were evaluated on the basis of whether they would appeal to the mechanics who would be using them. Wacker believed this was the way to beat his competitors. He did not believe in planned obsolescence. As a result the Ammco products continued to make a profit for their customers for a long time.

Ammco sold its products through warehouse distributors and automotive jobbers. Consequently warehouse distribution amounted to 50 to 55 percent of total sales. Wacker considered going directly to the consumer like Snap-On Tools, Inc., and Sun Electric. He believed that he could reduce the price of a lathe substantially if he went directly to the consumer. He was afraid, however, that doing this might have a negative effect on the company's other lines.

Wacker believed that a business could compete on price, promotion, advertising, service, quality, or product differentiation but that "you can't compete on all at the same time." He went on to say that "we compete on quality and service and try to be the highest-priced line, yet we give the best value per dollar spent. I care about profit, not volume." Wacker believed that salespeople focused too much on volume to the exclusion of relationship of a price charged and the service provided. It was his perception that he was not charging enough for the meters in LCC. "I have been trying to raise the price singlehandedly." He felt that while LCC devices cost more, the consumer got more value. "Salespeople always figure to sell on price." John Dragoni, the most recent vice president of sales has been asked to train the salespeople to look at sales from the company's point of view.

One of the problems that concerned Wacker was his belief that the new cars were more complicated than the old ones. Also, the older, heavier cars were more frequently in need of brake service than some of the newer, compact cars. The new brake repair machines had to be more complicated, yet perhaps would be used less frequently.

MARKETING WHEEL SERVICE PRODUCTS

Sales of the wheel service line, started in 1963, experienced uneven growth. Sales reached $306,453 in 1966, and fell to $177,983 in 1969 before recovering to $369,487 in 1974. A full line of products had been developed, which included: portable alignment testers, scuff detectors, wheel stand sets, four different types of drive-on rack sets, and a series of specific tools such as toe gauges, camber/caster gauges, and adjusting tools. The products were available, but the sales force ignored them and instead concentrated on selling the brake service line. Thus in November 1975, it was decided to introduce the Rent-Ammco program to gain a bigger share of the market in wheel alignment.

This program was a form of time payment which Ammo decided to finance internally as long as it was possible to do so. Ammco sold the wheel alignment equipment to a dealer and at the same time lent money to a buyer who would buy it from a dealer. The buyer would then pay back in installments. The buyer who decided not to keep the equipment could easily terminate the contract on short notice.

McPherson and Wacker did not interpret this program in the same way. For the general manager this was a very useful marketing tool which was designed to attract more customers by easing the terms of the purchase plan. Moreover he had always felt that this was a very flexible program which could easily be discontinued whenever necessary. Wacker, however, had always been reluctant to initiate this program, because of its possible drain on cash. He discovered somewhat later, by examining the financial statements in March 1977, that the effect of the Rent-Ammco program on the company was even worse than he had expected. The program had gone above the projected $800,000 level and was already causing a cash drain of more than $1 million by the end of February.

Although it was using cash, the program was instrumental in overcoming customer resistance and consequently helped increase sales. The idea had originated from the salespeople themselves, who had always said that it would be very helpful to have a financing plan to aid in overcoming buyers' resistance.

At the time the Rent-Ammco program was in progress, a second program was implemented to increase the sales of wheel alignment equipment. It was decided to put pressure on the sales force by increasing the number of salespersons and by redesigning and reducing sales territories. As a result the salesperson had to develop the sales of wheel alignment units in order to be able to increase his or her compensation.

Finally, in 1976, L. Monteith, a new, aggressive sales manager launched the VAN program. He persuaded McPherson to decide on that program without Wacker's final approval. Formerly, each of the 100 salespersons had a van or station wagon which carried a demonstration unit. Monteith wished to introduce a new slogan: "Call the Ammco man in the blue van," and thought that each saleperson should have a van with two brake lathes in the back. These completely equipped vans would permit salesmen to make product demonstrations in the presence of any potential buyer. According to this plan, the company would buy the vans at fleet prices, install the demonstrator units inside and carry the financing up to $7,000 a piece. Each salesperson had the choice to sign up for that program and acquire a new van (Dodge, Ford, or Chevrolet). The corresponding price would be deducted from salary and commissions over a two-year period. Wacker had been willing to consider this option, but only reluctantly. The program nevertheless was very popular, and about half the salespersons signed up for it. Since the company was cash-rich at that time, McPherson and Monteith had decided to finance the program directly.

PROBLEMS OF THE EXPANSION PROGRAM AND DECLINING SALES

Over the summer of 1976, Wacker got somewhat worried about the extent of the expansion program itself. Early in September, he called McPherson into his office to express his doubts:

Wacker: "What if anything goes wrong?"

McPherson: "Nothing will go wrong. The cash generated internally will be more than enough to finance our investment program."

Wacker: "Well, I don't want to get caught off guard. Why don't you go and talk to the three major banks in Chicago and check with them about obtaining a line of credit?"

A few weeks later, Wacker had not heard anything from McPherson about the line of credit. He asked him again. A few days later Wacker talked to McPherson about the problem and discovered he had sent the treasurer (Dennis Yankus) to check with the different banks on the possibility of obtaining that

EXHIBIT 7
Ammco Tools, Inc.
Monthly Income Statements
March 1976 to February 1977

	1976				
	Mar	**Apr**	**May**	**June**	**July**
AUTOMOTIVE					
Gross shipments	$1922.3	$2003.6	$2269.7	$2547.4	$1294.3
Less returns/allowances	32.6	23.0	41.8	23.0	30.8
Net shipments	1889.7	1980.6	2227.9	2524.4	1263.5
Cost of sales	920.4	926.5	983.2	1104.1	623.8
GROSS PROFIT	969.3	1054.1	1244.7	1420.3	639.7
Other costs					
Commissions	251.8	254.3	297.2	343.4	164.5
Freight out	31.7	29.1	28.0	32.4	24.0
Other	(6.2)	(3.0)	(3.2)	(2.7)	(4.2)
AUTOMOTIVE INCOME	692.0	773.7	922.7	1047.2	455.4
METER INCOME (LCC)	0.4	0.4	0.9	0.7	0.2
TOTAL INCOME	$ 692.4	$ 774.1	$ 923.6	$1047.9	$ 455.6
DEPARTMENTAL EXPENSE					
Engineering expense	58.3	53.1	54.1	54.2	60.1
Selling expense	127.7	149.0	113.4	109.6	116.7
Administrative expense	231.0	223.2	216.9	231.8	240.2
Other expense, net	10.4	19.0	17.3	23.7	24.6
Total departmental	427.4	444.3	401.7	419.3	441.6
OPERATING INCOME	265.0	329.8	521.9	628.6	14.0
Interest expense	–	–	–	–	–
NET INCOME	265.0	329.8	521.9	628.6	14.0
Tax provision	132.0	167.0	261.0	316.0	7.0
NET PROFIT	$ 133.0	$ 162.8	$ 260.9	$ 312.6	$ 7.0

line of credit. By mid-October, McPherson had not presented any option for a line of credit; so Wacker decided to check himself with Northern Trust, which was coexecutor of his father's estate. Northern Trust agreed to grant $1 million in revolving credit and a $0.5 million credit line.

In November, it was necessary to decide on the level of bonuses and dividends. The company had a fixed profit-sharing plan in which everybody participated. As usual Wacker asked McPherson for his recommendations. The general manager proposed an increase in bonus by 51 percent over the previous year. He also recommended $42,450 in additional dividend payments. These recommended increases would mean the outlay of an additional $171,303 in cash for 1976 over the $634,596 paid in 1975 (bonus and dividends). Wacker was assured that this could be done without "getting into the bank." The fol-

	1976					1977	
	Aug	Sept	Oct	Nov	Dec	Jan	Feb
	$2507.4	$2038.5	$2214.2	$2241.0	$1633.2	$1039.2	$2094.5
	46.8	32.6	36.0	34.1	46.3	36.2	58.6
	2460.6	2005.9	2178.2	2206.9	1586.9	1003.0	2035.9
	1087.3	951.8	1031.1	1090.6	788.6	727.1	926.7
	1373.3	1054.1	1147.1	1116.3	798.3	275.9	1109.2
	322.0	265.4	289.4	293.1	212.9	141.4	274.6
	26.4	41.6	25.4	31.8	32.2	22.0	24.7
	(7.9)	(4.2)	(3.9)	(4.3)	(3.4)	(3.7)	(5.1)
	1032.8	751.3	836.2	795.7	556.6	116.2	815.0
	0.4	0.4	0.3	0.4	0.4	0.4	2.0
	$1033.2	$ 751.7	$ 836.5	$ 796.1	$ 557.0	$ 116.6	$ 817.0
	57.4	63.2	66.3	73.9	74.2	67.4	67.3
	87.1	172.2	118.9	143.9	146.8	119.6	139.9
	232.4	226.0	234.4	252.9	378.8	273.7	275.6
	3.8	23.5	23.1	8.4	77.6	14.6	11.8
	380.7	484.9	442.7	479.1	677.4	475.3	494.6
	652.5	266.8	393.8	317.0	(120.4)	(358.7)	322.4
	(1.2)	–	–	–	(7.4)	–	(2.9)
	651.3	266.8	393.8	317.0	(137.8)	(358.7)	319.5
	326.0	134.0	195.0	158.0	(12.0)	(180.0)	163.0
	$ 325.3	$ 132.8	$ 198.8	$ 159.0	$ (125.8)	$ (178.7)	$ 156.5

lowing month, at the December meeting of the board of directors, Wacker proposed a resolution to increase the dividend and it was passed unanimously.

January 1977 proved to be a difficult period for the company. Although Ammco's sales were not significantly seasonal, January had traditionally been a weak month. Usually the two middle quarters accounted for about 53 percent of sales, whereas the winter and fall quarters only 47 percent. December, January, and February usually had lower sales. Sales in January 1977, however, were considerably below expectations. Net shipments amounted to only $1,003,038, a figure 5.5 percent lower than the corresponding figure a year before and 36.8 percent and 54.6 percent lower than net shipments for December 1976 and November 1976, respectively. Income statements and balance sheets for this period are shown in Exhibits 7 and 8.

EXHIBIT 8
Ammco Tools, Inc.
1977 Balance Sheet - Through June 30, 1977

	12-31-74	12-31-75	12-31-76
Cash	$ 178,198	$ 181,720	$ 11,869
Securities	325,000	1,600,000	–
Accounts receivable-net	1,930,580	1,819,056	2,513,216
Due from LCC	116,112	14,724	11,907
Inventories	2,830,364	2,648,480	3,464,989
Inventory reserve-LIFO	537,100-	639,000-	744,000-
Prepaid expenses	68,985	33,907	41,510
Total current assets	4,912,139	5,658,887	5,299,491
Investment-LCC	850,000	1,450,000	1,130,000
Investment-rent-Ammco	–	1,000	800,000
Cash value of life insurance	297,161	351,629	408,976
Note receivable-Dayco	248,669	238,699	227,848
Note receivable-JWB	–	–	480,710
Other investments	36,420	36,420	1,650
Total investments	1,432,250	2,077,748	3,049,184
Property, plant, and equipment	7,855,047	8,552,697	9,832,970
Accumulated depreciation	3,359,073-	3,985,257-	4,645,989-
Net plant and equipment	4,495,974	4,567,440	5,186,981
Patents and trademarks	13,015	13,078	12,911
Deferred federal income taxes	202,000	270,000	314,274
TOTAL ASSETS	11,055,378	12,587,153	13,862,841
Notes payable to bank	–	–	–
Accounts payable	459,866	410,362	717,780
Accrued expenses	692,239	730,575	730,466
Federal and state income taxes	126,345-	603,185	262,909
Total current liabilities	1,025,760	1,744,122	1,711,155
Long-term debt–Prud	650,000	–	–
Long-term debt–bank	–	–	–
Long-term debt–other	250,699	324,395	392,151
Capital stock	1,000,000	1,000,000	1,000,000
Earned surplus, Jan. 1	7,214,412	8,128,919	9,518,637
Year to date profit	1,254,107	1,771,768	1,665,400
Less dividends paid	339,600-	382,050-	424,500-
Other	–	–	–
Total equity	9,128,919	10,518,637	11,759,537
TOTAL LIABILITIES AND EQUITY	$11,055,378	$12,578,153	$13,862,841
Current ratio	4.8	3.0	2.9
Book value per share	107.53	123.89	138.51

	1-31-77	2-28-77	3-31-77	4-30-77	5-31-77	6-20-77
	$ 48,332	$ 152,000	$ 165,261	$ 41,004	$ 113,963	$ 214,758
	–	–	–	–	–	–
	1,894,005	2,492,754	2,890,416	3,440,843	3,586,485	3,260,186
	12,129	43,380	15,946	48,117	42,457	23,657
	3,877,347	4,074,120	4,273,603	4,061,599	3,735,342	3,533,871
	744,000-	780,000-	780,000-	780,000-	780,000-	780,000-
	26,022	64,133	519	172,517	158,744	170,460
	5,113,835	6,046,447	6,565,745	6,784,080	6,856,971	6,422,962
	1,120,000	1,110,000	1,060,000	1,060,000	1,060,000	1,060,000
	900,000	1,060,000	1,111,892	1,163,015	1,209,203	1,188,209
	408,976	408,976	408,976	408,976	408,976	408,976
	226,902	225,949	224,989	224,022	223,049	222,069
	559,621	618,525	677,422	851,312	850,195	954,071
	1,650	1,650	1,650	1,650	1,650	1,650
	3,217,149	3,425,100	3,484,929	3,708,975	3,753,073	3,834,979
	10,016,617	10,154,025	10,246,943	10,397,094	10,582,029	10,729,700
	4,720,909-	4,795,989-	4,870,989-	4,945,989-	5,020,989-	5,095,959-
	5,295,628	5,358,036	5,375,954	5,451,105	5,561,040	5,633,711
	12,811	12,711	12,611	12,511	12,411	12,311
	114,274	314,274	314,274	314,274	314,274	314,274
	13,953,697	15,156,568	15,753,513	16,270,945	16,497,769	16,278,253
	–	–	500,000	500,000	500,000	500,000
	1,234,893	1,083,443	740,683	949,892	440,854	456,872
	152,102	976,371	786,703	811,807	927,934	874,364
	14,298-	148,702	381,702	402,952	710,109	333,359
	1,972,697	2,208,516	2,409,088	2,664,651	2,578,897	2,164,595
	–	–	–	–	–	–
	–	800,000	1,000,000	1,000,000	1,000,000	1,000,000
	400,151	408,151	411,816	419,816	427,816	411,461
	1,000,000	1,000,000	1,000,000	1,000,000	1,000,000	1,000,000
	10,759,537	10,759,537	10,759,537	10,759,537	10,759,537	10,759,537
	78,687-	22,277-	257,973	511,843	816,420	1,032,321
	–	–	84,900-	84,900-	84,900-	169,800-
	–	–	–	–	–	–
	11,680,850	11,737,260	11,932,610	12,186,480	12,491,057	12,622,058
	$13,953,697	$15,156,568	$15,753,513	$16,270,945	$16,497,769	$16,218,233
	2.4	2.6	2.6	2.4	2.5	2.8
	136.41	138.25	140.55	143.54	147.13	148.67

Wacker tried to understand what went wrong. The explanation he received from his general manager was that external factors—not under company control—had caused very low sales and consequently very low shipments. Salespersons were just not bringing back any orders, and the few orders that were obtained could be processed at record speed.

Unshipped orders in December 1976 amounted to $858,514; at the end of January 1977 they were up to $886,149 but went back down to $537,978 at the end of February. At Ammco an average backlog of orders of $1 million was considered normal. It amounted to about two weeks worth of orders ($0.5 million was a minimum since it took about one week just to process an order).

In addition to weak demand, Yankus, the treasurer, felt that past increases in prices may have played a role. Prices might have been over competitive level at that time. In fact, after the freeze in prices and wages, the trend was reversed in 1974. Inflation set in and with newly liberated prices and wages, costs went up. In order to maintain the profit margin, Ammco started to raise its prices twice a year to recover cost increases. In 1974, the biggest increase amounted to 19 percent; then prices increased every 6 months at an average yearly rate of 8 to 12 percent until 1977 when they started to stabilize.

Wacker discovered that internal reasons also played a role in the low shipments. In a conversation with the plant manager, he found out that production had been stopped for a week in January in order to take a new inventory. The physical inventory figures did not match the computerized inventory figures. There were large discrepancies, apparently due to record-keeping problems with a new inventory control system.

On February 2, McPherson came to see Wacker and asked that $500,000 be borrowed as interim working capital in order to alleviate the consequences of the poor January sales performance. Wacker agreed, after being assured that this sum would be adequate for the foreseeable future. Three weeks later, McPherson asked that an additional $300,000 be borrowed. Again Wacker sought and received assurances that this amount would be sufficient. On March 3, McPherson asked that $200,000 more be borrowed. The following exchange ensued:

Wacker: "In September you said we would not need anything and did not even bother to go to the banks in order to ask for a line of credit. Then you said we had to borrow $500,000 and that this would be enough. Then $300,000 more, and now we are up to $1 million. Are you sure that this will be the last time."

McPherson: "Yes. This will be enough."

McPherson again explained that the problem in January could not have been foreseen and that borrowing money was the only way to reduce the adverse effects on the company's financial statements. Sales for February of $2,035,858 were much higher than in January. A loss of $178,687 in January and profit of $156,410 in February still left the company in a net loss position. On March 7, McPherson was again in Wacker's office:

McPherson: "Despite past projections, I think we're going to need to draw down another $500,000 from our line of credit."

OPERATING PROBLEMS—TURNAROUND EFFORTS

In March 1977, Wacker was concerned about the recent incorrect cash projections from his general manager. He decided to write him a letter indicating the specific objectives to be accomplished by the end of the year. (See Exhibit 9.) A copy of the letter was sent to the other top executives of the company in order to "bring Ammco's situation out in the open and in order that all will share in the responsibility of turning the company around."

Among the items mentioned were the following:

- Incur no additional debt and liquidate all existing debt.
- Incur no more capital expenditures without Wacker's approval.
- Increase shipments to $26 million a year, reduce inventory to $3.1 million, and increase inventory turnover to 3.8.
- Earn 9.6 percent on sales after tax by year end.

On the same list were other programs that Wacker wanted reduced or refinanced in order to decrease the financial burdens on the company.

In addition, Wacker had grown dissatisfied with the company's organization structure. All important information had been filtered to him through the general manager. He decided to reorganize his top corporate management team, and, at the same time take some responsibilities away from McPherson. Thus the responsibility of the plant was given entirely to Lenny Morrison, who was placed in charge of manufacturing and engineering. McPherson was assigned to a newly created position, vice president in charge of administration. An executive committee was also formed, composed of Wacker, McPherson (administration), Yankus (treasurer), Morrison (manufacturing and engineering), and Wally Mitchell (research and development).

Inventory problems continued throughout July of 1977. The difference between the physical inventory and computer inventory figure could not be reconciled. Wacker finally retained a consulting firm, which after review presented him with some preliminary conclusions and a list of recommendations.

Essentially these were:

1 The company was running too many computers. One would be enough. In fact there were three computers: One IBM 360-40 at Ammco and two IBM 360-30's—one at Liquid Controls, the other one reserved for programming tests. This was primarily due to the fact that during the sixties, Wacker was upset about Liquid Control's dependency on Ammco. In fact Liquid Controls was a second fiddle. Ammco's problems were always solved first. For this reason, the companies were completely separated in 1967 and were now in two separate buildings. Later on, the same decision was made for the computer.

EXHIBIT 9
AMMCO TOOLS, INC.
LETTER FROM WACKER TO McPHERSON

AMMCO TOOLS, INC/2100 COMMONWEALTH AVENUE/NORTH CHICAGO, ILLINOIS 60064

March 16, 1977

Tom McPherson
General Manager

Dear Tom:

In order that Ammco Tools, Inc., may eliminate its indebtedness to the Northern Trust Company before the end of this year, please make it your business to achieve the following objectives as soon as possible:

1. *Van Program*

No more vans to be ordered by Ammco after the 12 on order are delivered. Please attempt to refinance the 32 vans at the National Bank of North Chicago or elsewhere. The proposed van program desired by Mr. Cannistraro can be carried out and completed providing the financing is not done by Ammco. Please let me know as soon as this is completed.

2. *Rent-Ammco*

Please see that the Rent-Ammco program is discontinued immediately, and by that I mean: no more new business is to be written.

3. *Inventory*

Inventory to be reduced to $3,100,000, which should support shipments of $26,000,000 at 3.8 inventory turns per year at present prices.

4. No new obligations of any sort to be taken on without my approval.

5. I wish to sign all capital equipment or other requisitions for $500.00 or more. This does not include purchases for inventory, which will be controlled by item #3 above.

6. No additional employees to be hired other than sales representatives. Both attrition and terminations, as necessary, will serve to reduce work force in office and plant.

7. No salary increases are to be given, and I will approve none in any case, until our situation is turned around.

8. You have stated that you believe that our 9.6% after tax profit on sales is too high to achieve. I believe it's too low as an objective. With proper management we should be able to achieve it and go beyond it.

Please let me know if you have any questions with respect to any of the above as there should be no misunderstandings.

Fred G. Wacker, Jr.

cc: Mr. W. F. Mitchell
Mr. Len Morrison
Mr. Dennis Yankus

Source: Corporate Records

Liquid Controls would have its own computer so that it could get proper service and would not have to wait for Ammco's programs to be run first.

2 The company had too many people in both office and plant. A reduction of the size of the staff was needed. The consulting firm was proposing a $64,610 payroll reduction through the termination of four employees.

McPherson had been in close contact with the consultants since the beginning of the study and had been aware of their preliminary conclusions. Early in September the head of the consulting firm, Sam Rose, called Wacker about McPherson's lack of cooperation:

Rose: "Fred, we can't get anywhere. You paid for these studies. We proposed a few changes, but McPherson is still 'stonewalling' my recommendations for change."

On Friday, September 9, 1977, Wacker terminated McPherson's employment with Ammco. The following morning McPherson called him at home and wanted to see him. Wacker set up a Monday meeting.

At the meeting McPherson handed Wacker a letter. In the letter McPherson regretted the fact that he had disappointed Wacker, reviewed his work history, and argued that he would be the best individual to implement the recommendations from the computer consultants, Sam Rose and Company. McPherson concluded the letter:

You have many efforts going on to reach the objectives you have set for the company. When it comes to setting up and running internal controls systems in all of these areas, the best person you could have working to accomplish this is myself, simply because of my experience with both companies over the years. There is also the highly important fact that I am well liked and respected by most people in the company, which gives me the ability to work with them without representing an unknown or threatening force that any newcomer must necessarily overcome. While both of us do not subscribe to the indispensable-person theory, it is nevertheless true that someone other than myself would have to go through a familiarization period, both in learning how all things I have mentioned are done, and in working toward rapport with all the other people concerned.

To get the job done right and as expeditiously as possible, I believe I am your best man.

On the basis of McPherson's letter and their conference together on Monday morning, Wacker told McPherson a few days later that he could return.

After his return, McPherson let it be known that he did not agree with some of the consultant's proposals. He was particularly adamant about not changing either the computers and/or computer personnel. Wacker and Rose talked on the phone once more about the decisions that would have to be made and about McPherson's lack of flexibility in carrying them out. Wacker again asked for McPherson's resignation. McPherson left the company on September 30, 1977.

Reflecting on this event, Wacker said:

To this day I like Tom. I felt sorry about it, but there was no other way except to let him go. I told McPherson, "You got me in debt. I asked you to do some things and you didn't do them." He didn't follow through. He worked with me long enough. He knew what I wanted.

During the fall, they effectively started to do the work of two companies on a single computer (IBM 360-40), and the elimination of the two IBM 360-30's was effective as of October 12 for Ammco and November 12 for Liquid Controls. Wacker still received the same reports as he did before.

In terms of material management, Ammco's inventory reduction program proceeded on schedule. At a meeting with the consultant and Ammco's top executives on October 12, it was announced that coding had been completed for all manufactured parts and that appropriate run quantities (economic order quantities), as well as appropriate reorder points, would be calculated and available for review by October 17.

Following the consultant's recommendation three people were dismissed. At the same time Wacker felt that Ammco was slightly overstaffed in terms of production personnel; therefore no new people were added to the production floor in 1977, and consequently the size of the work force decreased from 211 persons in January to 196 at the end of December as a result of attrition.

In an interview Wacker made the following points:

- In April and May the company experienced record sales.
- In October monthly shipments exceeded $3 million for the first time.
- In March, April, and May the profit rate exceeded the 10 percent target.
- The last portion of the $1.5 million line of credit was paid back in October.

In reviewing the new organizational structure, Wacker felt that he had made a mistake earlier. He noted:

When Tom was general manager, he had, in fact, the position of an executive vice president. All the other executives reported to him instead of reporting directly to me. Therefore, I did not always get the whole story. I lost touch with what was going on. Now, in the new structure, everybody reports directly to me. There is no one in between. Communications are more direct, better, and more satisfying.

(See Exhibit 10.)

AMMCO'S DEVELOPMENT AFTER THE 1977 TURNAROUND

The departure of McPherson was followed by the appointment of J. Dragoni as sales manager replacing L. Monteith, who had initiated the VAN program. Wally Mitchell retired at 74 as director of research and development and was succeeded by Lenny Morrison.

Wacker ran the company through an informal executive group, consisting of Morrison, Yankus, and the vice president of sales and marketing, Dragoni. Morrison had gradually assumed responsibility for research and development as Mitchell moved toward retirement at the age of 74.

Wacker also changed Ammco's Canadian distribution, replacing an outside organization with direct Ammco people, as in the United States. The responsibility of sales and product distribution in Canada was taken over by an employee of Ammco's sales department in the headquarters office.

Ammco's new plant scheduled to open in 1980 was delayed until the spring of 1981 due to construction problems. Because of the delay, production at the

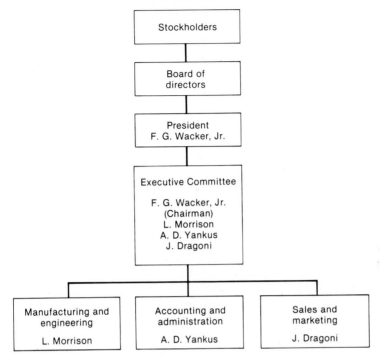

EXHIBIT 10
Ammco Tools, Inc. new organization chart. (*Source:* Corporate records.)

old plant had to be modified several times in the first quarter of 1980. Sales declined in the first quarter of 1980 after a strong fourth quarter in 1979. Inventory reached a level of $6.86 million. Wacker initially responded by putting the hourly workers on a four-day work week. He then let 15 employees go. Inventory levels remained high despite the reduced production, however, and an additional 100 employees were laid off before the problem was ultimately resolved.

After a number of years of touring the trade shows looking for companies to purchase, Wacker initiated discussions with four firms about the possibility of acquisition. Discussion with one company was ended when the owner kept increasing the price each time an agreement appeared imminent. A second set of negotiations was successful. In 1979 an agreement to purchase Magnum Corporation was completed approximately one year after negotiations were initiated. The final sales price was $2.5 million. Magnum was a small, family-run corporation. The owner and senior manager was an older man who ran the company with the assistance of his son-in-law. The Ohio-based company was roughly 10 years old. Its sole product was a patented, automatic tire changer.

In reflecting on the company's performance, Wacker wondered how effectively he had dealt with McPherson and the cash-drain problem which occurred in 1977. He was also concerned with immediate and future changes needed to be implemented to achieve his long-term goal of "staying alive" in a highly competitive and rapidly changing industry. While satisfied with the past financial performance of the company, he found the most recent financial data disappointing. (See Exhibits 1 and 2.)

The rapid increase in small cars also presented a challenge and market opportunity for Ammco. Small engines would have to be rebuilt, particularly if people tended to keep cars longer. This would result in an increased demand for engine-rebuilding tools. Brakes on smaller cars also tended to wear out sooner and would demand increased service. This also held true for tires and wheel alignment.

Management succession was also a matter Fred Wacker had given consideration. He expressed great confidence in Lenny Morrison as an executive who was adept in manufacturing, engineering, and product development. He stated that his son looked like the only real possibility to succeed him at this time. Although his son had worked in the plant for three summers while in college, Fred Wacker was not sure if he had made up his mind to commit himself to the business.

PART TWO

ANALYZING COMPETITIVE THREATS AND OPPORTUNITIES

Competitive Analysis: The Life Cycle of the Firm and Its Industry Environment

MONITORING THE ENVIRONMENT

Assessing and appraising the opportunities available for the business enterprise to effect profitability and growth constitutes a never-ending management task which is frequently overlooked or avoided in the day-to-day operations of the average firm. Sunk investment costs, successful entrenched business operations, the resistance to change, and the difficulty of challenging the short-run viewpoint of management and labor present formidable barriers to the search for new opportunities. This action is usually taken when decline has set in and the inroads of competitors are no longer a threat but a reality. Management acuity is not necessary to recognize "red ink," declining sales and profits, the loss of market share, and the threat of insolvency. One of the greatest barriers to change and adjustment is *past success—success sows the seeds of failure*. The successful concepts, technological breakthroughs, and the innovative or "better products" have a tendency to create "corporate complacency" and lull management into a state of euphoria. The duration of this state is usually determined by the degree of success and how firmly the company becomes entrenched in its industry position: as a market leader and an efficient low-cost producer, or as a market specialist with a specific focus on a higher-quality product or well-defined market segment.

Management must be constantly diagnosing, probing, analyzing, and interpreting significant internal and external events which affect the progress of the enterprise toward its preconceived objectives. Threats to the firm's competitive position, its product line, and its market scope must be detected and recognized before they take their toll and erode the basic core of the business operation. Monitoring the environment to determine potential technological breakthroughs which may change the composition of industries or create new industries, product innovations, and improvements which obsolete existing products and stimulate demand for "new products" is a complex and difficult task which few organizations accomplish with consistency.

The Life Cycle of the Firm

In seeking control measures to signal the need for reformulation and reappraisal of a threatened competitive position, management should direct its attention to the profile of the firm's life cycle in addition to the signs indicated in the external environment. Identifying the *phase* of the firm's life cycle can reveal management behavior which can be expected in the typical pattern of events likely to be associated with each separate and distinct evolving stage of the life cycle. Exhibit 3-1 depicts the four stages of the life cycle of the typically "successful" firm. It is apparent that this illustration parallels the often-used product life-cycle curve, which applies to a particular product of a company.[1] The life cycle of a particular product will be affected by a firm's strategic behavior depending on whether it is a "core product" which accounts for a significant

[1] P. Kotler, *Marketing Management,* 4th ed. (Englewood Cliffs, N.J.: Prentice-Hall, 1980).

EXHIBIT 3-1
Typical life cycle of the successful firm.

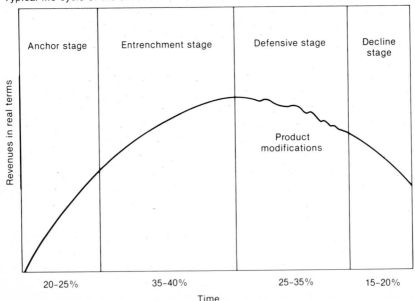

EXHIBIT 3-2
TYPICAL MANAGEMENT ACTION AND RESPONSE IN VARIOUS STAGES OF THE LIFE CYCLE OF THE FIRM

Anchor stage	Entrenchment stage	Defensive stage	Decline stage
1 Assess strengths and resources.	1 Build upon initial success.	1 Direct action toward maintaining market share and industrial position.	1 Product or products slip into commodity items.
2 Define "business it is in": nature, scope, and growth pattern.	2 Develop own industry dimensions or become part of on-going industry.	2 Attempt to expand served market: "new customers" for same product, demographic expansion.	2 Competition becomes intense.
3 Distinguish firm from competitors: technical breakthrough, innovative concept, "better product."	3 Allocate firm's skills and resources to build organization.	3 Attempt product modification, product-line proliferation.	3 Price cutting is frequently engaged in.
4 Develop defined product or product-line concept.	4 Pursue strategic thrust developed in anchor stage.	4 Attempt to improve quality, "outservice" competition, create and sell "improved product."	4 Seek tariff relief from foreign competition.
5 Develop an under-standing of the "art of business" it has entered, its market dimensions, and customers' wants and needs.	5 Establish firm on a broad market front or special market segment, or as market leader or one of market leaders.	5 Seek "missed market opportunities."	5 Engage in "segment retreat."
	6 Develop operating strategies for support of strategic thrust.	6 Use "excessive promotion" to establish or re-establish distinctive image among competitors.	6 Employ cost cutting, plant and facility closing, personnel reduction.
	7 Mold management and labor into organization unit dedicated to achieve firm's objectives.	7 Engage in pricing competition, special pricing strategies, to protect market share.	7 Sell off firm assets, divisions, companies, product lines.
	8 Seek to stabilize firm's skills and resources to establish market position.		8 Attempt intense diversification and/or mergers.
	9 Have root, operating, organizational, and control strategies become "corporate policy."		

99

amount of sales and profits or whether it is a less important product within a family of products or diversified offerings. The firm's or management's behavior and the structure of the industry *will always* affect the life cycle of the entire product market scope, particularly in the late maturity and declining stages. In some instances the failure of entrenched firms in mature industries to respond to change has prolonged the life of products beyond their time. Exhibit 3-2 outlines the expected management action and response in the life cycle of the firm. These responses are explained in greater detail in the following pages.

Anchor Stage   In this initial developing stage, the firm is seeking an *anchor,* a defined product or product-line concept, that identifies, as clearly as possible, the "business that it is in"—its nature, scope, and growth pattern. In the *anchor* stage management may be groping for identity to distinguish the firm in a sea of competitors or to establish a new concept, a technological breakthrough, or a "better product." It is in this period that the *mettle* of management is truly tested. We frequently hear it stated that in this stage the entrepreneur fares best: *the idea generator, the risk taker, the pioneer, the innovator,* the one with foresight and persistence. Most companies never emerge from this phase to become significant factors in the industrial world. Their *anchor* never takes hold to afford them the opportunity to pursue a profitable and successful life span. Recognition of this factor early in the anchor stage allows management to seek other opportunities and avoid the problems of attempting to keep a marginal business afloat. For every success story such as IBM, Polaroid, and McDonald's, there are innumerable examples of companies that never achieved profitable growth or, in many cases, survival. Failure to meet capital requirements, or undercapitalization, is a common cause of early failure. Underestimating capital needs or the inability to attract investment funds frequently hastens the demise of embryonic firms or prevents them from becoming securely anchored in a favorable position to allow for growth and a profitable life span.

Innovations and technological breakthroughs require more time and significantly more capital to *anchor* than the entry of a firm into an on-going industry with a "better product" that will establish a specific niche or meet perceived industrial or consumer wants or needs that have been neglected by the industry. Complete and unreserved commitment is required to successfully span the anchor stage. It is in this period that the business concept, breakthrough, or innovative product takes hold or falls by the wayside, or becomes an "also ran." At this phase, management must be particularly aware of its competitive position and its need to successfully manage growth to ensure survival in order to allow entry into the second stage of the life cycle. The firm must accurately assess its strengths and weaknesses and develop an understanding of the "art of the business" it has entered. Management must thoroughly understand the market it has entered and the wants and needs of the customers it has chosen to serve. In the anchor phase a firm is unencumbered by the past existing products or services, or a specific market position. Its opportunity to think strategically is unhampered; it can be inventive, innovative, and daring. In the later stages of its life cycle the firm will carry the burden of past success, established product lines, tradition, and conservatism. These trappings of comfortable survival can become shackles of resistance preventing change and disruptions to the status quo. Competitive threats can easily be dismissed or provoke defensive reaction rather than reformulation and assessment of needed strategic changes.

Entrenchment Stage   The companies that successfully anchor their position and provide for the initial growth to launch their concept or products usually enter a prolonged entrenchment stage where they build upon initial success and establish a new industry or a prominent place in an on-going industry. Management allocates the firm's skills and resources in this period to build the organization into an industrial force that pursues the strategic thrust developed in the anchor stage.

The firm may seek to entrench itself as a market leader on a broad front or within specific market segments. If the strategic thrust dictates the need for market leadership in a growth market, attempts will be made to gain a commanding market share, which may require significant capital investment, and in the long run cause capital intensity in specialized assets. Low-cost, efficient production will be pursued, and efforts will be directed toward channels of distribution to reach the broadest market. To attain industry leadership or to become one of the dominant firms within an industry group in the entrenchment stage, a strong commitment to quality and service must be instilled in the organization.

If a firm seeks to distinguish itself in a specific market segment, or develop products aimed at several specialized market niches, it must seek to dominate these market areas. Operating strategies for each marketing objective will be different and will require a different set of support functions from production, finance, and personnel. In the entrenchment stage the firm seeks to develop and stabilize the skills and resources needed to establish its market position. Attempts are made to develop and mold management and labor into an organizational unit dedicated to achieving the firm's objectives. The successful company achieves this position, if only for a short time period. But in this necessary process the organization frequently develops traditions and norms which militate against adaptation to change at a later stage in its life cycle.

Successful development of the firm in the entrenchment stage requires the attainment of market leadership on a broad front or within a segment of an industry. Profitable growth and survival is seldom, if ever, attained by companies which seek to "go in between"—not moving toward market leadership on a broad front or within any viable segment which would allow for growth and profitability. Firms which attempt to broaden their product market scope to seek a place as a market leader on a broad front and at the same time within a number of specialized market segments usually fail to become entrenched as a leader in any phase of the industry. Fragmentation of efforts is very costly and unproductive and dissipates the skills and resources of an organization.

Within the framework of our industrial complex we have many examples of companies which have anchored and entrenched their organizations by creating new industries or significantly changing on-going industries through market segmentation and specialization. IBM developed the "computer industry" through the successful introduction of the large mainframe computers. Other established companies in the electrical industry, such as General Electric (GE), Westinghouse, and RCA, did not expand upon their skills and resources to develop or anchor a position in this new high-growth industry, although GE and RCA entered the field after IBM was anchored and were forced to withdraw when they suffered significant losses. Polaroid entered the field of photography with an innovative instant camera and gained a foothold in an industry dominated by Kodak. McDonald's found a specialized niche in the staid restaurant business by developing an efficient and profitable fast-food service.

Defensive Stage   After a firm is firmly entrenched in an industry and has gained a viable market position, it stands ready to defend its hard-won gains. In the early period of the defensive stage, strategic action is most likely to be directed toward maintenance of market share to prevent encroachment by imitators, price cutters, and the new product lines which purport to offer better quality and service. Protection of market position requires strategic planning which takes into account the expected life cycle of the firm's product or products and hence, the firm, the potential growth in the firm's market areas, and the expected return on the sunk investment. The alternative investment opportunities must also be considered as part of a continuous environmental scanning process. The firm should not wait until the later period of the defensive stage, when it is about to enter the decline cycle, to start reformulation and seek diversification or necessary product-line changes. Stagnation can set in quickly and can easily force a crisis situation. In periods of stress and crisis, hastened and hurried decisions are made when corporate resources and strategic options are likely to be limited.

Most successful companies "slip" into the defensive stage after a long build-up in the entrenchment stage. Distinct production, marketing, financial, and organizational strategies which were formulated in the anchor and early periods of entrenchment have become "corporate policy." The image and character of the organization have been formed and are reflected in the culture of the firm and in management's behavior. Without a continuous strategic planning process, companies usually stay to fight too long in the defensive stage and run the risk of having not just specific products but the whole organization becoming mired in a decline cycle. Corporate history is replete with examples of companies that stayed too long with their basic core business. The Fortune 500 select list of the largest corporations reveals almost a 50 percent turnover in less than 20 years. In the forefront of today's corporate crises we find Chrysler fighting for survival and the entire U.S. automotive industry in a too-long-delayed reformulation as they try to cope with intense foreign competition, mainly the Japanese, and a rapidly changing environment which rendered their product-line concepts obsolete. The configuration of the world automotive industry has changed; whether or not U.S. producers will ever gain back their position of yesteryear is very doubtful.

Other companies that gained market leadership through innovative products and good management in the anchor and entrenchment stages find themselves faced with defending their position. Xerox, after many years of market dominance in the photocopy business, now finds itself faced with serious threats from several competitors. Xerox had exceptional growth and profits through a long time period as it pioneered and developed the photocopy industry as we know it today. The company chose to price for margin and left "an umbrella," which was inviting to skilled competitors. Some analysts suggest that Xerox might have staved off potential competitors by reducing prices to defend its market share.

American Telephone and Telegraph Co. (AT&T) for the first time in its long history as a telephone company finds its virtual monopoly position threatened by a number of competitors. Court decisions and advances in the electronic industry have changed the nature and dimensions of the industry. A new telecommunications industry has emerged which seemingly will also alter the configuration of several other industry complexes such as printing, airlines, newspapers, and book publishing. AT&T has been in a reformulation phase which is designed to develop new products and services in the telecommunications field and to develop a marketing concept within the organization. Attempts to defend its long-entrenched position in court have not staved off threatening competitors. The company has now chosen to take an aggressive stance to try to anchor a prominent position in the expanding telecommunications field.[2]

Defensive strategies can be many and varied depending on the stage of maturity of the firm and its product lines. The more solidly entrenched the company's product lines are and the more established its concept of business is in its culture, the longer it will try to defend its position before seeking new concepts and products or diversification. The fight to defend market share frequently goes on long after the prospects for growth and profitability for the core business of the firm has dimmed. The loss of market share and/or declining sales and profitability are frequently met by defensive strategies which call for the redesign of the existing product line, cosmetic improvements to the product, an overhaul of distribution channels, or attempts to improve product quality or to "outservice" competition. Some companies seek to improve their market base by attempting to expand their served market. At times they find it expedient to change an existing product line to attract a broader segment of the population or to aim an "improved product" at a different customer group than their traditional channels of distribution serve. Food producers with their major

[2] *Forbes*, Jan. 4, 1982, pp. 234–235.

thrust in the baby food market have modified their products to direct marketing efforts to dietary foods and an aging population. Management in the defensive stage usually directs its efforts to seek "missed market opportunities" which were not considered in the anchor and entrenchment stages, when emphasis was placed on growth and increasing market share in the more accessible and obvious market areas. This preoccupation with product-line modification usually produces "blips" or "ripples" in the firm's life cycle which prolongs the defensive stage and aids in postponing the decline stage. It does not, however, encourage management to stress the strategic process and seek new product lines and investment opportunities, which will prevent the company from entering the decline phase.

Decline Stage   How long should a company defend a market position it has developed and nurtured over a long time period? A simple answer, which unfortunately is used by many companies, is to stay as long as the business is profitable. This frequently is too long, because the longer the firm fights in the defensive stage the more likely it will enter the decline stage. When growth has slowed or stopped, an effort needs to be made to harvest the return from the ailing cash cows to increase cash flow into product development or diversification.

Eventually all products become commodity items, and as such only the strongest survive. Profitability in commodity products is limited or frequently nonexistent because of intense competition, which leads to price cutting and the consequent reduction of margins. Ease of entry, limited strategic options, and long product life in an industry create the condition for forcing products into commodities. Management should identify these factors before it is too late to engage in an orderly transfer of resources into more promising ventures. When to drop products and leave an industry requires special management skills derived from a well-defined strategic planning system. Products that yield cash flow and still provide reasonable margins, but show little or no growth, need constant surveillance, but should not be eliminated until alternative investments can take up the slack. Fighting for market share in a declining market dissipates funds and management resources which should be directed to product development or product diversification. Remaining in markets and industries that are in a definite state of decline may be prolonged by a market leader which can reap a slow harvest. The followers in such a market, however, will probably find it difficult to survive. The market leader is likely to have greater financial and managerial resources and thus be in a better position to protect market share in a declining market. Market leaders frequently jeopardize their survival by attempting to benefit from the last gasp of a dying company or industry. Strategic planning dictates seeking alternatives when the firm is still viable and has the resources to develop new concepts and products to keep the organization healthy and competitive.

Levi Strauss, the market leader in "blue jeans," has utilized its resources from the major product to seek diversification within a family of products, such as jackets, sportswear, men's suits, and women's wear. This action has taken place in a period when the sales of blue jeans as a newly found "uniform" for the young and those of college age added greatly to the long-existing traditional utilitarian demand for their basic product. The market expanded significantly as it became "fashionable" to wear blue jeans. In the expansion period there were new entrants which segmented the market by creating designer items out of the practical work garment. Many imitators also entered the market with lower-priced copies of Levi's products and the more expensive fashion jeans. Levi's management recognized that despite their market leadership in a resurging market, the firm could remain stagnant and subject to decline if it attempted to remain a single-product firm subject to the vagaries of consumer taste trends and a commodity product.[3]

Basic products and industries with a long life span are difficult to move to new opportunities and usually have a long decline stage. This can be said of the steel, shoe, and textile industries in the United States. The firms within these industries, with a few exceptions, have experienced a long decline stage in their life cycles. International competition has accentuated their problems and hastened the demise of some of the companies in these industries. In a not-too-unusual move, most of the U.S. companies in the industries have sought tariff relief as a protective measure to allow them to survive. This kind of action has been advocated in a number of cases throughout U.S. industrial history. It is both a defensive stage and decline stage action, or perhaps more accurately it can be described as a reaction to attempt to salvage a dying firm in a declining industry.

Companies in these industries suffer from "induced decline"; while their markets show little or no growth, their basic products are still produced and sold on a worldwide basis, and some companies show profitability and growth as distinct units in these industries. United States firms in shoes, textiles, and steel have entered the decline cycle partly because of foreign competition. As industry growth slowed and foreign competition entered with lower prices and higher-quality products, many of the firms in these industries had already entered the decline stage. Their unimpressive records were not an attraction for capital investment, and declining business decreased cash flow needed to provide new plants and equipment and to keep pace with technological developments. In periods of prosperity and high demand, which prevailed in a long postwar period, many companies became marginal producers sustained by increased demand and "umbrella pricing" by industry leaders. Management frequently made concessions to labor without receiving increased productivity. Product development and capital reinvestment were neglected; marginal plants continued to operate because of pent-up demand on a worldwide basis. The cold, grim realities of major foreign competitors such as West Germany and Japan and the arrival of developing countries into the industrial phase caught many in these industries with outmoded high-cost product lines in aging

[3] *Fortune,* Nov. 19, 1979, pp. 86–89.

businesses. These events cast their shadows long before they became a reality. Strategic planning may have softened their impact and allowed some of the firms to survive and seek new market positions. We can point to companies within these industries which have had profitable growth by segmenting their markets and developing innovative product lines.

The firms in the steel industry which dropped losing products and segmented their market into specialty steel have experienced higher returns on total invested capital and shareholders equity than the large basic steel producers which serve all facets of the market. As previously indicated, steel is a necessary and important worldwide commodity, and companies within the industry are still profitable and have shown a growth pattern despite the decline of a number of basic steel producers. Nucor provides an excellent example of profitability and growth in a U.S. industry considered to be stagnant and in decline. Started in 1969, this "minimill" producer is emerging as a national steel company with four plants geographically located to serve specific market needs. Since 1969 earnings have shown a compounded growth of 31 percent a year, and return on average equity in recent years has exceeded 28 percent. The company has employed the latest technology in the industry and developed some of its own. As a minimill producer the company melts scrap steel in electric furnaces and is able to produce a ton of steel aimed mainly at specialty markets, at a cost significantly lower than the Japanese and the large integrated U.S. producers.[4]

A strategy frequently employed in the decline stage is to engage in "segment retreat." Firms phase out of markets and try to "back up" into a market segment where they think they can compete. They marshal their skills and resources to build a fortress around one segment of the market to make a last ditch effort to survive; or they close plants, decrease labor and personnel, and significantly reduce their sales and presence in the industry. These measures may provide some temporary relief and prolong the decline stage. In other cases they may hasten the demise of companies. Sooner or later their assumed protected segments will be attacked by the industry leaders, foreign or domestic, as they seek to expand market share. Reduced output despite cost-cutting measures leaves the retreating firm with few options and high-cost products. In effect they are "chased back up" their experience curves.

This is happening in steel, automobiles, and textiles. Plants have been closed, output has been reduced, and costs per unit have increased as many companies in these industries have sought segment retreat. This market strategy must be distinguished from planned market segmentation where a company capitalizes on its resources to seek a niche where it can vigorously compete through strength, not through forced retreat. Shrinking the size of a company is not any guarantee of survival. At this stage the strengths and resources of the company are usually dissipated, and their ability to attract needed capital in-

[4]*Fortune,* April 6, 1981, pp. 43–46.

vestment to build a solid position in their chosen retreat segment is severely restricted.

Firms in the decline stage and fighting for survival cover a large cross section of industry; however, they all exhibit typical decline strategies. International Harvester, long a leader in the manufacture of farm implements, tractors, and motor trucks, is engaged in a fight for survival. The company is in the decline stage and is hampered in its efforts to survive by a severe recession in farm implement and truck sales. Management action has reduced the size of the company by sales of diversified units and parts of its core business. Plants have been closed, and labor and management personnel have been drastically reduced.[5]

Kroehler Manufacturing Company, a factor in the furniture industry, has been fighting to maintain a firm identity. In its decline stage it has closed and sold plants, sold off parts of its business, and retreated into its basic core business of manufacturing and selling medium-priced upholstered furniture, after a foray into higher-priced designer furniture.[6]

AMC, American Motors Corporation, is also in a survival situation after a long decline period. The problems of the U.S. auto industry has pushed the smallest of U.S. auto producers to the brink in its effort to stay alive. Renault, the French government-owned auto maker, has put $225.5 million into troubled AMC with a commitment to add $122.5 million at a later date. This financing has given Renault 46.4 percent of AMC's stock.[7]

Diversification usually starts in the later part of the defensive stage and frequently intensifies in the early part of the decline stage. Most diversification attempts in the decline stage are hampered by falling profits and reduced cash flow. As a consequence, weak acquisitions are often made which add to the problems of the firm rather than provide an avenue for relief. A more likely move by weaker firms in the decline stage is to seek a merger, which all too frequently may be with another weak company in the decline stage. The old adage "misery loves company" has been supported by the record of weak mergers. In the automotive industry, Hudson joined Nash to form American Motors. Ailing Pan American joined with a weak National Airlines. The railroads throughout their history have been merging weak lines, with few successful survivals.

Companies that have entered a decline stage and still have a good cash flow are in most instances part of basic capital-intensive industries and still enjoy liberal depreciation allowances. Their diversification efforts may be more selective. Such efforts, however, usually signal a retreat from the core business, which is declining due to competitive threats, domestic and foreign, and changes in the industry structure. Technological deficiencies which seem too

---

[5]*Chicago Tribune,* Dec. 27, 1981, sec. 5, pp. 1–2.
[6]See Kroehler Case, this edition.
[7]*Wall Street Journal,* Nov. 18, 1981, p. 2.

great to overcome are also a factor which drives capital-intensive companies to seek escape through diversification. Northwest Industries used the cash flow from North Western Railroad to develop a miniconglomerate with diverse interests and sold the core business of the railroad to the employees. IC Industries used the cash flow of the Illinois Central Railroad to form its miniconglomerate. Steel companies such as Allegheny Ludlum formed Allegheny Industries, which makes various products, from industrial to consumer items, with a minimum stake in the steel industry.[8] U.S. Steel has attracted attention and criticism because of its efforts to diversify into the petroleum business through Marathon Oil, a $6.4 billion purchase. It should be noted that U.S. Steel, the giant of the industry, through the acquisition would reduce its steel sales from 70 percent to about 40 percent of total sales, based on 1980 sales data.[9]

National Steel has diversified through the acquisition of several large savings and loan companies. Republic Steel has entered joint ventures to develop coal properties and has also purchased a property and casualty insurance company. The most successful companies in the steel industry have diversified out of basic steel into specialty steels and the fabrication of steel-related products which have different economic cycles and represent the entry into more than just a specialty segment of the steel industry.[10] The characteristics and dimensions of the products are sufficiently different to provide entry into a new industry.

Although industrial giants such as U.S. Steel with a significant entry into the petroleum business and Du Pont with its purchase of the large integrated oil producer, Conoco, may prove to be exceptions, diversification intensely pursued in the decline stage of a firm's life cycle seldom produces a viable entity that can embark on a new growth stage and anchor a position in another industry or competitive environment. Survival for the "shell of the company" may be attained, but it is usually without products that can provide a "critical mass" to gain a distinct strategic thrust and maintain the firm's image or establish a new identity as the forerunner in a new industrial endeavor. The basic tenets of diversification, the advantages and disadvantages, still apply to firms in the decline stage despite the fact that they are usually pursued in a constrained stage of urgency.

INDUSTRY CHARACTERISTICS AND DIMENSIONS

Industry Boundaries

After a firm has anchored itself with a successful introduction of its product line, its competitive fight has just begun. It may be fortunate enough to have a unique position, in which case it forges a new industry. However, it is more

---

[8] Allegheny Industries, Annual Report, 1980.
[9] *Business Week,* Dec. 7, 1981, pp. 34–35.
[10] *Forbes,* Jan. 4, 1982, pp. 120–124.

likely that an enterprise must entrench itself into an industrial complex which is on-going or in the formative stages. To analyze the opportunities and competitive threats to a firm, the nature and life cycle of its industry must be appraised. An organization must know and understand the characteristics of its industry. Defining an industry is not an easy task because of the substitutability of products and the fluid nature of many industries. The proliferation of products and the extensive product-line modifications which take place as industries mature further complicate forming a simple definition. The concept of perfect competition facilitates industry definition by stipulating a set of conditions whereby all firms produce identical products, there is complete freedom and exchange of information, there are no barriers to entry, and there are no special firm attributes to allow for bargaining power.

These conditions do not describe typical industrial complexes, although we do find intense competition a factor in many. The most frequently used industry classification is the Department of Commerce's Standard Industrial Classification (SIC) index. This broad categorization, however, still requires considerable refinement to position a firm for analysis. The usual industry definition provides for a group of firms which produce products that are similar in nature and are designed to satisfy a common defined demand. Therefore the group of products can easily be substituted one for another. Strategic action of an individual company within an industry, in effect, attempts to differentiate its product from competitors by stressing actual, perceived, or imagined differences calculated to stimulate demand.

Industry Concentration: Oligopolies

By their competitive action market leaders within a defined industry may seek to prevent entry. They can utilize strength to discourage new competition by their defensive pricing policies, based on accumulated experience and low unit costs, through judicious use of their resources to effect product improvements and advances, and by the accumulation of commanding market shares. When these conditions exist within an industry, they are likely to discourage entry unless a potential entrant has an innovative product or a technological breakthrough which may change the nature and dimensions of the industry. When firms are not among the market leaders under this type of industry structure, they very likely should attempt an orderly withdrawal. Intense competition over time usually turns all basic industries into oligopolies, where few firms remain and the industry leader or leaders have the major share of the market. At this level the industry's products have become commodities, vertical integration has occurred, and growth has been slowed. Top firms fight for market share, and price is the main competitive weapon. When the industry has settled down to a few top companies, overcapacity usually exists, except for peak-demand periods, and oligopolistic pricing through price leadership usually prevails.

In today's worldwide competitive pattern this industry condition can be altered by foreign competition. The domestic oligopolies of the steel and automotive industries have been jolted and changed in dimension by foreign competition. We also find that the U.S. oil industry has been changed in nature and dimension by the energy crisis, OPEC (Organization of Petroleum Exporting Countries) pricing, and the resultant flood of new entries.

Oligopolies and Limited Strategic Options

These basic industries, such as steel, aluminum, petroleum, copper, and other minerals, have long lives because of the nature of their products, and are not usually subject to dramatic external or internal shocks. All these industries have reached maturity and the inevitable stage of oligopoly; and the major market share of the core products of the industry are concentrated in a small number of vertically integrated firms. Such industries are characterized by capital intensity which, in addition to the product characteristics, protects the industry life cycle, acting as a barrier to entry.

Firms within industries that parallel this type of structure have *limited strategic options*. Over a long time period technological differences in mature industries are likely to be insignificant, and because of the nature of the basic product, differentiation is minimal or nonexistent. Corporate size, heavy, concentrated capital investment, antitrust threats, and government regulation limit or exclude alternative investment choices. In addition, years of organization building to effect efficient operations within the confines of a single industry tends to develop a corporate culture that thinks "steel," "oil," or other basic product lines. All these factors leave few options for revitalization or changes in the direction of the firm. When growth has ceased or declined, and the industry becomes labeled as matured or stagnant, investors seek alternatives and depress stock prices. Except for cyclical trends, stocks within these industries are not considered good investments and lack the vitality of firms in the anchor or entrenchment stages. Management is confronted with the perplexing questions: Where do we go from here? What are our viable options?

Diversification has usually been the most frequently employed option. This answer is not just in reply to the above questions but is also an outlet for embarrassingly high cash flows that are not reinvested in the unattractive core business. The worldwide problems of the petroleum business have prompted the industry leaders to acquire coal companies and seek other entries which would enhance their image and position as "energy companies," not just oil producers. Other companies, such as Mobil, have sought to gain entry into nonrelated fields. Mobil acquired Marcor, a merged company composed of the large retailer Montgomery Ward and Container Corporation, a packaging company.[11] U.S. Steel, as previously mentioned, acquired Marathon Oil at a time when the U.S. steel industry was in decline and suffering from a lack of investment in

---

[11]*Chicago Tribune,* Nov. 8, 1981, sec. 5, pp. 1–2.

new facilities and modern technology. Most of these diversification efforts, as previously discussed, have not met with great success and have not launched the companies on a new growth trajectory. Some of the acquisitions have only recently occurred or have not had sufficient time to provide the acquiring companies with the needed stimulus to revive profitable growth. It is not likely that diversification too far removed from the basic skills and resources of the large corporations engaged in a basic commodity industry will provide an outlet to duplicate the original growth and profit patterns. It is more likely to just maintain and prolong the firm's life cycle.

Industry Structure and Competitive Patterns

Industry structure is most frequently mentioned as a major factor in the determination and extent of competitive patterns among the firms that compete within a group. Like the life cycle of a company, an industry structure develops over time and frames its own life cycle. Similar to individual companies, some industries enter the decline stage and fade into oblivion. Their demise may be occasioned by distinct technological developments or gradual product developments and innovative changes which forge new industries or so distort the structure of existing industries that they are forced into new dimensions and designs. It is easy to identify the long life cycle of some business groups, such as the carriage and wagon industry, which was described in Chapter 2. It met its demise because of the motor car, a technological breakthrough which became commercially feasible in the early years of the twentieth century. This invention clearly gave rise to a new dominant industrial force through the creation of the automotive industry. Carriage and wagon producers faded into oblivion, although prominent names and companies in the automotive industry, such as Studebaker, Durant, and the Fisher Brothers, came from wagon and carriage shops. The new automotive industry also sent the bicycle industry into decline. Important figures in the bicycle industry, such as Nash, Barney Oldfield, John Willys, and the Dodge Brothers, left to enter the newly formed automotive industry. The bicycle in this period began a rapid decline as a transportation vehicle. Through the years in the United States it has had several resurgences as a children's toy and a sports recreation vehicle.

All industry life cycles are not as easily marked and traced as that of the wagon and carriage group. Nor is the technological development or innovation which disrupts the cycle and causes the decline as easily discernible as it was in this industry. Structural changes in industries are usually more subtle and often do not cause abrupt and noticeable declines. The typewriter industry went from mechanical to electric over a long time period. IBM became the dominant factor in the industry through its concentration and development of the electric typewriter. Market leaders such as Royal and Remington and others saw their market shares erode on a year-to-year basis. Their late entry into electric typewriters was no doubt due in part to the failure to recognize that a new force was changing the nature and dimensions of the industry and forcing them into a decline cycle. A study of this industry shows that the market leaders fought too long in the defensive stage rather than seeking a new competitive entry.

The fluid nature of industry structure is further illustrated by the new generation of typewriters which are electronic and will replace electric typewriters by about 1983. The expected capabilities of electronic typewriters will include data communicating capability and editing functions and will very likely serve as computer terminals. It will be difficult to reconcile this instrument with the typewriter industry or market as it has been known in the past. Word processing has invaded the office equipment market, and with storage capabilities it represents a significant departure from the standard use of typewriter, method of editing of copy, and the final printed form. The office equipment market in terms of the "office of the future" will be a combination of many single products which are parts and segments of the present industry combined in an electronic system. Single work stations will consolidate multiple functions and very likely replace the personal computer as well as typewriters and other equipment, in the office. The office equipment industry could easily become an adjunct of the computer industry.[12]

Determining the characteristics and boundaries of the office equipment industry and the computer industry in the future will be difficult, as it is now, or may be simplified if single companies produce a complete system combining multiple functions in one or several work stations. We can be certain, however, that old-line office form and equipment producers will not survive unless they have a firm foothold in the electronic office of the future.

When IBM developed its mainframe computer line, it also developed the computer industry. Its dominance of the market determined the dimensions of the industry and set the competitive pattern as imitators and followers sought special niches in segments of the industry in peripherals, plug-in compatibles, or varied accessory lines. The development of the small computer and the so-called personal computer is now challenging IBM's position. IBM made a late entry into this growth market. Semiconductor companies such as Intel have also entered the microcomputer market.[13] The characteristics and dimensions of the computer industry are rapidly changing and will continue to affect competitive patterns in the future. Firms that do not keep pace with the technological developments within the broad confines of this industry will miss the strategic options and will be constantly threatened by more aggressive foresighted competitors.

Multiple strategic options are not confined to the multifaceted computer industry. The research-oriented chemical industry is stretching into the pharmaceutical industry with preservatives and laboratory chemicals. Genetic engineering in the life sciences is offering great potential for product development and may significantly change industry dimensions. Oldline chemical companies

---

[12] *Forbes,* Jan. 4, 1982, pp. 148–150.
[13] *Forbes,* Jan. 4, 1982, pp. 144–147. Also see *Fortune,* June 29, 1981, pp. 84–92.

that continue to rely on commodity items in the bulk chemical line will have their future threatened and could easily slip into the decline stage.[14]

The drug industry, which has fluid boundaries, also has significant strategic options. Industry dimensions are constantly being stretched, and the possibility of new discoveries which could jar and change competitive patterns is constantly present.

Strategic Options in Fragmented Industries

The structure of many industries is fragmented without dominant industry leaders with commanding market shares. Various factors contribute to the development of this kind of industrial structure. Many of these factors are overlapping and are difficult to isolate; only the more distinctive and important will be considered.

The nature of the industry products may not lend itself to economies of scale and allow for the experience curve effect, thus inhibiting efforts to gain a commanding market share. This applies to products that require some degree of customizing and have a relatively high price, such as special types of machine tools, metalworking products, process machinery, and varieties of specialty-steel products. Another example is found in the furniture industry, which has traditionally been comprised of a number of small firms without an industry leader or company that had a long product line. Most firms in the industry specialized in a specific line such as upholstered furniture, dining room or bedroom furniture, office furniture, or specific furniture pieces such as chairs, tables, outdoor furniture, or other accessory items. Furniture production does not easily lend itself to mass production, and except for some specific pieces, has been resistant to technological advancements. The industry practice of selling on an order basis from trade shows and showrooms has also limited production for inventory.

Some industries are not concentrated because vertical integration may not be practical because of the raw material supply and/or the nature of the distribution channels. Carpeting is a product of a fragmented industry which is generally considered a commodity item. No firm has a commanding market share, and there are a number of companies with relatively small market shares which make up the industry. The traditional raw material of carpeting was wool, which was purchased on the open market by carpet manufacturers. This made any effort to gain an advantage by seeking some control over raw material supply impractical. Synthetic fibers have replaced wool as the basic raw material for carpeting. This material was developed by the major chemical companies after a long period of research and development and significant investment. This kind of project could not be undertaken by any of the carpet manufacturers because of the required scientific research personnel and the large capital outlays. The fragmented industry, with only a limited number of sup-

[14] *Forbes*, Jan. 4, 1982, pp. 110–116.

pliers, prevents the development of any buyer advantages. The advanced technology of the carpet industry became available to any entrant or manufacturer with the development of the tufting machine, which provided the same basic cost advantages to all industry firms. This added to the difficulty of gaining dominance in the industry.

The nature of the distribution channels in furniture and carpeting militate against forward integration. Like the bulk of consumer products in the household line, products of these industries are sold through a variety of channels such as large retail chains, small retailers, chain discount houses, and department stores.

Some products may discourage national distribution and size because of transport cost and geographical market preferences. This is true for dairy products such as milk, bakery products (with some exceptions), and candy producers. These factors also prevented the brewery industry from being concentrated. Local tastes and the "quality" of water were thought important in local and regional beer sales. Shipping beer on a national basis was costly and impractical. The development of brewing techniques allowing the use of any treated water supply changed the structure of this industry. Regional breweries were established with economies of scale and national promotion and advertising. This eliminated most of the small breweries and concentrated national market share in a small number of producers.

Some industries are populated with a large number of small to medium-sized firms because of ease of entry and a small initial investment. This is true of the apparel industry, which is frequently referred to as the "rag trade." Price competition is intense, product imitation is rampant, and entry and exit to the industry is numerous. The industry is also highly fragmented with few producers that approach a full product line. Most producers are in a segment of the market or have specialized products in a narrowly defined line.

Some products may not be easily adapted to the development of brand loyalty or the creation of "a product franchise." With some exceptions this is true of a good part of the apparel industry such as children's clothing, women's wear and accessories, and other smaller segments. Jewelry and other artisan products, most small-purchase household products, and most furniture products are difficult to establish as "national brands."

Some products may be highly dependent on creative effort and highly susceptible to fashion design; others may be an exclusive product aimed at a narrow market segment. Most products that fall into these categories are the result of entrepreneurial enterprise, where the owner or owners are guided by personal objectives in addition to profit. As a result, entry and exit may not fit the usual industrial pattern, which is guided by profitability, growth, and survival. "Psychic income" can be an important factor in inducing entrepreneurs to assume risks to gain entry into businesses of this nature, and can also be a powerful deterrent to leaving the business even if the returns are marginal and prospects are uncertain.

Gauging the Firm's Position in Its Industry and the Economy

The analysis of industry dimensions and structure indicates a number of significant factors that must be included in the appraisal of a firm's competitive position. Important external considerations which should be considered in examining the firm's competitive threats and opportunities include such questions as the following:

What is the current state of the economy?

What do forecasts seem to indicate about the immediate and long-range economic future?

Is there evidence of significant new technologies which could affect the company's position?

What is the nature of the company's industry?

What is the pattern of competition in the industry?

Is the tendency toward concentration? Growth patterns?

What is the extent of foreign competition with regard to the company's products?

What is the firm's position in internal markets?

How does the firm's products compare with major industry competitors in terms of market share? Product quality? Pricing strategy? Product style and design?

In relation to competitors how can the firm's market strengths be rated? Its market image? Its brand names? Its advertising and promotion? Its channels of distribution?

How does the firm appraise its major competitors' skills and resources? Their ability to respond to challenges in the marketplace in terms of asset strength, productive facilities, and cost structure? Their market strengths in terms of product lines, brand identification, market image, product market scope, and channels of distribution? Their financial strengths in terms of cash flow, profit patterns, and growth patterns? Their research and development capabilities?

How attractive is the company to the investing public?

What is the firm's public image?

How and to what extent does government regulation influence the company and its industry?

What is government regulation likely to be in the future?

What is the political and social environment in which the company operates? What is it likely to be in the future?

RISK OF MEETING COMPETITIVE THREATS AND|OPPORTUNITIES

The decline of a business or an industry as described in the preceding pages can be due to a number of factors both internal and external. The neglect of strategic planning, however, is the major cause of the failure of management to heed the signals of competitive threats and to capitalize on new opportunities which appear in the marketplace. Strategic planning is not review planning and necessitates a long-range viewpoint. Product improvement, product development, and major technological changes and innovations require significant research and development expenditures for the future without immediate payout in the present. The choice of direction and the expenditure of effort for research and development projects entails risk and uncertainty and an imperative need for a systematic scanning process built into a strategic plan. As it has been so often pointed out, U. S. business efforts all too frequently are short-run in their outlook. The need for the corporation to maximize shareholders' wealth, to provide respectable financial statistics, and to maintain a stock price which is acceptable are powerful deterrents to a long-range managerial outlook. The importance of economic objectives in the guidance and life cycle of the firm are discussed in greater detail in Chapter 6.

SUMMARY AND GENERAL COMMENTS

Assessing and appraising the opportunities available for the business enterprise to effect profitability and growth is a never-ending management task frequently overlooked or avoided in the day-to-day operations of the average firm. This action is usually taken when decline has set in and the inroads of competitors are no longer a threat but a reality. Successful concepts, innovations, and products have a tendency in the long run to create "corporate complacency." Management must be constantly diagnosing, probing, analyzing, and interpreting significant internal and external events which affect the progress of the enterprise.

Identifying the phase of the life cycle can reveal expected management behavior in the typical pattern of events likely to be associated with each separate evolving stage of the cycle.

In the *anchor stage* the firm seeks to identify the "business that it is in"; a defined product, or product-line concept; and its nature, scope, and growth pattern. In the anchor stage management may be groping for identity to distinguish the firm in a sea of competitors and to establish a new concept, a technological breakthrough, or a "better product."

Companies that successfully anchor their position and provide for the initial growth to launch their concept or products usually enter the *entrenchment stage*. At this phase they build upon their success and establish a new industry or prominent place in an on-going industry.

After a company is firmly entrenched in an industry and has gained a viable market position, it stands ready to defend its hard-won gains. Most companies "slip" into the defensive stage after a long buildup in the entrenchment stage. Distinct production, marketing, financial, and organizational strategies which were formulated in the anchor and early periods of the entrenchment stage become "corporate policy." Without a continuous strategic planning process, companies run the risk of having the whole organization becoming mired in a decline cycle.

Companies that do not develop new strategic thrusts in the defensive stage are forced into a decline phase. Ease of entry, limited strategic options, and long product life create the condition for forcing products into commodities. When to drop products and leave an industry requires special management skills derived from a well-defined strategic planning system. Many firms may seek tariff relief in the decline stage, shrink the size of the company, or seek segment retreat. At this stage the strengths and resources are usually dissipated, and the firm's ability to utilize recovery strategies is severely restricted. Diversification usually starts in the latter stages of the defensive stage and frequently intensifies in the early part of the decline stage. Weak acquisitions and mergers are often made in this period because of the lack of strategic options and a limited cash position.

To analyze the opportunities and competitive threats to a firm, the nature and life cycle of its industry must be appraised. An organization must know and understand the characteristics of its industry. By their competitive action market leaders within a defined industry may seek to prevent entry. They can utilize strength to discourage new competition. At this stage of development industry products have become commodities, vertical integration has occurred, and growth has been slowed. Basic industries that have reached the oligopoly stage have few strategic options to utilize for revitalizing the firm. Corporate size, heavy concentrated capital investment, antitrust threats, and government regulation limit or exclude alternative investment choices. Diversification has usually been the most frequently employed option. Diversification too far removed from the basic skills and resources of large corporations engaged in a basic commodity industry is not likely to return the firm to its original growth and profit patterns.

Industry structure is most frequently mentioned as a major factor in the determination and extent of competitive patterns. Like the life cycle of a company, an industry structure develops over time and frames its own life cycle. All industry life cycles are not easily marked and traced. Structural changes in industries can be subtle and not subject to abrupt and noticeable changes. Some industries are fluid in nature and present significant opportunities for strategic options, as contrasted to the basic heavy goods industries that are constrained in seeking alternative investment opportunities.

SELECTED REFERENCES

Abell, D. F., and J. S. Hammond: *Strategic Marketing Problems and Analytical Approaches* (Englewood Cliffs, N. J.: Prentice-Hall, 1979).

Ansoff, H. I.: *Corporate Strategy* (New York: McGraw-Hill, 1965).

Drucker, P. F.: *Managing In Turbulent Times* (New York: Harper & Row, 1980).

Lorange, P., and R. Vancil: *Strategic Planning Systems* (Englewood Cliffs, N.J.: Prentice-Hall, 1977).

McCarthy, E. J.: *Basic Marketing: A Managerial Approach* (Homewood, Ill.: Irwin, 1978).

Porter, M. E.: *Competitive Strategy* (New York: Free Press, Macmillan Publishing Company, 1980).

CHAPTER 4

Management Response to Environmental Change: Analysis of External Factors Affecting Strategic Planning

NEED TO MONITOR EXTERNAL ENVIRONMENT

Management must be constantly alerted to the potential impact on the organization of economic, political, and technological change in order to formulate the strategic decisions which will determine its future course. Its investment choices are commitments to the future and always involve uncertainty and a calculated degree of risk taking. Information systems are usually concentrated on the internal functions of the firm, with some attention directed to market changes and trends. As a result, as indicated in the case histories in preceding chapters, management usually reacts only belatedly to environmental impacts and changes. Searching the environment and identifying possible potential effects on the operations of an enterprise and formulating plans to cope with projected external threats or opportunities is a difficult task that is not usually effectively accomplished by most management groups.

Environmental Forecasting

Environmental forecasting has recently emerged as a recommended, orderly process to aid management in this formidable undertaking. It has been derived from environmental monitoring and has its roots in economic forecasting, which has long been part of management's decision-making process. Environmental forecasting represents an attempt to apply intellectual order to the process of determining vectors of future societal changes. It encompasses more than the traditional parameters of economic and technological forecasting—it also includes events in the social and political spheres which will shape the future course of our industrial society. In this process of environmental forecasting, management attempts to determine the significant and relevant events which are likely to occur within a specified time dimension and to anticipate the impact they will have on society and its institutions. Through an analysis of the presaged events and their interaction with each other, some assessment can be made regarding the future trend and development of industrial markets and potential consumer demands. It also provides some basis for anticipating problems and threats to existing industries, products, and methods of conducting business. In recent years such key events as public and political stress on ecology, pronounced changes in value systems, the trend toward zero population growth, and the rapid technological changes derived from the space program (such as miniaturization and complex telecommunication systems) have exerted a strong pressure for change in society and consequently in industry.

How well management forecasted these significant events and their effect on specific industries and businesses is difficult to determine. There is evidence to indicate that some have made decided advances utilizing the recently discovered technologies to develop new products for industrial and consumer use. Other firms have suffered as a result of failing to anticipate the effects of these events on their core businesses. How effective an environmental forecasting process can be is a matter of conjecture; it must still be classified as an experimental art, although its objectives are admirable and highly practical for the business enterprise. The best most organizations can hope for is to provide management with sufficient pertinent data to create an awareness of environmental trends which will have potential effects on their specific enterprises or offer possible opportunities for investment and the utilization of the firm's skills and resources. As previously indicated, management must incorporate environmental monitoring into the control and information system as part of its planning process. If this leads to a formalized environmental forecasting system which can be effectively staffed and financed, it will greatly aid decision makers in coping with the uncertainties of the future.

COMPETITIVE ANALYSIS AS A FACTOR IN ENVIRONMENTAL SCANNING

Monitoring Competition

In the previous chapters, competitive threats were stressed as a major factor affecting the progress and survival of the firm. The most immediate need is for continuous monitoring of competitors. This formidable task is not easily accomplished. While there are many visible indicators and signals of competitor behavior, competitors' strategic plans are usually well-kept secrets which outward surveillance is not likely to detect. Attempting to provide checklists for management to aid in industry and competitor analysis is not intended in this chapter. Some of the key factors affecting the firm's competitive environment will be considered.

Industry Factors in Environmental Scanning: Fragmented Industries

Industry analysis, as suggested in Chapter 3, is a vital ingredient in environmental scanning. Industry structure significantly affects the firm's competitive position. Fragmented industries with ease of entry complicate the task of monitoring competitors. It is also difficult to anticipate competitor moves. New entrants increase competition and jeopardize the profitability of the established firms. New entrants are likely to seek market share and as a result cause price instability. Apparel manufacturers fall into this category. They are also victims of changing fashions, which are difficult to predict and require quick response to competitors' actions in the marketplace.

The carpeting industry has also been plagued with many entrants and a pricing structure which has virtually reduced the product to a commodity item. Despite acquisitions of carpet manufacturers by large diversified companies, such as Armstrong World Industries, U.S. Gypsum, and RCA, the industry structure has not significantly changed. If and when consolidation and concentration occur in the manufacture of carpet, the competitive pattern will be altered and many of the present producers will be acquired or will drop out of the industry. With the entrance of large companies seeking diversification, the smaller producers will be forced to increase their efforts to monitor the industry environment. However, the structure of the industry may be a factor in causing divestitures by the acquiring companies which find a lack of profit potential in their acquisitions. The nature of the raw material supply has prevented backward vertical integration, and the multiple channels of distribution have prevented forward integration, which has been a factor in preventing concentration.

Fragmented industries in which no single firm or small number of firms hold commanding market shares usually lack distinctive market signals to alert companies to competitiors' moves. The number of competitors and the variation on product themes are difficult to track. Products that offer an opportunity for a producer to customize, such as machine tools and metalworking, process machinery, and specialty steels, form segments which may narrowly define industry boundaries and reduce the predictability of competitive strategies. Other highly specialized products such as jewelry, artisan products, many furniture products, and small-purchase household items are difficult if not impossible to monitor because of the extreme fragmentation. Producers in these areas are usually alerted to new competitive threats after they have entered the market.

Environmental Scanning: Oligopolies

Oligopolies in the capital-intensive industries have few producers, and their market positions are firmly established. Domestic monitoring, even for technological changes in the industry, are usually not too difficult to detect. However, such industries as steel, automotive, and television manufacture witnessed the decline and erosion of their established positions in the U.S. market because of foreign competition.

The supermarket industry, which is comprised mainly of regional oligopolies, have a need for constant competitor monitoring. The main competitive weapon to maintain and gain market share is price competition. The industry, as a consequence, has been subject to numerous price wars which have seriously impacted the profits of all participants as they struggled to maintain or increase their position. This has been true of retail gasoline distribution and a number of other commodity items in industries where price leadership does not exist.

The airline industry under deregulation has been subjected to price wars, particularly for long-distance flights. With only minor differences in service, airline transportation is a commodity item, and significant market-share increases can only be accomplished through price competition. How far this present trend of price cutting will extend is difficult to determine. Losses in the industry are prevalent, and leave little doubt that price wars are detrimental to all competitors. Deregulation has also resulted in a number of new entrants who have utilized the price mechanism to gain a foothold in the industry. This very recent change has increased the number of competitors and has increased the need for, and complicated, the environmental scanning process.

Companies in concentrated industries have posed a threat to other on-going industries because of their diversification efforts. Their large concentrations of capital and cash flow have enabled them to make significantly large acquisitions outside of their core businesses. The previously cited U.S. Steel's acquisition of Marathon Oil, Du Pont's purchase of Conoco, and Mobil's buy-out of Marcor are examples of unanticipated competitive threats to established firms in these industries. Entry through acquisition is a constant threat to any industry. If the acquiring firms have financial resources exceeding the average of companies in the industry, they can pose a serious threat to the incumbent firms by changing competitive patterns in the industry.

The entry of Procter and Gamble into the facial tissue market jolted Kimberly Clark, long the industry leader with its Kleenex brand. Procter and Gamble also disrupted the toothpaste market with its Crest entry, and became a factor in the coffee market through its purchase of Folgers. IBM's innovative electric typewriter changed the industry's dimensions. There are many other examples of unanticipated entries and acquisitions that changed industry competition and jarred entrenched producers, who considered only established companies within the industry as competitive threats.

Industries that have a number of strategic options and are driven by significant technological breakthroughs, such as the electronics industry and the pharmaceutical and drug industry, are fluid in nature. The dimensions of such industries are changing frequently due to new discoveries and research and development (R&D) breakthroughs. Environmental scanning for businesses in these industries will aid in detecting new developments spawned by private companies, universities, and foundations. However, only well-organized, productive R&D efforts will enable firms to keep pace in a rapidly changing scientific environment.

INTERPRETING ENVIRONMENTAL TRENDS

Economic and Demographic Factors

Despite the numerous events which have not been accurately predicted and acted upon by management, most coming events cast their shadow long before they have made a significant social and economic impact. In most instances the lack of data and sufficient information are not the major obstacles to environmental forecasting. The difficulty usually lies in management's interpretation and analysis of available information and its delay in making decisions about the future. The potential impact of change is usually evident years before the actual change takes a firm grip and affects all of society and its business institutions.

Demographic changes have had a pronounced effect on the economics of industry on a worldwide basis. The post-World War II period provided accelerated demand for many products in the area of home and family formation. The baby boom of the period offered significant opportunities in the areas associated with child rearing, education, and youth products. This wave has faded, and now most of the western world is faced with an aging population, with emphasis shifting from youth to the middle and older population. Such changing demographics have obvious implications for many industries and their products. Keeping pace with the demand for baby food products presented an opportunity and challenge for producers in this area. In the past decade they have been faced with declining demand and a need to seek new markets in different demographic sectors.

An aging work force and the government-mandated extension of retirement age in the United States to 70 years of age provide opportunities and threats to certain industries. The rising number of women in the work force has also been a factor in changing competitive patterns in industries as far-reaching as wearing apparel, fast-food chains, and convenience foods for home consumption. This movement may affect hospital care, health products, leisure-time products, and those products which appeal to the retired sector.

In Europe the retirement age has drifted downward, and while the number of women in the work force has not reached U.S. proportions, it has been steadily increasing. Thus, firms with international outlets face conflicting demand patterns.

Ford's Reaction to Environmental Changes

As discussed in previous chapters, Ford continued to produce his Model T long after the signs revealing decided demographic and social changes were clearly visible. Environmental trends indicated a continuing rise in disposable incomes, a shift of farm population to urban areas, and a change in consumer preferences from basic automotive transportation—represented by the Model T—to a car with more conveniences and style. General Motors detected these social and economic changes and accurately interpreted their significance in relation to the automobile market; therefore GM made inroads into Ford's commanding market position by introducing annual model changes, providing a choice of colors, and emphasizing styling and design. The Chevrolet, the company's entry into the low-price field, eventually surpassed the Ford as the sales leader.

Sears, Roebuck's Interpretation of Environmental Trends

General Wood of Sears, Roebuck is credited with recognizing the demographic changes which gained impetus after 1910 and the marked increase in the use of the automobile in the 1910-1920 period as potential threats to the mail-order business.[1] General Wood served in Panama after his graduation from West Point, helping to build the canal. In his off-duty hours he is said to have studiously read the *Statistical Abstract of United States* and noted emerging demographic trends which clearly indicated that the United States was rapidly changing from a rural, agrarian society to an urban, industrial society. He also became aware of the increase in the number of automobiles and what this meant in terms of mobility for both the farmer and the urban dweller. After World War I he accepted a position at Montgomery Ward and attempted to convince the executive group of the need to establish retail stores to offset the decline in mail-order sales and take advantage of the potential of well-located retail stores. His efforts met with little success, and he left Ward's to accept a position at Sears at the request of Julius Rosenwald, the head of the company. Wood was given the title of vice president in charge of factories and retail stores.

Despite opposition from mail-order executives, whose primary interest was in expanding the old, established core business, Wood started opening retail stores. After a slow start in 1925, a chain of Sears retail stores grew rapidly and established a new root strategy for the organization. The emphasis in distribution was shifted from mail order to retail department stores, which stressed a wider variety and higher quality of merchandise. Wood's awareness of the environmental trends and his ability to interpret their threat to established mail-order houses—as well as the opportunity they offered for retail merchandising—were major factors in providing Sears with the momentum which carried it to its position as the world's largest merchandiser.

In recent years, Sears has experienced significant losses in its core business, which some analysts attribute to the fact that the company misjudged its entrenched position as a retailer of lower- to medium-priced merchandise when it made efforts to upgrade its status by stocking higher-priced wares. This

---

[1] A. Chandler, *Strategy and Structure* (Cambridge, Mass., M.I.T., 1962).

provided an opportunity for competitors such as K mart and other discount chains to lure away many of Sears' traditional customers. The company experienced a decline in profits as the new entrants into "discount merchandising" had steady growth in sales and profits. Sears entered a retrenchment program and a strategic redesign. The company has diversified away from its core business by furthering its interests in financial services.

Environmental Trends: The Case of Volkswagen

Volkswagen represents the most recent victim of economic trends which increased its costs, increased the buying power in its major markets, and changed consumer preferences away from basic low-priced automotive transportation to cars that offered style and comfort. The VW story is a repeat of the Model-T syndrome. The high-quality, low-priced VW Beetle found ready acceptance in the post-World War II markets, and the company experienced spectacular growth. The special market niche at the low end of the automotive market was made possible in the early stages of VW's development by the relatively low wages in West Germany and the low value of the German mark in relation to the currencies of VW's major export markets. Rising income levels in West Germany increased labor costs to the point where VW no longer had an advantage in export markets. Concurrently, the value of the German mark in relation to other currencies in VW's major markets increased greatly, creating another export disadvantage. Rising income levels gave buyers who formerly sought the lowest-priced automotive transportation the opportunity to choose convenience, comfort, and style not offered by VW's basic Beetle. This combination of economic circumstances caused serious losses for VW and forced a change in its root strategy which included phasing out the Beetle and introducing a new line of cars.

Social and Political Factors Affecting the Environment

It is difficult to separate the economic, social, and political forces which affect the environment of business enterprises. They are interrelated and require an analysis of the cross-impacts they exert to clearly differentiate the extent and nature of their respective influences. It is clearly evident, however, how the dramatic events of recent years have accelerated change and have produced a profound effect on our industrial society. The vigilant quest for environmental quality has spawned numerous activist citizen groups which have exerted pressure in the political arena to effect legislation aimed at reducing pollution. This action, while designed to be universal in its application, has been directed mainly at industry. The impact of antipollution legislation and public pressure for cleaner air has been felt in many areas and particularly in those industries and companies which are classified as environmentally sensitive. The fortunes of some companies in the environmentally sensitive petroleum industry have been severely affected by recent legislation and social action. The Ethyl Corporation, producers of the lead additive for high octane gasoline, represents a practical example of a company pressured by environmental factors which seriously threatened its core business.

The Clark Oil Company Case

Clark Oil offers another example of a successful company which was forced to change its basic business thrust because of the antipollution campaign and the later effects of the energy crisis. Over the years, Clark had developed a well-defined root strategy as a semi-integrated marketer of high-grade premium gasoline distributed through a chain of regional service stations. The company had successfully nurtured the image of the "premium people," which distinguished its distribution outlets from the all-purpose service stations of competitors selling various grades of regular and premium gasoline. The ecological movement for cleaner air dictated the sale of no-lead gasoline, and the fuel crisis (precipitated by the oil embargo of the Middle Eastern oil-producing nations) directed attention to smaller cars which got better mileage and ran on regular gasoline. These factors forced Clark to abandon its long-standing root strategy predicated on the sale of only premium leaded gasoline. The company added no-lead gasoline (at considerable expense) and changed its advertising and company image to reflect its new position in the industry.

The Case of the Tobacco Industry

The social and political pressures exerted against the tobacco industry in the United States have forced the major companies into an orderly retreat from sole reliance on tobacco as a product. The link of cigarette smoking with lung cancer triggered legislation which forced the manufacturers to label their product as potentially dangerous and also restricted their advertising efforts. These actions and the potential threat of the barring of cigarette sales have caused most major producers to conduct diversification programs away from their core business. This defensive diversification move has led the firms to acquire a variety of companies in several different industries. R. J. Reynolds, the largest tobacco company, has interests in seagoing transport, petroleum, food and beverage companies, and packaging materials. Philip Morris, Inc., the second largest producer, has diversified into printing, land development, packaging materials, greeting cards, razor blades and shavers, and the brewing industry. Despite their numerous acquisitions, the dominant part of the sales and revenues of both companies still come from tobacco sales.

Government Regulation:
The Case of Procter and Gamble and Clorox

Government regulation and government action are important environmental factors associated with the political scene which can directly affect a company's strategic planning. The restriction of the antitrust laws and the uncertainty associated with their enforcement has been felt by policymakers in many different industries and has forced significant changes in the conduct of their businesses. The Clorox-P&G case is an excellent illustration of the impact of antitrust laws on the successful, innovative company intent on profitable growth. Procter and Gamble, the largest manufacturer of soap, detergents, and cleansers, acquired Clorox, the nation's largest producer of household liquid bleach. Liquid bleach, like P&G's product lines, was a low-priced, rapid-turnover household item sold mainly through grocery stores and super-markets. The products of both companies were presold through mass advertising and sales promotions. The acquisition of Clorox by P&G was a "perfect fit" and a logical extension of the company's product line, which offered financial, marketing, and production synergies. After protracted hearings, court proceedings, and appeals covering a period of 10 years, the Supreme Court upheld a Federal Trade Commission ruling which ordered P&G to divest itself of Clorox. The Commission described the merger as a "product-extension" merger and in violation of Section 7 of the Clayton Act. It was pointed out that P&G's products and Clorox's bleach were closely related products. Both were low-cost, high-turnover consumer products sold to the same customers at the same stores by the same merchandising methods. The merger, in the opinion of the Commission, which was upheld by the Supreme Court, offered possibilities for significant integration at both the marketing and distribution level. The large size of P&G and its dominant position in the industry plus the market dominance of Clorox were major factors in the Commission's findings. Discounting the market position of the two companies and P&G's size, an examination of the Commission's ruling suggests that the major reasons for disallowing the merger constitute the basic elements of a good merger involving compatability, fit, and synergy.

Technological Factors Affecting the Environment[2]

The technological advances of the past several decades have had a forceful impact on our industrial society. The computer has come of age in this period, developing from its early beginnings in the days of vacuum tubes to the utilization of electronic circuitry which has revolutionized information processing. The computer and electronic technology have been responsible for eliminating traditional markets and jobs and have caused severe dislocations for many companies. At the same time the new technology has initiated new businesses and created a demand for new jobs and skills. One of the most notable developments of the space age, miniaturization, has advanced computer technology and resulted in the growth of many scientific products. In addition, it has

[2] See James R. Bright and Milton E. F. Schoenman (eds.), *A Guide to Practical Technological Forecasting* (Englewood Cliffs, N. J.: Prentice-Hall, 1972).

spawned such popular products as the all-purpose electronic calculators and pocket calculators.

There is no doubt that technology is a constant threat to traditional industries and established product lines, but it is also an essential source of opportunity which must be nurtured and developed. The policymakers who monitor the environment and correctly interpret the ever-present signals which forecast coming events have the time to take action to avoid dislocating impacts on their enterprises, and they are also in a position to take advantage of new technologies. As previously indicated, environmental changes and technological developments in most instances cast long shadows and provide early and persistent warning signals before the events they forecast take hold and have a significant societal impact.[3]

Technological Change and the Railroad Industry

The history of the railroad industry illustrates the slow development of technology and environmental changes which severely affected their traditional business. Competition for the passenger and freight business of the railroads developed over a long time period. The usage of the automobile developed on a gradual basis, starting with the turn of the century and exploding at the end of the World War II period. The airline industry, which captured the bulk of the railroads' long-haul and business passenger travel, developed very slowly. It took a span of over 25 years before air-transport technology was sufficiently advanced to attract a significant number of travelers. The trucking industry grew with advances in automotive technology and the growth of the highway system. It took almost 30 years before trucks seriously hurt the railroad industry. Another environmental factor which affected the railroads was the serious burden of government regulations, which severely hampered their ability to respond to threats to their long-standing businesses. It is also interesting to note that while the traditional businesses of the railroads were being seriously affected, a technological development with a long history, the diesel-powered locomotive, was eliminating the steam locomotive.

Technological Change: Invention and Innovation

The invention and development of television also began a long time before its effect was felt in industry and society. The first important development of television can be traced to the period of the late 1920s, the time when another technological advance, radio, was enjoying its first commercial success. Television did not make a decided impact until the early 1950s. Despite its long period of development, the movie and magazine industries failed to heed the strong envi-

---

[3] See James R. Bright, "Evaluating Signals of Technological Change," *Harvard Business Review*, January-February 1970, pp. 62–70, and James R. Bright, "Opportunity and Threat in Technological Change," *Harvard Business Review*, November-December 1962.

ronmental signals that forecast television's potential success and the effects it would have on these businesses as well as society.

The often-repeated story of the development of the Xerox copying machine illustrates a very recent example of a technological development which changed the course of an important segment of industry.[4] The first patent on xerography was reported in *The New York Times* in 1940 and excited the interest of many people. An IBM marketing man is reputed to have tried to interest his company in the invention, but without success. An abstract of the patent also appeared in Kodak's technical report entitled *Patent Abstracts* in 1940; however, Kodak did not pursue the new process.

In 1948 Haloid, a small company, picked up the patent and developed it into the Xerox Copier, which revolutionized the duplicating and reproduction industry. Like the examples cited previously, the "Xerox revolution" was a long time in developing from an idea to a patent, and finally to commercial success. But during the course of this development many signals were emitted which could have been monitored by the managements of the many companies that were seriously affected by Xerox's success in the marketplace.

Technological development and progress is inextricably tied to the economic, social, and political factors which prevail in the environment. Technology has and will continue to create an impact on the environment and will also be a major change agent in our industrial society. Therefore management cannot afford to ignore technological advances. This was clearly delineated in the preceding accounts of the new industries and businesses created through technological discoveries and of the impact they have had on traditional businesses and product lines. Despite the imprecise nature of the embryonic science or art of technological forecasting, policymakers must keep pace with developing technologies in an effort to determine their importance and potential threat or opportunity to their enterprise.

International Dimensions of Environmental Scanning

Global competition is now a fact of life, and while it presents an opportunity and challenge to the firm, it complicates the task of environmental scanning. No longer can the companies of foreign countries be overlooked as competitive threats. The events of recent years have shown that long-held positions of leadership can be eroded by foreign competition. In the United States the steel industry has been shaken by foreign competitors. The U.S. automotive industry has lost its place as the number-one world producer to the Japanese, and have seen their market shares and profits eroded. Despite the fact that General Motors and Ford had established market positions in Europe, where they met the demand of different foreign markets, they became victims of competitors' imports into their home markets.

Japanese competition took over the major share of the radio industry in the

---

[4] Bright and Schoenman, op. cit., pp. 238–256.

United States over a decade ago. It has also acquired a dominant position in the production and sale of television sets, and a strong share in the electronics industry and a number of other associated industries. These industries were nurtured and developed in the United States and thought to be invulnerable to foreign competition.

The rise of OPEC on the international scene has created significant disruptions for domestic and multinational business. It has increased the world price of oil from a range of $6 to $12 a barrel to $34 to $40 a barrel. This cartel pricing has not only changed the dimensions of the petroleum industry but has affected the cost structure of practically all of U.S. industry. The surge in petroleum prices has not only threatened the survival of business on a worldwide basis but has also provided opportunities for firms in oil exploration and well-drilling services, and for manufacturers of products or product improvements directed to fuel conservation. Like other dramatic events the impact of OPEC was not foreseen by most companies, both multinational and domestic. The recent oversupply of oil, and the consequent softening of world prices, was also a surprise to many companies.

Oil is not the only strategic commodity that is subject to multinational economics and politics; many other strategic minerals necessary for industrial production are subject to global political shifts and economic changes which might disrupt the supply flow.

The extent of international trade, multinational monetary flows, and the trend to transnationalism, which involves a movement toward production sharing, strongly reinforce the interdependency of today's world.

Nations which have recently emerged into industrial states, such as South Korea, Singapore, Taiwan, Brazil, and the Crown Colony of Hong Kong, have shown that they can be formidable competitors. These emerging countries, with the support of their governments, have entered into more sophisticated industrial areas requiring large capital investment. The fluid nature of a global economy provides these countries with the opportunity to buy technology, and to seek joint ventures or licensing agreements. Countries in this stage of development are no longer restricted to labor-intensive industries or the shipping of raw materials. They can enter international competition in areas formerly reserved for the developed industrialized western nations. The impact of this global threat to the established producers of western nations, while recognized, has not been fully comprehended by many managers or incorporated into their environmental scanning systems.

Recent international movements, in part caused by the recession and intense global competition, have placed another burden on management already concerned about international environmental scanning. In Europe, where the United States has its most significant international investments, the climate for investment has been changing and threatens established positions in this market. Growing union pressures and restrictive labor laws of several European countries complicate the operations of established U.S. businesses and dampen their enthusiasm for increased investment in this large market area.

Growing nationalism, mainly emanating from the desire to gain position in high-technology industries of the future, has caused some European nations to "sponsor" companies or provide their own entries into these industries. These institutions are favored in their internal environment and are granted concessions denied foreign competitors.

Volatile exchange rates and increased currency exchange controls also complicate the determination of future opportunities and competitive threats.

Global European firms discouraged by potential problems in their home markets have extended their investments into the United States because of its stability and market attractiveness. This movement will no doubt increase and must be calculated into the assessment of the future competitive climate for all industries.

The need for global scanning is imperative for strategic planning. It is clear that while such environmental analysis must be incorporated within the firm's information system, it cannot be accomplished without a network of sources. Internal information flow from foreign subsidiaries must be evaluated at several corporate levels, and firms may have to rely heavily on outside information sources and special consulting reports.

Environmental Factors and Corporate Social Responsibility

Accurately assessing the environmental impacts and pressures on the business firm is a herculean task beyond the capabilities of any single executive group. This chapter has merely highlighted the environmental factors which influence policy formulation and has described some of the significant effects of external influences on management. It is difficult to separate the corporate response to the environment and the corporation's exercise of social responsibility. Some contend that rapid technological advance and industrial expansion have caused many of our environmental problems. The business community has frequently been called upon to solve many environmental difficulties, whether or not it was thought that business was the major cause of the problems. Since the business community is the energizing force of our free-enterprise society, many contend that the care, maintenance, and improvement of the environment in all its aspects is its social responsibility. The extent and limits of the social responsibilities of business enterprises have never been clearly defined. This question has long been the subject of considerable debate and controversy. The eminent economist Milton Friedman and other writers in the field contend that the sole and overriding objective of management is to maximize profits, which in turn will contribute to the efficient use of resources and to environmental improvement.[5] Friedman's argument also supports the enlightened-self-interest response which leads businesses into exercising social responsibilities to foster and protect their industrial status. It is difficult to determine whether the response of business to environmental problems stems from "a corporate con-

---

[5] See Milton F. Friedman, *Capitalism and Freedom* (Chicago: University of Chicago Press, 1962), pp. 133–136; Peter F. Drucker, *The Age of Discontinuity* (New York: Harper & Row, 1969), pp. 188–211; Paul F. Heyne, *Private Keepers of Public Interest* (New York: McGraw-Hill, 1968), pp. 107–110.

science" or a rational recognition of the need to exercise social responsibility in order to maximize long-run profit and growth potentials.

Regardless of the motives that have conditioned corporate responses to social problems, there has been a marked increase in the public's expectations of business in the solution of these problems. The public has come to expect corporate participation in support of education, charities, the arts, and the solution of minority and urban problems. These expectations are based on the contention that business in our highly industrialized free-enterprise society is too important a factor to confine itself to a basic overriding objective of maximizing shareholders' wealth. In its response to legal requirements to cease environmental abuses and correct their results, the corporation has little choice; but it does have the freedom to choose whether or not it will participate—by contributing funds and management time—in the solution of social problems. The extent and limits of corporate social responsibility remains an intensely debated question which has elicited serious and voluminous response in the literature.[6] An in-depth discussion of this subject area is beyond the scope of this chapter. The major emphasis has been on providing a basis for the recognition of the problems and dimensions of management's role in formulating a reasoned response to the pressing environmental and social problems of our industrial society.

SUMMARY AND GENERAL COMMENTS

Management must be constantly alerted to the potential impact on the organization of economic, political, and technological change in order to formulate the strategic decisions which will determine its future course. Environmental forecasting has recently emerged as a recommended orderly process to aid management in this necessary function. This process should be incorporated into the firm's information system as part of its strategic planning process.

Competitors within an industry constitute the greatest need for environmental scanning and continuous monitoring. Industry analysis is a vital ingredient in environmental monitoring. Industry structure significantly affects the firm's competitive position. Fragmented industries with ease of entry complicate the task of monitoring competitors. Oligopolies in capital-intensive industries are usually not too difficult to monitor. However, such industries have suffered decline and erosion of their established positions as a result of foreign competition in their home markets.

Regional oligopolies such as supermarkets need close competitor sur-

---

[6] See, for example, William J. Baumol et al., *A New Rationale for Corporate Social Power* (New York: Committee for Economic Development, 1970); Neil H. Chamberlain, *The Limits of Corporate Responsibility* (New York: Basic Books, 1973); John J. Corson and George A. Steiner, *Measuring Business's Social Performance: The Corporate Social Audit* (New York: Committee for Economic Development, 1974); Neil H. Jacoby, *Corporate Power and Social Responsibility; A Blueprint for the Future* (New York: Macmillan, 1973); and Lee E. Preston and James E. Post, *Private Management and Public Policy* (Englewood Cliffs, N.J.: Prentice-Hall, 1975).

veillance because of the tendency toward price cutting, the most frequently utilized weapon to hold and gain market share. Airlines with few differences in service, and under deregulation, have engaged in significant price wars to hold or gain market share, with unfortunate results. This has also been true of other industries with commodity products without price leadership.

Economic and demographic factors have the most significant impact on business. Population changes have altered demand schedules for numerous products and have also provided new opportunities for many firms. The shift from youth-oriented economics to a population growth of older people in the past decade affected significant industry changes. The aging work force, the influx of women into industry, and the raising of the retirement age in the United States provide opportunities and threats to certain industries.

Social and political factors have changed the industrial environment and affected the position of many companies. The impact of antipollution measures and public pressure for cleaner air seriously affected the automotive industry at a time when it was under severe pressure from foreign competition.

Antitrust laws have long been a threat to large concentrated companies, whose efforts to diversify have often been thwarted or aborted.

Technological breakthroughs have changed industries and disrupted the comfortable positions of many entrenched firms.

It is difficult to separate the corporation's response to the environment and its exercise of social responsibility. Since business is the energizing force of a free-enterprise society, many contend that the care, maintenance, and improvement of the environment in all its aspects is social responsibility. The extent and limits of the social responsibilities of business have never been clearly defined. Regardless of the motives that have conditioned corporate responses to social problems, there has been a marked increase in the public's expectations of business in the solution of these problems.

SELECTED REFERENCES

Abell, D., and J. Hammond: *Strategic Marketing Problems and Analytical Approaches* (Englewood Cliffs, N. J.: Prentice-Hall, 1979).

Aguilar, F. J.: *Scanning the Business Environment* (New York: Macmillan, 1967).

Drucker, P.: *Management In Turbulent Times* (New York: Harper & Row, 1980).

Fahey, L., and W. King: "Environmental Scanning for Corporate Planning," *Business Horizons,* February, 1973.

Keegan, W.: "Multinational Scanning: A Study of Information Sources Utilized by Headquarters Executives in Multinational Companies," *Administrative Science Quarterly,* 1974.

Lebell, D., and O. Krasner: "Selecting Environmental Forecasting Techniques from Business Planning Requirements," *Academy of Management Review,* 1977.

Lorange, P., and R. Vancil: *Strategic Planning Systems* (Englewood Cliffs, N.J.: Prentice-Hall, 1977).

Wall, J.: "What the Competition is Doing: You Need to Know," *Harvard Business Review,* November-December, 1974.

CHAPTER 5

The Firm as a System: Diagnosis and Analysis of Internal Business Problems

THE EXECUTIVE ROLE IN ANALYZING BUSINESS PROBLEMS: THE CONCEPTS OF FUNCTIONAL DYNAMICS

The diagnostic or problem-solving process is initiated when the firm's information system indicates that performance is not in accordance with its strategic plan. Deviations from expectations may be minor, or may be the forerunner of serious future problems. Performance gaps are usually detected by the monitoring of financial controls. These first signs may or may not signal the need for extensive probing of the firm's operations. The interpretation of control signals at the policymaking level will determine the extent of required internal analysis.

The strategic design illustrated in Exhibit 5-1 not only provides the basic guidelines for executive action but also serves as the framework for problem identification and situational analysis. The key to analysis of major business problems for the top management group is found in the continued recognition of the stated mission and purpose of the enterprise. In seeking the root cause of major problems and the focal point for the initiation of recovery strategies, policymakers must view the firm as a single system functioning as a whole unit through the interaction of its parts or subsystems.

As indicated in Chapter 1, it is not unusual for policymakers and members of the general management group to suffer from functional emotionalism, an affliction which causes them to view the problems of the organization as manifestations of functional maladjustments. This failure to view the firm as a whole usually results in attempts to assign business problems to separate categories and proceed to solve them one at a time in a piecemeal fashion. The principal of functional dynamics soon becomes apparent, however, when this approach is

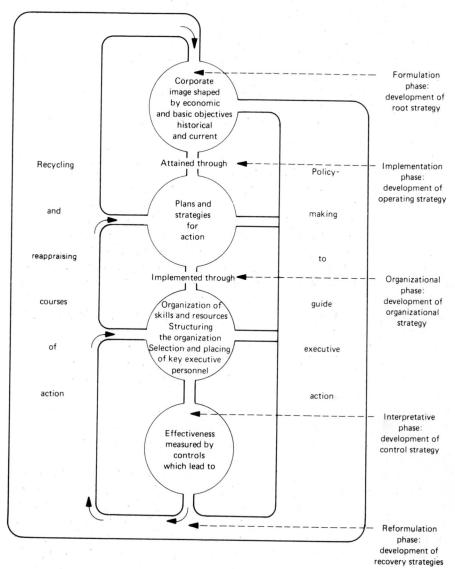

EXHIBIT 5-1
Flow of the policy formulation process and the development of the strategic design.

used. A decision to change a basic policy affects all enterprise functions to a greater or lesser degree; significant changes in the marketing function, like additions to or deletions from the product line, directly affect the production function and may require additional skills and resources or result in the reduction of management and labor. The interrelatedness of the operations of the enterprise must be taken into account in all management's deliberations, and the effect of decisions made to solve basic functional problems must be viewed in terms of both the internal and external environment of the firm.

THE RELATION OF THE LIFE CYCLE OF THE FIRM TO INTERNAL PROBLEMS

Internal analysis must include an examination of the firm's life cycle. The stage of its cycle is a factor which determines the action that must be taken to take advantage of a growth situation, protect a position, stave off a decline, or initiate a recovery strategy. (See Exhibits 3-1 and 3-2.)

The nature of internal problems will vary with the phase of the company's cycle and may be directly related to its life-cycle position. The problems likely to be encountered in the early phases of the firm's life cycle will involve capital shortages and financing difficulties which are commonly associated with attempts to entrench and establish a company within an industry. At this phase the firm is usually struggling to gain recognition and market position for its product line or concept. If it is an innovative product the missionary work must be undertaken and marketing campaigns initiated. Working capital to meet these requirements may be difficult for the embryonic firm to generate.

The functional problems of finance and marketing in such situations will be reflections of the company's stage of development, which should be recognized in analyzing its situation.

In the entrenchment stage the firm is seeking to establish its industry position earned in the anchor stage. The pressure of building market share, maintaining growth, and establishing organizational structure with the needed support functions can create significant internal problems. Recognizing the nature of these problems, which are likely to occur in the development of any company, is a formidable task for management. In seeking solutions to a myriad of problems which may seem interminable, management should not be deterred from the pursuit of their strategic plans. Once a viable strategic thrust has been established in the anchor stage it should be continued and exploited in the entrenchment stage to assure the firm's competitive position and industry status. Problems created by "growing pains" should be properly diagnosed as a "normal" and expected ingredient of the entrenchment stage. Seldom is drastic action needed in this phase of the corporate life cycle to correct deviations from stated objectives. Overreaction can lead to diminution of the firm's strategic thrust.

Companies which have entered the defensive phase will develop problems common to this stage of the corporate life cycle. In many respects this phase has characteristics similar to the anchor stage. Defensive action to protect market share and revive growth in a mature product line frequently results in expanding served markets and modifying old product lines to be promoted as "new." In the defensive stage product-line proliferation is not uncommon, nor is price competition designed to protect market share.

Working-capital needs can be just as acute as they frequently are in the anchor and entrenchment stages. Problems related to organizational structure and personnel are often experienced in this phase because of defensive action requiring structural realignments and personnel adjustments.

In the decline stage the functional problems are multiple and more difficult to solve. Product lines may have slipped into commodity items, causing the typical problems of low growth and low margins, excess price competition, and sometimes excess capacity. Financial problems are normal results of decline. Marketing problems, production problems, excess capacity, and personnel problems are factors which are not unusual but expected to be encountered in analyzing a company's situation in the decline stage.

INDUSTRY LIFE CYCLE AND STRUCTURE AS FACTORS IN INTERNAL ANALYSIS

In diagnosing a company's situation and seeking to understand the nature of its functional problems, management must have a thorough understanding of its industry.

Industry analysis is treated in some detail in Chapter 3. The major elements of this analysis are used here to support the problem-solving process.

The life cycle and structure of an industry are major factors determining competitive behavior. In the early stages of industry development firms are seeking to establish market position and competition is likely to be intense. New technologies and innovative products and concepts are vigorously pursued as companies seek competitive advantages to establish market share. The internal problems caused by this kind of industry environment will differ from the internal problems of a firm in a mature industry. In the early stages of an industry, while capital requirements will be high, market growth is likely to be rapid and provide room for many competitors. When growth slows and the industry matures, financing will be less of a problem, but competition can become intense as companies fight to maintain positions. Once the "sorting out" process begins, only the strong firms will survive. Eventually most industries become oligopolies, and the internal problems of the firms in the industry will reflect this change. Growth requirements in terms of capital, marketing expertise, and personnel will not be major considerations. Defensive tactics will take over, and survival will become a dominant management objective.

As industries pass maturity into decline, companies in the industry will have little choice but to pursue a holding action and seek to diversify into new industries. Internal problems caused by industry decline are not easily solved since they are out of the direct control of management. The decline phase of an industry will produce the same general problems for all the companies remaining in the industry, such as low margins and returns, deficits, no growth, inefficiency, excess productive capacity, and personnel problems.

As indicated in Chapter 3, industry structure can be a major determinant of the internal problems of the firm. The industry can be fragmented as a result of the nature of the products produced. In such industries management must recognize that no single firm has a significant market share. Attempts to alleviate internal problems through market growth are not likely to succeed. Product differentiation will also be difficult to attain. The industry is also likely to be fluid, with relatively easy entry and exit, which can cause surges of price cutting and intense competition. In diagnosing internal problems and assessing a firm's situation in a fragmented industry, management must be aware of the competitive characteristics. Firms within concentrated industries with few competitors will face a different pattern of internal problems. As previously stated, the industry will be mature, "shakeout" will have occurred, and growth will slow except for cyclical fluctuations. If price leadership does not exist in the industry, price cutting will be a constant threat.

Capital intensity and vertical integration will be factors in the industry. Cash flow, assets management, and problems of managing decentralized units will likely confront management.

There are a significant number of industry characteristics which have not been included in the brief treatment of this chapter. Chapter 3 provides greater detail and references which can be consulted for further analysis.

PROBLEM IDENTIFICATION

The first step in problem identification involves the fundamental process of examining all the facts and data available in a given situation. Before any action can be taken or any decision made, the policymaker must have as full an understanding as possible of the company's position and of the extent and nature of its problems. The dynamics of business and the changing economic scene make this analytical procedure a never-ending task. Management is almost invariably hampered in the diagnosis and decision-making process by an insufficiency of data. Therefore policymakers must learn to take action without perfect knowledge of the internal and external factors which could affect decision making; dealing with uncertainty and risk taking are essential skills the executive must acquire to prevent decline and stagnation of the enterprise. Each situation the policymakers encounter represents a particular complex of events at a point in time—a situation that is subject to change and to all the uncertainties and vagaries of a competitive business society. Managers must learn to recognize that, in the dynamics of the marketplace, strategies of long standing can become outmoded; successful product lines can mature and decline in sales and profitability; new technologies may change market patterns; and competitors' innovations may disrupt long-range plans and projections. External factors may also create or accentuate situational changes; the economic environment may change; new government regulations may restrict expansion and affect production, costs, and product lines. As a consequence, top management must retain flexibility and be constantly alert and sensitive to changes in the climate for decision making.

ANALYSIS OF BASIC DATA

The information system of the enterprise should provide the answer to basic questions designed to help the policymaker solve problems. The extent and scope of a company's information and control system may vary from simple, informal, internal communication lines to large, complex, computer-based operations. In each situation, however, there are basic factors to be considered and common questions to be asked. For example:

What facts, figures, and data are available to present the company's current position in all aspects of its operations?

What additional information will be needed to provide a complete picture of the company's situation?

What information is available about external factors which can affect the firm's current and future situation? Does the company engage in environmental scanning? Does it have any systematic way of reflecting environmental changes in its data base?

What sources can be utilized outside of the company's information system? Industry data? Governmental data? Consultants' reports?

The gathering, sorting, and assessing of information will lead to more specific questions related to the internal operations of the firm's functional areas.

Financial Analysis

Financial analysis should provide important information about progress toward economic objectives and the extent of deviation from preconceived targets. The financial strength of the firm is an important factor in determining its ability to maintain its market position or to initiate a recovery strategy. The difficulties of many companies is first signaled by declining earnings. The difficulties of Chrysler, International-Harvester, Itel, and a number of other large companies were portended by their financial indicators long before they reached a crisis situation. Their struggle to effect recoveries has been seriously affected by their financial weakness. Weak capital structures, high debt-to-equity ratios, and weak working-capital positions restrict their ability to regain market share and prevent further dilution of assets. As described in Chapter 3, companies in the decline phase turn to distress tactics such as seeking relief from the government, selling off assets, or resorting to more drastic measures provided by provisions of the bankruptcy act.

Important questions to consider in financial analysis should include:

I How well are the economic objectives of the company being met?

II What is its profitability rate? Profit patterns?
  A What are the company's capital structure proportions?
    1 Debt-to-equity ratio?
    2 Retained earnings position?
III What is its growth rate? Growth in earnings per share? Growth in dividends per share?
IV What is its internal cost of capital?
  V How efficiently is the company operating in terms of resource allocation? Asset management?
  A What is its working capital position?
    1 Current ratio?
    2 Accounts receivable turnover?
    3 Inventory turnover?
    4 Cash flow?
  B What is its turnover of operating assets?
VI Is the company financially sound enough to ensure long-run survival? Growth?

Marketing Analysis

The importance of the marketing function has been stressed throughout this book as an integral part of strategic planning. In addition to the information contained in Chapter 3, Chapter 7 provides the student with significant additional information related to market share brought out in the PIMS material (profit impact of market share), the analysis of the experience curve, and the review of the Boston Consulting Group's growth/share matrix. In attempting to assess the market strengths or weaknesses of the firm to support the problem-solving process, the following questions should be considered.

I What is the company's position in marketing and sales?
  A Scope of product line: Is it too extensive? Or too limited?
  B Market share?
  C Market direction? Proper segmentation? Product leadership?
  D Effectiveness of promotion and advertising?
  E Cost effectiveness?
  F Effectiveness of market research?
  G Effectiveness of sales force?
  H Effectiveness of the channels of distribution?
  I Product attractiveness? Packaging?

Production and Operations

The interrelationship of the marketing and production functions should be thoroughly understood in probing for problem areas. Significant questions that will aid in analysis of the production function include:

I Are there problems in manufacturing?
  A Lack of production and marketing coordination?
  B Slow and inefficient operations?
  C Outmoded equipment and facilities?
  D Need for new technologies and automated processes?
  E Sufficient capacity to meet demands?
  F Excess capacity problems?
  G Relation of total production costs to competition?
  H Adequate supply sources?

Allied Functional Analysis

The firm could be confronted with problems in other allied functional areas that may require analysis. Inquiries to initiate the diagnosis into other important functions of the company are suggested in the following guideline questions:

  I What are the nature and extent of personnel and labor problems?
 II Are there problems of organizational design and structure?
  A Is the company structure compatible with root and operating strategies?
  B Is there evidence of interpersonal relations problems? In the executive group? Within the employee group? Between the executive and employee group?
    1 Is there a lack of motivation? A lack of delegation and control?
    2 Is there evidence of a lack of information and feedback?
    3 Is the control system adequately reflecting warning signals to elicit early response by management?
    4 What is the overall quality of management and labor in relation to competition?

This list of questions which the policymaker might logically consider in analyzing the internal factors affecting the enterprise by no means exhausts the important queries which may be made. They are merely suggestive of a line of reasoning or a way of thinking which directs attention to significant problem areas.

APPRAISAL OF FIRM'S SKILLS AND RESOURCES

An appraisal of the company's skills and resources will aid in further defining the analytical process and will tend to integrate the internal and external factors which may affect its position. An inventory of specific assets, both tangible and intangible, is necessary to determine if the enterprise is capable of competing favorably and profitably and has the strength and vitality to attain its basic objectives. Specific questions which will aid in evaluating a company's position include the following:

Does the company enjoy a unique position in the industry?

Does it have competitive advantages in terms of brand names, patent position, trademarks, copyrights, market reputation, and company image?

Does the company have a strong and complete product line?

Is the product line diversified?

Does the company have a well-defined distribution system?

What is the state of product development?

Technological development?

Extent of research and development capability?

What specific fixed assets does the company own or lease? Property, plant, equipment?

What is the condition of the company's fixed assets? Age?

Are there any special or unique features about the assets which give the company competitive advantages?

Does the company have any locational advantages? Proximity to markets? To raw materials? To labor?

What personnel resources does the company have? An exceptional leader? Exceptional top and middle management groups? Skilled labor?

Does the company have good labor relations?

Does the company have sufficient financial resources to enable it to maintain its present position or acquire needed skills and resources?

Does the company have adequate working capital? Line of credit?

What prospects does it have for raising capital through the sale of securities? Equity financing? Debt financing?

DETERMINING THE ROOT CAUSE OF BUSINESS PROBLEMS

These questions, and many more that the manager will be likely to raise in the course of appraising the skills and resources of the firm in a particular business situation, will lead to a consideration of the basic processes of policy formulation. What objectives have been determined? What strategic plans have been developed? And most important, are the firm's basic objectives and strategic plans compatible with its skills and resources?

Engaging in the analytical process of appraising the functional areas of the business enterprise, examining the internal and external factors which affect decision making, and inventorying the company's skills and resources will afford the manager an insight into specific business problem situations from several angles. While there may be overlapping in the analytical procedures, multiple sightings from different vantage points will aid in putting problems in perspective and in assessing the validity and importance of the available information about the position and operation of the company being analyzed. The process of evaluating large amounts of data and separating the relevant from the irrelevant—as well as distinguishing between fact and assumption—is a constant one which must be engaged in throughout the analytical process. Out of this sifting and refining of the raw data, the significant problems of the company will emerge.

The next important step in the policymaking process involves the selection of the root cause of the major problem areas of the firm—the focal points for action. What should be done? Where should we begin? There may be distinct evidence of problems in marketing, production, finance, and other allied areas. These problems represent a collection of matters that need attention; separately they do not provide a clue to the order of needed executive action. The problems cannot be attacked in a piecemeal fashion because of the interrelationship of the functional areas. "Putting out the fire" in the sales area may only cause a new fire to flare up in production. The major problems of the firm cut across functional and departmental lines; there can be no separate, self-contained distress areas.

Functional and departmental problems are really symptoms or manifestations of a more deep-rooted difficulty that lies within the spectrum of the policymaking process and in the area of responsibility of top management. The analysis and judgment of the top management group, the policymakers of the firm, must therefore transcend functional and departmental lines and conceive of the entity as a single unit directed toward predetermined goals and guided by planned courses of action. Top management must direct its attention to the underlying problems of the firm and not to the surface indications.

TRANSLATING PROBLEMS INTO THE BASIC PROCESSES OF POLICY FORMULATION

The evidence of specific problems can, however, be translated into terms of basic processes of policy formulation. A more generalized diagnostic approach can then be applied to relate the symptoms to possible failures in one of the four basic areas of the policymaking process:

1 The formulation phase—Review of basic objectives and reformulation of root strategy
   2 The implementation phase—Redesign of operational strategy
   3 The organizational phase—Redesign of organizational strategy
   4 The interpretative phase—Redesign of control strategy

The four basic steps in the policy-formulation process are difficult to isolate in the going concern. They are interdependent and meld together to form a basic strategic design. However, in most instances it is possible to analyze each phase of the process against the background of the significant problems and difficulties of the enterprise in each particular business situation. Exhibit 5-2 illustrates the continuous flow of the policymaking process and the interdependence of each basic step in decision making and policy formulation.

ADAPTING THE SYSTEMS APPROACH TO THE ANALYSIS OF THE FIRM

The diagnostic process or situational analysis may or may not be perceived by the firm as an integral, formalized procedure which requires specific designations. There are few companies which engage in a constant search for warning

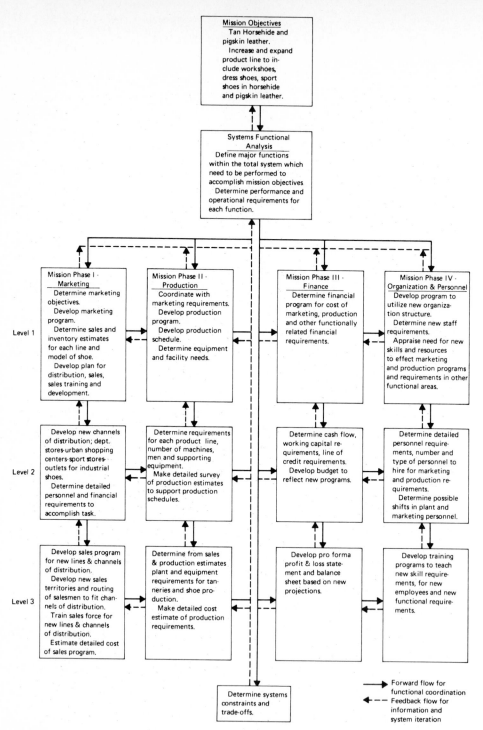

Mission Objectives
Tan Horsehide and pigskin leather.
Increase and expand product line to include workshoes, dress shoes, sport shoes in horsehide and pigskin leather.

Systems Functional Analysis
Define major functions within the total system which need to be performed to accomplish mission objectives
Determine performance and operational requirements for each function.

Mission Phase I - Marketing
Determine marketing objectives.
Develop marketing program.
Determine sales and inventory estimates for each line and model of shoe.
Develop plan for distribution, sales, sales training and development.

Mission Phase II - Production
Coordinate with marketing requirements.
Develop production program.
Develop production schedule.
Determine equipment and facility needs.

Mission Phase III - Finance
Determine financial program for cost of marketing, production and other functionally related financial requirements.

Mission Phase IV - Organization & Personnel
Develop program to utilize new organization structure.
Determine new staff requirements.
Appraise need for new skills and resources to effect marketing and production programs and requirements in other functional areas.

Level 1

Level 2

Develop new channels of distribution; dept. stores-urban shopping centers-sport stores-outlets for industrial shoes.
Determine detailed personnel and financial requirements to accomplish task.

Determine requirements for each product line, number of machines, men and supporting equipment.
Make detailed survey of production estimates to support production schedules.

Determine cash flow, working capital requirements, line of credit requirements.
Develop budget to reflect new programs.

Determine detailed personnel requirements, number and type of personnel to hire for marketing and production requirements.
Determine possible shifts in plant and marketing personnel.

Level 3

Develop sales program for new lines & channels of distribution.
Develop new sales territories and routing of salesmen to fit channels of distribution.
Train sales force for new lines & channels of distribution.
Estimate detailed cost of sales program.

Determine from sales & production estimates plant and equipment requirements for tanneries and shoe production.
Make detailed cost estimate of production requirements.

Develop pro forma profit & loss statement and balance sheet based on new projections.

Develop training programs to teach new skill requirements, for new employees and new functional requirements.

Determine systems constraints and trade-offs.

→ Forward flow for functional coordination
←-- Feedback flow for information and system iteration

EXHIBIT 5-2
Functional flow diagram illustrating the effects of reformulation based on situational analysis.

signals in the environment or monitor their information systems for signs in the internal operations which threaten their performance or the attainment of preconceived objectives. The problem-search process is usually initiated by functional response indicating a need for corrective action in the areas of production, marketing, finance, etc. Distress signals of malfunction are easiest to detect when problems are isolated or compartmentalized. Unfortunately, there are few functional problems of any magnitude which are isolated. As previously indicated, they are interrelated, and the principle of functional dynamics usually prevails because the business entity is a system. Specific functional problems confronting management represent one state or part of a total system which is constantly undergoing change through functional dynamics —responding to the force and pressure of other functions or parts of the system which are undergoing dynamic change.

The basic concept of the systems approach can be adapted to analyze the firm and evaluate its performance if we recognize some of the limitations of applying this technique to the nonstatic business enterprise which must remain flexible and dynamic if it is to cope with its competitive environment. Unlike most engineering tasks, to which the systems approach was originally applied, the mission objectives of individual business concerns can be and frequently are changed to meet the demands of the changing environment of the marketplace; consequently, design requirements and design constraints are not as rigidly defined or imposed, nor do they have the degree of permanence attached to the usual engineering assignment. Nevertheless, the elements of a system are contained within the business entity. *The business enterprise has relevant, related functions which are unified by the basic economic and business objectives of the firm. These objectives are expressed in its policy formulation process and in the development of its strategic design. There is a pattern and set of relationships through the flow of the specific functions from product inception to product consumption.*

Exhibit 5-1 utilizes the terminology of systems analysis to show the necessary functional flow and suppport of a reformulation or change in the mission objective of a manufacturing company resulting from a significant change in its product line. This reformulation required distinct changes in all of its functional areas and operations. The systems approach shows the effect of the change in mission objectives on marketing, production, finance, organization, and personnel.

The systems approach, despite some limitations which were previously mentioned, can be effectively utilized in diagnosing a company's situation and probing for significant problem areas. This method also clearly reinforces the concept of *functional dynamics* illustrating system iteration and the interaction of the functional areas. The block diagram provides a basis for following the functional flow from product inception to ultimate delivery to the customer.

SUMMARY AND GENERAL COMMENTS

The diagnostic or problem-solving process is initiated when the firm's information system indicates that performance is not in accordance with its strategic plans. The key to analysis of major business problems for the top management group is found in the continued recognition of the stated mission and purpose of the enterprise. In seeking the root cause of major problems and the focal point for the initiation of recovery strategies, management must view the company as a single system functioning as a whole unit through the interaction of its parts or subsystems. The system of functional dynamics must be understood. A decision to change a basic policy in one functional area affects all enterprise functions to a greater or lesser degree.

Internal analysis must include an examination of the firm's life cycle. The stage of its life cycle is a factor which determines the action which must be taken to take advantage of a growth situation, protect a position, stave off a decline, or initiate a recovery strategy. The nature of internal problems will vary with the phase of the company's life cycle and may be directly related to its life cycle. The problems likely to be encountered in the early phase of a firm's life cycle are likely to differ in nature from internal problems experienced in the defensive and decline stages.

In diagnosing a company's situation and seeking to analyze the nature of its functional problems, management must have a thorough understanding of its industry. The life cycle and structure of an industry are major factors determining competitive behavior. In the early stages of industry development growth requirements will preoccupy the firm. In the mature stage of industries defensive tactics are likely to be dominant. In declining industries management choice is restricted and management usually has little choice but to pursue a holding action and seek to diversify into new industries.

Industry structure can be a major determinant of the internal problems of the company. The nature of an industry's products are important determinants of industry structure. High technology, innovative products, and new concepts are associated with growth industries. Products which are difficult to differentiate and are not capital-intensive are usually found in fragmented industries. Products necessitating high capital requirements usually result in a concentrated industry structure with a small number of producers.

Functional analysis of finance, marketing, production, and other allied areas such as worker effectiveness, overall personnel relations, management effectiveness, and organizational design and structure should be undertaken to assure the detection of factors which may impede performance. This chapter includes a series of guideline questions directed to the examination and appraisal of the major functions of the firm.

The basic concept of the systems approach can be adapted to analyze the firm and evaluate its performance if we recognize some of the limitations of applying this technique to the nonstatic enterprise which must remain flexible and dynamic. The elements of a system are contained within the business entity. The business enterprise has relevant, related functions which are unified by the basic economics and business objectives of the firm. There is a pattern and set of relationships through the flow of the specific functions from product inception to product consumption. A flowchart diagram illustrating the adaptation of the systems approach is included in this chapter.

The evidence of specific functional area problems can be translated into terms of strategic planning and policy formulation. A more generalized diagnostic approach can be applied to functional symptoms which may point to potential breakdowns in one of the four basic areas of the policymaking process. Exhibit 5-1 illustrates the flow of policy formulation and strategic planning.

SELECTED REFERENCES

Andrews, K. R.: *The Concept of the Corporation* (Homewood, Ill.: Irwin, 1980).

Ansoff, Igor H.: *Corporate Strategy; An Analytical Approach to Business Policy* (New York: McGraw-Hill, 1965).

———, Roger DeClerck, and Robert Haynes: *From Strategic Planning to Strategic Management* (New York: Wiley, 1976).

Argenti, John: *Corporate Collapse: The Causes and Symptoms* (New York: Wiley, 1976).

Buchele, R.: "How to Evaluate a Firm," *California Management Review,* Fall 1962, pp. 5-16.

Cannon, J. T.: *Business Strategy and Policy* (New York: Harcourt, Brace & World, 1968).

Cleland, David, and William King: *Systems Analysis and Project Management* (New York: McGraw-Hill, 1968).

Coyle, R.: "Systems Dynamics: An Approach to Policy Formulation," *Journal of Business Policy,* Spring 1973.

Ferguson, Charles: *Measuring Corporate Strategy* (Homewood, Ill: Dow Jones-Irwin, 1974).

Hobbs, John, and Donald Heany: "Coupling Strategy to Operating Plans," *Harvard Business Review*, May-June 1977.

Hofer, Charles, and Dan Schendel: *Strategy Formulation: Analytical Concepts* (St. Paul, Minn.: West, 1978).

Kotler, Philip: *Marketing Management,* 4th ed. (Englewood Cliffs, N. J.: Prentice-Hall, 1980).

Lorange, Peter, and Richard Vancil: *Strategic Planning Systems* (Englewood Cliffs, N.J., Prentice-Hall, 1977).

Mintzberg, Henry: "The Manager's Job: Folklore and Fiction," *Harvard Business Review,* July-August 1975.

Munford, Enid, and Andrew Pettigrew: *Implementing Strategic Decisions* (London: Longmans, 1975).

Porter, Michael: *Competitive Strategy* (New York: The Free Press, a division of Macmillan, 1980).

Smith, Theodore: *Dynamic Strategic Planning: The Art of Planning for Success* (New York: McGraw-Hill, 1977).

Stevenson, Harold: "Defining Corporate Strengths and Weaknesses," *Sloan Management Review*, Spring 1976.

Tilles, Seymour: "How to Evaluate Corporate Strategy," *Harvard Business Review*, July-August 1963.

CASES ON BUSINESS POLICY FOR PART TWO

The cases in Part Two describe a variety of significant issues and challenges faced by management in a number of different businesses and industries. The many policy and functional problems presented in the cases provide the student with an opportunity to apply a systematic, organized approach to the analysis of complex business situations. The cases in this section also delineate the important role of general management in problem solving and illustrate for the student the need for a thorough understanding of the firm's operations and its environment as a necessary preliminary step in the development of a strategic plan.

The importance of the life cycle of the firm and its industry environment as factors which determine its competitive posture are clearly illustrated in several of the cases in this section. The environmental challenges to management pose a constant threat to the firm's survival. The cases in this part all indicate the need and importance for environmental scanning to assure effective management response to significant external changes and pressures which can affect the company's competitive position.

Medford Clothiers

THE COMPANY'S POSITION IN 1982

John Medford, Jr., assumed the chief executive role of Medford Clothiers in 1978 when his father retired because of health problems. Medford, Jr. joined the company in 1973, leaving a law practice in Chicago to become assistant to his father. John Medford, Sr., had been chairman and president of the company for over 40 years.

Medford Clothiers was considered to be a medium-sized company in the clothing industry. The firm was located in Chicago and was privately held by the Medford family, a small number of employees, relatives, and friends. The brand name of Medford had a long-standing reputation in the industry for quality men's clothing. The conservative approach of Medford to styling, fabric selection, and pricing was considered to be a deterrent to growth by many; however, John Medford, Sr., did not think so. He often reminded his management team that the company's customer group was composed mainly of conservative business men in the middle forties up to over sixty who could afford to pay the Medford price, which ranged from $275 to $400 for suits, $150 to $325 for jackets or sport coats, and from $60 to $100 for separate slacks or trousers. Medford had never been a leader in styling, and did not get heavily involved in knits or synthetic materials. Blends with wool and synthetics were used in Medford clothing but not heavily promoted by the company. The return of 100 percent wool suits in the late 1970s pleased management.

Medford casual clothes, separate jackets and pants, were of high quality and price. They appealed to the same customers who purchased their suits. Despite the increasing sales in men's casual wear, some of the management, particularly those that had long years of service with the company, were not enthused about having the separates replacing the standard suit as the company's leading product line.

In commenting on the company's position in the industry, Medford Jr., stated:

The men's clothing business has undergone considerable change in the past decade or two. Men's suits have come back and shown sales increases in the past several years, but casual wear is still the major growth area in the industry. Sport coats and slacks take up at least half of the display space in men's clothing stores or departments. In many cases suits account for one-third or less of the floor space. I expect this trend to continue. While we have a good line of clothing in this area, we are at the high price end. Competition in all phases of the men's clothing business is intense, particularly in the casual wear, men's sport jackets and separate trousers or coordinated jackets and pants. Small manufacturers can easily enter the field and copy almost any design with ease. Their clothing is priced at least 50 percent under ours. Usually they are not sold in the same area of a store as our merchandise; however, in many cases they can be found on display tables nearby.

We also have had recent entries into the men's clothing market with such firms as Levi Strauss, with suits and casual wear, and Blue Bell, with casual wear. These lines appeal to younger men who have purchased their jeans. But they still provide competition. Instead of moving up into one of our fine suits, the younger man might be inclined to buy two coordinated outfits for the price of one of our suits. The largest sales of men's suits is still in the $100 to $150 range. While the upper end of the market has picked up, it still is the smaller segment.

Our problem I guess is one of size. We haven't shown as much growth in the past five years as some of our big competitors, like Hart, Schaffner & Marx, and the specialty producers like Levi, Palm Beach, and others. However, we are still an independent business. We haven't gone bankrupt nor have we been acquired. We aren't big enough to be a real leader, and make any real moves, nor are we small enough to be flexible and move quickly into the newest fashions and rapid changes in the industry.

CONSUMERS AND RETAIL OUTLETS

The principal customers of Medford Clothiers were middle-aged men who resided in metropolitan areas and were employed in professional, business, or office occupations. They usually earned incomes in the upper-middle to high brackets. Management felt that, while people who worked in factories or as laborers also purchased some high-priced suits and topcoats to be worn when off the job, members of this group often found sport or casual clothing more to their liking and seldom purchased the more expensive suits.

Although every year brought new buyers into the market, replacement of worn garments was the prime cause for purchase of men's suits. Another important factor was the desire of certain customers to enlarge their wardrobes for social or occupational reasons. Because men had been traditionally more conservative in dress than women, attempts to create obsolescence by changing styles had not been important on a year-to-year basis until recently.

Men's clothing in the United States was distributed through a variety of outlets. Retail clothiers operated primarily as men's specialty stores but sometimes carried women's and children's wear as well. The salespeople in these stores were usually experienced, well trained, and competent to assist a customer; good tailors were also employed to make what alterations were needed. A store usually offered a range of prices and stocked suits made by several manufacturers. Sometimes a store carried clothing bearing its own label. Private labels were often used by stores to obtain higher markups. Business was generated by window displays, advertising in local papers, and direct mail. Other media, such as radio and television, had also been used. Medford Clothiers sold about 80 percent of its volume through retail clothiers.

Department stores varied somewhat in the emphasis given to men's clothing. Some department stores had a "men's shop" or "store for men" which featured an attractive assortment of suits and outer coats bearing labels of a number of manufacturers and the store's own brand. These stores for men had expert salespeople and tailors. In other department stores, however, men's clothing was less important and was not offered in such variety, nor were the salespeople particularly expert. The importance of department stores as outlets for men's clothing varied to some extent between geographical areas. In big-city areas, the department store tended to be more important. Medford Clothiers used department stores as a secondary channel of distribution and manufactured some suits to be sold under the private labels of certain high-grade department stores.

Medford's private brand sales had increased from 5 percent in 1976 to 35 percent in 1982. The declining sales in retail outlets was made up through the private sales but at a lower margin. The private brand sales were to department stores which had men's shops and catered to the middle-age executive group who purchased higher-priced clothing. Medford, Jr., felt that the company might have to eventually increase private brand sales to 40 percent or more because of declining sales in its retail store distribution system.

Medford's declining profits had decreased cash flow and caused the firm to reduce advertising and promotion expense. The lack of company-owned stores also contributed to declining retail sales for the Medford line. Independent dealers carrying the company's clothing also sold other labels, and many had decreased Medford stock in favor of lower-priced casual lines. Dealers also complained of Medford's decrease in advertising and promotional allowances.

Medford, Jr., had personally acquired 10 of the major private brand accounts. When he became the CEO, he made contact with leading department stores which had previously expressed an interest in buying Medford's quality suits for their own labels. John Medford, Sr., had turned down their requests on previous occasions because he thought the margins were too low and other producers with higher volume and lower cost structures would always be a threat to take the business away from his company. Others in management agreed with Medford, Sr.'s position. Charles Medford, the vice president of sales, stated that this hurt the independent dealers since there was little difference in the quality and styling of the private brands and the Medford line.

In some cases, chain stores were owned by a company which manufactured its own merchandise. Many of these chains sold suits and topcoats in the lower price classifications. Even though their prices were low, these chains often found it necessary to extend credit. Since volume was important and price was the determining factor, salespeople had to strive for high sales and did not spend as much time in rendering the kind of service needed to build up a personal clientele as did salespeople in the men's specialty stores. Large manufacturers making high-grade men's clothing did own stores in a number of large cities, and some of the stores did bear the manufacturer's name, such as Hart, Schaffner & Marx. One advantage of owning retail outlets was the ability to manufacture somewhat in advance with the knowledge that suits would be stocked. On the other hand, the problem of selling the garments was not solved simply by ownership of stores. Medford Clothiers had a policy of not owning stores.

While most manufacturers sold direct to the retail store, there were some jobbers who bought from those manufacturers who did not have sales organizations. Jobbers might also buy up lots of clothing from broken lines, distress merchandise, or other assorted lots of clothing, such as cancellations. Jobbers played a relatively minor role in the 1970s.

Store location was an important matter in the merchandising of men's clothing. The trend toward suburban living, changed buying habits, and the development of the large regional shopping centers led men to purchase most clothing in the suburbs. Since Medford did not own its own stores, it had to rely on its retail accounts for the suburban outlets. Many of the stores that carried Medford's line were late to enter the suburban shopping centers.

SALES PATTERNS

Until 1950, Medford Clothiers restricted its sales efforts to the territory east of the Mississippi. In this sales area, the company followed the practice of selecting an exclusive outlet in each city. It felt that better sales effort would result, that an exclusive outlet would enhance the prestige of its line, and that men who wanted the hand-tailored Medford clothing would seek out the store. This policy was continued after 1950, when the company expanded its sales west of the Mississippi. Medford's major competitors also had the policy of granting exclusive distribution to a retail outlet in a specified geographical area but in recent years had made many exceptions to this policy. John Medford, Sr., said, "The top-notch retailer has the power to demand exclusivity, and we manufacturers until recently have had little choice but to give it to him."

As a matter of policy, Medford Clothiers had always given much sales emphasis to small and medium-sized cities as well as concentrating on larger cities. Mr. Medford explained, "We like the stability of the smaller communities. Our kind of operation needs their stable influence as well as the business of the more fashion-minded customers of the big cities and surrounding suburban areas."

In 1976, Medford Clothiers had about 800 accounts; in 1982 they had been reduced to 630. These stores, however, did sell one or more lines of other clothing manufacturers. About 20 percent of these outlets were department stores. In all sales territories, unwritten agreements between the company and the store management provided for meeting quotas based on experience with stores of similar size in similar communities. The relationship between the Medford company and these store managements was in most cases a very friendly and personal one.

Over the years Medford Clothiers' outlets had experienced varying degrees of growth. Some had expanded with their areas; others had remained in the same locations with the same floor space.

The company had 25 salespeople who operated out of the New York and Chicago offices on extensive sales trips. Topcoats, overcoats, and winter suits were sold March through June; visits for reorders were made at other times. The spring and summer lines were sold September through February, with other visits for reorders. The salespeople had periods when not much selling could be done. At these times, they did their missionary work, visiting stores and acquainting each store's selling staff with sales ideas.

The average length of company service among the Medford salespeople was six years. Typically, a person was in training in the company's office for about a year before getting a field assignment. The salespeople turned in weekly reports on their activities with information about sales, style trends, etc. They also submitted weekly expense accounts. Each salesperson was given a territorial quota and was paid on a salary-and-commission basis.

Charles Medford, vice president in charge of sales, was required to select a number of store outlets every year to replace the stores that were dropped from the company's list. Sometimes a store was sold or liquidated when store owners decided to go out of business or seek a more popular line. Sometimes a franchise was taken away. For example, one store used the Medford trademark to get people into the store but then passed off its own brand as being of the same quality or even of the same manufacturer. Before selection of a store, a careful check was made of its credit, management, location, and facilities. It was not difficult to find a store eager to sell Medford clothing, which lent prestige to the merchandise line. The company was finding it very difficult to keep accounts and increase sales.

The Medford company from time to time had helped a new store get started in an area where there was no suitable outlet. Accommodation loans and open-book credit were extended. The company had also been under pressure recently from retail clothiers to assume responsibility for carrying a larger inventory. There had been suggestions by retailers generally that they should not be required to place firm orders for more than 50 percent of their season's business in advance of the season. Manufacturers generally felt that such a practice would work to the disadvantage of the industry. Medford, Jr., concurred in this belief. He felt that Medford Clothiers should resist the attempts of retailers to have the manufacturer increase his credit function.

William Medford, the vice president in charge of advertising, developed an advertising program that would assist the retail-store owner in every season of the year. For many years, Medford Clothiers had advertised in national magazines, but it concluded that the most effective results were obtained by helping each store with advertising in its own area. The company paid half the cost of advertising up to 3 percent of sales in each store. The company furnished ideas, copy, and mats which a store could use if it desired.

Sales for the fall and winter business amounted to 60 percent of the company's total business. The remaining 40 percent represented sales in spring and summer. These percentages had changed very little over the past several years. Management felt that the 60-40 relationship would remain relatively undisturbed despite manufacturers' efforts to minimize the seasonal production problems.

DESIGN AND PURCHASING

Medford's outstanding designer, Fred Jones, retired in 1978 at 68 years of age. He had been responsible for much of Medford's early success in setting fashion trends in conservative, high-priced men's wear. Jones was succeeded as chief designer by George Reese, 52 years old, who came from a clothing company in Rochester, New York, which was liquidated. Reese was of the opinion that the Medford line needed to reduce its dependence on conservative styling and conservative colored fabrics. He proposed introducing a new line of suits, jackets, and trousers that would have appeal to younger men. Medford, Jr., expressed an interest in his proposals, one of which recommended getting a prominent sports figure to endorse the line and possibly bear his name. John Medford, Sr., who still contributed to major decisions, and Charles Medford, the vice president of sales, were not in favor of Reese's suggestion. Medford, Jr., said he would seriously consider the proposal when business showed some signs of recovery.

The designer played an important role in the company's operations when a new model was approved. He helped develop the patterns needed for cutting the various sizes that would be made. Designing required a most exacting knowledge of clothing manufacture, since new ideas on style could only be carried out if they were feasible from a manufacturing standpoint.

The designer worked closely with Mr. Wilson, the woolens-purchasing vice president, in developing ideas for patterns, shades, and types of fabric. Mr. Wilson visited textile manufacturers to see new fabrics and also worked with one particular company in developing new fabrics. One recent innovation included a design in longer-wearing worsted which had the softness of tweed cloth plus a pattern with pleasing vitality. Since new designs and new fabrics could not be patented, it was expected that others would attempt to copy this development.

Purchasing was one of the key functions of the business. Mr. Wilson, the woolens-purchasing vice president, had to follow the trends of the wool and synthetic market as well as textile markets in this country and abroad. Some purchases were made in imported cloths from the United Kingdom and Ireland. Generally, in the men's clothing business imported fabrics tended to be used in the cheaper or more expensive suits, while suits in the middle ranges were usually made from domestic fabrics.

Since the company offered a wide selection of fabrics in many shades and patterns, some purchases involved small amounts, such as two or four "pieces" (40 to 80 suits), although there was usually a minimum-size order set by the seller. The company found that deliveries of small orders were apt to involve delays, since textile mills gave better service to large orders.

Final decisions about the line to be offered were made by the top officials—the president, vice presidents of production and sales, purchasing vice president, purchasing agent, and designer. After his trip to the textile markets, the purchasing department agent usually knew in March what fabrics were good buys. Decisions were made in April. Medford Clothiers followed the industry custom of reaching decisions about the next fall season's models in April, in order to provide sufficient time for designing, manufacturing, and distribution. New models were always made up and inspected carefully before being added to the line.

Reports from the field by salespeople were useful in forming decisions on the line, since there were regional differences throughout the country with respect to preference for style and shades. In the northeast, tastes were more conservative—darker tones, with style less pronounced. "In the west, men like clothes that 'glorify the man,' " said one Medford salesperson, "bolder colors and lots of styles."

In each of the two seasons, the company had about 700 to 1,000 different fabrics, with about 100 to 200 being the same for both seasons. Probably 200 fabrics were the same from one fall line to the next. A typical breakdown of the number of fabrics used in the two seasons was as follows:

	Spring	Fall
Regular-weight and tropical suits*	500	450
Topcoats	75	200
Overcoats	—	150
Sport coats	75	125
Slacks	100	75
	750	1,000

*Wools, synthetics, wool-synthetic combinations.

The company had about six basic models of suits in single-breasted styles. It also made a limited number of double-breasted suits, and many suits of the past eight years had vests. These basic models were given some regional differences to make some 18 models, counting modifications. These 18 were obtainable in an average of 152 different stock sizes and in some 450 different fall fabrics.

The company designed some lines to give service in a variety of situations and seasons. Some suits had enough pattern and vitality to make the coats useful as sport jackets when worn with slacks. Some suits were made of lightweight fabrics that permitted them to be worn in spring, summer, and autumn.

In all lines of suits and topcoats, a variety of fabrics and styles was offered to suit a wide range of preference. For example, the summer line included suits of light worsted, fabrics of wool and synthetics, and fabrics of wool and some silk. The company also offered some highly styled models in its line to appeal to those who like distinctive dress.

Forecasting was an ever-present problem. As John Medford, Jr., put it, "We're like the rest in the industry. We do our forecasting by the seat of the pants."

PRODUCTION PROCESS

When fabrics arrived at the main plant, the bolts were stored close to the inspection and shrinking departments. Cloth was run over rollers and was inspected under high-intensity special lighting by an operator who looked for irregularities and marked their location on the edge of the cloth with string. Since wool is an animal fiber, it was expected that there would be some irregularities, although they were not always considered as flaws. If more than 10 percent of a bolt was defective, it was returned. Synthetic fibers were also inspected for irregularities.

After inspection, the cloth was given alternate hot and cold baths, after which the cloth stayed wet for 24 to 48 hours before the final shrinking. Then the cloth was dried as it passed over rollers in a heated area. Although 3 to 5 percent of the bolt of cloth was lost in shrinkage, fabrics given this treatment could go through countless dry cleanings without shrinking. Adequate shrinking was omitted by manufacturers of cheaper-grade suits. Tape and other materials used in the inside construction were also shrunk to prevent shrinking that would pull the suit out of shape.

Shrunk fabrics were rolled on huge drums between layers of heavy, satin-smooth cloth; steam under pressure was forced through the layers to give the fabric a rich and lasting finish.

The cloth was then taken upstairs by elevator to the cutting room. Electric cutting knives could be used to cut as many as eight layers of cloth on which patterns had been marked out. Actually, the "lays" (layers cut) averaged around four because of many different patterns, sizes, and special orders. There were, of course, large, powerful cutters able to cut up to 50 lays of cloth, but they were economical only with large volume. Also, union rules did not permit this kind of equipment for the better grade of suit. One worker commented, "We never cut more than 20 lays at a time." Peak cutting for suits, separate coats, and trousers occurred in March through November, with a low in July when the plant shut down for vacation. Peak cuttings for outercoats occurred in August and September, with a low in January and February.

The company's designer worked with highly skilled draftspersons to create patterns for some 245 sizes. This work was performed in a special department, and over 19,000 patterns were stocked to make the company's line of models in all the various sizes. The company used separate patterns for each part of a suit, whereas concerns making cheaper grades might, for example, use the same size pocket for several different suit sizes. The cutters exercised great care in matching stripes and plaids, which was not done so carefully by makers of cheaper suits. Linings were also cut to specific patterns for each size, rather than using "averages" for several sizes, the latter being the practice for cheaper suits. Material used for linings was of high quality.

The Medford system for men's clothing manufacture required attention to "a thousand and one" details. There were close to 200 separate operations in making a suit coat and over 100 in making a pair of trousers. After the cloth was cut to a pattern, the pieces were bundled and placed in boxes. Trimmings and findings were also bundled and placed in boxes. Buttons, thread, and linings were, of course, carefully matched before being placed in the boxes. These boxes were taken down in an elevator and placed in trucks for transportation to the No. 2 plant, where the remainder of the manufacturing steps were carried out.

The company had long before outgrown the original plant, and a second building had been purchased four blocks away. In the No. 2 plant, the bundles from the cutting department were passed along a production line where the many operations were performed largely by hand, although some sewing machines were used. The linings were basted to the cloth—several thousand such basting stitches were used as a guide for hand-finishing tailors—and then the basting stitches were removed. Some 100 reinforcements were made in a suit at every point of strain. For example, stays and reinforcements prevented pockets from sagging; collars, lapels, edge seams, and armholes were carefully stitched with tape where needed. Only pure silk thread was used because of its strength and resistance to fading. At various stages there were many pressing operations to give the suit a lasting shapeliness. A suit coat had 36 pressings—at every seam, reinforcement, and joining. Of these pressings, 29 were "underpressing" (performed on inside parts). Cheaper suits may have flat-table pressing without the careful shaping of the hand-tailored suit, and they do not hold their form as well. Medford Clothiers had special presses for collars and shoulders to give suits proper form at those important points.

Buttonholes were sewn by hand, because machines could not match the strength and flexibility achieved by hand tailoring. Buttons were also sewn on by hand to give greater performance.

There were some 96 inspections along the way for each suit—over 70 of which were for tailoring operations. Twice a week top management inspected suits chosen at random from the line. The suits were modeled and were examined with great care. Following the completion of manufacturing, the suits were placed on hangers, hung on racks, and returned by truck to the main building where they were stored on racks, three levels high, prior to shipping. A movable ladder was used by the workers who transferred the suits to these racks in building No. 1. Suits were shipped, still on hangers, in cartons reinforced with wooden strips and especially designed to protect the suits in transit.

The use of artificial fibers presents a number of manufacturing problems for the men's clothing industry. Since synthetic fiber has different properties from wool, it is necessary to reduce shrinkage in trimmings to a minimum, and cutting cannot be done at great speed lest the layers of cloth fuse. Sewing and pressing requires extra care. For example, light sewing-thread tensions on machines were needed; high-speed sewing was not desirable; and in pressing, temperature had to be carefully controlled lest the fabric fuse under heat.

In such a competitive industry as men's clothing, every step of the production process needs to be done efficiently. Lost opportunities for savings narrow the profit margins. One of the officers pointed to some boxes containing scraps of cloth from the cutting room and said, "That's where we make our profit."

The Medford company also provided a special service for men who couldn't wear stock sizes or who preferred suits made to order. Each store selling Medford clothing was provided with forms on which measurements were to be indicated. A box of swatches, containing some fabrics used in suits and coats and some special fabrics used only in special orders, was likewise sent to the store. Thus the customer could select a fabric that appealed to him. These special orders were handled by a special department that cut the fabrics and bundled them to be sent to the other building where sewing operations were carried on. The company doubted that this business was very profitable but felt the service retained many customers who liked high-grade clothing and who would buy some Medford clothing, such as outercoats and topcoats, in stock sizes.

Since orders for a particular season's output came in a relatively short period, the production control department scheduled production with greater efficiency during peak periods of manufacture than at other times. Reorders and special orders, which were difficult to anticipate, were scheduled during the off-peak period. Orders were put on punched cards, which made it easy to accumulate orders for a particular model, size, and fabric. Tickets were made out showing specifications as to model, size, fabric, etc. Copies accompanied the bundles, as well as strips of small numbered tickets which were torn off and kept by operators to show the number of pieces worked on. Progress of manufacturing was noted by the return of copies to the production control department when an operation was completed.

Careful attention was given to inventory control over fabrics, trimmings, and findings. Inventory records for fabrics showed amounts on order, amounts received, and totals on hand and issued; a swatch of each fabric was attached to the inventory record. Iventory of buttons, thread, trimmings, etc., presented some problems because of the large number of items that were kept on hand. A man formerly in charge of those items had devised his own system. After his death, however, no one else could follow his scheme and a new system was devised.

The company maintained a small laboratory for testing the fabrics purchased. Such factors as resistance to fading, the proportion of wool in mixed fabrics, wearing qualities, etc., were investigated by a skilled technician.

Plant facilities included some 150,000 square feet of space in the main building, and 120,000 square feet in building No. 2. The plants had been modernized and were air-conditioned. Open areas in most departments permitted the supervisors a good view of all activities under their guidance. The executive officers and home office personnel were located in the main building.

EMPLOYEES

The employees of the company were all highly skilled and were considered by the management to be loyal to the company. The average age of the employees was rather high, and there was difficulty in recruiting new employees. The younger generation of clothing workers' families seemed to prefer other occupations. Those already employed in the men's clothing industry tended to stay, since they had acquired a skill valuable only in their own industry. The average employee had between 15 and 20 years of service with Medford Clothiers and was considered by management as resistant to most changes. The proportion of women employees had been increasing.

Employees in the men's clothing industry were unionized for the most part, and wage negotiations on an industry basis set the pattern for wages in various manufacturing areas. Local negotiations with the union did not produce any important variations in the wage between firms in a specific area, although there were some differentials between New York, Philadelphia, Chicago, etc.

Union agreements provided for employers to pay for benefits involving sickness, accidents, old age, and death. There was also a union social insurance program that gave limited payments for hospitalization, surgery, death, and retirement. One-week vacations were given to employees who had served for less than three years. In periods of low activity, work tended to be shared. While the terms of contracts specified a 36-hour week, in practice the week was 40 hours (8 hours for 5 days). The company operated cafeterias at both plants. The officers and other employees joined the same line to buy food and ate in the same room in the main building.

The average hourly rate was close to the average for all manufacturing, but the average weekly earnings tended to be larger because of the contract work week. Employees were paid according to a piece-rate system, with about 85 percent of the operations paid on that basis. The company was planning to add an industrial engineer to its factory staff, since none was presently employed.

Medford's management had seriously considered shutting down the older No. 1 plant and moving its offices to the second plant. Between 1977 and 1979 it had to temporarily lay off employees and operate plant No. 1 at half capacity. Union rules required lay-offs according to seniority. The acquisition of private-label business after Medford, Jr., became the CEO permitted running both plants at about full capacity. Management, however, was seriously considering remodeling plant No. 2 and moving all production to this unit.

MEDFORD'S ORGANIZATION

The top management group included eight men. Six of them had over 30 years experience with the company. Only Medford, Jr., and George Reese, the chief designer, had less time with the company. (See organization chart, Exhibit 1.) Medford, Sr. had always considered the experience of the management group to be a distinct asset to the company. The management relationship was very informal. Medford, Sr., although not active in the company, was still an important influence on the organization. He frequently held weekend meetings in his Lake Forest home to share his long experience with the executive group. He had spent his entire career in Medford and was respected by management and employees. Medford, Jr., tried to seek his advice on important decisions whenever possible. However, he assumed full control of day-to-day operations when he became the chief executive in 1978.

William Medford, vice president of advertising, and Charles Medford were brothers of Medford, Sr. Both had spent their entire careers in the company and were shareholders. They acted very independent in their positions, and Medford, Jr., seldom questioned their decisions. The other members of the management group, Robert Hill, vice president of production, Mike Wilson, vice president of purchasing, and Joe Allen, the controller, all had long years of service with Medford. Wilson spent several months in his Florida home each winter season. He frequently spoke of retiring. Hill and Allen were also beyond normal retirement age. They all held stock in the company and were of the opinion that they could aid Medford, Jr., by staying on and giving him the benefit of their years of experience. The board of directors was made up of Medford, Sr., Medford, Jr., Allen, Hill, and Charles Medford.

FINANCIAL POSITION

Medford, Jr., was concerned about the company's declining sales and profits. (See Exhibits 2 and 3.) In commenting on the situation, he stated:

> We still have a tenable financial position, but our sales and profits have shown a steady decline. How long can this last? We have little debt and are family-owned. This protects us and gives us assurance against a takeover. But declining dividends

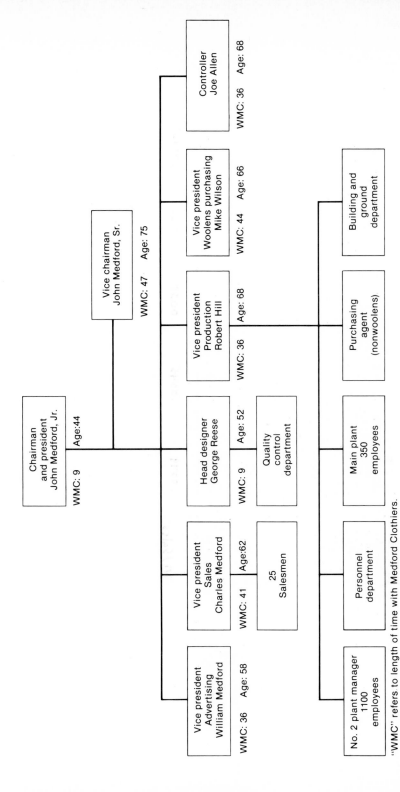

Chairman and president
John Medford, Jr.
WMC: 9   Age:44

Vice chairman
John Medford, Sr.
WMC: 47   Age: 75

Controller
Joe Allen
WMC: 36   Age: 68

Vice president
Woolens purchasing
Mike Wilson
WMC: 44   Age: 66

Vice president
Production
Robert Hill
WMC: 36   Age: 68

Head designer
George Reese
WMC: 9   Age: 52

Quality control department

Vice president
Sales
Charles Medford
WMC: 41   Age:62

25 Salesmen

Vice president
Advertising
William Medford
WMC: 36   Age: 58

Building and ground department

Purchasing agent (nonwoolens)

Main plant
350 employees

Personnel department

No. 2 plant manager
1100 employees

"WMC" refers to length of time with Medford Clothiers.

EXHIBIT 1
Medford Clothiers Organization Chart, 1982.

163

EXHIBIT 2
Medford Clothiers
Statement of Earnings 1978–1982
Years Ending June 30

	1978	1979	1980	1981	1982
Sales	$33,800,000	$32,785,000	$31,650,000	$30,950,000	$30,140,000
Less, cost of goods sold	21,600,000	22,153,000	21,150,000	21,427,000	20,890,000
Gross profit	12,200,000	10,632,000	10,500,000	9,523,000	9,250,000
Less, selling and administration expense	11,250,000	9,832,000	9,600,000	8,820,560	8,639,000
Operating profit	950,000	800,000	900,000	702,440	611,000
Less, interest expense	640,000	524,000	680,000	590,420	530,000
Profit before taxes	310,000	276,000	220,000	112,020	81,000
Federal and state taxes	145,700	126,960	101,214	49,380	34,500
Net profit	$ 164,300	$ 149,040	$ 118,786	$ 62,640	$ 46,500
Earnings per share	0.66	0.60	0.48	0.25	0.186
Dividends per common share	0.30	.20	.20	.10	
Net to retained earnings	$ 89,360	$ 99,080	$ 68,826	$ 37,692	$ 46,500

NI/Sales   .0048   .0045   .0038   .0020   .0015

164

EXHIBIT 3
Medford Clothiers
Balance Sheets
Years Ending June 30

	1978	1979	1980	1981	1982
Cash and marketable securities	$ 1,840,000	$ 1,790,000	$ 1,890,000	$ 2,140,000	$ 2,120,000
Accounts receivable, net	14,890,000	14,800,000	13,980,000	13,820,000	13,800,000
Inventories	10,760,000	10,250,000	10,710,948	9,680,000	9,750,000
Prepaid expenses	340,000	220,000	280,000	370,000	310,000
Total current assets	27,830,000	27,060,000	26,860,948	26,010,000	25,980,000
Property, plant and equipment	8,400,000	8,400,000	8,400,000	8,650,000	8,650,000
—Reserve for depreciation	3,250,000	3,600,000	3,950,000	4,380,000	4,816,000
Net fixed assets	5,150,000	4,800,000	4,450,000	4,270,000	3,834,000
Deferred charges	1,625,000	1,550,000	1,250,000	1,680,000	1,180,000
Total fixed assets	6,775,000	6,350,000	5,700,000	5,950,000	5,014,000
TOTAL ASSETS	$34,605,000	$33,410,000	$32,560,948	$32,160,000	$30,994,000
Liabilities and net worth					
Accounts payable	2,490,600	2,200,000	2,060,000	2,150,000	1,980,624
Notes payable to banks	6,200,564	4,815,000	4,160,000	4,250,000	3,509,000
Other current liabilities	1,101,000	1,483,020	1,359,964	741,324	440,000
Total current liabilities	9,792,164	8,498,020	7,579,964	7,141,324	5,929,624
Long-term debt					
7.5% Debenture bonds due 1986	2,700,000	2,700,000	2,700,000	2,700,000	2,700,000
Common stock outstanding					
249,800 Shares $10 par	2,498,800	2,498,800	2,498,800	2,498,800	2,498,800
Paid-in surplus	7,907,736	7,907,736	7,907,736	7,907,736	7,907,736
Retained earnings	13,300,000	13,399,154	13,468,148	13,505,840	13,552,340
Less treasury stock	1,593,700	1,593,700	1,593,700	1,593,700	1,593,700
TOTAL NET WORTH	22,112,836	22,211,990	22,280,984	22,318,676	22,364,376
TOTAL LIABILITIES AND NET WORTH	$34,605,000	$33,410,000	$32,560,948	$32,160,000	$30,994,000

and the omission of a dividend this year does not please our family stockholders, most of whom are active members of management. We are at a disadvantage without captive stores; we must depend on our independent dealer network, which is being inundated with competitive lines which offer attractive styling at lower prices. Our dependence on private branding has really kept us alive, but at much reduced margins.

THE OUTLOOK FOR MEDFORD

In commenting on the company's position, Medford, Sr., stated:

The men's clothing industry has changed greatly over the years, it's not like it was when I was a young man. There was a day when my family could look forward to several million dollars profit each year. But no more. The men's suit and outercoat business has great competition now from casual clothes, sport jackets and trousers, short outercoats and "car" coats, and raincoats with liners.

Medford, Jr., like his father, considered the company's cost of production to be too high. No one in the firm wanted to produce anything but a quality garment. To assure this, the company followed a process that few, if any, producers used. Medford's suits were of high quality, but other brand names carried a quality connotation as high or higher and their production costs tended to be lower. Medford's system of manufacture utilized very little automation and demanded highly trained tailors, which added to labor costs. The company also stressed wool and had been subject to vagaries of this market.

Medford, Jr., was concerned about declining sales, particularly in the dealer stores. Declining profits affected cash flow and restricted efforts to increase advertising expenses to promote the Medford brand name. Medford, Jr., spent a good part of his time trying to convince his father and the other members of the management group of the need to seek alternatives. He felt that the company was not progressing and in the not-too-distant future might face a crisis situation.

MEN'S APPAREL INDUSTRY

The men's clothing industry was a slow-growing industry with a relatively large number of producers. While not as volatile as the women's apparel business, the ease of entry and the ease of copying styles and designs made it very competitive. The largest growth in the past decade was made by the producers of jeans such as Levi Strauss, the largest firm in the industry with sales of $3.1 billion, and Blue Bell with sales of $1.5 billion in jeans, western clothes, and other accessories. Hart, Schaffner & Marx was the largest producer and seller of men's suits and other clothing, with sales of $875 million. Hart, Schaffner & Marx was the leader in branded, higher-priced men's clothing. The company owned 313 retail outlets and distributed through thousands of department stores and independent retail outlets. Hart, Schaffner & Marx had acquired a number of brand names through acquisitions. In addition to the Hart, Schaffner

& Marx brand it manufactured and sold 16 other brands ranging from high- to medium-priced suits and casuals to the high-priced top of the line. The company had also entered the women's apparel market, which accounted for approximately 23 percent of its total sales.

Palm Beach, which produced moderately priced suits mainly for summer and fall wear, had sales over $580 million. The firm also made casual clothes for men and had branded lines of women's apparel. Approximately 20 percent of its sales were for private-brand labels. Phillips Van Heusen, best known for men's shirts, also produced men's suits and had acquired several brand names. Its annual sales were approximately $500 million. Cluett Peabody, also a manufacturer of men's shirts, produced a line of men's suits, with sales of $800 million; 25 percent of its sales were on private labeling for men's suits, underwear, and shirts.

While the number of companies producing men's clothing was decreasing, well-known brand names were being acquired by larger firms or had gone out of business. The popularity of casual clothing, however, provided an opportunity for new companies to enter the industry. Their output was in the lower price range, and their main competition was from foreign producers. In men's suits and casuals, although some labels were well established, many customers made their purchases on the basis of style, quality, and price.

In addition to a number of middle-sized firms there were a large number of smaller companies. In 1981 producers of men's and boys' suits and coats numbered about 2,900. Cuttings in men's suits (see Exhibit 4) had declined since they peaked in 1978. The popularity of the three-piece suit (vests) increased cuttings in the 1970s. The three-piece suit, however, was declining in favor, and it was reflected in total cuttings in 1979 and 1980. Cuttings for the two-piece suit increased over 10 percent in 1981. Casual wear, separate dress and sport coats, increased about 35 percent in 1981. Cuttings for separate trousers had shown a decline; however, they still remained at a high level. The sales of men's apparel was dependent on the level of consumer income and, with the prevailing recession in 1981–1982, was not expected to show any significant increase. Men's clothes in the lower-priced category and the high-priced area, particularly the branded clothing, were expected to fare the best. There was a general feeling in the industry that suits in the middle-priced range of $100 to $150 were too high-priced for the average purchaser and lacked the appeal of the higher-priced branded clothing. Most of the growth in the industry was expected to continue to come from the casual clothing—the separates—as consumers became more cost-conscious. Separate coats and trousers provided more flexibility for the man's wardrobe and provided a better fit with lower alteration costs. Also, off sizes were easily accommodated.

Brand names seemed to be increasing in sales and were being given greater attention in the industry. The 35- to 39-year-old category was increasing, and the age group from 40 to 54 was expected to increase significantly in the period 1985–1990. (See Exhibit 5). These demographic factors had intensified the campaign of many producers to foster brand loyalty in the age groups of 25 to

EXHIBIT 4
CUTTINGS OF MEN'S APPAREL*

Year	Suits	Separate dress and sport coats	Separate dress and sport trousers	Shirts (all fabrics)			Dungarees and jeans	Sweaters (ship-ments)	Work pants (excl. overalls)
				Dress	Sport†	Work			
	In thousands of units			In thousands of dozens					
1980	14,471	17,985	122,399	7,671	5,961	3,681	11,611	3,096	3,597
1979	15,935	15,603	124,688	7,868	6,503	3,600	11,587	2,806	3,745
R1978	17,526	14,966	122,661	8,125	6,887	3,750	11,816	3,127	3,808
1977	17,333	14,729	128,840	9,226	8,983	3,950	17,429	3,283	3,513
1976	15,657	12,670	127,003	9,198	10,377	3,381	16,508	3,046	3,437
1975	14,380	10,599	118,944	8,935	7,033	2,642	14,866	2,525	3,482
1974	17,259	17,635	119,116	10,983	7,316	3,919	17,153	3,516	3,925
1973	16,701	18,801	149,746	13,316	7,784	4,316	17,780	4,527	3,721
1972	18,174	18,202	182,034	12,690	8,224	4,131	13,319	3,911	4,346
1971	16,477	14,403	183,738	12,148	8,647	3,936	12,375	3,535	4,005

*Data for 1976 and prior years not comparable because of a change in the number of establishments.
†Includes woven shirts only.
R—Revised
Note: Compiled from monthly data.
Source: Department of Commerce.

EXHIBIT 5
U.S. POPULATION PROJECTIONS
(IN THOUSANDS)

	1981		1985		1990	
	Number	**Percent of total**	**Number**	**Percent of total**	**Number**	**Percent of total**
Under 5	16,620	7.4	18,803	8.1	19,437	8.0
5–14	33,400	14.9	32,826	14.1	33,768	14.7
15–19	20,019	9.4	18,007	7.7	16,777	6.9
20–24	21,116	8.9	21,116	9.4	17,953	7.4
25–29	19,324	8.6	20,510	8.8	20,169	8.3
30–34	18,138	8.1	19,278	8.3	20,917	8.6
35–39	14,290	6.4	17,274	7.4	19,261	7.9
40–54	34,524	15.4	36,559	15.7	42,642	17.5
55–64	21,413	9.6	21,737	9.3	20,776	8.5
65+	25,368	11.3	27,305	11.08	29,824	12.2
All ages	224,212	100.0	232,880	100.00	248,513	100.0

Source: Department of Commerce, *Population Series,* July 1, 1977, p. 25.

34, before they entered the 40 to 54 bracket, with the expectation that brand identification would carry over.

While the increase in imports of men's clothing had slowed in the period of 1978–1982, they still accounted for 25 percent of men's suits. The decline in imports, however, was not expected to last. The success of imports resulted mainly from the fact that apparel production was one of the least automated and most labor-intensive manufacturing industries in the United States. Although U.S. apparel workers earned the equivalent of the average wage, or slightly over, for all manufacturing, their pay was considerably higher by $3.50 to $5.00 an hour than wages paid in the apparel industry in Hong Kong, Taiwan, South Korea, and Sri Lanka. Because of such economies, imported apparel, after duties of 16 to 32 percent, is sold at wholesale up to 20 percent less than clothing made in the United States. Since capital cost per employee in the clothing industry is approximately 50 percent less than that required in most manufacturing industries, it is easily entered by the less industrialized countries which seek investment in the less capital-intensive industries to promote employment.

A new source of foreign competition has emerged in China. Imports from China in men's suits and work trousers have risen 115 to 125 percent in the past several years. Wage rates in China are estimated at 20 cents per hour. Duties on Chinese goods are about twice those levied on other apparel imports. However, U.S. producers fear the effects of China's desire to increase its exports to the United States and obtain a most-favored-nation status, which would substantially reduce the tariffs. Some have expressed the concern that under these import conditions, the huge supply of cheap Chinese labor could inundate the United States with exported apparel. Apparel producers in the United States have responded to the import problem by seeking government aid. The 1.3 million U.S. apparel workers have a powerful lobby which has achieved a significant amount of protection. The U.S. government has negotiated 18 bilateral agreements designed to hold apparel imports to an annual growth rate of 6 percent. Producers, however, have claimed that bilaterals have not provided the answer since imports have risen above the quota levels. This is due to the fact that the industry in the United States has shown only a 2 percent growth rate.

Some large apparel producers such as Cluett Peabody have tried to remain competitive through automation. Automation in cutting and computer pattern design and producing systems are available. However, it is estimated that over 60 percent of the industry is "undermechanized." Smaller producers use little automation.

The larger producers have also established manufacturing operations in the low-labor-cost countries and in some cases have entered into joint ventures with foreign companies. Many producers think foreign ventures are too risky and require too much capital that could be better utilized in the United States. There is also a reservation about how long low wages in the foreign countries will prevail as they become more industrialized and economically developed.

Capital Carpets

In discussing the current situation of Capital, President Charles D. Parker stated:

> The slowdown in building and the decline in total carpet sales have affected us in the past two years; however, we have managed to more than hold our own because of our strong contract business. We, of course, aren't very big in the industry, which is part of our problem. We have also tried to be the Cadillac of the carpet industry. Capital makes fine-quality carpets and tries to use the best materials available. The industry projections, however, show only a small growth for this part of the carpet market. We also have traditionally been heavy in the contract carpet sales and have neglected, to some extent, the home market. These factors have prompted me to request Bob Hartley, our vice president of manufacturing, and John Prince, vice president of marketing [see Exhibit 1] to assess the feasibility of expanding our product line and our channels of distribution.
>
> The carpet industry's sales have declined in real terms, and our profits have been seriously affected at a time when we are badly in need of funds to put into effect our proposed changes in order to broaden our lines and sales outlets and to ensure more efficient production. We had two good years in 1972 and 1973, but carpet production, which had reached a total of 1.03 billion square yards in 1973, declined almost 7 percent in 1974 to 959 million square yards. In 1975, production declined still further, by 4.8 percent, to approximately 913 million square yards. We managed to produce a shade over our previous totals in these two years, but that was due mainly to our new tufting machinery at the Savannah plant which gave us longer runs and, I expect, more inventory than we needed. The last part of 1975 has given us a boost after the decline which started in the latter half of 1974 and continued into the first quarter of 1975, when we experienced a deficit in earnings. While our profits have declined drastically from 1972 to 1973, we have held on, and the increase in the last two

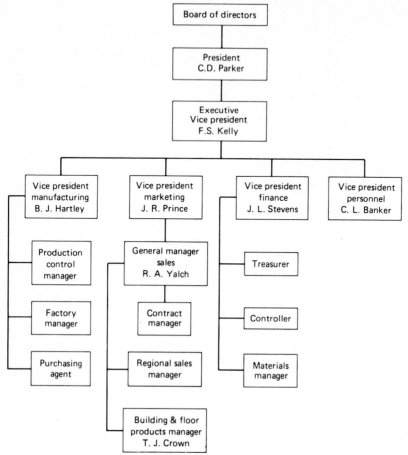

EXHIBIT 1
The Capital Carpet Company corporate organization chart, 1976.

quarters of 1975 is encouraging. [See Exhibits 2 and 3.] Forecasts for the carpet industry for 1976 look favorable. I still think this is a growth industry. Carpet production and sales have increased almost 200 percent in the past decade, and our production and sales have gone along with the industry. [See Exhibits 4 and 5.]

ORIGIN AND DEVELOPMENT OF CAPITAL

The company established its first sales office in Atlanta, Georgia, in 1908. In 1976, it operated three manufacturing facilities—a spinning plant and a tufting plant, both in Savannah, and a weaving plant in Atlanta. Capital's line included tufted and woven carpets made of both wool and synthetic fibers. Woven patterned and figured carpets, styled after oriental carpets, were Capital's

EXHIBIT 2
Capital Carpets
Statement of Income and Retained Earnings
December 31, 1975

Net sales		$33,241,500
Less: Cost of products sold	$24,385,000	
Depreciation expense	1,076,500	
Warehousing, shipping, selling, and administrative expense	5,033,241	30,494,741
Operating income		$ 2,746,759
Deduct interest on long-term debt	300,000	
Other interest	28,000	328,000
Net income before taxes		$ 2,418,759
Less: Income taxes		1,161,004
Net income		$ 1,257,755
Dividends paid at 20¢ a share on 2 milllion shares		400,000
Amount added to retained earnings 1975		$ 857,755
Retained earnings prior years		11,500,000
Total retained earnings		$12,357,755
Capital surplus		3,900,000
Capital stock		2,000,000

Five-Year Summary of Earnings

Year ending December 31	Sales	Net income	Earnings per share	Cash dividend	Common stock price range
1975	$33,241,500	$1,257,755	$0.628	$0.20	8–5
1974	30,460,500	1,131,068	0.565	0.20	12–7
1973	29,260,400	1,720,000	0.860	0.20	22–14
1972	24,750,350	1,575,000	0.787	0.15	20–11
1971	21,250,150	1,150,000	0.575	0.10	12–6

Capital Carpets
Statement of Income and Retained Earnings
December 31, 1974

Net sales		$30,460,500
Less: Cost of products sold	$22,000,500	
Depreciation expense	1,154,745	
Warehouse, shipping, selling, and administrative expense	4,800,125	$27,955,370
Operating income		$ 2,505,130
Deduct interest on long-term debt	300,000	
Other interest	30,000	330,000
Net income before taxes		$ 2,175,130
Less: Federal income taxes		1,044,062
Net income		$ 1,131,068
Dividends paid at 20¢ a share on 2 million shares		400,000
Amount added to retained earnings 1974		$ 731,068
Retained earnings prior years		10,768,932
Total retained earnings		$11,500,000
Capital surplus		$ 3,900,000
Capital stock		$ 2,000,000

EXHIBIT 3
Capital Carpets
Balance Sheet
Years Ending December 31

	1975		1974	
Current assets:				
Cash		$ 1,300,000		$ 1,100,000
Accounts receivable		4,550,000		3,750,000
Inventories (on LIFO basis)				
Finished goods	$ 5,225,250		$ 4,778,250	
Work in process	2,200,150		2,005,000	
Raw materials	950,125	8,375,250	875,125	7,658,375
Prepaid expenses and other current assets		638,800		345,000
Total current assets		$14,864,050		$12,853,375
Fixed assets:				
Property, plant, and equipment				
Land		$ 2,500,000		$ 2,500,000
Building and plants	$ 5,250,000		$ 5,512,500	
Equipment	10,175,000		9,989,000	
	$15,425,000		$15,501,500	
Less: Reserve for depreciation	6,250,000		5,173,500	
Net plant and equipment		$ 9,175,000		$10,328,000
Total assets		$26,539,050		$25,681,375
Liabilities and net worth:				
Accounts payable		$ 1,790,125		$ 1,500,000
Notes payable to bank		280,000		300,000
Federal income taxes payable		1,161,004		1,044,062
Accrued liabilities		650,166		637,313
Current portion of long-term debt		400,000		400,000
Total current liabilities		$ 4,281,295		$ 3,881,375
Long-term debt				
7.5% mortgage bonds		$ 4,000,000		$ 4,400,000
Net worth				
Common stock				
2 million shares $1 per value		2,000,000		2,000,000
Capital surplus		3,900,000		3,900,000
Retained earnings		12,357,755		11,500,000
Total liabilities and net worth		$26,539,050		$25,681,375

specialty. The company had 1,570 employees. Its 10 sales offices were located in New York, Boston, Atlanta, Pittsburgh, Chicago, Savannah, Cleveland, St. Louis, Detroit, and San Francisco. Capital followed a policy of maintaining quality production and concentrating on contract or commercial sales; as a consequence, its name was not well known to retail customers. Capital's carpet

EXHIBIT 4
CAPITAL CARPETS
CARPET PRODUCTION GROWTH RATES, 1964–1975

Year	Total carpet industry (millions of sq. yd.)	Total carpet industry growth rate
1964	374	18%
1965	432	15%
1966	469	9%
1967	483	3%
1968	580	20%
1969	640	10%
1970	705	10%
1971	770	9%
1972	847	10%
1973	1,030	21.6%
1974	959	−6.8%
1975	913	−4.8%

production was 30 percent in wool, compared with the industry average of 8 percent. The company used synthetics in its tufted carpets but was limited to stock-dyed fibers because it did not have piece-dying equipment.

Commenting on the manufacturing facilities and the organization of Capital, B. J. Hartley, vice president of manufacturing, stated:

> The Atlanta plant is used primarily for weaving and contains much equipment which is old and slow . . . . The spinning plant at Savannah, while operated efficiently, is bur-

EXHIBIT 5
CAPITAL CARPETS
PRODUCTION BY CAPITAL, 1963–1975
(Thousands of Yards)

Year	Tufted	Woven	Total	Percent of growth
1963		540	540	
1964		603	603	12
1965		488	488	−18
1966		498	498	2
1967	50	619	669	34
1968	89	620	709	6
1969	180	491	671	−5
1970	240	610	850	27
1971	550	654	1,204	42
1972	1,100	500	1,600	33
1973	1,600	400	2,000	25
1974	1,750	300	2,050	2.5
1975	1,900	200	2,100	2.4

dened with slow equipment . . . .The tufting plant at Savannah is new and the installed equipment is modern, but it is apparent to even a casual observer that the operators have much to learn about efficient output. Capital's equipment also includes several 60-year-old gripper looms which may be among the few remaining ones in the U.S. We propose to retain our present equipment but to emphasize tufting. We plan to expand to product lines, which are versatile and full, since our specialties—floral and abstract patterns—are no longer popular at retail.

Capital sold to wholesalers, to private retailers, and to the contract market at both wholesale and retail. Thirty-three percent of its sales were direct contract sales (and 70 percent contract in terms of end users), compared with the industry average of 20 percent.

Competitors believed that Capital built up considerable ill will among wholesalers by its pricing tactics of underbidding wholesalers for attractive contract jobs, leaving only less desirable business for wholesalers.

CAPITAL'S MARKET POSITION

The development of Capital's market position began in the 1950s, when most carpeting was woven (versus tufted) and the main fiber was wool (versus synthetics). Capital's lines consisted of wool friezes and plushes, both manufactured on Velvet looms; wool floral and abstract designs, made on Wilton looms; and wool orientals and specialties, manufactured on gripper Axminster looms. The company's sales through retailers were concentrated heavily on the wool friezes and the domestic orientals. At the time, contract carpeting was primarily for hotels and fashionable restaurants and the demand was not great.

In the carpet industry expansion of the late 1950s, the tufting process and synthetic fibers coupled with their relatively low price caused retail markets to expand. The institutional and commercial markets also expanded. These markets were traditionally higher-quality, higher-priced carpet markets.

As the retail demand moved away from high-quality woven wool carpeting, Capital concentrated upon the contract market. To achieve growth, the company adopted a strategy of outservicing and outpricing its competitors in the contract field. Capital's facilities enabled it to offer fast delivery and small production runs, both resulting in very low margins in a field which was generally less profitable than the retail field. As the dual market trend continued, Capital became isolated in the contract field, while its competitors, who had moved into tufting early, were able to sell all segments of the markets. The company's entry into tufting was limited and late.

THE CARPET INDUSTRY: COMPETITION AND MANUFACTURING

The rug and carpet industry was classified as highly competitive. Industry data indicated that there were over 250 individual companies with more than 200 plants manufacturing carpet and scatter rugs in the United States. The number of companies manufacturing tufted carpets had increased by 30 percent in the past 15 years, while the number of manufacturers of woven carpets declined by 25 percent. The number of carpet looms in place declined from 3,234 to approximately 1,500, and the number of tufting machines increased to 3,000. Competition existed not only among different companies producing the same types of rugs, but also among different types of rugs and carpets.

Major producers accounted for approximately 40 to 50 percent of the industry total. Mohasco was the leader; including Firth, acquired in 1962, its sales were estimated to account for about 11 percent. As a result of the acquisition of Lees by Burlington Industries in early 1960, it was difficult to make an accurate estimate of the company's share of total industry sales. However, it was believed that Lees probably accounted for about 10 percent. Bigelow-Sanford, 94 percent owned by Sperry and Hutchinson, was next in importance, accounting for about 9 percent. Other important producers included Coronet, a fast-growing concern almost wholly engaged in tufted carpeting, Masland (C. H.) & Sons, Roxbury Carpet, and Armstrong Cork (through its acquisition of E & B Carpet). E. T. Barwick Mills and Magee Carpet, both privately owned, were also important in the industry. Prices in the industry ranged from approximately $4 per square yard for the low-cost polyester to $35 or more for high-quality wool carpets. Because of the high cost of wool, retail sales of wool carpeting accounted for approximately 5 to 8 percent of total sales. Since Capital produced only wool, Acrilan, and nylon, its prices were in the medium to high range of $11.95 to $28 per square yard. Contract prices varied according to the specifications and order size; because much of Capital's contract business was in wool, its prices tended to be higher than the industry average.

Historically, all carpeting had been of woven construction, and most of it was woven from wool. In woven carpeting the pile and backing yarns were alternately jute or cotton thread. The most common types of woven carpeting were Velvet, Wilton, or Axminster. Velvet was used mostly for solid colors. Wilton was woven on a Jacquard loom which used a series of perforated cards similar to player-piano rolls, which regulated the feeding of different colors of yarn into the loom and made possible the introduction of intricate patterns which had great clarity. Axminster was woven on a special carpet loom which allowed an almost unlimited combination of design and color. The changing of patterns on all types of carpet construction was a slow, expensive process. The weaving was also slow, sometimes producing only 10 or 12 linear feet in a working day. Woven carpets were relatively high-priced, and their sale was tending to become limited to prestige installations.

The tufted method of producing carpet was introduced in 1949. In tufting, the machine acted as a mammoth sewing machine, with hundreds of needles aligned across the width of the machine. A yarn threaded through each needle eye was pierced through the backing fabric. As the needle was retracted, a loop (the tuft) was formed and held by the backing fabric. A heavy coating of latex was later applied to the back of the fabric to anchor the tufts permanently into place. Weaving machines fabricated the entire carpet, including the backing and pile; in tufting, only the pile was fabricated; the backing was prefabricated. Electronic control in both the yarn feed and the needle action permitted the creation of pattern textures. While any fiber could be tufted, most tufted carpets were made from synthetics. Tufting was a fast production process compared to weaving, and quality tufted carpets sold at prices which were considerably lower than those of woven carpets. In the relatively short period of its existence, tufted carpeting had taken over 80 percent of the U. S. market, and other markets were undergoing the same experience.

Until the advent of the broadloom tufted carpet machines, tufted output was limited to such items as small scatter rugs and bath mats. With the development of this machine, which did not require a large capital outlay or much skilled labor, the square-yard volume of tufted broadloom increased more than 50-fold from the early 1950s to 1976.

Total domestic broadloom shipments increased steadily from 64.7 million square yards (90 percent woven) in 1951 to over 400 million in 1975 (approximately 10 percent woven and knitted). The entire postwar gain was attributable to the tufted process, with shipments of woven rugs and carpets in 1975 less than in the 1950s. Tufted was able to achieve its rapid penetration of the market primarily because of significant cost saving in manufacture.

CAPITAL'S PRODUCT LINES

Capital had one of the few gripper Axminster operations in the United States. From a production scheduling standpoint, this permitted them to plan shorter runs and to produce a more clearly defined pattern. However, their gripper looms were 60 years old, and their production rate was only 18 linear inches per hour. A full working day was required to shift from one pattern to another. Until Capital added tufted carpeting to its line, the Axminster looms produced Capital's only significant retail line—their domestic oriental collection—and a collection of modern shag designs. Capital offered a wide range of patterns and sizes in its domestic orientals.

Although carpet industry members adopted tufting of synthetic fibers as early as 1950, Capital responded to the trend in 1964, when it built a tufting mill and introduced acrylic and nylon fibers into its weaving operations. Tufting produced carpeting much faster and at lower production cost than weaving machines. With synthetics, less yarn was required per square yard because synthetics had greater bulking capabilities. Since 80 percent of the cost of the carpet was in the yarn, the use of synthetics brought about further cost reductions, which quickly reduced the retail price of carpeting.

Capital's first tufting plant had three tufters, a scroll machine, a cut-pile machine, and a seven-roll loop machine. Production capacity was limited but permitted Capital to offer a diversified line.

Capital had equipment to blend, card, and spin raw wool. It could skein-dye a minimum of 1,000 pounds, which, in terms of 45- to 48-ounce cloth, would be approximately 250 square yards or two full rolls. This could be doubled by using dual kettles operating under the same dye lot for 2,200 pounds. However, in stock dyeing (yarn being dyed before blending, carding, and spinning), Capital was limited to a 5,000-pound minimum. Stock dyeing did not restrict them to a 1-yard count as did skein dyeing but committed them to a longer run of one color.

When considering their frieze patterns, Capital had to think in terms of minimum 5,000-pound runs because, in addition to dyeing their frieze yarn, they heat-set it in their stock-dye kettles. To offset their production run commitments, they offered frieze in several widths, which caused inventory problems. Capital also made proprietary lines for large-volume accounts, such as chain department stores and mail-order houses.

When Capital entered the tufting field, it encountered difficulties in fiber procurement. In the acrylic field, it started with Du Pont Orlon, which had to be spun and stock-dyed by an outside commission spinner and dyer, since Capital did not have sufficient capacity to handle its own spinning of synthetic fibers. Also, Orlon was considered to be of lower quality than Acrilan. (See Exhibit 6.)

In the summer of 1966, Capital was successful in negotiating a contract with Chemstrand for the use of Acrilan fiber. In the nylon field, the company resorted to buying from a continuous-filament nylon producer in Holland because it could supply solution-dyed material. Capital did not have facilities to do piece dyeing and as a result paid a high price for yarn.

Capital introduced one line made from staple nylon, which was purchased from Du Pont and spun and stock-dyed. This was the Cosmic line, which became one of the most successful sellers and one of the most profitable.

In 1976, Capital had ten running tufted lines; five were considered by management to be inferior to the competition in color, style, and price. This was primarily due to yarn source. When using solution-dyed continuous-filament nylon, creels had to be changed after every color run, which created inventory problems and resulted in higher costs. Capital was dependent upon the commission spinner and dyer as far as the preparation of acrylic yarn was concerned, and on its raw material supplier as far as solution-dyed continuous nylon filament was concerned. The company did not have the same capacity of yarn preparation and dyeing for synthetic fibers as it had had for wool.

Capital's product assortment in 1976, including both weaving and tufting, was 30 percent wool, 35 percent acrylic, and 35 percent nylon. The comparable assortment for the total U. S. carpet industry was 8 percent wool, 25 percent acrylic, and 55 percent nylon, with 12 percent in other fibers (polyester, polypropylene). Due to Capital's inability to piece-dye, it did not have products in the continuous-filament nylon lines, which were the most popular.

EXHIBIT 6
CARPET FIBER CHART*

Fiber	Plus qualities	Minus qualities	Cleanability
Wool	Excellent durability; springy and crush resistant; adaptable to styling; flame resistant.	Must be mothproofed; can be damaged by alkaline detergents; is expensive; waste or reprocessed wool is a poor choice.	Needs cleaning less frequently than synthetics, but is more difficult to clean.

Synthetic fibers
(All synthetic fibers are mothproof and resistant to mildew)

Fiber	Plus qualities	Minus qualities	Cleanability
Acrylic Trade names: Acrilan, Creslan, Orlon, Zefran, Sayelle, Zefkrome	Takes color well; springy and crush resistant; good resistance to soil and sunlight; is most wool-like in appearance; nonallergenic.	May "pill."	Cleans very easily.
Nylon Trade names: Anso, Antron, Cadon, Caprolan, Cumuloft Enkalure, Enka-loft	Springy and crush resistant; nonallergenic; considered by many to be the best-wearing of the synthetic fibers.	Soils easily in bright colors; pills in staple loop pile; some static electricity; fiber melts; cool to touch. Buy virgin, not waste, nylon.	Excellent.
Polyester Trade names: Avlin, Dacron, Fortrel, Kodel, Encron, Trevira	Excellent durability, Looks luxurious; resists spills and stains; nonallergenic.	Cool to touch; some pilling and static electricity. Does not wear as well as nylon or acrylic in high-traffic areas.	Excellent.

CAPITAL'S MARKETING PROGRAM

Traditionally the sales department had been told by manufacturing what products they had to sell. Prices were determined by the accounting department. Capital's top management set a sales budget each year, and the sales department was charged with meeting this budget. John Prince, vice president of marketing, was aware that Richard Yalch, general sales manager, was unhappy with the way the sales budget was determined. Yalch claimed that his organization was not given enough flexibility and that effective selling techniques and effective training programs cost more than he was getting. His argument bothered Charles Parker; however, Jay Stevens, vice president of finance,

Fiber	Plus qualities	Minus qualities	Cleanability
Synthetic fibers			
(All synthetic fibers are mothproof and resistant to mildew)			
Polypropylene (olefin) Trade names: Herculon, Vectra, Marvess, Polycrest	Wears extremely well; nonallergenic; lightweight; good resistance to soil and stains except grease.	Fiber melts in lower grades; is likely to crush.	Excellent, except for set-in grease stains.
Additional fibers used in carpeting to a limited degree			
Cotton	Excellent durability; soft; not subject to moths or mildew.	Fiber and color can be destroyed by bleach or lye.	Small rugs can be machine-washed, carpets shampooed successfully.
Rayon	Takes color well; is soft; good chemical resistance; not affected by moths.	In less dense pile, has poor flame resistance; crushes; poor durability and soil resistance.	As cleanable as cotton.
Modacrylics Trade names: Dynel, Elura, Verel	Used in blends for flame resistance; very durable; may be used in high-pile rugs.	Lacks good resilience; pills and shreds easily.	Cleans very well.

*This chart is adapted from *Buy It Right—The Shopper's Guide to Home Furnishings* by Jan Brown, published by the Consumer Services Division of Career Institute, Mundelein, Ill.

pointed out that Capital had been doing well with the present method and that sales departments in many firms perennially asked for more dollars.

Capital sold to wholesalers but at the same time sold directly to any retailer who was willing to buy from them. Many retailers were sold products at prices which were lower, in some cases, than prices for wholesalers.

Richard Yalch slanted his efforts toward woven carpet and contract work. He felt that the carpet business could not afford the luxury of a wholesaler's margin. Capital's salespeople were considered to be knowledgeable about carpets, but they were strongly oriented toward the contract field. All carpeting business other than private home installations was considered contract business. It typically included office buildings, banks, stores, schools, auditoriums, clubs, hotels, mortuaries, motels, churches, and apartment houses. While retail carpet sales had followed the trend toward synthetics, contract merchandise had not followed this trend to the same extent. Tufted synthetics were gaining a larger percentage of the growing contract market, but most of this gain was at the expense of installations which had formerly used hard-surfaced materials. Most public-space-area customers were still choosing woven fabrics of close construction in Velvet, Wilton, and Axminster weaves.

Capital's management believed that contract carpet selling was a special field. Typical contract carpetings were constructed to withstand heavy usage in public areas, and they were, in some instances, more expensive than retail carpeting. This called for technical manufacturing knowledge on the part of the salespeople in fabric selection. Furthermore, most large jobs were put out on the basis of open tender, which required that the salespeople produce complete technical specifications. The manufacturer's salesperson was also required to give advice on installation and maintenance. Careful cultivation of customer relations was required so that, if Capital was underbid on an open tender job, there might be a second opportunity to price the job, perhaps in a less expensive fabric, a mill second, or a discontinued line.

CAPITAL'S EXPANSION PLANS

In early 1976, Capital's business was 60 percent contract and 40 percent in other channels, with some 20 accounts generating 70 percent of Capital's sales. On this contract base, it was the intention of management to build two businesses: wholesale and retail.

It was Capital's stated aim to preserve the contract part of its business as the base for the development of the wholesale-retail business. The sales manager outlined the following policies to maintain the contract business:

   I Determine to remain price-competitive.
  II Keep Capital people imbued with the idea that the company intends to become even stronger in its contract position.
 III Specialize in contract sales management, with Capital people becoming the experts.
 IV Bring Capital's contract know-how to the industry through:
    A Technical information
    B Installation
    C Job organization
    D Contract leads and their pursuit
    E Job financing
    F Soliciting specifiers (architects, etc.) versus end-users
    G Catering to decorators, color consultants
    H Providing specifiers with miniature sample sets, etc.
    I Concentrated follow-up on lost jobs to discover the reasons why
   V Develop products and techniques unique to Capital.
  VI Develop tight technical specifications.
 VII Build a reputation as an innovator.

Early in 1976, Mr. F. S. Kelly, executive vice president, suggested to Mr. J.

R. Price, vice president of marketing, that selling and administrative expenses in the event of expansion would increase considerably. Assuming that Capital sales were at a level of $50 million, the following estimate was made of the additional personnel required for marketing and administration (see Exhibits 7 to 10):

    5 Commodity managers
    5 Field sales managers
  50 Salespeople
  25 Secretarial and clerical for sales
    5 Assistants in the bureau of merchandising
  25 Order department
  <u> 5</u> Installation instructors
120 Total marketing

Specific amounts were estimated for Capital advertising, samples, and wholesalers' convention.

In light of the proposal made by Mr. F. S. Kelly, Charles D. Parker, president, announced that the marketing organization was being restructured to enable the company to maintain its strong position in the contract field.

In accordance with the expansion plans, B. J. Hartley suggested that a 72,000-square-foot addition to the Savannah plant would be advantageous. The new plant would adjoin the existing building and would house piece-dyeing facilities, spinning equipment, and added warehouse space. An additional tufting machine would also be installed in the existing Savannah plant. Construction time was estimated to be about 14 to 16 months. An autoclave to heat-set a hard twist would be installed after construction, and an additional two cards and spinning frames would be installed in December. The enlarged facilities would permit Capital to process all their carpets from bulk fiber to the finished carpet with less dependence on outside spinners and dyers.

EXHIBIT 7
PROJECTED EXPANSION PROGRAM PLANNED FOR 1977–1981

Project	Amount	Recovery period	Added profit (average: 5 years)	Estimated return on added capital (average: 5 years)
Tufter, piece dyeing, and building	$ 675,000	1.5 years	$ 651,000	20.5%
Yarn preparation, stock dyeing, and building	1,082,000	3.0 years	1,281,000	30.0%
Autoclave	58,000	1.0 year	155,000	30.4%
	$1,815,000		$2,087,000	26.8%

EXHIBIT 8
EXPANSION PROGRAM, PART 2

Expansion funds

Funds needed for a cut-pile tufter and piece-dyeing equipment:

Items	Estimated cost
One cut-pile tufter	$ 98,100
Two 15' dye becks	86,000
One sample unit	1,200
Vacuum extracting equipment	38,200
12 wet carts	12,000
One 1,500-lb scale	2,500
Storage racks	4,500
Piece-dyeing installation costs	40,000
Manufacturing building—18,000 sq ft	266,000
Warehouse building—7,500 sq ft	89,500
Warehouse roll racks	15,000
Contingency for building	12,500
Contingency for machinery items	10,500
Total new capital required	$675,500

The building costs shown above are specific for the manufacturing area required for piece dyeing, and represent half of the costs for additional warehouse space included in the total building project.

This project is a combination cost-reduction and expanded-capacity job based on the following economic assumptions:

Capacity

The cut-pile tufter will enable us to produce an additional 200,000 square yards of tufted carpet per year. At our present average mix of nylon and acrylic fiber, this will produce $2,260,000 per year in additional net sales and $550,000 of gross margin.

The addition of piece-dyeing equipment will increase nylon sales and margin as shown below.

Five-year record of sales and margin

Year	Square yards (000)	Amount (000)	Gross margin
1977	1,000	$2,000	$333
1978	1,300	2,800	500
1979	1,500	3,000	684
1980	1,500	3,000	684
1981	1,500	3,000	684

EXHIBIT 9
EXPANSION PROGRAM, PART 3

Cost reduction

Piece dyeing will enable us to eliminate the need for commission dyers, and we will substitute continuous-filament nylon for staple, which will result in direct cost saving of 26 cents per pound for nylon. As a result of longer production runs using neutral color fiber, we also expect to improve manufacturing margins by 2% in 1975 and 1976 and 3% thereafter. The net manufacturing savings will accrue as follows:

Year	Direct cost savings, 26¢ per lb (000)	Production efficiency (000)	Added manufacturing expense (000)	Net savings (000)
1977	$143	$ 44	$(70)	$117
1978	208	64	(80)	192
1979	286	132	(85)	333
1980	286	132	(85)	333
1981	286	132	(85)	333
Average	$242	$101	$(81)	$262

Selling, administrative, and interest expenses

We have made provision for increased selling and administrative expenses at 4.5% of additional net sales. Interest costs calculated at 9.5% would be $64,125.

DISTRIBUTION CHANNELS

Contract carpeting was sold by manufacturer to several distinct classifications of customers:

1 Large department stores' contract divisions. These consisted of all larger jobs where the credit was secure.

2 Contract houses, specializing in contract but still doing some retail business. These also did the larger jobs, but they included apartment houses, etc., where the credit risk was often hard to determine.

3 Direct retail accounts, which often solicited and did a small amount of contract business on the side. These were typically small local jobs, where personal acquaintance with the customer was important.

4 Distributors who took jobs in their dealers' localities on the basis of personal connections, mutual church or club memberships, etc. Political connections accounted for a significant portion of this business.

Changing the distribution pattern would be slow for a number of reasons. The initial tufting capacity would not support an immediate all-out effort. It was believed that the Capital color line would need reworking because the colors were "hard" and considered to be poorly correlated, and some commercially dyed yards lacked color control; 65 percent of Capital's business was in Chicago and Detroit; 65 retail accounts there sold Capital carpets, and all of them at times bought directly. Wholesalers there also handled the Capital line, but their relationship was a tenuous one. Management believed that changing these relationships would require much time and tact.

Capital had 13 wholesale stocks across the country. After considerable investigation, it was concluded that it would be best to have the wholesaler establish selected distribution at retail. Since most retailers sold from samples, it was essential that they purchase sample books. It was felt that one wholesaler

EXHIBIT 10
EXPANSION PROGRAM, PART 4

Capital employed

Capital requirements for accounts receivable, inventories, and property, plant, and equipment (PP&E) are detailed below. We do not expect to increase cash or miscellaneous assets as a result of this project.

Year	Accounts receivable (45 days) (000)	Inventory (000)	PP&E (000)	Total increase (000)
1977	$258	$609	$451	$1,318
1978	307	669	423	1,399
1979	408	889	395	1,692
1980	408	889	367	1,664
1981	408	889	339	1,636
Average	$358	$789	$395	$1,542

Based on the foregoing assumptions, additional sales, net profit, capital, and return on capital employed (ROCE) for the 1976–1980 period are as follows:

Year	Net sales (000)	Net profits (000)	Capital employed (000)	(ROCE)
1977	$7,060	$463	$3,018	15.3%
1978	7,460	582	3,099	18.7
1979	8,260	737	3,292	22.5
1980	8,260	737	3,264	22.9
1981	8,260	737	3,236	23.4
Average	$7,860	$651	$3,182	20.5%

Recovery period

We will recover our fixed capital expenditures of $675,500 in 1.5 years. This employs the average method over the five-year period. Calculated on the specific method, our recovery period will be 2.1 years.

would be in a better position to offer semiexclusivity to a retailer, who would purchase a display of the new Capital Carpets sample books. Of the 13 distributor stocks, 8 were carrying complete competing lines. The distributor organization was reduced to 11 wholesale stocks.

For each wholesaler, Capital set up an exclusive territory based upon the trading zones normally covered by the wholesaler. A suggested zone selling price was established for each wholesaler, based upon landed cost, which would return a gross profit on full rolls of 17 percent and 25.5 percent on cut quantities. This margin was arrived at after a discussion with Capital wholesalers about the margins they were earning on their carpet lines. It was felt that if the margins originally set up were not attractive, Capital would not be able to set up the wholesaler organization.

As part of the new arrangements, the wholesalers would participate in contract business and their dealers would be bidding against the large contract houses which would be buying directly from Capital. Considering that every contract job was priced differently, depending upon its size and the carpet construction involved, it was expected that wholesalers would earn gross margins of 6 to 10 percent on this portion of their business.

Since the new wholesalers would represent the Capital line, it was expected that it would be possible for them to be somewhat flexible in their pricing. This would be especially true in the case of retail accounts which had previously purchased directly from Capital at prices lower than the wholesaler's cost. It was intended that they would be serviced in the interim by the wholesaler at prices which would be between the retailer's old buying price and the new suggested wholesaler selling price.

Capital did not arrange a volume rebate program for its wholesalers, but management intended to give consideration to this at a later date, after proper product lines had been established.

PRODUCT-LINE EXPANSION AND FUTURE PROSPECTS

Vice Presidents Prince and Hartley and General Manager of Sales Yalch, after a study and review of Capital's product line, recommended to President Parker that an effort be made to broaden the company's market offerings. They pointed out that the traditional wool, nylon, and Acrilan should be continued but that additional lines should be added using synthetic yarns, with a gradual decreasing of the production of wool carpeting.

The need for new patterns and designs was also emphasized, particularly for the residential or home markets.

Mr. Prince noted the need to attempt to match competition in terms of length and variety of product line. All members of the group agreed that Capital's line was not adequate. In reference to these statements, President Parker stated:

> We must be concerned about the cost and the length of time it would take to create a longer product line. Many of our competitors are doing a much larger volume than we

are, and they are in a position to support a long line on a profitable basis. What is economical for them, however, may not be right for us considering our resources and position in the industry. Nevertheless, I am concerned about our future plan of action for the expansion program and about your recommendations for product-line expansion. The carpet industry shows signs of picking up this year and next. The downtrend which began in the second half of 1974 has reversed itself. There are certainly signs of a rebound in the home furnishings business. Inventory gluts which became evident in the last quarter of 1974 have been substantially cleared. Residential building is expected to top $43 billion in 1976, up 37 percent from 1975, and 1977 should show continued improvement. Single-family units are projected to show a 30 percent increase in 1976 over 1975. I think we are going to have an enlarged market in 1976–1977, and the industry may return to its old growth rates, or at least show a growth trend. The demand for both retail and contract carpeting should be strong. In 1976, a 12.5 percent increase over 1975 is projected, with continuing growth in 1977. We must take advantage of our opportunities; however, we should proceed with caution. Production costs continue to increase and I doubt seriously whether our projected figures for the proposed expansion are valid today. What also concerns me is the continuing increase in the price of fibers. We may do a lot of business, but can we maintain our margins in the process?

Laura Lee

Samuel Fischer was chairman of the board and chief executive officer of Laura Lee. In reflecting on the company, he said:

> No doubt about it, inflation has eroded our margins, and the high cost of borrowing has prevented us from recovering increased operating costs. Almost everyone in the garment business has had their share of financial difficulties, and it looks as though this will continue for the rest of 1982. But the Laura Lee name is well known in the women's apparel field, despite severe problems. Our Laura Lee line has held up very well and is profitable. We can continue to grow in this market segment. We are making significant operating changes, and if this economy turns around, our reputation, brand names, and national network of stores carrying our lines are going to put us solidly in the profit column.

Laura Lee experienced a loss of $2.3 million on sales of $151 million in 1982. After marginal profits in 1977 the company recorded a significant loss of $3.5 million in 1978. Profitability returned in 1979 when the company earned $6.7 million, the most profitable year in its history. In 1980 profits slipped to $2.4 million. The U-Sew-It Division of the company incurred significant losses in 1981 and 1982. The recession, rising costs, and high interest rates all contributed to the corporate losses of $3.1 million in fiscal year 1981 and the loss in 1982. (See Exhibits 1, 2, and 3.)

In 1982 Laura Lee was engaged in the design, manufacture, and sale of women's wear through its Laura Lee Apparel Division, made up of six units. The company also operated a retail fabric division, U-Sew-It, which sold prepared patterns of their own fabrics for home sewing. L&L Transport was a separate division of Laura Lee which provided the trucking facilities for the

EXHIBIT 1

Laura Lee

Statement of Income for Fiscal Years Ending May 1

(in Thousands)

Sales	1982	1981	1980	1979	1978
Women's Wear	$133,000	$123,200	$112,400	$ 93,100	$ 78,300
L&L Transport	10,500	12,500	5,300	2,900	800
U-Sew-It	7,900	9,100	9,400	9,700	10,100
Net sales	151,400	144,800	127,100	105,700	89,200
Less cost of goods sold	116,600	108,700	91,500	71,400	62,300
Gross profit on sales	34,800	36,100	35,600	34,300	26,900
Less selling and administrative expense	33,200	34,800	30,400	24,100	27,350
Income from continuing operations	1,600	1,300	5,200	10,200	−450
Loss on discontinued operations	600	1,300	600	–	–
Interest expense	3,200	3,000	2,500	1,800	3,000
Other expense	60	40	70	60	50
Net income before taxes	(2,260)	(3,040)	2,130	8,340	(3,500)
Federal and state taxes	50	60	1,470	4,025	55
Tax credit—loss carry forward	–	–	1,155	2,400	–
Net income	(2,310)	(3,100)	2,445	6,715	(3,555)

company and also operated as a public licensed carrier. The Laura Lee
Division sold through 4,700 retail accounts on a national basis, including major
department stores and women's wear retail specialty shops. The sales force
numbered 90 in the Laura Lee Division and 25 in the U-Sew-It Division. The
company had 11 sales display spaces in six cities and operated seven plants in
six cities. Total employment in 1982 was 1,700; this included 1,150 production
workers in the Laura Lee Division, which also provided the fabrics for the U-
Sew-It Division, 250 workers in L&L Transport, and the remainder in executive, staff, and clerical positions.

ORIGIN AND DEVELOPMENT OF THE COMPANY

Early Growth

Laura Lee was started by Bernard Fischer in 1934 when he formed a partnership to sell wholesale women's apparel. After a few difficult years he gained
a following of independent department stores in the rural areas. In 1953 Laura
Lee was incorporated and began the manufacture of its own products. Through
the 1950s the company showed gradual growth manufacturing and marketing
moderate-priced apparel designed for the younger woman. The product line
was expanded, and a sales organization was developed to sell directly to retailers. When knitted fabrics became popular in the early 1960s, Laura Lee
decided to stress the polyester knits and developed a full line of budget garments in this fabric. The company set an objective of growth to attain a size sufficient to gain economies of scale in manufacture and to broaden its market
base.

Bernard Fischer set a goal of increasing sales 15 to 20 percent per year. His
ambition was to reach $200 to $250 million in sales. He also sought to expand
manufacturing into the central southern states, where labor was plentiful and
unions were not strong. He often expressed his hope to eventually get all manufacturing out of the New York garment district.

Sales increased to $4 million in 1962 and showed little growth for the next
two years. This turn of events discouraged Bernard Fischer, who was intent on
reaching his goal of 15 to 20 percent annual sales growth.

He continued to seek new approaches to selling the Laura Lee line and in his
words "stumbled on the key" while visiting a luggage maker in Kansas to shop
for moderate-priced carrying cases for his salespeople to use as sample cases.

Turn Around Year

In the luggage maker's display room he noticed a large wall map on which the
areas around cities like New York, Philadelphia, and Cleveland were studded
with colored pins, but there were no pins on the smaller cities, areas which he
had been trying to develop. The luggage maker said that these were his retail

EXHIBIT 2
Laura Lee
Consolidated Balance Sheets Fiscal Year Ending May 1
(in Thousands)

	1982	1981	1980	1979	1978
Cash and marketable securities	$ 60	$ 1,200	$ 2,700	$ 3,600	$ 1,300
Accounts receivable less allowance doubtful accounts	20,200	19,000	17,500	15,400	11,300
Inventories					
Raw materials	9,200	9,500	9,800	8,400	7,400
Goods-in-process	3,400	4,200	4,200	3,700	2,700
Finished goods	9,400	9,300	8,200	8,000	9,600
Total	22,000	23,000	22,200	20,100	19,700
U-Sew-It inventories	3,440	3,462	3,700	3,800	3,000
Total inventories	25,440	26,462	25,900	23,900	21,700
Prepaid expenses	3,400	3,000	3,400	2,800	1,700
Total current assets	49,100	49,662	49,500	45,700	35,000
Fixed assets					
Land	1,050	1,050	1,050	1,050	1,050
Buildings	6,700	6,700	6,700	8,400	8,400
Machinery and equipment	11,900	11,900	10,460	10,460	8,640
Leasehold improvements	1,600	1,600	1,400	1,200	1,100
Total	21,250	21,250	19,610	20,110	19,190
Less accumulated depreciation	11,120	9,640	8,490	7,100	5,860

Net fixed assets	$ 10,130	$ 11,610	$ 11,210	$ 13,010	$ 13,330
Other assets	120	–			
Total assets	59,350	61,272	60,620	58,710	48,330
Current liabilities	3,080	5,502	5,400	5,700	4,272
Current amount of long-term debt	1,487	1,062	1,500	1,100	1,600
Accounts payable	8,960	6,770	6,400	7,225	5,952
Accrued expenses	5,630	5,863	5,200	5,975	5,670
Total current liabilities	19,157	19,197	18,500	20,000	17,494
Long-term debt	17,000	16,500	13,500	13,000	11,900
Deferred charges	308	370	325	220	186
Stockholder's equity					
Common stock—par value $1.00					
Authorized 5 million shares					
Issued and outstanding	3,363	3,363	3,363	3,363	3,363
Capital paid in excess of par value	9,858	9,858	9,858	9,858	9,858
Retained earnings	9,664	11,974	15,074	12,269	5,529
Total liabilities and capital	22,885	25,195	28,295	25,490	18,750
Total	$ 59,350	$ 61,272	$ 60,620	$ 58,710	$ 48,330

EXHIBIT 3
Laura Lee Divisional Financial Data
(in Thousands)

Division	Year	Sales	Intracompany sales	Net sales	Profit from continuing operations	Consolidated income from continuing operations	Division identifiable assets
Women's Wear	1982	$133,000	—	$133,000	$1,550	$1,600	$46,866
	1981	123,200	—	123,200	1,000	1,300	49,618
	1980	112,400	—	112,400	5,040	5,200	48,677
	1979	93,100	—	93,100	9,440	10,200	48,729
	1978	78,300	—	78,300	1,810	1,800	41,340
L&L Transport	1982	8,715	$1,785	10,500	1,050	1,600	9,497
	1981	8,000	4,500	12,500	1,150	1,300	8,578
	1980	3,127	2,173	5,300	530	5,200	5,759
	1979	1,450	750	2,200	400	10,200	2,742
	1978	520	180	800	90	1,800	483
U-Sew-It	1982	7,900	—	7,900	(840)	1,600	2,967
	1981	9,100	—	9,100	(850)	1,300	3,676
	1980	9,400	—	9,400	(370)	5,200	6,181
	1979	9,700	—	9,700	50	10,200	7,339
	1978	10,100	—	10,100	80	1,800	6,527

dealers and that his line did not sell worth a darn in small cities and farm towns. "The realization hit like a clap of thunder," said Bernard Fischer. "Where moderate-priced luggage would sell, so would the Laura Lee line. I had been a damn fool! I had been plowing all over the hinterland, while there were acres of diamonds right in my own backyard."

On his return to New York, Bernard Fischer switched his sales effort. The existing Laura Lee retailers in small cities and rural areas were retained, but the effort to obtain new retailers was directed to metropolitan areas. "The pivotal year for our business was 1964," said Bernard Fischer. "It was our turning point. From then on sales shot up jet-propelled."

Acquisitions and Expansion

Until 1964 Laura Lee had grown significantly, but the growth had been entirely internal. In 1964 Laura Lee acquired the Derby Day line on an exchange-of-share basis. This was the first of a series of acquisitions which were to follow. In May, 1966, Laura Lee acquired Cantigny, Inc., which manufactured and wholesaled moderately priced knitted garments retailing at $30 to $50, under the brand name "Cantigny." Cantigny was a well-established brand, and for 18 years the company operated its own plant at Saratoga Springs, New York.

The Derby Day knitted line which Laura Lee acquired in 1964 was manufactured by Dressmakers Ltd. in its modern plant in Montreal. Bernard Fischer decided to shift all knitwear manufacture to the more efficient Montreal plant, and during the summer of 1966 the Dressmakers plant was enlarged for that purpose. The Cantigny Saratoga Springs equipment was sold at auction, and new equipment to produce the Cantigny line was installed in Montreal. From August to December the Saratoga plant was not producing, because of the move. In December the Saratoga plant began to produce some other Laura Lee lines, but these took only part of its capacity. "Immediately after we acquired Cantigny," said Bernard Fischer, "we switched its distribution from wholesalers to our direct-to-retailers system. Cantigny fulfilled our every expectation. It was enthusiastically accepted for its styling and price as one of the finest lines in the country."

Early in 1967 Bernard Fischer decided to sell all of Laura Lee's lines in Canada through Dressmakers Ltd.'s established distribution system. Laura Lee garments received immediate acceptance in Canada, and sales were over $450,000 the first five months of operation. However, introductory expenses and further import-duty difficulties resulted in a loss of sales for the spring of 1967.

In June, 1967, Laura Lee acquired the Cross Country and Princess Juniors brands. Both of these lines were produced in rented loft quarters in the New York garment district. Cross Country manufactured casual dresses, which its owners had sold in sportswear departments; Princess Juniors made dresses styled specifically for the mature woman who wore a junior size. "Princess," said Bernard Fischer, "will provide that look of youthfulness for our women's market that Laura Lee's misses lines provide for young ladies. It will widen our total line considerably." During 1968 Laura Lee acquired Buster Boy, which manufactured low-priced junior-size sportswear sold through specialty shops. It also acquired McLane, which made youthfully styled, highly sophisticated dresses specifically for women who wore sizes 8 to 16. Buster Boy became the bottom Laura Lee line, with retail prices of $7 to $12 for dresses; McLane became the top line, with $40 to $60 dresses. Both were manufactured in rented quarters.

In 1968 Bernard Fischer decided to enter the women's rainwear and outerwear business. He hired a sales manager and a plant superintendent who had experience in these lines, and working with these men, Noreen Mallory, the designer, designed a line which was produced in the Bridgeport plant. The introduction went moderately well.

During 1968 Bernard Fischer also bought Loraine & Company and its "Loraine" brand name. Operating from a leased plant in Hartford, Connecticut, Loraine produced garments which duplicated a large sector of the Laura Lee brand line but gave the company added plant capacity and significantly increased its retail organization.

Buster Boy continued to be manufactured under its former management, without any change in quality or price. Many Laura Lee retailers did not accept the "cheap" Buster Boy line, and many of those who did returned large portions of their purchases as being shoddy and not in keeping with Laura Lee standards. The McLane line was of excellent quality, but many Laura Lee dealers considered the prices to be above their range and did not take it on. After a year of effort, Bernard Fischer abruptly decided to discontinue both lines. The remaining inventories were sacrificed to jobbers, and their production equipment was sold. Laura Lee wrote off $345,000 on the two lines.

During 1969 Bernard Fischer, following the advice of industrial engineering consultants, made a major revision of Laura Lee's cutting, sewing, and shipping operations. The company also made substantial capital expenditures to expand its manufacturing capacity, its warehouse space, and its New York City showrooms. The total expansion added 139,000 square feet to the company's operating capacity. Further additional capacity was obtained when Laura Lee bought the Pied Piper Company, which made misses outerwear, and Calico Corner, which, in addition to dresses, made junior outerwear. With these companies Laura Lee acquired personnel experienced in the design, manufacture, and sale of outerwear and rainwear. Before the year ended, Laura Lee disposed of these companies' New York plants and moved their operations to a new plant which Laura Lee built for them in Columbia, North Carolina.

Facilities at Shelbyville, Tennessee, were expanded in 1970, a second plant was built at Bridgeport, and a new plant built at Warwick, Rhode Island. Bernard Fischer attributed the decline in profits in this year to disruptions caused by the expansions, to start-up costs at the new plants, and to temporary inefficiencies caused by the separation of the functions of cutting, sewing, and shipping.

Rationalization of Production

By 1968 Laura Lee was producing over 100 different garments at eight plants, and Bernard Fischer became convinced that the company was suffering from difficulties in coordinating production schedules and in integrating shipments. Following a study made by a national firm of industrial engineering consultants, he consented to a major revision of all Laura Lee operations. During 1968 all cutting operations (except those of Dressmakers Ltd.) were concentrated in the Bridgeport plants. All leased plants were disposed of, and all sewing operations were parceled out to Laura Lee's owned plants, with each plant specializing in one or several of the brand lines. All shipping was concentrated in the new Bridgeport plant. All operations were computerized to coordinate production, inventories, manufacturing schedules, and warehouse and plant loads. Purchasing, shipping, billing, and accounts receivable were also computerized.

The combined and coordinated total operations were made possible by the use of a fleet of semitrailer trucks, each capable of carrying a 12-ton load. Using alternating crews, these trucks operated 24 hours a day, picking up palletted loads of cut fabrics at Bridgeport and distributing them to the other plants, where the garments were sewn. The trucks then hauled the finished garments back to Bridgeport, which became Laura Lee's centralized shipping center for all orders. Each truck averaged a fully loaded round-trip haul every two days. Bernard Fischer stated that the new system minimized inventories, cut distribution costs, and gave retailers much faster service.

ORGANIZATIONAL DEVELOPMENT

Developments under Bernard Fischer

Bernard Fischer was the undisputed driving force of Laura Lee. He not only developed the company but dominated the organization and insisted on serving as the chief executive officer and the sales manager from the start of the company in 1934 until he retired in the role of vice chairman in 1974 at the age of 70. Although he appointed his son-in-law, Samuel Fischer, husband of his eldest daughter, Laura Lee, as president and general manager in 1967, he still dominated the business. Samuel Fischer left a law firm in 1965 to become vice president of administration in Laura Lee, a position which included everything except manufacturing and sales. When he assumed his role of president and general manager, he stated, "I see little difference in what I am doing now under the new title. Bernard still runs the shop. I handle the day-to-day operations, but he makes the big decisions."

Jacob Eisner was hired by Bernard Fischer as vice president of manufacturing in late 1964. He had 12 years experience in production management in the garment industry. Initially Eisner acted not only as production manager but he also had purchasing, order filling, billing, and mailing reporting to him. As the company expanded, he reluctantly relinquished these charges to Samuel Fischer and John Kaufman, the treasurer and chief financial officer. Kaufman joined Laura Lee in 1966 after serving for eight years in a C.P.A. firm. In 1968 he assumed the positions of controller and treasurer.

David Rose, a nephew of Bernard Fischer, was hired in 1966 as merchandise manager. He had 10 years experience in merchandising with a national mail-order house. He was 31 years old when he joined Laura Lee. His relatively high salary and his early inputs into company strategy were resented by some of the management and supervisory personnel.

Noreen Mallory was hired by Bernard Fischer in 1964. Although she was only 34 years of age at the time, she was appointed vice president of design. Her position was described as director of design personnel; however she assumed an important advisory position in product and marketing matters and was frequently consulted by Bernard Fischer. Her designs became an important factor in the development of the Laura Lee line.

Organizational relationships under Bernard Fischer were casual and informal. There were no distinct lines of authority. There was considerable overlap of functions. Noreen Mallory was often in conflict with David Rose over merchandising problems, and Jacob Eisner and John Kaufman had occasional disputes about the supervision of personnel in billing and shipping. Bernard Fischer, since he had hired all of the key management personnel, felt a close personal relationship to each of them. When he was not too involved with his marketing role, he concerned himself in settling internal disputes. His ability to reconcile the management differences was recognized by all in the group and particularly Samuel Fischer, who tried to remain aloof from the bickerings.

Developments under Samuel Fischer

From 1972 until he assumed an inactive role of vice chairman, Bernard Fischer gradually withdrew from his dominant management function. He was pleased that his son-in-law was willing to assume leadership of the organization.

Samuel Fischer built upon the reputation of the Laura Lee line and expanded both marketing and manufacturing operations. In 1973 he added to the firm's trucking equipment and facilities and began utilizing slack time of the equipment to transport under contract for soft-goods manufacturers in the Bridgeport area. By 1979 total revenues of L&L Transport had grown to $2.2 million, and the line was recognized as a profit center. It charged going rates for hauling to Laura Lee subsidiaries and actively competed as a commercial freight-transport company. John Reed, a former manager of a national trucking firm, was appointed vice president and manager of L&L in 1979.

Under Samuel Fischer, David Rose was appointed vice president of marketing and merged his former functions as merchandising manager into a single unit. Noreen Mallory's position was reduced in scope. She continued as vice president of design and styling but was not as involved in policymaking as she was under Bernard Fischer. She frequently talked of retiring from Laura Lee at 55 and becoming a design consultant to the high fashion houses in the garment industry.

To keep pace with an expanding organization, Samuel Fischer added new personnel and separated several of the major functions of the company into separate operating units. The expansion of L&L Transport created a new, separate profit center. The opening of company-owned U-Sew-It stores prompted the development of a separate U-Sew-It Division as a profit center. Richard Mayer, who had worked under David Rose in merchandising and marketing, was appointed vice president in charge of this operation. He built up a separate sales force to call on retail stores carrying the U-Sew-It line and to service the U-Sew-It company-owned stores. The sales force reached its peak in 1978 when 40 salespersons were employed. In 1982 this number was reduced to 25.

Each line in the Laura Lee Division retained its president and separate staffs as they did under Bernard Fischer. They reported to David Rose, the vice president of marketing and merchandising. (For a comparison of Laura Lee under Bernard Fischer and Samuel Fischer, see Exhibits 4 and 5.)

MARKETING AND SALES: LAURA LEE PRODUCT LINES

The Laura Lee women's wear lines were directed mainly to juniors or young adults—women in the 15- to 24-year-old bracket. The line also included products for women in the 25- to 45-year-old bracket who wore junior sizes. The main product included dresses of the "soft variety" (dress sales had been declining in importance in recent years) and sportswear and leisure wear represented mainly by "separates," i.e., tops or blouses and skirts and pants. Separates were the largest-selling segment of the line, accounting for over 40 percent of total sales. Tailored suits in the moderate price range accounted for approximately 20 percent of retail sales, rainwear and outerwear for 15 percent of sales, and dresses for about 25 percent. All of Laura Lee's apparel was in the "popular" price range of approximately $18 to $35 for separate pieces, $50 to $85 for tailored suits, $35 to $55 for rainwear, and $50 to $85 for outerwear.

Laura Lee Line

With the exception of the Laura Lee line, all the other product lines including the brand names had been purchased by the company. The Laura Lee label was the top of the line and was priced higher than any of the other apparel products. The label was used on dresses, outerwear, and tailored suits. A relatively high-priced limited group of separates also carried the Laura Lee label. This line was distributed through the better department stores and specialty apparel shops. The Loraine line was actually a duplicate of the Laura Lee line but did not carry all items in this line. Some designs were reserved for the better stores.

Loraine Line

The Loraine line was directed only to specialty apparel shops that needed a "touch of quality" to supplement their lower-priced merchandise.

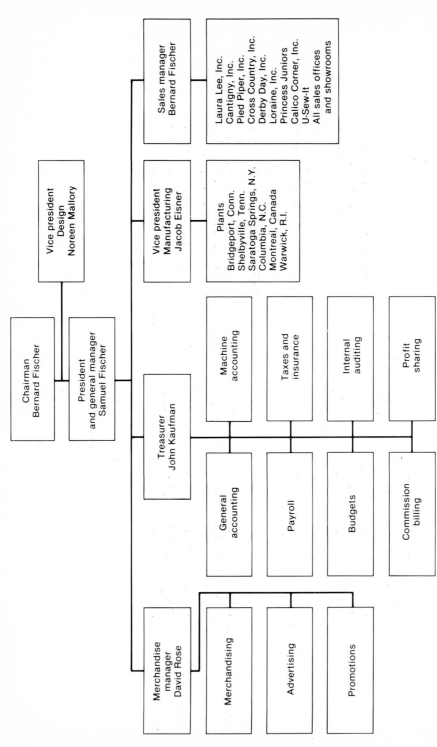

EXHIBIT 4
Organization chart of Laura Lee, Inc. under Bernard Fischer.

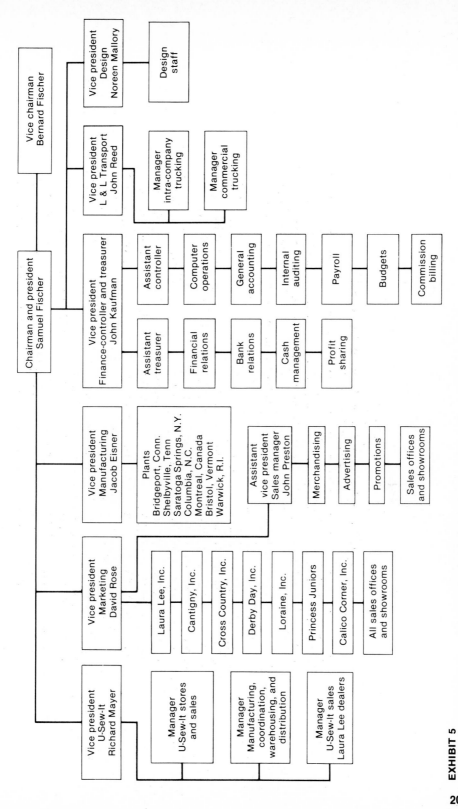

EXHIBIT 5
Organization chart of Laura Lee, Inc. under Samuel Fischer.

Management was careful to keep its Laura Lee line higher-priced apparel well distanced from the shops which carried the Loraine label.

Pied Piper Line

This product line was exclusively rainwear and outerwear, and was sold to all retailers, including those which carried the Laura Lee labels in rainwear and outerwear.

Derby Day and Cantigny Lines

These products were sold mainly in Canada; however they were also distributed in the United States in the better apparel specialty shops. Samuel Fischer drastically reduced the production of polyester knits in the Montreal plant when he became the chief executive, despite the objections of David Rose and John Preston. Samuel Fischer was of the opinion that they did not hold their shape and lacked "quality appeal." Noreen Mallory aided the Derby Day staff in designing a new line of wool knits which sold in the higher price range. This new line did not sell well, and David Rose thought that customers still remembered the lower-priced polyester knits which carried the Derby Day label and were reluctant to pay the higher price for wool knits with the same label.

The Cantigny line was concentrated in dresses and tailored suits with some separates. While sales of this moderate- to high-priced line were good in Canada, they did not sell well in U.S. department stores, and specialty shops claimed they only duplicated the Laura Lee and Loraine lines. As a result of declining sales, the Montreal plant had excess capacity and expanded its manufacture of the company's other lines. In the period of 1978–1982 it became increasingly difficult to transport fabric across the borders and to ship back the finished products. Increasing transport costs added to the problems of clearing custom requirements in Canada and caused Samuel Fischer to consider selling one of his most efficient production units. He thought this might also alleviate some of the company's pressing cash difficulties.

Calico Corners Line

Calico Corners was designed for the 15 to 18 year olds. The style was casual and included sportswear and separates, and outerwear for the younger set. The Calico line was the lowest priced of all the Laura Lee products. It was distributed in department stores and most of the specialty apparel shops which carried the company's products.

Cross Country Line

Cross Country produced separates for casual and sportswear. In 1978 Samuel Fischer decided to have this label devoted exclusively to separates. The line was distributed to specialty shops which catered to the teens and was not usually carried in the shops which served the more mature women. This line had an exceptional increase in sales since 1979. It was priced in the moderate range, and David Rose insisted that it be marketed as a "better quality" garment for girls in the 15- to 18-year-old range.

Princess Junior Line

This product line was designed for the so-called "misses" represented by women of about 24 to 45 that wore junior sizes and had difficulty being fitted in the average department store or specialty shop. The line was priced in the lower-moderate range to attract mature women that did not want to pay a higher price to be fitted in the better specialty apparel stores. David Rose was insistent that the line carry a variety of fabrics and styles. The president of Princess Juniors thought this merchandising policy added too much to cost for the additional sales it created. The line was sold in department stores and in the specialty shops except those which carried the Laura Lee line.

Private Labels

When Samuel Fischer became the chief executive officer, he immediately organized a special sales group working out of New York which sold Laura Lee products for private labeling to chain stores and mail-order houses. The customers included Sears, Penneys, Montgomery Ward, and a number of smaller accounts. Orders were taken through salespersons, the Laura Lee special catalog, and at the company's showrooms in New York. Since the chains had centralized purchasing, the major consideration of the sales staff was to court and convince the buyers of the merits of the lines which Laura Lee produced. Most of the company's designs and lines were made available for private-label sales. In most cases there had to be modifications to avoid direct duplication of the lines sold to Laura Lee dealers, and to meet specifications of the buyers.

From 1975 to 1982 sales of private brands increased over 10 times and represented approximately 18 to 29 percent of total apparel sales. Both Noreen Mallory and David Rose were very concerned about this rapid increase in private-brand sales and the amount of production time this activity absorbed. Noreen Mallory contended that the necessary modifications placed a strain on designers in the various lines, particularly Calico Corners and Cross Country. Jacob Eisner complained of the cost of making modifications in the production process.

Selling private brands required bidding against a number of competitors. Contracts were not awarded strictly on a price basis. Style, design, and fabric quality were always considered. The margins on each garment, however, were significantly lower than that received from the department stores and specialty shops. The order size was the factor which made private-brand sales attractive.

Returns were always a problem, and they usually had to be sold to "clearance dealers" who removed the labels and sold them off the rack. John Kaufman frequently questioned the profitability of this operation. He contended that to really take advantage of private-brand selling it would be necessary to dedicate 50 percent of the company's production to this activity. He and David Rose had reservations about what private-brand sales might do to the dealer network in the long run.

U-Sew-It Division

Bernard Fischer conceived the idea to start the U-Sew-It Division after observing an increased interest in home sewing in the late 1960s. When the company concentrated its cutting operations in the Bridgeport plant, it provided a ready supply of cut fabrics which could be utilized for home-sewing customers. The U-Sew-It Division was started in the summer of 1968 as a mail-order operation channeled through Laura Lee's retail outlets.

The new U-Sew-It Division offered the customer cut pieces of any Laura Lee garment (except knits) in her size, together with a pattern and directions for sewing. Customers were informed of the U-Sew-It plan through a full page in the Laura Lee catalog and by poster-sized showcards in Laura Lee retail shops. Each retailer was asked to buy a book of fabric swatches from which the customer could choose her preferred material. Retailers were supplied with order forms, which were mailed to the Bridgeport plant. A separate unit at Bridgeport filled each order singly and mailed it directly, on a C.O.D. basis, to the customer. Each order included buttons, thread, and bindings. Retailers received a percentage on every order. Billing, shipping, and retail commissions were computerized.

Bernard Fischer anticipated that the new division would bring a whole new group of customers who did their own sewing and would not buy the Laura Lee finished garments. He expected that the new customers would be attracted by the Laura Lee styles and selection of fabrics that they would not be likely to find in fabric or yard goods stores. Prices were set far enough below finished garment prices to be attractive to cost-conscious customers. Retailers were assured by the company that they would earn the same margin on U-Sew-It sales as on the sales of the finished products. Many retailers did not believe this and were of the opinion that the promotion of the U-Sew-It kits would cut into their garment trade and encourage customers to take up home sewing to supplement their wardrobes.

The U-Sew-It selections were advertised in national magazines utilizing coupons requesting a Laura Lee catalog. The advertisements also invited customers to visit Laura Lee retail shops to seek additional information about the U-Sew-It plans. This campaign increased sales but also increased resentment of Laura Lee retailers who objected to U-Sew-It. Eventually 75 of the company's retailers dropped the entire Laura Lee line.

In late 1970 Laura Lee opened six company-owned U-Sew-It stores in six cities: Ames, Iowa; Lancaster, Pennsylvania; South Bend, Indiana; Wheeling, West Virginia; Ironton, Ohio; and Paducah, Kentucky. The initial sites were selected because the company thought the stores would have particular appeal to the population in these areas. In the 1969 to 1970 period U-Sew-It recorded a loss of $48,000 on sales of $250,000. In 1971 a loss of $37,000 was experienced on sales of $684,000. The loss in 1971 forced Bernard Fischer and his staff to recalculate the pricing system for the U-Sew-It kits. As a result, prices for the kits were substantially increased in 1972, which resulted in a slight profit of $25,000 on sales of $650,000. In view of the low return the company decided to reduce the margins allotted to the retailers for selling the U-Sew-It plan. This resulted in the dropping of the plan from approximately 40 percent of the retail outlets.

Bernard Fischer, however, was still determined to make his idea a success. He was sure that the key to profitability was to be found in a widespread network of company-owned U-Sew-It outlets. In 1973 Laura Lee opened four new U-Sew-It stores, and five more were added in 1974 and 1975. Sales increased slowly, averaging about $400,000 per unit after the store network was operational. The division experienced losses of $55,000 and $72,000 in 1974 and 1975, followed by losses of $150,000 in 1976, $50,000 in 1977. $150,000 in 1976, $50,000 in 1977 and a profit of $80,000 in 1978 and a profit of $250,000 in 1979. (See Exhibit 3.)

Despite the profit of 1979 the retailers handling the U-Sew-It kits complained of the competition it created for the finished Laura Lee lines. They maintained that the sales increase in U-Sew-It kits was due to the lowering of the price on the kits and the lower dealer's margins. They also pointed out that the exceptionally attractive Laura Lee dresses and separates brought in customers who were frequently drawn to the U-Sew-It kits, which featured many of the top-selling Laura Lee lines at a significantly lower price and appealed to those inclined to make their own clothes. Many of the shop owners thought that the profit potential of the U-Sew-It kits would never be more than marginal and continued to carry the line because they thought that it might attract customers who could be traded up to the finished apparel.

In 1980, after reviewing the sales of the U-Sew-It division, Samuel Fischer decided to close the most unprofitable of the stores. John Kaufman indicated that the bulk of the division's sales were still coming from the retail shops which handled the Laura Lee line. Four of the 15 stores were closed in 1980. The closings cost was $600,000, due mainly to settlement of the leases on the stores. The operating loss of $370,000 in 1980 was followed by a loss of $850,000 in 1981 and $840,000 in 1982. Five stores were closed in 1981, and three smaller units were closed in 1982. (See Exhibit 3.)

Despite the lack of sales growth and profitability of the U-Sew-It Division, management was of the opinion that the operation had profit potential with the elimination of the unprofitable stores and a renewed campaign to push the line through Laura Lee retail stores. While there was some disagreement over the future of the U-Sew-It stores, Samuel Fischer made the decision to "wait and see" what would happen with the decreased number of outlets. Noreen Mallory and John Kaufman favored dropping the entire U-Sew-It line. David Rose and John Preston, the new sales manager, were in favor of trying to institute the initial mail-order arrangement with catalog distribution through the Laura Lee retailers. The number of retailers carrying the U-Sew-It kits had dropped to less than 1,000 stores out of the company's network of 4,700 stores.

Jacob Eisner, the vice president of manufacturing, cautioned management to carefully consider any effort to disband the operation entirely. He pointed out that shared costs were involved and the fabrics sold in the U-Sew-It kits, while they were the same as that contained in the finished goods, actually represented remnants of the cuttings for the Laura Lee patterns. He often stated that the costing of the material of the kits should not be done on the same basis as it was for the finished fabrics. Eisner and Kaufman, the financial officer, engaged in heated debates over this matter.

SELLING AND DISTRIBUTION

Apparel Sales

Ninety salespersons of Laura Lee were assigned to particular product-line divisions and operated out of their own offices. The sales representatives in the showrooms took orders for particular lines displayed at their location. The Laura Lee product-line catalog was distributed on a fee basis to all of the company's 4,700 retail outlets. Many orders were made directly to the product division sales offices or through corporate offices in New York City, using the catalog as the buying guide. This was especially true for stores located in rural areas and on the west coast, where Laura Lee had less sales concentration. The company's catalogs were very attractive and were printed in color on a glossy finish. The cost of each full catalog was about $2.50. The catalogs for each separate line were printed on standard grade paper and cost approximately 85 cents to print. The full-line catalog usually contained about 100 separate items. Only the major lines were featured in the photographs, and the others were line drawings. The special line catalogs for each division contained from 25 to 30 items. (See Exhibit 6 for the locations of sales offices.)

Selling Seasons

Sales were divided into separate seasons—spring, summer, fall, winter—and the holiday seasons of Christmas and Easter, when special selling efforts were made to accommodate the mood of these particular periods. The fall season, from August to the end of October, was the major selling season, followed by the spring season, from February 1 to April 30. Lines were sold at least one season in advance of the season for delivery. This was necessary because of the

EXHIBIT 6
PRINCIPAL SALES OFFICES AND SHOWROOMS

Office or Showroom	Lines carried
1700 Broadway, N.Y.C.	Laura Lee
1700 Broadway, N.Y.C.	Cross Country
1700 Broadway, N.Y.C.	Cantigny, Derby Day
398 Seventh Ave., N.Y.C.	Pied Piper
404 Seventh Ave., N.Y.C.	Loraine, Calico Corner, Princess Junior
8420 Dominion Blvd., Montreal	All lines
Houston Show Mark, Houston, Texas	All lines
Miami Exhibitors Mart, Miami, Florida	All lines
Pacific Apparel Mart, San Francisco	All lines
The Merchandise Mart, Chicago, Illinois	All lines

lead time needed to assure fabric delivery. This required a commitment for fabrics in sufficient quantities to meet projected sales in each line. Each product-line division ordered its fabrics through central purchasing at the corporate office in New York. Jacob Eisner supervised all purchases and coordinated production schedules. The Laura Lee line required commitments for fabrics more in advance than the other branded lines. Fabric orders for private label sales were contractual, and therefore it was easier to satisfy production requirements for these. Despite careful planning, each selling season Laura Lee had unsold finished goods and fabrics on hand. U-Sew-It took a good part of the excess fabrics but was never able to utilize all of it because the kits had to be prepared in advance of the selling season, going through much the same process as required for finished goods.

International Sales

Samuel Fischer stated:

> We do not make a great effort to sell internationally, because the competition has become very intense in the past five years. We do have an international export department operated out of our New York office. We license a number of foreign companies to produce some of our lines. The Laura Lee label attracts the most attention, although we sell several other of our products. The royalties from licensing do not contribute much to our revenues. I think we need to make a real effort to increase foreign sales or get out of international business.

PURCHASING AND MANUFACTURING

Plants

Laura Lee maintained seven manufacturing plants to produce its seven product lines, private-label lines, and U-Sew-It kits. Total manufacturing space was ap-

EXHIBIT 7
MANUFACTURING PLANTS

Plant	Area, square feet
Bridgeport, Connecticut	250,000
Bridgeport, Connecticut	70,000
Shelbyville, Tennessee	64,000
Saratoga Springs, New York	40,000
Columbia, North Carolina	45,000
Montreal, Canada	30,000
Warwick, Rhode Island	30,000

proximately 520,000 square feet. (See Exhibit 7.) All the plants were owned by the company and contained more space for production than required to support current sales levels. The plants were acquired or built under Bernard Fischer to accommodate his objective of reaching $250 million in sales. The Columbia, South Carolina, and the Montreal plants were the most efficient; however, they were both relatively small. The production workers in the company's plants were all members of the International Ladies Garment Worker's Union (ILGWU). Some of the L&L Transport workers were also members of the ILGWU.

The real estate of the plant locations was carried at cost. Samuel Fischer estimated their value to be at least five times book value, and the value of the buildings about four times book value. John Kaufman questioned these estimates, stating that many of the factories were not in especially attractive areas and the buildings were not easily convertible to other uses. The excess-capacity problem was a concern for all of management.

Fabric Purchasing

The raw materials used in Laura Lee's apparel manufacture were piece goods and yarns which were purchased from a number of textile mills. Noreen Mallory worked closely with Jacob Eisner to aid in fabric selection. She contended that she adhered to simple designs which aided in reducing manufacturing costs. Eisner required that each mill provide a liaison person to work with Noreen Mallory. Through this procedure he hoped to get immediate attention when fabrics proved to be unsatisfactory or in short supply.

Quality Control

Jacob Eisner worked with about 25 mills using 8 to 10 of these mills for the bulk of the company's purchases. When the fabric was selected, with the aid of the design staff and the purchasing department, arrangements were made with selected mills to produce and deliver the fabrics at specified dates. A pattern was produced from the selected designs. The pattern was then used as the guide for cutting the fabric into the proper components for sewing. Management felt that the close association of the design, production, and purchasing were the major factors in providing quality control.

Noreen Mallory insisted that all garments be full-cut to assure proper fit and to provide the touch of quality which management thought was essential for success. Eisner personally supervised quality control procedures in all the plants and frequently visited plant sites to make sure the pattern designs were being properly followed. The close attention to quality control was reflected in Laura Lee garments.

L&L TRANSPORT

Bernard Fischer conceived the idea of picking up cut fabrics at the Bridgeport plant and transporting them to the other Laura Lee plants for fabrication. The finished garments were hauled back to Bridgeport, which served as a central shipping point. The company's fleet of trucks grew as sales expanded. Samuel Fischer expanded the fleet in 1973 to enter the contract hauling business to take advantage of slack periods and eliminate "dead head" hauling. The division was organized as a separate profit center. Sales of L&L expanded from $800,000 in 1978 to $10.5 million in 1981, which included intracompany sales. Profits for L&L increased from $90,000 in 1978 to $1.1 million in 1981. Sales and profits declined in 1982; contract sales in this period increased, while intracompany sales declined. (See Exhibit 3.)

In 1982 L&L employed 250 full-time workers and a number of part-time workers hired from the union halls. The fleet included 210 trailers and 425 tractors, which were rotated on two to three shifts per day. Although carried on the books at a significantly lower figure, Samuel Fischer calculated the value of L&L at about $12 to $15 million. L&L's terminals and warehouses were in leased quarters which the company had improved to accommodate increased business.

THE WOMEN'S APPAREL INDUSTRY

Competitive Patterns

The garment industry has long been recognized as highly competitive and populated by a large number of small- to medium-sized firms. No single company accounts for more than a small percentage of the total market. Laura Lee could be considered in the middle to upper-middle of the industry in terms of size. There were several companies larger than Laura Lee but none had a large share of the total market. Imports, particularly from Hong Kong and recently from Korea, provided significant competition. After a steady increase in the

1970s, imports of wearing apparel showed a slight decline in the 1979 to 1982 period. Foreign manufacturers were losing their competitive edge because of rising labor costs.

Entry into the industry required little capital. As a consequence, firms were constantly moving in and out. The ease with which designs could be copied also added to the intensity of competition in the industry. There were many loft operations, mainly located in New York City, which produced low-priced copies of the better designs to sell to the wholesale trade. Some of the loft operations also did contract sewing for recognized brands in the industry.

Because of the fragmented nature of the industry, it was difficult to measure market shares. Except for the sales figures of publicly held companies, there was little data available to make significant comparisons in the women's apparel industry.

Trends in Fashion

The rapid change in women's fashions added to the risks and volatility in the industry. Many designs did not "catch on" and were returned by retailers. The seasonal nature of sales and the seasonal changes in apparel added to the risks and sales fluctuations of the firms in the industry. Despite recurring problems, the outlook for sales in women's apparel was considered to be good. The population group in the 24- to 40-year-old range was increasing and was expected to reach 25 percent of the total population by 1985. This age group accounts for the largest percentage of apparel sales, particularly in women's clothes.

Dresses have declined in sales from 1970 to 1979. The introduction of the "soft look" helped to boost sales of dresses in 1980 to 1982. The soft look was adopted for the more formal dresses, but it was also very evident in casual clothes and "dressed up" sportswear which provided for flexibility and could be worn for a variety of occasions.

The increased number of women entering the work force has been a factor in changing the kind of apparel sold in the industry. The trend to "tailored suits" has been apparent in recent years. While this kind of apparel is usually purchased by women in professional positions, there was also a marked increase in the sale of dressed-up casual wear and lower-priced suits with related separates which could lend a dressed-up look for working women. All styles of sportswear and "active wear" were expected to increase in sales. It was anticipated that pants suits would continue to decline in sales. Separates, i.e., separate pants and shirts to be worn with a variety of tops, replaced the pants suits in popularity. Coats were also expected to continue to decline in sales. The more flexible casual rainwear with liners had, to a large extent, replaced the more formal outerwear. The budget apparel in the $30 to $40 range was a large part of sales, and was expected to increase in importance. Jeans and "fashion jeans" had made significant inroads into the teen market and the casual market for young adults. Western-style clothes had also gained in importance. Some industry analysts, however, expected that their sales growth would taper off as the fad value diminished.

Labor and Manufacturing

Despite some advances in automation, the apparel industry was still considered labor-intensive. Much of the fine sewing and pattern cutting was still done by hand, particularly by the smaller firms. Most garment workers were union members and were employed by the more established and stable companies. Unions were very strong and usually had 100 percent representation in plants located in the northern states. The newer plants in the southern states were nonunion or only partly union. The loft operations which had grown in recent years, particularly in the New York City garment section, were not unionized. The increasing amount of women's wear being produced by nonunion workers placed some of the old established producers, which employed mainly union workers, at a cost disadvantage.

Approximately 50 percent of all wearing apparel produced in the United States is made from synthetic fabrics. The price of synthetic fiber produced in the United States is the lowest in the world, and price competition among suppliers of the fabric has facilitated the entry of loft operations into the industry. Despite the lowering of some material costs, the cost of goods sold in the industry continued to increase. Margins in the industry were expected to continue to remain low.

Financial Position of Laura Lee

Long-term debt consisted of subordinated debentures of $3.5 million at 10.5 percent interest due in 1984, with $1.2 million payable annually. In 1978 Laura Lee entered into a revolving credit arrangement with three New York banks to provide $15 million of both long-term and short-term credit. The seasonal nature of Laura Lee's business required loans for inventory and receivables at the peak of its selling period, mainly in the second and third quarters. The company's short-term loans reached $11 million in 1981.

This arrangement was changed in January 1982, when Laura Lee found it could not meet its repayment schedule under the revolving credit arrangement. The loan was changed to a five-year-term loan of $15 million at 2.5 percent above the prime rate. All of Laura Lee's owned real estate was pledged as mortgage collateral for the loan. The company was restricted from paying dividends and from acquiring any additional loans, either short- or long-term. Working capital of $3 million had to be maintained, and the current ratio had to be at least 1:1. Ten percent of the loan was due annually starting in 1983.

A short-term loan arrangement was entered into in January 1982, with a factoring firm granting up to $15 million. The accounts receivable were turned over to the factor at a discount equivalent to 3.7 percent over the prevailing prime rate.

Time for Decisions for Laura Lee

Samuel Fischer stated:

> Fiscal 1982 was certainly a disappointment. In our second quarter, which is always our best quarter, we had almost record sales and profits. Our new line of separates with the "soft look" caught on. We couldn't keep up with the orders. The need for financing of fabrics and inventory took us back into the banks, and we had to renegotiate our loans. Interest rates are damaging us severely. If they were anywhere near 10 percent, we would be in fair shape. From the second quarter on we began to feel the effects of the severe recession we are now in. The Laura Lee division did very well despite the drop-off from the second quarter. The press of our severe financial problems and the nagging high-interest-rate problems must be dealt with. We need to take some immediate action.

Clark Oil and Refining Corporation[1]

In the first quarter of 1981, Clark experienced a disappointing decline in earnings despite an increase in total revenues from $400.7 million in the fourth quarter of 1980 to $421.7 million early in 1981. Net income declined from $4.3 million to a loss of $4.4 million, and earnings per share declined from 30 cents to a deficit of 31 cents for the same period. (See Exhibit 1.)

Management stated that the decline in the first quarter of 1981 was due primarily to changes in overall market conditions and regulatory shifts which took place during the period. The Reagan administration's decontrol of oil prices was met with a marked fall-off in demand, and resulted in a substantial buildup of inventories. Oil prices had declined, and product oversupply continued. The company said that purchasing lead time presented some difficulty in achieving "a manageable balance" between supply and demand. With no crude oil production of its own, Clark was forced to purchase practically all its crude oil requirements either from domestic or foreign producers. This condition made the company especially sensitive to changes in crude oil costs. In the past, competitive conditions and federal government price freezes had prevented Clark from recovering the increases in crude oil through higher gasoline prices.

ORIGIN AND DEVELOPMENT

Clark Oil and Refining Corporation was founded by Emory T. Clark in 1932 with a $14 investment and a one-pump Milwaukee service station. Initially the

---

[1] This case represents a revision of the 1976 case originally prepared by David M. Vrooman. This updated version of the case was prepared by Albert W. Isenman under the direction of Professor Thomas J. McNichols from published sources and company annual reports.

EXHIBIT 1
SUMMARY OF 1981 FIRST
QUARTER ($000's)

Revenues	
Net Sales	$421,773
Dividends, interest	8,935
Total	$430,708
Costs	
Crude	$417,527
Selling	8,116
Taxes	10,153
Depreciation	3,795
Interest	1,205
Total	$441,468
Income (Pretax)	($10,760)
Tax	(6,291)
Total	($4,469)

company served exclusively as a marketing organization; Clark procured gasoline from the major refiners for distribution by semi-independent station operators, who in turn sold the gasoline under the Clark brand name. During 1939 and 1940, in conjunction with its expansion into Minnesota and Missouri, Clark began developing and leasing its own service stations. In 1943, the company acquired its first manufacturing facility, an oil refinery at Marrero, Louisiana. In 1945, Clark purchased a larger refinery at Blue Island, Illinois (a suburb of Chicago). The Marrero installation was converted to a bulk terminal in 1951.

The company's growth quickened during the 1950s. The expansion program called for the addition of 60 new stations per year, the improvement of 40 existing stations per year, modernizing and enlarging the Blue Island refinery, expanding the transportation system (particularly pipelines), and initiating efforts in exploration for crude oil and natural gas. By the end of the decade, Clark's marketing area included Illinois, Michigan, Indiana, Ohio, Iowa, eastern North Dakota, and eastern Kansas as well as its original territory of Wisconsin, Minnesota, and Missouri.

In 1957 an exploration and production office was opened in Denver in an effort to extend the integration of Clark's operations to include crude oil supply. Initial exploratory drilling was confined to the central Rocky Mountain region of the United States. These attempts were largely unsuccessful; exploration was gradually shifted to Alberta, New Mexico, Texas, and eventually Louisiana, where efforts proved to be more productive. In 1966 the exploration office was moved to Houston. During the late 1960s, the company's foreign division, established in 1962, participated in several largely unsuccessful exploratory ventures in Mozambique, Libya, and Brunei.

The 1960s saw a substantial expansion of Clark's production facilities. In 1964 the company completed a petrochemical complex, adjacent to its Blue Island refinery, designed principally to produce phenol and acetone for the plastics industry. In 1967 Clark purchased a refinery in Wood River, Illinois—near St. Louis—from Sinclair Oil Corporation. In 1968, the company purchased Colab Resin Corporation of Tewksbury, Massachusetts, and the liquid phenolic resins business of Allied Chemical Corporation; subsequently, Clark Chemical Corporation, a wholly owned subsidiary, was formed to operate all Clark's petrochemical and resin business. In 1973 Clark sold the Colab Resin business for $1.75 million.

Clark acquired the assets of the Owens Oil Companies of Bloomington, Illinois, in 1968. In this acquisition, Clark assumed ownership of and supplied product to 122 Owens service stations (primarily in Illinois, Indiana, and Michigan), all of which continued to carry the Owens name.

No further acquisitions of production or retail facilities were made in the 1970s, as the company focused its efforts on production efficiencies and trimness of operations. For example, major capital expenditures of its refineries resulted in refining capacity substantially over the amount for which the units were originally designed. Refineries were also improved to bring them in line with pollution requirements. At the same time, a program to close marginal service stations was instituted, bringing the total number of outlets down from 1,846 in 1976 to 1,400 by decade's end.

CLARK'S POSITION IN THE INDUSTRY

Through the 1970s, Clark was the largest "independent" oil company in the midwest. The company engaged in exploration, production, transportation, refining, and marketing; however, because of insufficiencies in the first two of these activities, Clark was not considered to be fully integrated. The large oil companies were formed following successful discoveries of great reservoirs of crude oil. Clark began as a marketing organization, and its attempts to acquire its own crude oil supply had not met with great success; as recently as 1978 the company was still pursuing exploration and development of several underwater tracts off the Gulf Coast. By this time, Clark ranked next to last among energy companies in its five-year return on equity, edging out Commonwealth Oil Company, which was undergoing bankruptcy. Its own exploration provided only 1 percent of its needs.

Clark built its reputation in the 25 years following World War II by concentrating its marketing efforts entirely upon the sale of premium (100 octane) gasoline; Clark "Super 100" was the only grade of gasoline sold by the company's outlets. However, in 1970, in response to rising concern over automobile emissions and the tendency of tetraethyl lead (the cheapest additive capable of raising a gasoline's octane rating) to foul emission-reducing catalytic converters,

Clark entered the "regular" gasoline market with a 93.5 octane fuel. In 1973, all Clark's service stations offered both premium and regular gasolines. In October 1974, Clark introduced a new no-lead premium to offset the phase-out of leaded premium and the disappointing sales of unleaded regular gasoline. At the time of its introduction, Clark's no-lead premium was unique in the company's marketing area.

MANAGEMENT AND ORGANIZATION

In 1973, Emory T. Clark, the company's founder and majority stockholder, held the position of chairman of the board of directors (as he had since the creation of the position in 1970). Although past the age at which many executives enter retirement, Clark retained an active role in the company's affairs, continuing to maintain both presence and authority at corporate headquarters in Milwaukee until December 24, 1974, when he retired as chairman of the board of directors but retained the chairmanship of the executive committee.

Clark's was an almost typical Horatio Alger story. He was born in relative poverty yet rose to wealth by personally and determinedly guiding his company throughout its history. All major decisions were made by—or were at least subject to the approval of—Clark, who still owned over 40 percent of the company's stock until mid-1980. Clark was not prone to take vacations or involve himself in the political or social circles of Milwaukee, his chief concerns being his family and his company. The latter was described by one executive as "a one-man show." None of Clark's three sons worked for the company.

In 1974 at the time of Clark's retirement to the executive committee, Owen L. Hill became chairman of the board and chief executive officer; George W. Jandacek became president and chief operations officer. The men had been top executives with Clark since 1959 and 1964, respectively.

Hill and Jandacek resigned in 1978 over a disagreement with Clark, who then came out of retirement to head the company again. Clark recruited Robert G. Reed, III, to become chairman of the board and chief executive officer the following year. Reed was a veteran of the oil industry, having been in top executive positions at Tesoro Petroleum Corporation since 1972.

CRUDE OIL PROCUREMENT

In 1978, Clark's refineries processed approximately 117,000 barrels of crude oil per day; the company's daily production of crude amounted to less than 2,000 barrels. For the remainder of its refinery input, Clark was dependent on external markets, both domestic and foreign. Management considered this situation undesirable because it subjected Clark to a considerable amount of uncertainty in the supply of its refineries. Not only was the existence of a constant and dependable input quantity uncertain but the availability of an appropriate quality of crude was not assured. The latter point was of particular importance because of Clark's former "premium only" policy; consistent with the output of a high-quality gasoline, both of Clark's refineries were equipped to handle only "sweet" (low-sulfur) crude.

Nonetheless, Clark was necessarily subject to the vagaries of the market for domestic crude on short-term (30-, 60-, 90-day) contracts with the larger American oil companies; negotiations in extending or modifying those contracts were frequent. On occasion the company sold previous purchases of crude in order to acquire a higher-grade supply.

By mid-1973 Clark was committed to markedly increasing its importation of foreign crude oil despite the acknowledged volatility of the market—domestic purchases had declined to 17 percent of Clark's total input. Management contended that the company had little choice: it had to rely on foreign oil for at least the foreseeable future. Other American oil companies were no longer willing to sell excess to Clark. The richest and most accessible oil fields in North America had already been extensively exploited, with the exception of the North Slope fields in Alaska. Existing plans to pipe the North Slope output directly to west coast refineries and markets appeared to eliminate the possibility of any direct supply to Clark.

The year 1973 saw long-dormant petroleum supply-and-demand problems develop into a serious energy crisis—an apparent chronic and substantial deficiency of refined petroleum supply in comparison to demand—brought about essentially by rapid demand increases, stable domestic crude oil production, and the Arab oil embargo consequent to the Middle Eastern war. The crisis affected Clark's supply of crude oil, although to a lesser initial degree than was the case with most other oil companies.

Clark was successful in supplying its refineries with nearly 100 percent of their throughput capacity until the embargo was imposed. Clark quickly looked for other sources and was able to purchase enough crude to hold throughput at 93 percent of capacity in 1974. Through much of the remainder of the 1970s, Clark's supply of crude was directly affected by negotiations with foreign sources and by domestic regulation of both supply and prices.

For example, in 1974, a federal allocation program designed to equalize crude supply to the various oil companies forced Clark to sell approximately 500,000 barrels of its crude oil monthly to other firms (including major, fully integrated companies such as Texaco), reducing its throughput to the national average of 77 percent of capacity. In March the embargo was lifted by all of the Arab oil-producing nations except Libya and Syria.

The most serious crude oil supply difficulty encountered by Clark in 1974 was one of cost instead of availability—the reverse of the problem faced by the company in 1973. Clark paid considerably more than the industry average of approximately $9 per barrel for its 1974 crude oil supply.

At the end of the year, the Federal Energy Administration (FEA) took action to alleviate this inequity, in effect enforced by its own action to freeze buyer-seller relationships in their 1973 state, through the establishment of a crude oil cost equalization program. Under this program, refiners whose crude inputs were composed of more than 40 percent price-controlled domestic oil (the approximate national average) were to purchase entitlements for their excess over 40 percent from refiners holding less than the national average. Clark, as a seller of entitlements, realized more than $36 million in 1975.

Clark's management was concerned about the Canadian government's reduction in the quantity of crude and condensate exported to the United States. In January 1976, the total was reduced to 510 thousand barrels per day (b/d) from 750 thousand b/d in December 1975. The export total was expected to be reduced to about 380 thousand b/d in the latter part of 1976. Clark received only 7,500 b/d of Canadian crude and condensate under the FEA allocation program. In order to sustain refinery runs, the lost Canadian crude had to be replaced by additional offshore foreign crude purchases. Clark protested the FEA allocation of Canadian crude imports, to no avail, as Canadian supply was ended after 1976.

In the latter half of the decade, the company continued to sharpen its skills in negotiating for crude supply from diverse foreign sources. During 1976, Clark purchased 65 percent of its crude from Abu Dhabi, Oman, Nigeria, Libya, North Sea, and Venezuela, more than doubling its dependence on these sources. In 1977, the foreign supply increased to 77 percent of the company input. Mexico became an important source of crude oil for Clark in 1978 with a significant contract.

Company management expected domestic demand to slacken and prices to continue to escalate, and so stabilized its foreign relationships with long-term contracts at the prevailing prices. Clark was one of the few energy companies not directly affected by the stoppage of Iranian supplies in 1979.

During the same period, improvements in production efficiency brought Clark's refinery capacity to an unprecedented 130,000 b/d in 1979.

EXPLORATION AND DEVELOPMENT

Owen Hill had considered the reliance on an external supply of crude to be unavoidable in the short run but by no means desirable. He felt that Clark's goal should be complete integration; a near-perfect balance of production, refining, and marketing. It was widely accepted in the industry that Texaco most closely exemplified this ideal. That company produced and refined roughly the same quantity that it sold. Because this characteristic assured a company of control or elimination of internal markets—and because the conventional wisdom postulated that the "real money" in the oil industry was in production—the objective of crude oil sufficiency was held by Clark through most of its history. Consequently, when Clark's earnings developed to the point that the company could support the necessary capital expenditures, Clark began to pursue its own exploration program.

Exploration continued through most of the decade, as Clark invested nearly $1 billion in an effort to become fully integrated. The investment in exploration and production was significant for Clark, but a pittance compared with the larger companies it was attempting to emulate.

Although a number of the company's on- and offshore developments were productive, none provided the "big strike" necessary to make a meaningful contribution to Clark's need for crude oil supply.

Clark sold all its productive oil and gas properties in Canada and all its interests in unproductive oil and gas acreage in the Arctic Islands of Canada for a cash consideration of $2.25 million in 1976. Management stated that because the company held carried interests in the Arctic Islands properties, carrying parties would have recovered all expenditures before Clark could realize any revenues. Assuming commercial discoveries of oil and gas, it would have been many years before the company could have received any return on its investment. Under these conditions, the board of directors elected to take an immediate profit on the venture.

The company's remaining exploratory and development activities were concentrated in offshore Louisiana and Texas. Gas and condensate production was established in three different reservoirs, and oil was encountered in a fourth. Semiproven gas reserves were estimated at 35 billion to 40 billion cubic feet.

In addition to closing its exploration office in Calgary, Alberta, Canada, and selling its Arctic Islands interests, Clark withdrew from the SCAND exploratory group in offshore Louisiana and abstained from participation in lease sales in the Gulf of Mexico in 1975 except for the purchase of one tract to protect established interests. Management stated that budgetary constraints and the rapidly escalating exploration and development costs offshore in relation to an unrealistically low controlled price for natural gas were major factors in making these decisions.

Clark's management believed in the mid-1970s that the deteriorating national energy supply would ultimately force natural gas prices to increase to permit recovery of higher costs and to be competitive with other sources of gas and other fuels. With higher natural gas prices, the company anticipated it could earn a fair rate of return on its offshore properties, which had been acquired at comparatively low average per-acre costs. Management contended that onshore exploration would have to be favorably considered despite the high cost of exploration and drilling and the difficulty of making "finds." Clark's management considered bidding for offshore leases risky and costly, particularly in view of the low price for natural gas and the environmental and regulatory complications.

Industry sources described Clark's exploration activities as "virtually fruitless."

MARKETING

As noted previously, Clark's traditional market image was based upon the "premium only" policy established early in the company's history. Especially in the late 1960s, Clark's advertising program was directed toward strongly reinforcing this image; the company's television spots, concentrated heavily in new market areas, vigorously identified Clark as "the premium people." It was therefore not without reluctance that in 1970 the company began the production and marketing of regular-grade gasoline.

Nonetheless, Clark's management saw the decision as inevitable—both environmental concerns and the rising popularity of the smaller automobiles seemed to present a shrinking market for premium-grade gasolines. In 1969, premium-grade gasolines constituted approximately 45 percent of all gasolines sold in the United States; by 1973 premium sales amounted to less than 35 percent of the total gasoline market. Clark's premium sales during the same period fell from 100 percent of its total sales to roughly 30 percent.

The full range of questions concerning product line had not been resolved, however. Under the provisions of the Environmental Protection Act of 1979, all oil companies were required to offer for sale at all their service stations a completely lead-free gasoline by July 1984. For Clark, this posed a problem. Its stations were equipped to accommodate just two grades of gasoline, so the company discontinued sales of its traditional premium gasoline, which at the time accounted for approximately 20 percent of Clark's gasoline sales.

Demand for the new unleaded regular proved to be disappointing. Consequently, in October, the company began phasing out that grade and began production and marketing of a 97.5-octane unleaded premium. The new gasoline grade satisfied the octane requirements of the automobiles of the vast majority of Clark's former premium customers as well as the requirements of the 1975-model automobiles equipped with catalytic converters and designed to operate with lead-free fuel. At the time of its introduction, Clark no-lead premium was unique in the company's marketing area. Management considered initial sales and projected demand of the new product to be very promising.

Gasolines sold under the Clark brand name were priced competitively with those of the major national companies. The same products sold by Owens stations generally were priced 2 to 3 cents per gallon lower.

The shortages that began to plague oil markets in early 1973, in addition to raising station operating costs, brought Clark's vigorous retail expansion program to a halt. In 1972 Clark built 84 new service stations; in 1973 it curtailed expansion. Oil shortages also forced the company to reduce its wholesale supply of gasoline to several small midwestern retailers.

Clark stations sold gasoline, motor oil, and a few incidental items (candy, cigarettes, soft drinks, and, most recently, milk and bread). They did not sell tires, batteries, accessories; neither did they offer lubrication, tire changing, or repairs of any kind.

Since late 1971, Clark had operated a few experimental self-service stations in Wisconsin, Missouri, and Kentucky. In 1972, these stations reported large gallonage gains. Further pursuit of this program was hampered by the fact that in the most populous midwestern states (Illinois, Ohio, and Michigan), self-service gasoline retailing was prohibited by law.

In 1973, Clark's retail gasoline sales rose by 23.8 percent despite the continuing substantial price increases (by early 1974, the retail price of 93.5-octane regular had risen above 60 cents per gallon in some areas). Given the nationwide petroleum shortage, the company was able to sell, without the assistance of any retail advertising, all the regular and premium (99-octane) gasolines which it produced. Primarily for financial reasons, Clark ceased all retail advertising in mid-1971. The tight supply in 1973 helped the company prosper, as it posted earnings of $30.5 million, or $4.29 per share.

As a result of the developing shortage, monthly supply allocations, based upon sales histories, were established in June 1973 for all Clark and Owens service stations. As demand continued to rise and supply began to fall, individual stations followed the general industry pattern of curtailing operating hours and restricting sales. With the imposition of the Federal Crude Oil Allocation Program in February of 1974, the shortage of supply at Clark pumps became even more acute; the company was forced to cut deliveries to its dealers by as much as 40 percent in relation to the similar period of the previous year.

The allocation program reduced retail deliveries not only by forcing sales of crude oil to other companies but also by diverting a percentage of refinery output to wholesale accounts (principally small independent retailers) in accordance with 1972 distribution patterns. This provision had the effect of increasing wholesale sales over 1973 levels at the expense of sales to Clark's own retailers.

Clark experienced a sharp decline in retail sales in 1974. Product shortages reduced sales volumes early in the year, while substantially increased crude oil costs and the discontinuance of its premium gasoline diminished Clark's competitiveness in the second half. The company's performance was noticeably below that of most of its competitors; according to the American Petroleum Institute, 1974 industry sales of gasoline and distillate fuel were down 2 and 4.3 percent, respectively, from 1973 levels.

Through 1977, Clark provided incentives for conversion of its outlets to self-service facilities, with one out of eight offering the option. Additionally, the company experimented with the expansion of service stations to include foods and convenience items. Clark designed and opened a combination grocerette/service station in 1976, and it was successful. Six more were developed the following year as customers responded favorably. By 1978, 22 such stations were in operation, and Clark returned to broadcast and print advertising to tout its premium-performance unleaded gasoline.

Clark's stations, located in over 650 north central cities, were both functional and attractive. They featured ample driveway area, spacious entrances and exits, and were laid out in such a way as to minimize congestion. Brightly colored orange, black, and white, most Clark stations made tasteful use of flower gardens and foundation plantings; their overall appearance was clean and uncluttered. Mr. Clark himself had devoted a considerable amount of time to station inspection tours to ensure that company standards were met by individual station operators.

Clark's station-construction efforts had been concentrated entirely in heavy traffic areas, particularly near main highway or expressway exits or on the "going home" side of major thoroughfares. Such a policy was of critical importance to Clark, since virtually all the company's retail sales were of gasoline only. The typical Clark station sold approximately twice as much gasoline as did the "industry average" station. Most Clark stations were open 24 hours a day. (See Exhibit 2.)

REFINING

Clark's two refineries had a combined crude oil processing capacity of 107,000 b/d in 1974. The rated production capacity of the Blue Island refinery was 70,000 b/d; the Wood River refinery accounted for the remainder.

The installation in Blue Island had been geared primarily for the production of premium-grade gasoline, although it was also capable of producing regular and unleaded gasolines. Sizable capital expenditures in 1969 and 1970 for modifications to the fluid catalytic cracker and crude processing units and for the addition of an 18,000 b/d platforming unit had significantly increased the refinery's efficiency and its potential output of high-octane gasoline.

The Wood River refinery was originally designed for the production of heavy heating oil. Shortly after purchasing the refinery from Sinclair, Clark began a substantial construction and modification program at the Wood River

EXHIBIT 2
1980 Marketing area.

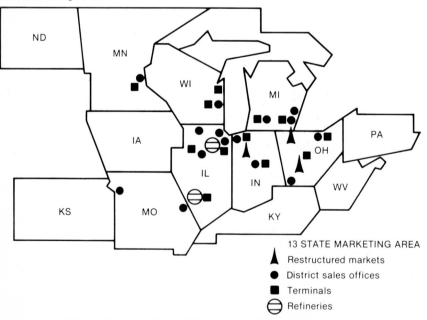

13 STATE MARKETING AREA
▲ Restructured markets
● District sales offices
■ Terminals
⊖ Refineries

facility, significantly shifting its potential output to greater quantities of gasoline (premium, regular, or unleaded), lighter fuel oils, and metallurgical coke.

During the third quarter of 1975, new crude and vacuum units designed for processing 45,000 b/d of crude were placed in operation at the Wood River refinery. Only high-sulfur crude oil was available for processing at this refinery. Lack of downstream distillate desulfurization capacity limited processing to approximately 45,000 b/d. A fluid catalytic cracking unit was converted to the hot regenerator mode of operation, the latest technology available.

In 1976, operation of the Wood River refinery exceeded its design capacity, producing as much as 55,000 b/d. The watchword became "efficiency," as Clark's refineries consumed 7 percent less energy to refine crude than in 1972.

In 1977, the refineries produced an average of 113,565 b/d, with energy consumption decreasing to 8 percent less than the 1972 per-barrel figure. The trend continued in 1978, with the refineries averaging 115,620 b/d and reducing consumption by 12.8 percent over 1972.

Revamping the Wood River plant began late in 1978, with a planned increase in its capacity to produce unleaded gasoline. Two million dollars was budgeted for this work in 1978. Prior to the planned improvements, Wood River had the capability to produce only 25 percent of its gasoline output as unleaded; 65 percent capability was expected to result from the improvements. Management saw these steps as necessary to meet increasing consumer demand for unleaded gasoline (expected to be 45 percent of all gasoline sold by the end of 1979) and to meet EPA requirements for lead phase-down. The Wood River project was also expected to increase its processing capacity to 65,000 b/d. (See Exhibit 3.)

TRANSPORTATION

Clark always had adhered to a policy of ensuring the existence of low-cost transportation in the development of its market areas. In 1943, the company began shipping all of its finished products by water from its Marrero refinery on the Mississippi. At that time all Clark's major markets were accessible to the Mississippi, the Illinois Canal, or the Great Lakes. After World War II, with the expansion of the industry's low-cost pipeline system, Clark shifted its transportation of both crude oil and finished products to pipelines, facilitating both the spread of the company's market and the relocation of the manufacturing operations.

Crude oil was transported from the oil fields or ports of entry to the refineries through a network of common carrier pipelines, several of which were partially owned by Clark. Through Southcap Pipe Line Company, Clark held a 9.8 percent interest in the Capline—a 40-inch (large-diameter) crude pipeline extending 630 miles from St. James, Louisiana, to Patoke, Illinois. At Patoke, the Capline connected with the Chicap line (205 miles of line from Pa-

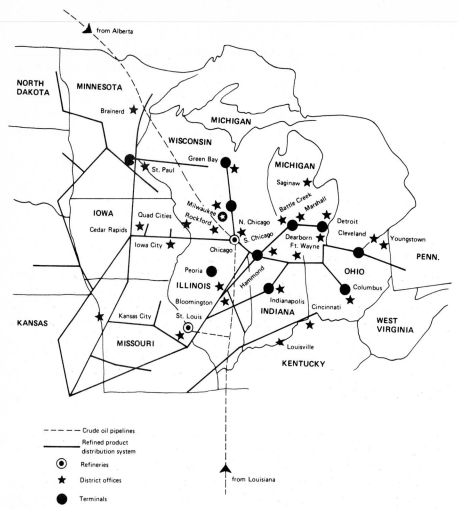

EXHIBIT 3
Supply and distribution system.

toke to Chicago, with a spur to the Blue Island refinery) and the Capwood line
(Patoke to the Wood River refinery, 55 miles). Clark made use of available
water transportation. The Wood River refinery and marine terminals in New
Orleans, Peoria, and St. Paul could be serviced either by moderate-sized ocean
tankers or by river barges.

In November 1973, Clark established a wholly-owned foreign subsidiary,
Clark Trading and Transport, Inc., to operate crude oil tankers. As of March
1974, the new subsidiary had under charter one small (50,000 deadweight tons)

tanker, and two new 250,000-ton very large crude carriers (VLCCs) on order and scheduled for delivery in 1974 and 1976. Additional capacity was supplied by the four 55,000-ton tankers chartered by the parent company in late 1972. The latter vessels were subchartered to other firms when not in use by Clark.

In the fall of 1974, coincident with delivery of its first VLCC, Clark was to implement a four-year agreement with another oil company for terminal rights at the deep-water port of Curacao in the West Indies. The VLCCs were to transport crude from the Persian Gulf to Curacao; from there the crude was to be transshipped in the smaller tankers to Louisiana. Eventual direct operation of the VLCCs between the Persian Gulf and the planned deep-water Louisiana Offshore Oil Port was desired; however, because of environmental consider- ations, federal legislation permitting construction of that port had not yet been passed and Clark had withdrawn from the project.

All the pipelines through which Clark received crude oil were increased in capacity during 1974. Except for this, the year was one of retrenchment for Clark's transport activities. Because of its reduced product sales, the company was forced to curtail refinery runs, which in turn reduced its need for crude oil tankers. The oil tanker market was depressed in 1975 and continued to be depressed in 1976. As a result, Clark reduced its tanker commitments wherev- er possible. Charters were terminated on the tankers Yanxillas, Ellen, and Er- cole, all in the 50,000- to 60,000-deadweight-ton class. Two similar-type tankers were still in service. The charters on these vessels expired in Sep- tember 1976 and January 1977. Two other crude carriers were under contract, one in service and one in lay-up, which was expected to go into service as a result of increasing dependence on offshore crude oil.

The world tanker market continued to be weak through 1978, and Clark in- curred operating losses on the ships. The company chartered the vessels to other companies whenever possible, but the depressed market caused one tanker to spend a portion of the year in lay-up again. Management concern for the cost of maintaining its shipping operations was partly alleviated with the ac- cidental sinking of one of the tankers in 1979.

PETROCHEMICALS AND RESINS

Clark Chemical's Blue Island petrochemical plant, adjacent to the Blue Island refinery, manufactured phenol and acetone from purchased benzene and from propylene, a product of Clark's refining operations. The plant had been enlarged in 1971; phenol production capacity had been raised from 68 million to 80 million pounds per year, and acetone pounds-per-year capacity had been increased from 34 million to 40 billion. Phenol was used in the manufacture of resins, nylon, detergents, pharmaceuticals, and fungicides. Acetone was used as a solvent in paints, varnishes, and certain pharmaceuticals.

Clark Chemical also operated resin plants in Blue Island and in Tewksbury, Massachusetts (up to the time of the sale). Both plants made use of portions of the Blue Island phenol in the manufacture of phenol-formaldehyde, urea-formaldehyde, and melamine-formaldehyde resins. These products were purchased primarily by the textile, paper, plywood, abrasives, and glass-cloth industries.

In 1973 chemical sales totaled 139,790,000 pounds of resin, phenol, and acetone. However, because of low sales growth and earnings, the Tewksbury resin plant was sold in June 1973. Performance of the Blue Island plant was considered satisfactory, and no disposition was scheduled. Despite raw materials shortages which forced an operations cutback to 70 percent of capacity during November and December, in 1973 the Blue Island chemical plant produced a record output: 79,479,561 pounds of acetone.

In contrast to the parent company's operations, in 1974 the Clark Chemical Corporation enjoyed its most profitable year.

The latter half of the decade was marked by increasing raw materials prices, which lowered earnings for the chemical subsidiary. In response, the company adopted improvements in production technology to increase both plant efficiency and the yield of phenol.

THE CHANGES OF 1979

The oil industry was surprised when, shortly after he became CEO at Clark, Robert G. Reed decided to sell the company's exploration and crude oil–producing properties. Given Clark's difficulties purchasing crude and the overall tight supplies in mid-1979, the decision provoked a minor controversy.

Management stated that the move marked a return to Clark's original strategy—refining and marketing—and that the cash generated by the sale would be invested specifically to improve production efficiency and marketing efforts. (See Exhibit 4.) The sale of the exploration and production operations to the Petro-Lewis Corporation of Denver for $89.8 million was completed near the end of 1979.

The sale placed the company in a cash-rich position to close the year, despite two other unexpected factors: a retroactive price increase by one of Clark's Mid-East suppliers, and Clark's decision to buy back the unexpired portion of its long-term tanker charter. (The other tanker sank during the year, so the company was able to direct its efforts at pipeline and spot-tankering to fulfill its transportation needs.) The company announced an extra year-end dividend of 20 cents per share.

At the time of the sale, Clark revealed its new corporate objectives:

1 To become one of the nation's most cost-efficient distributors of energy products to the American consumer

2 To make Clark a broadly diversified supplier of chemical products for industry

3 To attain a consistent 5 percent return on revenues, a 10 percent return on assets, and a 20 percent return on shareholder equity

Executives said that several strategies would be implemented to meet these objectives:

1 A strengthened management team and reorganized structure
2 Reduced tanker and pipeline costs
3 A restructured station network aimed at an operating cost ratio equal to or better than that of the most efficient competitor in each market
4 Continued upgrading of refinery yields, capitalizing on technology which already produced an above-average proportion of gasoline per barrel of crude and featured a capability for 90 percent unleaded fuel output
5 Expanded petrochemical operations, through enlarged facilities and acquisition
6 Deployment of Clark's current cash reserves to maximum advantage in the above activities and other opportunities then under study

The corporate structure was revised in light of the company's goals and product mix. The new organization was intended to assign performance accountability, decentralize decision making, and allow for future internal and external growth. (See Exhibits 5 and 6.)

The executive and operating roles of top management were distinguished. Corporate staff officers and managers of finance, government relations, general counsel, corporate planning, human resources, and internal audit reported to the chief executive officer.

All operating units were combined into the refined products group. Unit vice presidents and managers for refining operations, administration, crude oil supply and transportation, retail marketing, chemical products, and wholesale sales and refined products distribution were responsible to the executive vice president, who was in turn responsible to the president and chief operating officer (a position then unoccupied), who, in turn, reported to the chairman. Each unit was designed and structured as an independent activity with specific tasks and goals, as follows:

Crude oil supply and transportation: procure crude supplies, cultivating and securing new and established sources

Refinery operations: encompass all manufacturing, including refined petroleum products and chemical products, provide maximum production efficiency, and maintain and extend technological advantages

Wholesale sales and refined products distribution: include various marketing and supply and distribution activities formerly dispersed throughout the company, coordinate product availability with demand, increase terminal throughput and reduce unit costs

Retail marketing: Seek profit improvement opportunities through restructuring of mix of station formats and locations, efficient management of the retail network, and providing corollary real estate, construction, and sales training services.

EXHIBIT 4
SUMMARY OF CLARK'S 1979 STRATEGY REFORMULATION

1979 position	Facilities	Markets served
Petroleum operation sales rose 19.6% to $1,133 million.	Retail	Retail
Petroleum operating income up 115% to $68 million.	Service stations total 1,793 units, with 29 closed in 1979.	Grocerette station concept combining self-service gasoline and convenience foods expanded to 27 units.
Retail gasoline volume declined 7%.	74% are company-operated.	Regular and unleaded gas marketed at all stations.
Gasoline production totals 28 million barrels, down 7%.	40% self-service stations, 60% full-service.	Refining
Pipeline expanded and tanker costs reduced.	Refining	Clark's two refineries processed gasoline sold in 13-state market area.
Oil and gas exploration and production facilities sold for $89.8 million, with right to purchase production retained by Clark.	$10.3 million in capital completed or begun.	Unleaded gasoline production capacity increased to 90%, to serve changing consumer needs.
	Total refinery capacity increased 3.8% to 135,000 b/d.	Transportation
	Transportation	After buy-out of the VLCC and the sinking of the ULCC, Clark now has one 80,000-ton tanker in position to balance costs—charter vs. spot.
	Chicap pipeline system crude oil capacity increased to 485,000 b/d from 380,000 b/d. Clark pipeline ownership is 23%.	

Planned 1982 position	Facilities	Markets served
Objectives	Retail	Retail
Become one of the nation's more cost-efficient refiners and distributors of energy products.	Restructure service-station network.	Consolidate lower-volume stations.
	Construct additional superstations where appropriate.	Erect high-volume superstations in high-traffic metropolitan areas to meet changing driving patterns and shopping habits resulting from higher gasoline prices.
Obtain additional contract crude oil at competitive prices.	90% self-service stations, 10% full-service.	
Attain consistent:	Add new grocerette stations in rural and suburban areas.	Convert to cost-efficient self-service stations.
5% return on revenues	Upgrade refinery facilities to run sour and/or heavy crudes.	Refining
10% return on assets		
20% return on shareholders' equity		Continue production of all gasoline marketed at Clark stations.
	Transportation	Transportation
	Efficient and flexible use of long-term charter and spot tanker operations to transport any additional volumes of crude oil.	Reduce tanker costs.

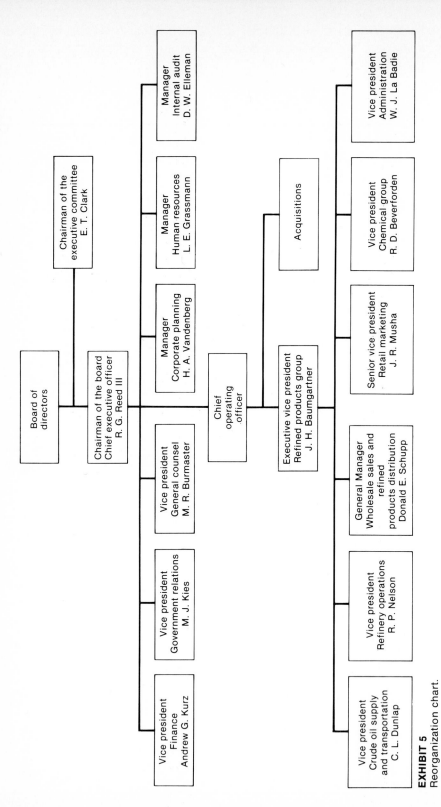

EXHIBIT 5
Reorganization chart.

230

EXHIBIT 6
CLARK OIL AND REFINING CORPORATION TOP MANAGEMENT

Name	Title	Age	With Clark since	Present post since	Formerly
Robert G. Reed, III	Chairman of the board Chief executive officer	53	1979	1979	Executive VP, Tesoro Petroleum
M. R. Burmaster	Vice president (VP) General counsel	46	1973	1975	Corporate secretary, Clark
Andrew G. Kurz	VP, finance	37	1981	1981	Major oil company
Harold J. Lessner	Secretary	37	1974	1979	Attorney, Clark legal dept.
Edward A. Maciejewski	Controller	56	1953	1975	Asst. controller, Clark
Michael J. Kies	VP, government relations	49	1957	1979	Mgr., energy regulations, Clark
Harold W. Simmons	Treasurer	46	1961	1975	Asst. treasurer, Clark
John H. Baumgartner	Executive VP, refined products group	45	1956	1980	Executive VP, Clark
Jacob R. Musha	VP, retail marketing	44	1968	1979	Sales mgr., Clark
Robert D. Beverforden	VP, chemical group	44	1968	1979	Sales mgr., Clark
C. L. Dunlap	VP, oil supply and transportation	37	1969	1979	Attorney, Clark legal dept.
Robert P. Nelson	VP, refineries	49	1961	1980	VP, manufacturing, Clark
Donald E. Schupp	VP, wholesale sales	34	1980	1980	Large independent oil company

Chemical products marketing: Expand and possibly divide into separate group, to develop new product ideas and expand market penetration

Administration: provide support services and systems necessary to operation of the Refined Products Group

Through 1979, the company continued to restructure its marketing program by consolidating lower volume locations. In one major metropolitan area that year, 30 stations out of 200 were closed. No material capital gain or loss from the sale of closed units in metropolitan areas was expected, but the company said that the consolidation phase would contribute materially to profitability goals since:

• The remaining units experienced a 40 percent gain in average monthly gallonage.
• Total volume was undiminished.
• Station operating cost for the two districts involved dropped several cents per gallon.

In general, older stations in high-risk urban areas had the highest costs and were to receive the earliest attention. Not all consolidations were to involve the same proportion of stations or yield the same cost reductions, since the operating environment varied. The consolidation phase was expected to generate several million dollars of cash for investment in more profitable formats like superstations, self-service stations, and grocerettes.

The short-run goal was to deliver the limited supply of product through the least number of the most efficient stations.

The long-term requirement was a station network positioned for:

• A more balanced competitive environment, through gradual alleviation of the current restricted crude oil supply situation
• The possible effect of much higher gasoline prices and/or rationing on driving patterns and shopping habits

At year's end, about 60 percent of the nearly 1,300 remaining company-operated stations were full-service. About 40 percent were self-service. By the end of 1980 as many as 200 more units were to be converted, and by the end of 1982, the proportion was expected to be 90 percent self-service, 10 percent full-service—a relationship that was expected to persist. The cost of conversion was relatively minor—about $15,000 per unit—and was only to involve a total of $4.5 million through 1982. The company also announced that capital improvements completed or begun in 1979 would maintain or extend the two principal advantages over other refiners: the ability to produce more gasoline per barrel and to produce a higher proportion of unleaded gasoline. Management felt that both would permit Clark to better meet future consumer demand during periods of tight as well as strong supply.

At the time Clark could make 90 percent of its gasoline in unleaded form, well ahead of the industry capacity in place. Industry sources projected

1980 national demand for unleaded gasoline at 47 percent of the total, compared with 75 percent for 1985.

INITIAL RESULTS

In 1980, Clark management concentrated its effort on implementing the strategy that had been announced during the previous year. The total number of service stations was brought down to 1,512, and marketing districts were reduced to 15 from 23. Conversion to self-service was completed at 109 stations, and selected sites were developed as grocerettes and "super-pumper," high-capacity stations. An 11 percent increase in retail volume to 1.2 billion gallons and an 8.5 percent reduction in station costs were realized. However, increasing prices for crude oil and lower margins on fuel oil and other refined products combined to produce a decline in operating earnings.

By early 1981, supplies of oil were again plentiful, yet consumer demand was down, a result of the mild winter that year and the fact that smaller cars were proliferating. Prices at the pumps were down as a result; but Clark's oil prices were fixed by long-term contract at rates substantially above the market.

FUTURE PROSPECTS

Clark posted a loss in the first quarter of 1981, but management insisted that its strategy was wise and that conditions would stabilize as excess supplies of crude oil inventories diminished (see Exhibits 7 to 9 for financial statements). Clark executives stated that efficient operations and carefully negotiated supply contracts would be the key to success. The continuing political volatility in the Middle East and the potential effects of the Reagan administration's deregulation of the oil industry were major concerns. It was not clear how these factors would impinge upon Clark.

EXHIBIT 7
SIX YEAR SUMMARY OF OPERATIONS

INCOME STATEMENT DATA ($ in millions)	1980	1979	1978	1977	1976	1975	Compound rate of change
Income							
Net sales and operating revenue	$1,623.2	$1,156.9	$960.0	$861.9	$706.8	$592.1	22%
Dividends, interest and other	34.4	18.1	8.6	9.0	5.7	14.8	18
	1,657.6	1,175.0	968.6	870.9	712.5	606.9	22
Costs and expenses							
Crude oil products, materials, and operating expense	1,492.3	1,022.1	869.5	784.8	640.1	545.1	22
Selling, administrative, and general expense	33.2	28.7	24.1	22.4	17.4	13.7	19
Taxes other than income taxes	38.4	29.1	26.9	22.0	16.5	17.4	17
Depreciation and amortization	14.5	14.2	14.3	14.3	13.8	12.6	3
Interest	4.7	6.0	9.4	12.2	13.6	14.4	(25)
	1,583.1	1,100.1	944.2	855.7	701.4	603.2	21
Income from continuing operations before income taxes	74.5	74.9	24.4	15.2	11.1	3.7	82
Income taxes (credits)	30.6	33.2	9.8	4.3	3.4	(2.1)	—
Net income from continuing operations	43.9	41.7	14.6	10.9	7.7	5.8	50
Discontinued operations							
Income (loss) from oil and gas production (less applicable income taxes)	—	.8	.4	5.5	1.2	(1.2)	—
Gain on disposal of oil and gas properties (less applicable income taxes)	—	34.9	—	—	—	—	—
Net income	$ 43.9	$ 77.4	$ 15.0	$ 16.4	$ 8.9	$ 4.6	57%

BALANCE SHEET DATA ($ in millions)

							%
Current assets	$ 332.2	$ 304.8	$143.8	$154.3	$150.7	$120.7	22%
Investments and other assets	9.9	7.9	5.4	6.0	5.6	6.4	9
Property, plant and equipment—gross	312.3	296.0	353.5	351.5	342.3	345.2	(2)
Less allowances for depreciation and amortization	167.5	155.5	167.0	154.3	134.3	119.7	7
Property, plant and equipment—net	144.8	140.5	186.5	197.2	208.0	225.5	(9)
Total assets	$ 486.9	$ 453.2	$335.7	$357.5	$364.3	$352.6	7
Current liabilities	198.7	195.4	109.6	118.1	113.8	97.7	15
Long-term debt	.5	.8	33.1	57.3	81.5	89.3	—
Long-term lease obligations	37.8	40.4	43.4	46.3	49.2	51.8	(7)
Other long-term and deferred items	22.9	21.1	25.4	22.5	19.2	18.5	4
Shareholders' equity	227.0	195.5	124.2	113.3	100.6	95.3	19
Total liabilities and shareholders' equity	$ 486.9	$ 453.2	$335.7	$357.7	$364.3	$352.6	7%

FINANCIAL POSITION DATA ($ in millions)

Funds provided						
Continuing operations	$ 59.6	$ 62.9	$ 32.7	$ 25.4	$ 18.3	$ 16.9
Discontinued operations	–	37.9	11.6	11.1	7.2	4.2
Other	2.6	39.3	0.7	1.9	14.9	35.4
Total funds provided	62.2	140.1	45.0	38.4	40.4	56.5
Funds used						
Capital expenditures	20.9	19.7	14.9	7.9	12.5	41.4
Debt reductions	4.0	36.4	27.8	27.5	10.4	3.3
Dividends	10.0	6.6	4.3	3.7	3.6	3.6
Other	3.2	2.3	–	–	–	.3
Total funds used	38.1	65.0	47.0	39.1	26.5	48.6
Increase (decrease) in working capital	$ 24.1	$ 75.1	$ (2.0)	$ (0.7)	$ 13.9	$ 7.9

EXHIBIT 7 (*continued*)
SIX YEAR SUMMARY OF OPERATIONS

	1980	1979	1978	1977	1976	1975	Compound rate of change
PER SHARE DATA							
Income							
Continuing operations	$ 3.03	$ 2.90	$ 1.02	$ .76	$ .54	$ .41	49%
Discontinued operations	—	.05	.03	.39	.09	(.08)	—
Disposal of oil and gas operations	—	2.43	—	—	—	—	—
Net income	$ 3.03	$ 5.38	$ 1.05	$ 1.15	$ .63	$ .33	56
Dividends	$ 0.70	$ 0.46	$ 0.30	$ 0.2625	$ 0.25	$ 0.25	23
Book value	$15.89	$ 13.63	$ 8.71	$ 7.97	$ 7.08	$ 6.70	19%
Year-end shares outstanding (thousands)	14,282	14,338	14,249	14,221	14,217	14,217	
Common shareholders (at year end)	6,537	7,273	8,114	8,652	9,133	9,,9	
RATE OF RETURN ANALYSIS							
Net margin (income % of net sales)							
Gross income	8.06%	11.65%	9.43%	8.94%	9.44%	7.94%	
Operating income	2.76	5.43	2.62	2.12	2.69	.55	
Pretax income	4.65	6.47	2.54	1.76	1.57	.63	
Net income	2.71	3.60	1.52	1.26	1.09	.98	
Asset turnover ($ net sales per $ of average assets)							
Current assets	$ 5.10	$ 5.16	$ 6.44	$ 5.65	$ 5.21	$ 4.52	
Property, plant & equipment—gross	5.34	3.56	2.72	2.48	2.06	1.91	
Total assets	3.45	2.93	2.77	2.39	1.97	1.69	
Return on assets (income % average total assets)							
Operating income	9.53%	15.91%	7.26%	5.07%	5.30%	.93%	
Pretax income	15.85	18.98	7.04	4.20	3.09	1.06	
Net income	9.34	10.56	4.20	3.01	2.15	1.65	
Financial leverage (per $ average shareholders' equity)							
Average total assets	$ 2.23	$ 2.47	$ 2.92	$ 3.37	$ 3.66	$ 3.70	

Average current liabilities	.93	1.21	.96	1.08	1.08	1.18
Average long-term debt	.01	.11	.38	.65	.87	.80
Average long-term obligations	.19	.26	.38	.47	.52	.56
Average other long-term and deferred items	.10	.15	.20	.19	.19	.16
Average total liabilities	1.23	1.47	1.92	2.37	2.66	2.70

Return on equity (income % of average shareholders' equity)

Operating income	21.20%	39.28%	21.18%	17.11%	19.40%	3.45%
Pretax income	35.28	46.84	20.54	14.18	11.31	3.92
Net income	20.79	26.07	12.25	10.14	7.86	6.12

EMPLOYEES AT YEAR-END

Company station employees	5,916	6,626	7,602	7,591	6,497	3,877
Administrative and other	1,263	1,249	1,226	1,275	1,225	1,168
Total	7,179	7,875	8,828	8,866	7,722	5,045

BUSINESS SEGMENT DATA
(in thousands of dollars)

Revenues						
Petroleum operations	$1,593,597	$1,133,557	$947,957	$848,513	$689,248	$588,041
Chemical	39,588	34,681	23,276	22,818	22,648	19,301
Other	31,355	13,417	3,857	3,651	3,205	2,568
Intercompany eliminations	(6,905)	(6,640)	(6,505)	(4,108)	(2,656)	(2,980)
Total	$1,657,635	$1,175,015	$968,585	$870,874	$712,445	$606,930
Operating income (loss)						
Petroleum operations	$ 48,991	$ 68,851	$ 31,906	$ 24,483	$ 20,615	$ 15,614
Chemical	12,518	9,658	6,133	6,612	7,664	6,655
Equity earnings	3,069	2,162	2,166	2,851	2,323	1,985
Unallocated overhead, interest expense, other income, and other deductions	9,941	(5,821)	(15,815)	(18,774)	(19,522)	(20,537)
Total income	$ 74,519	$ 74,850	$ 24,390	$ 15,172	$ 11,080	$ 3,717

EXHIBIT 7 *(continued)*
SIX YEAR SUMMARY OF OPERATIONS

	1980	1979	1978	1977	1976	1975	Compound rate of change
BUSINESS SEGMENT DATA (in thousands of dollars)							
Identifiable assets							
Petroleum operations	$ 273,015	$260,561	$279,176	$297,760	$305,793	$271,420	
Chemical	10,524	10,124	6,650	6,665	7,224	8,705	
Oil and gas production (sold in 1979)	—	—	45,775	48,659	47,499	55,496	
Equity in affiliates	6,938	3,249	3,048	3,152	2,602	3,122	
General corporate assets	196,396	179,281	1,051	1,233	1,233	13,845	
Total	$ 486,873	$ 453,215	$335,700	$357,469	$364,351	$352,588	
Depreciation and amortization							
Petroleum operations	$ 13,982	$ 13,604	$ 13,485	$ 13,588	$ 13,080	$ 11,908	
Chemical	292	450	653	644	640	619	
Other	180	172	120	116	112	116	
Total	$ 14,454	$ 14,226	$ 14,258	$ 14,348	$ 13,832	$ 12,643	
Operating margin (income as % of revenues)							
Petroleum operations	3.1%	6.1%	3.4%	2.9%	3.0%	2.7%	
Chemical	31.6%	27.9%	26.4%	29.0%	33.8%	34.5%	
Asset turnover (revenues ÷ beginning assets)							
Petroleum operations	6.12	4.06	3.18	2.78	2.54	2.22	
Chemical	3.91	5.22	3.49	3.16	2.60	2.26	
Return on assets (income as % of beginning assets)							
Petroleum operations	18.8%	24.7%	10.7%	8.0%	7.6%	5.9%	
Chemical	123.7%	145.2%	92.0%	91.5%	88.0%	78.1%	

EXHIBIT 8

CONSOLIDATED STATEMENTS OF CHANGES IN FINANCIAL POSITION
(Thousands of Dollars)

	1980	1979	1978
Funds provided			
Income from continuing operations	$43,920	$ 41,658	$14,541
Expense (income) not involving funds:			
Depreciation and amortization	14,454	14,226	14,258
Abandonment of property, plant and equipment		6,735	
Deferred income taxes	2,881	476	3,310
Other	(1,689)	(200)	604
Total from continuing operations	59,566	62,895	32,713
Income from discontinued operations		818	419
Gain on disposal of oil and gas properties		34,952	
Expense (income) not involving funds:			
Depreciation, depletion and amortization		5,842	10,831
Deferred income taxes		(3,759)	355
Total from discontinued operations	59,566	100,748	44,318
Proceeds from exercise of stock options	525	490	154
Disposals of property, plant and equipment	2,124	583	495
Carrying amount of property, plant and equipment of discontinued operations		38,338	
Total funds provided	62,215	140,159	44,967
Funds used			
Additions to property, plant and equipment	20,889	19,745	14,859
Decrease in advances on gas incentive contracts	1,085	1,049	713
Decrease in long-term debt and lease obligations	2,895	35,268	27,142
Cash dividends	10,047	6,623	4,267
Other changes—net	3,163	2,331	12
Total funds used	38,079	65,016	46,993
Increase (decrease) in working capital	$24,136	$ 75,143	($ 2,026)
Changes in components of working capital			
Increase (decrease) in current assets:			
Cash and short-term investments	$ 4,330	$171,273	($ 7,744)
Trade receivables	19,879	(15,129)	9,386
Inventories	4,303	1,707	(12,037)
Prepaid expenses and other	(1,143)	3,112	(56)
Increase (decrease) in current assets	27,369	160,963	(10,451)
Increase (decrease) in current liabilities:			
Accounts payable	35,061	45,038	(13,850)
Dividends payable	(1,434)	1,434	
Accrued liabilities	6,792	136	1,512
Taxes, other than income	4,246	(1,937)	481
Federal and state income taxes	(41,660)	44,785	2,640
Long-term obligations due within one year	228	(3,636)	792
Increase (decrease) in current liabilities	3,233	85,820	(8,425)
Increase (decrease) in working capital	$24,136	$ 75,143	($ 2,026)

EXHIBIT 9
EXCERPTS FROM NOTES TO CONSOLIDATED FINANCIAL STATEMENTS, DECEMBER 31, 1980

Note A—Accounting practices and principles

The accompanying consolidated financial statements include the accounts of the Company and its wholly-owned subsidiaries, except for an insurance subsidiary which is carried at equity. Investments in certain corporations (owned 23% to 50%) are also carried at equity. Under this method, equity in the earnings or losses of these corporations is reflected in the Company's earnings rather than when realized through dividends.

Short-term investments are stated at cost plus accrued interest, which approximates market value.

The Company values its inventory at the lower of cost or market. The Company's method of determining crude oil and refined products costs is the last-in, first-out (LIFO) method. All other inventories are stated at cost determined by the first-in, first-out (FIFO) or average cost methods. Crude oil and refined products inventories valued on the LIFO method were $227,400,000 and $156,200,000 less than they would have been if they had been valued on a current cost basis at December 31, 1980 and December 31, 1979, respectively.

Depreciation of plant and equipment is determined generally on the straight-line method over the estimated useful lives of the assets.

Note B—Sale of oil and gas properties

On October 31, 1979 the Company sold substantially all of the net assets of its subsidiary, Clark Oil Producing Co. for $89,800,000 in cash. Income and costs and expenses of oil and gas production for periods prior to date of disposition have been segregated in the statement of income. Amounts (in thousands of dollars) relating to the discontinued operations were as follows:

	1979*	1978	1977	1976	1975
Income	$12,332	$16,676	$16,383	$11,730	$ 8,553
Costs and expenses	10,551	16,971	11,490	9,872	11,757
Income taxes (credit)	963	(714)	1,814	618	(2,031)
Net income (loss) from operations	$ 818	$ 419	$ 3,079	$ 1,240	($ 1,173)

*Ten months

Note C—Advances on gas incentive contracts

The advances are payable, without interest, to a pipeline company in annual amounts of $1,085,000 in 1981, $3,821,000 in 1982, $7,030,000 in 1983 and $1,804,000 in 1984.

Note D—Shareholders' equity

On October 24, 1980 the board of directors declared a two-for-one stock split effected in the form of a 100% stock dividend payable to holders of record as of December 18, 1980, and on December 8, 1980 the shareholders approved an increase in the number of authorized shares of Common Stock to 30,000,000 shares.

Non-qualified options issued under a 1976 plan are exercisable after one year whereas qualified options under the plan are exercisable to the extent of 25% of such options after one year and an additional 25% every six months thereafter. All options expire five years from date of grant.

At December 31, 1980 the Company had reserved 402,700 shares of Common Stock for issuance in connection with the stock option plan. Stock option transactions during 1980 and 1979 are summarized as follows (14,000 shares at $11.00 were exercised in 1978):

	1980		1979	
	Shares	Option price	Shares	Option price
Outstanding—January 1	181,000	$5.50 to $14.00	226,000	$5.50
Granted	298,000	$17.50	50,000	$13.50 to $14.00
Exercised	(70,300)	$ 5.50	(89,000)	$5.50
Cancelled	(6,000)	$17.50	(6,000)	$5.50
Outstanding—December 31	402,700	$5.50 to $17.50	181,000	$ 5.50 to $14.00
Exercisable—December 31	54,700		181,00	
Available for grant—December 31	-0-		298,000	

Note E—Leases

The Company leases numerous properties (principally retail gasoline service stations owned by companies in which the Company is an investor) under initial terms of up to twenty-five years. The Company also leases a crude oil tanker and equipment under operating leases many of which are cancellable.

Marketing property, plant and equipment includes the following amounts which have been capitalized:

	December 31	
	1980	1979
	(in thousands of dollars)	
Cost	$67,570	$67,644
Less allowance for amortization	39,882	37,353
	$27,688	$30,291

Lease amortization is included in depreciation expense.

Future minimum payments under the capital leases and noncancellable operating leases with initial or remaining terms of one year or more consisted of the following:

	Capital leases	Operating leases
	(in thousands of dollars)	
1981	$ 7,497	$ 7,362
1982	7,406	5,107
1983	7,291	5,067
1984	7,176	4,897
1985	6,962	4,460
1986–1990	26,015	16,530
1991–1995	4,598	3,733
Thereafter		553
Total minimum lease payments	$66,945	$47,709
Less amounts representing interest	25,992	
Present value of net minimum lease payments	$40,953	

EXHIBIT 9 (*continued*)
EXCERPTS FROM NOTES TO CONSOLIDATED FINANCIAL STATEMENTS DECEMBER 31, 1980

Total rental expense for all operating leases including one tanker lease in 1980 and three tanker leases in 1979 and 1978, was $10,975,000 in 1980, $30,667,000 (including $5,300,000 for termination of a crude oil tanker lease) in 1979, and $25,263,000 in 1978.

Note F—Contingencies

The Internal Revenue Service has completed examinations of the Company's federal income tax returns for 1971 through 1975 and has proposed adjustments, certain of which the Company has protested. The Company believes the proposed adjustments and additional adjustments, if any, which might be proposed for subsequent years will not have a material effect on the Company's financial position.

The Company's operations are subject to various government regulatory controls, particularly those of the Department of Energy. The Department of Energy had been conducting a continuous audit of the Company's records, and in January 1981 issued a Notice of Probable Violation alleging apparent violation of regulations resulting in overstatement of base prices and understatement of cost recoveries approximating $298,000,000. The Company and its counsel believe the Company is in substantial compliance with all regulations as issued and that the Department of Energy's findings are without fact or basis, and, any liability which finally may be determined will not materially affect the financial position of the Company.

THREE

THE PURPOSE OF THE ORGANIZATION

CHAPTER 6

Determination of Basic Objectives: Developing the Root Strategy of the Firm

DETERMINATION OF BASIC ECONOMIC OBJECTIVES

The life cycle of a business with its typical four stages provides a basic framework for analysis that can be utilized to determine the firm's industry position, and facilitate detecting signs of stagnation and aging to prevent slipping into the decline stage. As indicated in Chapter 2, the development of a strategic design is a necessary factor in establishing the success of an enterprise. However, as illustrated in the previous chapters, the success of this development may well establish a corporate culture that entrenches the firm in a position of industry leadership so solidly that it reacts negatively to change and competitive threats, preventing or delaying reformulation and the recognition of a need for recycling its strategic design.

Each phase of a company's strategic design is developed in sequential order whether or not management has a formal or informal strategic planning system. To gain an understanding of the process and to facilitate analysis of the firm's strategic thrust, each phase should be appraised in relation to the skills and resources of the organization, its potential competitive advantages in the marketplace, and the strength of existing or potential competition. This chapter is concerned with an analysis of the primary stage of the strategic design—the development of the root strategy and the determination of the basic objectives of the organization.

In the initial stage of development of a business enterprise or in the reformulation phase of the on-going business entity, the policymaking group must appraise the skills and resources of the organization and determine the basic objectives which will shape the image and character of the company and provide the guidelines for developing a strategic design. The mission and purpose of all organizations, whether private or public, profit or nonprofit, must be clearly defined, communicated, and understood before meaningful executive action can take place.

The lack of clear-cut objectives will lead to uncertainty in planning, structuring, and staffing the organization and in developing an information and control system to measure the effectiveness of management decisions. It has frequently been stated that all organizations have a hierarchy of objectives which effectively determines priorities for investment decisions and management actions. At the policy level, these objectives are usually broadly stated and become embodied in the strategic design of the company. In the on-going business concern which is subject to the vagaries of the marketplace, basic economic objectives provide the initial guidelines and the unifying force which directs all action and forms the base for control and accountability.

OVERRIDING BASIC ECONOMIC OBJECTIVES: PROFITABILITY, GROWTH, AND SURVIVAL

In determining the root strategy of a business enterprise, it must be assumed that the elementary economic objectives of *profitability, growth,* and *survival* are paramount and supersede the basic "business objectives" which help shape the image of the firm and provide the base for the development of a strategic design. In the on-going company, it is sometimes difficult to determine the significance and relationship of the objective set; operating objectives such as market-share targets affect profitability, customer-service objectives affect profitability, objectives related to product market scope and diversification affect profitability, and the broad range of social objectives embraced by many organizations are directly related to profitability.

Constraints on profitability, growth, and the threat of failure are major factors in providing the thrust for companies to seek new product lines, expansion, and diversification. Businesses operating in a competitive environment must be profitable in order to survive. Thus the profit objective is taken for granted and is only subject to scrutiny in relation to specific goals and measures of profitability. If the management of a business enterprise does not consider survival—the continuity of the firm—as an elementary objective, then its whole strategic design will be directed toward terminal objectives, such as a limited venture in the terms of time—with foreseeable liquidation or sale—or "conditioning of a company" for a potential merger or acquisition by another firm. Once management has determined a terminal objective, the course of executive action will be directed toward that end and not the normative competitive strategy dictated by the survival objective; the economic objective of growth must follow from profitability and is necessary to ensure survival of the enterprise. While the old cliché that "no business stands still—it must either grow or perish" has frequently been contested, the argument has only been in terms of degrees. In today's competitive business society, growth over time is essential to survival. It is just a question of how much growth is necessary and manageable to maintain a dynamic business enterprise. Slowed growth usually signals the need to scrutinize the firm's life cycle to determine if it is entering a decline stage and requires a recycling and reformulation of its strategic design.

In the long run, profitability, growth, and survival must become the overriding basic objectives of the managers of business enterprises in our competitive, complex industrial society. The policymakers act as economic agents seeking to allocate the limited resources of the firm to business investments which will maximize the return to the shareholders or owners. This maximization principle is under continuous attack despite its groundings in basic economic theory. We frequently find maximization explained or defended in economic texts and business journals by thorough discussions of the short-run versus long-run profit goals of the enterprise. The threat of certain businesses to the ecology, the pressure of governmental regulations, antitrust action, taxation, and the pressure of public opinion are also taken into consideration in the adaptive economic model of the firm through recognition of the fact that the business enterprise which seeks to remain a viable entity for an indefinite period of time must forego opportunistic profit maximization in the short run. The continuity of the firm is the major concern of the policymakers, and consequently they must realistically adjust their profitability goals to correspond with environmental constraints. This does not deny the potential exceptional performance in terms of profitability in the life cycle of the enterprise.

MAXIMIZATION AND BOUNDED RATIONALITY

In seeking to reconcile the varied concepts of what constitutes the basic overriding objective of the business entity, the major considerations of the factors of time horizon, long run versus short run, perceived aspiration levels, what the policymaker decides will maximize income, and the nature and state of the industrial environments in which the firm operates must be taken into account. It is frequently stated that no firm ever optimizes or maximizes but rather "satisfices,"[1] reaching a compromise or satisfactory level of output or income. These contentions have to be true if for no other reason than that no entrepreneur in a dynamic industrial society would ever be aware of when or if the firm had reached optimal results. The multiproduct, diversified companies which account for the largest measure of economic activity in our industrial society may have thousands of strategic options available to them. Even if it were possible to measure and equate the almost infinite combinations of products, the projection of their revenue-producing potentials would be impossible in a dynamic economy. Bounded rationality[2] is no doubt a major factor in preventing profit maximization in the true sense.

Despite the impossibility of reaching optimal results because of the lack of

[1]J. March and H. Simon, *Organizations* (New York: Wiley, 1958).
[2]Ibid.

the predetermined conditions present in the classical theory of the firm, management is still intensely preoccupied with maximizing corporate revenues or—in our modern industrial society—in attempting to maximize shareholder's wealth.

THE CLASSICAL THEORY OF THE FIRM: USE AND LIMITATIONS

Despite its simplicity, the economic model, or the classical theory of the firm, has provided the policymaker with a basic concept that has had many successful applications in guiding the business enterprise. If we examine the concepts and functions used by students of business administration, we find that much of the material is an extension of the classical theory of the firm, and the so-called newer, sophisticated tools are applications of marginal analysis supplemented by calculus.

Like the economist, the policymaker is constantly attempting to allocate restricted resources among many competing investment opportunities. It can be argued that in the long run the entrepreneur, like the economist, assumes that profit maximization is the ultimate guide in resource allocation or in the choice among alternative investment opportunities. The major concern of economists has been with the optimal allocation of national resources. In the context of the economic model, the firm is viewed as a single decision-making unit addressing itself to the optimal allocation of its resources as a microunit in the national economy. This model of individual choice, from which the principle of profit maximization has been derived, has frequently been criticized as a basis for decision making because of its lack of realism and its restrictive assumptions. It is assumed in the classical theory that the firm constantly seeks an equilibrium level of output or production where its marginal costs are equated with its marginal revenues. When this point has been reached, profit maximization has been attained. If we assume explicit marginalism and profit maximization as the ultimate goal of the entrepreneur, then we must also recognize the following limiting bases of the classical theory of the firm:

1 Perfect competition with an industrywide homogeneous product; all products are equivalent and product superiority or inferiority is nonexistent.

2 There is perfect knowledge in the industry, and all producers have the equivalent production technology. There is also perfect market knowledge, and all consumers have complete product knowledge. Therefore all producers must meet the established market price.

3 There is free entry to all markets and freedom of exit from all markets, with no barriers. Firms can move freely from one industry to another as they seek to maximize profits.

4 There is atomistic competition with large numbers of buyers and sellers in each market who act independently, without collusion, and each firm is too small to be able to have more than a negligible effect on market price.

While the economic model of the firm has recognized limitations, it has made significant contributions to the policymaking process. Managers in our economy make decisions predicated on this hypothetical model more frequently than they do on any other concept of the enterprise. In spite of the simplicity of the economists' model and the continual reference to its lack of reality in relation to large-scale, multiproduct organizations which dominate our society, the economy of our system of relatively free enterprise is still closely patterned after the classical theory of the firm. The applications of this theory are evident in any study of the decision-making process of policymaking executives, and the derived concept of profit maximization is the one element of the economic model which has the most frequent application in business.

MAXIMIZATION OF SHAREHOLDERS' WEALTH: THE CONCEPT OF THE *k* FACTOR

In establishing basic economic objectives, the policymaker must seek a measure which will reflect the profitability, growth, and survival characteristics of the firm. In determining a criterion function or standard to judge the efficacy of enterprise performance, a valuation model which reflects the increase in the wealth of shareholders or owners of the firm is a logical choice. In the case of public corporations, shareholders provide the equity capital; as owners, they take the financial risks, sharing in the losses or profits of the firm. The most practical and comprehensive index management can utilize to measure the increase in shareholders' wealth is the market price of the company's stock. The higher the price, the greater command the shareholder has over economic goods. The stockholders have the option of selling their shares, so as to realize capital gains and increase their consumption or to seek alternative investments. In the event the stock has not performed to expectation, stockholders can sell their shares, thus in effect indicating dissatisfaction with management's performance.

If we accept the proposition that equity holders, the owners of public corporations, invest to increase their wealth or economic well-being, then all management decisions should be directed toward this end. Policymakers, in allocating the firm's scarce resources, must seek to maximize shareholders' wealth through the development of strategies that will ensure profitable growth and the survival of the firm. To influence stock value, management must command a positive price for its shares. This is accomplished by ensuring a stream of dividends and a sustained growth rate in earnings, which eventually is reflected in the dividend payouts.

The shareholder, as an investor in the capital market, will set a current market price for the securities of corporations by discounting or capitalizing future expected benefits from owning these securities. If the corporations pay dividends and increase the dividend payout at a constant rate, the following simplified, discounted cash-flow formula will provide an adequate guide for the internal cost of capital to the firm and the investor's discount of future benefits for holding a corporation's stock:

$$P = \frac{D}{k - g} \quad \text{or} \quad k = \frac{D}{P} + g$$

where P = current price of corporation stock
 D = current dividend rate
 g = expected rate of growth in dividends
 k = investor's discounted cost of capital

The k Factor and the Shareholders

The investors, in effect, set a discount rate (k) based on their assumptions about a company's future growth in dividends resulting from a corresponding growth in earnings. This discount rate equates the present value of all expected future dividends per share with the current market price of the company's stock. The k or discount rate for any particular investor would theoretically include allowances for the degree of business risk involved in the purchase of any company's shares. The greater the degree of risk associated with the future of the business venture in terms of its products and markets and the extent and nature of debt included in its capital structure, the greater the k discount rate the investor would ascribe to a company's share.

Expected growth in dividends is at best difficult for investors to estimate with any degree of accuracy. In the practical sense, the shareholders' use of the k factor and management's use of this measure are related to the past performance of the firm as a basis for judging future or expected results. In terms of dividend growth, g is usually taken as the compounded growth in dividends over the most recent five-year period. Many corporations, particularly in the early stages of their growth cycle, do not pay dividends. In terms of the valuation model, as previously stated, such cases would not produce a positive value. In these situations, g is taken as the compounded growth in earnings over the most recent five-year period. Since earnings must provide the basis for all dividend payments, management would use the compounded growth in earnings in computing its internal cost of capital. For example, if a company pays no dividend, its compounded growth in earnings for the most recent five-year period was 10 percent, and the current price of its stock was $30, then:

$$k = \frac{D}{P} + g$$

$$k = \frac{0}{30} + 0.10 = 0.10$$

The positive value of k in this case is a result of the compounded growth in earnings which would be recognized by a potential investor. It can logically be assumed that eventually all firms initiate a dividend policy, and the mix of dividends paid and the compounded growth in dividends, resulting from the compounded growth in earnings, are the major determinants of a company's stock price. This is illustrated in the following example where a company pays an annual dividend of $1.50 and the compounded growth in dividends is 15 percent:

$$k = \frac{1.50}{30} + 0.15 = 0.20$$

and

$$P = \frac{D}{k - g}$$

$$P = \frac{1.50}{20 - 15} = 0.30$$

The k Factor as a Measure of Expected Performance

The cost of capital then becomes a measure of actual and required or expected performance for management. k can be used as an analytical device as well as a measurement standard. Management provides information to the stockholder through its time path in earnings and through its dividend stream, and k serves management as a good financial standard or target rate to measure the results of performance for committed funds or funds about to be allocated to specific investment projects.

In determining basic objectives, management must first consider the firm's k factor, which will serve as a cutoff rate or a hurdle rate of return for evaluating investment projects. The k factor, as the firm's internal cost of capital, is the minimum rate of return that the company must have on its equity financing to leave unchanged the market price of its stock. In this sense, the internal cost of a firm's capital is its hurdle rate. If the per-share value of a firm's common stock will decrease if investments are made at 9 percent, and increase if they are made at 10 percent, then the cost of capital must be between 9 and 10 percent. For example, successful companies in the electronics field have enjoyed high k factors, and in the selection of investment projects for expansion or diversification have set target rates in the 25 to 30 percent range to maintain or increase their internal cost of capital and the price of their common stock. They also sought potential growth in earnings to maintain or enhance their position and set target rates above the cost of capital to sustain the increase in their k factor and stock price.

If the current k factor for a growth company which produces electronic products is 25 percent, then management cannot make major investments in projects which will produce a discount rate below 25 percent without effectively lowering the market price of the company's stock. Such action would signal to investors, who are seeking to maximize their wealth, a change in management's performance and expectations. In effect, the higher a firm's cost of capital is, the more difficult it is for management to make investments which will sustain a high k factor or increase the k through sustained growth in earnings. As companies mature and their growth slows, management usually pays out more of earnings in dividends. A high dividend payout also tends to counteract a lower g (growth in earnings or dividends), which may sustain or stabilize a company's k factor.

The k factor for industries in a growth cycle, as might be expected, is likely to be significantly higher than for industry as a whole. There may also be variance among the firms within an industry, with a range of k factors reflecting loss years for some companies and exceptional growth periods for others. If a company has a relatively low k in a growth industry, it may indicate poor management or unusual external factors which affected its earnings growth.

Mature industries and companies with product lines in the advanced stages of their life cycle are likely to have lower k factors, which are bolstered by more generous dividend policies than generally followed by growth companies.

The k Factor and Industry Characteristics

In determining basic economic objectives, the policymaker must take into consideration the characteristics of the industry or industries the company is in and the nature and extent of its product line in order to set realistic target rates for expected performance. Management must be constantly vigilant of its k as the internal cost of capital to serve as the guideline for project selection; such awareness must guide research and development policies, design for new-product developments, and expansion and diversification strategies. The important consideration for policymakers is to utilize the k factor, which, in addition to representing the firm's internal cost of capital, reflects the investor's valuation of the company and its future prospects in determining whether specific formulated strategies which will require the commitment of the corporation's funds are consistent with the economic objectives of the firm. When management sets its economic objectives for profitability, growth, and survival, these objectives must be consistent with the firm's skills and resources. As previously indicated, well-managed companies in growth industries or companies with well-defined research and development policies intent on new-product development can set high k factors and reasonably expect to attain them. Other firms in more mature industries and those without exceptional skills and resources realistically must set economic objectives at a low level. The knowledge of a declining k is a major factor in promoting growth and expansion through diversification, acquisitions, and mergers.

Limitations to the Use of the k Factor

There are recognized limitations to the use of the k factor which have been treated by various authors concerned with the cost of capital and with valuation models in general.[3] It is also well to recognize that this particular valuation model is, in effect, an extension of capital-budgeting models. If k is known, it becomes the required rate of return in the discounted-cash-flow approach to capital budgeting, substituting for r the rate used to discount the stream of future cash flows expected from a particular investment project which should equal the initial investment. The references made to the cost of capital have also been based on the assumption of static capital-structure proportions and have shown, in effect, the cost of equity capital. For firms that used varied equity and debt instruments in significant amounts, calculations should be made to determine costs of specific components of their capital structure. Once the costs had been calculated, a weighted average cost of capital would be computed. In the long run, however, firms usually maintain relatively constant capital-structure proportions, with expansion financed mainly out of retained earnings. In most cases, such firms are likely to utilize a manageable rather than optimal package of financing. Management efforts are directed toward selecting investment projects calculated to yield more than their weighted average cost of capital. If this is accomplished, the new investments will yield more than the cost of equity capital and eventually raise the firm's stock price by signaling to investors the potential of an increased stream of earnings and dividends.

There are other reference goals employed by management to set economic objectives which are perhaps more frequently used than the k factor. The most widely utilized of these measures is the concept of return on invested capital (ROI), which, taken for the firm as a whole, usually is the closest approximation of its cost of capital. This measure, while it has proved itself as a valuable management tool, is not predictive and does not embody the growth factor, which reflects investors' expectations of a firm's future performance. ROI is also not directly related to the market price of a firm's stock, which best reflects the shareholders' wealth. However, it is still a useful measure for internal use, particularly for multiproduct and multi-industry companies. The PIMS data (profit impact on market strategy) uses return on investment (ROI) as its measure for profit performance. This valuable data bank for strategic analyses is discussed in Chapter 7.

Survival Characteristics

As stressed previously, the k factor provides the best measure of profitability, growth, and survival, the major economic objectives of the firm. The logic of having to make a profit and at least grow in minimal terms to keep pace with inflation and the growth in gross national product in a free enterprise economy needs no explanation. However, there are considerable differences in the

[3]See E. Lerner, *Managerial Finance: A System Approach* (New York: Harcourt, Brace, 1971); Ezra Solomon, *The Theory of Financial Management* (New York: Columbia University Press, 1971); James C. Van Horne, *Fundamentals of Financial Management* (Englewood Cliffs, N. J.: Prentice-Hall, 1974); J. F. Weston and E. F. Brigham, *Managerial Finance,* 6th ed. (Hinsdale, Ill.: Dryden Press, 1978).

degrees of survival and the conditions of survival which any particular firm will tolerate or endure. For the organization which finds itself in a precarious position with technical insolvency or bankruptcy a potential threat, the need to have income exceed expenditures is imperative. The survival goal here is quite clear—it is at the minimal level. There is no need to consider varied levels of returns when the firm is scrambling to keep alive in the short run. If the company in this condition perceives any hope or possibility for a fair return on its future efforts, it is likely to utilize all practical and legal means to survive.

The significant problems of survival arise with the on-going firm which is not faced with imminent failure. All companies are confronted with determining the minimum amounts of profit and rates of return they will tolerate and still continue in a particular kind of business. This applies not only to the company as a whole but also to its divisions and product lines. The overall return of the firm should be looked at, and a goal or target rate should be determined which is compatible with the firm's capabilities and attainable within the constraints of the industry and the competitive environment.

Differences in Survival Rates

Companies which have had a long period of sustained growth in earnings, such as IBM, Xerox, Avon, and some of the successful pharmaceutical and proprietary drug firms and electronics manufacturers, have found their k factors to be very high and difficult to maintain. The higher their cost of capital, the higher their hurdle rate and the greater their difficulty in making investments to sustain their growth in earnings. No firm can be expected to maintain an exceptionally high growth rate for an indefinite period of time; consequently, management must expect to have a lower cost of capital as the firm, its products, and the industry mature. For many policymakers, the average industry k factor may not be sufficiently attractive or offer the incentive to keep the firm intact. Without the prospect of R&D innovations or technological breakthroughs, the management of such an enterprise usually seeks diversification or tries to effect some combination which will enhance its share price. Other management groups may find an 8 to 10 percent k factor acceptable within the bounds of the industry and environmental constraints and/or the firm's skills and resources. Consequently, there is a varied range of acceptable rates for the cost of capital within our industrial complex.

It is clear from an examination of the average cost of capital and the ROI rates of various industries that firms will of necessity have different survival rates (defined as the minimum rate below the firm's cost of capital which management will tolerate), just as they have different stated k factors or profit goals. Tradition, inertia, and the "hope for a better day" sometimes permit enterprises to survive despite an unattractive profitability rate. This kind of "entrepreneurial coasting" frequently leads the firm into difficulties with the passage of time. The lack of incentive and a dim future complicates the day-to-day management task. Unattractive investment returns have a tendency to forestall needed technological improvements and thus reduce the firm's competitive position. This lack of profitability may also complicate the task of recruiting and holding good managers.

Interdependence and Complementarity

Many of the pitfalls are also apparent in the case of divisions or product lines which fail to measure up to a company's k, or cost of capital. But here the problem is complicated by the frequent interdependence of divisions and product lines within an organization. Whether it is true or not, it is relatively easy to justify divisions or product lines which earn at a rate well below the company's stated survival rates on the basis of their contribution to overhead, space utilization, and vertical integration as well as the need for them to complement the company's other products and services. To effectively forestall the continuation of product lines and divisions which have a lower cost of capital than the firm as a whole, management should calculate a survival rate designed to include product or division complementarity. For example, if the return on product A is calculated at 15 percent and is above the cost of capital for the firm as whole, and if product B has a rate of 10 percent, which is below the cost of capital, the question of survival for product B must be considered by management. If the sales of product A are complemented by the market presence of product B, then management should calculate a complementary return for product A which incorporates the extent of dependence of product A on product B. This kind of calculation would lower product A's return but would be a more realistic appraisal of its earning power. It would also more clearly state the necessity for retaining product B, which earns at a rate below the cost of capital for the firm as a whole. If such analysis proved that the amount of complementarity product B extended to product A was minimal, then management would have to consider dropping product B.

In selecting survival rates, it must be pointed out that all multiproduct and divisionalized enterprises have an array of rates, with the likelihood of considerable variation. Companies of any size and complexity are constantly seeking new investment opportunities and facing the difficult decision of when to phase out product lines or even particular divisions or subsidiaries. A predetermined survival rate will serve as an effective guideline in constantly directing management's attention to its k factor.

Failure to Act on Survival Rates

There are many examples in industry of where policymakers waited too long to shift or change the nature of their businesses because of a low or declining rate of return. In the 1950s, prior to a wave of acquisitions and mergers, it was not uncommon to find clothing manufacturers earning less than 5 percent on invested capital. This toleration of a minimum survival rate was due in part to the attitude of managements which recognized the possibility of greater return in other ventures but were reluctant to liquidate or consolidate their enterprises because of personal objectives, tradition, and long memories of the excellent profits of bygone years. It was also not uncommon to find companies holding on to divisions or product lines which earned a return considerably less than the overall company rate. Sometimes this was due to the phasing-out concept, which some managements frequently mention as the reason for the continued existence of a below-average earning unit. Companies have been known to take 20 years to phase out a product or service. Attachment and personal interest may sometimes overrule good business judgment concerning a survival rate, particularly if a division or a product has had a long and profitable history prior to its decline.

> One large and prominent manufacturer, which was number one in several areas of its industry, entered a completely different business as a diversification move. The new division suffered losses for a period of years. Even after it made a profit, the return was in the 2 to 3 percent range, while the other divisions of the company consistently earned 11 to 14 percent on invested capital.
>
> Disposing of this division was the subject of frequent policy-level discussions. Efforts in this direction were always stymied, however, by the fact that the executive who directed the acquisition of the marginal division was revered in company history and had been credited with developing the other divisions to industry leadership. Twenty years after the acquisition, this division was finally sold, a belated recognition of the fact that it consistently earned at a rate 10 percent below the company's determined survival rate.

We can, of course, find many other examples of companies that liquidated businesses, divisions, or product lines because they did not measure up to the stated survival rate. This has been particularly true of growth companies which have measured their success in the marketplace on the basis of a stated sustained rate of growth in earnings and stock price.

Establishing the Use of the *k* Factor

The foregoing is not intended as a brief encounter with the fundamentals of financial management, which the student or manager can better acquire from any finance textbook, but rather to establish the often-used k factor as a tool for management decision making and relate it to the fundamentals of policy formulation. If we accept the maximization of the shareholders' wealth as the major mission of management, then the use of k becomes significant to the policymaker as an instrument which unifies the specific allocation of resources to various investment projects and provides a view of the value of the firm as a single entity.

DEVELOPING THE ROOT STRATEGY OF THE FIRM

The root strategy of an organization is determined over time and is a composite of basic economic and business objectives expressed in terms of the specific allocation of the firm's skills and resources in the marketplace. This primary, multifaceted phase of the policymaking process is undoubtedly more difficult to delineate and lends itself more to conceptualization than the more pragmatic phases of *implementation, organization,* and *interpretation,* where operating, organizational, and control strategies are developed. The root strategy describes the kind and type of business the enterprises will engage in and the nature and extent of the commitment of its skills and resources.

In the initial stages of development of the business enterprise, the root strategy is usually easily discernible. For example, the Polaroid Land Camera Company, which enjoys international success, was organized to exploit the invention of Dr. Land. He had created a camera which not only took photographs but also developed the pictures in a matter of seconds. This product was, of course, unique and warranted a distinct niche in the marketplace. The major skills and resources of the company at its inception were based on Dr. Land's invention and the obvious potential demand which existed for such a product. To be successful with its product, the Polaroid Company had to develop operational strategies in terms of production, marketing, and financing to support its root strategy. An organization had to be formed and structured to accomplish the expressed objectives of the newly formed company. While the root strategy of Polaroid was firmly determined by its innovative product, operational strategy had to be developed through time and experience in the marketplace.

Other large industrial organizations which are part of our economy today stemmed from a scientific method or discovery or from clearly discernible skills and resources. The formation of the Ethyl Corporation is an example which parallels Polaroid in terms of its initial stages of development. The company was formed originally as a joint venture of General Motors and the then Standard Oil Company of New Jersey to exploit the discovery of tetraethyl lead, a compound or gasoline additive which produced an even burning of fuel, thus reducing engine knocking and effectively raising the octane of the gasoline. The purpose and objective of this company at its formation were simply stated: "solely to produce and market lead additives for gasoline used in motor vehicles." The major skill and resource the company had, of course, was the chemical discovery of how to make tetraethyl into a compound which could be added to gasoline to produce the favorable market effect of enabling the fuel to burn evenly and thus more efficiently. Like Polaroid, the Ethyl Corporation had to develop operational strategies and an effective organization to support its root strategy.

It is not difficult to isolate the formulation phase or to delineate the root strategy of a firm in its initial stages of development. While a comprehensive plan may not be formalized in the formative stages of a business enterprise, the originators of any company must have a good idea of the basic niche they intend to occupy in the marketplace, whether it be for goods or services. The start of most business endeavors is based on specific skills and resources of the entrepreneurs, either real or imagined. In most instances, considerable thought is given in the formulation phase to the economic service or function the embryonic enterprise will provide for society. The strength or vitality of the need to be filled is the major external determining factor for the survival of the firm; the degree of "uniqueness" or extent of innovation present in the goods or services offered by a business enterprise in the primary phases of its life cycle will be readily apparent and will provide the foundation for the enterprise's successful operation.

An example of a well-defined root strategy and strategic design of a successful company is illustrated in a report to the shareholders of Medtronic Inc.,[4] an organization that can generally be classified as a health care company providing cardiac pacing and services (see Exhibit 6-1).

DEFINING THE ROOT STRATEGY IN THE ON-GOING FIRM

The necessity of defining the purpose and nature of a beginning business is evident. However, when the policymaker or student of business policy attempts to delineate the root strategy or basic characteristics of the going concern, the task becomes more complex and difficult. The size and maturity of the enterprise in many cases tend to obscure its original intent in entering the marketplace. The multiple stages of growth and the shifts in strategy and direction necessitated by the changing economic environment complicate the job of tracing the origin of specific strategies and differentiating between the various stages of the policymaking process.

For example, Sears, Roebuck and Company, the largest and one of the most successful merchandising organizations in the world, has enjoyed steady growth in sales and profits over the years. The success of Sears has been based

[4] From the *Annual Report to the Stockholders,* Medtronic Inc., 1980.

EXHIBIT 6-1
REPORT TO THE SHAREHOLDERS OF MEDTRONIC INC

DISCUSSION OF GOALS AND PERFORMANCE

The following business and financial goals have been published in our annual report for the past five years. They are important in planning and evaluating Medtronic performance over the longer-term and should not be viewed in the context of a single year. Thus, in any given year we can expect to exceed or fall short of some of the goals. They are subject to annual review and revision. Aspects of the goals are discussed throughout the report.

Business Goals
The bulk of our resources and energies—financial, technological and management—will be directed toward cardiac pacing products and services. The cardiac pacing industry is growing and changing rapidly due to major technological ad-

vances. Therefore, the majority of our research and development and capital expenditures are directed to this business area. Cardiac pacing related sales cover implantable pulse generators; pacing leads; instrumentation for diagnosis, analysis and programming; external pacemakers and patient follow-up services.

We must ensure that our position in this business is one of product and marketing leadership. Last year the market underwent a major transition to multiprogrammable pacemakers led by Medtronic's Spectrax^{TM}-SX system. We believe the next major shift will be toward physiologic pacing. Medtronic has advanced produced programs in clinical evaluation and production which will lead the market later this year in this highly sophisticated new market segment.

Compound annual revenue and earnings per share growth from our present business should be approximately 20 percent. Compound sales growth over the past five years is 19.3 percent. Earnings per share grew 25.1 percent over the same period. Last year sales increased 16 percent, while earnings per share were up seven percent.

Continued emphasis will be placed on the multinational character of our business with the long-term objective of achieving a stronger position in key market areas throughout the world. Medtronic is the leading cardiac pacing company worldwide. This position is manifested by holding the leading market share position in eight out of the ten largest markets in the world, including the top three. Programs are focused on enhancing our position in these and other countries with our entire range of products and services.

Diversification will be a major area of attention, with opportunities pursued through internal development and acquisitions, but limited to the health care field. Our diagnostic imaging, neurological device and heart valve business areas grew 44 percent last year. They reflect Medtronic diversification across a spectrum from screening and diagnosis to therapy and treatment and to monitoring and follow-up. The latter is represented by our Cardiocare heart monitoring service which is part of cardiovascular operations.

We will continue to invest in areas promising long-term commercial success. Our major thrusts are to expand pacing to a broader cardiovascular base, and to pursue new applications and implantology and electrical stimulation technologies. Major programs are well along in tachyarrhythmia control, defibrillation, drug administration, movement disorders and ambulatory monitoring.

Financial Goals

The return on average shareholders' equity is targeted to exceed 20 percent. The return on shareholders' equity for 1981 was 21.9 percent. Return on equity for the past five years has averaged 19.5 percent. Return on equity is calculated by dividing net earnings by average equity.

Growth in investment should approximate 20 percent annually, exclusive of acquisitions. Investment increased to $241 million from $206 million during the year, an increase of 17.4 percent. Over the past five years compound growth in investment was 20.1 percent. Investment is defined as year-end total assets less non-interest bearing liabilities and is not expected to increase at the same rate each year.

The capital structure will consist primarily of equity, with interest-bearing debt as an alternative which, over a period of years, should not exceed 20 percent of total investment. Total interest-bearing debt at year end was $32 million, down from $33 million last year. Debt was 13.3 percent of investment compared to 16.1 percent a year ago.

Dividends will be equal to approximately 20 percent of the previous year's net earnings. Four quarterly dividends of 12 cents were paid during the year. On June 24, 1981 Medtronic's board of directors raised the quarterly dividend to 14 cents per share.

on its long-standing root strategy of relatively low prices for quality merchandise and good service. In recent periods, however, Sears's growth has been slowed and profits have declined. While there were many problems affecting the company's growth, such as a recession and adjustments to sheer size, many observers have attributed Sears's slowdown to an identity crisis. The company has, in recent years, upgraded its merchandise to attract customers in the higher-income brackets and to take advantage of the increase in discretionary incomes on a national scale. While the higher-priced merchandise attracted some buyers, observers claimed it drove away traditional low-income shoppers and confused the image of Sears in the minds of many of its customers. Some retailers claimed that the buyers in the upper-income bracket did not associate Sears with higher-priced and fashion merchandise at competitively low prices. There is no doubt that Sears maintained many of its traditional customers and added new shoppers seeking quality merchandise in the higher-price brackets. The question for the student of business policy, however, is whether or not this change represented a transitional strategy which would eventually change Sears's root strategy into that of a distributor of higher-quality and higher-priced merchandise or whether it merely is indicative of a change to accommodate a broader segment of the buying public.

There is no doubt that K Mart discount stores, one of the fastest-growing retail chains, cut deeply into Sears's retail business. Other discount chains also attracted the "old line" Sears customers with their more attractive pricing. In recent years the profits of Sears have come mainly from its Allstate insurance subsidiary. This factor plus the decline in retail earnings and recent loss years prompted management to diversify heavily into financial services, which have been augmented by the recent acquisition of a large brokerage firm and the nation's largest real estate broker.

Acquisitions, mergers, diversification attempts, and product proliferation engaged in over time blur and confuse the image of the enterprise. Frequently attempts to describe and trace the root strategy of the large, multiproduct, multidivisional, and conglomerate-type corporations defy conventional analysis and necessitate reverting to basic economic objectives to find a unifying link for the varied enterpreneurial efforts. The task of defining root and operational strategies is frequently restricted to the separate companies, divisions, or product lines which make up the enterprise.

TRANSITIONAL STRATEGIES

As indicated in the Sears case, large, successful business organizations are constantly seeking new opportunities and reacting to environmental changes which call for the reformulation or redesign of their strategic plans. Consequently it is not unusual to find companies in a state of transition as they gradually move from one distinct root strategy of long standing to the development or formulation stages of a new root strategy. In this process, they usually devise a transitional strategy which will allow management to "test the water" in the marketplace to determine the feasibility of redesigning the firm's strategic plan through significant changes in product and/or market scope or distinct new ventures developed through expansion or acquisition. The gradual development of a strategic design change resulting in the redefining of a firm's root strategy through a transitional stage also allows a company to maintain a position in its markets of long standing and maintain a haven for retreat in the event a new venture proves to be unattractive or unsuccessful.

Northwest Industries offers an interesting example of a transitional strategy. The company was formed or developed out of the North Western Railroad and its properties. The railroad experienced the usual problems in the industry of low return on invested capital and a number of years with significant losses. New management took advantage of the railroad's high cash flow and loss carry-forward to acquire a number of independent companies producing such products as wearing apparel and footwear, automotive and industrial batteries, steel pipe and fluorescent lamp ballasts, and chemical products such as pesticides and flame retardants for agriculture and industry. Northwest also became the exclusive importer and selling agent of Cutty Sark brand Scotch whiskey and wines of the Baron Phillippe de Rothschild, S. A. These acquisitions, as indicated, made the organization a holding company of diverse operating subsidiaries including the railroad. When the new enterprise had been established and its direction firmly indicated, the railroad operation was sold to the railroad employees. The new highly diversified holding company operation was, of course, predicated on an entirely different root strategy from the strategy of operating a railroad.

TRANSITION FROM OPERATING TO ROOT STRATEGY

There are many examples of firms which through a gradual transition develop an operating strategy into a root strategy either by a distinct predetermined reformulation or by "drift strategy." Procter and Gamble,[5] the highly successful producer and marketer of household products, moved from the production and sale of soap, detergent, and cleanser products to the manufacture and distribution of a diversified line of cleansing products, food products, and paper products. P&G, as the largest manufacturer and marketer of cleansing products, was a major supplier to so-called grocery and drugstores. When supermarkets—mainly owned and operated by large regional and national chains—replaced the small grocery stores, P&G became a product supplier to these outlets. The concentration of the retail selling of food and other household products offered exceptional marketing opportunities to P&G, which already dominated the market in the soap-detergent-cleanser field.

As the supermarket distribution system grew nationally, P&G gradually

---

[5] See the *Clorox* case, Part Eight.

changed its basic root strategy through product-line extension from a producer and marketer of soaps, detergents, and cleansers into that of a mass marketer of household products distributed almost exclusively through supermarkets. This new articulation of a root strategy provided the impetus for acquisition and extension of the company's product lines into coffee, cake mixes, snack foods, and paper products to supplement the long line of cleansing products sold off the supermarket shelves. In effect, P&G converted what is normally thought of as an operating strategy, the distribution channel for its products, into a basic concept and distinct root strategy. After the conversion, the key to strategic planning for the growth and development of P&G was based on the concept of mass marketing a relatively low-priced quality consumer product line through supermarkets, the synergistic utilization of one of the nation's largest advertising budgets, plus the advantages of high manufacturing productivity and expertise in the purchasing of raw materials.

Avon products, a leading distributor of cosmetics and beauty care preparations, illustrates a case of transition from operating to root strategy which occurred early in the company's development.[6] Avon, like P&G, derived its distinctive root strategy from its distribution system. The firm originally began operations in 1866 as the California Perfume Company, and early in its history marketed its products on a door-to-door basis—a common and accepted form of distribution at the turn of the century. The president of Avon at the time was reputed to have given a sample case of perfume to a woman employee who, in effect, became the first "Avon lady," pioneering the selling network which eventually became a major asset.

Over time, the company developed a marketing concept with a highly specialized distribution system based on the Avon lady. The Avon lady was not considered an employee but rather a representative of the company, an independent businesswoman who made her own hours, received no salary, and was paid a flat commission based on sales. The concept made it clear that the Avon lady was more than a salesperson, she was the company's distribution system.

Each Avon lady had an exclusive sales territory in her own neighborhood, and, acting as an independent entrepreneur, she ordered merchandise from Avon, sold the products to her customers, delivered the orders to the customers, and collected the money. When the Avon lady delivered the orders and collected for them, she had another sales opportunity. The company developed a cycle of 26 two-week selling campaigns coinciding with the cycle of sales-delivery-reorder. Under this selling system, each Avon lady had 26 sales opportunities with each customer. Avon supported its sales network with attractively packaged, quality products, designed to please the large market segment of America's middle-class women.

Without its highly individualized distribution system, Avon's root strategy would have to be defined in much the same terms as the strategies of its major

[6] See *Forbes*, July 1, 1973, pp. 20–27.

competitors in the cosmetic and beauty care field, which normally distribute their products through department stores, drugstores, beauty shops, and supermarkets. Avon gained distinct advantages through its distribution concept. Its marketing costs were much lower than those of its competitors, who paid the retailer a margin of approximately 40 percent on top of salaries and commissions for salespeople and demonstrators and for free samples. The bulk of Avon's marketing costs were included in its commissions—of approximately 25 to 40 percent—to its salesladies, who constituted Avon's distribution system.

PERSONAL AND EXTERNAL FACTORS AFFECTING STRATEGIC PLANNING

Many additional factors are important in shaping the corporate image and guiding the direction of the company. The root strategy established over time develops a certain character and creates an image of the firm in the minds of its customers and competitors. Some companies are characterized as progressive, the forerunners in an industry, the firms most likely to develop new products and services. They seek and create new opportunities and assume the risks attached to the innovating process. Other companies develop a reputation for conservatism; they may be averse to taking risks and prefer to make changes and adaptations only when "the groundwork has been laid" and the element of risk in "plowing new ground" has been reasonably reduced by the market action of other enterprises.

The personal objectives of individuals in the hierarchy of management may also be a major factor in shaping the character of a company. For example, a desire to maintain ownership and management control may restrict the size and activities of a business by confining it to its own capital resources. Dominant individuals in management, even in large corporations, may be personally responsible for molding a particular reputation which a firm may enjoy or find a handicap.

The shaping of a corporate image is also inextricably tied to a company's relations with external groups. The manner and method it utilizes to attain its desired place in industry and the consequent institutional social philosophy it develops will have a profound effect on its employees, stockholders, customers, competitors, the government, and the general public. The importance, intensity, and scope of the external relations of business enterprises has significantly increased in the past decade. Ecological considerations, new and complex government regulations, and social constraints have complicated the management function.

EVALUATING BASIC OBJECTIVES AND ROOT STRATEGY

In the determination and analysis of the firm's basic objectives and root strategy, management must constantly keep in mind such questions as the following:

What are the firm's economic objectives? What is its cost of capital, k factor? What are its projected profitability, growth, and survival rates?

What place will the firm fill in the social order?

What need or service will it supply to society?

What market niche or industry position does the firm seek to attain?

What specific products or services is the firm going to make and sell?

Does the firm have a single-product line? Multiproduct line?

Will the firm enter or compete in a new or on-going industry?

What is the nature of the industry structure? Competitive patterns?

Will the company force a technological breakthrough with its product or products?

Will the firm pioneer a new industry?

Are the firm's products innovative and new to the marketplace?

What is the estimated size of the markets the firm is in or about to enter?

What are its growth prospects?

What decisions have been made about the size of the firm?

What share of the market does it seek?

How will it attempt to integrate? Horizontally? Vertically?

Are the firm's objectives compatible with its skills and resources?

What skills and resources does the firm have and need to accomplish its predetermined goals?

What are the strengths and limitations of its skills and resources?

Can it accomplish the stated goals with its financial resources? With its skills and resources in production and marketing? With its organization and personnel?

SUMMARY AND GENERAL COMMENTS

Each phase of a company's strategic design is developed in sequential order whether or not management has a formal or informal strategic planning system. In the initial stage of development of an enterprise the policymaking group must examine the skills and resources of the organization and determine the basic objectives which will shape the image and character of the company. In determining the root strategy of a business enterprise the elementary economic objectives of *profitability, growth,* and *survival* are paramount and supersede the "basic business objectives." The profit objective is taken for granted and is only subject to scrutiny in relation to specific goals and measures of profitability. If management does not consider survival—the continuity of the firm—as an elementary objective, then its strategy will be directed toward terminal objectives, such as a limited venture, liquidation or sale, or conditioning for a possible merger or acquisition.

In establishing basic economic objectives the policymaker must seek a measure which will reflect the profitability, growth, and survival characteristics of the firm. In determining a criterion function or standard of the efficacy of enterprise performance, a valuation model which reflects the increase in the wealth of shareholders or owners of the firm is a logical choice. The following simplified formula provides an adequate guide for the internal cost of capital to the firm and the investor's discount of future benefits for holding a corporation's stock:

$$P = \frac{D}{k - g} \quad \text{or} \quad k = \frac{D}{p} + g$$

where P = current price of corporation stock
D = current dividend rate
g = expected rate of growth in dividends
k = investor's discounted cost of capital

The cost of capital can be used as a measure of actual and required expected performance for management. k can be used as an analytical tool as well as a measurement standard; however, its limitations should be recognized. There are other reference goals utilized by management to set economic objectives which are perhaps more frequently employed than the k factor. The most widely used of these measures is the concept of return and invested capital (ROI), which, taken for the firm as a whole, is the closest approximation of the k factor. As stressed in the chapter, the k factor provides the best measure of profitability, growth, and survival, the major economic objectives of the firm.

The root strategy of a firm is determined over time and is a composite of basic economic and business objectives in terms of specific allocation of skills and resources. The root strategy describes the kind and type of business the enterprise will engage in and the nature and extent of the commitment of its skills and resources.

In the initial stages of the development of a business, the root strategy is easily discernible. Defining the root strategy of the on-going multiproduct, multidivisional company is a much more complex and difficult task. The multiple stages of growth and shifts in strategy and direction necessitated by the changing economic environment complicate the task of tracing the origin of specific strategies and differentiating between the various stages of the policymaking process.

Many additional factors are important in shaping the corporate image and guiding the direction of the company. The root strategy established over time develops a certain character and creates an image of the firm in the minds of its customers and competitors. The personal objectives of founders or the hierarchy of the firm may also be a major factor in shaping the character of an organization.

SELECTED REFERENCES

Andrews, K.: *The Concept of Corporate Strategy* (Homewood, Ill.: Dow Jones-Irwin, 1980).

Ansoff, I.: *Corporate Strategy* (New York: McGraw-Hill, 1965).

Chandler, A. D., Jr.: *Strategy and Structure* (Cambridge, Mass.: M.I.T., 1962).

Henderson, B. D.: *Henderson On Corporate Strategy* (Cambridge, Mass.: Abt Books, 1979).

Hofer, C. W., and Dan Schandel: *Strategic Management: A New View of Business Policy and Planning* (Boston: Little, Brown, 1979).

Uyterhoeven, H. E. R., R. W. Ackerman, and J. W. Rosenblum: *Strategy and Organization* (Homewood, Ill.: Irwin, 1977).

CASES ON BUSINESS POLICY FOR PART THREE

The cases in Part Three provide the student with an opportunity to review and analyze the economic objectives of a number of different companies and to apply the concept of profit maximization, discussed in Chapter 6, to their operations. The cases in this section also permit a thorough analysis of the development of basic business objectives and the formulation of root strategy in a number of diverse business situations in different industries. In the appraisal of the cases, the student should develop an appreciation for the complexity of the policy formulation process. The need to formulate a distinct root strategy becomes apparent in the analysis of cases on multiproduct and highly diversified companies. The cases also expose the student to the effects of personal management objectives and environmental factors on strategic planning.

Mint Flavors

John Reed, a midwest farmer, formed Mint Flavors in 1915 to expand his operations as a grower of peppermint and spearmint plants and distiller of commercial oils derived from these crops. In the early years of his farming he saw the need for an intermediary to provide essential services to growers and commercial users of peppermint and spearmint oils. He noted that the growers extracted and distilled the oil from the mint crops at their respective farms, producing a raw oil which had to be redistilled to meet the specifications for flavor and blendability of the end users. In addition to the problems of processing, Reed anticipated that demand for mint oils would increase significantly in the near future as a result of the continuing population growth and the increasing use of peppermint and spearmint flavors in chewing gum, candies, and various other products utilizing flavoring aids.

Reed reasoned that as the demand for mint oils increased it would no longer be practical for ultimate users to contact individual farmers, contract for their oil, and process and blend the oil for use in the end product. In addition, he thought that the seasonal mint crops were subject to the usual vagaries and uncertainties of any agricultural product, and increased demand would create a more volatile market which would be difficult to monitor for both the grower and commercial user of mint oils. Because of these factors, Reed calculated that there was an excellent opportunity to provide needed coordination of the flow of mint oils from the grower to the end user.

To capitalize on the future growth of the use of mint flavoring, Reed decided to set up his own business as an expert intermediary who would provide essential services to the suppliers and end users of the flavors. He outlined his potential services as follows:

1 He would purchase the raw oils from the growers. In this way, he would monitor the supply available in the season and aid growers by providing a more reliable market for the product.

2 He would inventory the raw oils and save users from having to search for the right amounts and blends. As users realized their needs, they could contact Reed and he could either provide the oils or indicate if they would be available from the next crop.

3 By inventorying the raw oils, Reed could provide any blend specified by the user, and could promise quicker and more reliable delivery of the product because it would be coming from one single source rather than several farmers.

4 He could utilize expertise in the oils from growth to blending, and provide a consistently superior product.

5 His knowledge of the growth of the plants would allow him to aid farmers in planting and spraying their crops and, subsequently, in developing superior plants of consistent quality.

6 He would aid ultimate users in developing the flavor and blendability they sought.

7 He would assume the risk inherent in the raw commodity by undertaking the "intermediary" position and thus gain potential return in the premium he could charge for reducing the risk of the end user and in providing a direct market for the increasing demand and supply.

Based on this concept of service to the grower and user of mint flavors, Reed's small privately owned intermediary operation was established and developed into a viable, profitable business.

OPERATIONS UNDER JOHN REED

Reed's farm was located in the center of the mint crop growing and thus provided him with an ideal gathering station at harvest time for the raw oil and an excellent distribution point for the distilled oils, which were shipped mainly to customers in the eastern part of the United States. The process of producing peppermint and spearmint oils was capital-intensive relative to the amount of labor required. The farmers in the midwest area shipped their raw oil to Reed, who processed the oil according to the needs of commercial users and shipped it to the various accounts. As the business developed, Reed employed his four sons to aid him in the growing enterprise. John Reed remained the primary field contact and salesman. Three of his sons, Tom, Lee, and Roy, worked with the father as field contacts and salesmen. The fourth son, Fred, who graduated from the University of Illinois with a degree in chemical engineering, assumed the production responsibilities and eventually took over the major task of fulfilling customers' exacting requirements for processing and blending of the mint oils.

After several years of operations the sons increased their responsibilities and Mint Flavors became recognized as a family-owned and managed business of the highest integrity with a reputation for efficient and honest operations. This was an attractive quality for both the farmer growers and the commercial buyers of mint oils.

The nature of the operations of Mint Flavors did not require an elaborate organization, and the close relations of the family members permitted informal organizational relationships and managerial style. The objectives of the company were simple since it was a family-owned enterprise. John Reed frequently stated:

> The prosperity of the family depends upon the prosperity of the company, and the prosperity of this company depends upon stable grower and buyer relations. We intend to maintain excellent relations by offering superior quality, not only in our end oil product, but also in quality advice to farmer and oil user.

John Reed did not consider growth as an important factor. He was mainly concerned with having the business produce a comfortable return for all the family members. He realized the uniqueness of the company, and he believed that any commercial user of mint flavors would eventually seek out his firm because of its solid, long-standing reputation. John Reed did not actively pursue new accounts; when requests were made to do business, he would accept the orders if delivery could be accomplished without interfering with the demands of his existing customers.

In line with his conservative approach to the business, John Reed financed all his requirements internally. This long-standing policy was changed only in the latter years of his tenure in the company. New products of existing customers increased demand for peppermint and spearmint oils. This increased demand forced the company to seek short-term financing for the harvest season when all the raw oil was shipped from the farmer suppliers. In this season Mint Flavors' cash outflow exceeded internal cash generation. The loans were paid back rapidly when the refined oil was shipped to the commercial users. John Reed still put strict constraints on the amount of funds borrowed and frequently had to increase his loans for a short period in the harvest season to keep pace with the increasing demand for mint oils from his regular customers. The company did not attempt to inventory oil in anticipation of increasing demand from commercial users.

EXPANSION AND STRATEGIC DEVELOPMENT

Until his death in 1968, John Reed not only ran Mint Flavors but he was also the sole owner. When he died, ownership was equally divided among his four sons and a change in strategy occurred. The sons realized that there was considerable growth potential for the company in new customers (those previously depending on competitors for supply), in existing customers, and in industries or companies previously depending on artificial flavorings, a type of flavoring which had developed prior to Reed's death. Moreover, there was an increasing demand for other oils, not unlike peppermint and spearmint, such as citrus oils, which was a potential area of expansion for the company.

The Reed brothers decided to actively pursue these opportunities since the expertise and funds were available for expansion. The brothers were insistent that Mint Flavors remain a family-owned and managed business. Like John Reed, they believed that they were accountable for profitability and growth only to the family. The projected profitability and growth appeared to them to be exceptionally good. The brothers were sure that continued and expanded uses of the flavor and fragrance of oils of peppermint and spearmint and the citrus oils (lemon, orange, and lime) were inevitable.

There were three domestic and five worldwide competitors of Mint Flavors, and the Reeds felt that the market would probably not support another domestic supplier or intermediary such as Mint Flavors. The basic raw material was restricted by the limited areas in which peppermint and spearmint would grow. Furthermore, the industry required a highly specialized knowledge, and the Reeds were certain that should any firm attempt to enter the market in competition with their company, they would be aware of such a move in advance because of the continuing close relations with both growers and users. This early warning system, they felt, would allow them to respond quickly to potential competitors. Finally, the amount of interaction among the growers, Mint Flavors, and users in search of better-quality plants and growing methods had fostered trustworthy relations which would be difficult for any potential competitor to overcome. The company believed that its market share, supplying approximately 38 percent of oil utilized in the domestic market, was stable and sales volume would increase in proportion to market expansion or remain relatively constant. The Reeds anticipated increased international market share since its competitors entered that market several years later than Mint Flavors.

John Reed was very successful in establishing strong supplier/buyer relations. He entered the market at a time when gum, candy, and toothpaste companies were beginning to realize the desirability and consumer acceptance of the natural mint flavoring. He was ready to supply high-quality, specification oil and was always ready to aid his customers with their blends to assure consumer acceptance of the flavor. This policy established the company favorably in users' opinions. Customer acceptance was a major factor in allowing the company to successfully enter the citrus oil market.

When John Reed died, three of the sons took over the purchasing and sales responsibilities, and Fred Reed, the fourth brother, continued as chemist and head of production. However, the company did not increase its personnel to the extent necessary to assume the additional responsibilities and sheer volume of work resulting from the expansion into citrus flavors and international markets. Mint Flavors did not have a formal personnel department or personnel training program.

EXECUTIVE RESPONSIBILITIES AND ORGANIZATIONAL RELATIONSHIPS

The four Reed brothers were responsible for the major functions of the company. The brothers ranged in age from 53 to 64 and had spent their entire career in the company. (See Exhibits 1 and 2.) Tom Reed acted in the role of the chief executive officer; however, most decisions were made by consensus. Significant decisions frequently took an inordinate amount of time because of some differences of opinion among the brothers concerning the extent of expansion the company should undertake. Roy Reed was interested in furthering expansion in citrus flavors and taking advantage of potential international sales. Tom Reed was not in favor of too rapid an expansion. He felt that the company had entered new markets since the death of their father, and had done very well. He stated:

> We have successfully entered the citrus oil market, and there no doubt is room for expansion for us in this market. We have the funds to carry us a good way; but we must be careful, we don't want to get into the banks and run the potential risk of losing control. I think we should take it easy, go slow for now, wait and see. There no doubt is room for the company to expand internationally, but we should be careful. We now deal with agents, and we have a European representative in London that deals mainly with our mint and citrus oils. We now have about 10% plus of our sales out of international markets.

EXHIBIT 1
Top management team: breakdown of individual responsibilities.

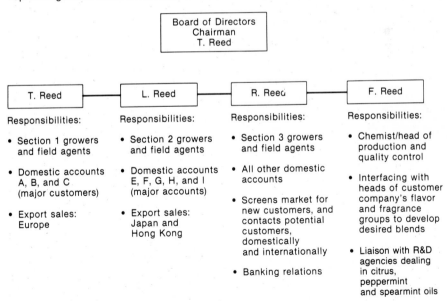

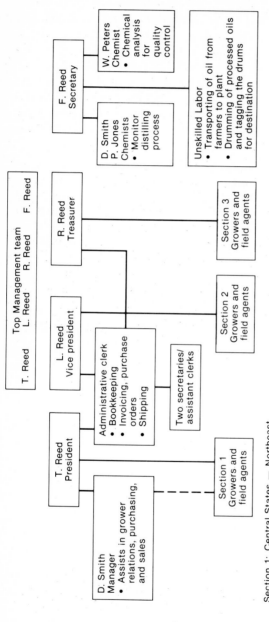

Section 1: Central States — Northeast
2: Southeast
3: West — Southwest

EXHIBIT 2
Mint Flavor, Inc. organization chart.

Roy Reed, as the major contact for new customers domestically and internationally, stated:

> I think we have exceptional opportunities because of our unique position in a unique industry. We can't allow our market share to drop; we must keep pace with the market expansion. While we have some foothold in citrus oils, we have not taken advantage of the real possibilities here, nor have we pushed our international efforts. We have a good cash flow, and no doubt we could always go public as a last resort. I must admit that the movement into citrus oils has severely strapped our executive group and work force. We still have a lot to learn about the citrus oil market. For years our expertise has been in mint flavors.

The board of directors of Mint Flavors was made up of the four Reeds and the company's lawyer. Tom Reed, age 58, was the chairman of the board as well as the chief executive officer. He was also responsible for all Section One growers and field agents, and handled the three largest accounts of the firm. In addition, he was responsible for export sales to Europe; however, Tom did not devote much of his time to this function. Roy Reed put a lot of his effort into promoting all export sales, and was particularly interested in European sales. Despite the titles of Tom Reed, the company operated in a very informal manner. The other brothers frequently made policy decisions which affected their areas of responsibility and often informed Tom and the executive group after the decisions were made.

Lee Reed, at 64 the oldest of the brothers, was responsible for all Section Two growers and field agents. He also personally handled five major accounts and assumed responsibility for export sales to Japan and Hong Kong. Although Lee was the oldest of the brothers, he was still the most aggressive and had developed a special rapport with the growers and consumers. All of the Reeds respected his sales ability. Lee usually expressed support for Tom Reed's views when the question of expansion was brought up.

Roy Reed, age 53, was considered to be the most assertive of the brothers. He was not reluctant to express his opinion about the need to continue the growth and expansion which started after the death of John Reed. Despite his feelings about the need to expand to maintain market share, Roy was an amicable and effective member of the executive group. His official responsibilities included all Section Three growers and field agents and all domestic accounts not covered by Tom and Lee. Roy frequently stated that he enjoyed and found the most challenge in promoting new business, particularly on the international fronts.

Fred Reed, age 55, since his graduation from the University of Illinois with a degree in chemical engineering, had eventually restricted his company activities to the technical side. He was in charge of chemistry and production and quality control. His long experience in the business and the quality of Mint Flavors products marked Fred as an expert in the field. His advice was frequently sought, and he made numerous appearances as a speaker at agricultural association meetings and agricultural courses in universities. The other

Reed brothers had great respect for his expertise. Fred's knowledge and experience was reflected in his success with customers in working on their blending problems and in acting as the company's liaison with both public and private research and development groups which concentrated on mint and citrus oils.

Dan Smith, 47 years of age, was the most important executive in the company outside of the Reed brothers. Smith was a graduate of Indiana University with a degree in business administration. He was born and raised on an Illinois farm near the Reed properties. In his 20 years of service with Mint Flavors he performed a variety of functions. For the past five years he worked closely with Tom Reed, frequently taking over his role when Tom was on extended trips to visit field agents.

Peter Jones and Bill Peters were chemical engineers who studied at the University of Illinois. Their functions were mainly technical, and they performed few supervisory functions other than directing laboratory assistants in monitoring the distilling process and performing chemical analysis for the quality control program.

OPERATIONAL PLANNING

Tom Reed stated:

> While we are in an unusual business, in many respects it is much the same as any other commodity. The market sets the price as soon as it becomes apparent what the crops will yield and what the quality of the harvest will be. While the cost of our raw material varies with the harvest, our selling and administrative costs, and that of our competitors, remain relatively constant as a percentage of sales. Our major problem is attempting to forecast demand for mint and citrus oils. I must admit that we rely to a great extent on our experience and intuition in doing our forecasting, we don't have a formal system, we just pool our best judgment. I don't know of a really formal system of forecasting that is used by any company in the industry. There are too many variables to contend with, so we have to depend on our many years of experience. I don't know how well we would do if we had to depend upon others to make our forecasts.

The Reed brothers were aware of the risks inherent in their business. In addition to the uncertainty of the growth and yield potential of the mint crop, there was also the problem of coping with the growers, who sought the highest price and waited to contract their oil until after the harvest. Estimating the supply, estimating the demand for oil quantities and specific oils, and estimating the price to the ultimate consumer to complete seasonal contracts were annual tasks which consumed a considerable amount of time of the whole executive group.

Beyond maintaining grower and consumer relations and forecasting crop yields and consumer demand for mint oils, the management function was not considered too challenging by the Reeds. The production function was highly automated, and the expertise was in the distilling process to produce the specifications of individual consumers. The raw oils could be held for an indefinite period and processed according to consumer needs when the individual orders were received. This aided the company in balancing their production schedule and reduced the total number of employees required in the plant. Mint Flavors employed a total of only 50 people at maximum, including field agents and the personnel in sales and administration.

The Reeds believed that not assigning specific functional responsibilities, except for production, aided the company in its planning and day-to-day operations. Roy Reed voiced the brothers' concept of management in these terms:

> Essentially we have developed the business, since our father's death, as a management team. All of us are aware of the strategic decisions that have to be made, and we all share in their deliberation. We are not bogged down or overwhelmed by functional responsibilities. We see the business as a whole run by a team of four informed owners and managers armed with years of invaluable experience. Our major problem is in attempting to cope with normal growth and trying to improve our position in citrus oils and international markets, where we have to operate mainly through agents. We must protect our market share and go along with the normal expansion in the flavor business. We have a good financial position (see Exhibits 3 and 4), but if we expand our business in the future, we are going to have to seek additional funds other than our own cash generation. We must pursue growth by anticipating user needs, expanding into new markets, mainly international, and seek out new products that can use our oils. Essentially we must keep up with growing markets and maintain our market share.

EXHIBIT 3
Mint Flavors, Inc. Statement of Earnings
(000 omitted)

	1981	1980	1979	1978	1977
Sales	$ 64,200	$ 59,800	$ 57,100	$ 54,244	$ 51,640
Less cost of goods sold	57,780	53,820	52,530	50,121	48,231
Gross profit	$ 6,420	$ 5,980	$ 4,570	$ 4,123	$ 3,409
Less selling and administrative expense	2,824	2,691	2,455	2,332	2,152
Operating income	$ 3,596	$ 3,289	$ 2,115	$ 1,791	$ 1,257
Short-term interest expense	122	117	95	80	91
	$ 3,474	$ 3,172	$ 2,020	$ 1,711	$ 1,166
Federal & state income taxes	1,667	1,522	970	821	560
Net income	$ 1,807	$ 1,650	$ 1,050	$ 890	$ 606
Dividends paid	$ 150	$ 100	$ 100	$ 90	$ 50

EXHIBIT 4
Mint Flavors, Inc. Balance Sheet 1976–1980
(000 omitted)

	1981	1980	1979	1978	1977
Current assets					
Cash & deposits	$ 784	$ 690	$ 693	$ 550	$ 550
Short-term marketable securities	680	650	580	400	350
Trade accounts receivable	3,410	2,110	2,250	1,825	1,230
Notes receivable, trade	720	787	420	350	335
Inventories, raw & blended oils	4,470	3,970	2,870	2,650	2,600
Prepaid and other assets	40	50	40	40	30
Total current assets	$10,104	$8,257	$6,853	$5,815	$5,095
Fixed assets					
Land, at cost	$ 100	$ 100	$ 100	$ 100	$ 100
Buildings, machinery & equipment	1,510	1,480	1,290	1,290	1,185
Office furniture & fixtures	70	70	50	50	50
Less, accumulated depreciation	(690)	(685)	(678)	(678)	(675)
Net fixed assets	$ 990	$ 965	$ 762	$ 762	$ 660
Total assets	$11,094	$9,222	$7,615	$6,577	$5,755
Current liabilities					
Trade accounts payable	$ 920	$ 895	$ 890	$ 870	$ 880
Notes payable	–	–	60	50	–
Accrued taxes payable	420	390	210	150	190
Other current liabilities	250	100	40	42	30
Total current liabilities	$1,590	$1,385	$1,200	$1,112	$1,100
Stockholders equity					
Common stock, $100; 170 thousand shares outstanding @ $1.00 par	$ 170	$ 170	170	$ 170	$ 170
Capital surplus	50	50	50	50	50
Retained earnings	9,284	7,617	6,195	5,245	4,435
Total stockholders equity	9,504	7,837	6,415	5,465	4,655
Total liabilities and stockholders equity	$11,094	$9,222	$7,615	$6,577	$5,755

Electrom Corporation

In early 1976 the management of Electrom was debating the desirability and practicality of further plant expansion to accommodate their requirements for the production of electronic calculators. The company had expanded its facilities in 1974 and anticipated that additional expansion would eliminate the necessity of subcontracting. Subcontracting had proved expensive to the company in two ways: it directly increased costs by 10 to 15 percent and additionally caused quality-control problems. Sales of electronic calculators—particularly the hand-held or pocket calculators—had steadily increased, and Electrom's share of this market had doubled. But profits in the industry were down because of severe price cutting. Electrom's management was concerned with keeping cost down and remaining in this rapidly expanding market. Despite the phenomenal sales growth of hand-held electronic calculators, the leading marketer in 1973 and 1974, Bowmar, filed to reorganize under Chapter XI of the Bankruptcy Act in 1975. Commodore Business Machines of Canada, another prominent producer of pocket electronic calculators, experienced losses in 1975 despite an increase in sales. Major adjustments were taking place in the electronic calculator industry because of overcapacity and aggressive price cutting. This situation occurred despite the continued growth in sales and an increasing penetration of United States producers into overseas markets.

"We have done well in producing private brands for chain stores, discount houses and other outlets," stated Mr. D. H. Pasall, president and chief executive officer of Electrom. He continued:

We have also expanded our business through distributors who sell private brands for premiums used by financial institutions, food chains, and various businesses. This has been mainly the simple four-function pocket calculators, which has not been our major market. It has enabled us, however, to weather a severe storm. While our margins have been affected, like everyone else's, our sales have increased and we have established an industry position. The demand for pocket calculators is still high and the market continues to grow—for example, sales to the student population jumped 40 per cent in 1975. This is a fantastic market. However, there are many pitfalls. Casio, the Japanese producer, entered the U. S. market in the second half of 1975. Others, no doubt, will follow. Casio came in big with a $19.95 model, but National Semiconductor introduced a similar unit for $16.95, and Commodore has a $10 pocket calculator. Even Texas Instruments, a leader in the field, has brought out a $16 model in an effort to keep pace after experiencing losses in their market. Price competition at the lower end of the scale for the four-function models is ridiculous. We have seen our business in this area decline rapidly since the latter part of 1975. Our profits have declined 45 percent despite an 8 percent increase in sales.[See Exhibits 1 and 2.] Our lowest-priced pocket calculator is $29.95, but it's quality and it shows. However, if we want to hold what business we have in this area, we are going to have to get the price down, at least under $25. Our quality and our models at the upper end of the scale, where the demand is for performance, have helped us to hold our position. Our integration also is a big factor. Unlike Bowmar and Commodore, we manufacture all the basic parts for the calculators. Our early entry into the field has helped us establish a good market position.

Our foreign sales are not significant at this time, but I notice there is considerable price cutting over there. I saw an advertisement for a pocket calculator for about $23 in a London paper the other day. If this is the case, you know a real price war is on and all of Europe will be affected. But like the U. S., it is a big market and believe me, it is going to expand. Despite the price cutting, we must remember we are in a fantastic growth market. We were early in the commercial application of semiconductors

EXHIBIT 1

SUMMARY STATEMENT OF EARNINGS, YEARS ENDING DECEMBER 31
(Thousands of Dollars)

	1975	1974	1973	1972	1971
Sales	$43,444	$39,923	$30,242	$23,007	$18,898
Cost of goods sold	29,871	25,868	17,985	13,948	12,775
Gross profit on sales	13,573	14,055	12,257	9,059	6,123
Selling, administrative, and general expenses	10,969	8,372	7,112	4,805	3,866
Operating profit	2,604	5,683	5,145	4,254	2,257
Add: other income (licensing)	667	515	420	380	350
Net income before taxes	3,271	6,198	5,565	4,634	2,607
Federal tax on income	1,570	3,080	2,675	2,224	1,255
Net income	1,701	3,118	2,890	2,410	1,352
Dividends	0	95	375	300	225
Net income per share	$ .556	$ 1.020	$ .945	$ .788	$ .442

EXHIBIT 2
ELECTROM CORPORATION
BALANCE SHEET, DECEMBER 31, 1975 AND 1974
(Thousands of Dollars)

	1975	1974
Current Assets:		
Cash	$ 2,067	$ 2,520
Securities: short term	200	200
Notes and accounts receivable	5,001	5,213
Inventories:		
Finished goods and work in process at LIFO cost	6,272	6,003
Raw materials, at lower of cost or market	2,573	3,614
Deposits and prepaid expenses	143	114
Total current assets	$16,256	$17,664
Property, plant, and equipment, at cost less accumulated	24,426	20,740
depreciation and amortization	10,100	8,292
Net plant and equipment	14,326	12,448
Other assets:		
Patents	600	600
Total assets	$31,182	$30,712

	1975	1974
Current Liabilities:		
Short-term notes payable	$ 2,800	$ 3,650
Long-term debt, payable in 1976	170	170
Accounts payable and accruals	5,310	5,510
Provision for federal taxes on income	1,570	1,496
Total current liabilities	9,850	10,826
Long-term debt		
Mortgage payable, 6.5% due 1983	560	30
Term note payable, 8.5% due 1978	350	450
Other	–	85
Total long-term debt	910	1,165
Capital stock and surplus		
Common stock, par value $1		
per share, authorized		
5,000,000 shares: reserved		
for stock options, 45,500 shares		
at Dec. 31, 1975; issued and		
outstanding 1975, 3,056,000 shares	$ 3,056	$ 3,056
Earned surplus	17,366	15,665
Total capital stock and surplus	20,422	18,721
Total liabilities and equity	$31,182	$30,712

and microcircuits and we have a continuing strong program of research and development in the field.

Electronic calculators accounted for 40 percent of Electrom's monthly sales volume of $3.62 million. The other major items were transistor radios, 20 per-

EXHIBIT 3
ELECTROM CORPORATION PRODUCT LINE

	Percent of sales		Percent of profits	
	1975	1974	1975	1974
Electronic calculators	40	35	40.0	38.2
Transistor radios	20	25	17.6	22.0
Transistors	13	13	10.4	10.6
Recording tapes	10	11	10.0	10.4
Ferrite cores	6	4	10.5	7.8
Miscellaneous electronic components	11	12	11.5	11.0

cent; transistors (excluding those used in the company's own products), 13 percent; recording tapes, 10 percent; ferrite cores 6 percent; and miscellaneous products, 11 percent. (See Exhibit 3.) Electrom's stock was selling at $14 per share in early 1976. Its 1975 range was 16$^{1}/_{2}$ to 8.

The Electrom plants were located in industrial parks in Cleveland, Baltimore, and Atlanta. Sales offices were located in Atlanta, New York, Los Angeles, and Chicago. Employment totaled 1,850 and the sales volume for the period ending December 1975 was $43.4 million. The company had already experienced three periods of rapid growth, and some members of management felt that Electrom might be on the verge of still another wave of rapid expansion.

ELECTROM'S GROWTH AND DEVELOPMENT

The formation of Electrom in 1955 brought together experienced personnel who provided business acumen and financial resources. Younger men who had already demonstrated promise in a scientific field to which electricity was related brought enthusiasm and scientific talent. Donald Pasall, the president, assembled the resources and provided the day-to-day leadership for the organization both commercially and in scientific product development. The company enjoyed early success through product development.

The company's first products were primarily related to the electrical equipment field and government communication needs. Among these products were inductors, capacitors, resistors, and transistors. Sales grew slowly but steadily in the early periods; by 1960 the company employed 130 people.

In the late 1950s President Pasall, Mr. Talbern, Mr. Smith, and others of the Electrom management gave close attention to technical reports on semiconductors and speculated among themselves on their implications. By that time knowledge of the field had progressed to the point where extensive commercial application seemed to depend upon price. Transistors were priced at $4 per unit in the United States and were used mainly in military applications. About the only commercial application was in hearing aids. Relying upon their experience with electronics, President Pasall and his management resolved to initiate a crash program to build a commercially acceptable transistor radio using Electrom-built transistors to be marketed under the Electrom name. All subsequent products were marketed under the Electrom name. In 1959, 60 percent of the Company's engineering force had been mobilized for the task. The first Electrom transistors were produced in late 1959, and the company's first all-transistor radio followed in early 1960. The necessary licensing arrangements had been made with the Western Electric Company, and preparations for commercial products were started. The first Electrom transistor radio, a five-transistor set, went on the market in October 1960. Sales were limited by the selling price, however, and no attempt was made to export the product to Europe.

Electrom scientists and engineers continued to work on improving the quality and size characteristics of the transistor radio. In April 1962 these efforts were rewarded with the company's first all-transistor superheterodyne radio with build-in dynamic speaker. It employed six transistors and retailed for $40. The growth of Electrom from April 1962 to April 1965 was almost wholly attributable to the company's output of both high-quality transistor radios and electrical and mechanical calculating machines. During these four years, Electrom production of radios tripled and production of calculating machines quadrupled. Sales volume increased from approximately $95,000 per month to over $835,000. To meet demand, the company's line of transistor radios was broadened and by April 1964 included 15 production models. Among these was a 12-transistor AM/FM model, one of the first commercial models of its kind. The new radio was introduced in the summer of 1963 and was well received in the marketplace.

Electrom's sales of transistor radios increased significantly until competition from imports, mainly Japanese, became too intense. The company had some competitive advantages, however, since it produced its own transistors and had established a position in the quality market. Electrom maintained a good market position until after 1966, when sales and profits for their transistor radio line declined. The import of radios increased steadily in this period and in 1976 accounted for over 95 percent of the home radio market in the United States. Many United States producers used overseas facilities for the manufacture of essential radio parts, such as transistors, and some also assembled radios in these facilities. Electrom preferred to use its own United States manufacturing facilities and concentrated on a small segment of the quality and specialty market. The company's experience with transistor radios proved to be very valuable in the manufacture and marketing of calculators.

The intensity of competition in the transistor and transistor radio market and management's awareness of opportunities in the electronic calculator field resulted in the company redirecting its research efforts.

Development of the Electronic Calculator Line

In 1966, Mr. Pasall became convinced of the commercial possibilities of electronic calculators and urged his management to mobilize a special research group to initiate designs and manufacturing processes for a new line of electronic calculators. A task force of physicists, mathematicians, electrical engineers, and mechanical engineers was assembled to develop a commercially feasible means of producing the new product. Since this group constituted about 50 percent of the company's engineering and scientific personnel at the time, the use of the task-force idea in the hope of achieving success ahead of competition represented something of a gamble on the part of management. Production of desk-top calculators in commercial quantities and quality was initiated in mid-1968.

The developments of Electrom's engineers were not immediately rewarded with success in the marketplace, however. Since competition was intense, a vigorous advertising campaign of approximately $620,000 was undertaken to gain acceptance by placing ads in technical, trade, and business magazines, as well as newspapers, and promoting sales to educational institutions. These campaigns were followed by products designed especially for use in office work in business and government. Particularly successful was the Electrom effort to apply electronic calculators to accounting and engineering education. This was followed by a broadening of the market as the "professional" models of electronic calculators were supplemented by lower-cost models designed for home use.

As a result of its efforts, Electrom was one of several domestic producers of five multipurpose electronic calculators in 1971. Competition was strong, and by early 1972 there were 40 producers of electronic calculators with essentially the same capabilities as Electrom's; in 1975 this number was down to 20. The five largest producers together supplied about 60 percent of the market for calculators. By 1975, Texas Instruments had gained control of 30 percent of the market for hand-held calculators.

Electrom produced a range of electronic calculators, from the simple, low-priced, four-function pocket calculators to the more sophisticated scientific pocket and desk-top models used for specific office work and in educational institutions. Pocket calculators accounted for over 60 percent of Electrom's total calculator sales, replacing the desk-top models as the sales leader. Electrom's calculators averaged approximately $90, with a range from $29.95 to $350 for its advanced multifunction scientific desk-top model. The average price received in 1974 for Electrom's calculators was $100. In this year Electrom had a greater percentage of sales at the upper range, and price cutting was far less severe than it was in 1975. Management expected the average unit price for its calculators to continue to decline, however. In addition to the four-function pocket model, Electrom produced four additional hand-held pocket units that performed multifunctions, had memories, and could display 10 significant digits as well as 2 exponential digits. The company had both pocket and desk-top models which performed arithmetic, trigonometric functions and conversions, and logarithmic and exponential functions and constants. Electrom, however, did not have any fully programmable calculators.

Continuing Research Efforts

As a corollary to its work with electronic calculators, Electrom developed a patented process for making high-quality ferrite cores for computer storage and other uses. Commercial production of these cores began in 1976 in a 15,000-square-foot factory which had been constructed for this purpose in an industrial park near Atlanta. The location was selected because of its proximity to a university where much of the research was undertaken and because of the availability of low-cost electric power needed in the ferrite reduction process. The company had limited success in marketing the cores; however, management felt it could, through increased effort, establish a market position.

As a result of its continued efforts, the company had new product lines in various stages of development, such as oscillators, voltmeters, wave-form analyzers, frequency measuring equipment, and microwave and waveguide test instruments. Developmental work under way in 1976 also included programmable calculators and computerized accounting and billing machines.

THE CALCULATOR INDUSTRY

The calculator industry in 1976 was segmented into three distinct markets: (1) general business, 12 percent; (2) scientific/technical, 12 percent; and (3) mass consumer or hand-held pocket calculators, 76 percent. Rapid technological advances in electronics led to development of ultrasophisticated machines that could be programmed to solve the most complex problems and to the creation of micro-mini hand-held units at prices most users could afford. Of the 20 companies marketing calculators, about three-fourths offered business and scientific units, while one-fourth sold only hand-held pocket calculators. (See Exhibit 4.)

Improved circuit technology and new high-speed printing mechanisms greatly improved capabilities while at the same time lowering prices of electronic calculators. In 1976, approximate costs for a digit, for example, was 30 cents to produce the answer display unit; a year earlier the cost was $1 a digit. The cost of the chip was down to $4, from around $20 in 1970. Assembly time was currently estimated at between 5 and 10 minutes, compared to 25 to 30 minutes three years ago. Although desk-top-size units predominated, there were also a number of high-quality pocket-size scientific and business calculators. Special-purpose preprogrammed calculators performed complex scientific and business computations. Models that could be programmed by magnetic cards or by director keyboard entry were fast becoming a factor. Although basically simple to operate, these machines required good software support programs.

The hand-held pocket calculator rapidly became one of the nation's fastest-growing sales items. (See Exhibit 5.) Demand for these units exceeded supply. Portability and low price tags were the prime appeals of the ac-battery operated models. The pocket calculator first emerged in 1970 in the $150 to $350 price

EXHIBIT 4
U.S. CALCULATOR PRODUCERS*
(Worldwide unit sales in thousands)

	1973	1974	
		Low	High
Semiconductor producers			
Texas Instruments	2,000	4,500	5,000
Rockwell International	820	1,500	1,700
National Semiconductor	160	1,000	1,500
Mostok	100	300	500
Nonintegrated producers			
Bowmar Instruments	1,200	1,800	2,200
Commodore Business Machines	950	1,200	1,300
Litronix	180	800	1,000
Summit International	400	600	700
APF	200	400	600
Hewlett-Packard	250	330	350

*Estimated from published data.

range. There were still units with scientific or business capabilities in this range, but the simple four-function units dropped to under $10. (See Exhibit 6.) Users were finding out that a $40 calculator might not serve their needs as well as a $75 or $200 model. Higher-priced, sophisticated models were generally available through traditional office equipment and stationery store outlets. The low-price, mass-market models were being featured by department and discount stores, hardware and drug chains, electronic component firms, appliance-TV stores, audio stores, catalogue showrooms, and variety and gift stores.

EXHIBIT 5
HAND-HELD CALCULATOR CONSUMPTION—CONSUMER AND SCIENTIFIC
(In Thousands)

	1972	1973	1974	1975	1976*
U.S.	3,200	8,700	12,500	15,000	18,000
Europe	400	1,500	3,000	4,000	6,000
Japan and the rest of the world	1,200	2,300	3,300	4,000	5,000
Total	4,800	12,500	18,800	23,000	29,000

*Estimated.
Source: Morgan Stanley Research Estimates.

EXHIBIT 6
AVERAGE SELLING PRICES OF
CALCULATORS ON THE UNITED
STATES MARKET
(Per Unit)

	Retail level	Factory level
1971	$200	$145
1972	125	87
1973	80	57
1974	47	34
1975	37	28
1976*	30	23

*Estimated.
Source: Morgan Stanley Research Estimates and Published Sources.

The vertically integrated manufacturers, such as Texas Instruments, National Semiconductor, and Rockwell International, pushed forward into end-use products such as pocket calculators to capitalize on their cost advantages through large-scale integration technology (LSI). Semiconductor circuits accounted for 70 percent of the material cost of a calculator.

Because of the economic advantages of microelectronics, the consumer market for calculators was considered to have high growth potential. The low end of the calculator market was considered to have the highest growth potential; however, the use of these units promoted the sale of more sophisticated models.

Electronic calculators utilized integrated circuits to perform the basic arithmetic functions, plus square root and memory functions to perform the functions of a small computer. Most units used a simple keyboard for entry, and they displayed entries and results through light-emitting diodes (LEDs), liquid crystal displays (LCDs), planar discharge displays, and fluorescent tube devices. Pocket calculators were available for engineering and scientific applications.

Some models could supply natural and base-10 logarithms, trigonometric functions, and numerous other statistical capabilities. Hewlett-Packard was dominant in the upper end of the calculator market and was the first to introduce a pocket version which had several memory units and could be programmed with magnetic cards. Desk-top and pocket calculators could be applied to a number of business applications such as calculation of bond yields, bond yields to maturity, means, standard deviations, and linear regression analysis.

The larger scientific and engineering calculators performed like small computers. Microcircuits enabled them to perform a larger number of functions than standard calculators. These units could be programmed, and some were capable of utilizing peripheral equipment such as tape drives, printers, and cathode-ray-tube display devices. Some units could transfer data directly to scientific measuring instruments. Major manufacturers in this area included Wang Laboratories, Hewlett-Packard, Textronix, Victor Comptometer, and Litton Industries.

Electric printing calculators were also available as replacements for electromechanical printing machines. Microelectronic components of these units replaced a mechanical calculating mechanism. Prices of these models declined to under $200 as the field developed.

In 1976, United States firms still dominated the electronic calculator market, accounting for approximately 50 percent of world sales. After the original desktop calculators were introduced in the mid-1960s, the Japanese dominated the market because of lower assembly costs. Breakthroughs by United States firms in the semiconductor field coupled with the upward reevaluation of the yen versus the dollar reversed this trend. The Japanese, however, were making a serious bid to recapture market share. Casio, after its entry in 1975 with a pocket calculator under $20 captured 12 to 15 percent of the low-price market. The company hoped to gain 25 to 30 percent within a few years.

Some producers were of the opinion that the calculator market was nearing a first stage of maturity and that it would reflect a seasonal variation in the future. The retailing seasons of Christmas, tax returns, graduation, and the return to school would, in the future, mark periods of peak demand.

ELECTRONIC COMPONENTS INDUSTRY

Electronic components served as building blocks for the production of a wide variety of electronic products for consumer, industry, and government needs. Almost the entire value of the components was included in the totals for these separate markets. Only the replacement part of the components industry represented an independent market not included in the other totals. Electronic components were vital parts of computers, test equipment, and analytical instruments. The large-scale minicomputers would not have existed without semiconductors and integrated circuits. The pocket calculator could not function without a specific metal-oxide–silicon semiconductor manufacturing process.

Component manufacturers had effected significant cost savings for equipment procedures through miniaturization, and the demand for their products had increased rapidly until the turndown in 1974-1975 (see Exhibit 7). Prospects for 1976 were considered to be more favorable. The recession also affected the consumer electronic equipment market as well as the industrial equipment sector in 1975. Government defense spending for electronic equipment, however, increased in this period. (See Exhibit 8.)

Electrom produced conventional electronic components in addition to transistors. These components, including transistors, were sold mainly on a contract basis by the technical and commercial sales staff to nonintegrated produc-

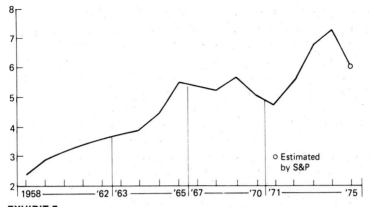

EXHIBIT 7
Electronic components (factory sales in billion dollars). (*Source:* Electronic Industries Association.)

ers of electronic products and equipment. In 1976 Electrom still produced passive electronic components such as inductors, capacitors, and resistors, all of which were basic to circuit design. These devices were discrete components and were not semiconductor devices or electron tubes. They were considered

EXHIBIT 8
FACTORY SALES OF ELECTRONIC EQUIPMENT
(Millions of Dollars)

Year	Con-sumer products*	Industrial products†	Govern-ment products	Replace-ment com-ponents	Total†
E1975	5,600	16,500	12,500	950	35,500
1974	6,185	17,191	11,050	960	35,386
1973	6,921	R15,091	10,800	920	R33,732
1972	6,642	R13,271	10,600	710	R31,223
1971	5,541	R10,891	10,700	634	R27,766
1970	3,683	R11,046	11,295	667	R26,691
1969	4,367	R10,874	12,287	718	R28,246
1968	4,157	9,940	12,563	675	27,335
1967	3,916	9,018	11,720	650	25,304
1966	4,130	5,842	10,330	640	20,942

*Prior to 1971, data reflected products either produced in the U.S. or imported by U.S. manufacturers for sale with their brand name, excluding foreign label imports. Data from 1971 on reflect products produced or purchased by U.S. manufacturers, plus those products imported directly by distributors or dealers for resale. Import statistics are adjusted to U.S. factory values, including U.S. import duties, freight charged from the foreign country to the U.S., and insurance. E-Estimated by S & P. R-Revised
†Telephone equipment sales included starting 1967
Source: Electronic Industries Association.

separate identifiable units which could be inserted into or removed from a system. Inductors were used to control the flow of current by inducing an electromotive force in a circuit to permit a lag in receiving the full force of current or to effectively reduce a current to zero when it was cut off. Capacitors were used to block the flow of direct current and to pass alternating current at a rate proportional to the capacitance value and frequency. Resistors were utilized to impede or limit current flow.

In 1975 the sale of passive devices dropped due to the general decline in the sale of electronic components and to the fact that discrete components were losing their identity by being incorporated in integrated circuits. Semiconductor producers were able to manufacture their own equivalents of these devices.

SEMICONDUCTORS

The semiconductor industry was characterized by significant technological advances and price cuts. New semiconductor devices sold initially at high prices and rapidly declined as production efficiency and competition increased. The average value of a digital integrated circuit, for example, dropped under $1 in 1975 from $17 in 1964, while the performance characteristics and the number of functions increased. This trend was expected to continue because of the emphasis the industry placed on developing new products and increasing yields.

Discrete semiconductor components were separate identifiable units, as contrasted to integrated circuits. These units were produced from silicon materials, which were processed with impurities to form transistors, diodes, zener diodes, rectifiers, thyristors, and other units. Transistors were used as solid-state devices, which employed the properties of semiconductor material to control the passage of electrical current, permitting amplification or switching of the current. Transistors were rapidly replacing tubes in microwave applications and were being employed in electronic automobile ignitions, seat-belt interlock systems, and household appliances. The market for discrete semiconductors declined over 20 percent in 1975, after several years of growth.

Integrated circuits (ICs) combined thousands of components into a single $1/4$-inch chip to perform as a complete circuit. This part of the components market had shown the greatest growth. Digital bipolar ICs, an important part of this sector, were sold to computer and computer peripheral producers and related industrial markets. Transistor-transistor logic components (TTLs) made up the major part of this area. Emitter-couple logic components (ECLs) were used for high-speed mainframe computer logic. Linear ICs were used in a number of applications such as stereo, television, and communications devices. ICs manufactured by the metal-oxide–silicon process (MOS) were an important part of a growing market due to the significant increase in the sale of pocket calculators. MOS devices were also used for core memory applications in some large-scale computers. The use of MOS memory units was increasing rapidly in the computer industry because they offered greater speed and used less space and power. The MOS process permitted more economical manufacturing of

EXHIBIT 9
WORLD SEMICONDUCTOR MARKETS—TOTAL
(Millions of Dollars)

	1973	1974	1975	1976
Transistor-transistor logic	$ 560	$ 700	$ 640	$ 750
Metal-oxide semiconductor	528	725	780	1,000
Emitter-coupled logic	65	75	90	120
Linear integrated circuits for specific application	415	490	490	570
Other—miscellaneous	190	185	170	170
Discretes—separate identifiable units of a single-action device	2,407	2,631	2,500	2,760
Totals	$4,165	$4,806	$4,670	$5,370
Percent change		15%	(3%)	15%

Sources: McGraw-Hill Survey, Morgan Stanley Research Estimates.

larger circuits than the bipolar method by decreased component size and the cost per bit of information.

In the early 1970s the semiconductor industry experienced rapid growth. In the third and fourth quarter of 1974, sales declined, and they continued to slide in 1975. Sales were expected to increase, however, in the first half of 1976 by approximately 15 percent. World markets were expected to expand, with United States producers maintaining their significant market share. (See Exhibits 9 and 10.)

A new development in ICs, the microprocessor, could be programmed like a computer and utilized for a number of electronic tasks. This device was a hybrid of several integrated circuits and/or related components combined into one package using microminiaturization techniques. Hybrids had shown unusual growth, and it was projected that this market would grow by 55 to 60 percent a year. At this rate of increase, hybrids would account for over one-fourth of United States sales of semiconductors by 1980. (See Exhibit 11.)

MANUFACTURING

Electrom added approximately 40,000 square feet to its main plant in the outskirts of Cleveland in 1974. The cost of the expansion was 200 percent greater than the cost of the original building constructed in 1965, when the company moved from rented quarters in Cleveland to establish its main plant and general offices in a new industrial park 12 miles from the heart of the city. It was anticipated that both land and building costs would continue to rise. However, because of Electrom's rapid growth, provision for adequate space for manufacturing, engineering, and research had been a problem, and it was expected that it would continue to be in the future.

The majority of the production operations conducted by Electrom consisted

EXHIBIT 10
ESTIMATED GEOGRAPHIC BREAKDOWN OF WORLD SEMICONDUCTOR
MARKET
(Millions of Dollars)

	1973	1974	1975	1976
North America	$1,907	$2,272	$2,190	$2,600
Transistor-transistor logic	405	530	490	560
Metal-oxide semiconductors	263	370	400	520
Emitter-coupled logic	35	45	45	60
Linear integrated circuits				
for specific application	205	235	230	270
Other—miscellaneous	95	95	85	90
Discretes—separate identifiable				
units of a single-action device	904	997	940	1,100
Europe	$1,004	$1,166	$1,140	$1,310
Transistor-transistor logic	95	110	90	120
Metal-oxide semiconductors	80	130	140	200
Emitter-coupled logic	20	20	30	40
Linear integrated circuits for				
specific application	100	120	120	140
Other—miscellaneous	60	55	50	50
Discretes—separate identifiable				
units of a single-action device	649	731	710	760
Rest of World	$1,254	$1,368	$1,340	$1,460
Transistor-transistor logic	60	60	60	70
Metal-oxide semiconductors	185	225	240	280
Emitter-coupled logic	10	10	15	20
Linear integrated circuits for				
specific application	110	135	140	160
Other—miscellaneous	35	35	35	30
Discretes—separate identifiable				
units of a single-action device	854	903	850	900

Source: Morgan Stanley Research Estimates.

of simple manual assembly work. Metal and plastic components, vacuum tubes, condensers, and resistors were purchased in finished form. These were redistributed (or delivered directly) to subcontractors for the preparation of subassemblies for radios and recording equipment. These subassemblies were then tested and incorporated into the final products by Electrom. A major exception to this pattern was the production of microcircuits and transistors, which were manufactured from basic materials at Electrom. Approximately 65 percent of manufactured cost represented purchased parts and materials, 25 percent wages, and 10 percent other expenses and overhead costs. All manufacturing operations except those involving the production of microcircuits were under the direction of Mr. Rockford, who was also in charge of employee relations and who had been in charge of factory supervision since the founding of

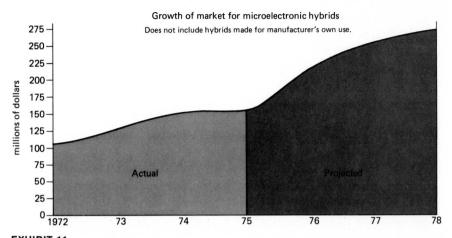

EXHIBIT 11
Projected growth for microelectronic hybrids. (*Source:* "U.S. Markets Forecasts,
1974 and 1975," *Electronics Magazine.*)

the company. The manufacture of microcircuits was under the direction of Mr.
G. Smith, who also directed research in the application of microcircuits.

In commenting upon the company's extensive use of subcontractors, Mr.
Rockford estimated that the organizations presently supplying Electrom had in
their employ about 1,000 persons who were wholly engaged in the manufacture
of components and subassemblies. The number of persons so engaged was approximately twice the size of Electrom's own factory force employed in transistors and microcircuit production. Mr. Rockford thought that the high cost of
land acquisition plus the relatively high wages which Electrom paid its factory
employees made it likely that the present scale of subcontracting would continue; that is, if production were to be expanded 100 percent, the use of subcontractors would expand 100 per cent. At the present level of production, however, Mr. Rockford thought it unlikely that the proportion of work allocated to
subcontractors would be expanded.

In the long run, Mr. Rockford desired to increase the proportion of work
performed within the Electrom organization in order to achieve better control
over quality. He observed that the X condensers were being made by three different small suppliers, and the characteristics of the product of each supplier
were sufficiently different to create performance variations in the final product.
Yet each supplier was producing an acceptable product according to the Electrom specifications and acceptance tests, and no one of the suppliers was large
enough to produce all of Electrom's requirements of condenser X. This was an
example, he said, of the additional type of production which the company
should undertake in its own plants.

Most of the subcontractors were small—the average employment was only
150—and their management had very limited technical and administrative

competence. Electrom had already assigned several industrial engineers to assist these suppliers with engineering design, manufacturing processes, and quality control. Financial assistance was also provided where necessary. Mr. Rockford thought that, in the future, even greater technical and administrative assistance would be required.

About 80 percent of the subcontractors were located within 10 miles. Delivery schedules were carefully coordinated to permit uninterrupted production at Electrom with very low inventories of subassemblies and components. Procurement, inventory control, and production control were consolidated in one section, where visual records of Electrom's schedules, subcontractors' schedules, and inventory levels were maintained.

Electrom subcontracted the servicing of its warranty agreements for radios and calculators on a regional basis. This had also proved to be a problem, and in 1974 the company had all warranty returns emanating in the eastern half of the country returned to its Cleveland factory. This added to the space problem.

The company's production schedules were "frozen" three months in advance of final assembly; that is, on April 1, orders were released for components for radios or calculators scheduled for assembly on July 1. These releases constituted authorization for vendor procurement and for subcontracting as well as for drawing materials, allocating personnel, and performing work within the Electrom organization.

OFFICERS, DIRECTORS, AND PRINCIPAL STOCKHOLDERS

Most of the officers and directors of Electrom Corporation in 1976 had been associated with the company since its establishment in 1955. (See organization chart, Exhibit 12.) Mr. C. Halver (71), chairman of the board of directors since 1960, had acted as an advisor to the company since its founding. Mr. Halver had been the chairman of a large Cleveland bank.

Donald Pasall (55), the president, was responsible for the initial founding of the company. A graduate engineer, Pasall had been involved in research and manufacturing of devices for recording, sorting, and transmitting data since 1946. His last association, prior to Electrom, had been as vice president and director of a company manufacturing measuring instruments. This company was dissolved and Mr. Pasall, Mr. Rockford, and a number of other engineers moved to Cleveland, where they started the research and manufacture of electrical communication equipment. John Talbern (47), general manager from 1955 to 1960 and vice president since 1960, also had been a principal in the founding of the company. A graduate in the physical sciences, Mr. Talbern had been a faculty member of a university prior to the establishment of Electrom.

Peter Doyle (53), vice president and director, was in charge of sales (professional items), patents, and public relations. A graduate of a business school, Mr. Doyle was one of the few members of top management who was not in science or engineering. Mr. Doyle however, had long been an enthusiastic member of the national electronics society and was active in the U.S. Amateur

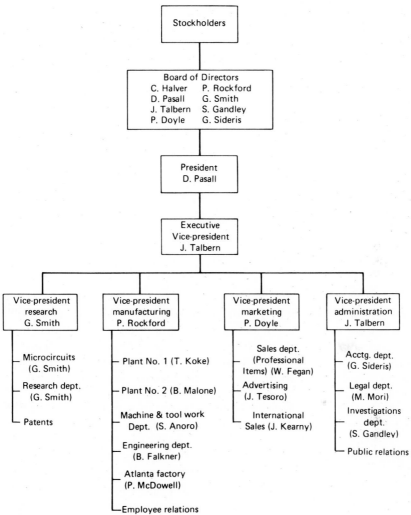

EXHIBIT 12
Organization chart, 1976.

Electronics League. Prior to his association with Electrom, Mr. Doyle had been an executive in the sales department of a large manufacturer of electrical goods.

Paul Rockford (51), vice president and executive director, was in charge of all manufacturing except microcircuits. Mr. Rockford was a graduate engineer who, prior to joining Electrom, had been associated with Mr. Pasall at the measuring instruments company.

Godfrey Smith (50), vice president and executive director, was in charge of the microcircuit division and the research department. A graduate of electrical engineering, Mr. Smith had been awarded a research assistantship at MIT following his graduation in 1946. From the time of his association with Electrom in 1955, Mr. Smith had contributed greatly to the company's programs of research and development, both as a scientist and as a supervisor of such activities.

Stephen Gandley (42), director and manager of the investigation department, and George Sideris (50), director and manager of the accounting department, had equally impressive backgrounds. Mr. Gandley had been an auditor of Electrom prior to becoming a director in 1964 and controller in 1968. Mr. Sideris had been a vice president at the main office of a large metropolitan bank before joining Electrom in 1962.

In 1976, officers and directors held about 40 percent of the company's stock with Halver, Pasall, and Talbern holding 20 percent, 10 percent, and 10 percent of this total respectively. Other stockholders included the Mortin Company and the Salter Company, a metropolitan bank, an insurance company, and an electrical manufacturing company.

EMPLOYEE RELATIONS

The usual personnel functions of hiring, training, promotion and transfer, wage and salary administration, health and safety activities, relations with the union, employee recreation, and other welfare programs were grouped in the employee relations department. Mr. Rockford, vice president for manufacturing, was in charge of this department. Members of the Electrom top management and particularly President Pasall, Mr. Talbern, and Mr. Rockford, were concerned about the future of the company's relations with the employees and their union, even though they considered the present relationship to be good.

Management was particularly concerned about two aspects of labor relations. The first was the increased difficulty of communication which resulted from the increased size of the organization. Only a few years earlier, in 1968, the employees had numbered less than 500; now there were over 1,850. The thought of dealing with another increase of similar magnitude within another three years was not very appealing. To maintain effective communication with even the present size of organization was difficult and time-consuming.

The specialized scientific and engineering personnel who had been brought into the company from time to time to help solve particularly difficult problems were also a matter of consideration. These men had made key contributions to recording tape production, ferrite development, and transistor development. In many instances they had been induced to leave companies or universities in which they had "permanent" status. Since their employment, the company's needs had shifted to other areas of research and development, and some of these specialists had either been unable to make or were uninterested in making a transition to the new fields of inquiry. Management was faced with the problem of how to motivate these men and use them effectively.

FINANCIAL MANAGEMENT

Electrom Corporation's rapid growth had required constant attention to financial planning. Earnings, although relatively good, were not sufficient to provide for expanded working capital requirements or for the necessary additions to plant and facilities.

Mr. C. Halver, chairman of the board, and Mr. G. Sideris, director and controller, had many years of experience in financial management. Their wide contacts in financial circles proved to be helpful. The company used short-term bank loans, regularly paying 1 percent over prime rate. Long-term funds were generated within the rule that at least half the funds should be provided by self-financing from retained earnings and the remainder by borrowing from various financial institutions.

To facilitate financial planning and operating control, a comprehensive budget was prepared annually. The budget was subdivided into semiannual and monthly periods and by departments and divisions. All department managers and division heads participated in both the budget preparation and the periodic review of operating results for their respective units.

The board of directors reviewed budget proposals and acted as the final approving body. The board received monthly reports of operating results, which were compared with the budget and with other measures such as return on sales and return on invested capital.

MARKETING

Sales of Electrom consumer products were made through its wholly owned subsidiary, Electrom Sales, Inc. This organization had its main office at the company's headquarters in Cleveland and branch offices in Atlanta, Los Angeles, Chicago, and New York. Each branch office sold to regional wholesalers who, in turn, provided a variety of electrical goods to shops in their cities.

The sales department was divided into two categories, technical and professional. Technical people sold transistors, ferrite products, and other electronic components directly to communication equipment manufacturers, research laboratories, and a variety of other producers. Professional salespeople sold electronic calculators and calculating machines to a wide variety of companies, the federal government, and educational institutions.

The policy of Electrom was to create a favorable impression as a producer of high-quality electronic products for both consumer and industrial users and to reflect the image of a leader in electronics applications. It was anticipated that Electrom would withdraw from a particular field when competition had driven profit margins down to a low level.

As a result of these policies, Electrom had entered the world market on a small scale. Approximately 5 to 6 percent of its total sales were to the export market. Due to the nature of the products, export sales were almost entirely to the more advanced countries. In 1975, 75 percent of its foreign sales came from Europe, 15 percent from Canada, and about 10 percent from other parts of the world. Electrom used sales agents in its export markets. Management decided that an effort would be made to establish additional distribution channels and to build the Electrom name abroad through advertising and sales promotion.

PRODUCT ENGINEERING, RESEARCH, AND DEVELOPMENT

Approximately 10 percent of sales revenue was budgeted to product engineering, research, and development. Of this sum, about 35 percent was marked for improvement of products already in commercial production, 25 percent was allocated to the application of new uses for microcircuits, 20 percent to the application of new uses for transistors, and the remainder to entirely new products or processing techniques. Perhaps the most publicized recent product of Electrom's research laboratories was a new type of microcircuit "bit." The principal benefit of this effort was expected to come from the lead which Electrom would have in the commercial application of the invention. If the lead pre   o be as great as it was in transistor radios, it was expected that the benefits would be substantial.

The general objectives of Electrom's research and development program, Mr. Pasall said, was to emphasize research of new products rather than products already on the market. In this regard he stated:

> One of the most important things that I learned at a recent conference was the research policy of the Du Pont Company. Du Pont has a clear-cut policy of always exploiting new products. . . . For example, when nylon, which that company had developed through its research, became popular, the company moved on into new fields, receiving patent fees for nylon manufacture. . . . Electrom had advanced by following this policy even before we were aware of its successful application by Du Pont. . . . From now on we plan to keep this policy and to exploit new technical fields. . . . We cannot be merely the keeper of a developed industry; we do not wish to become involved in trivial competition but plan to move on to new horizons.

PATENT POSITION

As a result of its research, Electrom had been granted more than 250 patents, nominally valued at approximately $0.6 million, and had more than 200 applications for additional patents pending. The company had experienced no difficulty in obtaining access to any patented manufacturing process which it had desired to use or to any patented product which it wished to manufacture. Electrom's experience in this regard was probably typical of the radio and electronics industry in the United States. The patents had been so widely dispersed that the industry had long ago been forced to adopt extensive cross-licensing arrangements and moderate fees in order to progress.

EXPANSION PROBLEMS AND FUTURE PLANS

According to President Pasall:

One of the major problems confronting Electrom is the need to establish new production goals for the company's line of electronic calculators. The tremendous scale of expansion achieved during the past year, from 10,000 per month to over 14,000 per month, has brought extensive changes in the composition of our organization, and all of our directors are concerned about the impact of another large-scale expansion and the long-run changes in the calculator market. A doubling of electronic calculator output means the addition of almost 500 people, together with the necessary space and equipment; a doubling of output a year ago meant adding only about one-fourth this amount of personnel, space, and equipment. The business has expanded at a rapid rate, but where are we going to be in the future?

Electrom's directors envisioned the company as an engineering research and development organization. They assumed that the company would progress and grow by moving from one new development or application to another. Mr. Pasall, commenting on this image and in assessing the firm's future, stated:

The success of the Electrom transistor radio and electronic calculator has involved the company in production of a type and a scale which has already altered the character of the organization by adding a large number of "permanent" employees whose skills are suitable only for mass production. Another such round of expansion would tie the company to mass production even more firmly. On the other hand, the sales of electronic calculators have contributed greatly to the company's expansion and profitability. The "sellers market" in high-quality, scientific, and business electronic calculators is of uncertain duration, however, and aggressive price competition both at home and abroad will probably continue. We have already experienced the drastic price drop in the simple four-function pocket calculator market, and it is spreading to the multifunction units. However, I have requested, and the directors have agreed, to omit dividend payments in anticipation of future capital expenditures.

The Trust Company

In January, 1967, the press announced that Mr. Howard Stokes had been elected chairman of the board of the Falls City Bank and Trust Company of Louisville, Kentucky. Mr. Stokes's election was the culmination of events which began in February, 1965, when Mrs. Beatrice Beaumont, the major stockholder in the bank, died. Inheritance tax demands made it necessary for her husband, Mr. John Jay Beaumont, to sell either his wife's stock or some of his substantial plantation properties. He chose to sell the stock. Shortly thereafter Mr. Beaumont, at the age of 68 and in ill health, resigned as president of the bank, an office he had held for 30 years. Following these events the bank's stock dropped to less than its book value. Ten months later Stokes Enterprises, headed by Howard Stokes, announced that it owned the controlling stock interest in the bank.

Howard Stokes, aged 58 and a native of Milwaukee, Wisconsin, was an entrepreneur with widely varied interests. He had started his business career as a proprietor of a dry goods store which he expanded into a department store that also did a mail-order business. Finding his strongest mail-order customer following was in Kentucky, Tennessee, and Missouri, he moved his business to Louisville in 1945. By 1966 he had a thriving mail-order business in the south central states, had 14 small department stores in Kentucky, and kept up side interests in supermarkets, motels, a catering service, a vending service, several real estate ventures, and an accident insurance company.

Mr. Stokes' immediate interest in the Fall City Bank stemmed from his accident insurance company, which sold policies via mail-order catalog and also from booths in each of his stores. The insurance company generated substantial funds for investment. Mr. Stokes had in mind annexing branch banking offices to each of his five department stores in Jefferson County, which he believed would be a ready-made vehicle for attracting depositors. He also had plans for granting consumer credit. In the first years of his ownership numerous changes took place in the Falls City Bank and Trust Company.

ORIGIN AND EARLY HISTORY OF THE BANK

The Falls City Bank and Trust Company was organized by a number of prominent Kentucky families in 1862 to engage in the trust business. These Kentuckians, realizing their tenuous position as a border state, deeded their properties to the Trust Company and made it the depository for their wills. Louisville, originally known as Falls City,[1] was a Union stores depot during the Civil War, an activity which brought it commercial prosperity.

Kentucky was a Union state, but many Kentuckians were southern in culture and sympathies. The original Falls City Trust Company was owned and staffed by Louisvillians of southern family backgrounds. Throughout the Confederacy there were southerners who feared that a northern victory would mean confiscation of their properties, and during the war they liquidated their wealth and deposited the proceeds in banks in Liverpool and Birmingham. In 1868, when the confiscation hazard had passed, the Falls City Trust Company amended its charter to become the Falls City Bank and Trust Company to enable it to accept the deposits of the substantial funds which were flowing back from England.

During the first years of its existence the bank attracted the trust patronage of the leading families of Kentucky. Its banking services were largely an offshoot of its trust connections and were rendered as an accommodation to its trust clientele. In later years its reputation as a trust company became so eminent that when Louisvillians said "the Trust Company" they meant the Falls City Bank and Trust Company. From its founding until 1966 the Trust Company was managed by members of its founding families.

THE LOUISVILLE COMMUNITY

Louisville was the largest city in Kentucky and the seat of government for Jefferson County. It had a population of 382,400, and Jefferson County had a population of 683,300. The metropolitan Louisville population was estimated to be over 800,000. Louisville was situated on the southern bank of the Ohio River and was the largest city close to southern Indiana and Illinois. By virtue of this it was the main wholesale and retail center for a trading area of 47 counties with a population of 1,575,300 and effective buying income of close to $4 billion.

The economy of Louisville was diversified and included industry, agricul-

---

[1] Louisville was originally called Falls City because it was located near a series of falls on the Ohio River which required boat traffic to be portaged. The transferring of passengers and freight gave birth to the city.

ture, commerce, and finance. Louisville was 50 miles from Frankfort, capital of the state, and was the regional headquarters for a number of federal agencies. Louisville was an educational center; it had 11 colleges and universities and was a regional center for the performing arts.

Agricultural activities in the area included tobacco raising, the breeding of beef cattle, and the siring and training of thoroughbred race horses. Churchill Downs, seat of the world-renowned Kentucky Derby, was in Louisville.

Louisville was the United States' largest producer of synthetic rubber, paint, varnish, and whiskey. It ranked second in cigarettes, home appliances, and aluminum for home use, and it was a large producer of farm tractors, household appliances, trucks, chemicals, furniture, printing, textiles, tools and dies, and food processing. In 1971 it had over 300,000 people employed in 850 manufacturing plants.

LOUISVILLE BANKING STRUCTURE

At the year-end in 1967 there were six banks in Jefferson County (see Exhibit 1). Three were considerably larger than the Trust Company. The Southland Bank and Trust Company was the youngest, founded in 1920, and it was the largest, with deposits of $517 million. The oldest, the Kentucky State Bank, was established in 1851 and had deposits of $453 million. The third, The Jefferson County Bank, a commercial bank since its origin, with deposits of $358 million, dated from 1862, as did the Trust Company. There were two small banks, both founded in 1900: the Bluegrass Trust Company, with $30 million in deposits, which did mainly trust business and was located in the affluent suburb of Saint Joan; and the Stockman's Bank, with deposits of $20 million, located at the thriving Louisville stockyards. The Trust Company, with deposits of $150 million, was ranked in size between the two small banks and the three large ones.

The larger banks were full-service banks and had numerous branches; the Trust Company did not have any branches. The larger banks offered extensive

EXHIBIT 1
MAJOR LOUISVILLE BANKS, 1967

	Date founded	Deposits (millions)	Loans (millions)	Branches
Southland Bank and Trust Company	1920	$517	$248	23
The Kentucky State Bank	1851	453	212	26
The Jefferson County Bank	1862	358	194	17
The Falls City Bank and Trust Company	1862	150	52	0
The Bluegrass Trust Company	1900	30	N.A.	0
The Stockman's Bank	1900	20	11	0

correspondent banking services to country banks in Kentucky and adjacent states. They had drive-in facilities and competed for consumer credit business. The larger banks were heavily oriented toward wholesale banking activities and extended sizable lines of credit to major corporations. All of them had divisions which offered full international banking services.

The Louisville banks had grown with the postwar boom in Jefferson County, especially the "young" Southland Bank and Trust Company, which was known to have aggressive management. The Trust Company had also grown during the postwar period, but at a considerably slower rate. Among the banks of Louisville, the Southland was said to have the largest share of large corporate accounts; the Jefferson County Bank was said to be the most liberal loan-maker and did the largest volume of consumer financing; the Kentucky State Bank was said to do a heavy mortgage loan business; and the Trust Company was said to have the most elegant and antiquated banking house and the most exclusive clientele.

THE TRUST COMPANY BUILDING

In 1892 the Trust Company had build a Greek Ionic banking edifice in Jefferson Shores, a prestige neighborhood, in the style which was in vogue for banks at the time. It was opposite the Jefferson County Courthouse. In 1971 the Trust Company, 10 times its 1892 size, was still housed in the same building. The original main banking floor, a showpiece of Victorian elegance at the time the bank was built, still had the same unchanged decor: the marble rails and columns, the plush upholstered furniture, heavy velvet portieres, an abundance of brass ornamentation, and deep-pile carpetings.

In 1938 the Trust Company built a plain, functional building to the west of its main building to house its enlarged clerical operations. It had three floors aboveground, was 12 times the area of the original building, and was connected to the front building by runways at the basement and second-floor levels. The public was admitted only to the front building.

In 1950 the Kentucky State Turnpike was built, crossing the Ohio River via the new Daniel Boone Bridge. The turnpike bisected Jefferson Shores, crossing the city in a way which cut off the Trust Company from central Louisville. This made Jefferson Shores difficult to reach. The area also showed signs of deteriorating.

JOHN JAY BEAUMONT

John Jay Beaumont, who had been president of the Trust Company for three decades, had been described by a friend as "a southern gentleman of wealth and good breeding, a patrician of cultured tastes—and an anachronism in the modern Kentucky scene of today." Mr. Beaumont was acquainted with every "old-line" family in northern Kentucky. He owned several thousand acres of bluegrass plantation land on which he bred Aberdeen Angus cattle and thoroughbred race horses. His wife had inherited a large single block of stock in the Trust Company. At age 38 John Jay became president, and he held the office for 30 years. The most important clients of the Trust Company did business with Mr. Beaumont on a personal-friendship basis. Mr. Beaumont came to be known as an authority on trust estates in Kentucky.

The Board of Directors and Staff under John Jay Beaumont

In Mr. Beaumont's day the chairman of the board had been Mr. Julian Johnstone, head of a chain of Kentucky supermarkets. Mr. Johnstone spent a considerable portion of his time on Trust Company business. He had been described as "a real working chairman, not just a figurehead." The Johnstone board had 17 members, whose average age was 63. Eight members seldom attended meetings; nine members attended every meeting. Among the nine were three senior officers of the bank.

Under Mr. Beaumont it had been the officers of the trust division who were looked upon as having higher status. Four-fifths of them were attorneys by profession; a number of them were considered wealthy. The officers in the banking department were a relatively smaller group and were varied in age and years of service with the Trust Company, as well as in personal backgrounds. Many had come to the Trust Company after learning their specialized functions in other banks. As a group, the Trust Company's officers were paid salaries which were 20% higher than those of the larger Louisville banks. Their caliber was considered to be excellent, but during the 1960s the Trust Company's high-pay policy was repeatedly being criticized by minority stockholders.

Until 1967 Mr. John Jay Beaumont had been president, chief executive officer, and chairman of the executive committee. He was active in banking matters but spent most of his time on trust activities, which he and Mr. William Shermington administered jointly. Mr. Beaumont had approved all lines of credit and loans and had passed on all personnel appointments.

Mr. Shermington, 64, an attorney, was a cousin of Mrs. Beaumont's. He had been with the Trust Company for 35 years and had headed the trust division since 1940. Under Mr. Shermington were six full vice presidents, each of whom was responsible for one or more types of trust accounts. When Mr. Shermington was absent from the bank, Mr. Beaumont assumed his duties as head of the trust division.

Mr. Reuben Daniels, 54, vice president, cashier, and a director, was a graduate of the Stonier Graduate School of Banking. He had come to the Trust Company at the age of 40 with extensive previous banking experience. Mr. Daniels supervised all banking operations but took almost no part in trust activities. He was seldom absent from the bank, he rarely traveled, and his outside activities were limited.

Since 1950 the Trust Company was managed by Messrs. Beaumont, Shermington, and Daniels as an executive team. The officers were sometimes consulted. So was Malcolm Pinney, the chief loan officer, who was the only commercial banker other than Mr. Daniels who was considered to have senior status. (See Exhibit 2.)

By virtue of its association with many influential Kentucky families, the Trust Company attracted to it employees of high caliber at all levels. Young

EXHIBIT 2
Organization chart of the Falls City Bank and Trust Company, 1966.

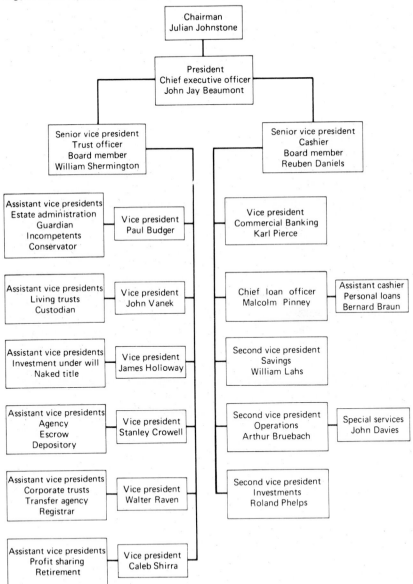

men from old Southern families came to it; many of them had independent means. As a result, there was also a steady departure of the Trust Company's young men, who left to take more responsible jobs with other banks. The bank also experienced a high rate of turnover among its female employees, most of whom worked there only a few years, until marriage. Mr. Beaumont had been proud to point out that the Trust Company had trained more trust officers than any other bank in Kentucky; he asserted that this gave it friendly and loyal connections with scores of other banks.

Savings

Over the years demand deposits had constituted a large part of the total deposits of the Trust Company, but after World War II time deposits had increased in importance. In 1954, savings made up 37% of the Trust Company's total deposits.

During the postwar period, savings and loan associations, which paid higher interest rates, had become popular. Other Louisville banks countered by mounting aggressive advertising campaigns directed at attracting savers. The Trust Company did not advertise, and at no time did it aggressively seek time deposits. After the new Kentucky Turnpike cut off the Trust Company from the traffic flow in the Louisville city center, its savings deposits declined.

Commercial Business

Throughout its history the inclinations of its owners, financial limitations, and lack of specialized personnel had prevented the Trust Company from offering comprehensive banking services with the same depth and breadth as competitive banks. Trust activities had always been considered primary. The Trust Company had developed few correspondent bank relationships. Its staff of savings and banking officers was capable but was much smaller than the staff in its trust division. Lack of branches and limited automation of operations had further restricted its banking activities.

"The Trust Company under Mr. Beaumont has not developed its commercial banking in keeping with the economic development of the region," said Mr. Reuben Daniels. "We have no intention of trying to become Louisville's largest bank. Every year we turned away enough business to keep a moderate-sized bank going. We turned them away because these accounts might require loan accommodations which we would not consider." Mr. Daniels said that there were whole categories of businesses whose patronage the Trust Company did not care to have at all because, as he put it, they were too "volatile." He cited as examples jewelers, taverns, night clubs, and furriers.

The Trust Company under Mr. Beaumont did not have a new-business department. Mr. Pinney, the chief loan officer, had a second vice president who assisted him and who spent about half of his time calling on prospective customers.

Personal Banking

Under Mr. Beaumont's management the Trust Company tended to discourage personal checking accounts. Accommodation accounts were granted to trust clients and the principals in its major commercial accounts. Others were required to make an initial deposit of $1,000 and to maintain minimum average balances of $500.

Personal loans were usually made only to important customers, and also on an accommodation basis. Most of these were collateralized by marketable securities. No consumer financing was done until 1950, when a Ford Motor Company regional truck dealer near Louisville requested some dealer financing. Retail financing was then extended to other auto agency accounts, and later to a large local International Harvester tractor dealer. Other commercial customers who did retail business were allowed to discount their customers' installment notes, but no customer loans were made directly to individuals. During Mr. Beaumont's day the Trust Company did not operate a consumer credit department.

Special Service

For many years the Trust Company had operated a special service department to perform accommodation services, such as clipping bond coupons, buying government bonds, and cashing matured securities. Under Mr. Beaumont these services had been expanded considerably, and customers were using it to purchase out-of-town theater tickets, to make hotel reservations, to anonymously purchase racehorse blood stock, and to purchase travel accommodations. All special services rendered had to be approved by a senior officer. All were gratis to customers of the Trust Company. The department had five employees.

Progress under Mr. Beaumont

During Mr. Beaumont's tenure the Trust Company's personal trust business grew, and corporate trust operations had an even larger growth. The Trust Company had also added a foreign department, which had become well established; most of its transactions were finalized through its correspondent connections in New York, Chicago, or San Francisco. Savings and commercial deposits had grown, but not in keeping with national growth rates. Greater Metropolitan Louisville had seen the most rapid growth in its history in the post-World War II period, and the larger Louisville banks had growth which had exceeded the national averages.

It was during Mr. Beaumont's administration that the clerical operations building had been built and some commercial and savings operations had been computerized. A parking lot had been added, and at the time of Mr. Beaumont's retirement a drive-in banking facility was being considered. A night depository had been installed in 1945. A Women's Finance Forum had been organized in 1952, and a Collective Investment Trust for Qualified Employees (mostly officers) had been started in 1958.

ORGANIZATIONAL CHANGES AFTER THE STOKES PURCHASE

"My interest in the Trust Company," said Mr. Stokes at the time of the purchase announcement, "stemmed primarily from the exceptional fund of talent it has in its staff of officers and employees. With these fine people we mean to make the Falls City Bank the leading Louisville bank, offering every modern banking service to its community." During the months which followed, there were many changes in the organization of the Trust Company.

The board of directors was reduced in size by the resignation of five members, including the chairman. Howard Stokes became the new chairman. Carsten Scheer, financial vice president of Stokes Enterprises, was made vice chairman, with the understanding that he would still continue to occupy his time as general financial director of Mr. Stokes' numerous business operations, spending about one day a week at the Trust Company. (See Exhibit 3.)

Reuben Daniels was elected president and chief executive officer of the bank with jurisdiction over both trust and banking activities. Upon announcement of this, Mr. Shermington took an early retirement. Byron Holowell, a young trust attorney, was advanced over the heads of several trust officers to become a senior vice president and head of the trust department, whereupon two trust officers resigned. Reuben Daniels continued to direct banking activities while Byron Holowell managed the trust department.

Frederick Gardiner, a junior vice president of the Home Acceptance Corporation, was brought into the bank to organize a consumer credit department. Spenser Speed, a 30-year-old assistant cashier, who Mr. Beaumont had described as a "precocious youngster, brimming with ideas and smoldering in frustration," was made a vice president and placed in charge of a newly created unit called the Personal Banking Division, which included personal checking accounts, savings, consumer credit, and branches. Walter Crowley, who was a junior vice president and assistant manager of the new-business department of the Southland Bank and Trust Company, was brought into the Trust Company as a vice president to organize a new-business department. It was rumored that he had been attracted by a high salary.

Under the new administration Mr. Daniels, who had only a passing knowledge of trust matters, tended to give prior attention to banking business and left the trust operations to Byron Holowell. Within the Trust Division there were indications that the vice presidents in charge of the sections—living trusts, corporate trusts, and so forth—were having little to do with Byron Holowell. No new vice presidents were named to replace those who had resigned; their previous assistants acted in their places.

Howard Stokes came to the bank only to officiate at board meetings; he seldom contacted any of the officers personally. Carsten Scheer appeared early every Friday morning, and after visiting with Byron Holowell for about a half-

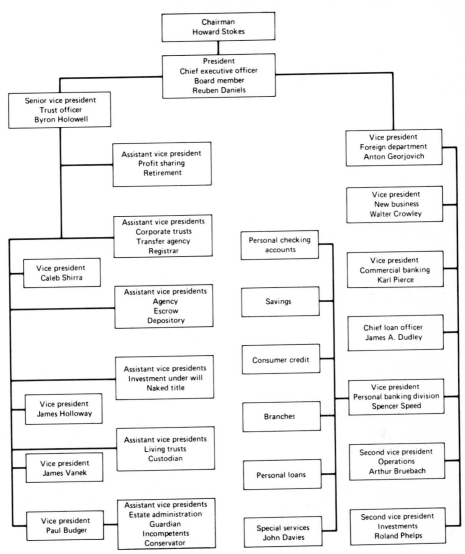

EXHIBIT 3
Organization chart of the Falls City Bank and Trust Company, 1971.

hour he spent the next hour or two with Reuben Daniels, reviewing what had been done in the banking division, studying loans and loan applications, looking over new accounts, and conveying to Mr. Daniels any new suggestions coming from Mr. Stokes. He then made his way through the bank, talking to officers in many departments. "It was a trying experience," said Mr. Daniels. "I was a career banker and I was being subjected to the advice of two men who had never had any banking experience. Often they suggested actions which were nonprofessional. Mr. Scheer's practice of talking to junior officers directly was highly unsettling."

During the period the Trust Company underwent what Mr. Daniels described as "an unreasonable series of audits by the bank examiners which were so severe that they amounted to harassment."[2] The third examination that year was in progress when Mr. Pinney, the chief loan officer, resigned. Two months later Mr. James Dudley, chief bank examiner of the District of Tennessee (which included all of Kentucky), resigned from his office and was elected vice president and chief loan officer of the Trust Company. Thereafter the Trust Company was managed by a triumvirate of Scheer, Daniels, and Dudley.

OPERATION OF THE TRUST COMPANY UNDER STOKES' MANAGEMENT

Two months after Stokes became chairman, the Trust Company opened its drive-in banking service. Three tellers' windows had been built as an annex to the operations building. During the first six months of their operation, two were usually in use. There was no significant change in deposits held.

In July, 1967, the Trust Company announced the opening of a consumer credit department as part of its personal banking service. Extensive advertising in the Louisville trading area invited the public to use the bank for its credit needs—"auto, furniture, signature loans—$25 to $5,000." Automatic credit arrangements were also made available.

During the postwar period Louisville had experienced a strong trend toward the suburbs. Suburban shopping centers mushroomed. During the first half of the 1960s five such centers, ranging from 12 to 70 acres, were built—The Mall, Westland, Roseland, Pleasure Ridge, and Oxmoor. Stokes Enterprises had one of its stores in the city. By the end of 1967 the Trust Company was prepared to open branches in annexes added to each of the Bargains Unlimited stores.

In April of 1967 word passed through the community that the Beaumont family trust accounts had been transferred to the Bluegrass Trust Company. During the following months a number of Louisville old-family estates—the John Hunt Morgans, the Breckenridges, the McDaniels, and the Hardins—followed suit. Howard Stokes remarked, "This does not cause any concern. The Trust Company has been operated as though it was an exclusive social club. But the dues it collected were low-income trust fees. We mean to earn high income from commercial banking."

During the spring and summer of 1967 a new advertising campaign was launched introducing "the new Trust Company *Bank*." The ads emphasized the banking, savings, loan, and branch services of the Trust Company and said little about its trust division. It was the first time in its history that the Trust Company had done such advertising, and the campaign used all available media—billboards, newspapers, radio, television, and direct mailings. Its

[2] The expenses of bank examinations are borne by the bank being examined.

printed ad themes featured "A Complete Banking Service—Where Parking Is No Problem—Checking Accounts, Time Deposits, Savings Accounts, Auto Loans, Consolidation Loans, Business, Collateral, and Real Estate Loans. Drive-In Banking Hours, 9 A.M. to 6 P.M., Monday through Friday."

During 1967 the number of savings accounts increased by 21 percent, but total savings deposits increased by only 7 percent. The number of personal checking accounts increased by 32 percent. "That was not really an impressive gain," said Mr. Scheer, "when you consider that we started from a very low base." Trust business declined. There was no appreciable change in demand deposits, despite vigorous solicitations made by the new five-man new-business department. "The banking business is slow-moving," said Mr. Scheer. "You don't have any spectaculars to bring the public rushing in, the way they do when we have giveaway sales at our Bargains Unlimited stores."

While the number of commercial accounts had increased by 6 percent, total demand deposits had declined by $1\frac{1}{2}$ percent. During the year Stokes Enterprises' deposits had added substantially to the Trust Company's assets. These gains were more than offset by the loss of local government deposits, due, Mr. Scheer said, "to the inordinate attention that was being paid to our affairs by the bank examiners."

For the year 1967 the Trust Company showed only a nominal profit and a drop from its long record of moderate but steady earnings. Mr. Scheer attributed the drop to reorganization expenses, the cost of new facilities (drive-in and branches), and the start-up expenses for the bank's new activities.

BANK LOCATION AND FUTURE FACILITIES

During the spring months of 1968 Mr. Scheer investigated the possibility of moving the Trust Company to a city-center location. There was a bank building in downtown Louisville which he thought was ideally located, quite central and close to the larger banks. Mr. Scheer came to the conclusion that it was too old and too small and it had no parking or drive-in possibilities. It was occupied by a finance company. Consideration was given to using it for a downtown branch, but projections indicated that a split operation would probably be at high cost.

A second possibility considered was an old department store in the city center. Built in 1933, the building was 12 stories in height and almost half a block square. The trend toward suburban shopping had caused its sales to decline to such an extent that it was known to be seeking a buyer. The store building required considerable remodeling to transform it into a banking facility, and the Trust Company would not use more than the lower five floors, leaving the question of how the upper floors might be used profitably. It was suggested that they might be used for a Bargains Unlimited store, but Mr. Stokes took a dim view of operating a department store which had no ground-floor level, even if the display windows would remain available. "That fine old store is dying from downtown-itis," said Mr. Stokes. "Our store would probably suffer from the same disease. We find the suburbs healthier."

The possibility of building a new structure had also been considered. No suitable vacant land was available, nor were desirable improved sites, and a new structure, it was conjectured, might cost approximately $6 to $7 million.

In their letter to shareholders which accompanied the year-end annual report for 1970, Messrs. Stokes and Scheer stated:

> For the year 1970 your bank enjoyed a continuing improving trend. Operating income was up from 1969, reflecting more commercial lending and higher lending rates. Consumer loans contributed significant earnings, but larger operating expenses and a 27 percent increase in interest expense held down the final net earnings. Last year's gain in net profits was achieved despite the surtax, which reduced net per share by 14 cents.
>
> New accounting regulations require banks to restate year-end results to include provisions for loan losses and profits and losses on securities transactions. This did not affect your bank's earnings significantly. Loan-loss experience and charge-offs were modest. There were virtually no changes in your bank's investment portfolio.
>
> Throughout its history your bank has been heavily engaged in trust business. Your new management intends to reorient your bank toward a major participation in wholesale banking activities. Recently your bank has been competing successfully with other large regional banks to participate in extending sizable lines of credit for major corporations. The opportunity was available to us because during the current period of money stringency, money center banks have been compelled by lack of funds or federal policy to turn away prospective borrowers. Loan-to-deposit ratios in many regional banks have been pushed to 80 percent or higher. Your bank's ratio has been about 50 percent or less for many years. Because regional banks have been experiencing a heavy runoff of commercial certificates of deposit, they have had to resort to other sources of high-cost funds, along with many money-market banks.
>
> During most of the past decade demand deposits were trending toward a higher percentage of your bank's total deposits while the percentage of time deposits declined. Due to the promotional efforts of your new management this trend has been reversed. At the close of 1970, on average balances, time deposits accounted for 40 percent of your bank's total deposits; by contrast, three years ago they represented less than 20 percent. Certificates of deposit account for much of the gain.

OPERATIONAL CHANGES

Early in 1971 the Trust Company entered the retail charge field with the initiation of the South Central Bank Americard Service, which was also available to other banks thoughout the South. Mr. Stokes had seen this move as a very promising supplemental means of granting credit in his chain of stores, which already had their own established credit-card system. At the year-end the Trust Company had generated only 7,500 accounts with receivables of $157,000 outstanding. In contrast, the largest Louisville bank, which had extensive correspondent connections with country banks, had 200,000 accounts with $6 million outstanding.

The charge-card start-up program involved large promotional expenses which caused the program to show a loss for the year. "We had anticipated a much larger acceptance," said Mr. Scheer. "Apparently the typical Trust Company client does not feel the need for a credit card, and the typical customer of our Bargains Unlimited stores is not a customer of the Trust Company." The credit-card department was later made a part of the newly formed travel service department. Mr. Scheer remarked, "The huge start-up costs are now over. We believe that by 1972 we will generate enough volume to reach the break-even point." He also pointed out that while credit-per-card had been small compared with national averages, so had the Trust Company's bad-debt losses.

A major event in 1971 was the expansion of the Trust Company's data processing operations, which, Mr. Scheer said, "offered significant growth potential." Up to this date the Trust Company had only a limited application of data processing applied to its banking operations. A data processing services department was now organized. All possible banking, savings, credit-card, and trust activities were tabulated, and the service was offered to the Trust Company's country bank correspondents. The latter were offered a wide range of services, including the processing of demand and savings deposits and installment loans.

During 1971 the Trust Company mounted a vigorous campaign to enlarge its correspondent banking connections, and the computer service was offered as a sales point. The project was only moderately successful; only a few new correspondents were acquired, and in no month did the services for outside customers increase by more than 2 percent. At the year-end the Trust Company's data processing services had three outside customers. A leading Louisville bank had 31 such customers. Mr. Scheer attributed this to the fact that the larger bank had a much larger correspondent following and more sophisticated, higher-capacity equipment. He thought that it would only require a higher volume to make the computer operation pay, and he was considering installing larger equipment and also processing the operations of the Bargains Unlimited stores.

In 1964 figures published by *The American Banker* had indicated that the Trust Company's Trust Division was the largest in the State of Kentucky from the standpoint of trust income. Since 1967 this trust business had been declining, both in terms of number of accounts and in terms of net income. "It isn't hard to see why," said Mr. Weldon, an old trust officer. "The new owners of the bank seem to be deliberately phasing out our fine trust business." He pointed out an ad theme, attributed to Mr. Scheer, which had been published widely:

You know us as
THE TRUST COMPANY
We would like you to think of us as
THE FALLS CITY BANK
A Full-Service Bank

At the end of 1971 trust accounts declined for the fifth straight year. "I don't think that the computers did us any good," said Mr. Weldon. "Some of our ads trumpeted that we now have a fully computerized trust service. I'm sure that many of our old customers didn't like to feel that they were fully computerized." In 1971 trust income fell to about 8 percent of total earnings. Since 1967 nine of the Trust Division's managerial personnel had left; they had been replaced by the promotion of juniors, and no additions had been made.

Historically, many of Trust Company's influential clientele had also held political office, and the Trust Company had become the obvious depository for the government funds which they controlled. In 1971 its total deposits of the state of Kentucky and political subdivisions constituted a much higher proportion of its demand deposits than any other Louisville bank. "It has become a tradition in Kentucky," said Mr. Reuben Daniels, "that the Trust Company is the leading depository of government funds."

During the 1960s the three largest Louisville banks had mounted aggressive campaigns to capture government accounts. One of the larger banks had engaged as a vice president a man who had formerly been Treasurer of the State of Kentucky. "This could hurt us," said Mr. Daniels. "That man knows where every vein of government gold lies. He also has connections which can open the right doors in the Capitol and in many a county courthouse and many a city hall."

FUTURE PROSPECTS

In the 1971 annual report Mr. Scheer said:

> Recently your bank has been working to improve its competitive position in the international banking arena. Our Foreign Department, established forty years ago, has now been enlarged to become our International Department, offering full international services. Previous voluntary restraint guidelines imposed by the federal government and our dependence upon our Chicago and New York correspondents placed a limit upon our ability to lend to foreign borrowers. A recent venture with leading regional banks across the country has led to the formation of Allied Bank International, which will make us fully competitive in international services with any other bank in our area.

In 1971 there were significant gains in consumer credit accounts. While operating income increased, net income showed a slight decline.

Mr. Scheer had been heavily occupied with Mr. Stokes' other interests, which were flourishing, and had not always been able to spend his usual Friday at the bank. In major matters none of the other officers acted without direction, and this had brought an increasing amount of banking questions to Mr. Stokes for decision. This was a development he had not anticipated and did not desire.

At the end of 1971 Mr. Stokes and Mr. Scheer were, themselves, still referring to the bank as The Trust Company. (See Exhibits 4 and 5.)

EXHIBIT 4
FALLS CITY BANK AND TRUST COMPANY COMPARATIVE INCOME STATEMENTS,
1967–1971 (Thousands of Dollars)

	Years ending December 31				
	1967	**1968**	**1969**	**1970**	**1971**
Operating income:					
Interest on loans and fees	$3,615	$4,065	$5,093	$ 5,212	$ 6,339
Interest on securities	1,800	1,840	1,035	2,567	2,889
Interest—political subdivisions	80	77	69	64	58
Trust department income	1,220	1,212	1,111	1,013	981
Other income	300	380	1,241	1,278	1,959
Total income	$7,015	$7,574	$8,549	$10,134	$12,226
Operating expenses:					
Salaries and wages	$1,479	$1,579	$1,778	$ 1,095	$ 2,369
Employee benefits (pension, etc.)	370	395	445	476	547
Interest on deposits	1,792	2,070	2,821	3,385	4,070
Provision for loan losses	60	44	24	46	60
Interest on borrowed money	30	17	20	34	51
Occupancy rentals (branches)	00	00	17	54	57
Other operating expenses	1,650	1,773	1,781	2,528	3,213
Total operating expenses	$5,381	$5,878	$6,886	$ 8,428	$10,367
Income taxes	374	520	442	418	600
Net securities gains (losses)	(2)	3	28	(6)	3
Net income	$1,258	$1,179	$1,249	$ 1,282	$ 1,262

EXHIBIT 5

FALLS CITY BANK AND TRUST COMPANY COMPARATIVE BALANCE SHEETS, 1967–1971
(Thousands of Dollars)

	Years ending December 31				
	1967	**1968**	**1969**	**1970**	**1971**
Resources:					
Cash and due from banks	$ 24,380	$ 26,050	$ 32,780	$ 41,902	$ 46,289
United States Government obligations	43,508	39,820	44,702	53,172	61,289
Federal funds sold	4,000	7,000	3,000	4,000	4,000
Government institution obligations	740	813	895	984	1,083
Municipal obligations	18,119	16,730	16,503	15,454	13,599
Federal Reserve Bank stock	300	300	300	300	300
Other investment securities	1,079	1,187	1,306	1,437	980
Loans and discounts	72,484	75,732	83,505	83,855	93,440
Building and equipment	999	1,099	1,209	1,330	1,463
Interest receivable	653	719	791	870	956
Other assets	422	464	510	561	617
Total	$166,684	$168,914	$185,501	$203,865	$224,016
Liabilities:					
Demand deposits	$120,471	$114,145	$116,491	$109,793	$118,146
Time deposits	29,940	37,548	50,225	73,662	83,630
Total deposits	$150,411	$151,693	$166,716	$183,455	$201,776
Interest collected but not earned	2,133	1,852	2,100	2,369	2,640
Other liabilities	612	673	740	814	902
Dividends payable	190	190	190	190	190
Capital stock	3,400	3,400	3,400	3,400	3,400
Surplus	6,200	6,200	6,200	6,200	7,194
Undivided profits	1,474	2,416	3,465	4,698	4,902
Reserves for loan losses and contingencies	2,264	2,490	2,690	2,739	3,012
Total	$166,684	$168,914	$185,501	$203,865	$224,016

Bartl's Brewery

CHANGES IN OWNERSHIP AND MANAGEMENT

> We certainly are not a factor in the brewing industry, although we have made some impact in the restaurant business. I am still confident we can continue to be a profitable enterprise. Despite our struggle to hold on in the brewing industry, I think it has been worthwhile, and we may soon be able to take advantage of the strengths we have and develop both businesses into viable entities.

Thus stated John Crawford, president and major stockholder of Bartl's Brewery. Crawford was the third president of Bartl's in the past eleven years. In 1977 he and a small group of investors purchased the company from the estate of George Schaefer, who had operated a small chain of fast-food restaurants in Dayton and the surrounding area. Schaefer purchased Bartl's from Royce Chandler and his associates. Chandler had rescued Bartl's from bankruptcy through a reorganization in 1965, when he and a group of investors, including employees, took over the company.

George Schaefer became the sole owner and president of Bartl's after he purchased the company in 1972. He bought the stock of Chandler and his group and also the shares of all other small holders, including Bartl's employees. Schaefer spent most of his money developing the restaurant business. He considered the brewery to be an adjunct to his proposed restaurant chain. However, upon the insistence of August Burg, Bartl's brewmaster, he made some efforts to make the brewery profitable. Schaefer died suddenly in 1976, and the brewery was operated under a trustee of his estate until it was sold to Crawford and his group in 1977.

Crawford was interested in Bartl's because of the brewery, and he was hopeful at the time of the purchase to develop the company into a strong regional brewery. Crawford had a long interest in breweries. As a young man he had acquired a large collection of beer cans and bottles, which he continued to add to through the years. The collection was on display in the lobby of the brewery office. Crawford had made it a point in his travels as an executive and part owner of a tool and die manufacturing firm to visit regional breweries in the United States. He also had visited a number of breweries in Europe and was particularly interested in small breweries. Crawford's associates accused him of having a romantic interest in breweries and viewing the business in this light, rather than in a pragmatic sense.

HISTORY AND DEVELOPMENT OF THE COMPANY

Bartl's, the oldest brewery in Ohio, was founded in 1862 by Bernhard Bartl, who learned brewing in Germany and emigrated to America in 1855. After working as a brewer in St. Louis and Milwaukee, he leased the plant of a defunct brewery on the site of the present Bartl's Brewery and began his own business. Success came quickly; when Bernhard Bartl died in 1898, he was reputed to be wealthy, and Bartl's was a thriving concern.

Bernhard Bartl, Jr., nicknamed "Judge" Bartl because he had studied law, followed his father as manager of the brewery. He preferred the brewing business to the practice of law and spent two years in Cincinnati studying "modern and scientific brewing techniques," then joined his father. Judge Bartl's management of the brewery was thrifty, conservative, and prudent. He added a chain of taverns which Bartl's began operating in 1900, introduced a limited line of bottled beer in 1913, switched to near beer during Prohibition, and enlarged the plant to double its capacity when Prohibition was repealed.

In 1935, Judge Bartl was joined by Bartl Koerner, the only son of the Judge's only sister, who shared equally with the Judge in the inheritance of the brewery. Bartl started as a salesman and subsequently held a number of offices in sales and operations. After five years he was sharing the management of the brewery with his uncle. The Judge supervised production; Bartl Koerner managed everything else. The joint management went smoothly for 11 years. During this period Bartl's was making a profit and continued to expand. Bartl Koerner extended sales into the periphery of the Dayton market, added canned beer, and in a single spectacular crash promotion entered Bartl's in the Indianapolis market, which eventually grew to be as large as Bartl's home market in Dayton.

Before World War II the large national brewers had operated from single central breweries because the lack of a uniform water supply would have caused beers brewed at other points to be "off flavor." Their strategy had been to produce beers which were presumably premium in quality and could command the higher prices which warranted the expense of shipping them to distant points. After the war new technologies solved the water problem, and national breweries proceeded to establish branch plants, brew locally, and sell at local prices. Canned beer became popular, and a myriad of competitive innovations were introduced by the nationals: "pop-tops," "rack-packs," "zip-caps," and "cold-packs." A wide variety of shapes and sizes appeared in cans, bottles, and widemouthed "mug-jugs." The total consumption of beer increased substantially, but the increase was in home consumption, while there was a trend away from tavern drinking. Throughout its history Bartl's had featured draft beer sold to the bar trade. Company profits declined from $1.7 million net in 1947 to $92,000 in 1951.

In 1952, Judge Bartl, then 81, became chairman of the board, and Bartl Koerner, who had been executive vice president for 11 years, was elected president. Judge Bartl brought in James Randall, a furniture executive, whom he made executive vice president and general manager. Bartl Koerner succeeded in ousting Mr. Randall and voiding his 10-year contract, publicly charging his uncle with senility and saying that "he never knew anything more than how to make beer the way it was made 60 years ago. . . ." Thereupon, the Judge forced Bartl Koerner from the presidency, stating that he had developed megalomania and believed himself capable of succeeding at anything, even converting Bartl's into a national brewery. For 15 months—January 1953 through March 1954 —the presidency remained vacant, and the company was managed by the sales manager. Backed by his mother and his wife, who was independently wealthy, Bartl Koerner appointed six board members who reelected him president. The next thing Bartl Koerner did was to fire the sales manager. The Judge tried again to oust Bartl, charging him with wasteful and extravagant management. Failing in this attempt, the Judge resigned from the board in 1956, leaving control of the company to Bartl Koerner. In 1957 Judge Bartl died.

Sales and profits continued to decline in the period from 1956 to 1962. Local retailers were not sure that Bartl's would survive the effects of the previous infighting for control. Within a year of Koerner's return in 1956, sales volume fell 45 percent. Koerner blamed his uncle, who, he said, had put all the company's capital into bricks and mortar. He launched a huge sales drive with little result, and after another five years of losses—January 1958 to December 1962—the company went into voluntary receivership. The first official act of the trustee was to dismiss Bartl Koerner.

In January, 1965, the reorganized company emerged, the trustee asserting: "We released many employees, cut salaries and wages, cut many expenses, and insisted on a general austerity program. Within a year we were no longer operating on a hand-to-mouth basis. We were able to make ends meet, were earning a profit, and didn't have to borrow additional funds from the banks." On January 1, 1965, the reorganized company was turned over to the group headed by Royce Chandler.

THE REORGANIZATION

Royce Chandler, who played the leading role in the reorganization, had been operating a Dayton advertising firm called Chandler and Associates. Bartl's

Brewery was one of his clients. Mr. Chandler was described as "a warm and enthusiastic man, always buoyant and with an ever-hopeful disposition." His agency had a reputation for creativity and had launched numerous successful advertising campaigns which were said to have made Mr. Chandler a millionaire. At the end of 1964, Bartl's owed Mr. Chandler a total of $70,000, an accumulation of approximately two years of fees.

Under the Chandler reorganization plan effected January 1, 1965, holders of the old preferred stock received, on a share-for-share basis, new preferred stock in the reorganized company. Holders of the old common stock received nothing. Five hundred thousand dollars in new common stock ($1 par) was subscribed and paid for. All delinquent accounts were paid in full; all other accounts were carried forward to the reorganized company.

Mr. Chandler called his plan the "Chandler-Dayton-Businessmen and Bartl's Brewery Employees' Reorganization Plan." "This is not just an ordinary business reorganization," said Mr. Chandler, "this is the fulfillment of an ideal."

BARTL'S ORGANIZATION UNDER CRAWFORD

Bartl's organizational relationship had been very informal since Chandler had taken over the company in reorganization. Many of the same employees continued to work through the changes in ownership and management. Schaefer brought in George Seitz from his restaurant chain. He was retained by Crawford as the vice president of the restaurant division. Seitz had spent 10 years with Schaefer's restaurant chain. He was considered to be very knowledgeable in the business. He disagreed with Crawford since he wanted to expand the restaurants and diminish the importance of beer in Bartl's strategy.

Fred Mayer, the vice president of brewery operations and sales was brought into Bartl's by Crawford. Under Schaefer both the manager of production and sales reported to him as the chief executive officer. Crawford was intent on increasing beer sales and felt that Mayer would provide marketing experience. He had 10 years experience with Falstaff and left the company in 1977 when offered a position by Bartl's. Crawford contacted Mayer through a mutual friend who was the president of a Dayton bank. Lotz, the manager of production, had been employed by Bartl's for 20 years. August Burg, the brewmaster, served under Chandler and Schaefer. He was recognized as one of the best regional brewmasters and was credited with creating the special draft beer which was the company's best-selling product. Burg was 68 years old but was still considered to be vigorous and energetic. Both Burg and Lotz did not see the need for a vice president of brewery operations and sales. Mayer admitted that he had trouble getting cooperation from both of them, but particularly from Burg whom he accused of arrogance. Burg frequently remarked that the brewmaster was the key to success and the beer producer depended on the taste of the product to gain profitability.

The purchasing agent, Lee Blum, was hired by Crawford in 1980 after some problems arose over purchase of restaurant supplies and inventory and brewery supplies. Central accounting maintained that it was not able to keep track of purchase orders and bills due suppliers because of the lack of coordination between the two divisions.

Each restaurant manager did his or her own purchasing but had to send a copy of the purchase order to Blum's office for checking and delivery to accounting. Blum also checked large purchases and recommended seeking other suppliers when he or his staff thought the cost of food or supplies were out of line with local prices. His office made a continuous effort to keep up with changing prices of items that were frequently purchased by the restaurants.

Beer ingredients were purchased through Blum, but solely on the demand of Burg or Mayer, who frequently disagreed over the designation of suppliers.

Both Mayer and Seitz felt that purchasing should be decentralized and handled through their offices. Simmonds, the chief financial officer, did not agree. He contended that the whole process was much more efficient and cost-effective since Blum had been made purchasing agent.

Peter Simmonds came to Bartl's shortly after Crawford assumed control of the company. He had formerly been controller of the tool and die company Crawford had been associated with. He also had some experience with a local certified public accounting (C.P.A.) firm. Simmonds was considered to be a good financial person, but on the conservative side. He had frequent discussions with Mayer and Seitz, the managers of the brewery and restaurant divisions, over overhead cost allocations. Burg, the brewmaster, also resented his probing into purchases of malts and hops. Simmonds argued that Burg ran too costly an operation. (See Exhibit 1 for Bartl's 1982 organization chart.)

BARTL'S RESTAURANTS

Development of the Restaurant Chain

At one time Bartl's operated, in the Dayton area, 28 taverns which served food. The major objective of the tavern-restaurants was to sell and promote Bartl's draft beer. Because of declining sales, the taverns had been gradually closed, and when Schaefer took over the company there were only two restaurants left. Both were in the downtown Dayton area.

Schaefer was attracted to the restaurants because of his background in the fast-food business. He noted that one of the restaurants was profitable, and the second marginally profitable. Under Schaefer's management, Bartl's expanded its restaurant chain from two to six. Two new restaurants were located on the outskirts of Dayton, one in Kettering, Ohio, in the Dayton metropolitan area, and one in Springfield, Ohio, on the road to Columbus, Ohio.

Schaefer placed emphasis on draft beer mainly because it complemented the menu of Bartl's restaurants. Each of the restaurants did an extensive lunch business and had special cocktail hours from 5:00 to 6:30 P.M. The restaurants located in the business district were closed on Sundays. Dinner business was slow in the downtown areas but very good in outlying areas. Schaefer

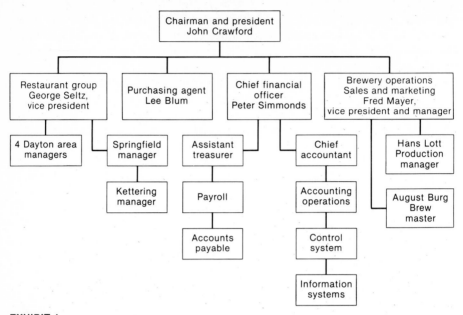

EXHIBIT 1
Bartl's organization chart, 1982.

borrowed from his fast-food restaurant menus. He successfully promoted a special high-quality beef hamburger served on dark bread baked especially for Bartl's at a Dayton bakery. According to Schaefer this "house special" was a major factor in selling Bartl's special draft beer. The menu was comprised mainly of German dishes, in keeping with Bartl's image as a brewer of good German draft beer. The outlying restaurants tended to vary this fare to cater to the suburban trade. The average meal price varied by location; however, it seldom exceeded $8.50. Beer was the main beverage sold in all of the restaurants.

The restaurant business increased substantially in volume from 1972 to 1976, and was the major factor in stemming Bartl's losses and providing its first profitable years in more than a decade.

Restaurants under Crawford

When Crawford took over Bartl's he was skeptical about the restaurants and their contribution to the company. He was primarily interested in maintaining Bartl's as a regional brewer. Crawford soon realized, however, that the restaurants were responsible for a significant amount of beer sales and had been responsible for the only profit the company had made since his group purchased Bartl's. Beer sales had shown a steady decline and did not return any profit to the company.

George Seitz, the vice president in charge of the restaurant operations, was in favor of building the restaurant chain. He had plans to enlarge the menu and increase the number of restaurants in selected outlying areas of Dayton, Springfield, Columbus, and possibly Indianapolis. Crawford and Peter Simmonds, the chief financial officer, took a more cautious view. They admitted that restaurant sales were profitable and showed promise but had questions about raising the capital to finance the expansion of a restaurant chain. The recession of 1981–1982 supported their views, despite the fact that Bartl's restaurant group was still profitable in the downturn.

The First Street restaurant in Dayton was the original restaurant in the Bartl chain. It moved its location several times in its 80-year history but remained within two blocks of its original location in downtown Dayton. This was the most profitable of the restaurant group with sales of $1.4 million. There were 250 seats with a long stand-up bar and stand-up tables for a "quick sandwich," which was served buffet style. Unlike the outlying restaurants, First Street featured baked ham and roast beef cut and served at the buffet. Most patrons were business people seeking a quick special lunch. Bartl's draft was served at the bar; the customer could eat there or go to a stand-up table. The dining area served all of Bartl's special German dishes, plus sandwiches, which could be ordered from the buffet.

Luncheon business was exceptionally good; dinner business was fair. Beer and liquor sales were very good. The special 5:00 to 6:30 P.M. cocktail hour was usually crowded. Beer was the popular choice. Mixed-drinks sales were not heavy. The restaurant was closed on Sundays.

Main Street, the second restaurant established by Bartl's, was on the fringes of the business district. It had moved several times in its 70-year history. It served the same menu as the First Street restaurant. Sales in the past year were $820,000. Management thought it was poorly located and received a good bit of its business from the overflow of the First Street restaurant. Liquor sales were good. Luncheon business was the main source of revenue. Dinner sales were poor, and management seriously considered closing the restaurant in the evening. Main Street did not have a stand-up serving area or a buffet line. The restaurant was too small to accommodate this type of arrangement. Rent was 15 percent lower than the First Street rental. The bar was about 60 percent the size of First Street. Main Street was also closed on Sundays.

Hills and Dales, on the outskirts of Dayton, was purchased by Schaefer. Sales in 1981 were $625,000 and seating capacity was 175. Schaefer had intended to enlarge the facility. The restaurant catered to a family trade. While the turnover was good, liquor sales were only fair. Luncheon trade was good because of several medium-sized office complexes in the area. Dinner business was excellent, but the average check was low because of the family trade.

Crow's Nest was the most recent and last acquisition of Schaefer. Seating capacity was 190. Business was marginally profitable. Sales were $610,000. Luncheon sales were only fair. Dinner trade was very good. Liquor sales were also good, but because of the small size of the restaurant, working areas were cramped and turnover was poor. The restaurant was open on weekends but closed on Mondays.

Kettering, within the Dayton metropolitan area, had been profitable two months after it opened. The site was in a former location of one of Schaefer's fast-food restaurants. Seating capacity was 225. Sales approximated $850,000. Luncheon business was fair; dinner business was good. Liquor sales were good, mainly at the cocktail hours of 5:00 to 6:30 P.M. Schaefer had tried to duplicate the decor of the First Street restaurant. The restaurant was open on weekends and closed on Mondays.

Springfield was located in an established mall. Rent was relatively high. Seating capacity was 230. Luncheon business was good and was composed of shoppers and business people in the vicinity. The menu varied slightly from the German fare. A salad bar was a main attraction. Dinner business was only fair, as were liquor sales. Annual sales approximated $750,000.

BARTL'S BEER OPERATIONS

Beer Sales

When George Schaefer purchased Bartl's from Royce Chandler and his group in 1972, the brewery was selling approximately 70,000 barrels a year. This represented a substantial decrease from the peak the company reached in 1968 when it sold 95,000 barrels. Beer sales continued to decline through 1977 except for 1976 when sales increased to 75,000 barrels from a low point of 64,000 barrels in 1975. In 1976, Bartl's conducted a series of sales campaigns which increased volume, but increased marketing expenses and promotion costs contributed to the company's loss of $150,000.

Bartl's beer sales continued to decline when Crawford took over the company (see Exhibit 2), and sales reached their lowest level in 1981. In the first half of 1982, beer sales continued their decline. Approximately 60 percent of total sales was in draft beer sold in kegs. Cans and bottles made up the remainder of sales with approximately 18 percent in bottles, sold mainly in taverns, and 22 percent in cans, which were distributed to supermarkets and packaged goods stores.

EXHIBIT 2
BARTL'S BEER SALES 1977–1982 (IN BARRELS)

Year	Draft	Cans	Bottles	Total
1977	26,000	14,000	12,000	52,000
1978	26,500	13,400	11,100	51,000
1979	26,900	12,000	10,100	49,000
1980	25,600	10,800	8,600	45,000
1981	25,800	10,700	8,500	43,000
1982 (to July 1)	13,300	3,400	2,300	19,000

The greatest margin was realized on draft sales, mainly because it was sold in Bartl's restaurants by the stein or glass, or by the pitcher. Restaurant beer sales accounted for over 60 percent of Bartl's draft beer sales.

Product Line

Bartl's had long produced a premium draft beer aimed at the discriminating beer drinker. It was generally agreed in the industry that draft beer was superior in taste to canned or bottled beer. Burg had frequently stated that:

> Packaged beers taste different from draft, as different as cabbage from sauerkraut. Can or bottle the beer, and it no longer is the real thing. But today people don't seem to care much about taste. Just give it to them cold; that seems to be all they ask. They will even drink bottled beer at a bar where the same beer is served on tap.

Through the years Bartl's had tried different kinds of premium beers. Velvet Gold was its most memorable effort.

In May, 1965, a faulty canning machine left too much air in the cans, allowing the beer to continue to ferment inside them and resulting in a beer that brewers termed "skunky" because its strong flavor gave the drinker "beer breath." In eliminating the trouble the Bartl brewers did two things: first, they adjusted the vacuum controls, and in doing so they inadvertently overcompensated; second, they removed the light brown crust of foam which appeared as a normal thing on the surface of all fermenting beer in the open fermentation process. To their surprise, they found that they had brewed a beer that was exceptionally light and pale, comparable to the highest-quality premium beers. Also, the new brew seemed to leave absolutely no aftertaste.

Mr. Chandler believed that they had chanced upon a revolutionary improvement in the age-old brewing process. In presenting their discovery to the board of directors, Mr. Chandler said, "Elimination of beer breath will put us leagues ahead of anyone in the industry, including the nationals."

Mr. Chandler proposed that Bartl's introduce the new brew as a fourth item in its line. He named it Velvet Gold and planned to market it in golden cans and gold-foil-sheathed bottles. The introduction was to be launched by heavy promotion and advertising on radio and television and in the regional editions of national magazines. His ad theme featured the slogan "Smooth as Velvet, Rich as Gold." Canned and bottled Velvet Gold was to be sold as a super-quality brew at prices which were higher than those of most premium beers. It was to be distributed through all channels, with heavy emphasis on grocery stores.

Mr. Chandler had the brewers condense the crust of foam which they removed and put it in pill-sized bottles labeled "slurge." These bottles were mounted on a placard which explained that the nauseous-looking moldy liquid in the little bottle was the dregs which other brewers left in their beers, giving the drinker beer breath, and that only Bartl's was purified of slurge. These exhibits were presented to taverns to be placed on bars.

In 1967 Chandler stopped the production and sales of Velvet Gold. However, his advertising and promotion campaign was remembered long after the beer was withdrawn from distribution. George Schaefer frequently remarked that Velvet Gold and the circus-like atmosphere surrounding its introduction and promotion made it difficult for Bartl's to introduce a new premium beer.

Bartl's also introduced a super-quality premium beer, Bartl's Bavarian, in 1965. It was well received, but in the course of two years sales began to decline. The nationals began pushing their premium beers in Bartl's area, and the imported premium beers became popular about this time. In the face of this kind of competition, Bavarian sales continued to decrease. When Schaefer took over the company, he eliminated the line entirely.

Bartl's bottled its premium draft beer and also produced a beer between premium and standard grade which was bottled. This was the only beer the company sold in cans. As previously indicated, draft beer, which accounted for 60 percent of total sales, was sold in Bartl's restaurants, which accounted for 60 percent of draft beer sales.

Draft beer was also sold to taverns in the area, which had been declining in number for over two decades. Bottled draft beer was sold in taverns, supermarkets, and package stores. It accounted for approximately 20 percent of bottle sales. Canned beer was distributed to supermarkets and package stores.

August Burg and John Mayer were both of the opinion that Bartl's needed a light beer and another special premium beer to be competitive and round out the line. Crawford was very interested in making such additions, but he was worried about risking any more capital in the highly competitive beer market when Bartl's sales were declining.

Burg continually extolled the quality of Bartl's draft beer. He stated that Bartl's aged their beer (lagering) an average of 55 days, over two times that of national beers, which usually were aged for about 20 to 24 days. Burg also stressed the fact that Bartl's used a natural process without using the chemicals which national brewers used to speed up the process. The ingredients were also costly. Burg used the best malts and hops available, and since Bartl's did not buy in large quantities, it was much more expensive to the company than it would be to a large brewery. The extended lagering time was also expensive since it restricted the batch turnover to less than six runs per year.

Seitz and Mayer both urged a cutting back of lagering time to approximately 35 days. But Burg objected strenuously, maintaining this would cause Bartl's to lose the only real competitive edge it had on the nationals. Crawford supported Burg. He also emphasized the matter of freshness. He said lager beer delivered short distances was less exposed to light and heat and thus maintained its freshness longer than beers delivered from a long distance.

Advertising and Promotion

Fred Mayer felt that Bartl's was at a severe disadvantage in terms of advertising and promotion when pitted against the nationals. Because of the restricted area of distribution, the company had to use TV spots, local newspapers, and billboards. Bartl's low volume made the cost of advertising and promotion per barrel of beer produced relatively high. Bartl's spent approximately $2.10 a barrel; the nationals spent $3.00 to $3.80 per barrel, and their advertising was judged to be two to three times more effective because of their national advertising and the size of the audience reached with TV commercials and other promotions. The amount of money spent for advertising by the nationals could range from $30 to $55 million per year, as contrasted to the less than $100,000 that Bartl's spent. Mayer estimated that the regionals selling in the Dayton area were spending over $400,000 on advertising.

Burg, the brewmaster, supported Mayer's position. He stated that Bartl's draft was as good a beer as you could find in the area and the lack of sales was due to a lack of promotion. George Seitz, the vice president of restaurant operations strongly disagreed with this position. He constantly reminded management that the restaurants were the major marketing force for beer sales. Seitz had proposed reducing brewery runs to accommodate only the restaurants. He thought the tavern sales and sales to other outlets was the major reason for losing money on beer sales. Seitz also pointed out that the restaurant advertising frequently featured Bartl's draft. Crawford said that reducing Bartl's beer sales would be a mistake and that the presence of Bartl's beer in taverns and other outlets aided the restaurant business. Crawford also stated that if beer sales had to be cut back any further he would consider contracting with a regional brewer in the area to make Bartl's beer for the restaurants. Crawford remembered and often repeated the statements that Schaefer had made to him when both were active in the local Rotary Club. "Increased promotion expenses produce increased volume, but they also decrease margins for the local brewer. Advertising can be risky. In a local area it may be better to depend on the reputation of your beer."

There were approximately 110 taverns in the Dayton area that Bartl's considered worth cultivating as customers. Bartl's beer was distributed on a regular basis to approximately 60 to 70 taverns. Some of the taverns carried more than one beer on tap. They also sold bottled beer produced by the nationals.

Bartl's also distributed to 60 supermarkets in the area and 50 package stores. Bartl's priced their canned beer about 10 percent under national competition but was frequently underpriced by other regional producers. Bartl's was also caught in price wars by the nationals and had to counter by reducing its prices and frequently taking a loss. In an effort to boost margins, Bartl's tried to push sales of its bottled premium draft beer but did not meet with much success. Seitz claimed that it was priced too high and suffered from comparison to their low-priced regular canned beer when sold in supermarkets and package stores.

Distribution

Bartl's had two of its own trucks for distribution of beer to its restaurants. The trucks also served taverns that were conveniently located en route to the various restaurants. These trucks were a source of irritation to the wholesalers which delivered Bartl's beer to taverns, supermarkets, and package stores. Fred Mayer frequently questioned the advisability of employing company-owned trucks. The drivers were union members and the helpers were also members of the teamster's union. Mayer maintained that upkeep and maintenance were very costly and offset any advantage Bartl's had in maintaining control over its own deliveries.

Crawford was of the opinion that in addition to delivery control it had significant advertising value since the trucks carried the Bartl's name painted on the side. He frequently pointed out what this kind of exposure would cost if the company had to lease advertising space on wholesaler's trucks. Crawford also indicated that this might not be possible anyway since Bartl's had to compete for space with larger brewers which used independent wholesalers in the same area.

Bartl's delivery costs were high. In addition to the cost of operating two trucks, they had to grant generous margins to the wholesalers because of their low volume.

The independent wholesalers which distributed Bartl's beer also distributed for a number of competing brands, including some of the largest national brewers. Fred Mayer frequently complained that Bartl's was often neglected in favor of the brewers which provided more volume to the distributors.

The Brewing Industry

The brewing industry was dominated by two large companies, Anheuser-Busch and Miller Brewing, a subsidiary of Philip Morris. Together they accounted for 53.4 percent of total industry sales in 1982. Four medium-sized producers accounted for 28.1 percent of sales; a number of smaller producers made up the remainder of the beer sales, accounting for 18.5 percent of the industry total. (See Exhibit 3.)

Beer consumption had shown a steady rise for the past two decades; the growth rate, however, was trending downward and was expected to be about 2.5 percent annually for the period of 1982–1987. The changing demographic pattern was a major factor in decreasing the rate of growth of beer sales. The population in the 18- to 24-year-old group, which drinks the most beer, is declining. (See Exhibit 4.) With the declining growth rate market-share gains would come mainly by one brewer capturing market share from another industry producer. This would no doubt add to the intensity of competition in an industry that was already considered highly competitive. The big two, Anheuser-Busch and Miller, had been actively engaged in a competitive battle for industry leadership. This intense struggle for market share left little room for the growth of medium-sized and small breweries. The industry, made up of about 60 companies, a decline from 450 several decades ago, was expected to continue to shrink through mergers and acquisitions, and failures. Small regional brewers were particularly vulnerable to the intense industry competi-

EXHIBIT 3
BREWING INDUSTRY SHIPMENTS (IN MILLIONS OF BARRELS)

	1977	1978	1979	1980	1981	1982	1984–86
Anheuser-Busch	36.6	41.6	46.2	50.2	54.5	59.0	70.0
Miller	24.2	31.3	35.8	37.2	40.2	42.5	46.5
Pabst	16.0	15.4	15.1	15.1	13.5	12.5	10.3
Schlitz	22.1	19.6	16.8	15.0	14.2	13.0	10.5
Coors	12.8	12.6	11.9	13.8	13.2	13.1	14.2
Heileman	6.2	7.1	11.2	13.3	14.1	14.8	17.5
Total, 6 major brewers	117.9	127.6	138.0	144.6	149.6	154.8	169.0
Next 5 brewers*	27.0	26.1	24.4	24.8	24.3	24.0	22.0
All other domestic brewers	12.1	9.0	8.4	6.8	6.0	5.8	5.0
Imports	2.5	3.5	4.4	4.8	5.3	5.5	8.0
Total	159.5	166.2	175.2	181.0	185.3	190.0	204.0

*Estimates for Stroh's, Olympia, Schmidt, Genesee, and Falstaff.
Source: Value Line, March 5, 1982.

tion, mainly from price cutting and the advertising blitzes of the major producers. The smaller breweries were no match for the big breweries which produced millions of barrels of beer annually (see Exhibit 5) at a much lower cost per barrel. Because of the shorter brewing process, the latest equipment, and the volume produced, productivity per worker in the large breweries could be eight to ten times greater than in the small breweries.

EXHIBIT 4
U.S. POPULATION PROJECTIONS (IN MILLIONS)

	1981		1985		1990	
Age	No.	Percent of total	No.	Percent of total	No.	Percent of total
Under 5	16,620	7.4	18,803	8.1	19,437	8.0
5–14	33,400	14.9	32,826	14.1	33,768	14.7
15–19	20,019	9.4	18,007	7.7	16,777	6.9
20–24	21,116	8.9	21,116	9.4	17,953	7.4
25–29	19,324	8.6	20,510	8.8	20,169	8.3
30–34	18,138	8.1	19,278	8.3	20,917	8.6
25–39	14,290	6.4	17,274	7.4	19,261	7.9
40–54	34,524	15.4	36,559	15.7	42,642	17.5
55–64	21,413	9.6	21,737	9.3	20,776	8.5
65+	25,368	11.3	27,305	11.08	29,824	12.2
All ages	224,212	100.0	232,880	100.00	248,513	100.00

Source: Department of Commmerce, Population Series, July 1, 1977, p. 25.

EXHIBIT 5
SALES OF LEADING BEER BRANDS (IN MILLIONS OF BARRELS)

Brand	1970	1978	1979	Percent change 1978—1979
Budweiser (Anheuser-Busch)	19.0	27.5	30.0	+ 9.1
High Life (Miller)	5.2	20.8	23.7	+13.9
Pabst Blue Ribbon	10.4	14.3	13.6	− 4.9
Coors	7.3	12.1	11.4	− 5.8
Schlitz	11.6	13.0	11.1	−14.6
Miller Lite		9.4	11.1	+18.1
Michelob (Anheuser-Busch)	1.1	7.5	8.3	+10.7
Stroh's	3.3	6.3	6.0	− 4.8
Olympia	3.4	5.4	4.8	−11.1
Old Style (Heileman)		3.1	4.0	+29.0
Old Milwaukee (Schlitz)	2.5	3.6	3.4	− 5.6
Total	63.8	123.0	127.4	

Source: *Impact*, July 15, 1980.

Smaller and regional brewers maintained that they gained a taste advantage by aging (called lagering) their beer up to two times as long as national brewers. Many local and regional brewers claimed they produced a distinctive taste in their beers which was designed to meet the taste preference of consumers in their areas. The national brewers were not in a position to cater to every local taste. In their mass brewing process they tried to strike a middle ground by brewing a good beer which would satisfy a lot of different tastes. Small regional brewers had been frequent winners over the nationals in beer taste tests held at fairs and expositions. These highly publicized events helped add to the mystique of local brands and aided many of them in their campaigns to sell their beer.

Beer taste was always a matter of intense discussion in the industry. The popularity of different kinds of beer varied over the years. As indicated in Exhibit 6, sales of premium beers and imported beers which were considered premium beers had shown an increase in recent years. Light beer had shown the greatest increase in sales since coming on the market. This lower-calorie beer was promoted and made popular by Miller Brewing Company, which conducted an extensive promotional campaign of "Miller Lite" after the brewery was purchased by Philip Morris, the large tobacco company which also owned Seven-Up, the soft drink producer. The surge in sales of Miller's light beer pushed the company into second place in the brewing industry and forced all of its major competitors to produce a light low-calorie beer to defend their position and stop the erosion of their market share. Local and regional brewers were slow to respond or did not make any effort to meet the demand for lighter beer. In addition to the cost involved in making a low-calorie beer, many of the brewers thought it would detract from their distinctive taste and dilute their major competitive edge over the nationals.

Production

Bartl's plant was very old, and parts of the building dated back over 75 years. Each recent president, Chandler, Schaefer, and Crawford, had made improvements and additions to the production facilities; however, Bartl's plant still could not be compared with the modern breweries or the two good regional breweries in Bartl's area. Crawford spent $50,000 in 1979 and $200,000 in 1980 on additions. He estimated, however, that it would take a minimum of $1 to $1.5 million to really make the plant modern. He cited the need for new kettles, instrumentation, a canning line, and significant improvements to the brewery building.

Bartl's brewing process—the 55-day aging process of 60 percent of Bartl's output—was a factor in the low productivity of the company. If lagering time were cut in half, Bartl's could double its output without any plant additions. Burg and Crawford felt that they could not take a chance on changing the taste of their premium beer. Burg said if they lost their different flavor, their individual character, they would lose what competitive edge they had. Seitz and Mayer disagreed. They were of the opinion that since the beer was served very cold coming out of the tap, the difference in taste would not be noticed. Seitz also pointed out that 60 percent of draft sales were made through the restaurants and consumed with meals, and therefore the taste factor was not as important as long as it met the same standards as the nationals.

Bartl's plant employed 40 workers who turned out 43,000 to 52,000 barrels a year depending on demand. The capacity of the brewery was about 120,000 barrels, a level Bartl's had not reached in over 25 years. National brewers with large regional breweries could produce over 7,000 barrels for each worker. The breweries with the most modern equipment and designed for output were said to produce 12,500 barrels annually, per worker. Bartl's averaged approxi-

EXHIBIT 6
APPARENT BEER CONSUMPTION BY TYPE (IN MILLIONS OF BARRELS)

Type	1970	1975	1976	1977	1978	1979	Percent change 1978–1979
Popular	71.9	65.4	61.1	57.1	51.8	38.8	−25.1
Premium	46.4	69.8	70.9	77.1	81.4	94.7	+16.3
Super-premium	1.1	5.0	6.1	7.8	9.7	10.5	+ 8.2
Light		2.8	6.5	10.2	15.2	19.1	+25.7
Imports	0.9	1.7	2.4	2.5	3.5	4.4	+25.7
Malt liquors	3.1	3.8	4.2	4.6	4.6	4.3	− 6.5
Total U.S.	123.4	148.5	151.3	159.3	166.2	171.8	
Annual percent change		+3.3	+1.8	+5.4	+4.3	+3.4	

Source: *Impact,* July 15, 1980.

mately 1,200 barrels per worker annually. The plant could produce up to 1,750 barrels per worker annually without additional workers if sales required this output.

The excess capacity of Bartl's was cited by Mayer as a reason to add a light beer and possibly another premium beer to the line. Burg was quick to caution management about the necessity of proper brewing to give a distinctive taste through the lagering process. He was fond of pointing out that the taste tests were usually won by the smaller breweries which lagered their beer over twice as long as the nationals. Burg was proud of the fact that Bartl's was lagered for 55 days, which he maintained was longer than any of their competitors, both national and regional. Burg was a firm advocate of a slow aging process; he claimed it let the flavor and body of the beer develop slowly and the brewer got the advantage of a natural process, rather than using chemicals to speed up lagering. Burg also claimed that he knew the preference of the consumers in Bartl's area and he aimed his beer taste at this target market. This approach pleased Crawford but was not so well received by Mayer. He thought the whole production process was too costly and time-consuming.

Bartl's canning was only 25,000 barrels per year. Mayer, however, contended that the effective capacity was only about 18,000 barrels per year because of a faulty canning line which was frequently inoperative. He was interested in increasing canning capacity if a decision was made to produce a light beer and another premium beer which could be sold in cans. The cost of installing a new canning line, however, could reach $200,000 or more. The old facilities of Bartl's required significant renovation to accommodate new modern machinery.

Replacing old equipment in the brewery with new could cost over $50 a barrel. Burg was of the opinion that much needed improvement could be purchased at far less from breweries that were leaving the industry or had significantly reduced their capacity. He figured that good equipment could be purchased for about $5 to $8 a barrel. He also reminded management that beer tanks had a 50-year life and 5- to 10-year-old tanks could be purchased for 10 cents on the dollar to replace some of Bartl's tanks which were 60 to 70 years old. The used equipment, Burg felt, if in good condition, could be operated efficiently since beer-making technology had changed little over the years. Burg said, "The new kettles and vats aren't any better, they are just more shiny. The only real change in this industry has been the substitution of chemicals for time in the lagering process."

Finance

Peter Simmonds, the chief financial officer, expressed some concern over Bartl's declining profits, which dropped from a high of $190,000 in 1978 to a low of $27,900 in 1980, with a slight increase in 1981 to $33,200. (See Exhibits 7A-E and 8A-E.) Restaurant sales had decreased to a five-year low in 1981, and brewery sales had shown a steady decline for the past 10 years. Bartl's continued to pay a dividend despite some decline in profits and the steady losses in the brewery. Crawford started dividend payments in 1978 and did not wish to discontinue at this time when the investing group was beginning to gain some confidence in the company. He thought it might be necessary to seek additional equity capital from the group at a future date.

Simmonds stated that the long-term debt was being reduced at $150,000 a year in accordance with the conditions of the term loan which was negotiated under Schaefer. The loan was originally for $3 million, with payments of $150,000 due annually starting in 1975. The loan was due to expire in 1985, when all of the remaining balance had to be paid. Simmonds found the low interest rate of 6.5 percent very attractive in view of the high interest rates in 1982. While the company was experiencing a decrease in profits, Simmonds was pleased that the equity was over three times the long-term debt. Operating profit for the restaurants was still 16 percent. The brewery losses, Simmonds asserted, were clouding the real earning power of Bartl's. He also was of the opinion that dividends should be omitted until profits were restored to their 1977–1978 levels.

CRAWFORD'S ASSESSMENT OF BARTL'S FUTURE

Sales of Bartl's continued their decline in July of 1982. Restaurant sales dropped 10 percent, continuing a slide which started early in the year. Crawford attributed this to the on-going recession and problems associated with the Main Street restaurant, which dropped in sales each month of 1982. In July the restaurant was showing a loss of $40,000 for the year to date. Crawford and Seitz thought the changing area around the restaurant and the overall drop in the restaurant business were the reasons for the decline in Main Street's business.

Beer sales continued their drop, recording a total of 19,000 barrels for the first half year. (See Exhibit 2.) Mayer said that increased expense for operations added to declining sales and would probably increase losses 20 to 30 percent for the brewery. In 1981, Bartl's lost $137,000 on sales of $1.8 million on the production of 43,000 barrels of beer.

Crawford was concerned about declining sales and the increasing losses on beer sales. He was still optimistic, however, about the future of Bartl's. He stated:

> Losses have to be a great disappointment to all of management and our group of investors. But I think a good deal of it can be attributed to the recession. We have made progress since we purchased Bartl's in 1977. We now have an organization and some good experienced executives running the company. Restaurants have a bright future, and we will probably expand this area in the future. The combination of Bartl's beer and the selected menu I think is a good attraction. Beer sales are suffering. But I believe this is only temporary. If we add to our product line and promote our

premium draft beer I know sales will increase. We must also seek to expand our selling territory beyond our immediate area. I think we can increase sales in Indiana and Kentucky. I understand Bartl's beer did fairly well there in past years. Chandler had extended sales as far as Oklahoma and Texas. This, of course, is not a good move; the distance is too great, and chances of market penetration are not very good. Bartl's eventually had to pull out of these markets, and when we took over, sales were pretty well confined to the Dayton area with some extensions into Indiana. We have a good beer, and I know it is going to sell. Regionals can compete with nationals in their home territory, particularly if they have the excellent outlet we have in our restaurants for beer sales. We have some plans for the brewery, and liquidation is not among them.

EXHIBIT 7A
Bartl's Brewery
Statement of Earnings
December 31, 1977

	Brewery	**Restaurants**	**Total**
Sales	$2,704,000	$4,970,000	$7,674,000
Less, excise tax	378,560		378,560
Total	$2,325,440	$4,970,000	$7,295,440
Less, cost of goods sold	1,770,330	4,101,200	5,871,530
Gross profit	$ 555,110	$ 868,800	$1,423,910
Less, selling, delivery, & administrative expense	505,000	370,500	875,500
Operating profit	$ 50,110	$ 498,300	$ 548,410
Less, interest expense			167,800
			$ 380,610
Less, other expense			60,610
Profit before taxes			$ 320,000
Taxes			153,600
Net profit			$ 166,400

EXHIBIT 7B
Bartl's Brewery
Statement of Earnings
December 31, 1978

	Brewery	Restaurants	Total
Sales	$2,652,000	$5,020,000	$7,672,000
Less, excise tax	371,280		371,280
Total	$2,280,720	$5,020,000	$7,300,720
Less, cost of goods sold	1,760,220	4,110,000	5,870,220
Gross profit	$ 520,500	$ 910,000	$1,430,500
Less, selling, delivery, & administrative expense	500,500	380,500	881,000
Operating profit	$ 20,000	$ 529,500	$ 549,500
Less, interest expense			162,500
			$ 387,000
Less, other expense			19,880
Profit before taxes			$ 367,120
Taxes			176,160
Net profit			$ 190,000
Dividends paid $1.00 per share			100,000
Net to retained earnings			$ 90,960

EXHIBIT 7C
Bartl's Brewery
Statement of Earnings
December 31, 1979

	Brewery	Restaurants	Total
Sales	$2,420,000	$4,970,000	$7,390,000
Less, excise tax	338,000		338,000
Total	$2,082,000	$4,970,000	$7,052,000
Less, cost of goods sold	1,680,000	4,105,740	5,785,740
Gross profit	$ 402,000	$ 864,260	$1,266,260
Less, selling, delivery, & administrative expense	472,000	370,260	842,260
Operating profit	($ 70,000)	$ 494,000	$ 424,000
Less, interest expense			127,800
			$ 296,200
Less, other expense			11,240
Profit before taxes			$ 284,960
Taxes			137,240
Net profit			$ 147,720
Dividends paid $1.00 per share			100,000
Net to retained earnings			$ 47,720

EXHIBIT 7D
Bartl's Brewery
Statement of Earnings
December 31, 1980

	Brewery	Restaurants	Total
Sales	$2,430,000	$5,010,000	$7,440,000
Less, excise tax	340,200	–	340,200
Total	$2,089,800	$5,010,000	$7,099,800
Less, cost of goods sold	1,679,600	4,140,000	5,819,600
Gross profit	$ 400,200	$ 870,000	$1,270,200
Less, selling, delivery, & administrative expense	490,100	375,600	865,700
Operating profit	($ 89,900)	$ 494,400	$ 404,400
Less, interest expense			137,700
			$ 266,700
Less, other expense			20,700
Profit before taxes			$ 246,000
Taxes			118,080
Net profit			$ 127,920
Dividends paid $1.00 per share			100,000
Net to retained earnings			$ 27,920

EXHIBIT 7E
Bartl's Brewery
Statement of Earnings
December 31, 1981

	Brewery	Restaurants	Total
Sales	$2,132,000	$4,885,000	$7,017,000
Less, excise tax	298,480	–	298,480
Total	$1,833,520	$4,885,000	$6,718,520
Less, cost of goods sold	1,660,520	4,045,000	5,705,520
Gross profit	$ 173,000	$ 840,000	$1,013,000
Less, selling, delivery, & administrative expense	310,000	380,500	690,500
Operating profit	($ 137,000)	$ 459,500	$ 322,500
Less, interest expense			130,500
			$ 192,000
Less, other expense			32,000
Profit before taxes			$ 160,000
Taxes			76,800
Net profit			$ 83,200
Dividends paid 50 cents per share			50,000
Net to retained earnings			$ 33,200

EXHIBIT 8A
Bartl's Brewery
Balance Sheet December 31, 1977

Current Assets

Cash			$358,000
Marketable securities			70,000
Accounts receivable, net			63,000
Inventories:			
Brewery	$148,000		
Restaurants	28,000		176,000
Prepaid expense			20,000
Total current assets			$687,000

Fixed assets	Brewery	Restaurants	
Land	$ 90,000	$1,500,000	$1,590,000
Building, machinery & equipment	3,150,000	1,980,000	5,130,000
Leasehold improvements		90,000	90,000
Cooperage & bottles	240,000		240,000
Total	$3,480,000	$3,570,000	$7,050,000
Less, reserve for depreciation	1,020,000	420,000	1,440,000
Total	$2,460,000	$3,150,000	$5,610,000
Deferred charges			10,000
Total fixed assets			$5,620,000
Total assets			$6,307,000

Current Liabilities

Accounts payable	$ 160,000
Notes payable	80,000
Current part of long-term debt	150,000
Fed. & state income taxes payable	170,000
Other current liabilities	17,000
Total current liabilities	$ 577,000
Long-term debt	$1,750,000

Stockholder's Equity

Common Stock, issued & outstanding, 100,000 shares @ $5.00	$ 500,000
Paid-in-surplus	3,400,000
Retained earnings	80,000
Total equity	$3,980,000
Total liabilities & net worth	$6,307,000 *

EXHIBIT 8B
Bartl's Brewery
Balance Sheet December 31, 1978

Current Assets			
Cash			$ 413,710
Marketable securities			80,000
Accounts receivable, net			85,000
Inventories:			
Brewery	$157,000		
Restaurants	32,000		189,000
Prepaid expense			60,000
Total current assets			$ 827,710

Fixed Assets	Brewery	Restaurants	
Land	$ 90,000	$1,500,000	$1,590,000
Building, machinery & equipment	3,150,000	1,980,000	5,130,000
Leasehold improvements		90,000	90,000
Cooperage & bottles	280,000		280,000
Total	$3,520,000	$3,570,000	$7,090,000
Less, reserve for depreciation	1,191,500	635,250	1,826,750
Total	$2,328,500	$2,934,750	$5,263,250
Deferred charges			70,000
Total fixed assets			$5,333,250
Total assets			$6,160,960

Current Liabilities			
Accounts payable			$ 85,000
Notes payable			60,000
Current part of long-term debt			150,000
Fed. & state income taxes payable			180,000
Other current liabilities			15,000
Total current liabilities			$ 490,000
Long-term debt			$1,600,000

Stockholder's Equity			
Common stock, issued & outstanding,			
100,000 shares @ $5.00			$ 500,000
Paid-in-surplus			3,400,000
Retained earnings			170,960
Total equity			$4,070,960
Total liabilities & net worth			$6,160,960

EXHIBIT 8C
Bartl's Brewery
Balance Sheet December 31, 1979

Current Assets			
Cash			$ 375,970
Marketable securities			80,000
Accounts receivable, net			76,000
Inventories:			
Brewery	$167,000		
Restaurants	40,000		207,000
Prepaid expense			35,000
Total current assets			$ 773,970

Fixed Assets	Brewery	Restaurants	
Land	$ 90,000	$1,500,000	$1,590,000
Building, machinery & equipment	3,200,000	2,130,000	5,330,000
Leasehold improvements		190,000	190,000
Cooperage & bottles	280,000	–	280,000
Total	$3,570,000	$3,820,000	$7,390,000
Less, reserve for depreciation	1,365,500	809,250	2,174,750
Total	$2,204,500	$3,010,750	$5,215,250
Deferred charges			40,000
Total fixed assets			$5,255,250
Total assets			$6,029,220

Current Liabilities	
Accounts payable	$ 80,000
Notes payable to bank	70,000
Current part of long-term debt	150,000
Fed. & state income taxes payable	140,500
Other current liabilities	20,000
Total current liabilities	$ 460,500
Long-term debt	$1,450,000

Stockholder's Equity	
Common stock issued and outstanding	
100,000 shares @ $5.00	$ 500,000
Paid-in-surplus	3,400,000
Retained earnings	218,720
Total equity	$4,118,720
Total liabilities and net worth	$6,029,220

EXHIBIT 8D
Bartl's Brewery
Balance Sheet December 31, 1980

	Brewery	Restaurants	
Current Assets			
Cash			$ 422,890
Marketable securities			190,000
Accounts receivable, net			87,000
Inventories:			
Brewery	$168,500		
Restaurants	42,000		210,500
Prepaid expense			60,000
Total current assets			$ 970,390
Fixed Assets	Brewery	Restaurants	
Land	$ 90,000	$1,500,000	$1,590,000
Building, machinery & equipment	3,200,000	2,130,000	5,330,000
Leasehold improvements		190,000	190,000
Cooperage & bottles	260,000		260,000
Total	$3,550,000	$3,820,000	$7,370,000
Less, reserve for depreciation	1,538,500	983,250	2,521,750
Total	$2,011,500	$2,836,750	$4,848,250
Deferred charges			60,000
Total fixed assets			$4,908,250
Total assets			$5,878,640
Current Liabilities			
Accounts payable			$ 82,000
Notes payable			67,000
Current part of long-term debt			150,000
Fed. & state income taxes payable			118,000
Other current liabilities			15,000
Total current liabilities			$ 432,000
Long-term debt			$1,300,000
Stockholder's Equity			
Common stock, issued & outstanding			
100,000 shares @ $5.00			$ 500,000
Paid-in-surplus			3,400,000
Retained earnings			246,640
Total equity			$4,146,640
Total liabilities & net worth			$5,878,640

EXHIBIT 8E
Bartl's Brewery
Balance Sheet December 31, 1981

Current Assets			
Cash			$ 484,890
Marketable securities			90,000
Accounts receivable, net			68,000
Inventories:			
Brewery	$166,200		
Restaurants	44,800		211,000
Prepaid expense			65,000
Total current assets			$ 918,890

	Brewery	Restaurants	
Fixed Assets			
Land	$ 90,000	$1,500,000	$1,590,000
Building, machinery & equipment	3,200,000	2,230,000	5,430,000
Leasehold improvements		290,000	290,000
Cooperage & bottles	270,000		270,000
Total	$3,560,000	$4,020,000	$7,580,000
Less, reserve for depreciation	1,712,000	1,097,250	2,809,250
Total	$1,848,000	$2,922,750	$4,770,750
Deferred charges			40,000
Total fixed assets			$4,810,750
Total assets			$5,729,640

Current Liabilities		
Accounts payable		$ 78,000
Notes payable		65,000
Current part of long-term debt		150,000
Fed. & state income taxes payable		76,800
Other current liabilities		30,000
Total current liabilities		$ 399,800
Long-term debt		$1,150,000
Stockholder's Equity		
Common stock, issued & outstanding		
100,000 shares @ $5.00		$ 500,000
Paid-in-surplus		3,400,000
Retained earnings		279,840
Total equity		$4,179,840
Total liabilities & net worth		$5,729,640

PART **FOUR**

THE PROCESS OF IMPLEMENTATION: EXECUTING THE STRATEGIC PLAN

CHAPTER 7

Development and Execution of Operating Strategies

OPERATING STRATEGIES

Defining Operating Strategies

Operating strategies set forth the general and specific action management intends to execute in the marketplace and in the management of the dominant functional areas of the business. The operating strategy of a firm is an essential part of its strategic design and flows from the root strategy. Like the root strategy it defines a clearly distinguishable course of action designed to gain a competitive advantage for the firm in the implementation phase. Of necessity, operating strategies must be flexible and subject to more changes and modifications than the root strategy, which has been "institutionalized" and nurtured over a period of time. The dynamics of the marketplace may force management to change operating strategies because of competitive action in terms of pricing, new product introductions, advertising and promotional campaigns, or any number of other unanticipated events. Environmental changes such as raw material and energy shortages, specific government actions such as increased or decreased regulation, or sudden economic changes may also be factors causing shifts in predetermined strategy.

It is essential to distinguish operating strategies from the routine operating plans or procedures which set guidelines for the day-to-day functions of the company's subunits. The term *operating strategy* is frequently used to define any kind of action taken by management without regard to the level or significance of the decision. In the context of this book operating strategy is considered as part of the firm's blueprint for action which should consistently reflect its root strategy. The efficacy of operating strategies must constantly be appraised in terms of their contribution to the progress of the company toward its stated basic economic and business objectives. We are concerned in this chapter with examining the broad scope of general and unique operating strategies which specifically define plans of action compatible with the firm's root strategy. In addition the transindustry and transcompany operating strategies, which can be multifunctional in scope, will also be considered. It is possible to distinguish a firm through a "unique" operating strategy which clearly differentiates it in the marketplace, or through the development of a clearly defined approach to functional management and the control of variables which are the key determinants of profitability.

Unique Operating Strategies

In any business venture there are no obvious courses of action which will lead to assured success. Management usually has a significant number of alternatives to choose from, and with time and experience develops an operating design which allocates the firm's skills and resources to specific courses of action. Some operating strategies are considered unique and do not follow usual industry patterns; however, when successful they clearly distinguish the firm from competition. Avon Products assumed a unique position in the cosmetic industry through its distribution system. Most cosmetic firms sell their products through drug stores, department stores, and supermarket chains. Avon, through a system of neighbor entrepreneurs, "Avon ladies," created a network of independent company representatives, thus avoiding the usual channels of distribution. The company accrued distinct advantages in a highly competitive industry through its home distribution. In addition to a number of personal-care products, Avon added a line of costume jewelry to its independently controlled distribution system. Today the company ranks as the world's largest manufacturer and marketer of cosmetics and costume jewelry. The operating strategy of Avon is closely intertwined with its root strategy, and in the minds of some may be defined as a root strategy.[1]

Nucor Steel, as described in Chapter 3, found a profitable niche in a declining U.S. industry by producing specialty steel in strategically located minimills using as raw material scrap iron and using efficient electric furnaces in production. While the company has judiciously chosen to serve a specific segment of the steel industry, its profitable growth comes mainly from its operating strategy, emphasizing the efficiency of its production process and the ability to service customers in the proximity of its mills.

Compatibility of Operating and Root Strategies

Regardless of how unique a specific operating strategy may be, it must be compatible with the root strategy of the enterprise. For example, a marketing

---

[1] See references to Avon, Chapters 3 and 8.

decision to sell a prestige consumer product through lower-level distribution channels, such as discount houses, may lead to economic disaster.

A production strategy or technology which does not meet the specifications of a product line in terms of style and design, quality and timing will not support a root strategy aimed at a specific market niche, although it may provide significant cost savings. An excellent example of this not-too-uncommon policy error is found in the Electric Steel case,[2] which also reinforces the basic requirement in the development of a root strategy of making a thorough and realistic appraisal of a firm's existing and projected skills and resources needed to attain predetermined basic objectives. The failure of many enterprises to execute a seemingly realistic strategy can be traced to an inadequate determination of the skills and resources required for implementation.

> The Electric Steel Corporation was formed to manufacture high-quality alloy steels using the Dornin process to produce the steel in electric furnaces. The original intent and the root strategy of the organizers of the firm was well defined. Management sought to satisfy the need for special-purpose alloy steels in a selected niche in the market, mainly for aircraft manufacturers and other highly specialized industrial users.
>
> Unfortunately, Electric Steel found itself in a precarious financial position shortly after its organization. The promoters miscalculated the amount of capital needed to put the corporation on a sound, going-concern basis and to put into effect its operating strategy. As a result, they had to resort to extensive borrowing, which proved to be a distinct disadvantage in light of subsequent operations. Because of the lack of capital, management was not able to complete the plant and facilities of the corporation according to their original plan. Inadequate production facilities in certain areas of the plant increased production costs and, to a great extent, nullified the advantages of the modern facilities which were present in the main area of the installation. Problems of finance also pressured the company to seek any type of order available on the steel market. Despite the original intention of producing and selling high-alloy steels, the firm, as an expedient measure, entered into the carbon-steel ingot trade, which eventually accounted for 30 percent of its total sales. This move was contrary to its root and operating strategies and brought Electric Steel into head-on competition with the larger and more efficient producers of the basic ingot and heavier steels. In this area, the firm had no competitive advantage but rather distinct competitive disadvantages.

The Electric Steel Corporation case presents a situation where the essential elements of policymaking were neglected and suitable alternative operating strategies were lacking. The company's hastily conceived, expedient operating strategies did not follow the root strategy, and the advantages of its product technology—its major competitive asset—was lost in its product-line selection and marketing efforts.

---

[2] See Thomas J. McNichols, *Policymaking and Executive Action*, 4th ed. (New York: McGraw-Hill, 1972), pp. 190–207.

Operating Strategies to Define Specific Action in the Marketplace

Operating strategies may define specific action in the marketplace. A major producer of floor coverings, for example, chose to distribute through wholesalers despite the fact that many of its competitors had abandoned this channel for direct distribution and the use of company-owned warehouses. IBM preferred to lease its products rather than make direct customer sales; this was not only a market strategy but a financial strategy as well. It also gave the company advantages in terms of maintenance and control of its products. Ford Motor Company, by virtue of its initial root strategy of producing and marketing a quality, low-price, standard automobile, was able to effect necessary operating strategies through the development of mass-production techniques which gave the firm competitive advantages in the industry for several decades. Capturing and maintaining market share or position is one of the most important elements of the implementation phase. Various operating strategies are utilized to attain this coveted goal; they may follow the pattern of price cutting, product-line proliferation, changes in channels of distribution, the utilization of new production technologies, and the use of financial power or techniques.

Operating Strategies to Gain and Maintain Market Position: The Clorox Case

Maintenance of market position may be an essential factor in effecting other operating strategies and in gaining essential competitive advantages. The largest producer of liquid bleach in the United States, Clorox (see case discussion in Part Eight of this volume), until recent years was a single-product company. Bleach is a relatively inexpensive product to manufacture and—because of a low sales price and high shipping costs—was not profitable to sell more than 300 miles from the point of manufacture. In addition, all liquid bleaches were chemically identical. To distinguish itself in this undistinguishable market, Clorox developed an operating strategy designed to capture market share and gain competitive advantages. The company eventually developed 13 strategically located plants which assured national distribution. Its closest competitor, Purex, had as many plants, but its bleach was available in less than half of the national market. Assured of national distribution, Clorox was able to develop a "long-continued mass advertising campaign" which made its product known to and preferred by the housewife as a premium brand. This national distribution and advertising enabled the company to differentiate its product and gain over 50 percent of the liquid bleach market. With its dominant market position, its bleach commanded a premium price.

This action by Clorox delineates the significant advantages accruing to a company through the successful execution of operating strategies aimed at increasing market share. The question could be raised, however, of whether or not the company's distinct operating strategies should have been considered as an integral part of its root strategy. However, if we recognize that it was a one-product company producing and selling only liquid bleach—essentially the same product sold by other, similar companies—then we have to look to the operating strategies of Clorox to trace the development of its dominant position.

A recent effort was initiated by Levi Strauss to gain market share and protect a position as the leading producer and marketer of "jeans" in the United States. Levi reached agreement to sell its famous product to Sears, Roebuck, the world's largest retailer, and to J. C. Penney, also a large mass merchandiser with a national chain of department stores. This represents a departure from Levi's long-standing policy of distributing through smaller, exclusive department stores and "jean boutiques." This move represents a distinct change in the company's operating strategy and is reported to have irritated Levi's traditional distributors.[3]

Generic Operating Strategies and Their Application

In recent years a number of significant strategic prescriptions have been developed which have provided a set of practical general strategies which can be applied across business lines and industry boundaries. The most prominent and widely used of these general or generic strategies are the *experience curve* and the *product portfolio matrix* initiated and utilized by the Boston Consulting Group (BCG), the various *industry attractiveness/business position matrices,* and the empirically based *market-strategy profitability analysis of PIMS.* These general strategies are interrelated and complementary and can be effectively used in determining and assessing the operating strategy of an on-going firm with a multiple product line or a number of subbusiness units (SBUs). In each of these strategic aids attention is directed to the functional dynamics of the firm and the monitoring of operational effectiveness under varying market and industry situations. In this section these concepts will be compared and contrasted, and their degree of complementarity and their usefulness in developing and executing operating strategies of the firm will be analyzed.

The Experience Curve as a Strategic Aid One of the "oldest" and most frequently referred to of the generic strategies is the "tired" experience curve. This useful strategic aid evolved from the learning curve, which was first observed in the aircraft industry by the commander of the Wright-Patterson Air Base in 1925. He calculated that the hours of labor it took to make one plane would predictably decline with the number of planes produced; thus the unit cost of production would decline with the accumulated units of production.

The learning curve has been applied to a number of industries where there is intense direct labor in the production process, such as the electronics, automo-

---

[3] See references to Levi Strauss, Chapter 3.

tive, and appliance industries. It has been used for internal analysis of assembly operations, cost-control decisions, and determination of pricing policies.

In 1966 the Boston Consulting Group through its founder, Bruce Henderson, expanded the learning curve to the more inclusive experience curve. In this concept firm activities other than just the direct cost of labor are taken into consideration in determining unit cost. The experience curve is based on the reasoning that the costs of any repetitive task, not just the direct labor costs of production, can be decreased, as the accumulated experience of performing the tasks increases. This would include all activities associated with a specific product, such as marketing, purchasing, and administration. The Boston Consulting Group maintains that the cost of most tasks and activities associated with adding value to a product will decrease approximately 20 to 30 percent each period the accumulated experience of performing these tasks and activities doubles.[4] In addition to direct labor associated with production, indirect labor tasks such as maintenance and material supply handling and delivery improve, overall supervision of the entire manufacturing process improves, and support staff as well as line management increase their efficiency.

The experience curve shown in Exhibit 7-1 follows the pattern of the learning curve. It is to be noted that the vertical axis measures cost per unit, in real terms, representing a composite of tasks performed, not just the direct labor costs associated with producing a product. The horizontal axis indicates the total experience associated with the product; this experience is usually stated as accumulated units produced. Following the BCG estimates that cost per unit decline approximately 20 to 30 percent each time accumulated units double, an average experience curve would be stated as a 70 to 80 percent (100—30 or 20) curve.[5]

The continued production of a specific product may also lead to product improvements and possibly innovations which not only increase demand but can also be a force in decreasing costs. It is also possible to develop lower-cost materials to incorporate into the products, thus effectively reducing unit costs.

Like the learning curve, the experience curve is more effectively used for standarized products with a distinct production process. As described in Chapter 2, Ford's objective to produce a low-priced quality automobile led to the standardization of the car to aid in effecting low unit costs of production. In the rapid growth period of Ford Motors, prices paralleled costs and enabled the company to gain the largest share of the automotive market. Volkswagen gained a major position in the automobile industry by producing the standarized, no-model-change Beetle. As to be expected, when the Model T and the Beetle reached maturity and entered a decline phase, the companies were forced by competition to produce a wider line of cars. The change from a single

[4] The Boston Consulting Group: "The Experience Curve Reviewed: I. The Concept," *Perspectives No. 124.*

[5] The Boston Consulting Group: "Experience Curves as a Planning Tool," reprinted from *IEEE Spectrum*, June 1970 (based on a speech by Dr. Patrick Conley, BCG, Feb. 1970).

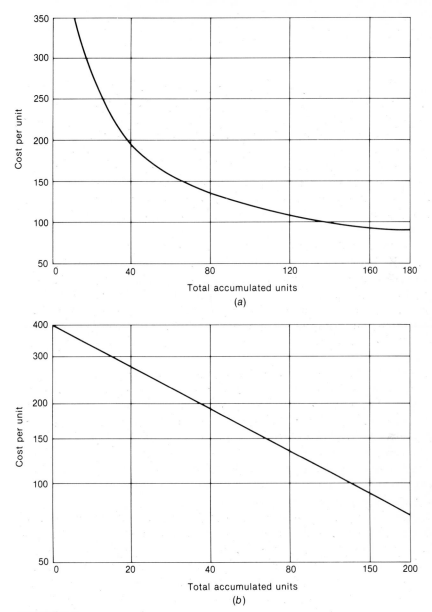

EXHIBIT 7-1
(a) Experience relationships on a linear scale; (b) experience relationships on a
log scale.

standardized product line to a broader line significantly reduced the effects of the
experience curve the firms enjoyed in their growth stages.

Strategic Implications of the Experience Curve   Although the experience
curve represents an approximation, it can be utilized as an effective strategic

aid. It is clear that if a firm has the lowest unit cost in an industry or segment of an industry, it also has achieved the highest production volume. Since it is rational to assume that a company would not produce a product unless it could be sold, then the highest-volume producer would have the largest market share. This relationship of total accumulated production and market share has been commonly observed. Market share and profitability are also equated, with some reservations. The following section discussing the PIMS material covers this relationship. Seeking to gain the most favorable position in a growth industry would require a producer to go down the experience curve as rapidly as possible to gain a dominant market share, and as a consequence high profits in relation to competitors. If a producer is seeking to gain market share from a market leader, the experience curve will signal the need to "close the gap" between the accumulated production of the leader and the challenger. This competitive action would require a thorough examination of the challenger's skills and resources to accomplish this task, and the skills and resources of the leaders, who may fight any effort to dislodge their company from its dominant market position.

In mature markets attempts to gain market share in a slow-growth market in most instances would not be worth the cost to increase capacity and attempt to lower marginal unit costs. At this stage the market leader or leaders will have the advantage of lower unit costs and be much better positioned to weather a price war.

If it is possible to have some knowledge of competitors' costs, and their accumulated production, the experience curve can be used to estimate the growth rate needed to attain parity with the competition. With high constant growth rates it is possible to overtake competitors in a short period of time, assuming they do not choose to protect their position because of complacency or a short-run outlook aimed at reaping profits. If pricing by the market-share leaders does not parallel their cost curve, it is to be assumed they are engaging in umbrella pricing. It is not likely they would price below the cost curve unless engaged in a serious price war.

The experience curve may also be a useful aid in cost control and pricing. Cost declines are predictable and consequently can aid in pricing. Texas Instruments, with leading market shares in semiconductors and handheld calculators, is said to have used "experience curve pricing" to gain an early foothold in these markets, and to aid in protecting their position against competitors. In adding new plant capacity for these products the company was able to predict its path along the experience curve and hence its unit costs, which allowed them to price their products on this basis before the new production came on stream.

Limitations of the Experience Curve   The use of the experience curve as a strategic aid is limited by a number of factors that have often plagued the use of accounting data: How can the product and its constituent elements be defined? How much overhead should be allocated to each product? All elements of costs related to a product will not have the same experience base. Several products may share costs of a common element included in each, such as an electric motor used in fans, drills, or paint sprayers. Calculating unit cost for each of these products with shared costs of the electric motor, however, should provide the company with a potential advantage over competitors since it would have gone down the experience curve with an essential element of the new products.

Scale effects are an important element in the utilization of the experience curve. It is estimated that approximately 10 to 15 percent of a typical experience curve is a result of direct labor saving and 10 to 15 percent results from task specialization. Increases in production result in increased workers, which permits the division of task assignments, thus increasing worker experience.[6] Unless there is market growth to support increasing capacity and work force, scale effects will not be attained. As in the case of calculating unit costs and shared costs, scale effects are very difficult to measure.

The experience curve is also a function of the rate of investment. Unless the firm has the capital or can gain it in the marketplace, it will not be able to build in the capacity and specialization required to finance growth and the resulting decline in marginal unit costs. These necessary requirements for gaining market share are not readily available to all entrants into an industry. As previously indicated the lack of capital is a common problem of embryonic firms seeking to gain an "anchor" in a growing industry. In corporations with a high "cutoff" rate for adding investment, cost declines along the experience curve will be slow; conversely if the cutoff rate is low, cost declines will be rapid. Without added investment capacity cannot be increased to gain the advantages of declining marginal unit costs.

It has been frequently mentioned that firms that build capital intensity by investing in plant and equipment to gain experience curve advantages may be severely reducing their flexibility. Gaining market share in products or industries that are subject to technological changes, or to the introduction of innovative products, may entail high risks. A new effort is being made to chart technology life cycles based on empirical data to aid in avoiding this pitfall of the experience curve, where a product is clearly identified with a specific technology. Before any company embarks on the pursuit of market share it should assess the nature of this risk, and also try to ascertain as accurately as possible where the products fit in terms of their life cycles.

Use of the experience curve has also been criticized because it in effect assumes that all products are, or become, commodity items, with little or no discernible differentiation among them. Since most examples of the successful use of the experience curve strategy involve high-value added products, there seems to be little application of this concept to the service industries, the fastest-growing sector of the economy. The use of the experience curve is also

---

[6]Boston Consulting Group: "The Experience Curve Reviewed: II. Why Does It Work?" *Perspectives No. 128.*

questioned because it is not logical to employ experience curve strategy in no-growth or slow-growth industries, which presently make up a substantial part of our economy.[7]

Despite these limitations, the experience curve can be effectively applied in many competitive situations as a strategic planning aid. It not only allows for internal analysis but can also be utilized to gain an understanding of competitors' positions and likely strategy.

PORTFOLIO ANALYSIS

Business-Product Analysis

The experience curve is based on the concept that costs are a direct function of accumulated market share. Market share equates to profitability and cash flow. The on-going firm that has successful SBUs (subbusiness units) and product lines will generate large cash flows as the SBUs or products move toward maturity as contrasted to the large cash requirements of SBUs and product lines in their growth and development stages. As SBUs and product lines decline, cash flow will diminish and fade away. Effective utilization of cash flows and the nurturing of the most productive units requires management's constant surveillance.

Unlike the single product firm, the diversified company with multiple SBUs or product lines has the opportunity to balance cash flows and channel investment into the most promising areas of its portfolio. Diversified portfolios enable a company to control its internal allocation of resources. The ability to utilize tax losses from one unit as an offset against a profitable one is an important advantage. Investing funds from a profitable maturing unit or product into the growing and cash-demanding part of the firm, which shows a tax loss, effectively lowers the cost of capital and provides an avenue for future growth through internally generated funds.

The basis for portfolio analysis and the channeling of available investment funds into the most promising and productive units of the firm is based on the structure and philosophy of management. Its approach to control of SBUs and product lines, its attitude toward risk and growth, and its interpretation of its life-cycle position are factors which have an impact on the effective use of portfolio management.

The company which structures its diversified units into separate independent profit center entities with each area depending on its own resources may factor out the flexibility and advantages inherent in its diversification. Concentration on short-run profits and ignoring the potential growth sectors of the portfolio because of their initial lack of cash flow and profitability can lead to cash-draining, last-ditch stands in the defensive stage of the firm's life cycle and eventual movement into the decline phase. Failure to nurture prospective in-

---

[7]See W. J. Abernathy, K. Wayne, "Limits of the Learning Curve," *Harvard Business Review,* September-October 1974, pp. 109–119.

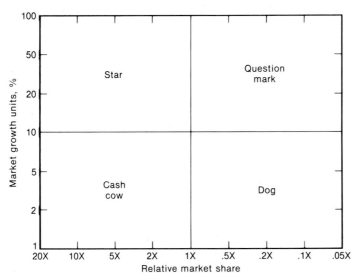

EXHIBIT 7-2
Boston consulting group (BCG) growth/share matrix.

vestments will eventually lead to a portfolio of mature, declining SBUs or product lines. This frequently leads to intensive acquisition and merger efforts as the firm seeks to employ the cash flows from mature businesses and product lines. The success of portfolio management is dependent on policymakers assuming the role of investors seeking to maximize long-run returns rather than a short-run position of operational managers.

Growth/Share Matrix

To aid in portfolio management BCG developed a four-cell business-product matrix which provides a display that can be utilized to make judgments about cash flow and the stage of growth, maturity, or decline of major SBUs or product lines.[8] Exhibit 7-2 shows BCG's frequently used and reproduced four-cell matrix. The horizontal axis indicates relative market share equivalent to cash generation and the vertical axis market or industry growth equivalent to cash use. A firm utilizing this matrix would plot its SBUs or product lines in one of the four quadrants depending upon the growth rate of the industry where its unit competes and the competitive position of the SBU or product based on market share. SBUs are frequently represented by circles with the size of the circle indicating the size of the business unit. SBUs or products falling within the lower left quadrant have low or stabilized market growth but high market share. These units produce or throw off more cash than can be effectively

[8]Boston Consulting Group: "The Experience Curve Reviewed: IV. The Growth Share Matrix or the Product Portfolio," *Perspectives No. 135*, 1973.

utilized to maintain their market position. These SBUs and product lines are labeled "cash cows" and can be milked to provide investment capital for promising growth businesses or embyronic product lines in the development stage. The SBUs or product lines which fall into the upper left quadrant are high growth units which are likely to provide sufficient cash flow to finance their requirements for market growth but not throw off cash for other investments. These units are designated the "stars" of the portfolio and represent the ultimate market position sought by management.

Units falling into the upper-right-hand quadrant are named "question marks." These SBUs or product lines are in the growth and development stage; their outcome in terms of long-run success is undetermined, although they have been selected as promising ventures worthy of capital investment. These units absorb cash; their cash requirements are likely to be high because of growth and development. They generate little cash and are presumed to be poised on the threshold waiting to enter the star category. A firm cannot support any significant number of SBUs or products in this cell, nor can it afford many failures or "also rans" which never emerge to the star category but fall into the kennel to become the "corporate dogs."

"Dogs" which fall into the lower right quadrant have low growth and low market share. Their "barking" resounds through the corporate halls since they are the cash traps that produce little or no profit. They entered the kennel through the cash cow or maturity cell as their market share and cash-generating ability diminished, or they dropped through the trap door of the question mark cell as failures. Units in the dog category are frequently the subject of much management discussion concerning how and when they should be phased out or if there is still any life left in "the old dog." This kind of management consideration is often a factor in producing the "blips" or "ripples" in the life cycle of an SBU or product line as a result of belated injections of capital for product modifications and promotions. Management usually finds it difficult to discard a business or product and direct its efforts to the promising growing ventures. This is particularly true if the units have had a long and profitable history.

Uses and Limitations of BCG's Growth/Share Matrix

The BCG four-cell matrix has the advantages previously discussed as an effective display to initiate portfolio analysis. Its major advantage is its simplicity. A visual display of the corporation's SBUs or product lines indicating their relative market share and growth can provide management with an initial starting point for developing or changing its strategic thrust. It allows management to track and balance cash flows from its diversified units. Cash providers and cash users can be distinguished. Policymakers can view their firm's position in its businesses and product lines and their relative industry status. The preparation and plotting of the SBUs and product lines on the matrix generally supplies much of the significant data needed for portfolio analysis and indicates additional information required for a thorough evaluation of the firm's overall position relative to its SBUs and product lines.

While the BCG matrix does provide a "quick glance" at the firm's position and an adaptable framework for considering investment alternatives, in the opinion of some analysts its major strength, simplicity, is also its main weakness. The extent of the relationship between cash flow and market share may be weak and difficult to determine in practice, and the correlation of industry growth and cash flow may also be questioned. Variations in industry structure, the difficulty of determining the dimensions of market segments, and a number of other interrelated variables may cause actual cash flow to deviate from predicted cash flows.

INDUSTRY OR MARKET ATTRACTIVENESS/BUSINESS POSITION MATRICES

Several multiple-celled matrices have been developed to enhance portfolio analysis. To an extent they eliminate some of the weaknesses attributed to BCG's growth/share matrix. These matrices are not based on quantitative measure of market share and industry or market growth, but utilize a number of qualitative factors which are significant in determining industry or market attractiveness and the relative competitive strengths and weaknesses of the firm. ROI (return on investment) is used as the basis for comparison of the business units represented in the displays. ROI measurement adds another dimension which may be more important in comparing investment options than market share, market growth, or cash flow.

A number of industry (or market) attractiveness/business (or competitive) position matrices are discussed in the literature and used in practice. Most of them represent adaptations or variations of the well-known *General Electric planning matrix* or the *Shell directional policy matrix*. These matrices will be discussed and analyzed as important examples of this popular strategic aid to portfolio management.

GE's Planning Grid

The General Electric screen shown in Exhibit 7-3 depicts industry or market attractiveness on the horizontal axis and business strengths or competitive position on the vertical axis. Each SBU is analyzed according to the criteria indicated in the exhibit and plotted on the screen to display its relative position. The strategic consideration for each SBU is determined by the position on the screen following the same general pattern suggested on the BCG growth share matrix. The lightly shaded areas in the upper left cells signal investment for growth and share building, the blank areas call for holding action and maintenance of position, and the black areas indicate a need for harvesting and phased divestment.[9]

---

[9] See "Not Recession Proof, but Recession Resistant," *Forbes*, March 15, 1975; W. K. Hall, "SBU's Hot, New Topic in the Management of Diversification," *Business Horizons*, vol. 23, no. 1, February 1978; C.H. Springer, "Strategic Management in General Electric," *Operations Research*, vol. 21, no. 6, November-December 1973, pp. 1177–1182.

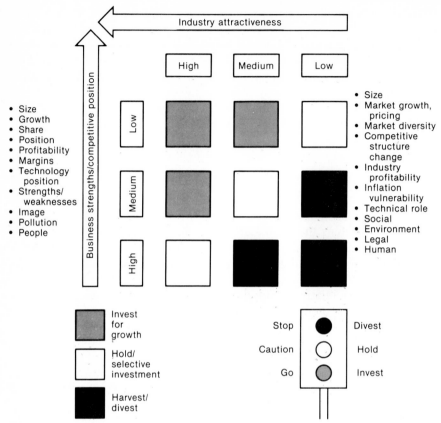

EXHIBIT 7-3
General Electric's planning grid.

A stoplight analogy has been applied to the planning grid to reinforce the strategic action suggested by the position of the SBUs on the screen. The lightly shaded areas represent a green light indicating a "go-ahead" for investment and development where business strength and industry attractiveness are high. The yellow light denotes caution for SBUs falling into the blank spaces of the grid. This suggests a holding action because business strength is low but the industry is attractive. Investment here is cautious and selective. The red light applies to the black areas where both business strength and industry attractiveness is low. SBUs in these cells are not candidates for further investment. Where possible they are "nursed along" for cash flow or gradually phased out or divested.

Shell Matrix

The Shell directional policy matrix shown in Exhibit 7-4 follows the same general pattern of the GE planning grid. Business attractiveness is plotted on the

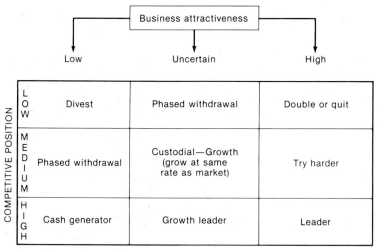

	Business attractiveness	
Low	Uncertain	High

COMPETITIVE POSITION		Low	Uncertain	High
	L O W	Divest	Phased withdrawal	Double or quit
	M E D I U M	Phased withdrawal	Custodial—Growth (grow at same rate as market)	Try harder
	H I G H	Cash generator	Growth leader	Leader

Evaluate criteria of business attractiveness—
evaluate competitive position
Use scale of 1–2–3–4

EXHIBIT 7-4
Shell directional policy matrix.

horizontal axis and competitive position on the vertical axis. Specific strategic action is recommended as shown in the exhibit for the units plotted in each of the nine cells.

The Shell matrix extends the utilization of the strategic planning grids by providing for the plotting of competitors' positions in each of the sectors of the matrix to enable management to compare its relative position with competitors. Terminology used in the Shell matrix differs in some respects from the BCG and GE matrices. The *disenvestment* cell corresponds to the *dog* in BCG and to the *harvest/divest* cells in the GE grid. The *phased withdrawal* cell would fall between the lines on the BCG matrix and equate to the *harvest/divest* position of GE. The *custodial* cell corresponds to the caution *hold position/selective investment* cell of GE. The four-cell BCG matrix does not provide for this distinction. The *double or quit* cell suggests the *question marks* in the BCG matrix or the *invest/growth* cells of GE. Units falling into this category are the ones to be selected for development into *leaders* or *stars*. The *try harder* cell includes units that have a position but if assigned more resources have the potential of becoming leaders in their sector. The *leader* cell corresponds to BCG's *star* and to GE's *invest/growth* cells. The *cash generator* category is related to BCG's *cash cow* and GE's *harvest/divest* cells.[10]

---

[10] See "The Directional Policy Matrix: A New Aid to Corporate Planning," *Shell Chemicals,* United Kingdom, November 1975; D. E. Hussey, "Portfolio Analysis: Practical Experiences with the Directional Policy Matrix," *Long-Range Planning,* vol. 11, no. 4, August 1978. See Also, S. J. D. Robinson, R. E. Hitchens, and D. P. Wade, "The Directional Policy Matrix: Tool for Strategic Planning," *Long-Range Planning,* vol. 11, no. 3, June 1978, pp. 8–15.

Use and Limitations of Industry Attractiveness/Business Position Matrices

The GE and Shell matrices add valuable dimensions to the BCG four-cell matrix. They allow for simultaneous comparison of several businesses in terms of the investment criteria of ROI. Like the BCG matrix they are particularly helpful in defining investment decisions at the corporate level for the varied units in the firm's portfolio. Their utility can also be extended to aid in determining the operating strategies to be pursued by each unit.

Developing the required data and criteria to make qualitative judgments about industry attractiveness and competitive strengths of the firm in order to plot the specific units on the matrix may be one of the most valuable contributions of this process. Projecting this analysis into the future to make judgments about where the industry will be in two to five years in terms of size, technology, the nature of competition, and industry structure provides the basis for assessing opportunities and competitive threats of the future. In this context the firm must also appraise its strengths and weaknesses and what its competitive position is likely to be in the future. Plotting the position of the firm and its major competitors on a matrix designed to reflect the characteristics of an industry in a designated future period provides a valuable strategic planning aid. It allows the firm to anticipate changes and to develop strategic responses.

The industry attractiveness/business position matrices, like the growth/share matrix, are basically simple displays or grids which can aid management in making strategic decisions. The judgments about what constitutes industry attractiveness and assessment of the competitive strengths of the firm are qualitative. While they can be weighted and tested over time, they still only represent the assessments of management. The required action necessary to implement the suggested signals of investing and expanding, holding a position, or divesting specific units may present a formidable complex task for management. Not many organizations have the stability and flexibility required to readily alter their strategic thrusts.

Long-held positions representing significant capital investments are not easily divested or "traded off." It is difficult to shift investment emphasis from the "tried and true" units to the promising ones that show potential. The decentralized structures of corporations and the general semiautonomous nature of SBUs in their portfolio of businesses is likely to be a strong deterrent to this kind of strategic action. As previously mentioned, in making strategic choices in portfolio management policymakers must think in terms of investment decisions, not operating decisions.

PIMS: PROFIT IMPACT OF MARKET SHARE

The PIMS Model

The nonprofit Strategic Planning Institute (SPI) has developed the largest data bank of information focused on the analysis of strategic business planning. Approximately 200 companies, representing over 2000 separate business units, participate.

In terms of a PIMS definition, a business unit is described:

> . . . as a division, product line, or other profit center within its parent company, selling a distinct set of products and/or services to a well-defined set of competitors and for which meaningful separation can be made of revenues, operating costs, investments and strategic plans.[11]

These SBUs form the data base providing information on about 100 items which describe market environment, the state of competition, the business strategies utilized, and the operating results. In PIMS evaluation, these factors account for 80 percent of the observed variation in the profitability of the SBUs included in the data base.

The PIMS program is divided into a profit-predicting model based on ROI, and a cash-flow–predicting model. The profit-predicting model is a function of 37 factors related to ROI, and the cash-flow–predicting model is a function of 19 variables or factors. Some of the factors are contained in each of the models. The variables used in this empirical model are isolated by utilizing multiple regression. The PIMS program also supplies a PAR report, which indicates the ROI that is considered normal for a business in a given industry situation with a particular set of characteristics which define its competitive position, its technology, and cost structure. The report also identifies the major strengths and weaknesses of the firm, which accounts for a high or low PAR. PAR data is developed from other businesses with similar characteristics.

Major Findings of PIMS

Market Share and Product Quality   The interrelationship of the experience curve and market share is clearly illustrated in the PIMS models. The importance and role of market share as a major factor influencing profitability is emphasized in the PIMS data. (Market share is defined as the firm's share as a percent of the three largest shareholders in the industry or market segment.) Their findings indicate that most high-share businesses have above-average rates of ROI and most small-share businesses have ROI below average. SBUs with large market shares tended to have above-average rates of investment turnover, and their ratio of marketing expense to sales was generally lower than that of firms with lower market shares. Product quality was closely related to market share. Firms with high quality and high market share recorded the highest ROIs. Quality of product was also found to partially offset low market share.[12]

[11] The PIMS Program, Strategic Planning Institute, 1977.

[12] See R. D. Buzzell and F. D. Wiersema, "Successful Share-Building Strategies," *Harvard Business Review,* January-February 1981, pp. 135–144; R. D. Buzzell, B. T. Gale, and R. G. M. Sultan, "Market Share Key to Profitability," *Harvard Business Review,* January-February 1975.

Analysis of the PIMS data revealed certain market patterns related to market share. The findings showed that in general if the second-ranking competitor was two-thirds as large as the leader, the third-ranked competitor was two-thirds as large as the second. These ratios continued down the line of market rankings. PIMS approximation of competitive ranking in a "natural structure" would be 40 percent share for the leader, the second-ranking firm would have 25 percent, the third 15 percent, and the fourth 10 percent.[13]

These data revealed that high marketing expenditures did not build market share for lower-quality products. The ROI of high-quality or average-quality products were also affected by high levels of marketing expenditures but not to the same extent as the lower-quality products. These findings suggest that strong firms with high market share could in the short-run increase marketing expenditures to gain additional market share to the detriment of their weaker competition.

Investment Intensity PIMS found that the most important impact on ROI after market share and product quality was investment intensity (defined as the ratio of total investment to sales). Analysis indicated that the higher the investment intensity the lower the ROI. It is assumed that these firms do not produce profit margins sufficient to offset the high investment in working assets. The nature of the industry, the state of its technology, and the extent of vertical integration are all factors contributing to investment intensity.[14]

Company Characteristics PIMS analysis showed that in general larger companies benefited most from large market share, and earned the highest ROI; average firms, in the middle, earned the lowest ROI. Larger companies received greater benefits from strong market positions than smaller firms. The smaller companies fared better, however, than the large firms in businesses with general low market shares. A number of other factors derived from the PIMS data were analyzed to determine their effect on ROI.[15]

Uses and Advantages of PIMS The PIMS program provides an exceptional data bank for analyzing the major factors affecting the profitability of the firm. It contains many more variables than the other matrices utilized in portfolio analysis and includes distinct measures of predicted ROI and cash flow. PIMS is applied to one business at a time, allowing a more thorough analysis of the strategy of an individual firm. Since the model is based on the data reported by approximately 2000 SBUs, it affords the opportunity to compare the results of the effects of strategic changes on ROI and cash flow of the single firm to what is considered normal or PAR for the companies included in the data bank. The

[13] R. D. Buzzell, B. T. Gale, and R. G. M. Sultan, op. cit.
[14] S. Schoeffler, R. D. Buzzell, and D. F. Heany, "Impact of Strategic Planning on Profit Performance," *Harvard Business Review*, March-April 1974.
[15] Ibid.

empirical data based on the past performances of companies involved in the PIMS program is diverse and cross-sectional, covering a variety of industrial classifications, and includes large, medium, and small firms.[16]

PIMS can be applied to the strategic planning process at several stages. ROI and cash-flow expectations can be analyzed in terms of the PAR reports, and shifts in operating strategies for SBUs can be quantitatively analyzed to determine the effects of changing key variables on ROI. PIMS provides analysis for the major classes of profit influences such as: industry/market environment, long-run industry growth rate, and short-run market growth; competitive position of the firm, market share, and product quality; capital structure, investment intensity, and fixed-capital intensity; the production process structure and the effects of vertical integration; company characteristics, corporate size, and degree of corporate diversity; budget allocation effects; and change-action factors.[17]

Limitations of PIMS   The multiplicity of variables utilized in PIMS provides many advantages for strategic analysis, but it may also be a limiting factor for precise and accurate appraisal. The statistical problems of multicollinearity caused by the relationship of the numerous variables prevents separating the effect of individual variables on the dependent variable.

PIMS developed independent clusters to facilitate separation of the effect of the variables on ROI and cash flow. However the individual variables are still difficult if not impossible to isolate. The inclusion of a large number of variables also makes the task of preparation difficult and time-consuming as compared with the other strategic aids for portfolio management. The understanding of this complex model may also be difficult and lead to incorrect interpretations. Analysis of future market changes and what they might mean to a firm's strategy are not provided by PIMS, with the exception of the impact on sales prices and costs. The major emphasis of PIMS is placed on the current operating strategy of the firm.[18] The association of ROI and market share may be the combined result of some unspecified third influence. Interpreting the direction of causation in PIMS models is still an open question. This argues for exercising considerable caution especially in using PIMS results to support untested policy prescriptions.

A number of other critical observations have been directed toward PIMS.[19] However, most critics of the program attest to its value and recognize it as the most comprehensive collection of empirical data available which can be effectively utilized as a strategic aid in business planning.

---

[16] Ibid.

[17] The PIMS Program, The Strategic Planning Institute, 1977.

[18] See D. F. Abell and J. S. Hammond, *Strategic Market Planning: Problems and Analytical Concepts* (Englewood Cliffs, N.J.: Prentice-Hall, 1979).

[19] See C. R. Anderson and F. T. Paine, "PIMS: A Reexamination," *Academy of Management Review*, July 1978, pp. 602–612.

OPERATING STRATEGY AND THE PLANNING FUNCTION

In each stage of the company's development and progress toward attaining its basic objectives, particular functional areas may require specific attention. The emphasis may shift from marketing to production and other areas of operation that require special consideration at a particular point in time to ensure conformity and coordination with the company's strategic design. In a dynamic business enterprise, particularly multiproduct companies and highly diversified organizations, it may be difficult to identify the operating phase of the strategic planning process. Most firms have a variety of operating plans in various stages of completion: long-range plans, short-range plans, special programs, and specific plans relating to subfunctions of the company. These plans outline a method or scheme of action or describe a program designed to effect particular operating strategies. In attempting to evaluate the operational strategy, it is convenient to think in terms of a master plan supplemented by detailed plans. The master plan should provide the overall blueprint or coordinating factor for the entire company program of action and should be the directing or guiding force for detailed functional planning. The master plan will be subject to numerous changes because of uncertainties and shifts in the marketplace. Long-range plans which outline action to be taken over a period of years, usually considered to be three to five years or longer, are subject to the greatest uncertainties and possibilities of change. Short-range plans, which are usually considered to run three months to a year or three years, are less likely to be changed. All plans must be flexible and should be backed by alternative plans. The ability to keep pace with trends in the market is a necessary element in the planning function. The shifting and adjusting of plans as part of the operating strategy may be required to cope with unanticipated moves by competitors or to keep pace with changes in economic conditions. The ability to meet the demands of particular situations and to provide the necessary flexibility to cope with change is a vital part of day-to-day planning.

EVALUATING OPERATING STRATEGY

The operating strategy should be designed to balance a company's skills and resources and to utilize them to the best possible advantage. All the functions of the business unit must be coordinated and conflicts of purpose between them resolved in terms of the overall basic objectives of the firm to eliminate suboptimization. The master plan should be designed to outline the comprehensive program and the principal steps in carrying this program into action to implement the operating strategy.

In the development of operating strategies designed to implement the firm's root strategy and to determine the plans to initiate action, the following questions may serve as guidelines:

1 Do the operating strategies best suit the company's skills and re-

sources? Marketing skills and resources? Production skills and resources? Personnel and labor skills?

2 Have the external factors been considered in the selection of operating strategies? Economic conditions? Competitive pattern? Industry factors?

3 Has the adopted plan been projected to determine extent of skill and resource utilization? Additional skills and resources needed? Possible effects of the plan on competitors? Potential customers and size of market?

4 Have the long-range and short-range plans been coordinated to effect operating strategies?

5 Has a range of alternative plans been considered?

6 Have well-defined alternative plans been drafted for use if needed?

7 Have divisional and departmental plans been coordinated in the overall program?

8 Has a time schedule been worked out for each step in the planned program of action?

9 Has economic forecasting been employed to aid in determining the market potential for each product line? Share of the market expected? Sales goal?

10 Have a master and detailed budget been prepared?

11 Have quantitative data been used and evaluated to determine the costs for each product line? Selling prices? Profit margins? Inventory requirements? Cash requirements? Profit goals? Expected return on investments? Breakeven point?

12 Has an adequate R&D program been set up?

13 Have specific and detailed programs been developed in the functional areas for each product line to carry out the master plan?

14 Are the company's operating strategies and plans flexible enough to allow for changes, adaptions, and strategic action to cope with unanticipated changes in the marketplace?

SUMMARY AND GENERAL COMMENTS

Operating strategies set forth the general and specific action management intends to execute in the marketplace and in the management of the dominant functional areas of the business. The operating strategy is an essential part of the strategic design and flows from the root strategy. The efficacy of operating strategies must be constantly appraised in terms of their contribution to the progress of the company toward stated economic and basic objectives.

Some operating strategies are considered unique and do not follow the usual industry patterns; however, when successful they clearly distinguish the firm from competition. Such companies as Avon and Nucor Steel have developed unique and successful operating strategies.

In recent years a number of significant prescriptions have been developed which can be applied across business lines and industry boundaries. These generic strategies are best represented by the *experience curve* developed by BCG and the *portfolio management matrices* of BCG, GE, and Shell. The experience curve is one of the oldest of the generic strategies and has been used in industry for a long period of time as a useful strategic aid to show the relationship of accumulated production and market share, to predict the expected decline in unit costs over time, to estimate the growth rate needed to attain parity with competition, and to aid in cost control and pricing. There are limitations to the use of the experience curve because of shared costs, scale effects, and the need for investment capital to provide the plant and equipment for increasing production. Capital intensity may reduce a firm's flexibility and make it vulnerable. The experience curve is based on the assumption that all products are commodities, and it has little relationship to service industries, the fastest-growing sector of the economy.

Portfolio analysis provides an important and added supplement to strategic analysis. The BCG *growth share matrix* is one of the most frequently used of these strategic aids. This four-celled matrix can be used to make judgments about the cash generation and cash use of SBUs or product lines and to analyze their competitive position. The growth/share matrix provides a convenient display to initiate portfolio analysis. One of its major advantages is its simplicity. In the opinion of some this is also its major weakness. The extent of the relationship of cash flow and market share can be weak and difficult to determine in practice, and the correlation of industry growth and cash flow may also be questioned.

The *GE planning grid* and the *Shell directional policy matrix* are representative of the many multiple-celled matrices developed to enhance portfolio analysis. They eliminate some of the weaknesses ascribed to the BCG matrix. ROI is used as the basis for comparison of the business units represented in these displays. Both matrices are based on qualitative judgments which are made to determine industry or business attractiveness, which is plotted on one axis, and business or competitive strengths of the firm, which is plotted on the other axis of the grid. Developing the data to plot these two factors on the matrix may be one of the most valuable contributions of the process. Projecting this analysis to make judgments about size, growth, technology, industry structure, and the nature of competition provides the basis for assessing opportunities and competitive threats of the future.

The weaknesses of these planning grids is found in the extent of qualitative judgments that have to be made about business attractiveness and the competitive strengths of the firm. The required action necessary to invest and grow, hold a position, or divest certain units may present a formidable, complex task for management. Not many organizations have the stability and flexibility to readily alter their strategic thrusts.

PIMS represents the largest data bank of information focused on the analysis of strategic business planning. The program is divided into a profit-predicting model based on ROI, and a cash-flow–predicting model. The interrelationship of the experience curve and market share is clearly illustrated in the PIMS data.

Market share is considered a major factor in influencing the profitability of the firm. Product quality was closely related to market share. Investment intensity and company characteristics were the next most important influences on the profitability of the firm. PIMS provides the basis for the analysis of the major classes of profit influences such as industry/market environment, the competitive position of the firm, fixed-capital intensity, the production process structure, the effects of vertical integration, and corporate size and diversity.

The multiplicity of variables used in PIMS may be one of its major weaknesses, limiting precise and accurate appraisal of the firm's strategies. Multicollinearity caused by the interrelationship of the numerous variables used in the models prevents isolating the effects of individual variables on the dependent variable, ROI. The inclusion of the numerous variables also makes the task of data preparation difficult and time-consuming compared with the other strategic aids used for portfolio management. Despite some limitations the PIMS program is recognized as the most comprehensive collection of empirical data available which can be effectively utilized as a strategic aid in business planning.

The operating strategy should be designed to balance a firm's skills and resources to utilize them to the best possible advantage. All the functions of the business should be coordinated in terms of the company's strategic design to minimize suboptimization.

SELECTED REFERENCES

Bloom, P. and P. Kotler: "Strategies for High Market Share Companies," *Harvard Business Review* (November-December 1975).

Fruhan, W., Jr.: "Pyrrhic Victories In Fights for Market Share," *Harvard Business Review* (September 24, 1972).

Hall, W.: "Survival Strategies In a Hostile Environment," *Harvard Business Review*, September-October 1980.

Hammermesh, R., M. Anderson, and J. Harris: "Strategies for Low Market Share Businesses," *Harvard Business Review*, May-June 1978.

Harvey, D. F.: *Business Policy and Strategic Management* (Columbus, Ohio: Merrill, 1982).

Haspeslagh, P.: "Portfolio Planning Uses and Limitations," *Harvard Business Review*, January-February 1982.

Hedley, B.: "Strategy and the Business Portfolio," *Long-Range Planning*, vol. 10, no. 1, February 1977.

———: "A Fundamental Approach to Strategy Development," *Long-Range Planning*, vol. 9, no. 1, December 1976, pp. 2–11.

Hofer, C.: "Toward a Contingency Theory of Business Strategy," *Academy of Management Journal*, vol. 18, no. 4, December 1975.

———, and D. Schendel: *Strategy Formulation: Analytical Concepts* (St. Paul, Minn.: West Publishing Company, 1978).

Kiechel, W.: "Planning by the Rules of the Corporate Strategy Game," *Fortune*, September 24, 1979, pp. 110–118.

————: "The Decline of the Experience Curve," *Fortune*, October 6, 1981, pp. 139–146.

————: "Oh, Where, Oh, Where Has My Little Dog Gone? Or My Cash Cow? Or My Star?" *Fortune*, November 2, 1981, pp. 148–154.

Lorange, P., and R. Vancil (eds.): *Strategic Planning Systems* (Englewood Cliffs, N.J.: Prentice-Hall, 1978).

Rothschild, W.: *Putting It All Together: A Guide to Strategic Thinking* (New York: AMACOM, 1976).

Rumelt, R.: *Strategy, Structure and Economic Performance* (Cambridge, Mass.: Graduate School of Business Administration, Harvard University, 1974).

CASES ON BUSINESS POLICY FOR PART FOUR

The cases in Part Four enable the student to acquire an overview of the importance of the implementation phase of the policymaking process. The necessity of committing the firm's skills and resources to an operating strategy and a determined plan of action becomes apparent to the student in the analysis of the varied case situations in this section.

The action taken by a firm to attempt to ensure success in the marketplace is guided by its operating strategy. As indicated in Chapter 7, the operating strategy flows from the determined root strategy and must be compatible with the root strategy. These important concepts can be readily analyzed and applied to the case situations in Part Four to aid in providing the student with an understanding of the pragmatic nature of the policymaker's role.

Frequently used strategic aids for the development and execution of operating strategies such as experience curves, growth/share matrices, and planning grids described in Chapter 7 can be applied in the analysis of cases in Part Four.

Gemini Optical

The Gemini Optical Company was formed, over a period of years, by the acquisition of locally owned and operated optical companies. Many of the owners of the acquired companies had stayed to manage various segments of Gemini's operations. Sales had shown moderate growth until 1978. However, the president, George Simmons, had not been able to reverse a decline in sales and losses for the period 1978–1980. The board of directors terminated Simmons and elected John Prince as president of Gemini in March 1980. Prince was charged with developing a plan of action to return the company to growth and profitability.

THE OPTICAL INDUSTRY

Prince was thoroughly familiar with the eyeglass industry in the United States. While the market's average unit growth rate had been approximately 3.5 percent over the last five years, the annual growth rate varied with the economy and the availability of consumer discretionary income. Prince estimated that the growth rate over the next three to five years would be in the area of 2.0 percent.

About half of the population (115 million) wore eyeglasses or contact lenses. Hard contact lenses were worn by 5 to 6 million people. Only 1.5 million people wore soft contact lenses. Approximately 50 million pairs of eyeglasses were purchased in 1980. The total size of the retail/dispensing market was approximately $3 billion. (See Exhibits 1 and 1A.)

A number of important trends had affected the industry in the period 1976–1980. One of these was the movement toward national health insurance.

371

EXHIBIT I

DEMOGRAPHY OF THE UNITED STATES, POPULATION REQUIRING CORRECTIVE EYEWEAR.

(a) Growth, 1950–2020; (b) characteristics of the U.S. population requiring corrective eyewear.*

(a)

Population	% Increase	Millions	
		1950	2020
Total	90	152	290
Corrective eyewear	120	73	161
Single vision	63	36	59
Multifocal	176	37	102
Postcataract	349	1.7	5.8

(b)

Year	Tot. pop.	EW pop.	% of tot.(1)	SV pop.	% of tot.(2)	MF pop.	% of tot.(3)	MF % EW	Cat. sur.	Cat. pop.	% of tot.(4)
1950	152.3	73.1	48.0	36.2	23.8	36.9	24.2	50.5	214.1	1,671.3	1.1
1955	165.9	79.1	47.7	38.0	22.9	41.1	24.8	52.0	244.5	1,939.0	1.2
1960	180.7	85.6	47.4	40.3	22.3	45.3	25.1	53.0	274.3	2,207.0	1.2
1965	194.3	92.3	47.5	43.1	22.2	49.3	25.4	53.4	301.6	2,436.4	1.3
1970	204.9	98.8	48.2	45.4	22.2	53.4	26.0	54.0	328.3	2,652.0	1.3
1975	213.5	105.2	49.2	48.2	22.6	56.9	26.6	54.1	359.2	2,937.2	1.4
1980	222.2	111.6	50.3	51.9	23.3	59.8	26.9	53.5	392.3	3,245.8	1.5
1985	232.9	118.1	50.7	55.8	24.0	62.3	26.8	52.8	420.6	3,528.2	1.5
1990	243.5	124.5	51.1	58.5	24.0	66.0	27.1	53.0	446.9	3,816.0	1.6
1995	252.7	131.1	51.9	59.7	23.6	71.5	28.3	54.5	468.9	4,012.9	1.6
2000	260.4	137.1	52.7	59.1	22.7	78.1	30.0	56.9	490.6	4,112.9	1.6
2005	267.6	143.7	53.7	57.9	21.6	85.8	32.1	59.7	523.6	4,263.0	1.6
2010	275.3	149.9	54.4	56.8	20.6	93.1	33.8	62.1	571.9	4,607.1	1.7
2015	283.2	155.5	54.9	57.2	20.2	98.4	34.7	63.2	635.1	5,185.5	1.8
2020	290.1	160.8	55.4	58.9	20.3	101.9	35.1	63.4	697.6	5,836.4	2.0

*NOTE: Tot. pop. = total population (millions); EW pop. = corrective eyewear population (millions); % of tot.(1) = EW population as % of total population; SV pop. = single vision population (millions); % of tot.(2) = SV population as % of total population; MF pop. = multifocal population (millions); % of tot.(3) = MF population as % of total population; MF % EW = MF population as % of EW population; Cat. sur. = cataract surgeries per year (thousands); Cat. pop. = postcataract population (thousands); % of tot.(4) = cataract population as % of total population.
Source: Optometric Monthly, February, 1980

While the specific implications would vary depending on the program enacted, the effect on the ophthalmic-goods industry could be significant. An increase in demand and government-mandated quality standards were likely, even though any such program would probably be implemented gradually.

Furthermore, not only was the federal government growing in importance as a third-party financier of eyeglass services, but labor unions, health maintenance organizations, and other third parties were also increasingly subsidizing eyeglass wearers.

The Federal Trade Commission (FTC) published a new trade regulation to eliminate various state bans on price advertising of eyeglasses. In addition, the FTC had proposed that optometrists and ophthalmologists be required to furnish patients with a copy of their prescription in order to allow the patient to purchase eyeglasses from any qualified source.

Both optometrists and ophthalmologists could write prescriptions for eyeglasses. However, an ophthalmologist was a licensed medical doctor, while an optometrist was not. Opticians could only sell and fit eyewear once a prescription was written. An FTC survey in one city had found price differences of 300 percent for the same pair of eyeglasses. Markups as high as 300 percent by independent opticians were not uncommon.

Regardless of the results of the FTC actions, the optical industry was becoming increasingly competitive. Both the retail and wholesale markets were very fragmented, with many competitors possessing a small market share. (See Exhibits 2 and 3.) Small and marginal businesses appeared likely to come under increasing pressure from larger, better-capitalized firms, mail-order houses, and strong local independents.

The industry consisted of three levels: the manufacturers, who produced the frames and lenses; the laboratories and wholesalers, who ground lenses and assembled glasses; and the retailers, who actually fitted the glasses to the customer. Manufacturers received roughly 15 percent, and the laboratory 20 to 27 percent of the consumer's dollar.

A number of large retail chains had entered the market in recent years. *Business Week* reported[1] that:

Independent opticians still hold 60% of the market—down from 86% five years ago—and as the chains become more aggressive, many predict that the ranks of the independents will dwindle rapidly. Some in the industry believe that the big drug and specialty chains will hold 75% of the market within five years.

According to a study sponsored by Dow Corning Corp., the average optical purchase is $50, and the gross margin to the retailer averages about 100%.

The average drug chain optical center should be able to generate $150,000 annually at margins averaging 50%, the Dow report continues. Opening an optical center, Dow says, costs about $10,000 for remodeling and inventory—more if the retailer adds his own laboratory.

---

[1] "Drugstores See a Boom in Eyeglasses," *Business Week*, February 13, 1978, pp. 116–120.

EXHIBIT 1A

DEMOGRAPHIC ANALYSIS OF EYEWEAR POPULATION

(a) State rankings by eyewear population; (b) increase in eyewear population, 1980–2000; (c) percentage increase in eyewear population, 1980–2000; (d) increase in multifocal population, 1980–2000.

(a) State	1980	2000	(b) Rank	State	Increase (1000s)
California	1	1	1	California	3203
New York	2	2	2	Florida	3086
Texas	3	3	3	Texas	2447
Pennsylvania	4	5	4	North Carolina	992
Illinois	5	6	5	Georgia	970
Ohio	6	7	6	Virginia	931
Florida	7	4	7	Arizona	762
Michigan	8	8	8	Maryland	688
New Jersey	9	9	9	Michigan	687
Massachusetts	10	11	10	Colorado	657
North Carolina	11	10	11	New Jersey	623
Indiana	12	14	12	Tennessee	598
Virginia	13	12	13	South Carolina	586
Georgia	14	13	14	Massachusetts	559
Missouri	15	16	15	Wisconsin	545
Wisconsin	16	15	16	Illinois	536
Tennessee	17	18	17	Pennsylvania	498
Maryland	18	17	18	Kentucky	497
Minnesota	19	19	19	Alabama	487
Louisiana	20	21	20	Ohio	436
Alabama	21	20	21	Louisiana	427
Washington	22	23	22	Oregon	412
Kentucky	23	22	23	Oklahoma	389
Connecticut	24	28	24	Minnesota	387
Iowa	25	29	25	Missouri	358
Oklahoma	26	27	26	Washington	349
South Carolina	27	24	27	Indiana	340
Colorado	28	26	28	Arkansas	331
Arizona	29	25	29	New York	290
Oregon	30	30	30	Mississippi	267
Kansas	31	33	31	Utah	257
Mississippi	32	32	32	New Mexico	256
Arkansas	33	31	33	Iowa	203
West Virginia	34	34	34	Connecticut	199
Nebraska	35	35	35	Idaho	190
New Mexico	36	36	36	Maine	186
Utah	37	37	37	West Virginia	185
Maine	38	38	38	Kansas	168
Rhode Island	39	42	39	Nebraska	167
Hawaii	40	40	40	Hawaii	163
Idaho	41	39	41	Nevada	160
New Hampshire	42	41	42	New Hampshire	156
Montana	43	43	43	Montana	127
South Dakota	44	45	44	Rhode Island	88
District of Columbia	45	48	45	Wyoming	79
Nevada	46	44	46	Alaska	76
North Dakota	47	46	47	Delaware	65
Delaware	48	47	48	Vermont	64
Vermont	49	49	49	North Dakota	61
Wyoming	50	50	50	South Dakota	50
Alaska	51	51	51	District of Columbia	−18

(c) Rank	State	%	(d) Rank	State	Increase (1000s)
1	Arizona	60.5	1	California	2254
2	Florida	58.9	2	Florida	2162
3	Colorado	48.8	3	Texas	1571
4	Nevada	48.8	4	North Carolina	710
5	Alaska	44.4	5	Georgia	629
6	Utah	43.9	6	Virginia	627
7	Idaho	43.9	7	Arizona	508
8	New Mexico	43.5	8	Michigan	487
9	South Carolina	40.8	9	Tennessee	450
10	Wyoming	39.5	10	Maryland	441
11	Texas	38.6	11	Colorado	427
12	Georgia	38.5	12	New Jersey	412
13	Hawaii	36.6	13	South Carolina	408
14	New Hampshire	36.1	14	Pennsylvania	392
15	Virginia	35.7	15	Ohio	388
16	North Carolina	34.9	16	Illinois	375
17	Oregon	33.2	17	Wisconsin	365
18	Maine	32.9	18	Alabama	352
19	Montana	32.4	19	Massachusetts	349
20	Maryland	32.3	20	Kentucky	338
21	Arkansas	29.1	21	Louisiana	304
22	California	28.6	22	New York	293
23	Kentucky	28.3	23	Oregon	290
24	Tennessee	27.3	24	Indiana	279
25	Oklahoma	26.8	25	Minnesota	272
26	Vermont	26.6	26	Washington	265
27	Alabama	26.1	27	Oklahoma	261
28	Wisconsin	23.0	28	Arkansas	242
29	Mississippi	23.0	29	Missouri	237
30	Louisiana	22.9	30	Mississippi	189
31	Delaware	22.2	31	New Mexico	180
32	Nebraska	20.8	32	Connecticut	158
33	West Virginia	19.5	33	Iowa	152
34	Minnesota	19.5	34	Utah	149
35	Washington	19.2	35	West Virginia	140
36	North Dakota	18.7	36	Idaho	127
37	Massachusetts	18.4	37	Maine	123
38	Rhode Island	17.8	38	Kansas	119
39	New Jersey	16.2	39	Nevada	119
40	Michigan	15.4	40	Hawaii	116
41	Missouri	14.5	41	Nebraska	107
42	South Dakota	14.3	42	New Hampshire	107
43	Kansas	14.2	43	Montana	88
44	Iowa	13.8	44	Wyoming	56
45	Indiana	12.9	45	Alaska	51
46	Connecticut	12.4	46	Delaware	48
47	Illinois	9.6	47	Rhode Island	46
48	Ohio	8.2	48	Vermont	46
49	Pennsylvania	8.0	49	North Dakota	44
50	New York	3.2	50	South Dakota	38
51	District of Columbia	−5.3	51	District of Columbia	−6

EXHIBIT 2
GEMINI-COMPETITIVE DATA* WHOLESALE MARKET SURVEY 1977–1978

	R$_x$ units	Percent of market	R$_x$ sales	Percent of market
Washington/Oregon				
Opticraft	190,000	19.9	$3,600,000	19.0
C.B. Optical	152,000	15.0	2,900,000	15.0
Northwest Northern	126,000	12.0	2,500,000	13.0
Northwest-Gemini	92,000	9.3	1,900,000	10.3
Georgia				
Williams Optical	36,400	20.0	800,000	20.0
Robertson Optical	20,800	15.0	520,000	15.0
Optical Service	36,000	20.0	540,000	20.0
Southern-Gemini	64,200	41.8	1,190,000	41.8
Maine, Massachusetts, Vermont, New Hampshire				
American Optical	222,000	6.8	4,000,000	5.6
McLeod Optical	156,000	4.5	2,800,000	3.9
Merrimack Optical	83,000	2.4	1,500,000	2.1
Eastern-Gemini	214,400	6.1	3,800,000	5.2
California				
American Optical	74,000	1.3	1,600,000	1.3
Optical Service	44,000	0.8	900,000	0.8
Heard Optical	43,500	0.7	915,000	0.7
California-Gemini	50,900	0.9	1,100,000	0.9
Midwest				
House of Vision	224,000	6.7	4,700,000	6.7
B&W	143,000	4.3	3,000,000	4.3
Grandview & Forecast	95,000	2.9	2,000,000	2.9
Midwest-Gemini	119,800	3.6	2,600,000	3.6

*Independent market survey conducted for Gemini. Does not include recent market entries of several divisions of large companies which gained significant market shares between 1978 and 1981.

The article had quoted Max Bunin, vice president of Revco D.S., Inc., as saying, "The key to it all is aggressive radio and television advertising with an emphasis on price."

While the chains appeared to possess many advantages, they had been criticized for poor product quality and for not providing the personalized service customary in the industry.

The wholesaling segment was dominated by independent firms, followed in importance by the larger mail-order operations located primarily in the sun belt. Some manufacturer-owned laboratories existed to supply retail locations, and an increasing number of third-party laboratories (operated by direct providers of health care) were appearing to serve captive markets. G. D. Searle & Co.,

EXHIBIT 3
GEMINI COMPETITIVE DATA* RETAIL MARKET SURVEY
1977–1978

	R$_x$ units	Percent of market	R$_x$ sales	Percent of market
Washington/Oregon				
Kaiser-Permanente	52,000	4.3	$2,400,000	2.9
Group Health	48,000	4.0	3,000,000	3.5
Western Optical	45,000	3.6	3,800,000	4.3
Northwest-Gemini	35,000	2.9	3,000,000	3.5
Tennessee				
Southern School of Optometry	13,500	30.0	878,000	35.1
Fisher Optical	5,600	12.4	364,000	14.6
Shipman Optical	2,700	6.0	176,000	7.0
Tennessee Optical	15,200	33.8	1,200,000	47.0
California				
Fedco	50,000	2.2	3,000,000	1.9
Superior Optical	31,250	1.4	2,500,000	1.6
Cole National	50,000	2.2	3,000,000	1.9
Southern California Optical	15,400	0.7	1,400,000	0.8
Midwest				
House of Vision	23,000	3.4	1,500,000	3.4
Almer Coe	27,700	4.1	1,800,000	4.1
Lee Optical	15,400	2.3	1,000,000	2.3
Midwest Optical	29,500	4.3	2,000,000	4.5

*Independent market survey conducted for Gemini. Does not include recent market entries of several divisions of large companies which gained significant market shares between 1978 and 1981.

Wall & Ochs, Giant Food, Inc., Peoples Drug Stores, Inc., and Jack Eckerd Corp., had all set up their own laboratories to support their retail outlets.

There appeared to be a trend in wholesale processing toward the well-financed larger-scale facilities. However, this segment of the industry was also suffering serious financial pressure due to overabundant processing capacity and increased asset bases caused by rapid product changes. While the chains were adding labs, the total number of laboratories was shrinking as smaller labs merged or went out of business. Bausch & Lomb, a manufacturer which once operated 130 labs, had reduced the total by one-third.

New products and new technologies had historically come from the manufacturing supplier. Prince expected this to remain the case in the future. While Gemini was not a manufacturer, they would have access to the new products. Recent and possible new products were:

Photochromic colored lenses
Hyperascheric cataract lenses

Polarized plastic lenses
Molded plastic prescription lenses
More designer fashion frames
Varilux II—varying-power, invisible bifocal lenses
Automatic refractors
Projection lensometers
Disposable soft contact lenses

Prince did not expect the new products to have a profound effect on the total market, but rather to replace existing products. He anticipated very little change in machinery technology.

Prince also was of the opinion that the industry had not fully exploited the potential for soft contact lenses. It was estimated that these lenses might be suitable for 35 million eyeglass wearers. Hard contact lenses cost the retailer $25 and sold for approximately $175. However, the fitting took considerable skill and patience and required about two hours cumulative time. The soft lenses cost about $75 and sold for $300, but only required about one-half hour fitting time.

GEMINI'S MARKET POSITION

Gemini competed in four segments of the business.

Wholesale Prescriptions

Prescription lenses, hard contact lenses, and frames were sold to optometrists, dispensing ophthalmologists, and other opticians who, in turn, dispensed these products directly to their patients. The prescriptions were fabricated in Gemini's 27 laboratories. (See Exhibit 4.) This segment represented approximately 40 percent of Gemini's total sales. (See Exhibit 5.)

EXHIBIT 4
GEMINI OPTICAL COMPANY RETAIL AND WHOLESALE OUTLETS

Companies	Coverage (states)	No. of retail outlets	No. of wholesale laboratories
Midwest-Gemini	6	20	6
N. California-Gemini	3	10	1
Northwest-Gemini	4	9	3
Southern-Gemini	5	8	6
Tennessee-Gemini	2	8	—
Eastern-Gemini	8	12	8
S. California-Gemini	1	9	3
Total	29	76	27

EXHIBIT 5
GEMINI OPTICAL COMPANY, PERIOD 1978–1980

	Sales in millions	Gross profit in millions	Gross profit margin, %
Wholesale prescriptions	$ 26.3	$ 8.6	32.6
Retail prescriptions	23.2	9.5	41.0
Wholesale stock	13.4	2.1	15.6
Equipment sales	3.2	0.3	18.2
Total	$ 66.1	$ 20.5	31.2

Retail Prescriptions

Eyeware was also sold directly to the consumer in accordance with ophthalmologists' or optometrists' prescriptions. These products were dispensed from Gemini's 76 retail locations. (See Exhibit 4.) This segment represented 35 percent of Gemini's total sales. (See Exhibit 5.)

Wholesale Stock

Optometrists, opticians, and dispensing ophthalmologists, in addition to buying finished prescriptions, also bought stock items such as uncut, finished, single-vision lenses, frame quantities, and plano sunglasses. These purchasers had their own finishing equipment, lens edgers, and tempering equipment to complete the prescriptions. Stock sales contributed 20 percent of total sales.

Equipment Sales

Instruments used in examining the eyes and chairs, units, and dispensing furniture were sold to professionals, hospitals, and educational institutions. This segment represented 5 percent of total sales.

Gemini was divided into seven profit centers to serve the national market. However, several geographic gaps existed because of either remoteness from existing laboratories or other business competitive reasons. David Brock, vice president of marketing, stated that the company's objectives had been to "position itself as a primary competitor in each of the markets it served and to improve its position where it was then dominant." Brock said Gemini hoped to achieve its objectives by:

1 Targeting to the middle to upper segment of the market
2 Offering a proliferation of the latest fashion and merchandising items
3 Serving customers through quality and efficient service
4 Opening or acquiring new retail outlets to reach various market niches
5 Locating wholesale laboratories in proximity to the buying accounts to meet customer demands

Gemini's market share was approximately 1.25 percent in 1980, and the company was striving to increase its share to 2.5 to 3.0 percent over the next three to five years.

Brock explained that the following strategies had been defined for each of the market segments:

Wholesale Prescriptions

1 Ophthalmologists, optometrists, and opticians bought on the basis of dependable quality and fast, reliable delivery. Gemini's normal delivery time was five days, which was considered excellent in comparison to the seven days which was considered standard.

2 As a result of the frequent introduction of both designer and basic frames and the enormous variety of lens materials, sizes, colors, and other physical properties, Gemini had attempted to stock most basic inventory. This proliferation of lenses and frames had resulted in reduced order time from the manufacturers.

3 Special prices and credit terms were given to high-volume customers and to attract new customers. Credit terms ranged from 5 percent/10 days/net 30 days, to 3 percent/20 days/net 60 days, to 2 percent/30 days/net 90 days.

4 Gemini employed 25 in-house salespersons to cover over 500 accounts. Stress was placed on building personal rapport with the account through frequent visits, favors, enhanced service, occasional entertainment, and special gratuities (free frames).

Retail Prescriptions

1 Gemini had 76 company-owned outlets (see Exhibit 4), and was constantly evaluating retail outlets, new openings, refurbishings, closures, and relocations.

2 Individual profit centers of Gemini advertised on radio, buses, billboards, and in trade publications. The amount expended was approximately 1.0 percent of sales.

3 Close interpersonal ties had been established over time between nondispensing doctors and retail optical outlets. Some retail prescriptions were secured by retail outlets located near the offices of nondispensing doctors, who referred their patients to those outlets for eyeglass and frame selection, fitting, and purchase.

4 Each retail outlet had a full-line inventory of fashionable designer frames and accessories to aid consumer choice.

5 Retail outlets had been designed professionally to enhance their image.

Wholesale Stock   The same salespersons that serviced the wholesale prescriptions also handled the sale of stock items. Marketing strategies were deployed in the same manner in this segment of the business.

Equipment Sales Each profit center had one equipment salesperson. Instruments had traditionally been low margin, but were considered important in establishing a good working relationship with professional customers.

MANUFACTURING OPERATIONS

When Prince discussed Gemini's manufacturing operations with Bill Jordan, vice president of production, he learned that the following production strategies had been developed with the goal of ensuring accurate and speedy fulfillment of customers' prescriptions by the laboratories.

1 Close proximity of the wholesale laboratories to the buying accounts had helped to fulfill market demands. Gemini had 27 wholesale laboratories supporting 76 retail outlets. (See Exhibit 4.) Major laboratories were located in Chicago, Atlanta, Concord (New Hampshire), Boston, Los Angeles, and Oakland. In addition, regional laboratories existed to supply groups of retail outlets.

2 Except for the Tennessee Optical Company, each of the other six profit centers had at least one wholesale laboratory. Heavy capital expenditures over the last three years had resulted, with the exception of a few small laboratories, in Gemini using the most up-to-date technology in the field.

3 Each profit center's wholesale laboratory capacity was flexible enough to meet increased growth of approximately 10 percent per year for the next three to five years.

4 Profit-center manufacturing executives had been upgraded in the hope that this would result in better-trained lab personnel and supervisors and consequently reduce the per unit costs.

FINANCIAL OPERATIONS

In line with the stated company objective "to position itself as a primary competitor in the markets it served and to improve its position in those markets it dominated," Bob Huff, the controller, outlined the following financial strategy to support the marketing and manufacturing strategies.

1 Inventory costs had been increased in order to carry a broader and more extensive line of designer frames and assorted lens requirements.

2 Carrying costs of the inventory, i.e., insurance, maintenance, storage, and capital costs, had been increased.

3 The ability to finance acquisitions of new retail outlets in prime locations with good accounts had been maintained.

4 Unprofitable retail outlets would be closed or relocated.

5 Cash flow was scheduled by each profit location, factoring in the higher inventory costs, slower collection of receivables resulting from granting liberal terms on wholesale accounts, and capital appropriation programs, in order to reduce short-term bank borrowings.

6 A capital expenditure program would be developed to constantly replace or supplement existing machinery and equipment to maintain high efficiency standards. At a minimum, an amount equal to depreciation expense was budgeted.

The financial strategies were quantified in the annual budget. Huff stated that each profit center submitted and performed against stated plans. Long-term financial goals were expressed in the annual five-year plan.

Gemini had increased its long-term capital base in the last three years by negotiating a term loan with a number of banks. The funds were used to pay for the extensive capital expenditures program and the increases in receivables and inventory. While this had resulted in reduced asset turnover in the short run, it was hoped that this would allow Gemini to become a primary competitor and thereby significantly more profitable in the future.

ORGANIZATION STRUCTURE AND CONTROL STRATEGIES

Prince's predecessor had implemented a decentralized organization structure to carry out the marketing, manufacturing, and financial strategies. (See Exhibit 6.)

Prince headed the operation as chief executive officer. Seven profit center general managers reported directly to Prince and were responsible for profits and losses of their operations.

Each profit center had its own functional staff, consisting of a vice president of marketing, a vice president of manufacturing, and a vice president-con-

EXHIBIT 6
Gemini Optical Company organization structure.

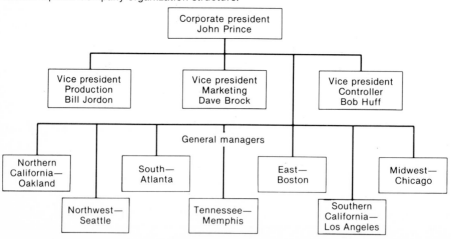

troller, all of whom reported directly to the general manager. In addition, the vice president-controller had dotted line responsibility to the corporate controller.

As president, Prince functioned principally as a policymaker, coordinator, and communications link between the general managers and the board of directors. A Gemini corporate staff was available to assist the profit centers in problem solving and special projects.

The decentralized structure was established to take advantage of the general managers' entrepreneurial knowledge of the business and to allow them flexibility in meeting competition.

Under the decentralized organization structure at Gemini, each profit center's progress towards its goals and objectives, as determined by its marketing, manufacturing, and financial strategies, was measured in the following manner.

A monthly management information system packet was prepared by each profit center. The packet contained the following reports:

1 Complete profit and loss statement including supporting pages itemizing selling, general, and administrative costs, cost of goods sold, and miscellaneous expenses. The actual results were compared to the budget and the prior year.

2 Balance sheet and analysis of all major balance sheet accounts, especially inventory turnover and receivables turnover.

3 Source and use of funds, and analysis of remittances to headquarters.

4 Analysis of retail store openings, closings, and relocations.

5 Sales in dollars and units by each retail outlet, with comparisons of actual results to budget.

6 Unit production at each wholesale laboratory, including such data as average per unit cost, breakage, absenteeism, turnover, and order backlog—all of which were compared with the budget.

Monthly executive committee meetings to discuss the prior month's performance were attended by the seven general managers, the Gemini chief executive officer and the corporate staff. Monthly board meetings were held at which the president discussed the company's performance to date. Weekly sales, order backlog, and cash position reports were submitted to Gemini headquarters.

Physical inventories were taken three times a year at each location. Adjustments were booked immediately, and a complete analysis of the variances submitted to headquarters.

Operational and financial audits were conducted twice annually. Each profit center was audited for approximately one week each year to ensure that records were kept according to the Gemini management guide and generally accepted accounting principles.

The corporate controller visited each profit center location at least once a month to assist the controller with various problem areas. More frequent visits from the president, as well as the staff, took place if problems persisted.

EXECUTIVE COMMITTEE MEETING—APRIL 1981

In 1978, for the first time in the company's history, Gemini experienced a loss of $80,000 on sales of $22.3 million. The sales decline and losses continued through 1980. On reviewing prior year's operations, it appeared to John Prince that *all* areas had contributed to the loss. Wholesale stock and equipment sales had only made a minimal contribution to gross profit (see Exhibit 5), while wholesale prescription's gross profit margin had declined to 32.6 percent from previous levels of 35 to 40 percent.

Because of the continuing nagging financial problems, John Prince called an executive committee meeting to try to ascertain the reasons for the continuing sales decline and losses from 1978–1980 and to discuss the pro forma income statement and balance sheet projections for the next three years which had been prepared by Bob Huff and the corporate staff. (See Exhibits 7, 8, and 9.)

Bill Jordon, vice president of manufacturing, stated, "One of the primary causes of the gross margin decline was the fact that Gemini's laboratories had operated at only 60 to 65 percent of capacity and the general managers had not reacted fast enough in cutting back labor when orders declined."

Harvey McIntosch, general manager of Northwest-Gemini, objected, stating that the real problem was the location of wholesale laboratories in cities where strong unions existed, while most of Gemini's competition had established so-called giant laboratories in the sun belt, where labor costs were considerably lower. McIntosch estimated that a $2.00 per unit cost differential existed between Gemini and their primary competitors.

Bill Jordon, vice president of production, said that high-volume companies in strong union territory had been able to negate the high labor cost. However, Gemini had been unable to achieve this benefit because of many laboratories sharing the business. Further, poor supervision had resulted in poor operating conditions as reflected in a high degree of breakage, turnover, and absenteeism.

Dave Brock, vice president of marketing, indicated that he felt Gemini's problems could be traced to the present decentralized organization structure in which each profit center general manager had his or her own procurement practices. Gemini brought lenses and frames from 54 separate vendors. This resulted in a loss of volume discounts of 3 to 5 percent given by large suppliers.

Bob Huff, vice president-controller, indicated that the earnings shortfall had strained Gemini's cash position, and argued further that the general managers had not reacted quickly in deferring purchases of inventory and equipment or to reduce operating expenses.

Several of the general managers complained heatedly that the corporate staff was trying to run their businesses, but didn't understand the problems they faced. They pointed out that they had been ordered to cut purchases even though new items were needed to maintain sales levels. At the same time, retail and wholesale inventory records were not computerized, contributing to $380,000 in unaccountable and obsolete inventory.

Huff countered that this did not explain the slow accounts receivable turnover. He indicated that it was not unusual for ophthalmologists, optometrists,

EXHIBIT 7
Gemini Optical Company
Income Statement
(000's)

	1973	1974	1975	1976	1977	1978	1979	1980
Net sales	$19,745	$20,054	$20,885	$21,236	$23,268	$22,345	$22,101	$21,732
Direct materials	8,052	8,256	8,781	8,919	9,842	9,659	9,592	9,432
Direct labor	1,619	1,704	1,817	1,869	2,094	2,066	2,033	2,021
Manufacturing expense	2,176	2,373	2,560	3,015	3,879	3,625	3,610	3,671
Total cost of sales	$11,847	$12,333	$13,158	$13,803	$15,815	$15,350	$15,235	$15,124
Gross profit	$ 7,898	$ 7,721	$ 7,727	$ 7,433	$ 7,453	$ 6,995	$ 6,866	$ 6,608
Prov. for bad debt	20	19	25	45	45	90	130	131
Selling expense	3,732	3,810	4,009	4,141	4,618	4,804	4,796	4,759
General and admin. expense	1,639	1,664	1,754	1,805	2,001	1,967	2,011	2,043
State taxes	84	66	35	54	70	–	–	40
Interest expense	260	285	294	295	240	254	268	240
Other expense (Income)	–	(34)	(44)	(107)	(67)	34	41	38
Total expense	$ 5,735	$ 5,810	$ 6,073	$ 6,233	$ 6,907	$ 7,149	$ 7,246	$ 7,251
Pretax profit (loss)	$ 2,163	$ 1,911	$ 1,654	$ 1,200	$ 546	$ (154)	$ (380)	$ (643)
Federal income taxes	1,038	917	794	576	262	(74)	(182)	(296)
Net income (loss)	$ 1,125	$ 994	$ 860	$ 624	$ 284	$ (80)	$ (198)	$ (347)
Summary: % to sales								
Direct materials	40.8	41.2	42.0	42.0	42.3	43.2	43.4	43.4
Direct labor	8.2	8.5	8.7	8.8	9.0	9.2	9.2	9.3
Gross profit	40.0	38.5	37.0	35.0	32.1	31.3	31.1	30.4
Selling exp.	18.9	19.0	19.2	19.5	19.8	21.5	21.7	21.9
General and admin. expense	8.3	8.3	8.4	8.5	8.1	8.8	9.1	9.4
Net income	5.7	4.9	4.1	2.9	1.2	(0.4)	(0.9)	(1.6)

EXHIBIT 8
Gemini Optical Company
Projected Income Statement
(000's)

	Projected		
	1981	**1982**	**1983**
Net sales	$21,114	$20,600	$19,975
Direct materials	8,889	8,622	8,330
Direct labor	1,858	1,782	1,718
Manufacturing expense	3,321	3,260	3,105
Total cost of sales	$14,068	$13,663	$13,153
Gross profit	$ 7,046	$ 6,937	$ 6,822
Bad debt expense	125	115	100
Selling expense	4,624	4,553	4,514
General and admin. expense	1,858	1,772	1,698
State & local taxes	61	50	25
Interest expense	246	250	225
Other expense (income)	100	–	–
Total expense	$ 7,014	$ 6,740	$ 6,562
Pretax profit (loss)	$ 32	$ 197	$ 260
Federal income taxes	15	91	120
Net income	$ 17	$ 106	$ 140
Summary: % to sales			
Direct materials	42.1	41.8	41.7
Direct labor	8.8	8.7	8.6
Gross profit	33.4	33.7	34.1
Selling expense	21.9	22.1	22.6
General and admin. expense	8.8	8.6	8.5
Net income	0.08	0.5	0.7

and opticians to be 180 days past due on wholesale prescriptions and equipment sales, and that over $350,000 of accounts receivable were now in that category.

The general managers replied that this was "part of being in the optical business," since these customers knew Gemini needed their wholesale prescriptions as well as their retail business.

Sidney Spelman, general manager of Tennessee Optical, complained that while his retail operation currently dominated the market, it was not positioned in the larger shopping malls and was coming under increasing pressure from the drug chains. Other general managers indicated that this problem also affected their operations.

Dave Brock proposed that a corporate program for coordinating marketing efforts should be installed. This would include training and incentive programs for salespersons, as well as regional or companywide advertising programs and promotional practices.

EXHIBIT 9
Gemini Optical Company
Projected Balance Sheet
(000's)

	Actual	Projected		
	1980	**1981**	**1982**	**1983**
Current Assets				
Cash	$ 993	$ 519	$ 322	$ 250
Trade receivables, net	2,350	2,256	2,150	2,210
Inventory	2,575	2,300	2,100	2,200
Prepaid and sundry	150	150	150	150
	$ 6,068	$ 5,225	$ 4,722	$ 4,810
Investments and other assets	500	560	600	600
Property, plant, and equipment, net	1,368	1,428	1,468	1,508
Total assets	$ 7,936	$ 7,213	$ 6,790	$ 6,918
Current liabilities				
Notes payable	$ 871	$ 301	$ 77	$ 240
Accounts payable	800	780	700	700
Accrued and other	400	450	425	450
Current maturities	200	200	200	200
	$ 2,271	$ 1,731	$ 1,402	$ 1,590
Long-term debt	2,500	2,300	2,100	1,900
Equity	3,165	3,182	3,288	3,428
Total liabilities and equity	$ 7,936	$ 7,213	$ 6,790	$ 6,918
Summary:				
Days sales in receivables	38	39	40	38
Inventory as percent of ongoing				
90 days sales	48.5	43.0	42.5	41.0
Capital expenditure	$113	$300	$300	$300
Depreciation	$244	$240	$260	$260
Return on equity, %	(2.15)	0.5	3.2	4.0

The general managers responded that too much paper work and too many reports were now required by corporate management, and that they would be more effective out in the field making sales calls. Joe Menna of Eastern-Gemini stated, "We are becoming a paper factory, let me go out and make sales!"

The meeting broke up late in the afternoon, since several of the general managers had to catch flights back to their regional offices. The proposed projections were not discussed.

JOHN PRINCE'S OBSERVATIONS

After reviewing his conversations with his corporate managers, Prince wondered if the decentralized organization structure was task-effective and if the profit center managers could be relied on to carry out any stated objectives.

EXHIBIT 10
CHANGING STRUCTURE OF THE OPTICAL INDUSTRY
(Major Producers and Subsidiaries; Stock Price Data, 1980)

Corporate name, subsidiaries, and affiliates	Ticker symbol	Market	Last 52-week period High	Low
ABBOTT LABORATORIES	ABT	NYSE	$43\frac{1}{8}$	$29\frac{1}{2}$
Murine Co., Inc.				
ALLERGAN PHARMACEUT.	AGN	NYSE	$57\frac{1}{2}$	24
Optik-Aids				
AMERICAN HOME PRODUCTS	AHP	NYSE	$29\frac{1}{2}$	$24\frac{3}{8}$
Ayerst Laboratories				
AMERICAN HOSPITAL SUPPLY CORP.	AHS	NYSE	$35\frac{3}{4}$	$23\frac{5}{8}$
Corneal Lens, Inc. Sauflon Intern'l				
Dade Div. Lens-Tec				
Heyer-Schulte Signet Optical Corp.				
AMERICAN STERILIZER	ASZ	NYSE	$10\frac{3}{4}$	$6\frac{3}{8}$
Lombart Lenses, Ltd.				
AMERICAN VISION CENTERS, INC.	AMVC	OTC	$2\frac{5}{8}$	1
Nat'l Contact Nat'l Contact Lens				
Lens Plan Distributors				
APOLLO LASERS	APLE	OTC	$8\frac{1}{8}$	3
BAUSCH & LOMB	BOL	NYSE	40	$23\frac{1}{2}$
Bushnell Opt. Ray-Ban				
Kenrex B & L Insur. Co.				
BEATRICE FOODS CO.	BRY	NYSE	$24\frac{1}{4}$	$19\frac{3}{4}$
James H. Rhodes & Co.				
BERKELEY BIO-MEDICAL	BBM	PS	$7\frac{1}{2}$	6
Berkeley Bio-Engineering				
BUCKBEE-MEARS	BBEE	OTC	$8\frac{1}{2}$	5
Vision-Ease Corp.				
CAVITRON	CAV	ASE	15	9
Biotronics Burton-Div.				
COHERENT, INC.	COHR	OTC	28	$17\frac{1}{2}$
Electro-Medical				
Technology				
COLE NATIONAL CORP.	CLE	NYSE	$16\frac{3}{8}$	$10\frac{1}{2}$
Bay Cities Opt. Gile Opt.				
Colston Opt. H & S Optics, Inc.				
Diederich Opt. Marco Opt. Co.				
Gate City Opt. Marston Opt.				
CONCEPT, INC.	CCPT	OTC	$7\frac{5}{8}$	4
CONTINUOUS CURVE	CURV	OTC	$40\frac{3}{4}$	$14\frac{3}{4}$
HydroCurve Soft Lenses, Inc.				
COOPER LABORATORIES	COO	NYSE	$26\frac{1}{4}$	$18\frac{7}{8}$
Flow Pharmaceuticals				
SMP Division				
CORNING GLASS WORKS	GLW	NYSE	65	$49\frac{5}{8}$
CREST ULTRASONICS		OTC	NA	NA
DANKER LABORATORIES	DANK	OTC	$8\frac{1}{2}$	4
Eye Con Lab. Optical Plastics				
Invisible Lens Co.				

Shares sold 100's (unofficial) 1/14–2/15	Closing 2/15/80	Net change since 1/11/80	% Change since 1/11/80	Price/ earnings ratio	Yield %	Dividend
18,228	$38^1/_4$	$-2^3/_4$	−6.6	13	2.6	1.00
7,737	$55^7/_8$	$-^7/_8$	−1.5	20	1.1	.60
75,264	$26^1/_8$	$-^5/_8$	−2.3	10	6.1	1.60
17,397	$31^1/_8$	$-2^1/_4$	−6.7	11	2.6	.80
6,742	$8^1/_8$	$-^7/_8$	−9.7	9	3.9	.32
2,284	$1^1/_2$	$+^1/_8$	+9.1	NA	NA	−
2,973	$7^1/_4$	$+^3/_8$	+5.5	NA	NA	−
10,440	38	$-^1/_2$	−1.3	12	2.6	1.00
24,297	$20^3/_8$	$-^1/_8$	−.6	7	5.9	1.20
NA	$6^1/_2$	$-^3/_4$	−10.3	NA	NA	−
2,872	$8^1/_8$	$+1^1/_4$	+18.2	NA	NA	.28
921	$14^1/_2$	$+1^1/_2$	+11.5	19	.8	.12
6,164	26	$+2^1/_2$	+10.6	NA	NA	−
510	$13^1/_4$	$-1^3/_4$	−11.7	6	5.4	.72
1,465	$5^1/_8$	$+^1/_4$	+5.1	NA	NA	.06
4,829	33	$+3^1/_4$	+10.9	NA	NA	−
4,912	23	$+1^3/_4$	+8.2	11	2.6	.60
12,376	$54^3/_8$	$+3^1/_4$	+6.4	8	3.9	2.12
NA	NA	NA	NA	NA	NA	NA
2,479	$7^1/_2$	$+1^3/_4$	+30.4	NA	NA	−

EXHIBIT 10 *(continued)*
CHANGING STRUCTURE OF THE OPTICAL INDUSTRY
(Major Producers and Subsidiaries; Stock Price Data, 1980)

Corporate name, subsidiaries, and affiliates		Ticker symbol	Market	Last 52-week period	
				High	Low
DENTSPLY		DSP	NYSE	20	$14^5/_8$
Denslite	Kindy				
Duling	Koenigkramer				
Imperial	Louisville Opt.				
U.S. Optical Frame					
EHRENREICH PHOTO OPT.		EHR	ASE	$14^7/_8$	$6^1/_8$
Nikon					
FERRO CORP.		FOE	NYSE	26	19
Transelco, Inc.					
FRIGITRONICS		FRG	NYSE	$18^1/_2$	$9^7/_8$
Benson	Ostertag Opt.				
Bisman Opt.	Owens Opt.				
Colonial Opt.	Park Central Opt.				
Criss	Parson's Optical				
FCL	Phoenix McLeod				
Frigi-Griffin	Precision-Cosmet				
Galleria Frame Fash.	Spartan Opt.				
Greenberg Opt.	Stereo Opt.				
Kamo Contacts	Valley Opt. Service				
FROST & SULLIVAN		FRSL	OTC	3	$1^1/_2$
W. R. GRACE & CO.		GRA	NYSE	$44^1/_2$	$25^7/_8$
Davison Chemical					
HOUSE OF VISION		HOV	ASE	$5^1/_8$	$2^3/_8$
E. H. Daniels Disp.	I-Framz				
Eye-Cen. Inc.	Jenkel-Davidson				
HOV Opticaleber	J. H. Penny				
Robinson-Houchin					
IPCO CORP.		IHS	NYSE	$6^5/_8$	$4^1/_8$
IPCO Optical	Sterling Optical				
ITEK		ITK	NYSE	$35^3/_8$	$19^1/_4$
Kelley & Hueber	Univis				
Merrimack Opt.	White-Haines				
Pennsylvania Optical					
KING OPTICAL		KNG	ASE	NA	NA
Capitol (Minnesota)	MSO				
Douglas (Kansas)	Opti-Cal				
King Opt. Lab.	Tough-Lite Lens				
Lee Opt.					
LIQUID AIR CORP. OF NORTH AMERICA		LANA	OTC	$28^3/_4$	$23^1/_2$
Techsight Corp.					
MARION LABS		MKC	NYSE	$16^1/_2$	$11^3/_8$
Apache Optical	Optico				
Lee Opt. (Ariz.)	Vista Opt.				
3M CO.		MMM	NYSE	$60^1/_4$	$46^5/_8$
Armorlite	Mcghan Medical Corp.				
NATIONAL PATENT DEV.		NPD	ASE	$10^7/_8$	$5^1/_4$
American Hydron	NPD Optics				

Shares sold 100's (unofficial) 1/14–2/15	Closing 2/15/80	Net change since 1/11/80	% Change since 1/11/80	Price/ earnings ratio	Yield %	Dividend
1,292	$17^7/_8$	$-^7/_8$	−4.9	10	5.2	.88
1,706	$10^1/_4$	$+3^1/_4$	+46.4	–	–	–
4,108	$21^1/_8$	$-1^3/_8$	−6.1	5	5.7	1.20
2,592	9	$-1^5/_8$	−14.1	9	3.0	.30
1,023	$2^3/_4$	$+^1/_4$	+10.0	NA	NA	.06
17,077	$41^1/_2$	−1	−2.4	8	4.9	2.05
552	$3^3/_4$	$+^3/_4$	+25.0	11	–	–
1,808	$5^3/_8$	$-^3/_8$	−6.5	19	2.2	.12
9,621	$29^1/_4$	$-1^5/_8$	−5.3	17	–	–
NA	NA	NA	NA	NA	NA	–
669	$24^1/_4$	$+^1/_2$	+2.1	NA	NA	1.40
5,726	$16^1/_4$	$+1^1/_2$	+10.2	22	3.9	.64
40,578	$52^3/_8$	$+2^5/_8$	+5.3	9	5.3	2.80
19,375	$10^7/_8$	$+2^1/_4$	+27.7	–	–	–

EXHIBIT 10 *(continued)*
CHANGING STRUCTURE OF THE OPTICAL INDUSTRY
(Major Producers and Subsidiaries; Stock Price Data, 1980)

Corporate name, subsidiaries, and affiliates		Ticker symbol	Market	Last 52-week period	
				High	Low
OMEGA OPTICAL		OMEG	OTC	$13\frac{1}{4}$	$7\frac{1}{2}$
Apollo	Milroy Optical				
Dennis Optical	Omega Contact Lens				
Hensel	Insurance Co.				
International Opt.	Optimum Optics, Inc.				
Master/Craft Contact	Precision Optics, Inc.				
Lens Lab					
OPTICAL RADIATION		ORCO	OTC	$17\frac{3}{4}$	$10\frac{1}{4}$
PFIZER, INC.		PFE	NYSE	$41\frac{3}{4}$	29
PPG INDUSTRIES		PPG	NYSE	$34\frac{1}{4}$	$25\frac{7}{8}$
REVLON		REV	NYSE	$54\frac{7}{8}$	39
Barnes-Hind	Coburn				
R. H. MEDICAL SERVICES		RHM	ASE	$21\frac{1}{4}$	$9\frac{1}{8}$
National Optical	Pan Optics, Inc.				
Swank Optical					
RLI CORP.		RLIC	OTC	$11\frac{1}{4}$	$7\frac{1}{2}$
Replacement Lens, Inc.					
R. P. SCHERER		SCHC	OTC	$13\frac{1}{4}$	$7\frac{3}{8}$
Storz Instruments	Surgical Mech. Res.				
RYNCO SCIENTIFIC CORP.			OTC	8	$3\frac{5}{8}$
Storz Instruments	Surgical Mech. Res.				
SEARLE, G. D.		SRL	NYSE	$23\frac{5}{8}$	$11\frac{1}{2}$
Hilman-Kohan	Searle Optical				
Opticks, Inc.	The Sunglass				
Pearle Optical	Vision Center				
SIMMONDS PRECISION PRODUCTS		SP	NYSE	$20\frac{3}{8}$	11
Acuity Systems					
SMITH KLINE CORP.		SKL	NYSE	$65\frac{1}{4}$	$38\frac{1}{2}$
Branson Ultrasonics	Humphrey Instru.				
STERNDENT		SDT	NYSE	$25\frac{1}{2}$	17
Unico, Inc.	Universal Opt.				
SYNTEX		SYN	ASE	$44\frac{1}{8}$	$30\frac{3}{8}$
Corneal Serv., Inc.	Syntex Ophthalmics				
Polymer Optics					
TEXTRON		TEXT	NYSE	30	$22\frac{3}{4}$
Shuron					
UNION CORP.		UCO	NYSE	$9\frac{1}{8}$	$4\frac{5}{8}$
Chandler Labs	Tex-O-Con				
Gordon Cont.	UCO Optics				
Lenses					
Morrison Labs	Union Optics Corp.				
U.S. INDUSTRIES		USI	NYSE	$10\frac{1}{2}$	$7\frac{3}{4}$
Columbian Opt.	Optimax				
Memphis Opt.	Spratt Opt.				
Northeast Opt.	Uhleman Opt.				
WARNER-LAMBERT		WLA	NYSE	$25\frac{5}{8}$	$17\frac{3}{8}$
American-Optical	Cool-Ray				

Source: Optical Index, March, 1980.

Shares sold 100's (unofficial) 1/14–2/15	Closing 2/15/80	Net change since 1/11/80	% Change since 1/11/80	Price/ earnings ratio	Yield %	Dividend
2,172	9	$-2^3/_4$	−23.4	NA	NA	.20
456	$11^1/_2$	$+^1/_2$	+4.5	NA	NA	–
29,479	$36^1/_4$	$-3^1/_2$	−8.8	11	3.6	1.32
6,944	32	$+2^7/_8$	+9.9	5	6.3	2.00
19,242	$40^7/_8$	−2	−4.7	10	3.8	1.56
421	$16^7/_8$	$-1^3/_8$	−7.5	8	1.2	.20
1,223	$9^7/_8$	$+^3/_8$	+3.9	NA	NA	.44
3,424	$7^3/_4$	$-^3/_8$	−4.6	NA	NA	.24
449	$5^3/_8$	$-^1/_8$	−2.3	NA	NA	–
45,896	$22^5/_8$	$+2^7/_8$	+1.6	14	2.3	.52
5,497	$14^3/_4$	$-1^1/_4$	−7.1	11	1.9	.28
32,804	$55^1/_2$	−9	−14.0	14	3.0	1.66
2,100	$17^7/_8$	$+^1/_8$	+.7	7	3.4	.60
12,076	$40^1/_8$	$-3^1/_8$	−7.2	11	3.2	1.30
10,306	$28^3/_4$	$+^3/_4$	+2.7	6	6.3	1.80
4,252	$6^3/_8$	$-^3/_8$	−5.6	7	5.0	.32
13,580	$9^3/_8$	$+^1/_4$	+2.7	5	8.1	.76
44,910	$21^1/_4$	$+^5/_8$	+3.0	10	6.2	1.32

The majority of the general managers were former entrepreneurs and had developed their skills through the sales end of the business. From his previous experience in the industry, Prince knew that competitors felt Gemini had experienced too many changes in strategy to be considered a serious threat. Further, vendors considered Gemini a "slow payer" and an "inefficient buyer."

Each profit center had its own chart of accounts and electronic data processing system (both hardware and software). The lack of a standard chart of accounts made meaningful comparisons of financial data next to impossible. In the period of time Prince had been with Gemini he had become unsure of whether the company knew its true product costs; as a consequence, he thought it might be giving away the goods in some instances and pricing them unrealistically high in others.

One month after the meeting, in going over Bob Huff's projections and the minutes of the meeting, Prince concluded that an alternative plan of action was

EXHIBIT 11
Gemini Optical Company
Revised Projected Income Statement
(000's)

	Projected		
	1981	1982	1983
Net sales	$28,311	$30,291	$33,471
Direct materials	10,786	11,450	12,585
Direct labor	2,435	2,544	2,745
Manufacturing expense	3,561	3,582	3,719
Total cost of sales	$16,782	$17,576	$19,049
Gross profit	$11,529	$12,715	$14,422
Bad debt expense	178	240	275
Selling expense	5,974	6,603	7,564
General and admin. expense	2,378	2,454	2,678
State and local taxes	207	251	271
Interest expense	359	400	425
Other expense (income)	–	150	175
Total expense	$ 9,096	$10,098	$11,388
Pretax profit (loss)	$ 2,433	$ 2,617	$ 3,034
Federal income taxes	1,119	1,203	1,396
Net income	$ 1,314	$ 1,414	$ 1,638
SUMMARY: % to sales			
Direct materials	38.1	37.8	37.6
Direct labor	8.6	8.4	8.2
Gross profit	40.8	42.0	43.1
Selling expense	21.2	21.8	22.6
General and admin. expense	8.4	8.1	8.0
Net income	4.7	4.7	4.9

needed and began to reflect on the action that should be taken. He was concerned about the changing structure of the industry (see Exhibit 10), with the large diversified firms continuing to gain market share with their numerous outlets. On the other hand he recognized the significant market opportunities that existed. With this in mind he asked Bob Huff to prepare projected financial statements which would reflect a more optimistic outlook (see Exhibits 11 and 12.) He wanted these to be distributed to all general managers and serve as new targets. Prince was of the opinion that the general managers needed to be more aggressive and strive for increased sales and profits rather than seeking to find excuses for their performance by blaming headquarters and the competitive environment.

EXHIBIT 12
Gemini Optical Company
Revised Projected Balance Sheet
(000's)

	Actual	Projected		
	1980	1981	1982	1983
Current Assets				
Cash	$ 993	$ 500	$ 500	$ 480
Trade receivables, net	2,350	2,870	2,685	3,156
Inventory	2,575	2,953	3,347	3,700
Prepaid and sundry	150	150	150	150
	6,068	6,473	6,682	7,486
Investments and other assets	500	560	600	600
Property, plant, and equipment, net	1,368	1,538	1,738	2,088
Total assets	$ 7,936	$ 8,571	$ 9,020	$10,174
Current liabilities				
Notes payable	$ 871	$ 301	77	–
Accounts payable	800	1,291	1,200	$ 1,350
Accrued and other	400	500	550	700
Current maturities	200	200	200	200
	2,271	2,292	2,027	2,250
Long-term debt	2,500	2,300	2,100	2,143
Equity	3,165	3,979	4,893	5,781
Total liabilities & equity	$ 7,936	$ 8,571	$ 9,020	$10,174
Summary:				
Days sales in receivables	38	37	34	32
Inventory as % of ongoing				
90 days sales	48.5	39.0	39.7	39.7
Capital expenditure	$113	$450	$500	$675
Depreciation	$244	$280	$300	$325
Return on equity, %	(2.5)	33.0	28.9	28.3
Dividend	–	$500	$600	$750

Federal Electronics

Tom Andreas returned from the corporate headquarters of Harrison Manufacturing Company in California in January of 1981 with mixed emotions. He had convinced the board of directors of the market potential of the CCD program (change-coupled device, an advanced integrated circuit) and the need for continued investment in this area, but he had also agreed to a goal of at least $100 million in sales by 1983. Since the sales of his Federal Division reached $39.5 million in 1980, it would not be easy to reach this target. The product lines of Federal were sold primarily to the Department of Defense. Tom Andreas considered the number of in-house projects awaiting completion and eventual sales, and the on-line products his division was now selling to the Defense Department, and concluded that the CCD program was the most promising project to exploit to expand sales.

DEVELOPMENT OF THE CCD PROJECT

Andreas was fascinated by the progress that Ben Bergman, one of his chief engineers, had been making with CCD and encouraged him to continue experiments with optical applications. Andreas considered Bergman an energetic salesman as well as a brilliant engineer (a rare combination in his eyes). Bergman, with difficulty, had acquired small research contracts out of various government agencies to finance his research. He developed a miniature TV camera, no larger than a pocket calculator. The CCD devices themselves were manufactured by the Harrison semiconductor facility in California. In 1975 a separate CCD product line was formed, and in 1976 demand for these TV cameras, which could be made in almost any configuration, could not be met because of difficulty of producing acceptable devices. Designing and building these devices was pushing technology to the brink because of their complexity (a device no larger than a fingernail contained over 200,000 components in seven layers). The west coast Harrison facility was more interested in commercial applications of CCD and less concerned with the imaging capabilities of the devices; this factor tended to hamper production.

Mr. Harrison had personally directed that all devices be manufactured on the west coast since he did not want to duplicate production facilities. Andreas had difficulty in resigning himself to reliance on California for device production. To offset this problem he offered to spend $1 million of his own R&D and capital allocation in return for a west coast facility dedicated to military optical uses of CCD devices. After much resistance his idea was accepted, and $200,000 was charged as proposal expenses to his 1979 operating results; another $300,000 was charged in 1980, as well as $500,000 for specialized equipment, which would be charged to his capital budget. In return for this investment, Federal would be entitled to all production of CCD devices. The operating results would be less severely impacted if the west coast could produce acceptable devices since Federal was under contract to several Department of Defense agencies to produce CCD-related products. Sales of device-related products would reduce the investment cost. In late 1977 a TV camera inside an artillery shell was demonstrated to the U.S. Army. The tests proved that surveillance of artillery strikes could be accomplished with a camera housed in a shell, transmitting photos back behind the lines. Several prototype cameras were sold in 1979, and in December of 1979 a quantity of 25 cameras at $15,000 each was ordered by the Army. If successfully completed, this contract would lead to a production award for thousands of cameras over a five-year period. The key factor was the availability of CCDs.

DEVELOPMENT OF THE FEDERAL DIVISION

The Federal Division of Harrison Manufacturing Company of Morristown, New Jersey developed from the original Harrison Aviation Company founded by Martin Harrison in 1938. In the early years Harrison was fascinated with both photography and aviation, and because of his interests, Harrison Aviation became a pioneer in the manufacture of precision aerial cameras. World War II led to spectacular growth for the company based on military uses of aerial cameras, and the company became a major supplier to the military of various specialized aerial cameras. Cameras were developed for reconnaissance, surveillance, mapping, and aircraft strike evaluation and sold in large quantities during the war.

At the end of the war the company branched out into various product lines, some of which had been developed prior to the war and some after. The name of the company was changed to Harrison Manufacturing Company, and growth was accomplished both from within and by acquisition. In the late 1950s and early 1960s the company became involved in electronics, and in 1968 Harrison and his staff decided that future company growth would be primarily in this field. The corporate headquarters was moved from Morristown to California, the heart of the burgeoning electronics industry and the site of Harrison electronics activity. At the time of the move, eleven separate divisions were operating in various fields on the east coast. In 1970 because of the need to conserve capital in order to become a factor in electronics, unprofitable divisions were either closed or sold. As a result only two divisions were left on the east coast. In addition to the Federal Division, the company operated an Industrial Division which manufactured audiovisual systems, aircraft galleys, and aviation fuel tank gauges. Both east coast operations were profitable. In 1970 Federal was approximately three times greater in sales volume than the Industrial Division.

OPERATIONS AND DEVELOPMENT OF PRODUCT LINES
OF THE FEDERAL DIVISION

At the time Tom Andreas took over operations in June of 1970, the division had plants in three locations. The main plant was in Morristown and housed the photographic (the line on which the company was founded), the reconnaissance (aerial), and the electronic data systems. Sales at this location were approximately $20 million. Sales of $8 million were generated by the facility at Clifton, New Jersey, where the product lines were radar systems, commercial television systems (CTS), and electronic jamming systems. Ordnance operation in Newark yielded sales of $6 million from the manufacture of electronic fuses (timing devices) for ordnance products such as bombs, missile warheads, artillery shells, and land mines. With the exception of the CTS line, all products were manufactured for the military. Total sales of the Federal Division were $35 million, and the overall operation showed a profit of $700,000 with a $1.2 million profit at Morristown offset by losses at the Clifton and Newark locations.

Following a loss of $350,000 in 1971 and at the urging of Tom Andreas, it was decided by the corporation to close the facility at Clifton. An attempt was made to sell the entire operation, but no deal could be consummated, so the CTS (Andreas was not comfortable with a losing commercial product) and the radar (Andreas felt that competition was too intense unless he had some technological edge) lines were sold to other companies. The electronic jamming line was transferred to the Morristown location. Included in the line transferred was an Army contract for $3.5 million for seven XLG-42 "state of the art" electronic jamming systems.

The ordnance operation had shown a loss of approximately $150,000 in 1970 primarily because the facility had been set up to run as a mass-production unit but had not been able to operate at capacity. In May of 1971 the U.S. Army awarded the ordnance operation a contract for 30,000 SG-56 timing devices at a cost of $775 each and deliverable at the rate of 1,000 per month starting in December 1971. The competition for this contract was intense, and competitors included Honeywell, Rockwell, Hughes, and Northrop. The award was made solely on the basis of price. Tom Andreas had personally decided on the final bid figure. In the eyes of the corporate officers, this contract, together with other existing contracts, provided the ordnance operation with enough business to warrant maintaining it as a separate division of the company. Andreas attempted to retain operational control of the new Ordnance Division, but was overruled; and effective June 1, 1972, the Ordnance Division became an autonomous division reporting directly to the corporate headquarters.

Material, production, personnel, and technical problems plagued the SG-56 program from inception, and the fledgling division took a write-off of $775,000 in 1972, which resulted in an operating loss for the year. In 1973, with a new general manager and controller, the division continued to sustain monthly operating losses. In the second quarter of 1973 an additional $500,000 write-off was made. At this point the division was three months behind schedule on delivery and was still experiencing operating difficulties. The division operating results were determined largely by the success of the SG-56 program since other new programs had not materialized. Tom Andreas was given operational control of the division in June of 1973 and appointed Roy Reed his chief of operations in an attempt to salvage the division. While the division still operated in the red for the remainder of 1973, no further write-offs were made. By April of 1974 the final shipment on the SG-56 program was made. Andreas convinced the board of directors that the remaining ordnance contracts should be completed at Morristown and the Newark facility should be closed down. The Army was awarding a follow-on production order for SG-56 devices, again on the basis of price. Andreas felt that the high-volume ordnance business did not represent a growth area; because of this impression he ordered the Ordnance Division to bid at $1,400 per unit. This was almost double the initial award price, and the Army awarded the follow-on contract to a competitor.

Shortly after Reed was assigned to "bail out" the Ordnance Division, the engineers at that division came up with a design change which increased the reliability of the SG-56 device as well as lowering its cost. Since it was anticipated that this change would save the Army significant amounts in future procurement costs, the Federal Division received a $1 million "Value Engineering Change" Award. In addition, royalties accrued to Federal from 1974 to 1975 based on the engineering change being incorporated into the follow-on contract. The contracts transferred to Morristown were completed during 1974 and 1975, and additional small-volume contracts were awarded for specialized devices. Despite this, sales of the Ordnance Division declined substantially.

In 1967 Harrison Manufacturing Company acquired a small business in Elmira, New York, which had some advanced designs on radio monitoring equipment. The division had never been profitable, and in September of 1973, Andreas was given control of the Elmira division, which was known as the

Electronic Measuring Division. The division sold primarily to the commercial market but had several small government contracts. By the end of 1974 the division was still not turning a profit and sales volume had not increased. Andreas recommended that the radio monitoring product line be transferred to Morristown, where military applications would be pursued and the remaining product lines sold. His recommendation was accepted, and the Elmira plant was closed in early 1975.

When Tom Andreas was appointed general manager in 1970 the Morristown operation was heavily "camera"-oriented and the photographic line accounted for approximately 30 percent of sales. Andreas sensed that mechanical equipment would soon be replaced in large part by electronics and tried to guide the Federal group into the military electronics market. An air-to-ground data transmission system, conceived and designed before Andreas took over, was sold to a major military aircraft producer, and in late 1970 Federal was awarded a sole-source subcontract from the producer for the system, for installation on all its future fighter aircraft, as well as for installation in 100 existing aircraft. Since 1971 Federal averaged shipments of 50 units per year at $200,000 per system. This product became the mainstay of the data systems product line and was the most profitable single product that Federal produced.

The electronic jamming equipment line transferred from Clifton was expanded, and in 1978 a $5 million contract was awarded by the U.S. Army for XLG-42A systems. The contract was completed in 1979, at a loss. Andreas considered the loss was more than offset in the operating results of the data transmission line, an investment in a technology that might bring future profitable contracts.

Radio monitoring systems transferred from the Elmira facility were likewise expanded and refined, and in 1979 an $8.5 million contract was awarded for MLG-71 systems. By the end of 1979 it was apparent that this would also be an unprofitable contract and $750,000 was written off as proposal expenses against 1979 operating results. While not happy with the loss, Andreas still considered it an investment in a technology which could provide as much as $100 million in sales over the next five years. Andreas was hopeful of being awarded a $20 million follow-on contract.

The original camera line had rapidly declined in importance, and by 1973 Andreas seriously considered discontinuing it altogether. He retained only a few of the key engineering personnel, and they proceeded to develop new film type cameras. Sudden interest by several foreign military buyers in standard product-line cameras resulted in increased sales in 1976 and 1977, and in 1978 a new long-range design camera, the FL-87, was developed. A $10 million order from a foreign customer was received for future delivery. In addition a new panoramic reconnaissance camera (LB-66) was developed through a $2.5 million cost-plus type contract from the U.S. Air Force. A production contract for additional units was expected. An updated version of the LB-66 was built concurrently with the LB-66 and became known as the LB-67. In effect two generations of cameras had been developed at the same time.

FEDERAL'S ORGANIZATION: EXECUTIVE GROUP

Andreas had spent his entire adult life in the defense industry, having worked for three large Department of Defense contractors in various engineering roles prior to joining the Federal Division as director of engineering in 1967. He had a reputation as a tough taskmaster and indeed had stepped on a lot of toes prior to becoming general manager of Federal in 1970. Andreas was a perfectionist who demanded a lot of his subordinates. When assigned a task by Andreas, a person would generally make every effort to accomplish the assignment since Andreas's wrath was legendary when he was confronted with failure.

To a large extent the current profitability of Federal was due to decisions Andreas had made on which markets he wanted to be in.

Mike Corboy joined Federal in 1970 as controller based on a recommendation of Tom Andreas to the board of directors. Andreas had liked Corboy when he interviewed him because of his assessment of Mike as a "pro." Mike had started out working for a C.P.A. firm but after several years had become an auditor for the Department of Defense, where he worked himself up to a supervisory position. Mike became fed up with the bureaucracy and served as controller of a major defense contractor before coming to Federal. Andreas had never had much use for "beancounters" before having Mike in the company, but over the years he had come to rely on and trust Mike more than any of his top people. Mike had an in-depth knowledge of financial practices in the industry. He made it a practice to hire the best help available regardless of cost.

> Let's face it. In a commercial organization I couldn't live with the accounting staff I have here. Hell, I've got more chiefs than indians. In fact this division couldn't survive in any commercial market with the organization chart we have. We duplicate functions and overpay a lot of people. Since most of our products don't compete on price, we wouldn't get much benefit out of being efficient.

With regard to Tom Andreas's commitment to achieve $100 million in sales by 1983, Mike had this to say:

> I don't know what Tom was thinking when he agreed to that one. It's not going to be easy talking him out of some of the schemes he's bound to consider, but I think one of my key functions is to protect Tom from himself. I'd love to reach that goal on a more gradual basis, but I know that is not Tom's style so I might as well resign myself to helping him in any way I can. If anyone can reach that goal, Tom can.

Other key management personnel are described in Exhibit 1. Federal's organization chart is shown in Exhibit 2.

FEDERAL'S POSITION IN 1981: PROSPECTS, PROJECTS, AND PRODUCT

A major aircraft producer had received contracts for continuing production of its fighter aircraft for the next three years. This assured that the data systems product line would be supplying the air-to-ground data transmission system for at least the next three years. In early 1981 Federal received a production award

EXHIBIT 1
FEDERAL ELECTRONICS KEY MANAGEMENT PERSONNEL DATA

Title	Name	Age	Education	Joined Federal
Corporate vice president and general manager, Federal Systems Division	Thomas Andreas	53	B.E.E., M.E.E., CCNY	1967
General manager, Communications Operation	Fred Herman	49	B.E.E., M.E.E., U.S.M.A., West Point	1969
General manager, Reconnaissance Operations	Anthony Franz	47	B.E.E., M.E.E., Columbia	1968
Director of Operations	Roy Reed	46	B.M.E., M.B.A., NYU	1970
Controller	Michael Corboy	54	B.S. (accounting), CCNY	1970
International Marketing	John Schneider	46	B.B.A., Fairleigh Dickinson	1967
Industrial Relations	Frank Sherman	43	B.A., M.B.A., Cornell	1972 1974

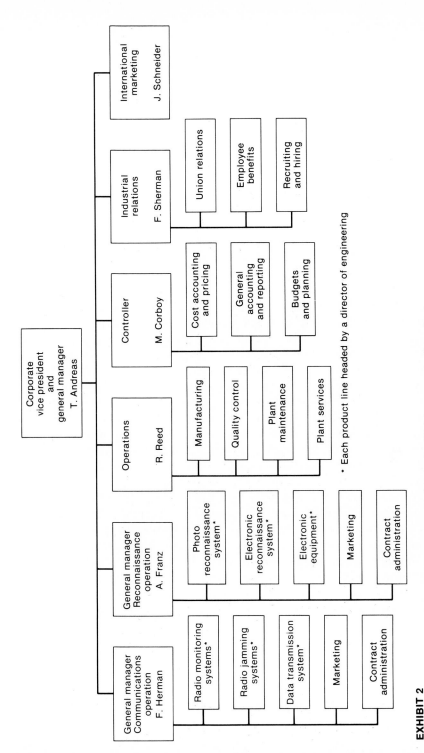

* Each product line is headed by a director of engineering

EXHIBIT 2
Harrison Manufacturing Company, Inc. Federal Electronics Division organization chart.

for the manufacture of fifty XLG-42A jamming systems totalling $8.8 million over the next two years. In addition, a $10 million award for modifying existing units in the field was anticipated within the next few months.

Andreas expected that Federal would receive an award for a minimum buy of fifteen LB-66 cameras at a cost of about $165,000 each. The LB-67, which Federal had built at its own expense while building the LB-66, was scheduled to be flight-tested by the Navy, and if successful a production award would be forthcoming. No other firms had anything comparable to the LB-67, so if the flight test was successful the FSD would have a potential "no competition" product usable for at least several more years. The FL-87 camera system currently being manufactured for a foreign customer was evoking interest from several Department of Defense agencies now that the "nonrecurring" costs had been charged to another customer.

The company which had tried the MLG-71 radio monitoring system had been pleased with the results of the units delivered. It was believed to be an exceptionally sensitive system. While no profit would accrue from the present contract because of the large overrun, future orders might prove to be more lucrative. A $20 million order would be awarded, presumably to Federal, sometime in 1981. Hopefully, technical problems would be solved by that time.

Several CCD devices had been produced by the Harrison facility in California in 1980. Customer inquiries about TV cameras using these devices were numerous. Because the devices could produce an image in low-light-level situations (the infrared range) and because of the extremely small size of the camera (it could be made as small as a disposable cigarette lighter), potential applications for the CCD cameras were numerous. Both domestic and foreign customers were eager to order cameras despite their current high price (minimum selling price was $6,000). However, production of the CCD devices in quantity was still not feasible. Competitors were also making progress with CCD, but their devices still did not match the quality of Harrison devices. One customer was interested in an FL-87 camera using CCD imaging instead of film.

The order for 25 artillery shell TV cameras was running behind schedule. Camera production was on schedule, but the CCD devices required were not. Large future orders were contingent on fulfilling this contract, and the Army relaxed the delivery schedule several times. Future orders were contingent on mass-producing the CCD devices and lowering the unit cost of the cameras from the current $15,000 level to less than $1,000 for the thousands of units potentially required in the future. The cost of the CCD devices was about one-third of the selling price. The market for this product was estimated to be as great as $100 million over the next seven years.

An R&D award for a reconnaissance system had been received by Federal. The system would use CCD-related technology in an attempt to design a real-time reconnaissance system capable of producing usable pictures in near zero light level conditions. While it was virtually sure that this system would never reach the production stage, completion of the contract would make Federal a factor in the real-time state of the art of reconnaissance systems. Andreas had agreed to invest (absorb an overrun) of $500,000 on this program, which was one of the reasons why Federal had received the award.

On his last visit to Harrison's California headquarters, Andreas had the go-ahead to search for possible companies with compatible product lines as possible acquisition candidates.

Expansion of Federal's current lines into commercial markets was not considered feasible by Andreas. The high proportion of skilled workers, engineers, scientists, and technicians and the specialized nature of the Federal facility would make it difficult to enter the price-competitive commercial world. In addition, he thought his marketing people were not attuned to the commercial markets, and Federal did not have the proper distribution channels. To Andreas, expansion or acquisitions into the commercial market seemed to present too many problems.

The Industrial Division had experienced some difficulty in 1978. Sales had remained level, but profitability was down for the first time in six years. In March 1979, Andreas was given operational control of the division. After this date the general manager of the Industrial Division reported to Andreas instead of directly to the corporate offices.

Andreas intended to schedule an all-day meeting with his top management group. He was well aware of the vagaries of the defense business, but he was also aware of the sales goal set by corporate headquarters for his division. A number of questions would have to be raised and hopefully answered in 1981. Was it possible for Federal to reach $100 million in sales by 1983? Would the CCD be a major factor in reaching this goal? What products and projects should be pushed? How do you effectively plan in the defense business when you don't have the benefit of commercial products? (See Exhibits 3, 4, and 5 for financial data of Federal.)

EXHIBIT 3
Harrison Manufacturing Company, Inc. (Parent Company)
Sales and Profit Summary
(000's)

	1976	1977	1978	1979	1980
Sales	$351,171	$384,933	$291,542	$443,221	$448,168
Net income	$ 26,318	$ 27,032	$ 10,424	$ 12,456	$ 11,162

EXHIBIT 4
Federal Division
of
Harrison Manufacturing Company, Inc.
Balance Sheet
(000's)

	1975	1976	1977	1978	1979	1980
Assets						
Cash (A)	$ (517)	$ (351)	$ (355)	$ (313)	$ (422)	$ (540)
Receivables	2,627	3,207	2,734	3,296	2,890	3,490
Inventory (net of progress payments)	1,571	715	1,661	845	1,424	1,750
Other assets	80	31	49	40	71	80
Total current assets	$3,761	$3,602	$4,089	$3,868	$3,963	$4,780
Property and equipment (net of depreciation)	3,653	2,859	2,753	3,213	3,483	3,640
Total assets	$7,414	$6,461	$6,842	$7,081	$7,446	$8,420
Liabilities						
Current portion of long-term debt					$ 15	$ 15
Customer deposits			520	885	2,378	3,060
Accounts payable, trade	$ 639	$ 539	$1,404	$1,000	1,426	1,600
Other payables	1,135	1,404	1,403	1,252	1,293	1,325
Total current long-term debt	$1,774	$1,943	$3,327	$3,127	$5,112	$6,000
				273	243	228
Advances from corporate	5,640	4,518	3,515	3,671	2,091	2,192
Total liabilities	$7,414	$6,461	$6,842	$7,081	$7,446	$8,420
Gross inventory	$3,434	$2,884*	$4,730	$5,975	$7,755	$9,600
Less: progress payments	1,863	2,169	3,069	5,130	6,331	7,850
Net inventory	$1,571	$ 715	$1,661	$ 845	$1,424	$1,750

(A) Cash balances are maintained only in Harrison Corporation home office accounts. Each day cash is charged to the corporate account and credited to each division's account for the amount of the division's "overdraft." The result is that every division of Harrison is in an overdraft position at the close of every business day.

*Adjusted (—482 thousand) to reflect change in accounting method for Internal Revenue Service purposes.

EXHIBIT 5

Federal Division
of
Harrison Manufacturing Company, Inc.
Income Statements
(000's)

	1975	1976	1977	1978	1979	1980
Sales	$22,563	$25,709	$23,148	$26,615	$31,805	$39,500
Cost of sales	17,163	19,079	15,969	18,647	22,989	27,550
Profit on sales	5,400	6,630	7,179	7,968	8,816	11,950
General & administrative	$ 964	$ 899	$ 750	$ 897	$ 938	$ 1,010
(A) Marketing	2,511	3,572	3,294	3,521	4,194	5,270
Research & development	112	53	—	143	—	240
Total expenses	$ 3,182	$ 4,524	$ 4,044	$ 4,561	$ 5,132	$ 6,520
Operating profit	$ 2,218	$ 2,106	$ 3,135	$ 3,407	$ 3,684	$ 5,430
Royalty income	42	48	56	—	—	52
Other income	65	111	3	33	(40)	15
Profit before corporate charges	$ 2,325	$ 2,265	$ 3,194	$ 3,440	$ 3,644	$ 5,497
Corporate gen. & adm.	$ 582	$ 719	$ 782	$ 619	$ 774	$ 850
Corporate interest	51	128	(15)	(190)	(295)	300
Profit before taxes	$ 1,692	$ 1,418	$ 2,427	$ 3,011	$ 3,165	$ 4,347

(A) Includes bid and proposal expenses. Unsolicited (by customer). Bid and proposal expenses account for approximately 40% of the total marketing expense. Such costs are considered a form of research and development.

APPENDIX: Notes on the Defense Industry

THE MARKET

The defense industry came into being following the end of the Korean war when it became apparent that the industry, and the high level of government spending in defense, was here to stay. Therefore, after the Korean war many firms remained in the defense "business." The fact that there was a shortage of qualified producers and that the industry was new as a peacetime entity led many commercial firms to enter the market.

Initially the large aircraft firms assumed the dominant role in the industry. However, the increased size and complexity of modern weapons systems made it obvious that no one firm could hope to develop technical competence in all areas. This led many firms to specialize in guidance, propulsion, nose cones, and other major components. Some contracts were handled by teams of contractors. In some cases the government contracted directly with each team member. In others, the prime contractor was selected and issued subcontracts to the other firms involved.

Over the years the percentage of the total U.S. government budget allocated to the military gradually declined, and the defense budget remained relatively constant. (See

Source: *Standard and Poor's Industrial Surveys, 1980–81*, Aerospace Industries Association, Bureau of Budget, Office of Management and Budget.

EXHIBIT 6
FEDERAL RESEARCH AND DEVELOPMENT EXPENDITURES
(In millions of dollars)

*Fis. Yr. End. Sept. 30	Total	DOD	NASA	AEC	Other
E1980	29,668	13,433	4,412	4,639	7,184
E1979	27,577	12,145	4,224	4,508	6,700
1978	24,532	10,726	3,833	3,925	6,048
1977	22,462	10,176	3,783	3,181	5,342
1976	20,233	9,329	3,521	2,225	5,158
1975	19,525	9,341	3,266	2,277	4,641
1974	18,239	8,958	3,258	1,825	4,202
1973	17,407	8,574	3,315	1,623	3,895
1972	16,629	8,275	3,422	1,552	3,380
1971	15,050	7,541	3,382	1,303	2,824
1970	15,632	7,588	3,753	1,616	2,695
1969	16,207	7,858	4,251	1,654	2,444

DOD—Department of Defense, NASA—National Aeronautics & Space Administration, AEC—Atomic Energy Commission. *Prior to 1977, fiscal yrs. ended June 30. E—Estimated. Note includes certain military personnel, procurement, civil functions, and some other items not included in other tables.
Sources: Bureau of the Budget and Aerospace Industries Association.

EXHIBIT 7
DEPARTMENT OF DEFENSE PROCUREMENT, RESEARCH,
DEVELOPMENT, TEST & EVALUATION, AND CONSTRUCTION
BUDGETS
(In millions of dollars: fiscal years to Sept. 30)

	1979	1980	1981
Procurement:			
Aircraft	12,224	13,462	14,446
Missiles	3,784	4,867	8,573
Ships	5,073	6,682	6,118
Combat Vehicles, Weapons and Torpedoes	1,977	2,325	3,079
Ordnance, Vehicles and Related Equip.	2,200	1,974	2,602
Electronics & Communications	2,749	2,772	3,300
Other	3,362	3,709	4,405
Total	31,368	35,792	40,524
Research, Development, Test & Evaluation:			
Technology Base	2,010	2,260	2,724
Advanced Technology Base	525	638	612
Strategic Programs	2,143	2,200	3,373
Tactical Programs	5,093	5,225	5,758
Intelligence & Communications	759	1,163	1,571
Management and Support	1,854	2,030	2,447
Total	12,383	13,517	16,488
Military Construction	2,523	2,295	3,251
Budget Authority	125,004	138,635	158,155

Source: Dept. of Defense as reported by *Aviation Week & Space Technology.*

Exhibits 6, 7, and 8.) While the budget remained constant, the individual weapons systems procured became more complex and costly; contracts were fewer in number but for larger dollar amounts. With a large number of firms competing for few contracts, the defense industry became extremely competitive.

The defense market may be broken down into three broad categories:

1 Procurements for items which are identical or closely related to civilian products. Examples would include trucks, fuels, lubricants, and textiles.

2 Procurements for items which are utilized exclusively by the government, such as tanks and artillery. While these items have no civilian counterpart, they do require utilization of manufacturing techniques similar to those used for civilian industrial products.

3 Procurements for defense or space products that are usually the result of a great deal of research. Such products tend to be both complex and costly, and production of such products often requires advanced specialized technical skills.

The Federal Division of Harrison Manufacturing Company supplied products for the third category of the defense industry. Some of the characteristics of this segment of the market were:

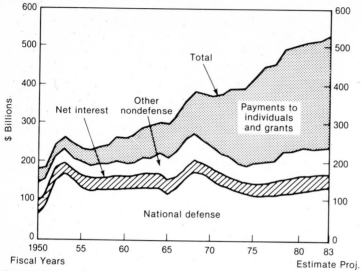

EXHIBIT 8
Federal outlays—constant 1979 dollars. (*Source*: Budget of the United States government, fiscal year 1980, 1981, Office of Management and Budget.)

1 It was no longer a growth market and had not been for several years. Pressure for social action by the government, as well as a perceived lessening of the Soviet military threat, has restricted the growth of the defense budget up to 1980.

2 Up to 1980 there was no indication of significant increases in research and development expenditures for new weapons systems.

3 Defense market requirements have changed rapidly and drastically because of changes in technology, a change in government priorities, or some combination of the two. Political, economic, and international factors all play a role in defining the market requirements. This was particularly evident when Salt II was not ratified and led to plans for increased defense spending.

4 There is usually a long planning cycle consisting of research, development, production, and support. It is not unusual for five to ten years to elapse between the time a product is conceived and the time it is produced. Some weapons systems have a life of 15 to 25 years, while others are obsolete by the time the first item is produced.

5 It is a market where technical achievement is often a major requirement. The customer's (Department of Defense) demand is contingent on the technological advances of potential enemies.

6 Highly specialized skills and facilities are often required.

7 It is a market where price is not the dominant factor. Despite budgetary pressure to rely more on cost than on technical excellence, many Department of Defense agencies apply their own criteria when making a procurement. In some markets price is not a factor at all; in other cases, it is the only criteria.

8 The customer (Department of Defense) regulates the terms of the procurement contract before, during, and after performance.

9 The customer in the form of various Department of Defense agencies has become increasingly sophisticated in both the selection of items to procure and in the ability to select and control the contractor.

10 A large percentage of items are procured by negotiation with selected suppliers. The competition for initial contracts for new items is therefore extremely intense.

11 Many firms are precluded from entering a specific market because they lack the technical competence or because of customer requirements for experience in that market.

12 Because of the characteristics of the defense market, firms within that market tend also to have some common characteristics.

13 Defense contractors tend to have a high degree of sophistication and to possess the extremely precise manufacturing capabilities needed to meet many design requirements.

14 Most firms are high R&D-oriented and pursue breakthroughs in the state of the art.

15 Most firms seek only a specialized segment of a market area. For example in the aircraft field there are firms that specialize in bombers, fighters, or helicopters, but few firms try to compete in all three categories. In specialized market areas there are usually fewer competitors and in some cases virtually no competitors. For example, only two firms supply steel for submarines, United States Steel and Lukens Steel. They have adequate output to supply the only customer, the U.S. Navy.

16 Markets tend to be cyclical in nature, owing to such factors as frequent program cancellations (e.g., the B-1 bomber) and failure to continue programs into production. In addition, there is an industry practice of establishing new divisions for new programs, and since many of these divisions are concerned with only one major project, they are difficult, if not impossible, to maintain when the program is complete.

17 Few firms have been able to successfully diversify into commercial markets.

INDUSTRY FINANCIAL STRUCTURE

In general, defense contractors work on a lower profit margin than their commercial counterparts. This situation is mitigated by the fact that when a contract is awarded the sale is guaranteed even before production has commenced. Even if a contract is cancelled, the contractor is entitled to termination expenses. In addition, particularly risky projects are awarded on a cost plus fixed-fee basis, which means that a contractor is guaranteed that all costs will be paid and the bill receive a negotiated fixed fee in addition.

While contractors tend to be in the forefront of technology, the customer frequently supplies specialized equipment and facilities for use on contracts. By so doing, the contractors utilize less of their own capital with the result that their return on assets is somewhat closer to their commercial counterparts.

Progress payments against work in process and relatively prompt payment of invoices when contracts are completed enable the contractor to minimize inventory and receivable problems. Commercial firms would welcome this system since these are two key areas of concern in most business ventures.

Accounting for costs, as well as all other aspects of defense contracting, is regulated by the Armed Services Procurement Regulations (ASPR). ASPR dictates which costs are allocable, allowable, and reasonable when charged to government contracts. Expenses such as entertainment and advertising may not be charged to a government contract. In addition all costs are audited regularly by the Defense Contract Audit Agency (DCAA). The Defense Contract Agency Services (DCAS) performs technical evaluation of contractor performance. Audits are performed before acceptance of a contractor's cost proposal, during the performance of the contract, and upon completion of the contract. ASPR dictates the maximum profit allowable to a contractor on all types of contracts. The fact is that when a contract is awarded either by negotiation or on the basis of competitive bidding, the contractor may exceed this profit limitation if the contractor does so by efficient performance. The Truth in Negotiations Act requires both the contractor and the government to disclose all known financial and technical information at the time of negotiation. If it is determined that excessive profits accrued to a contractor because of failure to disclose material data available at the time of negotiation, the contractor must refund the excessive profits to the customer. In all, the defense contractor is subject to close financial scrutiny in a regulated environment much the same as utilities, railroads, and airlines before deregulation.

MARKETING WITH THE GOVERNMENT

In the defense market the customer establishes the market and manages the channels of distribution. The defense contractor's marketing plan thus is indifferent to two areas of prime concern in the commercial field. Most products produced for the Department of Defense are accepted either at the contractor's plant or at a specified destination.

Marketing with the Department of Defense requires:

1 Identification of markets and potential customers and competitors within the market. Competitors will likely include at least one of the thirty largest contractors shown in Exhibit 9, since these companies account for almost 52 percent of all prime contracts awarded by the military.

2 Contact with key customer personnel in selected markets. The marketing effort requires demonstration to the customer of the capability of the contractor to perform. Technical and cost proposals are submitted, and the engineering people employed by the contractor generally work closely with the marketing people. Indeed, most top engineers spend a high percentage of their time on marketing efforts. The idea is to convince the customer that the company's unique technical approach to a system is the most effective both from a performance and from a cost viewpoint. Historically the contractor chosen for the development of a system was then awarded the initial production contract. There has been a trend recently to awarding contracts to two or more contractors who have differing technical proposals. After development of a system or product, the customer then chooses the one which most closely fits the technical and cost requirements and awards the production contract to that contractor. Now the award of a contract no longer virtually guarantees a production award, it only means that you are still in the running for the production award.

3 Posttransaction contact with customers to assure satisfaction with products procured and to solicit changes and recommendations for future procurements. Maintaining relations with various agencies is a key area of marketing. Gathering intelligence on potential new programs and on competitors' activities as well as discerning changes in the political philosophy are also vital aspects of the overall marketing effort. Such intelligence enables a firm to formulate its strategy and to decide whether it should go after a contract as a prime contractor or whether to team up with other contractors and receive a portion of a program as a subcontractor.

EXHIBIT 9
LEADING MILITARY PRIME CONTRACTORS (in millions of dollars)

Company	Contracts awarded		Company	Contracts awarded	
	1977	1978		1977	1978
General Dynamics	1,372	4,154	RCA	364	565
McDonnell Douglas	2,574	2,863	Honeywell	457	545
United Technologies	1,585	2,400	Westinghouse	802	539
Lockheed	1,673	2,226	Martin Marietta	426	539
General Electric	1,520	1,786	Fairchild Industries	429	508
Litton	609	1,557	AT&T	457	457
Boeing	1,580	1,525	Texas Instruments	324	434
Hughes A/C	1,093	1,489	Reynolds (RJ) Industries	*	421
Raytheon	1,041	1,307	General Motors	380	420
Grumman	1,428	1,180	Tenneco	745	407
Rockwell International	1,480	890	Ford Motor	352	406
Textron	455	868	IBM Corporation	547	396
Chrysler	620	743	LTV	*	384
Sperry Rand	652	612	Todd Shipyards	468	379
Northrop	1,047	586	FMC	*	361
			Total all contracts	50,385	59,582

*Not in list of major contractors for 1977.
Sources: Aerospace Industries Association, Department of Defense.

Jewel Companies, Inc.[1]

Jewel was a diversified national retailer which had recently repositioned itself both in geography and in business mix. As part of its planned repositioning, Jewel had acquired a major drugstore chain in the sun belt, increased its emphasis on the combination food-drug store as its primary investment vehicle, expanded its chain of limited-assortment discount grocery stores, and divested several unprofitable operations.

Founded in 1899, Jewel was by 1982 a coast-to-coast merchant doing business in 33 states. The company operated 1,224 retail outlets, which included supermarkets, food-drug stores, solo drugstores, convenience stores, limited-line discount food stores, and a franchised chain of ice cream–sandwich shops. Jewel was the seventh-largest food retailer in the nation, with sales of $4.2 billion in 1980 (see Exhibits 1, 2, and 3).

COMPANY HISTORY AND DEVELOPMENT

Direct Marketing

In 1899, Jewel Tea Company sold coffee, tea, and a limited line of groceries door to door in Chicago. This form of retailing was common at that time, and its most significant feature was the use of premiums in merchandising. Although the industry suffered from serious overcapacity, Jewel prospered, attributing its

---

[1] This case was prepared from published sources and the 1977 version of the case written by Curt Stiles. This version of the case was written by Ms. Judy Lipnick and Mr. Albert W. Isenman under the direction of Professor Thomas J. McNichols.

success in a highly competitive industry to two policies: (1) choosing premiums artfully and (2) providing the buyer with the premium before he or she had accumulated the required number of credits, a policy that Jewel called "advancing the premium."

Choice of a premium sensitive to the buying public's preference meant the difference between success and failure. Jewel demonstrated very early its mastery of premium selection, based upon two principles. First, quality premiums permitted Jewel to maintain prices that not only were higher than those of retail grocers but also were higher than those of most other home-service companies. Second, the premiums were part of a set, which tied the customer to acquiring not just one item but rather a whole set of items that could take years to complete.

Advancing the premium was crucial to Jewel as a promotional device because the industry was crowded with small, unstable operations with a high mortality. Whenever a company went out of business, all its customers working toward a premium had accumulated useless credits. Advancing the premium was promoted as a counter to this danger and proved to have great appeal with the public; it was probably the single most important factor leading to industry dominance by Jewel.

Growth

After going public in 1916, Jewel entered a period of rapid growth. The number of routes was doubled in a single year. Plans were to continue this expansion, but the social and economic conditions resulting from America's entry into World War I had adverse effects upon Jewel. Sales remained stable, but profits began to decline dramatically. In 1919, Jewel sustained a loss of $1.6 million on sales of $17.4 million. The loss worsened in 1920 to $2.0 million on sales of $18.0 million. To save the company, Jewel management began in 1920 to make major cutbacks in the size of the organization and the scope of operations and to enforce stringent cost-cutting measures.

By the end of 1921, it was clear that these measures were successful. Sales that year were reduced to only $11 million, but the large loss of 1920 had changed to a profit of $321,458. Sales and earnings continued to grow steadily over the next decade. By the end of 1931, Jewel possessed $3,220,284 in cash and marketable securities.

The seriousness of Jewel's situation in 1919 and 1920 led management to question whether home service was any longer a viable method of merchandising. It was subject to increasing costs of operations and increasingly large inroads into the market made by retail stores, particularly chain stores. To this was added, beginning in 1931, the spread of the Green River Ordinances. First passed in the small town of Green River, Wyoming, these municipal statutes, supported by local merchants, prohibited door-to-door selling. Although the Green River Ordinance was never a significant factor nationally, its mere existence clearly represented a possible threat to home-service routes. A third

EXHIBIT 1
Statement of Earnings
Jewel Companies, Inc.*
(in thousands except per share data)

	52 weeks ended Jan. 31, 1981
Sales	$4,267,922
Costs of doing business:	
Cost of goods sold	3,435,838
Selling, general, and administrative expenses	740,713
	4,176,551
Operating earnings	91,371
Losses on facility dispositions	—
Interest income	3,314
Interest expense:	
Jewel Companies, Inc.	(19,415)
Real estate affiliates	(10,897)
Earnings of U.S. companies from continuing operations before income taxes	64,373
Income taxes	24,242
Earnings of U.S. companies from continuing operations	40,131
Equity in net earnings of Aurrera, S.A.	24,416
Earnings from continuing operations	64,547
Earnings (loss) from operation subject to disposition, net of income taxes	(8,654)
Net earnings	$ 555,893
Primary earnings per average common share outstanding:	
Earnings of U.S. companies from continuing operations	$ 3.36
Equity in net earnings of Aurrera, S.A.	2.16
Earnings from continuing operations	5.52
Earnings (loss) from operation subject to disposition, net of income taxes	(0.76)
Net earnings	$ 4.76
Fully diluted earnings per share:	
Earnings from continuing operations	$ 5.31
Earnings (loss) from operation subject to disposition, net of income taxes	(0.71)
Net earnings	$ 4.60
STATEMENT OF RETAINED EARNINGS	
Balance, beginning of year	$ 303,346
Net earnings	55,893
Cash dividends declared:	
$3^1/_4$% preferred stock—$3.75 per share	(30)
Series A preferred stock—$0.56 per share	(2,161)
Common stock—$1.92 in 1980, $1.68 in 1979, $1.45 in 1978	(21,777)
Balance, end of year	$ 335,271

*1980 Annual Report, Jewel Companies, Inc.

52 weeks ended Feb. 2, 1980	52 weeks ended Feb. 3, 1979
$3,684,929	$3,434,113
2,939,007	2,728,352
664,544	630,512
3,603,551	3,358,864
81,378	75,249
–	(712)
2,356	2,945
(15,259)	(12,399)
(10,881)	(11,133)
57,594	53,950
22,824	21,851
34,770	32,099
14,543	8,476
49,313	40,575
1,373	567
$ 50,686	$ 41,142
$ 3.12	$ 280
1.30	.74
4.42	3.54
0.12	0.05
$ 4.54	$ 3.59
$ 4.34	$ 3.53
0.12	0.05
$ 4.46	$ 3.58
$ 271,458	$ 246,341
50,686	41,142
(40)	(47)
–	–
(18,758)	(15,978)
$ 303,346	$ 271,458

EXHIBIT 2
Statements of Financial Position
Jewel Companies*
(in thousands)

	January 31, 1981	February 2, 1980
Assets		
Current assets		
Cash	$ 17,853	$ 29,926
Short-term investments	20,133	10,760
Accounts receivable	42,005	37,709
Inventories	426,999	296,715
Prepaid expenses and other	18,909	17,381
Total current assets	525,899	392,491
Investments in Aurrera, S.A.	75,873	58,468
Land, buildings, and equipment, net:		
Jewel Companies, Inc.	471,743	356,734
Real estate affiliates	180,507	175,452
Total land, buildings, and equipment	652,250	532,186
Net assets of operation subject to disposition	–	13,967
Excess of cost over net assets acquired	17,095	–
Other assets	17,784	6,893
	$1,288,901	$1,004,005
Liabilities and shareholders' equity		
Current liabilities		
Accounts payable	$ 169,176	$ 127,601
Payrolls and other accrued expenses	166,046	123,931
Income taxes payable	4,489	4,936
Net liabilities of operation subject to disposition	2,450	–
Current maturities of long-term debt:		
Jewel Companies, Inc.	7,086	6,957
Real estate affiliates	7,523	7,535
Total current liabilities	356,770	270,960
Long-term debt, less current maturities:		
Jewel Companies, Inc.	230,525	159,624
Real estate affiliates	118,661	123,450
Deferred income taxes	46,879	50,141
Other deferred liabilities	25,060	22,195
Shareholders' equity:		
Preferred stock—3³/₄% cumulative $100 par value— authorized and issued 16,500 shares at January 31, 1981	1,650	1,650
Series A preferred stock—$2.31 cumulative convertible—$1 par value— authorized 5,000,000 shares, issued 3,854,201 shares at January 31, 1981	96,311	–
Common stock—$1 par value—authorized 25,000,000 shares, issued 11,678,441 shares at January 31, 1981	85,992	86,449
Retained earnings	335,271	303,346
Treasury stock, at cost	(8,218)	(13,810)
Total shareholders' equity	511,006	377,635
	$1,288,901	$1,004,005

*1980 Annual Report, Jewel Companies, Inc.

problem with home service lay in its limited growth potential. Jewel's management had learned in 1919 and 1920 the danger of too rapid addition of new routes. The company had a desire to expand and to use excess cash on hand, but it was doubtful that addition of routes at the maximum rate permitted by adequate planning and control could meet either desire. The home-service business apparently had the ability to generate more profit than it was able to reabsorb as investment.

Retail

In March 1932, Jewel purchased all 77 Chicago food stores of Loblaw, a Canadian firm caught by the Depression in an overexpanded position. The cost was $1 million. To obtain management for the chain, Jewel bought out a small four-store operation called Midwest Stores. The number of stores then totaled 81.

After two years of unprofitable operations, the former Midwest Stores management was dismissed and the food store operation was brought under Jewel management. A divisional structure was adopted, consisting of the Food Stores Department and the Home Services Department. A program of store modernization accompanied by very heavy promotion was pursued in an attempt to turn food operations around.

Diversification and Geographic Expansion

In the 1950s, an acquisition wave swept the chain supermarket industry. For example, in the period between 1951 and 1956 alone, there were approximately 40 acquisitions of substantial size, involving considerably more than a thousand stores. The effects of the acquisitions were both to increase the size of supermarket chains and to expand their geographic coverage. Most of the acquisitions were made by large chains of smaller chains.

Jewel made its first acquisition in 1957. At that time it consisted of two departments, the Food Stores Department with 184 stores in metropolitan Chicago and the Home Services Department with 2,000 routes (see Exhibit 4).

In the 1981 Corporate Profile the company described itself as ". . . a diversified national retailer with a new profile." In recent years sales and acquisitions were carefully planned to reposition the firm with respect to geography and business mix. Since 1978, this planned development had included the acquisition of Sav-On-Drugs, a major chain in the sun belt, and divestiture of several unprofitable operations.

Between 1978 and 1980, divestitures included Republic Lumber, Turn*Style, and the Milwaukee locations of Jewel Food Stores. In 1981, the company transferred the assets and business of the Jewel Home Shopping Service to a new cooperative organized by employees.

Further geographic expansion was evidenced by the planned growth of the Jewel T discount grocery store format. It was introduced in 1977 and operated 138 units in 8 states.

EXHIBIT 3A
Five Year Summary of Selected Financial Data
Jewel Companies*
(in thousands except per share data)

	1980	
	LIFO	FIFO
Operating results		
Sales	$4,267,922	$4,267,922
Earnings of U.S. companies from continuing operations	$ 40,131	$ 50,923
Equity in net earnings of Aurrera S.A.	24,416	24,416
Earnings from continuing operations	64,547	75,339
Operation subject to disposition	(8,654)	(8,654)
Net earnings	$ 55,893	$ 66,685
Earnings of U.S. companies from continuing operations as a percent of sales	.94%	1.19%
Earnings from continuing operations as a percent of shareholders' average equity	15.2%	17.7%
Per share results		
Primary earnings per common share		
Earnings from continuing operations	$ 5.52	$ 6.48
Operation subject to disposition	(.76)	(.76)
Net earnings	$ 4.76	$ 5.72
Fully diluted earnings per common share		
Earnings from continuing operations	$ 5.31	$ 6.20
Operation subject to disposition	(.71)	(.71)
Net earnings	$ 4.60	$ 5.49
Dividends declared per common share	$ 1.92	
Percent of net earnings	40%	
Equity per common share	$ 36.27	
Financial position		
Working capital	$ 169,129	
Total assets	1,288,901	
Long-term debt, less current maturities:		
Jewel Companies, Inc.	230,525	
Real estate affiliates	118,661	
Common shareholders' equity	413,893	
Other statistical data		
Employees (full-time equivalents)	39.0	
Square footage of retail stores:		
Supermarkets	10,255	
Drugstores	9,039	
Other operations	2,288	
Total at year end	21,582	

*19th Annual Report.

1979	1978	1977	1976
$3,684,929	$3,434,113	$3,195,146	$2,880,295
$ 34,770	$ 32,099	$ 21,013	$ 22,416
14,543	8,476	4,889	12,056
49,313	40,575	25,902	34,472
1,373	567	684	1,290
$ 50,686	$ 41,142	$ 26,586	$ 35,762
.94%	.93%	.66%	.78%
13.7%	12.0%	7.9%	11.0%
$ 4.42	$ 3.54	$ 2.23	$ 2.99
.12	.05	.06	.11
$ 4.54	$ 3.59	$ 2.29	$ 3.10
$ 4.34	$ 3.53	$ 2.22	$ 2.97
.12	.05	.06	.11
$ 4.46	$ 3.58	$ 2.28	$ 3.08
$ 1.68	$ 1.405	$ 1.30	$ 1.275
37%	57%	41%	
$ 33.69	$ 30.87	$ 28.58	$ 27.64
$ 121,531	$ 103,828	$ 107,460	$ 87,937
1,004,005	949,856	906,323	837,654
159,624	142,195	147,636	130,969
123,450	126,357	126,511	118,922
376,766	343,579	331,614	318,868
33.4	33.4	35.2	35.1
10,562	10,523	10,500	10,186
4,644	4,582	6,627	6,409
2,014	1,068	898	852
17,220	16,173	18,025	17,447

EXHIBIT 3B
TEN-YEAR SUMMARY OF SELECTED FINANCIAL DATA AND ANALYSIS

	Compound growth rate						Average value				
Period	Sales	Assets	Equity	Net income	Average shares	Earnings per share	Net margin ×	Asset turnover =	Return on assets	Financial × leverage =	Return on equity
1969–1974	12.1%	13.9%	11.5%	6.9%	2.6%	4.0%	1.39%	3.43	5.06%	2.50	12.4%
1974–1979	7.7	5.4	6.0	11.1	(.4)	11.6	1.11	3.56	4.09	2.72	11.1

Per Share Results

Fiscal year	Earnings	Change Due to				Percent increase (Dec.)	Retention rate	Dividends	
		Domestic earnings	Foreign investments	Outstanding shares	Total			Total	Increase (Dec.)
1969	$2.15	$ .05	$ .09	$ —	$ .14	7.0%	55%	$ .97	7.8%
1970	2.23	.04	.21	(.17)	.08	3.7	54	1.00	3.1
1971	2.40	.18	.07	(.08)	.17	7.6	56	1.03	3.0
1972	2.56	.16	.02	(.02)	.16	6.7	57	1.09	5.8
1973	2.60	(.06)	.11	(.01)	.04	1.6	58	1.11	1.8
1974	2.62	.07	(.01)	(.04)	.02	.8	56	1.15	3.6
1975	2.47	(.33)	.19	(.01)	(.15)	(5.7)	51	1.20	4.3
1976	3.10	.26	.39	(.02)	.63	25.5	60	1.25	4.2
1977	2.29	(.17)	(.62)	(.02)	(.81)	(26.1)	43	1.30	4.0
1978	3.59	.94	.32	.04	1.30	56.8	62	1.37	5.4
1979	4.54	.30	.56	.09	.95	26.5	64	1.62	18.2

Fiscal year	Book value		Price range	P/E range	Shareholders	Average shares outstanding	Average monthly volume
	Total	Increase (Dec.)				(000)	(000)
1969	$16.15	7.5%	37¹/₈ – 28⁵/₈	17–13	14,221	9,995	101.3
1970	18.06	11.8	36¹/₂ – 24³/₈	16–11	14,486	10,731	123.7

1971	19.51	8.0	44³/₈–34³/₈	18–11	14,165	11,099	147.2
1972	21.11	8.2	43¹/₈–27¹/₈	17–11	13,865	11,187	172.5
1973	23.25	10.1	34¹/₈–18⁵/₈	14–7	13,694	11,217	176.9
1974	24.60	5.8	29¹/₈–16⁵/₈	11–6	14,324	11,381	95.8
1975	25.84	5.0	25⁷/₈–16⁷/₈	10–7	14,746	11,452	184.2
1976	27.64	7.0	24¹/₄–19¹/₄	8–6	15,152	11,507	205.6
1977	28.58	3.4	26¹/₂–18¹/₈	11–8	14,973	11,576	240.2
1978	30.87	8.0	26–17¹/₂	7–5	14,596	11,442	244.2
1979	33.69	9.1	30¹/₈–20	7–4	13,925	11,155	242.5

Corporate growth and rate of return summary ($ in millions)

Fiscal year	Sales	Net earnings	Total assets	Common shareholders' equity	Net margin	Asset turnover	Return on assets	Financial leverage	Return on equity	Retention rate	Implied growth rate
1969	$1,469.6	$21.5	$406.5	$161.7	1.47%	3.62 ×	5.70%	2.48 ×	13.5%	55%	7.4%
1970	1,633.5	24.0	486.9	199.5	1.47	3.35	5.37	2.41	13.1	54	7.1
1971	1,815.2	26.7	520.0	217.5	1.47	3.49	5.30	2.38	12.7	56	7.1
1972	2,009.3	28.7	578.2	236.6	1.43	3.48	5.23	2.43	12.5	57	7.1
1973	2,219.6	29.6	671.6	261.2	1.32	3.30	4.69	2.56	11.8	58	6.8
1974	2,598.9	29.9	777.5	281.1	1.15	3.34	4.05	2.75	11.0	56	6.2
1975	2,817.8	28.3	804.1	296.9	1.00	3.50	3.58	2.70	9.7	51	4.9
1976	2,981.4	35.8	844.9	318.9	1.20	3.53	4.34	2.64	11.6	60	7.0
1977	3,277.7	26.6	914.2	331.6	.81	3.59	3.02	2.75	8.1	43	3.5
1978	3,516.4	41.1	958.1	343.6	1.17	3.67	4.39	2.78	12.1	62	7.5
1979	3,764.3	50.7	1,012.4	376.8	1.35	3.72	5.15	2.68	14.0	64	9.0

Net earnings ($ in millions)

Fiscal year	Sales	COS	Gross profit	SGA	Operating income	Net other increase (exp.)	Pretax income	Income taxes	Domestic earnings	Foreign earnings	Net earnings
1969	$1,469.6	$1,159.5	$310.1	$264.2	$45.9	$(5.7)	$40.2	$19.9	$20.3	$ 1.1	$21.4
1970	1,633.4	1,287.7	345.7	295.3	50.4	(8.1)	42.3	21.6	20.7	3.3	24.0
1971	1,815.2	1,425.3	389.9	339.4	50.5	(9.4)	41.2	18.5	22.6	4.1	26.7

EXHIBIT 3B *(continued)*
TEN-YEAR SUMMARY OF SELECTED FINANCIAL DATA AND ANALYSIS

Net earnings ($ in millions)

Fiscal year	Sales	COS	Gross profit	SGA	Operating income	Net other increase (exp.)	Pretax income	Income taxes	Domestic earnings	Foreign earnings	Net earnings
1972	2,009.3	1,578.8	430.5	376.9	53.6	(11.2)	42.4	18.0	24.4	4.3	28.7
1973	2,219.6	1,762.2	457.4	400.2	57.2	(14.9)	42.3	18.5	23.8	5.5	29.3
1974	2,598.9	2,054.3	544.6	480.6	64.0	(21.9)	42.1	17.6	24.5	5.4	29.9
1975	2,817.8	2,249.2	568.6	515.3	53.3	(21.3)	32.0	11.3	20.7	7.6	28.3
1976	2,981.4	2,353.8	627.6	565.7	61.9	(21.9)	40.0	16.3	23.7	12.1	35.8
1977	3,277.7	2,577.6	700.1	635.9	64.2	(31.3)	32.9	11.2	21.7	4.9	26.6
1978	3,516.4	2,768.7	747.7	671.5	76.2	(21.3)	54.9	22.2	32.7	8.4	41.1
1979	3,764.3	2,979.2	785.1	701.9	83.2	(23.8)	59.4	23.2	36.2	14.5	50.7

Net margin analysis (% of total sales)

Fiscal year	COS	Gross margin	SGA	Operating margin	Net other increase (exp.)	Pretax margin	Effective rate	Domestic margin	Foreign increment	Net margin
1969	78.89%	21.11%	17.98%	3.13%	(.39)%	2.74%	49.50%	1.38%	.07%	1.45%
1970	78.83	21.17	18.08	3.09	(.50)	2.59	51.06	1.27	.20	1.47
1971	78.52	21.48	18.70	2.78	(.52)	2.26	44.90	1.25	.23	1.48
1972	78.57	21.43	18.76	2.67	(.56)	2.11	42.45	1.21	.22	1.43
1973	79.39	20.61	18.03	2.58	(.67)	1.91	43.74	1.07	.25	1.32
1974	79.05	20.95	18.49	2.46	(.84)	1.62	41.81	.94	.21	1.15
1975	79.82	20.18	18.29	1.89	(.76)	1.13	35.31	.73	.27	1.00
1976	78.95	21.05	18.97	2.08	(.74)	1.34	40.75	.79	.41	1.20
1977	78.64	21.36	19.40	1.96	(.96)	1.00	34.04	.66	.15	.81
1978	78.74	21.26	19.09	2.17	(.61)	1.56	40.44	.93	.24	1.17
1979	79.14	20.86	18.65	2.21	(.63)	1.58	39.06	.96	.39	1.35

Investment of assets ($ in millions)

Fiscal year	Cash and equivalent	Accounts receivable	Inventories	Prepaid expenses	Current assets	Net plant and equip.		Foreign investment	Other assets	Total assets
						Jewel	R. E. affiliates			
1969	$41.2	$ 9.4	$110.1	$ 5.4	$166.1	$147.0	$ 64.3	$ 27.7	$1.4	$406.5
1970	54.9	22.4	121.4	4.9	203.6	166.1	83.9	30.4	2.9	486.9
1971	30.6	21.6	136.3	6.3	194.8	191.7	97.3	33.7	2.5	520.0
1972	21.0	24.6	151.0	6.5	203.1	224.9	113.3	33.6	3.3	578.2
1973	30.0	25.2	187.4	8.9	251.5	251.1	132.4	32.9	3.7	671.6
1974	33.7	31.7	208.0	9.5	282.9	301.2	151.4	38.7	3.3	777.5
1975	37.4	29.1	216.1	9.0	291.6	312.6	157.0	39.2	3.7	804.1
1976	32.6	34.4	239.8	11.2	318.0	312.1	165.1	46.2	3.5	844.9
1977	59.8	34.1	257.4	11.4	362.7	325.2	174.8	47.2	4.3	914.2
1978	65.6	43.5	271.9	11.4	392.4	334.0	177.7	48.7	5.3	958.1
1979	41.5	46.7	304.5	17.6	410.3	361.2	175.5	58.5	6.9	1,012.4

Sources of assets ($ in millions)

Fiscal year	Notes and accounts payable	Payroll and account expenses	Taxes payable	Current maturities		Current sources	Net long-term debt		Other noncurrent		Shareholders' equity
				Corporate	R. E. affil.		Corporate	R. E. affil.	Def.	Miscellaneous	
1969	$ N/A	$108.7	$ N/A	$1.5	$2.9	$113.1	59.0	$ 51.9	$13.6	$ 3.7	$165.2
1970	N/A	120.5	N/A	.7	3.3	124.5	76.8	61.6	17.0	4.3	202.7
1971	N/A	128.5	N/A	2.0	3.9	134.4	71.2	68.9	19.4	5.7	220.4
1972	81.2	51.0	8.8	2.0	4.6	147.6	77.7	83.5	24.7	6.6	238.1
1973	94.3	61.0	6.8	3.6	5.2	170.9	100.7	98.4	31.1	7.8	262.7
1974	104.2	70.5	5.0	6.7	5.7	192.1	146.5	114.0	33.7	8.7	282.5
1975	94.9	90.3	1.4	7.0	6.3	199.9	135.4	118.4	41.6	10.5	298.3
1976	100.6	95.8	11.1	7.2	6.7	221.4	131.0	118.9	40.2	13.1	320.3
1977	109.4	115.6	4.5	7.7	7.0	244.2	147.6	126.5	44.7	18.2	333.0
1978	127.0	131.0	4.7	6.9	7.3	277.9	142.2	126.4	47.2	19.7	344.7
1979	129.5	130.3	5.0	7.0	7.5	279.3	159.6	123.5	50.1	22.3	377.6

EXHIBIT 3B (continued)
TEN-YEAR SUMMARY OF SELECTED FINANCIAL DATA AND ANALYSIS

Interim Results

Fiscal period	Sales (millions)	Operating margin	Domestic earnings (000)	Foreign earnings (000)	Net earnings (000)	Net margin	Per share		
							Earnings	Dividend paid	Price range
1974 1	$ 550	2.29%	$ 4,570	$ 871	$ 5,441	.99%	$ .49	$ .277	29\frac{1}{8}$–24$\frac{1}{8}$
2	774	2.50	7,268	1,519	8,787	1.14	.77	.277	27$\frac{5}{8}$–19$\frac{1}{4}$
3	611	1.81	3,585	1,018	4,603	.75	.40	.30	22$\frac{1}{2}$–17$\frac{1}{4}$
4	664	3.16	9,075	1,985	11,060	1.67	.96	.30	22$\frac{3}{4}$–16$\frac{5}{8}$
Total	2,599	2.46	24,498	5,393	29,891	1.15	2.62	1.15	29$\frac{1}{8}$–16$\frac{5}{8}$
1975 1	602	1.75	3,450	1,338	4,788	.80	.43	.30	25$\frac{7}{8}$–20$\frac{1}{8}$
2	852	1.68	4,819	2,137	6,956	.82	.60	.30	24 –19$\frac{1}{8}$
3	654	1.57	3,190	1,733	4,923	.75	.43	.30	21$\frac{7}{8}$–16$\frac{7}{8}$
4	710	2.56	9,279	2,337	11,616	1.65	1.01	.30	22$\frac{1}{8}$–18$\frac{7}{8}$
Total	2,818	1.89	20,738	7,545	28,283	1.00	2.47	1.20	25$\frac{7}{8}$–16$\frac{7}{8}$
1976 1	647	1.38	3,165	1,785	4,949	.76	.43	.30	24$\frac{1}{4}$–20
2	892	1.87	5,907	3,448	9,355	1.05	.81	.30	23$\frac{3}{8}$–19$\frac{1}{4}$
3	673	1.55	3,485	5,204	8,689	1.29	.75	.335	24 –21$\frac{1}{4}$
4	769	3.16	11,150	1,619	12,769	1.66	1.11	.325	24 –21
Total	2,981	2.08	23,706	12,056	35,762	1.20	3.10	1.25	24$\frac{1}{4}$–19$\frac{1}{4}$
1977 1	720	1.74	5,269	280	5,549	.77	.48	.325	26$\frac{1}{2}$–22$\frac{7}{8}$
2	979	1.61	6,536	1,127	7,663	.78	.66	.325	24$\frac{3}{4}$–21$\frac{5}{8}$
3	749	.42	2,329	818	3,147	.42	.27	.325	23$\frac{3}{8}$–19$\frac{1}{4}$
4	830	3.01	7,563	2,664	10,227	1.23	.88	.325	20$\frac{1}{2}$–18$\frac{1}{8}$
Total	3,278	1.96	21,697	4,889	26,586	.81	2.29	1.300	26$\frac{1}{2}$–18$\frac{1}{8}$
1978 1	779	1.75	5,372	1,784	7,156	.92	.62	.325	20$\frac{1}{2}$–17$\frac{1}{2}$
2	1,015	2.18	8,888	1,935	10,823	1.07	.93	.325	23$\frac{3}{4}$–18$\frac{1}{8}$
3	769	1.50	5,145	1,374	6,519	.85	.57	.360	26 –20$\frac{1}{4}$
4	953	2.83	13,261	3,383	16,644	1.75	1.47	.360	21$\frac{3}{4}$–19
Total	3,516	2.17	32,666	8,476	41,142	1.17	3.59	1.370	26 –17$\frac{1}{2}$

1979 1	817	1.83	6,504	2,598	9,102	1.11	.82	.36	25 −20
2	1,131	2.18	10,429	3,670	14,099	1.25	1.26	.42	27 −22$^{3}/_{8}$
3	859	1.57	5,505	2,454	7,959	.93	.71	.42	26$^{3}/_{8}$−22$^{1}/_{2}$
4	957	3.14	13,705	5,821	19,526	2.04	1.75	.42	30$^{1}/_{8}$−22$^{7}/_{8}$
Total	3,764	2.21	36,143	14,543	50,686	1.35	4.54	1.62	30$^{1}/_{8}$−20
1980 1	901	2.03	7,348	4,024	11,372	1.26	1.01	.42	28$^{7}/_{8}$−22$^{1}/_{8}$
2	1,232	2.08	11,476	5,245	16,721	1.36	1.49	.48	32$^{1}/_{2}$−24$^{5}/_{8}$
3	966	2.10	9,163	4,083	13,246	1.37	1.17	.48	33$^{7}/_{8}$−29$^{1}/_{2}$

Note: In the charts and data: (1) fiscal years end on the Saturday nearest January 31 of the following year; (2) starting with 1974, figures are restated to reflect capital leases; (3) all share and per share data have been adjusted to reflect a 3-for-2 stock split in 1974; (4) earnings data excludes extraordinary income of $6.7 million or $.60 per share in 1973 and $1.2 million or $.11 per share in 1972.

EXHIBIT 4
JEWEL ACQUISITION AND SALES BY YEAR AND TYPE

Acquisitions

1957	Eisner Food Stores: A small supermarket chain operating in central Illinois and Indiana.
1960	Supermarches G. B.: A small Belgian supermarket chain founded by Jewel (36% interest) and a Belgian partner (36% interest).
1961	Super Bazaars: A small Belgian chain of self-service discount department stores founded by Jewel (18.75% interest) and three Belgian partners.
1961	Osco Drugs: A small self-service drugstore chain operating 31 stores in the midwest.
1962	Turn*Style: A small four-store chain of general merchandise stores located in the Boston area.
1964	Star Markets: A small supermarket chain operating in New England.
1964	Brighams: A small chain of ice cream and sandwich shops in New England, acquired by Star Markets in 1962.
1965	White Hen Pantry: A small chain of convenience food stores founded by Jewel as a franchise operation.
1966	Buttrey Super Stores: A small chain of combination supermarkets and general merchandise stores operating in Idaho and Montana.
1969	Aurerra, S.A.: A small (but Mexico's largest) chain of supermarkets, discount stores self-service department stores, restaurants, fashion apparel stores, and automobile service stations operating around Mexico City (Jewel had a 47% interest).
1970	Mass Feeding Corporation: A concern that packaged and distributed hot lunches to schools in Chicago and Detroit.
1972	Republic Lumber Company: A company that sold lumber and home-improvement supplies and contracted to build residential garages in Chicago.
1980	Sav-On-Drugs: A chain of 146 drugstores operating in Southern California, the San Jose area in northern California, Houston, and Las Vegas.

Divestitures

1973	Remaining interest in GB Enterprises, Belgium
1978	Turn*Style
1978	Republic Lumber Stores
1980	Milwaukee locations of Jewel Food Stores
1981	Jewel Home Shopping Service

THE JEWEL ORGANIZATION

In 1981, Jewel was in five businesses: retail groceries, restaurants, institutional catering, retail drugs and general merchandise stores, and manufacturing. Jewel had three franchise or agency store activities. These businesses were organized into 11 "companies," with the following characteristics:

Jewel Food Stores

Stores, December 1980	207
Total square foot (thousands)	6,472

Jewel Food Stores, the largest and most profitable division, served the Chicago metropolitan area, northern Illinois, northern Indiana, eastern Iowa, and Michigan. Most Jewel stores combined the sale of food and general merchandise.

Eisner Food and Agency Stores

Stores, December 1980	32
Total square feet (thousands)	787
Affiliated stores	59

Headquartered in Champaign, Illinois, Eisner operated in central Illinois and Indiana. It also franchised 59 independent stores and supplied them as a wholesaler.

Star Market Company

Stores, December 1980	53
Total square feet (thousands)	1,640

Star Market was headquartered in Cambridge, Massachusetts. It also served Maine, Rhode Island, New Hampshire, and Vermont. It was generally thought to be the sales leader among Boston supermarkets.

Buttrey Food Stores

Stores, December 1980	53
Total square feet (thousands)	1,356

Headquartered in Great Falls, Montana, Buttrey served Montana, Idaho, Minnesota, Oregon, Washington, Wyoming, and North Dakota. High quality and decentralization of management responsibility were given heavy emphasis.

White Hen Pantry

Stores, December 1980	244
Total square feet (thousands)	617

White Hen Pantry convenience stores were operated in the midwest and New England. Most of its outlets were franchised.

Brigham's

Stores, December 1980	95
Total square feet (thousands)	265

Brigham's was a franchise operation in the Boston area. It had a reputation for quality ice cream and sandwiches. Ice cream and candy were produced in a central manufacturing facility, and high quality was stressed.

Osco Drug

Stores, December 1980	280
Total square feet (thousands)	5,035

Osco operated drug and general merchandise stores in New England, the midwest, the middle south, and the northwest. Of the 280 units, 169 were located with Jewel, Eisner, Star, and Buttrey supermarkets.

Jewel T Discount Grocery

Stores, December 1980	138
Total square feet (thousands)	1,406

The Jewel T concept offered the customer a limited-line discount grocery store with the lowest possible prices and a no-frills approach. It operated in seven states.

Sav-On-Drugs

Stores, December 1980	146
Total square feet (thousands)	4,004

Sav-On operated in California, Las Vegas, and Houston. The stores offered a pharmacy and a wide variety of general merchandise. Twelve stores were home centers, which were combination drug and home-improvement centers.

Mass Feeding Corporation

Mass Feeding Corporation provided nutritional school lunches at affordable prices in fourteen states. Frozen meals were delivered to schools where they were reconstituted in high-speed convection ovens.

Park Corporation

The Park Corporation was engaged in manufacturing and selling a variety of private-label products not only to Jewel but to many outside customers.

At the beginning of 1981, the supermarket and drugstore operations were profitable and growing. Together, they constituted 91 percent of 1980 total sales. Park Corporation sales to Jewel Divisions had increased during the year, but operating earnings had fallen off due to flat sales to outside customers and price fluctuations of coffee and sugar. Mass Feeding Corporation experienced a 10 percent increase in operating earnings due to increased productivity and reduced overhead. White Hen Pantry showed a record 17 percent increase in operating earnings, and the outlook for growth was good providing real estate developers could secure acceptable financing. Jewel T had completed a major reshaping of operating and financing programs and was on sound footing for continued growth and operating improvement. Although Brigham's sales decreased 1 percent in 1980, operating earnings were up slightly. Consolidated performance data are presented in Exhibits 5A, B, and C.

JEWEL STRATEGY

At Jewel, organization values took on a particularly heavy emphasis, to the point that company philosophy was said to be the primary determinant of strategy. Jewel management stated that "strategy follows philosophy." Donald Perkins, former Jewel board chairman, defined strategy as "nothing more than an up-to-date plan that is consistent with the reputation-building goals of a company's basic philosophy."

Determinants of Jewel Strategies

The Jewel philosophy was embodied in 14 principles provided to everyone in contact with Jewel in the form of a printed booklet entitled "The Jewel Concepts: A Philosophy of Management." The 14 principles stressed such concepts as integrity, social responsibility, and motivation. In discussing strategy formulation at Jewel, four of these principles were cited as the determinants of recent Jewel strategic decisions.

1 Merchants of Empathy   "It is not groceries or merchandise we sell, as much as solutions to needs, problems, and the well-being of our customers." This principle was said to have motivated Jewel efforts in the area of consumerism.

2 The Spirit of Wanting To   "Individuals in Jewel have an emotional need to feel that their efforts serve a larger purpose . . .which benefits society." This principle was said to have motivated Jewel efforts to be effective in the ghetto market.

EXHIBIT 5A

CONSOLIDATED PERFORMANCE DATA—BUSINESS SEGMENTS
(in thousands)

	1980	1979	1978
Sales			
Supermarkets	$3,021,989	$2,817,944	$2,681,639
Drugstores*	859,903	608,304	584,889
Other operations	386,030	258,681	167,585
Total sales	$4,267,922	$3,684,929	$3,434,113
Operating earnings			
before unallocated expenses			
Supermarkets	$ 55,447	$ 57,496	$ 52,159
Drugstores*	31,459	21,312	15,971
Other operations	4,710	4,811	6,886
Total	91,616	81,619	75,016
Unallocated (net)†	(245)	(2,241)	233
Total operating earnings	$ 91,371	$ 81,378	$ 75,249
Identifiable assets			
Supermarkets	$ 613,379	$ 589,610	$ 550,463
Drugstores*	438,595	200,171	185,521
Other operations	85,200	67,657	41,276
Investment in Aurrera, S.A.	75,873	58,468	48,745
Unallocated	75,854	88,099	123,851
Total identifiable assets	$1,288,901	$1,004,005	$ 949,856
Capital expenditures (net)			
Supermarkets	$ 55,274	$ 53,571	$ 57,300
Drugstores*	25,286	14,641	12,402
Other operations	9,208	13,933	4,275
Unallocated	2,647	4,341	6,818
Total capital expenditures	$ 92,415	$ 86,486	$ 80,795
Depreciation expense			
Supermarkets	$ 41,446	$ 38,516	$ 36,219
Drugstores*	9,851	7,579	9,063
Other operations	5,381	3,957	3,044
Unallocated	5,135	5,414	4,197
Total depreciation expense	$ 61,814	$ 55,466	$ 52,523

*Includes Sav-On since its acquisition on November 6, 1980 and Turn*Style prior to its sale in June 1978.

†Unallocated consists principally of general corporate expenses and miscellaneous income.

3 Restless Unsatisfaction "In a rapidly changing world, with quickly shifting consumer needs and expectations, we dare not be too satisfied with anything we are doing. We dare not assume that what we are doing is all we might do." This principle was said to have motivated the Jewel move toward diversification.

Food/Drug

Emphasis on common location food and drug stores.

77	**$1,387	*$2,867
78	**$1,586	*$3,208
79	**$1,767	*$3,423
80	**$1,972	*$3,882

Food and Drug Sales—in millions of dollars
**Common Locations, *Total

Drug Stores

More solo drug stores in existing and new markets.

78	97
79	101
80	255
81 Plan	271

Units

Jewel T

Expansion of the Jewel T Discount Grocery Store chain.

78	29
79	100
80	138
81 Plan	187

Units

Franchising/Agency

Expansion of franchising and agency operations.

78	325
79	363
80	377
81 Plan	421

Franchise and Agency Units

Support Facilities

Increased investment in manufacturing and distribution support facilities.

78	$13.3
79	$14.7
80	$13.9
81 Plan	$20.6

Manufacturing and Distribution Investment—in millions of dollars

EXHIBIT 5B
Jewel Companies

Facility Improvements

Continued remodeling, enlargement and upgrading of existing retail facilities.

78	$24.2
79	$28.0
80	$31.2
81 Plan	$38.7

Investment in Remodeling, etc.—in millions of dollars

Aurrera

Continued investment in Aurrera, S.A.

77	$4.9
78	$8.5
79	$14.5
80	$24.4

Equity in Aurrera Earnings—in millions of dollars

Return on Equity

A 15% return on shareholders' equity from continuing operations.

77	8.1%	
78	12.0%	
79	13.7%	*17.7%
80	**15.2%	

Return on Shareholders' Equity
**LIFO, *FIFO

Return on Sales

U.S. earnings from continuing operations not less than 1% of sales.

77	.66%	
78	.93%	
79	.94%	
80	**.94%	*1.19%

U.S. Earnings as % of Sales
**LIFO, *FIFO

Dividends

Increased dividends for our stockholders.

77	$1.30
78	$1.37
79	$1.62
80	$1.86

Dividends Paid Per Share

4 Watching the Horizon "New forms of competition come over the horizon from time to time. This constantly changing business environment imposes on management the obligation to keep alert. But is is not enough merely to watch for new developments or to identify and study subtle trends. This identification of problems and opportunities must be matched with appropriate ac-

EXHIBIT 5C
PROJECTED STORE UNITS 1980–1983

Store Type	1980 Units	1980 Square feet (000)	1981 Units	1981 Square feet (000)	1982 Units	1982 Square feet (000)	1983 Units	1983 Square feet (000)	Percent change Units	Percent change Square feet (000)
Supermarkets	339	10,103	349	10,560	361	11,100	377	11,700	11.2	15.8
Drugstores	426	7,644	461	8,400	495	9,100	531	9,850	24.6	28.9
Discount grocery	138	1,470	194	1,990	245	2,450	310	3,040	124.6	106.8
Franchised units	341	893	369	960	403	1,040	438	1,120	28.4	25.4
Total	1,244	20,110	1,373	21,910	1,504	23,690	1,656	25,710	33.1	27.8

For several years, Jewel Companies' profitability and dividend goals have been:
• To produce a minimum return of 15 percent on net worth, compared with 14 percent in 1979 and an average of 11.2 percent over the past five years.
• To achieve and maintain a minimum net domestic earnings margin of 1.0 percent of sales, compared with 0.96 percent in 1979 and an average of 0.83 percent since 1974.

tion." This principle was said to have motivated the adoption by Jewel of four of the five types of retail outlets being considered by the industry.

ORGANIZATIONAL RELATIONSHIPS

Although corporate philosophy described Jewel as "an association of autonomous companies," in practice the 11 divisions were decentralized operating divisions and profit centers with which corporate headquarters was regularly involved. A statement of the relationship was contained in the corporate policy statement manual.

> Jewel's management style has evolved from a single corporate control center to today's concept of distinct operating companies, each with appropriate responsibilities and authority. But a strong philosophy of decentralization cannot survive without equally strong underlying principles that recognize the need to coordinate corporate responsibility with the individual profit center authority and responsibility. Thus, corporate policy statements are developed with this objective in mind.

The most important controlling policy statements were the following:

1 Each division was responsible for its own planning and strategy formulation, subject to review by corporate headquarters.

2 Each division was required to cooperate closely with other divisions. Company doctrine went so far as to say that a division's continued autonomy was dependent upon its ability and willingness to cooperate with other divisions.

3 Resources were allocated by corporate management based upon "(1) how well each division has been performing in comparison to approved plans and (2) how well each is expected to perform in the future, all balanced with (3) our overall financial strengths and marketing strategies."

4 Management personnel were moved, by corporate management, between divisions and between divisions and corporate headquarters.

5 Evaluations were conducted by corporate management of division and individual performances.

6 Total authority over and responsibility for the company were held by the chairman of the board and the president in the form of: (1) "their selection of individuals to whom decision-making authority is delegated" and (2) "their judgment of the degree to which and the speed by which that authority is spread."

Weston R. Christopherson, chairman of the board, and Richard G. Cline, chief operating officer, acted as a chief executive team. Corporate headquarters also contained a relatively small number of senior staff executives and their counterparts at each Jewel division.

At corporate headquarters there was a great deal of emphasis on what the management called "people strengths." Once a year, management reviewed talent with each of the company presidents to keep a spotlight on promising people. Christopherson stated, "One of Jewel's strengths is its reputation for quality, but an equal strength is its reputation for empathy."

JEWEL FOOD STORES

Geographic Coverage

Upon its entry into the supermarket industry in 1932, Jewel chose to concentrate its efforts in the Chicago area. This decision proved over time to be profitable for two reasons. First, it provided efficiencies and economies of scale. As one Jewel executive said, "Because of this concentration in one market, we get close supervision for less money and lower transportation and advertising costs." Second, concentration made Jewel the dominant food retailer in the Chicago market even though it was competing against larger chains such as A&P and Kroger. Local dominance meant that Jewel promotion and coverage of the market was much more effective, making possible the margins that Jewel found profitable.

In 1980, the Chicago food market was the third largest food market in the United States. It was approximately $6.5 billion per year and growing. A 1976 FTC study showed that the food chain holding the largest market share in a metropolitan area almost always had both a higher net profit rate and a higher gross margin. Jewel's share of the Chicago market was almost 40 percent.

The Chicago market was once considered to be an area of above-average profit margins. Its profit margins ranged between 1.0 and 1.5 percent, as compared with the national average of 0.9 percent. The higher profits could not avoid attracting competition. In the late 1960s, Fisher Foods of Detroit and Cleveland entered the Chicago market by purchasing Dominick's Stores, and California-based Lucky Stores entered with its Eagle Stores. As a result, by 1975 the Chicago market suffered from overcapacity. Margins were not allowed to decline, but volume dropped at all stores. Chicago chains began cutting prices to increase volume. It was uncertain whether the gains were enough to cover cuts. Finally competition forced National Tea out of the Chicago market.

Jewel followed the industry trend toward geographic expansion. Jewel's last move toward geographic expansion was made in 1971 when it took over five stores in Milwaukee from Kroger, which was leaving the Milwaukee market. Although the leader in Milwaukee held a 45 percent share of the market, Jewel thought that it could succeed where Kroger had failed. Jewel began to invest and promote heavily.

Donald Perkins, former chairman, defended the large expenditures in Milwaukee on the grounds that "Milwaukee is only 92 miles from downtown Chicago. Someday the two cities will be part of a big megalopolis. Now is the time to get in on the ground floor." Losses in Milwaukee were continuous, and in 1980 the Milwaukee stores were sold.

By the late 1970s, experience had shown that relevant markets were regional. In 1981, Jewel Food Stores was operating in Chicago, the upper midwest with the exception of Wisconsin, and eastern Iowa. It was planned that the number of stores would continue to grow in these areas, particularly in the smaller cities close to Chicago.

Sales

Over the years Jewel had built up a solid reputation for carrying top-quality products, for operating high-quality stores, and for having the highest concern for its customers. Company philosophy claimed that emphasis on quality came from Jewel's roots in direct marketing, where responsible routepeople dealt on a personal basis with individual customers that they came to know and deal with as friends. Whatever its source, the reputation for quality was intact in May 1981.

Jewel chose heavy promotion, both in-store promotion and media advertising, to be its primary competitive weapon. Most of the promotion focused on price specials, but always with an added emphasis on the Jewel reputation for quality. Confining promotion to price and quality gave Jewel a real competitive advantage in a number of situations. An example of one such situation was the promotional battle involving trading stamps. Jewel was the only major food chain not to espouse the trading stamp programs. In response to competitors' programs, Jewel increased price promotions and advertised them heavily. When the consumer's initial excitement over stamps diminished and the market settled down, Jewel returned to the original margin levels and promotional expenses. Competitors were still stuck with the cost of trading stamps.

Pricing

Possibly as a result of Jewel's quality image, the buying public always had the impression that Jewel charged premium prices. Jewel first discovered the existence of this impression in a 1934 market study. Although Jewel began at that time to try to change the impression, it persisted at the beginning of 1981. Attempts to change the public impression has taken three forms: the liberal use of price specials, private branding, and generic foods.

Price Specials   Vigorous promotion of a carefully selected assortment of staple items whose prices had been lowered was a standard policy at Jewel. These programs included a significant number of items (for example in 1966, the first year, 2,439 items out of approximately 9,000). Forbes called it "playing both ends of the supermarket pricing game." The purpose was to attract attention to the discount-level prices of the selected items while maintaining normal or higher-than-normal margins on all other items. Besides their great publicity value, the low-priced items attracted shoppers who might otherwise have shopped elsewhere. Since most consumers were one-store shoppers, they purchased the high-priced items along with low-priced items. This would probably have made the programs effective even if Jewel had lost money on the low-priced items. But in fact Jewel believed, and results seemed to confirm the belief, that it made even more money on the low-priced items than it did on those items with high prices. This resulted from the careful choice of the items to include in the program. Only those items were chosen that were price-sensitive staples. This meant that the reduction in the price of an item attracted a larger volume of sales to the degree that total revenue for that item was higher than it would have been if the item were sold for a high price.

Private Branding Jewel Companies entered the private brand (manufacturing) business shortly after 1900 because of the lack of suppliers who could meet Jewel's requirements for quality, cost, and service. Even though items were sold for a lower price, Jewel maintained average profit margins and sold a product of equal or better quality than the national brand. Great care had been taken to produce only items which met the above requirements.

If Jewel manufacturing operations were organized into one division, the division would have had 1979 sales of $367 million. Actually most manufacturing was done within two divisions—Jewel Food Stores and Park Manufacturing. The major items produced were coffee and tea, baking mixes, jams and jellies, potato chips, detergents, cosmetics, aerosol products, prepared meats, delicatessen items, bakery goods, and dairy products. Jewel sought to expand its manufacturing operations. In 1980, about 2 percent of Jewel's total manufacturing was sold to non-Jewel customers.

The use of private brands was not unique to Jewel. However, unlike A&P, Jewel has not allowed private brands to take preference over national brands. Most advertising and price specials were directed toward the promotion of national brands.

Generic Foods In 1976, Jewel Food Stores was the first to develop a generic label (no brand name) family of products. Originally these were introduced and demonstrated by Jewel's home economists in the larger stores. The company received a great deal of attention, including national media coverage, with this attempt at seeking "new ways to bring our customer greater value." By 1981, there were over 195 items in the stores.

The products were highly diversified, including food and nonfood items. The end-use quality of each item, such as nutrition and cleaning ability, was comparable to brand names. Packaging was completely unadorned, carrying only the name of the product. Generics have become a key part of Jewel Food Stores' overall marketing appeal. Entire sections of each store are devoted to generic displays.

Many food chains have watched Jewel's success and followed in the generic market. A study by *Supermarket Business* showed that generic labels were gaining market share (Exhibit 6). In dollar volume generics gained 30.1 percent from May 1979 to May 1980. The study showed that for the first time generic

EXHIBIT 6

PENETRATION AND TRENDS OF GENERIC LABELS
12-WEEK COMPARISONS–END MAY 2, 1980 VS. MAY 4,
1979

	Total	Shares
Generic labels		
Year ago: 12-week dollars ($000)	15,092.3	7.4%
Current: 12-week dollars ($000)	19,641.1	8.9%
Percent change	+30.1%	+1.5%
Year-ago units: 12 week (000)	32,291.4	10.2%
Current units: 12 week (000)	38,448.5	12.1%
Percent change	+19.1%	+1.9%
Regular private brands		
Year ago: 12-week dollars ($000)	34,344.0	16.9%
Current: 12-week dollars ($000)	35,517.5	16.2%
Percent change	+3.4%	−0.7%
Year-ago units: 12 week (000)	65,923.4	20.9%
Current units: 12 week (000)	65,516.5	20.6%
Percent change	−0.6%	−0.3%
All other brands		
Year ago: 12-week dollars ($000)	153,582.6	75.7%
Current: 12-week dollars ($000)	164,736.2	69.4%
Percent change	+7.3%	−0.8%
Year-ago units: 12 week (000)	217,088.4	68.8%
Current units: 12 week (000)	213,484.2	67.2%
Percent change	−1.7%	−1.6%

Source: Supermarket Business, November 1980.

labels share increased at the expense of "all other brands" rather than private-label brands. The market assumption is that the saturation levels for both food and nonfood generics has not been reached.

Retail Outlets

Donald Perkins, former chairman, liked to call Jewel a "location developer" rather than a builder of supermarkets. Company philosophy stressed a focus on providing whatever goods and services are required to meet the needs of a particular neighborhood. By 1980, approximately 48 percent of Jewel's outlets were combined food and general merchandise–drug configurations. Most of Jewel's competitors were conventional in the sense that they had only modest nonfood departments.

Much of Jewel's 1980 capacity in multipurpose stores was in the form of side-by-side combination stores in which a supermarket operated adjacent to an Osco. Jewel had been building these combination stores since 1962. Beginning in 1973, Jewel had also been building what the industry called *superstores* and Jewel called Grand Bazaar. By 1980, Jewel plans for the future were to continue to build these superstores, but not under the Grand Bazaar banner.

Jewel differed from its competitors in that it owned many of its facilities. Jewel justified this deviation from the industry trend of leasing on two grounds: first, it offered greater flexibility and control, and second, real estate was a good investment in a period of inflation.

Jewel Foods' Strategic Posture

The three major strategic actions cited in connection with a Jewel principle were described more fully in connection with their particular situations.

1 Consumerism Jewel was acknowledged by the Chicago area market to be the leader in meeting the following consumer demands:

- Attaching unit prices to all shelves
- Changing freshness dates from codes to easily understood calendar dates
- Hiring women and minorities (with special attention to accommodating foreign language difficulties)
- Providing information to permit price comparisons of prescription drugs

Jewel was moving toward full use of electronic scanning. At the beginning of 1981, the company had managed to avoid direct confrontation with consumer activist groups by marking prices on every item.

Although Jewel made efforts in the consumer field, it seemed in 1980 to remain the prime object of interest of consumer activist groups. However, the level of activity had been greatly reduced. The reason for the special interest in Jewel was that Jewel was the dominant supermarket in the Chicago market and therefore represented the greatest threat to consumers.

2 Minority Neighborhood Marketing At the beginning of 1981, Jewel had approximately forty stores in black and Hispanic neighborhoods. In 1980, Jewel built three new, larger stores, and planned to replace old stores with larger new stores. The total number of stores has decreased, but the total number of square footage has increased. In the future Jewel will continue to invest significant funds in the inner city serving blacks and Hispanics.

The most significantly growing segment of Chicago population was Hispanic. Jewel held the dominant share of the market, was working actively to fill specific food needs of the community, and hired Spanish-speaking employees.

Jewel's inner-city stores were heavily dependent upon food stamps; in many of the stores 30 to 40 percent of sales were paid for with food stamps. Although it cost more to operate in this area, Jewel claimed that its inner-city stores had sales 18 percent higher than its average store and that profit was satisfactory. Jewel also claimed that it was the most heavily shopped food retailer in the inner city and was the most respected by Chicago blacks and Hispanics.

3 Diverse Retail Outlets Five types of retail outlets were considered to be alternatives to the conventional supermarket: the discount food store, the combination store, the hypermarket, the superstore, and the minicenter. At the beginning of 1981, Jewel had stores in four of these configurations.

Discount Store   Jewel operated a warehouse store in the Chicago area for several years. It was closed when the company switched to a limited-assortment store called No-Frills. At the beginning of 1981, there were nine No-Frills stores in the Chicago market. The stores were similar to the Jewel T Discount Grocery Stores; however, in addition to dry groceries, they offered produce and dairy products.

Combination Store   Jewel was completely committed to this type of store, which combined the traditional supermarket with a drugstore offering both pharmaceutical services and general merchandise. Osco Drugs was combined with a supermarket in 100 of the 207 Jewel Food Stores. The 1980 Annual Report stated "As supermarkets are enlarged or relocated, it will almost always be to the combination-store format."

Superstore   Jewel Foods opened its first superstore in September 1973 and was the leader in building this type of store. A superstore was an expanded combination store offering more perishable sections such as fresh fish, fresh bakeries, delicatessens, and expanded drugstores. Although each store required enormous capital investments, Jewel claimed that they were successful. Jewel stated that "we feel that we have developed the store type in which the bulk of consumer grocery purchases will be made in the last two decades of this century."

Minicenter   In 1971, Jewel opened its one and only minicenter, called Jewel Village, in a Chicago suburb. It consisted of a combination store and a dozen Jewel-owned specialty shops under one roof. Although it still existed in 1981 there were no plans to build another one.

SUPERMARKET INDUSTRY

Industry Size and Structure

In 1980, the supermarket industry ended the year with sales of $170.7 billion. Inflation had frustrated the industry for the last decade. Raw sales numbers indicated an increase in sales from 1979 to 1980 of 10.5 percent mainly as a result of increased food prices (see Exhibit 7).

The supermarket industry was divided into two segments: chains and independents. The industry defined a chain as an operator of 11 or more supermarkets and an independent as an operator of fewer than 11 supermarkets. In 1980, chains took in six out of every ten sales dollars.

The supermarket industry could also be considered in terms of store size. A large supermarket was one with sales per year in excess of $1 million. A small supermarket was one with less than $1 million per year.

The level of concentration in the supermarket industry was not high. Unlike the general merchandise industry, where 10 to 20 top retailers completely dominated the market, there were hundreds of supermarket chains, and the number of independents was in the thousands. This low level of seller concentration in

EXHIBIT 7
THE ANNUAL AVERAGE FOOD PRICE INDEX OF
BUREAU OF LABOR STATISTICS (1967 = 100)
(INCLUDES FOOD AWAY FROM HOME)

Year	Food price index	Year	Food price index
1980	254.6	1968	103.6
1979	234.5	1967	100.0
1978	211.4	1965	94.5
1977	192.2	1960	88.0
1976	180.8	1955	81.6
1975	175.4	1950	74.5
1974	161.7	1945	50.7
1973	141.4	1940	35.2
1972	123.5	1935	36.5
1971	118.4	1930	45.9
1970	114.9	1925	48.4
1969	108.9	1920	61.5

the supermarket industry existed only on the national level. Not one of the chains was truly national. Therefore, geographic regions were usually dominated by a small number of supermarket companies.

Industry Growth

The effectiveness of cooperatives enabled even a small store representing a moderate investment to compete effectively with the stores of a chain. This fact led inevitably to a degree of overcapacity, which meant that most expansion must be external. External expansion, both within a firm's region and into another region, was achieved by buying a competitor's stores in that area. In addition to avoiding even greater overcapacity, this method avoided some start-up costs and operating problems. An industry belief held that any internal expansion should be into contiguous areas. These characteristics meant that there was a tendency for the growth of a firm to be at the expense of another firm.

Changing patterns of growth had started to create barriers to entry. Large chains which had often held small market shares in many regions, began to believe that greater profitability could be had by capturing larger market shares in fewer regions. This was done by operating fewer but much larger stores. At the same time average store size increased. The increased capital requirements of larger stores, between $1 and $2 million per store, together with the high interest rates of recent times, have presented higher barriers to entry to smaller and weaker companies, both chains and independents.

Operations

The supermarket industry believed profitability to be dependent upon two factors, volume and efficiency, providing the stores are in the right place. Undifferentiated products have led to unusually low margins, which have made the volume and efficiency criteria particularly important.

Volume was so important to the industry that it was measured in tonnage. This concern with volume, common to the entire industry, was known as "grocer's syndrome." According to an industry executive, "The secret to success is volume selling, and the profits will then come in—or are supposed to come in." Volume was believed by the industry to be the function of two elements, a broad product assortment and the rapid turnover of inventory.

Product Assortment

The number of different items carried by an average supermarket was large. It increased steadily from the end of World War II until the middle 1970s. The product assortment was classified as either foods or nonfoods. Tobacco products and cleaning and household supplies were traditionally included with food, leaving general merchandise and health and beauty aids as the only categories of nonfood items (see Exhibit 8).

Recently there has been a tendency toward a wider range of services and nonfood merchandise. Several facts supported this trend. Americans thought more before they drove, and found one-stop shopping a convenience—a "supermarket." Working women put a premium on time and convenience and didn't wish to make many stops. Many of these products had healthy margins and were likely to get shelf space. Finally, stores found that well-managed service departments, bakeries, and deli counters, in addition to being profitable, could build traffic and distinguish a store.

Inventory Turnover

A significant factor in supermarket operation was inventory control. Inventories in the industry were large. For instance, Jewel's inventory was equal to 81.2 percent of its total current assets (Exhibit 2). According to a Jewel spokesperson the company turns its inventory about 13 times a year—which is about the industry average (Exhibit 9). The industry had used the FIFO (first in, first out) method of valuing inventory, until the inflation of food prices and costs of 1973 and 1974 forced a shift to LIFO (last in, first out). During inflationary periods LIFO results in lower reported earnings (because of higher cost of goods sold) and therefore tax benefits. The high rate of inflation also caused the industry to talk of reducing the level of inventory. But with a turnover time of less than one month, this was not possible to any significant degree without improved methods of physical distribution.

Efficiency

Efficiency in the supermarket industry was concerned primarily with physical distribution. Effort focused on (1) obtaining a large volume of items in continuous supply, (2) preparing them for purchase by marking them with the prices,

EXHIBIT 8
SUMMARY OF 1979 FOOD STORE PRODUCTS (add 000 to all dollar figures)

	Value of total domestic consumption	Amount spent in grocery stores	Percent of food sales	Percent of total store	Percent groceries to total
Perishables					
Baked goods	$145,624,060	$ 91,989,210	66.50	51.18	63
Dairy section	18,651,040	10,873,760	7.86	6.05	58
Frozen foods	28,068,310	13,583,850	9.82	7.56	48
Fresh and cured meat, fish, and poultry	11,597,850	8,400,110	6.07	4.67	72
Produce	61,773,820	40,289,200	29.13	22.42	65
	25,533,040	18,842,290	13.62	10.48	74
Dry groceries	$ 78,919,040	$ 46,327,790	33.50	25.78	59
Baking needs	58,760	52,440	0.04	0.03	89
Beverages, alcoholic	26,119,580	9,132,770	6.60	5.08	35
Beverages, prepared	8,500,780	6,537,840	4.73	3.64	77
Beverages, soft drinks	7,558,350	4,395,260	3.18	2.45	58
Candy and chewing gum	6,349,430	1,895,550	1.37	1.05	30
Canned foods	12,299,380	10,234,310	7.40	5.69	83
Cereals, flour, macaroni	5,272,440	4,588,100	3.32	2.55	87
Condiments, dressings, spreads, relishes	3,880,770	2,948,770	2.13	1.64	76
Desserts	280,610	249,950	0.18	0.14	89
Dried foods	3,174,600	2,080,290	1.51	1.16	66
Fats and shortening	1,588,160	1,230,300	0.89	0.69	77
Jams, jellies, preserves	747,340	640,300	0.46	0.36	86
Sweeteners, flavors	2,169,860	1,708,690	1.23	0.93	79
All other dry groceries	1,289,050	918,450	0.67	0.51	71
Duplication (subtract)	-394,200	-285,240	-0.21	-0.16	—
Total foods	$224,543,100	$138,317,000	100.00	100.00	76.96

444

Other groceries	$ 34,852,780	54.96	12.66	65
Household supplies	15,260,260	30.25	6.97	82
Pet foods	3,152,620	6.97	1.61	92
Tobacco products	14,825,650	14.79	3.40	41
All other groceries n.e.c.	1,614,250	2.95	.68	76
Total foods & grocery products	$259,395,880	—	89.62	62
General merchandise	nd	45.04	10.38	nd
Health and beauty aids (non-R_x)	17,553,380	16.36	3.77	39
Prescriptions	11,381,350	2.14	.49	8
Flashlights & batteries	958,030	.74	.17	32
Greeting cards	2,138,170	.19	.04	4
Hosiery	3,360,910	1.20	.28	15
Household glassware	106,360	.26	.05	15
Housewares, other	nd	5.13	1.18	nd
Magazines and newspapers	5,127,010	1.89	.44	15
Motor oil and additives	986,320	.45	.45	19
Pet accessories	1,389,100	1.06	.24	32
Phonograph records	1,479,710	.35	.08	10
Photo products	4,011,810	1.18	.27	12
Stationery/writing implements	1,033,600	.38	.10	16
Toys	5,442,800	.33	.08	8
Other general merchandise	nd	13.38	3.08	nd
Total excluding HBA and R_x	nd	25.54	6.12	nd
Total nonfoods	nd	100.00	23.04	nd
Grand total	$179,717,000	—	100.00	nd

EXHIBIT 9
COMPOSITE CHAIN REPORT: MARGIN, EXPENSES, EARNINGS

	1974-1975	1975-1976	1976-1977	1977-1978
Gross margin	21.15%	21.22%	21.35%	21.74%
Expenses				
Payroll	11.71	11.68	12.03	12.34
Supplies	1.12	1.10	1.07	1.03
Utilities	0.94	1.05	1.02	1.08
Communications	0.09	0.10	0.09	0.08
Travel	0.09	0.09	0.09	0.09
Services purchased	1.21	1.31	1.26	1.29
Promotional activities	0.51	0.40	0.42	0.40
Professional services	0.08	0.07	0.06	0.06
Donations	0.01	0.01	0.01	0.01
Insurance	0.70	0.76	0.89	0.90
Taxes and licenses*	0.92	0.97	1.01	1.00
Property rentals	1.37	1.32	1.28	1.25
Equipment rentals	0.17	0.18	0.13	0.14
Depreciation & amortization	0.75	0.77	0.72	0.69
Repairs	0.64	0.64	0.61	0.61
Unclassified	0.92	0.89	0.95	0.97
Credits and allowances	(−0.70)	(−0.66)	(−0.71)	(−0.59)
Total expense before interest	20.52	20.70	20.93	21.40
Total interest	0.64	0.60	0.55	0.57
Total expense including interest	21.17	21.31	21,48	21.97
Net operating profit	(−0.02)	(−0.09)	(−0.13)	(−0.22)
Other income or deductions				
Credit for imputed interest	0.42	0.44	0.43	0.41
Cash discounts earned	0.67	0.65	0.64	0.59
Other revenue, net†	0.19	0.19	0.19	0.06
Total net other income	1.28	1.27	1.25	1.07
Total net earnings before income taxes	1.25	1.17	1.12	0.84
Total income taxes	0.57	0.55	0.45	0.33
Total net earnings after income taxes	0.67	0.62	0.66	0.51
Net earnings after taxes as a percent of net worth	9.61	8.56	9.38	7.48
Stockturns	12.61	12.76	12.59	12.43

*Except on income.
†Including profit or loss on real estate.
Source: Cornell University, "Operating Results of Food Chains."

(3) presenting them to the buyer's inspection in a manner to decrease the buyer's effort and increase his or her desire to purchase, and (4) calculating the cost, conducting the transaction, and releasing the items to the buyer. Each stage of this process required a large amount of labor. Therefore, any effort to increase efficiency involved the reduction of the amount of labor required. In 1980, labor was the greatest source of expense (see Exhibit 9).

1978-1979	1979-1980
21.50%	21.71%
12.23	12.39
0.99	1.06
1.04	1.04
0.07	
0.08	0.09
1.13	1.20
0.31	0.35
0.06	0.07
0.01	0.01
0.88	0.85
0.90	0.93
1.13	1.18
0.14	
0.81	0.79
0.63	0.59
1.19	1.09
(1.03)	(1.00)
20.57	20.84
0.61	0.56
21.18	21.40
0.32	0.32
0.42	0.41
0.61	0.52
0.34	0.14
1.37	1.07
1.70	1.39
0.77	0.59
0.93	0.80
13.27	11.66
13.54	12.77

The industry looked to increase efficiency by: (1) increasing the size of stores and (2) improving the technology of physical distribution. It was believed that larger but fewer stores would be more efficient in all respects. The plans assumed continued low-fuel costs. The same assumption was used in the calculation of the cost of transporting materials to larger but more widely dispersed stores and in the assessment of the likelihood of masses of buyers traveling to and from widely dispersed stores. In the future, increasing energy costs were expected to create a greater importance for energy management. During the year 1979–1980, the increase in energy and fuel costs was 34.9 percent, the largest factor increasing marketing costs all along the food chain.

The major improvement in the technology of physical distribution was in the form of electronic scanning which used the universal product code (UPC). This was a small symbol, of necessity no larger than 1.5 square inches, which contained up to a trillion machine-readable characters. It could be affixed to any kind of package, bag, bottle, box, can, jar, tube, etc. At the checkout stand, the item needed only to be passed in front of an electronic scanner for the nature of the item to be noted, the price to be obtained from the central computer, and the bill to be totaled. Receipts listed the price and name of each item. Besides greatly speeding up the checkout procedure, UPC provided numerous physical distribution efficiencies. Theoretically, items would no longer have to be individually marked with price. This meant that items could be packed in large bins by the manufacturer and shipped directly to the stores. The bins could be brought into the store by forklifts and placed on the aisles for consumer examination. The first time an item would be handled by store personnel would be at the checkout stand.

Unions, which feared job attrition, and consumers, who suspected chicanery, slowed most efforts to eliminate price marking. However, the major chains were recognizing other benefits of electronic scanning, and installations were increasing. These systems can reduce shrinkage from cashier errors and thefts, automate certain bookkeeping functions, and reduce the number of checkouts. Information could be generated to measure promotion effects, and slow-moving products could be identified.

Promotion

Promotion of supermarket products could be viewed as being conducted on two levels. One level was national. This type of promotion concerned only national brands. It was conducted by the manufacturer of a brand, and was in no way associated with a particular supermarket handling the brand. Such promotion usually stressed the quality and distinctive features of the item.

The other level was that of the supermarket. This promotion focused on the area in which the company operated. The item promoted was usually a national brand, although house brands and generics could be promoted, and promotion usually stressed price.

Price promotion took two forms. One was maintaining low prices across the board, a practice known as *discounting*. The other offered specials on selected items. According to *Progressive Grocer,* most companies preferred to stay competitive by offering specials on selected items rather than by discounting. This fact indicated the importance of promotion to supermarkets, because a policy of successfully offering periodic specials was much more dependent upon promotion than was a policy of continuous discounting.

The most important promotional medium for supermarkets was the daily newspaper. Advertisements were timed to precede the periods of heaviest shopping activity. Although the percentage of sales devoted to promotional activities declined from 1974 to 1980, the same period saw an increase in the use of coupons as a promotional device. The coupon was included in a newspaper ad and provided the special low price of an item only to those customers who returned the coupon to the store at the time of the purchase. This device saved for the supermarket that revenue which would have been lost by providing the lower price to those customers who had not seen the newspaper ad and therefore would presumably purchase the item at its regular price. The amount of revenue saved is believed to be significant, because only 10 percent of the coupons are ever redeemed.

Pricing

The prices of supermarket items were set to yield varying item margins. The margins are supposed to correspond roughly to the amount of value added in each item, but the exact value added in each item is not accurately known. Therefore, the setting of prices was somewhat arbitrary. Some studies showed that there were no standard prices, often even among the stores of the same company. The varying item margins made the total or gross margins subject to what was called the "supermarket mix problem." Supermarket gross margins could change significantly as a result of nothing more than a change in consumer attitudes independent to actions taken by the supermarket.

Although farm prices were substantially unchanged from 1930 to 1941, the gross margins of food chains in the same period showed a steady decline. The FTC attributed this decline to "the supermarket revolution," as small specialty stores were replaced by large, efficient, self-service stores combining all food sales under a single roof. This revolution was mostly complete by the late 1940s. The subsequent increase in gross margins was attributed by the FTC to "expensive merchandising practices such as the issuance of trading stamps, games of chance, carry-out and check-cashing services, more general use of advertised specials and price coupons (which require more labor), and over-building of stores."

Financing

A feature of the supermarket industry's financial structure was its high degree of leverage. This leverage was permitted by:

1 *High liquidity.* Accounts receivable were small; inventories and cash made up approximately 90 percent of current assets. Since inventory turnover was rapid, approximately 13 times a year, cash flow was very high. This makes it possible for the industry to maintain a current ratio of 1.37 (Exhibit 10).

2 *Noncyclicality.* Examination of the history of the supermarket industry

EXHIBIT 10

FINANCIAL RATIOS, DISTRIBUTION OF ASSETS, AND RATE OF RETURN ON
INVESTMENT OF GROCERY CHAINS

	50 chains 1976-1977	53 chains 1977-1978	48 chains 1978-1979	55 chains 1979—
Financial ratios				
Current assets to liabilities	1.50	1.44	1.34	1.37
Net sales to total assets	6.51	6.01	6.13	5.71
Net sales to net worth	14.11	14.58	14.28	14.64
Net worth to total assets	0.46	0.41	0.43	0.39
Distributions of assets				
Current	56.78	57.12	R53.96	53.43
Property and equipment	40.97	39.35	R43.38	42.84
Goodwill and intangibles	0.21	0.41	0.20	1.75
Other	3.00	3.12	R 2.48	1.98
Return on investment				
Net earnings, % of assets	4.33	3.08	5.70	4.55
Net earnings, % of net worth	9.38	7.48	13.27	11.68

R = Revised.

revealed no trace of any cycle. Neither depression nor economic boom, defla-
tion nor inflation, unduly affected the sale of basic foodstuffs.

3 *Basic stability.* The sale of food was not subject to wide swings, either random or due to identifiable causes. Sale of food was not subject to trends or
varying preferences, and an FTC study proved the absence of any seasonality.

Debt was of two types, loans and leases. Leases made up a large part of the
supermarket industry debt. If leases were not included, then debt as a percentage of capital (debt/total capital) was about 40 percent. When leases were
included, the supermarket industry had one of the highest debt-to-capitalization
(debt plus leases/total capital) ratios among retailers.

INDUSTRY TRENDS

Demographic

Supermarket industry growth was tied to population trends. The total U.S.
population growth averaged less than 1 percent in recent years. Opportunities
for growth were to be most likely in the areas benefiting from current migration
patterns.

There were two negative growth factors closely related to population trends.
First, according to the Department of Commerce, grocery store sales as a percentage of disposable income dropped from 11.9 percent in 1970 to 10.9 percent in 1979. This was not surprising, as there was a limit to the amount of food

that could be consumed regardless of income. Second, the growth of one- and two-person households increased the percentage of families who were inclined to eat out.

Inflation

Inflation appeared to be the cause of the primary problems facing supermarket operators at the beginning of the 1980s. In 1980, food marketing costs rose 13.5 percent, while farm costs rose only 6.4 percent (see Exhibit 11). Operators were most concerned with high interest rates, maintenance of current net profit margins, generation of sufficient capital internally to support growth, enough sales to offset inflation, and procurement of outside capital. Oil was the biggest single factor increasing distribution costs along the entire food chain. Many executives were worried that deregulation of transportation would put upward pressure on truck and rail rates, further increasing costs. Although it was felt that the new Reagan administration would help the country's economic fortunes overall, supermarket executives did not expect relief from double-digit inflation in the near future.

Consumer Buying Patterns

As a result of more consumer attention to spending, the supermarkets were facing a more segmented society. Consumer buying habits were splintering. While some consumers were trading down, others were showing a great fascination with nutrition and gourmet and ethnic cooking.

EXHIBIT 11
FARM COSTS

	1978	1979	1980
Marketing bill			
Labor	+ 9.9%	+ 8.8%	+10.1%
Packaging	+ 6.2	+11.6	+14.4
Energy and fuel	+ 6.7	+26.2	+34.9
Rail transportation	+ 7.5	+14.0	+18.5
Supplies	+ 4.8	+13.3	+15.4
Maintenance	+ 8.2	+10.3	+11.0
Interest	+42.4	+36.5	+12.6
Total marketing costs	+ 8.5%	+11.1%	+13.5%
Farm bill			
Raw farm product	+10.4%	+13.6%	+ 3.3%
Processed product	+ 8.9	+ 9.3	+ 8.3
Total farm costs	+ 9.4%	+11.2%	+ 6.4%

Note: Farm prices rise 6.4% while marketing costs climb 13.5%.
  Source: Progressive Grocer, April 1981.

The supermarkets were paying more attention to the lifestyles of each trading area. The trend was toward a wider variety of store formats. The no-frills limited-assortment warehouse supermarket was back on the scene as a response to budget-conscious families. At the other extreme, there was great confidence in the stores of over 30,000 square feet and 12,000 items to serve those with more eclectic tastes.

Consumer Movements

Consumer activist efforts were focused primarily on two issues: they were opposed to any further increases in food prices, and they were opposed to the universal product code (UPC). The opposition to increasing prices had little success.

Opposition to the universal product code was much more focused. Consumer activists objected to UPC in its entirety but seemed to have resigned themselves to its implementation. However, they refused to accept the removal of price markings from each individual item. Even though shelf price markings were to be available, consumer activists argued that the lack of item markings would make price-conscious shopping more difficult and would leave the shopper an easier victim of price changes.

In some communities, legislation had been passed to require the price marking of each individual item. The supermarket industry was concerned about such legislation. UPC was viewed as an important means of reducing costs. If each item had to be handled, the efficiency of the system would be much reduced and costs in the form of labor would be higher.

Market Uncertainty

The increasing uncertainty of the market, caused by changing consumer buying patterns and by increasing consumer resistance, was a source of great concern to the industry. The capital structure of the supermarket industry was one of high financial leverage. Debt capital had always been readily available at reasonable rates because the supermarket industry was characterized by being highly liquid with a high cash flow, by the stability of its sales and the resulting low level of risk, and by the lack of cyclicity in its sales. The industry feared that market uncertainty would result in lower cash flow, higher risk, and/or greater cyclicity with an undesirable effect upon the capital structure. The supermarket industry was itself contributing to the uncertainty by its move toward greater emphasis on convenience foods and nonfoods, since sales of both of these classes of goods were less stable and more cyclical than are sales of staple foods.

Energy Crisis

One of the greatest causes of concern at the beginning of the 1980s was the increasing costs and threatening shortages of energy. Average costs had increased 17 percent for chains and 18 percent for independents in 1980. The resulting uncertainty affected two areas: transportation and operation of the stores. Transportation costs included both the transport of goods to the stores and the travel of shoppers to the stores. The question was whether or not the costs and shortages would be aggravated by the industry trend toward fewer stores located at greater distances from sources of supply and homes of shoppers. The question concerning the operators of supermarkets was whether or not the industry trend toward larger stores would require greater amounts of energy. The answer to either question was not known, but the supermarket industry believed that both questions would be answered in the negative because of the economies of scale expected from fewer and larger stores.

Minority Neighborhood Marketing

By 1980, food stamps had become a way of life in supermarkets. After World War II cities experienced a constant inflow of nonwhite poor. Few of the chains were successful in trying to serve the new and very different shoppers. Stores in minority neighborhoods dropped in sales, deteriorated in operating standards, and became unprofitable. Most of the stores closed as the chains retreated from the inner city. Since most of these people lived in the inner city, a marketing void arose. The chains belatedly realized that they had abandoned a large and growing sector of the market.

Although minority neighborhood supermarkets usually had higher operating costs and lower sales, they could be profitable because they operated with a higher gross margin. A study of supermarketing in an Atlanta ghetto showed that the higher gross margin of stores in the inner city was not due to higher prices. It was instead due to the different product mix purchased in the inner city. Inner-city blacks regularly bought items that carried a higher markup than items most heavily purchased by suburban whites.

Government Pressures

Public concern for continuously rising prices was reflected in the government attitudes toward supermarkets. Legislation had been introduced in the U.S. Senate to authorize an investigation of all levels of the food industry. It was prompted by charges that food manufacturers and retailers were operating as monopolists with regard to pricing. The FTC was beginning an investigation into beef pricing, which was thought to be excessive.

Retailing Trends

1 Geographic Expansion   The acquisition movement of the 1950s and 1960s increased geographic expansion and was believed to correlate with size and success. But by the 1970s the supermarket industry appeared to have realized that in the sale of food the relevant market was regional, not national. A number of FTC studies showed that the most profitable company was almost invariably the one that dominated a regional or local market. There had been an uninterrupted decline in the number of supermarkets in operation since 1970. This was attributable to the recent emphasis on larger stores, the difficulty in operating older small units, as well as the drop in geographic expansion.

2 Price Competition Prices decreased consistently throughout the 1930s and early 1940s as a result of the "supermarket revolution." Retail prices were low enough to be a minor factor in the shopper's decision to buy, thus permitting the supermarkets to avoid unpleasant price competition and to rely instead on promotion as the primary competitive tool. In the late 1950s, farm prices had begun to rise, pushing up retail prices. By the late 1960s, retail food prices were high enough to make price competition a potentially effective, if not pleasant, competitive tool.

To be a profitable discounter, a supermarket had to increase efficiency by increasing size of stores and increasing automation, and decrease costs by eliminating frills and reducing the amount of personal service provided to the customer. Success in reduced-service formats was thought to depend on ability to consistently provide lower prices than traditional stores. It was speculated that further erosion of brand loyalties would make price the sole determinant in a purchase decision.

3 Nonfoods Retailing A major question that occupied the supermarket industry's attention all through the last two decades was whether or not the industry should diversify out of food retailing and adopt a broader product assortment. Interest in this issue was so high as to motivate a number of supermarket chains to acquire other chains that sold general merchandise, drugs, and other nonfood items or to develop divisions internally to handle such items.

Proponents of diversification into nonfood retailing believed that the following factors argued in its favor:

1 Consumers desired a broader product mix. Consumers' increased education, income, and leisure was believed to make them want a greater diversity of products available with the ease and efficiency provided by a shopping trip to a single location.

2 Larger metropolitan areas and increased consumer mobility make it possible for the consumer to reach the larger but fewer stores resulting from diversity.

3 Economies of scale would make all the diverse items less expensive.

4 A broad, diverse product mix would offer a company a means of attaining a competitive edge over companies slow to adopt the broader mix.

5 A broader mix offered a supermarket firm the opportunity to obtain higher margins available from nonfood items.

6 The diversity was believed to provide a synergy that would increase the sales of all items.

7 A broader product mix would offer a supermarket the opportunity both to utilize its merchandising capabilities more fully and to expand more rapidly than would be possible within the confines of the food-retailing business.

4 Store Configuration   A remaining question concerned the form to be adopted by the diversified retail outlet. The form chosen would be dependent upon how far a particular company wished to go in the direction of product diversification. A company that chose to move into a number of different product categories could become what one industry expert called a "conglomerchant." A conglomerchant was defined as "a multiline merchandising empire under central ownership, usually combining several styles of retailing with behind-the-scenes integration of some distribution and management functions." It was suggested that the multiline merchandising could encompass any or all of the following:

1 Food stores
2 General merchandise stores
3 Drugstores
4 Restaurants
5 Institutional catering
6 Specialty stores
7 Warehouse distribution centers
8 A wholesale division to serve independents
9 Service specialties
10 Foreign stores

The industry had developed three types of outlets to handle the diverse product assortment. All required high capital investments and high volume for their success.

Combination stores consisted of a food store combined with one or two other stores, such as a drugstore or a general merchandise store, under a common roof. The stores usually had a common entrance and often a common checkout area, but they were still separate stores. The belief was that the volume of one would increase the volume of the other.

The *minicenter* represented an elaboration of the combination store. It consisted of a number of distinct and separate specialty shops attached to the periphery of the major stores. It amounted to a small shopping center in which all the stores belonged to the same company. It was believed to attract shoppers who preferred to buy luxury and novelty items in a small-shop atmosphere. It was expected that shoppers attracted to the specialty shops would also add to the volume of the major stores.

Hypermarkets fused all the diverse products into one store. It might include all the items sold in the above two types of outlets but, instead of dividing the assortment of items into separate selling units, it combined them into a common display, maintained the display by a common support function, sold the diverse items through a common checkout counter, and put receipts into a common till. This type of retail outlet had been developed in Europe.

On the other hand, those companies that chose to diversify less than the conglomerchant could turn to what the industry had come to call the *superstore*. The superstore differed from the hypermarket in the degree of product diversity. While the hypermarket included as many different items as could be fitted into the selling space, the superstore included a more limited number of items whose diversity was controlled by the ruling concept of the superstore, the "serving of routine buying needs." What might be defined as a routine buying need could vary with place and time, but it was not likely to include such things as durable goods or major articles of clothing, both of which were sold in hypermarkets. Although large size was not required of the superstore, it was likely to be large in order to include all those items defined as routine needs, and it was likely to be even larger in the future as rising living standards increased the number of items defined as routine needs.

JEWEL COMPANIES, INC.: STRATEGIC POSTURE, 1981

In the 1980 Annual Report, Weston R. Christopherson, chairman of the board and chief executive officer, states, "During the latter half of the 1970s, Jewel management made an in-depth study of the company's strengths and weaknesses and of external influences with which we expected to deal in the years ahead." By 1981, Jewel Companies had developed an investment plan for the company through 1983. The plan is based on the following strategies and is depicted in Exhibit 12:

1 Jewel will continue emphasis on the combination food store-drugstore.

2 Jewel will continue emphasis on drug retailing. Osco and Sav-On divisions will continue to invest in new solo drugstores.

3 Jewel will continue its strong commitment to food retailing. There will be no new solo supermarkets, but present facilities will be kept in excellent condition. Enlargements or relocations will be in the combination store format. Convenience stores will continue to be a growth segment, and suitable acquisitions will be desirable. More discount stores will be opened to ensure service to the growing segment of shoppers who are willing to trade off convenience and service for 20 to 30 percent savings on basic food items.

4 Jewel will continue to diversify geographically into regions of the country which offer growth potential and will lessen the company's dependence on any one market.

5 Significant investments will be made in manufacturing facilities to support Jewel's own merchandising and marketing programs. Capital will be committed for new or modernization programs for support areas (warehousing, transportation, systems, and offices).

6 Interest will continue in mergers and acquisitions of other companies which are appropriate to the achievement of Jewel's goals.

The Jewel Companies, Inc., Corporate Profile published in January 1981 concludes with the statement that "...management believes the company has

EXHIBIT 12

JEWEL COMPANIES INVESTMENT PLAN THROUGH 1983

Strategy	
• Combined food/drug stores	• Merchandising
• Solo drug stores	• Manufacturing and distribution
• Jewel T. discount grocery stores	• Mexico
• Franchising and agency	• New facilities investment

New facilities

Year	Units	Square footage (000)	Year	Units	Square footage(000)
Supermarkets*			Drugstores*		
1976	378	10,186	1976	223	3,757
1977	374	10,500	1977	245	4,242
1978	364	10,523	1978	254	4,394
1979	357	10,562	1979	263	4,644
1980 est.	339	10,103	1980 est.	426	7,644
1981 est.	349	10,560	1981 est.	461	8,400
1982 est.	361	11,100	1982 est.	495	9,100
1983 est.	377	11,700	1983 est.	531	9,850
Discount grocery			Franchised and agency units		
1977	11	78	1976	260	839
1978	29	246	1977	277	868
1979	100	1,150	1978	325	1,108
1980 est.	138	1,470	1979	360	1,200
1981 est.	194	1,990	1980 est.	382	1,482
1982 est.	245	2,450	1981 est.	423	1,750
1983 est.	310	3,040	1982 est.	469	2,050
			1983 est.	517	2,350

*Includes food portion of food/drug units.

positioned its human and physical resources appropriately and has the financial strength to meet the challenges of the 1980s while increasing earnings and return on investment."

Specialty Candy

Specialty Candy Company produced four kinds of candy specialties: hard candies, jellies, mints, and caramels. The candies were produced and packaged in the company's plant in Franklin Park, Illinois, a suburb of Chicago. Initially the company sold only bulk candy, but competition forced Specialty to develop a line of packaged candies. The introduction of packaged specialty candies proved to be profitable for the company, and sales increases of approximately 10 percent had been experienced for the past 10 years. In the early stages of the company's development, Mr. Brooks, the president, handled the midwest sales territories from the Chicago office. His major efforts were made by soliciting the large accounts by telephone. Mr. Joe Mitchell, the vice president of sales, handled everything east of Chicago, with a few large accounts in the New York area and a number of accounts spread along the eastern seaboard. Mitchell was forced to do a good deal of traveling in an effort to build territories and open new accounts. Although he traveled extensively, Mitchell was in charge of production and shipping. These tasks were frequently delegated to the plant manager.

Specialty's packaged candies increased gradually as the accounts were developed for its new line. The company, however, remained a factor in the bulk-candy business. It sold most of the bulk candy to house accounts or "rebaggers," who bought the candy and bagged it for sale at retail. This included independent operators as well as supermarket chain stores. The district managers and the company's sales force handled most of these accounts. Candy sold to rebaggers accounted for approximately 35 to 40 percent of Specialty's sales. The margin on bulk-candy sales was lower than packaged goods but required less labor and production expense. It also did not require as much storage space since it was usually shipped soon after being produced to fill orders previously received. The packaged goods were sealed fresh in soft bags and stored in cases until shipment orders were received. Packaged seasonal candies had to be produced well in advance to meet heavy demands of the holiday seasons or special occasions.

As the packaged line developed and the customer base increased, the responsibilities and burdens on management increased significantly. Mr. Brooks and Mr. Mitchell remained heavily involved in sales and left the candy production to the director of manufacturing, Fred Kaminski. In the early years of the company, the major efforts of Brooks and Mitchell were directed to candy jobbers and chain-store accounts.

With the continued increase in sales, particularly in the east, John Brooks appointed a district manager for the eastern seaboard and added three new sales positions. As the company continued to expand, four additional district managers were hired for the central states, the western states, the southwest, and the southeast. (See Exhibit 1.) The sales force was gradually enlarged to include approximately 18 salespersons and 35 candy brokers, who replaced the jobbers the company utilized in its development stages.

As Specialty expanded, it decreased its reliance on the company sales force and employed candy brokers.[1] Most of the major producers of candy used brokers, who were directed and coordinated by national sales managers. Specialty's combination of a company sales force and brokers was not extensively used in the industry, particularly not by the large producers. The greatest concentration of Specialty's sales were in the central and eastern states and in the large cities such as New York, Chicago, Detroit, and Boston. Most of the company sales force was utilized in these areas. Brokers were employed mainly in the southern and western states. The company salespersons and the brokers covered all the major cities of the United States. The district sales managers were responsible for the direction and coordination of the company salespersons and brokers in their area.

John Brooks stated:

The major problems we have in this business is attempting to plan and forecast sales, which is not an easy task because our main thrust is in packaging candies for seasonal appeal. Sales management, our second major problem area, is of course directly related to forecasting demand. Even though our sales have increased over 10 percent for the past 10 years, I must admit that Joe Mitchell and I still have to do the forecasting. I am probably the final authority on how much we are going to produce. After all, I am the CEO and I guess sooner or later the buck stops here. Even Joe, although he is in everything up to his neck, including forecasting demand, likes to let me put down the final number of cases to produce and hopefully sell.

We need to package our candies in the summer months to meet our heaviest de-

---

[1] A broker, while an independent agent, did not take title or ownership of the candy, as jobbers or wholesalers did. Rather, a broker acted as a sales representative for the company for distribution to the retailer, in effect an extension of the company's own sales force. When jobbers and wholesalers sold to retailers, they were selling from stock they owned.

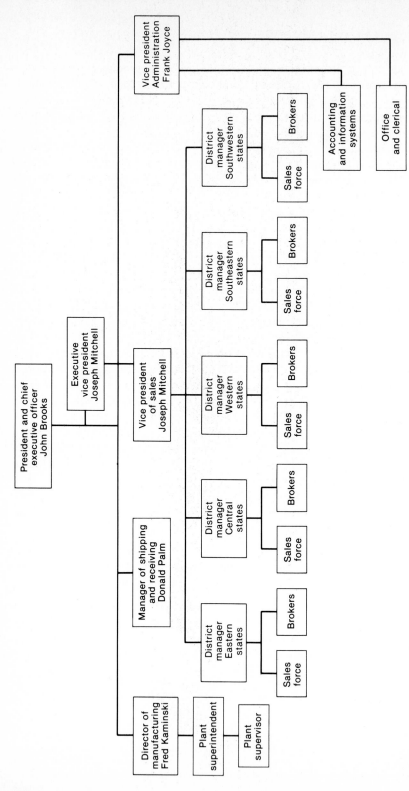

EXHIBIT 1
Organization chart of the Specialty Candy Company.

mand periods. This schedule also enables us to employ part-time help when we most need them. We use a lot of students for packaging and tending the automatic packaging equipment. We have to make our forecasts well in advance so production can do the scheduling, personnel can provide the needed help, and purchasing can have the necessary supply of ingredients available. We produce almost 6 million pounds of candy a year and use thousands of tons and gallons of varied ingredients in addition to carloads of sugar. We still produce over 35 percent of our candy for bulk sales. I must say we are able to forecast our bulk sales with greater accuracy than the packaged goods, although it's all the same candy. Having four basic candies with significant differences in ingredients requires detailed planning of purchases. We don't have as much space as we would like or really need. We have outgrown our facilities, and there is nowhere to expand in our present location. Cramped quarters makes it very difficult to store raw materials and finished product. We have got to produce our product and ship it fast. This means a lot of coordination between production and sales. Forecasting provides the basis for such coordination. Forecasting is the most stimulating part of my job, and I actually enjoy it, even though the pressure is on me, because if I am off by any significant margin, we can really be in trouble.

I must admit that I don't think anyone in the company really knows how forecasts are made. In many ways, the whole job of forecasting relies very heavily on guesswork. We don't base our findings on last year's figures because I have found what happened last year is no indication of what will happen this year. Actually, we base our forecast on the overall trend of our business in the present year. We consider such factors as the general outlook of competition in the industry, price lists of competitive companies, and the type of packaging and displays they are coming out with. We also look at many other factors. For example, on our Halloween forecast, we estimated sales of 120,000 cases as compared with 126,000 last year. I lowered the estimate because production of this type of candy had increased in the industry. Besides, some of the competitive packages and displays were very elaborate. We weren't able to go into extreme changes in packaging this year, since we don't have the facilities for it and I didn't feel it would be worth the investment at this time. After we consider all these things, I put down a figure which is our best guess of what the sales in each line will be.

For the last period we sent our forecast, which included the Halloween items plus other items to be produced in this period, to the production department. The production department then sent me a schedule of open time for the three-month period, based on our forecast. Open time is the number of unused worker-hours there will be in the department based on our forecast. We are seldom far off on this because of our experience in production. We know how much those machines can produce and what the workers can do. If there are unused worker-hours, we fill in the time with some other staple item which we can sell. If we are short of worker-hours, we must cut back our figures on certain items. We pay close attention to open time because we want our workers to keep busy. We want to avoid layoffs or too much overtime work.

In the middle of October John Brooks discovered that his final forecast for Halloween candy sales was off about 13 percent. The accepted procedure of Specialty was to sell the excess candy at the best price obtainable, which was usually a substantial discount. The stores purchasing the discounted merchandise counted on postholiday sales at substantial discounts in the event the candy was not sold prior to the holiday.

In explaining the forecast error, Brooks stated:

You can really get stuck on the forecasts. If we only had small brokers to deal with and lost one or two of them, we would pick up the business somewhere else. But we also work with large chain-store operations. If we lose one of them, we lose a lot of business. That's what happened on the Halloween forecast. Chain stores don't buy until late in the season, so there is no way of knowing what will happen until the last minute. And there is practically no way of predicting whether they will or will not buy. But when the forecast is off, profits are cut because we must dump the excess of stock at cost or lower. On the Halloween forecast, we hit very close on other items in the forecast. Only 8 cases were left on one item, 10 cases on another, and 31 cases on the last item. That's almost perfect. You can't get much closer. But 15,000 cases were left on the Halloween candy. Now, on most of our products if we find we are off on an item, we can change our forecast and we can switch over to something else. But the Halloween candy required special packaging and we had to complete it in the summer months when part-time help was available. There was no way of knowing that three large accounts wouldn't buy our product this year.

I have my district managers forecast items. We don't use their predictions, but by asking them to make the forecasts, we help them feel closer to the company. They don't know we don't use their predictions, and they never see my final forecast. Their job is to sell candy. My midwest manager was off close to 2,000 cases on one item and 800 on another. This sort of error is common in most of their forecasting. They haven't had much experience, and they aren't able to grasp the overall trends in sales as Joe and I can. They find selling bulk candy to rebaggers much easier, so they tend not to give the packaged goods the required attention. The district managers look at last year's sales and figure they can do better this year. As a result, their predictions are way off. We can see the overall trend and are able to grasp the total situation. As a result, we come much closer than they do. They haven't got the skill. But we do use their forecast to put pressure on them. We can get on them and tell them sales aren't coming near their predictions. This tends to jack them up a little—we can throw the ball their way. If I had my choice, I'd like to train someone to do the forecasting other than Joe and myself. We need the time to sell the big accounts. But as it is, it doesn't seem likely. No one has the experience to do it. And with all the guesswork involved, you have to be able to grasp the overall conditions in the industry.

Joe Mitchell, the vice president of sales, was also very involved in planning and forecasting product demand. He worked closely with John Brooks, and because of their long association he did not seem to mind Brooks making final decisions on production and product lines. His major complaint was about the same as that of Brooks—too much to do and too little time to plan. In discussing the day-to-day problems Joe stated:

I agree with John, forecasting is a very tricky business because there is a good deal of guesswork involved. I feel it when my guess is wrong. Besides all of this, I have to listen to the salespeople's and brokers' problems. They call in every Tuesday morning and bring up their problems. As if I haven't got enough problems of my own. I have to listen to theirs too. But today was even worse because I received some of the reports on our Halloween sales forecast. When we are off on these forecasts, I bear the brunt of the blame. The pressure is always on me. It's the old story, the ball bounces two ways, but in my position, I am the one who always catches it.

If you don't keep on the sales force, they slack off. You must jack them up or they fall into ruts and then sales drop off. By the same token, I have to keep on my district managers because they tend to take life easy and not spend enough time with the force and the brokers. When this happens, they fall into ruts. Salespeople get content with what they have too easily, and don't plug to get new accounts in the territory. And they don't spend enough time with established accounts. You have to keep on them all of the time so sales don't fall off.

If sales fall, our forecast suffers. Then I am in the middle. The district managers put on the pressure to change packages, put in new lines and promotions, and lower prices. John puts on the pressure when profits drop off, so I'm in the middle. I have to worry about the shipping department getting out orders on time, or the salespeople and customers start hollering. The shipping department keeps a perpetual inventory. If an order comes in and some of the items aren't in stock, they should cancel out those items, send the balance of the order to the shipping room and ask the customer to reorder. However, the shipping department often will sit on the order. Then the customer lets me know about it by complaining of poor service. Then we have a problem when a customer wants to make an adjustment because of overbuying.

The salesmen and brokers were considered an important part of Specialty because of the company's great reliance on candy packages which followed a holiday theme. The major sales effort was made in the fall and through the Christmas season. Valentines' Day and the Easter season were also important sales periods. The summer months were low periods which the company used to good advantage by producing and packaging for the fall and Christmas season. In the early years of the company salespersons were hired without much selection or training. In the past 10-year period, however, Specialty made a real effort to try to select the best people for the sales positions and give them fundamental initial training. In discussing the training and development of the sales force, Joe Mitchell said:

We don't have many dissatisfied salespeople. They begin their jobs at a good starting salary and are put through an extensive training program with the district manager. The district manager spends about three weeks with the salespersons, working with them in their territory. The manager outlines all company procedure to the salespersons. I send a notebook to each salesperson which contains all the instructions and company policies they have to know about. If they read the book, they shouldn't have any more questions, although we get some dillies now and then. There is no reason for some of the questions. All of our policy is written down in black and white. If they would only read the book, half of their problems would be answered. I tell them to look it up, and that ends that. I have enough problems of my own without having to answer questions which are already answered. Monthly dollar volume quotas of sales are set up for each territory, and a salesperson must meet this quota before he or she begins making commissions. The district managers are also responsible for the brokers, and we have twice as many brokers as we have salespersons. In many ways the brokers are easier to handle, since they are not our employees. If they are not producing, it is no problem to cut them off and engage another brokerage house. However, we try to maintain the same relations with our brokers as we do with our own salespeople. They are subject to the same treatment, and I see that they each get a notebook outlining all our company policies. The greatest difficulty we have with brokers is in trying to instill in them the need to develop a personal touch with the bigger accounts. This is a little hard to do since many of the houses may handle other merchandise and even other candies. That's why I, and to some extent John, try to get out to the big customers as often as we can. Of course, the district managers have that responsibility also. In the southern states and to a large extent in the western states, we use brokers almost exclusively.

Joe Mitchell was very pleased with the company's control system; he explained how he and John Brooks, the president, were able to keep close control over the sales force.

Our district managers keep close tabs on our sales force and the brokers. We have quite an ingenious system with our district managers which gives them added compensation and forces them to keep close watch on their sales force. If there weren't controls, they would get out of hand. We have figured what the cost of doing business is in each of our areas. For example, let's say it is 8 percent of net sales in the western area. We then raise that figure to 9 percent and tell the district manager he will make 20 percent of the savings realized under that 9 percent amount. Thus the manager will watch the costs very closely because it means money.

District managers keep in close touch with their sales force and brokers. They have to if they want extra money in their pockets. I also keep in close touch with the sales force so I know what's going on and so I can see if they are developing their territories. Each Tuesday morning, between 7 and 12, I can expect a telephone call from each district manager. They report on their progress, and we discuss any problems they may have. I am also able to find out where each district manager will be and what they will be doing for the rest of the week. I can keep close tabs on them and am able to determine whether they are covering their territories adequately. If a manager wants to take a day off to play golf with some business associates, I'll usually say go ahead. But at least I know where they are and that they are on the job and aren't letting any account get stale. On Thursday, my district managers talk to their salespeople and brokers, and I talk to the managers on Friday or Saturday to discuss problems in their areas. Thus, I can follow what they are doing.

I keep notebooks on the district managers. It's important to know where they are and what they are doing so I can be sure the job is being done. Every three weeks, each district manager sends me a calendar stating where he or she will be each day for the following three weeks. If I didn't know where they were, I wouldn't be able to determine whether they were spending enough time with their people. They wouldn't get out enough, and the sales would fall. So I know where they are all of the time. I know where I can reach them in case something comes up. If they're not where they said they would be, they will have some explaining to do.

I also hold periodic sales meetings throughout the year. A couple of weeks ago I held a meeting with the western district in Denver. Some of the sales force and brokers were upset because I messed up their Saturday. But we discussed the problems of the district, I took them all out to dinner, and then sent them on their way. Since I am always in touch with them, I can ask them about certain accounts which we haven't been receiving orders from. And we can also discuss areas which haven't been properly developed. We try to keep them on their toes.

We have increased our business about 10 percent each year for the past 10 years since we introduced our packaged lines. I think this says a good deal about our sales group. As a matter of fact, each territory has increased in sales each year. If there isn't an increase for the year, the district manager is going to have some explaining to do.

I also have another control over the sales operation. I thumb through the orders we receive from customers each day. This way I can keep a quick check on what the sales force is doing.

In reviewing the problems and challenges of being the chief executive officer of Specialty, John Brooks stated:

I find selling candy a very interesting business. We must come up with something new all the time. It seems as if we never stop planning or working on new ideas. If we didn't do this, we would be stuck. In the candy business, where you are dealing with an item picked up off a counter, you have to constantly come up with new gimmicks and packages to catch the public eye and to keep items appealing. What goes this year may fall flat on its face next year. So you must be on the lookout all the time in order to keep sales up. You have to offer new packages, displays, and promotional schemes to interest the brokers and chain-store outlets. If you let up for a minute, they will go over to a competitor. And not only must you sell your customers, but you have to sell your sales managers, too. If they're not sold on the product, they won't do a good job of selling it. We have to change our promotional schemes and packaging displays to keep ahead of our competitors. For example, we've been using a certain display box for our cheaper candies for about three years, and it has always sold very well. I made my forecast on the item this year and got stung. Our competitors came out with either the same idea or something better. It took them three years to discover that these display boxes were selling candy. But because we didn't have something new this year, sales suffered. In the middle of the season Joe and I had to come up with a promotional scheme to move the candy. We got rid of it, but there was a heck of a lot of detail and headache involved. Now I must begin working on a new idea for next year to push the cheaper lines. For example, right now our district managers are saying we have to start changing designs on our 80-cent package lines (7.5 ounces per package). They don't know the aggravation we have to go through in changing those packages. None of our people really understand it. And yet, they may be right. We've had our present package for over two years now.

Many times our planning is thrown way off because of a change in an item. We may predict it will sell more than it does, or we may underestimate the demand. For example, we came out with a new type of caramel candy last year. I didn't think it would do much, but it sold so well that we had a backlog of orders. So I cut out some of our other items for a while. Yet after watching the trend of sales on caramels over the first couple of months, I saw we weren't even going to hit 50,000 cases. I then noticed that a large chain store in Indianapolis wasn't buying the item this year. You see, chain operations buy late, so I am unable to learn what they will do until the last minute. Well, this store accounted for 4,000 cases last year. So I revised my forecast down to 45,000 cases, and we changed our production setup to fill in the open time with other items. This is a big job, but it pays off in the long run. And we're not stuck with candy.

But the problem didn't end there. Our salesperson in Indianapolis wasn't selling any caramel candy this year. As a matter of fact, except for that big account, this person didn't sell much last year. In general, other salespeople were doing as well or running ahead of last year. But discounting the large chain operations, the Indianapolis salesperson was doing nothing. Here was probably a problem of someone who just didn't like caramels and so had no desire to sell it. You have to get on such a person, or they will hurt your sales. We called and laid it on the line. I don't mean to imply that I do all the promotional work. We do hold periodic meetings with our district managers. Joe Mitchell and I bring in the district managers, and we usually spend the day with them. We try to make them feel a part of the organization by discussing promotional ideas with them. We listen to their suggestions, whatever they are worth, and then mull them over ourselves. I work on the ideas and future plans. Joe offers valuable assistance and contributes some good ideas. After we have formulated the plans, I usually have Joe inform the district managers what to expect in the future. I also do some traveling and call on our large accounts. Actually, I should do more than I do. I think Joe and I should be out a good deal of the time. If I could travel and call on our big accounts, I feel it would be a big help to Joe and the company. But it seems every time I plan to go, something comes up here and I'm stuck. Maybe I'm not a good organizer—I don't know. But it means a lot to some of the big accounts when a president or vice president calls on them. Well, I know if I were in their shoes, it would make a much greater impression if an officer called on me rather than a salesperson or broker or district manager. When I go to see our large accounts I am received in grand style. Besides, I get to know these people. I can call them by their first names, and it's easier to talk to people on the telephone once you have met them. A good example was the call I made to the purchasing agent at Smith's today. I knew the man, could speak to him frankly, and got an order for 400 cases of candy. You would be surprised how many orders Joe and I can get that our people and district managers cannot get from big accounts. And it's just as good for the sales force because they get their commissions if the account is in their territory. I did make one mistake about six months ago, however, on a trip to Philadelphia. I went there myself and opened a new chain-store account. But I neglected to take my Philadelphia salesperson or eastern district manager with me. It really didn't make too much difference to the salesperson, because credit for the new account meant more money. But it was a slap in the face for the district manager, because he had made unsuccessful attempts in the past to open the account, and then I went there and opened the account. It would have been better if I had taken him along. At least he would have then had the feeling he had participated, in some way, in getting the account, although we never would have opened it if I hadn't gone there. These people will ignore a district manager but not a president. I talked the matter over with Joe Mitchell, and he suggested I take the district manager with me when I call on these accounts. From now on, I'll have to make a point of having district managers with me when I make calls on the big accounts.

There are a few problems created when I go out, but I still think I should try to get out more often. The only trouble is it's too difficult to get away. We are approaching about $15 million in sales. This company is changing. There is always a good deal of detail that holds you back. I try to have Frank Joyce, our vice president of administration, and his staff handle details and most of the correspondence with customers, with suppliers, and for special situations. But when decisions have to be made, I must be here. After all, you have to keep up on things all the time, and I can't be in two places at once. As it is, I have to call the office at least once a day when I'm out. There are always a million questions to answer. Problems keep piling up, and I'm deluged when I return; and each time I plan to leave, something comes up to keep me here. How do you plan for expansion when you have a small staff and are in that no-man's land of less than $20 million in sales? Because of the niche we sought in this business, we have had to build it on personal contacts. Joe and I have virtually built this business ourselves. That's why we are so heavily involved in sales and promotion. When you have big chain operations and department stores as accounts, you need close and personal contact with the customer. I don't think we can afford to lose this. But I don't know how we can keep pace with the business. We both work 12 to 14 hours a day, and I am frequently in here on Saturday and Sunday.

APPENDIX: Some Notes on the Candy Industry*

INDUSTRY TRENDS

The shipments of all domestic confectionery products increased 8.6 percent to an all-time high of over $4.6 billion in 1980. Despite higher prices, which contributed to the increase, shipments in the industry increased 3.4 percent, measured in real terms, over 1972 constant dollars. (See Exhibit 1A.)

The confectionery industry has faced many challenges in the past five years. The costs of production have risen significantly, particularly the ingredients, due mainly to the increase in sugar and peanut prices. Producer prices continued to increase in 1980, rising 7 percent over the 1979 period. The increase in production costs was also due to a shift in demand for higher-priced candies of the chocolate variety. Per capita consumption continued to decline, dropping to 15.4 pounds in 1980 from 16.6 pounds in 1979. (See Exhibit 2.) This decline was due to the decrease in consumption of nonchocolate

*Source: Confectionery Manufacturers' Sales and Distribution, U.S. Dept. of Commerce: Bureau of Industrial Economics, March 1982.

EXHIBIT 1A
CONFECTIONERY PRODUCTS SHIPMENTS AND
VALUE OF SHIPMENTS IN CURRENT AND CONSTANT
DOLLARS 1972–1980 (in millions)

Year	Quantity, pounds	Current dollars	Constant dollars
1980	3,438	4,649	2,549
1979	3,673	4,281	2,465
1978	3,588	3,847	2,327
1977	3,700	3,675	2,264
1976	3,467	2,912	1,854
1975	3,357	2,830	1,957
1974	3,651	2,771	2,262
1973	3,807	2,141	2,141
1972	3,793	1,977	1,977
Compound annual percent change	−1.2	11.3	3.2

EXHIBIT 2
PER CAPITA CONSUMPTION AND EXPENDITURES, AND VALUE PER
POUND OF CONFECTIONERY PRODUCTS, 1972–1980

Year	Per capita consumption, pounds	Average unit value, cents/pound	Per capita expenditure, dollars/person
1980	15.4	135.2	20.82
1979	16.6	116.6	19.36
1978	16.5	107.2	17.69
1977	17.3	99.0	17.13
1976	16.8	84.0	14.11
1975	16.1	84.3	13.57
1974	17.6	75.9	13.36
1973	18.5	56.2	10.40
1972	18.7	52.1	9.74
Compound annual percent change	−2.4	12.7	10.0

candies, which dropped 15 percent in the period 1979–1980 to 1.4 billion pounds. (See Exhibit 3.)

Another adjustment facing candy manufacturers was the drop in population in the 5- to 17-year-old age group, which accounts for a significant amount of candy consumption. The industry has been able to offset this consumer change by changing their product mix. They have placed emphasis on higher-quality, higher-priced candies aimed at the adult group.

EXHIBIT 3
QUANTITY AND VALUE OF DOMESTIC CONFECTIONERY SHIPMENTS BY PRODUCT
CATEGORY, 1980 AND 1979 (thousands, except where noted)

Product category	Shipments, pounds		Change	
	1980	1979	Pounds	Percent
Total confectionery shipments	3,438,262	3,672,936	−234,674	−6.4
Confectionery, type not specified	139,370	148,792	−9,422	−6.3
Chocolate and nonchocolate types	3,298,892	3,524,144	−225,252	−6.4
Chocolate type confectionery	1,862,572	1,828,626	23,946	1.3
Nonchocolate type confectionery	1,436,320	1,685,515	−249,195	−14.8

Product category	Shipments, dollars		Change	
	1980	1979	Pounds	Percent
Total confectionery shipments	4,649,390	4,281,441	367,949	8.6
Confectionery, type not specified	187,341	171,111	16,230	9.5
Chocolate and nonchocolate types	4,462,049	4,110,330	351,719	8.6
Chocolate type confectionery	3,147,292	2,854,725	292,567	10.2
Nonchocolate type confectionery	1,314,757	1,255,605	59,152	4.7

This sales shift has been mainly centered in chocolate candies, which increased 10 percent in 1980 to $3.1 billion. The quantity of shipments also showed an increase, rising 1.3 percent to 1.9 billion pounds. The wholesale price of chocolate candy rose to $1.69 a pound in 1980, an increase of 8 percent over 1979. Nonchocolate candy rose in price to 92 cents during this period, an increase of 24 percent. This factor accounts for the increase in value of nonchocolate confections of 4.7 percent in 1980, despite a drop in shipments of 15 percent. (See Exhibits 4 and 5 for breakdown of candy sales and shipments by type.)

Employment in the industry increased very slightly in 1980 over 1979, rising to approximately 54 thousand persons. Average hourly wages for production workers increased 3 percent in this period to $5.68. Since 1972 employment in the industry has declined at a compound annual rate of 1.4 percent; according to the most recent data real output per worker in the industry has increased an average annual rate of 3 percent from 1972 to 1978.

DISTRIBUTION

Direct sales to retailers were almost $2.1 billion in 1980, accounting for 44 percent of total manufacturer's sales. Direct sales to retail grocery chains amounted to $1.1 billion,

EXHIBIT 4
QUANTITY, VALUE OF SHIPMENTS AND AVERAGE UNIT VALUE BY CONFECTIONERY PRODUCT TYPE, 1980 (thousands, except where noted)

	Shipments		Average unit value, cents/pound
Product type	Quantity, pounds	Value, dollars	
Total, all confectionery shipments	3,438,262	4,649,390	135.2
Confectionery, not specified by kind	139,370	187,341	134.4
Total, chocolate and nonchocolate confectionery	3,298,892	4,462,049	135.3
Chocolate and chocolate-type confectionery	1,862,572	3,147,292	169.0
Solid	165,472	319,634	193.2
Solid with inclusion	154,812	317,784	205.3
Enrobed or molded			
With candy, nut, or fruit centers	858,351	1,395,090	162.5
With bakery product center	103,245	197,007	190.8
Panned	305,810	493,523	161.4
Assortments and other	192,852	285,642	148.1
Chocolate-type, not specified	82,030	138,612	169.0
Nonchocolate-type confectionery	1,436,320	1,314,757	91.5
Hard candy	470,086	530,889	112.9
Chewy candy	266,029	226,387	85.1
Soft candy	347,852	254,911	73.3
Iced coated candy	15,497	21,092	136.1
Panned	175,165	154,878	88.4
Licorice and licorice type	98,530	68,787	69.8
Nonchocolate type, not specified	63,161	57,813	91.5

EXHIBIT 5

PERCENT DISTRIBUTION OF QUANTITY AND VALUE OF SHIPMENTS, BY
CONFECTIONERY PRODUCT TYPE, 1980

| | Percent distribution | | | |
| | All shipments | | Product type shipments | |
Product type	Quantity	Value	Quantity	Value
Total, all confectionery shipments	100.0	100.0	N.A.*	N.A.
Confectionery, not specified by kind	4.1	4.0	N.A.	N.A.
Total, chocolate and nonchocolate confectionery	95.9	96.0	N.A.	N.A.
Chocolate and chocolate-type confectionery	54.2	67.7	100.0	100.0
Solid	4.8	6.9	8.9	10.2
Solid with inclusion	4.5	6.8	8.3	10.1
Enrobed or molded				
With candy, nut, or fruit centers	25.0	30.0	46.1	44.3
With bakery product center	3.0	4.2	5.5	6.3
Panned	8.9	10.6	16.4	15.7
Assortments and others	5.6	6.1	10.4	9.1
Chocolate-type, not specified	2.4	3.0	4.4	4.4
Nonchocolate-type confectionery	41.8	28.3	100.0	100.0
Hard candy	13.7	12.5	32.7	40.4
Chewy candy	7.7	4.9	17.2	19.4
Soft candy	10.1	5.5	16.0	11.8
Ice coated candy	0.5	0.5	10.8	16.0
Panned	5.1	3.3	12.2	11.8
Licorice and licorice type	2.9	1.5	6.9	5.2
Nonchocolate type, not specified	1.8	1.2	4.4	4.4

*N.A. = not applicable.

a total of 23 percent of producer's sales. Direct sales to drug and general merchandise
stores was about $1 billion. (See Exhibit 6).

INGREDIENTS

Ingredient costs accounted for 48 percent of manufacturer's sales in 1980. The total
cost of all ingredients used was $2.2 billion. Cocoa-based inputs were 40 percent of all
ingredients purchased. Ingredient usage declined in most areas in 1980, reflecting the
overall decrease in production. (See Exhibit 7 for a breakdown of ingredients used.)

FOREIGN TRADE

The volume of exports totaled 51 million pounds in 1980, a 12 percent decline from
1979. The value of exports declined 2 percent to $58 million. Exports represented 1.3

EXHIBIT 6
CONFECTIONERY SALES BY TYPE OF OUTLET (thousands, except where noted)

1980 and 1979 summary comparison by type of outlet

	Value of shipments		
	1980	1979	Percent change
Total sales	4,745,105	4,411,550	7.6
Resales	95,715	130,109	−26.4
Total, shipments by outlet	4,649,390	4,281,441	8.6
Merchant wholesalers	1,606,996	1,615,994	−0.6
Retail stores, government, export, other	2,736,151	2,341,052	16.9
Outlet, not specified by kind	306,243	324,395	−5.6

Detail by type of outlet, 1980

Type of outlet	Value of shipments	Percentage total sales	Distribution shipments by outlet
Total sales	4,745,105	100.0	–
Resales	95,715	2.0	–
Total, sales by outlet	4,649,390	98.0	100.0
Merchant wholesaler	1,606,996	33.9	34.6
Direct to retailers	2,095,699	44.2	45.1
Grocery store chains, retail	1,088,098	22.9	23.4
Drugstore chains, retail	504,937	10.6	10.9
General merchandise stores	502,664	10.6	10.8
Manufacturer's own retail stores	152,143	3.2	3.3
Government/military	91,987	1.9	2.0
Other, including export	396,322	8.4	8.5
All other	338,071	7.1	7.3
Export	58,251	1.2	1.3
Type of outlet not specified by kind	306,243	6.5	6.6

percent of all confectionery sales and 1.5 percent of all poundage shipped. Canada and Mexico were the largest U.S. export markets, accounting for 40 percent of total confectionery exports. Far Eastern countries, mainly Hong Kong and Japan, took 20 percent of U.S. confectionery exports. The Caribbean area and the South American countries followed in importance. The decline in chocolate confectionery shipments to Canada accounted for the 1980 decline in total exports. (See Exhibit 8.)

The value imports of confectionery declined 21 percent in 1980; the quantity imported declined only 6 percent. The difference was due to the change in the currency exchange rate due to the strengthening of the dollar. Major suppliers of imported confectionery products into the United States were western European countries, Brazil, Canada, and Mexico. (See Exhibit 9.)

EXHIBIT 7
CONSUMPTION OF SELECTED INGREDIENTS BY CONFECTIONERY MANUFACTURERS,
1980 (thousands, except where noted)

Ingredients	Ingredient usage		Percent of total value	Unit value, cents/pound
	Pounds	Dollars		
Total materials consumed	N.A.*	2,242,223	100.0	N.A.
Materials not specified by kind	N.A.	221,264	9.9	N.A.
Total, materials specified by kind	N.A.	2,020,959	90.1	N.A.
Cocoa, chocolate, and cocoa composition	724,333	900,079	40.1	124.3
Cocoa beans	211,301	278,934	12.4	132.0
Cocoa butter	117,395	303,848	13.6	258.8
Cocoa powder composition coatings	24,865	24,737	1.1	99.5
Chocolate coatings, all	135,386	292,560	13.0	216.1
Milk chocolate	171,995	228,934	10.2	133.1
Other	63,391	63,626	2.8	100.4
Sweeteners	2,177,938	434,955	19.4	20.0
Sugar (cane-beet)	1,304,958	345,123	15.4	26.4
Corn syrup	872,980	89,832	4.0	10.3
Nut meats	272,261	190,584	8.5	70.0
Peanuts (shelled basis)	237,415	121,647	5.4	51.2
Almond kernels	22,580	44,427	2.0	196.8
Other nuts and nut meat	12,266	24,510	1.1	199.8
Coconut meats	18,220	12,457	0.6	68.4
Fats and oils, all	81,880	47,553	2.1	58.1
Milk products, all	N.A.	197,756	8.8	N.A.
Other edible materials†	N.A.	237,575	10.6	N.A.

*N.A. = not applicable.
†Includes corn starch, essential oils, flavorings, eggs and egg products, fruits, jams, and other materials on which specific data were not collected.

INDUSTRY STRUCTURE

The confectionery manufacturers in the United States continued their increase in size through 1980. The number of firms with sales greater than $18 million is rising, and firms in this category are attaining a large percentage of the industry's total sales. Companies reporting sales of $20 million number about 35. They account for approximately 80 percent of total industry sales. In 1970, twenty-one companies in the over $20 million category accounted for 55 percent of total industry sales. About 20 firms have sales between $10 and $20 million, which account for approximately 12.5 percent of total sales. The trend toward larger companies is expected to continue as inflation and mergers move many companies into larger sales volume. About 113 manufacturers reported sales between $1 and $10 million, accounting for 10 percent of industry sales. Approximately 63 firms have sales of $1 million or less; they represent less than 1 percent of the industry. There are frequent newcomers into the industry which go unrecorded until their sales volume is significant enough to be recognized. (See Exhibit 10.)

EXHIBIT 8
QUALITY AND VALUE OF CONFECTIONERY EXPORTS, BY COUNTRY AND PRODUCT CATEGORY, 1980 AND 1979
(thousands)

Source country	Chocolate confectionery				Nonchocolate confectionery			
	1980		1979		1980		1979	
	Pounds	Dollars	Pounds	Dollars	Pounds	Dollars	Pounds	Dollars
Total	16,421	22,563	29,802	33,761	28,906	29,624	30,091	28,629
Canada	4,765	4,939	14,067	11,768	8,639	7,127	8,745	5,680
Mexico	996	1,041	1,340	1,422	3,993	2,750	4,660	2,667
Argentina	467	780	21	31	704	1,793	259	1,521
Bahamas	275	329	262	288	1,605	1,076	542	473
Bermuda	86	150	92	140	150	193	216	257
Chile	709	982	572	623	131	142	89	191
Columbia	95	77	157	181	475	458	348	262
Dominican Rep.	745	916	539	481	553	305	100	78
Guatemala	233	350	104	146	298	336	224	179
Honduras	92	135	82	72	105	100	186	153
Netherlands Antilles	151	166	505	432	1,775	1,535	1,362	1,279
Panama	427	518	489	624	206	201	128	113
Trinidad	48	27	23	16	459	370	306	229
Venezuela	170	220	92	108	617	940	224	165
Belgium	34	52	3	7	219	178	39	39
West Germany	191	175	55	62	557	595	511	486
Iceland	240	384	80	125	24	36	28	43
Sweden	215	184	959	778	2	4	159	169
United Kingdom	252	261	139	114	251	349	775	734
Kuwait	198	185	80	69	124	128	581	172
Saudi Arabia	302	443	338	439	683	625	651	635
Australia	43	86	2,886	2,630	162	245	111	129
Taiwan	67	60	56	84	200	556	228	202
Hong Kong	1,010	2,274	1,108	1,668	1,151	2,398	830	1,631
Japan	3,612	6,205	4,723	8,974	3,276	4,235	6,299	8,135
Singapore	121	217	197	296	415	498	441	396
Other	877	1,407	833	1,183	2,132	2,387	2,048	2,221

Source: U.S. Department of Commerce, "U.S. Exports, F.T.-410."

473

EXHIBIT 9
QUANTITY AND VALUE OF CONFECTIONERY IMPORTS, BY COUNTRY AND PRODUCT CATEGORY, 1980 AND 1979 (thousands)

Source country	Chocolate confectionery				Nonchocolate confectionery			
	1980		1979		1980		1979	
	Pounds	Dollars	Pounds	Dollars	Pounds	Dollars	Pounds	Dollars
Total	27,729	40,326	27,924	38,319	87,854	80,078	92,827	89,483
Canada	8,043	10,520	6,296	7,108	5,837	3,937	5,094	2,653
Mexico	1,750	1,169	1,325	811	1,418	876	2,213	1,130
Argentina	6	17	195	136	2,394	1,341	4,803	2,189
Brazil	363	179	466	227	13,105	5,222	7,934	2,730
Columbia	132	77	272	168	7,370	2,903	7,358	2,674
Belgium	205	742	121	602	576	497	580	432
Denmark	378	466	374	456	1,393	1,159	1,870	1,375
Finland	667	677	662	617	728	724	907	790
France	187	580	144	350	601	1,107	936	1,486
West Germany	2,616	4,760	5,518	9,371	14,511	26,306	14,420	36,128
Ireland	97	102	459	729	67	46	40	59
Italy	1,292	3,463	1,353	3,033	3,897	3,640	4,644	5,421
Netherlands	903	1,303	1,134	1,357	5,031	4,645	5,172	4,412
Poland	534	335	451	307	2,541	980	2,315	856
Spain	100	171	107	261	1,173	3,086	1,169	3,301
Sweden	262	557	556	583	5,537	3,883	5,921	3,351
Switzerland	1,632	4,103	1,287	3,114	295	417	353	528
United Kingdom	7,316	9,743	6,007	7,927	14,705	14,236	19,458	14,997
Israel	372	462	405	385	881	484	1,267	435
South Africa, Rep. of	153	73	70	29	1,851	822	2,644	1,159
Australia	174	97	96	45	267	161	229	115
Taiwan	9	15	24	32	309	345	533	541
Hong Kong	85	157	116	84	1,222	1,232	1,525	1,111
Japan	8	24	5	14	468	851	418	807
Other countries	435	544	481	573	1,677	1,178	1,089	03

Source: U.S. Department of Commerce, "U.S. Imports, F.T.-246."

EXHIBIT 10
CONFECTIONERY MANUFACTURERS' SALES, GROUPED BY COMPANY SIZE, 1979

Sales size group	Number of companies	1979 Sales ($000)	Percent of sales
Total Sales	N.A.*	4,347,048	100.0
$20 million and over	35	3,410,321	78.5
$10 to $20 million	21	297,707	6.8
$3 to $10 million	52	316,464	7.3
$1 to $3 million	61	118,566	2.7
$500,000 to $1 million	33	26,027	0.6
Less than $500,000	30†	6,852	0.2
Size of company, n.s.k.‡	N.A.	171,111	3.9

*N.A. = not available.
†These figures include estimates for a large number of small companies that are not included in the annual mailing panel.
‡n.s.k. = not specified by kind.

INDUSTRY PROSPECTS

The value of 1981 shipments are expected to total $5.2 billion, an increase of 11 percent over 1980. Per capita consumption and the poundage shipped will show a slight increase. The decline of sugar and peanut prices in 1981 resulted in only a 4 percent increase in ingredient prices. Cocoa prices are also expected to continue to show less increase. These factors will be of substantial benefit to producers in the future.

The slowing population growth, smaller families, and the increased senior population level will continue in the next decade; U.S. population is expected to grow about 10 percent in the 1980s as contrasted to 11.4 percent growth in the 1970s. The 5- to 17-year-old group, an important candy-eating group, is expected to increase in number by 1985.

Confectionery manufacturers are expected to continue to develop their product lines to accommodate the changing population mix and the apparent shift in demand of higher-quality candies. Product development and packaging will be major matters of concern for candy producers in the future years.

ORGANIZATION AND CONTROL STRATEGIES

Development and Execution of Organization and Control Strategies: Organizational Design

TRANSITION TO ORGANIZATION STRATEGY

The transition from policy formulation and operational planning to executive action is accomplished through the essential step of developing an organizational strategy. The organizational design cannot be developed in isolation as a separate and distinct managerial effort. It must flow from the preceding phases of the strategic planning process and should reflect the basic economic and business objectives of the firm. The organizational strategy should also be interrelated and specifically aligned to the successive stage of the policymaking process—the control strategy. Organizational design and the choice of structure are distinct strategic decisions and an integral part of the firm's strategic design, logically following from its predetermined root and operating strategies.

CONCEPT OF ORGANIZATIONAL DEVELOPMENT

This concept of organizational development has been concisely and emphatically stated in the literature by several authors. Chandler, in his work *Strategy and Structure,* defined the sequential process as follows:[1]

> Strategy can be defined as the determination of basic long-term goals and objectives of an enterprise, and the adoption of courses of action and the allocation of resources necessary for carrying out these goals. Decisions to expand the volume of activities, to set up distant plants and offices, to move into new economic functions, or become diversified along many lines of business involve the defining of new basic goals. New

---

[1] A. D. Chandler, Jr., *Strategy and Structure* (Cambridge, Mass.: M.I.T., 1962), pp. 13–14.

479

courses of action must be devised and resources allocated and reallocated in order to achieve these goals. . . . As the adoption of a new strategy may add new types of personnel and alter the business horizon of the men responsible for the enterprise, it can have a profound effect on the form of its organization. . . . The thesis deduced from these several propositions is then that *structure follows strategy,* and that the most complex type of structure is the *result of the concatenation of several basic strategies.* [Italics added.]

Andrews, in *The Concept of Corporate Strategy,* states the same general proposition in a slightly different context:[2]

> . . . . The simple prescription we wish to add here is that the nature of corporate strategy *must be made to dominate the design of organizational structure and processes.* That is, the principal criterion for all decisions on organizational structure and behavior should be their relevance to the achievement of the organizational purpose, not to their conformity to the dictates of special disciplines.
>
> Thus, the theses we suggest for your consideration are first that conscious strategy can be consciously implemented through skills primarily administrative in nature, and second, the chief determinant of organizational structure and the processes by which tasks are assigned and performance motivated, rewarded, and controlled should be *the strategy of the firm,* not the history of the company, its position in the industry, the specialized background of its executives, the principles of organization as developed in textbooks, the recommendations of consultants, or the conviction that one form of organization is intrinsically better than another . . . .

ORGANIZATIONAL DESIGN AND CONTINGENCY THEORY

The proposition that strategy determines structure is to some extent based on contingency theory, which is prevalent in the literature of organization theory. Contingency theory as applied to the organization structure of a firm states that:[3]

1 There is no one best way to organize.

2 One form of organization may be better than another, depending upon the environmental factors and the firm's situation.

The first statement refers to research findings which conclude that there are no universal principles which will guide managers in developing an organization structure which will apply to different firms in different industries. This proposition is contrary to much of the earlier concepts expressed in management literature. The second proposition applies to findings related to empirical research which, succinctly stated, concluded that environmental conditions

[2] Kenneth R. Andrews, *The Concept of Corporate Strategy* (Homewood, Ill.: Dow-Jones-Irwin, 1971), p. 181.

[3] See J. W. Lawrence and P. R. Lorsch, *Organizational and Environment: Managing Differentiation and Integration* (Boston: Graduate School of Business, Harvard University, 1967). See also, F. E. Kast and J. E. Rosenzweig, *Contingency Views of Organization and Management* (Chicago: Science Research Associates, 1973).

and the individual situations of particular companies were key determinants in the selection of the most effective organizational design. This statement, however, does not contradict the first proposition that there is no one best way to organize. If an organization structure is designed that achieves the firm's stated economic and business objectives, it can be judged to be effective. This structure could be based on many variations; however, it would most likely follow basic patterns of structure which accommodate the strategic design of the firm. Effective organization strategies can cover a wide range of structures, but their design is not a random event. To be effective they must reflect the root and operating strategies of the firm which were developed to respond to opportunities and threats of the competitive environment as perceived by management.

CONTRASTING ORGANIZATIONAL STRATEGIES: FORD MOTOR

The strategic profiles of Ford Motor Company and General Motors which were delineated in Chapter 2 reinforce the preceding concepts of organizational design and structure and provide excellent illustrations of contrasting organizational strategies. Ford developed a highly centralized structure with authority centered in the chief executive and the production executives who implemented his policies. The company was organized along traditional functional lines, such as sales, production, finance, personnel, etc. There was no evidence of decentralized functions or decentralized authority in the early stages of the company's development. This centralized organization structure logically flowed from the concept of business developed by Ford—to manufacture a basic, standardized, low-priced car for the mass market. The one-model concept—with a single chassis for a few body styles, interchangeable parts, one color choice (black), and no accessories—facilitated the development of a centralized, ladderlike structure. Ford's concept of organization was logical and effective because of the simplicity of his standardized product, which eliminated the need for decentralization and the duplication of staff functions. In later years, however, after the company had grown to be the number-one producer of automobiles in the world, the centralized structure lacked the flexibility to provide for the delegation and control needed to permit effective management.

GENERAL MOTORS' ORGANIZATIONAL STRATEGY

The organizational strategy of General Motors developed under Sloan represents a significant contribution to the theory and concept of the management and control of complex decentralized companies. As the head of a special committee organized to study the company's product policy, Sloan developed the first definitive statement of a root strategy for the firm, which distinguished it from other car manufacturers. Essentially, the new statement of strategy placed General Motors in all segments of the automobile market where the company determined it could secure sufficient volume to profitably employ its resources from the low-priced end, represented by Chevrolet, to the high-priced quality market of Cadillac.

Sloan's major contribution in strategic development, however, was in the organization and control area. General Motors, with its root strategy of multiple car lines to satisfy each determined market segment and an operating strategy which included partial vertical integration and numerous subunits, required a highly decentralized organization with a well-defined control system to manage the company. Sloan provided a strong base to build a decentralized organization structure.[4] Sloan's organizational strategy was directed toward retaining the decentralization which existed under Durant. However, through the establishment of clear lines of authority and coordination and interrelation between various groups and divisions, he developed an effective management team directed toward the attainment of the corporate objectives. His concept gave substance to the loosely knit organization structure which had existed under Durant. He established separate profit centers for each division of the company and developed a strong central staff to handle corporate affairs. In addition, he devised a committee structure which served as an integrating and stabilizing factor for the organization. Sloan also, perhaps for the first time in corporate history, clearly outlined the functions and responsibilities of the chief executive officer in a highly decentralized, complex organization. Except for some variations and necessary changes to accommodate growth and expansion, General Motors' organizational strategy remains close to the original form which was developed by Sloan.

EFFECTS OF OPERATING STRATEGY ON ORGANIZATIONAL STRUCTURE

In addition to the obvious differences of centralization and decentralization illustrated in the case of Ford and General Motors, both companies utilized the franchised dealer system, which affected their organizational designs and set the trend for distribution in the industry. If the automobile industry had initially chosen to sell their product through their own retail units, their organization would have been significantly different than it is at present under the conceived strategy of selling through franchised dealers who operate their retail sales and service establishments under "guided independence." Not only would the structure of General Motors, Ford, Chrysler, and American Motors be substantially different in shape and size, but there would also be marked differences in organizational relationships. The functional dynamics vis-à-vis production-marketing would be more direct and pointed; the authority relationship would be direct; communication would be direct; and no doubt greater control would be exercised over selling policies, customer relations, and repair policies.

---

[4]Alfred P. Sloan, *My Years with General Motors* (New York: Doubleday, 1963).

EXAMPLES OF THE EFFECT OF ROOT AND OPERATING STRATEGY ON ORGANIZATIONAL DEVELOPMENT: AVON

Through analysis of specific companies in other industries, we can reinforce the effect of distinct root and operating strategies on the development of organizational strategy. For example, companies which sell through representatives, agents, or wholesalers rather than develop a complete sales force of their own will have a different composition and structure to their organization than firms which have chosen to market through their own sales group at all levels. For example, in the case of Avon Products,[5] the root and operating strategies were distinctly interrelated with the development of its organizational design and structure. The Avon lady was a representative of the company, not a salaried employee. She acted as a neighborhood entrepreneur with an exclusive sales territory, ordering products from Avon, selling to customers, delivering the product, and collecting payment. In effect, she was the distribution system. Each of the 275,000 Avon ladies was supervised by 2,254 district managers, controlled by 111 division managers who reported to general managers of branches, the latter serving as the distribution points for Avon Products. This organizational design gave Avon competitive advantages in terms of much lower marketing costs. Unlike its major competitors in the distribution and sale of cosmetics and beauty care products, Avon paid commissions only to the salesladies and did not have the added burden of paying salaries to sales personnel, discounts to retailers, and additional payments for demonstrators and free samples. This concept of distribution also provided the company with a simple, uncomplicated organization structure with few layers of management and a relatively small corporate headquarters staff.[6]

If we examine the product market scope of varied enterprises, we can identify significant organization structure and strategy differences between single-line product and multiproduct firms. The proliferation of product lines both horizontally and vertically has introduced product managers and brand managers. The tendency to give operating independence to divisional, product, and brand managers has significantly altered the authority control relations of many organizations. These shifts in operating strategy not only change the formal structure but also create a new informal structure and new organizational relationships.

PROCTER AND GAMBLE'S ORGANIZATIONAL STRATEGY

Procter and Gamble's strategic design, which was described in Chapter 4, provides an illustration of the effective utilization of brand managers as an integral part of an organizational design. The company is generally credited with initiating this organizational strategy in 1927 to more effectively manage its ex-

---

[5]See *Forbes,* July 1, 1973, pp. 20–26.
[6]*Ibid.*

panding product line of soaps, detergents, and cleansing agents. While P&G's proliferation of products provided for expansion and growth, it caused organization and control problems, placed branded products in competition with each other, and complicated the problem of monitoring and assessing marketing performance. The concept of brand management was built into the organization structure and refined over the years to decentralize the marketing function and provide control over individual branded products. Each brand manager had his own profit center and had the responsibility for the coordination of market planning, market research, sales, sales promotion, packaging and design, advertising, and manufacturing with a specific branded product or family of products.

This strategic concept of brand management became part of the basic business philosophy of P&G and influenced its root and operating strategies. It also gave the company competitive advantages and provided the organizational flexibility needed to attain its basic economic objectives of growth and expansion. The expansion of the organizational dimensions of P&G also gave the company the opportunity to enlarge its management group, thus creating opportunities and incentives for aspiring executives. Titles and management responsibilities could be bestowed on qualified members of management at a relatively early period in their careers. This advantage extended to the recruitment of potential management talent, who saw an opportunity to attain executive status at a relatively early date.[7]

GROWTH AND EXPANSION AS FACTORS IN ORGANIZATIONAL DEVELOPMENT

As illustrated in the preceding descriptions of corporate strategic development, in addition to the conceived root and operating strategies, growth and expansion can be major factors in influencing changes in organizational strategy. Each successive stage of growth places the corporation at a higher plateau which exerts new demands and pressures, not experienced previously, on the organization structure. Growth and expansion frequently create corporate crises because policymakers, as shown in the case of Ford and General Motors, fail to realize the increased complexity of their companies and attempt to manage with an organizational structure designed for a stage of enterprise development long since passed. The successful companies in our industrial society have experienced sustained periods of growth, particularly in the past two decades.

In addition to a prolonged expansionary cycle, many growth companies have gone through changes in their strategic design, usually on a transitional basis, by gradually shifting the allocation of their skills and resources to give the firm new form and direction, thus adding to the need for a reformulation of

[7]"Brand Manager-No Longer King," *Business Week,* June 9, 1973, pp. 58–63. See also "The Clorox Case" in Part Nine of this volume.

the organizational strategy. The growth process is likely to produce new functions, add new levels of management, and significantly increase staff as efforts are made by management to control an expanding, more complex organization.

GENERAL ELECTRIC'S ORGANIZATIONAL DESIGN

General Electric, the multi-billion-dollar producer of electrical products, appliances, and supplies and one of the world's most diversified companies, has, over time, made changes in its organizational strategy to respond to rapid growth and development.[8] The original company was formed in 1878 to finance Thomas Edison's experiments with the incandescent lamp, and in 1892 a number of pioneer companies in the electrical field incorporated as the General Electric Company. The newly formed organization expanded rapidly in its developmental period, and through the years its growth has paralleled the growth curve of the use of electricity in the United States. The growth of GE was internally generated through the development of new products and markets, which resulted in a highly diversified company. Until 1939, GE was able to operate with a centralized organization structure. From 1920 to 1939, the company's sales volume increased from $200 million to $342 million. Under pressure of war production, sales volume rapidly rose to $1.3 billion by 1943. Management became increasingly aware of the difficulties and virtual impossibility of operating a company with such growth characteristics under its highly centralized organization structure. Therefore a study was undertaken by GE under the direction of Ralph Cordiner, who later became the chief executive officer, to determine the best way to organize the rapidly growing industrial giant. As a result, a new, decentralized organizational strategy was effected in 1951, dividing the company in terms of products, geography, and functional types of work. Many positions and units were discontinued, and many new positions and components were added to the company's structure. Approximately 100 decentralized operating departments grouped under 21 operating divisions were set up, each as an independent profit center with full responsibility and authority for product engineering, manufacturing, and marketing. Many of the product lines competed with each other in the marketplace. Services were organized at the corporate level for the major functions of accounting, engineering, legal services, management consultation, manufacturing, marketing, public and employee relations, treasury, and research. The executive office provided leadership and long-range planning for the company as a whole. This office comprised a group of executives who shared the work of the president; it included the chairman of the board and five executive vice presidents. The president served as the chief executive officer; the chairman of the board represented the president in financial matters, public and government relations, and international matters;

---

[8]See Ralph Cordier, Jr., *New Frontiers for Professional Managers* (New York: McGraw-Hill, 1956).

and the executive vice presidents represented the president in relations with specific group operating divisions.

GE continued to grow and adapted this basic decentralized organization structure to accommodate product expansion. By 1968 the company had grown to about 170 departments arrayed into 50 divisions, which were organized into 10 groups. As growth and diversification substantially increased into the 1970s, it became evident to management that some businesses became fragmented among newly formed departments and created planning problems. The concept of each department being a separate profit center and business unit was in many cases lost, and a business identification problem developed. Management also became aware of the need to improve the planning function at both the corporate and operating levels. To solve these major problems and other difficulties that had developed within the system due to accelerated growth, the policymaking group initiated a study to aid in the development of a new organizational strategy.

A new strategy evolved from the study and reformulation process which retained the basic structure of group divisions and departments but superimposed on this design strategic business units (SBUs) for the purpose of developing strategic plans at the point in the organization where they could be most advantageously formulated. The components which made up the 43 newly designated SBUs were drawn from the group, division, or department level.[9] Essentially, each SBU was independent of other SBUs in the company, having its own collection of related businesses and its own mission and objectives, set of outside competitors, products, markets, and organization. It was intended that each SBU operate as much as possible as an independent business with a manager who had responsibility, accountability, and authority for the performance and profitability of the unit. The manager and the SBU's organization were responsible for developing a strategic plan for their unit which was subject to review in terms of balancing resource allocation for the best interests of the company as a whole. The operational planning function, which contributed to the strategic plan, was done by the components within the SBU. Specifically, this planning outlined the support the components were going to contribute to the SBU strategic plan and, at the same time, advanced strategies for the SBU's part of the business. The strategic plan of each SBU was subject to a strategic review at an organizational level above the SBU.

The concept of SBUs enabled the corporate executive office to better define the mission, objectives, and strategic plans for GE as a corporate entity. It also provided a major advantage to the corporation by reducing the complex task of resource allocation from 170 or more departments to 43 clearly identified business units.

---

[9] See C. H. Springer, "Strategic Management in General Electric," *Operations Research*, vol. 21, no. 6, November–December 1973, pp. 1177–1182. See also *GE's Evolving Management System*, unpublished internal report, January 18, 1972.

DEVELOPING THE ORGANIZATIONAL STRUCTURE

In the initial steps of organizational planning the firm attempts to develop an "ideal" structure which will provide the best possible grouping of projected activities. This "custom built" organization structure is designed to cover each phase and function of the firm's operations. It is intended to provide the most effective medium for harnessing and utilizing available skills and resources and for reflecting the firm's objectives and managerial philosophy.

The basic framework for decision making and action must establish the relationships between each level of the management job and clearly define authority links, spans, and limitations to permit executives and subordinates to understand the nature and extent of their responsibilities. In structuring a practical working organization, management will be confronted with many of the following problems:

How should operational activities be divided? By functional departments? By processes of production? By geographical location? Territories? Districts? Divisions? Product lines?

How should the lines of authority and responsibility be drawn?

How should relationships between units be defined to fix responsibilities and allow for delegation of authority?

What limits should be considered for the span of management control and the length of lines of communication?

To what extent should operations and lines of authority be centralized? Decentralized?

Does the structure allow for the use of specialized functional skills? For the use of substructures? Project management? Task forces?

How should the relationships between line and staff be defined?

Does the structure provide for balance and flexibility?

While an efficient organizational structure will be a major factor in determining successful operations, it still represents only the vehicle or means through which executive action is channeled. The most important and difficult task is the selection and placement of a working management team which will effectively guide the firm along the lines charted in the strategic planning stages. While the organizational structure should be initially based on an ideal framework, invariably it must be adapted for the human factor. In the final step of filling out the structure, modifications of the ideal organizational form will be necessary to fit the capabilities and limitations of available executive personnel.

ADAPTING ORGANIZATIONAL STRUCTURES

Despite necessary and inevitable deviations from initially drafted ideal structures, organizational planning will provide the firm with a standard which will afford sounder evaluation of personnel, control over organizational changes, and greater flexibility to adapt to environmental changes.

Executive personnel are charged with the responsibility of translating policies and plans into action and developing a smoothly functioning team out of the people within the organization. The personnel of many and varied skills must be properly administered in a great variety of functional activities on a day-to-day basis; their tasks and programs must be arranged and their activities coordinated and directed toward predetermined goals. The type and quality of executives required to perform these managerial functions may vary to a great extent according to the nature, objectives, and policies of the firm. Despite titles, management positions are not standardized. Similarly, management requirements within a firm are not static. Shifts and changes in objectives and plans, and the consequent demand for new and different skills, may require a redesign of the organization structure.

Corporate expansion, in addition to creating a need for increased executive personnel, will also undoubtedly cause shifts in management levels. Problems of line and staff, decentralization, and management training and development will become important factors in organizational planning. Adapting the organization to the dynamics of the business scene demands constant reappraisal of the interrelationship of the multitude of factors affecting the human forces guiding the destiny of the firm. Organizational design and structure should determine the flow of the decision-making process. When organizations are ill-designed and lag behind the conceived strategies of the firm, their ineffectiveness is quickly felt and usually results in frequent bypassing and reliance upon the informal organization structure. Reorganization to accommodate growth and expansion or alignment with changes in the root or operating strategies constitutes a formidable task for most companies. Restructuring usually involves eliminating specific positions and/or components of the organization and developing new units with different specifications and personnel requirements. As a consequence, management is frequently reluctant to accept the need for reorganization and to make the necessary personnel adjustments. It is almost axiomatic to state that the organizational design of all growing business enterprises lags behind their operating strategies, which are usually the most adaptable to environmental changes affecting the enterprise and its markets. There is always a search for the optimum organizational model and strategy—a fleeting goal that is seldom if ever attained.

INTERPRETATIVE PHASE: DEVELOPING CONTROL STRATEGIES

As an integral part of the firm's strategic design, the control function stems from, and is interrelated with, the organizational phase of the policymaking process. In this context, control strategies should constantly reflect the company's operations as a total system. Performance measures designed for subsidiaries, divisions, departments, and various other subunits should emanate from the basic objectives of the corporate enterprise. Management cannot devise a control system as an independent function; it must be part of the sequential process of strategic planning and be designed to evaluate and monitor the progress of the organization toward clear-cut economic and business objectives. This implies that management has a strategic choice in developing control systems and that control strategies are subject to reformulation in accord with shifts and changes in the direction of the firm. Our interest, as part of the analysis of the policymaking process, is focused on this concept and not on the techniques of control or the mechanics of the control function.

CONTROL STRATEGIES: FORD AND GENERAL MOTORS

The profiling of the various companies in the preceding chapters clearly indicated management's innovation and adaptation of control systems to reflect their strategic plans. In its early stages of development, the control system of Ford Motor was simple and direct to accommodate the centralized organization structure and virtual one-man rule. The rapid growth of the company and the automotive industry, however, rendered this initial system obsolete. It failed to provide the early-warning signals and information needed to detect marked changes in the environment and on the competitive scene. Minor changes were made in the control systems of Ford as the firm went through several reformulations. But it was not until 1945 that the company, under the direction of Henry Ford II and Ernest R. Breech, who came from General Motors, adopted control strategies suited to the firm's size and product-market scope.

General Motors' problems in the development of adequate control systems paralleled that of Ford although the company originally had a distinctly different mission in the industry. Will Durant, like Henry Ford, was a self-willed entrepreneur who organized General Motors as a loosely knit holding company without an adequate control system. Like Ford, Durant was content to utilize a simple, uncomplicated set of controls. His company, however, unlike Ford's, was a complex organization of a number of separate, independent, producing companies which lacked direction and control from the parent unit. It might be said that General Motors was a company out of control from its inception. In 1910, only two years after its organization, the firm experienced its first major financial crisis, which led to the removal of Durant from his executive functions. The second major crisis occurred in 1920, four years after Durant returned as chief executive officer, and for the same reason, the lack of an adequate control system designed to monitor a decentralized group of autonomous companies. A severe cash flow crisis and the lack of inventory control placed the company in jeopardy and led to the permanent removal of Durant from office. As related in Chapter 2, after the Du Ponts took over as major investors, Alfred Sloan eventually became the chief executive officer and was credited with giving the company its first well-defined root strategy. In addition to providing General Motors with a distinct mission and purpose in the automotive industry, Sloan devised the organizational and control strategies which allowed this complex, highly decentralized automotive giant to operate as a single corporate entity. A complete control system was devised over time to retain the independence of the various divisions but provide control and direction at the corporate level. In describing the system, Sloan stated, "It was on the financial side that the last necessary key to decentralization with coordinated control could be found. The key, in principle, was the concept, if we had the means to review and judge the effectiveness of operations, we could safely leave the prosecution of those operations to the men in charge of them." The principle of return on invested capital, which was originated at Du Pont, was the base used for measuring the performance of division operations and became the backbone of the company's control system. Through the years, this concept was modified to fit the General Motors strategic design. Sloan and his central staff also devised innovative financial techniques which aided in making the control system operate effectively. Sloan's committee structure was also a major factor in the development and operation of the company's control strategies.

INNOVATIVE CONTROL SYSTEMS: PROCTER AND GAMBLE AND AVON

Effective control systems, as described in the cases of Avon Products and P&G, frequently are the result of an innovative design derived out of the company's strategic structure. Avon, the manufacturer and distributor of cosmetics and beauty-care products, through the development of its Avon-lady concept, could afford the luxury of a simplified distribution system, a simplified organizational structure, and an uncomplicated control system. Since the Avon lady was the major factor in the distribution system, the company, unlike its main competitors, did not need all the attendant controls and organizational layers that go with retail distribution. Procter and Gamble, through its brand-manager system, was able to bring control and accountability closer to the consumer level at a key point in its organizational structure. This system also provided the company with more information and a more rapid way of transmitting vital product information to the policymaking level. As described in the foregoing section of this chapter, General Electric devised an innovative method of bringing its controls into focus through the concept of strategic business units. The company's size and complexity forced it to seek a more manageable way of controlling and allocating resources to its numerous and varied businesses. Each SBU manager operated an independent business and had profit responsibility for his or her unit. This concept relieved the executive group in corporate management from monitoring and evaluating 170 departments, committing them instead to the surveillance of only 43 SBUs.

ECONOMIC OBJECTIVES AND FINANCIAL CONTROLS

Controls are primarily developed around a financial system which measures inputs into the system—the allocation of skills and resources—and outputs from the system—profit or loss from operations expressed in terms of monetary units. Basic economic objectives provide the foundation for managerial control and the major quantitative measures of the effective performance of the firm. This statement is based on the assumption, emphasized in Chapter 6, that the primary objective of the business enterprise is to maximize the shareholders' or owners' wealth. As previously noted, this managerial action is taken over a long time horizon and within the context of governmental restrictions and the dictates of society and the environment. This simplified economic concept of the firm states that the enterprise must prosper and survive in order to contribute to the goals of society. The internal cost of capital and the discount rate (k) an investor would ascribe to a company's share of stock offers the best measure of the economic objectives of profitability, growth, and survival. The utilization of this criterion provides the policymaker with an effective way of controlling resource allocation and determining the overall effectiveness of the corporate entity in maximizing the shareholders' wealth, the primary objective of the business enterprise. As previously indicated in Chapter 6, the most practical and comprehensive index management can utilize to measure the increase in the shareholders' wealth is the market price of its stock. The internal cost of capital (k) of the firm can be used as an analytical tool, as well as a measurement standard. It serves as a good financial standard or target rate to measure the results of performance for invested funds, or for funds available for allocation to specific new investment projects. As a control measure, k serves as a cut-off rate or hurdle rate of return for the evaluation of investment projects selected to provide profitability and growth. If the cost of capital of a firm is declining, it signals to management the need to reexamine its basic strategic design, as well as its operating efficiency, to determine the need for reformulation. The use of k by management as an integral part of the control system can be a major factor in signaling a declining or mature product line, a mature industry, and of the need to consider seeking growth and expansion through diversification, acquisitions, or mergers.

Significant additional financial data and measures are usually derived from a control system. The extent depends on the complexity of the firm, and the judgment of management about the number of key control areas which need monitoring to assure effective operations. The budget in most organizations is a basic tool utilized by management to control resource allocation and day-to-day operations. It has the advantage of combining the planning function with the control function and also requires management at key levels to set objectives, usually in terms of product units and monetary units for specified budgetary periods. The budget also requires participation on the part of corporate managers and line managers and fixes responsibility for performance at the designated levels in the organization.

Responsibility levels in an organization will vary according to its size, complexity, and the extent of its product line. Common classifications are *expense centers,* where the input in terms of expenses but not the output is measured. Most production units, staff units, and special-project centers which are not considered permanent fall into this category. *Profit centers,* where both the inputs (costs) and the outputs (revenues) are measured, are usually departments which can, in effect, "sell" their services to other units in the company. Or they may be production units, such as plants, which can price a product to sell to the marketing unit. *Investment centers* are areas of the company where the manager is held accountable for the employment of the invested capital in the unit as well as for the unit's revenues.

The investment center is the most important to the top management group for purposes of judgment of performance and resource allocation. The unit of measure is termed *return on invested capital* or *return on capital employed;* it is expressed as a ratio of profit-revenue after expenses to invested capital or capital employed in the investment center. This concept has been utilized mainly by large, diversified, decentralized organizations. It is credited by many to be the single most important management tool for the control of performance and for effective management of decentralized operations. The investment center concept was considered a major factor by Sloan in the effective development of General Motors' decentralized organizational structure and also in the case of General Electric under Cordiner.

QUALITATIVE CONTROLS

The salient factors of leadership communication, motivation, delegation, compensation, incentive, and individual needs and differences are major considerations in the effective performance of the business enterprise. Quantitative measures will indicate good or poor performance in relation to a predetermined set of objectives, but they will not detect individual behavioral characteristics which contribute to or detract from the overall effectiveness of the firm. Goal conflict can be present in any company, but it is more likely to be evident in large, complex, decentralized organizations. Managers of subunits may and do frequently have personal objectives which conflict with the basic objectives of the firm and, as a result, tend to suboptimize. A well-defined control system will be structured to encourage rather than discourage goal congruence; the objectives of management and the workers should, within reasonable limits, be compatible with the objectives of the organization.

In addition to behavioral considerations and interpersonal relations which have a decided effect on management performance, the matter of qualitative controls must also be considered in judging the efficacy of a system. Personnel and management development, public responsibility, the long-run survival of the firm versus short-run expediency, and environmental and ecological considerations are all important matters that have to be managed to assure the success and well-being of the firm. Unfortunately, judgments about these factors are not built into quantitative control systems and are evaluated mainly on a subjective basis.

ASSESSING THE CONTROL SYSTEM

Once the organization has put into action the plans and strategies designed to attain the firm's objectives, management is confronted with the problem of controlling and appraising day-to-day operations. It must assess the soundness of its strategic plans and measure the performance of subordinates entrusted with the responsibility of putting specific programs into action. The review of the firm's operations requires a continuous flow of pertinent information through organization channels to enable management to make significant judgments regarding such questions as the following:

Does the control system reflect environmental trends? Competitive opportunities and threats?

How well is the firm doing in relation to its basic economic objectives? Profitability? Growth? Basic business objectives? In relation to industry trends?

What is the market share? Cost trends?

What is the relationship of progress to plan in the overall program? In the timing and execution of specific programs?

How effectively are subordinates performing specific functions in the execution of the firm's strategic plan?

The ability of management to answer important questions of this nature depends upon the adequacy of its system of controls. Ideally, control measures are based upon the objectives, plans, and strategies of the firm and are designed to reflect the action, efficiency, and progress the organization has made toward attaining its predetermined objectives. It is difficult, however, to examine the control function in isolation because it is so distinctly dependent upon and tied to the other phases of the policymaking process. Efficient controls are dependent, first of all, upon good planning, sound administrative policies, and a clearly defined organization structure. The firm's objectives and strategic plans may thus serve as control standards to measure and judge the efficiency of operations. Control measures may indicate that changes or refinements are necessary in these basic objectives, plans, and strategies.

Despite the fact that the control function is so enmeshed with the other processes of policymaking, it is necessary for management to analyze this function independently to determine whether or not it meets the requirements of the firm's operations. A well-conceived control system will reflect the organization structure and tie the control standards to individual responsibility. In essence, control always reflects individual performance, since specific functions are assigned and authority and responsibility are delegated to particular persons within the organizational unit. A clearly defined organization structure aids in focusing attention on the manager or managers responsible for meeting specific goals or standards of performance. The organization thus provides the vehicle not only for directing and coordinating action but also for maintaining control and appraising individual performance.

The following policy questions will aid in further testing the efficacy of a control system:

Have strategic control points been selected which will most accurately reflect the progress of the firm and the performance of management?

What measures will best reflect the progress toward overall company objectives? Toward the objectives of particular subunits? Divisions? Departments?

Can the controls be readily comprehended by the management personnel who will be expected to utilize them in the day-to-day operations?

Are the controls forward-looking, so that deviations from the charted course can be detected in sufficient time to apply corrective action?

Are the controls flexible enough to allow for necessary sudden shifts in planning and strategy?

Does the control system, in addition to detecting deviations from plan, provide the means to initiate corrective action?

CONTROL AS A SYSTEM

For control measures to be effective in determining the adequacy of the firm's strategic design, they must be conceived as a system and developed as a coordinated unit. It is useful to examine the control strategy in three phases:

1 Precontrol Phase In this phase the root strategy of the firm is analyzed in relation to the firm's capabilities—its skills and resources. Is the firm capable of attaining a specific niche in the marketplace? Is its product line or service competitive enough to assure a specified market share? Is it unique, innovative, or obsolete? Does the firm have the financial and personnel resources needed to attain its objectives of market penetration, profitability, and growth?

The determination of basic economic and business objectives must begin with an assessment of the skills and resources of the enterprise. Setting objectives or goals beyond the capabilities of the firm renders a control system ineffective from the start. Profitability and budgetary goals, which form the backbone of most business control systems, are frequently overstated and sometimes unrealistic in terms of the capabilities of the enterprise and the economic environment. To assure goal congruence, the root strategy and objectives of the organization must be realistically determined and measured against the inventory of skills and resources of the enterprise.

2 Continuing Control Phase The appraisal of the capabilities of the management group and operating personnel must be a continuous process and not relegated to infrequent reappraisals triggered by crisis situations. Management development and training are essential ingredients of a control system. Delegating authority and responsibility to managers not ready for or incapable of the tasks assigned them virtually assures that the enterprise objectives will not be attained. Continuing control suggests that a pro forma organization chart be maintained to indicate the specific kinds and types of management skills required to attain long-run and short-run objectives. Unless the management group is subject to continued evaluation and development, maintaining the firm's position—or reaching new goals in terms of profitability, growth, and expansion—becomes a difficult if not impossible task.

3 Postcontrol Phase   This phase of the control system usually receives the most attention and review on the part of management. While recording and interpreting results is an essential and important executive function, it is still based on past performance and the effectiveness of the information system. The objective of control measures is to provide the information to assess progress toward predetermined goals and to aid the policymaker in problem identification. It must be remembered that the most elaborate control systems will not correct the mistakes of the past but only aid in providing for more effective executive action in the future.

Interpretation of results is a demanding, on-going task of the policymaker. Failure to correctly interpret internal and external signs provided through the control system has led many a firm to failure or to slow, profitless readjustment periods. We can also find numerous examples of firms which operate on "strategy by drift" rather than utilizing planned strategy changes to correct and alter the course of the enterprise. The lack of an intelligent and decisive review of postcontrol information may lead to a do-nothing policy and permit the corporate ship to drift with the economic tide until a crisis situation arises and forces reformulation.

DYNAMIC CONTROL STRATEGIES

The use of general strategies discussed in Chapter 7 are frequently used as dynamic control measures, dynamic in the sense that they can be utilized to keep pace with the progress of significant strategic decisions in terms of product and business portfolios, and capital investments. The experience curve provides a display of accumulated units of production and costs per unit. The accumulated production is also an indication of market share. This measure combines cost control and market intelligence. The BCG business-product portfolio matrix reinforces the experience curve displaying market-share growth rate and relative market share. The corporate portfolio can be examined in its simplest form enabling management to make judgments about the need for further analysis of specific products or businesses. The portfolio can be judged in terms of cash flow from SBUs or products and cash requirements for growth of these segments and development of new corporate ventures.

The business-attractiveness measures are also related to portfolio analysis relating the business strengths to the scale of attractiveness and potential profit growth of business segments. These matrices provide a display in greater detail than that of BCG to enable management to make judgments about business performance in the marketplace and thus provide a guide to investment decisions.

The PIMS data bank and models provide a ready analysis of the factors influencing profitability and the extent of their influence on return on investment (ROI). The PIMS display provides further guidelines for management in terms of market share, product quality, marketing expenditures, R&D expenditures, investment intensity, and product quality.

SUMMARY AND GENERAL COMMENTS

The organizational design cannot be developed in isolation as a separate and distinct managerial effort. It must flow from the preceding phase of the strategic planning process and should reflect the basic economic and business objectives of the firm. This concept of strategy is based in part on contingency theory. Effective organization strategies can cover a wide range of structures developed to respond to opportunities and threats in the competitive environment, as perceived by management.

The contrasting organizational designs of Ford Motor Company and General Motors reinforce the concept that structure follows strategy. Ford's initial centralized structure was based on its root strategy of producing and marketing a basic, standardized, low-priced economy car. In contrast, General Motors developed a decentralized profit-center structure to accommodate a root strategy designed to produce and market automobiles for each viable market segment of the industry.

Growth and expansion can be major factors influencing organizational strategy. The growth process is likely to produce new functions, add new levels of management, and significantly increase staff as efforts are made by management to control an expanding, more complex organization.

The analysis of specific companies reinforces the effect of root and operational strategies on the development of organizational design. Companies which sell through representatives or wholesalers rather than develop their own sales force have a different organization composition and structure. Avon and Procter and Gamble developed unique organization structures to accommodate their root and operating strategies. Growth and expansion places stress on management by necessitating new levels of management and increased staff efforts to control a more complex organization. General Electric changed from a centralized organization to a decentralized structure and later adapted this structure to form strategic business units to better define the mission, objectives, and strategic plans of the company. This new structure reduced 170 or more departments to 43 clearly identified business units.

Restructuring usually creates the need for eliminating components and shifting personnel or eliminating specific positions. As a consequence, management is frequently reluctant to accept the need for reorganization and make the necessary adjustments.

The control strategy stems from and is interrelated with the organizational phase of the policymaking process. Control strategies should constantly reflect the company's operations as a total system encompassing precontrol, current control, and postcontrol.

Companies adapt their control systems to reflect their strategic design. Ford's highly centralized organization was managed by a simple and direct control system; General Motors' decentralized multiproduct organization demanded a complex profit-centered control system. The organization structures of Avon and Procter and Gamble resulted in the development of innovative control systems suited to their strategic designs.

Controls are primarily developed around the financial system which measures inputs into the organization. Basic economic objectives provide the basis for managerial control and the major quantitative measures of the effective performance of the firm.

SELECTED REFERENCES

Ansoff, H. I.: *Corporate Strategy* (New York: McGraw-Hill, 1965).

Duncan, R.: "Characteristics of Organizational Environments and Perceived Environmental Uncertainty," *Administrative Service Quarterly,* September 1972.

Galbraith, J.: *Designing Complex Organizations* (Reading, Mass.: Addison-Wesley, 1973).

Hofer, C. W.: "Toward A Contingency Theory of Business Strategy," *Academy of Management Journal,* December 1975.

Rumelt, R.: *Strategy, Structure, and Economic Performance* (Boston: Graduate School of Business Administration, Harvard University, 1974).

CASES ON BUSINESS POLICY FOR PART FIVE

The cases in Part Five emphasize the problems of organization and control confronted by policymakers in the management of diverse businesses and nonprofit institutions. In analyzing the cases in this section, the student has the opportunity to gain a better understanding of the development of organizational strategies and structures and of the design of control systems in both centralized and decentralized companies. The cases also stress the importance of the leadership role in the management of complex organizations and in the development of an effective management team to lead and guide the multiple subunits which make up large decentralized enterprises. Problems of growth and expansion and their effect on organization and control are also included in the case situations. In addition to the leadership function, the significant factors of executive motivation, compensation, and incentives are stressed in several of the cases.

Beta Electronics

The Beta Company was a leading producer of test and measuring equipment in the electronics field. Sales and earnings of the company had increased 18 to 20 percent each year for the past 10 years, and were expected to top $800 million within a few years. Beta employed approximately 7,500 people in the United States and 3,400 in Europe. The company was 27 years old, and from a humble beginning in a small 1,500-square-foot factory had grown to be a significant factor in a specialized sector of the electronics field. Beta's reputation was built on quality, and the entire organization was committed to excellence. The attention to product detail and reliability exhibited by the executives and work force was reflected in the industry's acceptance of the company's components.

Executives in Beta described the corporate culture as a "shirt-sleeve environment." Tom Beecher, one of the cofounders of the company, stated:

> We are literally a shirt-sleeve environment. That's how we started, and I see no reason to change. We built a solid reputation on getting out reliable, dependable products. I don't think requiring everybody to dress up is going to change our fortunes any.

The corporate culture extended beyond the "shirt-sleeve" philosophy. George Reynolds, vice president of operations, in discussing the environment of the company stated:

> The big bosses, Tom Beecher and Art Longstreet, have really worked at making this an egalitarian establishment. They want output and excellence, but no frills. There are no designated places in the parking lot except for visitors, and you can tell the cars of Tom and Art from the rest of the executives and work force, because they

drive Toyotas, one blue and one red. It's embarrassing for some of us that drive a Mercedes.

We don't even have an executive dining room. That's kind of ridiculous for a company our size. We have a stream of visitors every day, and most represent top-level companies. We have to take them down the freeway to Menlo Park or Palo Alto for lunch. It wastes a lot of time. Even if we had an executive dining room here, you still wouldn't be able to get a drink. Tom and Art don't go for that.

The most recent addition to the executive group, Ralph Rogers, came to Beta from a large electronics firm in the Palo Alto area, where he held the title of manager of human resources. He spent his first three months at Beta doing routine personnel functions and drafting a human resource plan. He held the title of vice president of human resources, and was surprised to find that the others in the executive group, while being friendly and supportive, did not seem to understand what his position entailed. Tom Beecher had hired him after several long interviews in which Tom did most of the talking, mainly relating his philosophy of the need for a clear expression of true moral values within the business enterprise, and in all dealings with customers.

After several months in the organization, Ralph became convinced that there was a distinct moral conviction that permeated the organization. He didn't know how to explain it, but he knew it was there. He attributed it, for the most part, to the founders of the company, Tom Beecher and Art Longstreet. In his study of the development of the company he found no evidence of any attempt to formalize management development within the organization. All management training was informal. There was no system or follow-up and appraisal. Art Longstreet had said:

> Let's not get formal about developing managers; this is too personal a matter. We have always used the buddy system here. Put the young exec with the older, experienced manager. Rotate him around to the various parts of the organization and then put him in the swim. If he's got it, he will survive and do a good job. Despite the size of the company Tom and I are always ready to help out executives. We are willing to listen, and we don't mind going down to the factory lines. Why in this main plant I think we know the names of all the managers and supervisors and a good number of the workers. We are committed to excellence at all levels, and most people around here know we better get it through performance. This includes the personal development of our executives. We are going to give all the help we can, but in the end, they are going to have to do it themselves.

Ralph Rogers didn't find anything particularly unusual in the backgrounds of the company founders to explain their dedication to creating an environment intent on fostering moral values and the pursuit of excellence. Both Beecher and Longstreet were graduates of M.I.T. (Massachusetts Institute of Technology) and came to California as young engineers on the staff of a large aerospace company. They did not have a strong religious background, but both attended church regularly and were active in promoting and contributing to social and charitable causes. When they started Beta, they encountered severe financial problems in their third year of operations. They elicited the cooperation and support of the executive staff and employee groups, who took significant salary cuts, and some contributed funds from their savings to aid the firm. Beecher and Longstreet never forgot this display of help and confidence, and were reputed to have made an almost religious vow to make Beta the finest company in the business. To show their appreciation they started a generous profit-sharing plan, paid exceptionally high salaries, and made it a practice to keep as close a contact with the entire employee group as possible. Despite the size of the company and the several plants and European operations, Rogers noted that both Beecher and Longstreet still made an heroic effort to keep close contact with all employee groups. This meant long hours and much traveling since they also were quite aware of their responsibilities as the chief executives of a company approaching a billion dollars in sales.

Through numerous discussions with the executive group and some of the key supervisors in the main plant, Rogers became aware of the fact that despite its size the company did not have a formal communications system. The informal atmosphere fostered person-to-person communications with the exception of significant changes and announcements which were accomplished through an official memo. There was also an in-house paper which was issued quarterly, although frequently it was issued only two times a year. This paper contained the usual personal announcements about the activities of the employees, and in every issue there were long statements from either Beecher or Longstreet, or both, about the importance of maintaining strong moral values as individuals and collectively as a company. The need for excellence in manufacture was detailed and stressed. In the articles that appeared in the company paper and in their executive meetings, both Beecher and Longstreet stressed the success of the Japanese and attributed this success to the strong commitment of the Japanese to the workers and their families and the pursuit of excellence.

Rogers found it difficult to secure the information he thought he needed to develop a human resources organization and plan for development. Part of his problem, he discovered, was due to the fact that the company did not have a formal organization chart which depicted the actual functioning of the company. There were no offices, except for three at the end of the spacious executive floor, two of which were used by Beecher and Longstreet, and the third for any executive that needed privacy for a visitor. These offices had large glass panels which gave a view of the "bull pen" where most headquarters executives worked.

There was a lack of formal systems throughout the company, and Rogers was convinced there was a lack of formal control over the executive group. He did find, however, that while the company did not have formal control systems or made much use of committees there was a Corporate Values Committee made up of the top 10 executives in the organization. This committee met once a month to discuss the "state of moral health" of the organization and in effect recommit themselves and Beta to maintaining the highest moral integrity. Various problems and situations of other corporations which exemplified high or low moral values were discussed at these meetings. The discourses frequently drifted into extolling the virtues of the "Japanese system." Tom Beecher, and occasionally Art Longstreet, were the leaders in directing the discussions in this vein.

Rogers was not sure that all the executives at the top, or for that matter supervisory and employee groups, "bought the Beta line." However, he did feel that there was a commitment to quality and a genuine sense of pride about being part of a successful organization dedicated to excellence and integrity. It was difficult to know how deep this feeling went, so Rogers accepted it as part of an unusual corporate culture—something that he had never experienced before.

The lack of formal systems was most evident in management development. Rogers was amazed at the decided lack of attention to management development in any formal sense. He had to admit that Beta had an excellent growth record that was not easily matched. He was also impressed with the caliber of the executive group and had to admit they were hard-working and dedicated. But he also detected an overwhelming preoccupation with the technical, production side of the business. It seemed to him that marketing and some facets of administration, including human resource development, were not given much attention or direction from the top. The engineer technicians were regarded as the most important people in the organization.

Prior to developing his human resource plan and recommendations for organizational changes, Rogers scheduled an interview of 30 minutes duration with Beecher and Longstreet. He knew he wouldn't have much time because Beecher was due to leave for Washington, D.C., and Longstreet had scheduled a trip to visit the European installations. Both were scheduled to leave in the early afternoon. Rogers had found that tight schedules were a way of life at Beta, so he felt fortunate to have some time alone with top management.

Rogers began the meeting by presenting his ideas about the need for a formal management development program and also offered some suggestions for organization changes. Tom Beecher replied to Roger's comments about the lack of systems in this fashion:

> Ralph, I appreciate the work you have been doing on this, but I also know that it takes some time to learn our system, and we do have a system. I admit it is very personal—actually person to person. We all try to keep track of each other. One helps the other, and we really get a lot done this way. You take our Corporate Values Committee; this is an excellent vehicle for communication. We can and do discuss important strategic problems at these meetings. This doesn't detract any from our dedication to maintaining true moral values in the organization. We do have control despite the way it looks when you are not familiar with the operations of the company. Our quality control systems in our plants are probably the best in the valley. Our production scheduling and manufacturing is second to none.

Art Longstreet added:

> Our management is tested by cost performance and schedule performance. We are all cost-conscious, as well as quality-conscious. I admit not many of the executive group

have direct profit responsibility. We limit that pretty much to the division vice presidents. Mostly our managers don't know what ROI (return on investment) means. We don't tamper with R&D either. They are given very explicit directives as to what we want and where we want to go; then they pretty much have a free hand.

Tom Beecher interjected:

As far as management development is concerned, Art and I have always believed that it was a personal matter. We as an organization had to offer help and encouragement and provide the opportunities, but the rest was up to the individual. We both realize that this company is changing rapidly because of growth. Something needs to be done about management development, our organization, and our internal systems. We must accept the needed changes. You have our full support, so continue with your planning. However, we don't want to destroy our value systems in this organization. Nor do we want to lose our person-to-person, first-name rapport with the executive groups.

The meeting abruptly ended when Beecher's secretary interrupted to remind him it was time to go to the airport.

Later in the day, while reviewing his notes on the meeting, Rogers wondered how to interpret the remarks of Beecher and Longstreet. How far could he go in recommending the needed organizational changes and getting a management development program under way? Where was the logical starting place?

Coastal Chemical

Dr. Raymond Wilson, chairman of the board and chief executive officer of Coastal Chemical, in commenting on the role of research and development in the company stated:

> We have always been committed to research in the chemical business. You don't have much choice if you intend to progress and keep pace with today's rapidly changing technology. In the past several years, however, Coastal, like many other chemical companies, has been placed in a cost squeeze. Our basic raw materials have increased significantly in price, and this has affected our margins. We are now at a crossroad, and we must reappraise our corporate objectives and align our R&D efforts to support and aid in the development of our overall company efforts. The price of feedstock for our petrochemical business has caused us to take a real hard look at our efforts in this area. We would like to move the company into high-value products rather than stress the commodity products, which have low margins and are intensely competitive. But we may have to do some retrenchment before we are in a position to move into the more promising fields. We need to change the direction of our present R&D efforts to put Coastal in a better competitive position.
>
> In recent years our rate of return has not been satisfactory. While we showed some improvement in 1981 over 1980, the company is significantly below our 1975 net earnings (see Exhibits 1 and 2). In the period 1975–1981 inflation has increased our costs of products and services and our petrochemical activities have been hampered by the OPEC pricing. But in this time period our R&D hasn't come up with new viable product lines that pay off on the bottom line. Our efforts in the last several years have been directed toward bringing our R&D activities in line with our economic objectives. We reduced our R&D budget in 1981 and showed increased net earnings.
>
> However, we are still faced with many important questions which are paramount

EXHIBIT 1
Coastal Chemical Company
Consolidated Statement of Net Earnings
Year Ended 31 December
($1,000)

	1975	1976	1977	1978	1979	1980	1981
Net sales & operating revenues	$405,445	$419,189	$488,931	$490,961	$526,919	$548,206	$569,000
Miscellaneous revenues	767	824	1,383	1,521	1,784	1,988	2,274
Total revenues	$406,212	$420,013	$490,314	$492,482	$528,703	$550,194	$571,274
Costs and expenses:							
Cost of products & services sold	$253,596	$261,752	$317,971	$318,610	$343,788	$359,721	$374,055
R&D expenses*	9,279	11,751	12,898	16,104	16,854	14,276	13,417*
Selling, administrative, and general expenses	65,469	67,669	73,207	73,599	80,114	85,199	89,893
Depreciation of property, plant, and equipment	28,627	30,501	43,104	44,817	46,618	47,073	48,569
Pension plans	6,447	6,331	6,913	6,986	7,871	6,477	5,997
Interest	46	1,416	2,904	3,623	2,650	–	–
Provision of bonus	1,811	1,300	1,678	1,768	1,995	2,149	2,296
Loss on disposal of property and equipment	68	–	–	–	–	–	21
Federal taxes on income	20,000	19,400	15,000	13,000	14,000	17,500	18,500
Total expenses	$385,343	$400,120	$473,675	$478,507	$513,890	$532,395	$552,748
Earnings from operations	$ 20,869	$ 19,893	$ 16,639	$ 13,975	$ 14,813	$ 17,799	$ 18,526
Extraneous gains or losses (after taxes)	2,481	–	–	–	–	–	–
Net earnings	$ 23,350	$ 19,893	$ 16,639	$ 13,975	$ 14,813	$ 17,799	$ 18,526

*Royalty income was offset against R&D expenses.

EXHIBIT 2
Consolidated Balance Sheet
Year Ended 31 December
($1,000)

	1975	1976
Current assets:		
Cash	$ 49,783	$ 16,271
U.S. government securities - at cost & accrued int. (approx. mkt.)	1,178	20,714
Marketable securities - at cost & accrued int. (approx. mkt.)	–	–
Trade accounts receivable, net	42,799	46,551
Other accounts and claims receivable, net	1,947	2,964
Inventories:		
Finished & in-process products & raw materials	47,741	48,499
Materials, repair parts, other supplies	6,695	6,767
Total inventories	$ 54,436	$ 55,266
Prepaid taxes, insurance, & other expenses	1,825	9,316
Total current assets	$151,968	$151,082
Investments and other assets:		
Long-term sulfur properties sale contract	$ 644	$ 545
Refundable federal taxes on income	2,791	2,791
Miscellaneous investments & other assets, including investments in foreign affiliates, at cost	4,333	4,313
Total investments and other assets	$ 7,768	$ 7,649
Property, plant, and equipment at cost, less accumulated depreciation:		
Land	$ 19,461	$ 20,706
Buildings, machinery, and equipment	585,561	680,395
Construction in progress	82,581	102,464
Total	$687,603	$803,563
Less accumulated depreciation	356,860	407,572
Total property, plant, & equipment	$330,743	$395,993
Total assets	$490,479	$554,724
Current liabilities:		
Trade accounts payable	$ 33,685	$ 30,508
Accrued pension plan costs	4,872	7,045
Salaries, wages, and amounts withheld from employees	10,827	10,624
Payroll, property, and other taxes	11,007	13,632
Provision for self-insurance	1,863	1,856
Income taxes payable	14,057	7,206
Portion of term loans payable within one year	–	–
Total current liabilities	$ 76,311	$ 70,871
Term loans payable to bank less amount due within one year	$ –	$ 56,601

1977	1978	1979	1980	1981
$ 17,053	$ 26,183	$ 18,623	$ 20,130	$ 16,206
18,501	398	–	–	–
–	–	14,359	10,813	10,136
37,115	59,872	52,925	60,536	65,907
3,364	3,056	1,782	1,746	2,988
69,157	61,861	62,084	62,546	66,597
7,491	7,496	7,896	8,109	7,910
$ 76,648	$ 69,357	$ 69,980	$ 70,655	$ 74,507
8,839	9,145	9,121	10,231	11,007
$161,520	$168,011	$ 166,790	$ 174,111	$ 180,751
$ 446	$ 347	$ 248	$ 149	$ –
–	–	–	–	–
3,311	2,747	4,412	9,302	19,551
$ 3,757	$ 3,094	$ 4,660	$ 9,451	$ 19,551
$ 24,182	$ 27,809	$ 28,826	$ 29,315	$ 29,259
826,482	861,704	981,009	1,026,096	1,065,561
19,379	62,129	10,158	13,991	9,911
$870,043	$951,642	$1,019,993	$1,069,402	$1,104,731
487,919	575,938	667,610	714,683	762,431
$382,124	$375,704	$ 352,383	$ 354,719	$ 342,300
$547,401	$546,809	$ 523,833	$ 538,281	$ 542,602
$ 28,695	$ 27,382	$ 26,286	$ 27,806	$ 21,087
6,568	8,071	7,804	6,076	7,244
12,078	14,716	16,031	16,189	16,593
20,482	22,222	22,110	23,898	20,651
1,855	1,675	1,584	1,618	–
14,351	9,569	14,306	12,260	15,503
11,011	29,183	–	–	–
$ 95,040	$112,818	$ 88,121	$ 87,847	$ 81,078
$ 72,542	$ 32,242	$ –	$ –	$ –

EXHIBIT 2 (*continued*)
Consolidated Balance Sheet
Year Ended 31 December
($1,000)

	1975	1976
Shareholders' investment:		
Preferred stock, $100 par value		
to be redeemed Dec. 31, 1976	$ 73,617	$ 72,101
Common stock, $1 par value*	7,897	7,907
Additional paid-in capital	160,206	160,974
Revaluation of sulfur properties	2,461	2,084
Retained earnings	169,987	184,186
Total shareholders' equity	$414,168	$427,252
Total liabilities	$490,479	$554,724

*10,000,000 shares authorized between 1975–1979;
50,000,000 shares authorized in 1979.

to our strategic planning. Some of these questions are:

1 Should the company try simply to maintain its present level of business and to become more and more efficient and profitable in its chosen field?
2 Should it try to expand within its current field and increase sales of existing products, at the same time developing new uses and new products in its basic line?
3 Should the company broaden its interests and move into entirely new fields, presumably of higher profitability?

Depending on the answer we reach in our corporate review, the R&D department should then be able to tailor its own objectives to meet the company objectives. There are four principal directions of activities that we think the R&D department should consider:

1 Concentrate research on those cost-reduction and product-improvement projects with the greatest remaining potential for profit.
2 Search for new ways for existing products.
3 Diversify through R&D into new fields.
4 Seek government research contracts in fields where technical skills of the department are particularly well adapted.

To accomplish these objectives we must be certain of our R&D expenditures producing results. We intend to exert stricter budgetary control over R&D. We need to show more immediate results; however, we realize we must also make long-range commitments.

CORPORATE DEVELOPMENT

The Coastal Chemical Company was organized for the purpose of manufacturing sulfuric and nitric acids for industrial use. The company survived the

1977	1978	1979	1980	1981
$ –	$ –	$ –	$ –	$ –
7,907	7,951	8,100	8,108	8,117
160,974	162,116	170,439	171,031	171,773
1,702	1,324	942	564	–
209,236	230,358	256,231	270,731	281,634
$379,819	$401,749	$435,712	$450,434	$461,524
$547,401	$546,809	$523,833	$538,281	$542,602

Great Depression of the 1930s and diversified its lines greatly during World War II, particularly in the field of industrial plastics. The development of petrochemicals, which first became important during the decade of the 1930s, began to offer increasing competition to the nonpetrochemical companies, particularly after the new and inexpensive methods of obtaining hydrogen from petroleum were invented.

In addition, the demands being made on the chemical industry for new synthetic materials, fuels, and lubes in connection with the missile rocket and space programs being promulgated after World War II by the U.S. Department of Defense, and later the National Aeronautical and Space Agency, offered new and lucrative markets for fundamental chemical research and development. Because of the intensive heat encountered on reentry of the missile or spacecraft into the earth's atmosphere and other hostile environmental factors encountered in space, all material for hardware, fuels, and lubes practically had to be revolutionized, and this required vast amounts of scientific research.

The chemical industry had been research-minded from its very inception, and the Coastal Chemical Company was no exception to the rule. As was stated in a company history written many years later, "... [the company's top management] became convinced that expenditures for research and development had cash value, and to lag behind in technical development was likely to cost heavily."

SCOPE OF COASTAL'S R&D ACTIVITIES

The basic long-standing R&D policy of the company was:

1 To help the manufacturing department solve problems resulting from the tremendous demand for industrial chemicals of all kinds

2 To learn how to make these products in improved quality from lower-grade raw materials as high-grade raw materials became scarce

The Coastal Chemical Company did not enter the petrochemical field until after World War II, when it purchased a small petrochemical company. The petrochemical company was a wartime project and had purchased its raw materials from a nearby oil refinery, converting them into a limited range of synthetic resins. This petrochemical company had already established a small research laboratory for the purpose of helping customers find uses for its products. This laboratory was taken over by the parent company's R&D department.

After the acquisition of the petrochemical laboratory the scope of the Coastal Chemical R&D department was expanded to include petrochemical research and development. The director of research, John Stearns, felt this expansion to be justified, as the company's overall objective was understood by top management to be " . . .in the development of any technically based operation or product which our capital, manufacturing, marketing, or technical assets render commercially attractive."

GROWTH OF R&D DEPARTMENT

Acting under this general policy, the Coastal Chemical Company rapidly expanded the scope of both the chemical and petrochemical research, with heavy emphasis on petrochemical research (see Exhibit 3). The director of research was elevated to the rank of vice president when petrochemical research and development was placed under his jurisdiction. He was also made a member of the "inside" board of directors of Coastal Chemical Company.[1] (The growth of Coastal Chemical's R&D department is shown in Exhibit 4).

COMMERCIAL VALUE OF R&D ACTIVITIES

The vice president of the parent company's R&D department had the economic section of the main laboratory prepare a five-year study of the estimated economic value[2] to the company of all chemical and petrochemical R&D. The study found that the economic value of the R&D work to the company averaged $60 million per year for the period (see Exhibit 5).

The report further pointed out that the estimated economic value to the company did not and could not show the intangible values derived from enhancing

---

[1]Coastal Chemical Company had long had an "inside" board of directors. Other members included the president, executive vice president, and the heads of the manufacturing, marketing, finance, and legal departments. In the 1970s, five outside directors were appointed.

[2]That amount of business activity created as a result of the activities of the R&D department. Net economic value is the total economic value minus the developmental costs involved. The value derived from R&D activities may not be traceable directly to a specific amount of sales increase or other indicators and/or a specific product. Other exogenous and endogenous variables, such as a new use created by the general public for the product in question, may have caused the observed increase.

EXHIBIT 3
PETROCHEMICAL PRODUCTS AND THEIR AREAS OF USE

End products

1 Basic chemicals:
  a Hydrogen
  b Chlorine
  c Hydrogen peroxide
  d etc.
2 Foams, both rigid & flexible
3 Fertilizers
4 Solid rocket fuel binder
5 Gasoline additives
6 Dry-cleaning chemicals
7 Rocket lubricants
8 Synthetic fibers
9 Hydraulic fluids
10 Cleaning compounds for machinery
11 Caulking compounds
12 Detergents & soaps
13 Swimming pool disinfectants
14 Cosmetics
15 Dye
16 Wrapping materials

Industries

Product	Agriculture	Automotive	Building & construction	Chemical	Cosmetic	Dyestuff	Ferrous metal	Food & beverages	Fuel & power	Glass & ceramic	Highway construction & maintenance	Leather processing	Nonferrous metal	Paint	Paper	Petroleum	Pharmaceutical	Plastics, resins, & film	Printing	Refrigeration & air conditioning	Rubber	Sanitation	Soap & surfactant	Textile	Water treating
Oxides:																									
Ethylene	×	×		×		×			×					×		×	×						×		
Propylene		×		×		×								×		×	×					×	×		
Glycols:																									
Ethylene	×	×	×	×		×		×	×	×	×			×	×	×	×	×	×	×	×				
Diethylene	×	×	×	×		×		×	×	×	×			×	×	×	×	×	×	×	×				
Polyethylene		×		×	×	×	×			×			×					×	×	×				×	
Polypropylene		×		×														×		×	×			×	
Glycerin:																									
Glycol ethers	×	×	×	×	×	×	×	×	×	×		×	×	×	×	×	×	×	×		×		×	×	
Surfactants	×	×	×	×	×	×	×	×	×			×	×	×	×	×	×	×			×	×	×	×	×
Chlorinated	×	×	×	×		×		×	×			×	×	×	×	×	×	×	×	×	×	×	×	×	×

513

EXHIBIT 4
TOTAL R&D EXPENSES AND PERSONNEL, 1972–1981

Year	Chemical R&D expense, $ million	Petrochemical R&D expense, $ million	Combined R&D expense, $ million	R&D personnel,* number		
				Professional†	Technical	Supplying
1972	8.48	0.80	9.28	380	640	165
1974	10.90	0.85	11.75	467	730	187
1976	11.70	1.20	12.90	476	730	178
1978	13.55	2.55	16.10‡	510	778	174
1981	13.45	3.40	16.85	459	608	140

*Includes the home and subsidiary plants R&D department personnel.
†The majority of professional workers had their Ph.D.s in chemistry or chemical engineering. All were college graduates with at least a bachelor's degree in these fields.
‡For the last three years of the period, 1979–81 inclusive, total research and development expenditures, including production research, were from $16 to $17 million per year. Of this amount about 80 percent was spent on chemical and 20 percent on petrochemical research and development.

the R&D stature of the company by the publication of professional papers, cooperative studies either through committees of professional societies or with other companies, or patents obtained as a result of either company or individual research.[3] The vice president of the R&D department felt that this department

[3] The policy of the department was to allow every professional employee up to 10 percent of his or her time for private research on any subject in which he or she was interested. It was not required that the private project have prospects of immediate economic value to the company, but the project had to be related to the general field of chemical product and process research. Many times private projects, if and when they showed promise of success, became company-sponsored projects.

EXHIBIT 5
PERCENTAGE BREAKDOWN OF ECONOMIC VALUE TO THE COMPANY FROM TOTAL
RESEARCH ACTIVITIES, 1977–1981

	Company's estimated breakdown of the economic value to the company derived from each type of research	R&D department's claimed share of the estimated economic value to the company
Products improvement research	16.64	25.2
Process improvement research	13.00	85.0
Product specification services	44.74	6.5
New product research	5.35	65.7
New process development	16.10	98.6
Investment analysis studies	3.91	65.0
Supporting activities	0.26	83.0
	100.00	40.0 (weighted average)

had achieved an outstanding reputation with respect to its professional capabilities (see Exhibit 6).

Although the company had never considered the procuring of United States or foreign patents as a primary objective of the R&D activities, such activity was bringing in relatively small but steady income from licenses. Income from royalty payments was treated as an offset to R&D expenditures.

Another direct source of income to the R&D department was reimbursements received under federal government contracts for expenses incurred in connection with government research projects. Such payments averaged about $750,000 annually and covered both synthetic materials and lube research work.

CHANGES IN COASTAL CHEMICAL COMPANY'S R&D ORGANIZATION, POLICIES, AND PROCEDURES

After the corporate review was completed in January of 1982, the board of directors announced a major corporate reorganization and realignment of operating functions of the consolidated group of companies, one of which was the newly formed Coastal Petrochemical Company. The purposes of this reorganization were: (1) to reduce the number of subsidiary companies, and (2) to realign the operating activities to increase the return on investment and increase profits.

The corporate reorganization was designed to create what the parent company called "two primary profit centers: (1) manufacturing and marketing of chemical products and (2) manufacturing and marketing of petrochemical products." The parent company retained direct financial control over the consolidated group of companies. The further expansion of the company into the petrochemical field was to be strictly limited for the ensuing five years, as capital available for such expansion was expected to be scarce.

In connection with the second objective, Dr. Wilson announced a new corporate policy for the consolidated group of companies. In brief, this policy stated that for the ensuing five years (unless changed by action of the board of directors of the parent company) the overall objective of the consolidated companies would be to lift the chemical business to a satisfactory return on invest-

EXHIBIT 6
OUTPUT OF PATENTS GRANTED, PAPERS PUBLISHED, AND
REPORTS ISSUED DURING THE PERIOD 1972–1980

	1972	1974	1976	1978	1980
Patents issued	62	87	131	118	122
Papers published	27	35	34	42	66
Reports issued	18	28	66	40	48

ment. Product diversification and exploitation of new products would be small for these years.

In April 1982, three months after the new corporate policy was announced, a new directive as to the objectives and function of the R&D departments of the parent and petrochemical companies was issued. The essential items in the directive were:

1 The research and development operation throughout the consolidated companies would be a "limited growth" operation for the next several years, or until modified by action of the parent company.

2 Technological research by the parent company would be maintained at a level sufficient to capitalize on present patent assets and service licenses. Diversification and exploitation of new chemical fields arising from new research would be small for the next five years.

3 The R&D department of the parent company would restrict its research primarily to relatively short-term product and process work,[4] and would aim it primarily at cost and profit improvement. Such long-term efforts as were appropriate should be directed primarily toward new concepts and uses for industrial chemicals and plastics.

4 The Government Contract Division of the parent company's R&D department would continue to conduct government contract research at its own laboratory or elsewhere as required.

5 The R&D department of the parent company no longer had any responsibility to conduct research for subsidiaries[5] unless specific project budgets were provided by the subsidiary company, even if the subsidiaries were doing R&D work for the parent company.

6 The R&D department of the parent company should complete its review of the R&D needs for manufacturing and marketing of nonpetroleum industrial chemicals and should establish programs at its laboratory which would satisfy the requirement of promoting the nonpetroleum business.

7 The R&D department of the Coastal Petrochemical Company (now independent) would be commensurate with the needs of the present product lines and level of sales.

8 Coastal Petrochemical Company's R&D department was charged with defensive research and technical service, but with a minimum of long-range or fundamental research.

9 Coastal Petrochemical Company's research in behalf of licensee support would be of two categories: (a) defensive work designed to fulfill existing commitments, and (b) offensive research explicitly pointed toward royalty income from new licensees.

10 The management of all subsidiaries should give serious thought to their technical needs, and, for the present, should put their R&D work on a contract

---

[4] For definitions of the various categories of research, see Appendix A.
[5] After the reorganization there were four subsidiary companies including foreign subsidiaries.

basis with the existing parent company's R&D department or if necessary with outside research institutions. (No more research laboratories were to be established.)

With reference to point 6 in the above directive, John Stearns, vice president of R&D, had initiated, prior to the issuance of the R&D directive but with the approval of the company, a departmental study of his own. The purpose of this study was to determine the changes required in research activities by the new company objectives. After the research directive was received, Stearns suggested and received the approval of Coastal's chairman, Raymond Wilson, to hire an outside business consulting firm which had specialized in studying R&D operations and objectives in order to check the department's own study and conclusions. The firm was immediately employed, and started its studies.

The consultant's report recommended somewhat more drastic and speedier action than the departmental report, although it was highly complimentary with respect to the caliber of the professional staff of Coastal Chemical Company's R&D department and the laboratory space and equipment provided by the company. The criticisms in the consultant's report were leveled at (1) the over-organization of the R&D department, (2) the lack of overall control provided under the program system, resulting in unnecessary increases in costs and delays in completing specific projects, and (3) the lack of effective and rapid communication between the lower supervisory and working levels of the R&D department and the user of the research results.

The consultant recommended: (1) that the maximum number of departmental supervisory levels between the professional worker and the vice president of the department be reduced from 7 to 4, and (2) that a "project" method of operation be substituted for the "program" method.

Under the project method a "project leader" would be appointed for each proposed project. The project leader would be provided with an adequate professional staff to perform the various phases of the work required, regardless of the location of workers in the department's formal organization structure. Also for each project team a "user representative" or "client" would be appointed to ensure direct and continuous contact between the using department or client company and the project researchers. The "project" method of operation would, therefore, satisfy both the second and third objections made by the consultant to current methods of organization.

Cost control would be exercised by monthly reports of actual project expenditures compared with budget authorizations. Copies of these monthly cost statements would be furnished to the vice president, the project leader, and the client representative. If it appeared that the objectives or budget of the project needed revision, it would be the responsibility of the project leader to prepare recommendations of such changes for the vice president and the client. This in effect would give continuous control over the project and enable client users to have a better understanding of the precise problems being encountered by the workers on the project. It was thought that this would decrease the criticism of "using" departments that the research process was so slow that the results had lost their timeliness before the program was completed.

In addition to these three main points, the consultant's report recommended a 25 percent cut in professional staff of the Coastal Chemical Company's department. (The consultant's report to the parent company did not indicate what the organization of an independent R&D department of the Coastal Petrochemical Company should be.)

While the departmental and consultant studies were being made, Raymond Wilson and the board decided that the branch laboratory at the petrochemical plant which had been maintained by the parent company's R&D department would be closed as soon as possible, leaving the Coastal Petrochemical Company with only a small R&D department, whose duties would be solely confined to assisting customers or licensees. It was also agreed between the Coastal Petrochemical Company and the Coastal Chemical Company that the former would contract with the parent company's R&D department for any long-range fundamental research it needed performed. Therefore, the parent company's R&D department would retain its petrochemical section, albeit with a reduced staff, at its main laboratory.

The parent company's research directive had authorized its R&D department to continue its U.S. government contract work and perform it either in its "propulsion" laboratory or subcontract it out to others, as required. Therefore, no changes were made in the laboratory facilities for this purpose.

The petrochemical laboratory at the petrochemical plant was closed. A few of the professional personnel remained to operate the Customer and Licensee Research Laboratory authorized to the Petrochemical Company. Some of the surplus professional personnel were moved to the main chemical laboratory, and a few were released. Surplus equipment no longer needed at the petrochemical laboratory was either sold or shipped to the parent company's laboratory.

Inasmuch as it was realized by the Coastal Chemical Company's R&D department that the chemical product and process research and development work would both be reduced in quantity and changed in direction, a departmental reorganization plan was submitted by both the departmental and consultant studies. After much heated debate, differences between the proposals were adjusted, and a departmental reorganization plan was announced and made effective (see Exhibit 7).

At the same time the new departmental organization was put into effect, the operating technique was changed from the "program" to the "project" method. Departmental officials had some skepticism as to how well the project system would work for long-range fundamental or exploratory research. On the other hand, they felt that the department had in fact been using the project method of operation for short-range product or process research, hence had no objection to the change in nomenclature. (For the form in which a research project was presented to the vice president of research for approval, see Appendix B.)

With respect to budget retrenchment, no serious attempt was made to

EXHIBIT 7
LINE OF AUTHORITY
COASTAL CHEMICAL COMPANY'S R&D DEPARTMENT BEFORE AND AFTER
DEPARTMENTAL REORGANIZATION

Before reorganization	After reorganization
Director-General	Vice president
Manager of chemical research laboratory	
Director of chemical research	Director of chemical research
Director of product research	
Area director	General supervisor
Division director	
Section leader	Project leader
Group leader	
Professional worker	Professional worker

rewrite the parent company's R&D departmental budget since it had been made up six months prior to the corporate reorganization. The consultant did, however, use the departmental budget as the basis for recommending both the changes in direction and total amount of expenditures to be made under the new parent company directives. The overall decrease recommended for chemical research was quite small (5.4 percent), but how and where the money was to be spent represented a significant change in direction (see Exhibit 8).

In his annual report to the president of his company and the board of directors, John Stearns, the vice president of R&D, stated that chemical research expenditures had increased about 3 percent but that owing to the removal of petrochemical research activities at the petrochemical plant, petrochemical research costs had declined 87.5 percent. After adjustments due to the transfer of the chemical laboratory at the petrochemical plant to the Coastal Chemical laboratory, the parent company's R&D department had lost 43 employees but had taken on 31 (most new employees) so that the net change was a decrease of 12. The professional staff of the R&D department numbered 386 and the technical and supporting staffs 629.

Preliminary budget forecasts for the years 1982–1984 indicated a decrease in research expenditures by the R&D department of 10 percent, with little or no further decrease to occur in 1985. Human power would also be reduced to what Stearns felt was an irreducible minimum of 300 professional employees. The technical staff would be reduced to a minimum in 1983, and might have to be increased slightly in 1984 to offset in part the reduction of professional workers.

JOHN STEARNS'S APPRAISAL OF COASTAL'S PROSPECTS

In reviewing the activities of the past year John Stearns, vice president of R&D, stated:

EXHIBIT 8
CHANGES IN DIRECTION OF RESEARCH

Type of activity	5-year average 1977–1981, %	Recommended distribution, %
Product improvement research	16.75	30.7
Process improvement research	11.10	51.1
Product specification services	8.00	6.7
New product research	21.25	2.8
New process development	20.80	4.1
Investment analysis studies	9.90	3.0
Supporting activities	12.20	1.6
	100.00	100.0

Type of activity	Recommended distribution,* %
Fundamental and/or exploratory research	4.0
Defensive research	49.0
Offensive research	5.6
Research technical service	6.4
Technical services (development)	28.5
Patents and licensing	6.5
	100.0

*Based on an offensive-defensive classification.

It is difficult to maintain a productive R&D department if the company policy has decreed a decrease in R&D expenditures at a time when efforts should be made to expand R&D activities to attain the announced objectives of the company. The dismantling of the petrochemical R&D facility will not enhance our position in this field. By our own admission we need to upgrade our product lines. Curtailing expenditures where they are most needed is not the answer to the development of new products and processes. Our petrochemical products have become too much of a commodity line.

I am not too enthused about the changes recommended by Chairman Wilson, or the consultant we hired to review the R&D department's organization. I need direct contact with the research staff, but at the same time I have to be a manager. I think we should be thinking about a new organizational design that will aid us and give the guidance needed to develop the products in the promising areas of chemicals and petrochemicals. Several of the major chemical companies have made a commitment to biotechnology, genetics, and industrial microbiology. In the area of petrochemicals we should use this base to consider enzymes, petroleeching and several other new areas that have recently been exploited. Our staff is competent, but they need support, not constantly shifting objectives. Several of the large chemical companies have made big commitments into the new exotic fields. This is not a time for contraction; the opportunities for expansion are tremendous in the field of chemistry and pharmaceuticals. In this company we have only touched on the surface of the new areas open to research and development.

APPENDIX A: Classifications of Research and Development Projects

R&D projects are classified in many different ways. Most industrial researchers tend to use the following threefold classification. Each classification overlaps the others, so the qualifying adjective(s) used is not necessarily the only one that could be applied.

I By length of time likely to be consumed in carrying out the research assignment

    A *Short-term.* A project likely to be completed in not more than one year, and certainly in less than two.

    B *Long-term.* A project which is likely to take from five to ten years to bring to completion.

II By type of competitive advantage sought

    A *Offensive.* Research that is directed toward finding entirely new products or processes including both manufacturing and marketing aspects.

    B *Defensive.* Research that is directed toward improving present products and/or processes for the purpose of keeping the company competitive in the existing marketplace.

III By objective of the research

    A *Pure or basic research.* This is research undertaken solely for the purpose of increasing the scientific knowledge of mankind, regardless of whether or not the project has economic or social value. It is the domain of the universities and scientific foundations. Little or no pure research is undertaken in industrial laboratories, but industrial firms can and do participate through grants and donations to universities and engineering schools.

    B *Fundamental research.*[1] It is sometimes known by empirical experience certain results can be attained under specified conditions, but the "why" or "how" they happen is not known. Fundamental research is undertaken to find the "why" or "how" the known result is obtained. It is generally long-term research, with a high degree of uncertainty as to the results which will be obtained from the project.

    C *Explanatory research.*[1] This takes the results of pure research and attempts to apply them to known products or processes to find out "what" will happen through the application of the pure research results to existing products or processes. It is considered to be somewhat more commercially oriented than fundamental research and to have somewhat better chances of profitable results. It is generally long-term research.

    D *Product and/or process research.* This may be either for the purpose (1) of discovering entirely new products or processes of commercial value, or (2) of improving existing products and processes. This type of research is closely allied to "offensive" research for (1) and "defensive research" for (2). Numerically speaking, most projects are short-term of themselves; but there is a continuing flow of projects, so that product or process research usually is the "bread and butter" work of many industrial research departments.

    E *Government research.* These projects have been mainly directed to defense and space projects. It is estimated that the government accounts for approximately 70 percent of total R&D spending in the United States. Total industrial R&D spending was approximately $28 billion in 1980. The chemical industry expended approximately $89.8 million in 1980.

---

[1] Fundamental and exploratory research are sometimes linked together under the name of "advanced technical" research.

APPENDIX B: Project Proposal
R&D Department–Coastal Chemical Co.

Project Title	Project No.	
	Project Leader	

Starting Date:	Estimated Controllable Costs	$M
	Estimated Overhead Costs	$M _____
Target Date:	Total	$M
	Estimated Capital Costs	$M

Urgency of Completion:

Technical Objective: (The technology to be acquired.)

Approach: (Main steps with key personnel and any major new equipment required.)

Prepared By: Date:

Commercial Objective and Benefits Expected:

Alternatives:

Our Strengths and Weaknesses:

What would be required for commercialization if technically successful?

Professional Team Members:

Client Department:
Client Representative:

Schedule of Reviews and Reports: (Types; Dates; To Whom Made)

Multitech International

"We are producing and selling approximately 75 percent of our product in overseas markets," stated Eric Nittzel, chairman of the board and chief executive officer of Multitech, a Swedish company with SKr 10.5 billion in sales (SKr. Swedish krona of 10.5 billion = approximately 2.3 billion dollars). Multitech produced a wide range of electrical, industrial, and commercial office products in 20 countries in various parts of the world. (See Exhibit 1.) Nittzell explained that he was in the process of bringing into the headquarters in Stockholm as many of his area and country managing directors as he could to discuss some of the problems being encountered between the headquarters office and the subsidiaries.

Nittzell said:

Our problem is probably not much different than that of many other companies in our same position. Communications are very difficult when you are dealing in great distances, different cultures, and different product lines. We sometimes forget that we have almost 400 companies in our organization. This perplexing problem of centralization vs. decentralization has been around a long time, and it is tough. You never know how far to go in either direction. Do you keep your hands off the subsidiaries? How far do you go? How much control should you exercise? It seems as though whatever position you adopt, you're bound to have problems. We have had declining profits in some of our subsidiaries in the past several years, and we have had to engage in recentralization to try to control costs and improve margins. Decentralization is great when it works, but unfortunately it doesn't always work smoothly. One of the real challenges is the difficulty of trying to instill into managing directors the need for strategic planning. We work hard trying to get our strategic thinking understood, but I am not so sure we are getting it across to the managing directors of our

EXHIBIT I

MULTITECH INTERNATIONAL WORLDWIDE SALES, PLANTS, AND FACILITIES

Country	Sales, billions, SKr	Plants and facilities
Europe		
Sweden - Domestic	2.240	30
France	1.400	5
United Kingdom	0.780	4
West Germany	0.500	4
Switzerland	0.460	4
Norway	0.450	1
Denmark	0.270	1
Finland	0.250	1
Italy	0.300	2
Holland	0.220	1
Spain	0.180	1
Other	0.300	–
Total Europe	7.350	54
North America		
United States	1.440	8
Canada	0.270	2
Mexico	0.490	3
Total North America	2.200	13
South America & Central America		
Brazil	0.190	3
Argentina	0.140	2
Columbia	0.050	1
Venezuela	0.038	1
Costa Rica	0.008	–
Guatemala	0.004	1
Total South & Central America	0.430	8
Oceania		
Australia	0.170	2
New Zealand	0.020	–
Singapore	0.040	1
Total Oceania	0.230	3
Asia	0.240	–
Africa	0.050	–
Total	10.500	78

subsidiaries. We spend a great deal of time on our planning here in Stockholm; we are not just reviewing last year's plans and budgets and making extrapolations for next year. We have attempted in the Swedish tradition to permit a great deal of autonomy to our foreign units. We really try to keep hands off unless they seek headquarters' help or a severe problem occurs. We want them to perform the day-to-day operations and implement the strategy developed here at headquarters. We give the area directors and managing directors a great deal of authority and responsibility, and we expect them to produce results.

Managers must realize, however, that all areas of the world are not the same, and our operations in various parts of the world are not similar in product line or sales turnover. Our operations in the United States, United Kingdom, and France are very large in relation to other foreign operations. By necessity, we must give them more attention and, while I don't like to say it, intervene more frequently than we do with our businesses in other countries. We don't want to get into the position of some other large European companies that have extensive operations in the United States. Their hands-off policy has been to the extreme. Sooner or later they will have to step in and provide stronger direction. I know, of course, that they have been deterred somewhat by the fear of possible antitrust action by the United States.

At the Stockholm meeting of area managers and managing directors, many complaints were made, particularly by the managing directors. The most common complaint centered on the strategic planning of headquarters. The managing director of the Swiss subsidiaries commented on the need for greater participation by the foreign companies in developing the overall strategy of the company. He stated:

Strategy should not be confined to headquarters. Management in the subsidiaries has something to contribute. Headquarters does not have the knowledge of the local situations. They don't have our every-day production problems, and they don't have the detailed knowledge of our markets that we possess.

Several managing directors of companies in the less-developed areas complained of headquarters' insistence on producing products too sophisticated and expensive for their market. They also mentioned headquarters' lack of knowledge and appreciation of the difficulty of dealing with severe inflation and devaluation.

The managing director of France, one of Multitech's largest subsidiary markets, said:

The majority of the managing directors are of the opinion that the headquarters' reporting system is far too time-consuming and demanding. It is not efficient and places a heavy load on the managing directors. Monthly reports requiring significant financial data, sales reports, and production data take up the time of the staff as well as the managing directors. Many subsidiary managers question if headquarters are really interested in the reports. Some managers claim headquarters is too bogged down in detail and fails to answer important questions concerning their development. Several managers maintained that headquarters did not read their five-year plans and frequently requested information from the subsidiaries which was explicitly stated in the plans.

The management of the Spanish subsidiary said that headquarters was too concerned about short-term profits and not sufficiently interested in seeking penetration in local markets. The managers cited the efforts of their subsidiary to maintain the largest customer for an electric product by taking a loss on a large order to prevent a competitor from getting the business. Headquarters

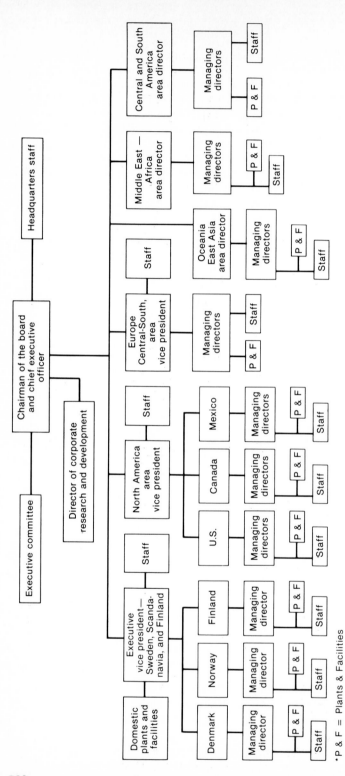

*P & F = Plants & Facilities

EXHIBIT 2
Multitech International organization.

demanded that the subsidiary renegotiate the contract. This led to a prolonged debate over the merits of profit on a single contract versus maintaining market share.

Many of the complaints about headquarters by the managing directors Eric Nittzell had heard before. He knew that many of them arose because of misunderstandings and a failure on the part of the managing directors to appreciate the role of the executive group in headquarters who were responsible for formulating the strategic plans for the whole organization, not just for a subunit. Nittzell also realized that despite the success of Multitech, which had shown substantial growth in sales and profits in the past decade, there was a need for strategic integration and a need to arrest the growing tendency of the subsidiaries to suboptimize at the expense of the corporate whole. No doubt a good part of the problem was due to the rapid expansion of the past decade when Multitech's sales increased 700 percent, with 70 percent of this increase in the foreign subsidiaries. Perhaps now was the time to effect a reorganization of the multinational operations. (See Exhibit 2.) Some of the product areas such as electrical equipment, computer peripherals, and packaging equipment had become very sophisticated and required headquarters' staff assistance at the subsidiary level. Nittzell had also been reminded by Eric Peterson that the attempts at rationalization had increased intersubsidiary sales of product and were causing disputes over transfer pricing. Nittzell had also discussed with his staff the problem of where to locate research and development facilities. They were now all concentrated in Sweden. The managing directors of the larger subsidiaries in the United States, the United Kingdom, and France had frequently requested that research and development facilities be placed in their country areas. Nittzell had also been reminded by the managing directors that the boards of directors of the subsidiaries were perfunctory, and in most cases were organized to meet the legal requirements of the country of residence.

Nittzell called a meeting of headquarters' staff to seek some possible solutions to the problems raised by the managing directors and the inevitable difficulties of multinational expansion.

ACOG[1]

Warren H. Pearse, M.D., executive director of the American College of Obstetricians and Gynecologists (ACOG), stated:

> Our staff and resources have grown rapidly and become more specialized over the past few years, yet we have a sense that there is some discontent among our members. That is why I've asked several staff members to study our committee/staff organization and suggest a way that we can make it more responsive.

Pearse, the newly appointed executive director, was chosen for the post after a year-long search for a director who would help ACOG become more vigorous, especially in the light of increasing government activity in health care. When Pearse took the post, he said: "An association has some of the features of a political party but also acts like a business in other ways."

Charted in 1951 as a nonprofit institution, ACOG established the following objectives:

• To foster and stimulate interest in obstetrics and gynecology and all aspects of the work for the welfare of women

• To establish and maintain the highest possible standards for obstetric and gynecologic education and postgraduate education in medical schools and hospitals, obstetric and gynecological practice and research

[1]This case was made possible by the cooperation of the American College of Obstetricians and Gynecologists. It was prepared by Mr. Albert W. Isenman under the direction of Prof. Thomas J. McNichols as the basis for class discussion rather than to illustrate effective or ineffective handling of an administrative situation.

• To promote publications and encourage contributions to medical and scientific literature pertaining to obstetrics and gynecology

ORGANIZATION: THE CONSTITUENCY

Any physician who completed a postgraduate residency and an examination in obstetrics and gynecology was eligible to be a member (fellow or junior fellow) of ACOG.

ACOG fellows paid annual dues of $125 each; junior fellows paid no dues (see Exhibit 1). Although the primary benefit of membership was a sense of peer affiliation, there were more tangible benefits:

• Group insurance and travel programs
• Subscription to a scientific journal
• Various other newsletters, bulletins, and technical brochures
• Admission to conventions and scientific meetings
• A book of standards by which most hospital ob-gyn departments were operated
• Part of the public "voice" of the specialty in the form of its position papers and policies
• The right to vote for officers and to hold office in the organization (each fellow had one vote)

About four-fifths of the members were engaged in private practice; the remainder included military, public health, academic, and administrative physicians.

The college was governed by an executive board comprised of the officers of the executive committee and chairpersons of the geographic districts. Candidates for office were selected at the district and national level by nominating committees, and customarily only one candidate was proposed for each vacant office. Fellows voted for, or against, the single nominee for office. There had never been an opposing candidate for national office, nor had any nominee ever failed to be elected. An examination of the roster of national officers, district officers, and nominating committee members revealed many of the same names appearing in these three capacities year after year. Moreover, high officers tended to be older fellows, with an average in the high fifties to low sixties.

The elective process was often criticized as being inbred and restrictive; and just as often it was defended as bringing about stability and mature leadership. "A constant dilemma in associations," said one manager, "is to balance the need for broad representation of the constituency with the need to develop capable senior officers over the years."

ORGANIZATION: THE COMMITTEES

One avenue for membership participation was through ACOG's standing committees (see Exhibit 2). The president annually appointed committee members

EXHIBIT 1

BY-LAWS OF THE AMERICAN COLLEGE OF OBSTETRICIANS AND GYNECOLOGISTS

Excerpts

Article II
Objectives and Powers

Section 1. In addition to the purposes named in the Certificate of Incorporation, the objectives of the corporation shall be to foster and stimulate improvements in all aspects of the health care of women which properly come within the scope of obstetrics and gynecology.

Section 2. The College shall have all the powers of a corporation, organized not for pecuniary profit, as are now or shall hereafter be conferred by the statutes of the State of Illinois.

Article III
Membership and Privileges

Section 1. Fellows.
  a. The active members of the College shall consist of and be known as Fellows. They shall be elected in accordance with the By-Laws of the College and with such additional rules which may from time to time be adopted.
  b. Fellows shall have the right to vote at general and special meetings of the College and to hold office therein.

Article IV
Fellows, Their Qualifications, Proposal, and Election

Section 1. Qualifications. A candidate for Fellowship in the American College of Obstetricians and Gynecologists must demonstrate the following qualifications and must meet the following requirements to the satisfaction of the Executive Board:
  a. Graduation from an acceptable medical school and the completion of graduate training.
  b. Continuous limitation of training and/or professional activities to obstetrics and/or gynecology for the five years immediately prior to the date of application. Exception may be made by the Executive Board when such specialized training and/or professional experience has been interrupted by military service or other exigency.
  c. Demonstration of evidence of high ethical and professional standing, including clinical ability and experience as determined by Fellows in the candidate's District, and successful completion of an examination in obstetrics and gynecology.

Section 2. Proposals for Fellowship. The name of a candidate for Fellowship shall be proposed by a Fellow and shall be endorsed by a second Fellow in the candidate's District, neither of whom is a College, District, or Section officer. Written statements certifying the candidate's qualifications and activities, made by both the proposer and endorser, shall be sent directly to the College office for filing with the completed official form of application for Fellowship.

Article V
Junior Fellows, Their Qualifications, Proposal, Election, and Organization

Section 1. Qualifications. A candidate for Junior Fellowship must meet the following requirements to the satisfaction of the Executive Board:
  a. Graduation from an acceptable medical school.
  b. Current participation in an acceptable residency program in obstetrics and gynecology; or, upon successful completion of such a program, immediate and continued limitation of professional activities exclusively to obstetrics and/or gynecology pending fulfillment of the requirements for Fellowship in the College.

Article XI
Officers

Section 1. Officers. The officers of the College shall consist of the following:

President	Treasurer
President Elect	Secretary
Immediate Past President	Assistant Secretary
Vice President	Executive Director

Section 2. Committee on Nominations.

  a. *Composition.*

    1. The Past President most recently retired from the Executive Board shall be an Ex Officio member of the committee and shall act as Chairman. The next two most recent available Past Presidents shall also be committee members.

    2. Each District shall have one representative as a member of the committee to be appointed in the following manner:

      (a). The three former District Chairmen most recently retired from the Executive Board shall serve as the representatives of their Districts on the committee.

      (b). A representative for each of the remaining six Districts shall be appointed by the President Elect, after consultation with the President and the Immediate Past President. The appointment shall be made from the list of names, provided by the District Chairmen, of at least three Fellows from the District.

  b. *Duties.* The duties of the Committee on Nominations shall be to prepare a slate of nominees for the elective offices, i.e., President Elect, Vice President, Treasurer, Secretary, and Assistant Secretary.

Section 3. Notification. The slate of nominees for all elective offices shall be submitted in writing to all voting Fellows at least one month before the Annual Meeting.

Section 4. Election. The election of all nominees shall be by majority vote of all Fellows, in person or by proxy, voting at the Annual Business Meeting.

Article XII
Executive Board

Section 1. Members. The Executive Board shall consist of the President, Immediate Past President, President Elect, Vice President, Treasurer, Secretary, Assistant Secretary, and the District Chairmen. The District Chairmen shall be elected by the Fellows of the College residing in their respective Districts as hereinafter provided.

Section 2. Powers and Duties. The general management of the College shall be vested in the Executive Board, whose powers and duties shall be those ordinarily held and performed by the board of directors of a corporation. It shall:

  a. Transact all business required to carry out the objectives of the organization arising in the interim between Annual Meetings.

  b. Manage, control, and conserve the property interests of the College.

  c. Elect Fellows, Junior Fellows, Honorary Fellows, Life Fellows, Associate Fellows, and Affiliate Fellows.

  d. Fix initiation fees, annual dues and special assessments of Fellows, Junior Fellows, Associate Fellows, Affiliate Fellows, and adjunct members of Sections.

  e. Fix boundaries of Districts and Sections and create new Districts and Sections when necessary.

  f. Call special meetings of the College.

  g. Create standing and temporary committees, designate in which category each committee shall be placed and provide whatever definition of committee duties is indicated.

  h. Vote by mail ballot when necessary.

  i. Transact all business, not otherwise provided for, that may pertain to the College.

EXHIBIT 2

ACOG COMMISSIONS AND COMMITTEES

Commission on education

Committees on:
Annual Clinical Meeting
Audiovisual Education
Continuing Education
Education in Family Life
Public Education and Com-
munication
Technical Bulletins
Terminology
Committees for Special Interest
Community Health
Endocrinology and Fertility
Maternal and Perinatal Medicine
Oncology
Pediatric and Adolescent Gynecol-
ogy
Psychosomatic Obstetrics and Gyne-
cology

General Committees:

Bio-ethics (Ad Hoc)
By-laws (Ad Hoc)
Credentials
Executive Committee of the Executive
Board
Finance

Future Development of the College
Higher Education Loan Program
Honors and Recognitions
Host Committee
Industrial Exhibits
Insurance
Liaison with International Federation
of Gynecology and Obstetrics
World Congress on Gynecology and
Obstetrics
Nominations
Recertification Procedures
College Representatives to Other Or-
ganizations

Commission on practice

Committee on:
American Indian Affairs
Gynecologic Practice
Health Care Delivery
Nutrition
Obstetric Practice
Professional Liability
Professional Personnel
Professional Standards

from the membership at large, usually to serve three-year terms. Each year, a few positions on each committee became vacant.

Annually, new standing committees were proposed and old committees were discontinued, subject to the approval of the executive board. Usually, committees were established whenever some issue—medical or political—became clear enough or bothersome enough to warrant some attention by the college. Thus, most committees began by addressing a purpose or objective at a specific point in time. Pearse explained further:

A lot of members have participated in the organization through the committee structure. But we're locked into the annual appointment cycle—if something important comes up quickly, like an issue needing a public statement, we may or may not have a committee assembled that can address the issue competently and quickly. Also, when the original purposes of committees are achieved or become obsolete, the committee nevertheless goes on. Its purposes may become unclear, and some of them spend a good deal of time and money just discussing what they might do. They're discontinued long after they have ceased to be useful.

In its history, the college had had over 150 committees come and go. ACOG fellows were sometimes critical of the preponderance of academic physicians who served on committees. Academicians tended to be more widely known than practicing physicians, and therefore were more likely to be selected. They also frequently had time available—committees met three or four times per year—while practicing physicians' time was more limited by the press of practice commitments.

ORGANIZATION: THE STAFF

The executive director of the college, appointed by the executive board, hired and supervised a full-time staff of about 100 persons (see Exhibit 3). Staff salary expenditures averaged about 41 percent of the total expenses of the organization, 79 percent of its net expenses (net expenses were the result of subtracting "related income" such as grants and royalties). The executive director and

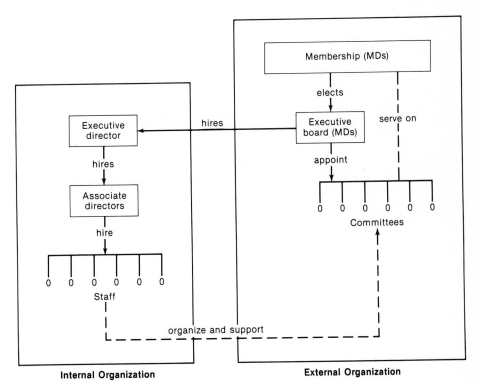

EXHIBIT 3
ACOG organization.

one or two associates were obstetrician-gynecologists; the other staff members were not physicians.

The staff was organized in functional fashion: there were staff members who provided operating support to the organization (records, data processing, accounting, payroll, convention management). Other staff members worked with the committees. Among them was found a variety of professional backgrounds, including law, statistics, management, education, and public administration.

The staff and membership worked together to create ACOG's position papers, policies, meetings, and educational materials. Any publication or statement must have wound its way through a tedious and circuitous path of inter-committee referrals, staff research, argument, and debate before being committed to final form by vote of the executive board. Some ideas never entered into the development stage, falling by the wayside at the lower staff or committee levels for lack of an advocate. Therefore, it often happened that new issues or problems were only addressed when they became "crises."

ENVIRONMENT

There were a half dozen or so other associations that addressed the obstetric-gynecologic field. Some were limited-membership academic societies; others were regional in scope; others limited their interest to some subfield. In no case did membership in one organization preclude one from joining ACOG. Most ACOG officers felt that as long as the organization appeared active and interesting, it would never want for membership support. The record tended to bear this out, as each year the number of new members slightly exceeded those lost by attrition (resignation, retirement, or death). It was estimated that about 92 percent of the eligible physicians did join the organization (see Exhibit 4).

The organization engaged in a limited formal scan of its environment. It exchanged representatives on committees of other organizations (mostly other medical associations). It maintained one staff person who monitored the *Congressional Record, Federal Register,* and other government publications, and who alerted officials if there were federal issues that might be addressed. It was tacitly assumed that the medical and scientific environment was monitored adequately simply because there were so many physicians in and around the organization.

FINANCIAL FACTORS

ACOG's controller, Len Bedsault, remarked:

> Our annual dues from membership average about $1.6 to $1.7 million. The annual clinical meeting generates enough in registration fees to more than offset the meeting cost. Our journal shows a slight surplus in subscriptions over publication cost and the Nurses Association shows a slight revenue of $17 to $18 thousand annually.

EXHIBIT 4
FELLOWSHIP DEFINITIONS

Fellows:	Fellows must be board-certified obstetrician-gynecologists who have applied to and been accepted by ACOG. Fellows pay full dues and receive full membership privileges. There were 12,861 fellows.
Junior fellows:	Junior fellows are physicians who are in residency training to become obstetrician-gynecologists. They pay nominal annual dues. Within ten years after beginning residency training, a junior fellow must apply for full fellowship or lose membership privileges. They numbered 4,982.
Life fellows:	Life fellows are retired or disabled physicians. They pay no dues. Life fellows numbered 954.
Others:	Honorary and affiliate fellows are of various professions and pay no dues. They totaled 154.

We can estimate accurately our dues revenue; our annual estimation of expenditures for salaried positions and for travel expenses needed to maintain the committees is also fairly accurate.

We appropriate budget levels in much the same way Congress appropriates expenditures relative to public undertakings. If the expenses are estimated to exceed the income, our Finance Committee may eliminate some committee projects and proposed staff positions until we get a good fit. If expenditures viewed as "essential" still exceed the estimated income, then debt service or a dues increase becomes necessary.

In the past, the college was able to meet its expenses without frequent dues increases. It maintained a very comfortable and well-equipped office, with staff salaries at a fairly competitive level. Some slack was always built into the budget each year to allow for unexpected projects or changes in direction that might occur during the year. But the rigidly defined committee structure usually restricted the possibility of getting a new project budgeted except annually.

THE ACTIVITIES OF THE STUDY GROUP

Three staff members and an associate director comprised the study group established by Pearse to examine the committee and staff organization. The group's attention first concentrated on staff responsibilities. One person recalled:

I staffed three committees which were all over the map with their interests and projects. Sometimes, easily 50 percent of the meeting time is spent discussing the role of the committee—where it should be going and what was expected of it. When they finally get around to drafting a paper or undertaking a research project, it may or may not be something I'm knowledgeable or interested in. So sometimes I'm able to do a lot of helpful research, and at other times I'm hardly able to do more than take notes.

Another said:

> I agree we ought to have clearer lines of responsibility for staff. But mostly our problem is with the committees. A lot of good ideas come up but never get acted on.

Relatively little progress was made by the study group until it began to think in somewhat larger terms. One member suggested that with a new director in place, "perhaps now is the time to really go on the offensive" and make some changes in the organization's basic staff structure and planning process. A note was sent to Pearse stating that, if authorized, the group would propose a redesigned system of staff assignments with the following objectives in mind:

1 To establish singular and clear staff autonomy in the management of committee-related projects

2 To identify ideas and projects worthy of pursuit and to allocate the staff and physical resources more efficiently to implement them

3 To react more quickly to the changing political and social environment, and more importantly to anticipate future environmental changes that impact upon ACOG

Pearse responded:

> I believe you should begin at point zero, and suggest a complete rebuilding of the staff and committee structure. A better organization might be more economical, if we can rid ourselves of some of the "dead wood" committees that eat up a large portion of the budget. Because we also invest so much in staff, it makes sense to try to get as much "product" as we can from staff and committees.

In endorsing the study group's goals as stated above, Pearse added the following objectives to his charge to the study group:

1 To maintain the widest possible membership participation in ACOG activities—in a geographic sense, in the sense of widely differing points of view—and to identify new talent among the membership

2 To maintain each president's prerogatives in appointing membership participants, and his or her prerogatives in influencing thematic goals and objectives of ACOG

3 To allocate staff and membership resources more efficiently

Over the course of several subsequent meetings, the study group developed a proposal for reorganizing the staff/committee structure which is summarized here:

First, it was recommended that the college establish two "resource commissions" to deal with matters pertaining to medical education and medical practice, respectively. They would be composed of ACOG members appointed by the president, and would serve as the overall planning and policymaking body for its area. Thus, there would be a Practice Resource Commission and an Education Resource Commission.

Second, a staff associate director (a physician reporting directly to the executive director) would serve as principal staff to each resource commission. Thus, there would be an associate director for the Education Resource Commission and an associate director for the Practice Resource Commission. Other staff members, reporting to these associate directors, would also serve as staff to the commissions.

Third, each resource commission would be responsible for identifying the problems and issues which may be addressed, arranging them in order of priority, and assigning task forces to deal with each problem or issue.

Fourth, members of task forces would be appointed by the president on the recommendation of the resource commission, and would be assigned a budget level and a staff member to act as project manager. The task force would function to meet a specified objective (or set of objectives) by a definite deadline.

Fifth, upon completion of the assigned activity, the task force would report its results directly to the executive board for formal ratification of recommendations. (During a task force's tenure, it would refer to the resource commission for additional advice or direction.) Task forces would be disbanded immediately upon completion of their assignments.

Thus, the existing array of standing committees could be disbanded. There was a small number of committees which were required by the bylaws or by conventional association management, and these would be retained unchanged. Examples were: Executive Committee, Nominations Committee, Finance Committee, Committee on Liaison with the International Federation of Gynecology and Obstetrics, and Committee on Honors and Recognition. This would represent a reduction in committees from 39 to about 6.

A staff member recalled:

> Since the average direct cost of a committee meeting was about $4,000 (not including staff time), and most committees met two or three times, this proposal was to free up well over $300,000 that could be applied to task forces. But beyond that, we liked the idea that the task forces could achieve "sunset" after doing their job.

Pearse and the associate directors of ACOG were intrigued by the idea, and asked for a more detailed functional description of the system.

THE RESOURCE COMMISSIONS AND HOW THEY WOULD FUNCTION

A resource commission of eight members would be appointed by the president-elect on a rotating basis: two new members each year with four-year terms. The two longest-tenured members of the resource commission would serve as cochairpersons of the group.

Members of the resource commission would be appointed on the basis of the special skills they would bring to the group—not on the basis of some constituency that they might represent. Since the main purpose of the resource commission was to identify problems, allocate resources, and conduct planning activities, members needed a familiarity with the college, a national perspective, and an established record of service in management and administrative functions, and needed to be active either in practice or in education (depending on which of the two commissions he or she was to serve on).

Each resource commission would meet relatively frequently (perhaps quarterly or even every other month). Its purpose was not to take on projects itself. Rather, it would review issues and problems presented by staff, or which came to the resource commission because of members' contact with other ACOG members; it would relate these problems to other ACOG goals and projects; it would identify experts from the membership at large to serve on task forces.

TASK FORCES

Task forces (see Exhibit 5) were to be recommended by the resource commissions and appointed by the president. Each would be composed of the

EXHIBIT 5
Organization of task forces (proposed).

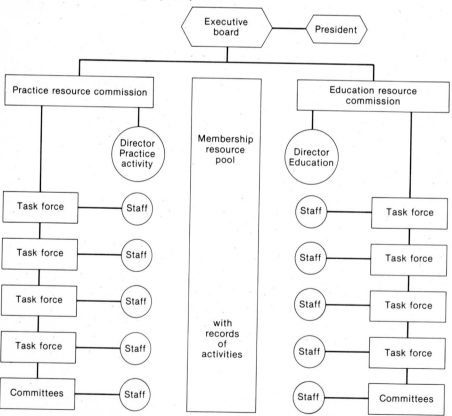

minimum number of members to deal with the task, and would be given a clear set of objectives, a budget, a deadline, and a staff manager. Members of the task force were to be drawn from a pool of ACOG members (and possibly persons from other organizations) who had relevant expertise. Task forces would frequently have one member who serves on the resource commission in order to provide cross-communication.

THE RESOURCE POOL

A file would be constructed of individuals who might be called upon to serve on task forces. A data profile listing their interests and areas of expertise could be built from a variety of sources with a view to expanding the potential number of participants.

STAFF ASSIGNMENTS

Staff assignments were to be made on the basis of staff competence. When particular staff expertise was needed but not available among existing staff members, consideration could be given to hiring consultants, medical students, Ph.D. candidates, or other short-term personnel to provide technical staff support to a task force (while management support would continue to be provided by a regular ACOG staff member).

The study group also developed a scenario describing how several problems might be addressed if the hypothetical new system were already in place.

SCENARIO: SPECIFIC EXAMPLES OF OPERATION

The resource commission might decide that the following were important issues with which the college could deal:

1 Childbirth education
2 Retention of fetal monitor records
3 Reference document on drugs in pregnancy
4 Establishment of maternal mortality registry
5 Deregulation of mandatory chest x-rays
6 Establishment of breast milk banks
7 Standards for prenatal care

(These were actual topics then under discussion by a standing committee.)

If the response of the resource commission to these issues indicated that items 2, 3, and 7 above were the priority items deserving immediate and concentrated attention, three task forces would then be established:

1 Task Force on Fetal Monitor Records
Staff person assigned along with a lawyer and two fellows to articulate the issues related to retention of fetal monitor records, including liability of

physicians years hence when clinical implications of monitor interpretation may be very different; storage problems; precedent in ECG or EEG tracings. They were to propose an ACOG policy and report back in no later than two months.

2 Task Force on Drugs in Pregnancy

Staff person assigned with three fellows including one with strong pharmacology background assigned to consider publishing an ACOG guide to important known drug-pregnancy interactions. They were to create a sample outline of contents, and an estimation of the degree of difficulty and length of time to produce the document, and describe the technical skills of persons necessary to produce the document. Two meetings are authorized, but the question of philanthropic support must be addressed prior to holding a second meeting. They were to report to the resource commission following each meeting, with final report expected within ten months.

3 Task Force on Prenatal Standards

The above examples would carry here also. Since it is a more complicated subject and one in which ACOG is not unilaterally interested, a task force might be assigned to investigate the objectives and work of other organizations (public health), the possibility of influencing or coopting that work, and then the procedures so.

Finally, the remaining issues not identified by the resource commission would probably be viewed as important but not deserving of immediate action or expenditure. The resource commission might then satisfy itself by appointing a:

4 Task Force on the Obstetric Practice Environment

Staff person assigned with two fellows and a junior fellow with a charge to review among themselves by mail and phone the pertinent literature related to topics 1, 4, 5, and 6 above, report on the expected impact if these issues were not dealt with, and determine whether any of these issues portends any new social-environmental-technical trend for which the college might begin to prepare itself.

COST

Budget planning for the proposed structure would fit within ACOG's current financial planning cycle and in some respects the new structure would make budgeting easier. Since task forces would be appointed at random times, and since project assignments would require varying lengths of time to complete, the result would be a year-round stream of start and stop dates for task forces. These dates would overlap the start and stop of ACOG's fiscal year, and so annual budget determinations would not be made for every task force from scratch.

The budget for committee and commission activities under practice totaled $99,650 and under education totaled $90,340. Under the proposed plan, the Practice Resource Commission would meet four times annually for two days

(8 × 4 × $350), costing $11,200, and the Education Resource Commission at comparable expense, $11,200.

Each resource commission would then be allotted, based on current activity levels, 150 person/meeting units (a one-person, two-day meeting average cost of $350 per member) or a total cost of $52,500.

If an average task force consisted of five individuals, who met together three times (probably an overestimate), each resource commission could direct *ten* task forces per year. The cost of each resource commission would be $30,000 to $40,000 less than at present.

NUMBERS

The number of individual fellows and junior fellows who serve on practice committees was 54—this plan would provide a minimum of 58. The number of individual fellows and junior fellows on education committees was 86 (larger because of six special interest committees). Again, the minimum under the new plan would be 58.

PRESENTATION OF THE PROPOSAL

The study group's proposal, as outlined in the foregoing, met with the approval of Pearse and his fellow directors. The next step was to present the proposal formally to the Executive Committee of the executive board. Presumably, that group's support would pave the way for formal ratification by the entire executive board. The proposal was one of the first major recommendations made to the executive board by Pearse in his brief tenure as executive director. Some staff felt that this enhanced the chances that the proposal would be endorsed as a symbol of the executive board's desire to support its new chief executive officer. Pearse reported the Executive Committee's response in a memo to the staff study group:

> The Executive Committee reaction to the proposed reorganization was predictable: it was too radical to abolish everyone's favorite committee. We have been asked to once again present proposals at the May meeting.
>
> There were two general suggestions. The first, championed only by one person, was that there should be a single resource commission to help identify and allocate issues. Apart from this there was much more general support for a plan which would retain administrative committees as we had proposed, but also retain several "absolutely essential" standing committees in both the practice and education areas. They suggested that we should retain standing committees that: (1) have a continuing related function; (2) need aggressive expertise; (3) serve a "watchdog" purpose.

Presenting the proposal to the executive board placed it in the public domain among members of ACOG. In the weeks following the presentation, many comments and criticisms were received by staff members and officers. Although many comments were favorable, most respondents suggested retaining this or that committee, or offered new features to the plan reflecting some personal interest. Additionally, there was strong opposition from some members and officers who alleged that the organization "amounted to nothing more than a staff attempt to take control of the committees away from the membership."

Another problem related to constituent interest emerged and was outlined in a memo by Pearse:

> The whole "committees for special interest" area remains a problem. One person would deal with it by making each one of these a separate functional committee. Others do not know how to deal with it, but we have now six special interest committees; three of these are represented by subspecialty boards, and three are not. On the outside, clamoring to be special interest committees, are a whole series of other groups, some of which are based largely on ability to use a single piece of equipment. Maybe we should have some kind of an overall subspecialty interest group or section?

Further concerns about the proposed reorganization were raised in the following comments by an influential senior member of the executive board:

> Unless an organized mechanism is developed for the planning of ACOG activities, a lack of coordinated effort may develop. Duplication of activities and resulting frustrations may develop.
>
> A defined procedure for the planning of ACOG activities is highly desirable if the committee-commission reorganization is to be accomplished without the impairment of the effectiveness of the college. The following items require clarification:
>
> **1** What is to be the method of choosing the representatives to serve on the resource commission and on task forces?
>
> **2** What is to be the relationship of any retained standing committee to the resource commission?
>
> **3** Is the selection of the subject for a task force to be at the discretion of the resource commission?
>
> **4** How are the task forces to be funded? If they are to be appointed on a short-term, ad hoc basis, it may be difficult to make satisfactory budget proposals for their activities.
>
> **5** How is the report of the task force to be presented? Is it to be made to the resource commission for its evaluation and revision, or is it to be made directly to the executive board?
>
> **6** Who is to be designated as responsible for the implementation of any action recommended by a task force?

Pearse reconvened the staff study group to revise the reorganization proposal in the light of the various criticisms:

> Implementation of these changes for the next year would require adoption no later than the September meeting of the Executive Committee. I would like to meet with you to discuss your suggestions. Should we revise the plan? If so, what is a good strategy for assuring its approval when we present it? Or do you think we should just try to work with the system we already have?

Illinois Masonic Medical Center[1]

When Gerald W. Mungerson began his career as executive director of Illinois Masonic Medical Center (IMMC) in July, 1972, he faced numerous immediate and long-term problems. The hospital was in the midst of a major expansion and modernization program which had compelled IMMC's administration to reevaluate virtually every aspect of the institution's operation and management. The construction of the W. Clement Stone Pavilion would increase IMMC's floor space by more than 50 percent to 500,000 square feet, and the administration had originally anticipated increasing the hospital's capacity by about 45 percent by 1980. However, as a result of a nationwide decline in hospital occupancy rates in 1971 and the development of an apparent oversupply of general medical bed space in the Chicago area, they decided instead to maintain the current capacity of 565 beds and to shift existing facilities to other uses as space in the Stone Pavilion became available. Because of this change in space utilization plans, IMMC's administration had undertaken an extensive review of the hospital's operations and had made or planned changes in the laundry, supply and distribution, and warehousing functions of the institution.

Among the first areas of concern for Mr. Mungerson was IMMC's budget for the 1973 fiscal year, which began October 1, 1972. Budgeting deliberations were in progress when he arrived in July, and within two months Mr. Mungerson would have to present the final proposals to the board of trustees for approval. It became evident to him that although several persons and committees

---

[1] This case was prepared by William Sandberg, research assistant, under the supervision of Assistant Professor Charles W. Hofer.

bore responsibilities for budgeting decisions, it was not until the budget reached him that a single person or office considered the total budget. While the determination of operating budgets was an important managerial function, Mr. Mungerson felt that capital budgeting, with its implications for long-range planning and fund requirements, demanded his attention. It was his impression that IMMC's capital budgeting process, particularly for medical equipment, sometimes applied the wrong criteria or inefficiently allocated resources and seldom showed regard for the availability of funds or for cash-flow management. Consequently, he sought to establish a permanent, coordinated capital budgeting system which would correct these deficiencies. He also hoped that more explicit criteria and priorities could be applied to both medical and nonmedical budget requests and that midyear supplementary appropriations could be eliminated.

In 1972, IMMC was organized by divisions, as indicated in Exhibit 1. The directors of the Finance, Operations, and Nursing Divisions[2] reported directly to the executive director. The director of professional services[3] reported to the medical director, while medical personnel reported to either the chief of staff (elected by the staff) or the medical director, both of whom were responsible to the executive director. In Mr. Mungerson's opinion, IMMC's administrative responsibilities could be divided into three basic categories:

1 Fund raising and long-range planning, which were the responsibilities of the board of trustees

2 Functional administration, short-range planning, and strategic implementation, which fell to the divisional directors

3 The dispensing of medical care, which was under the direction of the medical director and the chief of staff

FINANCIAL POLICIES OF IMMC

The traditional attitude of IMMC's administration toward the hospital's financial structure had been cautious. Following the 1926 construction of the hospital's School of Nursing with borrowed funds, the administration, headed by the late Judge Edgar Jonas, refrained from borrowing. It was a standing policy under Judge Jonas that all new construction should be financed entirely with cash. This debt-free policy was not abandoned until 1965.

During the latter 1960s, under Executive Director Allen M. Hicks, IMMC used mortgages, collateralized bank loans, and unsecured bank loans to meet both construction and operating requirements. Most of the funds obtained through these sources between 1967 and 1971 were secured by a mortgage on

[2] Referred to as "the functional departments."
[3] Considered "medical departments."

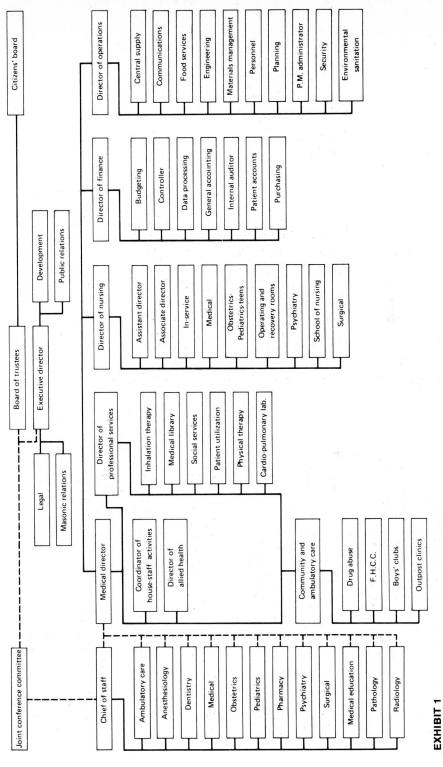

EXHIBIT 1
Organization of Illinois Masonic Medical Center—1973.

545

EXHIBIT 2
IMMC'S DEBT AND MORTGAGE FINANCING, 1967–1971

	1967	1968	1969	1970	1971
Secured bank loans (due on demand)	$144,000*	$144,000*	–	–	$ 900,000§
Unsecured bank loans	–	$240,000†	–	–	–
Stone Pavilion interim mortgage	–	–	–	$1,713,593‡	$2,509,701¶
Mortgage and real estate contracts payable	$ 73,752	$257,477	$186,209	$ 84,641	$ 64,914

*Borrowed at $4^1/_2$ percent from The Northern Trust Company, Chicago. Investments with a September 30, 1968 market value of $328,146 pledged as collateral.

†Borrowed at $5^1/_2$ percent from the First National Bank of Chicago. Due January 16, 1969.

‡Construction loan borrowed at 8.75 percent from The Northern Trust Company with substantially all of IMMC's buildings, including those under construction, pledged as collateral.

§Borrowed at 6 percent from The Northern Trust Company. IMMC's patient accounts receivable, valued at $3.8 million after deduction of provision for uncollectible accounts, pledged as collateral.

¶Construction loan borrowed at $7^1/_4$ percent from The Northern Trust Company with the same conditions as ‡.

substantially all of IMMC's buildings, including the Stone Pavilion. Exhibit 2 shows IMMC's debt and mortgage financing for these years.

During Mr. Hicks's tenure, IMMC's capital spending was governed by a different attitude than in Judge Jonas's years. According to one IMMC administrator, it was assumed that funds were available for any desirable project. If a medical department claimed that a proposed project would meet a medical need and/or improve patient care, the executive director and the trustees would appropriate the necessary funds.

During this period, requests for both capital and noncapital expenditures from medical and functional departments were made directly to the executive director, who selected projects for recommendation to the board of trustees. The board's approval, virtually assured by the recommendation of the executive director, authorized the immediate expenditure of the appropriated money. Under Judge Jonas and for the first five years under Mr. Hicks, there was neither a budgeting procedure nor a regular review of expenditures. Requests were made as needs arose and were approved without setting an overall spending limit. IMMC had no budget of any type prior to 1970 and no capital budget until 1971. Even with both operating and capital budgets, spending was not tightly controlled in the 1971 and 1972 fiscal years, according to IMMC's director of general accounting, since additional requests were made and approved throughout both years in the same fashion as in previous years. These informal, verbal requests to Mr. Hicks were unrecorded, which precluded detailed examination of deliberations on budgeting or authorization of capital spending.[4]

EFFECTS OF THE STONE PAVILION ON CAPITAL BUDGETING AT IMMC

Traditionally, IMMC's equipment needs and construction activities had been financed through four funds: the general fund, the plant fund, the development fund, and the specific-purpose funds. In 1971, a fifth designation, the endowment funds, was added to encourage bequests. (See Exhibit 4 for descriptions of the five fund categories used by IMMC in 1972.) Beginning in the 1968 fiscal year, when IMMC hired an architectural firm to design the Stone Pavilion, the development fund was used for financing the entire Stone Pavilion project. Other hospital equipment and building activities continued to be financed through combinations of the four funds then in existence. The creation of endowment funds in 1971 had no effect on the Stone Pavilion project, which continued to be financed through the development fund. Exhibit 5 provides the five funds' balances from 1967 through 1971, and Exhibit 6 details annual changes in these funds from 1968 through 1971.

The construction, equipping, and occupation of the Stone Pavilion presented an organizational challenge to IMMC, since the existing administrative structure lacked coordination among the departments involved in these activities. For example, each medical department submitted its own requests for equipment, independent of the requests from other departments. Similarly, furnishings and nonmedical equipment were obtained on a departmental need basis. When the Stone Pavilion was completed, many medical departments as well as functional departments would move to the new facility, thus raising the question of whether to transfer or replace equipment and furnishings. To provide centralized decision-making responsibility for the move into the new facilities, Mr. Hicks asked Wes McCormick (the director of operations) in January 1970 to manage all aspects of the move. Mr. McCormick's responsibilities included determining the medical equipment needs and forming a capital

---

[4]According to the director of general accounting during most of Mr. Hicks's tenure, there was no record of the number of requests made to Mr. Hicks or of the number that he approved, modified, or rejected. In the opinion of a current accounting department head, however, capital spending in an average year was probably roughly equal to IMMC's allowance for depreciation in that year. IMMC's allowances for depreciation for 1968–1971 were the following:

1968:	$334,999
1969:	$429,000
1970:	$469,000
1971:	$522,000

Because IMMC's records did not distinguish among types of expenditures for fixed assets, Exhibit 3 shows additions to fixed assets for 1967 through 1972.

EXHIBIT 3
ADDITIONS TO FIXED ASSETS, BY DIVISION, 1967–1972

Division	1967	1968	1969	1970	1971	1972
A.* Administrative functions†	$ 1,132	$ 13,810	$ 3,655	$ 9,139	$ 7,526	$ 19,444
B. Medical and nursing	24,000	302,514	110,107	269,450	142,461	162,741
C. Professional services	17,132	59,531	77,119	97,747	44,742	51,746
D. Finance	802	3,752	8,173	13,852	8,048	15,902
E. Operations	70,136	31,002	16,736	31,703	18,148	37,692
F. Building and land	132,566	908,505	947,485	452,633	516,607	737,979
	$245,768	$1,319,114	$1,163,275	$874,524	$737,532	$1,025,504

*See Exhibits 3A, 3B, . . . , 3F for detailed information concerning each division.
†Executive director, public relations, Masonic relations, fund raising, gift shop.

budget for the new facility. This move by Mr. Hicks created a second channel for medical department capital requests: if the department was to be included in the Stone Pavilion, Mr. McCormick developed its capital budget requests for submission to the trustees; otherwise, the existing procedure through Mr. Hicks's office continued.

THE 1970–1971 CRISES AND IMMC'S RESPONSE

A combination of events, including the federal government's unfavorable adjustment of Medicare account claims, contributed to a lower net income than had been expected for fiscal 1970. Capital budgeting for the medical departments, however, remained largely a question of filling stated medical needs until early 1971. At that time, the state government froze its payment level for

EXHIBIT 3A
ADDITIONS TO FIXED ASSETS

	1967	1968	1969	1970	1971	1972
Executive offices	$ 351	$10,511	$2,591	$5,944	$5,015	$19,444
Public relations		696	264	1,127	1,443	
Religious services						
Fund raising	510	1,685		1,738	368	
Masonic relations		415	500	330		
Gift shop		318			700	
Administration	271	185	300			
Total	$1,132	$13,810	$3,655	$9,139	$7,526	$19,444

EXHIBIT 3B
ADDITIONS TO FIXED ASSETS

	1967	1968	1969	1970	1971	1972
Resident interns	$	$	$ 217	$ 1,446	$ 1,171	$ 3,799
Medical education director				2,480	871	1,034
Medical education		1,028		3,003		318
Medical equipment	152	7,931	1,817	2,796	1,542	0
Doctors' offices		399	81	506	1,539	0
Nursing administration	1,139	1,572	190	2,557	1,679	0
Nurse training school	2,853	6,284	4,297	11,114	7,704	516
In-service education (nursing)		1,092				0
Inpatients	10,544	13,456	2,061	49,781	5,480	24,553
Outpatients	3,381	23,695	14,785	93,815	20,510	3,018
Emergency room	550					1,525
Bloodbank	50			1,351	7,046	1,123
Pharmacy		674	1,449	530	6,619	1,956
Nursery		1,577	3,516	4,928		686
Pediatrics		2,815	4,122	372	8,974	11,355
Obstetrics	688			637	2,570	590
Operating rooms	885	27,470	26,692	10,154	33,486	17,489
Delivery rooms	1,905	35,113		5,103	15,681	1,955
Recovery rooms		277				1,007
Intensive care		1,463	8,054	21,093	3,385	0
Cardiac unit	114	1,221	22,450	1,851	12,878	253
Isolation			762	1,031	209	0
Radiology	1,354	174,117	18,101	34,934	3,360	29,711
Cobalt therapy	385	228	353		6,654	47,313
Psychiatry		2,102	1,160	367	1,106	430
Internal medicine						6,100
Dental						4,835
Anesthesiology						3,175
Total	$24,000	$302,514	$110,107	$269,450	$142,461	$162,741

EXHIBIT 3C
ADDITIONS TO FIXED ASSETS

	1967	1968	1969	1970	1971	1972
Medical records	$ 5,065	$ 2,874	$ 2,465	$ 9,240	$10,236	$ 0
Medical library	0	0	6,377	488	445	1,468
Laboratory	6,705	18,026	51,953	26,225	3,945	10,342
Electrocardiology		306	2,366	933	1,481	
Electroencephalography		7,610		3,275	121	7,574
Cardiopulmonary lab	4,870	27,109	280	23,432	1,692	22,392
Physical therapy	195	2,011	910	11,162	4,384	1,945
Inhalation therapy	82	1,262	11,237	10,544	17,451	7,575
Occupational therapy	215					
Social services		303	1,531		1,192	283
Audiovisual				12,448	3,795	
Patient service administration						
Total	$17,132	$59,531	$77,119	$97,747	$44,742	$51,746

EXHIBIT 3D
ADDITIONS TO FIXED ASSETS

	1967	1968	1969	1970	1971	1972
Accounting	$	$1,423	$2,945	$ 5,284	$1,784	$ 2,992
Cashiering						
Payroll		325	221	500		
Accounts				476		
Admitting	490	44	349	3,507	3,104	1,913
Credits collection	312	1,001	539	138	520	5,588
Purchasing			3,756	1,374	610	1,600
Data processing		959	363	2,573	2,030	3,809
Total	$802	$3,752	$8,173	$13,852	$8,048	$15,902

EXHIBIT 3E
ADDITIONS TO FIXED ASSETS

	1967	1968	1969	1970	1971	1972
Personnel	$ 187	$ 801	$ 1,789	$ 698	$ 589	$ 1,069
Employee health		166	196	133		135
Maintenance of personnel						
Telephone service						246
Mail room		204				13,811
Messengers		61	692	194	629	
Communications		2,309	3,430	4,203		
Dietitians	456	353	430	4,737		
Kitchen	21,476	496	219	775		4,235
Special diet kitchen	254				1,517	
Cafeteria	28,153	3,787		1,100		
Dishwashing	14,475		367			
Floor kitchens	111			774		
Sanitation	910	2,682	2,644	9,071	2,448	436
Laundry		9,935	951	1,106	1,058	5,044
Heating plant (laundry)			409			
Linen						
Operation of plant	58			4,049		
Maintenance	814	6,122	1,520	514	1,364	8,622
Security	2,588	587	837		3,359	3,812
Central supply			2,230	741	5,210	
Storeroom	654	3,599	777	2,886	1,984	282
Planning			245	742		
Total	$70,136	$31,002	$16,736	$31,703	$18,148	$37,692

EXHIBIT 3F
ADDITIONS TO FIXED ASSETS

	1967	1968	1969	1970	1971	1972
Access space	$ 48	$ 332	$	$	$	$
Rental properties		18,406	6,411	3,132	2,196	
Power distribution					436,643	37,325
Land	34,500	327,268	112,130	4,200	33,300	371,215
Buildings A, B, C	54,891	234,154	53,209	14,212	13,527	324,801
Building D	35,227	13,368	752	19,805	3,604	
Building E			2,535	580	737	
Nurses' home (old)	5,060	659	412			2,065
Nurses' home (new)	2,541		651	1,917		
911-913 Wellington		72,500	48,189	29,756		573
887-889 Nelson	299	3,101	2,372	4,402		
900-906 Oakdale		152,939	4,611			
933 Wellington		87,578	610	373,400		2,000
937 Wellington			22,290	190	25,803	
New boiler house			693,313	1,039	797	
Total	$132,566	$908,505	$947,485	$452,633	$516,607	$737,979

EXHIBIT 4
DESCRIPTION OF IMMC USES AND SOURCES OF PERMANENT FUND
CLASSIFICATIONS

Fund	Uses	Sources
General	Transfers of cash to plant and to development; additions to fixed assets	Net income; depreciation
Plant	Additions to fixed assets; charge for depreciation	Transfers from all other funds
Development	Additions to fixed assets; fund-raising expenses	Transfers from general donations; Stone Foundation*; federal and state grants; other foundations; dividends and interest†; capital gains (losses); rental income; sundry
Specific purposes	Transfers to general fund to support services of hospital; scholarships; Katherine Wright Clinic (outpatient psychiatry)	Donations; foundations; interest
Endowment	None expended as yet; fund not begun until fiscal 1971	Donations; interest

*A total of $3.95 million through fiscal 1971.
†Approximately 83 percent interest and 17 percent dividends.

EXHIBIT 5
IMMC PERMANENT FUND BALANCES (thousands of dollars)

	1967	1968	1969	1970	1971
General	$ 1,724	$ 1,845	$ 1,945	$ 1,781	$ 1,803
Plant	7,295	8,117	9,083	9,519	9,790
Building and development	1,686	1,581	2,162	2,603	7,222
Special purpose	187	80	96	88	243
Endowment	–	–	–	–	8
Total	$10,892	$11,623	$13,286	$13,991	$19,066

EXHIBIT 6
ILLINOIS MASONIC MEDICAL CENTER, ANNUAL CHANGES IN FUND BALANCES
(thousands of dollars)

	1968	1969	1970	1971
General fund				
Additions				
Net income	$ 28	$ 531	$ 5	$ 51
Deductions				
Loss on abandonment	0	0	0	49
Net change before interfund transfers	$ 28	$ 531	$ 5	$ 2
Interfund transfers				
Provision for depreciation	$ 335	$ 429	$ 469	$ 522
Net book value, buildings razed	108			
Transfer of cash	(131)	(596)	(222)	(352)
Additions to fixed assets	(219)	(264)	(416)	(150)
Net effect of transfers	$ 93	$ (431)	$ (169)	$ 20
Net change in fund balance	121	100	(164)	22
Opening balance	1,724	1,845	1,945	1,781
Year-end balance	$1,845	$1,945	$1,781	$1,803
Plant				
Interfund transfers				
Provision for depreciation	$ (335)	$ (429)	$ (469)	$ (522)
Net book value, buildings razed	(108)	0	0	0
Additions to fixed assets	1,265	1,166	905	793
Net effect of transfers	$ 822	$ 737	$ 436	$ 271
Valuation adjustment	0	229	0	0
Net change in fund balance	$ 822	$ 966	$ 436	$ 271
Opening balance	7,295	8,117	9,083	9,519
Year-end balance	$8,117	$9,083	$9,519	$9,790

EXHIBIT 6 (*continued*)
ILLINOIS MASONIC MEDICAL CENTER, ANNUAL CHANGES IN FUND BALANCES
(thousands of dollars)

	1968	1969	1970	1971
Development				
Additions				
Donations	$ 659	$ 671	$ 706	$4,882
Dividends	16	10	2	6
Interest	52	53	10	29
Gain (loss), sales of investments	0	157	(2)	0
Net retail income	1	35	44	7
Total additions	$ 728	$ 926	$ 760	$4,924
Deductions				
Fund-raising expenses	$ 29	$ 30	$ 86	$ 33
Loss on sale of real estate	2	9	0	0
Total deductions	$ 31	$ 39	$ 86	$ 33
Net change before interfund transfers	697	887	674	4,891
Interfund transfers				
Transfer of cash	$ 131	$ 596	$ 222	$ 352
Additions to fixed assets	(1,044)	(902)	(455)	(624)
Additions of construction	111	0	0	0
Net effect of transfers	$ (802)	$ (306)	$ (233)	$ (272)
Net change in fund balance	(105)	581	441	4,619
Opening balance	1,686	1,581	2,162	2,603
Year-end balance	$1,581	$2,162	$2,603	$7,222
Specific purposes				
Additions				
Donations	$ 83	$ 60	$ 60	$ 368
Dividends and interest	4	1	1	1
Total additions	$ 87	$ 61	$ 61	$ 369
Deductions				
Transferred to general fund				
Free services	$ 32	$ 19	$ 0	$ 96
Medical library books, etc.	12	15	20	21
General operations	24	0	0	29
Scholarships	11	10	15	12
Katherine Wright Clinic	0	0	0	37
Adjustments to student loan received	2	0	0	0
Total deductions	$ 81	$ 44	$ 35	$ 195
Net change before interfund transfers	6	17	26	174
Interfund transfers				
Additions to fixed assets	$ (2)	$ (1)	$ (34)	$ (19)
Additions to construction	(111)	0	0	0
Net effect of transfers	$ (113)	$ (1)	$ (34)	$ (19)
Net change in fund balance	$ (107)	$ 16	$ (8)	$ 155
Opening balance	187	80	96	88
Year-end balance	$ 80	$ 96	$ 88	$ 243

Medicaid (welfare) patients, leaving IMMC an increasing deficit on each Medicaid patient. Combined with the earlier federal decision, this action reduced IMMC's net operating revenue by about $732,000 from the budgeted level for the 1971 fiscal year. To meet immediate cash-flow needs, IMMC secured a bank loan of $900,000 (see Exhibit 2) despite generally tight credit and also increased its mortgage. In February 1971, Mr. Hicks felt that IMMC had reached a critical financial situation. He decided to institute an austerity program immediately.

THE AUSTERITY COMMITTEES

To implement this program, Mr. Hicks created a standing review board, known as the Austerity Committee, to assign priorities to all departmental requests for funds. The committee consisted of the following IMMC administrators and officials:

Harvey Morowitz (chairperson)	Director of personnel
Sy Berebitsky	Director of general accounting
Bill Blessing	Director of professional services
Trudy Gorecki	Director of nursing
Dick Gustafson	Manager of medical transcriptions
Karen Heggen	Director of budgeting
Ted Leiterman	Director of Family Health Care Center
Wes McCormick	Director of operations
Jim Rozanski	Director of purchasing
Arnie Silver	Director of finance

The committee was responsible for reviewing both operating expenditures and capital investment requests made by the functional and the medical departments. Only funds budgeted for the Stone Pavilion were beyond the committee's purview—these continued to be approved by Wes McCormick. The Austerity Committee met weekly to rule on items submitted in advance of its meeting and placed on its agenda. Typically, five or six items would be considered at each meeting.

The committee's most serious decision, in Harvey Morowitz's opinion, came in late 1971. A continual decline in IMMC's occupancy rate through October had further reduced anticipated revenues and left IMMC with substantial idle capacity.[5] To reduce overhead and operating costs, the Austerity Committee suspended some programs, including the Family Health Care Center, and it laid off 87 employees in what the committee deemed to be noncritical areas. The projected cost reduction in fiscal 1972 from these actions was $500,000.

More typical of the decisions made by the Austerity Committee, according to Morowitz, was whether to appropriate $500 to purchase a pool table for use

[5] The average occupancy rate, which had been 86.5 percent in 1970, declined to 84.3 percent in mid-1971 and had fallen to less than 82 percent by October.

in the psychiatric ward. The committee assigned two members to investigate the existing recreational facilities at IMMC and, based on their recommendation, approved the request.

Despite the absence of a standard format or methodology, decisions affecting the functional departments were usually approached through cost/benefit analysis, with projects offering cash savings in operations given favorable reception by the committee. Capital allocation among medical departments, however, troubled the Austerity Committee. According to one member, the committee displayed an "arbitrariness" in handling medical department requests. He believed that most of the committee members felt that their lack of specialized knowledge in medical fields left them incapable of making sound decisions.

Therefore, at the request of the original Austerity Committee, a new Medical Austerity Committee was established in December 1971 to consider all funds requests of the medical departments. Mr. Blessing retained his membership on the original committee, now known as the Administrative Austerity Committee, and also served on the Medical Austerity Committee. He was unique in his dual membership and was expected to serve as a liaison between the two committees, although coordination between them was limited to his keeping each committee apprised of the other's decisions. The balance of the Medical Austerity Committee consisted of the chairpersons of IMMC's clinical medical departments, as indicated below:

T. Howard Clarke, M.D. (chairperson)	Medical director
J. Barton, M.D.	Obstetrics/gynecology
I. Belgrade, M.D.	Family medicine (F.H.C.C.)
W. Blessing	Director of professional services
L. Braudo, M.D.	Pediatrics
C. Drake, M.D.	Surgery
E. Feldman, M.D. (chief of staff)	Internal medicine
D. Frederickson, D.D.S.	Dentistry
G. Gyori, M.D.	Pathology
L. Hirsch, M.D.	Ambulatory care
R. Kelsey, M.D.	Pathology
D. Loomis, M.D.	Psychiatry
W. Meszaros, M.D.	Radiology

From its inception, the Medical Austerity Committee's deliberations were conducted as a part of the regular meetings of the medical department chairpersons led by Dr. T. Howard Clarke, medical director. Usually it considered two or three items each week as part of the order of business of these meetings. According to Mr. Blessing, the committee established no criteria for evaluating requests and did not attempt to assign priorities to those approved. He indicated that minor items typically received quick approval, while a $60,000 request would face tougher questioning.

Mr. Blessing also observed that Dr. Clarke, despite his medical experience, was unable to equal the specialized knowledge of his department chairpersons and therefore relied on their medical judgments concerning capital requests from their own departments. Because of the degree of specialized knowledge involved in many requests, each department chairperson was usually similarly dependent on his or her colleague's judgments regarding their respective departments. Thus, Mr. Blessing believed, committee members perceived the rejection of a capital request as a slap at the capabilities of a fellow department chairperson and would approve any request that seemed reasonable. Another deterrent to close scrutiny of requests was each committee member's realization that his own requests would be examined in turn by the committee. In Mr. Blessing's opinion, this created a reluctance to antagonize anyone possessing an opportunity to retaliate.

Assessments of the Austerity Committees and Their Accomplishments

According to Harvey Morowitz, the Administrative Austerity Committee seemed to "act as a psychological brake" on spending by the functional departments. He believed that prior to the committee's establishment there had been no central authority for authorizing expenditures, so departments had spent according to their own wishes. In 1971, when the Administrative Austerity Committee had jurisdiction over both medical and functional departments, IMMC's operating expenses were reduced to $22,151,472 from a budgeted level of $22,812,000.[6] The 1972 budget projected operating expenses of $24,314,000, of which $22,474,000 was for "hospital functions"[7] compared with $20,968,000 budgeted for those functions in 1971. Mr. Morowitz also believed that the committee had become an important communications link among the functional divisions and facilitated the determination of funding priorities on a hospitalwide basis. Mr. Morowitz noted an increasing pressure on his committee to consider a 10- to 15-year horizon in its deliberation. For example, in 1971, Mr. Hicks had requested a study to determine the types of services which IMMC should offer in the 1980s. Mr. Morowitz felt that the absence of explicit, written objectives for the committee left its responsibilities indefinite and subject to alteration by the executive director.

The Medical Austerity Committee did not recommend any cost-reduction program comparable to the lay-offs instituted by the administrative committee, nor did it refuse or reduce any major requests. Despite the infrequency of adverse action on medical departments' requests, the committee was credited by Dr. Clarke and Mr. Blessing with reducing the capital expenditures made by

---

[6]The recent trend in operating expenses at IMMC is evident in the annual operating expenses for 1967–1970 (in millions):

1967:	$10.30
1968:	$12.56
1969:	$15.25
1970:	$18.94

[7]Most of the remainder was for "medical functions" and "the family health function."

medical departments.[8] Dr. Clarke felt that medical department chairpersons were more careful about submitting requests for funds, knowing that their colleagues would examine them. He attributed the high rate of project approvals to more effective screening prior to the submission of requests.

Coordination of budgeting efforts by the two committees was largely informal and relied on the dual role of Bill Blessing. Neither committee was given a specific ceiling on spending nor was there an allocation of funds between the two committees. Instead, each committee was directed to minimize expenditures within its jurisdiction. The capital budgets approved for fiscal years 1971 and 1972 are shown in Exhibit 7.

CAPITAL BUDGETING FOR MEDICAL EQUIPMENT—1972

By the spring of 1972, IMMC's financial crises had eased and the urgency that once surrounded austerity committee proceedings abated. As the practice of annual budgeting became more familiar to IMMC department and division heads, interim requests for funds became less frequent.[9]

The two austerity committees, whose responsibilities had never been clearly defined or made permanent during Mr. Hicks's tenure, were less active as fewer items were submitted for their consideration. Departmental budgets and spending continued to be reviewed by the committees prior to being sent to the executive director for presentation to the board of trustees, but, as in 1970 and 1971, a major portion of the expenditures for medical equipment was devoted to equipping the Stone Pavilion. This portion, which totaled about $1.95

[8] Operating expenses for medical functions, however, had increased in 1971 by about 6.8 percent over their budgeted level of $1.20 million and were budgeted as $1.46 million in 1972.

[9] In the third quarter of fiscal 1972, the Medical Austerity Committee authorized the hiring of an additional secretary in one medical department. It also received a request from another department for a typewriter and suggested that the department apply directly to "the administration."

EXHIBIT 7
ILLINOIS MASONIC MEDICAL CENTER, CAPITAL BUDGETS, 1971–1972

	1971 funds budgeted	1971 approved (no funds available)	1972 funds budgeted
Nursing Division			
Administration	$ 1,310	$ 0	$ 1,566
Nursing education	1,030	0	12,600
Medical*	8,420	11,495	11,220
Surgical*	2,620	0	2,775
Psychiatric*	985	1,015	900
Operating room*	9,000	3,000	21,350
Obstetrics*	17,695	15,705	19,410
Subtotal	$ 41,060	$ 31,215	$ 69,821

EXHIBIT 7 *(continued)*

	1971 funds budgeted	1971 approved (no funds available)	1972 funds budgeted
Professional Services Division			
Laboratories	$ 15,000	$ 35,000	$ 0
Electrodiagnostics	15,000	12,735	11,800
Radiology	16,950	10,000	90,114
Anesthesiology	7,960	1,000	0
Inhalation therapy	2,500		21,336
Physical medicine	5,402	3,000	13,370
Social services	1,350	0	0
Community dentistry	0	0	31,317
Pathology	0	0	29,000
Ambulatory care	5,000	41,082	0
Pharmacy	(See Operations Division)		32,000
Medical records	7,820	3,000	0
Subtotal	$ 76,982	$105,817	$228,937
Operations Division			
Audiovisual	$ 8,350	$ 0	$ 0
Communications	0	11,000	0
Pharmacy	9,144	0	—
Medical transcriptions	20,000	0	0
Food service	10,400	0	0
Plant management	3,325	0	0
Sanitation	5,000	0	9,422
Personnel	2,100	400	2,305
Medical supply/equipment	5,111	4,889	0
Security	0	0	5,446
Legal/property administration	34,822	3,025	0
Subtotal	$ 98,252	$ 19,314	$ 17,173
Finance Division			
Administration	$ 2,000	$ 500	$ 0
Purchasing-warehouse	2,850	0	0
Data processing/information systems	1,400	0	250
Accounting	6,960	7,750	3,445
Subtotal	$ 13,210	$ 8,250	$ 3,695
Administration			
Executive office	$ 5,000	$ 0	$ 0
Masonic relations	218	0	0
Public relations	575	0	0
Subtotal	$ 5,793	$ 0	$ 0
Medical Division*			
Administration	$ 6,000	$ 0	$ 0
Obstetrics/gynecology	0	0	5,170
Pediatrics	0	0	14,000
Subtotal	$ 6,000	$ 0	$ 19,170
Planning department, project furnishings, and contingencies	$170,000	$497,500	$ 61,204
Total	$411,297	$662,096	$400,000

*Some medical departments' budgets are included under Nursing Division.

million over the three-year span,[10] remained under the supervision of Wes Mc-Cormick and bypassed both austerity committees.

Sources of Requests

Other requests from medical departments for capital expenditures in fiscal 1973 were to be sent to Dr. Clarke by July 1972. Almost all requests originated at the departmental level, either from physicians or from nurses. According to Mr. Blessing, the Department of Nursing suggested more projects than any other group. Typically, nurses who encountered difficulties in their daily work would advise Mrs. Gorecki, the director of nursing, of their needs. Mrs. Gorecki screened these requests and combined those which seemed reasonable into medical department totals. In Mr. Blessing's opinion, physicians accounted for the next largest number of requests. He believed that their requests often were prompted by their exposure to medical equipment through salespeople, journal advertising, displays at medical conventions, and at other hospitals. As was the case with nurses, physicians directed their suggestions to their respective department chairpersons, who considered them for inclusion in the departmental budget request to be submitted in July.

There were varying capital needs among the medical departments. Some, such as the cardiopulmonary laboratory, regularly exerted pressure for new testing devices as technological advances made possible more sophisticated analyses. Mr. Blessing attributed this pressure in part to the demands of the technicians working in such departments. Others, such as x-ray, had relatively low capital requirements beyond their initial setup costs. Regardless of the department involved, the medical professionals were accorded great influence because of the hospital administration's overriding commitment to patient care. This meant that the physicians had an advantage in any budgeting dispute, according to Mr. Blessing, because they could always cite improved patient care as a benefit of a proposed project.[11]

Information Gathering and Development

In most instances the department submitting a capital budget request would also indicate the type of equipment desired and would often specify a preferred manufacturer or model. Although there was no standard format for such reports, departments were encouraged to include cost estimates and both the projected usage and the likely benefits of the requested equipment. The IMMC

---

[10] Roughly one-third of this amount represented federal grants.

[11] Although IMMC's aggregation of the capital budgets for medical and nursing departments prevents the measurement of the percentage approved of each group's budget request, the actions of the Administrative Austerity Committee in approving operating budgets for fiscal 1972 indicate that administrative personnel viewed medical requests from the Department of Nursing as favorably as those from physicians. While denying about 5 percent of the combined Medical Department and house staff budget request, the committee approved all but 2 percent of the Nursing Service request and granted the entire request for Nursing Education.

administrators' chariness of intruding in the internal affairs of medical departments and thus violating their autonomy made it difficult for them to obtain such estimates or to verify estimates submitted by the medical departments.[12] Furthermore, even when such quantitative analysis was possible, challenging physicians' assertions as to the qualitative aspects of patient care often irritated the physicians.

If the particular needs of a department required unusual or custom-made equipment, that department was expected to include such requirements and to propose designs for what was needed. Specifications and designs sometimes were developed with the assistance of equipment manufacturers, since IMMC did not have staff engineers. Through this stage, personnel in the department making the request were responsible for any designs and specifications, since IMMC's specialized medical knowledge in any field was concentrated in the medical department.

The degree of specialization involved in equipment requests often prompted Dr. Clarke to seek expert advice about the likely costs and benefits of such equipment. Usually he sought information from hospitals or medical departments with situations comparable to IMMC's through his contacts with other medical directors and specialists not associated with IMMC. In this way he was able to determine whether particular equipment was necessary for the type or scale of departmental operations anticipated at IMMC and to obtain professional opinions on the merits of comparable equipment offered by various manufacturers. It was Dr. Clarke's opinion that meaningful, competitive bids were relatively unlikely when equipment was of a complex medical nature because competing equipment was seldom similar enough to permit decisions based mainly on price. In general, he was willing to pay a premium of 15 percent or more to obtain proved equipment rather than choose a riskier, less expensive alternative. Because of this preference for certainty in performance, he attached greater significance to the advice and guidance he received from his outside contacts than to the prices offered by manufacturers. Consulting with medical personnel outside IMMC was also advisable since it helped assure the approval of the board of trustees. The board was reluctant to approve the acquisition of experimental or prototypical equipment, so if Dr. Clarke could present evidence of equipment's success at similar institutions, delay or refusal of the request was much less likely.

CAPITAL BUDGETING FOR MEDICAL EQUIPMENT IN THE STONE PAVILION

Despite the existence of the austerity committees, Wes McCormick had retained responsibility for all plans involving the Stone Pavilion. His duties

---

[12] Although nursing departments were not conceded as much autonomy as medical departments, the operations of the two groups were frequently so interrelated that the administrators' acknowledged reluctance to intrude in medical department affairs hampered the gathering of information concerning nursing department requests.

included instituting color-coded interior decorating to simplify directing persons about the building, scheduling departmental moving dates to minimize the need for any shutdown of services, and developing operating plans for many of his operations departments (e.g., dietary, engineering, sanitation) to service the new pavilion. As mentioned previously, the inclusion of capital budgeting for the Stone Pavilion among Mr. McCormick's responsibilities was seen by Mr. Hicks as a way of avoiding confusion and duplication of effort among the various departments and divisions involved in moving to the new facility.

In January 1970, Mr. McCormick circulated questionnaires among the medical departments which were scheduled to be moved. He requested a complete listing of each department's equipment and furnishing needs, including minor noncapital items as well as major medical equipment. Great detail was required because of the provisions of the Hill-Burton Act, which controlled the $500,000 in federal funds that IMMC was granted toward furnishing the Stone Pavilion. Late in the year, Mr. McCormick received the department's responses. By considering the costs of moving revenue lost due to interrupted operation, the remaining useful life of existing equipment, and projected departmental patient volume, he and Dr. Clarke decided whether existing equipment should be moved or replaced. He also evaluated requests for new equipment or expanded facilities. If he doubted the medical practicability of a request, Mr. McCormick would confer with Dr. Clarke, but the decision was his responsibility. If a requested addition to IMMC's equipment seemed desirable and reasonable, Mr. McCormick would ask the department making the request to submit detailed specifications.

Upon receiving such specifications, Mr. McCormick would seek information from manufacturers of medical equipment and compare their products with the specifications written by IMMC's medical department. If there were no significant differences between the specifications and a reputable, existing product, Mr. McCormick and the medical department would settle on that one. If the department's specifications were not met by existing products, Mr. McCormick would "negotiate" with the department to achieve a compromise between their desired equipment capabilities and those of existing products. His objective in such negotiations was to eliminate "pie in the sky" specifications that might disqualify otherwise suitable equipment. During this stage of evaluation, Mr. McCormick sometimes sought the aid of outside consultants to gain acceptance of his suggestions, since he felt the medical specialists at IMMC gave more credence to the opinions of fellow professionals than to those of an administrator. If IMMC's needs could not be filled by existing products, Mr. McCormick would send the specifications to manufacturers for bids. This action was independent of any bids sought by Dr. Clarke on equipment requested by departments that were not moving to the Stone Pavilion. He participated in Stone Pavilion budgeting decisions only when Mr. McCormick sought his medical advice.

The Anesthesiology Department's Request

Among the equipment requests that Wes McCormick received in fiscal 1971 was one from the Anesthesiology Department for new electronic monitoring equipment for use in the operating rooms, recovery rooms, and intensive care section of the Stone Pavilion. Although there was no doubt in their minds that the equipment would cost more than $200,000, Dr. Rosenberg, the chairperson of the department, and his colleague, Dr. Heller, felt that the increasing level of patient monitoring made the equipment technologically desirable. Mr. McCormick and Dr. Clarke had already agreed that because of technological advances since IMMC last purchased such equipment, the hospital's existing equipment was outdated and that the Anesthesiology Department would be reequipped upon moving to the Stone Pavilion. Consequently, Mr. McCormick now had to consider only the number of monitoring units needed for the department and the types of equipment to be purchased rather than whether any purchases should be made. To this end, he asked Drs. Rosenberg and Heller to detail their request, e.g., to specify the desired number of units, the indicators to be monitored, and the data storage capacity required.

To comply with this request, Dr. Rosenberg sought help from a manufacturer of patient monitoring equipment. According to Dr. Rosenberg, he was forced to resort to the manufacturer because he was unable to write the specifications without engineering assistance, and no engineers were available to the medical staff at IMMC.

In March 1971, the Anesthesiology Department presented the proposed specifications to Wes McCormick. In addition to identifying the body functions to be monitored and recorded, the plans included one monitor for each bed in the recovery rooms and intensive care section and one for each operating room. The plans also included sufficient computer storage capacity to maintain records of the most recent four-hour period on each machine. Using these specifications, Wes McCormick sought bids from selected manufacturers of such equipment. The bids—which were received in August 1971—ranged from $215,000 to $280,000, with the low bid submitted by the company which had aided in writing the specifications.[13] Exhibit 8 shows a typical bid on these specifications. In September 1971, Mr. McCormick won the approval of the board of trustees to make the purchase within the range of bids received, since he felt that the low-bidding company had benefited from tailoring the specifications to fit its own equipment.

Having received preliminary bids but being unbound by any contract, Wes McCormick sought to lower the cost of the equipment by eliminating unnecessary or uneconomic capabilities. He had already persuaded the Anesthesiology Department to specify transistors rather than tubes for the monitoring equip-

---

[13] This was the only original bid of which records remained in 1972. The manufacturer submitting this bid did not submit a bid on the revised specifications in fiscal 1972.

EXHIBIT 8
TYPICAL BID ON ORIGINAL SPECIFICATIONS FOR
PATIENT MONITORING EQUIPMENT

Item	Price
Bedside and operating table monitors	$144,000
Nurses' consoles and display monitors	65,595
Recovery room central station	30,435
Intensive care unit central station	13,905
Accessories and installation	19,260
	$273,195

ment and now faced the task of proving the medical soundness as well as the financial merit of reducing the monitoring equipment's capabilities. The anesthesiologists remained firm in supporting their initial specifications and were buttressed in their arguments by the reports of a University of Illinois Medical School consultant whom they had hired. To counter their arguments and to have any hope of persuading the anesthesiologists that reduction of the monitoring equipment proposal was medically sound, Mr. McCormick turned to Dr. Clarke.

Through his contacts among hospital administrators, Dr. Clarke contacted and retained as a consultant an east coast anesthesiologist who had become a hospital administrator as well.[14] According to Mr. McCormick, this man enjoyed a reputation for knowledgeable and reasonable views in both anesthesiology and management fields and was well regarded among both medical professionals and administrators. After visiting IMMC to study the question, this consultant recommended several reductions in the scope of the monitoring project. Most prominent among his proposals were the limitations of recall capacity to about half the level proposed by the Anesthesiology Department ($1\frac{1}{2}$ or 2 hours rather than 4 hours) and the reduction of monitoring units from 44 to 36. The reduction in units was reasonable, he concluded, because there are always patients requiring less intensive monitoring who could be assigned to regular beds and checked periodically by the staff. With the consultant's support providing greater receptiveness among the anesthesiologists, Wes McCormick succeeded in winning their agreement to the changes. After working with IMMC's architects to ensure that the monitoring equipment would be compatible with other proposed equipment and consistent with available space, Wes McCormick solicited bids on the revised equipment package.

In August 1972, three manufacturers had responded to IMMC's invitation to bid. The range of the bids (from $211,673 to about $260,000[15]) reflected the savings accomplished by reducing the number of monitoring units and their

[14] The fees and expenses paid for the consultant were $1,200.
[15] Neither IMMC nor the manufacturer submitting the highest bid had retained any record of the details of the bid.

data storage capacity for the levels originally specified. Exhibit 9 included the two lowest bids on the revised specifications.

The anesthesiologists preferred the manufacturer submitting the middle bid (labeled Company A in Exhibit 9), who had assisted them in writing the original specifications. Dr. Clarke also preferred this manufacturer's equipment and had expressed his willingness to pay as much as a 15 percent premium for it. However, Dr. Clarke, Mr. McCormick, and the east coast consultant considered the equipment of the low bidder (labeled Company B in Exhibit 9) to be satisfactory for IMMC's purposes and to have been sufficiently proved elsewhere to satisfy the board of trustees. Therefore, Mr. McCormick's final decision would hinge on the weight given to the preferences of the medical staff in comparison to purely financial consideration.

Although Mr. Mungerson had joined IMMC while the decisions about the monitoring equipment were still in progress, his involvement had been limited to attending a meeting at which the east coast consultant had presented his recommendations to Dr. Rosenberg, Dr. Clarke, and Mr. McCormick. Mr. Mungerson attended the meeting as a moderator rather than as a decision maker because he had neither participated in the previous deliberations nor had the time to familiarize himself with the issues being discussed. He had decided to rely on Wes McCormick's judgment in this matter but felt that his presence at the meeting might bring a speedier agreement.

MR. MUNGERSON'S VIEWS ON IMMC'S CAPITAL BUDGETING PROCESS

Although he did not have to decide the fate of each capital budget request that came before him, Mr. Mungerson believed that the budgeting process at

EXHIBIT 9
LOWEST BIDS FOR PATIENT MONITORING EQUIPMENT, REVISED
SPECIFICATIONS

Component location	Company A	Company B
Cardiovascular operating room	$ 8,035	$ 8,620
Neurosurgery operating room	7,650	7,475
General surgery operating room	41,405	35,448
Cystoscopy operating room	6,280	6,040
Operating room central station	56,995	14,520
Recovery room	35,535	62,920
Recovery room central station	6,095	18,675
Intensive care unit	50,805	35,610
Intensive care unit central station	7,015	12,525
Accessories (data storage, transducer, miscellaneous equipment)	10,130	9,840
Total	$229,945	$211,673

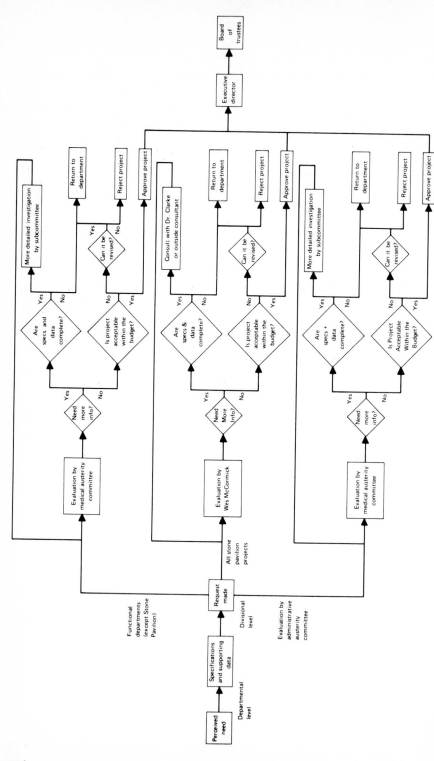

EXHIBIT 10
IMMC capital budgeting process (1972).

IMMC was a concern of the executive director. He also was of the opinion that the present process, depicted in Exhibit 10, required revision; before any revision could be made, however, he felt he would have to consider the following questions:

1 Should the austerity committee system be retained? If so, should it be modified?

2 How could IMMC's administrators exercise effective control over capital spending in medical departments without imposing laymen's "arbitrariness" on medical plans?

3 Should the changes be instituted for the 1973 fiscal year or delayed a year? Implementation of any changes would have to be coordinated with the schedule for budgeting for the fiscal year which would begin within two months. Departmental operating budgets had already been drawn. Would an interim system designed just for fiscal 1973 be possible, or should the process be changed just once and permanently?

REFORMULATION: RECYCLING THE POLICYMAKING PROCESS

The Process of Reformulation: Revising the Strategic Design; Developing Recovery Strategies

REFORMULATION: THE BASIS OF STRATEGIC PLANNING

Successful concepts, technological breakthroughs, and innovations reach maturity, and as products slip into commodity items, competition becomes intense and profitability is limited or nonexistent. Competitive forces can dislodge a market leader; a changing industry structure can erode a firm's profits and advantage. To prevent falling into a decline position, management must be constantly alert to its changing environment and identify the stage of the firm's life cycle to initiate reformulation and the necessary recovery strategies to engage in the orderly transfer of resources into the development of new concepts or product lines. This requires constant diagnosing, probing, analyzing, and interpreting significant internal and external events which may threaten the well-being and survival of the firm.

The on-going monitoring of the control system is a major function of management at all levels. The interpretation of information supplied by the system is a vital responsibility of the top management group, who must determine when and if reformulation should be initiated and to what extent the policymaking process should be recycled. The information system may reflect favorable signs indicating that the firm is performing according to expectations and the organization is functioning smoothly. Almost invariably, however, an organization attempting to implement a complex strategic plan will be subject to the vagaries of internal forces and pressures which will cause it to deviate from its charted course. In a dynamic business society corporate strategies and operating plans can easily be rendered obsolete by competitors' innovations, technological developments, and environmental influences which cause shifts in the marketplace. The control system may signal a need to recast the root strategy and thus require the development of a recovery strategy, a complete recycling of the policymaking process, and a redesign of the operating, organizational, and control strategies.

Drastic changes and a complete reformulation of the strategic design, however, are not generally dictated by the information derived from the control system. This action usually occurs over a long time period, on a transitional basis; it is a complicated and demanding task which frequently results in significant management personnel changes and distinct changes in the internal operations of the firm. In most instances the reformulation process will be centered on one or more of the successive phases of policymaking, calling for changes in operating strategies to cope with day-to-day changes in the marketplace, organizational adjustments or redesign to more effectively execute the strategic plan, or a bolstering or change in design of the control system to provide the information and vital signals needed to assure timely and effective reformulation.

REFORMULATION OF THE ROOT STRATEGY: FORD MOTOR

An example of a drastic reformulation is evident in the previously discussed Ford Motor Company case. Ford's decision to discontinue the famous and eminently successful Model T came abruptly in 1927. Despite the sudden decision on the part of Ford to abandon the Model T, the causes for the demise of his standardized one-model low-priced car were evident in the environment and industry trend for some period of time. Ford had refused to recognize the environmental changes which threatened his number-one market position and waited too long to begin the reformulation process and develop a recovery strategy. Before making his decision to discontinue production of the Model T, Ford attempted several unsuccessful recovery strategies. He tried to restyle the car through superficial changes and provided an option of four colors instead of the traditional single choice of black. When these attempts failed to recapture the loss of market share, Ford shut down all his plants and took the company out of the market for one year.

Ford's recovery strategy was based on a new car, the Model A. While the new model offered many improvements over the Model T and enjoyed an initial flush of success, it soon became evident that it could not keep pace with the strong competition of General Motors' Chevrolet and Chrysler's Plymouth. The company did not complete the reformulation process—it engaged in only partial reformulation. A complete recycling of the policymaking process to change root, operating, organizational, and control strategies was not undertaken. Basically the only change in Ford's strategic design was in substituting the Model A, with some improvements and a greater choice of variations in body styles, for the Model T. Instead of offering a variety of cars and model changes, as the competition did, the Model A remained unchanged for five years except for minor variations. In 1932 Ford dropped the Model A and brought out a completely new line of automobiles with V8 engines. It was not until 1945, when control of the company passed from its founder, Ford, that the company went through a complete reformulation, recycling each phase of the policymaking process.[1]

REFORMULATION: VOLKSWAGEN

The history of Volkswagen parallels Ford in many respects. The company's dedication to producing and marketing a quality low-priced automobile that appealed to the mass market never varied from its inception until recent years. Like Ford, VW's basic car, the Beetle, was mass-produced in a highly automated plant; a strong centralized organization and rigid cost controls were major factors in guiding the initial success of the company. VW's prolonged period of reformulation was similar to the experience of Ford. For a period of over 20 years, the Beetle was the company's major product, accounting for 70 percent or more of total production and the bulk of the profits. The various other models which the company introduced, with VW motors and basic engineering, were not particularly successful and contributed little to profits.

As a result, management sought to extend its product-line diversification and in 1965 purchased the Auto Union, which produced the Audi. In 1969 it arranged the merger of Auto Union with NSU Motorenwerke to form Audi-NSU. The products of this subsidiary placed the company in a higher-priced category and extended its marketing offerings. This also marked the first significant move VW made toward reformulation. Despite the introduction of many variations in both the Beetle and Audi models, the Beetle still remained the company's major product and profit contributor although it declined in percentage of total production.

Sales of the Beetle continued to decline, however, due to strong competition in Europe and the United States, its major export market. The rising costs of production in West Germany and the rising value of the Deutschmark on foreign exchanges priced the Beetle over much of its competition. Japanese entries into the small-car market and new United States entries, plus the competition of other European producers, added to the problems of VW. To stem this tide VW introduced the Passat (Dasher in the United States), a standard model with front engine and many accessories and options, and a new sports car, the Scirocco. Both these automobiles were in a price category well above the Beetle and above much of the competition. In 1975 VW introduced the Golf—named the Rabbit in the United States—and began to phase out the Beetle. This action, as in the case of the demise of the Model T, was a very difficult and wrenching decision on the part of management. The company experienced large losses in 1974 and 1975 and also lost its position as the leading foreign importer into the United States, its largest single market. As in the case of Ford, the company based its recovery strategy on a new model and diversification of its product line. The signs of the potential demise of the Beetle were present in the environment long before management made the decision to reformulate and finally abandon its very successful root strategy. Rising in-

[1] Ford Motor Company, see Chapter 2.

come levels and the desire for more than basic transportation, plus strong competition from many quarters, were indicated in the environment long before the management of VW made its decisions to phase out production of the Beetle and introduce a new, diversified line of automobiles.[2]

REFORMULATION: AMERICAN MOTORS

Another prominent example of a reformulation and recycling of the policymaking process resulting in a distinct change in root strategy is found in the action taken by American Motors in the 1950s. American Motors was formed in 1954 as a merger of Hudson and Nash, two financially distressed companies (misery loves company). This combination placed the newly formed organization and its product line in direct competition with the big three (General Motors, Ford, and Chrysler), which had decidedly more skills and resources. George Romney became the chief executive officer in 1954 and promoted a lightweight compact car named the Rambler, which had been in development since 1943 as a potential recovery strategy sorely needed by the newly formed company for survival. Romney's efforts initiated a reformulation in the company whose management group had carried over a big-car-market philosophy from the Nash and Hudson organizations. Romney gambled the future of the firm on seeking a special niche in the automotive industry which would initially avoid head-on competition with the big three. He discontinued the Nash and Hudson product lines and redirected the skills and resources of the company from the production and marketing of models in the lower-medium, medium, and higher-medium price range to the production and sale of the low-priced compact Rambler.

This reformulation guided by Romney necessitated significant changes in the company's strategic design. A new root strategy was developed through the reduction of the product line to a single entry in a specific segment of the automotive market. The operating, organizational design, and control strategies were also redefined to correspond to the new mission. Relations with dealers were changed; the advertising strategy dictated a new theme stressing price, size, "compactness," and economy of operation. According to Romney, it took seven years before the Rambler caught on and sales increased. While the reformulation process assured the survival of the firm and gave the company a short-term measure of success, it required a long time span to revitalize the organization and effect the new strategic design.[3]

REFORMULATION: LEATHERCRAFT

The Leathercraft case also illustrates a reformulation which resulted in a distinct change in root strategy. As in the Ford and VW cases, management did not interpret the signs which were evident in the environment and threatened the company's survival. Leathercraft produced and sold horsehide work shoes

---

[2] Volkswagen, see the case entitled *Volkswagenwerk* in Part Six, this volume.
[3] "AMC Gambles $60 Million on New Company," *Business Week*, Jan. 20, 1975.

in rural areas of the Midwest. The increasing cost of horsehide and the dwindling farm population eventually caused declining profits and a deficit year. The population shifts and the decline of the horse, their basic source of raw material, were evident long before management began the process of reformulation. The delayed introduction of a recovery strategy was done on a transitional basis through the gradual development of a process to tan pigskin leather to take the place of the dwindling and high-cost raw material of horsehide. The company introduced a line of dress shoes, casual shoes, golf shoes, and hunting boots utilizing both horsehide and pigskin. Despite Leathercraft's efforts to market its new line and expand out of the rural areas, approximately 60 percent of the sales remained in rural areas with populations of 1,000 or under, and horsehide work shoes continued to be the company's best seller. Leathercraft's management, as in the case of Ford, failed to complete the reformulation process, changing only the root strategy in terms of a new and expanded product line made of pigskin, an unproved basic raw material.

The company did not develop and utilize the necessary increased channels of distribution to sell their product line, which required expansion into the urban-suburban areas. It did not expand into new selling centers—such as department stores, sporting goods stores, independent shoestores, and special outlets for industrial shoes—to replace and supplement its distribution system, which was confined mainly to single stores in rural areas. Unanticipated production problems were encountered because of the failure to coordinate with the marketing efforts. Leathercraft expanded its line in a five-year period from 50 to 140 models of horsehide and from 15 to 90 models of pigskin. Production inefficiencies added to cost, and the company encountered significant returns due to the shipping of poor-quality merchandise. Management also neglected to change its organizational strategy to align it with its new product-market scope. The marketing and sales organization needed to be changed, and the sales force lacked training and incentives to sell the new products in the expanded distribution system. Leathercraft followed the pattern of Ford and VW in delaying too long in responding to the environmental factors and internal problems which affected the firm's survival. The definitive recovery strategy initiated by the company took a prolonged period, and the recycling process was incomplete. The operating strategy was not sufficiently redefined to follow the functional flow from the new product-line inception to the ultimate delivery to the customer, and the company did not tie its organizational and control strategies to its redefined root strategy.[4]

REFORMULATION OF OPERATING, ORGANIZATIONAL, AND CONTROL STRATEGIES: A&P'S RECOVERY STRATEGY

In most situations, reappraisal of a company's operations will not indicate a need for a drastic change in root strategy. The reformulation process is more

---

[4]See "Leathercraft Case," McNichols, *Policymaking and Executive Action* (New York: McGraw-Hill, 1972).

likely to focus on one or more of the successive phases of the policymaking process. Recovery strategies may be initiated through changes in operating, organizational, or control strategies.

A&P, long the leading supermarket chain in the United States, developed a distinct operating strategy in an effort to recover market share and profitability. The company, suffering intense competition, particularly from regional chains, lost its number-one position in the industry to Safeway while it sustained severe losses. A&P's management launched a major campaign termed "WEO—Where Economy Originates." This recovery strategy was directed at the operating level to underprice competition, and was supported by an intense advertising campaign stressing the WEO approach as assurance of low prices. This effort succeeded in restoring some lost market share; however, the severe price cutting which accompanied the campaign caused significant losses not only to A&P but to its competitors, who reacted with their own price-cutting campaigns in an effort to maintain their market share. The WEO campaign was eventually abandoned. A&P's problems were more deep-rooted than the loss of market share due to price competition. The company failed to keep pace with the move to the suburbs and to modernize and expand their supermarket facilities. A&P continued its decline despite a change in management, which purchased over 50 percent of its stock. The new management has significantly reduced the number of stores and withdrawn from several geographic areas where competition was intense.[5]

PROCTER AND GAMBLE'S REFORMULATION OF ORGANIZATION STRATEGY

The expansion of P&G's product line and market dominance through the years provided for growth but caused organization and control problems and complicated the monitoring and assessing of the performance of its many branded items. In its reformulation to correct this problem and to seek new strategies to facilitate continued growth and expansion, the management of P&G developed the brand-management concept. This organizational strategy changed the company's structure and design; it provided for the decentralization of the marketing function and tighter control over individual brand products. Each brand manager was given responsibility for the coordination of all the marketing functions for a given product and for the coordination with production for the manufacture of the given brand. This organizational strategy became part of P&G's basic business philosophy and influenced its root and operating strategies. The reformulation efforts at the organizational phase provided the company with the needed flexibility to attain its economic objectives of growth and expansion.[6]

---

[5]"The Food Giants Struggle to Stay in Step with Consumers," *Fortune*, Feb. 8, 1978.
[6]"Brand Manager—No Longer King," *Business Week*, June 9, 1973.

GENERAL MOTORS' REFORMULATION OF ORGANIZATION AND CONTROL STRATEGIES

While General Motors under Alfred Sloan went through a complete reformulation and recycled through each phase of the policymaking process, Sloan concentrated mainly on designing the company's organization and control strategies. His initial efforts toward reformulation were launched under Durant, the founder of General Motors, who requested him to study the organization of the company to seek possible solutions to the problems of rapid expansion which occurred after World War I. This resulted in his organization study, which defined the basis for operating a multiunit organization and established the principles for the management of complex, decentralized corporations. Sloan developed organizational and control strategies to give substance to the loosely knit group of companies which existed under Durant. His organizational design established separate profit centers for each division of the company and provided for the development of a strong central staff and a committee structure which served as a stabilizing and controlling influence on the company. His concept of organization and control made it possible for this large decentralized group of separate divisions to operate as a single corporate entity. A complete control system was developed under Sloan's guidance—a system which retained the independence of the divisions but established control and direction at the corporate level.

GENERAL ELECTRIC'S REFORMULATION OF ORGANIZATIONAL AND CONTROL STRATEGIES

Growth and expansion, as indicated in Chapter 8, were the vital factors which prompted a major reformulation in General Electric. The growth of the company was internally generated through the development of new products and markets, which resulted in a very diversified company. GE operated as a centralized organization through the early stages of its growth and through the World War II period, when its sales volume increased significantly. Management became increasingly aware of the problems and difficulties of operating a growth company under a centralized organization structure. As a result, a study was initiated under Ralph Cordiner, who later became chief executive officer, to determine the best method of organization to cope with the sustained and rapid growth of the company. As a result of Cordiner's study, a new organizational strategy was adopted in 1951. It provided for a decentralized organization in terms of product lines, geography, and functional types of work. Approximately 100 decentralized operating departments under 21 operating divisions were established as independent profit centers with full responsibility and authority for product engineering, manufacturing, and marketing.

This reformulation which resulted from Cordiner's study was directed to the organizational and control strategies of the company and did not materially affect its root and operating strategies. As in the case of Procter and Gamble and General Motors, GE was primarily concerned with the problems of management of growth and expansion and consequently concentrated its efforts at the organizational and control phases of the policymaking process.

This same basic reasoning, a need to reformulate at the organization and control levels, was evident in GE's development of its organizational concept of the strategic business unit (SBU) in the early 1970s. The company had grown to over 170 departments in 50 divisions organized into 10 groups. Management contended that the number of organizational units fragmented many of the separate businesses and created planning problems. The concept of each department standing as an independent profit center became obscured, and a business identification problem became apparent. To alleviate these difficulties and provide for continued growth and expansion, management went through a reformulation process and developed a new organizational strategy based on the SBUs. GE retained its basic structure of groups, divisions, and departments but superimposed on this the SBUs. Each SBU was designed as a collection of related businesses with its own mission and objectives and was operated as an independent profit center with the responsibility for strategic planning of the unit. This organizational strategy reduced corporate management's complex task of resource allocation from 170 or more departments to 43 clearly identified business units.[7]

REFORMULATION OF SEPARATE BUSINESS UNITS IN DECENTRALIZED ORGANIZATIONS

The complex, highly decentralized organizations that have many subsidiaries, divisions, and product lines are faced with the problem of reformulation at the corporate level for the total organization and the constant reappraisal of the separate and frequently distinct other operations or businesses which make up the total entity. Each situation has to be judged separately and in relation to the overall corporate objectives. The problem of maintaining profitable growth also complicates the reformulation process; judgments have to be made about the allocation of funds for expansion for each component or frequently for the phasing out or elimination of failing divisions or companies which do not meet the cutoff rates of return or internal cost of capital requirements set by the firm. This later result of reformulation is clearly illustrated in the much-publicized cases of the disposal of the computer divisions of GE and RCA.

The Case of General Electric's Computer Division

From 1957 through 1970 GE experienced losses of $162.7 million in its United States–based computer operations. The company had invested approximately

[7]See Ralph Cordiner, Jr., *New Frontiers for Professional Managers* (New York: McGraw-Hill, 1956). See also C. H. Springer, "Strategic Management in General Electric," *Operations Research*, vol. 21, no. 6, November–December 1973, pp. 1177–1182; also *GE's Evolving Management System*, unpublished internal report, January 18, 1972.

$472 million in this period in an effort to make it competitive with the giant of the industry, IBM, which had over 70 percent market share. In addition to IBM, GE and six other producers, known as the seven dwarfs, made up the computer industry in the United States. Not any of these companies had as much as 7 percent of the total market share, and GE had approximately 4 to 5 percent of the market.

Faced with the losses in the computer business and the cash drain of two other major losing ventures, nuclear power and jet engines, Fred Borch, GE's chairman, appointed a task force of three vice presidents to reappraise these businesses and provide the information needed to aid in the future allocation of corporate funds. The task force had to consider the computer groups' advanced product-line plan, known in the company as the APL, which proposed a new computer family that would have 20 to 40 percent better performance than IBM's existing line. APL's pro forma statements indicated that the new line would incur losses of approximately $538 million through 1973 before it would turn profitable. It was estimated that the line would turn a profit in 1974 and absorb the accumulated deficits by 1977. Total estimated revenues for the new line were placed at $8.2 billion for the period 1969 to 1981, with a pretax profit of $2.34 billion. The APL plan projected an increase in market share to 8 percent by 1975 and a rise to 10 percent shortly thereafter. GE's management estimated that the company would be required to raise a minimum of $500 million to put the APL plan into effect.

In early 1970 the task force reported to GE's corporate executive office that in their opinion the company could not undertake a $500 million venture that would incur substantial immediate losses. The task force pointed out that GE was under pressure to produce an immediate growth in earnings, was faced with increasing financial demands from its core businesses, and was suffering losses from its other major risk ventures, nuclear power and jet engines. The task force also expressed the opinion that the APL plan was risky and was based on the questionable assumption that GE had the capability to keep to the cost and time schedules of the APL plan. Concern was also expressed about the possible competitive reaction of IBM, which had strength in all technologies, including software (computer programming), as contrasted to GE, which was a generalist in the industry without a strong base for specialization and whose major product lines were obsolete. In addition, IBM had superior sales coverage, low manufacturing costs, and an exceptionally large customer base due to the fact that it had installed approximately 72 percent of the world's computers.

After a thorough reformulation of its three major losing ventures, GE decided to drop out of the computer business in 1970, since it was not considered vital to the company's success, and to continue in nuclear power and jet engines. Management reasoned that the latter two businesses were closely related to their core lines of electrical products and were sure to become profitable in the near future. In addition, GE had three- to five-year commitments to customers in these lines. GE sold its computer business to Honeywell for $110 million in notes and $124.5 million in Honeywell stock.[8]

The Case of RCA's Computer Division

Robert W. Sarnoff, chairman of the board and chief executive officer of RCA, stated on September 15, 1970, that "it is our intention to make RCA a major multinational enterprise doing business principally in computer-based information systems." Sarnoff, in introducing the most recent computers in the company's line at its new $22 million computer manufacturing plant in Marlboro, Massachusetts, also stated that the company was determined to attain an industry rank second only to IBM in the United States. In order to accomplish this goal, he would be prepared to commit whatever resources were necessary. These statements indicated the extent of RCA's commitment to the computer business and the intention of management to make a success of its efforts. RCA hoped to gain a 10 percent market share of the computer industry by 1975. RCA had been in the computer business through its computer systems division since it started developing its first computer in 1953. The company had a few minor successes but never gained over a 3 percent share of the computer market; like GE, RCA was a generalist in the field without any highly developed technical or specialist skills. In 1964, RCA decided to bring out a lower-cost model of IBM's 360 system. It was intended that the new line, named Spectra 70, be compatible with IBM's to permit use of IBM programs on the RCA model. It was hoped that this compatibility would gain some customers for RCA.

The Spectra 70 proved to have much in common with IBM's 360 line and encouraged management to push computers as a major product. Additional models of Spectra were produced, and the company made an entry into the time-sharing market, which required the use of a hardware-software device called virtual memory. Since there was no effective virtual memory system in the industry, RCA decided to concentrate its resources on developing such a system. But only a few of RCA's customers were ready for the virtual memory system; because much of its effort had been directed to this limited market, its Spectra system was somewhat neglected.

When IBM completed its software (programming system) for the 360, RCA's Spectra system was rendered noncompetitive. While there were delays in introducing new models of the Spectra, IBM announced its new 370 line, which had several innovations and competed very favorably in price with RCA's Spectra. IBM subsequently offered price cuts on its peripheral products, which reduced the overall cost of the IBM system and placed further pressure on RCA's computer lines.

RCA embarked on a new product line called New Technology Series

---

[8] See Scott R. Schmedel, "Why and How GE Left Computer Field: The Road is Marked in IBM Trial Record," *Wall Street Journal,* Jan. 12, 1976, p. 24.

(NTS), which proved to be expensive and difficult to make compatible with IBM's 370 and the earlier RCA models. Despite management changes and increased efforts to make the new line competitive, the company experienced severe losses. In view of the losses and lack of progress in making its computer line competitive, RCA went through a reappraisal of its position. On September 17, 1971, Sarnoff announced that RCA was discontinuing its computer business and was seeking to sell the division. This was one year after the company had announced its full commitment to making a success in the computer industry. RCA took an extraordinary loss of $490 million when it wrote off the computer division. Like GE, RCA had many other important, profitable divisions competing for corporate funds, and the cash drain caused by the losses in the computer division decreased their funds for investment. Another factor which prompted the decision to drop the computer business was the estimate made by management that to remain viable the division would require a $500 million investment (the same figure advanced by GE) over a five-year period.[9]

REFORMULATION AND THE LIFE CYCLE OF THE FIRM

Anchor Stage

Recovery strategies will vary according to the stage of the firm's life cycle. In the anchor and entrenchment stages if the firm encounters problems or difficulties it is likely to be in the financial area in terms of generating sufficient investment capital to establish a position or to maintain a position and develop an organization to assure growth. In these stages the industry growth rate is usually attractive, and the entering firms will be mainly concerned with gaining market share and industry position. Unless threatened by unusual environmental or industry changes such as technological breakthroughs or innovations which significantly change the dimensions of the industry, disruptions to a company's progress will be mainly functional in nature and not likely to be related to the root strategy. Changes in the operating strategy at this level usually will correct most problems or difficulties. If they do not, management is faced with a failing business and is forced to leave the industry.

Entrenchment Stage

Once the firm has experienced a period of successful entrenchment, it becomes subjected to new competitive threats and environmental shocks as its products and industry approach maturity. In this stage there is a need for constant surveillance of the environment to detect looming competitive threats or promising opportunities which will accommodate the utilization of the firm's skills and

---

[9] See Katharine Davis Fishman, "Programmed for Disaster, The Story of RCA's $490 Million Computer Debacle," *Atlantic Monthly,* May 1972, pp. 34–42.

resources. In the entrenchment stage, recycling of the policymaking process is likely to be concentrated at the operational and organizational levels as the firm seeks adjustments to correct deviations from stated objectives and action plans. The major concern of the firm in the latter stages of entrenchment is to be aware of its position in the life cycle and to initiate reformulation before decline sets in.

Defensive Stage

In the defensive stage the firm should concentrate on a thorough reformulation of the root strategy to determine the future prospects for existing product lines. At this stage intensive search for alternatives should be undertaken and new product development should be stressed. As stated in Chapter 3, unfortunately most firms concentrate on defensive action in an effort to maintain their position, rather than aggressively seek more viable opportunities.

Decline Stage

In the decline stage companies are forced into reformulation, usually at a time when resources have been depleted and options are severely limited. Firms in the latter stages of decline are frequently forced to sell off subsidiaries, product lines, and other resources to survive. Such efforts reduce the organization to a restricted segment of an industry accompanied by a loss of key personnel and strategic resources.

Diversification attempts are intensified in the latter stages of decline. Firms in serious trouble are forced to seek mergers, not acquisitions. Such mergers are likely to be with other companies suffering from the same kinds of problems. Firms in this stage of decline are targets for acquisition at a time when their bargaining power is at a minimum level. Companies which have sufficient cash flow and resources to allow their escape from dying businesses have more opportunities to reformulate through diversification. Such efforts are usually a retreat from the core business which is in decline because of competitive threats, domestic and foreign, and changes in the industry structure. As indicated in Chapter 3, technological deficiencies which seem too great to overcome may also be a factor which drives capital-intensive companies to seek escape through diversification. Diversification attempts intensively pursued in the decline stage seldom effect a successful reformulation which will provide the firm with the basis for a new growth stage and anchor a position in another industry or competitive environment. Survival may be attained, but usually without products that provide the critical mass needed to gain a new distinct strategic thrust.

Reformulation and Industry Structure

Industry structure is also an important consideration in reformulation. Like the life cycle of a company, an industry develops over time and frames its own life cycle. When industries fade into oblivion because of new technologies or in-novations, or changing environmental conditions, all firms are faced with reformulation. Some survive in other industries, but most go out of business. Basic industries such as steel, aluminum, petroleum, copper, and other miner-als have limited options. When faced with reformulation, they are inhibited by their long-established corporate culture and concentrated capital investment within a single industry. Diversification away from the core business has been the practice of the major producers, and segmentation has been the most com-mon pattern for smaller producers.

Fragmented industries such as apparel, jewelry, small household goods, or creative and fashion-designed products are populated with a large number of small to medium-sized firms. Ease of entry and difficulties in establishing na-tional brands, or gaining a "franchise" in these industries, lead to frequent reformulations and business failures.

Other industries, such as electronics, drugs, and pharmaceuticals, have fluid boundaries. These segments provide more significant strategic options. Their dimensions are constantly being expanded and stretched through new discover-ies. While offering multiple options, these factors also pose a competitive threat to the firm not alert to the changing industry environment.

As previously discussed, the decline of a business or industry can be due to a number of factors both internal and external. The neglect of strategic planning is usually the major cause of management failing to heed the need for reformulation. Product development, technological breakthrough, and innova-tions require research and development expenditures without immediate results or payout. These efforts entail risk and uncertainty. To ensure reformulation before the decline stage the firm must build a systematic scan-ning process into its strategic design.

THE REFORMULATION PROCESS AND MANAGEMENT REACTIONS

In each of the previous descriptions of the reformulation process, a common core is detectable. The companies all enjoyed periods of success and were confronted with a changing environment and different market conditions which stunted their growth and progress and, in some cases, threatened their survival. Ford, Leathercraft, and VW developed distinct root strategies which gave them a special market niche and were responsible for a sustained period of suc-cessful operation. In the case of Ford and VW, the root strategies led to spec-tacular growth. In each situation management was reluctant to recognize that its strategies of long standing were no longer adaptable to the changing market conditions. Although the companies, along with American Motors, eventually effected new strategic designs, they waited too long to take action. As a result, they incurred financial losses and the loss of market position.

This syndrome is very common in industry. It is not unusual to find very successful companies with recognized product and market positions which suf-fer declines in their fortunes because they waited too long to begin the painful reformulation process. It is in the periods of greatest success that the seeds of future failure or decline are sown. The old cliché that nothing succeeds like success has no doubt been used repeatedly to prevent some managements from facing the reality of a need for reformulation. It is very difficult to abandon a concept, a technology, a product, or an array of products responsible for providing the company with its measure of success over a long time period. Developing a new root strategy and phasing out the old is an extremely difficult assignment for the policymaking group. The transitional period is the most trying when the new concept or product line is being nurtured and the old concepts or product lines are still providing the greatest measure of sales and income to keep the company viable. The failure to complete the reformulation by recycling through each phase of the policymaking process is evident in most companies that initiate change. Upsetting well-established company practices and philosophies is not done easily and requires persistent effort and dedication to the need to change the corporate mission. The redesign of the organizational structure to align it with a newly formed root strategy is usually the most difficult and demanding task in the recycling process. Disrupting organizational relationships, eliminating positions, creating new areas of responsibility, and making the necessary managerial and personnel ' ¿es usually are treated with fear and caution. Rather than face this undesirable task head-on, many managements try to adapt an inefficient and unsuitable old organization structure to the new strategic design, or they delay in making the required organizational adjustments. As a result, the organization strategy and structure of most companies lag behind their operating and root strategies, and in large companies are frequently in a state of seemingly constant readjustment. Guaranteeing the success and, in many cases, the very survival of the firm is dependent upon the constant monitoring of an effective control system that has incorporated environmental scanning.

EXTERNAL MONITORING AND INTERNAL CONTROLS

The external monitoring system of the business enterprise should provide inputs to appraise the realism and potential of the root strategy and to signal the need to reformulate to meet the new challenges of the opportunities and problems found in the external environment or state of nature. Internal controls coupled with inputs from the environment should aid in determining the effectiveness of operating strategies. The organizational structure and design should also be tested against performance measures as the agent for executing the operating strategies and providing the basis for the functioning of the control strategies. Interpretation and judgment of the effectiveness of organizational performance are dependent upon the quality and significance of the information system and will determine the extent of executive action needed in the recycling process. This system must, of course, be interpreted by a management group that is not resistant to change and is not reluctant to throw off the shackles of past success and to adapt to new market situations.

The conceptual model of the policymaking process, which leads from the formulation phase through the reformulation phase, has been developed in Chapters 1 through 9 and is presented in outline form below:

OUTLINE OF THE CONCEPTUAL MODEL OF THE FIRM: THE POLICYMAKING PROCESS

I Formulation phase

A Determining the root strategy: Development of basic overall guiding policies which determine the economic, industrial, and geographic setting of the organization. The character of the business unit is molded through the deliberations of the formulation (or reformulation) phase. The following elementary economic objectives are determined:

1 Profitability—What is the k factor? Internal cost of capital? Rate?

2 Growth rate

3 Survival rates—Under what conditions does the firm wish to exist? What are its survival characteristics? What is the extent of complementarity? (How much does product B contribute to the sales of product A?) What is the firm's attitude? Dynamic? Conservative? Innovative? Follower?

B Forming the basic business strategy

1 What is the extent of the firm's skills and resources?

2 How does the firm intend to commit its skills and resources?

3 What are the practical alternatives?

4 What specific business or businesses will the firm pursue?

5 What market niche will the firm seek within the general framework of the industry?

II Implementation phase

A Development of operating strategy: The loose overall framework of the formulation phase should be the determining factor in developing the operating strategy of the firm. Functional strategies and policies are developed in this phase to guide the short-range planning and day-to-day operations of the enterprise. Marketing, production, finance, and personnel plans are coordinated with overall firm objectives through the formulation of coordinating subobjectives. Changes in the marketplace are met through flexible operating strategies which provide for adjustment and change.

1 Marketing considerations

  a Product line, extent, purpose

  b Pricing, packaging, design

  c Channels of distribution

2 Production considerations

  a Capital equipment expenditures

  b Plant sites, locations, size, etc.

  c Production methods

3 Financial considerations
  a Financial policies—aligned with corporate strategy
    1) Dividends
    2) Retained earnings
    3) Debt
    4) Cash flow
    5) Budgeting
    6) Long-range plans

III Organizational phase: Development of organizational strategy. The root and operating strategies determine organizational requirements and should be the major factors which shape the structure of the firm.
  A Strategic considerations in this area are
    1 Organizational design, structure
      a Communications net requirements
      b Skill requirements based on basic overall objectives and subobjectives
      c Staff requirements and relationships
      d Centralization versus decentralization
      e Product management versus plant and/or geographical management

IV Interpretative phase: Development of the control strategy. Interpretation of results must flow through the organizational net and must be based on responsibility and performance of individuals strategically placed in the organizational structure. The feedback mechanism is a function of the organizational structure and the intangible factors of organizational behavior. The control strategy must flow from the organizational design and must measure the progress toward the corporate objectives and subgoals determined through the root and operating strategies of the firm.
  A Factors to be considered in the development of control strategies
    1 Selection of key control variables
    2 Coordination of control measures
    3 Qualitative versus quantitative control measures
    4 Use of systems analysis in structuring a control system
    5 External monitoring system

V Reformulation or recycling phase: Development of recovery strategies. One of the major executive functions is the interpretation of the progress and health of the firm as measured against the conceived objectives and strategies of the firm. Constant reappraisal must be built into the system and should flow as an input from the control strategies employed by the firm. The external monitoring system should provide inputs to appraise the realism and potential of the root strategy and to signal the need to reformulate to meet the new challenges of the opportunities and problems found in the external environment or state of nature. Internal controls coupled with inputs from the environment should aid in determining the effectiveness of operating strategies. The organizational structure and design should also be tested against performance measures as the agent for executing the operating strategies and providing the basis for the functioning of the control strategies. Interpretation and judgment of the effectiveness of organizational performance are dependent upon the quality and significance of the information system and will determine the extent of executive action needed in the recycling process.

SUMMARY AND GENERAL COMMENTS

Successful concepts, technological breakthroughs, and innovations reach maturity, and as products slip into commodity items, competition becomes intense and profitability is limited or nonexistent. Competition can dislodge market leaders, and changing industry structure can erode a firm's profit. Management must be constantly alert to the changing environment to initiate reformulation and recovery strategies when necessary.

Drastic changes and complete reformulation of the strategic design are usually not necessary. In most instances the reformulation process will be centered on one or more of the successive phases of policymaking: the operating, organizational, and control strategies.

Significant examples of changes in root strategy are found in the history of Ford, General Motors, American Motors, and Volkswagen. All of these companies instituted recovery strategies which made distinct changes in the direction and structure of their organization.

Operating strategies are most frequently utilized for recovery in the reformulation phase. A&P attempted to recover its lost profitability and market share through a campaign termed "WEO—Where Economy Originates." This recovery strategy was based on underpricing competitors and an intensive advertising campaign. Counteraction by competitors prevented this strategy from attaining management's objectives. A&P continued to lose market share and sustained continued losses.

Organization and control strategies are frequently focused on in the recovery stage. Procter and Gamble developed a unique strategy to remedy problems caused by growth and expansion. P&G designed a brand management concept which provided for the decentralization of the marketing function and tighter control over individual brand products.

Sloan developed pioneering organization and control strategies to accomplish the thorough reformulation of General Motors. Sloan, through changes in the company's strategic design, gave substance to the loosely knit group of companies launched under Durant, the organizer of General Motors.

General Electric reorganized into groups of small business units (SBUs) to provide for strategic planning and control of its 170 departments, 50 divisions, and 10 groups. This organizational strategy reduced the 170 departments into 43 clearly identified SBUs.

The large decentralized organizations must look to the management of their separate units as distinct businesses and be prepared to initiate reformulation when problems or stagnation occurs.

To prevent falling into a decline position, management must be constantly alert to its changing environment and identify the stage of the firm's life cycle. Reformulation and the necessary recovery strategies must be started before the decline stage to assure the orderly transfer of resources into the development of new concepts and product lines. Recovery strategies will vary according to the stage of the company's life cycle.

In each of the descriptions of the reformulation process a common core is detectable. All of the companies enjoyed periods of success and were confronted with a changing environment and different market conditions which impeded their progress and in some cases threatened their survival. In each case management was reluctant to recognize that its strategies of long standing were no longer adaptable to the changing environment. It is not unusual to find companies with recognized product and market positions which experienced declines in their fortunes because they waited too long to begin the painful process of reformulation.

SELECTED REFERENCES

Abel, D., and J. Hammond: *Strategic Marketing Planning: Problems and Analytical Approaches* (Englewood Cliffs, N.J.: Prentice-Hall, 1979).

Andrews, K.: *The Concept of Corporate Strategy* (Homewood, Ill.: Irwin, 1980).

Ansoff, I.: "Managing Strategic Surprise by Response to Weak Signals," *California Management Review,* Winter 1976.

Chandler, A.: *Strategy and Structure* (Cambridge, Mass.: M.I.T., 1962).

Drucker, P.: *Management* (New York: Harper & Row, 1974).

———: *Management in Turbulent Times* (New York: Harper & Row, 1980).

Harrigan, K.: *Strategies for Declining Industries* (Lexington, Mass.: Heath, 1980).

Hofer, C. W., and D. E. Schandel: *Strategy Formulation: Analytical Concepts* (St. Paul, Minn.: West, 1978).

Kami, M. J., and J. E. Ross: *Corporate Management in Crisis: Why the Mighty Fall* (Englewood Cliffs, N.J.: Prentice-Hall, 1973).

Lorange, P., and R. Vancil (eds.): *Strategic Planning Systems* (Englewood Cliffs, N.J.: Prentice-Hall, 1978).

Porter, M.: *Competitive Strategy* (New York: Free Press, a division of Macmillan, 1980).

Schandel, D. E., R. Patton, and J. Riggs: "Corporate Turnaround Strategies: A Study of Profit Decline and Recovery," *Journal of General Management,* vol. 3, no. 3, Spring 1976.

CASES ON BUSINESS POLICY FOR PART SIX

The cases in Part Six are a vital link in the chain of the policymaking process and in effect represent the closing of the system to recycle the policymaking process and redesign the strategic plan. The examples of reformulation illustrated in the cases give the student the opportunity to reexamine and reinforce the conceptual framework delineated in other parts of the book and to recognize the necessity for the constant monitoring of the internal control system and the scanning of the environment to determine the need for reformulation and the development of recovery strategies.

The cases in this section also indicate the difficulty of initiating and completing the reformulation process by recycling through each phase of the policymaking process. The general reluctance of management to phase out a once-successful concept or product line and to launch a needed recovery strategy is also clearly illustrated in several of the cases.

Kroehler Manufacturing Company[1]

Kroehler experienced losses of $4.6 million in 1977, $9.5 million in 1978, and $18.4 million in 1979. The company's losses continued into 1980. Prior to experiencing this succession of loss years, Kroehler was recognized as one of the largest producers of good-quality, medium-priced upholstered and wood occasional tables in the United States and Canada. In 1976, the company's products were distributed in 4,175 retail furniture and department stores, including Sears, J. C. Penney, Montgomery Ward, and Levitz, with a total of 8,950 retail outlets in the United States and Canada. Kroehler's management engaged a consulting firm in 1976 to determine the future areas of growth for the home furnishing industry. In line with the recommendations of the consultant's study, Kroehler's management reformulated its strategy to seek a niche in the higher-priced design and fashion-conscious market served by prestige retail outlets. At the same time the company decided to focus upon upholstered furniture and sold its office furniture subsidiary.

DEVELOPMENT OF KROEHLER

The Kroehler Manufacturing Company had its beginning in 1893, in a small rural community 25 miles southwest of Chicago, as the Naperville Lounge Company. The firm was founded with $6,000 in total capital by 10 investors to produce and sell upholstered chaise lounges. Twenty-one-year-old Peter Kroehler was hired as a stenographer and general assistant. He did the buying

[1]This case is a revision of the 1978 version based on company annual reports and other published data.

and selling, wrote the first catalog, and packed the finished lounges for shipment by horse-drawn wagons to dealers.

In spite of diligence and hard work, the company lost money during its first two years, due in large part to the financial panic of 1893 and its aftermath. Peter Kroehler borrowed $500 from his father and bought out the interest of some of the original stockholders in 1895. As a new part-owner, Kroehler began to seek out new markets for his products in the late 1890s. Soon the P. K. Wrigley company was sending a new Naperville lounge with each order for $25 worth of chewing gum. A mail-order firm in the gold-mining town of Cripple Creek, Colorado was selling a silver-plated teapot at $9, for which the customer also received a Naperville lounge as a premium. The mail-order firm paid 85 cents for the teapot and $4 for the lounge. Orders for lounges were coming into the Naperville plant at the rate of 35 per day.

By 1902, Kroehler invented and patented a folding bed which converted into a davenport lounge. Demand for the Naperville standard and new convertible model lounges was such that by 1913 new production facilities had been built in Kankakee, Illinois, Binghamton, New York, and Cleveland, Ohio. In 1915 the four factories merged into one corporation, the Kroehler Manufacturing Company. During the same year, a two-thirds interest was acquired in the Kindel Bed Company, which had factories in Brooklyn, New York, Grand Rapids, Michigan, and Toronto, Canada.

At this point Peter Kroehler entered into a contract to buy Sears's half-interest in Kroehler Manufacturing Company. The price agreed upon was $1 million, and was to be paid at the rate of $100,000 per year, plus 6 percent interest on the unpaid balance.

By 1924 additional production plants had been purchased or leased in San Francisco and Los Angeles, California, and Dallas, Texas, in order to fill nationwide sales demands. With 10 plants in the United States and Canada, Kroehler had by 1940 become the world's largest furniture manufacturer. The company was producing upholstered and wood residential furniture, as well as the highly successful "push-back" theater seat, which had been designed by Peter Kroehler in 1930.

Further expansion into other segments of the domestic and international furniture business came in the 1960s. In an attempt to enter into the office furniture market, Kroehler purchased Murphy-Miller, Inc., in 1964 and operated the Owensboro, Kentucky, company as a wholly owned subsidiary. In 1966 Kroehler acquired, for cash, the Lexington Chair Division of Thomason Industries, the Welcome (North Carolina) Furniture Company, and the Colonial Manufacturing Company. In 1969 a half-interest was acquired in Colchones Principe (now Industrial Principe Kroehler, S.A.), a large manufacturer of mattresses and upholstered furniture in Mexico City. In the same year, the furniture division of Canadian Bedding and Furniture, Ltd., was purchased and operated as Kroehler Manufacturing Co., Ltd.

During 1970, the Lexington Chair Division and the Colonial Manufacturing Company facilities were sold. In April 1977, the Murphy-Miller office furniture subsidiary was sold. The Canadian subsidiary was sold in August 1979.

KROEHLER'S PRODUCTION METHODS AND FACILITIES

Furniture manufacturing methods were not easily automated, and the industry was labor-intensive. Productivity gains came in the areas of plant modernization and product design rather than the production process itself. Kroehler continued to search for improvements to increase productivity and lower unit costs. It spent over $2.5 million in 1978 and $1.7 million in 1979 on the development of new styles, production methods, and materials.

Kroehler implemented new computer-controlled fabric cutters to get the maximum cuts from increasingly expensive upholstery fabrics, implemented computer-generated production scheduling, and accomplished the standardization of springs used throughout the product lines to reduce the extent of required inventory. This standardization reduced the spring stock from over 1,800 items to just under 100 items.

Approximately 25 to 30 percent of the floor space in each Kroehler manufacturing facility was used for administrative offices and warehouse storage purposes. Plant layouts were product-oriented. The plants were operated at an average of 70 percent capacity and could increase output by 10 percent immediately, if required, through the use of overtime by production workers. In order to bring production up to 100 percent of capacity, it would be necessary to hire and train new workers.

Kroehler made most of the components it used in manufacturing furniture except for the mechanism in recliners and sleep sofas, polyurethane foam cushioning, and upholstery fabrics. However, the company did create its own fabric designs and worked with the fabric manufacturers to produce them. Polyurethane cushioning was purchased from suppliers located near the upholstered furniture plants because the foam was so light in weight and rail freight weights were based on shipment volumes. A few hundred pounds of material might completely fill a railroad box car.

Kroehler purchased steel wire and made coil springs at four plants. At one time the company investigated the possibility of making its own spring steel and upholstery fabric, but neither was economically feasible. The firm did have a cotton mill in Memphis which made cotton felt for lining upholstery fabrics, and processed cotton for sale to outside customers. Green hardwood logs were purchased from small loggers and obtained from government timberland cuttings.

Kroehler competed with other industries for raw materials. Besides the furniture makers, the largest purchaser of polyurethane foam and upholstery fabric was the automobile industry; and the largest buyer of wood was the housing industry. Kroehler had considered buying hardwood timberlands since new hybrids had been developed which matured in only 15 years, as compared with 40 years for traditional oak and walnut trees used in furniture. Kroehler did not buy lumber futures on the commodities markets.

At one time, Kroehler purchased its raw materials quarterly. In an attempt to lower inventory costs, the company began purchasing lot quantities for each material. In 1976, a "controlled centralized purchasing" function was initiated.

This office established sources for each plant's required raw materials, monitored material cost and availability, and placed orders. Transportation costs were often the most critical factor in purchasing decisions if the materials were available from several sources.

Some raw materials, for example, burlap, hardwoods such as teak and mahogany, and certain fabrics, were purchased from foreign suppliers since no domestic sources were available. Purchases of these imported materials were made up to six months in advance because of unreliable ocean transport schedules. Approximately 15 percent of Kroehler's raw material purchases were made abroad.

Wood had been the traditional frame material for upholstered furniture because of good availability, reasonable cost, high strength, and durability. Recent technological advances had brought about alternative materials. Welded steel frames had been developed for sofas, sleep sofas, chairs, and recliners. The steel frames were stronger and more durable than wooden ones, and were competitive in cost. However, the straight I-beam construction of the steel frames did not lend itself well to most styling designs.

Rigid plastic frames could be molded into any shape, but they were more expensive than standard wood frames. In addition, customer acceptance of plastic upholstered furniture frames was low because "plastic denoted cheapness." At one time Kroehler had a small capability for manufacturing decorative plastic parts but stopped producing and using them because of low popularity among furniture dealers and customers.

Kroehler intentionally tried to minimize its dependence on outside suppliers. Thus, although the company's principal products were sofas, chairs, sleeper sofas, and recliners for living room and leisure room use, and wood occasional tables, it also produced processed cotton and furniture frames. It sold excess cotton and frames to other manufacturers. Kroehler purchased lumber, steel wire, cotton, upholstery fabrics, polyurethane, plastic trim parts, polyester fiberfill, mattresses, and mechanisms for prevailing market prices. The company was not dependent on any one source for any raw material or component parts.

Kroehler's main problems in furniture production were in the areas of labor and logistics. The turnover rate among upholstered furniture workers was relatively high, and the constant change in style and design of furniture created considerable inventory problems. Of Kroehler's 450 furniture designs and 350 upholstery fabric patterns, half were changed every year.

Kroehler management had steadfastly held to the belief that maintaining production facilities throughout the country would result in a significant competitive advantage for the company. Manufacturing facilities close to major markets would minimize transportation costs of finished goods and provide Kroehler with a significant price advantage over other national or large regional manufacturers. However, as the result of increasing cost pressures, Kroehler found the overhead burden of maintaining a large number of plants too costly. Beginning in 1977, 10 facilities whose main products were upholstered furni-

EXHIBIT 1
PRODUCTION FACILITIES OF KROEHLER MANUFACTURING
COMPANY AND SUBSIDIARIES

Production plant location	Approximate floor area, square feet	Plant's principal output
Kankakee, Illinois (2)	338,000	Upholstered furniture
	227,000	Upholstered furniture
Binghamton, New York	467,000	Upholstered furniture
Charlotte, North Carolina	108,000	Upholstered furniture
Welcome, North Carolina (2)	76,000	Occasional tables and upholstered furniture
	137,500	Fabric warehouse and upholstered furniture
Memphis, Tennessee	47,000	Processed cotton
Newport, Tennessee	156,000*	Upholstered furniture
Dallas, Texas	158,000	Upholstered furniture
Mexico City, Mexico (2)	44,000	Mattresses
	60,000*	Upholstered furniture

*Leased.

ture were closed and sold. The production facilities still in operation in 1980 are shown in Exhibit 1.

In 1980, Kroehler employed approximately 2,400 employees in the United States and Mexico. The Kankakee, Illinois, Binghamton, New York, Charlotte, North Carolina, and Dallas, Texas, plants were closed for approximately two weeks in January 1980 because of a strike by local members of the Upholsterer's International Union of North America.

MARKETING AND DISTRIBUTION

In 1980, Kroehler sold its upholstered and wood furniture and occasional tables to 5,300 retail furniture and department stores and to national merchandising chains. Approximately 1,500 furniture dealers operating more than 2,600 retail outlets in nearly all the 300 major population centers in the United States constituted a network of dealers franchised by the Kroehler Company to sell one or more Kroehler product lines.

The national merchandising chains (Sears, Montgomery Ward, and Levitz Furniture Corp.) accounted for a lesser percentage of net sales than in prior years. Levitz accounted for approximately 13 percent of net sales, and Sears accounted for approximately 17 percent of net sales in 1979–1980. Each of the national merchandising chains sold an exclusive style group under its own private brand name, except Levitz, which sold the "Kroehler Royale" line. (See Exhibit 2 for a breakdown of sales by product line.)

As stated in its 1979 Annual Report:

> The company continues to emphasize the merchandising of upholstered products for the mass market at medium retail price points. Each product line has been restyled for broader appeal among the 25 to 44 year age groups, which represent the prime furniture-purchasing consumer segments. In addition, the company has broadened its offerings of casual styling directed at the fast-growing family room market. While these styling efforts have taken place, the number of product offerings has been reduced, along with a complete frame standardization program.

The name *Kroehler* was an internationally recognized brand name. It was a registered trademark in the United States (where it expires in 1992) and in Mexico in 1981 as well as in other countries. The U.S. and Mexican registrations were renewable for periods of 20 years and 5 years, respectively.

Kroehler's furniture was sold in the low and medium price brackets by retail dealers. The company's competition in the United States and Canada came from large nationwide manufacturers or the numerous small local furniture makers, depending upon the geographic market area. With a 3 percent market share in the United States it was the third largest U.S. producer of upholstered furniture. The 10 largest producers in the United States accounted for 25 percent of industry sales. (See the appendix for a review of the furniture industry.)

There appeared to be little brand-name loyalty among retail furniture customers. Shoppers tended to pick a store rather than a brand of furniture. However, furniture dealers had strong brand preferences and steered customers toward particular product lines. Consequently, Kroehler attempted to win the loyalty of its dealers with better dealer services.

Kroehler provided its retail dealers with an "ad-builder" kit, consisting of radio advertising scripts and all materials necessary for the preparation of custom newspaper ads by dealers. The only items which were left blank in the kit ads were the dealer's name and the sale prices.

Kroehler also provided a service warranty to dealers. Defective furniture could be returned to Kroehler for repair, or the problem corrected by Kroehler service representatives in the store.

The area of product warranties for furniture had not been a competitive factor in retail sales. Not many people would buy a new automobile or color television set, for example, without some kind of promise that the item would not fall apart 10 minutes after its purchase. Yet few customers, after buying hundreds or even thousands of dollars' worth of furniture, even asked for a warranty that the items would last through the day, or that the store or the manufacturer would provide any corrective service for defects.

La-Z-Boy Chair Company promoted a "lifetime warranty" on all parts of its patented reclining mechanism, but La-Z-Boy defined "lifetime" as the useful life of the chair as determined by the user. Frame parts were warranted for two

EXHIBIT 2
KROEHLER MANUFACTURING CO. BREAKDOWN OF NET SALES AND PRETAX INCOME BY PRODUCT AND BY LINE OF BUSINESS 1972–1979

Net sales attributed to	1979	1978	1977	1976	1975	1974	1973	1972
Upholstered furniture, %	90	89	91	91	92	89	89	92
Wood living room, dining room, and bedroom furniture, %	6	8	7	7	7	6	5	3
Office furniture, bedding, %	4*	3*	2*	2*	1*	5	6	5
Total, %	100	100	100	100	100	100	100	100

Pretax contribution to consolidated income (loss) attributed to	1979	1978	1977	1976	1975	1974	1973	1972
Household furniture, wood and upholstered, %	100	100	100	83	65	90	95	97
Office furniture, %	0	0	0	17	35	10	5	3
Total, %	100	100	100	100	100	100	100	100

*Excludes operating results of office furniture class of products, which was discontinued in 1977.

years. Monsanto offered a two-year warranty on certain fabrics used for upholstered furniture. Some retailers had their own product warranty or service programs, or guarantees of satisfaction on delivery of the furniture to the customer's home. The Norwalk Furniture Company offered a consumer warranty
more as a positive production quality control measure rather than as a competitive advantage or marketing point.

In 1975, Kroehler considered adopting an express consumer warranty for
its products, but decided instead to continue using a statement of product quality called the Kroehler "Word of Honor."

Kroehler's products competed in the marketplace with automobiles and
major appliances for consumer purchasing dollars. Higher purchases in these
durable goods areas could mean lower furniture sales in a level economy. In
periods of economic slowdown, a decision to buy new furniture was among the
first to be postponed, and one of the last to be renewed during an economic recovery. However, a portion of the furniture industry appeared to be "reces-
sion-proof." The sales of high-priced furniture, along with Cadillac automobiles, were not significantly affected during the recessions of the early and
mid-1970s.

As a means of controlling distribution of its products, Kroehler established
its franchised dealer network. A "franchise" was a written agreement between
Kroehler and the furniture dealer, specifying the following:

- Dealer sales goals
- Credit and financing requirements
- Percentage of store display space to be devoted to Kroehler product lines
- Advertising dollars to be spent by the dealer
- Amount of advertising rebates to be paid to the dealer by Kroehler
- The names of other area furniture dealers to which Kroehler sold the same
product lines

Each dealer was franchised by product line (recliners, for example), and was
expected to give special sales emphasis to the franchised lines. Very few
dealers were not franchised for all of Kroehler's lines, and most dealers who
applied for a Kroehler franchise received one. Kroehler did not operate its own
retail furniture outlets since the company felt this might antagonize dealers.

Furniture orders were placed by dealers either through the Kroehler
catalog, at one of the several furniture market trade shows held during the year,
at seven furniture showrooms in various cities, or through one of the 110
Kroehler sales representatives. A year-long study of costs and sales at all permanent Kroehler showrooms was conducted during 1975. Subsequently,
showrooms were closed in the New York Furniture Exchange, in Atlanta, and
in the American Furniture Mart in Chicago. (Peter Kroehler had helped to
build the American Furniture Mart in 1923, was the first chairman of its board
of governors, and served as a director until 1939.) Kroehler leased showrooms
in San Francisco and Inglewood, California, High Point, North Carolina, and

Dallas, Texas. An additional showroom was maintained at the Kroehler production plant in Mexico.

Ninety percent of Kroehler's production was delivered directly to dealers by the company's private truck fleet of 240 tractors and 480 trailers, apportioned among the eight furniture production plants near major markets. Kroehler relied on its own truck transport rather than common carriers in order to:

1 Maintain control over furniture deliveries and schedules
2 Make and keep close contact with the franchised dealers
3 Avoid the situation of commercial carriers not accepting unpacked furniture or partial loads for shipment, thus delaying orders

In the future, management indicated it would probably rely more on rail piggyback service. Kroehler did not ship to furniture dealers in Montana, northeastern Maine, or small dealers more than 50 miles off a route if shipping costs exceeded the potential profit from an order.

Mr. Kenneth Kroehler, chairman of the board of Kroehler Manufacturing Company, expressed the opinion that "economic indicators are not sufficient any more to tell us where the market is headed." The population of persons aged 25 to 34, when most people form their own households and acquire furniture, will increase markedly with the maturing of the post-World War II baby boom. And, with rising disposable income levels, more people in all socioeconomic levels have the purchasing power to buy the furniture they choose.

The Kroehler Company reevaluated its traditional bread-and-butter target-market demographics in 1976 with a study by Management Horizons of Columbus, Ohio. Changes were found to have taken place in income level, age segments, and housing patterns. The study concluded that for the next five-year period, Kroehler's target market would:

- Be predominantly female
- Be aged 25 to 45
- Have $12,000 to $25,000 in annual household income
- Have attained some college education, but less than a degree
- Be 50 percent working women with jobs outside the home
- Be value-oriented

However, Mr. Kroehler maintained that "demographics must be supplemented by life-style research." Attitudes and life-styles appeared to cut across traditional demographic category lines (see Exhibit 3), and all groups had become more conscious of furniture design and style than in the past.

Until 1976, Kroehler had directed its marketing efforts at three channels of retail outlets: the warehouse-showrooms, the large national merchandising chains, and the furniture stores. A fourth group, consisting of fine department stores and high-fashion "style stores," typically dealt in higher-priced furniture and did not carry the Kroehler product line. Beginning in 1977 Kroehler aggressively sought to expand its sales to this group.

EXHIBIT 3
MAJOR LIFE-STYLE SEGMENTS

Characteristics	Middle America	Younger trendsetters	Affluent middle-agers	Older sophisticates
Percentage of population	40%	20%	20%	11%
Amount of purchasing power	35%	24%	27%	12%
Orientation	Home	Job	Home and outside activity	Job and outside activity
Male dominance	Strong	No	Accepted	Neutral
Social values	Very conservative	Very liberal	Semiliberal	Conservative
Housekeeping	Pathological housekeepers	Very casual	Concerned	Concerned
Concern with appearance	Limited concern	Very concerned	Very concerned	Very concerned
Interest in fashion	Limited interest	Interested	Very interested	Very interested
Attitude toward change	Resists	Accepts	Accepts	Accepts
Inflation sensitivity	Very sensitive	Very sensitive	*Not sensitive	*Not sensitive
Dining/ entertaining	Very limited	Active	Very active	Very active
Age	Above average (47)	Young (33)	Above average (37)	Older (58)
Income	Lowest ($10,900)	Slightly above average ($14,400)	Highest ($17,900)	Second highest ($14,700)
Education	Lowest	Second highest	Above average	Highest
		*Woman works	*Woman works	

*Key differences.

Note: Singles, a growing category, are mainly in young trendsetters and older sophisticates groups. Young trendsetters and affluent middle-agers could very possibly be one store's target.

Each retail furniture sales channel tended to draw on one or two of the life-style segments profiled in Exhibit 3. "In servicing the needs of these four groups (of retail outlets), we need to create separate consumer identities in each," explained Terrence L. Henderson, Kroehler's then executive vice president for marketing. "This needs to be done not by whim or happenstance, but by deliberate programs." Accordingly, the traditional, colonial, and modern Kroehler Citation lines were upgraded with several new designs, and a new line of high-fashion upholstered furniture in the upper-middle price range was brought out as part of Kroehler's program to create a new image for itself among the fine department stores and their customers.

After an extensive search for a recognized fashion designer for its new line of furniture, Kroehler chose Angelo Donghia, an internationally known designer of interiors, furniture, and fabrics, and president of Donghia Associates, Inc., of New York. Donghia created a collection of 20 upholstered pieces and tables, plus more than two dozen fabrics. The sofas in the collection were priced to retail at approximately $1,000, the chairs at $500, and tables at $450. The designs and fabrics were interchangeable to enable pieces to be mixed or matched. Design patents for the collection were applied for by Kroehler.

"We want the Donghia line to stand on its own and to sell on its own. We are telling stores to measure the merchandise regardless of its price line, and if it can't compete, not to buy it. We are not trying to push Donghia on the strength of the Kroehler name," emphasized Mr. Henderson.

The collection was introduced in April 1977 at the Southern Furniture Market shown in High Point, North Carolina, and seemed to be successful in attracting that group of high-fashion stores which served sophisticated urban customers. The Donghia collection was intended to become Kroehler's top-of-the-line product with limited distribution. If sales justified it, the designs would filter down to other Kroehler product lines and franchised dealers. The second and third phases of the collection were introduced in October 1977 and April 1978, respectively. In early 1978, however, the company changed its marketing policy to emphasize products for the middle price range. The marketing pattern represented a return to the policies which had made Kroehler successful in the past.

More attention was focused on styling and price points where Kroehler had proven its leadership. In particular, recliners and sleep sofas received special attention and rejuvenation in 1978. "Basic" styles were revised, and trendy merchandise was dropped. On March 31, 1980, the company sold its reclining and occasional chair division to a corporation headed by a former officer, Gary Schroeder. A 15-year licensing agreement provided for the continued production of recliners and occasional chairs under the Kroehler name in return for minimum royalties of $50,000 per year.

ADVERTISING AND PROMOTION

Kroehler did some consumer advertising of its product lines, almost all of it in magazines. Kroehler placed these ads in shelter publications such as *House and Garden,* mass-circulation women's magazines such as *Woman's Day* and selected-market magazines such as *Apartment Life* to promote the Kroehler Citation line sold by furniture stores. Only occasionally would Kroehler place an "image" ad for top-of-the-line furniture such as the Donghia collection in *Vogue* or *The New Yorker* magazines.

Kroehler did not advertise in newspapers and typically placed only two 30-second television commercials during the year. These commercials were aired on the *Family Circle* annual tennis tournament, and were acquired as part of an advertising package purchase arrangement with *Family Circle* magazine.

In spite of relatively low consumer advertising expenditures, Kroehler enjoyed high brand-name recognition. This could be partly attributed to the inclusion of Kroehler products, by name, in the newspaper display advertising placed by furniture dealers. This exposure was partially subsidized by Kroehler. A sizable fraction of Kroehler's advertising budget (a flat amount per year, not tied to sales) was earmarked for rebates to franchised retail dealers. Most furniture stores did not advertise furniture by brand name, and the rebate was an incentive for dealers to actively promote the Kroehler name.

The remainder of Kroehler's advertising money went into furniture trade publication advertising. Ads were run every other month in *Professional Furniture* and *NHFA Reports,* two trade magazines Kroehler considered best in circulation and editorial content. The advertisements placed in these publications typically did not show Kroehler products. Instead the campaign was one of reminder advertising aimed at dealers. The ads listed specific points of Kroehler manufacture, such as a coil spring construction in upholstered furniture, or the benefits of buying from Kroehler. Supplemental trade ad announcements on new fabrics were made in trade weeklies. The Donghia collection, however, was one which Kroehler did promote in trade journal ads in order to heighten dealer interest before the 1977 Southern Furniture Market, when the collection was introduced.

At one time Kroehler's advertising was done by the Leo Brunett agency in Chicago. But for the period since 1973, Kroehler's in-house subsidiary, Ad Infinitum, Inc., had the account. The 15 percent fee normally paid to outside agencies was plowed back into the Kroehler advertising budget.

There was an annual management review of Ad Infinitum's problems and operations during which periodic presentations were made by outside agencies in an effort to land the Kroehler account. "An in-house agency was a lot of work," said Peter Alexander, Kroehler's advertising vice president, "and my life would be a lot easier if we had an outside agency again." However, lower advertising costs, advertising quality control, and better service to dealers were the reasons which Alexander cited for keeping advertising in-house.

Kroehler also had a house organ *(K-Line)* which was used to disseminate important company news (such as the good reception of the Donghia collection at the Southern Market) and to increase employees' interest in Kroehler product lines.

Market research for Kroehler was done by a full-time employee and occasionally by the Gallup polling organization on specific items.

KROEHLER'S FINANCIAL POSITION

Kroehler's consolidated net sales for 1979 were $116.3 million. The company showed a net loss of $18.4 million in 1979, almost double the 1978 loss. Management attributed the continuing losses to lower unit volume with national merchandise.

Gross profit was 5.9 percent of sales in 1979, compared with 9.4 percent in 1978 and 11.5 percent in 1977. The decrease in 1979 was primarily due to the adverse impact of lower volumes on overhead absorption, inefficiencies encountered in a plant that was closed in 1979, nonrecurring costs associated with increasing production at the Kankakee, Illinois, facility, and high material costs.

Selling and general and administrative expenses increased $336,000 in 1979 primarily as the result of increases in bad debt expenses of $1.1 million and increased advertising of $0.8 million. These increases were partially offset by decreased commission expenses (due to lower volumes) and the effects of the 1978 costs-reduction program.

Another factor affecting 1979 performance was nonrecurring expenses associated with plant closures and sales. Closed plant expenses increased $1.3 million over 1978, due to:

- Closing of San Bernardino, California, and Pontotoc, Mississippi, facilities
- Closing of Meridian, Mississippi, maxi-board operations
- Consolidation of two Kankakee, Illinois, plants into one
- Closing of the Naperville, Illinois, Shreveport, Louisiana, and Freemont, California, facilities in 1978
- Sale of the Canadian subsidiary

In addition, interest costs were up due to higher interest rates on increased levels of short-term borrowing.

On March 29, 1977, the company issued $20 million of $10\frac{1}{4}$ percent notes due March 1, 1992. In addition, in 1978 the company's cash requirements were partially met by short-term borrowings of up to $3 million from several banks and by the sale in April and June 1978 of approximately $1.5 million and $1.0 million, respectively, principal amounts of accounts receivable to a commercial finance company. In February 1979, the banks did not renew their short-term loans, and on March 21, 1979, Kroehler entered into a one-year agreement with a commercial finance company for a line of credit not to exceed $10 million, secured by accounts receivable. Also in March of 1979, a restrictive amendment was placed on the $10\frac{1}{4}$ percent notes. The company granted holders of the notes rights of first mortgage or deed of trust on all land and buildings as well as the stock of both the Canadian subsidiary and Mexican affiliate. The agreement also prevented payment of dividends to common shareholders unless earnings exceeded a stated level.

On March 28, 1980, Kroehler entered into an agreement with a commercial factor to collect all of the company's accounts receivable. Although Kroehler would pay a commission for these services, management anticipated that the arrangement would ultimately reduce the cost of collection by phasing out the company's own credit and collection operations. In addition, the agreement was a source of short-term funds for Kroehler in that up to 90 percent of the outstanding accounts receivable would be available to the company at $1^3/_4$ percent over the prime rate.

Kroehler's financial performance and industry comparisons are detailed in Exhibits 4 through 8.

KROEHLER'S EXECUTIVE GROUP AND ORGANIZATION

Kroehler comprised a group of separate companies. The parent company was principally engaged in the manufacture and sale of upholstered and wood residential furniture. All subsidiaries and the affiliate were also directly or indirectly in the furniture business. The Kroehler organization included the following entities in January 1980:

Name	State or country of record	Percent owned by parent
Kroehler Manufacturing Company (parent)	Delaware	
Subsidiaries:		
Basic Wood Products, Inc.	Mississippi	80
Ad Infinitum, Inc.	Illinois	100
Osiris, Inc.	Illinois	100
Affiliate:		
Industrias Principe Kroehler, S.A.	Mexico	50

Kroehler relied on decentralized management for its furniture-producing subsidiaries. The Mexican company competed in its own national market, completely separate from the parent company, except for the occasional use of some modified Kroehler designs. The Mexican affiliate manufactured upholstered furniture and mattresses. Basic Wood Products produced furniture frames for Kroehler. The subsidiary had its own sawmill and some timber holdings in Mississippi under the name of Osiris, Inc. Ad Infinitum, Inc., was the wholly owned in-house advertising agency for Kroehler.

The extent of recent reorganizations within the company was indicated in changes in top management. Only two of the eleven officers of the company held similar positions before Kroehler began experiencing losses in 1975 (see Exhibit 9). The average tenure of the other nine officers was only two years, compared with 10.4 years for the 1976 team. Many of the new officers were considerably younger as well (average age of 44.6 in 1980 compared with 51.8

EXHIBIT 4
Kroehler Manufacturing Co., Inc.
Consolidated Statement of Operations
(In Thousands of Dollars Except Where Noted)

	1979	1978	1977	1976	1975
Net sales and other operating revenues	116,264	141,951	152,769	157,156	134,726
Gross profit on sales	6,818	13,358	17,614	21,346	14,469
Less cost of sales	109,446	128,593	135,155	135,810	120,257
Selling, general, and administrative expenses	20,353	20,017	20,437	18,160	16,698
Operating income (loss)	(13,535)	(6,659)	(2,823)	3,186	(2,229)
Interest expenses	3,128	2,801	2,716	1,551	1,520
Other expenses	669	(186)	(312)	(742)	(304)
Income taxes	1,046	184	(647)	951	(1,738)
Extraordinary items (net)	—	—	—	—	—
Net income (Loss)	(18,37R)	(9,458)	(4,580)	1,426	(1,707)
Per share net income	($14.24)	($7.33)	($3.55)	$1.10	($1.33)
Dividends	—	—	—	—	—

EXHIBIT 5
Kroehler Manufacturing Co., Inc.
Consolidated Balance Sheets
(In Thousands of Dollars)

	1979	1978	1977	1976	1975
Assets					
Current:					
Cash	822	2,834	2,733	3,750	2,515
Restricted cash	2,029	—	—	—	—
Marketable securities	—	1,479	2,000	—	—
Accounts receivable	13,401	21,836	24,761	22,338	21,493
Inventories	12,456	26,704	28,649	27,031	27,904
Prepaid expenses	940	1,613	1,072	949	1,148
Miscellaneous	2,221*	195	594	422	1,837
Subtotal	31,869	54,661	59,849	54,490	54,897
Property and equipment:					
Land, buildings, and equipment	23,376	40,547	42,903	42,386	42,769
Accumulated depreciation	(14,605)	(22,086)	(23,396)	(23,142)	(22,501)
Net leases	970	2,135	2,076	1,413	1,623
Subtotal	9,741	20,596	21,583	20,657	21,891
Other:					
Deferred charges	1,778	2,025	2,027	1,749	1,555
Investment in foreign¹ affiliate	1,389	1,164	1,771	2,631	2,362
Miscellaneous	3,859	2,612	1,166	706	718
Subtotal	7,026	5,801	4,964	5,086	4,635
Total assets	48,636	81,058	86,396	80,233	81,423

	1979	1978	1977	1976	1975
Liabilities and stockholders' equity					
Current liabilities:					
Notes payable	2,110	3,404	1,297	814	394
Accounts payable	5,801	7,580	5,895	4,792	6,007
Accrued income and other taxes	459	1,023	1,120	1,612	1,231
Accrued compensation and other expenses	2,322	4,803	4,499	3,934	4,374
Current maturities of long-term debt	1,837	404	675	2,167	1,119
Subtotal	12,529	17,223	13,400	13,319	13,125
Long-term debt:					
Notes	12,000	20,000	20,000	11,000	12,500
Capital leases	2,131	2,553	2,379	1,176	1,921
Less current maturities	(1,837)	(404)	(675)	(2,167)	(1,119)
Miscellaneous	5	59	181	303	392
Subtotal	12,299	22,208	21,885	10,852	13,694
Deferred income taxes	312	—	29	71	89
Deferred employment benefits	3,251	3,004	2,915	2,725	2,663
Stockholders' equity:					
Common stock	1,290	1,290	1,290	1,290	1,290
Preferred conventional stock	—	—	—	271	271
Additional paid-in capital	14,109	14,109	14,109	14,118	14,118
Retained earnings	4,846	23,224	31,682	37,587	36,173
Subtotal	20,245	38,623	48,081	53,266	51,852
Total	48,636	81,058	86,396	80,233	81,423

*Includes $2,209 of assets under contract for sale through February 1980.

EXHIBIT 6
Kroehler Manufacturing Co. and Subsidiaries
Consolidated Statement of Changes in Financial Position
(In Thousands of Dollars)

	1979	1978	1977	1976	1975
Sources of working capital:					
Net income (loss)	(18,378)	(9,458)	(4,580)	1,426	(1,707)
Items which reduced (increased) income but did not require funds:					
Depreciation	(1,784)	(2,492)	2,550	2,594	2,645
Accrued pension costs	—	—	111	—	704
Equity in income of affiliate	357	143	(166)	124	(262)
Deferred income taxes and other items	(1,841)	(373)	(372)	86	(156)
Funds derived from operations	(15,110)	(6,736)	(2,457)	4,230	1,224
Proceeds from:					
Property and equipment sold	1,019	948	—	—	—
Long-term borrowing	64	972	23,040	6,500	163
Decrease in other assets and miscellaneous	3,087	285	232	—	864
Proceeds from sale of Canadian subsidiary	10,218	—	—	—	—
Total	(722)	(4,531)	20,815	10,730	2,251

EXHIBIT 6 (continued)

	1979	1978	1977	1976	
Uses of working capital:					
Cash dividends	—	—	325	12	.2
Purchase of property and equipment	537	3,716	3,040	1,738	1,768
Reduction in long-term debt	9,933	649	12,007	9,342	1,874
Increase in other assets and miscellaneous	—	—	280	239	—
Decrease in working capital	(11,192)	(8,896)	5,163	(601)	(1,403)
Changes in working capital items:					
Increase (decrease) in current assets:					
Cash and marketable securities	(1,462)	(460)	1,023	1,235	(1,258)
Receivables	3,076	2,925	2,423	845	602
Inventories	9,368	1,945	1,618	(873)	1,077
Prepaid expenses & income tax refunds	1,395	142	295	(1,614)	130
Total	(12,511)	(5,188)	5,359	(407)	551
Decrease (increase) in current liabilities:					
Notes payable to banks	890	(2,107)	(483)	(420)	1,727
Accounts payable	162	(1,685)	(1,103)	1,215	(2,215)
Accrued expenses	1,727	(187)	(102)	59	(609)
Current maturities of long-term debt	(1,460)	271	1,492	(1,048)	(857)
Total	1,319	(3,708)	(196)	(194)	(1,954)
Decrease in working capital	(11,192)	(8,896)	5,163	(601)	(1,403)

EXHIBIT 7
Kroehler Manufacturing Co. and Subsidiaries
Summary of Financial Performance 1966–1979

Year	Net sales ($ millions)	Net income	Earnings per share	Dividends per share	Stock price (low-high)	Price/earnings (low-high)
1966	$111.8	$ 2.8	$ 1.78	$0.96	$16 $-33^1/_8$	9–19
1967	107.0	2.1	0.85	0.25	16 $-25^1/_4$	19–30
1968	114.7	2.8	2.18	0.60	$19^3/_8-40^3/_4$	9–19
1969	106.9	1.8	1.36	1.00	20 $-39^1/_2$	15–29
1970	107.7	1.0	0.78	0.20	$11^1/_4-24^3/_8$	14–31
1971	120.0	2.6	2.04	0.20	$18^1/_2-36^1/_2$	9–18
1972	129.1	3.5	2.67	0.80	$23^1/_2-47^1/_4$	9–18
1973	143.4	3.4	2.63	1.00	$11^3/_8-27^1/_8$	4–10
1974	139.3	0.8	0.61	0.80	$7^1/_2-17^1/_2$	12–29
1975	134.7	(1.7)	(1.33)	0	8 $-13^1/_4$	—
1976	167.3	1.4	1.10	0	10 $-15^1/_4$	9–14
1977	152.9	(4.6)	(3.55)	0.25	$8^7/_8-14^5/_8$	—
1978	142.0	(9.5)	(7.33)	0	$7^7/_8-12^3/_4$	—
1979	116.3	(18.4)	(14.24)	0	$7^1/_2-13^1/_2$	—

EXHIBIT 8
COMPARATIVE FINANCIAL PERFORMANCE OF HOME FURNISHINGS INDUSTRY* VS. KROEHLER

Measure	1979 Industry	1979 Kroehler	1978 Industry	1978 Kroehler	1977 Industry	1977 Kroehler	1976 Industry	1976 Kroehler
Sales (1967 = 100)	402†	109	369	133	326	143	285	156
Net income (1967 = 100)	359†	def.	393	def.	294	def.	265	131
Net income (% of sales)	4.4†	NM	5/1	NM	4.5	NM	4.7	.9
Operating income (% of sales)	10.4†	NM	11.9	NM	11.2	NM	11.9	3.9
Five-year growth (%)	11.5‡	NM	—	—	—	—	—	—
Debt/equity ratio (%)	19.9†	—	17.6	36.5	18.3	31.3	19.2	16.9
Debt as % of net working capital	41.4†	—	35.0	59.2	39.0	47.2	40.6	26.5
Return on equity (%)	11.9†	NM	12.6	NM	11.2	NM	11.3	2.7

*Home furnishings industry averages computed using following firms: American Furniture, Bassett Furniture, Flexsteel Industries, Henredon Furniture, Lane Company, La-Z-Boy Chair, Leggett and Platt, Ludlow Corp., Mohasco Corp., Ohio-Sealy Mattress, Pulaski Furniture, Rowe Furniture, and Sperry & Hutchinson.
†Two firms not included due to missing data.
‡Based on nine firms showing positive growth in the last five years. (Four firms besides Kroehler have shown negative five-year growth.)
Source: Standard & Poor's Industry Surveys.

EXHIBIT 9
KROEHLER MANUFACTURING CO., INC. EXECUTIVE OFFICERS AS OF MARCH 11, 1980

Name	Office	First became elected officer	Age, years (Jan. 1, 1980)
Kenneth Kroehler	Director, chairman of the board	1946	62
William T. Welsh	President and chief executive officer	1980	59
Norman V. Chimenti	Vice president, operations	1976	39
Gene A. Davidsmeyer	Vice president, treasurer, and secretary	1976	42
Thomas C. Himes	Vice president, marketing	1977	36
James Hogan	Vice president, cotton processing	1977	50
Robert O'Meara	Vice president, sales	1980	51
Ben W. Nelson	Vice president, wood processing	1967	59
William Russell	Vice president, manufacturing	1979	41
Mark Seagle	Vice president, engineering	1979	30
Julian A. Voss	Controller	1978	54

EXHIBIT 10
KROEHLER MANUFACTURING CO., INC. BOARD OF DIRECTORS, APRIL 1980

Name	Principal occupation	Age, years	First became a director
Leo H. Arnstein	Lawyer-counsel, Arnstein, Gluck, Weitzenfeld & Minon; also director of PETX Petroleum Corp.	73	1968
Dan H. Edmonson	Former vice president of Kroehler Southwest	63	1964
John Kinsella	President and chief operating officer of Leo Burnett International (advertising agency)	51	1978
Kenneth Kroehler	Chairman of the board and former chief executive officer; also director of Protection Mutual Insurance	62	1941
Henry W. Meers	Managing director, Merrill Lynch White Weld Capital Markets Group; also director of DuKane Corp., Ill., Tool Works, Inc., International Minerals & Chemical Corp., Reliance Group, Inc., and Reliance Insurance Co.	71	1956
William J. Pfeif	Vice chairman of the board, Sunbeam Corp.; also director of Walter E. Heller International Corp.	62	1978
John E. Velde, Jr.	Private investor	62	1974

years in 1976.) A similar change had taken place in the board of directors. The number of directors had been reduced to seven from thirteen in 1977. Five of the seven current directors were on the board since at least 1974, and only one member of the new board was a member of the Kroehler family (four members of the Kroehler family were on the board in 1977). Similarly, only two present or former employees of the company were on the board, compared with eight in 1977. (See Exhibit 10).

Mr. William Welsh was appointed president and chief executive officer in 1980, for a one-year term, and Kenneth Kroehler retained his position as chairman of the board. Mr. Welsh was the first nonfamily member to head the company since its organization as the Kroehler Manufacturing Company. Mr. Welsh was confronted with the problem of returning the company to profitability at a time when Kroehler was consolidating its plants and effecting greater centralization of its production support functions, such as purchasing and fabric warehousing. As previously indicated, in its efforts to reduce costs, Kroehler sold its Canadian subsidiary and its newly constructed plant in San Bernardino, California, which eliminated much of its market in the west and Canada. (For a review of the furniture industry, see the appendix.)

APPENDIX: The Furniture Industry

The furniture industry was highly competitive and fragmented. An estimated 1,465 domestic manufacturers of upholstered furniture sold their output to both foreign and domestic customers. The capital requirements for entry were extremely low, and only a few firms reached $100 million sales per year. It was estimated that the ten largest producers of upholstered furniture in the United States accounted for approximately 25 percent of industry sales.

The furniture industry's products were generally divided into three major categories: upholstered furniture, metal furniture, and wood furniture or "case goods" (dining room tables, chairs, cabinets, bedroom sets, etc.). Other smaller categories included wood TV and radio cabinets, bedding and mattresses, and specialized furniture such as rattan. (See Exhibit 11.)

The household furniture industry suffered a decline in 1975 but rebounded again in 1976. Overall consumer expenditures for 1981 were expected to fall nearly 6 to 10 percent from 1980 levels. The decline was attributable to adverse economic conditions, particularly the recession in the housing industry.

FACTORS AFFECTING DEMAND

The primary factor behind the expected drop in furniture purchases was the declining rate of new housing starts brought on by the scarcity of mortgage money. (See Exhibit 12.) Seasonally adjusted housing starts fell 2.1 percent in April 1980, 42 percent lower than the previous year. Several projections pegged 1980 as the worst housing recession since World War II.

The rising prices of new homes also had a significant impact on the rate of home building. Inflationary pressures coupled with the higher costs of ownership, such as energy, taxes, and interest rates, eliminated certain income levels from the home buying market. High interest rates caused a major decline in existing home sales.

EXHIBIT 11
HOUSEHOLD FURNITURE INDUSTRY SHIPMENTS (IN MILLIONS OF CURRENT DOLLARS), EST.

	1972	1973	1974	1975	1976	1977	1978	1979	1980
Total shipments	7,416	8,216	8,365	7,770	9,041	10,372	11,460	12,800	12,150
Wood furniture	2,870	3,201	3,381	3,095	3,780	4,155	4,626	5,125	4,750
Upholstered	2,105	2,273	2,310	2,186	2,446	2,918	3,325	3,825	3,630
Metal	890	1,000	1,003	939	1,080	1,257	1,350	1,450	1,310
Other*	1,551	1,742	1,671	1,550	1,735	2,042	2,159	2,400	2,460

EST. = Estimated by Standard & Poor's.
*Includes bedding and mattresses, wood TV and radio cabinets, and other furniture.
Source: Department of Commerce and Federal Reserve Board.

The decline in real disposable income was also expected to continue to dramatically impact purchases of major home furnishings. Gains in personal income continued to lag behind increases in the consumer price index. In addition, inflation was pushing wage earners into higher tax brackets, further reducing real disposable income.

The long-term outlook for the industry was extremely favorable despite recent troubles. The number of people in the 36 to 44 age group (a key home buying segment of the population) is expected to increase 22 percent to 31.4 million by 1985, as compared with 25.7 million in this bracket in 1980. Individual households were expected to soar 20 percent, and the trend to increased home ownership was expected to continue (78 percent of married couples in 1979 versus 70 percent in 1970).

In addition, the rise in the number of two-income families made more income available for such items as household furnishings. Changing life-styles because of inflation and high energy costs would keep more people at home, who would be expected to spend more on making the home environment comfortable. The pent-up demand for new homes caused by the recession and inflationary pressures could significantly boost sales for the industry when those pressures eased.

MARKET CHARACTERISTICS

The domestic furniture manufacturers may be categorized according to:

1 Type of furniture. For example, La-Z-Boy made chairs and recliners primarily. Bassett made wood furniture primarily.

2 Price range. Henredon and Flexsteel were considered to be makers of high-priced furniture, while Kroehler historically produced mid-priced furniture.

3 Style. Ethan Allen was best known as a maker of colonial-style furniture.

The furniture industry was one in which manufacturers' innovations or designs were rapidly adopted by competitors. There were patents on furniture mechanisms; La-Z-Boy's recliner mechanisms were patented. Patents were also granted for furniture designs, if they were distinctive in the frame or covering fabric. Some patented furniture was manufactured under licensing agreements. However, this was not done to any significant extent. A patent did not provide any real protection to the inventor. A patented design needed only to be changed in some small respect to be manufactured almost at will by competitors.

Over the last two decades a marked change had quietly occurred in the furniture in-

EXHIBIT 12
FACTORS INFLUENCING DEMAND FOR HOME FURNISHINGS

Year	Gross national product Billions of 1972 dollars	Disposable personal income Total Billions of 1972 dollars	% of GNP	% Chg.	Consumer expenditures Total Billions of 1972 dollars	Furniture and household equipment Billions of 1972 dollars	% of total expenditures
E1980	1,422.0	980.0	68.9	−1.5	935.0	64.1	6.8
P1979	1,431.6	994.8	69.5	+2.3	924.0	63.2	6.8
1978	1,399.2	972.6	69.5	+4.6	900.8	60.3	6.7
1977	1,340.5	929.5	69.3	+4.2	861.7	57.3	6.6
1976	1,273.0	891.8	70.1	+3.7	820.5	53.1	6.5
1975	1,202.3	859.7	71.5	+2.1	774.6	49.9	6.4
1974	1,217.8	842.0	69.1	−1.5	760.7	50.7	6.7
1973	1,235.0	854.7	69.2	+6.7	767.7	49.9	6.5
1972	1,171.1	801.3	68.4	+4.2	733.0	44.8	6.1
1971	1,107.5	769.0	69.4	+3.7	691.9	39.9	5.8

†As of year end. P—Preliminary. E—Estimated by S&P.
Sources: Department of Commerce, Federal Reserve Board, Bureau of Labor Statistics, The Conference Board, and National Association of Realtors.

dustry in terms of retail sales and the product itself. In the past, most furniture was sold by relatively small to medium-sized furniture stores which had sample pieces on display and stocks of furniture in separately located warehouses available for delivery to customers. In an effort to reduce inventory storage and finance costs, smaller dealers kept only the sample display pieces. Customers placed special orders for fabrics or styles selected from a multitude of sample books. Only the large furniture warehouse-showrooms, such as Levitz, kept large quantities of inventory on hand, and most of that was picked up by the customers themselves. Traditional full-service furniture stores were still the most numerous, but they were losing sales to the large national merchandising chains, department stores, and furniture warehouse-showrooms. (See Exhibit 13.)

There was intense price competition among furniture retailers. While the large stores and warehouse-showrooms offered greater selection, they needed two to three times the profit on a sale of a living room or bedroom set that a small store required. The larger profit was needed to offset huge store rental and inventory costs as well as union-labor payroll expenses.

The retail prices for a new upholstered sofa ranged from $300 to over $2,500, depending to a large degree upon fabric selection. In the past, customers who were reluctant or unable to buy new furniture could have their old furniture refinished or reupholstered. However, prices for this service had increased to the point where it could cost $450 to $1,000 to reupholster an old sofa.

With prices for restored and brand new furniture increasing markedly, the alternative for price-conscious or mobile buyers could be in rental furniture. Previously concentrated in the south, low-income areas of major cities, and areas of highly mobile popula-

Consumer expenditures					
% of disposable income	New housing starts (thous.)	Sales of existing single-family homes (thous.)	†Installment credit outstanding		Consumer price index (1967 = 100)
			Limited $	% Chg.	
6.5	1,000	3,000	—	—	—
6.4	1,744	3,701	311,339	−13.0	217.7
6.2	2,020	3,563	275,629	−10.4	195.4
6.2	1,987	3,547	230,829	+19.0	181.5
6.0	1,538	3,002	193,977	+12.5	170.5
5.8	1,160	2,450	172,353	− 4.7	161.2
6.0	1,333	2,272	164,594	− 6.1	147.7
5.8	2,045	2,334	155,109	−16.5	133.1
5.6	2,357	2,252	133,178	−12.6	125.3
5.2	2,052	2,018	118,255	+12.1	121.3

tions such as California and Florida, furniture rental stores could carve out a larger market share in stable, working-class, suburban areas. Exhibit 14 details the characteristics of eight prototype furniture stores. Each type tends to focus on different target market segments and operates in different ways relative to merchandise, location, etc.

Most residential furniture can be categorized as traditional, modern (or contemporary), and early American (or colonial), with special categories for outdoor, Oriental, etc. These style categories were relatively unchanging. However, waves of style or fashion trends worked their way through furniture designs in approximately 8- to 9-year cycles. Demand in 1979–1980 remained the strongest for youth-oriented "life-style" home furnishings (which were part of the contemporary group), and this was expected to continue. The original mix-and-match, color-coordinated groups of portable, inexpensive furniture had been expanded to include "knock-down" furniture (requiring assembly by the buyer), modular pieces, wicker patio furniture, and waterbeds, combined with traditional styles of seating pieces and case goods. The "life-style" concept had also increased its appeal to other consumer groups, including the older and more affluent furniture purchasers. This style of furniture was sold primarily by specialized outlets or through newly developed department store boutiques. Major advances had also been made in using molded plastics and metal for outdoor furniture.

Furniture demand historically had been design-sensitive, and leading manufacturers had developed special design departments to strengthen their marketing efforts. Traditionally, when business activity was strong and order backlogs were growing, the regular showing of styles yielded good results. However, as competitive pressures mounted, particularly during periods of slower consumer buying, manufacturers were forced to come up with new ideas in styles, quality, and distribution to stimulate sales. For the

EXHIBIT 13
CLASSIFICATION OF FURNITURE RETAILERS

Classification	Market Share, %
Geographic location	
East	30.8%
Southeast	9.6%
Southwest	7.7%
Midwest	38.4%
West	13.5%
	100%
Annual sales volume	
Under $500,000	40.4%
$500,000 to $2 million	36.5%
$2 million to $5 million	19.2%
Over $5 million	3.9%
	100%
Number of stores	
Single store	67.4%
Two stores	23.1%
Three to five stores	5.7%
Six to 10 stores	1.9%
Over 11 stores	1.9%
	100%
Store type	
Sears, Penney's, Ward's	8%
Mass merchant (e.g., Levitz)	12%
Department stores and "style" furniture stores (e.g., Marshall Field, John M. Smyth)	21%
Specialty and other furniture stores	50%
Variety stores and miscellaneous	9%
	100%

Source: NHFA Reports, January 1977.

most part, products in the 1980s were expected to be of higher quality and of greater versatility, with an emphasis on contemporary and casual lines. Less-expensive lines tended to receive greater advertising and promotion during periods of slow demand.

Product lines for coming seasons were shown several times a year at wholesale exhibits, or "marts." The major marts were in High Point, North Carolina, and Chicago, Illinois. Other important exhibits were in New York City, Dallas, and Los Angeles. These shows were primarily attended by buyers from major retail stores. Sales were generally made in advance of production to avoid the likelihood of an unprofitable line and were based on the designs and models shown at the exhibits.

EXHIBIT 14
FURNITURE STORE PROTOTYPES

Store prototype	Target market segment(s)	Market positioning strategy	Physical size, square feet of selling area	Location	Advertising
Regular full-service furniture store	Age: 25-54 yr. olds Income: $10,000 to $20,000 Education: High school graduates or less Life-style: Dominant life-style profile (see Exhibit 3)	• Good selection of merchandise -at- • Reasonable prices	5,000 to 20,000	• Normally suburban orientation • Free-standing locations, perhaps in the vicinity of shopping centers • Average income areas	• Normal expenditure (4 to 6% of sales) • Primarily newspapers • Mass market to slightly up-scale image
Specialty store	Age: 25-54 yr. olds Income: Over $15,000 Education: High school graduates or more Life-style: Dominant to more sophisticated	• Unique merchandise -at- • Reasonable prices	3,000 to 50,000	• Normally suburban orientation • Free-standing locations or shopping center locations • Above-average income areas	• Normal to below-average expenditure • Primarily newspapers • Moderately sophisticated to sophisticated image
Showcase store	Age: 25-54 yr. olds Income: Over $15,000 Education: High school graduates or more Life-style: Dominant to more sophisticated	• Outstanding selection of merchandise -at- • Reasonable prices	35,000 to 100,000	• Normally suburban orientation • Free-standing locations adjacent to shopping centers • Above-average income areas	• Normal to below-average expenditure • Newspapers and maybe TV • Moderately sophisticated to sophisticated image

EXHIBIT 14 (*continued*)
FURNITURE STORE PROTOTYPES

Store prototype	Target market segment(s)	Market positioning strategy	Physical size, square feet of selling area	Location	Advertising
Furniture warehouse-showroom	Age: 25-54 yr. olds Income: Under $15,000 Education: High school graduates or less Life-style: Dominant to less sophisticated	• Popular styles and brands -at- • Low prices	30,000 to 60,000	• Normally suburban orientation • Free-standing locations adjacent to railroad tracks • Average to below-average income areas	• Normal to above-average expenditure • Newspapers and/or TV • Mass market to slightly down-scale image
Super store	Age: Under 35 Income: Under $20,000 Education: College graduates or less Life-style: New values	• "Now" furniture & furnishings -at- • Low prices	20,000 to 200,000	• Normally suburban orientation • Free-standing locations or abandoned supermarkets, discount department stores • Average to below-average income areas with high concentration of youth	• Normal to below-average expenditure • Newspapers and/or TV and/or radio • Contemporary/fun images
Catalog discount store	Age: 25-54, primarily under 35 Income: Under $20,000 Education: College graduate or less Life-style: Dominant to more sophisticated	• Outstanding selection -at- • Low prices	3,000 to 5,000	• Normally suburban orientation • Free-standing or shopping center location • Average income areas	• Limited to no advertising • Newspapers or TV or radio • Mass market to slightly up-scale image

Store type	Customer profile	Merchandise/price	Size (sq. ft.)	Location	Promotion
Budget/second-hand store	Age: Primarily under 35 Income: Primarily under $8,000 Education: Less than high school Life-style: Dominant to less sophisticated	• Unusual merchandise -at- • Low prices	3,000 to 20,000	• Central city orientation • Abandoned retail space • Below-average income areas	• Limited to no advertising • Newspapers or TV or radio • Mass market to slightly downscale image
Rental store	Age: Under 45 Income: Under $15,000 Education: High school graduate or less Life-style: Mobile, more sophisticated, new values	• Good selection of merchandise -at- • Affordable rates -which- • Can be returned or purchased	3,000 to 15,000	• Suburban and central city orientation • Free-standing • Average income locations	• Limited advertising • Newspapers • Mobile, special situation image

Source: Results of Profile V Research Program and Management Horizons, Inc.

PRODUCTIVITY TRENDS

The household furniture production index rose 3.3 percent in 1979 to a record 165.0, from 159.7 in the previous year (100 in 1967). For the period 1975–1979, the average annual rate of growth in the value of shipments was 9.9 percent, and employment only climbed 6 percent. Most of the gains in productivity reflected improvements in product design and equipment modernization.

FINANCIAL PRESSURES

Historically, the highly competitive nature of the household furniture industry had tended to limit profit margins. Profit margins quickly reflected changing demand patterns, narrowing when consumer spending shifted to other products and widening in response to changes in personal income levels and family formations. The current outlook for the industry was one of increasing pressures on margins as a result of declining demand, higher costs of raw materials and labor, and increased interest expense. The industry was not expected to be able to pass on these rising costs to consumers quickly enough to avoid price/cost pressures. These unfavorable trade conditions were likely to result in significant curtailment of production and more intense price and product competition.

Materials expense increased significantly in 1979–1980, coupled with periodic shortages of certain materials. Direct labor costs rose over 6 percent. In addition, the costs of complying with proposed government regulations adversely affected earnings.

PENDING GOVERNMENT REGULATIONS

One of the major problems of the 1980s could be how well the furniture industry coped with government regulations. A proposed regulation for mandatory care-labeling of household furniture was being finalized by the FTC. Once law, manufacturers would have six months to comply. This was not expected to be a major problem, however, as most firms were already providing the labeling voluntarily.

The Consumer Product Safety Commission (CPSC) had also proposed flammability standards for upholstered furniture to prevent an estimated 500 deaths a year caused by burning cigarettes. The proposed standards called for the elimination of highly flammable combinations of fabrics, filling materials, and construction materials.

In order to meet the proposed federal flammability standards, the furniture industry would have to rely on the following available methods:

1 Treating upholstery fabrics with fire-retardant chemicals
2 Adding fire-retardant chemicals to the polyurethane foam cushioning materials
3 Inserting a fire-resistant barrier called an interliner between the upholstery fabric covering and the cushioning materials

There were disadvantages to each alternative. The common disadvantage was increased cost of upholstered furniture. The only way to avoid substantial cost increases, in the range of 30 to 40 percent, was to apply a fire-retardant spray, which was still in the developmental stage.

The effectiveness of the interliner method, which was developed by Du Pont, varied with the type of upholstery fabric, furniture style, and the method of application. Some fabrics and constructions failed a cigarette ignition test even when the interliner was used properly. Furthermore, any effectiveness was diminished drastically if the interliner was ripped or cut, exposing flammable cushioning material beneath it. For this reason, interliners could not be used for upholstered public assembly or transit seating, where vandalism or arson was possible.

The CPSC projected the cost of compliance at $6.60 to $10.00 per sofa, but the industry estimated that it would be closer to $100. After considerable debate, the CPSC agreed in November 1979 to a one-year trial period in which voluntary guidelines established by the Upholstered Furniture Action Council (UFAC) would be tested. Under the agreement, the CPSC will monitor the impact of the UFAC guidelines and reach a final decision concerning mandatory standards, keeping in mind the results of voluntary compliance. The UFAC said that independent laboratory tests indicated that the possibility of cigarette ignition was reduced by 89 percent in UFAC-approved furniture.

In addition to regulations concerning care-labeling and flammability, other regulations pertaining to wood dust and hydrocarbon emissions from spraying and trucking industry deregulation were expected to have a major impact on the industry in the 1980s.

INDUSTRY CONSOLIDATION

One factor likely to impact the industry during the 1980s was the continuing trend toward consolidation. Bassett Furniture's acquisition of Weiman/Warren Lloyd, Ethan Allen's purchase of Knob Creek (Ethan Allen, in turn, was acquired by Interco in December 1979), and Broyhill's purchase of Woodward, Inc., were prime examples of a trend in which financially stronger firms were taking over weaker companies. For the industry in general, this trend was likely to improve operating efficiencies and, thus, profit margins in the long run.

Operating capacity was also expected to rise in the 1980s. It was estimated that most concerns operated at about 80 percent of capacity in 1979, but the level was likely to increase to as high as 90 percent in the next several years. In addition, standardization of furniture components (slides, cabinet doors, drawers, etc.) would help ease rising labor and raw material costs. Greater use of fiberboard and other wood substitutes, as well as injection molding, were also expected to moderate the rise in costs.

One aspect not expected to change was market concentration. Industry leaders would continue their strong expansion into the sun belt area, particularly Texas and Florida. Population growth in this fast-growing region was expected to continue in the 1980s, and a ready labor force was rapidly becoming available.

Manufacturers of household furniture were concentrated primarily in North Carolina, Tennessee, Virginia, New York, Pennsylvania, Indiana, Illinois, Michigan, and California. The industry consisted of more than 6,000 firms, many specializing in various product lines and employing approximately 308,000 workers.

The two major manufacturers of household furniture were Mohasco (sales of $325 million in 1979) and Bassett Furniture ($277 million). Both companies offered a broad range of wood and upholstered products. The other industry leaders were Interco ($227 million), Sperry & Hutchinson ($210 million), Armstrong World Industries (formerly Armstrong Cork) ($20 million), Lane Co. ($159 million), La-Z-Boy ($19 million), Burlington Industries ($152 million), and Singer ($151 million). Other important manufacturers were Broyhill and Drexel-Heritage, both privately owned.

Volkswagenwerk, AG[1]

In 1981, the Volkswagen (VW) group's earnings dropped 64 percent to DM 123.7 million from DM 193.0 million for 1980. Sales in this period, however, increased to DM 37.8 billion from DM 33.2 billion. VW's management expected to break even for 1982, with an expected drop in sales of about 5 percent from 2.5 million cars in 1980. (See Exhibits 1 to 5.)

VW management attributed the significant drop in profits to the worldwide automobile slump, particularly in the United States, West Germany, and Brazil. The company also experienced significant losses from its Triumph-Adler office equipment manufacturing subsidiary, which was purchased for $229 million in 1979 as a diversification effort. Triumph-Adler had a loss of DM 197 million in 1981.

In 1977, VW's management established a plant in the United States to assemble Rabbit models. The site selected was a partially completed Chrysler Corporation plant at New Stanton, Pennsylvania, 30 miles southeast of Pittsburgh. This decision had been long delayed by the supervisory board of VW and had been a matter of national controversy in West Germany.

VW'S POSITION IN THE UNITED STATES

When the automobile industry experienced difficulties on a worldwide scale in the latter part of the 1970s, VW was particularly hard hit because of the strong position of the German mark in relation to other currencies, particularly the

[1]This case was prepared from published sources including the 1977 version by Mr. Albert W. Isenman under the direction of Professor Thomas J. McNichols as a basis for class discussion rather than to illustrate effective or ineffective management.

U.S. dollar. The United States was the largest export market for VW, accounting for approximately one-third of the company's total export sales. VW sold 330,000 vehicles in the United States in 1981, while market share in the United States held at 3.3 percent. Management stated that VW had experienced greater difficulties in the United States than in the rest of the world. VW hoped to improve the trend in sales and market position with the acquisition of a second assembly plant in the United States, to be located near Detroit. Management was of the opinion that this facility would enable VW to become more competitive again in price as well as to diminish what remained of the exchange rate problem; the company anticipated lower overall production costs.

Erratic profits for several years following the large deficit of 1974 caused considerable unrest in the VW management ranks as well as in the labor unions and among employees in general. Since 40 percent of VW was owned by the West German government, the fate of the company was frequently debated in the Bundestag, the parliament of West Germany.

Mr. Rudolph Leiding had been chairman of VW since late 1972. As chairman of VW's Vorstand (board of management), which ran the company's day-to-day business, Mr. Leiding encountered opposition to some of his policies, particularly his efforts to get approval for the building of a plant in the United States. It was reported that some of his board members bitterly opposed this move, and they received support from some quarters because of the declining sales of VW and the recent layoffs of employees.

The Aufsichtsrat (a supervisory board made up of business people, labor representatives, and government officials), which oversaw the company's long-range strategies, was badly split on the issue and was unable to resolve the conflict. Mr. Leiding fought hard for the United States plant in the face of strong opposition. He finally resigned as chairman in 1975; the company officials cited ill health as the reason.

Mr. Toni Schmucker, the new chief executive of VW, faced serious problems of declining sales and profits. Rising production costs in Germany cut into margins, and increased competition from Japanese and other manufacturers in Europe affected sales. The devaluation of the dollar and the rising value of the mark severely affected VW's exports into the United States. In addition to losing a cost advantage it had held in the United States for a long time, the company was faced with increased competition from Japanese automobiles and the new entries into the small-car market of United States manufacturers. Mr. Schmucker was also confronted with reinforcing the product-line policy the company had embarked on under Mr. Leiding. Many new models had been added in an effort to reduce reliance on the Beetle, the basic VW, which had historically accounted for over 70 percent of production. While Beetle production had declined since 1967, in 1974 it still accounted for approximately 40 percent of total production. The Beetle was finally discontinued in 1978 (except in Mexico and Brazil). In addition, Schmucker had to contend with disputes on the management board, on the supervisory board, and with labor representatives.

EXHIBIT 1
CONSOLIDATED BALANCE SHEET—VW GROUP

Assets

Thousand DM

	Jan. 1, 1981	Amounts brought forward[3]	Additions	Disposals	Transfers	Write-ups	Depreciation	Dec. 31, 1981	Dec. 31, 1980
Fixed Assets and Investments									
A. Property, Plant, Equipment and Intangible Assets									
Real estate and land rights with office, factory and other buildings	2,939.009	—	295,972	18,697	189,222	—	213,632	3,191,874	2,939,009
with residential buildings	387,598	—	17,018	8,131	5,304	—	16,058	385,731	387,598
without buildings	153,577	—	11,202	5,813	1,568	—	535	159,999	153,577
Buildings on leased real estate	51,991	—	19,111	277	7,607	—	7,595	70,837	51,991
Machinery and fixtures	1,234,864	—	882,650	22,323	209,115	—	703,188	1,601,118	1,234,864
Plant and office equipment	2,401,440	1,412	1,845,978	355,520	463,175	—	1,390,600	2,965,885	2,401,440
Construction in progress and advance payments on fixed assets	1,151,045	—	1,701,379	43,551	(875,985)	—	107,205	1,825,683	1,151,045
Trademarks and the like	6,586	8	2,146	1,188	(6)	—	3,596	3,950	6,586
	8,326,110	1,420	4,775,456	455,500	—	—	2,442,409	10,205,077	8,326,110
B. Investments									
Investments in subsidiaries and affiliates	94,018	14	3,804	3,320	400	—	8,321	86,595	94,018
Other investment securities	14,060	—	398	881	5	—	89	13,493	14,060
Loans receivable with an initial term of four years or longer									
Par value at Dec. 31, 1981 256,910	172,119	—	44,276	15,070[2]	(1,191)	683	9,776	191,041	172,119
of which secured by mortgages 103,390									
loans in accordance with § 89 AktG 1,131									
loans in accordance with § 115 AktG 124									
Other investments	4,193	—	11,509	584	786	—	11,499	4,405	4,193
	284,390	14	59,987	19,855	—	683	29,685	295,534	284,390
	8,610,500	1,434	4,835,443	475,355	—	683	2,472,094	10,500,611	8,610,500

C. Adjustment Items Arising from Initial Consolidation		119,169	566,548
		10,619,780	**9,177,048**
Current Assets			
A. Inventories		**5,970,845**	**6,053,349**
B. Other Current Assets			
Advance payments to suppliers		25,143	23,693
Trade accounts receivable		1,533,090	1,277,706
of which amounts due in more than one year	2,601		
Trade acceptances		138,907	129,615
of which acceptances discountable at German Federal Bank	36,878		
Cheques on hand		45,005	52,758
Cash on hand, deposits at the German Federal Bank and in postal checking accounts		7,096	10,407
Cash in banks		2,630,910	3,784,888
Securities		1,107,477	1,141,021
Own stock (par value at Dec. 31, 1981 : 15,060)		21,235	21,235
Receivables from subsidiaries and affiliates		18,469	26,135
of which amounts for goods and services rendered	18,059		
Loans receivable in accordance with § 89 AktG		755	981
Miscellaneous other current assets		2,967,063	3,060,808
		8,495,150	**9,529,247**
		14,465,995	**15,582,596**
Prepaid and Deferred Expenses			
Discount on loans		135	8
Other items		286,701	196,661
of which commission	98,822		
		286,836	**196,669**
		25,372,611	**24,956,313**

(Continued on following page.)

EXHIBIT 1 *(continued)*
CONSOLIDATED BALANCE SHEET—VW GROUP

Stockholders' Equity and Liabilities

		Dec. 31, 1981	Dec. 31, 1980
Capital Stock of Volkswagenwerk AG		1,200,000	1,200,000
Consolidated Reserves			
Reserve from capital stock surplus[1]		589,407	550,707
Reserve of the Group arising from earnings[1]		4,216,443	4,037,941
Adjustment items arising from initial consolidation		37,272	37,115
		4,843,122	4,625,763
Minority Interest in Consolidated Subsidiaries		200,717	208,714
in net earnings	2,675		
in loss	90,312		
Reserves for Special Purposes			
Reserve for investment in developing countries in accordance with § 1 of the Developing Countries Tax Act		151,118	122,015
Reserve for price increases in accordance with § 74 of the Income Tax Regulation		39,884	33,736
Reserve in accordance with § 1 of the Foreign Investment Act		7,273	7,420
Reserve in accordance with § 3 of the Foreign Investment Act		97,462	101,685
Reserve in accordance with § 6b of the Income Tax Act		3,016	5,107
Reserves in accordance with French legislation		24,587	16,712
Reserve for replacement in accordance with section 35 of the Income Tax Guidelines		65	—
		323,405	286,675
Allowance for Doubtful Trade Acceptances and Accounts		35,397	159,061
Undetermined Liabilities			
Old-age pensions		3,475,496	3,106,752
Other undetermined liabilities			
Maintenance not performed during current year		30,862	46,586
Warranties without legal obligation		17,674	12,893
Other		4,006,440	4,111,682
		7,530,472	7,277,913
Liabilities with an Initial Term of Four Years or Longer			
Loans		518,220	513,606
of which secured by mortgages	180,000		
Due to banks		1,037,526	943,368
of which secured by mortgages	255,324		
Other liabilities		227,749	212,080
of which secured by mortgages	67,687		
		1,783,495	1,669,054
Of which amounts due within four years	734,298		
Other Liabilities			
Trade accounts payable		2,510,630	2,266,269
Liabilities resulting from the acceptance of bills drawn and the issuing of promissory notes		629,483	553,708
Due to banks		4,286,520	4,791,492
Advance payments from customers		77,903	63,417
Accounts payable to subsidiaries and affiliates		78	458
of which trade accounts payable	—		
Miscellaneous other liabilities		1,757,531	1,599,330
		9,262,145	9,274,674
Deferred Income		70,088	61,457
Net Earnings Available for Distribution		123,770	193,002
Contingent liabilities with respect to trade acceptances	25,710		
Contingent liabilities with respect to guaranty obligations	43,941		
Contingent liabilities with respect to warranties	6,187		
Other contingent liabilities	35,286		
		25,372,611	24,956,313

[1] These items include the legal reserve of the Volkswagenwerk AG in the amount of 843,387 thousand DM.
[2] Offset with foreign exchange adjustments in the amount of 7,194 thousand DM
[3] Amounts brought forward of companies consolidated for the first time

Mr. Schmucker guided VW back to profitability after the low years in 1974–1975, and was highly regarded in the European business community. In mid-1981, however, ill health forced Mr. Schmucker to resign. VW's finance director, Mr. Friedrich Thomee, 62, was appointed acting director but resigned a few months later when it became apparent that he would not be named CEO permanently. (Thomee had been criticized for recommending VW's purchase of Triumph-Adler.)

In January of 1982, Mr. Carl H. Hahn was appointed chairman and chief executive of VW. Mr. Hahn, an economist, had directed the U.S. marketing efforts for the Beetle from 1959–1964, but left VW in 1972 to become CEO of Germany's largest rubber company.

Despite current problems, VW enjoyed a worldwide reputation as a quality producer of economy cars. The company was the largest producer of automobiles in Europe and the third-largest auto maker in the world, surpassed only by General Motors and Ford. VW ranked fourth in size among European manufacturers, behind Royal Dutch Shell, Unilever, and Philips Gloeilampenfabrieken. At the beginning of 1982, VW employed 160,286 people in its German plants, up 0.9 percent from 1981. Worldwide, the VW group employed almost a quarter million persons. VW's multinational business extended to over 12,500 sales and service agencies located throughout the world. A chartered fleet of oceangoing vessels supplied completed automobiles, components for assembly, and replacement parts to world markets.

HISTORY AND DEVELOPMENT OF THE COMPANY

VW began with Ferdinand Porsche, a self-educated Austrian engineer, who was a world-famous pioneer designer of high-powered racing cars. Porsche wished to demonstrate his versatility by designing a low-cost, sturdy, utility automobile for the person of limited means. Since he was unable to interest German industrialists, Porsche brought his pioneering work to the attention of Adolph Hitler. Hitler immediately realized the potential appeal of a "people's car," the literal translation of the word "Volkswagen."

Hitler therefore ordered Porsche to develop the Volkswagen, for which Hitler set the specifications. It was to be a four-seat "family" auto with a two-cylinder, air-cooled 14-horsepower engine. It was to cruise at 100 kilometers per hour (65 miles per hour) and travel at 15 kilometers per liter of gasoline (about 32 miles per gallon). It was to be sturdy enough to need no repairs for 80,000 kilometers (50,000 miles), and it was to sell for DM 1,000 ($250). Porsche became convinced that Hitler's specifications were impractical and eventually designed an automobile that was closer to his original concept. He considered the 1,000-mark price unattainable and ignored it.

The first VW plant was built at Wolfsburg, between Hanover and Berlin. Only 210 of the original models were built, and none of these was ever sold to the public. Following the Wehrmacht occupation of Czechoslovakia, Hitler or-

EXHIBIT 2

CONSOLIDATED STATEMENT OF EARNINGS—VW GROUP

Year ended December 31, 1981

Thousand DM

	1981	1980
Sales	**37,878,488**	**33,288,039**
Decrease/Increase in inventories	(263,253)	1,262,484
	37,615,235	34,550,523
Material, wages and overhead capitalized as additions to plant and equipment	581,525	438,196
Gross Performance	**38,196,760**	**34,988,719**
Expenditures for raw materials, supplies and other materials	19,751,938	18,238,367
Excess of Gross Performance over Expenditures for Raw Materials, etc.	**18,444,822**	**16,750,352**
Income from profit and loss assumption agreements	100	130
Income from investments in subsidiaries and affiliates	43,444	43,402
Income from other financial investments	12,694	9,748
Other interest and similar income	1,153,060	919,776
Gains from disposal of fixed assets and investments and write-ups	148,442	97,855
Income from reduction of allowance for doubtful trade acceptances and accounts	123,664	3,686
Income from elimination of reserves for undetermined liabilities no longer required	194,346	288,275
Income from elimination of reserves for special purposes no longer required	9,455	22,529
Other income	1,693,906	1,010,767
of which extraordinary income 138,118		
	3,379,111	**2,396,168**
	21,823,933	**19,146,520**

Wages and salaries		9,795,476	8,961,483
Social expenditures – compulsory		1,429,364	1,290,529
Pension expenditures and voluntary payments		554,658	530,112
Depreciation of fixed assets and intangibles		2,442,409	2,063,014
Write-down of financial investments (in 1981 including investments in consolidated companies)		491,306	38,661
Write-down of other current assets		101,905	69,884
Losses on disposal of fixed assets and investments		47,329	24,523
Interest and similar charges		1,402,686	558,651
Taxes			
a) on income, earnings and property	771,507		1,329,261
b) other	76,735		70,414
		848,242	1,399,675
Expenses under profit and loss assumption agreements		913	367
Additions to reserves for special purposes		47,951	57,509
Other expenses		4,525,397	3,831,053
		21,687,636	**18,825,461**
Net Earnings		**136,297**	**321,059**
Volkswagenwerk AG's net earnings brought forward		3,411	3,207
		139,708	324,266
Change in consolidated reserves			
Transferred from reserves	20,021		59,624
Transferred to reserves	123,596		180,153
		103,575	120,529
Minority interest in net earnings of consolidated subsidiaries		2,675	14,401
Minority interest in losses of consolidated subsidiaries		90,312	3,666
Net Earnings Available for Distribution		**123,770**	**193,002**

EXHIBIT 3

BALANCE SHEET, VOLKSWAGENWERK AG

Assets

	Jan. 1, 1981 DM	Additions DM	Disposals DM	Transfers DM	Depreciation DM	Dec. 31, 1981 DM	Dec. 31, 1980 Thousand DM
Fixed Assets and Investments							
A. Property, Plant and Equipment							
Real estate and land rights with office, factory and other buildings	1,237,791,197	110,883,351	6,203,457	41,092,473	123,585,455	1,259,978,109	1,237,791
with residential buildings	7,918,409	1,320,729	3,962	2,549,250	430,586	11,353,840	7,918
without buildings	35,924,743	2,741,051	5,809	2,274,105	532,843	40,401,247	35,925
Buildings on leased real estate	18,128,113	14,533,283	—	3,821,111	4,670,878	31,811,629	18,128
Machinery and fixtures	433,847,336	389,273,923	13,524,167	49,486,604	418,950,432	440,133,264	433,847
Plant and office equipment	758,616,043	395,981,378	8,048,906	209,130,334	522,185,077	833,493,772	758,616
Construction in progress	256,585,152	360,675,026	17,543,107	(183,268,911)	78,750,000	337,698,160	256,585
Advance payments on fixed assets	145,482,531	61,487,937	18,203,825	(125,084,966)	8,850,000	54,831,677	145,483
	2,894,293,524	1,336,896,678	63,533,233	—	1,157,955,271	3,009,701,698	**2,894,293**
B. Investments							
Investments in subsidiaries and affiliates	2,207,497,776	803,837,196	506,600	—	823,394,877	2,187,433,495	2,207,498
Other investment securities	1	—	—	—		1	—
Loans receivable with an initial term of four years or longer Par value at Dec. 31, 1981 DM 248,958,185	118,807,000	41,435,050	18,608,593	—	10,014,966	131,618,491	118,807
of which secured by mortgages DM 122,231,517							
subsidiaries and affiliates DM 85,815,046							
loans in accordance with § 89 AktG DM 974,470							
loans in accordance with § 115 AktG DM 97,875							
	2,326,304,777	845,272,246	19,115,193	—	833,409,843	2,319,051,987	**2,326,305**
	5,220,598,301	2,182,168,924	82,648,426	—	1,991,365,114	5,328,753,685	**5,220,598**

Current Assets

A. Inventories

Raw materials and supplies	521,078.457	537,330
Work in progress	747,062.683	879,022
Finished products	745,318.654	842,703
	2,013,459.794	**2,259,055**

B. Other Current Assets

Advance payments to suppliers		7,435.633	24,730
Trade accounts receivable		415,380.613	397,160
of which amounts due in more than one year	DM –		2,196
Trade acceptances		10,602.796	
of which from subsidiaries and affiliates	DM 566,339		
of which acceptances discountable at German Federal Bank	DM –		
Cash on hand and deposits in postal checking accounts		2,333.074	5,180
Cash in banks		1,519,854.405	2,454,205
Securities		868,996.221	1,128,865
Own stock (par value at Dec. 31, 1981: DM 15,060,300)		21,234.776	21,235
Receivables from subsidiaries and affiliates		2,184,711.179	2,018,346
Miscellaneous other current assets		367,861.895	607,555
		5,398,410.592	**6,659,472**
		7,411,870.386	**8,918,527**

Prepaid and Deferred Expenses	**236,266**	**78**
	12,740,860.337	**14,139,203**

(Continued on following page.)

EXHIBIT 3 *(continued)*
BALANCE SHEET, VOLKSWAGENWERK AG

Stockholders' Equity and Liabilities

	Dec. 31, 1981 DM	Dec. 31, 1980 Thousand DM
Capital Stock	1,200,000,000	1,200,000
Reserves		
Legal reserve	843,387,000	843,387
Reserve for own stock	21,234,776	21,235
Other reserves	1,855,179,345	1,855,179
	2,719,801,121	2,719,801
Reserves for Special Purposes		
Reserve for investments in developing countries in accordance with § 1 of the Developing Countries Tax Act	151,118,056	122,015
Reserve in accordance with §§ 1 and 3 of the Foreign Investment Act	104,734,882	109,105
Reserve for price increases in accordance with § 74 of the Income Tax Regulation	35,208,199	29,759
Reserve in accordance with § 6b of the Income Tax Act	633,395	—
Reserve for replacement in accordance with section 35 of the Income Tax Guidelines	64,999	—
	291,759,531	260,879
Allowance for Doubtful Trade Acceptances and Accounts	4,130,000	72,468
Undetermined Liabilities		
Old-age pensions	2,836,300,000	2,532,728
Other undetermined liabilities		
Maintenance not performed during current year	16,800,000	30,900
Warranties without legal obligation	7,300,000	7,050
Other	2,817,869,782	3,152,581
	5,678,269,782	5,723,259
Liabilities with an Initial Term of Four Years or Longer		
Loans	180,000,000	210,000
of which secured by mortgages		
Due to banks	105,000,000	185,000
of which secured by mortgages DM 20,000,000		
Other liabilities	599,338	1,070
	285,599,338	396,070
Of which amounts due within four years DM 225,493,544		
Other Liabilities		
Trade accounts payable	1,081,850,413	1,087,463
Due to banks	293,536,293	431,898
Advance payments from customers	24,100,032	18,111
Accounts payable to subsidiaries and affiliates	93,140,792	1,083,367
Miscellaneous other liabilities	944,487,198	952,516
	2,437,114,728	3,573,355
Deferred Income	415,730	369
Net Earnings Available for Distribution	123,770,107	193,002
Contingent liabilities with respect to trade acceptances DM 687,556,385		
Contingent liabilities with respect to guaranty obligations DM 2,251,288,850		
Contingent liabilities with respect to warranties DM 410,006,298		
	12,740,860,337	14,139,203

dered the Volkswagenwerk converted to the war production. During the war the plant produced 70,000 cars for the German Army.

After the Germans surrendered, the British took over the Wolfsburg plant, only to find that 65 percent of the structure had been destroyed by Allied bombers. The British planned to reactivate the Volkswagenwerk to produce staff cars for a few years for their occupation forces and then to dismantle and appropriate the production equipment. But production lagged; only 1,785 cars were produced in 1945. Output rose to 10,020 in 1946 but declined to 8,973 in 1947. The British authorities came to the conclusion that the VW was not practical as a motor vehicle and that the production machinery was in such poor condition that it was not worth dismantling.

The British occupation forces concluded from their assessment that if the VW plant was returned to the Germans, "no undue competition on the world market against British products" was to be expected. Unable to find buyers for the factory among the Allied powers, the British invited Heinz Nordhoff, a German automotive engineer and an executive of General Motor's Opel Brandenburg operation, to take over direction of the Wolfsburg plant.

In Herr Nordhoff's first six months, production tripled; it totaled 19,244 for 1948 and 46,154 for 1949. In the following years, sales and production rose steadily; in 1950, 90,038 vehicles were produced, and in 1955 the one-millionth VW came off the assembly line. Production increases followed each year. Exporting had begun early and, as a matter of policy, export sales had been given priority. By 1957, over half of the company's production was sold abroad, and the VW was outselling all other cars in Germany, Belgium, Denmark, The Netherlands, Sweden, Switzerland, Austria, and Portugal. (See Exhibit 6.)

THE PUBLIC STOCK SALE

For over a decade following the end of the war, VW was under the aegis of the German government. The state of Lower Saxony appointed members to the Aufsichtsrat (the board of directors). All earnings were retained by VW for the purpose of expansion. In 1960, the Bundestag enacted a statute redefining the legal position of Volkswagenwerk GmbH and permitted the shares of the company to be transferred into private possession. In the ensuing stock sale, VW acquired $1\frac{1}{2}$ million shareholders. Capitalization was at DM 600 million ($150 million) divided into 6 million bearer shares of DM 100 ($25). Twenty percent of the stock went to the Federal Republic of Germany, 20 percent went to the state of Lower Saxony, and the 60 percent balance was allocated to German residents. The shares were offered at DM 350 ($87.50), and there were discounts of 10 to 25 percent, graded according to income and family status of the purchaser. The original rehabilitation of the VW had been financed by soliciting advances from prospective dealers. Thereafter, expansion had been financed out of earnings, all of which were retained by the theoretically ownerless organization.

EXHIBIT 4
STATEMENT OF EARNINGS, VOLKSWAGENWERK AG
Year ended December 31, 1981

	DM	1981 DM	1980 Thousand DM
Sales		**26,401,706,467**	**25,180,067**
Decrease/Increase in inventories		(176,854,027)	245,012
		26,224,852,440	25,425,079
Material, wages and overhead capitalized as additions to plant and equipment		190,894,929	197,937
Gross Performance		**26,415,747,369**	**25,623,016**
Expenditures for raw materials, supplies and other materials		16,609,541,708	15,809,408
Excess of Gross Performance over Expenditures for Raw Materials, etc.		**9,806,205,661**	**9,813,608**
Income from profit and loss assumption agreements		3,643,041	10,957
Income from investments in subsidiaries and affiliates		79,904,905	107,563
Income from other financial investments		2,540,829	1,858
Other interest and similar income		582,845,204	473,307
Gains from disposal of fixed assets and investments		41,977,607	20,624
Income from reduction of allowance for doubtful trade acceptances and accounts		68,338,000	5,157
Income from elimination of reserves for undetermined liabilities no longer required		109,617,448	75,935
Income from elimination of reserves for special purposes no longer required		4,369,995	22,130
Other income		1,237,789,781	776,862
of which extraordinary income	65,229,194		
		2,131,026,810	**1,494,393**
		11,937,232,471	**11,308,001**

Wages and salaries	5,413,495,428	5,406,638
Social expenditures – compulsory	754,980,560	728,115
Pension expenditures and voluntary payments	376,766,960	398,740
Depreciation of fixed assets	1,157,955,271	999,317
Write-down of financial investments	833,409,843	121,660
Write-down of other current assets	42,881,570	28,777
Losses on disposal of fixed assets and investments	7,830,652	662
Interest and similar charges	226,705,293	68,360
Taxes		
a) on income, earnings and property	474,014,590	1,133,653
b) other	2,649,356	3,322
	476,663,946	1,136,975
Expenses under profit and loss assumption agreements	275,027,894	1,052
Additions to reserves for special purposes	35,250,007	50,200
Other expenses	2,215,906,308	2,056,710
	11,816,873,732	**10,997,206**
Net Earnings	**120,358,739**	**310,795**
Net earnings brought forward from previous year	3,411,368	3,207
	123,770,107	314,002
Transfer from net earnings		121,000
to other reserves	—	121,000
Net Earnings Available for Distribution	**123,770,107**	**193,002**

During 1981 pension payments amounted to DM 69,760,274; payments during the next five years will be approximately 113, 124, 127, 132, 141 % of this amount.

According to our legally required audit, the accounting, the financial statements and the annual report comply with statutory provisions and the Company's articles of association.

EXHIBIT 5

TEN-YEAR SUMMARIES

Balance sheet and statement of earnings

	1972	1973	1974	1975	1976
	5,261	5,697	6,263	5,810	5,474
	585	554	636	524	560
	5,846	6,251	6,899	6,334	6,034
	2,338	3,489	4,117	2,949	3,267
	1,584	1,691	1,954	2,019	2,098
	1,038	1,151	472	1,619	2,888
	354	414	54	48	173
	5,314	6,745	6,597	6,635	8,426
	11,160	12,996	13,496	12,969	14,460
	900	900	900	900	900
	2,677	2,878	2,170	2,032	2,903
	209	230	188	186	198
	3,786	4,008	3,258	3,118	4,001

		1972	1973	1974	1975	1976
[1]	In the case of alterations to the items shown we have adjusted the figures for the previous year.	730	878	1,035	1,143	1,754
		1,604	1,623	1,507	1,740	2,109
		2,334	2,501	2,542	2,883	3,863
[2]	Decreased by the amounts shown under liabilities as allowance for doubtful trade acceptances and accounts (In previous years additional items on the assets side were affected.)	884	852	1,452	1,595	1,322
		366	448	581	666	952
		3,694	5,089	5,654	4,705	4,220
		4,944	6,389	7,687	6,966	6,494
[3]	Including stockholders' equity in reserves for special purposes	81	81	—	—	90
[4]	Excluding shares in net earnings to be distributed	15	17	9	2	12
		7,374	8,988	10,238	9,851	10,459
[5]	Including outside capital in reserves for special purposes	11,160	12,996	13,496	12,969	14,460
[6]	In 1977 for disposition by Annual Meeting of Stockholders, of which 144 million DM distributed as dividend (incl. bonus)	16,250	18,155	17,711	18,351	22,029
		9,098	9,850	10,068	10,066	11,598
		4,463	5,309	5,718	5,550	6,413
[7]	Up to 1976 only amounts intended for distribution	992	1,056	1,148	1,246	1,263
		600	483	305	404	486
		562	432	241	347	438
[8]	Not comparable with other years because of loss brought forward	891	1,127	1,279	1,242	1,265
		206	330	(807)	(157)	1,004[8]
		110	235	(262)	(14)	211

1977	1978	1979	1980	1981	In(De)crease 1981/80 in %	Balance Sheet (Structure) (million DM) December 31
						Assets
5,425	5,903	6,648	8,326	10,205	22.6	Property, plant and equipment
530	410	726	839	414	(50.6)	Investments
						Fixed Assets
5,955	6,313	7,374	9,165	10,619	15.9	and Investments
						Inventories and advance payments
3,180	3,491	4,400	6,073	5,996	(1.3)	to suppliers[2]
1,992	2,996	4,000	4,437	4,771	7.5	Receivables and the like[2]
3,837	4,364	4,781	3,971	2,822	(28.9)	Liquid funds, trade acceptances
560	1,016	1,123	1,151	1,129	(1.9)	Securities, own stock
9,569	11,867	14,304	15,632	14,718	(5.9)	Current Assets
15,524	18,180	21,678	24,797	25,337	2.2	Total Assets
						Stockholders' Equity and Liabilities
900	1,200	1,200	1,200	1,200	—	Capital stock
3,161	4,224	4,625	4,757	4,990	4.9	Reserves of the Group[3]
						Minority interest in consolidated
199	192	373	205	198	(3.3)	subsidiaries[4]
4,260	5,616	6,198	6,162	6,388	3.7	Stockholders' Equity
						Undetermined liabilities in respect
2,048	2,341	2,749	3,107	3,475	11.9	of old-age pensions
2,200	3,244	4,152	4,326	4,232	(2.2)	Other undetermined liabilities[5]
4,248	5,585	6,901	7,433	7,707	3.7	Undetermined Liabilities
						Liabilities payable within
1,450	1,284	1,273	1,161	1,053	(9.3)	more than 4 years
1,032	708	457	466	712	52.7	1 to 4 years
4,355	4,776	6,592	9,378	9,351	(0.3)	up to 1 year
6,837	6,768	8,322	11,005	11,116	1.0	Liabilities
						Net earnings available for distribution
173[6]	189	240	193	124	(35.9)	(Volkswagenwerk AG)[7]
						Minority interest in earnings
6	22	17	4	2	(30.6)	to be distributed
11,264	12,564	15,480	18,635	18,949	1.7	Outside Capital
15,524	18,180	21,678	24,797	25,337	2.2	Total Capital
						Statement of Earnings (Condensed) (million DM) January — December
24,503	27,285	31,638	34,989	38,197	9.2	Gross performance
12,746	14,099	15,835	18,238	19,752	8.3	Cost of materials
6,810	7,656	9,113	10,782	11,779	9.3	Labour cost
1,600	1,456	1,696	2,102	2,934	39.6	Depreciation and write-down
1,503	1,692	2,081	1,400	848	(39.4)	Taxes
1,454	1,624	2,004	1,329	772	(42.0)	on income, earnings and property
1,425	1,808	2,246	2,146	2,748	28.0	Sundry expenses less sundry income
419	574	667	321	136	(57.5)	Net earnings (Loss)
248	366	443	121	104	(14.1)	Increase (Decrease) in reserves

EXHIBIT 5A
VW GROUP IN FIGURES

	1981	1980	1979	1978	1977
Sales (million DM)	37,878	33,288	30,707	26,724	24,152
Increase (Decrease) on previous year in %	14	8	15	11	13
Domestic	12,064	11,850	12,499	11,229	9,714
Abroad	25,814	21,438	18,208	15,495	14,438
Export of domestic Group companies	14,957	14,102	12,337	10,932	9,914
Net contribution of foreign Group companies	12,398	8,733	7,398	5,970	5,634
Vehicle Sales (thousand units)	2,279	2,495	2,539	2,393	2,240
Increase (Decrease) on previous year in %	(9)	(2)	6	7	5
Domestic	738	788	901	895	811
Abroad	1,541	1,707	1,638	1,498	1,429
Production (thousand units)	2,246	2,574	2,542	2,385	2,219
Increase (Decrease) on previous year in %	(13)	1	7	7	2
Domestic	1,410	1,499	1,558	1,569	1,561
Abroad	836	1,075	984	816	658
Workforce at year end (thousand employees)	247	258	240	207	192
Increase (Decrease) on previous year in %	(4)	8	16	8	5
Domestic	160	159	157	139	133
Abroad	87	99	83	68	59
Capital Investments (million DM)	4,851	4,279	3,100	1,990	1,697
Increase (Decrease) on previous year in %	13	38	56	17	49
Domestic	3,089	3,163	2,374	1,559	969
Abroad	1,762	1,116	726	431	728
Cash Flow (million DM)	3,936	3,141	2,993	2,609	2,488
Increase (Decrease) on previous year in %	25	5	15	5	(19)
Net Earnings (million DM)	136	321	667	574	419
Dividend of Volkswagenwerk AG (million DM)	120	192	240	189	144[3]

1976	1975	1974	1973	1972
21,423	18,857	16,966	16,982	15,996
14	11	0	6	(3)
8,068	6,552	5,161	5,364	5,035
13,355	12,305	11,805	11,618	10,961
8,744	7,142	8,547	8,965	7,718
5,570	5,798	3,826	3,063	3,539
2,142	2,038	2,052	2,281	2,197
5	(1)	(10)	4	(5)
726	626	548	619	628
1,416	1,412	1,504	1,662	1,569
2,166	1,949	2,068	2,335	2,193
11	(6)	(11)	7	(7)
1,436	1,229	1,359	1,720	1,673
730	720	709	615	520
183	177	204	215	192
4	(13)	(5)	12	(5)
124	118	142	161	149
59	59	62	54	43
1,141	941	1,902	1,556	1,573
21	(51)	22	(1)	(19)
657	594	1,313	928	1,183
484	347	589	628	390
3,055	1,320	618	1,671	1,545
131	114	(63)	8	14
1,004[2]	(157)	(807)	330	206
90	—	—	81	81

[1] In the case of alterations to the items shown we have adjusted the figures for the previous year.

[2] Not comparable with other years because of loss brought forward

[3] Incl. bonus

EXHIBIT 6
VOLKSWAGEN TOTAL PRODUCTION
AND UNITED STATES SALES, 1945 TO
1981

Year	Total production	U.S. sales
1945	1,785	—
1946	10,020	—
1947	8,987	—
1948	19,244	—
1949	46,154	2
1950	90,038	157
1951	105,712	390
1952	136,013	611
1953	179,740	1,013
1954	242,373	6,614
1955	329,893	30,928
1956	395,690	55,690
1957	472,554	79,524
1958	553,399	104,306
1959	696,860	150,601
1960	865,858	191,372
1961	1,007,113	203,863
1962	1,184,675	222,740
1963	1,209,591	277,008
1964	1,410,715	343,263
1965	1,542,654	388,592
1966	1,583,239	423,645
1967	1,290,328	456,231
1968	1,707,402	567,975
1969	1,830,018	540,623
1970	1,898,422	571,441
1971	2,317,385	553,962
1972	2,192,524	529,587
1973	2,335,169	540,364
1974	2,067,980	401,101
1975	1,948,587	335,065
1976	2,165,627	238,167
1977	2,218,880	296,551
1978	2,384,563	256,860
1979	2,541,761	323,152
1980	2,573,871	336,078
1981	2,245,611	329,330
Total	43,810,435	8,556,668

EVOLUTION OF THE PRODUCT LINE

When Herr Nordhoff took charge of VW, he said, "The Volkswagen is a good auto. Therefore let us improve it." This became one of two basic VW policies.

The other Nordhoff maxim: "Let us continue with only one model, which we will constantly improve."

When critics were warning that VW was making the same mistake that Ford had made when he stayed with the Model T too long, VW management pointed out that there was a basic difference: Henry Ford had produced the same automobile, without any significant changes year after year. The VW, however, was constantly being improved. During the course of its history, hundreds of technical improvements were made in the VW—only the exterior body lines remained relatively unaltered.

In the early 1960s the company was meeting pressure from its dealers to increase the line of models. Management refused to change, pointing out the tremendous cost-price advantage inherent in the one-car, one-model strategy. Other auto makers made heavy capital expenditures for production equipment for their new models, with the result that the price of their $1\frac{1}{2}$ liter cars rose by DM 400 ($100). During the same period, the price of the Volkswagen was reduced by the same amount.

VW was not averse, however, to marketing variations on the basic Beetle theme. (See Exhibit 7.) In 1949, VW introduced the De Luxe Sedan, a slightly more elegant version of the standard Beetle. In 1950, the VW Commercial appeared. This was the basic VW power plant with "microbus" or "minivan" bodies of many types. In 1955, the Karmann-Ghia was added to the line, employing a two-seat coupe on the Beetle frame.

In 1961, when the VW growth rate declined, the company introduced the VW 1500, which had slimmer lines than the 1200, a 53-horsepower engine, and deluxe features. It was priced 50 percent over the Beetle. The next year VW brought out the Variant (known elsewhere as the Squareback), a small, sleek station wagon. Public reaction to this car was mixed, reception was slow, and the rate of growth continued to decline. In 1965, the 1300 line was introduced, which had the same basic styling as previous Beetle models but used a 60-horsepower engine. The same year VW brought out a 1600 version of the Squareback and its companion, the Fastback, both of which had 65-horsepower engines.

In 1968, the VW 411 entered the European market. This sedan with sleek lines was made available in both two- and four-door models. It had a four-cylinder air-cooled 80-horsepower engine, cruised at 90 miles per hour, and had deluxe appointments. It was replaced in 1969 by the 411E, a more powerful car with an 85-horsepower electronic fuel-injection engine. The company simultaneously introduced a station wagon version.

In 1970, VW introduced the Super Beetle. In outward styling the new model appeared to be the same as the Beetle, but it was three inches longer and had twice the luggage space, a 60-horsepower engine, a larger fuel tank, a blower-equipped ventilating system, and more elegant inside appointments than the Beetle. The company claimed it was different in 89 ways from the Beetle. It was priced at about DM 400 ($110) more than the conventional Beetle (VW 1600).

EXHIBIT 7
DEVELOPMENT OF VW's PRODUCT LINE

Volkswagen Beetle (Sedan and Convertible)
  1945 Volkswagen 1200 Standard 25 bhp DIN
  1954 bhp SAE; 1965 (VW 1200 A) 41.5 bhp SAE
  1949 Volkswagen 1200 De Luxe Sedan and 4-seater Convertible 25 bhp DIN
  1954 38 bhp SAE
  1960 41.5 bhp SAE
  1965 (as VW 1300) 50 bhp SAE
  1966 (as VW 1500) 53 bhp SAE
  1970 VW 1300 53 bhp SAE, VW 1302 bhp SAE, VW 1302 S 60 bhp SAE

VW-Karmann Ghia
  1955 Coupe, 1952 Convertible 36 bhp SAE; future development as for De Luxe Sedan

Volkswagen 1600
  1961 VW 1500 Sedan, VW 1500 Karmann Ghia Coupe 54 bhp SAE
  1962 VW Variant 54 bhp SAE
  1963 VW Sedan, Variant and Coupe 1500 S 65 SAE
  1965 VW 1600 TL Fastback (new), other models as VW 1600
  1966 VW 1600 I Notchback Sedan
  1969 VW 1600 L Karmann Ghia Coupe went out of production

VW 411
  1968 2- and 4-door Sedan (Normal and L) 76 bhp SAE
  1969 Sedan and Variant 411 E and LE 85 bhp SAE

VW Commercial
  1950 VW Commercial 25 bhp DIN
  1954 36 bhp SAE
  1960 41.5 bhp SAE
  1963 51 bhp SAE (One Tonner)
  1965 53 bhp SAE
  1967, 1968 VW Commercial 52 bhp SAE
  1970 60 bhp SAE

VW Micro Van
  1965 introduction; body by Westfalia, Wiendenbruck

VW 181
  1969 introduced as multipurpose vehicle; 53 bhp SAE

VW K 70
  1970 VW K 70 and VW K 70 L; 4-door Sedan, front-wheel drive, water-cooled; optional 88 (SAE) bhp or 105 (SAE) bhp engine

VW Passat (Dasher in U.S.)
  1973 VW Passat (Dasher in U.S.) Sedan; front engine; water-cooled; 4-cylinder; 90 cu in plus
  1978 improved engine to 97 cu in

VW Scirocco
  1973 VW Scirocco Sports Car; front engine; water-cooled; 4-cylinder; 90 cu in; front wheel drive
  1976 introduced larger engine, computer analysis
  1979 improvements in engine power

VW Golf (Rabbit in U.S.)
  1974-75 VW Golf (Rabbit in U.S.); front engine; water-cooled; 4-cylinder; 90 cu in; front wheel drive 1977 diesel motor
  1977 Rabbit increased horsepower to 78; fuel injected engine

VW Santana
  1981 limousine quality, npw 1.05-liter propulsion unit with high-compression technology

The conventional VW model, which had still, up to 1974, accounted for over 40 percent of the company's production, remained virtually unchanged from its original design by Ferdinand Porsche in the 1930s. It had a four-cylinder air-cooled rear "boxer-type" engine which developed 36 horsepower. It had minimum passing power—68 miles per hour (with a favorable tail wind). It traveled over 12 kilometers on a liter of gasoline (30 miles on a gallon). It had torsion bar instead of coil springs, at a considerable savings in space and weight. The basic VW had no fuel gauge. The complete engine weighed less than 100 kilograms (195 pounds), and changing engines took only half an hour. It had a four-speed floor shift, minimum of luggage space under the front bonnet and behind the rear seat, and it seated four passengers. Tires frequently lasted over 40,000 miles. The VW was unique in that it did not have a beamed chassis; the entire car was built upon a platform frame which provided a watertight underside for the body.

VW introduced its first conventional model in late 1973. Called the Passat, the new automobile featured a classic shape, was water-cooled, and had the engine in the front rather than in the rear (as did the Beetle and its variants). The Passat replaced the VW 1600, which went out of production in July 1973. The Passat was renamed the Dasher for the United States market and was introduced to buyers in early 1974. In the winter of 1973, VW's Scirocco was brought to the European market. This four-seat sports coupe entered the United States market in 1974. An additional model, called the Golf, was introduced in 1974 in Germany; management thought it would have potential as a new economy car capable of replacing the Beetle. This car entered the United States market as the Rabbit in late 1974 (see Exhibit 8). It was very well received in both Europe and the United States when it was introduced in 1975. However, it failed to produce sufficient sales in the United States to offset the decline of the Beetle. Management believed this was due mainly to its relatively high price in the small compact car market. In 1975, VW introduced the Polo at the Swiss Motor Show. This was its smallest car, similar to the Audi 50, with a 895-cc, 40-horsepower motor.

Through the late 1970s, improvements were made in the existing product line. In 1981, VW introduced the Santana, a limousine quality car designed as an entry into top-of-the line autos. The Jetta, a Rabbit model with a trunk, was introduced in 1980. (See Exhibit 11A for VW's full line of cars.)

The Audi was added to VW's line in 1965 with the acquisition of Auto Union which was merged with NSU to form Audi NSU Auto Union, AG. The car was developed through the years and represented VW's entry into middle-range high-performance cars, offering more options and luxury features. In 1981, Audi sales amounted to 329,246 units—an increase of 9.8 percent over 1980 sales. Audi produced four models but did not approach the volume sales of the basic VW line. Profits were nominal. In 1981 they amounted to DM 150,300 on sales of DM 5,774 million. Audi also produced 17,525 Porsche 924/944 models in 1981 for Porsche AG, Stuttgart. The Porsche units were not included in VW's production totals.

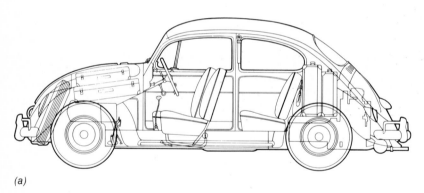

(a)

EXHIBIT 8
(a) The Beetle—the basic model; *(b)* the Rabbit; *(c)* the Scirocco.

LABOR FORCE AND AUTOMATION

After reaching a peak in 1974, sales declined, and VW was forced to utilize periodic layoffs in an effort to reduce excess production. The operation of plants at less than 60 percent of capacity caused the company to lose heavily (80 percent was considered break-even). Management attempted to avoid indefinite layoffs by putting workers on shortened schedules. Under this system, workers were paid nearly as much as they normally received. This action was not sufficient to adjust the overall labor force to the reduced level of output. (See Exhibit 9.)

(b)

(c)

The board of management approved a comprehensive personnel-reduction plan with the objective of achieving a total cut in jobs of nearly 25,000. There was fierce union opposition to this plan, and bargaining over the issues raised by the plan was protracted. During this period, the board and the union adopted a policy of *Mitbestimmung*, or codetermination of company policy. The union ultimately agreed that labor cuts were necessary to save the company, and so the labor force was reduced, through curtailing recruitment and cancelling contracts of employees who were willing to leave the company. By mid-1975, the labor force of VW was reduced to 94,980—26,984 less than the previous year.

EXHIBIT 9
WORK FORCE DEVELOPMENT AT VOLKSWAGENWERK AG

	Work force		Increase (decrease)	
	Dec. 31, 1981	Dec. 31, 1980	Absolute	Percent
Volkswagenwerk AG, total	120,071	118,766	1,305	1.1
Wolfsburg	58,876	57,927	949	1.6
Hanover	21,383	22,110	(727)	(3.3)
Brunswick	6,373	6,458	(85)	(1.3)
Kassel	16,665	16,681	(16)	0.1
Emden	9,341	8,338	1,003	12.0
Salzgitter	7,433	7,252	181	2.5
Wage earners	99,832	98,622	1,210	1.2
Salaried staff	20,239	20,144	95	0.05
Female employees	14,369	14,029	340	0.05
Foreign employees	11,323	11,643	(320)	(2.7)
Trainees	3,653	3,457	196	5.7

Additional cuts in the labor force were achieved through reduced reliance on foreign laborers. Foreign employees willing to return to their own countries received payments from VW and additional payments from a special fund set up by the state of Baden-Wuerttemberg. The proportion of foreign nationals in the labor force declined from 24.1 percent to 16.2 percent.

The question of importing labor from eastern Europe and North Africa was of great concern to government and business in western Europe. Prior to 1974, foreign workers represented 8.7 percent of the total work force in West Germany, 14.2 percent in France, and 29.6 percent in Switzerland. The cost advantage that used to accrue to companies hiring foreign labor was absorbed by increasing social costs. VW constructed 1,086 rental apartments for its employees in 1973 and granted loans of DM 17.2 million to its workers for housing needs. Since demands for apartments had been met and foreign workers were declining in number, no new plans for assistance were made after 1974. Foreign workers took the most menial jobs at low pay but often left when they had enough savings to return home. Foreign enclaves in major cities had become the scenes of conflict and posed problems for local governments. A more subtle problem was the tendency for management to disregard the need for modernization when cheap labor was available. It was widely agreed in many European Economic Community (EEC) countries that, because of these difficulties, the influx of foreign workers would have to be limited in the future. The recession reduced the need for any immediate action in this regard.

Union and political opposition to actual plant closings was very strong. Management decided to cut production and employment at plants sharply but to help the plants remain open. VW workers exerted a strong influence on the company's operations, since worker representatives constituted about one-third of the supervisory board. The worker representatives also exerted influence on the political representatives on the board who represented the government agencies, which owned 40 percent of VW. The planned readjustment measures at the beginning of 1975 entailed transferring the vehicle assembly from the Salzgitter plant to Wolfsburg. Necksarsulm and Brussels plants reduced operations to only one shift per day.

VW was able to automate its plants to a greater extent than its major competitors despite the large capital investment required. For several years the company had fabricated, assembled, and welded roof, front, and rear body sections in what was virtually a single mechanical operation. The extension of VW's product line required large capital expenditures to introduce new production technologies. (See Exhibit 10.)

In the latter part of the 1970s, VW's lead in automation was thought to be eroding, so the company announced plans to invest heavily through 1983 to increase the productivity and the flexibility of the production process. A dilemma in the automobile industry was maintaining mass-production efficiency while at the same time offering customization to the purchaser. In 1980, nearly 450,000 Golfs (Rabbits) were produced in Germany, of which about 340,000 had individualized equipment or other custom features dictated by the customer's order. By 1980, VW had also automated the transport and storage of assembled autos and parts, and was considered a leader in robot technology. (See Exhibit 11.)

The German unions did not oppose automation, although their concern for protection against job obsolescence was thought to have slowed it. VW management informed the unions of planned automation, so workers could be retrained for other positions or the labor requirement could be adjusted through ordinary attrition.

But the trend toward more automation was occurring in the United States and in Japan—both considered to be not far behind—and the auto industries of all three countries were experiencing complex problems of social dislocations in the labor force, government scrutiny, interest rates, and concern for energy efficiency.

VW had been generally free of domestic labor strife. Its employees earned more than the average of U.S. and German workers overall, and automation had considerably lightened the physical work load. Each VW worker received about an hour of paid breaks in the eight-hour workday, yet VW experienced nearly five times greater absenteeism than the Japanese auto makers.

INNOVATIONS IN ENGINES

In 1966, the NSU Spider, a small sports-type car, adopted the Wankel engine. Twelve companies in the United States, Britain, France, Italy, and Japan were experimenting with the engine. The Wankel engine, developed in 1954 by Felix Wankel, a German automotive engineer, replaced conventional cylinders and pistons with a triangular rotor. It had only two major moving parts and weighed considerably less than conventional engines. In France, Renault, in a joint

EXHIBIT 10
In 1974 there was a profound change to the makeup of the Volkswagenwerk AG's model range. A broader spectrum of models made it necessary to introduce new technical and organizational systems into the production process. Our picture shows the control center in the Wolfsburg plant's Press Shop. From here the optimum amount of control and supervision is exerted on the production process.

research contract with American Motors Corporation in the United States, was developing a rotary engine similar to the Wankel, but neither Renault nor American Motors put their engine into production. VW did not put its Wankel engine into commercial use.

EXHIBIT 11A
YEARLY PRODUCTION ACCORDING TO MODEL

Passenger cars	1981	1980
Golf	759,190	803,178
Jetta	198,622	176,063
Polo/Derby	117,099	160,813
Passat	261,835	265,627
Santana	3,913	—
Scirocco	46,945	62,827
Audi 80	180,109	225,914
Audi Coupe/Quattro	36,206	3,440
Audi 100	100,259	102,525
Audi 200	16,133	24,904
Beetle	157,505	236,177
Gol	31,976	61,698
Voyage	23,775	—
Brasilia	28,659	107,740
Other passenger cars	20,698	48,190

Commercial vehicles	1981	1980
Golf pick-up	40,097	28,349
Commercial	187,327	217,876
Heavy van (LT)	22,911	34,383
VW trucks (11/13 tonnes)	1,488	—
VW-M.A.N. trucks	1,885	3,021
Other commercial vehicles	8,979	11,155

In the United States, General Motors, Ford, and Chrysler have long been doing extensive research on new types of engines. One of these was the gas turbine engine, a rotary engine which could use any one of several common fuels, such as diesel oil, fuel oil, kerosene, or alcohol.

EXHIBIT 11B
AVERAGE DAILY PRODUCTION ACCORDING
TO GROUP COMPANY

Group company	Vehicles/day
Volkswagenwerk AG*	4,963
AUDI NSU AUTO UNION AG*	1,415
Volkswagen do Brasil*	1,287
Volkswagen of America	972
Volkswagen de Mexico	637
Volkswagen Bruxelles	586
Volkswagen of South Africa	265
Volkswagen Argentina	108
Volkswagen Caminhoes	48

*Excluding knocked-down vehicles delivered within the group; AUDI NSU AUTO UNION AG excluding Porsche 924/944.

The 1960s saw a sharp rise in interest in electric autos. All major United States auto makers were actively developing experimental models, and some of these were so advanced that they were being road-tested under practical driving conditions. None, however, had yet reached the stage of becoming a commercial reality.

The VW engine had been one of the critical items in Ferdinand Porsche's original design of the automobile. The basic Porsche-designed engine had been used in over 25 million VW vehicles of all body types, and it had achieved renown for its superior performance. From the beginning in 1948, it had been subjected to continuing research. During its history, more research had been expended upon it than on any other engine in the entire history of auto making. The engine remained virtually unchanged, however, the only changes being in technical refinements and increases in horsepower.

In 1973, VW introduced a radical departure for the company in engine design with the Passat (Dasher in the United States). This car was equipped with a transversely front-mounted water-cooled engine. The Scirocco and the Golf (Rabbit in the United States) were also powered with this new engine. This marked the first entry of VW into the standard motor field for its passenger-car line. The high-quality engine was also sold to Chrysler for use in its Omni and Horizon automobiles.

RESEARCH AND DEVELOPMENT

Historically, VW had always subscribed to a policy of extensive research activities. In earlier years, these efforts had been beamed largely at technical improvements in the Beetle. During the 1960s, the objective of the R&D activity was shifted. In 1972, VW's scientists and engineers were still pursuing the development of futuristic engineering principles, but they were also continuously adapting the current product line to changing market conditions.

The research activity included experimenting with novel propulsion methods. The principles of gas dynamics were used to determine the optimum of carbon dioxide mixtures and other harmful mixtures such as hydrocarbons and nitrous oxides.

To conduct these exhaustive research efforts effectively, new techniques were applied, using modern measuring and testing devices. Program-controlled simulators were used to produce in the laboratory the conditions to test the operational safety of vehicles under varying environmental conditions.

The R&D activities within the VW organization were not restricted to the Wolfsburg plant. Recently acquired subsidiaries still retained their specialized programs. NSU at Neckarsulm had the primary responsibility for the development of the rotary engine; the Audi 100 coupe was developed at Ingolstadt; another VW 1600 Squareback sedan was developed in Brazil. However, all R&D activities were centrally controlled and coordinated from Wolfsburg by Ernst Fiala, the director of R&D research and development.

Fiala, a member of the board of management, joined the company in 1970.

Initially he had the responsibility for the important ESV (experimental safety vehicle) project. This was a concept project to provide the means for learning how to improve the safety of occupants and road worthiness of future VW automobiles. The car was originally developed in cooperation with Germany's Department of Transportation and the U.S. Department of Transportation's National Highway Traffic Safety Administration. The program was financed entirely by VW. One of the major reasons for the extended research on the ESV was to attempt to develop a safer small car which could hold its own with the larger and heavier vehicles common in the United States. This was particularly important to VW, which had staked its future and reputation on small cars. The larger cars adapted more easily to safety devices, particularly those required under U.S. standards.

In addition to the area of safety, VW's R&D efforts were directed toward developing a prototype of a "mini city car," known unofficially as A-Zero. Like other automobile producers, VW had numerous technical projects on line such as restraint systems (including air bags), skid control, improved bumpers, fuel tanks, remote-control drive, antipollution devices, gas turbine and stratifed charge engines, and electric vehicles.

Management felt that R&D was necessary to keep up with or ahead of the competition, but that any competitive edge due to innovations was likely to be short-lived, as most could be quickly copied by competitors. In 1981, two developments were slated for introduction in the near future. One was the automatic cutoff device which stops and restarts the engine at traffic lights and improves fuel efficiency by one-fourth. Another was the direct-injection diesel engine. Both innovations were expected to appear in competitors' lines as well.

THE WORLD AUTOMOTIVE INDUSTRY

Six countries accounted for the bulk of the world's automotive production in 1980, which reached a grand total of approximately 38 million units. This was a distinct drop from 1978's record of 41 million units. (See Exhibit 12.) Automotive production had increased steadily since 1960, with the only decline prior to the precipitous drop in 1974 having occurred in 1967.

The United States was until 1980 the largest producer and consumer of automotive vehicles, and accounted for approximately 8.6 million units in 1980. Total U.S. production accounted for approximately one-fourth of world production, down from five years earlier when the United States garnered 30 to 31 percent of the world figure. The United States exported only a small amount of its production. However, U.S. subsidiaries abroad accounted for a large share of production in Europe.

Japan became the second largest auto producer in the world in 1967, and the largest in 1980 when production surpassed the 10 million mark. Japanese cars competed vigorously in most world markets and were particularly successful in the United States.

Among individual companies in 1980, General Motors remained the world

*Development of production in th t iative industries
in million vehicles (logarithmic sc le,*

(B) Great Britain
(I) Italy
(S) Soviet Union
(F) France

(G) Federal Republic of Germany
(U) USA
(J) Japan
(W) Worldwide

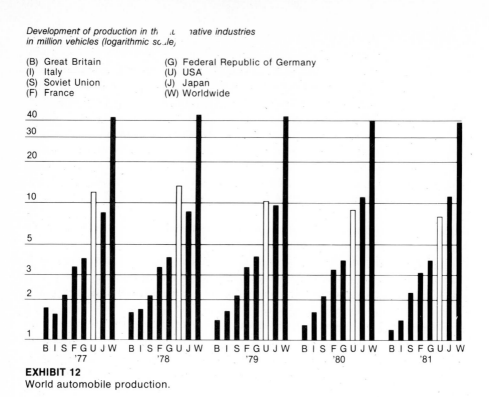

EXHIBIT 12
World automobile production.

leader with 6.8 million vehicles worldwide. By comparison, Ford produced 4.4 million, Toyota 3.2 million, Nissan 2.6 million, and VW 2.5 million.

Over the years, the Detroit headquarters management of the American big three had concentrated their efforts on the high-potential United States market and allowed themselves to be displaced in international trade by their European competitors, who were more export-minded and had the small economy cars which appealed to motorists in less-developed countries. Following the booming growth of the European auto market, General Motors' Opel and Ford Werke introduced economy models of their own design in the 1963 market—the Kadett and the Taunus (renamed the German Ford). These achieved immediate consumer acceptance, and both companies entered into expansion programs. It appeared that the Detroit managements had decided seriously to contend not only for a share of the European market, but for a position in the world market as well, mounting their campaign from their European subsidiaries. Within a five-year period the total production capacity of the big three in Europe was doubled. Together, they had an aggregate capacity over 3.5 million vehicles annually.

In Europe, American auto makers owned or controlled several major auto companies. These were Adam Opel AG (GM, Germany), Ford Werke (Ford

Motors, Germany), Vauxhall (GM, England), and Ford of England (Ford Motors, England). The European assets of these U.S. subsidiaries gave them the immense capital reserves and research and engineering facilities of their parent companies in Detroit. Nevertheless, VW still was a commanding force in European markets. Management attributed this to the introduction of its new vehicles, the Passat, Scirocco, and Golf. The good reception of the Passat and the renewed demand for the Beetle created by the need for economy and because of the energy crisis held VW's market share in Germany through the decade. The Golf (Rabbit in the United States) was the largest selling car in West Germany.

VW's foreign market difficulties arose in conjunction with the turmoil of the late 1960s in the international money markets. Speculative pressure against the dollar had led in part to the economic reforms initiated by President Nixon in August 1971. Besides freezing prices and wages for a temporary period, the President suspended the convertibility of the dollar into gold, imposed a 10 percent import surcharge until suitable exchange rates were agreed to by the major industrial powers of the West, and removed the 7 percent excise tax on domestic automobiles. The import surcharge was lifted by the Smithsonian Agreement of December 1971, when new parities were set. The dollar was devalued by 8 percent, and the yen and Deutschmark were revalued steeply against the dollar. The combined effect of these changes was to make U.S. goods cheaper overseas and to make imports into the United States costlier.

The devaluation of the dollar failed to reverse the U.S. balance-of-payments deficit, which in 1972 totaled $6.4 billion. An additional dollar devaluation of 10 percent was announced by the United States in February 1973. The final demise of the Bretton Woods system led to freely fluctuating exchange rates, which made exporting much more uncertain.

A more permanent monetary system was expected from a meeting of economic ministers of the International Monetary Fund in September 1973, but agreement was not reached. Plans for reform of the system appeared even further away following the petroleum price increases set by the Organization of Petroleum Exporting Countries (OPEC). The shift in resources from oil-consuming countries to oil-exporting countries involved such enormous funds transferred in such a short period of time that there was widespread doubt that the global monetary system could handle the stress.

The transfer of resources to OPEC countries was expected to result in many years of balance-of-payments deficits for the developed nations. It was certain that this new international situation made an immediate return to fixed or adjustable exchange rates impossible. Flexible rates allowed the international system the easiest means for currencies to adjust to great changes in trade and current accounts. But it was expected that short-term fluctuations would continue to vary greatly on the exchange markets as long as the massive balance-of-payments disequilibriums among the developed nations continued.

These changes had a negative effect on VW, which had already suffered considerably from monetary uncertainties before the OPEC price increases were introduced. The prices of VW models in the United States were especially affected, since the mark continued to appreciate against the dollar under flexible rates. From October 1972 to November 1973, the mark had appreciated 35 percent to the dollar. Volkswagen of America was forced to increase its prices to compensate, and did so four times in 1973. Price increases continued up to 1980. The significant increase in interest rates in the United States starting in 1979 and continuing into 1981 strengthened the dollar against foreign currencies. The German mark depreciated against the dollar 23 to 25 percent during the period.

VW IN EUROPE

The auto industry in Europe entered the 1970s with annual growth rates averaging 10 to 15 percent and with no decline in sight. Whereas European buyers had been accustomed to waiting long periods for delivery, increased capacity was eliminating waiting lines and the seller's market was becoming more discriminating and more demanding. The decline in 1974, however, forced all producers to revise their forecasts.

European auto makers had believed it to be axiomatic that production should always be at full plant capacity and, having until recently been chronically oversold, they were not inclined to risk overexpansion. Sources of capital for expansion were limited, and Europe did not have the sources of capital formation available to the U.S. producers. Expansion and modernization in Europe was customarily financed out of plowed-back earnings because there was no broad market for automobile securities. Also, in recent years price competition, Japanese success, overall evening of technological and design competencies, and rising costs had been depressing earnings.

In West Germany, annual new car registrations had been declining for several years. In 1981, VW sold 762,262 cars in West Germany (out of a total production of 2.25 million vehicles), down 3.2 percent from the previous year and 12 percent from 1979. VW's domestic market share was holding steady at between 29 and 30 percent, but there was a notable shift from upper to lower price ranges, as the Audi domestic market share declined from 9.5 percent to 8.8 percent. In the rest of Europe overall, VW sold 615,611 vehicles in 1981, which represented 85,422 more cars than the previous year.

Partly because of improvements in the franc-mark exchange rate, VW sales in France passed the 100,000-unit level for the first time in 1980, making France the largest European market for VW with sales of 135,000 cars in 1981. VW held a 5 percent market share in France.

Italy was the second largest market for VW, with nearly 130,000 units being delivered in 1981. The United Kingdom accounted for nearly 90,000 in VW sales, up slightly from the previous year. Denmark and the Netherlands were said to be declining markets.

OTHER MARKETS

Long an important market for VW, Brazil was troubled in 1981 by accelerating inflation, imbalance of payments, and tightening domestic credit, which made consumer auto purchases more difficult. This, combined with a two-month strike by metalworkers which halted VW's South American production, contributed to 185,940 fewer VW sales than in 1980, which also had been a decline year. The total sales of 205,203 units represented a 45.9 percent market share in cars and a 35.5 percent market share in commercial vehicles, on sales of 24,767 units, an increase over 1980. Export sales amounted to 83,296 units.

In Mexico, VW's 1981 market share climbed to 33.2 percent from 31 percent the previous year. Mexico was experiencing a general economic boom and favorable exchange rates, and there was a noticeable shift in purchase patterns toward heavier and higher-priced automobiles. VW sold 127,605 units in Mexico in 1981.

In South Africa, VW sold 60,618 units, the same as the previous year. This represented a 17.1 percent market share.

THE VW IN THE UNITED STATES

During the first few years of its history, the VW management had not found it difficult to develop export markets in European countries, especially those which did not have comparable auto production facilities. Sales in the United States, however, did not go well. A few hundred cars were shipped to the United States in 1953 and 1954, and these went begging for want of buyers. The United States sales representative was convinced that it would be possible to sell only about 800 cars a year in the United States. Nevertheless, VW decided to enter the American market. It founded a subsidiary called Volkswagen of America, Inc., which was to be the U.S. importing organization.

By 1955, 35,851 VWs were sold in the United States, and every year thereafter sales in the United States increased regardless of the fluctuations in sales of American automobiles. "In the United States we serve a distinct and separate market," said Herr Nordhoff. "We do not compete with American companies. This puts us completely outside the problems of the United States auto industry."

In 1964, VW built an assembly plant providing 2 million square feet of space at Emden, West Germany, a seaport on the North Sea coast. The plant was adjacent to the shiploading docks, and employed about 8,000 workers in 1971; it assembled West German-produced parts into Volkswagens specifically for shipment to the United States and Canada via VW's charter fleet of oceangoing automobile freighters.

Detroit did not seem concerned about foreign cars imported into the United States until the late 1950s. Then it responded to rising imports by producing a wide line of "compact" models, such as the Ford Falcon, the Chevrolet Corvair, and the Plymouth Valiant. All these were bigger, heavier, more luxurious, and about $250 higher in price than most imports. They did not match the imports in economy of operation. With the introduction of compacts, foreign imports dropped to about 340,000 in 1962, or half the 1959 volume. It was thought that this was the result of the poor quality of many of the imports and of their incompetent marketing and service organizations rather than because of competition from American compacts.

VW had set up a strong sales and service organization before it entered the U.S. market, and it offered a quality product. Its sales rose 60 percent during the period when its foreign competitors were losing ground.

Detroit responded by introducing new models such as Chevrolet's Vega and Chevette, the Ford Pinto, and American Motors' AMC Gremlin. With options such as automatic transmission, deluxe interior, and power steering, these two-door sedans were originally priced several hundred dollars more than the VW. But the continued decline of the dollar in relation to the DM lowered the prices of the smaller U.S. entries below that of VW's Beetle, the least expensive car sold in the United States. To cut production costs, Detroit adopted new approaches: the Vega was built in the most automated plant in the United States, capable of finishing 100 cars an hour; the new, smaller Chevette was introduced in 1975 at a lower price; the Pinto was made in only one model and its engine, fuel pump, steering gear, distributor, and transmission were imported. Ford and Chevrolet planned to keep their model style constant for five years. American Motors had always been slow to change its styling; however, the company's Pacer represented a distinct change.

In 1974, VW sales in the United States were adversely affected by price increases caused by changes in exchange rates and increased costs. The fuel shortage aided sales in the latter part of 1973; however, the company's market share for the year declined slightly from the 4.5 percent total of 1972; in 1974, VW's share of the U.S. market dropped to 3.8, from 4.4 of 1973. The new VW deliveries to customers slumped by 29.8 percent in 1974, with new car registrations of around 330,000. VW of America, Inc., suffered a $63.6 million loss.

In June 1975, VW's sales in the United States declined to 16.5 percent of the import market, and the company lost its long-standing first-place position to Toyota, the Japanese import, which accounted for 17.7 percent of the import market that year.

VW's share of the U.S. import market continued to decline through the latter half of the decade, and industry sources indicated that it would be very difficult for the company to regain its first-place position.

By the end of the decade, the American consumer's turning away from large automobiles was history, and foreign auto makers had continued to encroach upon the American market. The U.S. market share of foreign car makers rose to 28.8 percent in 1981 from 28.3 percent in 1980 and 23.2 percent in 1979.

VW sold 336,078 vehicles in the United States in 1980 and 329,330 in 1981. Of these, 204,990 were produced in VW's Pennsylvania plant, which was said to be operating at full capacity. VW management believed that the company lost money on cars which it exported to the United States and that future U.S.

sales growth depended on more production capacity. The company planned to begin production at a second plant, near Detroit, in 1982, later postponed to 1984. VW's U.S. market share was back up to 3.3 percent in 1980 and in 1981, and the company announced a goal of a 5 percent share of the market.

ORGANIZATIONAL CHANGES AND MANAGEMENT SUCCESSION

Heinz Nordhoff, who had guided VW since the end of the Second World War, had announced his intent to retire at the end of 1968. His death in April 1967 forced the board of directors to seek an immediate replacement, and they offered the position of chairman to Kurtz Lotz, 54, at that time the chairman of Brown, Boveri and Cie. Mr. Lotz accepted the position in April of that year and was to serve until October 1972.

Lotz's term was marked by extensive capital investment, largely in VW plants in West Germany. The purchase of Auto Union GmbH in 1965 was followed in 1969 by its merger, under chairman Lotz's promotion, with Audi NSU Auto Union AG. (See Exhibit 13.)

Of greatest concern to management was the steady decline in earnings during Mr. Lotz's tenure. In 1968, earnings as they related to gross output were at 4.3 percent; they fell to 3.1 percent in 1969; 1970 saw a further drop to 1.9 percent; and the year after earnings fell to 0.1 percent. Consolidated net earnings in 1972 increased to DM 205 million ($67.6 million), but no profits were recorded in VW's operations in Brussels, Indonesia, Spain, the United States, Canada, or France. With profits in 1972 being hampered by currency realignments, increased competition both in Europe and the Americas, and the poor showing of all the models in the VW line, Lotz's position was becoming increasingly tenuous. He was forced out in the fall of 1972, and the Aufsichtsrat began an immediate search for a new chairman.

His successor, named in October, was Rudolph Leiding. Unlike Lotz, Leiding had extensive experience in the automobile industry. Leiding had gained a favorable reputation during his tenure as director of VW of Brazil and had earlier, as Auto Union's director, turned the Bavarian subsidiary's $25 million loss into a profit.

The same problems which forced Chairman Lotz out of office faced Leiding at the beginning of 1973. Leiding was known to question the policy of heavy capital investment undertaken by Lotz and was critical of the diversity of the VW line. By the end of the first quarter of 1974, it was becoming evident that a loss for the year seemed inevitable. First-quarter consolidated sales were down 21.6 percent for VW; VW of America's sales were off 28 percent for the first quarter. Wage costs were expected to rise $221 million for the year, and material and shipping costs were expected to increase by $301 million. Chairman Leiding ascribed these declines to "a cost explosion of catastrophic dimensions."

As predicted, VW experienced its first loss since the company went public.

EXHIBIT 13
The major companies within the Volkswagen Group, Dec. 31, 1981.

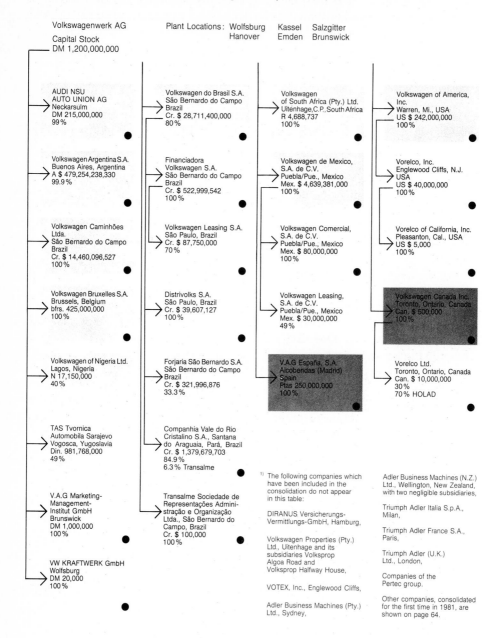

Volkswagenwerk AG

Capital Stock
DM 1,200,000,000

Plant Locations: Wolfsburg   Kassel   Salzgitter
                 Hanover   Emden   Brunswick

AUDI NSU
AUTO UNION AG
Neckarsulm
DM 215,000,000
99 %

Volkswagen do Brasil S.A.
São Bernardo do Campo
Brazil
Cr. $ 28,711,400,000
80 %

Volkswagen
of South Africa (Pty.) Ltd.
Uitenhage,C.P.,South Africa
R 4,688,737
100 %

Volkswagen of America,
Inc.
Warren, Mi., USA
US $ 242,000,000
100 %

Volkswagen Argentina S.A.
Buenos Aires, Argentina
A $ 479,254,238,330
99.9 %

Financiadora
Volkswagen S.A.
São Bernardo do Campo
Brazil
Cr. $ 522,999,542
100 %

Volkswagen de Mexico,
S.A. de C.V.
Puebla/Pue., Mexico
Mex. $ 4,639,381,000
100 %

Vorelco, Inc.
Englewood Cliffs, N.J.
USA
US $ 40,000,000
100 %

Volkswagen Caminhões
Ltda.
São Bernardo do Campo
Brazil
Cr. $ 14,460,096,527
100 %

Volkswagen Leasing S.A.
São Paulo, Brazil
Cr. $ 87,750,000
70 %

Volkswagen Comercial,
S.A. de C.V.
Puebla/Pue., Mexico
Mex. $ 80,000,000
100 %

Vorelco of California, Inc.
Pleasanton, Cal., USA
US $ 5,000
100 %

Volkswagen Bruxelles S.A.
Brussels, Belgium
bfrs. 425,000,000
100 %

Distrivolks S.A.
São Paulo, Brazil
Cr. $ 39,607,127
100 %

Volkswagen Leasing,
S.A. de C.V.
Puebla/Pue., Mexico
Mex. $ 30,000,000
49 %

Volkswagen Canada Inc.
Toronto, Ontario, Canada
Can. $ 500,000
100 %

Volkswagen of Nigeria Ltd.
Lagos, Nigeria
N 17,150,000
40 %

Forjaria São Bernardo S.A.
São Bernardo do Campo
Brazil
Cr. $ 321,996,876
33.3 %

V.A.G España, S.A.
Alcobendas (Madrid)
Spain
Ptas 250,000,000
100 %

Vorelco Ltd.
Toronto, Ontario, Canada
Can. $ 10,000,000
30 %
70 % HOLAD

TAS Tvornica
Automobila Sarajevo
Vogosca, Yugoslavia
Din. 981,768,000
49 %

Companhia Vale do Rio
Cristalino S.A., Santana
do Araguaia, Pará, Brazil
Cr. $ 1,379,679,703
84.9 %
6.3 % Transalme

1) The following companies which
have been included in the
consolidation do not appear
in this table:

DIRANUS Versicherungs-
Vermittlungs-GmbH, Hamburg,

Adler Business Machines (N.Z.)
Ltd., Wellington, New Zealand,
with two negligible subsidiaries,

Triumph Adler Italia S.p.A.,
Milan,

V.A.G Marketing-
Management-
Institut GmbH
Brunswick
DM 1,000,000
100 %

Transalme Sociedade de
Representações Admini-
stração e Organização
Ltda., São Bernardo do
Campo, Brazil
Cr. $ 100,000
100 %

Volkswagen Properties (Pty.)
Ltd., Uitenhage and its
subsidiaries Volksprop
Algoa Road and
Volksprop Halfway House,

Triumph Adler France S.A.,
Paris,

Triumph Adler (U.K.)
Ltd., London,

VW KRAFTWERK GmbH
Wolfsburg
DM 20,000
100 %

VOTEX, Inc., Englewood Cliffs,

Adler Business Machines (Pty.)
Ltd., Sydney,

Companies of the
Pertec group.

Other companies, consolidated
for the first time in 1981, are
shown on page 64.

Producing Companies
Distributing Companies
Other Companies

● Companies included in consolidated
financial statements[1]

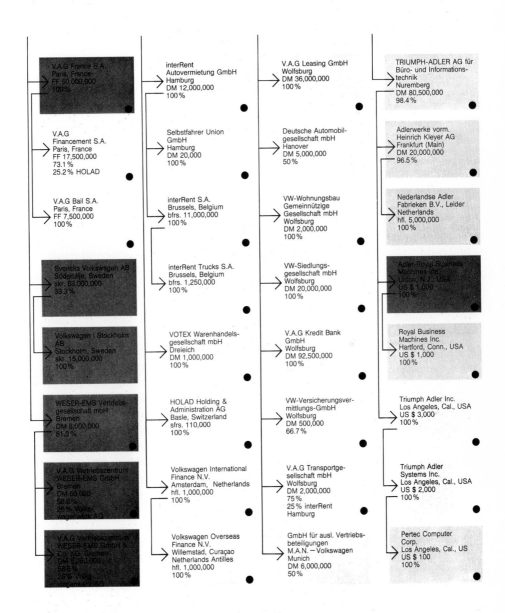

V.A.G France S.A.
Paris, France
FF 50,000,000
100%

V.A.G
Financement S.A.
Paris, France
FF 17,500,000
73.1%
25.2% HOLAD

V.A.G Bail S.A.
Paris, France
FF 7,500,000
100%

Svenska Volkswagen AB
Södertälje, Sweden
skr. 63,000,000
33.3%

Volkswagen i Stockholm
AB
Stockholm, Sweden
skr. 15,000,000
100%

WESER-EMS Vertriebs-
gesellschaft mbH
Bremen
DM 8,000,000
81.3%

V.A.G Vertriebszentrum
WESER-EMS GmbH
Bremen
DM 50,000
58.6%
26% Volks-
wagenwerk AG

V.A.G Vertriebszentrum
WESER-EMS GmbH &
Co. KG, Bremen
DM 5,250,000
58.6%
26% Volks-
wagenwerk AG

interRent
Autovermietung GmbH
Hamburg
DM 12,000,000
100%

Selbstfahrer Union
GmbH
Hamburg
DM 20,000
100%

interRent S.A.
Brussels, Belgium
bfrs. 11,000,000
100%

interRent Trucks S.A.
Brussels, Belgium
bfrs. 1,250,000
100%

VOTEX Warenhandels-
gesellschaft mbH
Dreieich
DM 1,000,000
100%

HOLAD Holding &
Administration AG
Basle, Switzerland
sfrs. 110,000
100%

Volkswagen International
Finance N.V.
Amsterdam, Netherlands
hfl. 1,000,000
100%

Volkswagen Overseas
Finance N.V.
Willemstad, Curaçao
Netherlands Antilles
hfl. 1,000,000
100%

V.A.G Leasing GmbH
Wolfsburg
DM 36,000,000
100%

Deutsche Automobil-
gesellschaft mbH
Hanover
DM 5,000,000
50%

VW-Wohnungsbau
Gemeinnützige
Gesellschaft mbH
Wolfsburg
DM 2,000,000
100%

VW-Siedlungs-
gesellschaft mbH
Wolfsburg
DM 20,000,000
100%

V.A.G Kredit Bank
GmbH
Wolfsburg
DM 92,500,000
100%

VW-Versicherungsver-
mittlungs-GmbH
Wolfsburg
DM 500,000
66.7%

V.A.G Transportge-
sellschaft mbH
Wolfsburg
DM 2,000,000
75%
25% interRent
Hamburg

GmbH für ausl. Vertriebs-
beteiligungen
M.A.N. — Volkswagen
Munich
DM 6,000,000
50%

TRIUMPH-ADLER AG für
Büro- und Informations-
technik
Nuremberg
DM 80,500,000
98.4%

Adlerwerke vorm.
Heinrich Kleyer AG
Frankfurt (Main)
DM 20,000,000
96.5%

Nederlandse Adler
Fabrieken B.V., Leider
Netherlands
hfl. 5,000,000
100%

Adler-Royal Business
Machines Inc.
Union, N.J., USA
US $ 1,000
100%

Royal Business
Machines Inc.
Hartford, Conn., USA
US $ 1,000
100%

Triumph Adler Inc.
Los Angeles, Cal., USA
US $ 3,000
100%

Triumph Adler
Systems Inc.
Los Angeles, Cal., USA
US $ 2,000
100%

Pertec Computer
Corp.
Los Angeles, Cal., US
US $ 100
100%

The magnitude of the 1974 loss ($313 million), however, created much concern on the part of the VW management group. Leiding's policies were questioned, particularly his strong advocacy of building a plant in the United States: the cuts in production, layoffs, and the move to close the Neckarsulm plant added to Leiding's problems. When the supervisory board could not resolve the issues of conflict of the management board, Leiding resigned as chairman of the management board.

Leiding was succeeded by Toni Schmucker, who had guided the large diversified steel producer Rheinstahl AG through some difficult problems not unlike VW's. While Schmucker had spent 30 years with Ford of Germany, rising to director of sales during his tenure, his reputation as an organizer was made at Rheinstahl, where he cut unprofitable operations, turned losses into profits, and then arranged the sale of the company in 1973 to August Thyssen-Huette AG, the large steel combine. Schmucker's management style was considered to be different from those of his predecessors, Nordhoff, Lotz, and Leiding. He had a reputation as a diplomat and an easy-to-work-with, although demanding, executive. His predecessors were generally considered to be hard-driving, authoritative, dominating executives, not given to diplomacy.

Mr. Schmucker acknowledged that his predecessor's capital investments and product-line redesign were strengths for VW. But costs were still rising and sales dropping, particularly in the United States. Mr. Schmucker achieved cost cutbacks through negotiated union cooperation on the issue of labor force reduction, and finally won approval for the VW plant in the United States.

Also during Mr. Schmucker's tenure, VW acquired control of Triumph-Adler, a German company which manufactured office equipment and marketed it worldwide. In 1981, Triumph-Adler lost DM 197 million on sales of DM 1.95 billion, and the company's chief executive resigned. VW had maintained a hands-off posture toward its subsidiary, believing that Triumph-Adler was a long-term investment and that Triumph-Adler executives knew the office equipment industry best. Pertec Computer Corporation, another Triumph-Adler subsidiary, was acquired by VW in 1979 for nearly $120 million, and lost $4.8 million on sales of $180 million in 1980. High interest rates in the United States were depressing the whole computer industry in the United States at this time. Meanwhile, Triumph-Adler's traditional strength in mechanical products (e.g., Royal typewriters) was being eroded by rapid gains of computer-based systems. Triumph-Adler had not possessed the capital or personnel to develop its own line of word-processing equipment.

Mr. Carl H. Hahn took over at VW in January 1982 after Mr. Schmucker's illness forced him to retire. Mr. Hahn had left VW in 1972 following disagreements with Rudolph Leiding. When Mr. Hahn returned to VW 10 years later, some VW executives resigned, fearing that old animosities might be rekindled. Mr. Hahn, as president of Continental, Germany's largest rubber company, had returned that company to profit after nine years of losses.

Like his predecessors, Hahn had to work within the VW organization, which was made up of the 21-member supervisory board of directors, which met normally about two times a year. (See Exhibits 14 and 15.) This group made or approved all major policy and strategic decisions of the company. It was composed of outside directors, including government members representing the 40 percent ownership by the government, labor or worker representatives authorized under the West German system of *Mitbestimmung* (codetermination), and business executives of prominent West German firms. Labor representatives on the board had been particularly influential in some policy matters, since they frequently could get support for their views from the political representatives on the board and thus gain a majority.

FUTURE PROSPECTS FOR VW

Hahn took over VW at a crucial period in the company's history. The problems of overcoming 1981's declining profits and the losses of Triumph-Adler and conserving VW's cash confronted him. Cost cutting, which resulted in layoffs and plant closings, brought severe labor and political protests. This matter was of particular concern, since both groups taken together comprised the majority on the supervisory board, which chose the chief executive officer of the company.

The new car line of the Passat (Dasher), Scirocco, and Golf (Rabbit) had set the direction of the company for the late 1970s. This move proved to be very beneficial to VW. The new cars had been very well received in the United States, Germany, and Europe and helped boost VW's sales despite the general decline in the automotive market.

The Rabbit had protected VW from the overall slowdown of the auto market in 1981, but by that time both the Japanese and American manufacturers had entered the market for small, fuel-efficient, front-wheel-drive vehicles. It appeared that VW was in a squeeze between lower-cost Japanese vehicles and similar units from the wealthier and, in the United States at least, more powerful Detroit auto makers. Technological advances by competitors had eroded the Rabbit's engineering edge, so that VW products were no longer the leaders in either quality or price. In world markets, Japanese auto makers had limited

EXHIBIT 14
THE STRUCTURE OF VOLKSWAGEN'S BOARD OF DIRECTORS

Supervisory Board (Aufsichtsrat)
20 members
Chairman Karl Gustav Ratjen
(authorizes major policy moves)

Board of Management (Vorstand)
10 members
Chairman Carl H. Hahn
(operating management decisions)

VW Group Subsidiary Companies

EXHIBIT 15
VW's SUPERVISORY BOARD AND BOARD OF DIRECTORS.

Supervisory board (Aufsichtsrat)

Karl Gustaf Ratjen (62), Frankfurt
  Chairman
  Chairman of the Board of
  Management of
  Metallgesellschaft AG

Eugen Loderer (61), Frankfurt
  Deputy Chairman
  Chairman of the
  Metalworkers' Union

Birgit Breuel (44), Hanover
  Minister for Economic Affairs and
  Transport of Lower Saxony

Dr. jur. F. Wilheim Christians (59),
  Dusseldorf
  Member of the Board of Management
  of Deutsche Bank AG

Siegfried Ehlers (57), Wolfsburg
  Chairman of the Group Works
  Council of Volkswagenwerk AG

Dr. rer. pol. Hans Friderichs (50)
  Frankfurt
  Member as of March 24, 1981
  Member of the Board of Management
  of the Dresdner Bank AG

Albert Hoffmeister (53), Wolfsburg
  Senior Executive of
  Volkswagenwerk AG

Hans-Gunter Hoppe (59), Berlin
  Former Member of the Berlin Senate

Walther Leisler Kiep (56), Hanover
  Member of the Federal
  German Parliament

Gerd Kuhl (59), Frankfurt
  Trade Union Secretary to the
  Executive Committee of the
  Metalworkers' Union

Walter Martius (62), Velbert-Langenberg
  Business Consultant

Hans L. Merkle (69)
  Gerlingen-Schillerhohe
  Chairman of the Management of
  Robert Bosch GmbH

Karl Heinrich Mirh (46), Kassel
  Chairman of Volkswagenwerk
  AG's Works Council representing
  the Kassel Plant

Gerhard Mogwitz (48), Hanover
  Chairman of Volkswagenwerk AG's
  Works Council representing the
  Hanover Plant

Walter Neuert (56), Ingolstadt
  Chairman of the Joint Works Council
  of AUDI NSU AUTO UNION AG

Manfred Pusch (43), Wolfsburg
  Deputy Chairman, Group Works
  Council of VW AG

Dr. rer. pol. Otto Schlecht (56),
  Bonn-Duisdorf
  Undersecretary of State in the
  Federal Ministry of Economics

Kurt Ernst Schmiedl (57), Emden
  Chairman of Volkswagenwerk AG's
  Works Council representing the
  Emden Plant

Dr. rer. pol. Horst Schulmann (48),
  Bonn
  Member as of January 1, 1981
  Undersecretary of State in the
  Federal Ministry of Finance

Dr. rer. pol. Albert Schunk (40),
  Frankfurt
  Trade Union Secretary to the
  Executive Committee of the
  Metalworkers' Union

EXHIBIT 15 *(continued)*

Board of management (Vorstand)

Carl H. Hahn (55)
   Chairman of the Board of
   Management
	Dr. jur. Peter Frerk (51)
	   Legal Matters, Auditing and Econ.

Horst Munzner (57)
   Deputy Chairman
   Purchasing and Material
	Dr. jur. Wolfgan R. Habbel (58)
	   AUDI NSU AUTO UNION AG
	
	Gunter Hartwich (46)
	   Production

Claus Borgward (43)
   Quality Assurance
	Dr. rer. pol. Verner P. Schmidt (49)
	   Sales

Karl-Heinz Briam (59)
   Personnel and Social Matters
   (Labour Director)
	Rolf Selowsky (51)
	   Finance and Business
	   Administration

Prof. Dr. techn. Ernst Fiala (53) Research and Development	

their American exports to the United States, and so in the 1980s were beginning to invade South America and third-world countries, which had been traditional strengths for VW.

Facing the 1980s, VW management foresaw a general slackening of world demand for motor vehicles, resulting in growth rates of about 2 to 3 percent, and expressed reluctance to predict how far it would be possible to improve the competitive position of the VW group. "The intensifying competition on the one hand and increased pressure of costs on the other," said management, "make it imperative to invest yet more than before in products and processes." Accordingly, VW scheduled investment for 1981–1983 at DM 13,000,000,000 for property, plant, and equipment. Management identified several major unpredictable forces which would have important impact on VW's competitive position: interest rates, exchange rates, fuel prices, competition from Japan worldwide, and competition from U.S. manufacturers in U.S. markets.

As he departed VW, Toni Schmucker voiced his concern that the very survival of the company was at stake in the short term.

British Leyland[1]

Sir Michael Edwardes, chairman of British Leyland (BL), is quite clear about the importance of the Metro, launched today, to the survival of the BL motor group. It is, he says, "the litmus test" of everything he has tried to do since he arrived at BL nearly three years ago.[2]

> It is not just the production of a new car to boost our depressed market share. Metro is a test of our ability to introduce entirely new standards of quality and reliability in a new plant with every automated advantage.
>
> The removal of restrictive practices, vastly improved industrial relations, demanning by 30,000 jobs in 30 months have enabled us to attain new levels of productivity to put us on a par with the best Europeans—in fact, it is a test of our ability to compete at every level.[3]

HISTORY

British Leyland is the end product of a series of mergers that go all the way back to the 1950s, when Austin and Morris combined to form British Motor Co. With the blessings of the Labor government B. M. C. combined with Leyland during the 1960s. Leyland was a profitable and well-managed producer of trucks and buses. By 1968, British Leyland had absorbed virtually all of the native segment of Britain's auto industry (subsidiaries of Detroit's big three

---

[1] This case was prepared from published sources by Kenneth Armstrong under the direction of Professor Thomas J. McNichols.

[2] Clifford Webb, "Can the Metro save BL," *New York Times*, June 10, 1980.

[3] Ibid.

make up about 42 percent of the industry). British Leyland produced a wide range of automobiles from the sporty Jaguar to the serviceable Mini. The idea behind these combinations was to create a British General Motors, but the parts were never successfully integrated into the whole. Instead, British Leyland turned out to be huge, clumsy, and uncoordinated.

Many of British Leyland's problems resulted from failure to successfully integrate its acquisitions. The economics of modern car production is built around the "building block" principle of using as many common elements as possible in a variety of models. However, this idea was never effectively implemented in the individual British Leyland companies. Labor-management relations also caused major problems for the company. Management was forced to deal with 58 different bargaining units in its 34 plants, and executives were involved in some kind of labor negotiation for nearly nine months of every year. Wage rates for a given job varied widely, and friction was always present.

On the production side of the business, model development lagged. The small Austin and Morris sedans finally disappeared from the U.S. market, giving up a firm foothold they had held since 1945. With the exception of the Mini—the last great British success—British Leyland's cars proved increasingly difficult to sell in continental Europe. To compound the problem, when Leyland dealers did have customers, they often did not have any cars because of production stoppages.

From the fall of 1973 onward, a succession of events, including the oil crisis, the three-day week, the weakening economic situation in the United Kingdom and worldwide, and the rapid increase in inflation, caused British Leyland's position to deteriorate markedly. The company has budgeted £68m pretax profit for 1973–1974, but a £16m loss was reported for the first half of the year ending in March, 1974.

This turnaround in profitability cast doubt upon BL's ability to finance its expansion, as well as weakening the case for investment in additional capacity. The original investment program for the following five to six years had been £900m. However, during the summer of 1974, it became obvious that this must be scaled down to a minimum level for maintaining a competitive position, and that even this level could not be financed from BL's own resources. Plans were thus scaled down, and a revised plan calling for £142m in expenditures by September 1974, and an additional £365m by September 1978, was presented to BL's principal bankers. To finance this modified plan, BL sought medium-term financing of £150m.[4]

However, the situation worsened, and 1974 results showed a year-end loss of £23.95m. BL was expected to reach the limit of its overdraft facilities by December, and it was becoming clear that in these circumstances, the banks were most unlikely to grant more.

After a series of meetings with government officials, the secretary of state

[4] *British Leyland: The Next Decade*, abridged version, The House of Commons, April 23, 1975, p. 11.

for industry announced on December 6th that:

> ... because of the company's position in the economy as a leading exporter and its importance to employment both directly and through the many firms that are dependent on it, the Government are informing the company's bankers that the approval of Parliament will be sought for a guarantee of the working capital required over and above existing facilities.
>
> In response to the company's request for support for its investment programme, the Government also intend to introduce longer-term arrangements, including a measure of public ownership. In order to help the Government in framing a scheme for this purpose, they propose to appoint a high level team, led by Sir Don Ryder, including members drawn from the Industrial Development Advisory Board, to advise on the company's situation and prospects, and the team will consult with the company and the trade unions in the course of its work.[5]

THE RYDER REPORT

The following is an abridged version of the Ryder report, *British Leyland: The Next Decade,* presented to the secretary of state for industry and dated April 23, 1975.

British Leyland: The Next Decade
Summary

We were appointed on 18th December 1974 "... to conduct, in consultation with the Corporation and the trade unions, an overall assessment of BLMC's present situation and future prospects, covering corporate strategy, investment, markets, organization, employment, productivity, management/labour relations, profitability and finance; and to report to the Government." At the same time the Government obtained Parliament's approval to a guarantee by the Government of lending by the banks to British Leyland of up to £50m.

Prospects for the Industry

We decided that, in assessing BL's situation and prospects, it would be useless to take a short-term view. In the motor industry three or four years must elapse between the decision to introduce a new model or to undertake a major plant modernisation and the completion of these projects. Once the new model is introduced and the new plant is in full operation, many more years must elapse before resources can be available to replace the model or renew the plant. Therefore decisions made now about a capital expenditure programme extending over five to seven years must take into account market prospects ten years from now.

Our starting point was therefore to examine world market prospects for the motor industry generally over the period to 1985. It is unusually difficult to make such an assessment at present. The past eighteen months have seen a sharp rise in the price of oil relative to other goods, historically high rates of inflation throughout the world, and a cutback in economic growth and consumer demand in the main industrial coun-

---

[5] British Leyland: The Next Decade, pp. 12–13.

tries. As a result car sales which had grown rapidly over the two decades up to 1973 fell abruptly in all major markets in 1974 and may be no higher and perhaps even somewhat lower this year. Along with more long term anxieties about the environment and congestion, the recent drop in demand has raised some doubts and uncertainties about future prospects for the motor industry.

Broadly our view is that while the world market for the motor industry over the next decade will undoubtedly be less buoyant than in the recent past and will be more fiercely competitive, particularly in the early years when there is likely to be excess capacity, it will remain a large and valuable market. Moreover, in some areas of the world and for some types of vehicles considerable growth in sales can be expected.

Nearly half the vehicles produced by BL are cars for the UK market. The UK market for cars depends mainly on trends in the economy, particularly in the growth of consumers' expenditure, and on action which Governments take to influence these trends. We think that the total UK car market should start to grow again in 1976, should by 1980 have recovered to the 1973 peak of 1.6m vehicles and should between 1980 and 1985 grow further to at least 1.7m vehicles and possibly a higher level.

In Western Europe (excluding the UK), which accounted for nearly 60 per cent (some 200,000) of BL's overseas car sales last year, we believe that total demand will start to recover next year, should reach around 9m cars in 1980 (13 per cent higher than in 1973) and at least 10m cars (26 per cent higher than in 1973) by 1985. In most other markets, including the USA, which last year accounted for about 15 per cent (some 52,000) of BL's overseas car sales, the pattern is expected to be more like that in the UK—a recovery to 1973 levels by 1980 and little growth between 1980 and 1985.

Partly as a result of the tendency to replace heavy trucks more frequently because of more stringent vehicle legislation and the cost and scarcity of qualified maintenance staff, total UK demand for heavy trucks seems likely to be about 30 per cent higher than last year by 1980 and there should be some further modest growth between 1980 and 1985. The prospects in overseas markets for heavy trucks are good. This is particularly true of those countries which either produce oil (Iran and Nigeria) or have good access to favourably priced oil (Turkey) and are growing fast. In these three countries it seems likely that demand for heavy trucks will more than double by 1985. There is also a large market for heavy trucks in Western Europe which shows modest but significant growth prospects over the next few years and where BL has a major opportunity for increasing its penetration.

In the UK BL is a dominant supplier of many types of bus (notably double deck buses) and operators seem likely to want to place large orders over the next few years which BL could not meet. We recommend that the Department of the Environment should as a matter of urgency hold discussions with BL and the major UK bus operators to work out arrangements for better co-ordination between the bus operators and BL to phase orders and deliveries. As capacity becomes available, both to meet home demand and to supply overseas markets on a more regular basis, BL will have to make a more systematic attempt to forecast overseas demand for buses.

The Right Strategy for BL

Against the background of this assessment of world market prospects we considered what strategy BL should follow over the next decade. We examined the following issues:

1 Whether there is a future for BL as a vehicle producer.

2 Whether BL should diversify into non-vehicle activities and divest itself of its existing peripheral activities.

3 Whether BL should remain a producer of both cars and commercial vehichles.

4 Whether BL should remain a producer of both volume and specialist cars.

5 In which geographical areas BL's marketing effort should be concentrated.

We concluded that there was undoubtedly a future for BL as a vehicle producer. Although competitive pressures will increase over the next decade, there is no reason why BL should despair of improving its position in this very valuable market. Vehicle production does not involve the kind of advanced technology which can only be financed in very strong and highly developed economies such as the United States. On the other hand, although there is likely to be an increasing trend towards local manufacture in the developing countries, there is enough scope for sophistication and refinement to give established producers with skilled labour forces a competitive edge in the developed countries. In general, therefore, vehicle production is the kind of industry which ought to remain an essential part of the UK's economic base. We believe, therefore, that BL should remain a major vehicle producer, although this means that urgent action must be taken to remedy the weaknesses which at present prevent it from competing effectively in world markets.

Since BL is already a very large company and needs to concentrate its managerial skills and resources on improving its competitive position as a major producer of vehicles, we concluded that it would not be wise for BL to diversify its activities into unrelated sectors of industry.

We concluded that BL should remain a producer both of cars and of trucks and buses, and also that BL should continue in both the "volume" and the "specialist" sectors of the car market. In particular we considered whether BL should abandon the "small/light" sector of the market. In practice, this would mean that BL would not provide for any replacement for the Mini in its future product plans. We concluded that there were strong arguments both on commercial grounds and on national economic grounds for BL to continue in the small/light sector of the market. In order to compete effectively in all the major sectors of the car market BL would have to cut out competition between models in the same sector, and reduce the number of different body-shells, engines, transmissions etc. Similar rationalisation would be necessary in trucks and buses. BL would also need to build on the reputation for quality and distinction which it enjoys in the more expensive sectors of the market. All its models, throughout the product range, should have sufficient distinction to ensure a competitive edge against the very high volume producers.

On markets we concluded that the main thrust of BL's marketing effort overseas should be to increase its present small share of the expanding Western European market both for cars (under 3 per cent at present) and for trucks and buses (about 1 per cent at present). BL should also continue to take full advantage of the very rapidly growing market for trucks and buses in certain developing countries such as Iran, Nigeria and Turkey.

Financial Position

An examination of past trading results shows that throughout the period since BL was formed in 1968, profits were wholly inadequate and insufficient to maintain the business on a viable basis. To make matters worse nearly all the profit was distributed as dividends instead of being retained to finance new capital investment. A substantial proportion of BL's fixed assets were old and had been fully written down. The depreciation charge was therefore an inadequate measure of what should have been spent on capital replacement. Working capital was also run down to a critical level.

We concluded therefore that BL's present levels of capital expenditure and working capital were far too low. Even to maintain these levels in real terms would, because of inflation, require BL to earn at least £100m a year profit, and much larger sums would need to be earned to make up for the capital rundown in the past. We concluded, therefore, that very large sums would be needed from external sources to finance the action required to make BL a viable business.

Engineering

We next examined BL's engineering resources and facilities to see whether they would be capable of carrying out an extensive program of product development and rationalisation. We consider that the dispersed and fragmented organisation of BL product development engineering is a serious weakness. We propose that the skills concerned with various aspects of product development—product planning, styling engineering and vehicle engineering—should be brought within a single product development organisation for cars and that there should be a similar organisation for trucks and buses. BL also needs new central laboratories and workshops for the design and development of new cars and components. We recommend that these should be built by 1979; as an interim measure, temporary facilities, probably at Solihull, should provide the centre of control for vehicle engineering personnel; the truck and bus facilities at Leyland should be extended as a matter of urgency.

Production

For historical reasons BL has a large number of plants scattered throughout the country. Although some progress has been made since the merger towards a more logical arrangement of manufacturing operations in the different locations, there is still too much movement of manufactured parts and subassemblies between plants. In body and assembly operations we recommend that individual plants should be associated with one or more model lines from the receipt of pressed out panels to final assembly. Likewise, plants should specialise in the production of engines, gearboxes and chassis without distinction by model type and without being involved in body assembly operations. Similar parts should be produced in the same location. A senior executive should be appointed to develop BL's parts manufacturing activities to improve costs and reduce the number of different parts. Substantial economies could and should be achieved quickly by a program to improve the layout of processes within plants.

The most serious feature of BL's production facilities is, however, that a large proportion of the plant and machinery is old, outdated and inefficient. BL's foundries are in urgent need of modernisation to bring them up to modern efficiency levels and safety and environmental standards. These serious deficiencies are the result of the lack of provision for capital expenditure. A massive program to modernise plant and equipment at BL must therefore be put in hand immediately in conjunction with the new product plan.

Organisation and Management

We then considered whether BL's existing organisation and management would be appropriate to carry out the strategy we had proposed and the necessary program of product rationalisation, reorganisation of production and engineering facilities, and new capital investment. We are convinced that BL's present organisational structure has harmful effects on the efficiency of BL's operations and is likely to impede its future development. It combines most of the disadvantages of both centralised and decentralised organisations with few of the advantages of either. There has been inadequate integration of the product planning, engineering, manufacturing and marketing of cars. The Managing Director has too many people reporting to him. The creation of a large corporate staff has undermined the authority and responsibility of line management.

Our approach has been to divide up BL's activities, within the overall corporate structure, into four separate businesses—British Leyland Cars, British Leyland Trucks and Buses, British Leyland Special Products and British Leyland International. Each would be a profit center in its own right with its own Managing Director. At corporate level there would be a non-executive Chairman and a Chief Executive and a corporate staff drastically reduced to the absolute minimum.

We considered and rejected the approach of dividing up BL's car operations into two or three separate divisions based on products (Austin Morris, Rover Triumph and Jaguar). We believe that this would impede the policies of product rationalisation and integration of design, engineering and production.

We attach the greatest importance to the maximum delegation of authority and responsibility within the new structure from the Chief Executive to the four Managing Directors and from them to the line management below them.

The most important proposals are those relating to British Leyland Cars where we recommend four line divisions—one dealing with product planning, development and engineering, one with manufacturing, one with sales and marketing, and one with parts and KD (knocked down) activities. This is a radical change from BL's present organisation which consists of separate divisions for different products dealing with their own engineering and marketing and, to some extent, manufacturing, co-ordinated by corporate staff.

Industrial Relations

Throughout our inquiry we were aware that, although we had many proposals to make BL more competitive—fewer and better models, improved facilities for design, engineering and production and changes in organisation and management—BL's success would depend most of all on the skills, efforts and attitudes of its 170,000 employees. We have therefore examined industrial relations at BL at some length. We do not subscribe to the view that all the ills of BL can be laid at the door of a strike-prone and work-shy labour force. Nevertheless, it is clear that if BL is to compete effectively there must be a reduction in the man-hours lost through industrial disputes. More productive use must also be made both of BL's existing capital investment and the planned additional capital investment and this must mean more realistic manning levels and more mobility and interchangeability of labour.

We found ample evidence that BL's employees at all levels want to make their contribution to solving BL's problems and we must therefore find ways of sustaining and developing this constructive approach. We consider it essential that the progress of the capital expenditure program and the injection of new finance by the Government should be staged and that each stage should depend on evidence of a tangible contribution by BL's work force and management to the reduction of industrial disputes and the improvement of productivity.

We consider that the multiplicity of bargaining units and renewal dates is an unsettling factor in BL's industrial relations. We therefore recommend that discussions should be held with the trade unions about a gradual but substantial reduction in the number of collective bargaining units with BL and about a reduction in the renewal dates for wage settlements.

The most crucial factor in improving industrial relations at BL and in creating the conditions in which productivity can be increased is, however, that there should be some significant progress towards industrial democracy. Means must be found to take advantage of the ideas, enthusiasm and energy of BL's workers in planning the future of the business on which their livelihood depends.

Cost of the Program

Inevitably, because of the backlog of past massive under-investment, the capital expenditure required is very large. In constant price terms it is £1,264m and in inflated price terms £2,090m over the eight years to end September 1982. There will also have to be an increased provision for working capital of around £260m in constant price terms or £750m in inflated price terms.

Our forecast is that BL's profits as a percentage of sales should improve to 11 per cent in 1981/82 compared with an average of 6.5% in the period 1968/69 to 1973/74. BL's return on capital employed is also forecast to improve to 19.6% in 81/82 compared with an average of 9.6% in the earlier period. After 1982 BL should start to reap the benefits of the new capital expenditure program.

Although BL is forecast to achieve a positive cash flow in 81/82 there is likely to be a requirement for funds from external sources during the period 74/75 to 80/81 of £1,300m to £1,400m in inflated price terms. In the period to end September 1978 the requirement is forecast to be £900m in inflated price terms.

Financing the Program

We therefore propose that the Government should be prepared to provide £200m in equity capital now and up to £500m in long term loan capital in stages over the period 1976 to 1978. The equity capital should be provided by the Government's underwriting of a rights issue to existing shareholders, following a capital reconstruction through a Scheme of Arrangement. It is likely that relatively few shareholders will take up these rights and the Government will therefore be left with most of the shares. The rights issue should be preceded by an offer by the Government to buy out existing shareholders at a price of 10p per share. On the inflation assumptions a further £500m is forecast to be required between end September 1978 and end September 1982. It is not possible to foresee the type of financing which will be appropriate for a period so far ahead but the Government must be prepared to make funds available either as loan capital or as a mixture of loan and equity capital.

We recommend that, following the initial injection of £200m of equity capital, there should be review points on each occasion when a further tranche of funds is provided to assess the contribution being made to the reduction of industrial disputes and the improvement in productivity.

OPERATIONS AFTER THE RYDER REPORT

As a result of the recommendations of the Ryder report, the British government bought 95 percent of British Leyland's stock. The company's 1974–1975 results showed a loss of £123.6m on sales of £1.87 billion. The two main planks of the Ryder plan were (1) that BL should retain a 33 percent market share in Britain and increase its exports, especially to the EEC, and (2) that BL should put up the bulk of the £2.8 billion in investment projected by Ryder over the next eight years, with the government's contribution limited to approximately £1 billion.

However, the historical problems of BL still remain. During the first half of the 1975–1976 fiscal year, strikes cost the company 700,000 worker hours. BL is still plagued with old plants and equipment, low morale, and an unwieldy range of 10 passenger-car models, none of which is selling particularly well. Its sports cars are more successful, as are its special-products division (a group of 10 companies that make refrigeration equipment, military vehicles, construction equipment, and other products) which made a 5 percent profit last year. Leyland's truck and bus operations also made a profit last year, and are in the black in the current year.[6]

Leyland's chief executive says that there is no way to avoid heavy losses this year, despite a recent 4.6 percent price increase in the car division, which accounts for two-thirds of sales. "The price increase is really meaningless because Leyland's problem is simply that it cannot produce cars that the public will buy," says Derek Glynn, economic director of the Confederation of British Industry.[7]

It is becoming apparent that the two major tenets of the Ryder plan are increasingly untenable. BL's share of the British market has already slipped 10 points (to 23 percent in October of 1977) since the Ryder report was published. Exports have fared no better. And far from generating investment funds internally, BL has had to use taxpayers' money, earmarked for investment, to pay its operating expenses. As December approaches, it appears that BL will need to draw another £35m of government cash to meet its December payroll.

In the midst of this continuing subpar performance, Sir Richard Dobson, who had become chairman of BL, ran into trouble with a tape recorder. Sir Richard, addressing what he thought was a private businessman's lunch,

---

[6] "Is British Leyland Worth the Money," *Business Week*, May 17, 1976, p. 36.
[7] Ibid.

made disparaging remarks about foreigners with whom BL was doing business in the Mideast; he referred to them as "wogs." One member in the audience recorded his words, and the transcript showed up in a left-wing London publication. Sir Richard was forced to resign, and this opened up the search for a new chairman.[8]

THE NEW CHAIRMAN

Sir Michael Edwardes is a pint-sized (5 ft 4 $\frac{1}{2}$ in) executive with a commanding personality. "People either adore him or dislike him intensely," says Jill Thompson, Edwardes's sister, who is director of a Johannesburg advertising agency.[9] She continues by saying that "he's been accused of having a Napoleon complex. He is hypercritical, sets high standards, and doesn't suffer fools gladly. We come from a very success-oriented family where there wasn't much patience for failure."[10] John Ray, Edwardes's successor as chief executive at Chloride points out that Edwardes would dominate any conversation "within about five minutes or sooner."[11]

The new BL chairman had an early start on a business career. At the upper-crust school in Grahamstown, he successfully bid for the job of leveling and grassing the school's playing fields. This led to a general contracting company after Edwardes graduated in law from Rhodes. Edwardes later sold his share of the business when he decided to pursue a career with Britain's Chloride.

Sir Michael joined Chloride's African subsidiary and achieved executive status in 1963 when he was put in charge of Chloride's Rhodesian operations. It was here that Edwardes developed the basic management philosophy he has followed since: analyzing management talent with the help of psychological testing, and decentralizing the business.[12]

Edwardes increased profits six times in Rhodesia before being transferred to Britain in 1966. He applied the same formula successfully to two struggling Chloride units, and was consequently named chief executive in 1972. In 1974 he added the title of chairman.

He has since established a "whiz kid" reputation at Chloride, which is Britain's largest battery maker. He has increased profits fivefold to $47.5 million, and in 1975 was named "Young Businessman of the Year" by the *Guardian* newspaper.

Edwardes, 47, expected to stay with Chloride till retirement, and probably would have if he hadn't agreed to become a part-time director of the newly formed National Enterprise Board in 1975. The NEB was formed by the Labor government as part of its "industrial strategy." The idea behind the NEB—to take an equity stake in struggling private enterprises and help them solve their

[8] Robert Ball, "Saving Leyland is a job for Hercules," *Fortune*, July 3, 1978, p. 58.
[9] "A New Prescription for British Leyland," *Business Week*, May 1, 1978, p. 104.
[10] Ibid.
[11] Ibid.
[12] Robert Ball, op. cit., p. 105.

problems—was not particularly popular with most business leaders. Edwardes's willingness to serve marked him as a businessman who in his words, "believes in a mixed economy."[13]

With BL in serious trouble, and the NEB looking around for a new management, attention soon centered on Edwardes. Sir Michael considered for about a month before deciding that he had an "absolute duty" to take the job. He is currently on a three-year leave from Chloride at a $93,000 salary equal to what he received at Chloride. The NEB has made it clear that these three years provide Edwardes with a "last chance" to save the company.

Edwardes's organizational formula continues to be similar to what has worked for him in the past. Though he must negotiate a companywide labor pact, Edwardes will push for decentralization. He promises to use "ruthless logic" in organizing teams of executives to run BL as a group of "profit centers." Sir Michael believes that "you must give people jobs they can get their arms around."[14] Edwardes also favors a strong board of directors. "If you've got a board that you know will dig in its heels on a matter of principle and will back the management, that transforms the morale of a company."[15]

The big question now is whether the Edwardes formula will work for BL. But as his sister points out: "One of the reasons he has such a success record is that he only tackles things he thinks he can master."[16] Adds Edwardes, "My long-term ambition is to get British Leyland right in three years. I don't think one minute beyond that."[17]

Prior to Edwardes's arrival, BL seemed to be driven by a death wish. The government's takeover in 1975 solved none of the company's fundamental problems. BL had ineffective management, unworkable organization, outdated models, and a reputation for poor quality. Edwardes's assessment as he took over was: "Nothing is more damning than our steady decline in market share against a rising market. People are literally walking past our showrooms without a second look."[18]

ORGANIZATION

Under the new structure proposed by Edwardes, BL Ltd. is merely a holding company with three major subsidiaries. The first, Leyland Vehicles, has regained its original identity as a truck and bus manufacturer. The second, Special Products Industries, brings together construction equipment, forklift trucks, and military vehicles. The third, BL Cars, is the automobile division and contains three separate subsidiaries: Austin-Morris, the volume car

---

[13] Robert Ball, op. cit., p. 59.
[14] Robert Ball, op. cit., p. 60.
[15] *Business Week*, May 1, 1978, p. 104.
[16] *Business Week*, May 1, 1978, p. 105.
[17] Ibid.
[18] Robert Ball, op. cit., p. 58.

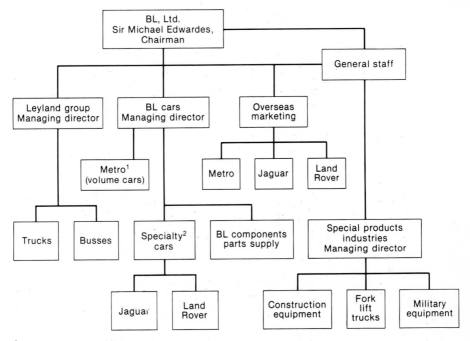

¹Metro replaced the Mini

²MG line — Triumph was dropped in October 1981

EXHIBIT 1
Operating structure—British Leyland (BL) Ltd.

division; Jaguar Rover Triumph, the specialist division; and BL Components, which supplies parts for the others. Overseas marketing has also been decentralized along product lines. (See Exhibit 1.)

Edwardes, while firmly believing that all of these parts are necessary to the future of BL, is trying to create five self-managing and identifiable profit centers. This should enable performance to be monitored more effectively. Several experts recommend that BL should always aim at a niche slightly above the cars offered by its much larger competitors, who produce more efficiently and mostly Europe-wide.[19] According to *The Economist,* "The correct BL strategy has always been to concentrate on the company's quality output (Rovers, Jaguars, and sports range) and slowly move away from the mass production of volume cars (in which productivity is at a premium, so BL cannot be expected to compete in the foreseeable future). There are waiting lists all over Europe for Rovers and Jaguars."[20]

[19]"New Look for Leyland," *The Economist,* March 19, 1977, p. 88.
[20]"A Slimmer British Leyland," *The Economist,* October 22, 1977, p. 86.

PRODUCTIVITY AND MANUFACTURING OPERATIONS

Productivity has always been a major problem area for BL. A joint union-management fact-finding team sent by the previous management to visit other European auto producers came back with the report that Leyland's output per person per year—currently 5.4 cars—is only one-half to two-thirds that of its European competitors like Volkswagen and Renault. Among the reasons given for Leyland's poor performance were shifts that started late and knocked off early, interruptions in the flow of parts, and extended rest breaks.[21]

Prospects for improved productivity occurred on Edwardes's first day on the job in November of 1977. On that day Leyland's 100,000 car workers voted 2 to 1 for a package of labor reforms, the most important of which was replacing the many individual labor pacts with a single, companywide labor pact to be negotiated by November 1979. The centralized agreement is to provide that all Leyland plants pay the same wage for comparable jobs. Edwardes, however, cannot take credit for this victory, as the government had passed the word that it would advance no more cash to Leyland if centralized bargaining were rejected.

Sir Michael's initial prescription was for a reduction of 12,500 jobs in 1978, most of these coming through attrition. Edwardes also was strong in dealing with manufacturing operations. For years, BL has been living with sloppy work, stoppages, and losses at its 3,000-worker Speke plant. Shortly after taking over, he announced that BL was closing the Speke plant and moving the work elsewhere. Actual cutbacks through August of 1979 reached 17,000, and reduced BL's work force to 165,000.

On September 9, 1979, Sir Michael announced that 25,000 additional employees would face unemployment. At least six BL plants would be closed in short order, and as many as seven more may face serious cutbacks. In November, workers gave their overwhelming (7 to 1) approval to Sir Michael's plan.

In April, 1980, management took the unprecedented step of unilaterally imposing a 5 percent increase subject to the union acceptance of sweeping changes in work rules. A strike by 18,500 workers at the giant Longbridge plant followed. Sir Michael threatened to fire all 18,500 if they were not back at work in five days, and when the workers realized he was not bluffing, they capitulated. There were several major concessions from the unions, including the elimination of trade barriers which prevented members of one union from removing as much as a screw or operating a switch in the territory of a rival union. Industrial engineers were also granted free access at all times, and maintenance teams have become more productive. An indicator of the progress being made is that in the first six months of 1980 BL experienced 126 strikes, compared with 234 in the same time period during the previous year.

On the new Metro assembly lines at the Longbridge plant, 38 workers and 28 robots do the work formerly done by 138 workers and conventional welding. The worker-hour content of a Metro is five hours—as good as any Europe-

---

[21] Robert Ball, op. cit., p. 61.

EXHIBIT 2
The new Metro. (*Source: Business Week,* April 6, 1981, McGraw-Hill Publication.)

an car maker and only one hour more than the Japanese.[22] Since the April settlement, there has been a 15 percent rise in productivity at the Longbridge plant. According to Clifford Webb, "For the first time since British Leyland was formed in 1968, it is now possible to see the outline of a rationalized production organization which lends itself to modern automated techniques."[23]

PRODUCTS AND PRODUCT DEVELOPMENT

When Edwardes took control of BL, the Mini, its best-selling nonfleet car, was nearly 20 years old, while BL's competitors had been consistently replacing their models every 4 or 5 years. BL was then producing some 14 different models in uneconomically small numbers while most of its competitors had two to five models. The Ryder plan called for scaling down to five models, and Sir Michael's plans were in line with this. However, the timetable was advanced two years so that the new Mini (now called Metro) would be introduced in 1980, which was about as fast as was possible. (See Exhibit 2.)

Perhaps the only real success story for BL is the Land Rover. The division that makes the Land Rover is the only vehicle-producing part of BL to generate

---

[22] "If BL Did Not Exist, Would Britain Have to Invent It," *The Economist,* November 8, 1980, p. 82.
[23] Clifford Webb, op. cit.

a profit. The division in 1980 chipped in approximately $100 million in profits on sales of $850 million. When Sir Michael took over he somehow got the necessary money to double the Land Rover capacity. Since that time productivity has risen 30 percent, output has been rising, and new models are rolling onto the market. Seven out of ten Land Rovers are sold to governments more concerned with their paramilitary reliability than the price. This has allowed Land Rover to remain profitable despite the ground it has lost to Japanese competitors in the pseudo-rugged four-wheel drive market. Even this division, however, has had its problems. The company stopped exporting Land Rovers to the United States in 1976, thus missing the U.S. boom in sales of off-the-road vehicles. And the first downturn in the world market for four-wheel drive vehicles since 1948, as well as the backwash of Britain's oil-buoyed currency, is causing even Land Rover to face possible cutbacks.

In the 1977 year, Leyland vehicles produced a pretax profit of £26.6m, but in 1978 it lost £5m. This division has also been short of capital. Several new models are scheduled for introduction during 1980 and 1981, but these will make their appearance in a declining market. 1979 was the banner year for trucks, and BL was too late with their new offerings.

Jaguar has long been one of the best known of the world's specialty cars. At the end of 1976, BL announced plans to spend £85m to expand and modernize two Jaguar factories over the next seven years. The investment will be used to increase production from 650 cars weekly, as well as to enhance the model range. However, Jaguar's market was hit hard when oil prices finally started hitting the upmarket end of cars in 1979. In September of 1980, Jaguar announced that it would seek 800 voluntary lay-offs because of declining auto sales. Only a month earlier it had announced plans to cut 300 white collar and 500 factory jobs by closing the Brown's Lane paint shop. Jaguar also projects that it needs £100m to bring in its new models by 1984.

These three areas, Land Rover, Leyland vehicles, and Jaguar accounted for 40 percent of BL by the end of 1980.[24]

After six years, the Metro is finally making it to dealer showrooms, and will be available in October of 1980. The Metro is a four-passenger, front-wheel drive hatchback that BL has invested with the latest in auto assembly technology. Initial dealer reaction has been positive. BL is hoping to capture 6 percent of the U.K. market with the Metro.[25] The Metro brings BL up against the competition of well-established cars such as the Ford Fiesta and the Datsun Cherry.

The Metro is to be followed in 1981 by the Honda Acclaim. This is a joint venture with Honda and will give BL a new midsized car. The Acclaim's engine and other key components will be imported from Honda, but BL claims that 70 percent of the value of the new car will be European. BL also says the deal will save it $350 million in development costs and produce a needed new model more quickly than it could have produced alone.[26] The first of three LC-10 midrange models is due to be launched in the spring of 1983, with all

[24] *The Economist*, November 8, 1980, p. 82.
[25] "BL is betting its life on the Metro Minicar," *Business Week*, September 29, 1980, p. 58.
[26] "Honda helps BL rebuild market share," *Business Week*, September 28, 1981, p. 47.

three on the market by 1985. The LC-10 series is aimed at a larger market segment (55 percent) and has a bigger profit potential than the Metro.

While BL's need for this infusion of new models is obvious, the wisdom of the financially strapped auto maker attempting to introduce five models in five years is open to question. BL will need to spend at least £300m annually to bring these models on stream.[27]

[27] "One Last Try, Then," *The Economist*, October 20, 1979, p. 83.

MARKET POSITION: AUTOS

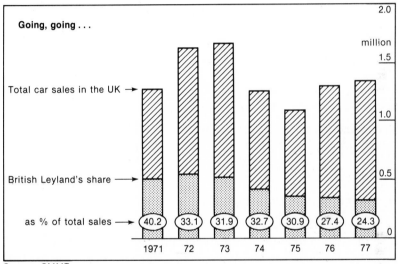

Source: SMMT

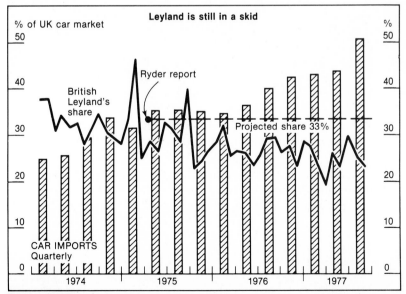

Source: SMMT

The Ryder plan was based upon the assumption that BL could hold onto its 33 percent share of the U.K. market. The accompanying charts show that this did not happen, and that market share had fallen about 10 points by the time Sir Michael had taken control of BL. However, the slide continued. Edwardes's recovery plan was based on BL regaining and holding 26 to 27 percent of the market. However, this too proved not to be feasible as market share slipped to 21 percent in 1978, and finally below 20 percent by 1979, hitting a low of 16 percent in June of 1980. Present plans are based on BL maintaining a 20 percent market share.

But even if it is able to introduce attractive enough models to hold 20 percent of the British market and hold onto its miniscule (0.4 percent in West Germany to 2 percent in Belgium) portion of the remaining European market, BL will still struggle to survive. It is only thirteenth in the world car league, and well below half the 2 million annual volume often regarded as the floor for staying in the mass-car market.[28] Sir Michael must find innovative ways of overcoming this major handicap.

FINANCIAL POSITION

The attached financial statements present the position of BL. By June of 1980, BL had already received £75m more than the £1000m requested by the original Ryder report. And still the losses persisted. (See Exhibits 3 and 4.)

CLOSING COMMENTS: 1981 UPDATE

• On January 26, 1981, the British government approved £990m ($2.376 billion) in emergency aid over the next two years for BL. £620m is earmarked for 1981–1982, and £370m for 1982–1983. BL chairman Sir Michael Edwardes welcomed the move but warned: "It will still be a hard slog for BL, which faces difficulties, as do all Western motor manufacturers."[29]

• The Metro hatchback has stopped the erosion of BL's British market share. The Metro has captured 7 percent of the market so far in 1981 and helped BL's total British market share climb to 19 percent through August—BL's first upswing in several years. BL hopes the Honda Acclaim, due in dealer showrooms on October 7, will increase market share another 1 $\frac{1}{2}$ to 2 percent.[30]

• BL's worst-hit operation in 1981 was its commercial vehicles division. Leyland Group, after showing a small profit in the first half of 1980, plummeted to a $91.6 million loss for the first half of 1981. The major problem with the truck group is that demand has dropped from 73,000 to 45,000 units between 1980 and 1981. Leyland Group has shed a quarter of its work force since the slide began, and promises further actions shortly. BL estimates that the

[28] *The Economist*, November 8, 1980, p. 82.
[29] "Britain Aids Ailing Leyland," *Chicago Tribune*, January 27, 1981.
[30] *Business Week*, September 28, 1981, p. 47.

EXHIBIT 3
BL Ltd.
Consolidated Income Account
(in £1000)

	1980	1979	1978	1977	1976*	1975†	1974‡
Sales	2,877,100	2,990,300	3,072,700	2,602,000	2,892,341	1,867,599	1,594,830
Trading profit	(293,900)	(46,200)	71,300	56,700	117,796	(38,117)	19,331
Interest payments	93,600	66,000	56,000	53,600	47,224	37,985	17,066
Taxation	3,200	6,300	12,600	8,100	25,922	(12,864)	9,000
Exceptional manpower reduction	—	10,000	13,600	—	—	—	—
Minority interest	5,800	3,000	2,100	3,000	2,274	713	1,525
Earnings before extras	(396,500)	(131,500)	(13,000)	(8,000)	42,376	(63,951)	(8,260)
Extra items	139,000	13,000	24,700	43,900	—	56,619	15,692
Net profit	(535,500)	(144,500)	(37,700)	(51,900)	42,376	(123,570)	(23,952)
Earnings per ordinary share	(26.2p)	(12.0p)	(7.8p)	(20.0p)	16.4p	(108.0p)	N/A

*15 months to 12-31-76.
†FY 10/1 to 9/30.
‡FY 10/1 to 9/30.

EXHIBIT 4
BL Ltd.
Consolidated Balance Sheet
(in £1000)

	1980	1979	1978	1977	1976	1975	1974
Assets							
Cash	18,900	24,800	86,700	59,949	86,167	61,091	78,427
Securities	—	—	—	—	—	—	16,661
Inventories	946,000	1,040,700	1,024,000	988,113	800,637	531,161	512,286
Receivables	433,600	447,600	397,000	356,289	311,406	254,276	191,855
Total current	1,398,500	1,513,100	1,508,600	1,404,351	1,198,210	846,528	799,229
Fixed assets (net)	768,900	655,700	517,600	383,326	310,924	257,464	239,907
Tools, dies, jigs	92,700	61,600	42,300	27,959	34,844	47,501	45,773
Investments	13,000	12,600	16,600	13,609	15,436	10,900	10,712
Total	2,273,100	2,243,000	2,094,100	1,829,245	1,559,414	1,162,393	1,095,621
Liabilities							
Creditors	758,000	733,600	691,400	647,071	518,448	450,357	478,931
Bills payable	224,500	86,900	97,700	162,232	196,165	143,042	42,791
Taxes	6,700	6,800	9,700	9,772	15,663	7,283	43,345
Bank loans	323,000	270,300	238,400	387,687	316,215	309,413	130,300
Total current	1,312,200	1,097,600	1,037,200	1,206,762	1,046,491	910,095	695,367
Capital stock	1,178,100	728,100	587,700	129,637	129,637	29,635	29,635
Reserves	(530,500)	9,600	155,600	198,039	247,488	108,481	118,701
Converted debt	26,700	26,700	26,700	26,749	26,749	26,749	26,767
Minority interest	32,100	24,300	22,100	21,593	8,739	6,422	11,224
Loan capital	203,300	355,400	263,000	240,635	90,720	77,899	73,248
Financial lease liabilities	51,200	—	—	—	—	—	—
Deferred exchange	—	—	—	3,258	4,599	2,132	6,374
Deferred tax	—	1,300	1,800	2,572	4,991	980	22,428
Total	2,273,100	2,243,000	2,094,100	1,829,245	1,559,414	1,162,393	1,095,621

Leyland Group has 30 percent to 40 percent excess capacity. By comparison, the loss of the car and parts units narrowed to $303 million from $510 million. These numbers helped push BL into its biggest ever first-half pretax loss—$370.4 million on sales of $2.7 billion.

• Jaguar sales to the United States increased over the previous year every month in 1981, with total 1981 unit sales of 4,695. Officials are predicting 1982 sales will break Jaguar's previous U.S. record of 7,384 set in 1976. The United States is now Jaguar's number-one world market.[31] (See Exhibit 5.)

• MG production ceased at the end of 1980, and the last Triumph was built in October of 1981, leaving Jaguar as the only luxury/sports car remaining for BL.

• BL blames the postponement from 1981 to 1983 of its break-even point on the side effects of the government's policies, particularly the high exchange rate.[32]

• In October, workers demanded an 11.5 percent annual pay increase. Edwardes countered with an offer of only 3.8 percent, and finally forced the workers to accept it. However, the British custom of daily "tea breaks" is now threatening the company's future. The unions had earlier agreed to reduce daily tea and rest breaks from 51 to 40 minutes in exchange for a cutback in the work week from 40 to 39 hours. But 2,200 workers, angry over their defeat on wages, decided to walk out. The strike halted production of 1,200 cars a day.[33]

[31] Jaguar News Release, February 5, 1982.
[32] *The Economist*, November 8, 1980, p. 60.
[33] "Those BL Blues," *Time*, December 8, 1981, p. 60.

EXHIBIT 5
The new Jaguar—1981.

PART SEVEN

MANAGING DIVERSIFICATION: EXPANSION, ACQUISITIONS, AND MERGERS

CHAPTER 10

The Strategy and Management of Expansion, Acquisitions, and Mergers

GROWTH THROUGH EXPANSION

Survival in a complex industrial society requires a business enterprise to have average annual growth in real terms at least equal to the growth in gross national product. While some positive growth would be indicated below this criterion, it would signal that the firm was not keeping pace with the national economy and may be approaching the decline stage.

How long a business will survive under these conditions is a function of its size and resources. The predetermined economic objectives of profitability, growth, and survival will serve as the guidelines in determining the firm's growth and expansion strategy. The skills and resources of the company, the characteristics of its products, its product-market scope, and the nature of its competitive environment are factors which may be favorable or detrimental to growth and expansion. Management's ability to assess these variables accurately is the major determining factor in the successful expansion of the enterprise.

Growth through expansion relies on the extension of the firm's product lines and the enlargement of its product-market scope. The average successful company that survives will gradually evolve into an organization with a family of related products which provided the impetus for growth and expansion. These changes are likely to result from R&D efforts for new product developments and changes and product adaptations and improvements to meet shifts in demand. These natural changes in the dimensions of the company may be gradual, routine, and unspectacular, and accomplished without significant strategic changes. All products, however, become commodity items, reach a stage of obsolescence, and if unchanged move the company toward the decline stage.

In the reformulation phase, the policymakers are constantly confronted with the nagging problem of growth: how to sustain a favorable growth rate, how to reformulate to attain a former favorable growth rate, or how to manage growth which has caused the company to lose control and profitability. We frequently hear the term "growth company" applied to firms that are current market favorites in a variety of industries, particularly in the pharmaceutical, electronic, office copier, and computer fields. Conversely, the term "no growth" has been applied from time to time to railroads, steel companies, and coal producers (until the recent energy crisis). A number of other prominent companies have been classified in the latter category because their products or services have been superseded by innovations or newly developed products or services which compete more favorably in the marketplace. Not all companies that have at one time or another been placed in the growth category have been able to sustain or manage their growth and expansion successfully, and many companies which were classified "no growth" have successfully diversified or relieved their reliance on products or services which were in decline.

Strategic Design and Potential Size

The strategic design of the enterprise is a major determinant of its potential size. If a company chooses to direct its efforts to a particular segment of the market rather than seek to span several or all phases of a specific market, it has effectively placed a limit on its size and growth. We can cite the case of Volkswagen, with its concept of a single car design for the lower end of the automobile market, as contrasted to General Motors, which covered all segments of the automotive market. VW's growth was limited to the growth in its market segment and its ability to expand its market share of this segment. General Motors, on the other hand, could increase its market share in all segments; its potential growth was limited only by the growth of the automobile industry. Ford Motor Company experienced the same market limitations after its first phase of development, during which it enjoyed spectacular and profitable growth. As previously described, Ford, a pioneer in the industry, struck on the concept of the all-purpose, high-quality, low-priced one-model car which suited the times and needs of the nation. Once the need for basic automotive transportation had been satisfied, however, Ford was faced with a decline in growth and a loss of position. After several reformulations, the company produced and marketed a number of models in various segments of the automotive market. This is essentially the same process of reformulation that VW has gone through in the past several years. The company phased out its famous Beetle and now offers a substantially expanded product line which spans several segments of the automobile market.[1]

[1]See Chapter 2, and the Volkswagen case in Part Six.

Size and Growth—Too Small

Size is always of major concern to the policymaker. The lack of production capacity and market strength can seriously restrict growth. The automobile industry can be referred to again for an example of size that restricts strategy. American Motors has been constantly plagued by its relatively small size in the automotive industry despite the fact that the company represents a merger between two former car producers, Nash and Hudson. American Motors has never gained the size in the industry to compete effectively and consistently against General Motors, Ford, and Chrysler. The company's product line and dealer organization has not been extensive enough to provide sustained profitable growth and allow the accumulation of capital necessary for expansion.[2]

Some established industries, because of their development patterns and degree of concentration, may permit easy entry for companies in certain industry segments but restrict growth beyond a certain size. The petroleum, brewing, automobile, and steel industries exhibit these characteristics. In the case of petroleum, the large, integrated producers which have sufficient crude oil to supply a substantial portion of their refinery and marketing needs are the key factors in the industry. The so-called independents in the industry range from relatively small marketing organizations to semi-integrated producers which have production, transportation, refinery, and marketing operations but lack sufficient crude oil supply of their own to assure the maintenance of market position or sustained growth. Clark Oil Company illustrates a case of an independent in this category. It began as a one-pump service station in 1932.

Clark performed only the marketing function in the early stages of its development, procuring its gasoline supply from major refiners. The company developed a network of service stations in the north central region of the country through franchised dealers using the Clark name and a smaller number of company-owned and operated facilities. Clark experienced rapid and profitable growth which enabled it to build refineries and a transportation system. Management realized, however, that its growth was limited by its lack of crude oil supply. A decision was made to explore for crude in 1957, but the company's initial attempts were unsuccessful. Clark has continued through the years to seek an adequate supply of crude oil of its own but did not have much success because of its late entry and the large capital outlays necessary for exploration and drilling. The financial risks involved in the search for crude oil on a worldwide basis are difficult if not impossible for any but the largest integrated producers which already have a substantial degree of crude oil sufficiency. Clark's need to rely on other producers for its basic raw material of crude oil is a major factor deterring its future growth and development, despite the fact that its management expertise has nurtured the company from a one-pump station to the largest independent petroleum company in the midwest.[3]

Brewing offers another example of a highly concentrated industry in which

[2] See Chapter 7.
[3] See the Clark Oil Company case in Part Six.

the lack of size can be a factor restricting growth and development. A small number of national brewers have the dominant market share, and a diminishing number of regional and local brewers make up the industry. The national brewers benefit from their large markets, which enable them to advertise nationally on radio and television and ensure long production runs at their strategically located plants serving specific areas of the country. The large sales volumes of the nationals enables them to reduce their costs of production, advertising, and promotion on a unit basis far below the costs of local or regional breweries. The small-size brewery which serves a limited market must seek expansion by market penetration (and head-on confrontation with the nationals) or through geographic expansion of its market without the production and marketing advantages of the nationals, which are entrenched in any regional area the small firm may enter. Many successful local or regional brewers have tried both options or a combination of the two to effect growth. Some have had a limited measure of success and others have failed as a result of the effort.

Coors provides an example of a strong and successful regional brewery which enjoyed growth and expansion through market penetration and limited geographic expansion. The company's root strategy dictated the brewing of a nonpasteurized beer at a single plant location in Golden, Colorado. The company claimed the water at this location was a major factor in the taste of its beer. The one-plant location and the limited shipping radius imposed by its non-pasteurized beer, which needed constant refrigeration, restricted Coor's entry in all national markets. As a result the company successfully gained impressive market shares in western and southwestern states.

The large national brewers initiated heavy advertising and price-cutting campaigns to regain market share lost to Coors. To prevent this encroachment and to seek greater market share, Coors started their own marketing campaigns in 1978. Despite their $145 million expenditure, only slight gains were made in overall market share, and net income dropped 70 percent on a 2 percent increase in volume in 1980 and continued to drop in 1981.

Coors lost significant share in California, the largest beer-drinking state, dropping from 35.8 percent to 22.5 percent of the market.

The company sells in 20 western and southern states. To gain any national distribution or significant increase in market share it will have to invade the midwest and the east coast, which accounts for two-thirds of all the beer sold in the United States. This move will mean abandoning their single brewery, striking out from their regional stronghold, and entering the price-cutting, highly competitive national markets, where the largest brewers are firmly entrenched.[4]

Size and Growth—Too Large

Size can be a restriction to growth in either of two ways: (1) if a company gets too large to be manageable or (2) if it is too small to compete and develop effec-

[4] *Wall Street Journal,* July 10, 1981.

tively in certain industries. There are practical limitations to growth which all expanding firms experience in the course of time. If the growth favorites of the stock market (such as IBM, Xerox, Avon, and a number of others) continued the spectacular compounded growth rate of their early stages of development, they would now exceed the gross national product. The question of when a company is too big to be effective or manageable is difficult to answer. When diminishing returns are reached in the production phase, it is evident that the advantage of size has run its course. Most companies of large size, however, are multiplant, multiproduct organizations, and their constraints on growth are reached because the size of the firm makes it unmanageable. Many analysts have questioned the management effectiveness of General Motors, General Electric, Exxon, U.S. Steel, and a number of other industrial giants because of their size. They have claimed that a breakup of these organizations into several separate economic units would provide for more effective management and more efficient operations. The recent court decision which resulted in a proposed divorce of AT&T from its operating telephone companies may provide a test of this hypothesis.

The question of how big is too big is not easily answered. There is evidence to indicate that some of the largest companies in U.S. industry are among the best managed. Whether they would be better managed if they were broken up into smaller economic units is still a controversial issue. The effective operation of large companies depends primarily on their ability to develop organizational and control strategies designed to keep pace with their growth. There is no question that bigness creates complex organizations and significantly complicates the management task. The problems of the auto and steel industry have been attributed by some analysts to the size of the leading producers and the fact that there were few competitors in industries dominated by the largest producer.

General Motors' highly decentralized organization was unmanageable and out of control under Will Durant. The development of a decentralized divisional organization of profit centers by Alfred Sloan enabled the company to prosper and develop into one of the world's largest business enterprises.[5]

Significant organizational changes were made by General Electric to keep pace with the company's rapid growth and expansion in the post-World War II period. A decentralized organizational strategy was put into effect in the company in 1951, after several years of study and preparation. This concept divided the organization in terms of products, geography, and functional assignments. Approximately 100 decentralized operating departments grouped under 21 operating divisions were established as independent profit centers. The continued growth of GE forced the company to seek a refinement of this organizational concept to cope with its expansion into 170 departments and 50 divisions. In 1972 the company established 43 strategic business units made up of related businesses for the purpose of strategic planning. Each SBU operated

---

[5] See Chapter 2.

as an independent business with a manager who had responsibility, accountability, and authority for the performance and profitability of the unit. The SBUs reduced the complex task of resource allocation from 170 or more departments to 43 clearly identified business units.[6]

Procter and Gamble offers another example of a large growth company which developed an organizational strategy to cope with its rapid expansion. P&G initiated the concept of brand management to effectively manage its expanding line of soaps, detergents, and cleansing agents. Each brand manager is responsible for the coordination of market planning, market research, sales, sales promotion, packaging and design, advertising, and manufacturing with a specific branded product or family of products. This strategic concept of brand management gave the company competitive advantages and provided the organizational flexibility needed to attain its economic objectives of growth and expansion.[7]

Most companies have grown by expanding their core business through market penetration, market development, and product-line expansion. The highly publicized growth companies such as IBM, Xerox, and Polaroid and the ones with a longer history of stable growth such as General Motors and Eastman Kodak have all developed and expanded on the basis of a single product or technology or a group of related products which reflected their basic technical skills and resources and were directed toward a common market area. General Electric's growth has also been internally generated, its broad scope of business being based primarily on its core business of products related to electricity, although the company is highly diversified and also produces jet engines and nuclear power plants.

The single-purpose business has many advantages in terms of defining distinct and clear-cut objectives, developing organizational relationships, and maintaining effective communications and control measures. Multipurpose businesses introduce complexities; their strategic design is frequently clouded and lacks the clarity that the design of a single-purpose firm has. The communications networks of multipurpose businesses are complicated and widespread, their organizational structures have more layers of management, and they find it more difficult to measure and appraise the results of their enterprise. There is no doubt that it is less difficult to attain success in a single-product, one-technology, one-market business than in complex, diverse, multifaceted businesses.

THE LIFE CYCLE OF THE FIRM AS A FACTOR IN GROWTH, EXPANSIONS, ACQUISITIONS, AND MERGERS

Anchor Stage

The life cycle of the firm described in Chapter 3 is a dominant factor in determining the pattern of growth and expansion and the nature and extent of

---

[6] See Chapter 6.
[7] See Chapter 6.

acquisitions and mergers. In the anchor stage, in the early period of growth, the company is likely to be preoccupied with establishing its identity and image as a viable part of a new or on-going industry. The cash flow of the enterprise will be directed toward financing the concept, "new or better" product, or technological breakthrough the firm has introduced to the marketplace. Management's concern is concentrated on guiding the new enterprise through the initial risk stage, establishing market position, and conserving and effectively using a minimum amount of working capital. Except for unusual "marriages" of compatible organizations that will mutually benefit from combining in the anchor stage, most companies in this phase will grow and expand by utilizing their own resources. Expansion will take place through market growth and possibly horizontally to enlarge product-market scope; acquisitions and merger are not likely to occur.

Entrenchment Stage

When a company enters the entrenchment stage, it has firmly anchored a place in the industrial complex and is seeking to enhance its position to assure profitable growth and expansion. At this phase a firm may seek to entrench itself as a market leader on a broad front, or within a specific market segment. If market leadership is pursued, the company, depending on its product, will have to make large investments to reinforce the investment started in the anchor stage. Significant capital investment may position the firm as a low-cost producer and a market leader. However, it could also result in capital intensity in specialized assets.

In a growing industry the firm will seek to establish a critical mass in the shortest time possible; as indicated in the PIMS data, a primary objective should be the establishment of market share as the forerunner of profitable performance. Most successful businesses establish an identity, a presence, in an industry with a single product in their initial development stages and with a family of related products as they expand their market position. Internal expansion is likely to prevail in the early period of the entrenchment phase. If the company is committed to technological development in a specific area, its product development will come from "within." Such successful companies as IBM, Xerox, Kodak, and Polaroid followed this pattern. When companies in the entrenchment stage enlarge their product-market scope, they are faced with decisions about continuing internal growth or seeking compatible acquisitions, or some combination of these two thrusts. This usually does not occur until the later stages of the entrenchment phase.

If the industry environment is volatile, and exhibits rapid change as well as rapid growth, the entrenched companies probably will rely heavily on their own resources for product expansion. This has been true of the electronics and pharmaceutical industries, which are fluid in nature and subject to frequent technological breakthroughs and new discoveries. Companies in these industries must rely on their R&D capabilities to keep pace with competitors and to assure continued growth and expansion.

Texas Instruments utilized its technological advances in chips to venture into consumer products such as handheld calculators and digital watches. This move forced significant expansion but did not deter the company's R&D efforts. IBM continued its growth and expansion by developing successive stages of advanced computer generations. It also fostered expansion and growth by extending its expertise into other product lines such as the electric typewriters, office copiers, and the most recent extension into robots.

When new products are introduced as a part of the firm's product-market scope, or related to a planned family of products, the firm may be confronted with establishing a position in a new industry, or developing a position in an on-going industry not associated with their core products. In long-lived industries with basic products such as steel, aluminum, copper, and other metals, growth and expansion in the entrenchment stage was accomplished to a great extent through vertical integration. Large companies in these industries sought control of their raw material supply and may have also integrated forward to market finished products. The oil industry and the steel, aluminum, and other basic product producers also expanded into transportation and other peripheral support systems. This type of expansion required significant investment and a different management perspective; however, it did not entail a need to build a position in an industry.

In the latter part of the entrenchment stage diversification and acquisitions may accelerate. It is in this phase that the firm will seek to make strategic changes to sustain growth and to prevent slipping into the defensive stage. This may call for a minor or drastic realignment of the company's product-market scope. As indicated in the previous examples of the growth in the fluid industries, and the basic industries, expansion can be attained through horizontal expansion or vertical integration, by building on a family of related products or developing necessary support businesses for core products.

Diversification will usually occur when the firm no longer considers that their expansion through their existing product-market scope will sustain their growth objectives. The company may also be prompted by a concern about approaching obsolescence or maturing products.

Defensive Stage

When a company enters into the defensive phase, it is concerned with protecting an entrenched market position to prevent encroachment by imitators, price cutters, and new product lines which purport to offer a better quality and service. Growth at this stage has slowed or the market has stabilized with no appreciable growth. As pointed out in Chapter 3, most companies, when they lose market share and experience declining sales and profits, devise defensive strategies. These strategies may prompt a redesign of the existing product lines, cosmetic improvements to the products, or an overhaul of distribution channels. Efforts are made to improve product quality or "outservice" competition, and some seek to expand their served market to attract a broader segment of consumers. Product modifications usually produce only "blips" or "ripples" in the firm's life cycle.

The successful firm that survives seeks new product lines and investment opportunities particularly in the later phases of the entrenchment stage and the early part of the defensive state. A well-defined strategic design will dictate any diversification plan by authorizing product areas or acquisitions compatible with the firm's skills and resources. Expansion through diversification may or may not entail acquisitions. In the later part of the defensive stage acquisitions are likely to accelerate because companies have exhausted their expertise in seeking a change in their strategic thrust through internal development efforts. The "rush" to utilize the cash flow from declining products through acceptable acquisitions is prompted in a large part by the fear of slipping into a decline phase.

Many companies overextend their capabilities in their acquisition efforts in the defensive stage. Control is often lost through extensive acquisition efforts. Firms are slow to adapt to the required restructuring of their organizations and the management of decentralized units. Lack of fit and compatibility of the parent company's skills and resources with those of the acquired companies or with product lines frequently leads to serious operating problems. The failure to acquire a critical mass that will provide a strong market position and profitable returns is also a common failing of many acquisitions at this stage.

In this phase of the firm's life cycle the acquisition pattern may completely reorient its strategic thrust and change the corporate form. This is the point where many companies change from an operating unit within an industry to a multiproduct multi-industry organization. With many diverse acquisitions, some firms have developed into conglomerates or holding companies.

Decline Stage

As previously stated, diversification is started in the later part of the defensive stage and intensifies in the early part of the decline phase. Most diversification efforts in the decline stage are hampered by falling profits, reduced cash flow, and limited acquisition options. Firms facing the severe problems of the latter decline stage are not likely to seek acquisitions or be in a position to diversify. Their efforts will be directed toward retrenchment; through segment retreat companies phase out of markets or try to revert into a market segment where they think they can compete, or they close plants, decrease labor and personnel, and significantly reduce their sales and presence in an industry.

When acquisitions are made in this phase of the company's life cycle, they will probably be weak and add to the problems of the firm rather than provide an avenue of relief. A more likely move by companies in this stage of decline is to seek a merger with another ailing firm.

Companies in the decline stage with a good cash position can make more selective acquisitions. Most firms in this position are in basic capital-intensive industries. Their diversification efforts usually indicate a retreat from the core business, which is declining because of competitive threats, domestic and foreign, and changes in the industry structure. Technological deficiencies which seem too great to overcome are also a factor in the decision of capital-intensive companies to seek diversification. The acquisitions of Marathon Oil by U.S. Steel and the numerous acquisitions made by Republic Steel and other similar firms provide examples of this kind of diversification strategy.

DIVERSIFICATION THROUGH ACQUISITIONS AND MERGERS

The Growth Objective

Despite the evidence, which indicates that the most successful cases of profitable growth and expansion have been based on a core business of a single product line or a family of related product lines, there is significant pressure on most policymakers to seek diversification. Management may reach the judgment that its basic core business is no longer capable of providing profitable growth and expansion and that the maintenance of economic objectives in terms of a high k factor is no longer possible without diversification. This fundamental economic objective and the desire to provide a change in the product-market scope of the enterprise have been the major reasons for the initiation of diversification programs in most businesses.

The formulation of a strategy for diversification must begin with an examination of the firm's basic objectives, skills, and resources and an appraisal of its strategic design. The movement into diversification usually necessitates a change in the company's root strategy and a complete recycling of the policymaking process. Prior to initiating an expansion program based on diversification, management must commit the firm to the growth objective specifying desired size, structure, and strategic design. This thorough reformulation process and appraisal is an essential preliminary step, since diversification is a risky venture representing strategic change for the firm and a significant departure from its traditional product lines and its form and structure of business. While there are some notable exceptions in industry—such as 3M, GE, IBM, Xerox, and others—which have R&D capability and strong staff support to develop products for diversification, most firms seek diversification through acquisitions and mergers.

In seeking diversification the firm must try to project its desired identity as a viable competitor in the marketplace of the future. The following questions should serve as the basis for analytical probing of diversification.

What are our strengths and weaknesses? Our skills and resources?

Do they position our firm for projected changes in technology, knowledge, demographics, world competition, new market dimensions?

What are our unique skills?

What do we do well that will afford the firm a competitive advantage?

Will we have the right concepts and products for the future?

Will the proposed expansion project the firm into the future or leave it in the past?

Will proposed new products or businesses be compatible with our skills and resources?

Will the proposed expansion require new technology, new skills and resources, and/or significant organizational changes?

Expansion by Vertical Integration

Acquisitions and mergers may be prompted by more than just the expansion objective. A firm may consider vertical integration a necessary step to ensure a viable competitive position. The integrated petroleum companies have made acquisitions through the years to give them "balance" in relation to production, transportation, refining, and marketing. Many of the semi-integrated companies in the industry are still seeking acquisitions or mergers to accomplish vertical integration. The large integrated steel companies have reached back to secure their supply of iron ore and other necessary raw materials utilized in steel production. They have also expanded into transportation for internal use and a number of other areas related to steel production and marketing. This type of acquisition is in effect "natural" and to an extent defensive. There are many other examples of vertical integration, such as large shoe manufacturers expanding into retail outlets, automobile producers acquiring parts manufacturers, and supermarket chains acquiring food-producing units. Regardless of how effective backward or forward vertical integration may be, it still complicates the management task and requires organizational adjustments to provide the necessary control. Unless management can reasonably make a case for vertical integration as a necessary economic decision to protect its core business, it must be viewed and evaluated like any other investment alternative and related to the firm's k factor.

Expansion by Horizontal Acquisitions and Mergers

Horizontal acquisitions and mergers are the most common in industry. They represent a product-line extension which in the opinion of management can be better effected through acquisition or merger than by internal expansion. Horizontal acquisitions and mergers usually represent market extensions within the same industry rather than product extension into other industries or efforts to support existing technologies. The acquisition and merger wave of the 1960s resulted in a large number of horizontal acquisitions and mergers. We find examples in textbook publishing, where companies established in the elementary and high school field acquired publishers in the college field to extend their product line and to defend themselves from the expected decline in elementary and high school enrollments. There were also a number of mergers of smaller textbook publishers who sought to combine to seek the "right size" to effectively compete in the industry. Large food producers such as Consolidated Foods, Beatrice Foods, and Pillsbury acquired a number of producers of varied food products to extend their product lines and take advantage of marketing synergies.

Diversification as a Seasonal or Cyclical Balancing Factor

In explaining diversification, the early economics textbooks almost invariably used the example of the local coal company which sold coal in the winter, as a home heating fuel, and diversified by selling ice in the summertime to supply the necessary refrigerant for the home icebox. The simple example aptly illustrates one of the basic reasons for the diversification of many businesses—to escape the reliance on one product which was sold on a seasonal basis. We find many current examples of this type of diversification—for example, that of a prominent producer of ski equipment who diversified into the manufacture and sale of tennis racquets to bridge the gap over the seasons. While there were differences in the manufacturing processes, the ski company was able to utilize most of its marketing concepts and channels of distribution for the newly added product. A producer of golf carts recently diversified into snowmobiles but found little synergy in marketing and distribution of these products, although they provided seasonal fits.

There are numerous examples of one-product-line seasonal businesses which found or developed good fits through diversification, thus enabling them to avoid or alleviate the problems of seasonality. There are, of course, many other examples of firms which, confronted with seasonal cycles, entered into businesses which bridged the seasonal gap but did not fit the skills and resources of the company and proved to be a drain rather than providing a source of profitable growth. We find recent evidence of diversification in the toy industry which produced these results. Several prominent firms sought to "diversify out" of almost total reliance on the Christmas buying season, but they lacked the resources and managerial know-how to cope with the unfamiliar new businesses which were acquired to accomplish this purpose.

Defense against Cyclical Declines

Diversification through acquisition and mergers has frequently been effected to provide the firm with a defense against cyclical declines in its core business or industry. A commonly cited example for textbook purposes is that of capital goods producers diversifying into consumer goods markets. As previously discussed, most producers of capital goods are rendered somewhat inflexible because of their degree of specialization and heavy investment in fixed assets. General Electric, however, is an example of a producer of capital goods in many areas of the electrical field and also of home appliances for the consumer goods market. Companies in the building products field have made many contracyclical acquisitions in attempts to offset the pronounced cyclical swings in the building industry.

Although there is evidence of relatively successful contracyclical diversification acquisitions and mergers, for the most part they are difficult for management to accomplish. In addition to the general lack of flexibility of the companies most affected by cyclical swings, there is the problem of attaining a "critical mass"—sufficient market penetration—in a contracyclical industry to assure successful operation. Many attempts at diversification to alleviate cyclical swings resulted in the acquisition or merger of small units which did not provide the thrust needed to acquire a viable market share. Management of the acquiring firms, in such cases, generally represented large producers steeped in specialized businesses—producers who did not have a knowledge of the "art of the business" of the newly acquired companies and who were preoccupied with the task of running their major traditional operations.

Pressure for, and Deterrents to, Diversification

A common pressure or incentive for diversification through acquisition is an embarrassing accumulation of cash. If management does not find investment opportunities in its core business because of market saturation, lack of adequate return on investment, or fear of antitrust action if greater market share is attained, there will be pressure to seek diversification. This is particularly true if the core business generates a significant cash flow. There is a tendency on the part of many management groups to make opportunistic acquisitions if cash is readily available. The railroads offer a prime example of this set of preconditions for acquisitions or mergers. The rate of return for most railroads has been low or actually nonexistent. Because of large investments in rolling stock and other fixed assets, however, railroads have generated significant cash flow through the years due to depreciation charges against revenues. This capital, plus tax credits for possible earnings shelters, has been utilized to diversify into conglomerate types of investments. For example, the management of North Western Railroad formed Northwest Industries as a separate entity holding the stock of the railroad and then diversified through acquisition. The newly formed company acquired a number of independent producers of wearing apparel and footwear, automotive and industrial batteries, steel pipe and fluorescent lamp ballasts, and chemical products for agriculture and industry. Northwest Industries went further afield by becoming the exclusive importer and selling agent of Cutty Sark brand Scotch whiskey and wines of Baron Phillipe de Rothschild, S.A. Northwest Industries eventually sold the railroad to an employee group.

The Illinois Central Railroad followed the same conglomerate pattern. The railroad management organized IC Industries as a separate corporate entity to hold the railroad stock and proceeded to make acquisitions. The new firm used its common, preferred stock and cash to acquire Pepsi-Cola General Bottlers; Dad's Root Beer and Bubble-Up; Midas-International, a producer of mufflers; plus producers of equipment for trucks, buses, and railroad cars. In addition, IC Industries developed real estate in Chicago's downtown lakefront areas. The holding company has been seeking to sell its railroad properties. The Penn Central Railroad, at a much earlier date, followed a pattern somewhat similar to that of Northwest and IC. The company's wide diversification moves were a major factor in developing the severe cash crisis which led the holding company into bankruptcy proceedings.

It is interesting to note that the railroads described above found their way out of a "stagnant industry" through the conglomerate process. Railroads, steel companies, coal producers, and others have frequently been placed in the no-growth, stagnant, or declining industry category. We find continued references in the business literature to a need not only for reformulation under these conditions but also an admonition to get out of these businesses and reinvest in more profitable enterprises. Their declining position has often been derisively compared to the growth of glamour companies in the field of electronics, pharmaceuticals, computers, and office copiers. The difficulty or in some cases the impossibility of orderly industry change or rapid diversification for many of the lumbering giants in the so-called stagnant industries is frequently overlooked. Companies with billions of dollars invested in steelmaking, which have predicated their past success on knowing the "art of steel business" and whose executive group "thinks steel," cannot readily shift their skills and resources to electronics or other glamour industries without potentially painful or disastrous results.

The railroads are in a similar position, without resorting to the conglomerate option. To change their root strategy to that of a transportation company covering all facets of the field provides material for a lively discussion of the marketing concept but ignores the implications of the antitrust laws and the virtual impossibility of an orderly conversion of specialized assets. Recycling of the policymaking process in these industries has been for the most part forced into the implementation phase, dictating the need for changes in operating strategy rather than drastic action involving abrupt shifts of resources into new businesses. This is illustrated by the recent history of the coal industry, long considered a declining business, which was revitalized before the energy crisis by improving operating efficiency through mechanization and the use of new mining techniques.

Diversification and High Internal Cost of Capital

Diversification can be a problem for firms with a high k factor and good growth rates as well as for companies which have low rates of return and no growth. Diversification becomes a problem for such companies because finding business opportunities to match or exceed their internal cost of capital is very difficult. IBM has enjoyed a high k factor for a sustained period of time and has approximately 70 percent of the computer market. IBM's management is confronted with maintaining its high k and sustaining its growth record. Because of the extent of its market penetration, it is not reasonable to expect continued growth through the increase in market share. The other alternative, of course, is to develop new products in other areas on an internal basis or to seek diversification through acquisitions and mergers. Diversification attempts present a problem in terms of obtaining a fit and matching IBM's skills and resources without violating antitrust laws and also in terms of matching or exceeding the high k factor which investors have come to expect from this market favorite. As a result, despite some recent attempts at diversification, IBM has placed a great deal of reliance on its R&D capability and technological excellence, attempting to maintain industry leadership by making its own products obsolete.

Xerox, with its strong grip on the office copier market, is in much the same position as IBM in terms of sustained growth and a high k factor, although the company does not have the number of products IBM has in the office equipment and supply field. Its spectacular growth has been based on a single product, the Xerox copying machine. Like IBM, the company is faced with the difficulty of finding matching products to continue its growth and maintain its high k factor. It is interesting to note that Xerox diversified into the computer field while IBM developed a copying machine to add to its office product line.

Defensive Mergers

The wave of acquisitions and mergers which was dominant in the 1960s created a number of "takeovers," many of which were vigorously fought by the management of companies targeted for acquisition. The threat of takeover was more likely for companies which had low price/earnings ratios. The relatively low prices of the stock of these companies in relation to their earnings was attractive to the aggressive expanding enterprises, particularly the conglomerates. These predicated their growth mainly on effecting financial synergy by trading their stock, which had high multiples of price to earnings, for the stock of companies with significantly lower price/earnings ratios. Many defensive strategies were developed by vulnerable companies to prevent unwanted takeovers. There were a number of "arranged" mergers between such companies which enabled the merging parties to select their own partners rather than be prey to a raid or takeover by an undesirable acquiring firm.

The Marcor case is a classic example of this defensive strategy. In 1968 Montgomery Ward, one of the nation's largest merchandising organizations and one which had been threatened by takeovers in the past, merged with Container Corporation of America, a leading firm in the packaging industry, which was also considered vulnerable to a takeover. The new enterprise, Marcor, Inc., represented two dissimilar operating companies with little evidence of synergy except for some distinct financial advantages in the form of tax deferrals, generated by Ward's credit sales, which could be utilized to offset earnings of Container Corporation. Ward experienced a decided drop in earnings in 1966, after several years of earnings growth. This slump depressed the company's stock price and made it an inviting prospect for a takeover. Container Corporation, despite a good earnings record, had a relatively low price/earnings ratio of 10. Management attributed this market rating to the fact that Wall Street incorrectly lumped the company into the paper industry, which was generally given a low multiple of stock price to earnings. In view of this situation, which had existed for some years, Container's management considered the company vulnerable to a takeover. Both firms saw advantages in a "friendly" merger which would avoid potential raids and allow them to retain their identity and continue individual operations with the same management under a holding-company organization. A Ward executive succinctly expressed one of the major purposes of this defensive merger in these terms: "We wanted to make a whale too big to get through the door."[8] The whale, however, wasn't big enough. Mobil Oil acquired Marcor in 1975.

Evaluating Expansion by Acquisitions and Mergers

Acquisitions and mergers may be described in a variety of ways and classified in a number of categories and subcategories other than vertical, horizontal, concentric, and conglomerate (which will be discussed in the latter part of this chapter). Our major interest is in the strategic implications for the policymaker in expansion by acquisition and merger. In addition to the strategic examples previously cited, there are several factors related to acquisitions and mergers which have been noted and analyzed in the literature for some time. In this context it has been stated that firms in the heavy industries (such as steel and other basic metals) and companies with large investments in virtual single-product lines (such as transportation, tires, oil, and other extractive industries) have not engaged in extensive diversification programs. It is to be noted, however, that in addition to the size of the leaders in these fields and their dominant market shares and investment requirements, there is also the problem in recent decades of a restraint on expansion because of potential violation of antitrust laws. Conversely, the study of acquisitions and mergers indicates that when an industry seems somewhat stagnant and internal growth risky, intraindustry merger is likely to take place. Compatible mergers in such instances may provide an increase in the economies of scale and an increase in market share for the combined unit without the fear of cutthroat competition. The nature of the industry is an important factor determining the likelihood of acquisitions and mergers. The mature industries, which are generally dominated by very large companies, are less likely to have intraindustry acquisitions and mergers. The new growing industries, which still lack dominant size in individual companies and are technologically oriented, are most likely to have intraindustry acquisitions and mergers.

Synergy and Fit

In approaching any acquisition or merger prospect, management, in addition to the important financial considerations, must determine if there is a "fit" between their firm and the company to be acquired. In measuring a fit there are a number of factors to be taken into consideration. The ideal acquisition or merger is based on compatibility between the companies involved. This has frequently been expressed in terms of synergy. *Synergy* in the initial stages of the usage of this term in relation to combinations was expressed as $2 + 2 = 5$,

---

[8] See the Marcor case in Part Seven.

with obvious reference to the fact that if you merged two firms with a fit, the new firm would be something greater than the sum of the two merging firms. *Synergy* in this case means that the combination of the skills and resources of two merging firms would provide for a potentially more effective enterprise with a product-market scope permitting greater market penetration and development. *Synergy* in this analysis is taken to mean a measure of the compatibility of the skills and resources of the combining companies, a measure of the degree of fit, and the potential effect of the companies' joint efforts after the acquisition or merger. As previously indicated, acquisitions and mergers involving product-line expansion have greater potential synergy than expansion by diversification.

Problems of Synergy and Fit

RCA with its numerous acquisitions encountered the common difficulties of diversification with its ventures into rental cars, financial services, publishing, broadcasting, home furnishings, some miscellaneous manufacturing, and the food business. These acquisitions did not fit with RCA's core businesses of TV receivers, broadcasting equipment, electronic components, and circuits. Banquet Foods, which RCA acquired in 1970 and disposed of a decade later, sets forth the difficulties of coping with the lack of synergy and fit. The acquisition cost RCA stock valued at more than $140 million. Banquet was a major poultry and frozen foods supplier and did not fit into RCA's core businesses, which relied on high technology, or the other major branch of TV broadcasting represented by the NBC network.

After 10 years of poor results and little growth, RCA sold Banquet to ConAgra for $45 to $55 million based on future profits of the acquired company. ConAgra, with a foothold in the chicken and food processing businesses, was able to utilize its knowledge of the agricultural business to provide improvements in production and marketing. The effects of this synergy raised Banquet's profits and market share, something RCA was not able to do after a decade of ownership.[9]

Procter and Gamble and Clorox—A Good Fit

The Procter and Gamble–Clorox acquisition effected in 1957 is an excellent example of a good fit or a synergistic acquisition. In analyzing this case, we can develop a framework for the evaluation of acquisitions and mergers. It is to be noted that despite the apparent success and duration of the merger, the Supreme Court in 1967 ordered the divestiture of Clorox and the return of the company to an independent status.

Procter and Gamble, the nation's largest manufacturer of soap, detergent, and cleansing products, acquired the assets of Clorox in exchange for stock

[9] *Fortune,* March 22, 1982, and the *Wall Street Journal,* Feb. 8, 1982.

having a market value of approximately $30.3 million. Clorox was the largest producer of household liquid bleach in the United States. Liquid bleach, like P&G's product lines, was a rapid-turnover household item sold mainly through grocery stores and supermarkets and presold through mass advertising and sales promotions. At the time of the merger, P&G had assets of $500 million and annual sales of $1.5 billion. More than half of P&G's sales ($514 million) were in the soap-detergent-cleanser field and $414 million were in packaged detergents, which accounted for 54.4 percent of this market. In addition, P&G was the largest advertiser in the United States, spending $80 million in advertising in 1957, the year of the merger, and $47 million on sales promotions.

Clorox had assets of $12 million and annual sales of approximately $40 million. The company had almost 50 percent of the liquid bleach market; and it spent $3.7 million on advertising, and $1.7 million on sales promotion in 1957. The company had no salespeople but sold through brokers and distributors. It is evident from the profiles of P&G and Clorox that there was an exceptional fit between the firms and that functional synergy was readily apparent. The joining of these two leaders in their closely allied product areas provides a classic example of the necessary prerequisites for the ideal merger. In the analysis of this merger the local starting point is the "make or buy" choice (to utilize this prevalent term in a slightly different way) which P&G's management had to make. The company calculated that their entry into the liquid bleach business through internal expansion would require a heavy investment to acquire a satisfactory market share. Procter and Gamble's management reasoned that taking over the Clorox business could be a way of achieving a dominant position in the liquid bleach market quickly, and one that would pay out reasonably well. The company promotion department's report predicted that P&G's sales, distributing, and manufacturing facilities and know-how could increase Clorox's market share in areas where it was low. It would also effect savings, thus increasing the profits of the business significantly. The merger provided exceptional marketing synergies. Procter and Gamble's packaged detergents and Clorox's liquid bleach were used complementarily; the consumer considered them to be closely related products. Both were low-unit-cost and high-turnover items which were sold to the same customers at the same stores. Clorox was also in a position to take advantage of P&G's well-developed and controlled national distribution system. Clorox had not developed its own distribution system but had used brokers and independent distributors. Product-line synergy was a major factor in advancing the merger. Procter and Gamble was not diversifying its interests by expanding into a substantially different, unfamiliar market or industry. Rather, it was entering an adjoining market identical to the markets in which it was already established and one which had much the same problems and opportunities and used the same methods and techniques of marketing the product to the ultimate consumer.

Clorox also fitted into P&G's long-standing policy of establishing brand preference in the markets it served. Clorox had established its liquid bleach as a premium brand despite the fact that all liquid bleaches were chemically identical. This brand identification was accomplished in much the same manner utilized by P&G for its products: intensive, long-continued mass advertising. The multiproduct brand-oriented P&G, with its huge advertising budget, was in a position to fit Clorox into its network television programs, which promoted several brands at a single showing. The large volume of P&G's television advertising gave the company significant discounts which Clorox could not achieve. There were also the advantages and savings to be accrued through joint advertising and sales promotions of P&G's detergent products, which complemented Clorox's liquid bleach.

Clorox's 13 plants scattered throughout the United States, which enabled the company to distribute its product nationally, also offered production synergies to tie in with P&G's national distribution system. Clorox could also fit into P&G's organizational strategy, which stressed brand management. Clorox's single product of liquid bleach could be managed and controlled by a brand manager in the same manner as the other branded items in P&G's product line.[10]

Conglomerate Acquisitions and Mergers

As previously indicated, the growth of most corporate enterprises has been internally generated through product development, product extension, and market penetration. The companies which have experienced the most profitable growth through internal expansion have had a single product line or a family of related products. Historically, mergers had not been a major factor in corporate expansion until the recent period of the 1960s. Most mergers prior to that involved vertical integration or horizontal expansion, generally within the same industrial category. Vertical integration was usually undertaken to ensure a viable competitive position to guarantee a source of raw material supply or a market for an end product. However, in most cases, vertical integration restricted a firm's expansion, increasing its dependence on its core business and thus reducing its flexibility, although it may have produced synergy through related technologies or markets. Horizontal mergers were usually product-line extensions within the same industry, which fitted the acquiring firm's skills and resources and broadened its product-market scope but also limited its flexibility.

The wave of acquisitions and mergers of the 1960s, in contrast, was dominated by the concentric firms and the conglomerate enterprises. These sought flexibility and did not restrict their acquisitions to companies with a single industry; instead, they expanded by crossing industry boundaries. There is a fine line between the highly diversified firms placed in the concentric category and the conglomerate enterprises. The distinction between these two forms of diversification strategy is usually expressed in terms of the degree of relatedness or fit that exists between the various units or subunits making up the

[10]See "The Clorox Case," Part Eight.

total enterprise. The concentric forms of diversification are predicated on extending the firm's skills and resources in technology, markets, or some combination of the two to effect synergistic expansion. The conglomerate form of diversification results in a combination of unrelated businesses which were acquired without regard to fit or synergy.

The relationships of technology, markets, and products in the concentric firm may be difficult to detect at times, despite management's talk of the degree of relatedness and synergy existing between the various companies and operations included in its multi-industry corporate entities. The search for unity has not been restricted to borderline concentric firms; it has also been actively pursued by companies classified as "pure conglomerates." The decline of the conglomerates in the eyes of the investors in the 1970s and the near disaster experienced by several market favorites, plus the serious question of how the large conglomerates can be effectively managed, have changed the conglomerate theme of $2 + 2 = 5$ to $2 + 2 = 3$. These factors have prompted highly diversified concentric companies and conglomerates to seek to avoid or discard the conglomerate label. Various corporate "unity themes" have been developed to mask the variety of acquisitions conglomerated under the ownership of a single corporate entity. We hear such terms as *high technology, marine systems, leisure industries, advanced materials systems,* and a host of others to describe companies engaged in such varied businesses as shipbuilding, movie production, chemicals, fertilizers, auto parts, electronic components, typewriters, food processing, and others too numerous to mention. These terms are intended to describe the root strategy of the "conceptually oriented conglomerate." The managements of some of the prominent conglomerates prefer to describe their enterprises as "free-form growth companies."

Advantages of the Conglomerate Form

Despite the fact that the companies which have shown the greatest profitable growth have produced a basic single-product line or a family of related products and it has been noted that diversification complicates the management task, a significant number of companies have adopted the conglomerate strategy. The period of the 1960s was characterized by an extensive wave of mergers dominated by the conglomerates, which achieved growth and size in a short time by diversifying into a multiplicity of different businesses. This movement reached its peak in 1968 and 1969, with 4,400 and 5,300 mergers taking place. It is interesting to note that when the mergers of this period tapered off, there was a wave of divestitures by many of the companies which were most active in the merger period. The purchasers were most often firms wishing to buy companies that were closely related to their own technologies and/or markets. Nevertheless, the conglomerate is an established form of enterprise in United States industry with its own concept of strategy.

It has often been stated that conglomerates defy conventional analysis because they lack a specific, identifiable root strategy. There is no question that the conglomerate enterprise has some advantages over conventional multiproduct or concentric firms. The most frequently mentioned advantages of the conglomerate are the following:[11]

1 The conglomerate has financial synergy. It usually has lower overall capital costs and can raise required funds on debt or equity at lower cost than the firms which make up the enterprise can on an individual basis. It also has better access to capital markets than would be possible for the conglomerate subsidiaries on an individual basis.

2 The conglomerate can gain the advantages of portfolio investment by balancing operating losses and gains of its subsidiaries to stabilize overall earnings. Portfolio investment should also be a stabilizing factor over time.

3 The conglomerate usually manages with a smaller headquarters staff, as contrasted to the large staffs of specialists usually associated with multiproduct and concentric organizations.

4 The number of diversified businesses in the conglomerate enterprise enable it to spread a skilled management headquarters team and a group of functional specialists over a much wider base than is possible for the average corporate enterprise.

Proving the Worth of the Conglomerate Form

Despite these advantages, the success of the conglomerate form is still a matter for discussion. The intense reaction to the rise and fall of the conglomerate in the 1960s has subsided, but it has placed the management of these multi-industry companies in the position of proving the worth of their organizations on the basis of growth in earnings from operations rather than from financial trading. Some of the major conglomerates, such as ITT and Textron, and others which have tended toward a more unifying theme of operation, such as Gulf and Western and Teledyne, have apparently made progress toward managing diversity. A number of others have not fared as well. The success of the conglomerates is still based upon their organizational and control strategies. Their basic unifying theme and root strategy is found in their economic objectives of profitability, growth, and survival. Strict financial controls and the ability to sever businesses which do not meet economic objectives still remain the key to success in any highly diversified organization.

In the future, the conglomerate is most likely to continue to move toward developing a more common thread—a stronger unifying theme—in its enterprise operations. The lack of apparent direction has no doubt contributed greatly to the diminished interest of investors in the conglomerate entity.

---

[11] I. Ansoff, *Corporate Strategy* (New York: McGraw-Hill, 1965); N. Berg, "What's Different About Conglomerate Management," *Harvard Business Review,* November–December, 1969; N. Jacoby, *The Conglomerate Corporation,* The Center for the Study of Democratic Institutions, a Center Magazine reprint, vol. 2, no. 4, July 1969.

SUMMARY AND GENERAL COMMENTS

In a complex industrial society a firm must show an average annual growth at least equal to the growth in gross national product. Growth through expansion relies on the extension of the firm's product lines and the enlargement of its product-market scope. The strategic design of the enterprise is a major determinant of its potential size. If a company chooses to direct its effort to a particular segment of the market rather than span several or all phases of a specific market, it effectively places a limit on its size and growth. Size is always of major concern to the policymaker. The lack of production capacity and market strength can seriously restrict growth. Industry structure can restrict the growth of smaller firms because of concentration and the dominance of the industry leaders.

Growth may also be restricted when a firm becomes too large to be manageable. When maturity is reached, growth becomes difficult. Many analysts have questioned the management effectiveness of the corporate giants. These firms are also subject to potential antitrust action which may be a factor in limiting their growth.

The life cycle of the firm is also a determinant of growth, expansion, acquisitions, and mergers. In the early stages of development, growth will most likely occur from internal expansion. Diversification and acquisitions at this phase are not likely to occur. Internal expansion will be a major factor in growth in the entrenchment stage. Diversification will occur in the later part of entrenchment. In the defensive stage companies usually diversify and may seek acquisitions as they seek to protect their entrenched positions. In this phase of the firm's life cycle, the diversification and acquisition pattern may completely reorient its strategic thrust and change the corporate form. In the early part of the decline stage, diversification and acquisition will intensify. In the latter part, diversification efforts will probably be impaired by falling profits, reduced cash flow, and limited acquisition prospects. A more likely move by companies in the later stages of decline is to seek a merger with another ailing firm.

When management judges that its basic core business is no longer capable of providing profitable growth and expansion, it will seek diversification. The movement into diversification usually necessitates a change in a company's root strategy and a complete recycling of the policymaking process. Vertical integration and horizontal acquisitions and mergers are methods of diversification and expansion utilized to implement strategic plans designed to bolster the company's market position. Diversification is also a measure employed to offset seasonal or cyclical swings.

Firms may be pressured into diversification through acquisitions because of an embarrassing accumulation of cash, a saturation of market opportunities in their core business, or a declining return in their basic businesses.

Diversification can be a problem for firms with a high k factor and good growth rates as well as for companies which have low rates of return and no growth. Firms with a high k factor have difficulty finding businesses to match or exceed their internal cost of capital.

Acquisitions and mergers are frequently the subject of corporate wars as the firm to be acquired resists an unfriendly takeover. This has led to corporate management seeking to be acquired by firms of their choice or attempting to find a compatible merger partner to fend off an unwanted suitor.

In approaching any acquisition or merger prospect, management, in addition to the important financial considerations, must determine if there is potential synergy and a fit between their firm and the company to be acquired or merged. The ideal combination is based on the compatibility between the companies involved.

The growth of most corporate enterprises have been internally generated through product development, product extension, and market penetration. However, significant acquisition and merger activity has occurred in recent decades. The acquisitions and mergers of the 1960s were made by concentric firms and conglomerate enterprises. The conglomerate form of diversification usually results in a combination of unrelated businesses which were acquired without regard to fit or synergy. There are some distinct advantages to the conglomerate form. However, the lack of synergy and fit usually leads to organization and control problems. With disappointing profit records, many conglomerates have sought to develop a common thread—a stronger unifying theme—in their operations.

SELECTED REFERENCES

K. Andrews: *The Concept of Corporate Strategy* (Homewood, Ill.: Irwin, 1980).

A. Chandler: *Strategy and Structure* (Cambridge, Mass.: M.I.T., 1962).

P. Drucker: *Management* (New York: Harper & Row, 1974).

————: *Management In Turbulent Times* (New York: Harper & Row, 1980).

P. Lorange and R. Vancil: *Strategic Planning Systems* (Englewood Cliffs, N.J.: Prentice-Hall, 1977).

E. Malmlow: "Corporate Strategic Planning In Practice," *Long Range Planning,* vol. 5, no. 3, 1972.

M. Porter: *Competitive Strategy* (New York: Free Press, a division of Macmillan, 1980).

R. Rumelt: *Strategy Structure and Economic Performance* (Boston: Graduate School of Business Administration, Harvard University, 1974).

CASES ON BUSINESS
POLICY FOR PART SEVEN

The cases in Part Seven clearly illustrate the strategic implications of growth and expansion for the policymaker seeking to improve the firm's competitive position and attain its predetermined economic objectives. The cases also provide the student with the opportunity to examine and analyze the significant effects of size on the competitive posture of companies in different industry settings. The effects of size on the organizational and control strategies of the firm are apparent in the cases.

The company situations also delineate the complex problems of developing a diversification strategy and the difficulties of managing complex organizations. The process of merger negotiations and the unification problems of the postmerger period are described in the Tandy and Marcor cases. Through the analysis of the data presented in these cases, students can determine the extent of degree of fit and synergy involved in the combinations.

Wilkinson Match[1]

In 1979 Wilkinson's profits were £19,002,000, up from £14,304,000 in 1978. The 1979 earnings were based on a turnover (sales) of £271,686,000, a 70 percent increase over the 1978 sales of £192,310,000, largely the result of the first full year's performance of True Temper Hardware, acquired in 1978. During 1979 Wilkinson's principal divisions had shown varying results. The large Consumer Products Division—which included matches and lighters, personal products, hardware and housewares, and writing instruments—posted a profit of £17,798,000. This was a substantial increase over 1978's £11,659,000. Hardware and housewares accounted for £7,220,000 and matches and lighters recorded £12,641,000 of the profit total, offsetting losses in writing instruments and in the company's long-standing mainstay, personal products.

Despite the varying divisional performance, the company felt that it had moved in a relatively short time from being the "David of the razor blade industry" to a Goliath in world markets. The 1979 net cash flow was a positive £2 million, and management had authorized £9 million in capital investment on new product development and in efforts to increase productivity and reduce costs (see Exhibits 1 to 6).

COMPANY HISTORY AND DEVELOPMENT

The Wilkinson Sword Company Limited traced its origins to Henry Nock, a gunsmith who established one of the largest gun and bayonet factories in the

---

[1] This case, revised from the 1977 version, was prepared from published sources by Mr. Albert W. Isenman under the direction of Professor Thomas J. McNichols as a basis for class discussion rather than to illustrate effective or ineffective handling of an administrative situation.

EXHIBIT 1
GROUP PROFIT AND LOSS ACCOUNT 1972–1979 (£ 000'S)

	1979	1978	1977	1976	1975	1974	1973	1972
Turnover	271,686	192,310	182,698	151,001	145,156	131,934	76,840	71,728
Operating profit	24,902	17,642	15,289	12,813	11,110	13,113	8,584	6,222
Interest	5,900	3,338	2,943	3,307	3,344	1,830	710	788
Profit before taxation	19,002	14,304	12,346	9,506	7,766	11,283	7,874	5,434
Taxation	7,839	6,065	6,318	4,781	3,567	5,058	3,109	2,126
Profit after taxation	11,163	8,239	6,028	4,725	4,197	6,225	4,765	3,308
Minority interests	1,264	1,539	1,448	1,008	916	935	785	421
Profit attributable to shareholders before extraordinary items	9,899	6,700	4,580	3,717	3,281	5,290	3,980	2,887
Extraordinary items	193	(739)	4	(1,618)	(3,605)	—	—	—
Attributable to shareholders	10,092	5,961	4,584	2,099	(324)	5,290	3,980	2,887
Preference dividends	63	63	63	63	63	63	90	90
Attributable to ordinary shareholders	10,029	5,898	4,521	2,036	(387)	5,227	3,890	2,797
Ordinary dividends	3,250	2,256	1,844	1,676	1,542	1,599	1,531	1,771
Retained profit	6,779	3,642	2,677	360	(1,929)	3,628	2,359	1,026
Earnings per ordinary share								
Basic	34.40p	29.65p	20.18p	16.33p	14.38p	23.4p	18.5p	13.7p
Fully diluted	31.40p	26.73p	18.83p	15.61p	13.98p	21.5p	—	—
Earnings per ordinary share on a fully deferred tax basis								
Basic	26.44p	22.85p	N/A	N/A	N/A	N/A	N/A	N/A
Fully diluted	24.51p	21.06p	N/A	N/A	N/A	N/A	N/A	N/A

Source: Wilkinson annual reports.

EXHIBIT 2
TURNOVER (IN £ 000'S)

By class of business

	1979		1978		1977		1976		1975	
Matches and lighters	75,143	27.7%	73,459	38.2%	71,520	39.1%	58,550	38.8%	56,905	39.2%
Personal products	45,067	16.6	46,261	24.0	41,154	22.5	33,698	22.3	27,199	18.7
Hardware and housewares	88,892	32.7	8,413	4.4	6,577	3.6	6,306	4.1	6,113	4.2
Writing instruments	12,907	4.7	15,033	7.8	15,613	8.6	12,342	8.2	7,384	5.1
Safety and protection	27,130	10.0	26,389	13.7	23,116	12.7	19,338	12.8	15,151	10.4
Packaging	20,889	7.7	20,668	10.8	20,833	11.4	14,901	9.9	15,881	10.9
Other	1,658	0.6	2,087	1.1	3,885	2.1	5,866	3.9	16,523	11.5
Total	271,686	100.0	192,310	100.0	182,698	100.0	151,001	100.0	145,156	100.0

By area

	1979		1978		1977		1976		1975	
United Kingdom	67,733	24.9%	66,831	34.8%	57,591	31.5%	45,217	29.9%	56,159	38.7%
Western hemisphere	126,201	46.5	50,855	26.4	55,720	30.5	46,795	31.0	42,195	29.1
Europe	27,078	10.0	26,402	13.7	23,494	12.9	21,699	14.4	15,171	10.4
Africa and Middle East	29,123	10.7	28,236	14.7	26,801	14.7	19,893	13.2	16,344	11.3
Pacific	21,551	7.9	19,986	10.7	19,092	10.4	17,397	11.5	15,287	10.5
Total	271,686	100.0	192,310	100.0	182,698	100.0	151,001	100.0	145,156	100.0

Source: Wilkinson annual reports.

713

EXHIBIT 3
OPERATING PROFIT (IN £000'S)

	1979		1978		1977		1976		1975	
By class of business										
Matches and lighters	12,641	50.8%	10,505	59.5%	7,533	49.3%	6,584	51.4%	5,093	45.8%
Personal products	(1,167)	(4.7)	735	4.2	3,562	23.3	3,296	25.7	3,286	29.6
Hardware and housewares	7,220	29.0	971	5.5	282	1.8	124	1.0	72	0.7
Writing instruments	(896)	(3.6)	(556)	(3.1)	(205)	(1.3)	(142)	(1.1)	(689)	(6.2)
Safety and protection	5,059	20.3	4,074	23.1	2,452	16.0	1,626	12.7	984	8.9
Packaging	1,740	7.0	1,740	9.9	1,600	10.5	1,160	9.0	2,269	20.4
Other	305	1.2	169	0.9	65	0.4	165	1.3	95	0.8
Total	24,902	100.0	17,642	100.0	15,289	100.0	12,813	100.0	11,110	100.0
By area										
United Kingdom	6,070	24.4%	9,120	51.7%	6,389	41.8%	4,882	38.1%	3,466	31.2%
Western hemisphere	6,240	25.0	525	3.0	1,416	9.3	1,618	12.6	1,559	14.0
Europe	3,449	13.9	1,582	9.0	2,578	17.1	2,188	16.9	1,918	17.3
Africa and Middle East	4,709	18.9	3,785	21.4	3,048	19.9	2,513	19.6	2,760	24.8
Pacific	4,434	17.8	2,630	14.9	1,858	12.1	1,612	12.6	1,407	12.7
Total	24,902	100.0	17,642	100.0	15,289	100.0	12,813	100.0	11,110	100.0

Source: Wilkinson annual reports.

EXHIBIT 4
Wilkinson Match Ltd.
Balance Sheets
1975–1979
(£000's)

	1979	1978	1977	1976	1975
Assets employed					
Stocks	—	—	—	—	—
Debtors	1,405	1,578	2,207	2,855	4,007
Short-term deposits and bank balances	646	565	54	1,665	1
Current assets	2,051	2,143	2,261	4,520	4,008
Bank loans and overdrafts	500	500	—	—	7
Creditors	2,725	3,047	2,198	1,829	1,682
Taxation	—	—	—	—	—
Dividends	3,250	2,239	1,844	1,676	1,542
Current liabilities	6,475	5,786	4,042	3,505	3,231
Net current assets	(4,424)	(3,643)	(1,781)	1,015	777
Investments	80	80	131	85	1,085
Interests in subsidiaries	56,985	47,996	56,910	51,746	52,096
Standing timber	—	—	—	—	—
Fixed assets	—	—	—	—	—
	52,641	44,433	55,260	52,846	53,958
Financed by					
Share capital	30,223	24,018	24,012	24,008	24,008
Reserves	11,357	9,341	15,160	12,239	10,103
	41,580	33,359	39,172	36,247	34,111
Minority interests	—	—	—	—	—
	41,580	33,359	39,172	36,247	34,111
Convertible loan stock	11,061	11,074	11,088	11,099	11,099
Loans	—	—	5,000	5,500	8,748
Deferred taxation	—	—	—	—	—
Deferred liabilities	—	—	—	—	—
	52,641	44,433	55,260	52,846	53,958

Source: Wilkinson annual reports.

city of London in 1772 (see Exhibit 7). Nock had an enterprising apprentice named James Wilkinson, who married his daughter and became his partner. When Nock died in 1804, Wilkinson took over and in 1820 added swordmaking for navy and army officers to his gunmaking activities. His son Henry, who succeeded him, moved the business to Pall Mall in central London, close to the Admiralty and War offices in Whitehall. James Wilkinson had secured an appointment as gunmaker to King George III, the first of nine royal appointments to British sovereigns which were to follow. Sword production was at its peak during the latter decades of the nineteenth century, when the Wilkinson firm

EXHIBIT 5
Wilkinson Group
Balance Sheets
1975–1979
(£ 000's)

	1979	1978	1977	1976	1975
Assets employed					
Stocks	71,265	44,978	38,967	32,961	33,511
Debtors	66,078	43,794	39,304	31,973	31,366
Short term deposits and bank balances	9,031	6,781	6,880	9,256	7,549
Current Assets	146,374	95,553	85,151	74,190	72,426
Bank loans and overdrafts	17,560	13,486	7,319	7,989	11,892
Creditors	53,595	36,917	37,049	29,180	24,772
Taxation	5,481	4,531	2,662	3,418	3,136
Dividends	3,250	2,239	1,844	1,676	1,542
Current Liabilities	79,886	57,173	48,874	42,263	41,342
Net current assets	66,488	38,380	36,277	31,927	31,084
Investments	2,434	1,626	1,584	1,176	2,297
Interests in subsidiaries	—	—	—	—	—
Standing timber	7,626	6,038	4,726	4,414	4,157
Fixed assets	78,280	60,892	68,857	48,437	47,587
	154,828	106,936	111,444	85,954	85,125
Financed by					
Share capital	30,223	24,018	24,012	24,008	24,008
Reserves	60,912	38,818	34,705	20,824	20,003
	91,135	62,836	58,717	44,832	44,011
Minority interests	15,176	15,804	16,335	12,451	13,214
	106,311	78,640	75,052	57,283	57,225
Convertible loan stock	11,061	11,074	11,088	11,099	11,099
Loans	30,041	16,669	18,199	16,176	14,932
Deferred taxation	546	553	7,105	1,396	1,869
Deferred liabilities	6,869	—	—	—	—
	154,828	106,936	111,444	85,954	85,125

Source: Wilkinson annual reports.

supplied arms for the Crimean and Boer wars and for the vast British armies throughout the Empire. In addition to making swords, cutlasses, sabers, and boarding pikes, the company also made lances. By the close of the century cavalry sword production alone was between 30,000 and 60,000 a year, and it was estimated that at any time Queen Victoria's armed forces had in use about half a million Wilkinson weapons.

The reign of Edward VII was peaceful, and production dropped sharply. Under George V during World War I, the Wilkinson factory moved to larger quarters in the Acton area of London, converted to emergency production, and

EXHIBIT 6
Wilkinson Match Limited and Subsidiaries
Source and Application of Funds
Year to 31st March 1979
(£ 000's)

	1979	1978	1977	1976	1975
Profit before taxation and					
extraordinary items	19,002	14,304	12,346	9,506	7,766
Depreciation	6,720	5,534	5,264	4,319	3,892
Other items	—	—	330	—	—
Total generated from trading	25,722	19,838	17,940	13,825	11,658
Extraordinary items before taxation					
and minorities	(117)	(918)	1,000	(2,801)	(4,623)
Shares issued at a premium in part					
consideration for the acquisition of					
True Temper Corporation	10,974	—	—	—	—
Subscription for shares in					
subsidiaries by minorities	1,103	—	—	—	—
Disposal of					
Fixed assets	3,218	3,319	1,631	1,202	1,655
Investments	966	—	769	1,121	246
Other sources	224	46	—	2,646	9,255
	42,090	22,285	21,340	15,993	18,191
Acquisition of					
Businesses	15,707	230	1,297	5	4,048
Fixed assets	8,817	5,420	8,985	7,295	10,536
Investments	1,670	192	408	—	—
Taxes	6,837	4,940	5,265	3,860	2,982
Dividends paid					
By Wilkinson Match Ltd.	2,302	1,923	1,739	1,605	988
By subsidiaries to minority					
shareholders	1,359	1,018	1,141	659	357
Standing timber (decrease)/increase	(1,126)	540	406	257	355
Deferred liabilities reduction	303	—	—	—	—
	35,869	14,263	19,241	13,681	19,266
Increase in working capital	4,390	14,145	5,817	(2,054)	3,748
Stocks	9,909	8,087	6,223	(1,054)	3,742
Debtors	2,092	6,936	7,339	1,839	3,828
Creditors	(7,611)	(878)	(7,745)	(4,947)	(3,822)
	40,259	28,408	25,058	11,627	23,014
Net inflow/(outflow) of funds	1,831	(6,123)	(3,718)	4,366	(4,823)
Increase/(decrease) in loans	4,009	(172)	2,012	1,244	5,572
Increase/(decrease) in cash balances	5,840	(6,295)	(1,706)	5,610	749

Source: Wilkinson annual reports.

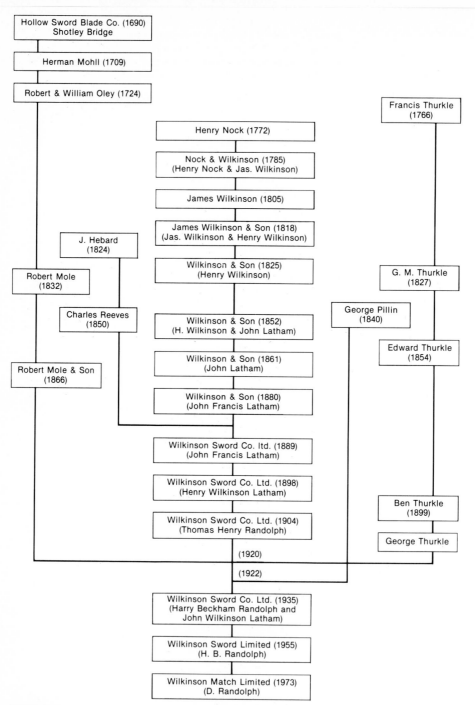

EXHIBIT 7
Development of Wilkinson Sword Limited. (*Source:* Wilkinson annual reports.)

turned out 2.5 million bayonets in addition to capacity production of swords. After the war, production virtually ceased, and the company reverted to the making of a hollow-ground straight-edged razor which it had been producing in modest quantities since 1890. At the turn of the century the company developed a safety razor which could be stropped automatically. In 1920 it began to make pruning shears, and it soon became the leader in the British Isles. During the 1930s it also had fleeting experiences in the making of nail clippers, scissors, table cutlery, and other cutting tools. At one time it manufactured the Wilkinson Touring Autocycle and the Pall Mall bicycle. The company began, in 1938, the manufacture of fire detection and protection equipment for aircraft, a joint venture with the Graviner Manufacturing Company Limited.

During World War II Wilkinson again converted entirely to war work, producing for the allied armies millions of bayonets, swords, commando knives, armor-piercing shot, flak suits, and bulletproof waistcoats. During the war the Graviner Company installed its firefighting equipment in a vast fleet of allied aircraft.

With the cessation of hostilities the Wilkinson plants were again abruptly idled. Safety-razor production was later resumed, but was slowed up by the postwar shortage of brass. There was some activity in Graviner fire protection equipment, which was adopted for use by the commercial airlines, then a fledgling industry. Garden tools became a major product, with the line expanded to include all garden tools with cutting edges, both clippers and cultivating tools. Sword production slowly picked up with the change of the army to its peacetime role.

In 1956 Wilkinson brought out its first stainless steel razor blade. In 1961 it introduced its historic Teflon-coated Wilkinson Sword Blade; in 1970 the chromium-coated blade; in 1972 the bonded blade; in 1976 the twin-blade and a disposable; and in 1979 the pivot-head blade.

ORGANIZATIONAL STRUCTURE AND POLICY

"Years ago," said Mr. Denys Randolph, chairman, "we were a little company with a total employee strength of 750, and we were owner-managed. Direct control of all sides of the business was possible by the chairman and the managing director."

With the rapid expansion of the business through acquisitions in the sixties, the management undertook a series of organizational moves to effect more decentralization. As a result the company was divided into six major product divisions: matches and lighters, personal products, hardware and housewares, writing instruments, packaging, and safety and protection.

In 1976 the company was restructured again, this time on a geographic basis. "The objective," said Christopher Lewinton, group managing director, "was to create a unified consumer product business in each territory out of the old separate product divisions. This will permit a strengthening of the local management and a decentralization of administrative support for the regions, where it can contribute more effectively to the efficient running of the business. In addition ... three product directors have been appointed. Their function is to maintain a worldwide overview of their product category with emphasis on marketing and product development." The new structure is depicted in Exhibit 8 (Wilkinson annual report).

Each of the subsidiary companies had its own board. Many of the boards were interlocking, with some individual directors sitting on many boards. Most

EXHIBIT 8
Wilkinson Match Organization.

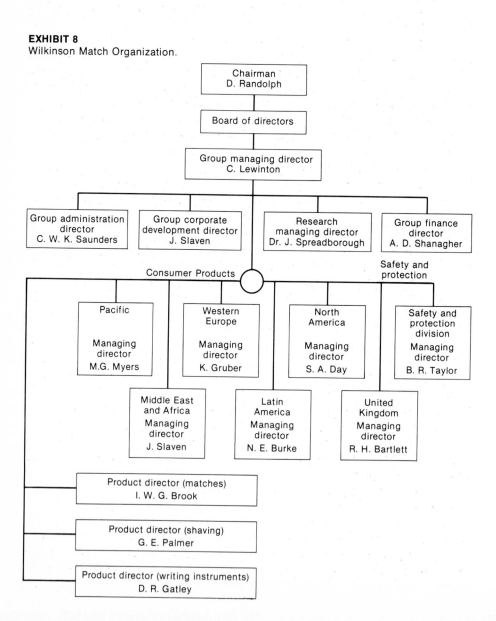

of the subsidiary companies were wholly owned. Wilkinson's interest in the subsidiary companies is depicted in Exhibit 9.

The parent board met monthly and controlled overall policy, but the day-to-day business of the group was managed by the international board, which acted as a management committee. The international board met every two weeks and made the operating decisions, which the parent board usually approved at its monthly meetings. The Randolph family held $97\frac{1}{2}$ percent of the nonpublic capital stock.

Several members of the Randolph family had served in various executive and board capacities during the twentieth century, with control passing to Mr. Denys Randolph in 1976.

> His climb to the top of the company, he comments with a smile, was helped by "being in the right place at the right time, but I've worked hard at it too." Made chairman and managing director of Wilkinson Sword in 1971, he was executive deputy chairman of British Match Corporation (subsequently Wilkinson Match) in 1973–1975, before taking the chairman's seat at Wilkinson Match in 1976.

> "My responsibilities are to the board, the shareholders and the executives. I must help plan strategy and watch performance. The managing director's job is to carry out the strategy...."

> Relaxed, carefully dressed, and confident ("I've a democratic style, but I'm a bit of an autocrat"), Randolph puts the idea of "quality" at the forefront of his thinking. "Our emphasis at Wilkinson Match is on quality of service and product. There was always that tradition in the old family firm—look at a book of matches and compare it with others round the world. In the UK, there's still a lot of high quality in production, and we have some of the finest management brains in the world: we are still the great innovators. But I'm afraid we have slipped back too far ... we will have to suffer for this in the future and it will be many years, if ever, before we catch up with the rest of Europe in our standards of living...."

> *--The Director (UK)*, July 1976

PRODUCT DIVISIONS: SALES AND PROFIT CONTRIBUTION

Personal Products Division

Razor Blades Wilkinson dated its entry into the razor blade business back to 1890. In 1898 the company introduced its first safety razor. While Wilkinson became a factor in the razor blade industry in Great Britain in this venture, the company was only moderately successful.

Production of razor blades was suspended in World Wars I and II. In the post-World War II period Wilkinson Sword decided to become a major producer in the razor blade market. In pursuing this policy it developed a revolutionary coated stainless steel blade which was introduced in 1961. The new blade proved to be successful almost instantly and catapulted the firm into a position of market leadership rivaling the international giant, Gillette, of the United States.

		Group percentage of issued shares	Activity
United Kingdom	Bryant & May Ltd.	100	a
	Graviner Ltd.	100	e
	H. W. Chapman Ltd.	100	f
	J. John Masters & Co. Ltd.	100	a
	Pains-Wessex Ltd.	100	e
	Schermuly Ltd.	100	e
	Stephenson, Mills Ltd.	100	c
	Thomas M. Nutbrown Ltd.	100	c
	Wilkinson Sword Ltd.	100	bc
	Wolverhampton Box Co. Ltd.	100	f
Australia	Wilkinson Match Australia Ltd.	100	g
	Bryant & May Pty. Ltd.	79	a
	A Preference	95	
	B Preference	100	
	Graviner (Australia) Pty. Ltd.	100	e
	Wilkinson Sword Pty. Ltd.	100	b
Brazil	Wilkinson Fiat Lux A & P. Ltd.	100	g
	Cia Fiat Lux de Fosforos de Segurance	97	a
	Preference	80	
	Cia Brasileira de Fosforos	63	a
	Preference	63	
	Fosforos do Norte S.A.	93	a
	A Preference	30	
	C Preference	56	
Canada	Eddy Match Co. Ltd.	100	ab
	True Temper Canada Ltd.	100	c
Egypt	Wilkinson Sword Middle East S.A.E.	51	b
Eire	True Temper (Ireland) Ltd.	100	c
Italy	Wilkinson Sword S.p.A.	100	b
Malawi	The Match Co. (Malawi) Ltd.	45	a
New Zealand	Bryant & May (N.Z.) Ltd.	100	a
	Graviner (New Zealand) Ltd.	100	e
	Wilkinson Sword (New Zealand) Ltd.	100	b
Papua New Guinea	Melanesian Matches Pty. Ltd.	79	a
	Preference	79	
South Africa	The Lion Match Co. Ltd.	64	a
	Interpak Holdings (Pty.) Ltd.	64	f
	Wilkinson Sword (South Africa)(Pty.) Ltd.	64	b
	Graviner (South Africa)(Pty.) Ltd.	100	e
Spain	Wilkinson Sword S.A.E.	85	b
United States	Graviner Inc.	100	e
	Scripto Inc.	56	d
	True Temper Corporation	100	c
	Wilkinson Match (U.S.A.) Inc.	100	g
	Wilkinson Sword Inc.	100	b
West Germany	Wilkinson Sword Europe GmbH	100	g
	Deugra GmbH.	100	e
	Wilkinson Sword GmbH.	67	b
Zimbabwe Rhodesia	Lion Match Ltd.	64	a

Note: Holdings are of ordinary shares or common stock except where indicated, and are all held by subsidiaries of Wilkinson Match Limited.

Key to Principal Activity

a Matches and Lighters
b Personal Products
c Hardware and Housewares
d Writing Instruments

e Safety and Protection
f Packaging
g Holding Company

EXHIBIT 9
Wilkinson's principal subsidiaries. (*Source:* Wilkinson annual reports.)

Stainless steel had long been known to razor blade manufacturers, who had avoided it because it posed technical and commercial problems. The Wilkinson management was aware of these problems, but it believed that there were possibilities in stainless which the industry had not explored. After years of development with a company, in Solingen, West Germany, Wilkinson introduced its phenomenally keen and long-lasting stainless steel blade, which was clearly an advance over any existing competitive blade.

News of the new blade's remarkable sharpness and durability spread rapidly by word of mouth as one shaver told another of its wonderful qualities. One London barrister commented, in a widely publicized quotation: "It doesn't just shave off your whiskers, it *breathes* them off." As the whispering campaign gained momentum, demand soared far beyond the company's capacity to produce.

While sales continued to increase, profits were declining largely because Wilkinson now needed to advertise. "We made certain forecasts, and we geared our output to them," Denys Randolph stated. "But we underestimated the marketing resources of our competitors, our blue friends. Well, it has proved more difficult than we expected. Believe me, though, we don't intend to stand still."

In the period 1964–1970 Wilkinson's profits had risen and fallen twice. Lower profit margins had been caused primarily by increasing market expenses. The costs involved in the worldwide promotion of consumer products had not been offset by substantial increases in sales.

When Wilkinson made its postwar reentrance into the razor blade business, it made only its coated stainless steel blade. Gillette did not have a steel blade in its line but placed heavy emphasis on its highly profitable Super Blue Blade. For three years Wilkinson and others, with their new stainless steel blades, cut deeply into Gillette's market share. During these years, as one commentator put it, Gillette literally sat back and thought. Factors considered by razor blade manufacturers were: stainless steel cost three times as much as carbon, and production costs were higher, but there were no additional expenses. All told, stainless blades did not cost three times as much as carbon blades, while the price of the stainless blade would be about 15 cents versus 6.7 cents for the Super Blue Blade.

The World Razor Blade Market   Until Wilkinson became a major producer, the world razor blade industry had consisted of (1) three large American producers which had international plants and markets, and (2) numerous small producers who manufactured and sold nationally or regionally.

The big three were Gillette, which produced the Blue Blade and the Super Blue Blade and later produced the Silver Stainless; the American Safety Razor Company of Philip Morris, which made the Gem (carbon) and later the Personna (stainless); and the Schick Safety Razor Company Division of Eversharp, Inc., which made the Pal (carbon) and later the Krona-Plus (stainless). Each of the big three had long experience in the razor blade business.

After the introduction of the teflon coated stainless steel razor blade in 1961 Wilkinson developed a global market for its razor blades. In several areas of the world Wilkinson was the market leader. In 1979 the company had 50 percent of the blade market in the UK, 34 percent of the West German market, 20 percent of the Italian market, and 25 percent of the Australian and South African markets. The company was well-positioned in other markets of the world. In the United States it maintained a market position which was estimated at about 8 to 10 percent. Because of Gillette and the other U.S. producers, competition for the American market was very intense. Wilkinson's shaving products were being subjected to changes in the industry and increased costs of manufacture, distribution, and new product development. Disposable razors were a competitive force of recent origin. This product, which was made prominent by BIC of France, had made inroads into the world blade market. These factors had made an impact on the profitability of Wilkinson's shaving products and contributed to losses in the personal products division of Wilkinson in 1979.

Development and current status of the personal products line In the 1970s Wilkinson changed the name of the Shaving Division to the Consumer Products Division and later to the Personal Products Division in order to reflect a broader base resulting from an extended line of products. In addition to the Teflon-coated stainless steel double-edged blade designed to last longer than the original stainless steel blade, there was a double-edged razor to fit both blades, a bonded blade and razor, a "fixed geometry" or twin blade, a pivot-head blade, a shaving soap aerosol, and a men's toilet soap. The company also manufactured a line of scissors and other cutting tools which drew on its traditional manufacturing strengths, and distributed Foster Grant sunglasses in the UK.

Scissors were introduced into Wilkinson's personal products line in 1974. The scissors were a high-quality product which rapidly gained market share in the UK. The company had plans to broaden its market through expanding the product line and entering global markets. Although volume was small, management considered it to be a profitable product.

Foster Grant sunglasses were also brought into Wilkinson's personal products line in 1974. This product gained an immediate market share of 15 percent in the UK. This success was short-lived, however, because the expense of attempting to develop an international market, and unfavorable summer weather created a loss for this product in 1979. Wilkinson added Revin International of Australia to its sunglasses product line in 1979.

Group Managing Director Lewinton explained that in 1979 the Personal Products Division accounted for 17 percent of the company's sales, but operated at a loss:

> Among the factors contributing to the operating loss was the continuing expenditure on developing our sunglasses market position internationally, while profits were badly affected by poor summer weather. Shaving results were also disappointing.

The shaving business is going through a period of change as manufacturers compete to win over traditional double-edge blade users to disposable products and introduce advanced systems which have improved characteristics of closeness and comfort. While this process is taking place, costs are inevitably incurred both in the design and introduction of new products and the redesign of production facilities.

We have recently launched "Profile," our new pivot-head razor, among the most advanced shaving systems in the world. While initial launch costs will affect profitability in the short term, we are confident that the introduction of new products will help restore the shaving business to its former position as an important contributor to group profits.[2]

Razor Blade Manufacture   A razor blade is a highly engineered product, mass-produced on automated machinery at the rate of 700 blades a minute, yet precise to tolerances of a millionth of an inch. The ultra-high-precision requirements, when combined with high-speed mass production, presented continuing problems in quality control.

In manufacturing there were nine main processes: perforating, hardening, normalizing, polishing, cleaning and drying, etching, grinding and honing, stropping, and coating. There were numerous detailed inspections during production, including the use of microscopes and blue lights. Over 20 percent of the razor blade work force was engaged in quality control. "If a man happens to get a bad blade," said a production executive, "he remembers it." In its early experiences, Wilkinson had critical manufacturing problems, sometimes scrapping over 20 percent of production.

In order to manufacture razor blades properly, Wilkinson believed that sophisticated research concerning the nature of shaving techniques and beards was important. Research findings, according to company officers, showed that men's beards differed, as did their standards for a good shave. The age of the shaver made a difference, and hair thickness varied from person to person. The technique of shaving had a decided effect: the heat of the shaving water, the soap used, and the time allowed for the soap to soften the beard were all factors that influenced blade performance. Because of this, Wilkinson was not satisfied that razor blades lent themselves entirely to objective testing. Therefore, it subjected its daily production of blades to an actual shaving test. In a test-shaving room at the plant, numerous staff members shaved every day, using soaps or creams of their own choice and their own personal techniques of shaving. Their opinions were recorded and the blades checked microscopically after use. Only after these final user tests was any batch of blades released for sale.

In 1979 Wilkinson manufactured razor blades in eight plants located in the U.S., Brazil, England, Germany, South Africa, and Zimbabwe (Rhodesia).

Sword Manufacture   "In understanding our company position," said one company executive, "you must be aware of the important role the sword has

---

[2]Wilkinson annual report.

played throughout our development. I think it is fair to say that the sword image and craftmanship have been key factors in our marketing policy through the years and explain a good deal our company's approach."

Over the thousands of years of sword history there had come to be an endless variety of swords, and Wilkinson took pride in the claim that it could make any sword in the world. There were blades with cutting edges on both sides, single-edged blades, straight blades, curved blades, and blades purely for thrusting. Hilts varied from simple grip and cross-guard to complicated basket hilts. The parts might be fine-plated with gold, silver, nickel, or rhodium, and handles might be set with jewels. The 1908 British cavalry trooper's sword, which is reputed to be the best sword ever designed, came at a time when the sword, as a weapon of war, was completely outmoded. "It is also a bit of an anomaly," reflected the executive, "that the swords Wilkinson turns out today, thanks to modern metallurgy and forging techniques, are better fighting weapons than the swords it made in the days when its swords were actually used as fighting weapons."

Wilkinson still produced swords of all types, although sales amounted to less than one-half of 1 percent of the group's turnover. Approximately 80 percent of the swords were sold overseas. Twenty-five percent were "cheap" swords—Masonic, cadet, lodge, and dancing swords—which were made of quality materials, but not subjected to rigorous tests. These sold for about $20 to $25. Sixty percent were regulation swords for armies, navies, and air forces. These sold for $60 to $110. Some 15 percent were custom-built. These were literally handcrafted, and the cost ranged from $500 to $10,000, depending on finishes and jeweling. In this category were the sword of honor presented to General Eisenhower after V-E Day, the sword of Stalingrad presented to Stalin by Winston Churchill, and the sword forged for the Queen's jubilee in 1977 (see Exhibit 10).

The heyday of the sword had been in the latter part of the nineteenth century when it served as a fighting weapon, was a regulation part of army and navy dress, and was also a part of a fashionable man's clothing, as the umbrella today is part of the proper attire of a London city man. Although the sword was largely an anachronism in the 1970s there was, nevertheless, still a world sword industry, with competing producers in England, Germany, Spain, France, and Japan. The greatest demand was for low-priced cadet, ceremonial, and stage swords, in which Wilkinson found itself unable to compete with the low prices offered by foreign producers, even the high-quality producers in Solingen and Toledo. As a matter of policy Wilkinson declined to lower its quality standards, and so an increasing part of the world sword trade was preempted by the Spaniards and the Japanese. The swords which Wilkinson once made for the American cadets at West Point, Annapolis, and Quantico now came mostly from Germany and Japan.

Sword demand had increased significantly in recent years, the chief demand coming from the emerging nations in Africa and Asia. "These nations are

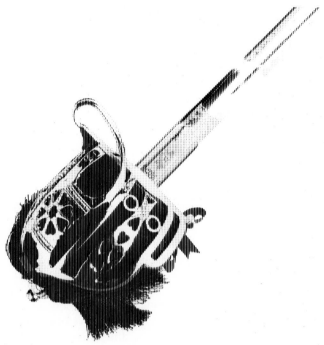

EXHIBIT 10
Wilkinson sword.

newly sovereign," said management, "and they place a high premium on cere-
mony. What can be more ceremonious than flourishing a hand-tooled sword?
There is a growing demand for them from African and Asian government officials who wear them with their ornate ceremonial dress uniforms." Wilkinson
frequently had orders from Sudan, the Hashimite kingdom of Jordan, Kuwait,
Israel, Ghana, Canada, Australia, Singapore, Bahrein, and Venezuela. "Today,
even though swords are less than 1 percent of our company's business, we still
do considerably better than breaking even. Swords have always paid their way,
and if this activity were a completely separate unit we would make a very tidy
profit. But swords are the traditional product of our company, and as a prestige
item they mean much more to us than their profitability. The public relations
aspect of our swords is fantastic, and we look upon our sword business as having far greater value to us than its monetary value. It has given Wilkinson
worldwide publicity. Our competitors in any of our lines have nothing like it."

Safety and Protection Division

Early in the 1930s a retired officer, Captain Salmon, invented an inertia switch
which triggered automatically to extinguish crash fires in automobiles. The

switch was developed by an engineer named Mathison who later adapted it to aircraft. Mathison's switch proved to be reliable and was in demand, but he lacked sufficient funds and so was embarrassed by sizable orders tendered to him by the British government. Mutual acquaintances introduced him to Mr. H. B. Randolph, and an arrangement was made whereby Mathison's Graviner Company (gravity-inertia) did the selling and Wilkinson did the developing and manufacturing.

Expansion of the Graviner business continued steadily, and Graviner equipment became increasingly complex. In 1958 working in cooperation with the Royal Aeronautical Establishment at Farnborough, Graviner developed an explosion-suppression system designed to prevent explosions of the fuel tanks in case of an incendiary strike on bombers. Graviner supplied protective equipment for most British military aircraft. Its equipment was also fitted to all British civil aircraft, including the Comet, Britannia, Viscount, and Vanguard. The company also developed adaptations of its equipment for other types of fighting vehicles and for railroad equipment and oceangoing ships.

Prior to 1964 Graviner and Wilkinson had been separate, privately owned companies, each operating from the site at Colnbrook. The relationship was harmonious, but there were problems of communications between the two companies, and occasionally conflict of opinion over product development and investment. In 1964 it was decided to eliminate these difficulties by merging the two companies. A new company, Graviner (Colnbrook) Limited was formed, with Wilkinson Sword owning two-thirds of the stock and Graviner one-third. This operation was designated as the Graviner Division and was independent in operations except for capital expenditures, personnel policies, legal matters, and building and site locations. It followed very wide policy guidelines laid down by the headquarters management, though its products were to be limited to safety and control equipment. In 1972 the division became a wholly owned Wilkinson subsidiary.

Since the Graviner facilities were geographically separate from the others in the Wilkinson group, most of which were 10 miles away at Acton, the Graviner Division tended to be especially autonomous. The Graviner Division made capital equipment, whereas the other Wilkinson divisions made consumer products.

By the 1970s Graviner had a world reputation for its special skills and technologies associated with protection of aircraft and missiles, cars, armored fighting vehicles, oceangoing freighters, tankers, passenger ships, small boats, Hovercraft, industrial plants, and stationary engine rooms. It was also producing general-purpose, handheld fire extinguishers.

Because there was a growing tendency for the British government and others to buy American airplanes or American airframes in which were installed home-manufactured engines, Graviner had formed a subsidiary company to represent it in Washington, D.C. Graviner equipment was being used increasingly in German military equipment, so Graviner formed a German company, Deugra Gmbh, to exploit Germany and the Common Market. It acquired a German plant site in expectation of the entrance of the UK into the Common Market which was utilized after the UK gained entrance. A policy decision was made to manufacture in Australia to circumvent the 30 percent Australian import duty. Subsidiaries were also formed in New Zealand and Hong Kong, and consideration was being given to establishing a Graviner subsidiary in France.

The Graviner manufacturing processes tended to be job-shop in nature, with some 400 products in production at almost any time, and only a few in batches of 1,000 or more on a single order. There was a great amount of product design and development engineering, which required a high order of engineering skill. Eighty percent of materials were purchased on a "released" basis, which required strict conformance and certified compliance with mechanical specifications. Graviner equipment included many microminiaturized electrical and electronic components, many of which had been in existence for only a few years. Graviner had, for example, been using transistors long before they were popularly used in radios.

Graviner had continued to maintain its position as a quality producer of basic fire protection equipment for aircraft and general use throughout the years. It had established itself as the supplier to most of the British aircraft industry. Graviner had also strengthened its position in the United States with the installation of its equipment on Boeing 747 aircraft. Since most of the world aircraft production in the future would take place in the United States, Graviner had taken steps to strengthen its sales efforts in the United States. The division also received contracts for the safety and arming devices of the Swingfire and Sea Dart missiles. Service to customers was provided around the world through Graviner subsidiaries and distributors.

By the end of the 1970s Graviner was the acknowledged leader in the field of aerospace fire protection. Graviner fire extinguishers had been approved by the Minister of Public Building and Works and had been chosen by the post office and the British railroad system. Growth in the field of industrial fire protection continued to expand with the development and sale of smoke detection and flame detection systems for factories. Several orders had been immediately placed for Graviner's fire protection equipment for ships with automatic engine room operation.

The product line continued to expand through the 1970s. An ultraviolet flame detector was viewed with considerable interest by the North Sea oil industry, while fire and smoke detection equipment commanded a 20 percent share of the UK market. Pains-Wessex/Schermuly Corporation, a manufacturer of fireworks and pyrotechnics, was acquired, adding specialty products such as distress signals and antiriot devices to the division. Military as well as civil marine interests were major customers. (The division provided the major fireworks displays for the Queen's jubilee celebrations in 1977.) Jointly with Allegheny-Ludlum, Wilkinson acquired HTL Industries of California, a manufacturer of aircraft fire-extinguishing systems. (Allegheny held 80 percent of the HTL stock, Wilkinson the balance.)

In 1979 Graviner operated seven plants, five in the UK, one in Australia, and one in Germany. HTL had six plants, five in the U.S. and one in Puerto Rico.

Hardware and Housewares Division

"We believe," said Mr. Denys Randolph, "that the best way to get into any line is to make the best quality products in the world. There weren't any quality garden tools in England until we introduced our line. Now customers are demanding quality tools. In pruners, shears, and cultivators we have creamed 80 to 90 percent of the top price market in England."

Wilkinson first introduced their line of pruning shears in 1920 to combat the post-World War I depression. Moderately successful, the garden tool activities were virtually discontinued during World War II, only to be revived again in 1948 when Wilkinson concentrated seriously on making a relatively complete line. "The Wilkinson management keeps in mind," said Mr. Denys Randolph, "that garden tools tided the company over after each world war."

Wilkinson considered that its special talents lay in design and in the processing of the cutting edges. Prices were based upon a cost formula and were shaded somewhat to make them competitive. The resulting prices and gross profit were high, but the final net return was low. Approximately 30 percent of the garden tool sales were exports, a large share going to the United States, Canada, and Australia. The remaining exported products were distributed to Europe, South Africa, and New Zealand.

The sale of garden tools in the United States was initiated in 1960. The development of distributors for the garden tool line was tied to the introduction of the company's Teflon-coated stainless steel blade introduced in 1961. The popular razor blades were offered as an incentive to the garden tool dealers, who soon became engrossed in selling the limited supply of razor blades they could obtain and relegated the garden tool line of Wilkinson Sword to a secondary position. The razor blades were withdrawn from the garden shops in 1963 and 1964 and distributed through the conventional channels of drugstores and supermarkets. In 1964 the garden tool line was separated from the company's other products in both manufacturing and sales. "Wilkinson, as a whole, has smarted under the 'one product' criticism," said Mr. Denys Randolph. "We mean to correct this image. Recreational spending is growing, but gardening seems to be diminishing because people are tending toward recreation which takes them away from home."

The line was expanded in the 1970s to include power tools (such as a cordless electric shrub trimmer), which subsequently maintained market leadership in the UK. The Nutbrown Company, manufacturer of housewares, was another acquisition during the decade.

Late in 1977 a series of negotiations and stock transactions which would permit Wilkinson to acquire True Temper Corporation from Allegheny-Ludlum, an American specialty steel company, neared completion. A relationship between Allegheny and Wilkinson had existed for several years, as Allegheny had been supplying shovels and other metal implements to round out Wilkinson's line of tools. True Temper manufactured garden tools and other consumer items.

Executives of Allegheny and Wilkinson had developed a certain rapport, and Allegheny president Robert Buckley said he was "impressed how they handled their safety and protection equipment business."[3] Allegheny had previously acquired the Chemetron Corporation, which manufactured chemicals and industrial gases and was thought to parallel the distribution channels of Wilkinson's safety equipment.

The deal was to provide joint appointments to Wilkinson's and Allegheny's boards, and Allegheny would have received over 50 percent of Wilkinson's stock for True Temper.

The first step was Allegheny-Ludlum's agreement to buy 6.5 million shares or 29% of Wilkinson's 22.4 million shares, from Swedish Match Co. Allegheny paid the equivalent of $4.85 per share, a hefty 30% premium over the trading price on the London Stock Exchange. Just two days later, Allegheny signed another agreement to sell its True Temper Corporation subsidiary, which manufactures garden and hand tools, to Wilkinson for 10.5 million newly issued shares. Together with the shares acquired from Swedish Match, Allegheny would have had working control of both Wilkinson and True Temper.

The dealings, however, left London institutional investors feeling frozen out. Under British takeover law, an acquisitor tendering for more than 30% of a publicly traded company's stock must make the offer available to all shareholders. But the deal with Swedish Match involved just 29% of Wilkinson's stock.

--Business Week, February 27, 1978.

Public outcry, institutional wrath that control of Wilkinson would pass to Allegheny with nobody but Swedish Match receiving a penny, and a report on True Temper by Wilkinson's accountants forced a revision of the terms of the deal. Allegheny-Ludlum effectively dropped the asking price for True Temper by agreeing to settle for cash ($8m paid over two years) and shares, which would lift its stake in Wilkinson to 44.4%; Allegheny-Ludlum also agreed not to increase its holding without making an offer to other shareholders.

--The Economist (UK), February 18, 1978.

Wilkinson management felt that the True Temper deal would "give us a substantial base in the U.S. which would help us do more business in North America, (and) a truly international garden products business to put alongside our other consumer categories. . . ." The exchange was approved in March at an extraordinary meeting of Wilkinson stockholders.

True Temper added a number of products to Wilkinson's line which ex-

---

[3] *Business Week,* January 9, 1978.

tended beyond garden tools. In addition to being one of the world's largest manufacturers of garden and hand tools, it was the world's largest producer of steel shafts for golf clubs and metal frames for tennis racquets and racketball racquets. The company was also a major supplier of products for the railroad industry which included railway wheels, axles, and continuous welded rail services and rail anchors.

The addition of True Temper in 1979 increased Wilkinson's hardware and houseware sales from £8.4 million in 1978 to more than £88.9 million. It also increased Wilkinson's Western Hemisphere sales from £30.8 million to £126.1 million.

Matches and Lighters, Writing Instruments

The relationship between Wilkinson and the match industry reportedly arose out of an almost accidental luncheon discussion in 1973 between Mr. Denys Randolph and the chairman of the British Match Corporation, Mr. I. H. Gilbert. The idea of a merger between the two companies struck both executives as a convenient way to escape the limitations of a narrow product line, but which more importantly would provide advantages of size and complementary international operations. (Additionally, British Match was said to be critically short of top management resources.) Announcement of the proposed merger was viewed as a puzzlement in the British financial press:

> ... The only common interest that British Match and Wilkinson Sword might have for promoting a merger is that both are involved in combustion—one as a promoter and the other as a preventor.
>
> --*London Times*, May 24, 1973

> ... (The merger) should be about as fertile as a coupling between a dromedary and a poodle. The two companies' businesses, it is claimed, are broadly compatible and have complementary skills—perhaps a reference to Wilkinson's production of fire protection equipment.
>
> --*The Economist*, May 26, 1973

Like Wilkinson, British Match was an old and respected company, having grown out of the development of a wax-covered safety match by a pharmacist in 1827. British Match held a virtual monopoly in the UK and dominated the world match market through the twentieth century. It marketed a variety of safety matches with various applications and colorful names: Swan Vestas, Bryant & May, Cap'n Webb, Scottish Bluebells, Redheads, and others. Over the years, British Match had added other enterprises to its portfolio, and was involved in ticket machines, fans, printing, and road-surfacing and building materials.

Shortly before the British Match–Wilkinson proposal was announced, word came from the United States that a new line of gas-fueled fashionable lighters which had been designed by Braun of Germany was about to be launched by Gillette.

The merger proposal drew an inquiry from the government's Monopolies Commission, portending a protracted and costly legal wrangling under Britain's recently toughened regulations on monopolies and mergers. Usually, merger proposals were withdrawn rather than face an inquiry, but Messrs. Gilbert and Randolph decided to press on. Eventually the merger was the first ever to be examined and cleared under the government's new rules.

But the degree to which the two firms' marketing operations could be dovetailed beneficially was still in question:

> ... There is uncertainty over Swedish Match, which owns one-third of its British cousin and does the selling in Europe.... It might now ... compete with Wilkinson Match.

> *--The Economist*, May 26, 1973.

In early 1974 Wilkinson acquired controlling interest (56 percent) in Scripto, Inc., manufacturer of pens and lighters. The two companies had had a joint distribution arrangement for slightly over a year.

Later that year Swedish Match and Wilkinson announced an unusual exchange of operating units.

> ... Swedish Match will sell 75% of its Genoud-Feudor disposable lighter business to Wilkinson for the equivalent of almost $9 million. Wilkinson will, in turn, sell to Swedish Match a 75% interest in its Weyroc building materials unit for $10.4 million.

> ... Sverker Ovesson, deputy director of Swedish Match, asserted the (arrangement) should be a significant asset in the competitive battle with Gillette, which has set its sights on overtaking Genoud-Feudor as number one in the lighter field.

> "Gillette had a good combination" marketing lighters and razor blades to ... retail outlets. "Now we think we have an even better combination" ... with Wilkinson marketing lighters, Wilkinson razor blades, and Scripto pens and lighters to retail outlets.

> *--Wall Street Journal*, July 24, 1974.

The match business continued to operate at profitable levels through the decade. According to Wilkinson's management, this was the result of specific efforts made during the past two years to improve manufacturing efficiency, marketing, and the management team.

For lighters and pens, the story was not so bright. By 1976 management recognized that the lighter industry was suffering from excess production capacity coupled with deep price cutting. Wilkinson maintained its market position but did not increase its investment. Large losses were posted in 1977 and 1978, with all Scripto USA lighter manufacturing facilities being closed in the latter year. Large losses were recorded in 1979 and management made the decision to import all lighters.

The writing instrument business was unprofitable until 1976, when it made a modest contribution. At that time, Christopher Lewinton stated, "this is a very large product category where, we believe, considerable opportunity exists and we are at the stage of establishing a base for the future." The following years, Scripto was reported to be growing profitably in the USA but suffering losses in the UK which put this activity overall into a loss. Consequently, management decided to terminate Scripto's UK operations and to undertake a costly reorganization of U.S. operations intended to leave the company "better placed to compete in this business." By 1979 Scripto USA was again operating at a loss, at which time Wilkinson appointed a new president to strengthen the management team, and improved results were anticipated. The company operated four plants for writing instruments, all in the U.S. In 1979 Scripto announced the introduction of the first erasable ball point pen which management hoped would be a major factor in returning Scripto to profitability.

Packaging

Wilkinson entered into the packaging business through acquisition in 1974. The packaging group included two plants in the UK at Wellingbrough and Wolverhampton, and the Interpack group which had four plants in South Africa. Wilkinson also owned Tanco, a profitable packaging operation in Australia which produced plastic mouldings. In 1979 packaging contributed 7.7 percent of sales and 70 percent of operating profit.

RESEARCH DIVISION AND PRODUCT POLICIES

Mr. Peter Randolph, the late chairman of the board, had stated:

> A company that is not looking ahead will die. A growing public company must constantly conceive what might be described as industrial children, new products, new processes, new divisions, acquisitions, mergers, even new top executives, if it is to be dynamic and interesting enough to employ the best brains at any level.

The Wilkinson management believed that the key to the company's future prosperity lay in new products and developments founded on research. This meant an investment in people as well as in facilities. The management believed that no less than 10 percent of its work force should be engaged in some form of research, and it usually had over 300 people engaged in research activities. The company provided university scholarships for postgraduate research students, retained senior faculty members of leading universities as consultants, and also used professional consultants. As a matter of policy it chose high-priced professional consultants on the assumption that by paying high fees to consultants who had established reputations it ensured good advice.

The Wilkinson management saw the distinction between research and engineering as being threefold: First, the time scale was different, research being

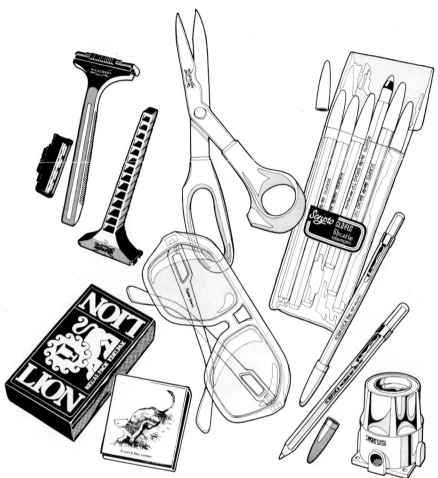

EXHIBIT 11
Wilkinson's diversified product line.

directed to the activities of future years, rather than to the urgent problems of manufacturing today. Second, the emphasis on equipment was different, enabling research to investigate much more radical changes than would be feasible in the engineering departments. Third, some projects involved such depth of scientific investigation that specialist teams had to be recruited and provided with elaborate apparatus. By integrating a number of such teams it was believed that a proper continuity of interest and utilization of equipment could be maintained, which was especially important to Wilkinson, with its diversity of products.

A Wilkinson research executive said:

We need more scientific investigation in depth. We suddenly find ourselves in a large business, and we need to defend it. To find out what a razor really does, we think we ought to investigate the whole process of shaving. What is hair? How is hair cut? What happens when any kind of blade cuts any kind of material? Does the edge go between the molecules? Does the edge go through individual molecules? The tip of a razor blade is one-millionth of an inch wide. Viewing it requires an electronic microscope, which is laboratory equipment. Engineers can't handle that small a dimension, can only work in thousandths. Wilkinson now has blades that cut very well. If they failed to do so tomorrow, would we know why?

In past years we had no shortage of research problems. We listed them, weighted them roughly for priorities. Now we have a research planning team which formulates research policies and makes recommendations to the board. We now have three research groups—Graviner, consumer products, and hand tools—and we are thinking of forming a group for developing new product lines which would not necessarily be related in any way to our present ones.

THE OUTLOOK

In viewing the outlook for the near future, management stated:

The world economic climate is becoming increasingly unfavourable and we are bound to view the immediate future with some caution. The problems we experienced in the second half of last year are persisting and we expect the figures for the first six months to be less good than those for the corresponding period of last year. Looking further ahead, we have a sound business with good prospects for growth worldwide and are well placed to take advantage of favourable changes in the world economic situation.[4]

(See Wilkinson's product line in Exhibit 11.)

[4]Wilkinson annual report, 1979.

Tandy Corporation

ACQUISITION PROPOSAL

In July of 1967, Charles D. Tandy, chairman of the board and chief executive officer of Tandy Corporation, learned that Leonards Department Store, a privately held department store complex in Fort Worth, Texas, might be for sale. Four years earlier, Charles Tandy had approached Leonards's owners with an offer to purchase the Leonard Company in order to have an immediate profit offset to a sizable tax loss carryover from the then recently acquired Radio Shack Corporation. No deal was made at that time because of a very high asking price on the part of Leonards's owners ($20 to $21 million cash) and the reluctance of Tandy Corporation bankers to finance an acquisition of that size.

Charles Tandy, however, retained an interest in acquiring Leonards, and in order to maintain a close contact with the company, Paul Leonard, president of Leonards and son of one of the founders of the company, was asked in 1965 to become a director of the Tandy Corporation. In July of 1967, Paul Leonard informed Charles Tandy that there had been some discussion by members of the Leonard families of the desirability of selling the company because of anticipated future estate problems. This discussion was precipitated by concern for the health of Mr. O. P. Leonard (age 70), one of the cofounders and principal owner of Leonards. Subsequent discussion with Paul Leonard indicated to Charles Tandy that an acquisition might be feasible, and then requested that financial information be prepared by Leonards for evaluation by Tandy Corporation personnel.

THE TANDY CORPORATION: HISTORY AND DEVELOPMENT

The Tandy Leather Company, a predecessor company of the Tandy Corporation, was cofounded in 1919 by Dave L. Tandy to supply shoe findings to the boot and shoe repair industry. During World War II, Dave Tandy became aware of the acute need by veterans' rehabilitation centers for materials which, with elementary skills and tools, could be assembled into useful and attractive items. Knowing from experience how difficult leather crafters found it to obtain leather, supplies, and tools, he offered a specialized range of products to meet this need. When Charles Tandy, Dave Tandy's son, returned home from the Navy in 1947 at the age of 29, he joined the family firm and concentrated his efforts on the sale of leather-working materials. While in Hawaii, Charles Tandy had observed the large quantities of leathercraft supplies being used in the hospitals and recreation centers and envisioned a national chain of leathercraft stores to meet the needs of leathercraft users.

In 1947, Charles Tandy opened two small retail stores specializing exclusively in leathercraft supplies in El Paso and San Antonio, Texas to develop and test sales and operation concepts for the proposed specialty leathercraft store chain. Both these ventures netted over a 100 percent return on investment in their first year of operation. According to Charles Tandy, three key concepts of store management and control were tested and proven successful in the operation of the first two stores:

1 *Catalog Support of a Specialty Product Line* To increase a store's sales range and to bring customers back to the store, a leathercraft catalog was prepared and mailed out in response to inquiries derived from small classified advertisements placed in national magazines. These inquiries were found to be the primary source of new business for the company. Each store specialized only in leathercraft, and their personnel became experts in the product line.

2 *Employee Participation* Charles Tandy and his management group believed that developing competent people was as vital to an organization as a good product, and that without incentives, neither the people nor the company could grow. A profit-sharing plan was implemented which allowed each store manager to receive a share of the pretax profits of his store. Also, employees of the company were allowed to buy into each new operation in the initial stages and to share in its growth.

3 *Control* To meet the needs of the profit-sharing program and for management information and control, the "profit center" (or control center) accounting technique was implemented, where each store was treated as a separate and distinct business operation, with all expenses and material purchases charged to that center at actual cost. This control system, although developed by necessity for the stores, was also implemented for internal control and overhead operations (accounting, advertising, etc.). The manager of each center was treated as an enterpreneur in the real sense: he or she was held responsible for maximization of profits. To accomplish this, the manager had to strive to maximize income by providing satisfactory service at a competitive price and to control expenses to a minimum acceptable level. A complete monthly profit and loss statement was prepared and made available to the manager no later than the fourteenth of the following month, showing the success or lack of success of his or her activities. Included on this statement were total income, itemized expenses by natural categories, and net profit. Consolidated results were prepared for each management level.

Through the use of the control center concept, each divisional unit and each subunit level was held accountable for the profit it earned and the loss it sustained. In this way, the burden of relating revenue and costs was shifted downward from top management to the lowest control unit.

The basic control procedures, merchandising concepts, and management methods developed in the first two Tandy stores were applied to all expansion areas in the ensuing years, and the plan was rated by Charles Tandy as the main reason for the success of the corporation.

The initial success of the first two stores encouraged Charles Tandy to open an additional 13 leathercraft stores by 1949, all of which were successful. A central warehouse was added. Additional items extending the product line included the "U-Do-It" line, which consisted of a kit containing complete material for a leather project. Factories were established to produce the products sold. Tandy management then evaluated other product lines which could be adapted to its type of marketing and operating procedures. In 1950, the Tandy organization acquired the American Handicraft Company of East Orange, New Jersey, a company with an excellent line of do-it-yourself handicraft products, two established retail stores in the New York market, and useful knowledge of school and institutional markets.

In the period 1950 to 1955, sales increased to approximately $8 million with after-tax earnings of $523,000. The company had leased stores in 75 cities.

In 1955, because of possible estate problems of David L. Tandy, who had been ill during the preceding year, the Tandy management sold the Tandy Leather Company to the American Hide and Leather Company of Boston, Massachusetts.

AMERICAN HIDE AND LEATHER COMPANY

The American Hide and Leather Company was incorporated in 1899 under the laws of the state of New Jersey. Its principal business was the tanning, finishing, and sale of calf leather and cattle-side upper leather. In 1955, after several years of substantial losses and at a time when the tanning industry in general was in a depressed condition, its directors decided that diversification was essential for the survival of the company. In mid-1955, it acquired all the outstanding stock of Tandy Leather Company of Fort Worth, Texas, and certain associated corporations. The Tandy group received $230,000 cash, fixed interest rate notes totaling $2 million, and options to purchase 500,000 shares of American Hide and Leather Company stock at $4 a share distributed over a four-year period.

On June 30, 1956, the company included two operating units: Tandy Industries, Inc., of Fort Worth, Texas, and a large tannery operation in Lowell, Massachusetts. The Lowell tannery was not profitable, and with the excess of productive capacity, the intense competition prevailing in the industry, and unsatisfactory labor relations, company management stated that they could see little likelihood that its operation could be greatly improved. During the latter part of 1956, the company disposed of the inventories and all physical assets pertaining to the tanning operation. The funds received were used to retire debt, to increase working capital, and to acquire new companies.

Three new companies were acquired in fields wholly unrelated to the leather industry. On July 1, 1956, the Musgrove Petroleum Corporation, Inc., of Wichita, Kansas, became a wholly owned subsidiary through the exchange of 196,028 shares of the company's stock for all the outstanding stock of Musgrove. On September 21, 1956, the company purchased for cash the assets and name of Shain & Company, Inc., of Boston, Massachusetts, a leading converter and distributor of fabrics and meshes for the shoe industry. On October 1, 1956, Dunbar Kapple, Inc., of Geneva, Illinois, became a wholly owned subsidiary through the exchange of 294,342 shares of the company's common stock for all of their outstanding stock. On December 31, 1956, the assets and name of Tex Tan of Yoakum, Texas, was acquired for cash and notes.

In December of 1956, following approval by the stockholders, the name of the company was changed from American Hide and Leather Company to General American Industries, Inc., to more clearly reflect the activities of the company and the expected pattern for its future.

PROBLEMS OF THE 1955–1959 PERIOD

The period from 1955 to 1959 was a troubled one for General American Industries. Musgrove Petroleum experienced a decline in profits as excessive domestic inventories and imports of foreign oil drastically reduced both the demand for domestic oil and its selling price. The low selling price in turn made it uneconomical to continue development and exploration work on sites which were not conveniently located in relation to pipelines and refineries. Thus, both the production and drilling divisions of Musgrove Petroleum Corporation were faced with substantially reduced demand for their products and services. As a result, the original development and exploration program had to be substantially curtailed.

During this same period, an abrupt change in military policy regarding expenditures for aircraft and missiles (which occurred in the fall of 1957), combined with the economic recession, seriously disrupted the Dunbar Kapple production and delivery schedules. Since Dunbar Kapple engineered and tested most of the items which it made for the aircraft industry and for missiles, a process which required several months before production could be started, the sudden change in military policy reduced production schedules below profitable levels. As a result, the Dunbar Kapple sales and earnings were well below the levels anticipated at the beginning of that year.

In Shain & Company, gross profit margins were reduced because of intensive competition, and profits were adversely affected by some unusual expense inherent in the building and promoting of new lines. Only the Tandy and Tex Tan groups were profitable.

It became apparent to the Tandy management that further dilution of the Tandy group interests would take place unless immediate corrective action was taken. This triggered a successful takeover bid of the parent corporation by the Tandy-Tex Tan groups, and in November, 1959, a new board of directors composed of Tandy supporters replaced the previous board (see Exhibit 1). The new board immediately implemented a study of the past history and the future prospects of the various divisions of the company. This study revealed that only two of the five divisions of General American Industries had a record of constant growth. After consideration of these facts, the board of directors authorized the company to sell the remaining three divisions. The two divisions retained were Tandy Industries and Tex Tan of Yoakum, Texas. The divisions sold were Musgrove Petroleum Corporation, Dunbar Kapple, Inc., and Shain & Company. The sale of these three divisions was accomplished during the first six months of 1960. A substantial loss was incurred on the sale of these

EXHIBIT 1
GENERAL AMERICAN INDUSTRIES, BOARD OF DIRECTORS

1958–1959 Board of Directors	1959–1960 Board of Directors

Charles D. Tandy
  Chairman of the board and president,
  Tandy Industries
	Charles D. Tandy
	  Chairman of the board and president
	  of the company

Stanley M. Rowland
  President and treasurer of the
  company
	Carl C. Welhausen
	  Vice president of the company and
	  general manager, Tex Tan

John B. Collier, Jr.
  President, Fort Worth Poultry & Egg
  Company
	John B. Collier, Jr.
	  President, Fort Worth Poultry & Egg
	  Company

James H. Dunbar, Jr.
  President, Dunbar Kapple, Inc.
	A. H. Hauser
	  Vice president, Chemical Bank
	  New York Trust Company

Philip A. Russell
  Stone & Webster Securities
  Corporation
	J. S. Nye
	  Partner, Nye & Whitehead

John Slezak
  Chairman, Kable Printing Company
	J. L. West
	  President, Tandy Leather Company

Pierce C. Musgrove
  President, Musgrove Petroleum
  Corporation, Inc.
	L. A. Henderson
	  Secretary-treasurer of the company,
	  vice president of Tandy Leather
	  Company

divisions. The Tandy and Tex Tan Companies' net sales and income over the preceding 10 years had shown substantial growth and profitability.

Charles Tandy, the new chairman of the board and president of General American Industries, stated that "while the operations, customer service, and sales programs of the two divisions were entirely independent, the Tandy and Tex Tan Companies supplemented each other in production facilities, distribution methods, and coverage of markets, and this favorable combination lent itself to a sound, integrated expansion program."

ACQUISITIONS AND EXPANSIONS, 1959–1967

During the 1960–1961 fiscal year, the name of the corporation was changed from General American Industries to Tandy Corporation to reflect, according to Charles Tandy, the new direction of the company and to allow the company to benefit from identification with the many Tandy stores throughout the country.

At the end of 1961, 125 leathercraft stores were operating in 105 cities of the United States and Canada. The acquisition of Clarke and Clarke, a leathercraft supplier in Ontario, Canada, provided the company an entry into the Canadian market. It was apparent to Charles Tandy, however, that cash flow was in excess of the expansion requirements of the corporation and that the company would need to acquire additional operations in order to maximize growth. In late 1962, this search resulted in three acquisitions, each of which was related to and/or supported existing company operations. Sturdy Die and Machine, Inc., of South Gate, California (a manufacturer of leathercraft tools); Corral Sportswear Company, of Ardmore, Oklahoma, a manufacturer of leather sport and casual clothing; and Cleveland Crafts, Inc., a retailer and manufacturer of arts and crafts material and supplies, were all acquired for cash.

Two growth opportunities were developed during the 1962–1963 fiscal year through negotiations with Cost Plus, Inc., of San Francisco and with Radio Shack Corporation of Boston, Massachusetts. According to Charles Tandy, "the agreements reached enabled the Tandy Corporation to measure the earning ability of both companies prior to making an equity investment in them and in their market fields." Options held by Tandy Corporation, if exercised, would give it a 38% interest in Cost Plus, Inc., and a 62 percent interest in Radio Shack Corporation.

COST PLUS IMPORTS

Cost Plus, Inc., was an importer and retailer of home furnishings, decorations, housewares, and gifts. Its overseas buyers made merchandise selections in many of the established and remote producing centers of the world, and sales were made to the public from one retail location in San Francisco. This importer-direct-to-consumer marketing plan offered the attraction of extremely low selling prices for tastefully chosen merchandise of a unique and handcrafted character which could not be readily duplicated. Annual sales volume at the San Francisco Fisherman's Wharf location had grown from $650,000 in 1958 to more than $3 million in 1963.

In September of 1962, Tandy, through a financial and distribution agreement, obtained an option to acquire an equity in Cost Plus, Inc., and the rights to establish additional Cost Plus stores in other cities. Stores were opened in early 1963 in San Mateo and Richmond, California, and in Fort Worth, Dallas, and San Antonio, Texas. With the opening of stores in Houston, Texas, and San Leandro and San Jose, California, a total of eight Cost Plus stores were in operation in late 1963.

RADIO SHACK CORPORATION

As early as 1961, Charles Tandy felt that the consumer electronics business might lend itself to the marketing techniques, control methods, and merchandising skills that had been developed in the other specialty businesses operated by Tandy. Late in 1961, Tandy Corporation acquired the consumer inventory of the Sweico Corporation, a small electronics supplier located in Fort Worth, to use as a pilot operation to learn the business. It became obvious to management, however, that to move forward in this area, a greater variety of merchandise and manpower talent was needed. This was made available in April of 1963, when Tandy Corporation acquired an option to purchase a majority interest at book value in Radio Shack Corporation of Boston, Massachusetts.

Radio Shack Corporation was a distributor of consumer and industrial electronic components, equipment, and parts with sales in 12 New England stores, a mail-order division, and an industrial division, with sales of approximately $15 million in fiscal 1963. In April of 1963, Tandy Corporation concluded an agreement which granted it immediate management control and options to acquire a majority interest in the company. Radio Shack in the years immediately preceding 1963 experienced rapid growth but recorded substantial operating losses, and immediate corrective action was needed to save the company from imminent bankruptcy.

Because of the potential importance of this acquisition to the future growth of Tandy Corporation, Charles Tandy personally assumed responsibility for its operations. At the same time, he remained the chief executive officer of Tandy Corporation. Charles Tandy confided at that time that he considered this new job one of the biggest and most difficult challenges of his career up to that date. He had to recast every aspect of the company: the distribution system, the advertising, and the merchandising program that could be expanded across the nation. In two years the Radio Shack division began to show profits. By 1967, sales had climbed to $29,702,000 and profits to $860,000 with 156 stores in operation nationwide (see Exhibit 2).

During fiscal 1965, 96,000 shares of Tandy Corporation common stock were issued to State Mutual Life Assurance Company in exchange for the outstanding preferred stock of Radio Shack Corporation. Conversion of the

EXHIBIT 2
STORES IN OPERATION BY DIVISION

	1967	1966	1965	1964	1963	1962	1961	1960
Tandy Leather Company	120	117	114	115	124	108	102	97
American Handicraft Company	42	35	27	26	24	23	18	18
Western Saddlery	—	—	—	—	6	5	5	5
Meribee Needle Arts	1	1	1	8	3	—	—	—
Cost Plus Imports	—	—	15	9	4	—	—	—
Tandy Electronic Stores	—	—	—	—	5	—	—	—
Radio Shack Stores	156	87	59	36	12	—	—	—
Wolfe Nursery	1	—	—	—	—	—	—	—
Total	320	240	216	189	183	140	125	118

preferred stock in June of 1965, together with the exercise of a stock purchase option during that month, brought Tandy Corporation's holdings of Radio Shack Corporation common stock to 85 percent of the outstanding shares. A series of financial moves and reorganizations increased their percentage ownership, and in June, 1967, Tandy Corporation acquired the remaining outstanding stock of Radio Shack Corporation (3.8 percent) for 32,172 shares of the common stock of Tandy Corporation, thus becoming the owners of 100 percent of the outstanding shares. This company was then merged into Tandy Corporation, and the corporate structure was dissolved.

During fiscal year 1967, Tandy Corporation acquired Wolfe Nursery, Inc., which put the Tandy Corporation in the garden supply and household plantings business. The corporation hoped to expand this operation into a store chain.

Early in 1967, in a speech given before a group of security analysts, Charles Tandy stated that his personal goal for Tandy Corporation was to increase its sales threefold every five years, as he had done in the past years. When asked if this would still be possible with the company sales now in the multi-million-dollar range. Charles Tandy replied that this same question was raised many times over the past years when sales were at lower levels and he could not then or now see where size could affect the ability to achieve his objective. (See Exhibits 5 to 8 at the end of the case.)

TANDY CORPORATION OPERATING DIVISIONS, 1967

The annual report of 1967 described the divisions as follows:

Tandy Corporation is presently composed of eight divisions whose operations include manufacturing and distribution, integrated retailing, and direct-mail sales of products keyed to educational and recreational markets.

Each operating division serves the needs of a distinctive and fast-growing area of modern educational and recreational activity, and each is benefiting from increased leisure time, higher income, and broadening public interest in the production and creative use of nonworking hours.

The growth experienced by Tandy Corporation in its operation during the uncertain economic climate of 1966 is evidence of the continued dramatic expansion in the educational and recreational requirements of our modern society.

Tandy Corporation's eight operating divisions were described in Tandy's annual report for 1967 as follows:

Tandy Leather Company The Tandy Leather Company subsidiary markets materials, equipment, and kits used in producing artistic and functional items of genuine leather through its 120 company-owned retail and mail-order stores in the United States and Canada. Primary lines of merchandise are footwear kits, handbag and wallet projects, parts and materials for the assembly and finishing of personal accessories, specialized tools, leathers, and hardware. More than half of the product mix is manufactured or assembled in its own integrated factories in Fort Worth, thus assuring a controlled supply of proprietary merchandise designed especially for the needs of schools, hospitals, recreational organizations, and other institutional establishments. Sales to semiprofessionals and hobbyist leather craftspeople make up a significant and growing portion of the business of the division.

Wolfe Nursery, Inc. The acquisition of Wolfe Nursery, Inc., of Stephenville, Texas, in the fall of 1966 introduced Tandy Corporation into still another major recreational and leisure-time market. The care and maintenance of garden and household plantings and grounds is a popular activity for men and women of all ages, particularly in surburban residential areas. The increasing number of garden clubs, flower shows, and neighborhood beautification programs is ample evidence of this trend. Wolfe Nursery, with its 40 years of experience in supplying live nursery plants, fruit trees, insecticides, fertilizers, garden equipment, and related items at wholesale and by mail order, is now increasing its retail garden centers, with eight in operation in Texas at the year-end. Nursery-farming operations in Stephenville and production contracts with other growers assure an adequate supply system for the anticipated retail expansion.

Tex Tan Welhausen Company The Tex Tan Welhausen Division manufactures distinctive leather accessories and markets them through a growing dealer organization now consisting of more than 12,000 retail outlets in the United States and seven foreign countries. At its plant in Yoakum, Texas, Tex Tan Welhausen produces wallets, travel kits, and belts of the highest quality through a combination of imaginative design, use of the finest leathers, and the maintenance of a traditional pride in their craft dating back many years. The division's products are sold in leading department stores, men's stores, and gift shops and are featured in popular men's magazines. A cooperative advertising program with dealers makes extensive seasonal use of metropolitan newspaper and television media.

Tex Tan Western Leather Company The Tex Tan Western Leather Company Division is considered to be the largest manufacturer of saddlery and riding equipment in the United States marketing under its own brand names. The division distributes its products through more than 8,000 ranch supply, outdoor stores, and "Western" outfitters throughout the country. From its origin as a supplier to ranchers and stockpersons, Tex Tan Western Leather Company has expanded its markets to include riding clubs, boarding stables, and camping and other modern outdoor recreational activities. The product line has been expanded further with the addition of personal accessories of Western design manufactured with the same care and skill developed over many years of saddlery production in the company plant in Yoakum.

Radio Shack Division The Radio Shack Division now operates 156 company-owned consumer electronics supply stores in the United States. This was an increase of 69 retail outlets during the past 12 months. The Radio Shack product line includes parts and circuitry components used extensively in educational and experimental work; audio system components for entertainment; communications equipment for commercial and recreational use; and associated supplies and equipment. Sales emphasis is placed upon the division's private brands and trademark items which are engineered by Radio Shack and produced under contract by manufacturing firms both domestically and abroad. The technological instruction given by schools, industry, and the military services has created an interest in and an understanding of electronics and its practical everyday applications among a rapidly increasing portion of the population. Considerably more than one million individual names appear on the Radio Shack customer list, in addition to thousands of commercial and institutional accounts.

Corral Sportswear Company   The Corral Sportswear Company subsidiary manufactures and distributes fine leather sportswear designed to serve the markets for both traditional and contemporary fashions in leather garments. Suedes, "roughout," and other specialty leathers are worked into attractively styled jackets for men, women, and children and are sold through the more than 4,000 outlets which now carry the "Jo-O-Kay" brand. During the year a second production facility was added to the company plant in Ardmore, Oklahoma, and a line of women's leather handbags and accessories was introduced, resulting in a sharp increase in the number and type of sales outlets which the company may now serve. Continuous emphasis on the use of genuine fine leathers has assured the Corral Sportswear Company a distinctive place in the very competitive outerwear industry.

American Handicrafts Company   The American Handicrafts Company subsidiary serves educational and recreational institutions and hundreds of thousands of individuals who perform creative crafts work for pleasure or profit through its 42 retail and mail-order stores operated nationally. The division markets materials and equipment, in bulk as well as in kit form, for use in over 30 fields of handcraft and art work other than leathercraft. Craft supplies are assembled in the Fort Worth facility from sources all over the world and are processed or packaged for distribution through the store system and by mail order. Basketry materials from Malaysia, mosaic tile from the Orient and Southern Europe, art metals from Scandinavia, and artist supplies from the United States and Europe are typical of the merchandise lines in which this division specializes.

Merribee Company   The Merribee Company Division sells needlecraft materials, kits, and supplies to individual and institutional customers nationally, distributing solely by mail order from its warehouse and assembly rooms in Fort Worth. Domestic and imported yarns for knitting, Irish linen for embroidery work, garment kits, instructions, patterns, and sewing and weaving equipment make up the essential merchandise lines. Needlework, in its various forms, is one of the oldest of handcraft activities and continues to rank among the highest in popular interest, year after year. The Merribee consumer catalog and other direct-mail sales literature reach and serve thousands of customers, mostly women, who live in suburban and rural areas where a full selection of needlework materials is not readily available. The Merribee division fills the needs of one of the many specialized fields of recreational and educational interest.

LEONARDS DEPARTMENT STORE

In July of 1967, at the request of Charles Tandy, financial information was furnished by Leonard Brothers for evaluation as a possible acquisition. In subsequent conversations with the Leonard family, they indicated that they would be flexible in working out a formula which the Tandy Corporation could accept for the purchase of Leonard operations. It was stated that the Leonard family might consider reducing the capital investment required if they were able to retain ownership of the buildings used by the department store. Leonards would then rent the properties to the purchaser of the business. To further reduce capital requirements and provide a more adequate return on investment to the Tandy Corporation, Charles Tandy also discussed the possibility of the selling of the accounts receivable of Leonards to a financial institution.

In 1967 Leonards Department Store was the largest retailer in the Greater Fort Worth trading area. Leonards was founded in 1918 by J. Marvin Leonard in a small, rustic one-room store 20 feet wide with about 1,500 square feet of space. Counters were boards on barrels; display cases were wash tubs. Two years later, Marvin's brother, Obadiah P. Leonard, joined him in the venture. Both men were in their early twenties. The first store was outgrown within two years, and the Leonards added the 15 feet next door, then the next 25 feet, then a two-story building. The products sold included groceries, meats, fruits, vegetables, auto accessories, hardware, notions, and seeds at wholesale and retail. In 1967 Leonards Department Store operated over 500,000 square feet of sales area covering a six-block area in downtown Fort Worth. With over 2,000 employees, it was one of the 10 largest employers in Fort Worth. (See Exhibits 9 to 12 for financial data.) Leonards retained its sales volume despite a general trend toward decreasing sales volume in most inner cities. This was due primarily to a convenient 29-acre 5,000-car parking lot located on the outskirts of the central business district which provided essential free parking for Leonards's customers. The parking area was connected to the retail store by a private subway system, the only subway owned and operated by a private corporation in the world. This subway operated early in the morning to provide persons working in downtown Fort Worth with free parking. As the only downtown terminal for the subway system was Leonards Department

Leonards

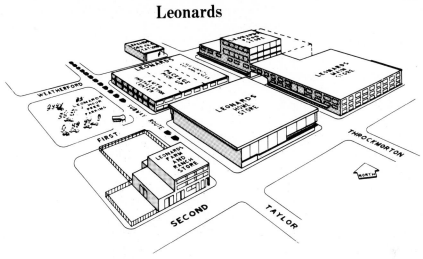

EXHIBIT 3
Layout of Leonards in 1967.

Store, there was subtle encouragement for the subway patrons to shop at Leonards. Over 7 million riders used this subway each year (see Exhibit 3).

Leonards's 108 separate merchandising departments offered products ranging from huge farm tractors to exquisite mink coats. In addition to traditional department store product lines, Leonards operated a food supermarket, a complete farm and ranch store, a service station, and an autoservice center. Leonards's customer base was made up primarily of middle-class, lower middle-class, and low-class population groups for apparel merchandise; however, all income classes were considered as potential purchasers of their hard goods lines. Leonards had the reputation for being an in-depth merchandiser, offering the widest selection of merchandise of all retailers in the trading area. In recent years, Leonards had moved to upgrade its overall image in order to increase its sales to the upper middle-class population.

Leonards's organizational structure was typical of most department stores. The company's operations were divided into two divisions: the merchandise division, responsible for sales and inventories, and the operating division, responsible for all other functions, including the physical store plant, customer service, credit, maintenance, subway, parking lots, etc. The accounting control system was also typical of department stores. Department managers were responsible for and received feedback information on sales, returns, gross margins, salary expense, miscellaneous selling expense, and the net contribution to corporate overhead and administrative expenses (defined as net sales less total expenses). Primary emphasis was placed on net sales and gross sales margins.

Paul Leonard, the president of Leonards, at 42 years of age was recognized by the industry as one of the top retailers in the United States. Mr. Leonard expressed an interest in remaining with Leonards as president if the Tandy Corporation decided to acquire the company. The other members of the Leonards management team were also considered competent retailers and experts in their respective fields.

To maximize sales opportunity and protect existing sales levels in the Fort Worth trading area, Leonards's management felt that expansion into the suburbs was essential. With this objective, an option to purchase land in northeast Fort Worth was pending and another potential location in Arlington, Texas, was under negotiation. Arlington was a community to the southeast of Fort Worth but within the Fort Worth trading area (located approximately halfway between Fort Worth and Dallas). It was contemplated that these new operations would be full-line stores and would be designed to appeal to the middle high-income groups as well as to the traditional customers of Leonards, thus upgrading the overall image of the company in the trading area. It was expected that both stores together would have approximately 250,000 square feet of floor space.

FORT WORTH, TEXAS, TRADING AREA

Leonards Department Store sales were closely linked to the economy of the Fort Worth, Texas, retail trading area. In 1967, Fort Worth, with a population of approximately 745,000 in the two-county metropolitan area, was the mercantile, commercial, and industrial headquarters for much of west Texas.

Fort Worth prided itself on being the city "where the west begins." It was established as a frontier army post in 1849 by Major Ripley Arnold and named for General Jenkins Worth, who distinguished himself in the Mexican War. The outpost became a stopping place on the storied Old Chisholm Trail and a shipping point for the great herds of Longhorn cattle being sent to northern markets. Progressive city leadership brought the first nine railroads to Fort Worth in 1876 and, with the subsequent west Texas oil boom, made the city an important metropolitan entity. (See Exhibit 4.)

Historically, Fort Worth's economy had been based on agriculture-oriented industries with major livestock marketing facilities, grain, manufacturing firms, and services. In 1967, the Fort Worth employment base was well diversified with strong representation in the aircraft industry. General Dynamics, Fort Worth Division, manufactured the F-111 jet for the Defense Department, and the Bell Helicopter Company built helicopters for both military and civilian use. A total of 25 manufacturing firms were located in the area, including producers of food and beverages, mobile homes, automobiles, and medical supplies. Fort Worth was also a center for higher education: the seven local college and university campuses had an enrollment in excess of 33,000 students. The Fort Worth area was also the location of 16 state government offices, 14 federal government offices, and 8 military installations.

EXHIBIT 4
FORT WORTH METROPOLITAN AREA

City of Fort Worth, incorporated area	212 square miles
Tarrant County	860 square miles
Standard Metropolitan Statistical Area	1,600 square miles

(The U.S. Bureau of the Budget has defined the Fort Worth Standard Metropolitan Statistical Area to include Tarrant and Johnson Counties—an area covering 1,600 square miles. Cleburne is the county seat of Johnson County.)

Population

Year	Fort Worth	Tarrant County	SMSA
1967	375,000	700,000	745,000
1960	356,268	538,495	573,215
1950	277,047	361,253	392,643
1940	177,662	255,521	255,905

Employment

	1957	1967	% Increase
Total civilian labor force	222,140	316,200	42.3
Employment total	212,840	307,500	44.5
Agricultural	3,900	3,150	−19.2
Nonagricultural	208,940	30,350	45.6
Manufacturing	55,215	93,350	69.1
Mining	3,535	2,020	−42.9
Construction	13,250	15,270	15.3
Transportation, communications, and utilities	16,620	16,190	− 2.6
Trades	52,630	73,600	39.8
Finance, insurance, and real estate	9,290	13,350	43.7
Services and misc.	34,940	55,200	57.9
Government	23,260	34,980	50.4

CONSIDERATION OF THE ACQUISITION

The Tandy Corporation management gave serious consideration to the proposed acquisition of Leonards Department Store. In an effort to reach a conclusion, several lengthy discussions were carried on with the top management group of Leonards. Both parties hoped to reach a conclusion about the acquisition as soon as possible. Mr. James L. West, president of Tandy Corporation, pointed out several factors concerning the proposed acquisition that needed to be considered, especially the matters of price, adaptability, and organizational relationship.

EXHIBIT 5

TANDY CORPORATION—SEVEN-YEAR STATISTICAL SUMMARY, YEAR ENDED JUNE 30

	1967	1966*	1965†	1964	1963	1962	1961
Net sales	$60,703,805	$49,875,701	$42,784,605	$23,853,039	$20,310,127	$17,693,507	$15,961,250
Earnings before federal income tax	3,542,277	3,225,029	2,261,962	1,498,818	1,117,522	1,226,259	964,603
Federal income tax	930,779	929,887	760,540	55,631	409,089	245,794	245,051
Net earnings	2,611,498	2,295,142	1,501,422	943,187	708,433	980,465	719,552
Net earnings as percent of sales	4.3%	4.6%	3.5%	4%	3.5%	5.5%	4.5%
Net earnings as percent of stock-holders' equity at beginning of year	28%	33%	36%	30%	12%	20%	16%
Current assets	22,039,768	18,635,429	17,505,413	9,130,686	8,409,197	7,343,739	6,883,451
Current liabilities	4,938,411	4,869,522	4,838,228	2,036,025	2,330,573	1,212,656	1,656,126
Current ratio	4.5 to 1	3.8 to 1	3.7 to 1	4.5 to 1	3.6 to 1	6.1 to 1	4.2 to 1
Net working capital	17,101,357	13,765,907	12,667,185	7,094,661	6,078,624	6,131,083	5,227,325
Long-term liabilities	10,906,691	8,429,027	8,590,011	5,188,125	5,450,484†	2,133,280	2,372,473
Net property and equipment	3,617,741	2,130,992	1,670,695	674,118	753,259	698,917	588,307
Earnings per common share	2.06	1.80	1.21	.89	.67	.63	.46
Common shares outstanding	1,267,858	1,272,462	1,243,376	1,060,938	1,060,938‡	1,561,061	1,527,398
Stockholders' equity	11,982,359	9,359,778	7,058,428	4,112,958	3,169,771‡	5,962,199	4,744,838
Net worth per common share	9.45	7.36	5.68	3.88	2.99	3.82	3.11
Retain earnings	9,858,938	7,247,440	5,091,395	3,633,115	2,689,928	1,981,495	990,153
Stockholders and nominees	2,231	2,472	2,465	2,297	2,479	3,004	2,666

*Restated to reflect pooling of interests resulting from merger of Radio Shack Corporation.
†Includes Radio Shack Corporation subsidiary which was consolidated effective July 1, 1964.
‡Reflects issuance of $3,500,000 of debentures in exchange for 500,123 shares of outstanding common stock in 1963.

EXHIBIT 6
TANDY CORPORATION AND SUBSIDIARIES—CONSOLIDATED
STATEMENT OF INCOME AND RETAINED EARNINGS

	1967	1966
Net sales	$60,703,805	$49,875,701
Other income	370,532	407,249
	61,074,337	50,282,950
Cost and expenses:		
Cost of products sold	33,835,258	28,262,875
Selling and administrative	22,772,766	18,070,717
Depreciation	339,160	263,927
Interest on debentures	226,756	227,253
Other interest charges, less interest income	357,018	158,067
	57,530,958	46,982,839
Income before federal income tax and minority interest	3,543,379	3,300,111
Provision for federal income tax (Note 4)	930,779	929,887
Net income before monthly interest	2,612,600	2,370,224
Minority interest in net income	1,102	75,082
Net income	2,611,498	2,295,142
Retained earnings—beginning of year (Note 1)	7,247,440	4,952,298
Retained earnings—end of year	$ 9,858,938	$ 7,247,440
Net income per share of common stock:		
Average outstanding shares	$2.06	$1.80
Pro forma, assuming conversion of warrants (Note 7)	$1.78	$1.55

EXHIBIT 7
Tandy Corporation and Subsidiaries—Consolidated Balance Sheet

Assets

	1967	1966
Current assets:		
Cash	$ 3,221,220	$ 1,171,461
Accounts and notes receivable:		
Trade, less allowance for doubtful accounts	4,202,751	5,084,148
Other	236,924	81,659
Inventories, at lower of approximate cost (substantially on a first-in, first-out basis) or market:		
Finished merchandise	12,678,552	10,388,261
Raw materials and work in process	1,322,943	1,531,707
Other current assets	377,378	378,193
Total current assets	22,039,768	18,635,429
Property and equipment, at cost less accumulated depreciation (Note 2)	3,617,741	2,130,992
Other assets, including deferred charges	707,901	769,992
Unamortized excess cost of investment (Note 3)	1,462,051	1,391,780
	$27,827,461	$22,928,193

EXHIBIT 7 (*continued*)

Liabilities And Stockholders' Equity

	1967	1966 (Restated, see Note 1)
Current liabilities:		
Notes payable to banks (Note 5)	$ 332,202	$ 466,145
Purchase obligations due within one year	121,281	150,660
Accounts payable	1,562,732	1,407,616
Accrued expenses	2,086,487	1,708,084
Federal income tax (Note 4)	835,709	1,137,017
Total current liabilities	4,938,411	4,869,522
Other liabilities:		
Notes payable to banks (Note 5)	6,553,267	4,149,155
Purchase obligations due after one year (Note 5)	760,508	444,650
6½% Subordinated debentures, due 1978 (Note 6)	3,482,900	3,494,500
Other noncurrent liabilities	110,016	340,723
	10,906,691	8,429,028
Equity of minority stockholders in Radio Shack Corporation (Note 1)		269,865
Stockholders' equity (Notes 1, 7, 8, and 9)		
Common stock, $1 par value:		
2,000,000 shares authorized		
1,696,574 shares issued	1,696,574	1,696,574
Capital surplus	3,651,473	3,306,293
Retained earnings	9,858,938	7,247,440
	15,206,985	12,250,307
Less—Common stock in treasury at cost—428,716 shares (1967) and 424,112 shares (1966)	3,224,626	2,890,529
	11,982,359	9,359,778
Commitments (Note 10)		
	$27,827,461	$22,928,193

EXHIBIT 8

TANDY CORPORATION AND SUBSIDIARIES—NOTES TO FINANCIAL STATEMENTS, JUNE 30, 1967

Note 1—principles of consolidation and merger of Radio Shack Corporation

The accompanying consolidated financial statements include the accounts of the parent company, Tandy Corporation, and its subsidiaries.

As of June 30, 1966, Tandy Corporation owned 269,357 shares (85.47%) of the outstanding common stock of Radio Shack Corporation. In fiscal 1967, Radio Shack issued to all its stockholders rights to purchase at $8 per share three new shares of common stock for each share previously owned. Tandy exercised its right and purchased 808,071 Radio Shack shares. As authorized by Radio Shack stockholders, Tandy also purchased at $8 per share 133,755 additional shares under rights granted to, but not exercised by, other stockholders. Furthermore, during the year Tandy purchased 1,090 Radio Shack shares directly from a stockholder. The foregoing transactions brought Tandy's ownership interest in Radio Shack to 96.2%, comprising 1,212,273 common shares.

Effective June 30, 1967, Tandy acquired the remaining minority interest (3.8%) in Radio Shack through a statutory merger of the latter company into Tandy, in connection with which Radio Shack minority stockholders received two Tandy shares for each three Radio Shack shares previously owned. This transaction was treated as a pooling of interests for financial accounting purposes and the accompanying financial statements give effect to the pooling on a retroactive basis.

As a result of giving retroactive effect to the pooling transaction, the consolidated financial statements for the year ended June 30, 1966 have been restated as follows:

	Amount of restatement (debit) credit
Minority interest in Radio Shack	($ 96,596)
Treasury stock (32,172 shares issued)	241,933
Capital surplus	(33,116)
Retained earnings:	
Balance at July 1, 1965	(139,097)
1966 net income	26,875

Note 2—property and equipment

	June 30,	
	1967	**1966**
Buildings	$ 539,262	$ 522,570
Machinery, equipment, furniture, and fixtures	4,785,820	3,434,520
	5,325,082	3,957,090
Less accumulated depreciation	2,062,643	1,853,900
	3,262,439	2,103,190
Land	355,302	27,802
	$3,617,741	$2,130,992

Certain of the purchase obligations referred to in Note 5 with unpaid balances aggregating $570,589 are secured by the mortgage of property and equipment carried in the consolidated balance sheet at a net amount of approximately $762,556.

EXHIBIT 8 (*continued*)

Note 3—unamortized excess cost of investment

During the fiscal year ended June 30, 1960, $1,000,000 was paid in final settlement of the purchase price of certain subsidiaries acquired in 1955. This final settlement was capitalized as goodwill, the excess cost of the subsidiaries arising from prior purchase payments having been amortized during the period from acquisition through June 30, 1960.

Tandy Corporation's aggregate cost of investment in Radio Shack Corporation exceeded its aggregate equity in book value of net assets at dates of acquisition by $376,896. As stated in Note 1, Radio Shack was merged into Tandy Corporation as of June 30, 1967.

In connection with the tax settlement described in Note 4, an amount of $85,155 was transferred during 1967 from property and equipment accounts to excess cost. Such amount arose in connection with several acquisitions of businesses during the early 1960's.

The Board of Directors has adopted the policy of reviewing these excess costs annually and the full amount will continue to be carried as an asset unless the Board determines that there has been a decline or a limitation in the value, at which time an appropriate amortization policy will be adopted.

Note 4—federal income tax

Federal income tax has been provided on the basis of separate returns to be filed for each corporation.

In fiscal 1967 and 1966, Radio Shack Corporation's net income was not subject to federal income tax due to the application of loss carry-overs. Had such loss carry-overs not been available, consolidated net income would have been reduced by approximately $400,000 in 1967 and $300,000 in 1966. As stated in Note 1, Radio Shack was merged into Tandy Corporation as of June 30, 1967. At that date Radio Shack had loss carry-overs for federal income tax purposes aggregating approximately $4,000,000, which in the opinion of the company's legal counsel may be applied against the taxable income of the parent company over the next two years.

A settlement of certain prior years' income tax disputes was effected and the resulting adjustments were recorded during 1967. The effect of these adjustments upon the accompanying consolidated financial statements was immaterial.

Note 5—purchase obligations and bank loans

Purchase obligations		
	Portion due within one year	**Portion due after one year**
Note payable to profit-sharing trusts of Tex Tan Division, 5¹/₂%, payable in eight installments, secured (Note 2)	$ 24,200	$ 169,400
Notes payable in connection with purchase of building, 6%, payable in monthly installments until January, 1985, secured (Note 2)	2,381	66,608
Note payable in connection with acquisition of assets in 1965, 6%, payable in three installments	35,200	76,000
Note payable in connection with purchase of assets in 1967, 6¹/₄%, first principal payment in 1973, secured (Note 2)		232,000
Note payable in connection with purchase of building by Radio Shack, 5%, payable in eight installments, secured (Note 2)	9,500	66,500
Note payable in connection with acquisition of a company in 1967, payable in four installments	50,000	150,000
Total purchase obligations	$121,281	$ 760,508

EXHIBIT 8 *(continued)*

TANDY CORPORATION AND SUBSIDIARIES—NOTES TO FINANCIAL STATEMENTS, JUNE 30, 1967

Notes payable to banks		
5% note	$300,000	$3,850,000
5¹/₂% note due December 26, 1968 (Paid in August, 1967 from proceeds of new financing described in second succeeding paragraph)		2,700,000
Others	32,202	3,267
Total notes payable to banks	$332,202	$6,553,267

The 5% bank loan ($4,150,000) is payable in four annual installments of $300,000 and a final installment of $2,950,000 in 1972.

In August, 1967, Tandy arranged for $6,000,000 in additional long-term financing of which $3,000,000 was received in August with the remaining $3,000,000 to be received in January, 1968. The loan is payable over 14 years with the first payment due in January, 1971 and bears interest at the rate of 6%.

Note 6—6¹/₂% subordinated debentures

The debentures are subordinate to all "senior indebtedness" (as defined in the indenture), including purchase and borrowed money obligations, and may be redeemed by the company in whole or in part at any time at principal amount and accrued interest or surrendered by the holders at any time until December 31, 1969 in payment for common stock purchased upon exercise of warrants described in Note 7.

Note 7—common stock

Warrants for the purchase of 219,677 shares of common stock were outstanding at June 30, 1967. These warrants were issued in connection with the 6¹/₂% subordinated debentures and entitle the holder to purchase common stock at $7.50 per share until December 31, 1967 or $9.00 per share from January 1, 1968 through December 31, 1969. Warrants were exercised for the purchase of 19,996 shares of stock during the year. The pro forma per share data in the statement of income is based on the assumption that all such warrants were exercised as of July 1, 1965 and the related proceeds applied against outstanding debt.

Changes in treasury stock during the year ended June 30, 1967 consisted of the following:

	Number of shares	Cost or average cost
Purchased on the open market	39,600	$586,035
Issued upon acquisition of net assets of Wolfe Nursery Co.	(15,000)	(102,150)
Issued upon exercise of stock purchase warrants	(19,996)	(149,788)
Net increase during fiscal 1967	4,604	$334,097

Note 8—capital surplus

The increase of $345,180 in capital surplus during the year ended June 30, 1967 is comprised of:

EXHIBIT 8 (*continued*)

Excess of proceeds from exercise of warrants for purchase of 19,996 shares of capital stock over average cost of treasury shares issued	$ 182
Excess of market value over average cost of treasury shares issued in connection with the Wolfe Nursery acquisition	78,553
1967 increase in capital surplus resulting from pooling of Radio Shack	266,445
	$345,180

Note 9—dividend and other restrictions

The indenture covering the company's debenture issue and the 5% bank loan agreement impose, under certain conditions, requirements or restrictions relating to minimum working capital, net worth, payment of dividends (other than dividends payable in capital stock of the company), and purchase, redemption, or other retirement by the company of any shares of its capital stock. Under the most restrictive provisions such payments are limited to approximately $2,200,000 as of June 30, 1967.

Note 10—commitments

The company leases property, which includes stores, administrative offices, and warehouses, under leases expiring between 1968 and 1983. Approximate minimum annual rentals under such leases are summarized below:

Fiscal year	Amount
1968	$1,950,000
1969	1,750,000
1970	1,500,000
1971	1,200,000
1972–1975	1,050,000
1976–1979	900,000
1980–1983	50,000

EXHIBIT 9

LEONARDS INC.—CONSOLIDATED STATEMENT OF INCOME

	Nine months ended		Years ended				
	October 28, 1967	October 30, 1966 (unaudited)	January 29, 1967	January 30, 1966	January 31, 1965 (unaudited)	December 29, 1963 (unaudited)	December 29, 1962 (unaudited)
Revenues							
Net sales (exclusive of sales of leased departments)	$26,082,770	$24,178,549	$34,353,272	$31,433,938	$31,086,829	$30,129,633	$32,272,503
Carrying and service charges	974,832	724,692	1,080,193	885,712	785,775	737,352	664,543
Commissions—leased departments	201,872	171,934	243,425	239,012	187,198	145,765	118,344
Interest income (principally from stockholders and affiliates)	26,425	6,127	8,169	55,353	153,238	108,710	39,133
Other income	35,959	39,283	47,419	110,593	67,970	13,590	40,160
	27,321,858	25,120,585	35,732,478	32,724,608	32,281,010	31,135,050	33,134,683
Costs and expenses							
Cost of goods sold (Notes 2&8)	17,535,547	16,590,622	23,337,039	21,494,892	21,336,052	20,916,476	23,063,031
Selling, general, and administrative expenses (b)	7,565,218	7,118,574	9,658,406	9,077,338	9,068,228	8,574,558	8,737,380
Depreciation	251,757	264,465	340,614	354,658	392,585	375,933	223,596
Provision for doubtful accounts	218,964	133,849	382,325	424,241	—	372,965	500,471
Interest:							
Long-term debt	50,471	57,040	76,053	69,904	—	308	5,363
Other	200,094	146,520	205,174	92,799	221,155	348,456	184,663
Minority interest in net income (loss) subsidiary	20,207	7,849	14,699	9,922	13,787	8,272	(691)
Provisions for income taxes (c) (d):							
Current	2,163,442	133,853	275,411	(390,196)	589,050	221,985	179,445
Deferred	(1,485,884)	273,757	535,981	949,903			
	677,558	407,610	811,392	559,707	589,050	221,985	179,445
	26,519,816	24,726,529	34,825,702	32,083,461	31,620,857	30,818,953	32,893,258
Income before extraordinary items	802,042	394,056	906,776	641,147	660,153	316,097	241,425

Extraordinary items:

Moving and temporary relocation expense, less applicable income tax reduction of $64,779			
Loss on sale of accounts receivable in connection with discontinuance of department store operations of Everybodys, less applicable income tax reduction of $72,296			(66,735)
Gain on sale of real estate, less applicable income tax of $36,585		109,756	
Discount on sale of accounts receivable, less applicable income tax reduction of $100,806		(100,807)	
Loss on sale of marketable securities, with no income tax effect	(478,882)		
Provision for loss on sale of accounts receivable, less applicable income tax reduction of $112,362 (c)	(121,725)		
Gain on sale of assets and business, less applicable income tax of $162,861 (a)	171,411		
	$ 851,728	$ 394,056	$ 906,776	$ 162,265	$ 559,346	$ 425,853	$ 114,894

Net income

Notes To Consolidated Statement of Income:

(a) During the year ended January 30, 1966, Leonards issued 352,946 shares of its common stock in exchange for all the outstanding shares of Everybodys. This transaction has been accounted for as a "pooling of interests" and accordingly the operations of Everybodys have been included in the above statement for the entire period of September 22, 1967, when Everybodys was merged into the Company. In the year ended December 29, 1962, Everybodys had sales of approximately $2,300,000 prior to discontinuing department store operations; subsequent revenues, principally from investments, have not been material.

At February 2, 1964 Leonards changed its fiscal year from the 52–53 weeks ending nearest December 31 to the corresponding period ending nearest January 31. As a result, operations, including sales and net income of $2,174,887 and $5,514, respectively, for the period December 30, 1963 to February 2, 1964, have been omitted from the above statement.

The consolidated statement of income for the year ended January 30, 1966 has been restated, principally to include the loss on sale of marketable securities, as recommended by opinion No. 9 of the Accounting Principles Board.

(b) See Note 6 to financial statements for lease obligations.

(c) Beginning with the year end January 30, 1966, Leonards has reported income from certain sales on the installment method for federal income tax purposes and has provided deferred income taxes on the difference between income reported for financial statement purposes and that reported for income tax purposes. As a result of a change in policy relating to option and contract accounts receivable (see Note 3 to financial statements), the deferred federal income tax became payable currently.

(d) Leonards deducts investment tax credits from the current federal income tax provision in the years in which it is applied to reduce taxes otherwise payable. The amount of such credits applied was: 1962—$28,042; 1963—$31,067; 1965—$11,933; 1966—$1,612; 1967—$18,483 and the nine months ended October 30, 1966 and October 28, 1967—$17,083 and none, respectively.

EXHIBIT 10
Leonards Inc. Balance Sheet
October 28, 1967

Assets

Current assets:

Cash	$ 1,078,247
U. S. Treasury bills, at cost which approximates market value	494,388
Inventory (Note 2)	7,042,244
Accounts receivable, less allowance for losses of $870,034	9,251,885
Due from stockholders, affiliates, and others	3,137,924
Prepaid expenses and other assets	151,932
Total current assets	21,156,620

Property and equipment, at cost (Note 3):

Building and improvements	$ 3,731,192	
Furniture, fixtures, and equipment	36,358	
	3,767,550	
Less accumulated depreciation and amortization	1,595,072	
	2,172,478	
Land	589,559	
Net property and equipment		2,762,037
		$23,918,657

Liabilities and Stockholders' Equity

Current liabilities:

Accounts payable		$ 1,299,332
Accrued expenses		576,074
Federal income tax (Note 4)		2,126,957
Long-term debt due within one year		121,484
Total current liabilities		4,123,847
Long-term debt due after one year (Note 5)		8,150,886

Commitments (Note 6)

Stockholders' equity:

Common stock: $1 par value, 2,500,000 shares authorized and issued, including shares in treasury	$ 2,500,000	
Capital in excess of par value (Note 7)	200,537	
Retained earnings	12,331,589	
	15,032,120	
Less cost of common stock held in treasury—870,329 shares (Note 7)	3,388,202	
Total stockholders' equity		11,643,924
		$23,918,657

EXHIBIT 11
LEONARDS INC., CONSOLIDATED STATEMENT OF RETAINED EARNINGS

	Year ended			Nine months ended October 28, 1967
	January 31, 1965 (unaudited)	January 30, 1966	January 29, 1967	
Balance at beginning of period	$11,970,066	$12,413,237	$10,656,694	$11,479,861
Net income	559,346	162,265	906,776	851,728
Retained earnings of Everybodys applicable to 293, 484 shares of common stock acquired for its treasury (Note 7)		(877,601)		
Excess of cost over par value of 352,946 shares of treasury stock issued in exchange for all of the outstanding stock of Everybodys (Note 7)		(1,020,349)		
Dividends paid:				
1965 and 1966—$.01 per share	(25,000)	(20,858)		
1967—$.05 per share			(83,609)	
Everybodys, prior to pooling of interests	(91,175)			
Balance at end of period	$12,413,237	$10,656,694	$11,479,861	$12,331,589

EXHIBIT 12

LEONARDS INC.—NOTES TO FINANCIAL STATEMENTS, OCTOBER 28, 1967

---

1. Basis of consolidated statements of income and of retained earnings

The consolidated statements of income and of retained earnings include the accounts of the Company, its wholly owned subsidiary, Everybodys (see Note (a) to consolidated statement of income), to September 22, 1967, when it was merged into the Company, and its majority-owned subsidiary, Mitchells of Fort Worth, Inc. Intercompany accounts and transactions have been eliminated.

2. Inventories

Inventories were valued principally at the lower of average cost or market determined by the retail inventory method. The amounts of inventories used in the computation of cost of goods sold for the three years and nine months ended October 28, 1967 were as follows:

February 3, 1964	$5,615,434
January 31, 1965	5,289,516
January 30, 1966	5,413,387
January 29, 1967	5,645,795
October 28, 1967	7,042,244

3. Property and equipment

Depreciation has been provided on the straight-line or declining-balance methods at annual rates based on the estimated remaining useful lives of the depreciable assets as follows:

Building and building improvements	4–50 years
Furniture and fixtures	5–12$\frac{1}{2}$ years
Automotive equipment	3–6 years
Subway and tunnel	5–17 years

Maintenance, repairs, and renewals of a minor nature have been charged to expense as incurred. Betterments and major renewals which extend the useful life of fixed assets have been capitalized.

Upon sale of property and equipment, the cost and accumulated depreciation applicable thereto have been removed from the accounts and any resulting profit or loss reflected in income.

4. Federal income tax

See Notes (c) and (d) to consolidated statement of income.

5. Long-term debt

Long-term debt at October 28, 1967 consisted of:

5$\frac{1}{2}$% secured promissory note due April 15, 1975	$7,042,250
5$\frac{1}{2}$% unsecured promissory notes due in annual installments of $100,260 including interest to April 15, 1975	640,576
5$\frac{1}{2}$% unsecured promissory notes due in annual installments of $92,272 including interest to April 15, 1975	468,060

The aggregate amount of maturities for each of the five years subsequent to October 28, 1967 were: 1968—$121,484; 1969—$131,742; 1970—$138,988; 1971—$146,632; 1972—$154,697. These notes have subsequently been paid in full.

EXHIBIT 12 *(continued)*

6. Lease obligations

The Company was obligated for minimum annual rentals of approximately $524,000, plus additional rents contingent on sales volume, under long-term leases with affiliated organizations.

7. Stockholders' equity

There were no changes in capital in excess of par value during the three years and nine months ended October 28, 1967.

On April 15, 1965 the Company acquired 414,167 shares of its common stock for $1,597,581, of which 352,946 shares costing $1,373,295 were later used in the acquisition of Everybodys (see Note (a) to consolidated statement of income). On the same date Everybodys acquired 293,484 shares of its common stock for $1,207,703. Everybodys also acquired, at the same date, 766,608 shares of the Company's common stock for $2,982,833, which shares are held in the treasury.

During the year ended January 29, 1967, the Company acquired an additional 42,500 shares for $169,219 and, during the nine months ended October 28, 1967, incurred additional costs of $11,864 in connection with shares previously acquired.

8. Supplementary information

All of the following were charged to profit and loss accounts other than cost of goods sold:

	Year ended			Nine months ended October 28, 1967
	January 31, 1965 (unaudited)	January 30, 1966	January 29, 1967	
Maintenance and repairs	$110,900	$124,509	$162,774	$ 94,988
Depreciation and amortization of property and equipment	$392,585	$354,658	$340,614	$251,757
Taxes other than income taxes:				
Payroll	$216,812	$232,485	$275,522	$220,239
Ad valorem and other	105,188	107,572	108,901	96,038
Franchise	50,684	42,424	34,009	36,185
	$372,684	$382,481	$418,432	$352,462
Rents	$720,378	$724,547	$747,142	$558,416

No management and service contract fees or royalties were incurred.

Marcor, Inc. — A Merger

On October 31, 1968, the stockholders of Montgomery Ward and Container Corporation of America voted to combine assets and managements of the two companies into Marcor, Inc. This merger resulted in a marketing-oriented, diversified, multi-billion-dollar company composed of leaders in the merchandising and packaging industries.

MONTGOMERY WARD

For the fiscal year ending January 31, 1970, Wards had over $2 billion in sales, making it the third largest general merchandising operation in the United States. Sales outlets were comprised of retail department stores (approximately 500) and catalog sales agencies or departments. Approximately 95 percent of all merchandise was sold under the company's private label; credit sales contributed about one-half of total sales.

Products and Services

Wards's larger retail department stores carried a full line of products:

1 Soft goods—apparel and accessories, piece goods, notions, linen, and bedding

2 Home furnishings—furniture, draperies, floor coverings, housewares, and table appliances

3 Major household appliances—stereo phonographs, television sets, air conditioners, refrigerators, freezers, and laundry equipment

4 Automotive equipment—tires, batteries, and accessories

5 Miscellaneous hard goods—hardware, power tools, sporting goods, toys, building supplies, and lawn, garden, and farm equipment and supplies

In addition to the above products, most stores provided services for delivery, installation, and repair of merchandise sold. Many of the larger stores contained departments such as beauty salons, optical and hearing aid centers, and "boutique" shops designed to serve customers by carrying full families of products, such as the Ski Chalet, Golf Pro Shop, International Gourmet Shop, Fur Salon, and Television Salon. Wards also provided professional advice in planning and remodeling kitchens and bathrooms and installing central heating and air conditioning. Accommodation centers were available to customers (for paying utility bills, cashing checks, and photocopying), as were cafeterias, home decorating and sewing courses, and self-development programs for young girls.

Subsidiaries

Wards operated the following subsidiaries:

1 Standard T Chemical Company, Inc., developed, manufactured, and sold consumer and commercial paints, household detergents, industrial coatings, floor maintenance products, paper coatings, and resins. Sales were made to Wards's merchandise departments, as well as to other companies.

2 The Ajax Manufacturing Division, formerly a manufacturer of fence and farm products, was acquired in 1924. It produced camper and utility trailers and tool stands. All the products were sold through Wards's retail and catalog outlets under the private brand names "Riverside," "Western Field," and "Power-Kraft."

3 Wards organized Montgomery Ward Life Insurance Company in 1966. In less than two years of operation, life insurance in force had exceeded $665 million, including a $300 million group policy covering Wards's employees and $200 million in credit accounts. Life insurance in force had increased to over $1 billion by 1970.

4 A 98 percent interest in Pioneer Trust and Savings Bank, Chicago, was acquired by Wards in 1966.

5 Associated Sand and Gravel Company, a producer of concrete pipe, concrete products, and paving materials was acquired early in 1968. This acquisition complemented Wards's ownership of Hydro Conduit Corporation and its affiliates (the latter company has since been sold by Wards to Marcor). Associated Sand and Gravel was also engaged in the installation of asphalt paving and the extraction, processing, and sale of sand and gravel.

Company History

Wards was founded in 1872 by Aaron Montgomery Ward and his brother-in-law, George R. Thorne. The company was exclusively a mail-order sales firm until 1926, when it opened the first of its chain of retail stores in Marysville, Kansas. Until 1958, Wards retail stores were located in a large number of separate markets, most of which were rural. Since 1958, Wards had been engaged in a program designed to shift the focus of its operations from the rural and single-store urban markets to multiple store metropolitan markets.

Much of the company's early sales difficulty was attributed to Sewell L. Avery, chief executive officer of Wards from 1931 to 1955. Known as a strict disciplinarian, Avery kept the company basically sound during the depression, and in the late 1930s developed a program for opening new retail stores and closing old ones. From 1941 to 1955, however, Avery hoarded funds in anticipation of a second great depression and refused to open any new stores. At the time of Avery's departure in 1955, the company had (1) accumulated $327 million in cash and securities, (2) became known as a "bank with a store front," and (3) remained a rural-oriented mail-order business with an outmoded store organization concentrated in small towns in the midwest.

Avery's successor was John Barr, former legal counsel to Wards. Barr spent $154 million for expansion and modernization of facilities between 1957 and 1961, opening a total of 58 new stores; several old stores were closed during the same period. Robert Brooker, former vice president in charge of manufacturing at Sears, Roebuck and Co. and president of Whirlpool, accepted the post as president and chief operating officer of Wards in 1961.

Brooker's Strategy   One of Brooker's first moves was to recruit key executives experienced in mass merchandising—many of whom came from Sears. Around 30 key individuals made a commitment to join and stay with Wards in the attempt to implement a new concept of mass distribution. Working with these key people, along with some talented holdovers from Wards, Brooker developed a plan for expansion which could be implemented while maintaining a degree of profitability.

Brooker conceived that, externally, Wards's strategic situation was the opposite of Sears's. Historically, Wards had been in small towns and had not moved into the new urban markets. On the other hand, Sears originally had big-city markets and had also expanded into most of the major new markets. In addition, many other competitors had moved into the newer urban markets, including J. C. Penney, some department stores, and various discount houses. Consequently, Wards was at a strategic disadvantage in almost every market because of the advantages accruing to established retailers in the form of customer loyalty, higher volume, and greater exposure.

The basic strategy developed for retail store location revolved around three key points of action: closing of smaller unprofitable stores, relocation of smaller stores, and opening of new stores in the major urban markets. The basic objective was to make the transition from small stores to large stores without having costs jeopardize earnings. Two elements of cost were present: start-up costs for new stores and closing costs for old stores. The latter cost items (employee transfers, uncollected accounts which must be forfeited, and so forth) were estimated to total $30,000 to $40,000 for each store closed.

Operating within the cost constraint, Brooker worked out a plan for relocation, closing, and expansion with two Wards executives, Harold Dysart and Howard Green. The programming of store relocations in areas where the company already had acceptance was a key element of the plan, as was the opening of new stores based on the "metro district" concept—the latter term referred to the establishment of a central management team for each major metropolitan market to coordinate buying, promoting, and selling activities of all stores within the district.

Brooker also implemented a new procurement and inventory control system, cut the number of supply sources in half, initiated computer applications in various operations, and developed new policies and modes of operations for catalog and credit sales. The net result of these changes was an increase in profitability up through 1965.

1966: A Setback In the plan developed by Brooker, it was anticipated that earnings per share would grow by roughly 15 percent a year after 1962. The projection turned out to be fairly accurate up through 1965, but instead of realizing the projected $2.30 a share in 1966, earnings fell to $1.24. Two major reasons for the setback given by Brooker were overconfidence in operations and a credit squeeze.

The plan had gone reasonably well in the relocation of stores and in the development of some major metro markets. The trouble came, according to Brooker, "in metro markets where we were the invaders." Major losses were incurred in the Los Angeles and Chicago markets where the "basic mistake . . . was in deciding that since we were doing so well on the schedule we'd set up, we could add more on—and it was just too much for us to digest." There were not enough people trained in the metro organization concept, and the net result was a deficiency of managerial skills. The credit squeeze problem resulted from too great a reliance on short-term borrowing in the immediately preceding years. Brooker had to choose whether to maintain receivables and borrow more money or to tighten credit terms to customers and lose sales. The final decision was to cut back on credit terms to customers, and according to Brooker, "that subsequently hurt our sales and profits. . .we were a little too conservative, but at least we were prudent."

Financial Position Exhibit 1 presents a five-year summary of financial information for Wards as of January 31, 1968; the data indicate Wards's financial position prior to the beginning of merger negotiations with Container Corporation.

CONTAINER CORPORATION OF AMERICA

Container Corporation was founded in 1926 by Walter P. Paepcke, who served as chief executive officer for more than 30 years. To form the company, Mr. Paepcke combined the paperboard packaging facilities of Chicago Mill and

EXHIBIT 1
WARDS AND SUBSIDIARIES, STATISTICAL SUMMARY (Thousands of Dollars)*

	1963	1964	1965	1966	1967
Operations					
Net sales	$1,500,112	$1,697,390	$1,748,360	$1,894,123	$1,879,009
Net earnings	20,967	21,865	23,963	16,528	17,425
Federal income taxes	17,353	17,300	17,748	10,939	13,357
Dividends	13,880	13,550	13,555	13,556	13,555
Earnings reinvested from previous years	7,087	8,316	10,408	2,972	3,870
Additions to properties and equipment	74,093	73,023	68,203	57,866	26,654
Depreciation and amortization	13,347	17,143	19,152	22,058	23,906
Number of retail stores	512	502	502	493	475
Number of catalog stores	737	818	864	793	719
Number of catalog sales agencies	—	108	287	569	632
Average number of employees	83	94	98	105	101
Financial position					
Working capital	$ 566,831	$ 588,516	$ 702,628	$ 651,017	$ 704,525
Accounts receivable	573,363	717,379	834,953	832,599	848,908
Inventories	328,564	349,867	400,206	408,433	401,043
Net investments in properties & equipment	216,757	269,146	311,576	344,212	338,409
Long-term debt	128,652	200,288	349,383	350,599	414,665
Stockholders' interest:					
Capital stock & earnings reinvested	637,936	646,250	656,733	659,818	662,073
Investment per common share	49.63	50.27	51.09	51.32	51.61
Earnings per common share	1.57	1.66	1.83	1.24	1.31
Dividends per common share	1.00	1.00	1.00	1.00	1.00
Shares outstanding:					
Class A	141	139	139	139	125
Common	12,569	12,579	12,581	12,586	12,586
Number of stockholders	97	92	87	88	85

*Except for figures on number of retail stores, catalog stores, and catalog sales agencies; and on investment, earnings, and dividends-per-common-share items.

Lumber Company with the plants and facilities of several other paperboard-fabricating firms.

In 1970 the company was the largest manufacturer of paperboard packaging (shipping containers and folding cartons) in the United States, and the second largest manufacturer of paperboard. Container and its subsidiaries manufactured and sold corrugated and solid-fiber shipping containers, folding cartons, fiber cans and drums, paper bags, plastic packaging, and paperboard in the form of containerboard and boxboard. The company's domestic shipments of shipping containers and folding cartons represented approximately 6 and 9 percent, respectively, of the totals of these industries; its domestic production of paperboard represented approximately 6 percent of the total production of that industry in 1970.

Container's products were used extensively in the packaging and shipping of food products, canned goods, clothing, soaps, beverages, furniture, automotive products and accessories, petroleum products, electrical equipment, household items, textiles, drugs, tobacco, and many other products. The increased use of packaging in recent years had been attributed to factors such as low cost, light weight, design techniques, improved protection and display characteristics, and the adaptability of products to mechanical packaging machinery and methods of industrial customers.

Manufacturing

In 1970 manufacturing operations were carried out in 83 packaging plants and mills in the United States and in 52 plants overseas. In the United States, there were 14 paperboard mills, 30 shipping containers, 14 folding cartons, 10 fiber cans, and 6 plastic packaging plants. Production operations were highly integrated. Overseas, Container's facilities consisted of 6 paperboard mills and the following fabricating plants: 13 shipping containers, 5 folding cartons, 3 fiber cans, 1 plastic packaging, and 2 paper bag plants.

As the company continued to expand its end-use markets, the packaging plants created a growing demand for the paperboard produced in company mills, which, in turn, drew upon substantial timber holdings owned by Container. In 1970 the company owned, leased, or had cutting rights on 779,000 acres of timberland. It also had a 49 percent equity in the T.R. Miller Mill Company, which owned an additional 194,000 acres.

Financial position

Exhibit 2 presents a five-year summary of financial information for Container Corporation as of December 31, 1967; the data indicate Container's financial position prior to the beginning of merger negotiations with Wards.

Earnings increased more than 70 percent from 1963 through 1967. Profits (after taxes) for 1968 were anticipated, at the time of negotiations, to be about 2 percent off from 1967. Dividends had kept pace with earnings over the 1963–1967 period, increasing from 92.5 cents per share in 1963 to $1.30 in 1967. Sales had grown 35 percent in the same period, with over $463 million in net sales realized during 1967. Return on shareholders' equity improved from 11.4 percent in 1963 to 14.7 percent in 1967. This return on equity measure had traditionally been used by Container in the measurement of performance

EXHIBIT 2

CONTAINER AND SUBSIDIARIES, STATISTICAL SUMMARY (Thousands of Dollars)*

	1963	1964	1965	1966	1967
Net sales	$356,814	$390,575	$405,689	$460,365	$463,135
Net earnings	19,125	23,140	27,301	34,231	32,906
Earnings per share	$ 1.71	$ 2.06	$ 2.42	$ 3.06	$ 2.95
Percent return on share- holders' equity	11.4	12.9	14.2	16.8	14.7
Common stock dividends	$ 10,003	$ 11,055	$ 12,848	$ 13,996	$ 14,555
Property additions and improvements	36,545	30,373	36,540	44,032	50,060
Depreciation & depletion	15,831	17,353	18,454	19,593	20,752
Current assets	103,226	118,478	114,279	133,214	125,230
Current liabilities	47,577	45,357	48,583	67,971	53,725
Working capital	55,649	73,121	65,696	65,243	71,505
Current ratio	2.17:1	2.61:1	2.35:1	1.96:1	2.33:1
Property, less reserve	$183,678	$192,661	$211,866	$236,251	$247,401
Deferred income taxes and other liabilities	8,661	8,823	12,850	17,421	19,660
Long-term debt	62,487	63,343	59,832	69,484	71,882
Shareholders' equity	179,926	191,943	203,717	223,417	241,105
Book value per share	15.79	16.89	18.19	19.95	21.64

*Except for figures on earnings per share, percent returns, book value per share, and current ratio items.

of individual plant managers; managers were given considerable autonomy in developing local markets and in gearing production to meet local needs under the "profit center" concept.

Container's recent growth was almost entirely internal and a result of "business as usual." According to Leo Schoenhofen, then the president of Container: "All we did was concentrate on manufacturing quality paperboard and plastic packaging products—on developing outstanding creative services for our customers—doing what we know how to do best—analyzing the needs of a market and finding a way to meet those needs—at a profit!" Schoenhofen also noted at the time, "Container has had an extremely successful modernization and expansion program—which has been financed primarily through retained earnings. And if this program continues as planned, we can look forward to continued growth in sales and earnings in the next five to ten years and beyond."

REASONS FOR THE MERGER

"We wanted to make a whale too big to get through the door." This was the explanation given by a Wards executive as to why the giant retailer and Container Corporation decided to merge into a holding company named Marcor, Inc., in November of 1968. Both companies felt vulnerable to a takeover, and, in large part, the merger was designed as a defense against this threat. Circumstances peculiar to each company, however, have also been cited as reasons for the merger.

Montgomery Ward

The following reasons have been given by Wards's management as justification for the merger in 1968:

1 The slump of Wards in 1966 resulted in depressed stock prices, and rumors began to circulate that the company was a prime candidate for a take-over. When queried about such a threat, Brooker replied: "... It was impossible to avoid recognizing that we were exposed. It is true that we were behind our planned level of progress, the price of our stock was down, and there were some rumors. Every so often we'd hear that someone was going to make a pass at us, though there was never anyone who approached us directly. This was a problem throughout the business community, and we were no exception. You know when you take charge of a company that is in trouble, you may have this problem somewhere along the line. You become most vulnerable when raiders see that you have solved your basic problems and are about to turn around.... As I thought about it then, I could see that some conglomerates, Litton and Gulf & Western, for example, were successful—they convinced managements that it was good to join them. A number of conglomerators— Ling, for example—had a sense of timing, had paper, and could buy almost anything. They could borrow to pay cash. But some failed at takeover because they didn't have management in their corner. A raider—as I used the term—tries to divide a company by moving without consulting its management or board."

On the subject of whether some powerful acquisitor could have accomplished a takeover, Brooker stated: "... We were an inviting prospect, but the management of Montgomery Ward in 1966 and 1967 was not easy prey to anyone. We would have been willing to talk to anyone legitimate if it would have been good for the stockholders. But it would also have to have been good for the management team, because they were under no obligation to stay if the top structure changed. All of them—the twenty or thirty key men—were basically independent people. They didn't have to work at Montgomery Ward. It wasn't a captive management. The people weren't chattels of the company. They were people who had come here, taken the risk, and done well.... It was to the shareholders' advantage to have these men running the company.... Most people who are interested in making a take-over want to get the management, too. Legitimate people want to arrange an acquisition on a basis that will get management support. If I had been faced with someone who sought management's agreement for a takeover, I would have had to go back to the people I had brought in and see what they wanted to do. That goes back to the commitments I made to them and they made to me at the beginning of my administration. That doesn't mean a tender offer couldn't have won, but if one had come along, we'd have fought it." Management also felt that Wards was about ready to turn the corner—a feeling apparently shared by outside financial analysts. Thus the combination with Container was consummated, in part, to gain the defensive value of increased size.

2 "One of the things that made this deal," said Gordon R. Worley, financial vice president of both Wards and Marcor, "was the tax deferral available to Montgomery Ward. Our earnings were not sufficient to utilize our full tax deferral. With this combination, we'll be in a position to bring the Container earnings under this tax-deferral umbrella, and, in effect, we will be able to defer the federal income tax on Container's earnings for a considerable period of time." The tax deferrals were a result of the federal tax laws as they applied to Wards's credit business; credit sales were reported, but the gross income on them did not have to be reported until collection was completed. "Since we are in the consumer-credit business and our receivables are constantly turned over," Worley explained, "as we collect $1 million we generate another $1 million to replace it. As long as we continue to stay in business and as long as our receivables continue to exist, we have what amounts to a permanent deferral of this gross income." In January, 1970, total tax deferrals available to Marcor from 1970 through 1973 were projected at $210 million. This source of funds could be used by Marcor in any way—to expand Container's operations, to expand Wards's operations, or to make acquisitions.

3 As stated by Brooker, "The combination of Container talents will bring to Wards a new look at the way we handle retailing and the way we handle the catalog. . . . If you bring in individuals who are competent and have ideas in other fields, they challenge your ways of doing business." Also, Brooker noted, "They have some skills in direct mail that I have been very interested in. We have a strong feeling that there is an opportunity in direct mail." Container's expertise in graphics was expected to play a major role in improving this and other forms of advertising. The fact that both companies were strongly marketing-oriented also contributed, in management's opinion, to a degree of "fit" between the two companies, and management expected it would produce synergistic effects. Some synergism was also anticipated management-wise, in that top managers in manufacturing, distribution, and sales could be brought together as a creative management team.

4 Another major attraction to Wards's management was the gaining of an experienced top management man of good age (54) in Leo Schoenhofen, then the chief executive officer of Container, who later became chairman of Marcor (upon Brooker's retirement from that position in May, 1970). Also, Wards was basically only one-deep in people with top management experience, as was Container. It was believed that the merger would result in two-deep at the Marcor level—a buying of time in order to further develop the human resources in each organization.

5 Finally, the fact that both Container and Wards were Chicago-based companies meant that no Wards or Container people would have to be moved around to different geographical areas.

Container Corporation

Container also had a number of reasons for merging with Wards:

1 Schoenhofen stated, "To be very plain, the basic advantage to Container Corporation from the stockholders' standpoint is that it enables us to extend our activity. There was some question in our mind in looking over the next ten years as to whether we would be able to finance our expansion just to keep our market position, not necessarily to increase it." The additional cash flow, emanating from Wards's tax-deferral benefits, would thus enable Container to maintain and improve its market position.

2 Because Wall Street had always lumped Container with the bulk of the paper industry (incorrectly so, in the opinion of the management), the company had a low price/earnings ratio of 10. Container's management felt that its creativity in design and marketing warranted a better evaluation—one which could be achieved with the merger. Also, the low price/earnings ratio made Container vulnerable to a takeover.

3 Container had been seeking ways to diversify into other areas of packaging and related fields that seemed to offer profit potential. The company had found, however, that it generally could not afford to acquire the kinds of companies which appeared attractive. In the early part of 1968, Container's management was also approached by a half-dozen acquisition-minded companies and had extensive exploratory conversations with them. As stated by Schoenhofen, "These were all situations in which one and one added up to two—or two and two added up to four—but no more. We felt we needed some synergism—a situation that we could contribute to and benefit from. We think we found this in the marketing orientation that is common to the Marcor companies."

4 Container's management was also reluctant to merge with another company for fear that the company would lose its identity—and perhaps even lose control of its organization. By joining with Wards in the formation of Marcor, Container had the opportunity to keep its own organization intact and to maintain its identity. The merger was made with the understanding that the Marcor management would maintain and strengthen the identity of each of the Marcor subsidiaries. Associated with this advantage was the feeling that Container would have a much better chance of pursuing and achieving its individual corporate objectives than ever before.

5 Another stated advantage of the merger to Container was that the deal was consummated with the understanding that Schoenhofen would move up to be chief executive officer of Marcor when Robert Brooker retired in 1970. This fact further assured Container's management that the company's aspirations would not be neglected even though it was expected that Wards would account for approximately 80 percent of Marcor's total sales in the near future. Also, Wards and Container agreed that the two firms would be equals in policy making via membership on a joint committee composed of senior executives divorced from line responsibilities.

6 As in the case of Wards, Container was also only one-deep in top management experience at the policy level.

FINANCIAL ANALYSIS AND TERMS OF THE MERGER

When asked how Container and Wards reached agreement on the exchange of stock for the merger, Brooker replied: "Obviously, during the period of talking you establish certain criteria that enable you to make an agreeable offer. We wanted to buy at the best price we could and at a ratio that would appeal to Container. But we didn't really have to bargain in the usual sense. We worked out a ratio that they thought was very fair, so there wasn't anything to bargain in it. They tried it out on Al Gordon, their financial adviser and a member of their board. He gave some practical advice that involved adjusting some of the relationships of the securities but not the ultimate value. In a tax-free merger, more than half of the exchange has to be for equity. For some technical reason, it's not good to have fifty-fifty, so what we wanted was to get no more than 49 percent of the Container stock tendered for debentures. Actually we got between 41 and 42 percent." The accounting for Marcor was on the basis of a partial pooling of interests.[1] Since all of Wards's shares of common stock were exchanged for shares of Marcor (one for one), all of Wards's earnings could be pooled into Marcor. Because, however, only 59 percent of Container's shares were exchanged for preferred shares of Marcor (one for one), only 59 percent of Container's earnings could be pooled by Marcor. The remaining 41 percent of Container's shares were purchased through the issuance of Marcor 6.5 percent subordinated debentures. Accordingly, these earnings were not available to Marcor prior to November 1, 1968, the effective date of the merger; thus 41 percent of Container's earnings through October 31, 1968, could not be included in Marcor's 1968 reported earnings.

Prior to the actual merger, financial analysts at Wards performed several analyses to indicate the potential benefits of the merger. Using 1968 earnings projections, and assuming that the merger had occurred at the beginning of fiscal 1967, analysts prepared the statement of pro forma earnings shown in Exhibit 3.

Analysts also prepared a pro forma consolidated balance sheet (Exhibit 4) for the end of fiscal 1968. One of the more important indications of the pro forma balance sheet was a projected borrowing base of $1,072 million. This compared with senior long-term debt of $551 million (the remainder of the long-term debt was subordinated) plus short-term debt of $413 million for a total debt of $964 million—a debt-to-equity-plus-subordinated-debt ratio of slightly better than one to one. Eliminating Montgomery Ward Credit Corporation (the financing vehicle for credit sales) would result in a total senior debt of

---

[1] "Pooling of interests" purchase agreement enables the parent corporation to treat new acquisitions as if they have always been a part of the parent insofar as reporting of earnings is concerned; the alternative, "purchasing accounting," allows the parent to take credit for an acquired company's profits only from the date of the acquisition.

EXHIBIT 3
PRO FORMA EARNINGS (Thousands of Dollars)

	Pro forma		Partial pooling to be reported	
	1967	**1968**	**1967**	**1968**
Wards and subsidiaries	$17,425	$30,000	$17,425	$30,000
Container Corporation	33,971	32,400	20,017	22,716
Total	51,396	62,400	37,442	52,716
Less: Interest (after taxes) on 6.5% subordinated debentures	9,115	8,273	—	2,082
Net earnings	$42,281	$54,127	37,442	$50,634
Less: Dividends—				
$2 convertible preferred	13,186	13,166	13,186	13,166
Wards's Class A Stock	—	—	968	643
Net earnings available to common stock	$29,095	$40,961	$23,288	$36,825
Earnings per share	$2.31	$3.25	$1.85	$2.93
Earnings per share assuming full conversion of convertible preferred	$2.20	$2.82	$1.90	$2.61

$321 million and equity and subordinated debt of $819 million—better than a 2.5 to 1 ratio (debt to equity plus subordinated debt). This was considered a most satisfactory ratio by management, who felt that it should enable Marcor and its subsidiaries to leverage their business still further with substantial amounts of additional debts.

EXHIBIT 4
Pro Forma Balance Sheet
(Thousands of Dollars)

Assets		Liabilities	
Cash	$ 65,000	Notes payable	$ 413,000
Receivables	1,008,000	Accounts payable	162,000
Inventories	444,000	Accrued expenses	86,000
Prepaid & other	54,000	Federal taxes:	
Total current assets	1,571,000	Currently payable	10,000
Investment in subsidiaries	91,000	Deferred	106,000
Properties & equip. (net)	648,000	Total current liabilities	$ 777,000
Deferred charges	9,000	Deferred federal taxes	13,000
Excess cost of subsidiaries		Long-term debt	846,000
over book value at date of		Minority interest	12,000
acquisition	$ 148,000	Equity	819,000
	$2,467,000		$2,467,000

Looking at the cash flow and deferred taxes available to Marcor, it was projected that $170 million would be generated from earnings, depreciation and amortization, and deferred federal income taxes in fiscal 1969. The pro forma cash-flow statement (Exhibit 5) was developed.

The $49 million represented estimated excess cash flow before consideration of any increase in customer receivables. Since Wards elected the installment basis for paying its federal taxes in 1963 and also elected to file a consolidated tax return in 1965, it was able to defer the payment of federal income taxes on the gross profit contained in uncollected customer receivables at the end of each tax year. It was also predicted that Wards would have $945 million of customer receivables as of January 31, 1969 (the company actually had $990 million of receivables at that date); the receivables was estimated to be 40 percent—which meant that Marcor could defer for tax purposes $370 million of taxable income, representing $184 million of taxes which would normally be payable. Wards's earnings through October 31, 1968, and Marcor earnings through January 31, 1969 (the end of fiscal 1968), were projected to utilize $210 million of the tax deferral, permitting the deferral of $106 million for fiscal 1968. The balance of $78 million (Exhibit 6) would be available for use by the combined companies of Marcor, since Container and its earnings would be included in the consolidated tax return of Marcor beginning November 1, 1968. Exhibit 6 summarizes the tax-deferral position estimated for fiscal 1968 and through fiscal 1973.

The projections indicated that Marcor would be able to defer upward of $60 million a year in federal income taxes through 1971, at which time the excess deferral would probably be fully used. The amount of the annual tax deferral was expected to rise thereafter, however, based on the estimated growth in Wards's outstanding receivables. As indicated in the previous exhibit, the annual tax deferrals were expected to total $300 million at the end of the five-year period.

The foregoing data indicated to both Wards and Container that each would

EXHIBIT 5
PRO FORMA CASH FLOW STATEMENT—FISCAL 1969
(Thousands of Dollars)

Net earnings before dividends	$ 60,000
Depreciation and amortization	53,000
Federal taxes (deferrable)	57,000
Total funds from operations	$170,000
Deduct:	
Capital expenditures	95,000
Dividends	26,000
Total funds required	$121,000
Funds available after operating requirements	$ 49,000

EXHIBIT 6
TAX DEFERRAL—FISCAL 1968–1973 (Thousands of Dollars)

	Fiscal 1968	Through fiscal 1973
Customer receivable balances	$945,000	$1,500,000
Deferred gross profit on credit sales	370,000	600,000
Total tax liability deferrable	184,000	300,000
Utilization in reduction of taxes payable	106,000	300,000
Available to offset future taxes payable	$ 78,000	—
Estimated net increase in deferred taxes in the five-year period		$ 194,000

be able to finance a greater rate of growth, as a result of the merger, than was possible to either company on an individual basis. Wards's earnings had not been sufficient to fully utilize the tax deferral in the past, and such a benefit had not been available to Container.

MARCOR: OBJECTIVES, ORGANIZATION, AND RESULTS

When Marcor came into existence in November, 1968, its basic objective was to "achieve growth through marketing concepts." It was anticipated that the holding company would finance the growth and provide coordinating plans for its subsidiaries. No basic changes in the name, administration, or operation of Montgomery Ward and Container were anticipated. Each of the companies would continue to have its own board of directors, officers, administrative staffs, and service functions; also, each was to continue its own programs of growth and expansion in merchandising, marketing, and manufacturing.

Objectives

Marcor's objectives, as stated in January 1970, were to:

1 Provide a financial structure which would make possible the physical investment needed to achieve sales and profits objectives.

2 Help all segments achieve their objectives by providing financial control and accountability in all company operations and in the measuring of performance at all levels.

3 Further develop personnel resources within the corporation with programs which would assure a successful future management, and to maintain a balance of programs for systems research and product development.

4 Diversify through internal development and acquisition into related and compatible areas in which Marcor's marketing capabilities, technical competence, and management skills could make significant contributions to sales and profit growth greater than established corporate norms.

5 Achieve an average annual sales growth of 8.5 percent and average annual net earnings growth of 14 percent through 1974. Container's goal was to achieve an average annual increase of 10 percent in both sales and earnings through 1974, while Montgomery Ward expected an average increase in sales of 9.5 percent per year over the same period.

Top Management Organization

The coordination of planning and management of Wards and Container was accomplished primarily through overlapping boards of directors. The board of directors for Wards included the president of Container; similarly, Wards's president sat on the board of directors for Container. The board of directors for Marcor included five of Wards's top officers and four of Container's, in addition to the normal representation of outside individuals.

The top operating executive officers for Marcor as of October 1970 were:

1 Leo Schoenhofen, chairman of the board and chief executive officer of Marcor.

2 Robert Brooker, chairman of the executive committee.

3 Gordon Worley, vice president of finance for both Marcor and Wards.

4 Daniel Walker, vice president and general counsel of both Marcor and Wards; secretary of Wards.

5 Richard Kelly, secretary of Marcor; assistant general counsel of both Marcor and Container.

Brooker, upon his retirement as chairman of Marcor in May 1970, assumed the chairmanship of the executive committee of both Marcor and Wards. The executive committee determined matters of policy between the quarterly board meetings and was influential in all major capital investment decisions. In addition to Brooker, the executive committee included Schoenhofen, Edward Donnell (Wards's president), and Henry Van der Eb (Container's president). Exhibit 7 presents the top organizational relationships as of January 1971.

Role of Top Management

The role of Marcor's operating executives in the operation of Wards and Container was to be a blend of "outside counselor and parent." The executives expected to preserve what was best at each of the companies, but they also believed that they would introduce a new degree of objectivity and independent scrutiny, permitting a fresh look at both operations.

Marcor's management expected to remain small and flexible so that it could respond quickly and effectively to new problems. It planned to draw freely on the management capabilities of both Wards and Container from time to time, assembling task forces to tackle particular projects and disbanding or reshaping the force as each problem was solved or redefined. The top executives also expected that Marcor would experience almost continuous restructuring and augmentation as its role evolved.

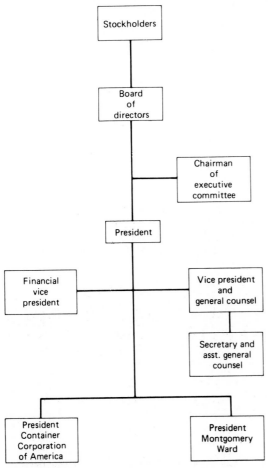

EXHIBIT 7
Marcor organization as of January 1971.

One of the most direct and immediate benefits seen by the Marcor management was the infusion of many of the specialized management skills and techniques of each company into the other's management force. Available management talent would be directed into critical areas first while additional opportunities in all parts of both operations were evaluated. This process, it was hoped, would involve the introduction of new management techniques and the temporary or permanent shifting of personnel within and between the two operations.

Marcor executives also saw, as one of their major tasks, the combining of development programs of each company to provide "cross-training" of the managements of Wards and Container. It was anticipated that Marcor could strengthen its continuing development program for management personnel in this way.

Administrative Functions

Except for the policy-level decisions, the primary functions of Marcor were performed by personnel from both Wards and Container. Wards personnel prepared the analyses and reports necessary for the coordination of financial planning, budgetary administration, accounting, and investor relations for Marcor. Wards people also performed the public relations function at the Marcor level, although Container handled all advertising. No administrative services were performed at the Marcor level for either Wards or Container. Both companies continued to perform their own legal, accounting, personnel, public relations, and other staff functions independently. Some thought had been given to centralizing these types of services (not only for Wards and Container, but also for their individual subsidiaries), but no action had been taken as of January, 1971. The major reason given for the lack of centralization was the desire to maintain the autonomy of Wards and Container; both companies preferred to move slowly toward establishing formal intercompany ties as opposed to informal working relationships and sharing of expertise.

Joint Task Forces

Very few joint operating forces were established to achieve the synergistic effects anticipated in the combination. One task force composed of Container's carton and packaging experts and Wards personnel was established to work on the protective packing of products received from Ward's suppliers. The project was expected to result in a substantial reduction in product damage and, consequently, in increased customer satisfaction.

Another task force was appointed to study how the retirement plans of the two companies might be integrated. This problem, as a part of the larger question of equalization of total compensation structures, revealed basic differences in industry practices which mitigated against common compensatory arrangements. The major result after nine months of study indicated that control should not emphasize equalization between similar positions in the two companies; rather, control should seek to ensure that each company remained competitive in salary, retirement plans, and other benefits with firms in the particular industry in which it operated.

Although few formal task forces had been assembled, informal sharing of ideas and expertise was encouraged by top management. Planning staffs from the two companies held meetings to discuss new approaches and common denominators in planning. Similarly, purchasing, traffic, and personnel department heads informally discussed common problems. This approach emanated from the emphasis on retention of autonomy and the desire of top management to avoid conflict at an early stage in the merged firm's life cycle; Marcor officials preferred to move slowly to ensure cross-fertilization of ideas and techniques in a conflict-free environment.

Personnel Transfers

In the first two years after the merger, only one incident occurred where personnel were formally transferred from one company to the other. At the time of the merger, Wards operated four IBM 360s in its computer processing center, while Container had only one 360 computer. The computing facilities were physically combined, although Wards and Container continued to perform systems analysis and programming independently. All keypunch and other operations were performed by Wards for both companies; this involved the transferring of around 20 keypunch operators and clerks from Container's payroll to Wards's. One systems analyst was transferred from Wards to Container at the same time.

Financial Results

Exhibit 8 presents a five-year statistical summary for Marcor, and assumes that the merger occurred before fiscal 1965. The actual postmerger results for a complete year of operation are reflected in the fiscal 1969 column.

Marcor net sales rose to $2.7 billion in 1969, an increase of 8.6 percent over 1968. Both Wards and Container posted record sales during the year; Wards sales improved 8.5 percent from $1.99 billion to $2.16 billion, and Container increased sales 8.6 percent from $469 million in 1968 to $510 million in 1969.

During the five years, consolidated net sales of Marcor increased at a compound annual rate of 5.4 percent. During the same period, sales of Wards increased at a compound annual rate of 4.9 percent, while the sales of Container increased at a rate of 5.5 percent.

Earnings for 1969 were $67 million, up 24.4 percent over $53.8 million in 1968, on a partial pooling basis. Had the merger occurred on February 1, 1968 (the beginning of fiscal 1968), Marcor 1969 earnings would show a 16.1 percent rise from $57.7 million in 1968, on a comparable pro forma basis. Earnings per share for 1969 would be up 19.7 percent from $3.50 in 1968; fully diluted 1969 earnings were $3.43, against $2.95 in 1968 on a comparable pro forma basis.

FUTURE GROWTH PHILOSOPHY

"We have no reluctance to achieve growth through acquisition. But growth through acquisition is not essential . . . we should concentrate on accelerating the growth of our present business to achieve the greatest profitability within the company and the maximum benefit for shareholders." These words by Brooker summarized Marcor's basic growth philosophy. The company would acquire another on-going concern if two major conditions were met. First and foremost, a company would not be acquired unless it provided a degree of "fit" with Marcor's operations. Secondly, the potential acquisition should be undervalued in terms of current market price.

EXHIBIT 8
MARCOR, INCORPORATED, FIVE-YEAR STATISTICAL SUMMARY (Thousands of Dollars)

	1969	1968	1967	1966	1965
Operations					
Net sales	$ 2,715,150	$ 2,500,705	$ 2,352,293	$ 2,354,488	$ 2,154,049
Net earnings*	66,950	53,810	37,443	36,699	40,050
Taxes on income (including all subsidiaries)*	58,417	49,920	27,582	26,527	30,685
Dividends*	25,701	25,265	22,131	21,803	21,215
Additions to properties and equipment	136,328	99,722	95,945	101,898	104,743
Depreciation and amortization	50,226	47,432	45,417	41,651	37,606
Financial position					
Working capital	$ 869,574	$ 842,784	$ 778,639	$ 711,842	$ 765,108
Accounts receivable	1,176,410	1,047,823	900,348	879,475	875,792
Inventories	530,819	499,448	447,955	457,120	445,173
Net investment in properties and equipment	750,372	706,491	602,279	580,463	523,442
Long-term debt—Senior	630,788	603,734	469,898	395,082	384,215
—Subordinated	295,472	299,181	29,950	25,000	25,000
Stockholders' interest					
Stockholders' equity*	$ 859,347	$ 817,615	$ 791,675	$ 777,544	$ 762,851
Investment per common share (book value of shares outstanding at end of year)	44.13	41.23	39.42	38.19	37.03
Earnings per common share and common equivalent share	4.19	3.14	1.85	1.79	2.04
Earnings per common share assuming full dilution	3.43	2.72	1.85	1.79	2.03
Shares outstanding:					
Preferred (pro forma prior to 1968)	6,558,072	6,612,352	6,566,049	6,597,704	6,598,680
Common	12,751,264	12,613,392	12,586,557	12,586,557	12,581,422
Number of stockholders	80,862	88,248	104,661	104,456	102,902

*Amounts prior to November 1, 1968, have been reduced by the portions applicable to Container Corporation shares exchanged for debentures at that date.

Wards and Container each had human power designated to evaluate potential acquisitions. Prospects were generally identified informally—by top corporate officers, by "marriage" brokers who contacted the companies, or by a multitude of other personnel or published sources. Once a potential acquisition had been identified, evaluations were conducted to determine degree of fit, future earnings prospects, and management capabilities. No formal criteria were employed; individual cases were judged according to different standards, as appropriate. In addition to the "degree of fit" criterion, however, much emphasis was to be placed on good management, as it was expected that any acquired companies would continue to operate rather autonomously. Neither Wards nor Container had any desire to be a conglomerate.

PART **EIGHT**

DETERMINATION AND ANALYSIS OF MANAGEMENT RESPONSIBILITIES AND THEIR LIMITS

CASES ON BUSINESS POLICY FOR PART EIGHT

External factors beyond the direct control of management can be major determinants of the profitability and survival of the firm.

The extent of corporate responsibilities and their limits are major factors constantly confronting the executive. Government regulation, antitrust laws, affirmative action and business ethics in foreign countries represent some of the challenges which are contained in the cases in Part Eight.

Through the analysis of the cases in Part Eight, the student should acquire an appreciation of the necessity for the importance of this dimension of the executive role.

United Brands

At 8:20 A.M. on February 3, 1975, Eli M. Black, chairman of United Brands Company, locked the doors to his 44th floor mid-Manhattan office in the Pan American Building, smashed his attaché case through his office window, and jumped to his death.

He left no suicide note, no word to explain his death.

That afternoon United Brands issued a statement in which a family spokesperson said Mr. Black had been under "great strain during the past several weeks because of business pressures. He had been working 16 to 18 hours a day and had become severely depressed because of the tension."[1]

Edward Gelsthorpe, executive vice president of the company, said that 1974 had been an "extremely difficult year for the company." Mr. Gelsthorpe added

This case was prepared from published sources by James C. Shaffer, National Association of Blue Shield Plans, with contributions from Peter C. Pierce, Lawrence D. Chrzanowski, and Professor Lawrence G. Lavengood. It was prepared as a basis for class discussion under the supervision of Professor Ram Charan.

[1]"United Brands Chairman, Eli M. Black, Plunges to His Death in Apparent Suicide," *Wall St. Journal*, Midwest edition, February 4, 1975.

that there were not any additional business or personal financial problems that could have contributed to Mr. Black's depression. "The great tragedy of Eli Black's death at this time," Mr. Gelsthorpe said, "is that under his leadership the company was on its way to overcoming several crises. We were convinced the traumatic period was behind us."[2]

The company's traumatic period was not behind it. Later it would be revealed that United Brands bribed a foreign government official in exchange for favorable tax treatment.

Three days after Eli Black's death, the United Brands board met and decided that for an interim period two board-appointed committees would be responsible for running the company. An executive search firm was enlisted to help choose a successor to Mr. Black. Approximately three months later, Wallace W. Booth, a former top executive with Ford Motor Company and Rockwell International Corporation, became president and chief executive officer of United Brands and faced the problems of running United Brands Company.

UNITED BRANDS COMPANY

United Brands Company, a conglomerate ranked by *Fortune* magazine as the eighty-fourth largest corporation in the United States in 1974, grew out of a merger between AMK Corporation and United Fruit Company (see Exhibits 1, 1A, and 1B).

United Brands is engaged principally in the food products business through its Agrimark Group, one of the world's largest producers and marketers of bananas, and through its wholly owned subsidiary John Morrell & Co., one of the largest meat packers in the United States on the basis of sales. Through its Diversified Capital Group, United Brands is involved in other activities including food processing, food services, and domestic agriculture (see Exhibit 2).

Bananas and Related Products

The Agrimark Group is engaged in producing, purchasing, transporting, and marketing bananas, which are grown and purchased primarily in Central and South America and the Philippines and then transported to the United States, Canada, Europe, and Japan primarily on United Brands' own and chartered ships. They are sold predominantly to independent wholesalers who resell to retail food stores and chains. The company, which advertises and maintains sales offices in the United States and other countries, uses the trademarks Chiquita, Fyffes, and Amigo.

Bananas are a highly perishable commodity. The crops are subject to disease

---

[2] Ibid.

and destruction by natural forces, particularly high winds and floods. Once harvested, they must be transported under controlled temperature conditions. Strikes and other transportation delays and diversions increase the possibility of fruit ripening and spoiling prior to delivery.

United Brands transports a substantial portion of its bananas in ships owned or chartered by the company; it operates owned and leased loading and unloading facilities in Latin American and most major ports of destination. When feasible, United Brands carries cargo, primarily backhaul, for third parties (see Exhibit 3).

Meat Packing and Related Products (Morrell)

Morrell is engaged primarily in operating meat-packing plants which slaughter and process hogs, cattle, and lambs and distribute meat products in fresh, frozen, and processed forms in most of the United States. Morrell produces and distributes animal feeds and animal products. They also import and distribute food products.

Morrell products are marketed in most of the United States under the name Morrell Pride and in various marketing areas under other brand names including Morrell Yorkshire, Hunter, Partridge, Rode, Broadcast, Peyton, Scott Petersen, Bob Ostrow, Tom Sawyer, and Greentree. Its animal feeds are sold under the label Golden Sun. Morrell boxed beef in vacuum is marketed under the trade name E-Z Redi Beef.

Morrell is subject to strict inspection, packaging, processing, and environmental regulations by the federal government and the various state governments in which it operates packing plants. It is affected by the weather, policies implemented by the U. S. Department of Agriculture, the supply of feed grains, and the supply and demand of the cattle market.

1972 was a difficult year for the entire meat industry; while John Morrell's sales were up substantially in that year, earnings declined from the prior year due in part to the shorter supply of hogs and adverse effects of Phase II price controls. It was in 1972 that the federal government implemented a number of policies to encourage higher farm prices. Coincident with these efforts was a worldwide shortage of feed grains and livestock, resulting in record-breaking livestock prices. While encouraging higher farm prices, the federal government pressured the retail trade to hold down food prices, especially meat. While meat prices did rise to all-time highs, they did not go up enough to offset the increased cost of livestock.

During that same year, earnings declined substantially in fresh pork and processed pork. The hog supply was down approximately 9 percent for the year in response to a short corn crop in 1970. Due to the reduced supply of hogs, there was a corresponding reduction in the number of hams available for processing and an equivalent reduction in the raw materials for producing

EXHIBIT 1
CONSOLIDATED STATEMENT OF INCOME (Thousands of Dollars Except Per Share Amounts)

	Year ended December 31				
	1970	1971	1972	1973*	1974
Net sales	$1,383,605	$1,373,027	$1,586,747	$1,841,738	$2,020,526
Operating costs and expenses					
Cost of sales	1,225,235	1,215,013	1,402,851	1,640,252	1,855,395
Selling, general, and administrative expenses	105,532	106,590	112,672	117,351	131,164
Depreciation	25,562	28,007	30,479	29,523	31,877
	1,356,329	1,349,610	1,546,002	1,787,126	2,018,436
Operating income	27,276	23,417	40,745	54,612	2,090
Interest and amortization of debt expense	(21,733)	(26,667)	(26,449)	(29,585)	(37,080)
Interest and other income-net	3,752	6,366	7,903	7,952	2,488
Income (loss) from continuing operations before items shown below	9,295	3,116	22,199	32,979	(32,502)
Unusual or infrequently occurring items	—	—	—	—	(26,808)
Income (loss) from continuing operations before income taxes	9,295	3,116	22,199	32,979	(59,310)
Estimated US and foreign income taxes	(6,492)	(7,945)	(12,970)	(15,250)	(12,000)
Income (loss) from continuing operations	2,803	(4,829)	9,229	17,729	(71,310)
Income from discontinued operations, net of applicable taxes	1,514	3,135	1,508	741	13,768

Gains on disposals of discontinued operations, net of US income taxes of $2,412 in 1973	—	—	—	7,238	10,704
Income (loss), before extraordinary items	4,317	(1,694)	10,737	25,708	(46,838)
Extraordinary items	(6,408)	(22,318)	6,971	(345)	3,231
Net income (loss)	$ (2,091)	$ (24,012)	$ 17,708	$ 25,363	$ (43,607)
Average number of primary shares outstanding	10,766	10,779	11,194	11,193	10,775
Earnings (loss) per share Primary and Fully Diluted: Income (loss) from continuing operations	$.06	$(.65)	$.67	$1.42	$(6.82)
Income from discontinued operations	.14	.29	.13	.07	1.28
Gains on disposals of discontinued operations	—	—	—	.65	.99
Income (loss) before extraordinary items	.20	(.36)	.80	2.14	(4.55)
Extraordinary items	(.59)	(2.07)	.62	(.03)	.30
Net income (loss)	$(.39)	$(2.43)	$1.42	$2.11	$(4.25)
Dividends per capital share	$ .30	$ .15	-0-	-0-	-0-

*Restated

Source: From 10-K United Brands has filed with the Securities Exchange Commission in 1975.

EXHIBIT 1A

BREAKDOWN OF UNITED BRANDS' CONTINUING OPERATIONS FOR THE FIVE YEARS ENDING DECEMBER 31, 1974 (Thousands of Dollars)

Net sales

	1970	1971	1972	1973	1974
Bananas and related products	$ 379,558	$ 397,551	$ 450,662	$ 449,971	$ 549,440
Meat packing and related products	898,916	847,056	1,012,175	1,258,415	1,288,996
Food processing and food services	66,555	74,001	68,280	67,624	103,525
United States agriculture and floriculture	29,615	42,587	42,461	48,426	51,003
Other	8,961	11,832	13,169	17,302	27,562
	$1,383,605	$1,373,027	$1,586,747	$1,841,738	$2,020,526

Contribution to operating income

	1970	1971	1972	1973	1974
Bananas and related products	$ 27,441	$ 11,170	$ 34,685	$ 26,323	$ (7,523)
Meat packing and related products	13,810	10,417	6,708	23,687	3,765
Food processing and food services	(1,387)	275	3,160	4,900	1,576
United States agriculture and floriculture	(11,028)	1,830	(2,473)	2,011	2,450
Other	2,394	3,223	1,698	1,143	5,349
	31,230	26,915	43,778	58,064	5,617
Less: corporate overhead	(3,954)	(3,498)	(3,033)	(3,537)	(3,527)
Operating income	$ 27,276	$ 23,417	$ 40,745	$ 54,612	$ 2,090

sliced bacon, frankfurters, sliced luncheon meat, and other sausage items. With both reduced volume and reduced margins, these items contributed less to overall profits than they had in the previous several years.

Morrell had a difficult time again in 1973. Consumer boycotts of beef, wage and price controls, ceiling prices on meat, livestock shortages, major labor negotiations, plant closings, and start-up problems at new facilities made 1973 a challenging year for Morrell. While it was anticipated early in the year that beef volume would increase in 1973, the high price of grain and government price controls caused producers to cut back dramatically, and that year ended with beef production in the United States down 6 percent from 1972.

In 1974 Morrell was forced to make approximately $4 million in capital expenditures in order to comply with various federally imposed environmental regulations.

Diversified Group

United Brands, through various subsidiaries and divisions, is involved in a number of food processing and food service activities:

1 The Unimark group, with plants in Costa Rica, Honduras, and Nicaragua, purchases palm oil from the Agrimark Group and uses this oil and other raw materials not purchased from the company to produce cooking and salad oil, margarine, and other products which it sells in the Central American markets.

2 A&W International, Inc., franchises a chain of drive-in restaurants in the United States.

3 J. Hungerford Smith Company, Inc., manufactures syrups, fudges, toppings, and beverage bases for the industrial and institutional food trade.

4 A&W Distributing markets canned and bottled root beer in certain regions of the United States.

5 Clemente Jacques is a food processing company in Mexico.

6 Inter-Harvest subsidiary grows lettuce, celery, and other vegetables on 25,000 acres of leased land in California and Arizona.

7 United Brands' Floriculture, Inc., produces and finishes foliage plants which are sold principally in the eastern and southeastern United States.

8 TRT Telecommunications Company is an international communications carrier subject to Federal Communications Commission jurisdiction.

9 Polymer United manufactures extruded and molded plastic products. It has plants in Panama, Costa Rica, and Honduras. Some of Polymer's products are sold to United Brands' subsidiaries.

Employees

United Brands employs approximately 50,000 persons, 34,000 of whom are employed by the Agrimark Group. Morrell employs 9,500 persons, and 6,500

EXHIBIT 1B
CONSOLIDATED BALANCE SHEETS, 1974–1974 (Thousands of Dollars)

	As of December 31				
	1970	1971	1972	1973	1974
Assets					
Current assets:					
Cash	$ 55,573	$ 21,514	$ 18,894	$ 20,986	$ 98,976
Marketable securities, at cost which approximates market	35,772	49,082	64,225	20,363	540
Accounts receivable, net	88,185	92,289	119,847	174,135	163,565
Inventories	72,892	83,696	94,412	210,689	176,891
Growing crops	28,084	31,885	29,678	—	—
Materials and supplies	30,120	28,441	25,331	—	—
Prepaid expenses	8,538	11,593	10,997	10,876	9,223
Total current assets	319,164	318,500	363,384	433,049	449,195
Investments and long-term receivables	54,920	44,324	67,417	55,072	32,822
Deferred charges	27,742	12,736	11,197	12,769	4,905
Property, plant, and equipment—net	360,008	334,530	331,018	403,128	350,921
Trademarks and leaseholds	46,071	49,882	50,249	47,004	45,031
Excess cost over fair value of net assets acquired	282,112	285,255	279,069	276,639	272,146
Assets held for disposal, at estimated realizable value	—	24,000	15,505	10,247	6,062
Total assets	$1,090,017	$1,069,227	$1,117,839	$1,237,908	$1,161,082
Liabilities and shareholders' equity					
Current liabilities:					
Notes and loans payable to banks	$ 48,092	$ 28,933	$ 43,419	$ 62,117	$ 70,459
Accounts payable and accrued liabilities	75,899	92,806	87,692	124,887	127,755

Long-term debt due within one year	8,144	7,656	14,719	11,326	9,905
U.S. and foreign income taxes	19,166	19,874	22,820	23,511	18,994
Deferred U.S. and foreign income taxes	10,607	11,436	10,882	11,102	11,108
Total current liabilities	161,908	160,705	179,532	232,943	238,221
Long-term debt	372,131	380,280	402,487	396,237	383,100
Accrued severance and other social benefits	33,949	37,095	34,596	54,369	63,395
Other liabilities and deferred credits	16,275	13,158	7,689	9,040	2,509
Total liabilities	584,263	591,238	624,304	692,589†	687,225*
Shareholders' equity:					
$3.00 Cumulative convertible preferred stock	2,876	2,769	2,738	2,723	2,715
$1.20 Cumulative convertible preferred stock	29,613	29,610	29,610	29,610	29,610
$3.20 Cumulative convertible preferred stock	7,452	7,452	7,452	7,421	7,420
Capital stock, $1 par value	10,775	10,781	10,773	10,775	10,776
Warrants and options to purchase capital stock	—	—	—	—	—
Capital surplus	366,192	366,303	366,322	366,367	366,375
Income retained in the business	88,846	61,074	76,640	99,863	54,651
	505,754	477,989	493,535	516,759	471,547
Total shareholders' equity	$1,090,017	$1,069,227	$1,117,839	$1,209,348†	$1,158,772*

*Minority interests in net assets of subsidiaries ($2,310) not included.
†Minority interests in net assets of subsidiaries ($28,560) not included.

EXHIBIT 2

PARENTS AND SUBSIDIARIES

(As of December 31, 1974, the Subsidiaries of United Brands and of Its
Subsidiaries, the Jurisdiction in which Organized and the Percent of Voting
Securities Owned by the Immediate Parent Corporation)

Company	Organized under laws of	Percent of voting securities owned by immediate parent
A&W Distributing Company	Delaware	100%
A&W International, Inc.	California	100%
Aceitera Corona, S.A.	Nicaragua	76%
Caribbean Enterprises, Inc.	Delaware	100%
Chiquita Brands Limited	Canada	100%
Chiquita Brands, Inc.	Delaware	100%
Chiriqui Land Company	Delaware	100%
Clemente Jacques y Cia., S.A.	Mexico	100%
Compania Agricola de Guatemala	Delaware	100%
Compania Agricola de Rio Tinto	Delaware	100%
Compania Bananera de Costa Rica	Delaware	100%
Compania Frutera de Sevilla	Delaware	100%
Compagnia Italiana della Frutta, S.P.A.	Italy	100%
Compania Numar, S.A.	Costa Rica	100%
Compania Procesadora de Frutas	Delaware	100%
Empresa Hondurena de Vapores, S.A.	Honduras	100%
Fyffes Group, Ltd.	England	100%
Inter-Harvest, Inc.	California	100%
J. Hungerford Smith Co., Inc.	Delaware	100%
J. Hungerford Smith, Ltd.	Canada	100%
La Compagnie des Bananes, S.A.	France	100%
Maritrop Trading Corporation	Delaware	100%
John Morrell & Co.	Delaware	100%
Ark Valley Feeders, Inc.	Kansas	100%
Golden Sun Feeds, Inc.	Iowa	100%
Farmers Grain & Supply Co.	Iowa	85%
M.H. Greenebaum, Inc.	New York	100%
John Morrell & Co., Ltd.	England	85%
Roberts and Oake, Inc.	Illinois	100%
Omer-Decugis et Fils	France	81%
Polymer United	Gran Cayman, Cayman Is.	100%
Spiers B.V.	Belgium	100%
Stuart Investments, Inc.	Delaware	100%
Surrey Shipping Company, Ltd.	Bermuda	100%
Tela Railroad Company	Delaware	100%
TRT Telecommunications Corporation	Delaware	100%
United Brands Floriculture, Inc.	Florida	100%
United Brands Continental, B.V.	Netherlands	100%
United Brands Overseas Finance Corp. N.V.	Netherlands Antilles	100%
Renco Limonadefabrieken B.V.	Netherlands	100%
Caraibische Scheepvaart Maatschappij B.V.	Netherlands	100%
United Fruit Jamaica Company	Delaware	100%
United Fruit Japan, Inc.	Delaware	100%
Far East Fruit Company, Ltd.	Japan	89%

are employed by the Diversified Group. Approximately 28,000 employees are employed in agricultural activities in Latin America.

United Brands maintains approximately fifty contracts with labor organizations in Latin America and the United States.

Eli M. Black

The driving force behind United Brands was Eli M. Black, who grew up in a poor family on Manhattan's Lower East Side. A descendant of 10 generations of rabbis and scholars, Mr. Black was graduated from Yeshiva University in 1940, was ordained, and served a Long Island congregation for four years.

Because he believed his position as a rabbi "was very unfulfilling" and "that sermons didn't change anyone's attitude about anything," according to a friend,

EXHIBIT 3
BANANA SHIPMENTS AND SALES

During the five years ending December 31, 1974, United Brands imported and sold the percentages indicated below of all bananas imported into the United States and Canada, Europe, and Japan:

	1970	1971	1972	1973	1974
United States & Canada	45%	47%	44%	35%	37%
Europe	40%	41%	39%	42%	44%
Japan	13%	11%	10%	11%	13%

The following table sets forth the distribution of the company's dollar sales of bananas, net of import duties for such years:

	1970	1971	1972	1973	1974
United States & Canada	50%	49%	49%	40%	38%
Europe	43%	45%	46%	52%	52%
Japan	7%	6%	5%	8%	10%

The preceding table excludes sales by British and European subsidiaries acting as distributors of bananas, substantially all of which are grown by third parties.

Boxes of bananas, each containing approximately 40 pounds, imported by the company into the areas indicated for such years were as follows (in thousands):

	1970	1971	1972	1973	1974
United States & Canada	44,730	48,671	45,758	36,408	39,141
Europe	37,207	43,975	46,754	44,290	43,290
Japan	5,960	6,056	5,831	5,492	6,213
Total	87,897	98,702	98,343	86,190	88,644

EXHIBIT 3 *(Continued)*
BANANA SHIPMENTS AND SALES

During the five years ended December 31, 1974, the percent of the company's total banana shipments attributable to bananas produced and purchased by United Brands in each country where it obtains bananas were as follows:

	1970	1971	1972	1973	1974
Panama					
Produced	27%	25%	25%	27%	20%
Purchased	9	8	7	6	5
	36	33	32	33	25
Honduras					
Produced	17	23	20	16	17
Purchased	7	7	6	6	5
	24	30	26	22	22
Costa Rica					
Produced	19	18	18	19	16
Purchased	—	—	1	1	—
	19	18	19	20	16
Guatemala					
Produced	9	9	11	—	—
Purchased	1	2	1	4	3
	10	11	12	4	3
Ecuador—purchased	1	2	4	11	13
Colombia—purchased	8	3	2	3	11
Philippines—purchased	—	1	2	4	7
Other—purchased	2	2	3	3	3
	100%	100%	100%	100%	100%

Note: Data for 1973 and 1974 reflect the effects of natural disasters in the Company's Honduran operation and sale of the Company's Guatemala properties in 1972.

he left his congregation.[3] First he joined Lehman Brothers investment house and later American Securities Corporation, where part of his responsibilities involved handling the financing for an old-line $5-million producer of milk bottle caps, American Seal-Kap Corporation.

In 1954 Mr. Black became chairman and chief executive officer of American Seal-Kap Corporation. In 1965, after weeding out the company's unprofitable lines, expanding others, and buying out other concerns, Mr. Black renamed the company AMK Corporation.

In late 1966, AMK Corporation acquired 33 percent of John Morrell & Company, a major meat packer located in Chicago. On December 31, 1967, AMK Corporation acquired the remaining 67 percent in John Morrell & Company, a company 20 times bigger than AMK Corporation.

In 1968, AMK purchased 9 percent of United Fruit Company; on February 13, 1969, Eli Black became a director of United Fruit.

[3]"Was Eli Black's Suicide Caused by the Tensions of Conflicting Worlds?" *Wall Street Journal,* Midwest Edition, February 14, 1975.

Black, according to associates and friends, was a reserved, formal man who frequently smiled but rarely laughed. "He was a very serious man. There was no small talk," said a business associate.[4] Black is described by former business associates as an autocrat who maintained tight personal control of his businesses. Eli Black was a sagacious businessman, an asset manager, whose "ability lies in uncovering value on a large scale, getting control of it and putting it to work uncovering more assets," according to *Fortune* magazine.[5]

One executive officer who worked under Black said, "Mr. Black wasn't comfortable with people who disagreed with his views."[6]

Mr. Black's recreation was his business and social causes, and he endeavored to combine the two (see Exhibit 4). He played no sports and rarely took part in vacations unless they were connected with business.

Friends say Mr. Black attracted people who had troubles and that he took other people's troubles on as though they were his own.

Leon Black recalled his father's vision that "a man's reach must extend beyond his grasp." He went on to add, "he internalized so many problems—the economic condition of the country, the energy crisis, the state of Israel (he was a director for PEC Israel Economics Company) and certainly his own business. He was used to being able by the force of his intellect to get through problems to solve them."[7] He was so confident that he could solve the pressing problems of the day that he sent Senator Abraham Ribicoff of Connecticut, a friend, his formula for getting the United States through the energy shortage.

According to *The Wall Street Journal,* he also took on smaller burdens of his friends. One person who visited him just before his death told of Mr. Black's greeting him with the words, "What can I do for you?"[8]

"When I heard that story, I began to realize the pressures Eli was under," said Bernard Fischman, a long-time friend of Mr. Black and his widow Shirley. "That was his topic sentence for starting a conversation."[9]

In 1969, Mr. Black turned his attention from the manufacturing industries with which he had been involved in the past to a food concern—United Fruit Company. As he considered acquiring United Fruit Company, he conducted a thorough examination of its past. In part, here is what he learned.

UNITED FRUIT COMPANY

United Fruit Company was incorporated in New Jersey in March 1899. Soon after its incorporation, it acquired numerous other fruit companies and some transportation companies with land in South and Central America and the West

---

[4] Ibid.

[5] "United Fruit's Shotgun Marriage," *Fortune,* April 1969, p. 122.

[6] "At United Brands Co., Fight for Control Came after Honduran Payoff," *Wall Street Journal,* Midwest Edition, May 7, 1975.

[7] "Was Eli Black's Suicide Caused by the Tensions of Conflicting Worlds?" *Wall Street Journal,* Midwest Edition, February 14, 1975.

[8] Ibid.

[9] Ibid.

EXHIBIT 4

ELI BLACK'S ACTION ON SOCIAL RESPONSIBILITY

The following appeared in the 1972 annual report of the United Brands Company:

Every public company has more than one constituency. Its management must answer to the shareholders, but it must also be responsive to the needs of its markets, the aspirations of its employees, and the interests of the general public. The larger the scope of the company, the more numerous those constituencies can become. In the case of an organization with the geographically widespread and varied business interests of United Brands, they can embrace a significant portion of the world.

We have very real responsibilities in each of those areas. They demand more than words; they demand substance. Companies can no longer deal with their responsibilities at the level of appearances only; they can no longer be satisfied with the treatment of effects. We must concern ourselves with causes and United Brands does.

It is because of the successful application of these principles that the Chicago Daily News in a story on the Company last year reported, "It may well be the most socially conscious American company in the hemisphere." The Company's social policies and practices have also led The New York Times to report in a recent front page story, "What emerges from talks with labor, management and government is a picture of a company that anticipated the changes that have swept Latin America and has quietly set about adjusting to them."

Judgments like these have been earned. They reflect substantial, long-term commitments which United Brands has made to all of the people to whom the Company is responsible. In some instances, this has meant the deliberate evolution away from traditional policies and practices. And in others, it has entailed creative vigilance to unexpected needs which the Company is equipped to answer.

Our Company's Responses to the Nicaraguan Earthquake Disaster

The most recent example of this kind of responsiveness was provided by the tragedy which took place during Christmas Week in Nicaragua. On the morning of December 23, in a series of three devastating shocks, most of the city of Managua was destroyed, countless thousands of men, women, and children were killed, including one Company employee, Humberto Vivas, a carpenter at the Corona plant. Thousands more were injured and made homeless. It was one of the most destructive earthquakes in Central American history. Within hours, your Company—itself no stranger to various kinds of devastation by nature—had begun to respond.

Because one of the first requirements in dealing effectively with disaster is communication, we immediately reopened the Managua office of TRT, United Brands tropical telecommunications subsidiary. TRT remained on the air round the clock for the next several days, providing critical information on the extent of the disaster for the guidance of relief efforts, and informing concerned families and friends of the whereabouts and condition of individuals known to have been in the area at the time of the disaster. During the first, frightening hours, TRT provided the only communications link between the stricken city and the outside world.

We then turned to the task of looking after our employees in the area—seeing that they were safe and that they and their families had the necessities of life.

In those first grim days following the earthquake, United Brands personnel witnessed and participated in a great many poignant episodes. One such was the story of a Company executive, John Young and his wife Barbara and their two children. Hours before the disaster struck, Mrs. Young had given birth to their first son, David. She was nursing David when the first tremors occurred. Two hours later the hospital had to be evacuated and Mrs. Young made her way to the nursery, carried the infant down the hospital stairs, and stood in front of the hospital for two hours before John came and led her and the baby to safety through the ruins of Managua. Meanwhile, two thousand miles away, the family of John and Barbara

EXHIBIT 4 *(Continued)*

Young were desperately trying to get some word about them, but communications were presumably nonexistent. Finally, Barbara's mother called New York State Assemblyman Stephen Solarz, who, in turn called United Brands Chairman E. M. Black. Mr. Black contacted the Company's office in San Jose, Costa Rica, and a Company plane was dispatched to Managua. Within hours Mr. Black was able to pass the word back that not only were the Youngs safe and on their way back to the United States, but also the news that Barbara had delivered their second child. The Youngs arrived home in time for Christmas and their story had a happy ending; not all the stories out of Managua had happy endings.

We offered the full help of our Company and its personnel to the Nicaraguan Government and we began to lay out a plan of assistance. On Christmas day we began the organization of what may be the most comprehensive relief program ever mounted by a private corporation on behalf of the people of another land. NEED, the Nicaraguan Earthquake Emergency Drive, was created by the Company and officially registered later that week as a non-profit corporation and staffed by volunteers from United Brands. The Company then produced a series of newspaper advertisements and radio and television spots featuring an appeal by Bill Russell, the well-known basketball star and television personality who had previously visited the city of Managua (also under Company sponsorship, as a representative of the Middle American Sports Foundation). Those advertisements appeared throughout the country during the week of January 15, in paid space and sponsored time, in the place of United Brands and Chiquita Products commercial messages. They were then repeated as public service announcements on 200 television stations, 400 radio stations, and are scheduled to appear in regional editions of such publications as *Time, Newsweek, Fortune, Sports Illustrated, Nation's Business,* and *U.S. News & World Report.* Thousands of dollars in contributions poured into NEED from every corner of the country. The advertisements and other announcements pledged that every cent collected will be used to aid the victims of the Managua disaster.

In addition, the Company set up a national telephone network, called the "Nicaraguan Lifeline," for telling Americans what they could do, what was needed, and directing them to the various agencies collecting relief supplies.

Donations are still coming in and United Brands shareholders wishing to participate in this historic effort should mail their contributions, in any amount to:

> NEED
> Box 1
> Boston, Massachusetts 02199

This is only one example of how the Company discharges its obligation. The real significance of NEED is the accurate reflection it provides of a far-reaching corporate policy commitment: to carefully examine all dimensions of our operating practices and management decisions, and to measure them against their potential impact . . . on the environment, on the cultural and social climates in which we operate, on our collective consciences, and on the quality of our lives.

Indies. Most of the company's operations were in Central America (see Exhibits 5, 5A, 5B, and 5C).

History

There are three principal periods in United Fruit Company's relationship with Central American banana producing countries.

EXHIBIT 5
IMPROVED AND UNIMPROVED ACREAGE AS OF DECEMBER 31, 1968

	Improved acreage					Total improved	Unimproved acreage	Total
	Bananas	Sugar	Cocoa	Oil palm	Other			
Colombia					1,118	1,118	15,963	17,081
Costa Rica	23,761		20,945	25,326	20,526	90,288	166,111	256,399
Guatemala	7,649				7,630	15,279	57,444	72,723
Honduras	20,637			9,652	28,819	59,108	128,739	187,847
Jamaica	66	8,708			1,745	10,519	3,773	14,292
Panama	26,615		4,486		15,197	46,298	64,334	110,632
Other (Including the United States, Europe, and Africa)	220				2,382	2,602	72,689	75,291
Grand total								734,649

EXHIBIT 5A
CENTRAL AMERICA—SOCIOECONOMIC CHARACTERISTICS

Country	Total number of households	Urban households (percent)	Rural households (percent)	Class A–B (percent)	Class C (percent)	Class D (percent)	Literacy rate (percent)	Average income per capita 1961, U.S. dollars	Average income per household 1961, U.S. dollars
Panama	200,000								
Guatemala	764,000	35	65	10	35	55	25	$176	$ 985
El Salvador	502,000	39	61	10	30	60	47	220	1,100
Honduras	367,000	23	77	5	30	65	47	207	1,180
Nicaragua	258,000	41	59	5	25	70	38	213	1,300
Costa Rica	243,000	34	66	10	40	50	88	344	2,000

*Approximate incomes in each class: Class A–B—more than $300/month.
Class C— $100–$300/month.
Class D— less than $100/month.

Source: Compiled from industry records and from information contained in *Proposed Mutual Defense and Assistance FY 1964*, Agency for International Development (Washington, D.C.: Government Printing Office, 1963).

EXHIBIT 5B
CENTRAL AMERICA—SOCIOECONOMIC DATA, 1971

	Guatemala	El Salvador	Honduras	Nicaragua	Costa Rica	Central America	Panama
Populations (millions)	5.2	3.4	2.6	2.0	1.8	15.0	1.5
Area (thousands of square kilometers)	108.9	21.4	112.1	148.0	50.9	441.3	77.1
Roads (thousands of kilometers)	12.3	8.7	5.2	11.4	20.5	58.1	6.8
Currency exchange	Quetzal	Colon	Lempira	Cordoba	Colon		Balboa
Rate in relation with the United States dollar	1:1	2.5:1	2:1	7:1	8.60:1		1:1
Capital city	Guatemala	San Salvador	Tegucigalpa	Managua	San Jose		Panama City
Metropolitan population	730,000	323,000	232,000	374,000	450,000		200,000

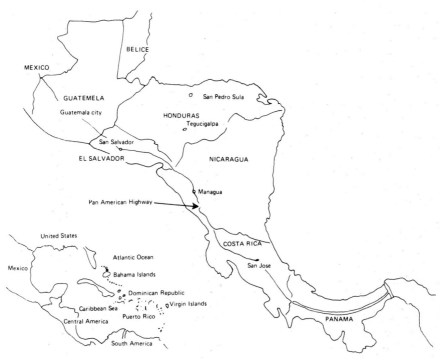

EXHIBIT 5C
United Brands, Central American territories.

The first period in United Fruit's relationship with Central America opened when the company was born and closed with the end of World War I. When United Fruit entered Latin America, the countries were disorganized, poor, and underdeveloped. The governments, which rested in the hands of a few powerful families, were weak, unstable, and unable to help the countries progress.

United Fruit Company entered the banana republics with offers to exchange tangible benefits—i.e., major developments such as seaports, railroads, hospitals, schools, farms, utilities, and homes—for a major part of the banana concession, about which the nations' citizens knew very little.

In the first contracts, negotiated between the company and the countries between 1903 and 1913, the governments wanted promises of specific benefits plus a 1 cent-per-bunch export tax on the bananas. In return, United Fruit Company received government land, permission to grow bananas, and an exemption from all other taxes.

Because there were few trained Central American nationals available to administer the company's operations, United Fruit Company relied primarily on executives and supervisors from the United States. The company also supplemented the needed work force in Latin America with United States laborers.

The second period of the company's history was between the two world wars, during which time the Central American nations became more aware of the values of the banana concession that they had given to the company. Consequently, some contractual terms were renegotiated and amended.

During this period, some Latin Americans began to view the favors United Fruit Company received via the contracts and the fact that United Fruit relied primarily on executives from the United States as threats to their nations' sovereignty and as a source of economic exploitation.

But despite these growing dissatisfactions with the United Fruit Company, the Latin American governments, when deeply in debt during the depression, borrowed money from United Fruit in order to survive. And, despite the depression and the disease which destroyed many plantations in Central America, United Fruit continued to invest in these countries.

The third period in United Fruit Company's history was after World War II. Earlier-negotiated contracts were rewritten to allow greater revenues to the countries; statutory minimum wages were instituted, and a program for transferring many of United Fruit Company's social services to government hands began.

By the start of this third period, Latin American peasants had learned what it meant to hold a regular job and to have money in their pockets. They had become skilled and learned how to operate complex machinery. A few learned to fill administrative, technical, and managerial positions. Latin America, with American money, could buy goods and services on the world market. Its standard of living had by this time been significantly enhanced.

In response to local pressure for more landownership by Latin American citizens, United Fruit Company developed an Associate Producer Program in the early 1960s. Under this program, company land was—through contract arrangement, sale, or lease—turned over to local banana growers; the company supervised the growing practices and then purchased the bananas from the local citizens. By the late 1960s, the bananas grown and shipped under this program constituted between 25 and 50 percent of the total banana shipments; however, there were problems. Local producers allowed working conditions and health and social services to deteriorate; trade unions found it difficult to organize banana workers under the program; and United Fruit Company had difficulty enforcing and maintaining quality standards. In 1969 United Fruit Company began modernizing its more outdated installations and turning over some of these facilities to local management, including a labor union.

As the countries developed, more powerful Central Americans began looking forward to the day when the company would be completely eliminated as a producer and when its activities would be limited to transportation and distribution. Some Central American political figures publicly expressed the belief that at some time the countries' bananas would be grown only by the countries' citizens and that the government would administer the heavy investment needed for irrigation, disease control, drainage, and collecting the fruit. These government leaders believed their countries' people possessed the skills necessary to undertake these projects and that the investments for the project could be fully recovered by profits. It was their belief that the profits would be used for investment and to assist the independent national worker on a greater scale than did his present wages.

During this third period in the company's history, it found the negotiating process with the Latin American countries more complex because the governments of these countries became more sophisticated.

The Power of Latin American Countries

Regardless of the degree to which the banana-producing republics are developed or literate, these nations have their sovereignty. Emanating from that sovereignty are two principal powers: expropriation, which means at any time these countries can legally expropriate any portion of the company's property,[10] and taxation, which can affect corporate profits. International law offers only two limitations on expropriation: those imposed by freely signed contracts and a requirement that a country compensate the companies fairly, adequately, and promptly. The taxing powers of the governments have been severely limited by contracts that United Fruit Company has maintained with the countries.

Even stronger is the power the various banana republics wield jointly against the company. This power, of course, undercuts the company's defensive ability to shift production from one country to another in order to avoid pressures placed upon it by a single country.

United Fruit Company and the United States Government

United Fruit Company moved very quickly into a position of supremacy in the banana business. At the outset, the United States government took very little action to regulate its growth, but as the company grew and became stronger, it opened itself to governmental tax laws.

Competing firms entering the banana market found the market already under the control of United Fruit Company, because United Fruit (1) had entered the market first, (2) had maintained a high quality of service, and (3) had implemented advanced production techniques which created better-quality bananas.

The company's size enabled it to make up losses from isolated producing areas with bananas from another area. Because United Fruit Company had in-

---

[10]In 1953 and 1954, Guatemala expropriated more than 370,000 acres of United Fruit Company's holdings. The U.S. State Department served a formal claim on the Guatemalan charge d'affaires in Washington, D.C., demanding payment to that company of more than $15 million for part of the expropriation. At first Guatemala denied the right of the United States government to intervene because the intervention was against the nation's sovereign rights. But in December 1954 an agreement was made with the Guatemalan government whereby the seized lands were returned to the company and the company agreed to (1) transfer to the government within six months, 100,000 acres on the Guatemalan west coast and to (2) pay the government a 30 percent tax on income from the west coast operations. Two years later, United Fruit Company and the Guatemalan government signed a new agreement.

tegrated much of its production, transportation, and marketing facilities, the company could sell its bananas at a lower price. Because of these factors, new competitors often sold out or joined United Fruit Company.

Despite the fact that the proportion of the world banana trade handled by United Fruit declined significantly between 1910 and 1955, the United States government filed two major antitrust suits in the 1950s. The federal government accused United Fruit of monopolizing the banana market because the company still controlled more than half the North American market for bananas.

In a 1958 consent decree entered into with the U.S. Department of Justice, United Fruit was ordered to give up one-third of its importing and all of its jobbing functions to newly created competitors. The company also was ordered to sell all but 100 shares of its International Railways of Central America stock.[11]

Other United Fruit Activity

Aside from its operations in Latin America during this period, United Fruit Company in the late 1950s began branching out into other operations, including petroleum and natural gas. In 1962 it acquired a Belgian fruit, fish, and vegetable distributor and in 1966 it acquired A&W Drive-Ins of Canada, Ltd. The following year it acquired Baskin-Robbins Ice Cream Company of Burbank, California.

ELI BLACK MERGES AMK AND UNITED FRUIT COMPANY

After Eli Black reviewed United Fruit's political and financial histories, AMK Corporation in 1969 acquired a majority interest in United Fruit Company. In June 1970, despite Federal Trade Commission warnings, AMK Corporation voted to merge with United Fruit. (The FTC had issued notices that it intended to institute proceedings against AMK, compelling it to divest itself of its 83 percent interest in United Fruit, and against United Fruit, compelling it to divest itself of interest in the domestic fresh produce business, primarily iceberg lettuce. At that point, United Fruit was facing the 1958 Justice Department decree to divest itself of 17 percent of its banana business during 1970.)

Prior to the merger, United Fruit's earnings were dwindling, but it did have cash reserves of about $100 million and no debt (see Exhibit 6). Some time in early 1967, the management of United Fruit Company agreed to let Donaldson, Lufkin, and Jenrette (hereafter referred to as DLJ), an upcoming and

---

[11] In 1933, the IRCA was near bankruptcy. Eventually the IRCA and United Fruit Company became partners. The company paid the railway's debts in exchange for 42.6 percent of the stock of the railroad company. It bought $5 million worth of freight cars and locomotives to haul bananas, but when not hauling bananas they would be used for other freight. The IRCA paid no rent on the equipment. Instead, it allowed the company to ship bananas for less than half the rate its competitors paid. This, of course, gave United Fruit Company a distinct advantage over its competitors.

aggressive Wall Street investment banking firm managed by young Harvard Business School graduates, evaluate the company's underlying value and report that information to the interested investing public. DLJ, indeed, according to some sources, discovered a gold mine with no long-term debt, very little preferred stock, and some $100 million in liquid assets. They considered it a superb opportunity for a conglomerate acquisition and it was DLJ which brought United Fruit Company to the attention of Mr. Black and made arrangements for his purchase of 9 percent of the company's stock on the open market without United Fruit Company's management knowing anything about it.

It was at 5 P.M., after the close of the stock market on September 24, 1968, that Mr. John M. Fox, then chairman of United Fruit Company, received the word from Mr. Black of what had happened. It was one of the largest single transactions ever to appear on the tape and reportedly one of the most financially rewarding company analyses ever made by DLJ. The management and board of United Fruit Company reportedly were stunned and they felt betrayed by DLJ. Subsequently, they fought Eli Black's overtures bitterly. Directors tried to find other suitors, but eventually they gave in and fell victim to his net. Black had successfully outbid two other conglomerates, Zapata Noreness and Textron, and AMK and United Fruit became United Brands.

UNITED BRANDS—HISTORY FROM MERGER TO BLACK'S DEATH

After Eli Black had created United Brands, he continued during the 1970s to buy and sell major concerns throughout the world.

In 1970, Mr. Black personally negotiated on behalf of the company's lettuce subsidiary, Inter-Harvest, Inc., with Cesar Chavez's United Farm Workers Union. Mr. Black was the first and only major lettuce grower to sign with the union. At the signing of that contract, Mr. Black invited Mr. Chavez to his Rosh Hashanah services, where Mr. Chavez read a prayer.

"You should have seen it," said a friend of Mr. Black who also attended the services. "It was something you could point out to your kids and say—see, business and social conscience do mix."[12]

In December 1972, United Brands sold its Guatemalan banana operation to Del Monte Corporation for more than $20 million. A year later it sold its 83 percent interest in Baskin-Robbins Ice Cream Company. In the latter part of 1972, United Brands began acquiring the Foster Grant Company, Inc., a major producer of styrene monomer, polystyrene products, and sunglasses. But after owning as much as 69 percent of Foster Grant, United Brands sold all its Foster Grant interests in January 1975 for nearly $70 million to American Hoechst Corporation, a United States subsidiary of Hoechst AG of West Germany.

[12] Ibid.

EXHIBIT 6A

UNITED FRUIT COMPANY AND SUBSIDIARIES, STATEMENT OF CONSOLIDATED EARNINGS, YEAR ENDED DECEMBER 31 (Thousands of Dollars)

	1963	1964	1965	1966	1967
Sales of products	$309,160	$316,828	$363,963	$398,251	$438,505
Services to customers	37,204	35,099	37,465	41,512	50,379
	346,364	351,927	399,428	439,763	488,884
Costs and expenses:					
Costs of sales and services to customers, excl. depreciation	293,917	293,827	314,029	345,465	379,903
Selling, general and admin. expenses, excl. depreciation	33,213	35,206	34,504	39,138	43,731
Depreciation	17,148	18,513	18,685	16,943	17,593
Property losses (gains), net	156	(847)	827	(215)	449
Provision for doubtful accounts	715	1,787	1,036	1,083	697
	345,149	348,486	369,081	402,414	442,373
Income from operations	1,215	3,441	30,347	37,349	46,511
Other income—net:					
Interest	2,250	2,515	3,342	4,616	4,855
Other	136	(477)	(2,484)	(296)	185
Earnings before taxes and extraordinary items	3,601	5,479	31,205	41,669	51,551
Provision for U.S. and foreign income taxes	3,031	3,552	12,686	16,654	19,438
Earnings before extraordinary items	570	1,927	18,519	25,015	32,113
Extraordinary items:					
Profits (losses), net after taxes, from sales of properties (less related costs of closing divisions in 1964 and 1965*	1,180	2,193	(3,465)	—	—

814

Reduction in anticipated tax benefits due to change in rates	—	(1,155)	—	—	—
Total extraordinary items	1,180	1,038	(3,465)	—	—
Net earnings for the period	$1,750	$2,965	$15,054	$25,015	$32,113
Per Share of common stock†:					
Earnings (loss) before extraordinary items	$ (.03)	$ .13	$2.21	$3.06	$4.00
Extraordinary items, net after taxes	.14	.13	(.43)	—	—
Net earnings for the period	$ .11	$ .26	$1.78	$3.06	$4.00
Pro forma earnings assuming conversion of convertible preferred shares outstanding and exercise of stock options	$ .21	$ .45	$ .15	$ .75	$1.10
Cash dividends declared	$ .60	$ .45	$ .15	$ .75	$1.10
Average number of common shares outstanding during the period	8,091,871	8,022,925	7,978,394	7,900,878	7,816,453‡

*After taxes: 1963—$365. 1964—$121. 1965—$2,048.

†Per share data are based on the weighted average number of common shares at the close of each month during the period, after recognition of the dividend requirements on the $2 convertible preferred stock ($850 in 1963, 1964 and 1965; $847 in 1966; $816 in 1967; $623 and $529 for the unaudited nine month periods ended September 30, 1967 and September 28, 1968 respectively.)

‡Includes the common share equivalent of preferred shares which became residual securities in September 1968.

EXHIBIT 6B
United Fruit Company Consolidated Balance Sheet
December 31, 1967
(Thousands of Dollars)

Assets	
Cash and marketable securities	$ 96,338
Accounts receivable, net	30,767
Inventories of products	19,615
Prepaid expenses	2,224
Total current assets	148,944
Material and supplies	18,943
Long-term loans and other noncurrent receivables	10,665
Fixed assets	412,978
Less: Accumulated depreciation	(226,909)
Net fixed assets	186,069
Deferred charges	11,962
Other assets	22,125
Total assets	$398,708

Liabilities	
Accounts payable	$ 12,817
Accrued liabilities	17,549
United States and foreign income taxes	14,908
Total current liabilities	45,274
Deferred income	1,513
Deferred European income taxes	3,972
Provision for severance and other social benefits, Net after taxes	15,976
Total liabilities	66,735
Cumulative preferred stock	8,511
Common stock	8,831
Paid in capital	184,782
Retained earnings	154,093
Less: Common stock reacquired for stock option incentive plans and other purposes	(24,244)
Total shareholders' equity	331,973
Total liability and equity	$398,078

UNITED BRANDS'S BANANA BUSINESS

It has been the banana business that has caused troubles for United Brands. In 1973 a windstorm swept through Honduras, curtailing the company's production there for some time. Early in 1974, the banana difficulties were further complicated. United Brands increased its exports from Honduras to the United States; meanwhile, its competitors also sharply raised their banana shipments to the United States. These factors combined to create an oversupply of bananas which severely depressed banana prices and produced what United Brands called "unsatisfactory banana operations" during the first quarter of 1974.[13]

While all the banana producers—including United Brands—were suffering from an oversupply of bananas, seven banana republics in Central and South America formed a Union of Banana Exporting Countries and pushed for higher fruit prices. The plan called for the banana exporting countries to levy a tax of $1 per 40-pound box of bananas. The banana republics said the tax was to offset increasing fuel costs.

The effort to impose these taxes began "the banana war." United Brands and other major banana exporting companies quickly protested this tax, and the banana war was quickly reduced to skirmishes involving just a few countries.

In April 1974, the Republic of Honduras enacted a 50-cent tax on each 40-pound box of bananas. It deferred payment on this tax, however, until June. In August, Eli Black wrote a letter to United Brands' shareholders in which he said that the Panamanian tax of $1 a box, the Costa Rican tax of 25 cents a box, and the Honduran tax of 50 cents a box "violated and breached the provisions of existing agreements with these countries." But he also wrote that the company realized the countries' need for additional revenue and said that he intended to negotiate with the countries to attempt to arrive at a reasonable formula.[14]

Later that same month, United Brands announced it had reached an "understanding with the Republic of Honduras" for a tax of 25 cents a box with gradual increases beginning in 1975 depending in part on the banana market at the time.[15] The 25-cents-a-box tax in 1974 would have reduced United Brands' costs by approximately $7.5 million over the 50-cents-a-box tax Honduras initially announced it would levy.

A month after this announcement, United Brands and Honduras suffered a devastating loss from Hurricane Fifi. The hurricane destroyed approximately 70 percent of United Brands' plantations in Honduras and caused a $20-million loss to crops and company facilities.

In January 1975, United Brands announced it had suffered a 1974 fourth-quarter loss from continuing operations of nearly $15 million compared with $3 million in earnings during the 1973 fourth quarter.

On February 6, after Eli Black's death, United Brands' board (see Exhibit 7) announced that, for an interim period, two committees—an executive committee and a management committee—jointly would assume the responsibilities of running the company (see Exhibit 7A).

---

[13] United Brands Company, Securities and Exchange Commission Form 10-K for fiscal year ending December 31, 1974, as amended April 10, 1975.

[14] In 1974 United Brands incurred a charge of more than $11 million because of banana export taxes imposed on Honduras, Panama, and Costa Rica. A 50-cents-a-box tax would have cost United Brands an estimated $15 million.

[15] At United Brands Co., Fight for Control Came after Honduran Payoff." *Wall Street Journal*, Midwest Edition, May 7, 1975.

EXHIBIT 7A

BACKGROUND OF BOARD OF DIRECTORS—PRE AND POST BLACK'S DEATH

Eli M. Black (elected 1970). He was a trustee for Alfred University and a Director of the Lincoln Center for the Performing Arts.

*Norman Alexander** (elected 1975). He was born in New York City in 1914. He received his A.B. from Columbia in 1934 and his L.L.B. in 1936, also from Columbia. He is currently president and a director of Sun Chemical Corp.; he is also president of Ampacet Corp. He is a member of the board of directors of the following companies: Standard Kollsman Industries, Inc.; Walter Kidde & Co.; and Dictaphone Corp. He is also on the board of overseers of Albert Einstein College of Medicine and a trustee of the Bronx-Lebanon Hospital.

*Wallace Booth** (elected 1975). He is presently president and chief executive officer of United Brands Co. He was born in Nashville, Tenn., in 1922. He received his B.A. and M.B.A. from the University of Chicago in 1948. He was with Ford Motor Co. from 1948–1968, where he held the following positions: manager in Dearborn Mich.; director of finance, vice president for finance, and treasurer of Ford Motor Co. Ltd., Canada; managing director, chief executive officer, Ford Motor Co., Australia; and vice president corporate staffs, Philco Ford, Philadelphia. From 1968–1974, he was vice president for finance for North American Rockwell Corp., California. He is a member of the board of directors of the following companies: Collins Radio Co.; American Data Systems, Inc.; and North American Rockwell Corp.

George F. Doriot† (elected 1975). He was born in 1899 and he received his B.S. from the University of Paris in 1915. He was assistant dean of Harvard Business School from 1926 to 1931. He is the founder of American Research and Development Corp. He is a director of the following companies: American Research and Development Corp.; National Shawmut Bank, Boston; The Boston Co., Inc.; Canadian Enterprise Development Corp.; European Enterprise Development Co.; Ionics, Inc.; Sun Life Assurance Co.; Textron Atlantic, Inc.; and Tech Studies, Inc.

*Max M. Fisher** (elected 1975). Born 1908; graduated Ohio State University in 1930. He is currently chairman of the board of Sefran Printing Co. He is on the board of the following companies: Dayco Corp.; Fruehauf Corp.; Manufacturers National Bank; Michigan Bell Telephone Co.; Michigan Consolidated Gas Co.; Owens Illinois, Inc.; and Taubman, Inc.

*Robert M. Gallop** (elected 1957‡). He was born in 1908 and graduated from City College of New York in 1928. He received a law degree from N.Y.U. in 1931. He is currently senior vice president and general counsel for United Brands Co. He is a director of Foster Grant Co.

*Donald R. Gant**† (elected 1972). He was born in 1928, graduated from the University of Pennsylvania in 1952, and received his M.B.A. from Harvard in 1954. He is currently a partner in Goldman, Sachs, and Co. He is a director of the following companies: Sperry & Hutchinson Co.; Liquid Air Corp. of North America; J.B. Ivey & Co.; and Amcord, Inc.

*George P. Gardner, Jr.**† (elected 1953§). He was born in 1917 and received his B.A. from Harvard in 1939. He is currently senior vice president and a director of Paine Webber, Inc. He is also a director of the following companies: Instron Corp.; Stanley Home Products, Inc.; New England Enterprises Capital Corp.; Ritz Carlton Hotel Co.; W.R. Grace & Co.; and Barry Wright Corp.

F. Mark Garlinghouse† (elected 1975). He was born in 1914, graduated from the University of Chicago in 1936, and received a law degree from Washburn University in 1939. He is currently vice president and general counsel for American Telephone and Telegraph Co. He is a director for the following companies: Ohio Bell Telephone Co.; L.F. Garlinghouse Co. (chairman); Polo Plastics, Inc.; M-C Industries, Inc.; Sun Chemical Corp.; and Chesapeake & Potomac Telephone Co.

Edward Gelsthorpe† (elected 1975). He was born in 1921 and graduated from Hamilton College in 1942. He is currently executive vice president of United Brands Co. He is a director of Gillette and Prudential Tower Building.

Dr. J. E. Goldman*† (elected 1970). He was born in New York City in 1921. He received degrees from Yeshiva College in 1940 and the University of Pennsylvania in 1943. He is senior vice president, chief scientist, and a director of Xerox Corp. He is also a director of Burndy Corp.

Maurice C. Kaplan*† (elected 1969‡). He received his A.B. from the University of Illinois and his J.D. from Northwestern University. He has been a Sterling Fellow at Yale, a visiting associate attorney at Stanford, a teacher at George Washington University Law School, an assistant director of the Securities and Exchange Commission, president of Starwood Corp., and chairman of the board of American Dual Vest Fund, Inc. He is also a director of American Research and Development Corp., George D. Ruper Corp., Welch's Grape Juice, and General Corp.

Samuel D. Lunt, Sr.*† (elected 1956‡). Born in 1905, he graduated from Hobart College in 1927 and received his M.B.A. from Harvard in 1929. He is a partner in S.D. Lunt and Co. and a director of the following companies: CF&I Steel Corp.; Aegis Corp. (chairman); Houdaille Industries, Inc.; Hudson General Corp.; and Margaret L. Wendt Foundation (chairman).

Joseph M. McDaniel, Jr.*† (elected 1957‡). Born in 1902, he received degrees from Johns Hopkins University in 1924 and 1930. He is a director of the following companies: Andrew-Hart Corp. (chairman); Oppenheimer Fund, Ind.; Kane-Miller Corp.; Reuco, D.C., Inc.; Cadence Industries Corp.; Oppenheimer A.I.M. Fund; Oppenheimer Time Fund; Oppenheimer Income Fund; Oppenheimer Special Fund. He is a trustee of Johns Hopkins University.

Seymour Milstein† (elected 1975). Private investor.

Elias Paul*† (elected 1971). Born in 1919, he graduated from the University of Illinois in 1947. He is president and chief executive officer of John Morrell & Co. He is a director of Golden Sun Feed Co. (chairman), Foster Grant, and John Horreu & Co., Ltd.

Simon H. Rifkind‡ (elected 1975). Born in 1901 in Russia, he graduated from City College of New York in 1922 and received a law degree from Columbia University in 1925. He is a partner in Paul Weiss, Rifkind, Wharton & Garrison. He is a director of Sterling Nat'l Bank, Revlon, Inc., and Hoeco's Corp.

Norman I. Schafler*† (elected 1958‡). He was born in 1917. He is a director of the following companies: Condec Corp. (chairman); Condelco; Lunkenheimer Co.; NRM Corp. (chairman); Consolidated Controls Corp; Lima Electric Motor Co.; Consolidated Diesel Electric Co.; Hammond Valve Co.; Unimation, Inc. (vice chairman); United Aircraft Products, Inc.; and ABC Air Land Freight Co.

John A. Taylor*† (elected 1973). Senior vice president, United Brands Co., and president of Agrimark Group.

David W. Wallace*† (elected 1960‡). Born in 1924, he received his B.S. from Yale in 1948 and his L.L.B. from Harvard in 1951. After spending three years with White & Case in New York, he joined Alleghany Corp. as general counsel in 1954. He then became secretary-treasurer, vice president, and executive vice president of Alleghany Corp. He later became executive vice president of AMK Corp., and he is currently president of Bangor Punta Corp. He is a director of the following companies: Smith & Wesson, Producers Cotton Oil Co., Piper Aircraft Corp., Lone Star Industries Corp.; and he is vice president and trustee of the Robert R. Young Foundation.

Jay Wells*† (elected 1965‡). Born in 1916, he graduated from Western Reserve University in 1936. He is chairman of the Board of Wells National Services Corp., and lessor of Hospital Communication System.

---

*Member of the Board after Black's death
†Member of the Board prior to Black's death
‡Nominee first became director of AMK Corp.
§Nominee first became director of United Fruit Co.

EXHIBIT 7B
EXECUTIVE AND MANAGEMENT COMMITTEES AFTER
BLACK'S DEATH

Executive Committee	**Management Committee**
George P. Gardner, Jr.	Norman E. Alexander
Edward Gelsthorpe	Donald R. Gant
Dr. J. E. Goldman, Chairman	George P. Gardner
Maurice C. Kaplan	Dr. J. E. Goldman
Elias Paul	Norman I. Schafler, Chairman
Simon H. Rifkind	David W. Wallace
	Jay Wells

Dr. Jacob E. Goldman, 53, a United Brands director and group vice president who also was chief scientist and director of the Xerox Corporation, became chairman of both committees at the outset; however, he later chaired only the executive committee. All company operating and staff groups within the company reported directly to the management committee. The executive committee was responsible for corporate policy.

Initially, Goldman indicated that the interim committee arrangement would last for at least two months. Immediate speculation about Mr. Black's successor centered on Edward Gelsthorpe,[16] executive vice president for the company. United Brands enlisted the services of an executive search company to help the company find a successor for Mr. Black.

CHRONOLOGY OF EVENTS

On March 28, 1975, United Brands announced that it had had a $71.3 million loss in 1974 from continuing operations. It reported a net loss after extraordinary items of $43.6 million, compared with the 1973 net income of $17.7 million or $1.42 a share. The company experienced a heavy fourth-quarter loss which, according to the company, was principally due to unfavorable banana operations, the termination of certain food processing and food service activity, interest charges, and income taxes. The fourth-quarter loss from continuing operations totaled $14.9 million, compared with year-before earnings of $3.1

---

[16] Edward Gelsthorpe joined United Brands in June 1974, after resigning as president and chief operating officer of the Gillette Company. Gelsthorpe joined United Brands as senior vice president, marketing. When Gelsthorpe departed the Gillette Company, it ended two months of speculation among securities analysts and gossip within Gillette about a growing "palace revolt" against Gelsthorpe, who was brought into the company in 1972 over the heads of long-time senior executives, as heir apparent to Vincent C. Ziegler, chairman and chief executive of Gillette. Before joining Gillette, Gelsthorpe rose swiftly through marketing ranks at Bristol-Myers Company and Colgate-Palmolive. He went on to build a reputation as a shrewd, innovative executive as president of Ocean Spray Cranberries, Inc., and as president of Hunt-Wesson Foods, Inc., a Norton Simon, Inc., subsidiary. Gelsthorpe was based in Boston, the traditional headquarters for the former United Fruit Company.

million. The company blamed the losses on Hurricane Fifi and on banana export taxes.

On April 2, Max M. Fisher, an independent investor and chairman of Detroit Renaissance, Inc., a group of businesspersons whose avowed goal was to revitalize downtown Detroit, was elected to the United Brands board. Also added to the board in April were F. Mark Garlinghouse, vice president and general counsel of American Telephone & Telegraph Co., and Seymour Milstein, a New York financier.

On April 8, 1975, United Brands disclosed it had paid a $1.25 million bribe in 1974 to an official of Honduras to win concessions from that country on the banana export tax.

On April 9, the Securities and Exchange Commission (SEC) formally accused United Brands of issuing false reports to hide more than $2 million in payoffs which were intended to win favorable business treatment by two governments. *The Wall Street Journal* named Italy as the second government, although the SEC civil suit did not reveal the country's identity.[17]

The SEC suit was the result of a routine investigation it customarily opens after an unusual death of a chief executive officer.

The SEC charged that the company issued reports that were false because they covered up the Honduras payments as well as "cash payments approximating $750,000 to officials of a foreign government in Europe in connection with securing of favorable business opportunities."[18] The SEC also suspended trading in United Brands shares until the following Monday. The SEC asked the court to appoint a special master to examine the company's records and to give the commission and United Brands shareholders a report "detailing all corporate funds which may have been used for improper payment to government officials foreign or domestic or for other improper purposes"[19] and stating the company's financial condition. The SEC's charges indicated that the company agreed to pay $2.5 million to bribe government officials of the Republic of Honduras in exchange for favorable government export tax treatment.

The SEC charged that after the alleged agreement, "United Brands deposited $1.25 million in accounts of the designated government officials in Swiss banks and agreed to pay an additional $1.25 million in the spring of 1975. The $1.25 million in corporate funds was obtained from certain foreign subsidiaries of United Brands which falsified its books and records to disguise the payment."[20]

A statement issued by United Brands on the same day it revealed the alleged bribes said the United Brands board of directors had learned that the company in 1974 paid "an official of the Republic of Honduras" $1.25 million to win

---

[17]"United Brands Paid Bribe of $1.25 Million to Honduran Official," *Wall Street Journal,* Midwest Edition, April 9, 1975.

[18]*Securities and Exchange Commission v. United Brands Company,* United States District Court for the District of Columbia (Litigation Release No. 6827).

[19]Ibid.

[20]Ibid.

reduction of the Honduran export tax on bananas.[21] The company said the payment was authorized by Eli Black and that the payment was made through foreign subsidiaries of the company and was not accurately identified on company books and records.

In the statement, United Brands said it was part of the original understanding with the Honduran official that an additional payment of $1.25 million would be made at a later date.

Although the company did not reveal the bribed Honduran official's identity, sources close to the investigation revealed the official as General Oswaldo Lopez, president of Honduras. Lopez immediately denied the charge.[22]

Immediately after Lopez denied he had been bribed by United Brands, he met with his cabinet and formed a blue-ribbon commission to investigate the allegations. The commission was given $100,000 to conduct its investigation inside and outside Honduras. "The commission is to discover the origin of this information, and if any Honduran official is found to be involved, he will be punished to the fullest extent of the law," a Lopez spokesperson said.

Meanwhile, United Brands' board appointed a special committee to investigate and report to it circumstances connected with the Honduran payment as well as "certain other payments in countries outside the Western Hemisphere."[23] The company said that, on the basis of the information it had, the "other payments" could be approximately $750,000.

A United Brands competitor told *The Wall Street Journal* that the revelations constituted "a deplorable development" and that it had never made payments similar to those allegedly made by United Brands.[24]

On April 10, a United Brands company stockholder filed a derivative and class action suit against United Brands charging it with mismanaging corporate assets and violating the Securities Exchange Act of 1934. The suit, filed in the U. S. District Court, Southern District of New York, was the first of several to be brought against the company as a result of its admission that it paid a bribe to a Honduran official.

On April 11, *The Wall Street Journal* reported that Price Waterhouse & Company, the outside auditor of United Brands, knew of the $1.25 million bribe paid by United Brands, but Price Waterhouse did not require disclosure

---

[21] "United Brands Paid Bribe of $1.25 Million to Honduran Official," *Wall Street Journal,* Midwest Edition, April 9, 1975.

[22] Lopez first came to power by overthrowing the liberal government of Dr. Ramon Villeda Morales in a bloody 1963 coup. From 1972, he ruled Honduras by decree and without a Congress. During his only elected term in office, from 1965 to 1971, Lopez led his troops in the 1969 four-day "soccer war" with neighboring El Salvador, a bloody conflict that claimed more than 2,000 lives and devastated the nation's economy. He returned to power in 1972 by ousting the elderly, constitutionally elected President Ramon Ernesto Cruz. A week prior to the bribe relevation, Lopez for reasons unexplained by the Honduran government, was stripped of his post as commander in chief of the Honduran Armed Forces; however, he retained his post as president.

[23] "United Brands Accused by SEC of Second Payoff," *Wall Street Journal,* Midwest Edition, April 10, 1975.

[24] "United Brands Paid Bribe of $1.25 Million to Honduran Official," *Wall Street Journal,* Midwest Edition, April 9, 1975.

for fear of jeopardizing the company's operations, thereby embarrassing the Latin American nation's government. Walton W. Kingsbery, partner in charge of auditing United Brands, said Price Waterhouse concluded it had no duty to override United Brands' decision to ask the Securities and Exchange Commission to keep the bribe secret. "We believed the route they were taking was reasonable."[25] Mr. Kingsbery said. He also said Price Waterhouse discussed its decision with the SEC, which raised no objection. The SEC did not charge Price Waterhouse with acting improperly.[26]

Although in Honduras political and public reactions on the surface were relatively calm, there was considerable confusion among the Honduran people. As one person said, "First we had a war, then a hurricane, now this."[27] This person's feeling that the poorest of Central American countries once again had been singled out for suffering was apparently widespread.

On April 16, 1975, it was revealed that federal prosecutors were investigating whether United Brands or its officers had violated criminal laws in connection with the company's $1.25 million payment to the Honduran government official. While it is not illegal under federal law for a United States company to bribe a foreign official, the prosecutors were apparently considering whether the company violated United States securities and tax laws in connection with the payments.

Investigators said possible violations included securities fraud which resulted from issuing allegedly false reports to shareholders to cover up the payments. According to one government official, United States tax laws specify that a bribe—even one that isn't illegal under United States law—cannot be treated as ordinary business expense for tax purposes. Therefore, United Brands could incur a tax liability and face a possible tax fraud charge if it treated as legitimate business expenses on its tax return the $1.25 million Honduran payoff or the $750,000 in payoffs that it admitted making to other government officials outside the Republic of Honduras.

On April 22, General Oswaldo Lopez was ousted as president in a bloodless takeover. Honduras' Supreme Military Council removed General Lopez and named Colonel Juan Alberto Melgar, commander in chief of the Honduran Armed Forces, as the country's new president.

---

[25] "Price Waterhouse Knew UB Paid Bribe but Didn't Require Disclosure," *Wall Street Journal,* Midwest Edition, April 11, 1975.

[26] It should be noted that the accounting profession is uncertain over its responsibility for reporting improper payments by corporations they audit. This concern was brought to the fore by the discovery of illegal campaign contributions by a number of well-known corporations. They of course included the discovery of a $10 million political slush fund at Gulf Oil Corporation, also a major Price Waterhouse client. One point of concern in the auditing profession is what chance a routine audit has of bringing such payments to light. Beyond that, however, audit docrine gives little guidance on what an auditor should do even if he stumbles upon an improper payment. According to *The Wall Street Journal,* the sums are typically small by normal audit standards and often are defended as necessary to the company's best interests. Regulatory authorities have given auditors very little guidance.

[27] "Banana Flap—Honduras Ready for Political Turmoil—UB Scandal," *Wall Street Journal,* Midwest Edition, April 14, 1975.

Lopez was ousted soon after he apparently refused to allow the Honduran commission investigating the United Brands payment to examine his foreign bank accounts. All other cabinet-level ministers granted the commission authorization to examine personal financial records and bank accounts in Honduras and other countries. (Most of the Lopez cabinet ministers, however, eventually were ousted.)

Despite the Lopez ouster, observers in Honduras described the country as "calm and tranquil."[28]

On the same day (April 22), United Brands reported a first-quarter net loss of nearly $4 million, compared with a net loss of $1.5 million the year earlier. Sales went down to $480.4 million from $491.3 million the previous year.

Also on this day, Simon H. Rifkind announced he had resigned from the United Brands board. The reason Mr. Rifkind gave for his resignation was that he could not devote the time to running the company that board members were required to devote since Eli Black's death. It was later speculated that the real reason Rifkind left was that he was unable to maintain peace among other United Brands board members, who were quarreling among themselves concerning the company's future. (See the appendix.)

On May 1, 1975, Costa Rica announced it was raising its export tax on bananas to $1 per 40-pound box. This was up from 25 cents for a 40-pound box. On the day before this announcement, Costa Rican Vice President Carlos Manuel said that other members of the Union of Banana Exporting Countries—Panama, Guatemala, Columbia, and Honduras—also were being asked to raise their export taxes.

During the week of April 28, the European Common Market accused United Brands of antitrust violations in the European banana market. The European Common Market sources said the accusation "definitely had no connection" with the United States government's investigation of bribery allegations against United Brands.[29]

By May 5, no formal charges had been filed against Mr. Lopez; however, he and his family were reportedly prepared to fly to exile in Madrid.

On May 15, the Honduras government commission appointed by Lopez reported that former Economic Minister Abraham Bennaton, not Lopez, was the official who received the $1.25 million bribe from United Brands to lower the banana export tax. Later it was speculated that Bennaton served as a middleman in the payoff to Lopez. Bennaton denied this charge.

Also on May 15, *The Wall Street Journal*[30] reported that United Brands made payoffs to officials not only in Honduras but also Costa Rica, Panama, Italy, and West Germany. In response to this *Journal* report, Costa Rican President Daniel Oduber gave United Brands 24 hours to disclose to which Costa Rican officials it paid bribes. Oduber said if United Brands did not name

---

[28] Ibid.

[29] *United Press International Dispatch* (Brussels), May 6, 1975.

[30] "United Brands Company Rejects SEC Terms of Settlement Offer," *Wall Street Journal*, Midwest Edition, May 15, 1975.

the officials involved, he would send a bill to his national assembly canceling the operating contract of United Brands's Costa Rican subsidiary and banning its operations permanently.

On May 16, it was learned that in Washington a federal grand jury was weighing possible criminal charges against United Brands and its top executives.

In Honduras, George Jorge Arturo Reina, the head of the investigative commission, said in a nationwide broadcast that United Brands executive John Taylor paid the bribe money to Bennaton at a meeting September 3 and 4, 1974, in Zurich, Switzerland. He said Bennaton denied the charges when he came before the commission.

WALLACE W. BOOTH

On May 12, Wallace W. Booth became president and chief executive officer of United Brands.

Booth, who spent 20 years with Ford Motor Company, played a major role in setting up Ford's financial control system. He became a director of and eventually headed Ford's Australian subsidiary. In 1968, Booth joined the Rockwell International Corporation; after seven years with Rockwell, he resigned as a senior vice president, director, and member of the executive committee. Two months after his resignation from Rockwell, he accepted the United Brands position.

Also on May 12, Max M. Fisher, a multimillionaire independent investor and a United Brands board member, was appointed acting chairman of the board at United Brands.

APPENDIX: Securities & Exchange Commission v. United Brands (United States District Court for the District of Columbia)

On April 9, 1975, the United States Securities and Exchange Commission commenced an action against United Brands in the United States District Court for the District of Columbia. The complaint alleges violations of Sections 10(b) and 13(a) of the Securities Exchange Act of 1934 and the Commission's Rules 10 b-5, and 13 a-1, 13 a-11, and 13 a-13, thereunder by reason of filing misleading annual and periodic reports filed with the Commission and in a letter to stockholders issued by the company of facts with respect to improper cash payments made by the company to officials of certain foreign countries. Selected excerpts from the Commission's complaint from its Litigation Release No. 6827/April 10, 1975 are:

> ... United Brand Form 8-K filed on September 13, 1974, with the Commission violated the anti-fraud and reporting provisions of the Exchange Act by omitting to disclose a method of business whereby in August, 1974, an arrangement was entered

into, pursuant to which United Brands agreed to pay $2.5 million to high government officials of the Republic of Honduras in exchange for favorable governmental action with respect to the imposition by Honduras of substantial taxes on the exportation of bananas. Additionally, the Form 8-K filing omits to disclose that United Brands deposited $1.25 million in Swiss bank accounts of designated government officials of the Republic of Honduras in September of 1974, and had agreed to pay an additional $1.25 million in the spring, 1975. The complaint also alleges that the $1.25 million in corporate funds was obtained from certain foreign subsidiaries of United Brands and that the company's books and records were falsified to conceal this.

Additionally, the complaint alleges that United Brands by means of false entries on the books and records of United Brands, caused to be disbursed approximately $759,000 in corporate funds over a five year period to officials of a foreign government in Europe in connection with the securing of favorable business opportunities.

*   *   *

On or about September 6, 1974, Defendant United Brands disseminated to its shareholders and others a letter which, in describing a favorable settlement with the Republic of Honduras with respect to its export taxes on bananas, stated: ". . . Some days ago, the company reached an understanding with the Government of Honduras, under which the tax situation in that country was settled on the basis of company paying a tax of $.25 per box, with yearly escalations beginning in 1975, which may depend, in part, on the banana market at the relevant times. There are other terms involved in the settlement, but the significant item is that the tax for the balance of this year was fixed at $.25 per box . . . . "

The complaint seeks: (*a*) a finding of violation of the above cited statutory sections and rules; (*b*) a permanent injunction restraining the company, its officers, directors and employees from misstating material facts or omitting to state material facts relating, among other things, to reporting as bona fide expenses disbursement of funds for improper payments to government officials for other improper purposes, the nature and extent of any such expenditures; the extent to which any officer, director or employee of the company has caused corporate funds to be used for such purposes; the fact that false entries have been made in the books and records of the company; the establishment of any secret or unrecorded fund or that payments have been made therefrom and the extent to which any director, officer or employee of the company has made false or fictitious entries, has maintained secret funds or made payments therefrom and the identity of such persons; (*c*) and injunction restraining the company, its officers, directors and employees (i) from filing annual, periodic or current reports which misstate or omit material facts and (ii) from using corporate funds for improper payments to government officials for other improper purposes; (*d*) a mandatory injunction compelling correction of annual and periodic reports heretofore filled; and (*e*) the appointment of a Special Master to inquire into such matters and report thereon to the Court, the plaintiff Commission, and the company's shareholders, and that the company pay the expenses of such inquiry and report.

A complaint was served on April 10, 1975, in an action brought by Henry Neugarten, named in the complaint as a stockholder, against the company and certain officers and directors alleging in Count I (a derivative count) that payment of $1,250,000 made to an official of the Republic of Honduras was in violation of law and caused damage to the company for which a judgment against the individual defendants is sought; and alleging in Count II that the defendants made untrue statements and failed to state material facts which had the effect of inflating the price of the company's stock and therefore damages are claimed from the defendants, including the company, for loss suffered thereby by the plaintiff and members of the class described in the complaint, being those persons who purchased common stock during the period from on or about April 1, 1974 to on or about April 8, 1975.

Litigation Commenced Subsequent to Date of Report of Independent Accountants   During April 1975, six additional federal or state court actions were commenced in New York against the company, certain officers and directors, and others. Four of the actions appear to state only derivative claims on behalf of the company, based upon allegedly wrongful payments to foreign officials, and one is a class action against the company and the individuals based upon alleged deception of the public by nondisclosure of such payments; in one action the complaint has not yet been served.

Eastman Kodak
and FIGHT

For Rochester, New York, the long, hot summer came in July of 1964. Four days of rioting and violence, set off by the arrest of a 17-year-old black on charges of drunkenness, ended with four persons dead, hundreds injured, a thousand arrested, and property damage totaling $1 million.

Rochester is described as a proud city—"proud of its tradition of abundant, locally provided social services, proud of its reputation as a clean, progressive community"[1]—and so, for many Rochesterites, finding an answer to the question "Why?" was not so easy. Some, of course, had no difficulty at all spotting the source of the trouble. Said one civic leader:

> This city seems to have become a victim of its own generosity. Rochester is known as a soft touch for welfare and relief chiselers. As a result, there has been a large influx of shiftless Negroes with no real desire to work for a living.
>
> In 1950, there were only about 6,500 Negroes in Rochester. Now there are 33,000. Many of the newcomers are ne'er-do-wells. They are the people who live in squalor, who won't try to better themselves, whose main interest seems to be where the next bottle of booze is coming from.[2]

Outsiders, on the other hand, tended to look for the seeds of violence in a complex of causes—the blacks' segregated and run-down housing; their lack of education, lack of job skills, and lack of motivation; their frustration and sense of hopelessness in the face of poverty; their animus against the police—in gen-

[1]Patrick Anderson, "Making Trouble Is Alinsky's Business." *The New York Times Magazine*, October 9, 1966.

[2]*U.S. News & World Report*, August 10, 1964, p. 38.

eral, the smoldering resentment which alienated blacks felt toward a prosperous white community. But whatever the cause or causes of the racial explosion, the disastrous results left little doubt that there was a "new, angry, combustible force" in the city's midst.

Rochester is a thriving industrial area, with such firms as Eastman Kodak, Xerox, Bausch & Lomb, Taylor Instruments, and divisions of General Motors and General Dynamics offering well-paid jobs to highly skilled workers, and the city speaks of itself in glowing terms:

> A community of more than 700,000 people with the highest percentage of skilled, technical, and professional employees of any major U.S. metropolitan area; more engineers than any one of 23 States; the highest median family income of any city in the State, sixth highest in the nation...67 percent of the residents owning their own houses.[3]

Understandably, the scars have been erased from this public relations picture; for Rochester, along with the rest of urban America, is afflicted with mounting "inner city" problems.

In 1964, Rochester's 35,000 blacks accounted for about one-tenth of the city's population.[4] Living in a slum area, they worked at construction or low-pay service jobs or were on relief.[5] For, although the city's major industries adhered to equal-opportunity policies, blacks, with their minimum skills and education, could not meet most job requirements. Eastman Kodak, the largest employer of all, had recently begun to actively recruit black workers; but, after the riot, its industrial relations director pointed out to a *New York Times* reporter: "We're not in the habit of hiring bodies. We need skills. We don't grow many peanuts in Eastman Kodak."[6]

Following the summer's outburst of violence, the Rochester Area Council of Churches (a Protestant group) had brought in two members of Dr. Martin Luther King's Southern Christian Leadership Conference to see what could be done about easing conditions in the poverty-stricken black areas. But after several weeks, and for reasons which have never been clearly explained, the SCLC representatives departed. The Council then invited Saul Alinsky, the "middle-aged deus ex machina of American slum agitation,"[7] to Rochester. And, predictably, a cry of outrage went up. The city's two Gannet-owned newspapers immediately denounced the church leaders' move; a local radio station told the clergy that in the future they would have to pay for their Sunday morning radio time, which, up to that point, had been free; and the Community Chest hastened to invite the Urban League to set up shop in Rochester.

---

[3] From a full-page ad run in the February 5, 1967, issue of *The New York Times* and quoted in Raymond A. Schroth, "Self-Doubt and Black Pride," *America,* April 1, 1967, p. 503.

[4] The total population of Rochester decreased from 332,488 in 1950 to 318,611 in 1960, while its black population grew from 7,590 to 23, 586.

[5] *Business Week,* August 1, 1964, p. 24.

[6] Quoted in *Newsweek,* August 10, 1964, p. 27.

[7] *The New York Times Magazine,* October 9, 1966, p. 28.

SAUL ALINSKY AND "FIGHT"

Acid-tongued and voluble, Saul Alinsky makes good copy, but mention of his name alone is sufficient to set the teeth of dozens of American communities on edge. Alinsky, who believes that the poor (because they are not a power bloc) are cut off from any meaningful participation in the democratic process, has spent three decades organizing slum communnities throughout the United States. In 1940, with the financial backing of Marshall Field III, he set up the Industrial Areas Foundation, "a kind of training school for agitators," in Chicago. Soon other philanthropists and foundations and several church groups (particularly the Catholic Archdiocese of Chicago)[8] were contributing money to IAF's work. Alinsky, who borrowed many of his techniques from the American labor movement, spent the 1940s and 1950s organizing Mexican-American slums in California and various other slum districts in Chicago, Detroit, and New York. He came into national prominence in the early 1960s when he put together the Woodlawn Organization of Chicago's south side.

The aim of an Alinsky project is to create a "disciplined, broad-based power organization capable of wringing concessions—better jobs, better schools, better garbage collection, better housing—from the local establishment."[9] Through organization, the IAF seeks to replace the slum resident's alienation with participation in the decision-making process. "The hell with charity," says Alinsky. "It's self-determination that counts."

When invited to a community, the IAF sends in an organizer who scouts around churches, barbershops, and pool halls looking for potential slum leaders and for any existing organizations which might be welded into a power bloc. Once an effective combination has been set up, the IAF pulls out and the organization is on its own. This generally takes two or three years, and the Foundation charges $50,000 a year for its services.[10] "One thing we instill in all our organizations," Alinsky says, "is that old Spanish civil war slogan, 'Better to die on your feet than to live on your knees.' Social scientists don't like to think in these terms. They would rather talk about politics being a matter of accomodation, consensus—not this conflict business. This is typical academic drivel. How do you have a consensus before you have a conflict? There has to be a rearrangement of power and then you get consensus."[11] But Alinsky disclaims any interest in imposing values or political goals on slum residents—"We're just technicians trying to organize people" is Alinsky's approach to a project.

In Rochester, the IAF project became known as FIGHT (Freedom, Integration, God, Honor—Today).[12] Alinsky sent Edward Chambers, his top

[8] Bishop Bernard Sheil of Chicago was a strong Alinsky supporter, and it was he who introduced Alinsky to Marshall Field.

[9] *The New York Times Magazine,* October 9, 1966.

[10] Alinsky draws a $25,000-a-year salary from the Foundation; organizers are paid $15,000.

[11] *The New York Times Magazine,* October 9, 1966.

[12] This acronym prompted the publishers of the Gannet newspapers to offer a few "less offensive" names. "How about W-O-R-K instead of F-I-G-H-T, how about L-O-V-E, how about T-R-Y, how about D-E-E-D-S?" See the *New Republic,* January 21, 1967, pp. 11-13.

organizer, to the city in the spring of 1965, and in June of that year, FIGHT adopted a constitution and elected its first president, the Reverend Franklin Florence. Reverend Florence, a Church of Christ minister, is

> very much the New Negro. He is angry and articulate. He wears a "Black Power" button, reveres the memory of Malcolm X and is studiously rude to most whites.... Florence's relationship with Alinsky and Chambers is a delicate one. He clearly resents the fact that he needs their help. In Rochester, as elsewhere, the days are numbered when white men can lead the black man's revolt.[13]

But Alinsky believes that the black needs white allies, and so a "separate but not quite equal" group called the "Friends of FIGHT" was organized to provide money, legal expertise, and tutors for various FIGHT programs.

FIGHT's biggest success since its founding involved the city's urban renewal plan; there, the black organization won provision for construction of new housing on vacant land before destruction of the old, as well as low-rise public housing on scattered sites, nonprofit public housing corporations, and 250 units of public housing where only two units had been planned.

In its first efforts to tackle the unemployment problem, FIGHT had arranged an on-the-job training program with Xerox for 15 blacks; but by September, 1966, it had broadened its sights considerably when it began negotiating with Eastman Kodak for the recruitment, training, and hiring of 600 blacks. Taking on Kodak was something that just wasn't done in Rochester, Reverend Florence explained, "but we knew if we could get Kodak in line, every other business would follow."[14]

THE COMPANY

Rochester has often been called the Kodak City, for profitable Eastman Kodak, with 41,000 people on its local payroll, is by far the largest employer in the Rochester area and a dominant influence on community life.[15] Over the years, Kodak has projected a quality image—in product and in management—and the company has long been known as a good place to work. Its personnel turnover is one-fourth the national industrial average, and none of its U.S. plants has ever been unionized.

Much of "the Kodak way" is derivative of founder George Eastman's approach to company management; and at his death in 1932, "his three closest associates took over more or less as a team, with considerable commingling of responsibility and a singularity of purpose: to do as Mr. Eastman would have done."[16] A "philosopher-tinkerer," Kodak's founder pioneered in several areas

---

[13] *The New York Times Magazine,* October 9, 1966.

[14] The Binghamton, New York, *Sunday Press,* April 23, 1967.

[15] Kodak employs about 13 percent of the area's labor force and about one out of three in industry.

[16] Robert Sheehan, "The Kodak Picture—Sunshine and Shadow," *Fortune,* May, 1965, p. 129.

of industrial relations.[17] By 1903, his company had worked out an employment stabilization program to overcome seasonal variations in labor needs and to cut down on lay-offs; in 1911, it created a benefit, accident, and pension fund for employees; and in 1912, it established its unique wage-dividend policy whereby the rate of dividends to workers is scaled to the rate of cash dividends paid to stockholders. In 1966, for example, a wage dividend of $69.3 million was paid in cash to approximately 63,000 Kodak employees in the United States, or contributed for their benefit to the employees' savings and investment plan. This was $39.50 for each $1,000 earned over the previous five-year period.

George Eastman was also a firm believer in hiring the best brains available; and with nearly 450 of its employees holding doctorates, Kodak, it is said, appears to have more Ph.D.s running around the shop than office boys.[18] A glance at the credentials of several of its executives quickly confirms the fact that Kodak has, for some time, stressed formal academic training and intellectual achievement. Albert Chapman, who joined Kodak in 1919 and who retired as chairman of the board at the end of 1966, was a Phi Beta Kappa, with a doctorate in physics from Princeton. William Vaughn, Chapman's successor, is a Phi Beta Kappa also. After receiving an "A" in every course he took at Vanderbilt University, Vaughn went on for a master's degree in mathematics at Rice Institute, received a second bachelor's degree at Oxford (where he studied as a Rhodes Scholar), and started to work for Kodak in 1928. Louis Eilers, who succeeded Vaughn as president, began his Kodak career as a research chemist in 1934 after receiving a Ph.D. from Northwestern University.[19]

Financially, too, Kodak is an impressive company. The world's largest supplier of photographic materials and a leading manufacturer of chemicals, plastics, and synthetic fibers, it ranked thirty-fifth in size among U.S. industrial corporations in 1966.

> During the past decade, operations showed uninterrupted gains, sales growing at a 7.4% compound annual rate, while earnings advanced at an 11.5% compound annual rate. Focusing on the period starting in 1962 to the present, the picture gets even better. Overall sales crossed the billion-dollar mark for the first time in 1962. But, with 1966 sales estimated at roughly $1.7 billion, we see a gain of almost 70% .... From a financial point of view, Kodak is extremely strong. It has no long-term debt, while cash and marketable securities exceed its current liabilities.[20]

---

[17] Mr. Eastman was also a philanthropist par excellence. In 1924, he gave away half of his fortune. His total gifts amounted to more than $75 million, with the University of Rochester and the Massachusetts Institute of Technology the leading beneficiaries. Kodak has continued the philanthropic tradition. In the last decade, the company has given $22 million to Rochester's hospitals, schools, and Community Chest (of which Eastman was founder).

[18] Philip A. Cavalier, "Kodak's Growth: Never Out of Focus," *The Magazine of Wall Street,* November 26, 1966, p. 246.

[19] Mr. Eilers returned to Rochester as an executive vice president in 1964, after serving five years in Kingsport, Tennessee, first as vice president and later as president of Kodak's Tennessee Eastman and Texas Eastman companies.

[20] *The Magazine of Wall Street,* November 26, 1966, pp. 277–278.

KODAK UNDER FIRE

It was somewhat surprising, in the fall of 1966, to find seemingly imperturbable Eastman Kodak smack in the center of a mushrooming controversy. In September, the company was asked by FIGHT if it would consider setting up a training program (to include such fundamentals as reading and arithmetic) for some 500 to 600 blacks. "We're not talking about the man who can compete," Reverend Florence pointed out to Kodak officials. "We're talking about the down-and-out, the man crushed by this evil system, the man emasculated, who can't make it on his own. He has a right to work."[21] And he went on to propose that FIGHT recruit and Kodak train these unemployables over an 18-month period for entry-level jobs with the company. When FIGHT approached Kodak, its main argument was that in the past the company had ignored Rochester's blacks and had hired white workers from other cities—that now it should give favored treatment to local blacks regardless of the expense. "If Kodak can take pictures of the moon," Florence contended, "it can create 500 jobs for our people."

"We were sympathetic and open-minded," said William Vaughn, who was president at the time. "We realize this is a civic problem and a national problem that has to be solved."[22] Therefore, Vaughn did not expressly turn down Florence's idea, but agreed to further talks. At a second meeting on September 14, FIGHT presented its proposal in writing, and Vaughn distributed a statement which outlined Kodak's plans for expanding training programs and invited FIGHT to refer possible applicants. After this meeting, Vaughn turned future discussions[23] over to Kenneth Howard of the industrial relations department.

Representatives of Kodak and FIGHT met twice again in September, but the meetings never got off the ground. Back and forth went letters between Kodak and FIGHT, with neither side agreeing on what had taken place.[24] Reverend Florence refused to discuss anything but the FIGHT proposal, while Kodak continued to argue that FIGHT should cooperate, as other organizations were doing, by referring candidates for the company's expanding training programs for the unskilled and uneducated.

The previous spring, Kodak issued a management letter setting forth a change in emphasis in the company's employment policies.

> ...our policy had been simply to try to employ the person best fitted to do the work available without regard for his or her background. We have moved actively beyond that position. We now seek to help the individual who lacks the necessary qualifications to become qualified. In other words, we are contributing to the training of the individual so that he or she can qualify for employment. . . .
>
> Overall, it appears that industry must look less critically at the individual's school record and work experience and more at his potential. Frustration and unfa-

---

[21] *Business Week*, April 29, 1967, p. 38.

[22] *Ibid.*, pp. 38–39.

[23] Nonunion Kodak carefully avoided the use of the word "negotiations" in describing its dealings with FIGHT.

[24] For copies of two of the letters included in this correspondence, see Appendix A.

vorable circumstances in early life often result in a school record far below the person's actual potential.

The letter went on to describe several special training programs which Kodak was already operating and those which were in the process of development. But FIGHT contended that these "limited" programs encompassed "neither the imagination nor boldness required to tackle the serious employment problems of Rochester."

Throughout the September meetings, both Kodak and FIGHT had refused to budge an inch, and

> the situation was aggravated by the fact that the FIGHT negotiators did not trust Howard. The formidable Rev. Florence is quick to sense when a white man is ill at ease in his presence, and he could not respect a man who seemed afraid of him. But perhaps nonunion Kodak was not accustomed to bargaining with another "power" organization.[25]

In television and newspaper conferences, Reverend Florence promised to keep pressuring Kodak until it "woke up and came into the twentieth century," while Saul Alinsky called Kodak's attitude "arrogant" and typical of Rochester's "self-righteousness." Alinsky further accused the company of playing a public relations "con game" with FIGHT, when in October it announced the hiring of the Indiana-based Board of Fundamental Education to help expand its remedial education programs. The new programs were to have an initial enrollment of 100, but, as it turned out, the trainees had already been selected. Sixty had recently been hired by Kodak and 40 were regular employees.[26]

For its part, Kodak showed determination to stick by its position that FIGHT should cooperate with Kodak's plans, and in November it sent a letter to company supervisors explaining its stand on the FIGHT proposal:

> We [cannot] enter into an arrangement exclusively with any organization to recruit candidates for employment and still be fair to the thousands of people who apply on their own initiative or are referred by others.

> We [cannot] agree to a program which would commit Kodak to hire and train a specific and substantial number of people in a period which would extend so far into the future.

> ...we responded by telling FIGHT that we would expand and broaden certain special training activities, and we expressed the hope that they would refer candidates to us.... At the same time, we have affirmed that we cannot delegate decisions on recruitment, selection, and training for KODAK jobs to any outside group. Other organizations with whom we have worked readily understand this.

Despite a background of deadlocks, discussions were eventually resumed in December as a result of a luncheon conversation between John G. Mulder, a

---

[25]*America*, April 1, 1967, p. 503.
[26]See the *Rochester Democrat*, October 26, 1966, and the *Rochester Times-Union*, October 24, 1966.

Kodak assistant vice president,[27] and an acquaintance of his, the Rev. Marvin Chandler, who was an official of FIGHT. During the course of their talk about possible ways to resolve the dispute, Chandler told Mulder that FIGHT would prefer a new negotiating team. The two men next discussed the matter at an unannounced meeting in Kodak's board room on December 16, and Vaughn (who hoped "there was a new deal here") gave Mulder the go-ahead to meet with FIGHT representatives. Kodak had expected to deal with Chandler, but Reverend Florence attended the two-day meetings which followed; and on December 20, he and Mulder signed a joint statement to the effect that FIGHT and Kodak had agreed to "an objective of the recruitment and referral (to include screening and selection) of 600 unemployed people over a 24-month period, barring unforeseen economic changes affecting the Rochester community. FIGHT, at its own expense, would provide counseling for the employees selected by Kodak." (For the full text of the statement, see Appendix B.)

According to reports, Kodak's president-elect Louis Eilers[28] exploded when he heard of the signing. The next morning Kodak's executive committee voted to repudiate the agreement, and the following day the board of directors agreed. A statement was then drafted, and Eilers informed reporters that the agreement was invalid because Mulder had no authority to sign any document on Kodak's behalf. He told newsmen that Kodak had neither intended nor authorized such an arrangement and that when management heard about it, "We all expressed the greatest of displeasure at the signing." Asked why Mulder would sign the statement if he had no authority to do so, Eilers could only reply that the assistant vice president had "apparently not been informed of company policies."[29] He added, however, that he "didn't envision any change in Mulder's job." Mulder himself declined to comment on the dispute, saying he was "in no position to talk," but he personally had gone to Reverend Chandler's home to break the news that Kodak would not honor the agreement. As for FIGHT's president, he announced that his organization would demand that the agreement be put into effect. "They've shown they're no good and deceitful. Obviously, there are people in Kodak who know what such a program can mean, yet there are hard-line people who don't care a thing about partnership with the poor." Florence insisted that he had asked Mulder three times if he had the authority to sign the agreement.

In the midst of the uproar that followed, Kodak ran a conciliatory two-page ad in the local morning and afternoon newspapers stating it "sincerely regret

[27]Mr. Mulder, the assistant general manager of Kodak Park Works, the company's largest installation in the Rochester area, was also president of the city's Council of Social Agencies. His wife is a member of the Friends of FIGHT.

[28]In November 1966, Kodak had announced Mr. Chapman's resignation as board chairman, effective January 1, 1967, Mr. Vaughn's election to the chairmanship, and Mr. Eilers's election to the presidency.

[29]*The New York Times*, January 7, 1967. While the public probably will never know what Vaughn's directions to Mulder were, Vaughn insists that the assistant vice president exceeded his instructions, feeling that "he got trapped, or rather trapped himself." See *Business Week*, April 29, 1967, p. 40.

[ted] any misunderstanding," but it could not "discriminate by having an exclusive recruiting arrangement with any organization. Nor, owing to the uncertainties of economic conditions [could] the company commit itself on a long-term basis to employ a specific number of people." Kodak was "deeply concerned to do all that [it] reasonably can to meet a pressing social need in this community, namely, to try to develop employment opportunities," and management was taking "many positive steps" in this direction.

But the tone of remarks made by Kodak's president at a news conference on January 6 was decidedly bitter. Eilers took the occasion to fire off a succession of charges against FIGHT. Its "talk about employment," he said, was "being used as a screen for making a power drive" in the community, and its demands were "arbitrary and unreasonable."

> Since the Alinsky forces were brought to Rochester, FIGHT has run a continuing war against numerous Rochester institutions that help build Rochester—the school system, the community chest, the city government, and even organizations especially set up to help solve minority group problems.
> Kodak's turn came last September. A savage attack has been directed at us since that time.[30]

FIGHT, he charged, was trying to gain an exclusive hold on 600 jobs, and the training and hiring programs which it insisted the company agree to would require Kodak management to surrender its prerogative to determine whom to hire and when. This the company neither could nor would do. Eilers pointed out that Kodak had some 1,200 to 1,500 blacks among its Rochester employees, several hundred of whom had been hired in the last few months,[31] and the company already had special training and employment programs for the unskilled and uneducated, with which FIGHT had repeatedly refused to cooperate. Later, Eilers was to say:

> To tell the truth, I don't know what they want. Certainly not jobs—they could have had those, and still can. Every one of the other 10 referring agencies in Rochester has placed people in jobs at Kodak and none has asked for an exclusive deal.
> This year we'll have about 300 more in our training program. It's too bad FIGHT doesn't want to participate.[32]

A COMMUNITY DIVIDED

Between 1960 and 1967, Rochester had accomplished far more than the country as a whole in increasing black employment, but an unrelenting influx of unskilled and uneducated southern blacks had completely wiped out the city's gains. While black employment in the area had risen 43 percent (more than four times the national average), there had been a 46 percent increase in the black

---

[30] *The New York Times,* January 7, 1967.
[31] "Kodak's Vaughn grants that FIGHT pressure led Kodak to hire more Negroes," *Business Week,* April 29, 1967, pp. 39–40.
[32] The Binghamton *Sunday Press,* April 23, 1967.

population of working age. Availability of jobs was not the problem. At the beginning of 1967, there were 10,000 job openings in the Rochester area, but 60 percent of these openings required a high school education and more than 15 percent required a college degree. Yet 54 percent of Rochester's unemployed black males had less than a ninth-grade education.

The Rochester community, already confronted with an uphill situation and the specter of another racial explosion, was splintered in its reaction to the Kodak-FIGHT dispute. "Kodak made FIGHT look good," a University of Rochester professor said. "If I were Alinsky," said the acting president of Friends of FIGHT, "I would have bribed Eilers to repudiate the agreement."[33] To add to the tension, a number of Kodak employees were members of Friends of FIGHT, and there were rumors of an ideological split within the company itself. For weeks following Kodak's repudiation of the agreement, sermons for and against FIGHT and the Council of Churches were heard at Sunday services. And the publisher of Rochester's newspapers excoriated the Council for widening the "gulf between the pulpit and pew" by bringing in a divisive force which had attacked a "company famed the world over for its sometimes ponderous but ever humane approach to all things." The president (a Kodak employee) and two members of the board of directors of the Council resigned in protest against its continued support of FIGHT. Still, the Council gained an ally in Fulton J. Sheen, the newly appointed bishop of the Rochester Catholic diocese, who, in his first appointment, named a highly vocal FIGHT supporter and Kodak critic as his special vicar to minister to the poor of the city. And representatives of the National Council of Churches, the United Presbyterian Church, and the United Church of Christ came out in support of FIGHT.

Within the black community itself, there was a mixed reaction to FIGHT's abrasive tactics. The head of the local Urban League attacked Reverend Florence's "irresponsibility" and questioned whether "FIGHT and only FIGHT should be the spokesman for the 'poor' black man in the Rochester community." A supporter of FIGHT ("Negroes must have a militant organization"), he objected to Florence's followers calling him a traitor to the cause because he did not "necessarily follow the FIGHT philosophy as projected by Minister Florence."[34] The Urban League also took strong exception to Florence's statement that it would be joining a "conspiracy" if it referred any applicants to Kodak's training programs.

On the whole, most Rochesterites seemed anxious to get Kodak and FIGHT "unhooked" from their dispute, and a group of industrial and religious leaders set about organizing Rochester Jobs, Inc., to provide work for 1,500 hard-core unemployed. The organization received commitments from 40 companies (including Kodak) to provide on-the-job training, remedial education, and counseling, with jobs to be divided on a quota basis.

---

[33] Barbara Carter, "The FIGHT against Kodak," *The Reporter*, April 20, 1967, p. 30. There was some feeling in Rochester that FIGHT would have been hard put to produce the 600 Negroes its proposal called for.

[34] *The Reporter*, April 20, 1967, p. 31.

Determined to hold Kodak to the signed agreement, however, Reverend Florence did nothing throughout the uneasy winter to lessen the mounting tension. In January, he invited Stokely Carmichael to speak to a FIGHT rally. Promising a national boycott which would bring Kodak to its knees, Carmichael predicted that "When we're through, Florence will say 'Jump,' and Kodak will ask 'How high?'"[35] Florence next fired off a telegram to Kodak's president, warning: "The cold of February will give way to the warm of spring, and eventually to the long hot summer. What will happen in Rochester in the summer of 1967 is at the doorstep of the Eastman Kodak Company. . . . You'll be hearing from us, and it won't be in black and white."[36]

And Kodak did hear from FIGHT—at its annual meeting on April 25. The entire two-and-three-quarters hour meeting (except for a brief review of operating results) was devoted to the Kodak-FIGHT dispute. Reverend Florence (the owner of one share of Kodak stock)[37] took the floor to demand that the company reinstate the December 20 agreement, and when Chairman Vaughn refused, Florence, together with 25 FIGHT supporters, walked out of the meeting, declaring, "This is war—and I state it again—war." Florence told 600 demonstrators waiting outside, "Racial war has been declared on American Negroes by Eastman Kodak. Kodak has shown American Negroes that powerful companies can't be trusted." He promised the crowd that FIGHT would conduct a national campaign against Kodak, including a "candlelight service" in Rochester on July 24, the third anniversary of the city's race riot.

To stockholders remaining in the meeting (including representatives of several church groups who had withheld their proxies from management),[38] Vaughn explained that Kodak refused to honor the December 20 agreement because it was unauthorized. "In his overzealousness to resolve the controversy, Mr. Mulder put his name to a document prepared by FIGHT," the Chairman said. "The incident was most unfortunate and regrettable. We have acknowledged it was a mistake and have apologized for it ever since." (Vaughn later told reporters that Mulder was still an assistant vice president and would not be penalized for his action.)

FIGHT, in the meantime, increased its request to Kodak and asked the company to provide 2,000 jobs, and Saul Alinsky gave Kodak warning of what to expect in the future. "The battle," said he, "will be in Eastman Kodak's arena—the nation from Harlem to Watts."

Looking back over the long-drawn-out dispute, Kodak's president opined: "I think we used too much patience."[39]

---

[35] *Ibid.*, p. 28.

[36] *The Reporter,* April 20, 1967, p. 31.

[37] In anticipation of the annual meeting, Florence and each of nine other FIGHT officials had purchased a share of Kodak stock, for a total of ten shares.

[38] FIGHT had succeeded in getting stockholders to withhold proxies for about 40,000 shares. At the meeting, 84 percent of Kodak's 80,772,718 shares outstanding were voted for management. Reverend Florence had also filed suit to get the company to give him access to its list of stockholders, but a New York State court denied the request.

[39] *Business Week,* April 29, 1967, p. 41.

APPENDIX A

EASTMAN KODAK COMPANY
Rochester, New York 14650

September 28, 1966

Minister Franklin Florence, President
FIGHT
FIGHT Headquarters
86 Prospect Street
Rochester, New York 14608

Dear Minister Florence:

I have your letter of September 26 from which I note that apparently considerable misunderstandings still exist as to what we tried to convey to you and your associates in FIGHT at our meeting on September 14.

In the first place, Kodak's programs and plans described at that meeting, in response to your verbal proposal of September 2, were *not* simply "a repeat of your limited special training programs," as you state in your letter. If you will reread, closely and carefully, the second paragraph on page 2 of the statement handed to you at our meeting on September 14 you will see that we are talking of "an *expanded* concept of on-the-job training," which we go on to describe in general terms. We went on to say that we hoped "to benefit from suggestions which FIGHT may offer," as well as from those of other organizations interested in these matters.

Since the goals of "the FIGHT proposal" seemed to be so close to the aims of our programs, we assumed that you wanted to cooperate in making our efforts more successful.

We have indicated to you on several occasions that we cannot accept your "proposal," which is, quoting from your September 14 memorandum, as follows: "Kodak would train over an 18-month period between 500 and 600 persons so that they qualify for entry level positions across the board. FIGHT would recruit and counsel trainees and offer advice, consultation, and assistance in the project." Your memorandum also states that the project "...would be geared to individuals with limited education and skills..." and that "...areas to be worked out would include selection criteria, recruitment, training needs..." and that "programs should include remedial reading and arithmetic; industrial orientation and training to afford a basic understanding of industrial processes, tools, machinery, and work rules; basic skills training like material handling, blueprint reading, and mechanical principle; others." In addition, you have indicated that you expect this company to undertake all this exclusively in cooperation with FIGHT.

We have tried to make clear to you why we cannot accept the "FIGHT proposal." Apparently, it is necessary at this time for me to restate our position.

1 In light of the company's legal obligations and its responsibilities to Kodak customers, employees, stockholders, other applicants for employment, and the community, the company obviously cannot discriminate by granting any one organization an exclusive or monopolistic position in the recruitment, selection, or training of Kodak people.

2 We are not in a position to establish any statistical objective or quota for any special training programs which we undertake. Our ability to hire a person at Kodak depends first on the existence of a job opening and, second, on the availability of a person qualified to fill that opening.

During the last several months, we have hired a good many people, among whom were many Negroes. We hope we can continue to provide additional job opportunities in the future. But it is impossible for us to say how many, if any, such opportunities will be available at Kodak six months, a year, or 18 months hence. It would be an inexcusable deception on our part to promise something we cannot be sure of honoring.

You are quoted in this morning's paper as having said last evening, "I hate to believe a company of this stature would misguide poor people." We have no intention of misguiding anyone and it is precisely for this reason we cannot promise a given number of jobs at some future date when we do not control the economic and other factors which create the job opportunities.

I think both you and we are concerned with a problem to which no one has yet found a satisfactory solution—that is, how to motivate people to prepare themselves for job openings, and how to train people for industrial jobs who are lacking in such fundamental skills as reading, writing, and arithmetic. Certainly it would be dishonest and unfair to the people involved if we were to suggest that we have the knowledge or manpower to take on such a complete job where, so far as I know, no others have succeeded. However, as we have told you, we are planning to expand our special training efforts to see what further we can do. We are naturally anxious that any program we undertake have some reasonable chance of success.

What we are trying to do is to see what we can accomplish, by special training programs, to upgrade persons who are willing to try to improve themselves so they can qualify for the kinds of jobs we have. In doing this, we will seek the assistance of interested organizations which are willing to cooperate in constructive ways.

If FIGHT is interested in cooperating on this basis by making suggestions for the programs or referring applicants for them, I would again suggest that you resume discussions with Mr. Howard. If, on the other hand, your interest is solely in talking further about "the FIGHT proposal," I doubt that anything very useful could come from just going over the same ground that has been covered in the several talks that have already taken place.

Yours very truly,
/s/ W. S. Vaughn
President

WSVaughn:eml

FIGHT

October 7, 1966
Mr. W. S. Vaughn, President
Eastman Kodak Company
343 State Street
Rochester, New York 14650

Dear Mr. Vaughn:

I have your letter of September 28th and offer at this time the following observations.

An American economy which is in the first stages of inflation and which has shown an accompanying rising employment rate finds itself threatened by an alarming increase in unemployment among Negroes. The last figure issued by our government pointed to 8.3% of all employable Negroes were unemployed. It is clear to all students and observers of economic conditions among the Negroes of America that the employment rate in the various ghettos from Harlem to Watts are substantially higher. This dangerous condition not only for the Negro population but the general American public becomes particularly ominous since it follows on the heels of civil rights legislation, extensive job retraining programs, and a convergence of public opinion and government pressure upon private industry and organized labor to drop their discriminatory hiring practices and to open jobs for Negro fellow Americans. So, we are confronted with the strange and frightening anomaly of increasing employment for whites occurring simultaneously with decreasing employment for Negroes.

There are a number of reasons for this kind of economic sickness and one of the major ones is the fact that large industries such as Eastman Kodak persist in employing the same testing procedures for hiring eligibility to Negro applicants as they do with white applicants. The pursuit of this practice indicates an extraordinary insensitivity to the social and educational circumstances which have prevailed in our country for many years: circumstances of limited opportunities, economy-wise, education-wise, and in almost every other sector of our life which all Americans today are fully cognizant of and are moving toward their correction. It is clear that a Negro of the same age as that of a white has not had the academic opportunities to qualify for the same test. It is clear that if there is to be an intelligent approach to this issue that those factors must be taken into consideration in terms of equity as well as the practical politics of keeping a healthy American way for all people. The obvious remedy lies in avoidance in the trap of this discriminatory test and hiring of Negroes for jobs where they will not only receive on-the-job training, but also special educational programs to bring them up to the point where they could then qualify under the test. Any employer who would regard this as discrimination in reverse would be guilty of an extraordinary shortsightedness and unawareness of the general situation prevailing in our nation today.

This has been the issue in our approach to Eastman Kodak. With it has gone our own feelings that if private industry does not meet this challenge that we will of necessity have to assume that there is no other recourse but massive governmental public projects and we have nowhere else to turn except to our government. Paradoxically, major industries in America, including Eastman Kodak, have always expressed concern for the ever expanding encroachment by government in various areas of our life. They have regarded this with a great deal of alarm. Some of the most conservative of them have denounced it as creeping socialism. We, ourselves, believe that the democratic way of life would hold to most problems being met and resolved on a local community basis and that there is that kind of free initiate in various sectors of our society: that government should not move in unless local communities are obviously unable, incapable, or unwilling, to meet their own problems. Eastman Kodak has the opportunity to make a significant contribution by cooperating with FIGHT's proposal. But, if FIGHT continues to be stalled and politely rejected as it has been to this date, then we must conclude that while industry talks about government encroaching upon all spheres of the American scene that in fact, it is just talk and that it is coming because industry refuses to act. We, like all other Americans, prefer to be employed by our government, to have our dignity, to have a job and to have an economic future rather than to have a basket full of empty generalities and unemployment by private industry which is immobilized by its own straightjacket antiquated definitions of discrimination and by an astounding blindness to their own self-interest.

Use of terms like "exclusively," "monopolistic," "arbitrary demands," etc., in reference to the FIGHT proposal does an injustice to the careful thought and consideration that has gone into our suggestions. We have not even had the opportunity to discuss the details of our approach with Eastman Kodak.

Sincerely,
/s/ Franklin Florence
      Minister Franklin Florence
FF:ks

APPENDIX B

December 20, 1966

A special committee appointed by Eastman Kodak president, William Vaughn, has been meeting Monday and Tuesday with officers of the FIGHT organization.

Kodak representatives stated that they have not employed traditional standards of hiring for the last two years. FIGHT hailed this as a step in the right direction as well as Kodak officers' statement that they will deal with the problem of hard-core unemployed.

Job openings, specifications and hourly rates were discussed and agreed upon by the joint group.

January 15th was agreed upon as the date for a beginning of the referral of 600 employees, the bulk of which would be hard-core unemployed (unattached, uninvolved with traditional institutions).

Under the agreement, the FIGHT organization and Kodak agreed to an objective of the recruitment and referral (to include screening and selection) of 600 unemployed people over a 24-month period, barring unforeseen economic changes affecting the Rochester community. FIGHT, at its own expense, would provide counseling for the employees selected by Kodak.

Kodak agrees to the following: join with FIGHT in a firm agreement to

A. Continue semi-monthly meetings between Kodak and FIGHT to increase the effectiveness of the program.

B. Kodak will familiarize FIGHT counselors with the foremen and work skills required, and in turn FIGHT will familiarize Kodak foremen with the life and environment of poor people.

C. Kodak and FIGHT will share information on the referrals.

D. Kodak and FIGHT will issue a 60-day community progress report.

John Mulder
Asst. Vice President, Eastman Kodak
Asst. General Manager, Kodak Park Works
Franklin D. R. Florence
President of FIGHT

The Clorox Case

The owners of Clorox Chemical Company, nearing retirement age and wanting to sell the company, approached Procter & Gamble with the idea of a merger.[1] At the time, Clorox was the nation's largest producer of household liquid bleach, and P&G the leading U.S. manufacturer of soap, detergent, and cleanser products. Liquid bleach, like Procter's product lines, was a low-priced, rapid-turnover household item sold mainly through grocery stores and supermarkets and presold through mass advertising and sales promotions. After studying the liquid bleach market for two years, Procter's promotion department recommended that the company buy Clorox rather than bring out a bleach of its own. Since a "very heavy investment" would be required to obtain a satisfactory market share for a new bleach, "taking over the Clorox business . . . could be a way of achieving a dominant position in the liquid bleach market quickly, which would pay out reasonably well." The promotion department's report predicted that P&G's sales, distributing, and manufacturing setup could up Clorox's market share in areas where it was low and make a number of savings which would increase the profits of the business considerably. Additionally, the department pointed out that P&G could make more effective use of Clorox's advertising budget and achieve substantial advertising economies.

---

[1] In argument before the United States Supreme Court, P&G's attorneys said that initiative for the merger rested solely with Clorox owners, who wanted to dispose of their business for estate purposes "in exchange for the marketable securities of a big company." See *Advertising Age,* February 20, 1967, p. 194.

Procter decided to go ahead with the merger, and on August 1, 1957, acquired the assets of Clorox in exchange for stock of Procter having a market value of approximately $30.3 million. Two months later, on October 7, 1957, the Federal Trade Commission filed a complaint charging that Procter's purchase of Clorox might substantially lessen competition, or tend to create a monopoly in the production and sale of household liquid bleaches, in violation of Section 7 of the Clayton Act.[2]

At the time of the acquisition, P&G had assets in excess of one-half billion dollars and annual sales of $1.15 billion. More than half ($514 million) of its total domestic sales were in the soap-detergent-cleanser field, and in packaged detergents alone its sales were $414 million. Procter held 54.4 percent of the packaged detergent market, and, together with Colgate-Palmolive and Lever Brothers, accounted for more than 80 percent of this market. In 1957, P&G's percentages of national sales lined up as follows: 54.4 percent of packaged detergents; 31 percent of toilet soap; 30 percent of lard and shortening; and 19 percent of shampoo. In addition, the company was a major producer of food and paper products. The giant soap company was also the nation's largest advertiser and in 1957 spent more than $80 million on advertising and an additional $47 million on sales promotion.

In the liquid bleach industry, Clorox, with almost 50 percent of the market, was by far the leader. The company (which in the five years prior to the merger had experienced a steady and continuing growth in sales, profits, and net worth) had assets of over $12 million and annual sales of slightly less than $40 million. In 1957, Clorox spent nearly $3.7 million on advertising and $1.7 million for promotional activities. The company had no salespeople but sold its products through brokers and distributors.

Household liquid bleach ($5\frac{1}{4}$ percent sodium hypocholorite and $94\frac{3}{4}$ percent water) was a relatively inexpensive item to manufacture, but because of high shipping costs and a low sales price, it was not profitable to sell the bleach more than 300 miles from the point of manufacture. And Clorox, with 13 plants scattered throughout the United States, was the only company in the industry distributing its product nationally. Purex, its closest rival,[3] had as many plants, but its bleach was available on less than half the national market, and most other manufacturers, having but one plant, were limited to a regional market. In 1957, the six leading producers of household liquid bleach held the following market shares:

---

[2] "No corporation engaged in commerce shall acquire, directly or indirectly, the whole or any part of the stock or other share capital and no corporation subject to the jurisdiction of the Federal Trade Commission shall acquire the whole or any part of the assets of another corporation engaged also in commerce, where in any line of commerce in any section of the country, the effect of such acquisition may be substantially to lessen competition, or to tend to create a monopoly."

[3] While Clorox produced only liquid bleach, Purex manufactured other products, including abrasive cleaners, toilet soap, and detergents. Total sales of all Purex products were approximately $50 million in 1957.

Brand	Percent of total U.S. sales
Clorox	48.8
Purex	15.7
Roman Cleanser	5.9
Fleecy White	4.0
Hilex	3.3
Linco	2.1
	79.8
All other brands (about 200 producers)	20.2

Only eight bleach manufacturers had assets in excess of $1 million; very few had assets of more than $75,000; and total industry sales were less than $100 million annually (less than 10 percent of Procter's annual sales).

PROCEEDINGS BEFORE THE FEDERAL TRADE COMMISSION

The Procter-Clorox case became something of a football before the Federal Trade Commission.

June 7, 1960   Following a series of hearings which extended over a 14-month period, the hearing examiner issued his initial decision finding the acquisition violative of Section 7 and ordering divestiture.[4]

June 15, 1961   On appeal, the Commission set aside the initial decision and remanded the matter to the hearing examiner for the purpose of taking additional evidence on the post-merger situation in the liquid bleach industry.[5]

> As the hearing examiner has pointed out, this case involves a conglomerate acquisition and is therefore one of first impression .... [S]ince a conglomerate acquisition does not have the ..."automatic" effects of a vertical or horizontal merger, ... a consideration of post-acquisition factors is appropriate.

The record, as presently constituted, the Commission held, did not provide "an adequate basis for determining the legality" of the acquisition and a remand would provide "a more complete and detailed post-acquisition picture ... allowing the Commission an informed hindsight upon which it can act rather than placing too strong a reliance upon treacherous conjecture."

February 28, 1962   The remand hearing took only two days, and the hearing examiner then rendered a second decision, again finding against P&G and ordering divestiture.

---

[4] A brief description of the procedural steps involved in a Federal Trade Commission case is found in the appendix.

[5] 58 F. T. C. 1203.

December 15, 1963   On a second appeal, the Commission affirmed the hearing examiner's decision and ordered divestiture.[6] In this second decision, the Commission held the post-merger evidence irrelevant. (In the interim between the two decisions, the personnel on the Commission had changed, so that only one Commissioner participated in both decisions.) The admission of post-acquisition data, the Commission wrote,

> is proper only in the unusual case in which the structure of the market has changed radically since the merger . . . or in the perhaps still more unusual case in which the adverse effects of the merger on competition have already become manifest in the behavior of the firms in the market. If post-acquisition data are to be allowed any broader role in Section 7 proceedings, a [company], so long as the merger is the subject of an investigation or proceeding deliberately, may refrain from anti-competitive conduct—may sheathe, as it were, the market power conferred by the merger—and build instead, a record of good behavior to be used in rebuttal in the proceeding.

But more important, said the Commission,

> if a market structure conducive to non-competitive practices or adverse competitive effects is shown to have been created or aggravated by a merger, it is surely immaterial that specific behavioral manifestations have not yet appeared.[7]

THE FINAL DECISION OF THE FEDERAL TRADE COMMISSION

Keenly aware that the legality of Procter's purchase of Clorox was a question largely of first impression ("The absence of authoritative, specific precedents in this area compels us to look to basic principles in the interpretation and application of Section 7"), the Commission described the acquisition as a "product-expansion" merger.[8] Packaged detergents and household liquid bleach are used complementarily, the Commission pointed out, and from the homemaker's point of view are closely related products. Moreover, since detergents and bleach are low-cost, high-turnover consumer products, sold to the same cus-

---

[6] In ordering the divestiture, however, the Commission said that Procter might spin off the acquired assets to a new corporation owned by P&G stockholders but under separate management.

[7] *1963 Trade Cases* 16, 673.

[8] Here, the Commission wrote: "Another variant of the conventional horizontal merger is the merger of sellers of functionally closely related products which are not, however, close substitutes. This may be called a product-extension merger. The expression 'functionally closely related,' as used here, is not meant to carry any very precise connotation, but only to suggest the kind of merger that may enable significant integration in the production, distribution or marketing activities of the merging firms. . . . Only when the various subcategories of horizontal and vertical mergers have been exhausted do we reach the true diversification or conglomerate merger, involving firms which deal in unrelated products." But all mergers, said the Commission, "whether they be classified as horizontal, vertical or conglomerate, are within the reach of Section 7, and all are to be tested by the same standard." Definitional distinctions, the Commission continued, "import no legal distinctions under Section 7. The legal test of every merger, of whatever kind, is whether its effect may be substantially to lessen competition, or tend to create a monopoly, in any line of commerce in any section of the country."

tomers, at the same stores, and by the same merchandising methods, the merger offered possibilities for significant integration at both marketing and distribution levels.

> By this acquisition, then, Procter has not diversified its interest in the sense of expanding into a substantially different, unfamiliar market or industry. Rather, it has entered a market which adjoins, as it were, those markets in which it is already established, and which is virtually indistinguishable from them insofar as the problems and techniques of marketing the product to the ultimate consumer are concerned.

Taking a look at the pre-merger liquid bleach industry, the Commission called it highly concentrated, oligopolistic, strongly characterized by product differentiation through advertising, and barricaded to new entry, to a degree inconsistent with effectively competitive conditions. Between them, Clorox and Purex accounted for almost 65 percent of liquid bleach sales and, together with four other firms, for almost 80 percent—and of these six companies, a single one, Clorox, was dominant.[9] Only Purex could be considered to have been a significant competitor of Clorox, and its bleach was not sold in half of the country; in fact, in several areas, Clorox faced no competition whatever from the leading firms in the industry.

Since all liquid bleaches were chemically identical, the success of Clorox, a premium brand, was obviously due to the company's "long-continued mass advertising," whereby its name had become widely known to and preferred by the homemaker, "notwithstanding its high price and lack of superior quality." Most bleach manufacturers, the Commission observed, could not afford to advertise extensively, and although Purex was a large advertiser, its advertising was "very possibly less effective" than Clorox's because of its geographically limited market. Thus, the chief effect of Clorox's "intensive" advertising had been to gain a large share of the market at a higher price to the consumer. Given the importance of product differentiation in the bleach industry, advertising outlays were a formidable barrier to entry even before the merger, because any outsider who hoped to capture a satisfactory share of the market would have to incur a very heavy initial investment to promote its brand.

Having described the liquid bleach industry in these terms, the Commission went on to find that the substitution of multiproduct P&G, with its huge assets and enormous advertising power, for the dominant, but relatively small, single-product Clorox would lend further rigidity to an almost oligopolistic industry by scaring off potential competitors and inhibiting active competition from those firms already in the industry.

First, the Commission tried to ferret out the consequences for competition if P&G replaced Clorox in the bleach industry. Pinning much of its argument

---

[9] According to the Commission, Clorox's dominant position was "dramatically" shown by the fact that Procter "preferred to pay a very large premium for the good will of Clorox (the $17.7 million difference between the purchase price of Clorox, $30.3 million, and the valuation of Clorox's assets, $12.6 million, suggests the size of this premium), rather than enter the industry on its own."

against the merger on P&G's advertising and promotional power and the cost savings and other advantages resulting therefrom, the Commission found that post-merger Clorox could obtain $33^1/_3$ percent more network TV advertising for the same amount of money it had spent prior to the acquisition. This was due to the discounts which Procter received on its tremendous volume of TV advertising, and, the Commission noted, similar advertising discounts were available to P&G in the other media. But the advertising advantages of the merger were not limited to volume discounts. For example, P&G could afford to buy entire network TV programs on behalf of several of its products— something which pre-merger Clorox could not have done unless it were willing to put a disproportionate amount of its advertising budget into a single project. Also, if Procter felt that Clorox faced stiff competition in a particular locality, it could run a TV commercial in that area alone, while the rest of the country watched an ad for other Procter products. Thus, Clorox, the Commission pointed out, could gain the advantage of association with network TV, while limiting its advertising outlays to selected regional markets. Additional competitive advantages could be gained by including Clorox in P&G's sales promotion campaigns, cutting down greatly on Clorox's processing and mailing costs. And joint advertising in newspapers and magazines offered further possibilities for considerable cost savings.

The Commission went on to speculate that P&G's sales force might be able to induce retailers to give Clorox more and better shelf space, and that, as a multiproduct firm operating in a market of single-product firms, Procter might engage in systematic underpricing, subsidizing such action with profits from its other markets. And, the Commission continued,

> the conditions which retard competition in an industry are to an important degree psychological. They stem from competitors' appraisal of each other's intentions, rather than from the intentions—or the actions taken upon them—themselves. The appropriate standpoint for appraising the impact of this merger is, then, that of Clorox's rivals and of the firms which might contemplate entering the liquid bleach industry. To such firms, it is probably a matter of relative indifference, in setting business policy, how actively a Procter-owned Clorox pursues its opportunities for aggressive, market-dominating conduct. The firm confined by the high costs of shipping liquid bleach, and the high costs of national or regional advertising, within a geographically small area, cannot ignore the ability of a firm of Procter's size and experience to drive it out of business (not necessarily deliberately) by a sustained local campaign of advertising, sales promotions and other efforts. . . . A small or medium-sized firm contemplating entry cannot ignore the fact that Procter is a billion-dollar corporation whose marketing experience extends far beyond the limited horizons of the liquid bleach industry and whose aggregate operations are several times greater than those of all firms in the industry combined. Even a large firm contemplating entry into such an industry must find itself loath to challenging a brand as well-established as Clorox bleach, when that brand is backed by the powerful marketing capacities of a firm such as Procter. If we consider, in other words, not what Procter will in fact do to exploit the power conferred on it by the merger, or has done, but what it can and is reasonably likely to do in the event of a

challenge to its dominant market position in the liquid bleach industry, we are constrained to conclude that the merger has increased the power of Clorox, by dominating its competitors and discouraging new entry, to foreclose effective competition in the industry.

Turning next to the substantiality of the merger's anticompetitive effects, the Commission said that the five factors taken together persuaded it that Procter's purchase of Clorox violated Section 7:[10]

1 The relative disparity in size and strength as between Procter and the largest firms of the bleach industry

2 The excessive concentration in the industry at the time of the merger, and Clorox's dominant position in the industry

3 The elimination, brought about by the merger, of Procter as a potential competitor of Clorox

4 The position of Procter in other markets

5 The nature of the "economics" made possible by the merger

Procter's financial resources and scale of operations, the decision pointed out, overshadowed the entire liquid bleach industry, and the cost advantages made possible by the merger would substantially affect competitive conditions in the market. And the barriers to entry, "already formidable, become virtually insurmountable when the prospective entrant must reckon not with Clorox, but with Procter."

By the merger, P&G obtained a protected market position. Clorox's substantial market power might enable Procter to strengthen its position in other industries. And since Clorox and Procter manufacture closely related products, P&G might use Clorox bleach as a tie-in product, loss leader, or cross-coupon offering to promote other Procter products.

Still another important factor to consider about the merger was that it eliminated the "salutary" effect of Procter as a potential competitor of Clorox. In the past, the Commission reasoned, P&G had frequently extended its product lines by going into industries in which it had not been active before; it was one of the very few manufacturers of household cleaning products powerful enough to successfully challenge Clorox's position; and it had actually thought about the possibility of going into the liquid bleach business on its own. Therefore, Procter "must have figured as a tangible influence on Clorox's policies," and was, though in absentia, "by reason of its proximity, size, and probable line of growth, a substantial competitive factor" in the bleach industry. Before the acquisition, Procter "was not only a likely prospect for new entry into the bleach market, it was virtually the only such prospect." Thus, the merger by eliminating Procter as a potential entrant removed "one of the last factors tend-

---

[10] Here, the Commission noted: "We need not, and do not, consider whether one or more of these factors, taken separately, would be dispositive of the case."

ing to preserve a modicum of competitive pricing and business policies" in the bleach industry.[11]

Moving on to P&G's strong market position in other product areas, the Commission asserted that Procter's manifest strength rebutted any inference that it could not bring the enormous financial resources to bear on the liquid bleach industry. If P&G were spread thin over its other markets, it might be a different story; but such was not the case. Procter was a highly profitable company with demonstrated ability to mobilize and use its financial strength.

> Just as ownership of Clorox may enable Procter to enhance its competitive edge in other markets, so Procter's position in other markets may enhance its dominance, through its acquisition of Clorox, of the liquid bleach industry. . . .
> The short of it is that a conglomerate merger involving firms which have dominant power in their respective markets tends to reinforce and augment such power.

And, finally, in answer to Procter's arguments that the merger should be upheld on grounds of "efficiencies" (cost savings in advertising and sales promotions), the Commission found that in the instant case this type of "efficiency . . . hurts, not helps, a competitive economy and burdens, not benefits, the consuming public." For while "marketing economies, including those of advertising and sales promotion, are as desirable as economies in production and physical distribution," the point had been reached in the liquid bleach industry where advertising had lost its informative aspect and merely entrenched the market leader.

> The undue emphasis on advertising which characterized the liquid bleach industry is itself a symptom of and a contributing cause to the sickness of competition in the industry. Price competition, beneficial to the consumer, has given way to brand competition in a form beneficial only to the seller. In such an industry, cost advantages that enable still more extensive advertising only impair price competition further; they do not benefit the consumer.

Though the Commission rejected the post-merger evidence, it noted that Clorox's market share in 1961 was 51.5 percent, compared with its 48.8 percent share in 1957. And it concluded:

> Had Procter in fact fully integrated the marketing and other activities of Clorox in its overall organization, perhaps dramatic post-acquisition changes, directly traceable to the merger, would have occurred. But, save for taking advantage of certain advertising cost advantages and introducing sales promotions, Procter in the period covered by the post-acquisition evidence has carefully refrained from changing the nature of

---

[11] Here, the decision noted: "We have no occasion to speculate on such questions as whether or not Procter, had its acquisition of Clorox been blocked, would in fact have entered the bleach industry on its own, or whether or not it had done so, the result would have been to increase competition in the industry—although, with reference to the second question, we note the Supreme Court's recent observation that 'one premise of an antimerger statute such as § 7 is that corporate growth by internal expansion is socially preferable to growth by acquisition.'"

the operation; even the network of independent brokers has been retained. Such restraint appears to be motivated by a general Procter policy of moving slowly and cautiously in a new field until the Procter management feels totally acclimated to it. It is possible, as well, that the pendency of the instant proceeding has had a deterrent effect upon expansionist activities by Procter in the liquid bleach industry.

BEFORE THE U.S. COURT OF APPEALS
FOR THE SIXTH CIRCUIT[12]

Procter appealed the Commission's order and, in a unanimous decision, the circuit court upheld the acquisition and directed dismissal of the complaint.

> The Commission recognized that complete guidelines for this type of merger have not yet been developed and that the case presented a challenge to it and to the courts "to devise tests more precisely adjusted to the special dangers to a competitive economy posed by the conglomerate merger." We do not believe these tests should involve application of a per se rule.
>
> The Supreme Court has not ruled that bigness is unlawful, or that a large company may not merge with a smaller one in a different market field. Yet the size of Procter and its legitimate, successful operations in related fields pervades the entire opinion of the Commission, and seems to be the motivating factor which influenced the Commission to rule that the acquisition was illegal.

Findings of illegality, the appellate court observed, "may not be based upon 'treacherous conjecture,' possibility, or suspicion. And yet this is exactly what the second Commission indulged in. . . . "

Noting the Commission's opinion that the liquid bleach industry was highly concentrated, with virtually insurmountable barriers to entry on a national scale, the three-judge panel said that, while it probably would be difficult to break into the market on a national basis without expending a large sum of money, there was no evidence that anyone had ever tried to do so. And, the court continued, the fact that, in addition to the six leading bleach manufacturers, there were 200 smaller companies, both before and after the merger, "would not seem to indicate anything unhealthy about the market conditions."

The justices gave short shrift to the Commission's lengthy discourse on P&G's advertising might:

> Doubtless Procter could advertise more extensively than Clorox, but there is such a thing as saturating the market. We find it difficult to base a finding of illegality on discounts in advertising. . . . The fact that a merger may result in some economies is no reason to condemn it.

Nor did the appellate court find any merit to the Commission's claim that multiproduct Procter might be able to obtain more shelf space for Clorox. The

[12]*Procter & Gamble Company v. F.T.C.*, 358 F. 2d 74 (1966).

evidence was clear, the Court wrote, that pre-merger Clorox obtained very adequate shelf space.

Turning to the Commission's findings that the merger eliminated P&G as a potential competitor,[13] the judges held that there was no evidence tending to prove that Procter ever intended to enter the bleach business on its own; in fact, its promotion department had recommended against such a move. Therefore, the Commission's finding, the Court held, was based on "mere possibility and conjecture."

> Household liquid bleach is an old product; Procter is an old company. If Procter were on the brink [of entering the market on its own], it is surprising that it never lost its balance and fell in during the many years in which such bleach was on the market. It had never threatened to enter the market.

The reviewing court did not engage in any discussion as to the type of merger involved, but simply stated: "The merger in the present case was neither vertical nor horizontal, but conglomerate. The second Commission has characterized it as product extension." Under Section 7, the Court continued,

> it is necessary to determine whether there is a reasonable probability that the merger may result in a substantial lessening of competition. Amended Section 7 was intended to arrest anticompetitive tendencies in their incipiency. A mere possibility is not enough. [Citations omitted.]

P&G, according to the Court, "merely stepped into the shoes of Clorox," and whether it could do better than Clorox remained to be seen.

> The Nielsen tables ... for a period of five years prior to the merger and four years after, do not reveal any significant change in the rate of growth of Clorox.
> ... subsequent to the merger, competitors of Clorox sold substantially more bleach for more money than prior thereto. This evidence certainly does not prove anticompetitive effects of the merger. The Commission gave it no consideration.

The Sixth Circuit held the Commission in error in ruling that post-merger evidence was admissible only in unusual cases. Since a Section 7 proceeding involves the "drastic remedy of divestiture," said the justices, "any relevant evidence must be considered." The extent of the inquiry into post-merger conditions and the weight to be attached to the evidence may well depend on the circumstances of the case, they wrote, but where, as here, the evidence has been obtained, it should not be ignored. As for the contention that P&G's post-merger behavior may have been influenced by the pending litigation, this again, said the Court, was "pure conjecture." If, in the future, Procter engaged in predatory practices, the Federal Trade Commission had ample powers to deal with it.

---

[13] The Court noted that this issue had not been raised until after all the evidence was in and the appeal taken to the second Commission.

And, finally, the Court observed, Clorox wanted to sell its assets. A small company could not qualify; it "had to sell to a larger company or not sell at all."

BEFORE THE SUPREME COURT OF THE UNITED STATES[14]

The Federal Trade Commission appealed the Sixth Circuit's ruling, and, with Mr. Justice Douglas delivering the opinion (dated April 11, 1967), the Supreme Court in a 7 to 0 decision reversed the judgment of the court of appeals and remanded, with instructions to affirm and enforce the Commission's order.[15]

In essence, the Court said "Amen" to the Federal Trade Commission's exhaustive opinion. It adopted the Commission's product-extension merger characterization,[16] agreeing that it did not "aid analysis to talk of this merger in conventional terms, namely, horizontal or vertical or conglomerate"; and it repeated the Commission's statement that "all mergers are within reach of § 7, and all must be tested by the same standard, whether they are classified as horizontal, vertical, conglomerate or other."

The majority opinion declared: "The anticompetitive effects with which this product-extension merger is fraught can easily be seen: (1) the substitution of the powerful acquiring firm for the smaller, but already dominant, firm may substantially reduce the competitive structure of the industry by raising entry barriers and by dissuading the smaller firms from aggressively competing; (2) the acquisition eliminates the potential competition of the acquiring firm." The pre-merger liquid bleach industry, Justice Douglas wrote, was already oligopolistic. Clorox held a dominant position nationally, and in certain localities its position approached monopoly proportions. Thus, with P&G replacing Clorox, it was probable that Procter would become the price leader, causing the oligopoly to become more rigid, and smaller firms would probably become more cautious in competing because of a fear of P&G.

Additionally, the merger "may have the tendency" to raise the entry barriers, for Procter's tremendous advertising budget would enable it to divert advertising monies to meet the short-term threat of a newcomer. And the substantial advertising discounts which Procter enjoyed might put off potential competitors. Regarding this latter point, the opinion flatly stated: "Possible economies cannot be used as a defense to illegality."

In reversing the judgment of the court of appeals, the Court upheld the Federal Trade Commission's finding that the merger eliminated P&G as a potential competitor.

The evidence . . . clearly shows that Procter was the most likely entrant. . . . Procter was engaged in a vigorous program of diversifying into product lines closely related

---

[14]35 LW 4329.

[15]Mr. Justice Stewart and Mr. Justice Fortas did not participate in the decision. Mr. Justice Harlan wrote a concurring opinion.

[16]The opinion noted: "Since the products of the acquired company are complementary to those of the acquiring company and may be produced with similar facilities, marketed through the same channels and in the same manner, and advertised by the same media, the Commission aptly called the acquisition a 'product-extension merger.'"

to its basic products. Liquid bleach was a natural avenue of diversification since it is complementary to Procter's products, is sold to the customers through the same channels, and is advertised and merchandized in the same manner.

In its reliance upon post-merger evidence, Justice Douglas wrote, the court of appeals "misapprehended" the standards that were applicable in a Section 7 proceeding.

> Section . . . was intended to arrest the anticompetitive effects of market power in their incipiency. The core question is whether a merger may substantially lessen competition, and necessarily requires a prediction of the merger's impact on competition, present and future. The section can deal only with probabilities, not certainties. And there is certainly no requirement that the anticompetitive power manifest itself in anticompetitive action before § 7 can be called into play. [Citations omitted.]

CONCURRING OPINION OF MR. JUSTICE HARLAN

While agreeing that the Federal Trade Commission's order should be sustained, Justice Harlan took issue with the majority opinion because it made no effort to formulate standards for the application of Section 7 to mergers "which are neither horizontal nor vertical and which previously have not been considered in depth by the Court."

> It is regrettable to see this Court as it enters this comparatively new field of economic adjudication starting off with what has almost become a kind of *res ipsa loquitur* approach to antitrust cases.

The majority opinion "leaves the Commission, lawyers, and businessmen at large as to what is to be expected of them in the future cases of this kind." And while the Court declares that all mergers (no matter what they are called) must be tested by the same standard, it is equally important, Justice Harlan wrote, "to recognize that different sets of circumstances may call for fundamentally different tests of substantial anticompetitive effect."

The Justice agreed with the Commission's finding that the post-merger evidence was irrelevant and that in conglomerate or product-extension merger cases inquiry "should be directed toward reasonably probable changes in market structure," for "only by focusing on market structure can we begin to formulate standards which will allow the responsible agencies to give proper consideration to such mergers and allow businessmen to plan their actions with a fair degree of certainty."

Justice Harlan gave the following summary of four guides for determining the legality of conglomerate or product-extension mergers:

> First, the decision can rest on analysis of market structure without resort to evidence of post-merger anticompetitive behavior.
>
> Second, the operation of the pre-merger market must be understood as the foundation of successful analysis. The responsible agency may presume that the market operates in accord with generally accepted principles of economic theory, but the presumption must be open to challenge of alternative operational formulations.

Third, if it is reasonably probable that there will be a change in market structure which will allow the exercise of substantially greater market power, then a prima facie case has been made out under § 7.

Fourth, where the case against the merger rests on the probability of increased market power, the merging companies may attempt to prove that there are countervailing economies reasonably probable which should be weighed against the adverse effects.

And he found that the Commission's opinion conformed to this analysis.

While agreeing that the Commission was justified in giving no weight to P&G's efficiency defense (because discounts on large advertising outlays are not "true efficiencies"), Justice Harlan felt that the Commission's view on advertising economies was "overstated and oversimplified."

> Undeniably advertising may sometimes be used to create irrational brand preferences and mislead consumers as to the actual differences between products, but it is very difficult to discover at what point advertising ceases to be an aspect of healthy competition. It is not the Commission's function to decide which lawful elements of the "product" offered the consumer should be considered useful and which should be considered the symptoms of industrial "sickness." It is the consumer who must make that selection through the exercise of his purchasing power.

ADDENDUM

In February of 1967, nearly two months before the Supreme Court handed down its ruling on the Clorox merger, the Federal Trade Commission split 3 to 2 in accepting a consent settlement,[17] by which Procter & Gamble (in exchange for being allowed to keep the Folger Coffee Company, which it had purchased in 1963[18]) promised not to buy any domestic grocery products companies in the next seven years without prior FTC approval and further promised not to engage in any additional coffee mergers for the next ten years. P&G also agreed that during the next ten years it would report all incipient mergers involving any kind of product in the domestic market to the Commission.

The consent settlement further provided that P&G would not accept any media discounts or rate reductions on coffee advertising during the next five years when such discounts or reductions are based on advertising of other

---

[17] Under the Commission's rules, a party against whom the FTC had decided to issue a complaint is served with notice of the Commission's intention and receives a copy of the intended complaint and order. The party served may file a reply indicating willingness to have the proceeding disposed of by entry of an agreement containing a consent order. When such a reply is received, the party served, its counsel, and members of the Commission's Division of Consent Orders participate in the preparation and execution of an agreement containing a consent order. If the Commission subsequently determines that the proposed agreement should be accepted, it issues its complaint and simultaneously enters its decision and order.

[18] In a ten-year period, P&G had acquired five grocery product companies: W. T. Young Foods, Inc., (peanut butter and peanut products), 1955; prepared mix division of Nebraska Consolidated Mills (cake mixes), 1956; Charmin Paper Mills (paper tissues and related products), 1957; Clorox, 1957; and J. A. Folger & Co. (coffee), 1963.

Procter products, and that it would not conduct any coffee promotion in conjunction with its other products during the same period.

The majority, which included Commissioner Philip Elman, who had written the Commission's ruling against the Clorox merger, did not give any explanation for its acceptance of the settlement. But Commissioner Mary Gardiner Jones, who dissented on the grounds that regulation was inadequate and the FTC should have sought divestiture, said: "Instead of seeking divestiture, the order seeks to regulate, in a quite direct manner and for a five-year period, certain aspects of P&G's conduct of joint promotions involving coffee, and its other products and P&G's ability to exact reductions in media rates because of the magnitude of its several expenditures on advertising."[19]

The text of the FTC's complaint, which was released publicly with the announcement of the consent settlement, contended that the merger between P&G and Folger, the nation's second largest nonretailer of regular coffee and fourth in soluble coffee, might substantially lessen competition in the coffee business. Like Clorox, P&G was entering a new product field with its purchase of Folger.

The Commission had notified P&G in June of 1966 that it intended to challenge the Folger purchase and to seek divestiture, and its complaint stressed P&G's advertising and promotional strength and its ability to "achieve significant cost reductions" in: the buying of green coffee; the procuring of financing; the buying and placement of advertising; the conducting of consumer and sales promotions; the buying of containers and packaging materials; and the procuring of warehousing and transportation.[20]

APPENDIX

Under the Administrative Procedure Act and the Federal Trade Commission's rules, the initial decision of a hearing examiner becomes the decision of the Commission 30 days after it has been served upon the parties to the proceeding unless prior thereto (i) an appeal is made to the Commission; (ii) the Commission by order stays the effective date of the decision; or (iii) the Commission issues an order placing the case on its own docket for review. In rendering its decision on appeal or review, the Commission may adopt, modify, or set aside the findings, conclusions, and order of the initial decision.

A final decision by the Commission results in a dismissal or a cease and desist order. If the Commission issues a dismissal, the proceedings are at an end, for counsel supporting the complaint may not petition the courts for review. If the Commission issues a cease and desist order, this order may be appealed to a United States Court of Appeals, which may affirm, enforce, modify, or set aside the order. The judgment and decree of a Court of Appeals are subject to review by the United States Supreme Court upon certiorari.

[19] *Advertising Age,* February 27, 1967, p. 36.
[20] *Ibid.*

Managing Affirmative Action at National Union Bank

EXECUTIVE COMMITTEE MEETING ON AFFIRMATIVE ACTION

On Monday morning three members of the executive committee of National Union Bank held a special meeting to discuss a pressing problem. The committee included Theodore George, the chairman of the bank's board of directors; Donald Paige, vice chairman; and Walter Betsford, president. Also at the meeting was a group from the bank's human resources department. Roger Young, department head, human resources, led the group which also included John Thompson, group head, recruitment/employee affairs, and Alice Mitton, unit head, EEO/affirmative action (see Exhibit 1).

Young opened the meeting: "Gentlemen, our purpose for being here today is to recommend that the bank conduct an affected class analysis of its work force. Alice Mitton, who handles EEO/affirmative action for the bank, will present the details of the recommendation." Young nodded to Mitton, who began her presentation by first defining the term *affected class* according to the federal government affirmative action compliance manual:

> One or more employees, former employees, or applicants who have been denied employment opportunities or benefits because of discriminatory practices and/or policies by a federal contractor, its employees or agents. Evidence of an affected class requires: (1) identification of the discriminatory practices; (2) identification of the effects of discrimination; (3) identification of those suffering from the effects of discrimination.

Mitton distributed a hypothetical example of a government finding of an affected class, which read as follows:

858

Ten years ago a bank hired 25 individuals—10 females and 15 males—who were all fresh college graduates with liberal arts degrees. Now, 10 years later, a federal government agency during an affirmative action compliance review compares the average salary of the remaining females with the average salary of the remaining males. There is a significant difference. The agency looks to see if there are differences in performance or in education subsequent to hire and finds none. The agency concludes that the females were discriminated against in placement and promotion due to their sex and the result was the salary discrepancy. Since the bank cannot disprove the claim, it pays out a significant amount of money to "make whole" the individuals discriminated against.

Mitton continued:

Mr. George, Mr. Paige, Mr. Betsford, as you know, National Union is in the first stage of a federal government affirmative action compliance review. I believe that as part of that review the federal government will conduct an affected class analysis and ask for a substantial monetary settlement. My recommendation is that National Union should hire a consultant to conduct our own affected class analysis so that if, as a result of the compliance review, the government claims to have found an affected class we can refute or at least mitigate the claim. I must point out that if an affected class is found as a result of our own analysis, the bank must address it or else be in more jeopardy than when it started. Not dealing with known discrimination is unacceptable in the eyes of the government compliance agency.

Paige broke in and asked, "Why do we need a consultant to do this, and if we do, what is your cost estimate?"

EXHIBIT 1
Organization chart.

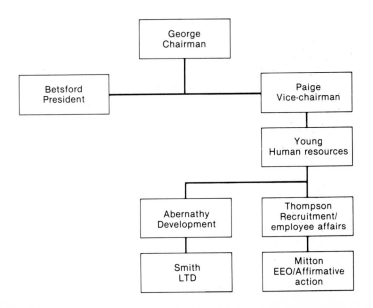

Mitton responded:

> The consultant is needed because an affected class analysis involves sophisticated multivariate statistical methods in which neither I nor anyone else in the human resources department is skilled.

Estimated Cost of Conducting an Affected Cost Analysis

Mitton continued:

> The cost to do our own affected class analysis is substantial. I estimate $200,000. The figure includes the cost of computer programming and processing, clerical and managerial time, as well as consultant's fees. We will have to create a data base using information gathered from our personnel files. Developing such a data base is labor-intensive and thus expensive. However, the data is essential to the success of the analysis. In one of the few published affected class analyses, a researcher needed eight variables to explain male/female salary differences in a bank (Exhibit 2). Only five of those variables are in our current computer system, and the other three must be developed by gathering data from the personnel files.

Betsford squirmed in his chair and finally spoke, "You realize that because of the recession the bank's profits have been declining. An expenditure like this would only add fuel to the fire. From what you said the $200,000 is only the beginning. If you find your affected class, the total cost could be more!"

Mitton was taken aback but composed herself and responded, "Yes, Mr. Betsford, I estimate the cost could run anywhere from $200,000 to $1 million. It is a substantial amount, but if we don't do it, we may have to pay out even more. Affected class settlements often run into the millions of dollars, and that is not even taking the adverse publicity into account."

Theodore George was well aware of adverse publicity, having suffered for almost a year with the publicity stemming from National Union's falling profits. He was, however, puzzled by some seemingly contradictory facts. George stated, "Since the bank had its first affirmative action plan in 1974, I believe there has been substantial progress in minority and female representation in our work force. I also understand that in our previous reviews in 1975 and 1977, the bank was found to be in compliance with the relevant regulations. How is it that now the bank can be liable for such huge claims of discrimination given the previous findings of nondiscrimination?"

"Mr. George, the regulatory environment in which we are operating has changed during the last few years," replied Mitton.

Regulatory Environment of Affirmative Action

Mitton began by pointing out that although affirmative action became prominent during the 1970s, its base lays squarely in the Civil Rights Act of 1964, Title VII of which makes it an "unlawful employment practice" for an employer to discriminate against any person in hiring, in discharge, or with respect to

EXHIBIT 2

MULTIPLE REGRESSION ANALYSIS OF SEX-RELATED CURRENT PAY DISPARITIES AMONG EMPLOYEES HIRED INTO NONPROFESSIONAL JOBS*

Dependent Variable-Natural Logarithm of Salary at Year-End 1979

Variables controlled cumulatively	Female/ male pay disparity (percent) (1)	t statistic (2)	R^2 (proportion) (3)	Adjusted R^2 (proportion) (4)
• Sex (1 = female) unadjusted	−10.45	−4.25†	0.05	0.05
Sex (1 = female) adjusted for:				
• Length of service at bank	−5.43	−2.82†	0.48	0.47
• Highest education level	−4.61	−2.50†	0.52	0.51
• Banking major	−3.86	−2.09‡	0.56	0.54
• Length and type of prior experience	−4.97	−2.53†	0.58	0.56
• Nonproductive time out of labor force	−3.72	−1.83‡	0.59	0.57
• Investments in bank career	−3.05	−1.49	0.60	0.58
• Career motivation factors	−1.35	−0.65	0.66	0.62
Sample size	313			
Number of females	207			

*By Judith Stoikov, vice president, National Economic Research Associates, Inc., from a speech before the American Bankers Association National Personnel Conference, Seattle, Washington, September 23, 1980.

†Statistically significant at the 1 percent level; one-tail test.

‡Statistically significant at the 5 percent level; one-tail test.

Source: NERA Regression Analysis.

"compensation, terms, conditions, or privileges of employment on the basis of race, color, religion, sex, or national origin." It has developed that if an employer is charged by either an individual or a government agency with an unlawful employment practice under Title VII, the employer has the burden of proving the absence of unlawful discrimination.

Title VII was followed by Lyndon Johnson's Executive Order 11246 (effective October 24, 1965) which required all government contractors and subcontractors, including persons or organizations acting as fund depositories, to commit themselves to equal employment opportunity and to take affirmative action to achieve it. Executive Order 11246 provides that affirmative action "shall include, but not be limited to, the following: employment, upgrading, demotion, or transfers; recruitment or recruitment advertising; layoff or termination; rates of pay or other forms of compensation; and selection for training, including apprenticeship."

Other statutes related to equality in employment opportunity include the Equal Pay Act of 1963, the Age Discrimination in Employment Act of 1967, the Rehabilitation Act of 1973, and the Vietnam-Era Veterans Readjustment Assistance Act of 1974. Most of this legislation has, in much of the country, a state counterpart which mirrors the federal law and is administered by state agencies which themselves usually have power to initiate lawsuits.

In December 1971 Executive Order 11246 was amended by Revised Order #4. The executive order as revised is administered by the Office of Contract Compliance Programs (OFCCP) in the U.S. Department of Labor. The revised order requires government contractors to set up affirmative action programs setting forth "specific and result-oriented procedures" by which the contractor promises to apply "every good-faith effort" to obtain equal employment opportunity. The contractor must take an analysis of its work force in all job categories, departments, and salary ranges, and identify the areas within which it is deficient. The contractor is required, moreover, to specify goals and timetables to which its good-faith effort will be directed to correct the deficiencies and to achieve full use of minorities and females. The categories of people that must be considered in setting goals for equal employment depend upon the representation of various minority groups and females in the community surrounding the employer's facility. The community is usually understood to be the standard metropolitan statistical area (SMSA), the county, or the city.

Until 1978, each federal agency reviewed the affirmative action compliance of the contractors it did business with. The OFCCP had authority for final approval of the contractors' affirmative action plans, but each agency conducted compliance reviews separately. Banks were reviewed by the Treasury Department which was considered to be one of the more lenient agencies. However in 1978 the Carter administration reorganized federal affirmative action compliance activity. All compliance reviews were to be conducted by a centralized office, the OFCCP. The change was made for the sake of both efficiency and effectiveness.

In addition to centralizing affirmative action compliance activity, the Carter administration set up a competition between the Equal Employment Opportunity Commission (EEOC) and the OFCCP. The EEOC enforces Title VII of the Civil Rights Act mainly through three methods: investigation of individual discrimination charges, investigation of class action charges, and investigation of discrimination charges initiated by the commissioners. The OFCCP, as previously mentioned, conducts affirmative action compliance reviews. The administration hinted that sometime in the future all federal equal employment activity would be centralized in one agency. The competition is to see which agency, the OFCCP or the EEOC, will be dominant.

The result has been an added emphasis during OFCCP affirmative action compliance reviews. There is, in addition to traditional strong emphasis on goals and timetables and programs to meet the goals, an added emphasis on finding affected classes. The reason is that affected classes are usually remedied with some sort of monetary payment. The OFCCP appears to be trying to prove its worth by the amount of dollars in affected class settlements it can obtain.

OFCCP's Targets

The banking industry is one of the OFCCP's main targets. Chase Manhattan in New York signed a conciliation agreement following a compliance review which called for $2 million in incentive promotion payments and development programs aimed specifically at females and minorities. Harris Bank in Chicago could not reach conciliation with the OFCCP after a compliance review initiated in 1977. The review went before a Department of Labor administrative law judge who ruled that Harris should pay $12 million in back pay to females to remedy systematic discrimination. The Harris review is still in court. Harris believes it is innocent and will contest the judgment.

"Mr. George, the OFCCP is after large monetary settlements," Mitton concluded, "and as a large bank, National Union is a target."

"Thank you, Miss Mitton," Mr. George replied, "if there aren't any more questions from either Don or Walt, I would like to have some time to ponder this situation. I believe your presentation and the memo you prepared will be enough information for me to make a decision. I'll let you know when I have decided."

As Young, Thompson, and Mitton waited for the elevator which would take them down to the human resources area, Young spoke. "John, Alice, I usually know which way Ted will go on an issue after a meeting, but this time I don't know. I'm sure the cost of the analysis and its effect on profitability will be an important issue."

NATIONAL UNION BANK'S POSITION AND BACKGROUND OF EEO

National Union Bank is one of the country's larger commercial banks. It serves a major metropolitan area in the mid-Atlantic region of the country. It employs approximately 6,000 persons in its central and branch offices. The affirmative action plan for the central office covers approximately 5,000 of the employees. The bank's business covers the full range of banking services, including some federal government business and a substantial amount of state and city business.

The structure of the bank is comparable to that of any large organization. It is subdivided into functional departments. With other banks, however, National Union shares a major difference from the more general pyramidal structure of organizations. The bank's structure has approximately half of its employees in the lower, nonexempt levels and half of its employees in the upper, exempt levels (Exhibit 3).

National Union's history related to affirmative action, according to Charles Loring, a personal banking manager who remembers it well, dates back to 1959, when the first black employee was hired by the bank. At that time Loring, who has been with the bank for almost 20 years, was working in the human resources area, from which he moved in 1971.

"The first blacks hired had a rough time," Loring recalled, "the problem being with first-line supervision." Loring calculated that between 1961 and 1965 the bank upped its percentage of minorities to between 1 and 2 percent of what was then a work force of about 3,600. He said that now managers hire minorities without question.

EXHIBIT 3
NATIONAL UNION BANK WORK FORCE STATISTICS:
JOB CLASSIFICATION

	Salary grade	Clerical	Professionals/ technicians/ sales	Managers/ supervisors
Nonexempt	1	74	—	—
	2	99	—	—
	3	257	—	—
	4	447	—	—
	5	555	—	—
	6	540	—	—
	7	540	252	65
Exempt	11	—	90	88
	12	—	306	134
	13	—	209	66
	14	—	195	133
	15	—	99	122
	16	—	—	102
	17	—	—	78
	Total	2,517	1,151	788

Note: Exempt Employees are salaried and generally do not receive overtime payments. Most exempts are professionals, salespeople, or managers.

Pointing to the line of teller windows across the floor from his office, Loring added, "Why, right over there is one of the black girls hired as a teller around 1964, and she's been great, just great. However, between 1965 and 1971, which was before I left personnel, our major question was how to develop a black labor pool. As far as this was concerned, the labor supply of these persons possessing the requisite skills was very small, and we weren't going to distort our whole salary structure just to hire some black people. The problem was that most of them could make more money elsewhere than we could pay them, so there wasn't any incentive for them to work here. Gradually we did have some success at the lower levels."

Loring also pointed out that females have progressed in the bank's structure. Although females have always been well represented in the nonexempt work force, female representation in the exempt work force was sparse in the early 1960s.

"Now," said Loring, "it seems that almost half of the lenders are female, at least the young ones. I'll bet in a few years one of the department heads will be a woman."

A MEETING WITH JOHN ABERNATHY

Alice Mitton had scheduled busy day for herself. At 10:00 A.M. was a meeting with John Abernathy, group head, development, and at 1:00 P.M. was lunch with Murray Smith, unit head, Lender Training Program (LTP).

Mitton had just sat down in John Abernathy's office when Abernathy entered and said, "Sorry to keep you waiting; I was with Roger. Well, you're here to tell me about this year's affirmative action goals and to find out what I plan to do to meet them."

"Yes, Jack, your group plays an important role in our affirmative action program. This sheet shows how well the bank's current work force stacks up against this year's goals [Exhibit 4]," Mitton said as she handed him the sheet. "You see that we still have work to do at the upper exempt salary grades for females and in the middle and upper exempt grades for minorities. We're OK in the nonexempt grades."

Abernathy responded, "Alice, would you refresh my memory on the logic behind the goals."

"The goals are based on an analysis of eight factors as specified by the OFCCP, the federal compliance agency for affirmative action. The factors include the general population, the labor force, the unemployed, the population with requisite skills, and the promotable or transferable population in the organization. The concept behind the goals as I have developed them is that the goal is the minimum percentage for minority or female representation—its floor. If there is a higher percentage, fine, but we want to make every good-faith effort to at least match the floor percentage." responded Mitton.

"So far, we have met our goals without lowering our standards for hiring or promotion. I'm grateful for that," Abernathy pointed out. "Next year we will

EXHIBIT 4
NATIONAL UNION BANK WORK FORCE PERCENTAGES AND GOALS

Job classification	Salary grade	Females		Minorities	
		Actual (%)	Goal (%)	Actual (%)	Goal (%)
Clerical	1	57	36	72	19
	2	83	36	68	19
	3	75	36	61	19
	4	81	36	54	19
	5	82	36	45	19
	6	81	36	40	19
	7	69	36	23	19
Professionals/	7	51	36	23	19
technicians/	11	58	30	13	15
sales	12	44	30	12	15
	13	31	30	8	15
	14	14	30	5	15
	15	13	30	2	15
Managers/	7	32	36	19	19
supervisors	11	43	17	18	8
	12	32	17	15	8
	13	33	17	9	8
	14	23	17	5	8
	15	8	17	3	8
	16	2	17	2	8
	17	0	19	1	8

continue to provide our development programs such as training courses, career counseling, job posting, educational assistance, and professional seminars. I think these programs will help but I still believe we are at the mercy of the two-tiered internal labor market as far as meeting minority exempt goals. Until we get a better minority flow into the exempt level, there is really no way we can ever meet those unachieved goals."

"I am going to talk to Murray Smith at lunch about that very problem," Mitton responded, "he does some of the key exempt-level hiring."

Abernathy's view of the two-tier internal labor market is depicted in Exhibit 5. Essentially, in his opinion there was only a small flow of nonexempts into exempt salary grades. In addition, those nonexempts who make the jump tend to stay in the lower-level exempt salary grades rather than continue to move up. The commonly accepted reason for the two-tier internal labor market is that exempt positions require skills and experience which nonexempts generally do not possess. Thus, the exempt positions from which an individual can advance are generally filled from external sources.

Abernathy said:

Alice, before you go, here's a copy of my proposal for a formal exempt development system. I'd appreciate your comments. The system would require each manager of

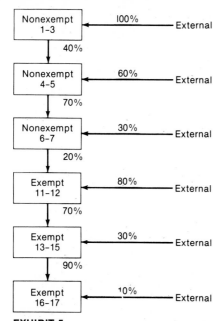

EXHIBIT 5
National Union Bank sources of placements into
salary grades.

exempt employees to produce a formal plan for the development of each subordinate. The plan is to be developed by the manager and the subordinate in conjunction with the Development Group. It should result in better development of the high-potential minorities we do have. Managers will be formally evaluated on the quality of these plans—that's the incentive. I find most managers won't do this type of thing unless their career and salary depends on it.

"Thanks, Jack," Mitton said as she rose from her chair and left Abernathy's office.

LUNCH WITH MURRAY SMITH

Mitton liked working with Murray Smith. He was a results-oriented individual who seemed to be successful at anything he set out to do. He graduated from the University of Michigan with a B.A. in economics and an M.B.A. with concentration in finance. Smith entered the Lender Training Program (LTP) upon graduation. He now manages that program. His first five years of permanent assignments were spent in lending positions. He saw his position as manager of the LTP as a broadening experience. Smith intends to return to lending in a year or so. Highly placed individuals in the bank consider Smith to be a "superstar." He is also a black man.

The LTP lasts one year and is intended to orient individuals for eventual placement into assignments in commercial banking and real estate. The trainees are first given three months of classroom training in accounting, finance, and management specifically as it relates to lending. The trainees then receive rotating assignments in various lending areas. After the nine months of temporary assignments the individuals are placed in permanent assignments based on interests and abilities.

Alice Mitton arrived at the executive dining room and found Murray Smith waiting in the lobby.

"Hello, Alice, right on time as usual," Smith said in greeting.

After they had sat down and ordered lunch, Mitton spoke about the purpose of the meeting, "Murray, do you think you can improve on the job you did last year—affirmative action-wise?"

"Well, Alice, last year out of 41 entrants into the LTP, 22 were female and 6 were minority. I won't take credit for a great effort in getting the females, but I did bust my tail in getting those six minorities. I'd say about 40 to 50 percent of all our interviewees were female, while only 10 to 15 percent were minority."

Mitton agreed, "Getting qualified minorities is a tough nut to crack."

Smith responded:

> You'd better believe it. The minorities who have the capacity to make it in the bank are also attractive to the IBMs, GMs, and Procter & Gambles of the world. I can't even dream of matching those salaries. The only ones I have a chance at are the ones specifically interested in banking, and then I am competing against the New York banks.

"Where will you be recruiting this season?" Mitton asked.

Smith's response:

> Oh, the usual places, of course, the eastern schools; Michigan, Indiana, and Northwestern in the Big Ten; a couple of other state universities—Virginia and North Carolina; top-notch private universities like Stanford, Chicago, and Washington U. I'll be recruiting both B.B.A.s and M.B.A.s.

"You sure are getting around," Mitton commented.

"I have to recruit nationwide to get the type of individuals the bank needs. Poised, self-confident, bright, polished, articulate individuals are hard to come by, and it takes a lot of work to find them and bring them in," Smith replied. "Alice, you'll recruit for me again this year, won't you?"

"Sure will; I would especially like to go to Washington U., you know it's my alma mater," Mitton said.

"No problem," said Smith.

As they left the dining room, Smith asked Mitton, "How is the compliance review going?"

Mitton's smile left her face as she replied,

> Well, I think it's going to be a tough one. You know, if you read the executive order, we do almost everything that is recommended. I don't think the government can ask

for more from us in that regard. As far as the affected class analysis goes, we'll have to play that one by ear.

"I remember last week you said you wanted to hire a consultant to help out. Did you get the OK?" Smith asked.

"It's with the chairman. I should find out this week," Mitton said.

When Mitton arrived at her office she was greeted by her secretary, "Young called, you are supposed to meet him in the chairman's office immediately."

CHARACTERISTICS OF THE CHIEF EXECUTIVE: HIS ROLE IN DEVELOPING THE CULTURE OF THE ORGANIZATION

CASES ON BUSINESS
POLICY FOR PART NINE

Top management leadership is a major factor in the success of any organization. The chief executive must provide the motivation and leadership for the entire organization and particularly for the management group. His executive style, personal philosophy, and behavioral patterns are reflected in the performance and effectiveness of the organization. The cases in Part Nine, Barrett Trumble, and Scandia, describe different executive characteristics, their philosophies and behavioral traits. Through the analysis of these case situations, the student should acquire some appreciation for the importance of human factors in the determination and execution of corporate policy.

Barrett Trumble

Professor Floyd Hall of Bristol University was visiting his old friend Barrett Trumble, president of Green & Richards, the leading quality department store in Gulf City, one of the fastest-growing metropolitan centers of the south. Hall read at breakfast of Trumble's election as president of the Community Fund.

Trumble said, "You might wonder, Floyd, why I would accept this job. I've already done my stint as general campaign manager for the Fund. I guess most people consider this kind of work an important community responsibility but, at the same time, enough of a headache to expect others to take over after you've done your share. I feel differently about it. Unless business leaders continue to spearhead the private sponsorship of needed community agencies, their functions, which must be performed by someone, will more and more be taken over by the federal, state, and municipal governments."

Trumble went on to say, "I played hard to get for quite a while. I told the boys I wouldn't take the job till we had firmed up our plans to raise funds for the next three years, including agreement on and acceptance by three executives who will take over successively as general campaign manager. Also, I insisted on the Fund setting up an advisory council of business executives, consisting of company presidents. I find that if we are going to get anything done around Gulf City, the way to do it is through the top brass. Now we have 20 business leaders on this council, and I am sure there is nothing we want to have done that we can't swing through this group. Then again, I think it's good for G&R for me to be out front in this type of job. As you can see from the morning's paper, we get pretty good publicity. In addition, I intend to have all meetings of the council and some meetings of the more important committees in our executive dining room in the store. And I am sure it won't turn out to be too much work. A job like this is just a job of getting it organized."

TRUMBLE'S OUTSIDE ACTIVITIES

Professor Hall suggested, "It sounds as though you have it well organized. However, don't you think you will still be harassed by personal appeals and requests from all the other agencies in Gulf City and from others who are interested in community welfare?"

Trumble replied, "Frankly, Floyd, I wouldn't tell this to anyone else, but I must confess that if I didn't have these outside interests, I'd just be twiddling my thumbs down at the store."

Hall was surprised. He knew that Trumble served on the boards of five other businesses: the First Federal Savings and Loan Association, the Commercial National Bank, the Equitable Casualty Insurance Company, Intercontinental Textile Products Corporation, and National Laboratories. He was also a trustee of the Franklin Museum of Modern Art, the Gulf City Symphony Orchestra, Hambletonian College, and the National Retail Merchants Association. Barrett was also a member of the business advisory committee to the Department of Commerce and the treasurer of the Gulf States' Republican Committee.

Barrett explained, "But these other activities don't really take much of my time. Most of these boards have no more than one meeting per month, and they are not very active during the summer months. Of course, when I am on any board committees, it takes a little more time. Then, down at the store, we have things so well organized that the operation pretty well runs itself. Ever since I brought in Tom Jenkins as executive vice president. I only find it necessary to get into things at the overall policy level."

TRUMBLE AND HIS VICE PRESIDENTS

Hall recalled that when Jenkins joined Green & Richards, the vice presidents in charge of customer relations and store operations had resigned to go with other merchandising firms. Trumble pointed out, "Of course, their resignations made it possible for us to promote two outstanding junior executives who were coming along so fast that we couldn't have kept them in the business if we hadn't been able to move them up the ladder. We now have eight vice presidents reporting to Jenkins; one each for ready-to-wear merchandising, home-furnishings merchandising, store operations, personnel relations, customer relations, control, advertising, and research. Tom and his eight vice presidents constitute an executive council which meets twice a week. I sit in on all the meetings and have an opportunity to keep in touch with major policy questions. Once in a while I find it necessary to step in where there is a strong difference of opinion, but I can usually rely on Tom to straighten things out without my intervention."

Hall asked, "Don't you find it necessary, as president, to meet with the heads of other businesses in town on questions which involve all the stores in town? For example, don't you have common problems like retaining the importance of the central business district as a shopping center or instituting charges for customer services which you can no longer render free of charge?"

"Yes, you have a point there. I could spend a lot of my time doing this, but the other boys are really better qualified than I am to make a contribution to joint meetings with other stores. For example, take the question of charging for deliveries, which is a hot subject right now. I think it is something all the stores must consider seriously. But why should I spend the time sitting in on the series of harangues among the other merchants in town when Jack Ogleby (vice president for store operations) is really up to date on this question and can quote chapter and verse when they get down to brass tacks in their discussions? Anyway, before anybody does anything about this, the question will come before our executive council, and I will get in on it at that point."

HOW TRUMBLE SPENDS HIS TIME

Hall wondered how Trumble used the rest of his time in directing the operations of Green & Richards. "Well, I guess I spend a good 10 percent of my time with the board of directors—in regular meetings of the board, in preparing for these meetings, and in individual conferences with some of the more interested members of the board. For example, Fredric Pellham (senior partner of the leading law firm in Gulf City) is on my neck now, pressing us to come up with a 10-year plan for our business. He thinks we should be looking to the future growth and development of G&R rather than concentrating on today's profits alone. However, the board as a whole now has enough confidence in me so that the others don't needle me the way Fred does.

"Also, the Green family is concerned with maintaining a good steady return on their investment. They aren't interested in spending the kind of money we would need over the next few years if we were going all out to become the largest department store in the south, which is what Fred would like to see.

"Then, I meet with the executive council twice a week. I have a regular meeting every Monday morning with Tom Jenkins. I am always available to talk with the other vice presidents about any of their problems. They know that I won't make any decisions on the matters they bring to me, but I am always glad to toss ideas around with them for whatever help that may be. But I guess I would have to say that most of my time in the store is spent just going through the business as much as I can. I spend between three and four hours a day walking through the store, particularly in the sales departments, just seeing how things are going, chatting with the people as I go, doing everything I can to help give people a lift. It helps keep me in touch with the ways things are moving out on the selling floor, and I am sure that the people down the line feel better to see me around, because they know that I am not trying to run things from an ivory tower."

OPERATING RESULTS OF G&R

"How has the store been doing the last couple of years, Barrett?"

"I certainly can't complain, Floyd. I would say our sales and profits are excellent. Every quarter, for the last three years, we have done better than our budgeted dollar sales, gross profit, and net profit. By the way, I have always found it useful to present to the board of directors a highly conservative sales and profit plan so there won't be any unpleasant surprises when the final reports are in. Our reports are better than the Federal Reserve reports for Gulf City as a whole and better than the National Retail Merchants Association averages. Looking ahead, with defense spending the way it is, creeping inflation, population trends in general, and the growth curve of Gulf City, I don't see how we can miss. Sometimes I wonder if we might show even better results if I put a little more pressure on the boys or if I spent a little more time myself in some of our major problem areas. But here we are, the major downtown store, with three surburban stores (two of which we did not have six years ago) and with our sales increasing every year somewhere between 4 and 6 percent. Our operating profits before income taxes have averaged 7.6 percent of sales for the last five years."[1]

DELEGATION AND MANAGEMENT DEVELOPMENT

"And now I have built a team. As I see my job, it is to help select and develop competent people for our key jobs and then let them go ahead and do the things they are qualified to do and for which they are being well paid. It seems to me you either delegate responsibility and authority or you don't. The trouble with most store heads with whom I am familiar is that they talk a lot about delegation but they spend a lot of their own personal time going around and asking the department heads why they bought this, what they think of that, why don't they do so and so. One of our mutual friends, who runs a store up north, tells me that he thinks his job is one of constantly impressing department heads with the fact that he is thoroughly familiar with the way things are going in each department. He watches each department's figures like a hawk and calls people on the phone or on the carpet to discuss what they have in mind to correct things in the future. I don't see why we spend a lot of time developing people and pay them the money that we do if we don't rely on them to take the kind of action that is good for business and therefore for themselves."

Floyd asked Barrett if he was satisfied with his executive staff. "I would think you would have problems from time to time, humans being what they are."

Trumble replied, "Sure, like any other big happy family, we have our troubles from time to time. For example, Malcolm Donaldson (vice president for personnel) gets himself steamed up on a special training course for executives

---

[1] The National Industrial Conference Board had reported that the previous year's operating profits of large department stores averaged 5.6 percent of sales.

and makes the mistake of bringing it up cold at the executive council meeting. The boys kick it around but finally decide that department heads have too many pressing problems confronting them, that it would be unwise to take them away from their operations for extended training sessions. Mal's idea gets voted down. Then, later in the day, he comes to me to see if he can get my backing for the idea, knowing that I am all for more and more executive training.

"What Mal ought to do is talk with some of the other vice presidents ahead of time and get them interested in the idea and at least briefed to the point where they understand thoroughly what Mal has in mind. Most things get settled in our business outside of council meetings; the interested executives are covered individually or in small groups ahead of time, so that when the issue comes to a vote at the council meeting, it is pretty much a matter of rubber-stamping the proposal.

"Mal really needs a lot of help, anyway. We have just employed a personnel consulting firm, with an annual retainer of $60,000. They keep us in touch with what is going on in other businesses, union trends, etc.; they work with Mal on employee training courses and do a lot of other things for us. For example, I learned the other day that one of their communications specialists is helping Mal write employee bulletins before they come to me for my signature."

BOARD RELATIONS

"You were saying, Barrett, that you don't have much trouble with the board of directors."

"No, except for Fred Pellham, who is a little troublesome from time to time. He has made it a point to dig into our business more deeply than the other directors. He gets his own industry figures direct from the Fed, National Retail Merchants, and Harvard Business School, so that he can compare our operations with what others are doing. As I told you, he is trying to get us to think further ahead and anticipate the changes that are likely to happen 10 years from now, so that we will be able to make the necessary moves today in terms of what is going to happen then, instead of struggling year by year to keep abreast as things shift. Of course, most merchants realize that department store business is, at best, a 90-day business; we have to be quick on our feet to meet day-to-day changes. No one has a good enough crystal ball to be able to forecast several years ahead.

"The other directors now accept almost anything I propose as a sound idea. Over the last five or six years, I have been careful to make sure that the things that I brought before the board were thoroughly explored and based on conservative projections. As a result, I no longer find it necessary to justify most of the things I want to do. Sometimes I wonder if they are a little too easy on me. However, I don't know; it is certainly a lot more comfortable this way. I can't say that I would like to repeat the struggles that I had in selling the board this idea or that idea during the first year or two I was in this job. I guess no president wants a board of directors that is as active in the business as their own stockholders expect them to be. From my own experience in serving as a director on these other boards, I find it pretty easy to put the management on the spot by raising questions which are not self-evident from the figures presented to the board. Before every board meeting in these other concerns, I spend a lot of time going over the material they send us ahead of time, because I think I have the responsibility, both legal and moral, as a director to serve as His Majesty's loyal opposition, so to speak."

OTHER ACTIVITIES

"By and large, it looks to me as though things are in pretty good shape at Green & Richards, but every once in a while I wonder where I am going. Here I am, close to 50, doing well financially—my directorships alone give me a pretty good income. Of course, income is not important in my tax bracket, and I definitely feel that my serving on these outside boards is a good thing for the store. Too many of my retailer friends aren't in touch with the methods and viewpoints of other businesspeople. I think I have the advantage over them as a result of these contacts outside our own trade.

"Apart from these business and community activities, I seem to have plenty of time for golf; I get in three rounds a week on the average, except when Jane and I are away on vacation. I guess I told you that we are leaving the middle of next month for a cruise around the world. In a way, this will combine business and vacation. It will give me an opportunity to touch base with some of our important resources from whom we import in the Far East and Europe. Our merchants are over there regularly, but I think it means something from time to time to have the head of the business pay them a visit. I get a real kick out of meeting their families, going through their operations, and talking about the problems they are up against. It seems to me that they get something out of it, too. In one sense, it does the same thing I try to do when I walk around the store each day—and maintaining good relations with our key resources, both domestic and foreign, is almost as important as good employee relations, I think. I also try to spend as much time as I can in our domestic markets—especially in New York and on the west coast."

Since Trumble was thoroughly wound up, Hall continued to listen without comment.

SATISFACTION THROUGH CONTRIBUTION

"I get a good deal of satisfaction out of things I am doing. I thoroughly enjoy my regular job. I feel that Green & Richards is making an important contribution to our growing community.

"I am convinced we help raise the cultural standards of Gulf City through our emphasis on quality merchandise and good taste; through constantly making available to our customers exciting new items, many of them exclusive with us; through concerts, Christmas and Easter festivities, art shows, and many other events throughout the year. I think our reputation for courteous service (and there is nothing more important), for making good on all commitments, for integrity and fairness in all dealings with customers, resources, and employees, sets an example for others in the community. And I believe that my chief contribution to Green & Richards is to help other people understand, believe in, and apply these principles to their day-to-day problems. My job is to help our executives grow and develop to the full limit of their capacities, to the point where they can operate on their own, within our guiding policies and principles. To the extent I am successful in doing this, I not only improve the sales and profits of the store but also feel, in some degree, the kind of satisfaction you derive from your teaching—the satisfaction which one gets from helping others.

"I would hate to give up any of my outside business interests or directorships. As for the Community Fund, the museum, and the other community service activities, I consider them too important to give up—they make it possible for me, in a small way, to repay the community for my own good fortune. You said you wanted to talk with me, Floyd, about the kind of problems I find most troublesome. I guess my problem is that I don't have any real problems at the present time. Of course, if we had a real recession, I would have my hands full down at the store without any of these outside interests. However, from the looks of things, there isn't going to be much for me to sink my teeth into in the near future."

EARLIER PROBLEMS AS GENERAL MERCHANDISE MANAGER

"Sometimes I find it hard to look back to nine years ago with G&R. I'm sure you remember how Jane used to complain about the way I worked around the clock and never had any time for her or the youngsters. At that time, we were in really bad shape. During the preceding five years, the store had slipped from first position to a shaky fourth in relation to the other stores in Gulf City. Someone had to get in and work closely with the buyers, one after another. I practically lived with each merchant, helping get his or her department back on its feet. In some cases, we found it necessary to replace them with seasoned buyers from other stores. I hated to bring in so many executives from the outside, but we simply didn't have enough good people coming along at the lower levels to do much promoting from within.

"And the store had developed such a poor reputation in some markets that I was forced to work personally with many leading apparel, accessories, and home furnishings resources before we were in a position to carry their lines again. With conditions as they were and with our competitors doing everything they could to keep us from regaining our No. 1 spot, this was a job I had to tackle myself, as general merchandise manager. The divisional supervisors and buyers just weren't strong enough to deal with the presidents and owners of some of the finest manufacturing establishments in this country and abroad. It was hard work, but it was also a lot of fun."

WHERE DO I GO FROM HERE?

"I can't help wondering what the next stop should be. Young Barrett and Sheila are well along in college and, except for summers, have flown the nest. The only way I can continue to grow is to keep on tackling new, challenging problems. I know that some of my friends think I'm already spreading myself too thin. From the look on your face, Floyd, it may be in your mind, too. I think I am pretty close to the boys down at the store, but it may be that they, too, think I am becoming an absentee president. However, as I have already said, I believe thoroughly in the significance of the causes for which I am working out-side of the business, and I also believe each of them, in one way or another, helps contribute to the success of Green & Richards. Besides, I just can't see myself sitting in the office down at the store, reading a newspaper and waiting for someone to come in with a problem.

"Every so often, I have thought about trying a few years of government ser-vice. Through my work on the business advisory council of the Department of Commerce, I am in touch with a good many of the key people in the administra-tion. If they knew that I might be available, I suspect there would be an oppor-tunity for me to move in at a level challenging enough to be more than just another bureaucratic job. Several of my friends have even had the temerity to suggest my name for governor, but in this state, a Republican candidate has lost the race before it starts. I think what I would really like to do is talk with you a little bit about your own experiences as a teacher. Perhaps, at this point in my career, I could get the greatest satisfaction from helping pass on to young peo-ple coming along some of the things I think I have learned in business. What do you think, Floyd?"

Hall arose as the two wives entered the room and said, "Why don't we let things soak a bit? You've given me so much to think about I hardly know where to begin."

TRUMBLE'S BACKGROUND

Floyd Hall recalled that Trumble had graduated from Hambletonian College. With business conditions as they were at the time, he had gone on to take his M.B.A. at the Tuck School of Business Administration at Dartmouth. All of his business life had been spent in retailing. Barrett had started as an assistant buyer of women's ready-to-wear at Fisk Brothers in Buffalo, New York. He progressed rapidly to the place where he was merchandising their entire ready-to-wear line. After eight years, he left Fisk to become divisional merchandise manager of a leading southeast department store. Four years later, he became assistant general merchandise manager of a nationally known high-quality store on the east coast. He joined Green & Richards as vice president and general merchandise manager and became president two years later. Hall recalled that Trumble had always been active in community affairs, wherever he worked. In the 20-odd years Hall had known him, Trumble had never shown any evi-dence of being under pressure. Hall considered this unusual in an industry noted for heavy demands it made on its executives. Trumble had always had time for a full social life and an opportunity to take advantage of his consuming interest in golf. Barrett had been runner-up twice in the national intercollegiate golf championship while in college. He continued to play top-drawer golf after graduation, reaching the quarter finals of the National Amateur in his mid-40s. Two years earlier, he had been runner-up for the Gulf State Championship and had been club champion of the Jefferson Davis Country Club for six years running.

THE "SERMON"

Floyd Hall remembered that Trumble had sent him a copy of a talk he had given before the Parkville Presbyterian Church shortly after he became president of G&R. When he returned to Bristol, he found it was still in his files.

THE OPPORTUNITIES AND RESPONSIBILITIES OF THE CHRISTIAN LAYMAN IN THE COMMUNITY

Excerpts from Barrett Trumble's Talk

Parkville Presbyterian Church

Wednesday Evening—November 28

It is very good to be with you, and I am sure that you understand that I am not here to preach. . . . But I thought that perhaps we could all think out loud, in an informal way, about the subject at hand, namely, the layman's opportunity and responsibility in the community.

The first thing we should ask ourselves is: What is a Christian layman? Obviously, a Christian layman is a follower of Jesus Christ and, in essence, stands for and believes, with his heart, in the teachings of Jesus. In this conjunction, it might be interesting to point out that Jesus Himself was a layman. Although he was called Rabbi (that is to say, teacher), there is no record of His attending a theological school. Further, Jesus surrounded Himself with laymen from the common walks of life, and although the message came down out of Heaven through Christ into the church, it was carried out of the church into life by laymen who preached the Gospel. There was really no other way to do this. . . .

. . . We might stress the qualities Jesus stands for and the kind of person He wants the Christian layman to be.

Taking great liberties with Matthew: In Chapter 5, Verse 3, which begins, "Blessed are the poor in spirit for theirs is the kingdom of Heaven" and goes on through the various beatitudes that Jesus mentioned, it seems quite clear that (1) kindness and consideration for others—giving the other fellow a second chance, (2) aggressive courage—going the second mile for good causes, (3) courtesy—coming from the heart, (4) thoughtfulness and understanding, (5) fairness, (6) integrity and vision, and (7) faith are some of the vital qualities that we should strive to possess in our everyday living if we would measure up to Jesus' standards.

. . . These very same qualities that Christ taught us to strive and stand for are the ones that make for true success in everyday life. I think it important to emphasize here that I am talking about inner spiritual, rather than material, success—the sort which would lead a man such as Disraeli to want to be a great *man* rather than a great *lawyer.* These qualities make for true success in every walk of life, whether one is engaged in teaching, farming, a profession, business, or household duties. The old idea that to be successful one had to be ruthless, unscrupulous. and tough with people just doesn't stand up today and it is my honest opinion that the inability to handle, work with, and influence people is probably the cause of the greatest number of personal failures in life. Time and time again, I have—and I am sure you have—seen brilliant people who appeared to have just what it takes for success fail utterly because they overlooked the fact that one rarely succeeds alone but rather succeeds because others make one successful. . . .

I have been very fortunate in my life to have met and watched a great number of prominent people at work. I think you will agree with me when I say that a Charles Wilson or a George Marshall or a Dwight Eisenhower exemplifies fully these qualities that I have listed. I have never met a more humble, homespun, or thoughtful man than Charles Wilson; nor a more kind, considerate, and honest one than Marshall; nor a more thoughtful, fair, or courageous man than Eisenhower. As a matter of fact, it seems to me that the greater the man, the fewer the pretenses and the more down-to-Christian-fundamentals he is. . . .

Let me quote, again, from the text: Ephesians 4:32—"Be ye kind one to another, tender-hearted, forgiving." In Barrie's play, *Little White Bird,* a young husband is waiting at the hospital for his child to be born. He has never been unkind to his wife, but he wonders if he has been as kind as he might have been. "Let us make a new rule from tonight," he says, "always to be a little kinder than is necessary." . . . "Somehow, I never thought it paid," said Lincoln, when his friends urged him to make a stinging reply to a bitter, untrue word spoken about him. In the end, kindness, even to those who have been unkind to us, is never regretted. "A little kinder than is necessary" is the finest of the little arts of life, if not its final joy. The only things we are never sorry for are the kind things said and done to others. They make a soft pillow at the end.

. . . What are the obligations of the layman to his business or profession? In this regard, we have a great obligation to attempt to do the best possible job that we can in the field we are in, whatever that field might be. I believe it was Plato who said, "The source of the greatest happiness is in a job well done." Furthermore, by doing a good job in our field, whether it be as a mother in the home, a teacher in the school, a doctor in the hospital, or a businessman, we raise the standard of living and happiness of all those around us, and I am sure you will agree this is a most worthwhile goal.

Then there is the obligation of the layman to his fellow worker. To realize the dignity of man, to make his working and living conditions as pleasant as possible, to treat him with inner courtesy—coming from the heart. . . .

More directly and to the point of our subject, there is the obligation of the layman to his community, and I mean this in the large sense—the community being either local, national, or worldwide. Now, this interest in the obligation to the community can take the form of helping to improve the school system, of working with the sick and needy through the hospitals and in other ways helping to take care of the less fortunate. It can take the form of interest in striving for better, more enlightened, and honest government or in working for world peace. And finally, it can take the shape of interest in the church and in what the church stands for. Certainly, in some small way to help improve the lot of one or all of these five community efforts would be a most Christian thing to do—certainly something that Jesus urges us to pursue.

Schools need better facilities, and teachers need more pay; the sick need care—the needy, relief from want; the government needs to understand and work for world peace and tolerance. And, certainly, the church, of all these community needs, should always be in our minds as an ever-present source of spiritual guidance, helping us to live every day a better and more Christian life. As I see it, going to church once a week isn't enough. We must also strive in our everyday living to *live* by the examples and teachings of Jesus. . . . It is not enough to just accept these teachings of Jesus. We must make these teachings work for us in our daily life.

. . . A Christian church is not a religion of monuments, but a religion of life. Of course, all of us must work for the physical needs of the church. But we must realize that the human race can never be saved by priests and monks and ministers alone, but rather by the Christian layman courageously setting a living example and aggressively selling, if you please, the teachings of Christ in his community. Every great idea must express itself in form. There must be an organization, but organization alone is not enough. Any religion worth having must demonstrate a power that makes changes in the lives of people who profess it. . . .

In conclusion—so many times I have heard people say that working for all these causes is fine, but what can I do about it—I am only one individual. . . . Of course, if everyone lived as Jesus taught us to live, there would probably not be need for helping other people. . . . If we solve our problems from a Christian and spiritual standpoint, we have taken a great step toward helping to solve the world's problems. Secondly, one doesn't have to head up organizations to be helpful. There are all levels of responsibility in community work for . . . anyone who wants to help. Finally, the argument that one is too busy would seem highly unjustified when the old expression, "When you want a job done, give it to a busy man," is so true.

Scandia Radio

Mr. Nels Pearson, president of Scandia Radio AB of Malmö, Sweden, had announced to the board of directors that, for personal reasons, he had decided to take retirement at age 63 and sever all of his connections with the company. The board had asked Mr. Pearson to remain for another year to give the company time to find a suitable successor who would be able to carry on Mr. Pearson's responsibilities, but Mr. Pearson agreed to remain for only six months. His leaving presented the board with the problem of replacing him with an executive skilled in the management of an international business.

Mr. Pearson had been with Scandia since the inception of the business. His schooling had been meager. As a youth, he learned radio technology in a home workshop. He joined the young Scandia organization as a vocational electrician. At Scandia young Pearson impressed Mr. Per Holm, then president, with his engaging personality and his knowledge of radio technology. Mr. Holm took him out of the shop and made him his office assistant. Mr. Pearson, over the years, took on many of Mr. Holm's administrative duties and in time became a senior executive with many responsibilities, including the direction of sales, both domestic and export.

In recognition of his performance, Mr. Pearson was named executive vice president. Two years later he became president, and Mr. Per Holm became chairman of the board. The export business, which he had started, remained one of Mr. Pearson's responsibilities. Mr. Pearson eventually became the sole director of the foreign business, which had grown from a simple operation of selling finished radios on the continent to an intricate complex which covered the globe and included wholly owned plants and subsidiary companies, partnership arrangements, trading agents, wholesaling arrangements, royalty and licensing contracts, selling components to local assemblers, and the custom manufacture of parts for competitive manufacturers. Mr. Pearson managed this business with the help of only three assistants, who had never assumed much authority.

The Scandia management had never looked upon its international business as being a separate entity. The foreign business had been treated as an arm of the domestic business without a separate division, although over two-thirds of Scandia's income came from international sales.

THE COMPANY'S HISTORY AND POSITION

Scandia Radio Aktiebolaget of Malmö, Sweden (SRA), had been organized in 1917 to manufacture Edison-type phonographs under license for the Scandinavian market. In 1926 it dropped phonograph production in favor of manufacturing a quality radio of its own design, which was so well received in Sweden, Norway, and Denmark that SRA became the leading radio manufacturer in Scandanavia. During the 1930s Scandia began an export program, and at the start of World War II over half of Scandia's production was sold in markets outside of Scandinavia. After 1945 Scandia added some phonographs to its product line and later some television sets, and it continued to expand its foreign radio trade.

Scandia was recognized as the largest radio producer in Sweden and a leading communications producer in Europe. It was also a leader in the world communications trade, with 70 percent of its total production being sold abroad. Its emphasis had always been on high-quality products; radio communications constituted 85 percent of its total sales volume. Approximately 90 percent of Scandia's radios were being sold in foreign markets. Almost all of its television sets, phonographs, and console combinations were sold within Scandinavia.

During the decade of the 1950s, the company experienced a major shift in its business. Its radio sales within Scandinavia dropped below the 1950 level. The management attributed the decline to two causes: (1) the advent of television, which competed directly with radios, and (2) the fast-rising general prosperity of Sweden, which provided Swedish consumers with the means to buy items previously beyond their reach. Scandia's radios now competed for the Swedish consumer's kroner with such items as automobiles, refrigerators, motorcycles, and washing machines. By the 1960s, radio sets were commonplace and unexciting in Sweden; many other products had more attraction.

At the same time that Scandia's home market was declining, its European markets were undergoing a similar decline, and for similar reasons. In the Common Market area the decline was accelerated by the new competition of Grundig in Germany and Philips of the Netherlands, both of which made excellent radios and electronic products, had much wider product lines, and had the advantage of being EEC members.

Outside of Europe, the various market area potentials presented a mixed picture. In the United States, which was by far the largest and most prosperous market, national competition, mainly on a price basis, was intense. Everywhere in the world competition from other exporting manufacturers was growing, especially from the Japanese, who sold at prices too low for Scandia to meet.

While radios were a mature or declining product in most industrialized countries, there was a growing market for them in undeveloped areas of the world, where many people had yet to buy their first radio set. However, the standard of living in these areas was usually so low that many people could not afford to buy even the cheapest radio set, much less a Scandia. The potential in these areas was not clear, but it could be enormous. The situation was further complicated by the threat of nationalization in some of the developing countries.

SEARCH FOR A NEW PRESIDENT

"Mr. Pearson grew up with our company," said Mr. Holm, "and as our company grew, he grew with it. This made it possible for him to handle our foreign affairs with his left hand, so to speak, while with his right hand he handled many other matters. He still does that today, despite our large volume of overseas business. Now we will need a person who will devote a considerable amount of time to directing our international activities. The person will need to have many skills and talents. At this stage of our history, it is hard to say just what these skills and talents should be."

The board of directors,[1] at the request of Per Holm (chairman of the board), had studied the problem of replacing Mr. Pearson and had come to three preliminary conclusions. First, that a formal search should be made, using management consultants, to find a new president; second, that the new president should be a person of proven performance in managing an international business; third, that consideration should be given to consolidating all of Scandia's international business in a newly created International Division, headed by a senior executive with appropriate staff support.

With the help of personnel consultants, the search had been narrowed down to three men, all of whom happened to be Scandia senior executives. The consultants advised that any one of the three was capable of holding the office, and they recommended that the board make the final selection, basing its choice upon the needs of Scandia. The board then decided that it would interview each of the three candidates personally before making its decision. Dr. Curt Scheer was the first candidate to be interviewed by the board. He was followed by Herr Heinrich Diederich and Mr. George Boyd.

Vita
Dr. Curt Scheer
Director of Finance and Administration, Scandia Radio AB
Age: 48

---

[1] See Exhibit 1 on p. 889.

EXHIBIT 1

THE MEMBERS OF THE BOARD OF DIRECTORS

Per Holm, chairman, Scandia Radio (Swedish)
Nels Pearson, president, Scandia Radio (Swedish)
Sture Andersson (banker) (Swiss)
Jan Aström (lawyer) (Swedish)
Francois DuBois (advertising agency executive) (Canadian)
Rune Gylling (president, International Paper Products Company) (Norwegian)
Lars Hägglund (executive vice president, international pharmaceutical manufacturer) (Swedish)
Ingemar Holmlind (president, Stockholm Department Stores) (Swedish)
Gunnar Swenson (international shipping firm) (Swedish)
Rolf Deinlund (president, machine tool company) (Danish)

Place of Birth: Basel, Switzerland
Nationality: Swiss
Citizenship: Swiss
Religion: Roman Catholic
Parentage: Father—Swiss
            Mother—Austrian
Height: 1 meter, 75 (5 ft 9 in)
Weight: 77.2 kilos (170 lb)
General health: Average good. Eyesight corrected by bifocals. Major impairment in
     hearing in the left ear.
Residence in childhood and youth: Basel, Switzerland
                                    Mannheim, Germany
                                    Geneva, Switzerland
Education: Volksschule, Gymnasium (public grade and high school),
            Basel, Switzerland
            Wirtsschafts Hochschule (Vocational Business College),
            Mannheim, Germany
            University of Geneva, Geneva, Switzerland
Diplomas, Degrees: Vereidigter Buchprüfer (Chartered Accountant),
                      Wirtsschafts Hochschule, Mannheim
                      Dr. Rer. Oec. (Doctorate in Economics), University of
                      Geneva (Majored in International Finance and Trade)
                      Dr. Rer. Pol. (Honorary Doctorate in Political Science),
                      University of Uppsala, Sweden
Experience:
     2 years with Swiss-American Chamber of Commerce, New York City, U.S.A.
     2 years with Schweizerbank (Swiss Bank), Bern, Switzerland (as Economist, International Dept.)
     Scandia, 21 years:
         Geneva Office, as financial executive and tax adviser, 3 years
         Scandia headquarters, Malmö, Finance Dept., 5 years
         Director of Finance, 5 years
         Director of Finance and Administration, 8 years

Languages:
  Switzer-Deutsch and German (native tongues)
  French (learned in school)
  English (learned during two years in New York, U.S.A.)
  Swedish (learned while with Scandia)
  Some Danish (learned from Danish-born wife)
Marital Status: Married
Nationality of Spouse: Danish born, of Swedish parentage. Long-time resident of
    Malmö
Citizenship of Spouse: Swedish
Family: 4 children, ages 13 to 18
Business and Professional Associations:
  International Association for Research into Income and Wealth
  Fellow: Econometric Society
  International Institute of Administrative Societies
  European Union of Accountants
  Member: International Committee for Historical Sciences
  Associate Member, Scandinavian Historical Society, Malmö
Outside Interests:
  Member, Malmö Civic Symphony Orchestra Board
  Amateur musician (violoncello)
  Sailing (yacht)
  Author of numerous scholarly articles on international trade, world political
    trends, international finance, the free trade areas, international corporate taxa-
    tion, Swiss cantons as tax havens, the Hanseatic League in Europe, the Viking
    Period in Scandinavian history, the coming of the Free Trade Era, and
    Sweden's capitalistic social-welfare state.

PER HOLM'S REMARKS ABOUT DR. SCHEER

"Dr. Scheer is our scholar. He is exceptionally able in statistical and financial
analysis. People are apt to describe him as 'figure-minded.' He has a long memory for precise data, and without referring to records he can quote significant financial data 10 years old. That once made me nervous; however, I've never
found his figures to be far off.

"People usually see Curt Scheer as just an informed accountant, but that is
really a surface impression. He is responsible for all of the company's money
management, accounting and paperwork, and many other administrative matters. As our treasurer, I rely on him as the final authority in financial matters.
He is Scandia's economist, and makes up our annual general economic
forecasts by world areas. He oversees all our domestic and international tax
matters. He is not a lawyer, but somewhere along the line he acquired a good
deal of corporate legal knowledge, and so he has become our liaison with our
company's attorneys. Curt also oversees all of our company's insurance matters, including the employees' group insurance and pension plan. He is also
our link with the government on such things as import and export duties and
restrictions, social welfare insurance, labor legislation, and income tax.

"Curt knows as much about Scandia in general as any one of us. He still supervises the costing system which he installed in our plants, and this has given him a good knowledge of our factory operations. He personally works with George Boyd on finalizing sales forecasts—in fact, he furnishes Boyd with the forecasts. He and Boyd jointly work out our pricing programs. And being the company's de facto legal officer has gotten him into anything and everything that the company does. What I'm saying, I guess, is that Curt Scheer is an economic and financial specialist who is really a broad-gauge generalist.

"Curt looks mild-mannered and easygoing, but underneath he's as tough as leather—a thorough workman who can handle a multitude of problems. He can have a dozen things going at once—union problems, court trials, insurance claims, new bond issues, tax appeals—like a juggler with a dozen balls in the air at the same time—and it doesn't seem to confuse him a bit, or to hurry his pace.

"People don't dislike Curt, but he's not likely to be the most popular one in a group. I've heard snide remarks about his being the company's efficiency expert, a typical auditor, always looking at the financial data. Actually, he's not unfriendly, but he's cool and reserved by nature. Maybe that goes with being an intellectual—what the Americans call an 'egghead.' They don't usually win popularity contests.

"Curt is definitely an international executive. He does a lot of reading, keeps up with world events, and travels a lot. Any installation we have, anywhere, he's been there, knows it first hand. He's more of a linguist than any of us, too. In fact, we look upon him as being *the* linguist for our headquarters office.

"For recreation, Curt plays a violin in an amateur symphony orchestra, and also sails a yacht. Strange combination. His yacht is a big one—sleeps six. On his vacations he cruises the Mediterranean.

"Curt isn't a Swede, you know. He's Swiss, and he's kept his Swiss citizenship. His wife is Swedish, and the Scheer family seems to be Swedish in every way. I tend to think of him as being a Swede—he's been here so long and he fits in so well.

"Now, let's call him in so you can talk to him yourselves."

Dr. Scheer enters. Quitely smiling, he casually greets each director in turn. His dress has a slightly rumpled appearance. His soft bow tie and his gnarled thornbriar pipe, which he puffs at with deliberation, add to his casual effect. He wears bifocal eyeglasses. At times, he absently fingers the hearing aid in his left ear, as though he is preoccupied in searching for an answer, but most of his replies are prompt and incisive. His manner is relaxed, and his replies give the impression of complete candor. Mr. Holm leads the discussion:

Holm: Dr. Scheer—you know of course, that you are being considered for the presidency of our company. This means general management of our international business. Would that have appeal to you?

Scheer: I would have no objection to the appointment. I am already heavily involved in our international business.

Holm: You are aware that we are being advised by consultants in our search. Our consultants have asked that each of the candidates answer certain questions to the board. Is this agreeable to you?

Scheer: Certainly.

Holm: Tell us about your career—as you have seen it.

Scheer: You already have my vita, so I take it you want my view of my career. My father was Oberstudierot (educational counselor) at a Basel gymnasium. Before that he had taught economics. My mother was also a bookish kind of person. I was an only child, and I wasn't robust and spent a good deal of my childhood at home. As far back as I can remember I was among the literati, the cognoscenti, and the intelligentsia. As a boy I got it from both sides, from my father and mother, and so it couldn't help but rub off on me. It was always assumed that I would go the full route through university studies. I passed my Abitur without difficulty. My parents didn't have a lot of money, and from there on I went just about all the way through university on scholarships. My father was an economist, and at one time he taught political economy, as it was called in those days. I had intended to become a teacher—had hopes of becoming a professor of economics—but would even have been satisfied to live out my life as a humble docent. Working at something economic, you enjoy the fruits of the economy more than if you teach economics to others. I liked the fruits. It wasn't long before I connected with SRA, and from then on my life seems to have been Scandia Radio, all the way. I'm satisfied with the way it's gone.

Holm: We all know that you have contributed greatly to Scandia. What do you see as your contribution?

Scheer: Inaugurating a "systems" approach to our international financing. Scandia, like many other international companies, drifted into making investments abroad. You might say it even backed into that position, because it was compelled by competitive forces. Our investments were sporadic; there was no master plan. By the time I came to Scandia, our foreign commitment was so large that a continuation of such a policy would have been intolerable. The sheer size of our foreign operations demanded that we rationalize our financial systems.

Holm: Could you be more specific? Give us examples?

Scheer: Yes, several. During the last twenty years Scandia has increased its operations abroad tenfold. Considering the vagaries of foreign political actions, equity investments would have been perilous. It was obvious to me that foreign leaders would often be willing to provide us with a very high percentage of debt capital in proportion to our equity, and so that became our policy in new ventures: a limited amount of equity and a generous proportion of debt.

Now I know that Banker Andersson at this very moment is thinking of the high interest costs. But we have deliberately used our multiple foreign subsidiaries to keep down our money costs, by taking advantage of the low interest rates in one country to supply the capital needs of operations in high-interest areas. This is simple if the money can be freely shifted between countries. If it is restricted by local governments, then we simply delay or accelerate the payment on the intersubsidiary sale of raw materials, components, or finished goods between the companies within the Scandia family. For example: One of our Danish subsidiaries had a cash surplus, which it lent to another Danish subsidiary which was receiving goods from one of our Swedish subsidiaries. The

Danish company prepaid its account with the Swedish subsidiary, and this money financed the movement of Swedish products into our Finnish subsidiary. Now here is what we accomplished:

If Finland had been required to pay for the goods, it would have had to borrow at the high going Finnish rate. If the Swedish subsidiary had financed the sale, it would have had to borrow at a high rate. But cash in Denmark was at a lower rate. Moreover, Danish currency was weak compared with the Swedish. By speeding up payments to Sweden, we not only obtained the money cheaper, but we hedged our position in Danish kroner at the same time.

Being as international as we are, we have also found it possible to adjust prices on intracompany sales according to a deliberate plan. If a country is in foreign exchange difficulties, it may earmark the scarce exchange for imports and not permit dividends to be remitted abroad. But in Scandia's case, I found it possible to take out our dividends, so to speak, by raising prices on intracompany sales proportionately.

Transfer prices are also a useful device for keeping down the overall corporate tax liability. We have found it possible to instruct our subsidiaries to set high prices on intracorporate shipments to high-tax countries and low prices on those low-cost countries.

I think that we ought to similarly systematize exchange-rate planning. We were well prepared when the English pound was devalued, by deferring payments and switching purchases to other countries. But we ought to set up a system of continuing studies which will scan all of our markets for fluctuations in exchange rate and for impending devaluations, so that we can take full advantage of them whenever and wherever they occur.

Holm: What are your strong points as an executive?

Scheer: I think that I have more respect for facts than most executives. Most situations that call for decisions lend themselves to quantification. I think of decision making as a syllogism. If you take the pains to do so, you can almost always spell out the major and minor premises in terms of concrete data. The conclusion then usually becomes obvious. You have only to calculate it, as you would in solving an equation. People may not always like it, when faced with these kinds of calculated consequences. But they can hardly argue. The results are self-evident.

Holm: Do you feel deficient in any way?

Scheer: (smiling wryly) The more I learn, the more I come to realize how little I know. That's not my pearl of wisdom, of course—I'm quoting. But as far as Scandia is concerned, I feel pretty well equipped. I say this in all due modesty.

Holm: What do you think of Scandia's past performance?

Scheer: Scandia has generally been considered a highly successful company, and so its past history has been chronicled as a success story. But what is success in an economic enterprise? Is it what the balance sheets and the income statements show? Can you measure it by any objective standards? I think that success is a relative thing, and I'm not sure to what you could definitely attribute the source. It might be the management, but management is a compound of the artful and the scientific and subject to good or bad fortune. For Scandia, fortune has been mostly good. As to our management, I think it's been good but primitive—competent in its rudimentary way, and effective, but rugged and unrefined. We've been like the old salt of a sea captain who roared at his young mate: "To hell with your barometers and weather gauges! When my bunions ache, there's a storm brewing, and we trim sail!"

Holm: What do you think of Scandia as it is today?

Scheer: I can give you three answers to that question. By any popular measure, Scandia is "prima"—in the money markets, in engineering circles and in the marketplace. That's what the public thinks. I don't think we can afford the luxury of basking in that glow. Which brings me to my second answer. If we take an introspective look at ourselves, we can hardly agree with the public's "prima" opinion. I'd say that the "prima" opinion is actually a "prima facie" opinion—one taken at face value. If we could only stand aside and take a detached look at ourselves, we'd see that our way of management is an anachronism—outmoded and outdated. If we continue to use present techniques, then we have reached our zenith. My third answer is that we are now at a stage in our history in which we have arrived at a point of divergence. We must conscientiously address ourselves to the question of choosing what we wish Scandia to be in the era of our posterity. If we resolve to determine that now, we probably can choose among a number of options still available to us at this time. If we ignore the dilemma, we will lose the initiative and thereafter experience stagnation.

Holm: Which leads right into my next question. What do you see as the company's future?

Scheer: We have our problems of the moment, but I see these as being eclipsed by the opportunities. Our future depends upon the attitude with which we face it. We can be reactionary, or conservative, or progressive. We are fortunate. We have many options.

Holm: Could you be more explicit?

Scheer: Some think that we have pushed too far, too fast, abroad, and that even in Scandinavia we will never again use our full capacity. We could retrench—cut back to our home market, survive there by eliminating ourselves of every last inefficiency, practicing Spartan economy to meet price competition. That would be reactionary. Taking that course, we would resign ourselves to remaining forever a relatively large producer in a radio market which is relatively small and might become smaller. No one could accuse us of being rashly ambitious, but no one could guarantee that it would be a sinecure. The conservative route would call for holding our present position, rationalizing, and consolidating as much as possible. In my opinion, our present position is untenable—we are beset by so many forces which are beyond our control, such as changes in customers' preferences, or the shifting world economy. There are so many self-seeking governments with narrow perspectives. And always, the whimsical, the unpredictable vicissitudes of politics. In our blind campaign for more sales, we have pushed ahead wherever we found an opening, and now our most advanced positions have weak lifelines. As conservatives, we would often find ourselves fighting rear-guard actions.

As progressives, we would have a number of attractive choices. It would depend on how we wished to be—what stance we chose in the expanding field of electronic communications.

Holm: Along which of the three routes would you lead the company?

Scheer: (curtly) That kind of decision should be reserved to the board of directors.

Holm: Are you in agreement with the plan to set up an International Division?

Scheer: There will be organizational difficulties. Henceforth, we will have a chief of the International Division, and a president. Over three-quarters of our business is now international. Who will actually be the chief executive?

Holm: Do you want the office of president?

Scheer: I am already so heavily involved in companywide foreign affairs that international business takes up most of my time. Therefore, it might make things easier to handle if I had full direction of our business. I, of course, would be honored to accept the office if it is offered to me. I am enthusiastic about expanding our international business.

Holm: Where will you live when you retire?

Scheer: Right here, in all likelihood. My Swedish family won't let me move, and I don't care to move, either. I guess I've become Swedish by marriage. *(Facetiously)* I thought we were talking about a promotion. Am I being fired? *(laughter)*.

Holm: Thank you very much for cooperating, Dr. Scheer.

Vita
Herr Heinrich Diederich
Director of Manufacturing, Scandia Radio AB
Age: 54
Place of Birth: Braunschweig, West Germany
Citizenship: German
Religion: Lutheran
Nationality of parents: Father: German
                                  Mother: Polish/German (Danzig)
General health: Good. Vision corrected by reading glasses
Height: 1 meter, 90 (6 ft 3 in)
Weight: 99.9 kilos (220 lb)
Residence in childhood and youth: Braunschweig, Germany
Education: Volksschule, Braunschweig
            Gymnasium, Braunschweig
            University, Braunschweig Technische Hochschule
Diplomas, Degrees: Degree in Electrical Engineering
Experience:
      Blaupunkt Radio, Braunschweig—8 years
        Design Engineer, electronics—2 years

Production Engineer, car radios (for Volkswagens)—4 years
Assistant Production Superintendent, radios—2 years
Scandia Radio—22 years
Assistant Plant Superintendent, Denmark—2 years
Plant Manager, Austria—3 years
Assistant Plant Manager, Malmö—3 years
Plant Manager, Malmö—4 years
Director of Manufacturing, Scandia Radio—10 years
Languages: German—native tongue
English—learned in school
Swedish—learned while with Scandia
Marital Status: Married
Nationality of Spouse: German
Citizenship of Spouse: German
Family: 8 children, ages 8 to 22
4 grandchildren
Business and Professional Organizations:
Vice President: International Scientific Radio Union
Chairman: Nordic Association of Radio Manufacturers
Council of Nordic Master Craftsmen
International Council of Societies of Industrial Design
International Electronics Assocaition
International Esperantist Chess League
Outside Interests:
Amateur radio operator
Malmö Civic Men's Choral Society
Home gardening
Chess

PER HOLM'S REMARKS ABOUT
HEINRICH (HEINZ) DIEDERICH

"Heinz Diederich is our technical man. I believe that he knows as much about radio technology and audio amplification as anyone in the world today. He's lived close to radios since his early boyhood. We have Diederich to thank for a number of our patents.

"Heinrich looks like the old Prussian ramrod type of plant manager, and sometimes I believe that he is. But for assistants, he chooses modern youngsters who are college-bred technicians. They are as much organization people as engineers. Two of his present staff are engineers who have American M.B.A. degrees. Sometimes I wonder if these youngsters are accountants, or finance people, or production engineers.

"It caused a ruffle of ill will when we made Diederich, who is German, production chief of Scandia. There were some career Swedes in the Malmö plant who felt that they had prior rights. We are an international company now, and our people are going to have to learn to forget their Swedish origins, or any other kind of origins, for that matter. You could look at it another way: I didn't choose Diederich because he was non-Swedish. I chose him because he knows radio design and he knows how to turn out radios.

"Heinz will give you the impression of being slow-moving. He *is* slow-moving; but when he does move into something, you can be pretty sure that he's thought about it. I've heard that no one in Malmö has ever beaten him at chess. That's not because of his brilliant moves. He simply takes his time and wears out his opponent.

"Diederich acts like a growly old bear—sometimes he even roars a little—but that is a surface impression and a cover. He actually is a kind man. He treats people fairly, without any grinning or backslapping. His people like him. Even the Swedes who were jealous of him didn't quit, and they are loyal to him now.

"Diederich has been a ham radio operator since he was eight years old. I'm told that the antenna for his home broadcasting outfit is the tallest and longest in Malmö. But radios aren't all of his life. At home he's all wrapped up in his kids, and by this time there are a few grandkids. In summer he spends his evenings weeding his roses and rutabagas. Heinrich doesn't travel much. He'd rather be at home than anywhere else—except in the plant.

"Diederich is a shirt-sleeved shop man. *(Ruefully)* I sometimes wish he were more of the executive type. I don't think he spends a fourth of his time at his desk. At most any time I'll find him hunched over a drawing board with some young draftsperson, or he'll be out patrolling the plant. He likes to feel the thump of the punch presses or hear the sputtering of the soldering irons and the whine of the circle saws. That races his pulse; that's life to him. Once when I almost choked on the smell of acid fumes in our electroplating shop, he laughed and called it the perfume of production. It smelled as sweet to him as his begonias.

"Now let's have Heinrich in and talk to him."

Heinrich Diederich enters and nods to the group of directors. He is a big, portly man. His steel-gray hair is a stiff, crew-cut bristle. His manner is stolid, impassive.

Holm: Herr Diederich, you know that you are being considered to head our company. Would the office of president have appeal to you?

Diederich: Yes, if the board determined that I was best man for the job at this time.

(Pause)

Holm: Would you explain, please?

Diederich: As you know, I find my present job very challenging. However, if it is the decision of you gentlemen *(nodding toward the board)* that I can better serve the company as the chief executive officer, I would exert every effort to move the company forward.

Holm: Our consultants have proposed certain questions which we would like to ask you.

Diederich: Feel free.

Holm: Please tell us about your career—as you have seen it.

Diederich: My father was a tool and diemaker by vocation. When I was a little boy he told me that he was making the dies which punched out the condenser plates for the radios being made by an early Braunschweig radio manufacturer. I found that exciting. Radio was the rage in those days, in the early 20s. As a 10-year-old I built my first headphone set out of a few wires and a cardboard oatmeal carton, and I was proud to get reception from Hanover, which was over 30 kilometers away. I have always found technical and scientific things interesting. While the other boys were playing soccer, I was in my home workshop tinkering with the new neutrodyne and superheterodyne tube radios. When the other boys were fascinated with athletic and military heroes, my heroes were Ferdinand Porsche and Thomas Edison, Marconi, Morse, and Alexander Graham Bell. We were not poor—my father earned good wages, and he determined that I would do better than he had done. There was no tradition of schooling in our family, but he and my mother encouraged me and helped me. I am the first one in our family to achieve a university education. I liked the natural sciences best. They came easy to me. If I had been allowed to do so, I would have studied only science—I would never have opened a book on history, or economics, or government, or anthropology. I took my degree just in time to become a soldier. I didn't do much soldiering. I was assigned to a specialist post at an army headquarters unit as a radio technician. I never saw any heavy action. After the war, I was lucky again. I got a job with a radio company right in my home city of Braunschweig. I did well there, and then Scandia offered me a better job in Denmark. I married early at the end of the war, and there were getting to be quite a few little Diederichs about. I couldn't afford to turn down raises. Besides, Scandia's excellent technology appealed to me. So I came to Scandia. I have not regretted it. I think that for an electronics engineer, I have had an ideal career.

Holm: We all know that you have contributed a great deal to Scandia. What do you see as your contribution?

Diederich: Three things. First, maintaining the high quality of our product line.

(Pause)

Holm: How, specifically?

Diederich: It is related to my other two points. My second point was the establishment of a spread of plants which virtually blanket the globe. My third point was the firm adoption of a policy of centralization of product planning, standardization of products, and quality control, with decentralization of production but with the overall production still directed centrally.

Holm: Would you explain, please?

Diederich: As our sales abroad increased, the pressure to establish local plants became strong. For example, our distributor in Canada, where we had a ten-week delivery schedule, didn't like predicting sales maybe six months in advance and maintaining a three-month supply in inventory. He wanted to draw from a plant in Montreal from which he could get deliveries within a week. So we built a small plant in Montreal. There are offsetting disadvantages to building small plants abroad. You lose the efficiencies of truly mass production that you get in a centralized home plant, which might more than offset duties and freight. And plants in developing countries might be very inefficient. For example, the radio which we produced in Columbia at \$41 might be produced in Mexico for \$32 and it might be produced in Malmö for only \$18! But nevertheless, we went the route of building small plants abroad to give better service and to satisfy the demands for nationalization of production.

Now, along with the pressure to build plants abroad comes pressure to modify our products to suit the tastes and preferences of the new market. The pressure comes not only from our salespeople; it comes from our engineers abroad, too. I have resisted this pressure, and insisted on uniformity, on standardization of our products, and even of our production processes, everywhere. This is the only way we can maintain quality and cost control. Now, while we have decentralized production in the sense of spreading it to dozens of plants abroad and giving local plant managers a free hand when it comes to labor relations and working conditions and many other things, we still are working at achieving a coordinated centralization of production planning. Scheer is much more advanced with his centralized financial planning than we are in production planning. We are just beginning to shape up. It does not make sense to try to produce our total product at each location. This is obvious. Many of our plants are located in countries which don't have the basic raw materials, such as wood, or aluminum, or steel, or copper, yet they insist, for purposes of nationalizing production, on making as much of the product as possible. Therefore, we find ourselves making stereo cabinets, or at least the veneers, in Arkansas and Canada and Sweden; in stamping chassis in Sweden, Germany, Holland, and the United States; in making components in Paris; and so on with other essentials. Often only assembly is done locally. Now, when you have this kind of operation, it must necessarily be integrated and coordinated by centralization of production planning, which we do here at Malmö. We don't yet have as smooth an operation here as I would like it to be, but I have some sharp young American industrial engineers who are studying the possibility of computerizing production schedules. But we have no intention of trying to run our individual plants on a day-to-day basis.

Holm: Do you feel deficient in any way?

Diederich: I have been a technical man, and in my end of the business I feel very confident. I am sure, however, that I would need to broaden my perspective in the president's role.

Holm: What do you think of Scandia's past performance?

Diederich: It has been excellent. SRA has always made as fine a communications product as anyone in the world. We deserve our good reputation.

Holm: What do you think of Scandia as it is today?

Diederich: I think we are in excellent condition, as least as far as our Malmö production and our continental plants are concerned. I am not that proud about what is coming out of our plants in Calcutta, or Zanzibar, or Buenos Aires, other than radios and some parts.

(Pause)

Holm: Why not?

Diederich: I should think that if developing nations want to get into production, they ought to begin with simple products—like shoes or furniture. A radio is a complex instrument. People cannot be cow herders today and radio makers tomorrow.

Holm: What do you see as Scandia's future?

Diederich: Well, I know that most people don't get very excited about radios and stereos any more. They are "old hat," as the English say. To my teenage daughter, they are as outdated as stereoscopes. I see it differently. There are great opportunities ahead for us. With our superior know-how, there are great areas that we have not even tried to exploit: the specialized kind of equipment needed by armies, by air forces, and in seagoing vessels, the highly refined equipment needed by commercial aircraft; and the use of radio in many industrial and commercial applications, where satellite radio might be much more practical than the equipment that we use today. The world today is so flooded with cheap radios that compete on a price basis that I think Scandia would do well to stay away from the general market. We ought to be doing what only *we* can do—making the superior-quality commercial sets that require superior talent in the making. It would mean cutting down on volume production, but we would then be in a field where we would have few competitors and where price, of course, would be a secondary consideration. It would be the answer to most of our world marketing problems. Products that are clearly superior —in the tehnical sense—vault right over the trade walls—the duties, the quotas, the nationalistic restrictions. Look at Swedish steel, or the Volkswagen, or Leica cameras, or Scotch whisky, or Wilkinson Sword razor blades, or Swiss watches, or Danish pottery.

Holm: (laughing) You've made your point. Are you in agreement with the plan to set up an international division?

Diederich: I am not sure how the International Division would work, but I cannot see that it would affect my end of the business very much. We already have full exchange of technical information, internationaliy. We also exchange personnel between all our foreign plants, as much as it is practical to do so. Our research and development will go right on as it is now, regardless of how you change the management. The new International Division might make quite a difference to Scheer and Boyd, but not to me.

Holm: Do you want the office of president?

Diederich: I would be honored, of course. While I am well situated in my present position, I still enjoy a challenge. I am interested in what is best for the company. I definitely would like the chance to be president.

Holm: Where will you live when you retire?

Diederich: I'm still a long way from retirement and hadn't really given it much thought. I assumed I would stay here until I retire, and maybe even stay here beyond 65, if it might be permitted. Most foreigners newly abroad tend to assume that their stay is temporary and that they will sooner or later go "home." But the longer you stay abroad, the more you get to be at home away from home. If I went home at age 65, I probably wouldn't feel at home there. I honestly cannot answer that question. Perhaps my wife can answer it.

Vita

Mr. George Boyd

Director of Marketing, Scandia Radio AB

Age: 51

Place of Birth: Blue Earth, Minnesota, U.S.A.

Nationality: American

Citizenship: U.S.A.

Religion: Protestant (nondenominational)

Parentage: Father: John Boyd, third-generation American of English-Irish ancestry
        Mother: Elise Schmidt, fourth-generation American of German ancestry

General Health: Good. No physical infirmities.

Height: 5 ft 10 in (1 meter, 78)

Weight: 175 lb (72.5 kilos)

Residence in childhood and youth: State of Minnesota, U.S.A.
                                Korean War
                                Lived in Chicago, Illinois, U.S.A.

Education: P.S. 4, Blue Earth, Minnesota
            Blue Earth Public High School
            Two years at Winona State College
            Night School in Chicago—selected subjects in salesmanship, advertising, merchandising, retailing, market research, sales supervision, etc.

Diplomas, Degrees: 4-year High School Diploma
                        60-hour Business Diploma, Northwestern University Evening Division

Experience:
    2 years U.S. Army, Infantry, Honorable Discharge; Rank, 1st Lieut.
    2 years Salesman, Home Beautiful Furniture Co., Chicago, Ill., U.S.A.
    3 years Lyric Radio Company, Chicago Area Sales Supervisor
  18 years Scandia Radio:
      6 years Lyric-Scandia, Midwest Sales Manager
      5 years Scandia Radio, Inc., Sales Manager, United States and Canada.
      2 years Assistant General Sales Manager, Scandia Radio AB, Malmö
      5 years Director of Sales, Scandia Radio AB, Malmö

Languages: English—Native tongue
           Swedish—Learned since 1965 with Scandia

Marital Status: Married

Nationality of Spouse: American, of English-Irish parentage

Citizenship of Spouse: U.S.A.

Family: No children

Business and Professional Associations: Delegate: International Marketing Federation.

Outside Interests: Spectator sports
                Reading
                World travel

PER HOLM'S REMARKS ABOUT GEORGE BOYD

"I once heard a man who disliked George Boyd describe him, nevertheless, as the world's greatest salesman. That might be a little overdone, but not much. You may not believe it when you first see him, because he's not the gladhandling type. George can melt ice when he wants to turn on the charm, but he's not by nature a gusher. He doesn't even do much smiling. He plays his own personality straight. I think of him as being aggressive, first of all, and second, I think of him as a maker of deals.

"George is always out to capture something, or to talk somebody into some kind of a horse trade. He is an honest trader, but when he charges after something he get it, just about every time. What he goes after, he brings home.

"Boyd drives himself hard. Even when he is relaxing, he's probably planning the next coup he's going to make. He drives his subordinates hard, too. Maybe too hard. He expects them to dedicate their total lives to Scandia, just as he does. I know that some of his people don't like him, but he gets things done.

"The Boyds have no children. He and his wife Ruth are a devoted couple. I sometimes think that Ruth works as hard at George's job as he does, and she enjoys it as much, too. She knows everyone who ever had anything to do with Scandia, and its competitors, and she knows their cousins and their uncles and their aunts. She's a living directory, and she helps George immensely. They are an excellent married working team.

"The Boyds are well off financially. Both of them had inheritances from their parents. They could live in style on income from investments if they cared to do so. Instead, they both work hard at George's job and live modestly in a seaside apartment near Malmö. You'd think that as sales chief he would have to do a lot of wining and dining, but they live quietly and only entertain when they need to do so.

"George is a talker. He can hold forth on most any subject, and he does—at length. He'll tell you—in no uncertain terms—what's wrong in the world and how to straighten it out. He'll tell you where world Christendom is heading, and what should be done about apartheid in South Africa. And when George has the floor, he holds it. He's pretty dogmatic.

"As you will see for yourselves. Let's have him in and talk to him."

George Boyd strides purposefully into the board room, nods unsmilingly in the direction of the directors, and says, simply, "Gentlemen." He makes a trim, well-tailored impression. Boyd has dark, piercing eyes and black hair and looks younger than his age. He declines a proffered chair, says that he would prefer to stand, and addresses the group:

Boyd: I understand that you wish me to answer certain questions. I will be pleased to do so. In fact, I have been looking forward to this session.

Holm: Would the office of president have appeal to you—especially in view of the fact that we are heavily international?

Boyd: It certainly would. Our international activities need unified direction.

Our international business needs leadership—strong leadership—and I believe I can supply it.

Holm: Please tell us about your life—from your own viewpoint.

Boyd: My father was a small-town merchant. He had the largest general store in Blue Earth, Minnesota, which was a prosperous farming community, and he did very well. My father was born on a farm in Minnesota. His parents came from England and Ireland.

My mother was American-born of German ancestry. Her parents were born in the United States and were proud of their ancestry in the United States dating back to the early 1800s.

My mother wanted me to become a teacher. She thought of that as a proud profession, and so I was sent to the state college. I really wasn't much interested in becoming a teacher. I had been helping my father in his store since I was a little boy, and I thought that the traveling salespeople who called on him led much more interesting lives than schoolteachers. There was one especially, who drove an old Dusenberg automobile, who was my boyhood hero. He sold underwear.

At state college I met my wife. We were married during my army service. Ruth and I have never regretted it. She has been a great help to me in my positions.

My parents were well off financially. They could easily have afforded to finance all of my schooling, but both of them believed in industry and thrift, and so they paid only for my tuition and board. If I wanted any spending money, I would have to earn that myself. At first I did odd jobs. They didn't pay well. Then I heard of a fraternity that wanted to buy new dishes and silver for its dining room. I got a special deal through a salesman who sold to my father, and I made the sale to the fraternity at a neat profit. Next I got the staple-food accounts for two fraternities, and later a laundry concession for the entire college. By my second year I was doing all kinds of business and earning big money for a young boy. I even sold the college itself a big order of furniture, and that "big-ticket" item was what led me into the furniture business in later years. My business dealings didn't do my grades any good, but they earned a lot of money, and inadvertently they became the most vital part of the education I received at that college. It saddened my mother, but my father was proud of me. Also, I got a taste for money early in life, and that was not good for a boy who was supposed to become a schoolteacher.

In the Korean war, I volunteered for service in the infantry at the end of my third year in college. After the war I didn't go back to school. A friend of mine got a job for me as a salesman in his father's wholesale business in Chicago. After a few months I was put in charge of radio sales. Three years later I accepted an offer to become Chicago sales manager of Lyric Radio, which was later bought by Scandia as a sales outlet. Scandia reorganized Lyric and made it a distributor, and I became North American sales manager. After a while I was invited to Malmö, and after a few years there, I became sales chief.

During my Chicago years, I had the opportunity to go to night school at a leading university, where I absorbed all the textbook knowledge I could find about selling and sales management. I already knew how to bargain—that seemed to be an inborn talent. I think I've led a charmed life. Except for the Korean War years, I've always been doing what I like and what I'm best at—managing a sales operation.

Holm: We all know that our sales have increased substantially in the years that you have directed our marketing. What do you see as your contribution to Scandia?

Boyd: Often when companies get into foreign operations, they do so rather aimlessly, without any real knowledge of their markets, which are quite likely to be very different in advanced countries versus developing countries or undeveloped areas. They lack sales sophistication.

I think this was especially true of Scandia. It sold abroad on the basis of old-established connections which it had developed haphazardly, on a sort of homespun who-knew-who basis.

I think I've modernized our sales tactics. Sales promotions abroad are now made on the basis of the most solid research which is available in each area, rather than according to "Who is our friend there?" Hunches have now been replaced with statistics, which we get not only from market researchers, but from economists, sociologists, and even political analysts. Sometimes our future in a country will depend upon an economic decision made by a politician, and then we even zero our investigations in on the politician personally, to try to get "inside" to anticipate which way his or her thinking is going. Our marketing decisions are now worked out systematically, where before they were based on "gut" feeling.

Holm: What do you think of the company's past performances?

Boyd: The rest of the world thinks that our company has performed superbly. I think that it has done very well, too, but I think that we have patches on the seat of our pants. We are still operating as though we were a Swedish company which is selling its radios abroad. This—at a time when only one in four of our products is sold in Scandinavia. Actually, we are an international company, or a multinational company, as some call it. We are not a truly "multinational" company. That name is usually reserved for companies that are truly global in production, sales, financing, and management. We haven't reached that stage yet. We sell in some markets; we have some production abroad; we have more debt financing abroad than we have equity investments; our top management is an international mix, but from that level down it's still mostly Swedes at home and locals abroad. And what's more significant, I think, is that our board is mostly Swedish and most of our thinking and our policies have a Scandinavian flavor.

Holm: What do you think of the company's present position?

Boyd: I think that we have reached the proverbial fork in the road, and at this time we must be decisive. In the beginning Scandia looked upon its foreign sales as something it did with its left hand when both hands weren't needed to work on the home business. Exporting was a sideshow; the main act was in Sweden. The export sales went well and they earned money. But Scandia treated these earnings as something it did on the side, like a person who bets a few idle kroner on the racehorses and when he or she wins says, well, I'll bet it all again, and if I'm lucky, I may double my money once more.

It did this without much regard to alternative opportunities abroad elsewhere on the international scene which might have been more profitable. And Scandia is now almost a global corporation.

Holm: What do you see as the company's future?

Boyd: Scandia has a very promising future. It is already an excellent company, but its present position could be merely the platform from which it steps into true global greatness. It could do that if we properly exploit the vast untapped potential for our products that lies waiting in the world market.

Holm: Could you expand on that?

Boyd: We are already an international company, not a Swedish company selling in foreign markets; but we have never formulated a definitely defined strategy that would make the best use of our competitive advantages. And we have advantages—in technology, in reputation, in our brand name, in competent management, and in an established customer following.

We ought to face the fact that we are on the threshold of becoming a truly global company, and we ought to act like one. We ought to establish our production deliberately in areas where the costs are lowest, and that would mean shifting it away from Sweden, where the level of the economy is very high, resulting in high costs. We should shift production to areas such as the Far East, where labor is plentiful and wages are low. Many U.S. electronics manufacturers are now doing this and selling their products in the high-price United States market. We ought to build up sales where the market has the most potential and is most rewarding in profits. This would mean adding cheaper-quality products to our present line, ones that could be sold to the vast masses who still live in darkness and are just emerging into the light of civilization and are hungry for radios but cannot afford our expensive ones. If we were to operate as a true global corporation should, we could find a glittering array of opportunities to buy cheap and sell dear, what with our many differing markets, varying labor conditions, market demands, political influences, and money markets—provided that we can properly coordinate the total into an integrated and smoothly functioning operation. We are not operating that way today. Today we still treat overseas business on a sort of happenstance basis, as though it was a side issue.

Holm: What are your strong points as an executive?

Boyd: I've heard, via the grapevine, that I'm a tiger in the jungle, and I'm proud of that criticism. Until lately Scandia subscribed to the philosophy of building the better mousetrap, and some of the world did actually beat a path to its door, but this won't work any longer in today's world market. You must drive hard, and you must wheel and deal.

Holm: Wheel and deal?

Boyd: Yes. Get trading advantages wherever and however we can. Through natural economic advantages, or political influence, or systematically using the power structure that exists in every country. For example: We can make some electronic products economically in Sweden or the United States; we can make radio and phono components more economically in Taiwan or Ireland, where labor rates are low. It might even be to our advantage, in some countries, to have competitors make some of our parts and electronic components for us. We might do all that and assemble them in England for sale in the United Kingdom and Commonwealth markets. These intercountry exports and imports often amount to a significant percentage of these countries' foreign trade and give us a good deal of political influence.

Holm: Do you feel deficient in any way?

Boyd: Not especially, except that I play the game to win, which means I play the game for blood, not for fun, and that's left a trail of people in my wake who aren't especially fond of me. Oddly enough, while many of these don't like me personally, they are still quite willing to do business with me because I make deals on the basis of having something that they want, and I'm willing to bargain.

Holm: How do you rate the other contenders for the job?

Boyd: They are all competent executives. I wouldn't care to make any other public appraisal of the men whose help and loyalty I would expect to enlist if I were to become chief.

Holm: Why do you want the job of president?

Boyd: Because I believe that Scandia's future lies in the direction of continued expansion of sales globally, and doing so profitably, and I would lead it to that goal.

Holm: Where will you live when you retire, and what do you intend to do?

Boyd: (after a blank pause) Frankly, your question puzzles me. I have never given any serious thought to retiring. I guess that means I feel I will go right on doing what I'm doing now, and die with my boots on, as they say in the States. As to where I'll live, that will be wherever my work takes me.

Holm: Thank you very much. You have been very candid and most helpful.

Holm: Well, gentlemen, that concludes our interviews. What do you think?

Jan Aström (lawyer): Gentlemen, in view of our line of questioning, I wonder if we have approached this in the wrong way. What are we really looking for? What talents should our new president have? What special qualification? How should he be different from our other executives? Do you think we would know a good international executive if we saw one?

Sture Andersson (banker): I don't think our man needs to be an experienced internationalist. Any good broad-gauge executive could be competent in the job, even if he speaks only Swedish and has never been outside of Malmö.

Ingemar Holmlind (department stores): How can he make major decisions about Scandia's world trade if he hasn't had experience as a world trader?

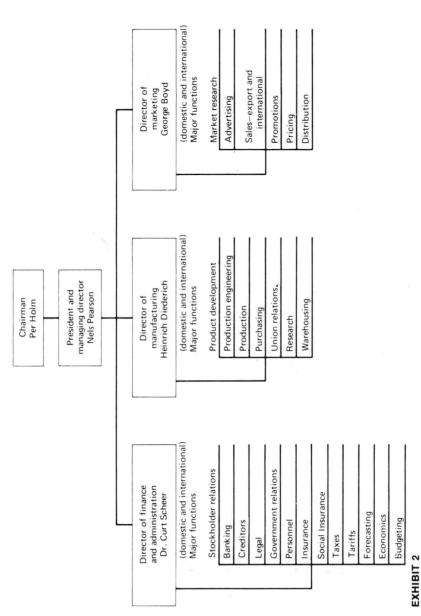

EXHIBIT 2

Scandia Radio AB, Malmö, Sweden, organization chart.

Chairman
Per Holm

President and
managing director
Nels Pearson

**Director of finance
and administration
Dr. Curt Scheer**

(domestic and international)
Major functions

Stockholder relations

Banking

Creditors

Legal

Government relations

Personnel

Insurance

Social Insurance

Taxes

Tariffs

Forecasting

Economics

Budgeting

**Director of
manufacturing
Heinrich Diederich**

(domestic and international)
Major functions

Product development

Production engineering

Production

Purchasing

Union relations

Research

Warehousing

**Director of
marketing
George Boyd**

(domestic and international)
Major functions

Market research

Advertising

Sales—export and
international

Promotions

Pricing

Distribution

Sture Andersson: I make decisions every day about fisheries and flour mills—and *(looking pointedly at Holmlind)* even department stores—and I am neither a fisherman nor a miller nor a merchant.

Ingemar Holmlind: But your decisions are financial ones.

Sture Andersson: Scandia *is* a commercial enterprise. It certainly isn't non-financial.

Holm: Well, gentlemen, we have had a busy day. I would suggest that we now adjourn and meet again a month from now. We must choose our new chief executive at our next meeting.